Notes on the New Testament

Albert Barnes

Edited by

Robert Frew

MATTHEW AND MARK

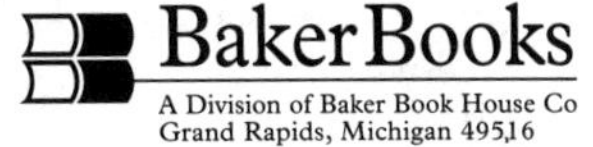

A Division of Baker Book House Co
Grand Rapids, Michigan 49516

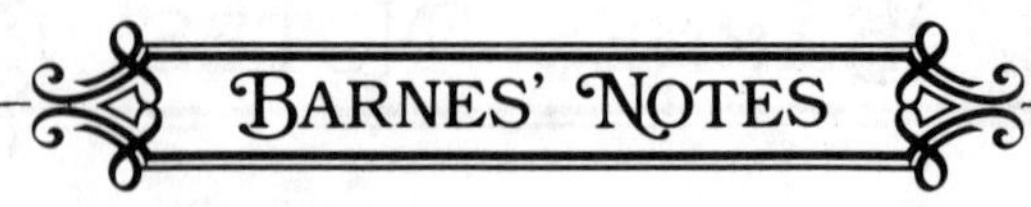

Heritage Edition

Fourteen Volumes 0834-4

1. Genesis (Murphy)	0835-2	8. Minor Prophets (Pusey)	0842-5
2. Exodus to Esther (Cook)	0836-0	9. The Gospels	0843-3
3. Job	0837-9	10. Acts and Romans	0844-1
4. Psalms	0838-7	11. I Corinthians to Galatians	0846-8
5. Proverbs to Ezekiel (Cook)	0839-5	12. Ephesians to Philemon	0847-6
6. Isaiah	0840-9	13. Hebrews to Jude	0848-4
7. Daniel	0841-7	14. Revelation	0849-2

When ordering by ISBN (International Standard Book Number), numbers listed above should be preceded by 0-8010-.

Reprinted from the 1847 edition published
by Blackie & Son, London

Reprinted 2005 by Baker Books
a division of Baker Book House Company
P.O. Box 6287, Grand Rapids, MI 49516-6287

Printed in the United States of America

PREFACE

TO THE REVISED EDITION OF THE NOTES ON THE NEW TESTAMENT

THE first volumes of these Notes on the New Testament—those on the Gospels—were published in 1832. The other volumes were published at intervals between that year and 1851, when the Notes on the Book of Revelation were published.

In 1840 the stereotype plates of the Gospels had become greatly worn, and it was found necessary to recast them, and a careful revision of the Notes was made. In that edition many errors were corrected; in some places the notes were enlarged, and at the close of the second volume a chronological table and an index, which it was supposed would be of value to the teachers in Sabbath-schools, were appended.

Since that time more than a quarter of a century has elapsed, and the Notes on the Gospels, as well as on other parts of the New Testament, have passed through numerous editions. During that time, also, great advances have been made in all the departments of knowledge necessary to a proper illustration of the Scriptures. Palestine has been explored more accurately than before; a better knowledge of Oriental manners and customs has been obtained; more accurate maps and illustrations have been published; and the best minds in Europe and in this country have been employed in illustrating the language employed and the manners and customs referred to in the New Testament. The means of explaining the Bible have fully kept up with the progress of the world in other things, and it is every way desirable that a commentary on the Scriptures should be such as to meet the wants of society as it advances in other respects.

In the revision the essential character of the work has not been changed. It would have been easy to have enlarged it very greatly, and by one competent to the task it might have been made much more learned; but it was supposed that the fact that since the first edition of the Gospels was issued more than five hundred and fifty thousand volumes have been sold in this country, and probably a larger number in Great Britain, and that it has been translated, in whole or in part, into the Welsh, French, and Tamil languages, and that numerous imitations of the general form and style of the work have been made in different religious denominations in this country, has shown that the plan of the work met a *want* in the public mind, and was adapted in some measure to supply that want, and that no essential change in its plan and character should be attempted. As the usefulness of the work, it is believed, has been much promoted by the fact that it was at first issued in small and convenient volumes, especially adapted to the use of Sabbath-schools and Bible-classes, that form of publication has not been changed.

While, however, no material change has been made in the character and plan of the work, I have endeavoured to improve it in every way in my power. In some places it has been abridged, but new matter has been added that will possibly somewhat enlarge the size of the volume. I have availed myself freely of such works as have been published bearing on the subject since the first edition was issued.

In now finishing my labours on the New Testament, after so many years, I cannot better express my emotions than in the words which I used when, in 1840, I sent forth the revised edition of the Gospels to the world, and which I supposed then would be the last time that I should address the public on the subject:

"I dismiss the work, therefore, finally, with deep feeling; feeling more deep by far than when I first submitted it to the press. I cannot be insensible to the fact that I have been, by my expositions of the New Testament, doing something—and it may be much—to mould the hearts and intellects of thousands of the rising generation in regard to the great doctrines and duties of religion—thousands who are to act their parts, and to develop these principles, when I am dead. Nor can I be insensible to the fact that in the form in which these volumes now go forth to the public, I may continue, though dead, to speak to the living; and that the work may be exerting an influence on immortal minds when I am in the eternal world. I need not say that, while I am sensitive to this consideration, I earnestly desire it. There are no sentiments in these volumes which I wish to alter; none that I do not believe to be truth that will abide the investigations of the great day; none of which I am ashamed. That I *may* be in error I know; that a better work than this might be prepared by a more gifted mind and a better heart, I know; but the truths here set forth are, I am persuaded, those which are destined to abide, and to be the means of saving millions of souls, and of ultimately converting this whole world to God. That these volumes may have a part in this great work is my earnest prayer; and with many thanks to the public for its favours, and to God, the Great Source of all blessings, I send them forth again, commending them to *his* care, and asking in a special manner the continued favour of Sabbath-school teachers and of the young."

ALBERT BARNES.

Washington Square, Philadelphia, Dec., 1868.

ORIGINAL PREFACE

TO THE NOTES ON THE GOSPELS.

In the preparation of the following Notes, free use has been made of all the helps within the reach of the author. . . . The object has been to express, in as few words as possible, the *real meaning* of the Gospels; the *results* of their critical study, rather than the *process* by which these results were reached.

This work is designed to occupy a place which is supposed to be unappropriated in attempts to explain the New Testament. It was my wish to present to Sunday-school teachers a plain and simple *explanation* of the more common difficulties of the book which it is their province to teach. This wish has given character to the work. If it should occur to anyone that more minute explanations of *words, phrases*, and *customs* have been attempted than might seem to them desirable, it will be recollected that many Sunday-school teachers have little access to means of information, and that no small part of their success is dependent on the *minuteness* and *correctness* of the explanation which is given to children.

This work is designed also to be a *Harmony of the Gospels*. Particular attention has been bestowed, especially in the Notes on Matthew, to bring the different narratives of the Evangelists together, and to show that, in their narration of the same events, there is no real contradiction. It will be recollected that *the sacred narrative of an event is what it is reported to be by all the Evangelists*. It will also be recollected that the most plausible objections to the New Testament have been drawn from the apparent contradictions in the Gospels. The importance of meeting these difficulties in the education of the young, and of showing that these objections are not well founded, will be apparent to all.

Particular attention has been paid to the *references* to parallel passages of Scripture. *In all instances in these Notes they are an essential part of the explanation of the text.* The authority of the Bible has been deemed the only authority that was necessary in such cases; and it is hoped that no one will condemn any explanation offered without a candid examination of the *real* meaning of the passages referred to.

The main design of these notes will be accomplished if they furnish a just *explanation* of the text. Practical remarks could not have been more full without materially increasing the size of the book, and, as was supposed, without essentially limiting its circulation and its usefulness. All that has been attempted, therefore, in this part of the work, has been to furnish *leading thoughts*, or heads of practical remark, to be enlarged on at the discretion of the teacher.

These Notes have been prepared amid the pressing and anxious cares of a responsible pastoral charge. Of their imperfection no one can be more sensible than the author. Of the time and patience indispensable in preparing even such brief Notes on the Bible, under the conviction that the opinions expressed *may* form the sentiments of the young on the subject of the Book of God, and determine their eternal destiny, no one can be sensible who has not made the experiment. The great truth is becoming more and more impressed on the minds of this generation that the Bible is the only authoritative source of religious belief; and if there is any institution pre-eminently calculated to deepen this impression, and fix it permanently in the minds of the coming age, it is the Sunday-school. Every minister of the gospel, every parent, every Christian, must therefore feel it important that *just views of interpretation* should be imbibed in these schools. I have felt more deeply than I have any other sentiment the importance of inculcating on the young proper modes of explaining the sacred Scriptures. If I can be one of the instruments, however humble, in extending such views through the community, my wish in this work will be accomplished. I commit it, therefore, to the blessing of the God of the Bible, with the prayer that it may be one among many instruments of forming correct religious views, and promoting the practical love of God and man, among the youth of this country.

ALBERT BARNES.

Philadelphia, August 25th, 1832.

INTRODUCTION

The writings which are regarded by Christians as the sole standard of faith and practice have been designated at various periods by different names. They are frequently called *The Scriptures*, to denote that they are the most important of all *writings; The Holy Scriptures*, because composed by persons divinely inspired, and containing sacred truth; and *The Canonical Scriptures.* The word *canon* means a *rule*, and it was applied by the Christian fathers to the books of the Bible because they were regarded as *an authoritative rule* of faith and practice; and also to distinguish them from certain *spurious* or *apocryphal* books, which, although some of them might be true as matter of history, or correct in doctrine, were not regarded as a *rule* of faith, and were therefore considered as not *canonical.*

But the most common appellation given now to these writings is The Bible. This is a Greek word signifying *book.* It is given to the Scriptures by way of eminence, to denote that this is the Book of books, as being infinitely superior to every unassisted production of the human mind. In the same way, the name *Koran* or *reading* is given to the writings of Mohammed, denoting that they are the chief writings to be *read*, or eminently the *reading.*

The most common and general division of the Bible is into the Old and New Testaments. The word *testament* with us means a *will;* an instrument in writing, by which a person declares his *will* in relation to his property after his death. This is not, however, its meaning when applied to the Scriptures. It is taken from the Greek translation of the Hebrew word meaning *covenant*, *compact*, or *agreement.* The word is applied to the *covenant* or *compact* which God made with the Jews to be their God, and thus primarily denotes the agreement, the compact, the promises, the institutions of the old dispensation, and then the *record* of that compact in the writings of Moses and the Prophets. The name "Old Testament," or "Old Covenant," therefore, denotes the books containing the records of God's covenant with his people, or his dispensations under the Mosaic or Jewish state. The phrase New Covenant, or Testament, denotes the books which contain the record of his *new* covenant or compact with his people under the Messiah, or since Christ came. We find mention made of *the Book of the Covenant* in Ex. xxiv. 7, and in the New Testament the word is once used (2 Co. iii. 14) with an undoubted reference to the sacred books of the Jews. By whom, or at what time, these terms were first used to designate the two divisions of the sacred Scriptures, is not certainly known. There can be no doubt, however, of the great antiquity of the application.

The Jews divided the Old Testament into three parts, called The Law, The Prophets, and The Hagiographa, or the holy writings.

This division is noticed by our Saviour in Lu. xxiv. 44,[1] "All things must be fulfilled which were written in the law of Moses and in the Prophets, and in the Psalms, concerning me." Josephus, the Jewish historian, also makes mention of the same division.[2] "We have," says he, "only twenty-two books which are to be believed to be of divine authority; of which five are the books of Moses. From the death of Moses to the reign of Artaxerxes, son of Xerxes, king of Persia, the prophets who were the successors of Moses have written in thirteen books. The remaining four books contain hymns to God and documents of life for the use of men." It is probable that precisely the same books were not always included in the same division; but there can be no doubt that the *division* itself was always retained. The division into twenty-two books was made partly, no doubt, for the convenience of the memory. This was the number of letters in the Hebrew alphabet. The English Bible contains thirty-nine instead of twenty-two books in the Old Testament. The number which Josephus reckons may be accurately made out as follows: The first division, comprehending the five books of Moses, or THE LAW. The second, including 1st, Joshua; 2d, Judges, with Ruth; 3d, Samuel; 4th, Kings; 5th, Isaiah; 6th, Jeremiah, with Lamenations; 7th, Ezekiel; 8th, Daniel; 9th, the twelve minor prophets; 10th, Job; 11th, Ezra, including Nehemiah; 12th, Esther; 13th, Chronicles: these thirteen books were called THE PROPHETS. The four remaining will be Psalms, Proverbs, Ecclesiastes, and the Song of Solomon. In regard to the second division, it is a fact well known that the twelve smaller prophets, from Hosea to Malachi, were for convenience uniformly united in one volume; that the small books of Ruth and Lamentations were attached to the larger works mentioned, and that Ezra and Nehemiah were long reckoned as one book.

The arrangement of the books of the Bible has not always been the same. The order followed in the English Bible is taken from the Greek translation called the Septuagint. Probably the best way to read the Bible is to read the books as nearly as possible in the order in which they were written. Thus Isaiah informs us (Is. i. 1) that his prophecies were delivered in the reigns of Uzziah, Jotham, Ahaz, and Hezekiah; and, to be correctly understood, they should be read in connection with the record of those reigns in Kings and Chronicles.

The names of most of the books in the Bible are taken from the Greek translation above mentioned.

The books of the Bible were anciently written without any breaks, or divisions into chapters and verses. For convenience the Jews early divided the Old Testament into greater and smaller sections. These sections in the law and prophets were read in the worship of the synagogues. The New Testament was also early divided in a similar manner.

The division into chapters and verses is of recent origin. It was first adopted in the 13th century by Cardinal Hugo, who wrote a celebrated commentary on the Scriptures. He divided the Latin Vulgate, the version used in the Church of Rome, into chapters nearly the same as those which now exist in our English translation. These chapters

[1] See Note on that place.

[2] *Against Apion.*

he divided into smaller sections by placing the letters A, B, C, &c., at equal distances from each other in the margin.

The division into verses was not made until a still later period. The division of Cardinal Hugo into chapters became known to Rabbi Nathan, a distinguished Jew, who adopted it for the Hebrew Bible, and placed the Hebrew letters, used also as numerals, in the margin. This was used by Rabbi Nathan in publishing a concordance, and adopted by Athias in a printed edition of the Hebrew Bible in 1661.

The verses into which the New Testament is divided are still more modern, and are an imitation of those used by Rabbi Nathan in the fifteenth century. This division was invented and first used by Stephens in an edition of the New Testament printed in 1551. The division was made as an amusement while he was on a journey from Lyons to Paris, during the intervals in which he rested in travelling. It has been adopted in all the subsequent editions of the Bible.

In regard to this division into chapters and verses, it is clear that they are of no authority whatever. It has been doubted whether the sacred writers used *any* points or divisions of any kind. It is certain that they were wholly unacquainted with those now in use. It is farther evident that these divisions have not been judiciously made in all cases. The sense is often interrupted by the close of a chapter, and still oftener by the break in the verses. In *reading* the Scriptures little regard should be had to this division. It is of use now only for reference; and, inaccurate as it is, it must evidently be substantially retained. All the books that have been printed for three hundred years, which refer to the Bible, have made their references to these chapters and verses; and to attempt any change now would be to render almost useless a great part of the religious books in our language, and to introduce inextricable confusion in all attempts to quote the Bible.

The first translation of the Old Testament was made about the year 270 before the Christian era. It was made at Alexandria in Egypt into the Greek language, and probably for the use of the Jews who were scattered among Pagan nations. Ancient writers inform us, indeed, that it was made at the command of Ptolemy Philadelphus, to be deposited in the Library at Alexandria. It bears internal marks of having been made by different individuals, and no doubt at different times. It came to be extensively used in Judea, and no small part of the quotations in the New Testament were taken from it. There is no doubt that the apostles were familiar with it; and as it had obtained general currency, they chose to quote it rather than translate the Hebrew for themselves. It is called the Septuagint, or the version by the seventy, from a tradition that seventy elders of Israel, deputed for that purpose, were employed in making the translation.[1]

The language spoken by our Saviour and his apostles was a corruption of the Hebrew, a mixture of that and the language spoken in Chaldee, called Syro-Chaldaic, or more commonly the Syriac. The reason why the New Testament was not written in this language was, that the Greek had become the common language used throughout

[1] For an account of this translation, see Introduction to my Notes on Isaiah, vol. i. pages 46, 47.

the Eastern nations subject to the Romans. This general use of the Greek language was produced by the invasion and conquest of those nations by Alexander the Great, about 330 years before Christ. The New Testament was, however, early translated into the Syriac language. A translation is now extant in that language, held in great veneration by Syrian Christians, said to have been made in the first century, or in the age of the apostles, and acknowledged by all to have been made before the close of the second century, and is one of the most valuable translations of the New Testament ever made. It has been translated into English by the late Dr. Murdock.

About the beginning of the fourth century the Bible was translated into Latin by Jerome. This translation was made in consequence, as he says, of the incorrectness of a version then in use, called the *Italic.* The translation made by Jerome, now called the Latin Vulgate, is the authorized version of the Church of Rome.[1]

The Bible was translated by Luther in the beginning of the Reformation. This translation has done much to fix the German language, and is now the received version among the Lutheran churches.

There have been many other translations of the Bible, and there are many more still in progress. More than one hundred and fifty translations of the whole Bible, or parts of it, have been made during the last half century. Those which have been mentioned, together with the English, have been, however, the principal, and are most relied on as faithful exhibitions of the meaning of the sacred Scriptures.

The English translation of the Bible now in use was made in the reign of James I. This translation was intended only as an improvement of those previously in existence. A short account of the translation of the Bible into our own language cannot fail to be interesting.

It is not easy to ascertain the precise time when the gospel was introduced into Britain, or when the inhabitants were first in possession of the Bible. The earliest version of which we have any account is a translation of the Psalms into the Saxon language about the year 706; but the principal translation at that early period was made by the "venerable Bede," about the year 730. He translated the whole Bible into the Saxon language.

The first English translation of the Bible was executed about the year 1290, by some unknown individual. About the year 1380, John Wickliffe, the morning star of the Reformation, translated the entire Bible into English from the Latin. The great labour and expense of transcribing books before the invention of printing probably prevented a very extensive circulation of the Scriptures among the people.[2] Yet the translation of Wickliffe is known to have produced a vast effect on the minds of the people. Knowledge was sought for with avidity. The minds of the people were beginning to be opened to the abominations of the Church of Rome, and the national mind was preparing for the great change which followed in the days of Luther. So deep was the impression made by Wickliffe's translation, and so dan-

[1] For an account of this version, see also my Notes on Isaiah, vol. i. pages 47, 48.

[2] So great was the expense of transcribing the Bible at that time, that the price of one of Wickliffe's New Testaments was not less than forty pounds sterling, or one hundred and seventy-seven dollars seventy-eight cents of our money. And it should be matter of devout gratitude to God that, by the art of printing, the New Testament can now be obtained for the trifling sum of ten cents, and the entire Bible for twenty-five.

gerous was it thought to be to the interest of the Romish religion, that a bill was brought into the House of Lords for the purpose of suppressing it. The bill was rejected through the influence of the Duke of Lancaster, and this gave encouragement to the friends of Wickliffe to publish a more correct translation of the Bible. At a convocation, however, held at Oxford in 1408, it was decreed that no one should translate any text of the Holy Scripture into English by way of a book, or little book, or tract, and that no book of this kind should be read that was composed in the time of John Wickliffe, or since his death. This decree led the way to a great persecution, and many persons were punished severely, and some even with death, for reading the Bible in English. The *Bible* translated by Wickliffe was never printed. Some years since the New Testament was printed in England.[1]

For the first printed English translation of the Scriptures we are indebted to William Tindal. He printed this translation at Antwerp in Flanders, and the copies were brought thence into England. So great was the opposition to this by the Roman Catholic clergy, that the Bishop of London endeavoured to buy up whole editions as fast as they were printed, to burn them. This, however, produced little effect. Copies of the New Testament were multiplied. It is said that on one occasion Sir Thomas More, then Chancellor of England, asked how Tindal contrived to maintain himself abroad: to which it was replied that the Bishop of London supported him by purchasing the Scriptures as fast as they could be printed.

In 1535 the whole Bible, translated into English, was printed in folio, and dedicated to the king, by Miles Coverdale. This was the first English translation of the Bible allowed by royal authority.

Various editions and translations of the Scriptures, with various degrees of correctness, were printed in successive years, till, in 1568, the edition appeared which was called "the Bishop's Bible," or "the great English Bible." This was prepared by royal authority. It was the work of much care. Different learned men undertook to translate different parts of the Bible, and after those portions had been carefully

[1] The following is a specimen of this translation:—

Matthew, chap. v.—And Jhesus seynge the people, went up into an hil; and whanne he was sett, his disciplis camen to him. And he openyde his mouthe, and taughte them; and seide, Blessid be pore men in spirit; for the kyngdom of hevenes is hereun.* Blessid ben mylde men: for thei schulen weelde the erthe. Blessid ben thei that mournen: for thei schal be comfortid. Blessid be thei that hungren and thirsten rigtwisnesse:† for thei schal be fulfilled. Blessid ben merciful men: for thei schul gete mercy. Blessid ben thei that ben of clene herte: for thei schulen se god. Blessid ben pesible men: for thei schulen be clepid goddis children. Blessid ben thei that suffren persecucioun for rightwisnesse: for the kyngdom of hevenes is hern. Ye schul be blessid whanne men schul curse you, and schul pursue you: and schul seye al yvel agens you liynge for me. Joie ye and be ye glade: for your meede is plenteous in hevenes: for so thei han pursued also prophets that weren bifore you. Ye ben salt of the erthe, that if the salt vanishe awey wherynne schal it be salted? to nothing it is worth over, no but it be cast out, and be defoulid of men. Ye ben light of the world, a citee sett on an hill may not be hid. Ne me teendith not a lanterne and puttith it under a bushel; but on a candlestik that it give light to alle that ben in the hous. So, schyne your light bifore men, that thei see youre gode workis, and glorifie your fadir that is in hevenes. Nyle ghe deme that I cam to undo the Lawe or the prophetis, I cam not to undo the lawe but to fulfille. Forsothe I sey to you till hevene and erthe passe, oon lettre, or oon title, schal not passe fro the Lawe till alle thingis be don. Therefore he that brekith oon of these leeste maundementis, and techith thus men, schal be clepid the Leest in the rewme of hevenes; but he that doth and techith, schal be clepid greet in the kyngdom of hevenes.—*Baber's Edit.*

* Theirs.] † Rightfulnesse, MS. *plures.*

compared, the whole was printed, and directed to be used as an authorized English translation of the Scriptures. This, after being reprinted many times, and after being in use for half a century, was succeeded by the translation at present in use.

As this is, in many respects, the most important of all English translations of the sacred Scriptures, it is proper to dwell more fully on the circumstances under which it was made.

It was undertaken by the authority of King James I. of England. He came to the throne in 1603. Several objections having been made to the "Bishop's Bible," then in general use, he ordered a new translation to be made. This work he committed to fifty-four men; but, before the translation was commenced, seven of them had either died or had declined the task, so that it was actually accomplished by forty-seven. All of them were eminently distinguished for their piety, and for their profound acquaintance with the original languages. This company of men was divided into six classes, and to each class was allotted a distinct part of the Bible to be translated. "Ten were to meet at Westminster, and to translate from Genesis to the end of the second book of Kings. Eight assembled at Cambridge, and were to translate the remaining historical books, the Psalms, Job, Canticles, and Ecclesiastes. At Oxford seven were to translate the four greater Prophets, the Lamentations of Jeremiah, and the twelve minor Prophets. The four Gospels, the Acts of the Apostles, and the Revelation, were assigned to another company of eight at Oxford, and the Epistles were allotted to a company of seven at Westminster. Lastly, another company at Cambridge were to translate the Apocrypha."

To these companies the king gave instructions to guide them in their work, of which the following is the substance:

The Bishop's Bible, then used, to be followed, and to be altered as little as the original would permit.

The names of the sacred writers to be retained as they were commonly used.

When a word had different significations, that to be kept which had been most commonly used by the fathers and most eminent writers.

No alteration to be made in the chapters and verses. No marginal notes to be affixed, except to explain the Greek and Hebrew words that could not be briefly and fitly explained in the text. Reference to parallel places to be set down in the margin.

Each man of a company to take the same chapters and translate them according to the best of his abilities; and when this was done all were to meet together and compare their translations, and agree which should be regarded as correct.

Each book, when thus translated and approved, to be sent to every other company for their approbation.

Besides this, the translators were authorized, in cases of great difficulty, to send letters to any learned men in the kingdom to obtain their opinion.

In this manner the Bible was translated into English. First, each individual translated each book allotted to his company. Second, the readings to be adopted were agreed upon by that company assembled together. Third, the book thus finished was sent to each of the other companies to be examined. At these meetings one read the English, and the rest held in their hands some Bible of Hebrew, Greek, Latin, French, Spanish, &c. If they found any fault, says Selden, they spoke; if not, he read on.

The translation was commenced in 1607, and completed in about three years. At the end of that time three copies of it were sent to London. Here a committee of six revised the work, which was afterward revised by Dr. Smith, who wrote the preface, and by Dr. Bilson. It was first printed in 1611 at London by Robert Barker.

From this account it is clear that no ordinary care was taken to furnish to English readers a correct translation of the sacred Scriptures. No version of the Bible was ever made under more happy auspices, and it would now be impossible to furnish another translation in our language under circumstances so propitious. Whether we contemplate the number, the learning, or the piety of the men employed in it; the cool deliberation with which it was executed; the care taken that it should secure the approbation of the most learned men in a country that embosomed a vast amount of literature; the harmony with which they conducted their work, or the comparative perfection of the translation, we see equal cause of gratitude to the great Author of the Bible that we have so pure a translation of his word.

From this time the English language became fixed. More than two hundred years have elapsed, and yet the simple and majestic purity and power of the English tongue is expressed in the English translation of the Bible as clearly as when it was given to the world. It has become the standard of our language, and nowhere can the purity and expressive dignity of this language be so fully found as in the sacred Scriptures.

The friends of this translation have never claimed for it inspiration or infallibility. Yet it is the concurrent testimony of all who are competent to express an opinion, that no translation of the Bible into any language has preserved so faithfully the sense of the original as the English. Phrases there may be, and it is confessed there are, which modern criticism has shown not to express the exact meaning of the original; but, as a whole, it indubitably stands unrivalled. Nor is it probable that any translation can now supply its place, or improve upon its substantial correctness. The fact that it has for two hundred years poured light into the minds of millions, and guided the steps of generation after generation in the way to heaven, has given to it somewhat of the venerableness which appropriately belongs to a book of God. Successive ages may correct some of its few unimportant errors, may throw light on some of its obscure passages; but to the consummation of all things it must stand, wherever the English language is spoken, as the purest specimen of its power to give utterance to the meaning of ancient tongues, and of the simple and pure majesty of the language which we speak.

These remarks are made, because it is easy for men who dislike the plain doctrines of the Bible, and for those ignorant of the true history of its translation, to throw out insinuations of its unfaithfulness. From various quarters are often heard demands for a new translation. I by no means assert the entire infallibility, much less the inspiration, of the English translation of the Bible; yet of its general faithfulness to the original there can be no doubt. It would be easy to multiply testimonies of the highest authority to this fact. But the general testimony of the world; the profound regard paid to it by men of the purest character and most extensive learning; the fact that it has warmed the hearts of the pious, ministered to the comforts of the wretched and the dying, and guided the steps of millions to glory for two hundred years, and that it now commands the high regard of Christians of so many different denominations, evinces that it is to no ordinary extent faithful to the original, and has a claim on the continued regard of coming generations.

It is perfectly clear, also, that it would be impossible *now* to translate the Scriptures into the English language under so favourable circumstances as those which attended the translation in the time of James I. No set of men could so command the confidence of the Christian world; no convention who claim the Christian name could be formed competent to the task, or if formed, could prosecute the work with harmony; no single denomination could make a translation that would secure the undisputed respect of others. The probability is, therefore, that while the English language is spoken, and as far as it is used, the English Bible will continue to form the faith and direct the lives of those who use that language, and that the words which now pour light into *our* minds will continue to illuminate the understandings and mould the feelings of unnumbered millions in their path to immortal life.

PREFACE

TO THE GOSPEL ACCORDING TO MATTHEW

THE word Gospel means *good news*, or *a joyful message*. It commonly signifies the message itself; but it is here used to denote *the book* containing the record of the message. The title "saint," given to the sacred writers of the New Testament, is of Roman Catholic origin, and is of no authority.

It has been pretty generally believed that Matthew wrote his Gospel in his native tongue; that is, the language of Palestine. That language was not pure Hebrew, but a mixture of the Hebrew, Chaldaic, and Syriac, commonly called *Syro-Chaldaic* or *Aramæan*. This language our Saviour undoubtedly used in his conversation;[1] and his disciples would naturally use this language also, unless there were good reasons why they should write in a foreign tongue. It is agreed that the remainder of the New Testament was written in Greek. The reason for this, in preference to the native language of the writers, was that Greek was the language then generally spoken and understood throughout the eastern countries conquered by Alexander the Great, and particularly in Judea, and in the regions where the apostles first laboured.

The Christian fathers, without any exception, assert that Matthew wrote his Gospel for the use of the Christians in Palestine, and say that it was written in the Hebrew dialect. It should be remarked, however, that many modern critics of much eminence do not suppose the evidence that Matthew wrote in Hebrew to be decisive, and believe that there is sufficient proof that, like the other writers of the New Testament, Matthew wrote in Greek. See Lardner's Works, vol. v. p. 308–318, London edition, 1829.

The Gospel of Matthew exists now, however, only in Greek. The original Hebrew, or Syro-Chaldaic, if it was written in that language, has been designedly laid aside or undesignedly lost. The question, then, naturally arises, Who is the author of the *Greek* translation which we possess? and is it to be regarded as of divine authority?

It has been conjectured by some that Matthew himself furnished a Greek translation of the Hebrew. This conjecture, in itself probable enough, is destitute, however, of testimony to support it. Athanasius, one of the early fathers, says that it was translated by "James, the brother of our Lord according to the flesh." Papias, another of the early fathers, says that "each one translated it as he was able." If James translated it, there can be no question about its inspiration and canonical authority. Nor does it affect the question of its inspiration, even if we are ignorant of the name of the translator. The proper

[1] See instances in Mar. vii. 34, and Mat. xxvii. 46.

inquiry is whether it had such evidence of inspiration as to be satisfactory to the Church in the times when they were under the direction of the apostles. That it *had* such evidence, none acquainted with ancient history will doubt.

Epiphanius says that the Gospel by Matthew was written while Peter and Paul were preaching at Rome. This was about the year of our Lord 63, about the time of the destruction of Jerusalem. It is now generally supposed that this Gospel was written about this time. There is very clear evidence *in* the Gospel that it was written before the destruction of Jerusalem. The destruction of the Holy City is clearly and minutely foretold, but there is not the slightest intimation in it that these predictions had been accomplished—a thing which we should naturally expect if the Gospel was not written until after these calamities came upon the Jews. Comp. Ac. xi. 28. It has been till lately uniformly regarded as having been written before either of the other evangelists. Some of late have, however, endeavoured to show that the Gospel by Luke was written first. All testimony, and all ancient arrangements of the books, are against the opinion; and when such is the fact, it is of little consequence to attend to other arguments.

In all copies of the New Testament, and in all translations, this Gospel has been placed first. This, it is probable, would not have been done had not Matthew published his Gospel before any other was written.

Matthew, the writer of this Gospel, called also Levi, son of Alphæus, was a publican, or tax-gatherer, under the Romans. See Notes on Mat. ix. 9; Lu. v. 27. Of his life and death little is certainly known. Socrates, a writer of the fifth century, says that he went to Ethiopia after the apostles were scattered abroad from Judea, and died a martyr in a city called Nadebbar, but by what kind of death is altogether uncertain. However, others speak of his preaching and dying in Parthia or Persia, and the diversity of their accounts seems to show that they are all without good foundation. See Lardner's Works, vol. v. p. 296, 297.

THE
GOSPEL ACCORDING TO MATTHEW

CHAPTER I.

THE book of the [a]generation of
Jesus Christ, the [b]son of David, [c]the son of Abraham.

a Lu.3.23, &c. *b* Ps.132.11; ch.22.45; Ac.2.30. *c* Ge.22.18; Ga.3.16.

2 Abraham[d] begat Isaac; and
[e]Isaac begat Jacob; and [f]Jacob begat Judas and his brethren;
3 And [g]Judas begat Phares and

d Ge.21.2-5. *e* Ge.25.26. *f* Ge.29.35, &c. *g* Ge. 38.29,30, &c.

1. *The book of the generation.* This is the proper title of the chapter. It is the same as to say, "the account of the ancestry or family, or the genealogical table of Jesus Christ." The phrase is common in Jewish writings. Compare Ge. v. 1. "This is the book of the generations of Adam," *i.e.* the genealogical table of the family or descendants of Adam. See also Ge. vi. 9. The Jews, moreover, as we do, kept such tables of their own families, and it is probable that this was copied from the record of the family of Joseph. ¶ *Jesus.* See Notes on ver. 21. ¶ *Christ.* The word *Christ* is a Greek word, signifying *anointed.* The Hebrew word signifying the same is *Messiah.* Hence, Jesus is called either the *Messiah*, or the *Christ*, meaning the same thing. The Jews speak of *the Messiah;* Christians speak of him as *the Christ.* Anciently, when kings and priests were set apart to their office, they were *anointed with oil*, Le. iv. 3; vi. 20; Ex. xxviii. 41; xxix. 7; 1 Sa. ix. 16; xv. 1; 2 Sa. xxiii. 1. To *anoint*, therefore, means often the same as to *consecrate*, or to set apart to an office. Hence those thus set apart are said to be *anointed*, or to be the anointed of God. It is for this reason that the name is given to the Lord Jesus. Comp. Notes on Da. ix. 24. He was set apart by God to be the King, and High-priest, and Prophet of his people. Anointing with oil was, moreover, supposed to be emblematic of the influences of the Holy Spirit; and as God gave him the Spirit *without measure* (Jn. iii. 34), so he is called peculiarly the Anointed of God. ¶ *The Son of David.* The word *son* among the Jews had a great variety of significations. It means literally a son; then a grandson; a descendant; an adopted son; a disciple, or one who is an object of tender affection—one who is to us *as a son.* In this place it means a *descendant* of David; or one who was of the *family* of David. It was important to trace the genealogy of Jesus up to David, because the promise had been made that the Messiah should be of his family, and all the Jews expected that it would be so. It would be impossible, therefore, to convince a *Jew* that Jesus was the Messiah, unless it could be shown that he was descended from *David.* See Je. xxiii. 5; Ps. cxxxii. 10, 11, compared with Ac. xiii. 23, and Jn. vii. 42. ¶ *The son of Abraham.* The descendant of Abraham. The promise was made to Abraham also. See Ge. xii. 3; xxi. 12; compare He. xi. 13; Ga. iii. 16. The Jews expected that the Messiah would be descended from him; and it was important, therefore, to trace the genealogy up to him also. Though Jesus was of humble birth, yet he was descended from most illustrious ancestors. Abraham, the father of the faithful—"the beauteous model of an Eastern prince," and David, the sweet psalmist of Israel, the conqueror, the magnificent and victorious leader of the people of God, were both among his ancestors. From these two persons, the most eminent for piety, and the most renowned for their excellencies of all the men of antiquity, sacred or profane, the Lord Jesus was descended; and though his birth and life were humble, yet they who regard an illustrious descent as of value, may find here all that is to be admired in piety, purity, patriotism, splendour, dignity, and renown.

2–16. These verses contain the genealogy of Jesus. Luke also (ch. iii.) gives a genealogy of the Messiah. No two passages of Scripture have caused more difficulty than these, and various attempts have been made to explain them. There are two sources of difficulty in these catalogues. 1st. Many

Zara of Thamar; and [h]Phares begat
Esrom; and [i]Esrom begat Aram;
4 And Aram begat Aminadab;
and [k]Aminadab begat Naasson;
and [l]Naasson begat Salmon;
5 And [m]Salmon begat Booz of
Rachab; and [n]Booz begat Obed
of Ruth; and Obed begat Jesse;
6 And [o]Jesse begat David the
king; and [p]David the king begat
Solomon of her *that had been the
wife* of Urias;
7 And [q]Solomon begat Roboam;
and Roboam begat Abia; and Abia
begat Asa;
8 And Asa begat Josaphat; and
Josaphat begat Joram; and Joram
begat Ozias;
9 And Ozias begat Joatham; and
Joatham begat Achaz; and Achaz
begat Ezekias;
10 And [r]Ezekias begat Manasses;
and Manasses begat Amon; and
Amon begat Josias;

h Ge.46.12. *i* Ru.4.19. *k* 1 Ch.2.10; Nu.1.7. *l* Ru.4.20. *m* Jos.6.25; Ru.4.21. *n* Ru.4.13. *o* 1 Sa.17.12. *p* 2 Sa.12.24. *q* 1 Ch.3.10, &c. *r* 2 Ki.20.21; 1 Ch.3.13.

names that are found in the Old Testament are here omitted; and, 2d, the tables of Matthew and Luke appear in many points to be different. From Adam to Abraham Matthew has mentioned no names, and Luke only has given the record. From Abraham to David the two tables are alike. Of course there is no difficulty in reconciling these two parts of the tables. The difficulty lies in that part of the genealogy from David to Christ. There they are entirely different. They are manifestly different lines. Not only are the *names* different, but Luke has mentioned, in this part of the genealogy, no less than forty-two names, while Matthew has recorded but twenty-seven.

Various ways have been proposed to explain this difficulty, but it must be admitted that none of them is perfectly satisfactory. It does not comport with the design of these Notes to enter minutely into an explanation of the perplexities of these passages. All that can be done is to suggest the various ways in which attempts have been made to explain them. 1. It is remarked that in nothing are mistakes more likely to occur than in such tables. From the similarity of names, and the different names by which the same person is often called, and from many other causes, errors would be more likely to creep into genealogical tables than in other writings. Some of the difficulties may have possibly occurred from this cause. 2. Most interpreters have supposed that Matthew gives the genealogy of *Joseph*, and Luke that of *Mary*. They were both descended from David, but in different lines. This solution derives some plausibility from the fact that the promise was made to *David*, and as Jesus was not the son of Joseph, it was important to show that *Mary* was also descended from him. But though this solution is plausible, and *may be* true, yet it wants evidence. It cannot, however, be proved that this was *not* the design of Luke. 3. It has been said also that Joseph was the *legal* son and heir of *Heli*, though the *real* son of Jacob, and that thus the two lines terminated in him. This was the explanation suggested by most of the Christian fathers, and on the whole is the most satisfactory. It was a law of the Jews that if a man died without children, his brother should marry his widow. Thus the two lines might have been intermingled. According to this solution, which was first proposed by Africanus, Matthan, descended from Solomon, married Estha, of whom was born Jacob. After Matthan's death, Matthat being of the same tribe, but of another family, married his widow, and of this marriage Heli was born. Jacob and Heli were therefore children of the same mother. Heli dying without children, his brother Jacob married his widow, and begat *Joseph*, who was thus the *legal* son of Heli. This is agreeable to the account in the two evangelists. Matthew says that *Jacob begat Joseph;* Luke says that Joseph was *the son of Heli*, i. e. was his *legal* heir, or was reckoned in law to be his son. This can be seen by the plan on the next page, showing the nature of the connection.

Though these solutions may not seem to be entirely satisfactory, yet there are two additional considerations which should set the matter at rest, and lead to the conclusion that the narratives are not really inconsistent. 1. No difficulty was ever found, or alleged, in regard to them, by any of the early enemies of

11 And [1]Josias begat Jechonias
and his brethren, about the time
they were carried away to Babylon;

[1] Some read *Josias begat Jakim, and Jakim begat Jechonias.*

12 And after they were brought
to Babylon, [s]Jechonias begat Salathiel; and [t]Salathiel begat Zorobabel;

s 1 Ch.3.17, &c. t Ne.12.1.

Christianity. There is no evidence that they ever adduced them as containing a contradiction. Many of those enemies were acute, learned, and able; and they show by their writings that they were not *indisposed* to detect all the errors that could possibly be found in the sacred narrative. Now it is to be remembered that the *Jews* were fully competent to show that these tables were incorrect, if they were really so; and it is clear that they were fully disposed, if possible, to do it. The fact, therefore, that it is not done, is clear evidence that *they* thought it to be correct. The same may be said of the acute pagans who wrote against Christianity. None of them have called in question the correctness of these tables. This is full proof that, in a time when it was easy to understand these tables, they were believed to be correct. 2. The evangelists are not responsible for the *correctness* of these tables. They are responsible only for what was their real and professed object to do. What was

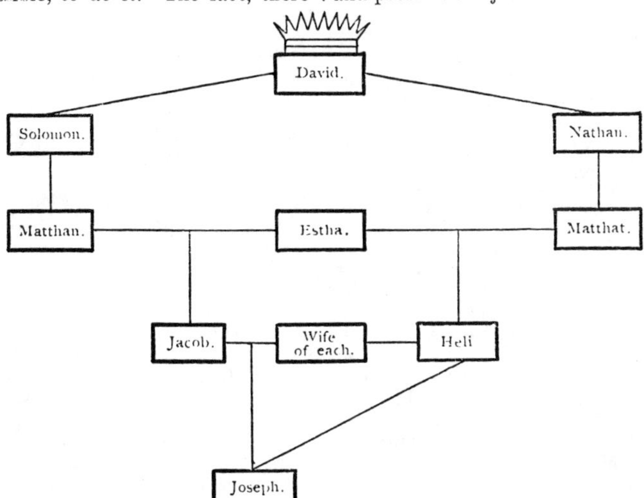

that object? It was to prove to the satisfaction of *the Jews* that Jesus was descended from *David*, and therefore that there was no argument from his ancestry that he was not the promised Messiah. Now to make this out, it was not necessary, nor would it have conduced to their argument, to have formed a *new* table of genealogy. All that could be done was to go to the *family records*—to the *public tables*, and copy them as they were *actually* kept, and show that, *according to the records of the nation*, Jesus was descended from David. This, among the Jews, would be full and decided testimony in the case. And this was doubtless done. In the same way, the records of a family among us, as they are kept by the family, are proof in courts of justice now of the birth, names, &c., of individuals. Nor is it necessary or proper for a court to call them in question or to attempt to correct them. So the tables here are good evidence to the only point that the writers wished to establish: that is, *to show to the Jews that Jesus of Nazareth was descended from David*. The only inquiry which can *now* be fairly made is whether they copied those tables *correctly*. It is clear that no man can prove that they did *not* so copy them, and therefore that no one can adduce them as an argument against the correctness of the New Testament.

17. *So all the generations*, &c. This

13 And Zorobabel begat Abiud;
and Abiud begat Eliakim; and
Eliakim begat Azor;
14 And Azor begat Sadoc; and
Sadoc begat Achim; and Achim
begat Eliud;
15 And Eliud begat Eleazar;
and Eleazar begat Matthan; and
Matthan begat Jacob;
16 And Jacob begat Joseph the
husband of Mary, of whom was
born Jesus, who is called Christ.
17 So all the generations from
Abraham to David *are* fourteen
generations; and from David until
the carrying away into Babylon
are fourteen generations; and from
the carrying away into Babylon

---

division of the names in the genealogical tables was doubtless adopted for the purpose of aiding the memory. It was common among the Jews; and other similar instances are preserved. The Jews were destitute of books besides the Old Testament, and they had but few copies of that among them, and those chiefly in their synagogues. They would therefore naturally devise plans to keep up the remembrance of the principal facts in their history. One method of doing this was to *divide* the tables of genealogy into portions of equal length, to be committed to memory. This greatly facilitated the remembrance of the names. A man who wished to commit to memory the names of a regiment of soldiers would naturally divide it into companies and platoons, and this would greatly facilitate his work. This was doubtless the reason in the case before us. And, though it is not strictly accurate, yet it was the *Jewish* way of keeping their records, and answered their purpose. There were three leading persons and events that nearly, or quite, divided their history into equal portions: Abraham, David, and the Babylonish captivity. From one to the other was *about* fourteen generations, and by omitting a few names it was sufficiently accurate to be made a general guide or directory in recalling the principal events in their history.

In counting these divisions, however, it will be seen that there is some difficulty in making out the number *fourteen* in each division. This may be explained in the following manner: In the first division, Abraham is the first and David the last, making together fourteen. In the second series, David would naturally be placed first, and the fourteen was completed in *Josiah*, about the time of the captivity, as sufficiently near for the purpose of convenient computation, 2 Ch. xxxv. In the third division Josiah would naturally be placed first, and the number was completed in Joseph; so that David and Josiah would be reckoned twice. This may be shown by the following table of the names:—

First division.	*Second division.*	*Third division.*
Abraham,	David,	Josias,
Isaac,	Solomon,	Jechonias,
Jacob,	Roboam,	Salathiel,
Judas,	Abia,	Zorobabel,
Phares,	Asa,	Abiud,
Esrom,	Josaphat,	Eliakim,
Aram,	Joram,	Azor,
Aminadab,	Ozias,	Sadoc,
Naasson,	Joatham,	Achim,
Salmon,	Achaz,	Eliud,
Booz,	Ezekias,	Eleazar,
Obed,	Manasses,	Matthan,
Jesse,	Amon,	Jacob,
David.	Josias.	Joseph.
——14	——14	——14

¶ *Carrying away into Babylon.* This refers to the captivity of Jerusalem, and the removal of the Jews to Babylon by Nebuchadnezzar, 588 years before Christ. See 2 Ch. xxxvi. Josiah was king when these calamities began to come upon the Jews, but the exact time of the seventy years of captivity did not commence until the eleventh year of Zedekiah's reign, or 32 years after the death of Josiah. Babylon was situated on the Euphrates, and was encompassed with walls which were about 60 miles in circuit, 87 feet broad, and 350 feet high, and the city was entered by a hundred brazen gates, 25 on each side. It was the capital of a vast empire, and the Jews remained there for seventy years. See my Notes on Isaiah xiii.

18. *Now the birth of Jesus Christ.* The circumstances attending his birth. ¶ *Was on this wise.* In this manner. ¶ *Espoused.* Betrothed, or engaged to be married. There was commonly an interval of ten or twevle months, among the Jews, between the contract of marriage and the celebration of the nuptials

unto Christ *are* fourteen generations.

18 Now the [u]birth of Jesus Christ was on this wise: When as his mother Mary was espoused to Joseph, *before they came together, she was found with child of the Holy Ghost.

19 Then Joseph her husband, being a just *man*, and not willing to make her a public example, was minded [v]to put her away privily.

20 But while he thought on these things, behold, the angel of the Lord appeared unto him in a dream, saying, [w]Joseph, thou son

u Lu.1.27, &c.
* 5th year before the account called *A.D.*

v De.24.1.
w ver.16.

(see Ge. xxiv. 55; Ju. xiv. 8; De. xx. 7), yet such was the nature of this engagement, that unfaithfulness to each other was deemed adultery. See De. xxii. 25, 28. ¶ *With child by the Holy Ghost.* See Note, Lu. i. 35.

19. *Her husband.* The word in the original does not imply that they were married. It means here the man to whom she was espoused. ¶ *A just* man. *Justice* consists in rendering to every man his own. Yet this is evidently not the character intended to be given here of Joseph. The meaning is that he was kind, tender, merciful; that he was so attached to Mary that he was not willing that she should be exposed to public shame. He sought, therefore, secretly to dissolve the connection, and to restore her to her friends without the punishment commonly inflicted on adultery. The word *just* has not unfrequently this meaning of mildness, or mercy. See 1 Jn. i. 9.; comp. Cicero, *De Fin.* 5, 23. ¶ *A public example.* To expose her to public shame or infamy. Adultery has always been considered a crime of a very heinous nature. In Egypt it was punished by cutting off the nose of the adulteress; in Persia the nose and ears were cut off; in Judea the punishment was death by stoning, Le. xx. 10; Eze. xvi. 38, 40; Jn. viii. 5. This punishment was also inflicted where the person was not married, but betrothed, De. xxi. 23, 24. In this case, therefore, the regular punishment would have been death in this painful and ignominious manner. Yet Joseph was a religious man—mild and tender; and he was not willing to *complain* of her to the magistrate, and expose her to death, but sought to avoid the shame, and to put her away privately. ¶ *Put her away privily.* The law of Moses gave the husband the power of divorce, De. xxiv. 1. It was customary in a bill of divorce to specify the causes for which the divorce was made, and witnesses were also present to testify to the divorce. But in this case, it seems, Joseph resolved to put her away *without specifying the cause;* for he was not willing to make her a public example. This is the meaning here of *privily.* Both to Joseph and Mary this must have been a great trial. Joseph was ardently attached to her, but her character was likely to be ruined, and he deemed it proper to separate her from him. Mary was innocent, but Joseph was not yet satisfied of her innocence. We may learn from this to put our trust in God. He will defend the innocent. Mary was in danger of being exposed to shame. Had she been connected with a cruel, passionate, and violent man, she would have died in disgrace. But God had so ordered it that she was betrothed to a man mild, amiable, and tender; and in due time Joseph was apprised of the truth in the case, and took his faithful and beloved wife to his bosom. Thus our only aim should be to preserve a conscience void of offence, and God will guard our reputation. We may be assailed by slander; circumstances may be against us; but in due time God will take care to vindicate our character and save us from ruin. See Ps. xxxvii. 5, 6.

20. *He thought on these things.* He did not act hastily. He did not take the course which the law would have *permitted* him to do, if he had been hasty, violent, or unjust. It was a case deeply affecting his happiness, his character, and the reputation and character of his chosen companion. God will guide the thoughtful and the anxious. And when *we* have looked patiently at a perplexed subject, and know not what to do, then God, as in the case of Joseph will interpose to lead us and direct our way. Ps. xxv. 9. ¶ *The angel of the Lord.* The word *angel* literally means a *messenger.* It is applied chiefly in the Scriptures to those invisible holy beings who have not fallen into sin; who live in heaven (1 Ti. v. 21; compare Jude 6);

of David, fear not to take unto thee Mary thy wife; for that which is [2]conceived in her is of the Holy Ghost.

21 And she shall bring forth a son, and thou shalt call his name [3]JESUS: for [x]he shall save his people from their sins.

22 Now all this was done, that it might be fulfilled which was

[2] begotten.

[3] i.e. *Saviour.* *x* Ac.5.31; 13.23,38.

and who are sent forth to minister to those who shall be heirs of salvation. See Notes on He. i. 13, 14, and on Da. ix. 21. The word is sometimes applied to *men*, as messengers (Lu. vii. 24; ix. 52; Ja. ii. 25); to the winds (Ps. civ. 4); to the pestilence (Ps. lxxviii. 49); or to whatever is appointed to *make known* or *to execute* the will of God. It is commonly applied, however, to the unfallen, happy spirits that are in heaven, whose dignity and pleasure it is to do the will of God. Various ways were employed by them in making known the will of God, by dreams, visions, assuming a human appearance, &c. ¶ *In a dream.* This was a common way of making known the will of God to the ancient prophets and people of God, Ge. xx. 3; xxx. 1, 11, 24; xxxvii. 5; xli. 1; 1 Ki. iii. 5: Dan. vii. 1; Job iv. 13-15; compare my Notes on Isaiah, vol. i. p. xi, xii, xiii. In what way it was ascertained that these dreams were from God cannot now be ascertained. It is sufficient for us to know that in this way many of the prophecies were communicated, and to remark that there is no evidence that we are to put reliance on *our* dreams. Dreams are wild, irregular movements of the mind when it is unshackled by reason, and it is mere superstition to suppose that God *now* makes known his will in this way. ¶ *Son of David.* Descendant of David. See ver. 1. The angel put him in mind of his relation to *David* perhaps to prepare him for the intelligence that Mary was to be the mother of the Messiah—the promised heir of David. ¶ *Fear not.* Do not hesitate, or have any apprehensions about her virtue and purity. Do not fear that she will be unworthy of you, or will disgrace you. ¶ *To take unto thee Mary thy wife.* To take her *as* thy wife; to recognize her as such, and to treat her as such. ¶ *For that which is conceived in her is of the Holy Ghost.* Is the direct creation of divine power. A body was thus prepared pure and holy, and free from the corruption of sin, in order that he might be qualified for his great work—the offering of a pure sacrifice to God. As this was necessary in order to the great work which he came to perform, Joseph is directed by an angel to receive her as pure and virtuous, and as every way worthy of his love. Comp. Notes on He. x. 5.

21. *His name JESUS.* The name *Jesus* is the same as *Saviour*. It is derived from the verb signifying *to save*. In Hebrew it is the same as *Joshua*. In two places in the New Testament it is used where it means Joshua, the leader of the Jews into Canaan, and in our translation the name *Joshua* should have been retained, Ac. vii. 45; He. iv. 8. It was a very common name among the Jews. ¶ *He shall save.* This expresses the same as the name, and on this account the name was given to him. He saves men by dying to redeem them; by giving the Holy Spirit to renew them (Jn. xvi. 7, 8); by his power in enabling them to overcome their spiritual enemies, in defending them from danger, in guiding them in the path of duty, in sustaining them in trials and in death; and he will raise them up at the last day, and exalt them to a world of purity and love. ¶ *His people.* Those whom the Father has given to him. The Jews were called the people of God because he had chosen them to himself, and regarded them as his peculiar and beloved people, separate from all the nations of the earth. Christians are called the people of Christ because it was the purpose of the Father to give them to him (Is. liii. 11; Jn. vi. 37); and because in due time he came to redeem them to himself, Tit. ii. 14; 1 Pe. i. 2. ¶ *From their sins.* This was the great business of Jesus in coming and dying. It was not to save men IN their sins, but FROM their sins. Sinners could not be happy in heaven. It would be a place of wretchedness to the guilty. The design of Jesus was, therefore, to save them *from* sin; and from this we may learn, 1st, That Jesus had a *design* in coming into the world. He came to save *his people;* and that design will surely be accomplished. It is impossible that in any part of it he should

spoken[y] of the Lord by the prophet, saying,
23 Behold, a virgin shall be with child, and shall bring forth a son, and [4]they shall call his name Emmanuel; which being interpreted, is, [z]God with us.
24 Then Joseph, being raised

y Is.7.14. 4 or, *his name shall be called.* z Jn. 1.14.

fail. 2d. We have no evidence that we are his people unless we are saved from the power and dominion of sin. A mere *profession* of being his people will not answer. Unless we give up our sins; unless we renounce the pride, pomp, and pleasure of the world, we have no evidence that we are the children of God. It is impossible that we should be Christians if we indulge in sin and live in the practice of any known iniquity. See 1 Jn. iii. 7, 8. 3d. That all professing Christians should feel that there is no salvation unless it is *from sin*, and that they can never be admitted to a holy heaven hereafter unless they are made pure, by the blood of Jesus, here.

22. *Now all this was done.* The prophecy here quoted is recorded in Is. vii. 14. See Notes on that passage. The prophecy was delivered about 740 years before Christ, in the reign of Ahaz, king of Judah. The land of Judea was threatened with an invasion by the united armies of Syria and Israel, under the command of Rezin and Pekah. Ahaz was alarmed, and seems to have contemplated calling in aid from Assyria to defend him. Isaiah was directed, in his consternation, to go to Ahaz, and tell him to ask a sign from God (Is. vii. 10, 11); that is, to look to *God* rather than to Assyria for aid. This he refused to do. He had not confidence in God, but feared that the land would be overrun by the armies of Syria (ver. 12), and relied only on the aid which he hoped to receive from Assyria. Isaiah answered that, in these circumstances, the Lord would himself give a sign, or a pledge, that the land should be delivered. The sign was, that a virgin should have a son, and that before that son would arrive to years of discretion, the land would be forsaken by these hostile kings. The prophecy was therefore designed *originally* to signify to Ahaz that the land would *certainly* be delivered from its calamities and dangers, and that the deliverance would not be long delayed. The land of *Syria* and *Israel, united* now in confederation, would be deprived of both their kings, and thus the land of Judah would be freed from the threatening danger. This appears to be the *literal* fulfilment of the passage in Isaiah. ¶ *Might be fulfilled.* It is more difficult to know in what sense this could be said to be *fulfilled* in the birth of Christ. To understand this, it may be remarked that the word *fulfilled* is used in the Scriptures and in other writings in many senses, of which the following are some: 1st. When a thing is *clearly predicted*, and comes to pass, as the destruction of Babylon, foretold in Is. xiii. 19–22; and of Jerusalem, in Mat. xxiv. 2d. When one thing is *typified* or shadowed forth by another, and when the event occurs, the type is said to be fulfilled. This was the case in regard to the types and sacrifices in the Old Testament, which were *fulfilled* by the coming of Christ. See He. ix. 3d. When prophecies of future events are expressed in language more elevated and full than the particular thing, at first denoted, demands. Or, in other words, when the language, though it may express one event, is also so full and rich as *appropriately* to express other events *in similar circumstances* and of similar import, they may be said to be *fulfilled.* Thus, *e.g.*, the last chapters of Isaiah, from the fortieth chapter, foretell the return of the Jews into Babylon, and every circumstance mentioned occurred in their return. But the language is more expanded and sublime than was necessary to express their return. It will also *express appropriately* a much more important and magnificent deliverance—that of the redeemed under the Messiah; and the return of the people of God to him, and the universal spread of the gospel; and therefore it may be said *to be fulfilled* in the coming of Jesus and the spread of the gospel. So, if there were any other magnificent and glorious events, still, *in similar circumstances*, and of like character, it might be said also that these prophecies were fulfilled in all of them. The language is so full and rich, and the promises are so grand, that they may appropriately express *all* these deliverances. This may be the sense in which

from sleep, did as the angel of the Lord had bidden him, and took unto him his wife:

25 And knew her not till she had brought [a]forth her first-born son: and he called his name [b]JESUS.

a Ex.13.2. b Lu.2.21.

---

the prophecy now under consideration may be said to have been fulfilled. 4th. Language is said to be fulfilled when, though it was used to express one event, it may be used also to express another. Thus a *fable* may be said to be fulfilled when an event occurs similar to the one concerning which it was first spoken. A parable has its fulfilment in all the cases to which it is applicable; and the same remark applies to a proverb, or to a declaration respecting human nature. The statement that "there is none that doeth good" (Ps. xiv. 3) was at first spoken of a particular race of wicked men. Yet it is applicable to others, and in this sense may be said to have been fulfilled. See Ro. iii. 10. In this use of the word *fulfilled*, it means, not that the passage was at first *intended* to apply *to this particular thing*, but that the words aptly or appropriately express the thing spoken of, and *may* be applied to it. We may say the same of this which was said of another thing, and thus the words express *both*, or *are fulfilled.* The writers of the New Testament seem occasionally to have used the word in this sense.

23. *Behold, a virgin shall be with child.* Matthew clearly understands this as applying literally *to a virgin.* Compare Lu. i. 34. It thus implies that the conception of Christ was *miraculous*, or that the body of the Messiah was *created* directly by the power of God, agreeably to the declaration in He. x. 5: "Wherefore, when he cometh into the world, he saith, Sacrifice and offering thou wouldest not, *but a body hast thou prepared me.*" ¶ *And they shall call his name Emmanuel.* That is, his name shall be so called. See Notes on Is. vii. 14. The word *Immanuel* is a Hebrew word, and means literally *God with us.* Matthew doubtless understands it as denoting that the Messiah was really "God with us," or that the divine nature was united with the human. He does not affirm that this was its meaning when used in reference to the child to whom it was first applied, but this is its signification as applicable to the Messiah. *It was fitly expressive of his character;* and in this sense it was fulfilled. When *first* used by Isaiah, it denoted simply that the birth of the child was a sign that God was with the Jews to deliver them. The Hebrews often incorporated the name of Jehovah, or God, into their proper names. Thus, Isaiah means "the salvation of Jehovah;" Eleazer, "help of God;" Eli, "my God," &c. But Matthew evidently intends more than was denoted by the simple use of such names. He had just given an account of the miraculous conception of Jesus; of his being begotten by the Holy Ghost. God was therefore his Father. He was divine as well as human. His appropriate name, therefore, was "God with us." And though the mere use of such a name would not prove that he had a divine nature, yet as *Matthew uses it*, and meant evidently to apply it, it *does* prove that Jesus was more than a man; that he was God as well as man. And it is this which gives glory to the plan of redemption. It is this which is the wonder of angels. It is this which makes the plan so vast, so grand, so full of instruction and comfort to Christians. See Phi. ii. 6–8. It is this which sheds such peace and joy into the sinner's heart; which gives him such security of salvation, and which renders the condescension of God in the work of redemption so great and his character so lovely.

"Till God in human flesh I see,
My thoughts no comfort find,
The holy, just, and sacred Three
Are terror to my mind.

"But if IMMANUEL's face appears,
My hope, my joy, begins.
His grace removes my slavish fears,
His blood removes my sins.'

For a full examination of the passage, see my Notes on Is. vii. 14.

24. *Being raised from sleep.* Having fully awoke. ¶ *Did as the angel of the Lord had bidden him.* That is, he took Mary to wife. Probably this was done immediately, as he was now convinced of her innocence, and he would not by delay leave any ground of suspicion that he had not confidence in her.

25. *Knew her not.* The doctrine of the virginity of Mary *before* the birth of Jesus is a doctrine of the Scriptures, and is very important to be believed. But the Bible does not affirm that she had no children afterward. Indeed, all

CHAPTER II.

NOW when Jesus was born* in Bethlehem of Judea, in the days of Herod the king, behold, there came wise men from the east to Jerusalem,

* 4th year before the account called *A.D.*

the accounts in the New Testament lead us to suppose that she had. See Notes on Mat. xiii. 55, 56. The language here evidently implies that she lived as the wife of Joseph after the birth of Jesus. ¶ *Her first-born son.* Her eldest son, or he that by the law had the privilege of birthright. This does not *of necessity* imply that she had other children, though it seems probable. It was the name given to the son which was first born, whether there were others or not. ¶ *His name JESUS.* This was given by divine appointment, ver. 21. It was conferred on him on the eighth day, at the time of his circumcision, Lu. ii. 21.

CHAPTER II.

1. *When Jesus was born.* See the full account of his birth in Lu. ii. 1–20. ¶ *In Bethlehem of Judea.* Bethlehem, the birthplace of Christ, was a small town about six miles south of Jerusalem. The word *Bethlehem* denotes "house of bread"—perhaps given to the place on account of its great fertility. It was also called *Ephrata*, a word supposed likewise to signify fertility, Ge. xxxv. 19; Ru. iv. 11; Ps. cxxxii. 6. It was called the city of David (Lu. ii. 4), because it was the city of his nativity, 1 Sa. xvi. 1, 18. It was called Bethlehem *of Judea*, to distinguish it from a town of the same name in Galilee, Jos. xix. 15. The soil of Bethlehem was noted for its fertility. Ancient travellers frequently spoke of its productions. The town is situated on an eminence, in the midst of hills and vales. At present it contains about two hundred houses, inhabited chiefly by Christians and Mohammedans, who live together in peace. About two hundred paces east of Bethlehem the place is still shown where our Saviour is supposed to have been born. There is a church and a convent there; and beneath the church a subterranean chapel, which is lighted by thirty-two lamps, which is said to be the place where was the stable in which Jesus was born, though no certain reliance is to be placed on the tradition which makes this the birthplace of the Saviour. ¶ *Herod the king.* Judea, where our Saviour was born, was a province of the Roman Empire. It was taken about 63 years before his birth by Pompey, and placed under tribute. Herod received his appointment from the Romans, and had reigned at the time of the birth of Jesus thirty-four years. Though he was permitted to be called *king*, yet he was in all respects dependent on the Roman emperor. He was commonly called Herod the Great because he had distinguished himself in the wars with Antigonus and his other enemies, and because he had evinced great talents in governing and defending his country, in repairing the temple, and in building and ornamenting the cities of his kingdom. He was, however, as much distinguished for his cruelty and his crimes as he was for his greatness. At this time Augustus was Emperor of Rome. The world was at peace. A large part of the known nations of the earth was united under the Roman emperor. Intercourse between different nations was easy and safe. Similar laws prevailed. The use of the Greek language was general throughout the world. All these circumstances combined to render this a favourable time to introduce the gospel, and to spread it through the earth; and the providence of God was remarkable in preparing the nations in this manner for the easy and rapid spread of the Christian religion. ¶ *Wise men.* The original word here is *magoi*, from which comes our word *magician*, now used in a bad sense, but not so in the original. The persons here denoted were philosophers, priests, or astronomers. They dwelt chiefly in Persia and Arabia. They were the learned men of the Eastern nations, devoted to astronomy, to religion, and to medicine. They were held in high esteem by the Persian court, were admitted as counsellors, and followed the camps in war to give advice. ¶ *From the east.* It is not known whether they came from Persia or Arabia. Both countries might be denoted by the word East—that is, east from Judea. ¶ *Jerusalem.* The capital of Judea. As there is frequent reference in the New Testament to Jerusalem; as it was the place of the

public worship of God; as it was the place where many important transactions in the life of the Saviour occurred, and where he died; and as no Sabbath-school teacher can intelligently explain the New Testament without some knowledge of that city, it seems desirable to present a brief description of it. A more full description may be seen in Calmet's *Dictionary*, and in the common works on Jewish antiquities. Jerusalem was the capital of the kingdom of Judah, and was built on the line dividing that tribe from the tribe of Benjamin. It was once called *Salem* (Ge. xiv. 18; Ps. lxxvi. 2), and in the days of Abraham was the abode of Melchizedek. When the Israelites took possession of the promised land, they found this stronghold in the possession of the *Jebusites*, by whom it was called *Jebus* or *Jebusi*, Jos. xviii. 28. The name *Jerusalem* was probably compounded of the two by changing a single letter, and calling it, for the sake of the sound, *Jerusalem* instead of *Jebusalem.* The ancient Salem was probably built on Mount Moriah or Acra—the eastern and western mountains on which Jerusalem was subsequently built. When the Jebusites became masters of the place, they erected a fortress in the southern quarter of the city, which was subsequently called Mount Zion, but which they called *Jebus;* and although the Israelites took possession of the adjacent territory (Jos. xviii. 28), the Jebusites still held this fortress or upper town until the time of David, who wrested it from them (2 Sa. v. 7–9), and then removed his court from Hebron to Jerusalem, which was thenceforward known as the city of David, 2 Sa. vi. 10, 12; 1 Ki. viii. 1. Jerusalem was built on several hills—Mount Zion on the south, Mount Moriah on the east, on which the temple was subsequently built (see Notes on ch. xxi. 12), Mount Acra on the west, and Mount Bezetha on the north. Mount Moriah and Mount Zion were separated by a valley, called by Josephus the *Valley of Cheesemongers*, over which there was a bridge or raised way leading from the one to the other. On the south-east of Mount Moriah, and between that and Mount Zion, there was a bluff or high rock capable of strong fortification, called *Ophel.* The city was encompassed by hills. On the west there were hills which overlooked the city; on the south was the valley of Jehoshaphat, or the valley of Hinnom (see Notes on Mat. v. 22), separating it from what is called the *Mount of Corruption;* on the east was the valley or the brook Kedron, dividing the city from the Mount of Olives. On the north the country was more level, though it was a broken or *rolling* country. On the south-east the valleys of the Kedron and Jehoshaphat united, and the waters flowed through the broken mountains in a south-easterly direction to the Dead Sea, some fifteen miles distant. The city of Jerusalem stands in 31° 50′ north latitude, and 35° 20′ east longitude from Greenwich. It is thirty-four miles south-easterly from Jaffa—the ancient Joppa—which is its seaport, and one hundred and twenty miles south-westerly from Damascus. The best view of the city of Jerusalem is from Mount Olivet on the east (comp. Notes on Mat. xxi. 1), the mountains in the east being somewhat higher than those on the west. The city was anciently inclosed within walls, a part of which are still standing. The position of the walls has been at various times changed, as the city has been larger or smaller, or as it has extended in different directions. The wall on the south formerly included the whole of Mount Zion, though the modern wall runs over the summit, including about half of the mountain. In the time of the Saviour the northern wall inclosed only Mounts Acra and Moriah north, though after his death Agrippa extended the wall so as to include Mount Bezetha on the north. About half of that is included in the present wall. The limits of the city on the east and the west, being more determined by the nature of the place, have been more fixed and permanent. The city was watered in part by the fountain of Siloam on the east (for a description of which, see Notes on Lu. xiii. 4, and on Is. vii. 3), and in part by the fountain of Gihon on the west of the city, which flowed into the vale of Jehoshaphat; and in the time of Solomon by an aqueduct, part of which is still remaining, by which water was brought from the vicinity of Bethlehem. The "pools of Solomon," three in number, one rising above another, and adapted to hold a large quantity of water, are still remaining in the vicinity of Bethlehem. The fountain of Siloam still flows freely (see Note on Is. vii. 3), though the fountain of Gihon is commonly dry. A reservoir or tank, how-

2 Saying, Where is he that is born [a]King of the Jews? for we have seen [b]his star in the east, and are come to [c]worship him.

a Zec.9.9. b Nu.24.17; Is.60 3. c Jn.5.23.

---

ever, remains at Gihon. Jerusalem had, probably, its highest degree of splendour in the time of Solomon. About four hundred years after, it was wholly destroyed by Nebuchadnezzar. It lay utterly desolate during the seventy years of the Jewish captivity. Then it was rebuilt, and restored to some degree of its former magnificence, and remained about six hundred years, when it was utterly destroyed by Titus, A.D. 70. In the reign of Adrian the city was partly rebuilt under the name of Ælia. The monuments of Pagan idolatry were erected in it, and it remained under Pagan jurisdiction until Helena, the mother of Constantine, overthrew the memorials of idolatry, and erected a magnificent church over the spot which was supposed to be the place of the Redeemer's sufferings and burial. Julian, the apostate, with the design to destroy the credit of the prophecy of the Saviour that the temple should remain in ruins (Mat. xxiv.), endeavoured to rebuild the temple. His own historian, Ammianus Marcellinus (see Warburton's *Divine Legation of Moses*), says that the workmen were impeded by balls of fire coming from the earth, and that he was compelled to abandon the undertaking. Jerusalem continued in the power of the Eastern emperors till the reign of the Caliph *Omar*, the third in succession from Mohammed, who reduced it under his control about the year 640. The Saracens continued masters of Jerusalem until the year 1099, when it was taken by the Crusaders under Godfrey of Bouillon. They founded a new kingdom, of which Jerusalem was the capital, which continued eighty-eight years under nine kings. At last this kingdom was utterly ruined by Saladin; and though the Christians once more obtained possession of the city, yet they were obliged again to relinquish it. In 1217 the Saracens were expelled by the Turks, who have ever since continued in possession of it. Jerusalem has been taken and pillaged seventeen times, and millions of men have been slaughtered within its walls. At present there is a splendid mosque—the mosque of Omar—on the site of the temple. The present population of Jerusalem is variously estimated at from 15,000 to 30,000. Turner estimates it at 26,000; Richardson, 20,000; Jowett, 15,000; Dr. Robinson at 11,000, viz., Mohammedans 4500, Jews 3000, Christians 3500.—*Biblical Researches*, vol. ii. p. 83, 84. The Jews have a number of synagogues. The Roman Catholics have a convent, and have the control of the church of the Holy Sepulchre. The Greeks have twelve convents; the Armenians have three convents on Mount Zion and one in the city; the Copts, Syrians, and Abyssinians have each of them one convent. The streets are narrow, and the houses are of stone, most of them low and irregular, with flat roofs or terraces, and with small windows only toward the street, usually protected by iron grates. The above description has been obtained from a great variety of sources, and it would be useless to refer to the works where the facts have been obtained.

2. *Where is he*, &c. There was at that time a prevalent expectation that some remarkable personage was about to appear in Judea. The Jews were anxiously looking for the coming of the Messiah. By computing the time mentioned by Daniel (ch. ix. 25-27), they knew that the period was approaching when he would appear. This personage, *they* supposed, would be a temporal prince, and they were expecting that he would deliver them from Roman bondage. It was natural that this expectation should spread into other countries. Many Jews at that time dwelt in Egypt, in Rome, and in Greece; many, also, had gone to Eastern countries, and in every place they carried their sacred writings, and diffused the expectation that some remarkable person was about to appear. Suetonius, a Roman historian, speaking of this rumour, says: "An ancient and settled persuasion prevailed throughout the East that the Fates had decreed some one to proceed from Judea who should attain universal empire."* Tacitus, another Roman historian, says: "Many were persuaded that it was contained in the ancient books of their priests, that at that very time the East should

* Vespasian, ch. 4.

3 When Herod the king had heard *these things*, he was troubled, and all Jerusalem with him.
4 And when he had [d]gathered all the chief priests and scribes of the people together, he demanded of them where Christ should be born.

d Ps.2.2.

prevail, and that some one should proceed from Judea and possess the dominion."* Josephus also, and Philo, two Jewish historians, make mention of the same expectation.† The *fact* that such a person was expected is clearly attested. Under this expectation these wise men came to do him homage, and inquired anxiously *where he was born?* ¶ *His star*. Among the ancients the appearance of a new star or comet was regarded as an omen of some remarkable event. Many such appearances are recorded by the Roman historians at the birth or death of distinguished men. Thus they say that at the death of Julius Cæsar a comet appeared in the heavens and shone seven days. These wise men also considered this as an evidence that the long-expected Prince was born. It is possible that they had been led to this belief by the prophecy of Balaam, Nu. xxiv. 17: "There shall come a *star* out of Jacob," &c. What this star was is not known. There have been many conjectures respecting it, but nothing is revealed concerning it. We are not to suppose that it was what *we* commonly mean by a *star*. The stars are vast bodies fixed in the heavens, and it is absurd to suppose that one of them was sent to guide the wise men. It is most probable that it was a luminous appearance, or meteor, such as we now see sometimes shoot from the sky, which the wise men saw, and which directed them to Jerusalem. It is possible that the same thing is meant which is mentioned by Lu. ii. 9: "*The glory of the Lord shone round about them;*" i.e. (see Note on this place), a great *light* appeared shining around them. That *light* might have been visible from afar, and *might* have been seen by the wise men in the East. ¶ *In the East*. This does not mean that they had seen the star to the east of themselves, but that, when *they* were in the East, they had seen this star. As this star was in the direction of Jerusalem, it must have been *west* of them. It might be translated, "We, being in the East, have seen his star." It is called *his* star, because they supposed it to be intended to indicate the time and place of his birth. ¶ *To worship him*. This does not mean that they had come to pay him *religious* homage, or to *adore* him. They regarded him as the King of the Jews, but there is no evidence that they supposed that he was divine. They came to honour him as *a Prince*, or a king, not as God. The original word implies no more than this. It means to prostrate one's self before another; to fall down and pay homage to another. This was the mode in which homage was paid to earthly kings, and this they wished to pay to the new-born King of the Jews. See the same meaning of the word in Mat. xx. 20; xviii. 26; Ac. x. 25; Lu. xiv. 10. The English word *worship* also meant formerly "to respect, to honour, to treat with civil reverence" (Webster).

3. *Had heard* these things. Had heard of their coming, and of the star, and of the design of their coming. ¶ *He was troubled*. Herod had obtained the kingdom by great crimes, and by shedding much blood. He was therefore easily alarmed by any remarkable appearances; and the fact that this star appeared, and that it was regarded as proof that a King of the Jews was born, alarmed him. Besides, it was a common expectation that the Messiah was about to appear, and he feared that his reign was about to come to an end. He therefore began to inquire in what way he might secure his own safety and the permanency of his government. ¶ *All Jerusalem*. The people of Jerusalem, and particularly the friends of Herod. There were many in Jerusalem to whom the coming of the Messiah would be a matter of joy; but all of Herod's friends would doubtless be alarmed at his coming.

4. *The chief priests*. By the *chief priests* here are meant not only the high-priest and his deputy, but also the heads or chiefs of the twenty-four classes into which David had divided the sacerdotal families, 1 Ch. xxiii. 6; xxiv.; 2 Ch. viii. 14; Ezr. viii. 24. ¶ *Scribes*. By the *scribes*, in the New Testament, are meant learned men; men skilled in the law, or the lawyers

* Annals, 5. 13. † Josephus, b. 1. 5. 5. 7. 31.

5 And they said unto him, In
Bethlehem of Judea: for thus it is
written by the prophet;
6 And[e] thou Bethlehem, *in* the
land of Juda, art not the least
among the princes of Juda: for
out of thee shall come a Govern-
or, [f]that shall [1]rule my people Israel.
7 Then Herod, when he had
privily called the wise men, inquired of them diligently what
time the star appeared.
8 And he sent them to Bethle-

e Mi.5.2; Jn.7.42. f Re.2 27. 1 or, *feed*, Is.40.11.

of the nation. They kept the records of the courts of justice, the registers of the synagogues, wrote articles of contract and sale, bills of divorce, &c. They were also called *lawyers*, Mat. xxii. 35, and *doctors of the law*, Lu. v. 17. They were called *scribes*, from the fact of their *writing* the public records. They were not, however, a *religious* sect, but might be either Pharisees or Sadducees. By *the chief priests and scribes* here mentioned is denoted the *Sanhedrim* or great council of the nation. This was composed of seventy-two men, who had the charge of the civil and religious affairs of the Jews. On this occasion Herod, in alarm, called them together, professedly to make inquiry respecting the birth of the Messiah. ¶ *Demanded of them.* Inquired, or asked of them. As they were the learned men of the nation, and as it was their business to study and explain the Old Testament, they were presumed to know what the prophecies had declared on that point. His object was to ascertain from prophecy *where* he was born, that he might put him to death, and thus calm the anxieties of his own mind. He seems not to have had any doubt about the *time when* he would be born. He was satisfied that the time had come.

5, 6. *By the prophet.* The Sanhedrim answered without hesitation. The question where he would be born had been settled by prophecy. This prophecy is found in Mi. v. 2. In that prophecy both the place of his birth and the character of the Messiah are so clearly set forth that there was no room to doubt. It will be observed that there is a considerable difference between the passage as quoted by the Sanhedrim and as it stands in Micah. The *main point*, however, is retained—the place of his birth. We are not concerned, therefore, in showing how these passages can be reconciled. Matthew, moreover, is not responsible for the correctness of the quotation. He affirms only that *the chief priests and scribes gave this answer to Herod*, and that Herod was satisfied. Admitting that *they* did not quote the passage correctly, it does not prove that Matthew has not reported *their answer* as they gave it, and this is all that he pretends to give. ¶ *Art not the least.* In Micah, "though thou be little." Though a small place so far as population is concerned, yet it shall *not* be small, or be the least in honour; for the Messiah shall be born there. His birth gave the place an honour which could not be conferred on the larger cities by all their numbers, their splendour, and their wealth. The birth of a distinguished personage was always supposed to give honour and importance to a city or country. Thus seven cities contended for the honour of giving birth to Homer; Stratford-upon-Avon is distinguished as the birthplace of Shakspeare; and Corsica as the birthplace of Napoleon. ¶ *A Governor.* A ruler. This is one of the characters of the Messiah, who is the king of his people, Jn. xviii. 37. The word *rule* here means to rule as a shepherd does his flock, in faithfulness and tenderness. Comp. Jn. x. 11; Is. xl. 10, 11; ix. 7.

7. *Privily.* Secretly, privately. He did this to ascertain the *time* when Jesus was born. ¶ *Diligently.* Accurately, exactly. He took pains to learn the precise time when the star appeared. He did this because he naturally concluded that the star appeared just at the time of his birth, and he wished to know precisely how old the child was.

8. *Go, and search diligently*, &c. Herod took all possible means to obtain accurate information respecting the child, that he might be sure of destroying him. He not only ascertained the probable time of his birth, and the *place* where he would be born, but he sent the wise men that they might actually see him, and bring him word. All this might have looked suspicious if he had not clothed it with the appearance of religion. He said to them, therefore, that he did it that he might go and worship him also. From this we may

hem; and said, Go and search diligently for the young child; and when ye have found *him*, bring me word again, that I may come and[g] worship him also.

9 When they had heard the king, they departed: and, lo, the star, which they saw [h]in the east, went before them, till it came and stood over where the young child was.

10 When they saw the star, they [i]rejoiced with exceeding great joy.

11 And when they were come into the house, they saw the young child with Mary his mother, and fell down, and worshipped him:

g Pr.26.24. *h* ver.2. *i* Ps.67.4.

learn, 1. That wicked men often cloak their evil designs under the appearance of religion. They attempt to deceive those who are really good, and to make them suppose that they have the same design. 2. Wicked men often attempt to make use of the pious to advance their evil purposes. Men like Herod will stop at nothing if they can carry their ends. They endeavour to deceive the simple, to allure the unsuspecting, and to beguile the weak, in order to accomplish their own purposes of wickedness. 3. The plans of wicked men are often well laid. Those plans occupy a long time. Such men make diligent inquiry, and all of it has the appearance of religion. But God sees the design; and though *men* are deceived, yet *God* cannot be, Pr. xv. 3.

9, 10. *The star—went before them.* From this it appears that the *star* was a luminous meteor, perhaps at no great distance from the ground. It is not unlikely that they lost sight of it after they had commenced their journey from the East. It is probable that it appeared to them first in the direction of Jerusalem. They concluded that the expected King had been born, and immediately commenced their journey to Jerusalem. When they arrived there, it was important that they should be directed to the very place where he was, and the star again appeared. It was for this reason that they rejoiced. They felt assured that they were under a heavenly guidance, and would be conducted to the new-born King of the Jews. And this shows, 1. That the birth of Jesus was an event of great moment, worthy of the divine interposition in directing these men to find the place of his nativity. 2. God will guide those who are disposed to find the Saviour. Even if for a time the light should be withdrawn, yet it will again appear, and direct us in the way to the Redeemer. 3. Our being led to Christ should fill us with joy. He is the way, the truth, and the life; the Saviour, the friend, the all in all; there is no other way of life, and there is no peace to the soul till he is found. When we are guided to *him*, therefore, our hearts should overflow with joy and praise; and we should humbly and thankfully follow every direction that leads to the Son of God, Jn. xii. 35, 36.

11. *The house.* The place where he was born, or the place where they lived at that time. ¶ *Fell down.* This was the usual way of showing respect or homage among the Jews, Es. viii. 3; Job i. 20; Da. iii. 7; Ps. lxxii. 11; Is. xlvi. 6. ¶ *Worshipped him.* Did him homage as King of the Jews. See Notes on ver. 2. ¶ *Had opened their treasures.* The treasures which they had brought, or the boxes, &c., in which they had brought their gold, &c. ¶ *They presented unto him gifts.* These were presented to him as King of the Jews, because they supposed he was to be a distinguished prince and conqueror. It was customary in the East to show respect for persons of distinction by making presents or offerings of this kind. See Ge. xxxii. 14; xliii. 11; 1 Sa. x. 27; 1 Ki. x. 2; Ps. lxxii. 10–15. This custom is still common in the East, and it is everywhere there unusual to approach a person of distinguished rank without a valuable present. ¶ *Frankincense.* Frankincense is a white resin or gum. It is obtained from a tree by making incisions in the bark, and suffering the gum to flow out. It is highly odoriferous or fragrant when burned, and was therefore used in worship, where it was burned as a pleasant offering to God. See Ex. xxx. 8; Le. xvi. 12. It is found in the East Indies, but chiefly in Arabia; and hence it has been supposed probable that the wise men came from Arabia. ¶ *Myrrh.* This was also a production of Arabia, and was obtained from a tree in the same

and when they had opened their
treasures, [k]they [2]presented unto
him gifts; gold, and frankincense,
and myrrh.
12 And [l]being warned of God
in a dream that they should not
return to Herod, they departed
into their own country another
way.
13 And when they were departed, behold, the angel of the Lord
appeareth to Joseph in a dream,
saying, Arise, and take the young
child and his mother, and flee into
Egypt, and be thou there until I
bring thee word: for Herod [m]will
seek the young child, to destroy
him.
14 When he arose, he took the
young child and his mother by
night, and departed into Egypt:
15 And was there until the death

k Ps.72.10; Is.60.6. 2 or, *offered.* *l* ch.1.20.

m Job 33.15,17.

manner as frankincense. The name denotes *bitterness*, and was given to it on account of its great bitterness. It was used chiefly in embalming the dead, because it had the property of preserving dead bodies from putrefaction. Compare Jn. xix. 39. It was much used in Egypt and in Judea. It was obtained from a thorny tree, which grows 8 or 9 feet high. It was at an early period an article of commerce (Ge. xxxvii. 25), and was an ingredient of the holy ointment, Ex. xxx. 23. It was also used as an agreeable perfume, Es. ii. 12; Ps. xlv. 8; Pr. vii. 17. It was also sometimes mingled with wine to form an article of drink. Such a drink was given to our Saviour, when about to be crucified, as a stupefying potion, Mar. xv. 23; compare Mat. xxvii. 34. The offerings here referred to were made because they were the most valuable which the country of the Magi or wise men produced. They were tokens of respect and homage which they paid to the new-born King of the Jews. They evinced their high regard for him, and their belief that he was to be an illustrious prince; and the fact that their deed is recorded with approbation shows us that we should offer *our* most valuable possessions, our all, to the Lord Jesus Christ. Wise men came from far to do him homage, and bowed down, and presented their best gifts and offerings. It is right that *we* give to him also our hearts, our property, our all.

12. *Warned of God.* This was done, doubtless, because, if they had given Herod precise information where he was, it would have been easy for him to send forth and slay him. And from this we learn that God will watch over those whom he loves; that he knows how to foil the purposes of the wicked, and to deliver his own out of the hands of those who would destroy them. ¶ *In a dream.* See Note on ch. i. 20.

13. *The angel appeareth to Joseph in a dream.* See ch. i. 20. ¶ *Flee into Egypt.* Egypt is situated to the south-west of Judea, and is distant from Bethlehem perhaps about 60 miles. It was at this time a Roman province. There were many Jews there, who had a temple and synagogues (see Notes on Is. xix. 18), and Joseph, therefore, would be among his own countrymen, and yet beyond the reach of Herod. The jurisdiction of Herod extended only to the River Sihon, or "river of Egypt," and, of course, beyond that Joseph was safe from his designs. For a description of Egypt, see Notes on Is. xix. It is remarkable that this is the only time in which our Saviour was out of Palestine, and that this was in the land where the children of Israel had suffered so much and so long under the oppression of the Egyptian kings. The very land which was the land of bondage and groaning for the Jews, became now the land of refuge and safety for the new-born King of Judea. God can overturn nations and kingdoms, so that those whom he loves shall be safe anywhere.

14. *When he arose.* Having arisen; that is, he arose immediately after awaking from his dream, and prepared at once to obey the command. ¶ *By night.* Thus he showed his prompt obedience to the command, and at the same time so concealed his departure as to render himself and Mary and the child safe from pursuit.

15. *The death of Herod.* Herod died in the thirty-seventh year of his reign. It is not certainly known in what year he began his reign, and hence it is impossible to determine the time that Joseph remained in Egypt. The best chronologers have supposed that he

of Herod, that it might be fulfilled which was spoken of the Lord by the prophet, saying, [n]Out of Egypt have I called my son.

16 Then Herod, when he saw that he was mocked of the wise men, was exceeding wroth, and sent forth, and slew all the chil-

n Ho.11.1.

died somewhere between two and four years after the birth of Christ, but at what particular time cannot now be determined. Nor can it be ascertained at what age Jesus was taken into Egypt. It seems probable that he was supposed to be a year old (see ver. 16), and of course the time that he remained in Egypt was not long. Herod died of a most painful and loathsome disease in Jericho. See Notes on ver. 16; also Josephus, *Ant.* xvii. 6. 5. ¶ *That it might be fulfilled*, &c. This language is recorded in Ho. xi. 1. It there evidently speaks of God's calling his people out of Egypt, under Moses. See Ex. iv. 22, 23. It might be said to be *fulfilled* in his calling Jesus from Egypt, because the words in Hosea aptly expressed this also. The same love which led him to deliver his people Israel from the land of Egypt, now led him also to deliver his Son from that place. The words used by Hosea would express both events. See Notes on ch. i. 22. Perhaps, also, the place in Hosea became *a proverb*, to express any great deliverance from danger; and thus it could be said to be *fulfilled* in Christ, as other proverbs are in cases to which they are applicable. It cannot be supposed that the passage in Hosea was a *prophecy* of the Messiah. It is evidently used by Matthew only because the *language* is appropriate to *express* the event.

16. *Then Herod, when he saw that he was mocked of the wise men.* When he saw that he had been deceived by them; that is, that they did not return as he had expected. It does not mean that they did it *for the purpose* of mocking or deriding him, but that he was *disappointed* in their not returning, or that he had been trifled with. ¶ *Exceeding wroth.* Very angry. He had been disappointed and deceived. He expected to send an executioner and kill Jesus alone. But, since he was disappointed in this, he thought he would accomplish the same thing, and be sure to destroy him, if he sent forth and put *all the children in the place* to death.—This is an illustration of the power of anger. It stops at nothing. If it cannot accomplish *just what* it wishes, it does not hesitate to go much farther, and accomplish much more evil than it at first designed. He that has a wicked heart, and indulges in anger, knows not where it will end, and will commonly commit far more evil than he at first intended. ¶ *Slew all the children.* That is, all the *male* children. This is implied in the original. The design of Herod was to cut off him that had been born *king* of the Jews. His purpose, therefore, did not require that he should slay the female children; and though he was cruel, yet we have no right to think that he attempted anything except what he thought to be for his own safety, and to secure himself from a rival. ¶ *In all the coasts thereof.* The word *coast* is commonly applied now to the regions around the sea, as the *seacoast.* Here it means the adjacent places, the settlements or hamlets around Bethlehem—all that were in that neighbourhood. We do not know how large a place Bethlehem was, nor, of course, how many were slain; but it was never a large town, and the number could not be very great. It is not probable that it contained more than one or two thousand inhabitants, and in this case the number of children slain was not over twenty or thirty. ¶ *From two years old and under.* Some writers have said that this does not mean, in the original, that they had *completed* two years; but that they had *entered* on the second year, or had completed about one year, and entered on the second. But the meaning of the word is doubtful. It is quite probable that they would not be particular about the *exact* age, but slew all that were about that age. ¶ *According to the time*, &c. He had endeavoured to ascertain of the wise men the exact time of his birth. He supposed he knew the age of Jesus. He slew, therefore, all that were of his age; that is, all that were born *about* the time when the star appeared—perhaps from six months old to two years. There is no reason to think that he would command those to be slain who had been born *after* the star appeared.

This destruction of the infants of

dren that were in Bethlehem, and in all the coasts thereof, from two years old and under, according to the time which he had [o]diligently inquired of the wise men.

17 Then was fulfilled that which

o ver. 7.

Bethlehem is not mentioned by Josephus, but for this omission three reasons may be given. 1. Josephus, a Jewish historian and a *Jew*, would not be likely to record anything that would appear to confirm the truth of Christianity. 2. This act of Herod was really so small, compared with his other crimes, that the historian might not think it worthy of record. Bethlehem was a small and obscure village, and the other crimes of Herod were so great and so public, that it is not to be wondered at that the Jewish historian has passed over this. 3. The order was probably given in secret, and might not have been known to Josephus. It pertained to the Christian history; and if the evangelists had not recorded it, it might have been unknown or forgotten. Besides, no argument can be drawn from the silence of the Jewish historian. No reason can be given why Matthew should not be considered to be as fully entitled to credit as Josephus. Yet there is no improbability in the account given by Matthew. Herod was an odious and bloody tyrant, and the facts of his reign prove that he was abundantly capable of this wickedness. The following bloody deeds will show that the slaying of the infants was in perfect accordance with his character. The account is taken from Josephus, as arranged by Dr. Lardner. Aristobulus, brother of his wife Mariamne, was murdered by his direction at eighteen years of age, because the people of Jerusalem had shown some affection for his person. —In the seventh year of his reign, he put to death Hyrcanus, grandfather of Mariamne, then eighty years of age, and who had formerly saved Herod's life; a man who had, in every revolution of fortune, shown a mild and peaceable disposition. — His beloved and beautiful wife, Mariamne, had a public execution, and her mother Alexandra followed soon after.—Alexander and Aristobulus, his two sons by Mariamne, were strangled in prison by his orders upon groundless suspicions, as it seems, when they were at man's estate, were married, and had children. —In his last sickness, a little before he died, he sent orders throughout Judea requiring the presence of all the chief men of the nation at Jericho. His orders were obeyed, for they were enforced with no less penalty than that of death. When they were come to Jericho he had them all shut up in the circus, and calling for his sister Salome and her husband Alexis, he said to them, "My life is now short. I know the Jewish people, and nothing will please them better than my death. You have them now in your custody. As soon as the breath is out of my body, and before my death can be known, do you let in the soldiers upon them and kill them. All Judea, then, and every family, will, though unwillingly, mourn at my death." Nay, Josephus says that with tears in his eyes he conjured them, by their love to him and their fidelity to God, not to fail of doing him this honour.—What objection, after this account, can there be to the account of his murdering the infants at Bethlehem? Surely there could be no cruelty, barbarity, or horrid crime which such a man was not capable of perpetrating.

17. *Then was fulfilled.* The word "fulfilled," here, is used evidently in the sense that the words in Jeremiah *aptly express* the event which Matthew was recording. Compare Notes on ch. i. 22. ¶ *That which was spoken by Jeremy the prophet.* Jeremiah. This quotation is taken from Je. xxxi. 15. The original design of the prophecy was to describe the sorrowful departure of the people of Israel into captivity after the conquest of Jerusalem by Nebuzaradan. The captives were assembled at Rama, Jeremiah himself being in chains, and there the fate of those who had escaped in the destruction of the city was decided at the will of the conqueror, Je. xl. 1. The nobles had been slain; the sons of the king had been murdered in his presence; the eyes of the king had been put out, and the people were then gathered at Rama in chains, whence they were to start on their mournful journey, slaves to a cruel monarch, leaving behind them all that was dear in life. The sadness of such a scene is well expressed in the language of the prophet, and it no less beautifully and fitly applies to the melancholy event which the evangelist records, and there

was spoken by [p]Jeremy the prophet, saying,

18 In Rama was there a voice heard, lamentation, and weeping, and great mourning, Rachel weeping *for* her children, and would not be comforted because they are not.

p Je.31.15.

could be no impropriety in his using it as a quotation.

18. *In Rama was there a voice heard.* Rama was a small town in the tribe of Benjamin. Rachel was the mother of Benjamin, and was buried near to Bethlehem, Ge. xxxv. 16–19. Rama was about 6 miles north-west of Jerusalem, near Bethel, and was some 10 or 12 miles from Bethlehem. The name *Rama* signifies *an eminence*, and was given to the town because it was situated on a hill. Rama is commonly supposed to be the same as the Arimathea of the New Testament—the place where Joseph lived who begged the body of Jesus. See Mat. xxvii. 57. This is also the same place in which Samuel was born, where he resided, died, and was buried, and where he anointed Saul as king, 1 Sa. i. 1, 19; ii. 11; viii. 4; xix. 18; xxv. 1. Mr. King, an American missionary, was at Rama—now called *Romba*—in 1824; and Mr. Whiting, another American missionary, was there in 1835. Mr. Whiting says: "The situation is exceedingly beautiful. It is about two hours distant from Jerusalem to the north-west, on an eminence commanding a view of a wide extent of beautiful diversified country. Hills, plains, and valleys, highly cultivated fields of wheat and barley, vineyards and oliveyards, are spread out before you as on a map, and numerous villages are scattered here and there over the whole view. To the west and north-west, beyond the hill-country, appears the vast plain of Sharon, and farther still you look out upon the *great and wide sea*. It occurred to me as not improbable that in the days of David and Solomon this place may have been a favourite retreat during the heat of summer, and that here the former may have often struck his sacred lyre. Some of the Psalms, or at least one of them (see Ps. civ. 25), seem to have been composed in some place which commanded a view of the Mediterranean; and this is the only place, I believe, in the vicinity of Jerusalem that affords such a view."

Rama was once a strongly fortified city, but there is no city here at present. A half-ruined Mohammedan mosque, which was originally a Christian church, stands over the tomb of the prophet; besides which, a few miserable dwellings are the only buildings that remain on this once-celebrated spot. Comp. Notes on Is. x. 29. The tomb of Rachel, which is supposed to mark the precise spot where Rachel was buried (comp. Ge. xxxv. 18–20; xlviii. 7), is near to Bethlehem, and she is represented as rising and weeping again over her children. "The tomb is a plain Saracenic mausoleum, having no claims to antiquity in its present form, but deeply interesting in sacred associations; for, by the singular consent of all authorities in such questions, it marks the actual site of her grave."—*The Land and the Book*, vol. ii. 501.

By a beautiful figure of speech, the prophet introduces the mother weeping over the tribe, her children, and with them weeping over the fallen destiny of Israel, and over the calamities about to come upon the land. Few images could be more striking than thus to introduce a mother, long dead, whose sepulchre was near, weeping bitterly over the terrible calamities that befell her descendants. The language and the image also aptly and beautifully expressed the sorrows of the mothers in Bethlehem when Herod slew their infant children. Under the cruelty of the tyrant almost every family was a family of tears, and well might there be lamentation, and weeping, and great mourning.

We may remark here that the sacred writers were cautious of speaking of the characters of wicked men. Here was one of the worst men in the world, committing one of the most awful crimes, and yet there is not a single mark of exclamation; there is not a single reference to any other part of his conduct; there is nothing that could lead to the knowledge that his character in other respects was not upright. There is no wanton and malignant *dragging him* into the narrative that they might gratify malice in making free with a very bad character. What was to their purpose, they recorded; what was not, they left to others. This is the nature

19 But when Herod was dead, behold, an angel of the Lord appeareth in a dream to Joseph in Egypt,
20 Saying, Arise, and take the young child and his mother, and go into the land of Israel: [q]for they are dead which sought the young child's life.
21 And he arose, and took the young child and his mother, and came into the land of Israel.
22 But when he heard that Archelaus did reign in Judea in the room of his father Herod, he was afraid to go thither: notwithstanding, being warned of God in

q Ex.4.19.

of religion. It does not speak evil of others except when necessary, nor then does it take pleasure in it.

19. *Herod was dead.* See Notes on ver. 15. Herod left three sons, and the kingdom was at his death divided between them. To Archelaus was given Judea, Idumea, and Samaria; to Philip, Batanea and Trachonitis; to Antipas, Galilee and Perea. Each of these was

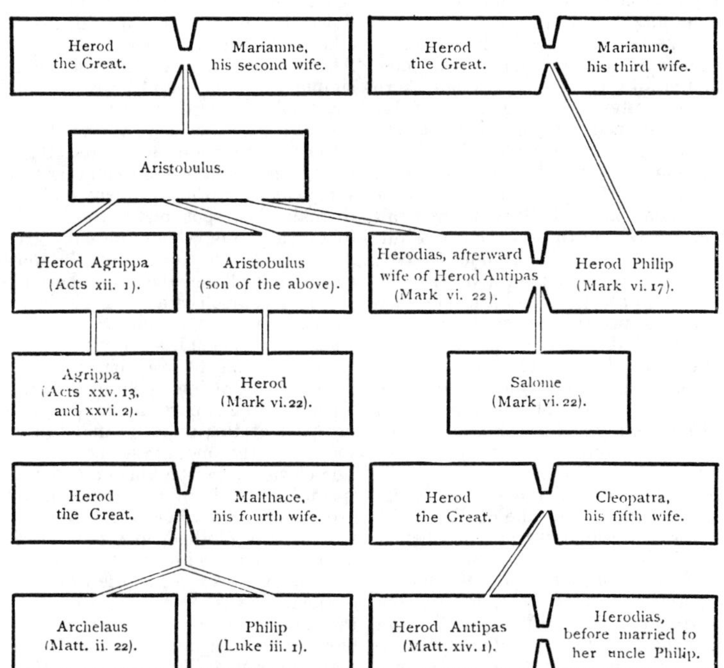

also called *Herod*, and these are the individuals who are so frequently referred to in the New Testament during the ministry of the Saviour and the labours of the apostles. The above table will show at a glance the chief connections of this family, as far as they are mentioned in the sacred history.

20. *They are dead who sought*, &c. This either refers to Herod alone, as is not uncommon, using the plural number for the singular; or it may refer to Herod and his son *Antipater*. He was of the same cruel disposition as his father, and was put to death by his father about five days before his own death.

22. *He heard that Archelaus did reign.* Archelaus possessed a cruel and tyrannical disposition similar to his father. At one of the Passovers he caused 3000 of the people to be put to death in the temple and city. For his crimes, after he had reigned nine years, he was banished by Augustus, the Ro-

a dream, he turned aside [r]into the parts of Galilee:

r ch.3.13; Lu.2.39.

23 And he came and dwelt in a city called [s]Nazareth: that it might

s Jn.1.45.

man emperor, to Gaul, where he died. Knowing his character, and fearing that he would not be safe, Joseph hesitated about going there, and was directed by God to go to Galilee, a place of safety. ¶ *The parts of Galilee.* The country of Galilee. At this time the land of Palestine was divided into three parts: GALILEE, on the north; SAMARIA, in the middle; and JUDEA, on the south. Galilee was under the government of Herod Antipas, who was comparatively a mild prince, and in his dominions Joseph might find safety.

23. *And he came and dwelt.* That is, he made it his permanent residence. The Lord Jesus, in fact, resided there until he entered on the work of his ministry—until he was about thirty years of age. ¶ *In a city called Nazareth.* This was a small town, situated in Galilee, west of Capernaum, and not far from Cana. It was built partly in a valley and partly on the declivity of a hill, Lu. iv. 29. A hill is yet pointed out, to the south of Nazareth, as the one from which the people of the place attempted to precipitate the Saviour. It was a place, at that time, proverbial for wickedness, Jn. iv. 46. It is now a large village, with a convent and two churches. One of the churches, called *the Church of the Annunciation*, is the finest in the Holy Land, except that of the Holy Sepulchre in Jerusalem.

A modern traveller describes Nazareth as situated upon the declivity of a hill, the vale which spreads out before it resembling a circular basin encompassed by mountains. Fifteen mountains appear to meet to form an inclosure for this beautiful spot, around which they rise like the edge of a shell, to guard it against intrusion. It is a rich and beautiful field, in the midst of barren mountains.

Another traveller speaks of the streets as narrow and steep. The houses, which are flat-roofed, are about two hundred and fifty in number, and the inhabitants he estimates at 2000. The population of the place is variously stated, though the average estimate is 3000, of whom about 500 are Turks, and the residue nominal Christians.

As all testimony to the truth and fidelity of the sacred narrative is important, I will here introduce a passage from the journal of Mr. Jowett, an intelligent modern traveller, especially as it is so full an illustration of the passage of Luke already cited.

"Nazareth is situated on the side, and extends nearly to the foot, of a hill, which, though not very high, is rather steep and overhanging. The eye naturally wanders over its summit in quest of some point from which it might probably be that the men of this place endeavoured to cast our Saviour down (Lu. iv. 29), but in vain; no rock adapted to such an object appears here. At the foot of the hill is a modest, simple plain, surrounded by low hills, reaching in length nearly a mile; in breadth, near the city, 150 yards; but farther south, about 400 yards. On this plain there are a few olive and fig trees, sufficient, or rather scarcely sufficient, to make the spot picturesque. Then follows a ravine, which gradually grows deeper and narrower toward the south; till, after walking about another mile, you find yourself in an immense chasm, with steep rocks on either side, from whence you behold, as it were beneath your feet and before you, the noble plain of Esdraelon. Nothing can be finer than the apparently immeasurable prospect of this plain, bounded on the south by the mountains of Samaria. The elevation of the hills on which the spectator stands in this ravine is very great; and the whole scene, when we saw it, was clothed in the most rich mountain-blue colour that can be conceived. At this spot, on the right hand of the ravine, is shown the rock to which the men of Nazareth are supposed to have conducted our Lord for the purpose of throwing him down. With the Testament in our hands we endeavoured to examine the probabilities of the spot; and I confess there is nothing in it which excites a scruple of incredulity in my mind. The rock here is perpendicular for about fifty feet, down which space it would be easy to hurl a person who should be unawares brought to the summit, and his perishing would be a very certain consequence. That the spot might be at a considerable distance from the city is an idea not inconsistent with St. Luke's account; for the expres-

be fulfilled which was spoken by the prophets, He shall be called a Nazarene.[t]

t Nu.6.13; Ju.13.5; 1 Sa.1.11; Am.2.10-12; Ac.24.5.

CHAPTER III.

IN those days came [a]John the Baptist, preaching in the wilderness of Judea,

a Lu.3.2; Jn. 1.28.

---

sion, *thrusting Jesus out of the city, and leading him to the brow of the hill on which their city was built*, gives fair scope for imagining that in their rage and debate the Nazarenes might, without originally intending his murder, press upon him for a considerable distance after they had quitted the synagogue. The distance, as already noticed, from modern Nazareth to the spot is scarcely two miles; a space which, in the fury of persecution, might soon be passed over. Or, should this appear too considerable, it is by no means certain but that Nazareth may at that time have extended through the principal part of the plain, which I have described as lying before the modern town. In this case, the distance passed over might not exceed a mile. I can see, therefore, no reason for thinking otherwise than that this may be the real scene where our divine prophet Jesus received so great a dishonour from the men of his own country and of his own kindred."

Mr. Fisk, an American missionary, was at Nazareth in the autumn of 1823. His description corresponds generally with that of Mr. Jowett. He estimates the population to be from 3000 to 5000, viz. Greeks, three hundred or four hundred families; Turks, two hundred; Catholics, one hundred; Greek Catholics, forty or fifty; Maronites, twenty or thirty; say in all seven hundred families. ¶ *That it might be fulfilled which was spoken*, &c. The words here are not found in any of the books of the Old Testament, and there has been much difficulty in ascertaining the meaning of this passage. Some have supposed that Matthew meant to refer to Ju. xiii. 5, to Samson as a type of Christ; others that he refers to Is. xi. 1, where the descendant of Jesse is called "a Branch;" in the Hebrew *Netzer*. Some have supposed that he refers to some prophecy which was not recorded, but handed down by tradition. But these suppositions are not satisfactory. It is much more probable that Matthew refers not to any particular place, but to the *leading characteristics* of the prophecies respecting him. The following remarks may make this clear: 1st. He does not say "by the *prophet*," as in ch. i. 22; ii. 5, 15, but "by the *prophets*," meaning no one particularly, but the general character of the prophecies. 2d. The leading and most prominent prophecies respecting him were, that he was to be of humble life; to be despised and rejected. See Is. liii. 2, 3, 7, 8, 9, 12; Ps. xxii. 3d. The phrase "he shall be called" means the same as *he shall be*. 4th. The character of the people of Nazareth was such that they were proverbially despised and contemned, Jn. i. 46; vii. 52. To come from Nazareth, therefore, or *to be a Nazarene*, was the same as to be despised, or to be esteemed of low birth; *to be a root out of dry ground, having no form or comeliness*. This was what had been predicted by all the prophets. When Matthew says, therefore, that the prophecies were "*fulfilled*," his meaning is, *that the predictions of the prophets that he would be of a low and despised condition, and would be rejected, were fully accomplished in his being an inhabitant of Nazareth, and despised as such.*

CHAPTER III.

1. *In those days.* The days here referred to cannot be those mentioned in the preceding chapter, for John was but six months older than Christ. Perhaps Matthew intended to embrace in his narrative the *whole time* that Jesus dwelt at Nazareth; and the meaning is, "*in those days while Jesus still dwelt at Nazareth*," John began to preach. It is not probable that John began to baptize or preach long before the Saviour entered on his ministry; and, consequently, from the time that is mentioned in the close of the second chapter to that mentioned in the beginning of the third, an interval of twenty-five or more years elapsed. ¶ *John the Baptist.* Or John *the baptizer*—so called from his principal office, that of baptizing. Baptism, or the application of water, was a rite well known to the Jews, and practised when they admitted proselytes to their religion from heathenism.—*Lightfoot.* ¶ *Preaching.* The word rendered *preach* means to proclaim in the manner of a public crier; to make proclamation. The discourses recorded in the New

2 And saying, Repent ye: for the kingdom of heaven is at hand.

Testament are mostly brief, sometimes consisting only of a single sentence. They were public proclamations of some great truth. Such appear to have been the discourses of John, calling men to repentance. ¶ *In the wilderness of Judea.* This country was situated along the Jordan and the Dead Sea, to the east of Jerusalem. The word translated *wilderness* does not denote, as with us, a place of boundless forests, entirely destitute of inhabitants; but a mountainous, rough, and thinly settled country, covered to some considerable extent with forests and rocks, and better fitted for pasture than for tilling. There were inhabitants in those places, and even villages, but they were the comparatively *unsettled* portions of the country, 1 Sa. xxv. 1, 2. In the time of Joshua there were six cities in what was then called *a wilderness*, Jos. xv. 61, 62.

2. *Repent ye.* Repentance implies sorrow for past offences (2 Co. vii. 10); a deep sense of the evil of sin as committed against God (Ps. li. 4); and a full purpose to turn from transgression and to lead a holy life. A true penitent has sorrow for sin, not only because it is ruinous to his soul, but chiefly because it is an offence against God, and is that abominable thing which he hates, Je. xliv. 4. It is produced by seeing the great danger and misery to which it exposes us; by seeing the justice and holiness of God (Job xlii. 6); and by seeing that our sins have been committed against *Christ*, and were the cause of his death, Ze. xii. 10; Lu. xxii. 61, 62. There are two words in the New Testament translated *repentance*, one of which denotes a *change of mind*, or a *reformation* of life; and the other, *sorrow* or *regret* that sin has been committed. The word used here is the former, calling the Jews to a change of life, or a *reformation* of conduct. In the time of John the nation had become extremely wicked and corrupt, perhaps more so than at any preceding period. Hence both he and Christ began their ministry by calling the nation to repentance. ¶ *The kingdom of heaven is at hand.* The phrases kingdom of heaven, kingdom of Christ, kingdom of God, are of frequent occurrence in the Bible. They all refer to the same thing. The expectation of such a kingdom was taken from the Old Testament, and especially from Daniel, ch. vii. 13, 14. The prophets had told of a successor to David that should sit on his throne, 1 Ki. ii. 4; viii. 25; Je. xxxiii. 17. The Jews expected a great national deliverer. They supposed that when the Messiah should appear, all the dead would be raised; that the judgment would take place; and that the enemies of the Jews would be destroyed, and that they themselves would be advanced to great national dignity and honour.

The *language* in which they were accustomed to describe this event was retained by our Saviour and his apostles. Yet they early attempted to correct the common notions respecting his reign. This was one design, doubtless, of John in preaching repentance. Instead of summoning them to *military exercises*, and collecting an army, which would have been in accordance with the expectations of the nation, he called them *to a change of life;* to the doctrine of repentance—a state of things far more accordant with the approach of a kingdom of purity.

The phrases "kingdom of God" and "kingdom of heaven" have been supposed to have a considerable variety of meaning. Some have supposed that they refer to the state of things in heaven; others, to the personal reign of Christ on earth; others, that they mean the church, or the reign of Christ in the hearts of his people. There can be no doubt that there is reference in the words to the condition of things in heaven after this life. But the church of God is a preparatory state to that beyond the grave—a state in which Christ pre-eminently rules and reigns—and there is no doubt that the phrases sometimes refer to the state of things in the church; and that they may refer, therefore, to the state of things which the Messiah was to set up—*his spiritual reign begun in the church on earth, and completed in heaven.*

The expression "the kingdom of heaven is at hand" would be best translated, "the *reign* of God draws near." We do not say commonly of a *kingdom* that it is *movable*, or that it *approaches*. A *reign* may be said to be at hand; and it may be said with propriety that the time when Christ would

3 For this is he that was spoken of by the prophet Esaias, saying, The[b] voice of one crying in the wilderness, Prepare ye the way of the Lord, make his paths straight.
4 And the same John [c]had his

b Is.40.3.

c 2 Ki.1.8; ch.11.8.

reign was at hand. In this sense it is meant that the time when Christ should *reign*, or set up his kingdom, or *begin* his dominion on earth, under the Christian economy, was about to commence. The phrase, then, should not be confined to any period of that reign, but includes his whole dominion over his people on earth and in heaven.

In the passage here it clearly means that the coming of the Messiah was near, or that the time of the reign of God which the Jews had expected was coming.

The word *heaven*, or *heavens*, as it is in the original, means sometimes the *place* so called; and sometimes it is, by a figure of speech, put for the Great Being whose residence is there, as in Da. iv. 26: "the *Heavens* do rule." See also Mar. xi. 30; Lu. xv. 18. As that kingdom was one of purity, it was proper that the people should prepare themselves for it by turning from their sins, and by bringing their hearts into a state suitable to his reign.

3. *The prophet Esaias.* The prophet *Isaiah.* Esaias is the Greek mode of writing the name. This passage is taken from Is. xl. 3. It is here said to have been spoken in reference to John, the forerunner of Christ. The language is such as was familiar to the Jews, and such as they would understand. It was spoken at first with reference to the return from the captivity at Babylon. Anciently it was customary in the march of armies to send messengers, or pioneers, before them to proclaim their approach; to provide for them; to remove obstructions; to make roads, level hills, fill up valleys, &c. Isaiah, describing the return from Babylon, uses language taken from that custom. A crier, or herald, is introduced. In the vast deserts that lay between Babylon and Judea he is represented as lifting up his voice, and, with authority, commanding a public road to be made for the return of the captive Jews, with the Lord as their deliverer. "Prepare his ways, make them straight," says he. The meaning in Isaiah is, "Let the valleys be exalted, or filled up, and the hills be levelled, and a straight, level highway be prepared, that they may march with ease and safety." See Notes on Is. xl. 3, 4. The custom here referred to is continued in the East at the present time. "When Ibrahim Pasha proposed to visit certain places on Lebanon, the emeers and sheiks sent forth a general proclamation, somewhat in the style of Isaiah's exhortation, to all the inhabitants, to assemble along the proposed route and prepare the way before him. The same was done in 1845, on a grand scale, when the present sultan visited Brousa. The stones were gathered out, the crooked places straightened, and the rough ones made level and smooth."—*The Land and the Book*, vol. i. p. 105, 106.

As applied to John, the passage means that he was sent to remove obstructions, and to prepare the people for the coming of the Messiah, like a herald going before an army on the march, to make preparations for its coming.

4. *His raiment of camel's hair.* His clothing. This is not the fine hair of the camel from which our elegant cloth is made called *camlet*, nor the more elegant stuff brought from the East Indies under the name of camel's hair, but the long shaggy hair of the camel, from which a coarse cheap cloth is made, still worn by the poorer classes in the East, and by monks. This dress of the camel's hair, and a leathern girdle, it seems, was the common dress of the prophets, 2 Ki. i. 8; Zec. xiii. 4. ¶ *His meat was locusts.* His food. These constituted the food of the common people. Among the Greeks the vilest of the people used to eat them; and the fact that John made his food of them is significant of his great poverty and humble life. The Jews were allowed to eat them, Le. xi. 22. Locusts are flying insects, and are of various kinds. The green locusts are about 2 inches in length and about the thickness of a man's finger. The common brown locust is about 3 inches long. The general form and appearance of the locust is not unlike the grasshopper. They were one of the plagues of Egypt (Ex. x.). In Eastern countries they are very numerous. They appear in such quantities as to darken the sky, and devour in a short time every green thing.

raiment of camel's hair, and a leathern girdle about his loins: and his meat was [d]locusts and wild honey.

d Le.11.22.

The whole earth is sometimes covered with them for many leagues, Joel i. 4; Is. xxxiii. 4, 5. "Some species of the locust are eaten at this day in Eastern countries, and are even esteemed a delicacy when properly cooked. After tearing off the legs and wings, and taking out the entrails, they stick them in long rows upon wooden spits, roast them at the fire, and then proceed to devour them with great zest. There are also other ways of preparing them. For example: they cook them and dress them in oil; or, having dried them, they pulverize them, and, when other food is scarce, make bread of the meal. The Bedouins pack them with salt in close masses, which they carry in their leathern sacks. From these they cut slices as they may need them. It is singular that even learned men have suffered themselves to hesitate about understanding these passages of the literal locust, when the fact that these are eaten by the Orientals is so abundantly proved by the concurrent testimony of travellers. One of them says they are brought to market on strings in all the cities of Arabia, and that he saw an Arab on Mount Sumara who had collected a sackful of them. They are prepared in different ways. An Arab in Egypt, of whom he requested that he would immediately eat locusts in his presence, threw them upon the glowing coals; and after he supposed they were roasted enough, he took them by the legs and head, and devoured the remainder at one mouthful. When the Arabs have them in quantities they roast or dry them in an oven, or boil them and eat them with salt. The Arabs in the kingdom of Morocco boil the locusts; and the Bedouins eat locusts, which are collected in great quantities in the beginning of April, when they are easily caught. After having been roasted a little upon the iron plate on which bread is baked, they are dried in the sun, and then put into large sacks, with the mixture of a little salt. They are never served up as a dish, but every one takes a handful of them when hungry" (*Un. Bib. Dic.*). Burckhardt, one of the most trustworthy of travellers, says: "*All* the Bedawins of Arabia and the inhabitants of towns in Nejd and Hedjaz are accustomed to eat locusts." "I have seen at Medina and Tayf *locust-shops*, where these animals were sold by *measure*. In Egypt and Nubia they are only eaten by the poorest beggars" (*The Land and the Book*, ii. 107). "Locusts," says Dr. Thomson (*The Land and the Book*, ii. 108), "are not eaten in Syria by any but the Bedawin on the extreme frontiers, and it is always spoken of as an inferior article of food, and regarded by most with disgust and loathing—tolerated only by the very poorest people. John the Baptist, however, was of this class either from necessity or election." It is remarkable that not only in respect to his food, but also in other respects, the peculiarities in John's mode of life have their counterparts in the present habits of the same class of persons. "The coat or mantle of camel's hair is seen still on the shoulders of the Arab who escorts the traveller through the desert, or of the shepherd who tends his flocks on the hills of Judea or in the valley of the Jordan. It is made of the thin, coarse hair of the camel, and not of the fine hair, which is manufactured into a species of rich cloth. I was told that both kinds of raiment are made on a large scale at Nablus, the ancient Shechem. The 'leathern girdle' may be seen around the body of the common labourer, when fully dressed, almost anywhere; whereas men of wealth take special pride in displaying a rich sash of silk or some other costly fabric" (Hackett's *Illustrations of Scripture*, p. 104). ¶ *Wild honey.* This was probably the honey that he found in the rocks of the wilderness. Palestine was often called the land flowing with milk and honey, Ex. iii. 8, 17; xiii. 5. Bees were kept with great care, and great numbers of them abounded in the fissures of trees and the clefts of rocks. "Bees abound there still, not only wild, but hived, as with us. I saw a great number of hives in the old castle near the Pools of Solomon; several, also, at Deburieh, at the foot of Tabor; and again at Mejdel, the Magdala of the New Testament, on the Lake of Tiberias. Maundrell says that he saw 'bees very industrious about the blossoms' between Jericho and the Dead Sea, which must have been within the limits of the very 'desert' in which John 'did eat locusts and

5 Then went out to him Jerusalem, and all Judea, and all the region round about Jordan,

6 And were baptized of him in Jordan, [e]confessing their sins.

e Ac.1.5; 2.38; 19.4,15,18.

wild honey'" (Hackett's *Illustrations of Scripture*, p. 104). There is also a species of honey called wild honey, or *wood honey* (1 Sa. xiv. 27, margin), or honey-dew, produced by certain little insects, and deposited on the leaves of trees, and flowing from them in great quantities to the ground. See 1 Sa. xiv. 24–27. This is said to be produced still in Arabia, and perhaps it was this which John lived upon.

5. *Jerusalem.* The people of Jerusalem. ¶ *All Judea.* Many people from Judea. It does not mean that literally *all* the people went, but that great multitudes went. It was general. Jerusalem was in the part of the country called Judea. Judea was situated on the *west* side of the Jordan. See Notes on Mat. ii. 22. ¶ *Region about Jordan.* On the east and west side of the river. Near to Jordan.

6. *Were baptized.* The word *baptize* signifies originally to *tinge*, to *dye*, to *stain*, as those who *dye* clothes. It here means to cleanse or wash anything by the application of water. See Notes on Mar. vii. 4. Washing, or ablution, was much in use among the Jews, as one of the rites of their religion, Nu. xix. 7; He. ix. 10. It was not customary, however, among them to *baptize* those who were converted to the Jewish religion until after the Babylonish captivity. At the time of John, and for some time previous, they had been accustomed to administer a rite of *baptism*, or *washing*, to those who became proselytes to their religion; that is, to those who were converted from being Gentiles. This was done to signify that they renounced the errors and worship of the Pagans, and as significant of their becoming *pure* by embracing a new religion. It was a solemn rite of *washing*, significant of *cleansing* from their former sins, and purifying them for the peculiar service of Jehovah. John found this custom in use; and as he was calling the Jews to a *new dispensation*—to a change in their form of religion—he administered this rite of *baptism*, or washing, to signify the cleansing from sin, the adopting of the new dispensation, or the fitness for the pure reign of the Messiah. He applied an old ordinance to a new purpose. As it was used by him it was a significant rite, or ceremony, intended to denote the putting away of impurity, and a purpose to be pure in heart and life. The Hebrew word (*Tabal*) which is rendered by the word baptize, occurs in the Old Testament in the following places, viz.: Le. iv. 6; xiv. 6, 51; Nu. xix. 18; Ru. ii. 14; Ex. xii. 22; De. xxxiii. 24; Ezr. xxiii. 15; Job ix. 31; Le. ix. 9; 1 Sa. xiv. 27 (*twice*); 2 Ki. v. 14; viii. 15; Ge. xxxvii. 31; Jos. iii. 15. It occurs in no other places; and from a careful examination of these passages its meaning among the Jews is to be derived. From these passages it will be seen that its radical meaning is neither to sprinkle nor to immerse. It is to *dip*, commonly for the purpose of sprinkling, or for some other purpose. Thus, to dip the *finger*, *i.e.* a part of the finger, in blood—enough to sprinkle with, Le. iv. 6. To dip a living bird, *and* cedar wood, and scarlet, and hyssop, in the blood of the bird that was killed, for the purpose of sprinkling; where it could *not* be that *all these* would be *immersed* in the blood of a single bird, Le. xiv. 6. To dip hyssop in the water, to sprinkle with, Nu. xix. 18. To dip a portion of bread in vinegar, Ru. ii. 14. To dip the feet in oil—an emblem of plenty, De. xxxiii. 24. To *dye*, or stain, Eze. xxiii. 15. To plunge into a ditch, so as to defile the clothes, Job ix. 31. To dip the *end* of a staff in honey, 1 Sa. xiv. 27. To dip in Jordan—a declaration respecting Naaman the Syrian, 2 Ki. v. 14. The direction of the prophet was to wash himself (ver. 10), and this shows that he understood *washing* and *baptizing* to mean the same thing. To dip a *towel*, or *quilt*, so as to spread it on the face of a man to smother him, 2 Ki. viii. 15. In none of these cases can it be shown that the meaning of the word is to *immerse* entirely. But in nearly all the cases the notion of applying the water to a part only of the person or object, though it was by dipping, is necessarily to be supposed.

In the New Testament the word, in various forms, occurs eighty times; fifty-seven with reference to *persons*. Of these fifty-seven times, it is followed by "in" (ἐν) eighteen times, as *in* water, *in* the desert, *in* Jordan; nine times by

7 But when he saw many of the Pharisees and Sadducees come to his baptism, he said unto them, [f]O generation of vipers, who hath warned you to [g]flee from the wrath to come?

f Is.59.5; ch.12.34; 23.33; Lu.3.7.

g Je.51.6; Ro.1.18.

"into" (εις), as *into* the name, &c., *into* Christ; once it is followed by επι (Ac. ii. 38), and twice by "for" (υπερ), 1 Cor. xv. 29.

The following remarks may be made in view of the investigation of the meaning of this word: 1st. That in baptism it is possible, perhaps probable, that the notion of dipping would be the one that would occur to a Jew. 2d. It would *not* occur to him that the word meant of necessity to dip entirely, or completely to immerse. 3d. The notion of *washing* would be the one which would most readily occur, as connected with a religious rite. See the cases of Naaman, and Mar. vii. 4 (Greek). 4th. It cannot be proved from an examination of the passages in the Old and New Testaments that the idea of a complete immersion *ever* was connected with the word, or that it *ever* in any case occurred. If those who were baptized went into the water, still it is not proved by that that the *only* mode of baptism was by immersion, as it might have been by *pouring*, though they were in the water. 5th. It is not positively enjoined anywhere in the New Testament that the only mode of baptism shall be by an entire submersion of the body under water. Without such a precept it cannot be made obligatory on people of all ages, nations, and climes, even if it were probable that in the mild climate of Judea it was the usual mode. ¶ *In Jordan.* The River Jordan is the eastern boundary of Palestine or Judea. It rises in Mount Lebanon, on the north of Palestine, and runs in a southerly direction, *underground*, for 13 miles, and then bursts forth with a great noise at Cesarea Philippi. It then unites with two small streams, and runs some miles farther, and empties into the Lake *Merom.* From this small lake it flows 13 miles, and then falls into the Lake Gennesareth, otherwise called the Sea of Tiberias or the Sea of Galilee. Through the middle of this lake, which is 15 miles long and from 6 to 9 broad, it flows undisturbed, and preserves a southerly direction for about 70 miles, and then falls into the Dead Sea. The Jordan, at its entrance into the Dead Sea, is about 90 feet wide. It flows in many places with great rapidity, and when swollen by rains pours like an impetuous torrent. It formerly regularly overflowed its banks in time of harvest, that is, in March, in some places 600 paces, Jos. iii. 15; 1 Ch. xii. 15. These banks are covered with small trees and shrubs, and afford a convenient dwelling for wild beasts. Allusion is often made to these thickets in the sacred Scriptures, Je. xlix. 19; l. 44. On the reason why a river, or a place abounding in water, was selected for administering baptism, see Notes on Jn. iii. 23.

7. *Pharisees and Sadducees.* The Jews were divided into three great sects—the Pharisees, the Sadducees, and the Essenes. In addition to these, some smaller sects are mentioned in the New Testament and by Josephus: the Herodians, probably political friends of Herod; the Galileans, a branch of the Pharisees; and the Therapeutæ, a branch of the Essenes, but converts from the Greeks. The three principal sects are supposed to have originated about 150 years before Christ, as they are mentioned by Josephus at that time in his history. Of course nothing is said of them in the Old Testament, as that was finished about 400 years before the Christian era.

I. THE PHARISEES were the most numerous and wealthy sect of the Jews. They derived their name from the Hebrew word *Pharash,* which signifies to set apart, or to separate, because they *separated* themselves from the rest of their countrymen, and professedly devoted themselves to peculiar strictness in religion. Their leading tenets were the following: that the world was governed by fate, or by a fixed decree of God; that the souls of men were immortal, and were either eternally happy or miserable beyond the grave; that the dead would be raised; that there were angels, good and bad; that God was under obligation to bestow peculiar favour on the Jews; and that they were justified by their own conformity to the law. They were proud, haughty, self-righteous, and held the common people in great disrespect, Jn.

vii. 49. They sought the offices of the state, and affected great dignity. They were ostentatious in their religious worship, praying in the corners of the streets, and seeking publicity in the bestowment of alms. They sought principally external cleanliness, and dealt much in ceremonial ablutions and washing.

Some of the laws of Moses they maintained very strictly. In addition to the written laws, they held to a multitude which they maintained had come down from Moses by tradition. These they felt themselves as much bound to observe as the written law. Under the influence of these laws they washed themselves before meals with great scrupulousness; they fasted twice a week—on Thursday, when they supposed Moses ascended Mount Sinai, and on Monday, when he descended; they wore broad phylacteries, and enlarged the fringe or borders of their garments; they loved the chief rooms at feasts, and the chief seats in the synagogues. They were in general a corrupt, hypocritical, office-seeking, haughty class of men. There are, however, some honourable exceptions recorded, Ac. v. 34; perhaps, also, Mar. xv. 43; Lu. ii. 25; xxiii. 51; Jn. xix. 38, 39–42; iii. 1; vii. 50.

II. THE SADDUCEES are supposed to have taken their name from Sadok, who flourished about 260 years before the Christian era. He was a pupil of Antigonus Sochæus, president of the sanhedrim, or great council of the nation. He had taught the duty of serving God *disinterestedly*, without the hope of reward or the fear of punishment. Sadok, not properly understanding the doctrine of his master, drew the inference that there was no future state of rewards or punishments, and on this belief he founded the sect. The other notions which they held, all to be traced to this leading doctrine, were: 1st. That there is no resurrection, neither angel nor spirit (Mat. xxii. 23; Ac. xxiii. 8); and that the soul of man perishes with the body. 2d. They rejected the doctrine of fate or decrees. 3d. They rejected all traditions, and professed to receive only the books of the Old Testament. They were far less numerous than the Pharisees, but their want of numbers was compensated, in some degree, by their wealth and standing in society. Though they did not generally *seek* office, yet several of them were advanced to the high-priesthood.

III. THE ESSENES, a third sect of the Jews, are not mentioned in the New Testament. They differed from both the Pharisees and the Sadducees. They were Jewish monks or hermits, passing their time little in society, but mostly in places of obscurity and retirement. It is not probable, therefore, that our Saviour often, if ever, encountered them; and this, it is supposed, is the reason why they are not mentioned in the New Testament. They were a contemplative sect, having little to do with the common business of life. The property which they possessed they held *in common*. They denied themselves, in a great measure, the usual comforts of life, and were exceedingly strict in the observance of the duties of religion. They were generally more pure than the rest of the Jews, and appear to have been an unambitious, a modest, and retiring sort of people. The two sexes were not in company except on the Sabbath, when they partook of their coarse fare, bread and salt only, together. They practised dancing in their worship. Few of them were married; they were opposed to oaths, and they asserted that *slavery* was repugnant to nature. In regard to doctrine, they did not differ materially from the Pharisees, except that they objected to the sacrifices of slain animals, and of course did not visit the temple, and were not, therefore, likely to come into public contact with the Saviour. They perpetuated their sect by proselytes, and by taking orphan children to train up.

The other sects of the Jews were too insignificant to demand any particular notice here. It may be said of the Jews generally that they possessed little of the spirit of religion; that they had corrupted some of the most important doctrines of the Bible; and that they were an ignorant, proud, ambitious, and sensual people. There was great propriety, therefore, in John's proclaiming to them the necessity of *repentance*.

Generation of vipers. Vipers are a species of serpents, from 2 to 5 feet in length and about an inch thick, with a flat head. They are of an ash or yellowish colour, speckled with long brown spots. There is no serpent that is more poisonous. The person bitten by them swells up almost immediately, and falls down dead. See Ac. xxviii. 6. The word *serpent*, or *viper*, is used to denote

8 Bring forth therefore fruits
meet for repentance[1]:
9 And think not to say within
yourselves, We have Abraham to
our father: for I say unto you, that
God is able of these stones to raise
up children unto Abraham.
10 And now also the axe is laid
unto the root of the trees: therefore every tree which bringeth not
forth good fruit, [h]is hewn down,
and cast into the fire.
11 I[i] indeed baptize you with
water unto repentance: but he

1 or, *answerable to amendment of life*.

h Jn.15.6. *i* Lu.3.16; Ac.19.4.

both cunning and malignancy. In the phrase "be ye wise as serpents" (Mat. x. 16), it means be prudent, or wise, referring to the account in Ge. iii. 1-6. Among the Jews the serpent was regarded as the symbol of cunning, circumspection, and prudence. It was so regarded in the Egyptian hieroglyphics. In the phrase "generation of vipers" (Mat. xii. 34), the viper is the symbol of wickedness, of envenomed malice—a symbol drawn from the *venom* of the serpent. It is not quite certain in which of these senses the phrase is used in this place. Probably it is used to denote their malignancy and wickedness. ¶ *Wrath to come.* John expresses his astonishment that sinners so hardened and so hypocritical as they were should have been induced to flee from coming wrath. The wrath to come means the divine indignation, or the punishment that will come on the guilty. See 1 Th. i. 10; 2 Th. i. 8, 9.

8. *Bring forth therefore fruits*, &c. That is, the proper fruits of reformation; the proper evidence that you are sincere. Do not bring your cunning and dissimulation to this work; carry not your hypocrisy into your professed repentance, but evince your sincerity by forsaking sin, and thus give evidence that this coming to Jordan to be baptized is not an act of dissimulation. No discourse could have been more appropriate or more *cutting*. ¶ *Fruits.* Conduct. See Mat. vii. 16-19. ¶ *Meet for repentance.* Fit for repentance; appropriate to it—the proper expression of repentance.

9. *And think not to say*, &c. They regarded it as sufficient righteousness that they were descended from so holy a man as Abraham. Comp. Jn. viii. 33-37, 53. John assured them that this was a matter of small consequence in the sight of God. Of the very stones of the Jordan he could raise up children to Abraham. The meaning seems to be this: God, from these stones, could more easily raise up those who should be *worthy* children of Abraham, or be *like him*, than simply, because you are descendants of Abraham, make you, who are proud and hypocritical, subjects of the Messiah's kingdom. Or, in other words, mere *nativity*, or the privileges of birth, avail nothing where there is not righteousness of life. Some have supposed, however, that by *these stones* he meant the Roman soldiers, or the heathen, who might also have attended on his ministry; and that God could *of them* raise up children to Abraham.

10. *The axe is laid at the root of the tree.* Laying the axe at the root of a tree is intended to denote that the tree is to be cut down. It was not merely to be *trimmed*, or to be cut *about the limbs*, but the very *tree* itself was to be struck. That is, a searching, trying kind of preaching has been commenced. A kingdom of justice is to be set up. Principles and conduct are to be investigated. No art, no dissimulation, will be successful. Men are to be tried by their lives, not by birth or profession. They who are not found to bear this test are to be rejected. The very *root* shall feel the *blow*, and the fruitless tree shall fall. This is a beautiful and very striking figure of speech, and a very direct threatening of future wrath. John regarded them as making a fair and promising profession, as trees do in *blossom*. But he told them, also, that they should bear *fruit* as well as *flowers*. Their *professions* of repentance were not enough. They should show, by a holy life, that their profession was genuine.

11. *Whose shoes I am not worthy to bear.* The word here translated *shoes* has a signification different from what it has in our language. At first, in order to keep the feet from the sharp stones or the burning sand, small pieces of wood were fastened to the soles of the feet, called *sandals*. Leather, or skins of beasts dressed, afterward were used. The foot was not covered at all, but the sandal, or piece of leather or wood, was bound by thongs. The people put off these when they enter

that cometh after me is mightier
than I, whose shoes I am not worthy to bear: [k]he shall baptize you
with the Holy Ghost, and *with*
fire:

k Ac.1.5.

12 Whose[l] fan *is* in his hand, and
he will thoroughly purge his floor,
and gather his wheat into the garner; but he will [m]burn up the chaff
with unquenchable fire.

l Mal.3.2,3. m Ps.1.4; Mal.4.1; Mar.9.44.

---

a house, and put them on when they leave it. To unloose and bind on sandals, on such occasions, was formerly

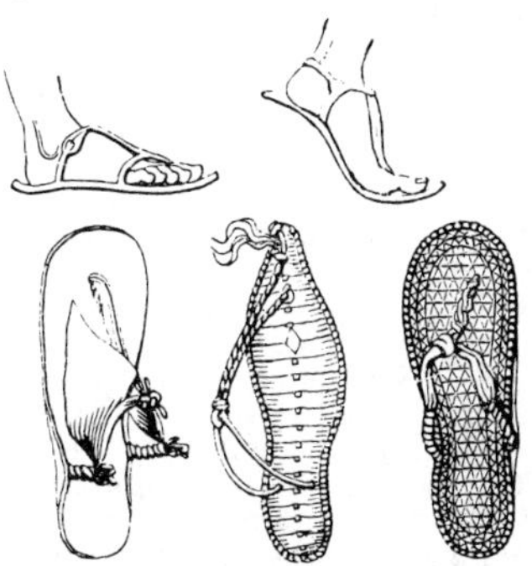

Egyptian Sandals.

the business of the lowest servants. The expression in this place, therefore, denotes great humility, and John says that he was not worthy to be the servant of him who should come after him. ¶ *Shall baptize you.* Shall send upon you the Holy Spirit. The Spirit of God is frequently represented as being poured out upon his people, Pr. i. 23; Is. xliv. 3; Joel ii. 28, 29; Ac. ii. 17, 18. The baptism of the Holy Spirit is the same, therefore, as the sending of his influences to convert, purify, and guide the soul. ¶ *The Holy Ghost.* The third person of the adorable Trinity, whose office it is to enlighten, renew, sanctify, and comfort the soul. He was promised by the Saviour *to convince* of sin, Jn. xvi. 8; to enlighten or teach the disciples, Jn. xiv. 26; xvi. 13; to comfort them in the absence of the Saviour, Jn. xiv. 18; xvi. 7; to change the heart, Tit. iii. 5. To be baptized with the Holy Ghost means that the Messiah would send upon the world a far more powerful and mighty influence than had attended the preaching of John. Many more would be converted. A mighty change would take place. His ministry would not affect the external life only, but *the heart, the motives, the soul;* and would produce rapid and permanent changes in the lives of men. See Ac. ii. 17, 18. ¶ With *fire.* This expression has been variously understood. Some have supposed that John refers to the afflictions and persecutions with which men would be tried under the Gospel; others, that the word *fire* means *judgment* or wrath. According to this latter interpretation, the meaning is that he would baptize a portion of mankind—those who were willing to be his followers—with the Holy Ghost, but the rest of mankind—the wicked—with fire; that is, with judgment and wrath. Fire is a symbol of vengeance. See Is. v. 24; lxi. 2; lxvi. 24. If this be the meaning, as seems to be probable, then John says that the ministry of the Messiah would be far more powerful than his was. It would be more searching and trying; and they who were not fitted to abide the test would be cast into eternal fire. Others have supposed, however, that by *fire*, here, John intends to express the idea that the preaching of the Messiah would be refining, powerful, purifying, as fire is sometimes an emblem of purity, Mal. iii. 2. It is difficult to ascertain the precise meaning farther than that his ministry would be very trying, purifying, searching. Multitudes would be converted; and those who were not true penitents would not be able to abide the trial, and would be driven away.

12. *His fan.* The word here used and rendered *fan* rather means a *winnowing shovel*, used for throwing the grain, after it was threshed, into the air, that the chaff might be driven away by the wind. This mode of separating the grain from the chaff is still practised in the East. It is not probable that the *fan*, as the term is now used, was known to the Orientals as an instrument for cleaning grain. See Notes on Is. xxx. 24. ¶ *His floor.* The threshing-floor was an open space, or area, in the field, usually on an elevated part of the land, Ge. l. 10. It had no covering or walls. It was a space of ground thirty or forty paces in diameter, and made smooth by rolling it or treading it hard. A high place

13 Then[n] cometh Jesus from Galilee to Jordan, unto John to be baptized of him.
14 But John forbade him, saying, I have need to be baptized of thee, and comest thou to me?
15 And Jesus answering said unto him, Suffer *it to be so* now: for thus it becometh us to fulfil all righteousness. Then he suffered him.
16 And Jesus, when he was baptized, went up straightway out of the water: and, lo, the heavens

n Mar.1.9; Lu.3.21.

was selected for the purpose of keeping it dry, and for the convenience of winnowing the grain by the wind. The grain was usually trodden out by oxen. Sometimes it was beaten with flails, as with us; and sometimes with a sharp threshing instrument, made to roll over the grain and to cut the straw at the same time. See Notes on Is. xli. 15. ¶ *Shall purge.* Shall cleanse or purify. Shall remove the chaff, &c. ¶ *The garner.* The granary, or place to deposit the wheat. ¶ *Unquenchable fire.* Fire that shall not be extinguished, that will utterly consume it. By the *floor*, here, is represented the Jewish people. By the *wheat*, the righteous, or the people of God. By the *chaff*, the wicked. They are often represented as being driven away like chaff before the wind, Job xxi. 18; Ps. i. 4; Is. xvii. 13; Ho. xiii. 13. They are also represented as chaff which the fire consumes, Is. v. 24. This image is often used to express judgments, Is. xli. 15: "Thou shall thresh the mountains and beat them small, and shalt make the hills as chaff." By the unquenchable fire is meant the eternal suffering of the wicked in hell, 2 Th. i. 8, 9; Mar. ix. 48; Mat. xxv. 41.

13. *Then cometh Jesus.* The Saviour is now introduced as about to enter on his work, or as about to be solemnly set apart to his great office of Messiah and Redeemer. The expression "cometh" implies that the act was voluntary on his part; that he went for that purpose and for no other. He left the part of Galilee—Nazareth—where he had lived for nearly thirty years, and went to the vicinity of the Jordan, where John was baptizing the people in great numbers, that he might be set apart to his work. The occasion was doubtless chosen in order that it might be as public and solemn as possible. It is to be remembered, also, that it was the *main* purpose of John's appointment to *introduce* the Messiah to the world, ver. 3. ¶ *To be baptized of him. By* him. Baptism was not in his case a symbol of personal reformation and repentance, for he was sinless; but it was a solemn rite by which he was set apart to his great office. It is true, also, that although he was personally holy, and that the baptism in his case had a different signification, in this respect, from that which is implied when it is administered now, yet that even in *his* case the great idea always implied in the ordinance of baptism had a place; for it was a symbol of *holiness* or *purity* in that great system of religion which he was about to set up in the world.

14. *John forbade him.* Refused him. ¶ *I have need.* It is more fit that *I* should be baptized with *thy* baptism, the Holy Ghost, than that thou shouldest be baptized in water by me. I am a sinner, and unworthy to administer this to the Messiah.

15. *Thus it becometh us.* It is fit and proper. And though you may feel yourself unworthy, yet it is proper it should be done. ¶ *All righteousness.* There was no particular precept in the Old Testament requiring this, but he chose to give the sanction of his example to the baptism of John, as to a divine ordinance. The phrase "all righteousness," here, is the same as *a righteous institution or appointment.* Jesus had no sin. But he was about to enter on his great work. It was proper that he should be set apart by his forerunner, and show his connection with him, and give his approbation to what John had done. He submitted to the ordinance of baptism, also, in order that occasion might be taken, at the commencement of his work, for God publicly to declare his approbation of him, and his solemn appointment to the office of the Messiah.

16. *Out of the water.* This shows that he had descended *to* the river. It literally means, "he went up directly FROM *the water.*" The original does not imply that they had descended *into* the river, and it cannot be *proved*, therefore, from this passage, that *his* baptism was by *immersion;* nor can it be proved that even *if* his baptism was by immersion,

were opened unto him, and he saw the[o] Spirit of God descending like a dove, and lighting upon him:

o Is.11.2; 42.1; 61.1; Jn.3.34.

17 And, lo, a voice from heaven, saying, [p]This is my beloved Son, in whom I am well pleased.

p Ps.2.7; Lu.9.35; Ep.1.6; 2 Pe.1.17.

---

that *therefore* the same mode is binding on men now. In order to demonstrate from this passage that immersion is *essential*, it is necessary to demonstrate, (*a*) that he went *into* the river; (*b*) that, being there, he was wholly immersed; (*c*) that the fact that *he* was immersed, if he was, proves that all others *must be*, in order that there could be a valid baptism. Neither of these three things has ever been demonstrated from this passage, nor can they be. ¶ *The heavens were opened unto him.* This was done while he was praying, Lu. iii. 21. The ordinances of religion will be commonly ineffectual without prayer. If in those ordinances we look to God, we may expect that he will bless us; the heavens will be opened, light will shine upon our path, and we shall meet with the approbation of God. The expression, "the heavens were opened," is one that commonly denotes the appearance of the clouds when it lightens. The heavens appear to open or give way. Something of this kind probably appeared to John at this time. The same appearance took place at Stephen's death, Ac. vii. 56. The expression means, he was permitted to see far into the heavens beyond what the natural vision would allow. ¶ *To him.* Some have referred this to Jesus, others to John. It probably refers to John. See Jn. i. 33. It was a testimony given to *John* that this was the Messiah. ¶ *He saw.* John saw. ¶ *The Spirit of God.* See ver. 11. This was the third person of the Trinity, descending upon him in the form of a dove, Lu. iii. 22. The *dove*, among the Jews, was the symbol of purity of heart, harmlessness, and gentleness, Mat. x. 16; comp. Ps. lv. 6, 7. The form chosen here was doubtless an emblem of the innocence, meekness, and tenderness of the Saviour. The gift of the Holy Spirit, in this manner, was the public approbation of Jesus (Jn. i. 33), and a sign of his being set apart to the office of the Messiah. We are not to suppose that there was any change wrought in the moral character of Jesus, but only that he was publicly set apart to his work, and solemnly approved by God in the office to which he was appointed.

17. *A voice from heaven.* A voice from God. Probably this was heard by all who were present. This voice, or sound, was repeated on the mount of transfiguration, Mat. xvii. 5; Lu. ix. 35, 36; 2 Pe. i. 17. It was also heard just before his death, and was then supposed by many to be thunder, Jn. xii. 28–30. It was a public declaration that Jesus was the Messiah. ¶ *My beloved Son.* This is the title which God himself gave to Jesus. It denotes the nearness of his relation to God, and the love of God for him, He. i. 2. It implies that he was equal with God, He. i. 5–8; Jn. x. 29–33; xix. 7. The term *Son* is expressive of love—of the nearness of his relation to God, and of his dignity and equality with God. ¶ *Am well pleased.* Am ever delighted. The language implies that he was constantly or uniformly well pleased with him; and in this solemn and public manner he expressed his approbation of him as the Redeemer of the world.

The baptism of Jesus has usually been regarded as a striking manifestation of the doctrine of the Trinity, or the doctrine that there are three persons in the divine nature. (1.) There is the person of *Jesus Christ*, the Son of God, baptized in Jordan, elsewhere declared to be equal with God, Jn. x. 30. (2.) *The Holy Spirit* descending in a bodily form upon the Saviour. The Holy Spirit is also equal with the Father, or is also God, Ac. v. 3, 4. (3.) The *Father*, addressing the Son, and declaring that he was well pleased with him. It is impossible to explain this transaction consistently in any other way than by supposing that there are three equal persons in the divine nature or essence, and that each of these sustains an important part in the work of redeeming men.

In the preaching of John the Baptist we are presented with an example of a faithful minister of God. Neither the wealth, the dignity, nor the power of his auditors deterred him from fearlessly declaring the truth respecting their character. He called things by their right names. He did not apologize for their sins. He set their transgressions fairly before them, and

CHAPTER IV.

THEN was Jesus [a]led up of the Spirit into the wilderness, [b]to be tempted of the devil.

2 And when he had fasted forty days and forty nights, he was afterward an hungered.

3 And when the tempter came

a 1 Ki.18.12; Eze.11.1,24; Ac.8.39. *b* Mar.1.12; Lu.4.1.

showed them faithfully and fearlessly what must be the consequence of a life of sin. So should all ministers of the Gospel preach. Rank, riches, and power should have nothing to do in shaping and gauging their ministry. In respectful terms, but without shrinking, all the truth of the Gospel must be spoken, or woe will follow the ambassador of Christ, 1 Cor. ix. 16.

In John we have also an example of humility. Blessed with great success, attended by the great and noble, and with nothing but *principle* to keep him from turning it to his advantage, he still kept himself out of view, and pointed to a far greater personage at hand. So should every minister of Jesus, however successful, keep the Lamb of God in his eye, and be willing —nay, rejoice—to lay all his success and honours at his feet.

Everything about the work of Jesus was wonderful. No person had before come into the world under such circumstances. God would not have attended the commencement of his life with such wonderful events if it had not been of the greatest moment to our race, and if he had not possessed a dignity above all prophets, kings, and priests. His "name" was to be called "Wonderful, Councillor, The mighty God, The everlasting Father, The Prince of Peace;" "of the increase of his government and peace" there was to be "no end;" "upon the throne of David and of his kingdom, to order it, and to establish it with judgment and with justice forever" (Is. ix. 6, 7); and it was proper that a voice from heaven should declare that he was the long-promised prince and Saviour; that the angels should attend him, and the Holy Spirit signalize his baptism by his personal presence. And it is proper that *we*, for whom he came, should give to him our undivided affections, our time, our influence, our hearts, and our lives.

CHAPTER IV.

1. *Then was Jesus led up of the Spirit.* Led up *by* the Spirit. Luke says (iv. 1) that Jesus was "full of the Holy Ghost;" and it was by his influence, therefore, that he went into the desert to be tempted. It was not done by presumption on the part of Jesus, nor was it for a mere display of his power in resisting temptation; but it was evidently that it might be seen that his holiness was such that he *could not* be seduced from allegiance to God. When the first Adam was created he was subjected to the temptation of the devil, and he fell and involved the race in ruin: it was not improper that the second Adam—the Redeemer of the race—should be subjected to temptation, in order that it might be seen that there was no power that could alienate him from God; that there *was* a kind and a degree of holiness which no art or power could estrange from allegiance. Mark (i. 12) says that this occurred "immediately" after his baptism; that is, in his case, as not unfrequently happens, the great temptation followed *immediately* the remarkable manifestation of the divine approbation and favour. In the clearest manifestations of the divine favour to us we may not be far from most powerful temptations, and then may be the time when it is necessary to be most carefully on our guard. ¶ *Into the wilderness.* See Notes on ch. iii. 1. ¶ *To be tempted.* The word *tempt*, in the original, means to try, to endeavour, to attempt to do a thing; then, to try the nature of a thing, as metals by fire; then, to test moral qualities by *trying* them, to see how they will endure; then, to endeavour to draw men away from virtue by suggesting motives to evil. This is the meaning here, and this is now the established sense of the word in the English language. ¶ *The devil.* This word originally means an adversary, or an accuser; then, any one opposed to us; then, an enemy of any kind. It is given in the Scriptures, by way of eminence, to the leader of evil angels —a being characterized as full of subtlety, envy, art, and hatred of mankind. He is known, also, by the name *Satan*, Job i. 6–12; Mat. xii. 26; *Beelzebub*, Mat. xii. 24; *the old Serpent*, Re. xii. 9; and *the Prince of the power of the air*, Ep. ii. 2. The name is once given

to him, he said, If thou be the Son of God, command that these stones be made bread.

4 But he answered and said, It is written, [c]Man shall not live by bread alone, but by every word that proceedeth out of the mouth of God.

c De.8.3.

to women (1 Ti. iii. 11): "Even so must their wives be grave, not *slanderers;*" in the original, *devils.*

2. *Had fasted.* Abstained from food. ¶ *Forty days and forty nights.* It has been questioned by some whether Christ abstained wholly from food, or only from the food to which he was accustomed. Luke says (ch. iv. 2) that he *ate nothing.* This settles the question. Mark says (ch. i. 13) that angels came and ministered unto him. At first view this would seem to imply that he did eat during that time. But Mark does not mention the *time* when the angels performed this office of kindness, and we are at liberty to suppose that he means to say that it was done at the close of the forty days; and the rather as Matthew, after giving an account of the temptation, says the same thing (ch. iv. 2). There are other instances of persons fasting forty days recorded in the Scriptures. Thus Moses fasted forty days, Ex. xxxiv. 28. Elijah also fasted the same length of time, 1 Ki. xix. 8. In these cases they were no doubt miraculously supported.

3. *The tempter.* The devil, or Satan. See ver. 1. ¶ *If thou be the Son of God.* If thou art God's own Son, then thou hast power to work a miracle, and here is a fit opportunity to try thy power, and show that thou art sent from God. ¶ *Command that these stones,* &c. The stones that were lying around him in the wilderness. No temptation could have been more plausible, or more likely to succeed, than this. He had just been *declared* to be the Son of God (ch. iii. 17), and here was an opportunity to show that he was *really* so. The circumstances were such as to make it appear plausible and proper to work this miracle. "Here you are," was the language of Satan, "hungry, cast out, alone, needy, poor, and yet the Son of God! If you have this power, how easy could you satisfy your wants! How foolish is it, then, for the Son of God, having all power, to be starving in this manner, when by a *word* he could *show* his power and relieve his wants, and when *in the thing itself* there could be nothing wrong!"

4. *But he answered and said,* &c. In reply to this artful temptation Christ answered by a quotation from the Old Testament. The passage is found in De. viii. 3. In that place the discourse is respecting *manna.* Moses says that the Lord humbled the people, and fed them with manna, an unusual kind of food, that they might learn that man did not live by *bread* only, but that there were other things to support life, and that everything which God had commanded was proper for this. The term "word," used in this place, means very often, in Hebrew, *thing,* and clearly in this place has that meaning. Neither Moses nor our Saviour had any reference to *spiritual food,* or to the *doctrines* necessary to support the faith of believers; but they simply meant that God could support life by other things than *bread;* that man was to live, not by *that* only, but by every other thing which proceeded out of his mouth; that is, which he chose to command men to eat. The substance of his answer, then, is: "It is not so imperiously necessary that I should have *bread* as to make a miracle proper to procure it. Life depends on the will of God. He can support it in other ways as well as by *bread.* He has created other things to be eaten, and man may live by everything that his Maker has commanded." And from this temptation we may learn: 1. That Satan oftens takes advantage of our circumstances and wants to tempt us. The poor, the hungry, and the naked he often tempts to repine and complain, and to be dishonest in order to supply their necessities. 2. Satan's temptations are often the strongest immediately after we have been remarkably favoured. Jesus had just been called the Son of God, and Satan took this opportunity to try him. He often attempts to fill us with pride and vain self-conceit when we have been favoured with any peace of mind, or any new view of God, and endeavours to urge us to do something which may bring us low and lead us to sin. 3. His temptations are plausible. They often seem to be only urging us to do what is good and proper. They seem even to urge us to promote

5 Then the devil taketh him up into [d]the holy city, and setteth him on a pinnacle of the temple,
6 And saith unto him, If thou be the Son of God, cast thyself down: for it is written, [e]He shall give his angels charge concerning thee: and in *their* hands they shall bear

d Ne.11.1; ch.27.53.

e Ps.91.11,12.

the glory of God, and to honour him. We are not to think, therefore, that because a thing *may seem to be good in itself*, that therefore it is to be done. Some of the most powerful temptations of Satan occur when he seems to be urging us to do what shall be for the glory of God. 4. We are to meet the temptations of Satan, as the Saviour did, with the plain and positive declarations of Scripture. We are to inquire whether the thing is *commanded*, and whether, therefore, it is right to do it, and not trust to our own feelings, or even our *wishes*, in the matter.

5. *Then the devil taketh him up.* This does not mean that he bore him through the air, or that he *compelled* him to go against his will, or that he wrought a miracle in any way to place him there. There is no evidence that Satan had *power* to do any of these things, and the word translated *taketh him up* does not imply any such thing. It means to conduct one; to lead one; to attend or accompany one; or to induce one to go. It is used in the following places in the same sense: Nu. xxiii. 14: "And he (Balak) *brought him* (Balaam) into the field of Zophim," &c. That is, he *led him*, or induced him to go there. Mat. xvii. 1: "And after six days Jesus *taketh* Peter, James," &c.; that is, led or conducted them—not by any means implying that he bore them by force. Mat. xx. 17: "Jesus, going to Jerusalem, *took* the twelve disciples apart," &c. See also Mat. xxvi. 37; xxvii. 27; Mar. v. 40. From these passages, and many more, it appears that all that is meant here is, that Satan *conducted* Jesus, or *accompanied* him; but not that this was done against the *will of Jesus.* ¶ *The holy city.* Jerusalem, called *holy* because the temple was there, and because it was the place of religious solemnities. ¶ *Setteth him on a pinnacle of the temple.* It is not perfectly certain to what part of the temple the sacred writer here refers. It has been supposed by some that he means the roof. But Josephus says that the roof was covered by spikes of gold, to prevent its being polluted by birds; and such a place would have been very inconvenient to stand upon. Others suppose that it was the top of the porch or entrance to the temple. But it is more than probable that the porch leading to the temple was not as high as the main building. It is more probable that he refers to that part of the sacred edifice which was called Solomon's Porch. The temple was built on the top of Mount Moriah. The temple itself, together with the courts and porches, occupied a large space of ground. See Notes on Mat. xxi. 12. To secure a level spot sufficiently large, it was necessary to put up a high wall on the east. The temple was surrounded with porches or piazzas 50 feet broad and 75 feet high. The porch on the south side was, however, 67 feet broad and 150 high. From the top of this to the bottom of the valley below was more than 700 feet, and Josephus says that one could scarcely look down without dizziness. The word *pinnacle* does not quite express the force of the original. It is a word given usually to *birds*, and denotes *wings*, or anything in the form of wings, and was given to the roof of this porch because it resembled a bird *dropping its wings.* It was on this place, doubtless, that Christ was placed.

6. *And saith unto him, If thou be the Son of God, cast thyself down.* The temptation here was, that he should at once avail himself of the protection of a promise of safety made to him, and thus demonstrate that he was the Messiah. If he was the true Messiah he had a certain assurance of protection, a promise that no harm could befall him; and thus, by so surprising a miracle, and such a clear proof of the divine interposition, he could at once establish his claim to the Messiahship. How much more easy would this be than to engage in a slow work of years to establish that claim; to encounter fatigue, and want, and poverty, and persecution, before that claim would be admitted! And where could be a more fit place for thus at once demonstrating that he was the Son of God, than on this pinnacle of the temple, in the very midst of Jerusalem, and perhaps in the presence of thousands who would see the wonderful performance? The *temp-*

thee up, lest at any time thou dash
thy foot against a stone.
7 Jesus said unto him, It is written again, [f]Thou shalt not tempt
the Lord thy God.

[f] De.6.16.

8 Again, the devil taketh him
up into an exceeding high mountain, and showeth him all the kingdoms of the world, and the glory
of them;
9 And saith unto him, All these

---

tation, therefore, in this case was, that by thus establishing his claim he would avoid all the obloquy, persecution, and suffering which he must otherwise endure if he attempted to prove that he was the Son of God by a life of toil and privation. ¶ *It is written.* That is, there is a passage of Scripture which promises special protection in such a case, and on which you may rely. The argument was not, perhaps, that this applied *exclusively* to the Messiah, but that, if applicable in any case, it would be in this; if *any* one could plead this promise, assuredly he could who claimed to be the Son of God. ¶ *He shall give his angels charge concerning thee*, &c. That is, they shall protect thee. ¶ *And in* their *hands they shall bear thee up.* They shall sustain thee, or hold thee up, so that thou shalt not be endangered by the fall. ¶ *Lest at any time thou dash thy foot against a stone.* This would be peculiarly appropriate in such a case. The promise, as Satan applied it, was that he should not be injured by the stones lying at the bottom of the wall or in the valley below. The case, therefore, seemed to be one that was especially contemplated by the promise.

7. *Jesus said unto him, It is written again.* Again the Saviour replied to Satan by a text of Scripture—a passage which expressly forbade an act like this. ¶ *Thou shalt not tempt the Lord thy God.* This is quoted literally from De. vi. 16. The meaning is, thou shalt not *try* him; or, thou shalt not, by throwing thyself into voluntary and uncommanded dangers, appeal to God for protection, or trifle with the promises made to those who are thrown into danger *by his providence.* It is true, indeed, that God aids those of his people who are placed *by him* in trial or danger; but it is *not* true that the promise was meant to extend to those who wantonly provoke him and trifle with the promised help. Thus Satan, artfully using and perverting Scripture, was met and repelled by Scripture rightly applied.

8. *An exceeding high mountain.* It is not known what mountain this was. It was probably some elevated place in the vicinity of Jerusalem, from the top of which could be seen no small part of the land of Palestine. The Abbé Mariti speaks of a mountain on which he was, which answers to the description here. "This part of the mountain," says he, "overlooks the mountains of Arabia, the country of Gilead, the country of the Amorites, the plains of Moab, the plains of Jericho, the River Jordan, and the whole extent of the Dead Sea." So Moses, before he died, went up into Mount Nebo, and from it God showed him "all the land of Gilead unto Dan, and all Naphtali, and the land of Ephraim and Manasseh, and all the land of Judah, unto the utmost sea, and the south, and the plain of the valley of Jericho, and the city of palm-trees, unto Zoar," De. xxxiv. 1–3. This shows that there were mountains from which no small part of the land of Canaan could be seen; and we need not suppose that there was any miracle when they were shown to the Saviour. ¶ *All the kingdoms of the world.* It is not probable that anything more is intended here than the kingdoms of Palestine, or of the land of Canaan, and those in the immediate vicinity. Judea was divided into three parts, and those parts were called *kingdoms;* and the sons of Herod, who presided over them, were called *kings.* The term *world* is often used in this limited sense to denote a part or a large part of the world, particularly the land of Canaan. See Ro. iv. 13, where it means *the land of Judah;* also Lu. ii. 1, and the Note on the place. ¶ *The glory of them.* The riches, splendour, towns, cities, mountains, &c., of this beautiful land.

9. *All these things*, &c. All these kingdoms. All these dominions Satan claimed a right to bestow on whom he pleased, and with considerable justice. They were excessively wicked; and with no small degree of propriety, therefore, he asserted his claim to give them away. This temptation had much plausibility. Satan regarded Jesus as the king of the Jews. As the Messiah he supposed he had come to take possession of all that country. He was poor, and unarmed,

things will I give thee, if thou wilt fall down and worship me.

10 Then saith Jesus unto him, Get thee hence, Satan: for it is written, [g]Thou shalt worship the Lord thy God, and him only shalt thou serve.

11 Then the devil leaveth him, and, behold, [h]angels came and ministered unto him.

12 Now when Jesus had heard

g De.6.13; 1 Sa.7.3.

h He.1.6,14.

and without followers or armies. Satan proposed to put him in possession of it *at once*, without any difficulty, if he would acknowledge *him* as the proper *lord* and disposer of that country; if he would trust to *him* rather than *to God*. ¶ *Worship me.* See Notes on Mat. ii. 2. The word here seems to mean, to acknowledge Satan as having a right to give these kingdoms to him; to acknowledge his dependence on him rather than God; that is, really to render *religious* homage. We may be surprised at his boldness. But he had been twice foiled. He supposed it was an object dear to the heart of the Messiah to obtain these kingdoms. He claimed a *right* over them; and he *seemed* not to be asking too much, if he *gave* them to Jesus, that Jesus should be willing to *acknowledge* the gift and express *gratitude* for it. So plausible are Satan's temptations, even when they are blasphemous; and so artfully does he present his allurements to the mind.

10. *Get thee hence.* These temptations, and this one especially, the Saviour met with a decided rebuke. This was a bolder attack than any which had been made before. The other temptations had been founded on an appeal to his necessities, and an offer of the protection of God in great danger; in both cases plausible, and in neither a direct violation of the law of God. Here was a higher attempt, a more decided and deadly thrust at the piety of the Saviour. It was a proposition that the Son of God should *worship* the devil, instead of honouring and adoring Him who made heaven and earth; that he should bow down before the Prince of wickedness and give him homage. ¶ *It is written.* In De. vi. 13. Satan asked him to worship him. This was expressly forbidden, and Jesus therefore drove him from his presence.

11. *Then the devil leaveth him.* He left him for a time, Lu. iv. 13. He intended to return again to the temptation, and, if possible, to seduce him yet from God. Comp. Jn. xiv. 30; Lu. xxii. 53. See Notes on He. xii. 4. ¶ *The angels came and ministered.* See Notes on ch. i. 20. They came and supplied his wants and comforted him. From this narrative we may learn:

(*a.*) That no one is so *holy* as to be free from temptation, for even the Son of God was sorely tempted.

(*b.*) That when God permits a temptation or trial to come upon us, he will, if we look to him, give us grace to resist and overcome it, 1 Co. x. 13.

(*c.*) We see the *art* of the tempter. His temptations are adapted to times and circumstances. They are plausible. What could have been more plausible than his suggestions to Christ? They were applicable to his circumstances. They had the appearance of much piety. They were backed by passages of Scripture—misapplied, but still most artfully presented. Satan never comes boldly and tempts men to sin, telling them that they are committing sin. Such a mode would defeat his design. It would put people on their guard. He commences, therefore, artfully and plausibly, and the real purpose does not appear till he has prepared the mind for it. This is the way with all temptation. No wicked man would *at once* tempt another to be profane, to be drunk, to be an infidel, or to commit adultery. The *principles* are first corrupted. The confidence is secured. The affections are won. And then the allurement is by little and little presented, till the victim falls. How should every one be on his guard at the very *first appearance* of evil, at the first suggestion that may possibly lead to sin!

(*d.*) One of the best ways of meeting temptation is by applying Scripture. So our Saviour did, and they will always best succeed who best wield the sword of the Spirit, which is the word of God, Ep. vi. 17.

12. *John was cast into prison.* For an account of the imprisonment of John see Mat. xiv. 1–13. ¶ *He departed into Galilee.* See Mat. ii. 22. The reasons why Jesus then went into Galilee were probably: 1st. Because the attention of the people had been much excited by John's preaching, and things seemed to

that John was [1]cast into prison, he
departed into Galilee:
13 And leaving Nazareth, he
came and dwelt in Capernaum,
which is upon the sea coast, in
the borders of Zabulon and Nephthalim:
14 That it might be fulfilled
which was spoken by Esaias the
prophet, saying,
15 The[i] land of Zabulon, and the
land of Nephthalim, *by* the way
of the sea, beyond Jordan, Galilee
of the Gentiles:
16 The[k] people which sat in darkness saw great light: and to them

1 or, *delivered up*.

i Is.9.1,2. *k* Is.42.6,7; Lu.2.32.

be favourable for success in his own ministry. 2d. It appeared desirable to have some one to second John in the work of reformation. 3d. It was less dangerous for him to commence his labours *there* than near Jerusalem. Judea was under the dominion of the scribes, and Pharisees, and priests. They would naturally look with envy on any one who set himself up for a public teacher, and who should attract much attention there. It was important, therefore, that the work of Jesus should begin in Galilee, and become somewhat established and known before he went to Jerusalem.

13. *Leaving Nazareth.* Because his townsmen cast him out, and rejected him. See Lu. iv. 14–30. ¶ *Came and dwelt in Capernaum.* This was a city on the north-west corner of the Sea of Tiberias. It is not mentioned in the Old Testament, but is repeatedly referred to in the Gospels. Though it was once a city of renown, and the metropolis of all Galilee, the site it occupied is now uncertain. When Mr. Fisk, an American missionary, travelled in Syria in 1823, he found twenty or thirty uninhabited Arab huts occupying what are supposed to be the ruins of the once-celebrated city of Capernaum.

The exact site of this ancient city has been a question of much interest, and is not supposed to be as yet fully settled; perhaps it is not possible that it should be. Dr. Robinson (*Biblical Researches*, iii. p. 283, 284, 288–295) supposes that the site of the ancient city is a place now called Khan Minyeh. Dr. Thomson (*The Land and the Book*, vol. ii. p. 542–547) supposes that it was at a place now called Tell Hum. This place is a short distance *north* of Khan Minyeh, or the site supposed by Dr. Robinson to be Capernaum. It is at the north-west corner of the Sea of Tiberias.

In this place and its neighbourhood Jesus spent no small part of the three years of his public ministry. It is hence called *his own city*, Mat. ix. 1. Here he healed the nobleman's son (Jn. iv. 47); Peter's wife's mother (Mat. viii. 14); the centurion's servant (Mat. viii. 5–13); and the ruler's daughter (Mat. ix. 23–25). ¶ *Upon the sea coast.* The Sea of Tiberias. ¶ *In the borders of Zabulon and Nephthalim.* These were two tribes of the children of Israel which were located in this part of the land of Canaan, and constituted in the time of Christ a part of Galilee. Comp. Ge. xlix. 13; Jos. xix. 10, 32. The word *borders* here means *boundaries.* Jesus came and dwelt in the *boundaries* or *regions* of Zabulon and Naphthali.

14–16. *That it might be fulfilled*, &c. This place is recorded in Is. ix. 1, 2. Matthew has given the *sense*, but not the very words of the prophet. For the meaning of the passage as employed by Isaiah, see Notes on Is. ix. 1, 2. ¶ *By the way of the sea.* Which is *near to* the sea, or in the vicinity of the sea. ¶ *Beyond Jordan.* This does not mean to the *east* of Jordan, as the phrase sometimes denotes, but rather in the vicinity of the Jordan, or perhaps in the vicinity of the sources of the Jordan. See De. i. 1; iv. 49. ¶ *Galilee of the Gentiles.* Galilee was divided into *upper* and *lower* Galilee. Upper Galilee was called *Galilee of the Gentiles*, because it was occupied chiefly by Gentiles. It was in the neighbourhood of Tyre, Sidon, &c. The word *Gentiles* includes in the Scriptures all who are not Jews. It means the same as *nations*, or, as we should say, the *heathen nations.*

16. *The people which sat in darkness.* This is an expression denoting great ignorance. As in darkness or night we can see nothing, and know not where to go, so those who are ignorant of God and their duty are said to be in darkness. The instruction which removes this ignorance is called *light.* See Jn. iii. 19; 1 Pe. ii. 9; 1 Jn. i. 5; ii. 8. As ignorance is often connected with crime and vice, so *darkness* is sometimes used

which sat in the region and shadow of death, light is sprung up.

17 From that time Jesus began to preach, and to say, [l]Repent: for the kingdom of heaven is at hand.

l ch.3.2; 10.7.

18 And Jesus, walking by the sea of Galilee, saw two brethren, Simon [m]called Peter, and Andrew his brother, casting a net into the sea: for they were fishers.

m Jn.1.42.

to denote sin, 1 Th. v. 5; Ep. v. 11; Lu. xxii. 53. ¶ *Saw great light.* That is, as the passage is employed by Matthew, the light under the Messiah would spring up among them. In that region he grew up, and in that region he preached a great part of his discourses and performed a great part of his miracles. ¶ *The region and shadow of death.* This is a forcible and beautiful image, designed also to denote ignorance and sin. It is often used in the Bible, and is very expressive. A *shadow* is caused by an object coming between us and the sun. So the Hebrews imaged death as standing between us and the sun, and casting a long, dark, and baleful shadow abroad on the face of the nations, denoting their great ignorance, sin, and woe. It denotes a dismal, gloomy, and dreadful shade, where death and sin reign, like the chills, damps, and horrors of the dwelling-place of the dead. See Job x. 21; xvi. 16; xxxiv. 22; Ps. xxiii. 4; Je. ii. 6. See also Notes on Is. ix. 2. These expressions denote that the country of Galilee was peculiarly dark. We know that the people were proverbially ignorant and stupid. They were distinguished for a coarse, outlandish manner of speech (Mar. xiv. 70), and are represented as having been also distinguished by a general profligacy of morals and manners. It shows the great compassion of the Saviour, that he went to preach to such poor and despised sinners. Instead of seeking the rich and the learned, he chose to minister to the needy, the ignorant, and the contemned. His office is to enlighten the ignorant; his delight to guide the wandering, and to raise up those that are in the shadow of death. In doing this, Jesus set an example for all his followers. It is their duty to seek out those who are sitting in the shadow of death, and to send the gospel to them. No small part of the world is still lying in wickedness—as wicked and wretched as was the land of Zabulon and Naphthali in the time of Jesus. The Lord Jesus is able to enlighten them also, and every Christian should regard it a privilege, as well as a duty, to imitate his Saviour in this, and to be permitted to send to them the light of life. See Mat. xxviii. 19.

17. See Notes on Mat. iii. 2.

18. *Sea of Galilee.* This was also called the Sea of Tiberias and the Lake of Gennesareth, and also the Sea of Chinnereth, Nu. xxxiv. 11; De. iii. 17; Jos. xii. 3. Its form is an irregular *oval*, with the large end to the north. It is about 14 miles in length, and from 6 to 9 in width. It is about 600 feet lower than the Mediterranean, and this great depression accounts for some of its peculiar phenomena. There is no part of Palestine, it is said, which can be compared in beauty with the environs of this lake. Many populous cities once stood on its shores, such as Tiberias, Bethsaida, Capernaum, Chorazin, Hippo, &c. The shores are described by Josephus as a perfect paradise, producing every luxury under heaven at all seasons of the year, and its remarkable beauty is still noticed by the traveller. "Seen from any point of the surrounding heights, it is a fine sheet of water—a burnished mirror set in a framework of surrounding hills and rugged mountains, which rise and roll backward and upward to where hoary Hermon hangs the picture on the blue vault of heaven." The lake is fed mainly by the Jordan; but besides this there are several great fountains and streams emptying into it during the rainy seasons, which pour an immense amount of water into it, raising its level several feet above the ordinary mark. See *The Land and the Book* (Thomson), vol. ii. p. 77. Lieutenant Lynch reports its greatest ascertained depth at 165 feet. The waters of the lake are sweet and pleasant to the taste, and clear. The lake still abounds with fish, and gives employment, as it did in the time of our Saviour, to those who live on its shores. It is, however, stormy, owing probably to the high hills by which it is surrounded. ¶ *Simon called Peter.* The name *Peter* means a rock, and is the same as *Cephas.* See Notes on Mat. xvi. 18; also Jn. i. 42; 1 Co. xv. 5.

19 And he saith unto them, Follow me, and I will make you [n]fish-
ers of men.
20 And they straightway [o]left
their nets, and followed him.
21 And going on from thence,
he saw other two brethren, [p]James
the son of Zebedee, and John his
brother, in a ship with Zebedee
their father, mending their nets:
and he called them.
22 And they immediately left
the ship and their father, and followed him.
23 And Jesus went about all
Galilee, [q]teaching in their synagogues, and preaching [r]the gospel
of the kingdom, and [s]healing all

n Lu.5.10; 1 Co.9.20-22; 2 Co.12.16. *o* Mar.10. 28-31. *p* Mar.1.19,20.

q ch.9.35; Lu.4.15,44. *r* ch.24.14; Mar.1.14. *s* Ps. 103.3; ch.8.16,17.

---

19. *Fishers of men.* Ministers or preachers of the gospel, whose business it shall be to win souls to Christ.

20. *Straightway.* Immediately—as all should do when the Lord Jesus calls them. ¶ *Left* their *nets.* Their nets were the means of their living, perhaps all their property. By leaving them immediately, and following him, they gave every evidence of sincerity. They showed, what we should, that they were willing to forsake *all* for the sake of Jesus, and to follow him wherever he should lead them. They went forth to persecution and death for his sake; but also to the honour of saving souls from death, and establishing a church that shall continue to the end of time. Little did they know what awaited them when they left their unmended nets to rot on the beach, and followed the unknown and unhonoured Jesus of Nazareth. So we know not what awaits us when we become his followers; but we should cheerfully go when our Saviour calls, willing to commit all into his hands—come honour or dishonour, sickness or health, riches or poverty, life or death. Be it ours to do our duty at once, and to commit the result to the great Redeemer who has called us. Comp. Mat. vi. 33; viii. 21, 22; Jn. xxi. 21, 22. ¶ *Follow him.* This is an expression denoting that they became his disciples, 2 Ki. vi. 19.

21. *And going on from thence.* From the place where he had found Peter and Andrew, ver. 18. ¶ *Saw two other brothers.* They were men engaged in the same employment, as it is probable that there were many such in the neighbourhood of the lake. ¶ *In a ship.* A small vessel. In fact, it was little more, probably, than a sail-boat. ¶ *Mending their nets.* A very common employment when they were not actually engaged in fishing.

22. *Left their father.* This showed how willing they were to follow Jesus. They showed us what we ought to do. If necessary, we should leave father, and mother, and every friend, Lu. xiv. 26. If they will go with us, and be Christians, it is well; if not, yet they should not hinder us. We should be the followers of Jesus. And, while in doing it we should treat our friends kindly and tenderly, yet we ought at all hazards to obey God, and do our duty to him. We may add that many, very many children, since Sabbath-schools have commenced, have been the means of their parents' conversion. Many children have spoken to their parents, or read the Bible to them, or other books, and prayed for them, and God has blessed them and converted them. Every child in a Sunday-school ought to be a Christian; and then should strive and pray that God would convert his parents, and make them Christians too. We see here, too, what humble instruments God makes use of to convert men. He chose fishermen to convert the world. He chooses the foolish to confound the wise. And it shows that religion is true, and is the power of God, when he makes use of such instruments to change the hearts of men and save their souls. See Notes on 1 Co. i. 26-28.

23. *All Galilee.* See Notes on ch. ii. 22. ¶ *Synagogues.* Places of worship, or places where the people *assembled* together to worship God. The origin of synagogues is involved in much obscurity. The *sacrifices* of the Jews were appointed to be held in *one* place, at Jerusalem. But there was nothing to forbid the other services of religion to be performed at any other place. Accordingly the praises of God were sung in the schools of the prophets; and those who chose were assembled by the prophets and seers on the Sabbath, and the new moons, for religious worship,

manner of sickness, and all manner of disease among the people.

24 And his fame went throughout all Syria: and they brought unto him all sick people that were taken with divers diseases and tor-

---

2 Ki. iv. 23; 1 Sa. x. 5–11. The people would soon see the necessity of providing convenient places for their services, to shelter them from storms and from the heat, and this was probably the origin of synagogues. At what time they were commenced is unknown. They are mentioned by Josephus a considerable time before the coming of Christ; and in his time they were multiplied, not only in Judea, but wherever there were Jews. There were no less than 480 in Jerusalem alone before it was taken by the Romans.

Synagogues were built in any place where ten men were found who were willing to associate for the purpose, and were the regular customary places of worship. In them the *law*, *i.e.* the Old Testament, divided into suitable portions, was read, prayers were offered, and the Scriptures were expounded. The law was so divided that the five books of Moses, and portions of the prophets, could be read through each year. The Scriptures, after being read, were expounded. This was done, either by the officers of the synagogue, or by any person who might be invited by the officiating minister. Our Saviour and the apostles were in the habit of attending at those places continually, and of speaking to the people, Lu. iv. 15–27; Ac. xiii. 14, 15.

The synagogues were built in imitation of the temple, with a centre building, supported by pillars, and a *court* surrounding it. See Notes on Mat. xxi. 12. In the centre building, or chapel, was a place prepared for the reading of the law. The law was kept in a chest, or ark, near to the pulpit. The uppermost seats (Mat. xxiii. 6) were those nearest to the pulpit. The people sat round, facing the pulpit. When the law was read, the officiating person rose; when it was expounded, he was seated. Our Saviour imitated their example, and was commonly seated in addressing the people, Mat. v. 1; xiii. 1. ¶ *Teaching.* Instructing the people, or explaining the gospel. ¶ *The gospel of the kingdom.* The good news respecting the kingdom he was about to set up; or the good news respecting the coming of the Messiah and the nature of his kingdom. ¶ *Preaching.* See Notes on ch. iii. 1. ¶ *All manner of sickness.* All kinds of sickness.

24. *And his fame went throughout all Syria.* It is not easy to fix the exact bounds of Syria in the time of our Saviour. It was, perhaps, the general name for the country lying between the Euphrates on the east, and the Mediterranean on the west; and between Mount Taurus on the north, and Arabia on the south. Through all this region his celebrity was spread by his power of working miracles; and, as might be expected, the sick from every quarter were brought to him, in the hope that he would give relief. ¶ *Those possessed with devils.* Much difficulty exists, and much has been written respecting those in the New Testament said to be possessed with the devil. It has been maintained by many that the sacred writers only meant by this expression to denote those who were *melancholy* or *epileptic*, or afflicted with some other grievous disease. This opinion has been supported by arguments too long to be repeated here. On the other hand, it has been supposed that the persons so described were under the influence of evil spirits, who had complete possession of the faculties, and who produced many symptoms of disease not unlike melancholy, madness, and epilepsy. That such was the fact will appear from the following considerations: 1st. Christ and the apostles spoke *to* them and *of* them *as such;* they addressed them, and managed them, precisely *as if* they were so possessed, leaving their hearers to infer beyond a doubt that such was their real opinion. 2d. Those who were thus possessed spake, conversed, asked questions, gave answers, and expressed their knowledge of Christ, and their fear of him—things that certainly could not be said of *diseases*, Mat. viii. 28; Lu. viii. 27. 3d. The devils, or evil spirits, are represented as going out of the persons possessed, and entering the bodies of others, Mat. viii. 32. 4th. Jesus spake to them, and asked their name, and they answered him. He threatened them, commanded them to be silent, to depart, and not to return, Mar. i. 25; v. 8; ix. 25. 5th. Those possessed are said *to know Christ; to be acquainted with the Son of God*, Lu. iv. 34;

ments, and those which were possessed with devils, and those which were lunatic, and those that had the palsy; and he healed them.

Mar. i. 24. This could not be said of diseases. 6th. The early fathers of the Church interpreted these passages in the same way. They derived their opinions probably from the apostles themselves, and their opinions are a fair interpretation of the apostles' sentiments. 7th. If it is denied that Christ believed in such possessions, it does not appear why any other clearly-expressed sentiment of his may not in the same way be disputed. There is, perhaps, no subject on which he expressed himself more clearly, or acted more uniformly, or which he left more clearly impressed on the minds of his disciples.

Nor is there any absurdity in the opinion that those persons were really under the influence of devils. For, 1st, It is no more absurd to suppose that an angel, or many angels, should have *fallen* and become wicked than that so many *men* should. 2d. It is no more absurd that Satan should have possession of the human faculties, or inflict diseases, than that *men* should do it—a thing which is done every day. What is more common than for a wicked man to corrupt the morals of others, or, by inducing them to become intemperate, to produce a state of body and mind quite as bad as to be possessed with the devil? 3d. We still see a multitude of cases that no man can prove *not* to be produced by the presence of an evil spirit. Who would attempt to say that some evil being may not have much to do in the case of madmen? 4th. It afforded an opportunity for Christ to show his power over the enemies of himself and of man, and thus to evince himself qualified to meet every enemy of the race, and triumphantly to redeem his people. He came to destroy the power of Satan, Ac. xxvi. 18; Ro. xvi. 20, 21. ¶ *Those which were lunatic.* This name is given to the disease from the Latin name of the *moon* (Luna). It has the same origin in Greek. It was given because it was formerly imagined that the patient was affected by the increase or the decrease of the moon. The name is still retained, although it is certain that the moon has no effect on the disease. The disease is mentioned only in this place, and in Mat. xvii. 15. It was probably the *falling-sickness* or *epilepsy*, the same as the disease mentioned Mar. ix. 18–20; Lu. ix. 39, 40. ¶ *And those that had the palsy.* Many infirmities were included under the general name of *palsy* in the New Testament. 1st. The paralytic shock, affecting the whole body. 2d. The hemiplegy, affecting only one side of the body; the most frequent form of the disease. 3d. The paraplegy, affecting all the system below the neck. 4th. The catalepsy. This is caused by a contraction of the muscles in the whole or a part of the body, and is very dangerous. The effects are very violent and fatal. For instance, if, when a person is struck, he happens to have his hand extended, he is unable to draw it back; if not extended, he is unable to stretch it out. It gradually becomes diminished in size, and dried up in appearance. Hence it was called *the withered hand*, Mat. xii. 10–13. 5th. The cramp. This, in Eastern countries, is a fearful malady, and by no means unfrequent. It originates from chills in the night. The limbs, when seized by it, remain unmovable, and the person afflicted with it resembles one undergoing a torture. This was probably the disease of the servant of the centurion, Mat. viii. 6; Lu. vii. 2. Death follows from this disease in a few days. ¶ *And he healed them.* This was done evidently by miraculous power. A miracle is an effect produced by divine power above, or opposed to, what are regular effects of the laws of nature. It is not a *violation* of the laws of nature, but is a suspension of their *usual operation*, for some important purpose. For instance, the regular effect of death is that the body returns to corruption. The ordinary laws of chemistry had been suspended by the operation of *life* — a power superior to those laws, and producing new combinations of matter in the animal or vegetable organization. When life is extinct those laws act in their proper power, and the body is *decomposed;* that is, the materials of which it is composed, under chemical laws, return to their natural forms of gases and earths. When one who claims to be from God suspends that regular effect, and gives life to a dead body for some important purpose, it is a miracle. Such an effect is clearly the result of divine power. No other being

25 And there followed him [t]great multitudes of people from Galilee, and *from* Decapolis, and *from* Jerusalem, and *from* Judea, and *from* beyond Jordan.

t Lu.6.17,19.

CHAPTER V.

AND seeing the multitudes, he went up into a mountain: and when he was set, his disciples came unto him:

---

but God can do it. When, therefore, Christ and the apostles exercised this power, it was clear evidence that God *approved* of their doctrines; that he had commissioned them; and that they were authorized to declare his will. He would not give this attestation to a false doctrine. Most or all of these diseases were incurable. When Christ cured them *by a word*, it was the clearest of all proofs that he was sent from heaven. This is one of the strong arguments for Christianity.

25. From *Decapolis*. *Decapolis* was the name of a region of country in the bounds of the half-tribe of Manasseh, mainly on the east of Jordan. It was so called because it included *ten cities*—the meaning of the word Decapolis in Greek. Geographers generally agree that Scythopolis was the chief of these cities, and was the only one of them west of the Jordan; that Hippo (Hippos), Gadara, Dion (or Dios), Pelea (or Pella), Gerasa (or Gergesa), Philadelphia, and Raphana (or Raphanæ), were seven of the remaining nine, and the other two were either Kanatha and Capitolias, or Damascus and Otopos. These cities were inhabited chiefly by foreigners (Greeks) in the days of our Saviour, and not by Jews. Hence the keeping of swine by the Gergesenes (Mat. viii. 30–33), which was forbidden by the Jewish law.

CHAPTER V.

1. *And seeing the multitudes.* The great numbers that came to attend on his ministry. The substance of this discourse is recorded also in Lu. vi. It is commonly called the Sermon on the Mount. It is not improbable that it was repeated, in substance, on different occasions, and to different people. At those times parts of it may have been omitted, and Luke may have recorded it as it was pronounced on one of those occasions. See Notes on Lu. vi. 17–20. ¶ *Went up into a mountain.* This mountain, or hill, was somewhere in the vicinity of Capernaum, but where precisely is not mentioned. He ascended the hill, doubtless, because it was more convenient to address the multitude from an eminence than if he were on the same level with them. A hill or mountain is still shown a short distance to the north-west of the ancient site of Capernaum, which tradition reports to have been the place where this sermon was delivered, and which is called on the maps the *Mount of Beatitudes.* The hill commonly believed to be that on which the sermon was delivered is on the road from Nazareth to Tiberias, not far from the latter place. The hill is known by the name of Kuran Huttin, the Horns of Huttin. Of this hill Professor Hackett (*Illustrations of Scripture*, p. 323, 324) says: "Though a noontide heat was beating down upon us with scorching power, I could not resist the temptation to turn aside and examine a place for which such a claim has been set up, though I cannot say that I have any great confidence in it. The hill referred to is rocky, and rises steeply to a moderate height above the plain. It has two summits, with a slight depression between them, and it is from these projecting points, or horns, that it receives the name given to it. From the top the observer has a full view of the Sea of Tiberias. The most pleasing feature of the landscape is that presented by the diversified appearance of the fields. The different plots of ground exhibit various colours, according to the state of cultivation: some of them are red, where the land has been newly ploughed up, the natural appearance of the soil; others yellow or white, where the harvest is beginning to ripen, or is already ripe; and others green, being covered with grass or springing grain. As they are contiguous to each other, or intermixed, these particoloured plots present at some distance an appearance of gay chequered work, which is really beautiful.

"In rhetorical descriptions of the delivery of the Sermon on the Mount, we often hear the people represented as looking up to the speaker from the sides of the hill, or listening to him from the plain. This would not be possible with reference to the present locality; for it is too precipitous and

2 And he opened his mouth, and
taught them, saying,
3 Blessed[a] *are* the [b]poor in spirit:
[c]for theirs is the kingdom of
heaven.
4 Blessed[d] *are* they that mourn:
[e]for they shall be comforted.

a Lu.6.20,&c. *b* Is.57.15; 66.2. *c* Ja.2.5. *d* Is.61.3; Eze.7.16. *e* Jn.16.20; 2 Co.1.7.

too elevated to allow of such a position. The Saviour could have sat there, however, in the midst of his hearers, for it affords a platform amply large enough for the accommodation of the hundreds who may have been present on that occasion." ¶ *And when he was set.* This was the common mode of teaching among the Jews, Lu. iv. 20; v. 3; Jn. viii. 2; Ac. xiii. 14; xvi. 13. ¶ *His disciples came unto him.* The word *disciples* means *learners,* those who are taught. Here it is put for those who attended on the ministry of Jesus, and does not imply that they were all Christians. See Jn. vi. 66.

3. *Blessed* are *the poor in spirit.* The word *blessed* means *happy,* referring to that which produces felicity, from whatever quarter it may come. ¶ *Poor in spirit.* Luke says simply, *Blessed are* THE POOR. It has been disputed whether Christ meant the *poor* in reference to the things of this life, or to *the humble.* The gospel is said to be preached to the poor, Lu. iv. 18; Mat. xi. 5. It was predicted that the Messiah would preach to the poor, Is. lxi. 1. It is said that they have peculiar facilities for being saved, Mat. xix. 23; Lu. xviii. 24. The state of such persons is therefore comparatively blessed, or happy. Riches produce care, anxiety, and dangers, and not the least is the danger of losing heaven by them. To be poor *in spirit* is to have a humble opinion of ourselves; to be sensible that we are sinners, and have no righteousness of our own; to be willing to be saved only by the rich grace and mercy of God; to be willing to be where God places us, to bear what he lays on us, to go where he bids us, and to die when he commands; to be willing to be in his hands, and to feel that we deserve no favour from him. It is opposed to pride, and vanity, and ambition. Such are happy: 1st. Because there is more real enjoyment in thinking of ourselves *as we are,* than in being filled with pride and vanity. 2d. Because such Jesus chooses to bless, and on them he confers his favours here. 3d. Because theirs will be the kingdom of heaven hereafter. It is remarkable that Jesus began his ministry in this manner, so unlike all others. Other teachers had taught that happiness was to be found in honour, or riches, or splendour, or sensual pleasure. Jesus overlooked all those things, and fixed his eye on the poor and the humble, and said that happiness was to be found in the lowly vale of poverty more than in the pomp and splendours of life. ¶ *Theirs is the kingdom of heaven.* That is, either they have peculiar facilities for entering the kingdom of heaven, and of *becoming Christians* here, or they shall enter heaven hereafter. Both these ideas are probably included. A state of poverty—a state where we are despised or unhonoured by men—is a state where men are most ready to seek the comforts of religion here, and a home in the heavens hereafter. See Notes on ch. ii. 2.

4. *Blessed* are *they that mourn.* This is capable of two meanings: either, that those are blessed who are afflicted with the loss of friends or possessions, or that they who mourn over *sin* are blessed. As Christ came to preach repentance, to induce men to mourn over their sins and to forsake them, it is probable that he had the latter particularly in view. Comp. 2 Cor. vii. 10. At the same time, it is true that the gospel only can give true comfort to those in affliction, Is. lxi. 1–3; Lu. iv. 18. Other sources of consolation do not reach the deep sorrows of the soul. They may blunt the sensibilities of the mind; they may produce a sullen and reluctant submission to what we cannot help; but they do not point to the true source of comfort. In the God of mercy only; in the Saviour; in the peace that flows from the hope of a better world, and there only, is there consolation, 2 Co. iii. 17, 18; v. 1. Those that mourn thus shall be comforted. So those that grieve over sin; that sorrow that they have committed it, and are afflicted and wounded that they have offended God, shall find comfort in the gospel. Through the merciful Saviour those sins may be forgiven. In him the weary and heavy-laden soul shall find peace (Mat. xi. 28–30); and the presence of the *Comforter,* the Holy Ghost, shall sustain them

5 Blessed *are* the meek: [f]for they shall inherit the earth.

f Ps.37.11.

6 Blessed *are* they which do hunger and thirst after righteousness: [g]for they shall be filled.

g Ps.145.19; Is.65.13.

here (Jn. xiv. 26, 27), and in heaven all their tears shall be wiped away, Re. xxi. 4.

5. *The meek.* Meekness is patience in the reception of injuries. It is neither meanness nor a surrender of our rights, nor cowardice; but it is the opposite of sudden anger, of malice, of long-harboured vengeance. Christ insisted on his right when he said, "If I have done evil, bear witness of the evil; but if well, why smitest thou me?" Jn. xviii. 23. Paul asserted his right when he said, "They have beaten us openly uncondemned, being Romans, and have cast us into prison; and now do they thrust us out privily? nay, verily; but let them come themselves, and fetch us out," Ac. xvi. 37. And yet Christ was the very model of meekness. It was one of his characteristics, "I am meek," Mat. xi. 29. So of Paul. No man endured more wrong, or endured it more patiently than he. Yet the Saviour and the apostle were not passionate. They bore all patiently. They did not press their rights through thick and thin, or trample down the rights of others to secure their own.

Meekness is the reception of injuries with a belief that God will vindicate us. "Vengeance is his; he will repay," Ro. xii. 19. It little becomes us to take his place, and to do what he has promised to do.

Meekness produces peace. It is proof of true greatness of soul. It comes from a heart too great to be moved by little insults. It looks upon those who offer them with pity. He that is constantly ruffled; that suffers every little insult or injury to throw him off his guard and to raise a storm of passion within, is at the mercy of every mortal that chooses to disturb him. He is like "the troubled sea that cannot rest, whose waters cast up mire and dirt." ¶ *They shall inherit the earth.* This might have been translated *the land.* It is probable that here is a reference to the manner in which the Jews commonly expressed themselves to denote any great blessing. It was promised to them that they should inherit the *land* of Canaan. For a long time the patriarchs looked forward to this, Ge. xv. 7, 8; Ex. xxxii. 13. They regarded it as a great blessing. It was so spoken of in the journey in the wilderness, and their hopes were crowned when they took possession of the promised land, De. i. 38; xvi. 20. In the time of our Saviour they were in the constant habit of using the Old Testament, where this promise perpetually occurs, and they used it *as a proverbial expression to denote any great blessing, perhaps as the sum of all blessings,* Ps. xxxvii. 20; Is. lx. 21. Our Saviour used it in this sense, and meant to say, not that the meek would own *great property* or have many lands, but that they would possess peculiar blessings. The Jews also considered the land of Canaan as a type of heaven, and of the blessings under the Messiah. To *inherit the land* became, therefore, an expression denoting those blessings. When our Saviour uses this language here, he means that the meek shall be received into his kingdom, and partake of its blessings here, and of the glories of the heavenly Canaan hereafter.—The value of *meekness,* even in regard to worldly property and success in life, is often exhibited in the Scriptures, Pr. xxii. 24, 25; xv. 1; xxv. 8, 15. It is also seen in common life that a meek, patient, mild man is the most prospered. An impatient and quarrelsome man raises up enemies; often loses property in lawsuits; spends his time in disputes and broils rather than in sober, honest industry; and is harassed, vexed, and unsuccessful in all that he does. "Godliness is profitable unto all things, having promise of the life that now is, and of that which is to come," 1 Ti. iv. 8. Comp. 1 Ti. vi. 3–6.

6. *Blessed* are *they which do hunger,* &c. Hunger and thirst, here, are expressive of strong desire. Nothing would better express the strong desire which we *ought* to feel to obtain righteousness than hunger and thirst. No wants are so keen, none so imperiously demand supply, as these. They occur daily, and when long continued, as in case of those shipwrecked, and doomed to wander months or years over burning sands, with scarcely any drink or food, nothing is more distressing. An ardent *desire* for anything is often represented in the Scriptures by hunger and thirst,

7 Blessed *are* the merciful: [h]for they shall obtain mercy.

h Ps.41.1,2.

8 Blessed[i] *are* the pure in heart: for they shall see God.

9 Blessed[k] *are* the peacemakers:

i Ps.24.3.4; Heb.12.14; 1 Jn.3.2,3. k Ps.34.14.

Ps. xlii. 1, 2; lxiii. 1, 2. A desire for the blessings of pardon and peace; a deep sense of sin, and want, and wretchedness, is also represented by thirsting, Is. lv. 1, 2. ¶ *They shall be filled.* They shall be satisfied—as a hungry man is when supplied with food, or a thirsty man when supplied with drink. Those who are perishing for want of righteousness; those who feel that they are lost sinners and strongly desire to be holy, shall be thus satisfied. Never was there a desire to be *holy* which God was not willing to gratify, and the gospel of Christ has made provision to satisfy all who truly desire to be holy. See Is. lv. 1-3, and lxv. 13; Jn. iv. 14; vi. 35; vii. 37, 38; Ps. xvii. 15.

7. *Blessed* are *the merciful.* That is, those who are so affected by the *sufferings* of others as to be disposed to alleviate them. This is given as an evidence of piety, and it is said that they who show mercy to others shall obtain it. The same sentiment is found in Mat. x. 42: "Whosoever shall give to drink unto one of these little ones a cup of cold water only, *in the name of a disciple*, verily I say unto you he shall in no wise lose his reward." See also Mat. xxv. 34-40. This should be done with a wish to glorify God; that is, in obedience to his commandments, and with a desire that he should be honoured, and with a feeling that we are benefiting one of his creatures. Then he will regard it as done *to him*, and will reward us. See the sentiment of this verse, that the merciful shall obtain mercy, more fully expressed in 2 Sa. xxii. 26, 27; and in Ps. xviii. 25, 26.

Nowhere do we imitate God more than in showing mercy. In nothing does God more delight than in the exercise of mercy, Ex. xxxiv. 6; Eze. xxxiii. 11; 1 Ti. ii. 4; 2 Pe. iii. 9. To us, guilty sinners; to us, wretched, dying, and exposed to eternal woe, he has shown his mercy by giving his Son to die for us; by expressing his willingness to pardon and save us; and by sending his Spirit to renew and sanctify our hearts. Each day of our life, each hour, and each moment, we partake of his undeserved mercy. All the blessings we enjoy are proofs of his mercy. If *we*, then, show mercy to the poor, the wretched, the guilty, it shows that we are *like God.* We have his spirit, and shall not lose our reward. And we have abundant opportunity to do it. Our world is full of guilt and woe, which we may help to relieve; and every day of our lives we have opportunity, by helping the poor and wretched, and by forgiving those who injure us, to show that we are like God. See Notes on ch. vi. 14, 15.

8. *Blessed* are *the pure in heart.* That is, whose minds, motives, and principles are pure; who seek not only to have the *external actions* correct, but who desire to be holy *in heart*, and who *are so.* Man looks on the outward appearance, but God looks on the heart. ¶ *They shall see God.* There is a sense in which *all* will see God, Re. i. 7. That is, they will behold him as a *Judge*, not as a *Friend.* In this place it is spoken of as a peculiar favour. So also in Re. xxii. 4: "And they shall *see his face.*" To see the face of one, or to be in the presence of any one, were terms among the Jews expressive of great favour. It was regarded as a high honour to be in the presence of kings and princes, and to be permitted to see them, Pr. xxii. 29: "He shall stand *before kings.*" See also 2 Ki. xxv. 19: "Those that stood in the king's presence;" in the Hebrew, those that saw the *face* of the king; that is, who were his favourites and friends. So here, to see God, means to be his friends and favourites, and to dwell with him in his kingdom.

9. *Blessed* are *the peacemakers.* Those who strive to prevent contention, strife, and war; who use their influence to reconcile opposing parties, and to prevent lawsuits and hostilities in families and neighbourhoods. Every man may do *something* of this; and no man is more like God than he who does it. There ought not to be unlawful and officious interference in that which is none of our business; but without any danger of acquiring this character, every man has many opportunities of reconciling opposing parties. Friends, neighbours, men of influence, lawyers, physicians, ministers of the gospel, may do much to promote peace. And it should be taken in hand in the beginning. "The

for they shall be called the children of God.

10 Blessed[l] *are* they which are persecuted for righteousness' sake: for theirs is the kingdom of heaven.

11 Blessed are ye when *men* shall revile you, and persecute *you*, and shall say all manner of evil against you [1]falsely for my sake.

12 Rejoice, and be exceeding

l 1 Pe.3.13,14.

1 *lying.*

---

beginning of strife," says Solomon, "is like the letting out of water." "An ounce of prevention," says the English proverb, "is worth a pound of cure." Long and most deadly quarrels might often be prevented by a little kind interference in the beginning. ¶ *Children of God.* See Notes on Mat. i. 1. Those who *resemble* God, or who manifest a spirit like his. He is the Author of peace (1 Co. xiv. 33); and all those who endeavour to promote peace are *like* him, and are worthy to be called his children.

10. *Blessed* are *they which are persecuted.* To *persecute* means literally to pursue, follow after, as one does a flying enemy. Here it means to vex, or oppress one, on account of his religion. They persecute others who injure their names, reputation, property, or who endanger or take their life, on account of their religious opinions. ¶ *For righteousness' sake.* Because they are righteous, or are the friends of God. We are not to seek persecution. We are not to provoke it by strange sentiments or conduct; by violating the laws of civil society, or by modes of speech that are unnecessarily offensive to others. But if, in the honest effort to be Christians, and to live the life of Christians, others persecute and revile us, we are to consider this as a blessing. It is an evidence that we are the children of God, and that he will defend us. "All that live godly in Christ Jesus shall suffer persecution," 2 Ti. iii. 12. ¶ *Theirs is the kingdom of heaven.* They have evidence that they are Christians, and that they will be brought to heaven.

11. *Blessed are ye when* men *shall revile you.* Reproach you; call you by evil and contemptuous names; ridicule you because you are Christians. Thus they said of Jesus that he was a Samaritan and had a devil (Jn. viii. 48); that he was mad (Jn. x. 20); and thus they reviled and mocked him on the cross, Mat. xxvii. 39–44. But, being reviled, he reviled not again (1 Pe. ii. 23); and thus being reviled, we should bless (1 Co. iv. 12); and thus, though the contempt of the world is not in itself desirable, yet it is blessed to tread in the footsteps of Jesus, to imitate his example, and even to suffer for his sake, Phi. i. 29. ¶ *All manner of evil against you falsely.* An emphasis should be laid on the word *falsely* in this passage. It is not blessed to have evil spoken of us if we *deserve it;* but if we deserve it not, then we should not consider it as a calamity. We should take it patiently, and show how much the Christian, under the consciousness of innocence, can bear, 1 Pe. iii. 13–18. ¶ *For my sake.* Because you are attached to me; because you are Christians. We are not to *seek* such things. We are not to do things to offend others; to treat them harshly or unkindly, and to *court* revilings. We are not to say or do things, though they may be on the subject of religion, designed to disgust or offend. But if, in the faithful endeavour to be Christians, we are reviled, as our Master was, then we are to take it with patience, and to remember that thousands before us have been treated in like manner. When thus reviled or persecuted, we are to be meek, patient, humble; not angry; not reviling again; but endeavouring to do good to our persecutors and slanderers, 2 Ti. ii. 24, 25. In this way many have been convinced of the power and excellence of that religion which they were persecuting and reviling. They have seen that nothing else *but* Christianity could impart such patience and meekness to the persecuted; and have, by this means, been constrained to submit themselves to the gospel of Jesus. Long since it became a proverb, "that the blood of the martyrs is the seed of the church."

12. *Rejoice, and be exceeding glad.* Regard it as a great privilege thus to be persecuted and to suffer—a thing not to be mourned over, but as among the chief blessings of life. ¶ *For great* is *your reward in heaven.* That is, your reward *will be* great in the future world. To those who suffer most, God imparts the highest rewards. Hence the crown of martyrdom has been thought to be the brightest that any of the redeemed

glad: for [m]great *is* your reward in heaven: for so persecuted they the prophets which were before you.

13 Ye are the [n]salt of the earth: but if the salt have lost his savour, wherewith shall it be salted? it is

m 2 Co.4.17.

n Mar.9.50.

shall wear; and hence many of the early Christians *sought* to become martyrs, and threw themselves in the way of their persecutors, that they might be put to death. They literally rejoiced, and leaped for joy, at the prospect of death for the sake of Jesus. Though God does not require us to *seek* persecution, yet all this shows that there is something in religion to sustain the soul which the world does not possess. Nothing but the consciousness of innocence, and the presence of God, could bear up the sufferers in the midst of these trials; and the flame, therefore, kindled to consume the martyr, has also been a bright light, showing the truth and power of the gospel of Jesus. ¶ *The prophets*, &c. The holy men who came to predict future events, and who were the religious teachers of the Jews. For an account of their persecution, see He. xi.

13. *Ye are the salt of the earth.* Salt renders food pleasant and palatable, and preserves from putrefaction. So Christians, by their lives and instructions, are to keep the world from entire moral corruption. By bringing down the blessing of God in answer to their prayers, and by their influence and example, they save the world from universal vice and crime. ¶ *Salt have lost its savour.* That is, if it has become tasteless, or has lost its preserving properties. The salt used in this country is a chemical compound—chloride of sodium—and if the *saltness* were lost, or it were to lose its *savour*, there would be nothing remaining. It enters into the very *nature* of the substance. In eastern countries, however, the salt used was impure, or mingled with vegetable or earthy substances, so that it might lose the whole of its saltness, and a considerable quantity of earthy matter remain. This was good for nothing, except that it was used to place in paths, or walks, as we use gravel. This kind of salt is common still in that country. It is found in the earth in veins or layers, and when exposed to the sun and rain, loses its saltness entirely. Maundrell says, "I broke a piece of it, of which that part that was exposed to the rain, sun, and air, though it had the sparks and particles of salt, yet it had perfectly lost its savour. The inner part, which was connected to the rock, retained its savour, as I found by proof." So Dr. Thomson (*The Land and the Book*, vol. ii. p. 43, 44) says, "I have often seen just such salt, and the identical disposition of it that our Lord has mentioned. A merchant of Sidon having farmed of the government the revenue from the importation of salt, brought over an immense quantity from the marshes of Cyprus—enough, in fact, to supply the whole province for at least twenty years. This he had transferred to the mountains, to cheat the government out of some small percentage. Sixty-five houses in Jûne—Lady Stanhope's village—were rented and filled with salt. These houses have merely earthen floors, and the salt next the ground, in a few years, entirely spoiled. I saw large quantities of it literally thrown into the street, to be trodden under foot of men and beasts. It was 'good for nothing.'

"It should be stated in this connection that the salt used in this country is not manufactured by boiling clean salt water, nor quarried from mines, but is obtained from marshes along the sea-shore, as in Cyprus, or from salt lakes in the interior, which dry up in summer, as the one in the desert north of Palmyra, and the great lake of Jebbûl, south-east of Aleppo.

"Maundrell, who visited the lake at Jebbûl, tells us that he found salt there which had entirely 'lost its savour,' and the same abounds among the debris at Usdum, and in other localities of rock-salt at the south end of the Dead Sea. Indeed, it is a well-known fact that the salt of *this country*, when in contact with the ground, or exposed to rain and sun, does become insipid and useless. From the manner in which it is gathered, much earth and other impurities are necessarily collected with it. Not a little of it is so impure that it cannot be used at all, and such salt soon effloresces and turns to dust—not to fruitful soil, however. It is not only good for nothing itself, but it actually destroys all fertility wherever it is thrown; and this is the reason why it is

thenceforth good for nothing, but to be cast out, and to be trodden under foot of men.

14 Ye are the [o]light of the world. A city that is set on an hill cannot be hid.

15 Neither do men light a candle, and put it under a [2]bushel, but on

o Phi.2.15.

2 The word in the original signifieth *a measure containing about a pint less than a peck.*

---

cast into the street. There is a sort of verbal verisimilitude in the manner in which our Lord alludes to the act: 'it is cast out' and 'trodden under foot;' so troublesome is this corrupted salt, that it is carefully swept up, carried forth, and thrown into the street. There is no place about the house, yard, or garden where it can be tolerated. No man will allow it to be thrown on to his field, and the only place for it is the street, and there it is cast to be trodden under foot of men."

14. *The light of the world.* The light of the world often denotes the *sun*, Jn. xi. 9. The sun renders objects visible, shows their form, their nature, their beauties, their deformities. The term *light* is often applied to religious teachers. See Mat. iv. 16; Lu. ii. 32; Jn. i. 4; viii. 12; Is. xlix. 6. It is pre-eminently applied to Jesus in these places, because he is, in the moral world, what the sun is in the natural world. The apostles, Christian ministers, and all Christians, are lights of the world, because they, by their instructions and example, show what God requires, what is the condition of man, what is the way of duty, peace, and happiness—the way that leads to heaven. ¶ *A city that is set on a hill*, &c. Many of the cities of Judea were placed on the summits or sides of mountains, and could be seen from afar. Perhaps Jesus *pointed* to such a city, and told his disciples that they were like it. Their actions could not be hid. The eyes of the world were upon them. They *must be seen;* and as this was the case, they ought to be holy, harmless, and undefiled.

Maundrell, Jowett, and others suppose that the Sermon on the Mount was delivered in the vicinity of the present city of *Safed*, or "the Horns of Huttin" (see Notes on ver. 1), and that this city may have been in his eye, and may have been directly referred to by the Saviour when he uttered this sentiment. It would give additional force and beauty to the passage to suppose that he pointed to the city. Of this Dr. Thomson (*The Land and the Book*, vol. i. p. 420, 421) says, "The shape of the hill is a well-described oval, and the wall corresponds to it. The bottom of the outer ditch is now a very flourishing vineyard, and the entire circuit is not far from half a mile. The wall is mostly modern, but built on one more ancient, portions of which can be seen on the east side. The interior summit rises about a hundred feet higher than this wall, and was a separate castle, strongly defended. Here are *bevelled* stones, as heavy, and as aged in appearance, as those of the most celebrated ruins in the country; and they prove that this has been a place of importance from a remote age. These ancient parts of the castle render it all but certain that there was then a city or citadel on this most conspicuous 'hill' top; and our Lord might well point to it to illustrate and confirm his precept. The present Hebrew name is Zephath, and may either refer to its elevation like a watch-tower, or to the beauty and grandeur of the surrounding prospects. Certainly they are quite sufficient to suggest the name. There lies Gennesaret, like a mirror set in framework of dark mountains and many-faced hills. Beyond is the vast plateau of the Hauran, faintly shading with its rocky ranges the utmost horizon eastward. Thence the eye sweeps over Gilead and Bashan, Samaria and Carmel, the plains of Galilee, the coasts of Phœnicia, the hills of Naphtali, the long line of Lebanon, and the lofty head of Hermon—a vast panorama, embracing a thousand points of historic and sacred interest."

15. *Neither do men light a candle*, &c. The word rendered *candle* means any portable light, as a lamp, candle, lantern. Comp. Mar. iv. 21; Lu. viii. 16; xii. 35. Jesus proceeded here to show them that the very reason why they were enlightened was that others might also see the light, and be benefited by it. When men light a candle, they do not *conceal* the light, but place it where it may be of use. So it is with religion. It is given that we may benefit others. It is not to be concealed, but suffered to show itself, and to shed light on a surrounding wicked world. ¶ *A bushel. Greek*, a measure containing nearly a

a candlestick; and it giveth light
unto all that are in the house.
16 Let your light so shine before
men, that they may see your good
works, and [p]glorify your Father
which is in heaven.

p 1 Pe.2.12.

17 Think not that I am come to
[q]destroy the law or the prophets:
I am not come to destroy, [r]but to
fulfil.
18 For verily I say unto you,
[s]Till heaven and earth pass, one jot

q ch.3.15. r Is.42.21; Ps.40.6,8. s Lu.16.17.

---

peck. It denotes anything, here, that might *conceal the light*.

16. *Let your light so shine*, &c. Let your holy life, your pure conversation, and your faithful instructions, be everywhere seen and known. Always, in all societies, in all business, at home and abroad, in prosperity and adversity, let it be seen that you are real Christians. ¶ *That they may see your good works.* The proper *motive* to influence us is not simply that we *may be seen* (comp. ch. vi. 1), but it should be that our heavenly Father may be glorified. The Pharisees acted to be *seen of men;* true Christians act to glorify God, and care little what *men* may think of them, except as by their conduct others may be brought to honour God, yet they should so live that men *may* see from their conduct what is the proper nature of their religion. ¶ *Glorify your Father.* Praise, or honour God, or be led to worship him. Seeing in your lives the excellency of religion, and the power and purity of the gospel, they may be won to be Christians also, and give praise and glory to God for his mercy to a lost world.

We learn here, 1. That religion, if it exist, cannot be concealed. 2. That where it is not manifest in the life, it does not exist. 3. That professors of religion, who live like other men, give evidence that they have never been truly converted. 4. That to attempt to conceal or hide our Christian knowledge or experience is to betray our trust, injure the cause of piety, and to render our lives useless. And, 5. That good actions will be seen, and will lead men to honour God. If we have no other way of doing good—if we are poor, and unlearned, and unknown—yet we may do good by our lives. No sincere and humble Christian lives in vain. The feeblest light at midnight is of use.

"How far the little candle throws his beams!
So shines a good deed in a naughty world!"

17. *Think not that I am come*, &c. Our Saviour was just entering on his work. It was important for him to state what he came to do. By his setting up to be a teacher in opposition to the scribes and Pharisees, some might charge him with an intention to destroy their law, and to abolish the customs of the nation. He therefore told them that he did not come for that end, but really to *fulfil* or accomplish what was in the law and the prophets. ¶ *To destroy.* To abrogate; to deny their divine authority; to set men free from the obligation to obey them. ¶ *The law.* The five books of Moses called the law. See Notes on Lu. xxiv. 44. ¶ *The prophets.* The books which the prophets wrote. These two divisions here seem to comprehend the Old Testament, and Jesus says that he came not to do away or destroy the authority of the Old Testament. ¶ *But to fulfil.* To complete the design; to fill up what was predicted; to accomplish what was intended in them. The word fulfil also means sometimes to *teach* or inculcate, Col. i. 25. The law of Moses contained many sacrifices and rites which were designed to shadow forth the Messiah. See Notes on He. ix. These were *fulfilled* when he came and offered himself a sacrifice to God,

"A sacrifice of nobler name,
And richer blood than they."

The prophets contained many predictions respecting his coming and death. These were all to be fulfilled and fully accomplished by his life and his sufferings.

18. *Verily.* Truly, certainly. A word of strong affirmation. ¶ *Till heaven and earth pass.* This expression denotes that the law *never would be destroyed* till it should be *all* fulfilled. It is the same as saying everything else may change; the very earth and heaven may pass away, but the law of God shall not be destroyed till its whole design has been accomplished. ¶ *One jot.* The word *jot*, or *yod*—'—is the name of the Hebrew letter *I*, the smallest letter in the Hebrew alphabet. ¶ *One tittle.* The word here used, in the Greek, means literally *a little horn*, then *a point*, *an extremity*. Several of

or one tittle shall in no wise pass
from the law, till all be fulfilled.
19 Whosoever therefore shall
break one of these least commandments, and shall teach men so, he
shall be called the least in the
kingdom of heaven: but whosoever shall do and teach *them*, the

---

the Hebrew letters were written with small points or apices, as in the letter *schin*—שׁ—or *sin*—שׂ—which serve to distinguish one letter from another. To change a small point of one letter, therefore, might vary the meaning of a word, and destroy the sense. The name "little horn" was given to these points probably from the manner in which they were written, resembling *a little horn*. Professor Hackett says of a manuscript which he saw a Jew transcribing: "One peculiarity, that struck me at once as I cast my eye over the parchment, was the horn-like appearance attached to some of the letters. I had seen the same mark, before this, in Hebrew manuscripts, but never where it was so prominent as here. The sign in question, as connected with the Hebrew Letter Lamedh in particular, had almost the appearance of an intentional imitation of a ram's head. It was to that appendage of the Hebrew letters that the Saviour referred when he said, 'Not one jot or little horn' (as the Greek term signifies, which our version renders 'tittle,') 'shall pass from the law until all be fulfilled.'"—*Illustrations of Scripture*, p. 234. Hence the Jews were exceedingly cautious in writing those letters, and considered the smallest change or omission a reason for destroying the whole manuscript when they were transcribing the Old Testament. The expression, "one jot or tittle," became proverbial, and means that the *smallest part* of the law should not be destroyed.

The laws of the Jews are commonly divided into moral, ceremonial, and judicial. The moral laws are such as grow out of the *nature of things*, and which cannot, therefore, be changed—such as the duty of loving God and his creatures. These cannot be abolished, as it can never be made right to *hate* God, or to hate our fellow-men. Of this kind are the ten commandments, and these our Saviour has neither abolished nor superseded.—The ceremonial laws are such as are appointed to meet certain states of society, or to regulate the religious rites and ceremonies of a people. These can be changed when circumstances are changed, and yet the moral law be untouched. A general in an army may command his soldiers to appear sometimes in a red coat and sometimes in blue or in yellow. This would be a *ceremonial* law, and might be changed as he pleased. The duty of *obeying him*, and of being faithful to his country, could not be changed. This is a moral law. A parent might suffer his children to have fifty different dresses at different times, and love them equally in all. The dress is a mere matter of *ceremony*, and may be changed. The child, in all these garments, is bound to *love* and *obey* his father. This is a *moral* law, and cannot be changed. So the laws of the Jews. Those designed to regulate mere matters of ceremony and rites of worship might be changed. Those requiring *love and obedience to God* and love to men could not be changed, and Christ did not attempt it, Mat. xix. 19; xxii. 37-39; Lu. x. 27; Ro. xiii. 9.—A third species of law was the *judicial*, or those laws regulating courts of justice which are contained in the Old Testament. These were of the nature of the ceremonial law, and might also be changed at pleasure. The *judicial* law of the Hebrews was adapted to their own civil society. When the form of their polity was changed this was of course no longer binding. The *ceremonial* law was *fulfilled* by the coming of Christ: the shadow was lost in the substance, and ceased to be binding. The *moral* law was confirmed and unchanged.

19. *Whosoever therefore shall break.* Shall violate or disobey. ¶ *One of these least commandments.* The Pharisees, it is probable, divided the precepts of the law into *lesser* and *greater*, teaching that they who violated the former were guilty of a trivial offence only. See Mat. xxiii. 23. Christ teaches that in his kingdom they who make this distinction, or who taught that any laws of God might be violated with impunity, should be called *least;* while *they* should be held in high regard who observed *all* the laws of God without distinction. ¶ *Shall be called least.* That is, shall *be* least. See ver. 9. The meaning of this passage seems to be

same shall be [t]called great in the kingdom of heaven.

20 For I say unto you, That except your righteousness shall exceed [u]*the righteousness* of the scribes and Pharisees, ye shall in no case enter into the kingdom of heaven.

21 Ye have heard that it was said [3]by them of old time, [v]Thou shalt not kill; and whosoever shall

t 1 Sa.2.30. *u* ch.23.23-28; Phi.3.9. [3] or, *to them.* *v* Ex.20.13; De.5.17.

this: in the kingdom of heaven, that is, in the kingdom of the Messiah, or in the church which he is about to establish (see Notes on Mat. iii. 2), he that breaks the least of these commandments shall be in no *esteem*, or shall not be regarded *as a proper religious teacher.* The Pharisees, by dividing the law into *greater* and *lesser* precepts, made no small part of it void by their traditions and divisions, Mat. xxiii. 23; xv. 3–6. Jesus says that in his kingdom all this vain division and tradition would cease. Such divisions and distinctions would be a small matter. He that attempted it should be the *least* of all. Men would be engaged in yielding obedience to *all* the law of God without any such vain distinctions. ¶ *Shall be called great.* He that teaches that *all* the law of God is binding, and that *the whole* of it should be obeyed, without attempting to specify what is most important, shall be a teacher worthy of his office, and shall be called great. We learn hence, 1. That *all* the law of God is binding on Christians. Comp. Ja. ii. 10. 2. That all the commands of God should be preached, in their proper place, by Christian ministers. 3. That they who pretend that there are any laws of God so small that they need not obey them, are unworthy of his kingdom. And, 4. That true piety has respect to *all* the commandments of God. Comp. Ps. cxix. 6.

20. *Your righteousness.* Your holiness; your *views* of the nature of righteousness, and your conduct and lives. Unless you are more holy than they are, you cannot be saved. ¶ *Shall exceed.* Shall excel, or *abound* more. The righteousness of true Christians is seated in the *heart*, and is therefore genuine. Jesus means that unless they had more *real* holiness of character than the scribes and Pharisees, they could not be saved. ¶ The righteousness *of the scribes and Pharisees.* See Notes on ch. iii. 7. Their righteousness consisted in *outward* observances of the ceremonial and traditional law. They offered sacrifices, fasted often, prayed much, were punctilious about ablutions, and tithes, and the ceremonies of religion, but neglected justice, truth, purity, and holiness of heart. See Mat. xxiii. 13–33. The righteousness that Jesus required in his kingdom was purity, chastity, honesty, temperance, the fear of God, and the love of man. It is pure, eternal, reaching the motives, and making the life holy. ¶ *The kingdom of heaven.* See Notes on ch. iii. 2. Shall not be a fit subject of his kingdom here, or saved in the world to come.

21. *Ye have heard.* Or, this is the common interpretation among the Jews. Jesus proceeds here to comment on some prevailing opinions among the Jews; to show that the righteousness of the scribes and Pharisees was defective; and that men needed a better righteousness, or they could not be saved. He illustrates what he meant by that better righteousness by showing that the common opinions of the scribes were erroneous. ¶ *By them of old time.* This *might* be translated *to the ancients*, referring to Moses and the prophets. But it is more probable that Jesus here refers to the *interpreters* of the law and the prophets. He did not set himself against the law of Moses, but against the false and pernicious interpretations of the law prevalent in his time. ¶ *Thou shalt not kill.* See Ex. xx. 13. This properly denotes taking the life of another with malice, or with an intention to murder him. The Jews understood it as meaning no more. The comment of our Saviour shows that it was spiritual, and was designed to extend to the *thoughts* and *feelings* as well as the external act. ¶ *Shall be in danger of.* Shall be held guilty, and be punished by. The law of Moses declared that the murderer should be put to death, Le. xxiv. 21; Nu. xxxv. 16. It did not say, however, by whom this should be done, and it was left to the Jews to organize courts to have cognizance of such crimes, De. xvi. 18. ¶ *The judgment.* This was the tribunal that had cognizance of cases of murder, &c. It was a *court* that sat in each city or town, and consisted

kill shall be in danger of the judgment:

22 But I say unto you, That[w] whosoever is angry with his brother without a cause, shall be in danger of the judgment: and whosoever shall say to his brother, [4]Raca, shall be in danger of the council:

w 1 Jn.3.15.

4 i.e. *vain fellow*, 2 Sa.6.20.

commonly of seven members. It was the lowest court among the Jews, and from it an appeal might be taken to the Sanhedrim.

22. *But I say unto you.* Jesus being God as well as man (Jn. i. 1, 14), and therefore, being the original giver of the law, had a right to expound it or change it as he pleased. Comp. Mat. xii. 6, 8. He therefore spoke here and elsewhere as *having authority*, and not as the scribes. It may be added here that no mere man ever spake as Jesus did, when explaining or enforcing the law. He did it as having a *right* to do it; and he that has a right to ordain and change laws in the government of God must be himself divine. ¶ *Is angry with his brother without a cause.* Anger, or that feeling which we have when we are injured, and which prompts us to defend ourselves when in danger, is a natural feeling, given to us—1st. As a proper expression of our disapprobation of a course of evil conduct; and 2d. That we may defend ourselves when suddenly attacked. When excited against sin, it is lawful. God is angry with the wicked, Ps. vii. 11. Jesus looked on the hypocritical Pharisees *with anger*, Mar. iii. 5. So it is said, "Be ye angry, and sin not," Ep. iv. 26. This anger, or indignation against *sin*, is not what our Saviour speaks of here. What he condemns here is anger *without a cause;* that is, unjustly, rashly, hastily, where no offence has been given or intended. In that case it is evil; and it is a violation of the sixth commandment, because *he that hateth his brother is a murderer*, 1 Jn. iii. 15. He has a feeling which would lead him to *commit* murder, if it were fully acted out. The word *brother* here refers not merely to one to whom we are nearly related, having the same parent or parents, as the word is commonly used, but includes also a neighbour, or perhaps anyone with whom we may be associated. As all men are descended from one Father and are all the creatures of the same God, so they are all brethren; and so every man should be regarded and treated as a brother, He. xi. 16. ¶ *Raca.* This is a Syriac word, expressive of great contempt. It comes from a verb signifying to be *empty*, *vain;* and hence, as a word of contempt, denotes *senseless*, *stupid*, *shallow-brains.* Jesus teaches here that to use such words is a violation of the *spirit* of the sixth commandment, and if indulged, may lead to a more open and dreadful infraction of that law. Children should learn that to use such words is highly offensive to God, for we must give an account for every *idle word* which we speak in the day of judgment, Mat. xii. 36. ¶ *In danger of the council.* The word translated *council* is in the original *Sanhedrim*, and there can be no doubt that the Saviour refers to the Jewish tribunal of that name. This was instituted in the time of the Maccabees, probably about 200 years before Christ. It was composed of seventy-two judges; the high-priest was the president of this tribunal. The seventy-two members were made up of the chief priests and elders of the people and the scribes. The chief priests were such as had discharged the office of the high-priest, and those who were the *heads* of the twenty-four classes of priests, who were called in an honorary way *high* or *chief* priests. See Mat. ii. 4. The *elders* were the princes of the tribes or heads of the family associations. It is not to be supposed that *all* the elders had a right to a seat here, but such only as were *elected* to the office. The *scribes* were learned men of the nation elected to this tribunal, being neither of the rank of priests or elders. This tribunal had cognizance of the great affairs of the nation. Till the time when Judea was subjected to the Romans, it had the power of life and death. It still retained the power of passing *sentence*, though the Roman magistrate held the right of execution. It usually sat in Jerusalem, in a room near the temple. It was before this tribunal that our Saviour was tried. It was then assembled in the palace of the high-priest, Mat. xxvi. 3–57; Jn. xviii. 24. ¶ *Thou fool.* This term expressed *more* than want of wisdom. It was expressive of the highest guilt. It had been commonly used to denote those who were idolaters (De. xxii. 21), and also one

but whosoever shall say, Thou fool, shall be in danger of hell fire.

23 Therefore, [x]if thou bring thy gift to the altar, and there rememberest that thy brother hath aught against thee,

24 Leave there thy gift before the altar, and go thy way; first be

x De.16.16,17.

who is guilty of great crimes, Jos. vii. 15; Ps. xiv. 1. ¶ *Hell fire.* The original of this is "*the* GEHENNAH *of fire.*" The word GEHENNA, commonly translated *hell*, is made up of two Hebrew words, and signifies the *valley of Hinnom.* This was formerly a pleasant valley near to Jerusalem, on the south. A small brook or torrent usually ran through it and partly encompassed the city. This valley the idolatrous Israelites devoted formerly to the horrid worship of Moloch, 2 Ki. xvi. 3; 2 Ch. xxviii. 3. In that worship, the ancient Jewish writers inform us, the idol of Moloch was of brass, adorned with a royal crown, having the head of a calf, and his arms extended as if to embrace anyone. When they offered children to him they heated the statue within by a great fire, and when it was burning hot they put the miserable child into his arms, where it was soon consumed by the heat; and, in order that the cries of the child might not be heard, they made a great noise with drums and other instruments about the idol. These drums were called TOPH, and hence a common name of the place was TOPHET, Je. vii. 31, 32.

After the return of the Jews from captivity, this place was held in such abhorrence that, by the example of Josiah (2 Ki. xxiii. 10), it was made the place where to throw all the dead carcasses and filth of the city, and was not unfrequently the place of public executions. It became, therefore, extremely offensive; the sight was terrific; the air was polluted and pestilential; and to preserve it in any manner pure, it was necessary to keep fires continually burning there. The extreme loathsomeness of the place; the filth and putrefaction; the corruption of the atmosphere, and the lurid fires blazing by day and night, made it one of the most appalling and terrific objects with which a Jew was acquainted. It was called the GEHENNA *of fire*, and was the image which our Saviour often employed to denote the future punishment of the wicked.

In this verse it denotes a degree of suffering higher than the punishment inflicted by the *court of seventy*, or the *Sanhedrim*, and the whole verse may therefore mean, "He that hates his brother without a cause is guilty of a violation of the sixth commandment, and shall be punished with a severity similar to that inflicted by the *court of judgment.* He that shall suffer his passions to transport him still farther, so that he shall make his brother an object of derision and contempt, shall be exposed to severer punishment, corresponding to that which the *Sanhedrim*, or *council*, inflicts. But he who shall load his brother with odious appellations and abusive language shall incur the severest degree of punishment, represented by being burned alive in the horrid and awful valley of Hinnom."

The amount, then, of this difficult and important verse is this: The Jews considered but *one crime* a violation of the sixth commandment, viz. actual murder, or wilful, unlawful taking *life.* Jesus says that the commandment is much broader. It relates not only to the *external* act, but to the feelings and words. He specifies three forms of such violation. 1st. Unjust *anger.* 2d. Anger accompanied with an expression of *contempt.* 3d. Anger, with an expression not only of contempt, but *wickedness.* Among the Jews there were three degrees of condemnation: that by the "judgment," the "council," and the "fire of Hinnom." Jesus says likewise there shall be grades of condemnation for the different ways of violating the sixth commandment. Not only *murder* shall be punished by God, but *anger* and *contempt* shall be regarded by him as a violation of the law, and punished according to the offence. As these offences were not actually cognizable before the Jewish tribunals, he must mean that they will be punished *hereafter*, and *all* these expressions therefore relate to *degrees of punishment* proportionate to crime in the future world—the world of justice and of woe.

23, 24. *Therefore, if thou bring thy gift to the altar*, &c. The Pharisees were intent only on the *external* act in worship. They looked not at all to the internal state of the mind. If a man conformed to the *external* rites of religion, however much envy, and malice, and secret ha-

reconciled to thy brother, and then
come and offer thy gift.

25 Agree[y] with thine adversary
quickly, whiles thou art in the way
with him; lest at any time the adversary deliver thee to the judge,
and the judge deliver thee to the
officer, and thou be cast into prison.

26 Verily I say unto thee, Thou
shalt by no means come out thence,

y Pr.25.8; Lu.12.58,59.

---

tred he might have, they thought he was doing well. Our Saviour taught a different doctrine. It was of more consequence to have the *heart* right than to perform the outward act. If, therefore, says he, a man has gone so far as to bring his gift *to the very altar*, and should remember that anyone had anything against him, it was his duty there to leave his offering and go and be reconciled. While a difference of this nature existed, his offering could not be acceptable. He was not to *wait* till the offended brother should come to him; he was to *go* and seek him out, and be reconciled. So now the worship of God will not be acceptable, however well performed *externally*, until we are at peace with those that we have injured. "To obey is better than sacrifice," 1 Sa. xv. 22. He that comes to worship his Maker filled with malice, and hatred, and envy, and *at war with his brethren*, is a hypocritical worshipper, and must meet with God's displeasure. God is not deceived, and he will not be mocked. ¶ *Thy gift.* Thy sacrifice. What thou art about to devote to God as an offering. ¶ *To the altar.* The altar was situated in front of the temple, and was the place on which sacrifices were made. See the Notes on plan, Mat. xxi. 12. To bring a gift to the altar was expressive of worshipping God, for this was the way in which he was formerly worshipped. ¶ *Thy brother.* Any man, especially any fellow-worshipper. Anyone of the same religious society. ¶ *Hath aught.* Is offended, or thinks he has been injured by you in any manner. ¶ *First be reconciled.* This means to settle the difficulty; to make proper acknowledgment or satisfaction for the injury. If you have wronged him, make restitution. If you owe him a debt which ought to be paid, pay it. If you have injured his character, confess it and seek pardon. If he is under an erroneous impression, if your conduct has been such as to *lead* him to suspect that you have injured him, make an explanation. Do all *in your power*, and all you *ought to do*, to have the matter settled. From this we learn: 1st. That, in order to worship God acceptably, we must do justice to our fellow-men. 2d. Our worship will not be acceptable unless we do all we can to live *peaceably* with others. 3d. It is our duty to *seek* reconciliation with others when we have injured them. 4th. This should be done *before* we attempt to worship God. 5th. This is often the reason why God does not accept our offerings, and we go empty away from our devotions. We do not do what we ought to others; we cherish improper feelings or refuse to make proper acknowledgments, and God *will not* accept such attempts to worship him.

25, 26. *Agree with thine adversary quickly.* This is still an illustration of the sixth commandment. To be in hostility, to go to law, to be litigious, is a violation always, on one side or the other, of the law requiring us to love our neighbour, and our Saviour regards it as a violation of the sixth commandment. While you are in the *way* with him, says he, that is, while you are *going* to the court, *before the trial has taken place*, it is your duty, if possible, to come to an agreement. It is wrong to carry the contention to a court of law. See 1 Co. vi. 6, 7. The consequence of *not* being reconciled, he expresses in the language of courts. The adversary shall deliver to the judge, and he to the executioner, and he shall throw you into prison. He did not mean to say that this would be *literally* the way with God, but that *His* dealings with those that harboured these feelings, and would not be *reconciled* with their brethren, were *represented* by the punishment inflicted by human tribunals. That is, he would hold all such as *violators* of the sixth commandment, and would punish them accordingly.

There is no propriety in the use sometimes made of this verse, in representing *God* as the "adversary" of the sinner, and urging him to be reconciled to God while in the way to judgment. Nor does the phrase "thou shalt by no means come out thence till thou hast paid the uttermost farthing" refer to the *eternity* of future punishment. It is language taken from courts of justice,

till thou hast paid the uttermost
farthing.
27 Ye have heard that it was
said by them of old time, Thou
shalt not commit adultery:
28 But I say unto you, That whosoever [2]looketh on a woman to lust
after her hath committed adultery
with her already in his heart.
29 And if thy right eye [5]offend
thee, pluck it out, and cast *it* from
thee: for it is profitable for thee

2 Job 31.1; Pr.6.25. 5 or, *do cause thee to offend.*

to illustrate the truth that God will *punish* men according to *justice* for not being reconciled to him. The punishment in the future world will be eternal indeed (Mat. xxv. 46), but *this* passage does not prove it. ¶ *Thine adversary.* A man that is opposed to us in law. It here means a *creditor;* a man who has a just claim on us. ¶ *In the way with him.* While you are going before the court. Before the trial comes on. It is remarkable that this *very direction* is found in the Roman law of the Twelve Tables, which expressly directed the plaintiff and defendant to make up the matter while they were *in the way,* or going to the prætor—*in via, rem uti pacunt orato.—Blackstone's Comm.,* iii. p. 299. Whether the Saviour had any reference to this cannot be determined. As the Roman laws prevailed to some extent in Palestine, however, it is possible that there was such an allusion. ¶ *The officer.* The executioner; or, as we should say, the sheriff. ¶ *The uttermost farthing.* The last farthing. All that is due. The *farthing* was a small coin used in Judea, equal to two *mites.* It was not quite equal to half a farthing of English money.

27, 28. *Ye have heard that it was said by them of old time, Thou shalt not commit adultery.* See Notes on ver. 21. Our Saviour in these verses explains the seventh commandment. It is probable that the Pharisees had explained this commandment, as they had the *sixth,* as extending only to the external act; and that they regarded evil thoughts and a wanton imagination as of little consequence, or as not forbidden by the law. Our Saviour assures them that the commandment did not regard the external act merely, but the secrets of the heart, and the movements of the *eye.* He declares that they who indulge a wanton desire, that they who *look* on a woman to increase their lust, have already, in the sight of God, violated the commandment, and committed adultery in the heart. Such was the guilt of David, whose deep and awful crime fully shows the danger of indulging in evil desires, and in the rovings of a wanton eye. See 2 Sa. xi.; Ps. li. See also 2 Pe. ii. 14. So exceeding strict and broad is the law of God! And so heinous in *his* sight are thoughts and feelings which may be for ever concealed from the world!

29. *Thy right eye.* The Hebrews, like others, were accustomed to represent the affections of the mind by the members or parts of the body, Ro. vii. 23; vi. 13. Thus the *bowels* denoted compassion; the *heart,* affection or feeling; the *reins,* understanding, secret purpose. An *evil eye* denotes sometimes *envy* (Mat. xx. 15), and sometimes an evil passion, or sin in general. Mar. vii. 21, 22: "Out of the heart proceedeth an *evil eye.*" In this place, as in 2 Pe. ii. 14, the expression is used to denote strong adulterous passion, unlawful desire, or wicked inclination. The *right* eye and hand are mentioned, because they are of most *use* to us, and denote that, however *strong* the passion may be, or difficult to part with, yet that we should do it. ¶ *Offend thee.* The noun from which the verb "offend," in the original, is derived, commonly means a *stumbling-block,* or a *stone* placed in the way, over which one might fall. It also means a *net,* or a certain part of a net against which, if a *bird* strikes, it springs the net, and is taken. It comes to signify, therefore, anything by which we fall, or are ensnared; and applied to *morals,* means anything by which we *fall* into sin, or by which we are *ensnared.* The English word *offend* means now, commonly, to displease; to make angry; to affront. This is by no means the sense of the word in Scripture. It means to cause to fall *into sin.* The eye does this when it wantonly *looks* on a woman to lust after her. ¶ *Pluck it out,* &c. It cannot be supposed that Christ intended this to be taken literally. His design was to teach that the *dearest* objects, if they cause us to sin, are to be abandoned; that by all sacrifices and self-denials we must overcome the evil propensities of our nature, and resist our wanton imaginations. Some of

that one of thy members should
perish, and not *that* thy whole
body should be [a]cast into hell.
30 And if thy right hand offend
thee, cut it off, and cast *it* from
thee: for it is profitable for thee
that one of thy members should
perish, and not *that* thy whole
body should be cast into hell.
31 It hath been said, [b]Whosoever
shall put away his wife, let him
give her a writing of divorcement:
32 But I say unto you, That [c]who-
soever shall put away his wife,
saving for the cause of fornication,
causeth her to commit adultery:
and whosoever shall marry her that
is divorced committeth adultery.
33 Again, ye have heard that it
hath been said by them of old

a Ro.8.13; 1 Co.9.27. *b* De.24.1; Je.3.1; Mar.10.2-9. *c* ch.19.9; 1 Co.7.10,11.

the fathers, however, took this commandment literally. Our Saviour several times repeated this sentiment. See Mat. xviii. 9; Mar. ix. 43–47. Comp. also Col. iii. 5. ¶ *It is profitable for thee.* It is *better* for thee. You will be a gainer by it. ¶ *One of thy members perish.* It is better to deny yourself the gratification of an evil passion here, however much it may cost you, than to go down to hell for ever. ¶ *Thy whole body should be cast into hell.* Thy body, with all its unsubdued and vicious propensities. This will constitute no small part of the misery of hell. The sinner will be sent there *as he is*, with every evil desire, every unsubdued propensity, every wicked and troublesome passion, and yet with no possibility of gratification. It constitutes our highest notions of misery when we think of a man filled with anger, pride, malice, avarice, envy and lust, and with no opportunity of gratifying them for ever. This is all that is necessary to make an eternal hell. On the word *hell*, see Notes on ver. 22.

30. *And if thy right hand offend thee.* The right hand is selected for the same reason as the right eye, because it is one of the most important members of the human body. The idea is, that the dearest earthly objects are to be sacrificed rather than that we should commit sin; that the most rigid self-denial should be practised, and that the most absolute self-government should be maintained at any sacrifice, rather than that we should suffer the mind to be polluted by unholy thoughts and impure desires.

31, 32. *It hath been said*, &c. That is, by Moses, De. xxiv. 1, 2. The husband was directed, if he put his wife away, to give her a bill of divorce, that is a certificate of the fact she had been his wife, and that he had dissolved the marriage. There was considerable difference of opinion among the Jews for what *causes* the husband was permitted to do this. One of their famous schools maintained that it might be done for any cause, however *trivial*. The other maintained that *adultery* only could justify it. The truth was, however, that the husband exercised this right at pleasure; that he was judge in the case, and dismissed his wife when and for what cause he chose. And this seems to be agreeable to the law in Deuteronomy. Our Saviour in Mar. x. 1–12, says that this was permitted on account of the hardness of their hearts, but that in the beginning it was not so. God made a single pair, and ordained marriage for life. But Moses found the people so much hardened; so long accustomed to the practice, and so rebellious, that, as a matter of *civil* appointment, he thought it best not to attempt any change. Our Saviour brought marriage back to its original intention, and declared that whosoever put away his wife henceforward, except for one offence, should be guilty of adultery. This is now the law of God. This was the original institution. This is the *only* law that is productive of peace and good morals, and that secures the respect due to a wife, and the good of children. Nor has any man or set of men—any legislature or any court, civil or ecclesiastical—a right to interfere, and declare that divorces may be granted for any other cause. They, therefore, whoever they may be, who are divorced for any cause except the single one of adultery, if they marry again, are, according to the Scriptures, living in adultery. No earthly laws can trample down the laws of God, or make that *right* which he has solemnly pronounced *wrong*.

33. *Thou shalt not forswear thyself.* Christ here proceeds to correct another false interpretation of the law. The

time, [d]Thou shalt not forswear thyself, but shalt perform unto the Lord thine oaths:
34 But I say unto you, [e]Swear not at all: neither by heaven; for it is God's throne:
35 Nor by the earth; for it is his footstool: neither by Jerusalem; for it is [f]the city of the great King.

d Le.19.12; Nu.30.2; De.23.23. e ch.23.16-22; Ja.5.12. f Re.21.2,10.

law respecting oaths is found in Le. xix. 12, and De. xxiii. 23. By those laws men were forbid to perjure themselves, or to *forswear*, that is, swear falsely. ¶ *Perform unto the Lord.* Perform literally, really, and religiously what is promised in an oath. ¶ *Thine oaths.* An oath is a solemn affirmation or declaration, made with an appeal to God for the truth of what is affirmed, and imprecating his vengeance, and renouncing his favour if what is affirmed is false. A false oath is called perjury, or, as in this place, *forswearing*.

It appears, however, from this passage, as well as from the ancient writings of the Jewish rabbins, that while the Jews professedly adhered to the law, they had introduced a number of oaths *in common conversation*, and oaths which they by no means considered to be binding. For example, they would swear by the temple, by the head, by heaven, by the earth. So long as they kept from swearing by the name *Jehovah*, and so long as they observed the oaths *publicly* taken, they seemed to consider all others as allowable, and allowedly broken. This is the abuse which Christ wished to correct. *It was the practice of swearing in common conversation, and especially swearing by created things.* To do this, he said that they were mistaken in their views of the *sacredness* of such oaths. They were very closely connected with God; and to *trifle* with them was a species of trifling with God. Heaven is *his* throne; the earth *his* footstool; Jerusalem *his* peculiar abode; the head was made *by him*, and was so much under his control that we could not make one hair white or black. To swear by these things, therefore, was to treat irreverently objects *created* by God, and could not be without guilt. It is remarkable that the sin here condemned by the Saviour prevails still in Palestine in the same form and manner referred to here. Dr. Thomson (*The Land and the Book*, vol. ii. p. 284) says, "The people now use the very same sort of oaths that are mentioned and condemned by our Lord. They swear by the head, by their life, by heaven, and by the temple, or what is in its place, the church. The forms of cursing and swearing, however, are almost infinite, and fall on the pained ear all day long."

Our Saviour here evidently had no reference to *judicial* oaths, or oaths taken in a court of justice. It was merely the foolish and wicked habit of swearing in private conversation; of swearing on every occasion and by everything that he condemned. This he *does* condemn in a most unqualified manner. He himself, however, did not refuse to take an oath in a court of law, Mat. xxvi. 63, 64. So Paul often *called God to witness* his sincerity, which is all that is meant by an oath. See Ro. i. 9; ix. 1; Ga. i. 20; He. vi. 16. Oaths were, moreover, prescribed in the law of Moses, and Christ did not come to repeal those laws. See Ex. xxii. 11; Le. v. 1; Nu. v. 19; De. xxix. 12, 14.

34, 35. *But I say unto you, Swear not at all.* That is, in the manner which he proceeds to specify. Swear not in any of the common and profane ways customary at that time. ¶ *By heaven; for it is God's throne.* To swear by that was, if it meant anything, *to swear by Him that sitteth thereon*, Mat. xxiii. 22. ¶ *Nor by the earth; for it is his footstool.* Swearing by that, therefore, is really swearing by God. Or perhaps it means, 1st. We have no right to *pledge*, or swear by, what belongs to God; and, 2d. That oaths by inanimate objects are unmeaning and wicked. If they are *real* oaths, they are by a living Being, who has power to take vengeance. A *footstool* is that on which the feet rest when sitting. The term is applied *to the earth* to denote how lowly and humble an object it is when compared with God. ¶ *Jerusalem.* See Notes on ch. ii. 1. ¶ *City of the Great King.* That is, of *God;* called the Great King because he was the King of the Israelites, and Jerusalem was the capital of the nation, and the place where he was peculiarly honoured *as king.* Comp. Ps. xlvi. 4; xlviii. 1, 2; lxxxvii. 3.

36. *Neither shalt thou swear by thy*

36 Neither shalt thou swear by thy head, because thou canst not make one hair white or black.

37 But [g]let your communication be, Yea, yea; Nay, nay: for whatsoever is more than these cometh of evil.

38 Ye have heard that it hath been said, [h]An eye for an eye, and a tooth for a tooth:

39 But I say unto you, [i]That ye resist not evil: [k]but whosoever shall smite thee on the right cheek, turn to him the other also.

g Ja.5.12.

h Ex.21.24. i Pr.20.22; 24.29; Ro.12.17-19. k Is.50.6.

head. This was a common oath. The Gentiles also used this oath. To swear by the *head* was the same as to swear by the *life;* or to say, I will forfeit my *life* if what I say is not true. God is the author of the life, and to swear by *that*, therefore, is the same as to swear by *him.* ¶ *Because thou canst not make one hair white or black.* You have no control or right over your own life. You cannot even change one single *hair. God* has all that control; and it is therefore *improper* and profane to pledge what is God's gift and God's property; and it is the same as swearing by God himself.

37. *But let your communication. Your word;* what you say. ¶ *Be, Yea.* Yes. This does not mean that we should always use the word *yea*, for it might as well have been translated *yes;* but it means that we should simply *affirm* or *declare* that a thing is so. ¶ *More than these.* More than these *affirmations.* ¶ *Cometh of evil.* Is evil. Proceeds from some evil disposition or purpose. And from this we may learn: 1st. That profane swearing is always the evidence of a depraved heart. To trifle with the name of God, or with any of his works, is itself most decided proof of depravity. 2d. That no man is believed any sooner in common conversation because he *swears* to a thing. When we hear a man swear to a thing, it is pretty good evidence that he knows what he is saying to be false, and we should be on our guard. He that will break the third commandment will not hesitate to break the ninth also. And this explains the fact that profane swearers are seldom believed. The man who is *always* believed is he whose character is beyond suspicion in all things, who obeys *all* the laws of God, and whose simple declaration, therefore, is enough. A man that is truly a Christian, and leads a Christian life, does not need oaths and profaneness to make him believed. 3d. It is no mark of a gentleman to swear. The most worthless and vile, the refuse of mankind, the drunkard and the prostitute, swear as well as the best dressed and educated *gentleman.* No particular endowments are requisite to give a *finish* to the art of cursing. The basest and meanest of mankind swear with as much tact and skill as the most refined, and he that wishes to degrade himself to the very lowest level of pollution and shame should learn to be a common swearer. Any man has talents enough to learn to curse God and his fellow-men, and to *pray*—for every man who swears prays—that God would sink him and others into hell. No profane man knows but that God will *hear his prayer*, and send him to the regions of woe. 4th. Profaneness does no man any good. No man is the richer, or wiser, or happier for it. It helps no one's morals or manners. It commends no one to any society. The profane man *must be*, of course, shut out from female society, and no refined intercourse can consist with it. It is disgusting to the refined; abominable to the good; insulting to those with whom we associate; degrading to the mind; unprofitable, needless, and injurious in society; and awful in the sight of God. 5th. God will not hold the profane swearer guiltless. Wantonly to profane his name, to call his vengeance down, to curse him on his throne, to invoke damnation, is perhaps of all offences the most awful. And there is not in the universe more cause of amazement at his forbearance, than that God does not rise in vengeance, and smite the profane swearer at once to hell. Verily, in a world like this, where his name is profaned every day, and hour, and moment by thousands, God shows that he is slow to anger, and that his mercy is without bounds!

38–41. *An eye for an eye*, &c. This command is found in Ex. xxi. 24; Le. xxiv. 20, and De. xix. 21. In these places it was given as a rule *to regulate the decisions of judges.* They were to take eye for eye, and tooth for tooth, and to inflict burning for burning. As a *judicial rule* it is not unjust. Christ

40 And if any man will sue thee at the law, and take away thy coat, let him have *thy* cloak also.

41 And whosoever shall compel thee to go a mile, go with him twain.

---

finds no fault with the rule as applied to *magistrates*, and does not take upon himself to repeal it. But instead of confining it to magistrates, the Jews had extended it to *private* conduct, and made it the rule by which to take *revenge*. They considered themselves justified by this rule to inflict the same injury on others that they had received. Against this our Saviour remonstrates. He declares that the law had no reference to private revenge, that it was given only to regulate the magistrate, and that their private conduct was to be governed by different principles.

The general principle which he laid down was, that we are not *to resist evil;* that is, as it is in the Greek, not to set ourselves against an evil person who is injuring us. But even this general direction is not to be pressed too strictly. Christ did not intend to teach that we are to see our families murdered, or be murdered ourselves, rather than to make resistance. The law of nature, and all laws, human and divine, justify self-defence when *life* is in danger. It cannot surely be the intention to teach that a father should sit by coolly and see his family butchered by savages, and not be allowed to defend them. Neither natural nor revealed religion ever did, or ever can, inculcate this doctrine. Our Saviour immediately explains what *he* means by it. Had he intended to refer it to a case where *life* is in danger, he would most surely have mentioned it. Such a case was far more worthy of statement than those which he *did* mention. A doctrine so unusual, so unlike all that the world had believed, and that the best men had acted on, deserved to be formally stated. Instead of doing this, however, he confines himself to smaller matters, to things of comparatively trivial interest, and says that in these we had better take wrong than to enter into strife and lawsuits. The first case is where we are smitten on the cheek. Rather than contend and fight, we should take it patiently, and turn the other cheek. This does not, however, prevent our remonstrating firmly yet mildly on the injustice of the thing, and insisting that justice should be done us, as is evident from the example of the Saviour himself. See Jn. xviii. 23. The second evil mentioned is where a man is *litigious* and determined to take all the advantage the law can give him, following us with vexatious and expensive lawsuits. Our Saviour directs us, rather than to imitate him—rather than to contend with a revengeful spirit in courts of justice—to take a trifling injury, and yield to him. This is merely a question about property, and not about conscience and life.

"*Coat.*" The Jews wore two principal garments, an interior and an exterior. The *interior*, here called the "*coat*," or the tunic, was made commonly of linen, and encircled the whole body, extending down to the knees. Sometimes beneath this garment, as in the case of the priests, there was another garment corresponding to pantaloons. The coat, or tunic, was extended to the neck, and had long or short sleeves. *Over* this was commonly worn an upper garment, here called "*cloak*," or mantle. It was made commonly nearly square, of different sizes, 5 or 6 cubits long and as many broad, and was wrapped around the body, and was thrown off when labour was performed. *If*, said Christ, an adversary wished to obtain, *at law*, *one* of these garments, rather than contend with him let him have the other also. A reference to various articles of apparel occurs frequently in the New Testament, and it is desirable to have a correct view of the ancient mode of dress, in order to a proper understanding of the Bible. The Asiatic modes of dress are nearly the same from age to age, and hence it is not difficult to illustrate the passages where such a reference occurs. The ordinary dress consisted of the inner garment, the outer garment, the girdle, and the sandals. In regard to the *sandals*, see Notes on ch. iii. 11.

In the girdle was the place of the purse (Mat. x. 9), and to it the sword and dirk were commonly attached. Comp. 2 Sa. xx. 8. In modern times the pistols are also fastened to the girdle. It is the usual place for the handkerchief, smoking materials, inkhorn, and, in general, the implements of one's profession. The girdle served to confine the loose flowing robe or

42 Give to him that asketh thee, and [l]from him that would borrow of thee turn not thou away.

43 Ye have heard that it hath been said, [m]Thou shalt love thy neighbour, and hate thine enemy:

44 But I say unto you, [n]Love your enemies, bless them that curse you, do good to them that hate you, and [o]pray for them which despitefully use you, and persecute you;

l De.15.7,11. m De.23.6. n Ro.12.14,20. o Lu.23.34; Ac.7.60.

outer garment to the body. It held the garment when it was tucked up, as it was usually in walking or in labour. Hence *to gird up the loins* became a significant figurative expression, denoting readiness for service, activity, labour, and watchfulness; and *to loose the loins* denoted the giving way to repose and indolence, 2 Ki. iv. 29; Job xxxviii. 3; Is. v. 27; Lu. xii. 35; Jn. xxi. 7.

Whosoever shall compel thee to go a mile. The word translated *shall compel* is of Persian origin. Post-offices were then unknown. In order that the royal commands might be delivered with safety and despatch in different parts of the empire, Cyrus stationed horsemen at proper intervals on all the great public highways. One of those delivered the message to another, and intelligence was thus rapidly and safely communicated. These heralds were permitted to *compel* any person, or to press any horse, boat, ship, or other vehicle that they might need for the quick transmission of the king's commandments. It was to this custom that our Saviour refers. Rather, says he, than *resist* a public authority requiring your attendance and aid for a certain distance, go peaceably twice the distance. ¶ *A mile.* A Roman *mile* was a thousand paces. ¶ *Twain.* Two.

42. *Give to him that asketh thee.* This is the general rule. It is better to give sometimes to an undeserving person than to turn away one really necessitous. It is good to be *in the habit* of giving. At the same time, the rule must be interpreted so as to be consistent with our duty to our families (1 Ti. v. 8) and with other objects of justice and charity. It is seldom, perhaps never, good to give to a man that is able to work, 2 Th. iii. 10. To give to such is to encourage laziness, and to support the idle at the expense of the industrious. If such a man is indeed hungry, feed him; if he wants anything farther, give him employment. If a widow, an orphan, a man of misfortune, or a man infirm, lame, or sick, is at your door, never send any of them away empty. See He. xiii. 2; Mat. xxv. 35–45. So of a poor and needy friend that wishes to borrow. We are not to turn away or deny him. This deserves, however, some limitation. It must be done in consistency with other duties. To lend to every worthless man would be to throw away our property, encourage laziness and crime, and ruin our families. It should be done consistently with every other obligation, and of this every man is to be the judge. Perhaps our Saviour meant to teach that where there was a *deserving* friend or brother in want, we should *lend* to him without usury, and without *standing much* about the security.

43. *Ye have heard that it hath been said, Thou shalt love thy neighbour, and hate thine enemy.* The command to love our neighbour was a law of God, Le. xix. 18. That we must therefore hate our enemy was an inference drawn from it by the Jews. They supposed that if we loved the one, we must of course hate the other. They were total strangers to that great, peculiar law of religion which requires us to love both. *A neighbour* is literally one that *lives* near to us; then, one that *is near* to us by acts of kindness and friendship. This is its meaning here. See also Lu. x. 36.

44. *Love your enemies.* There are two kinds of love, involving the same general feeling, or springing from the same fountain of good-will to all mankind, but differing so far as to admit of separation in idea. The one is that feeling by which we *approve of the conduct* of another, commonly called *the love of complacency;* the other, that by which we wish well to the *person* of another, though we cannot approve *his conduct.* This is *the love of benevolence*, and this love we are to bear toward our enemies. It is impossible to love the *conduct* of a man that curses and reviles us, that injures our person or property, or that violates all the laws of God; but, though

45 That ye may be the children of your Father which is in heaven: for [p]he maketh his sun to rise on the evil and on the good, and sendeth rain on the just and on the unjust.

46 For if ye love them which love you, what reward have ye? do not even the publicans the same?

47 And if ye salute your brethren only, what do ye more *than others?* do not even the publicans so?

48 Be ye therefore [q]perfect, even as your Father which is in heaven is perfect.

p Job 25.3.

q Ge.17.1; De.18.13; Lu.6.36,40; Col.1.28.

we may hate his conduct, and suffer keenly when *we* are affected by it, yet we may still wish well to the *person;* we may pity his madness and folly; we may speak kindly *of* him and *to* him; we may return good for evil; we may aid him in the time of trial; we may seek to do him good here and to promote his eternal welfare hereafter, Ro. xii. 17–20. This seems to be what is meant by loving our enemies; and this is a peculiar law of Christianity, and the highest possible test of piety, and probably the most difficult of all duties to be performed. ¶ *Bless them that curse you.* The word *bless* here means to *speak well of* or *to:*—not to curse again or to slander, but to speak of those things which we can *commend* in an enemy; or, if there is nothing that we can commend, to say nothing about him. The word *bless*, spoken of God, means to regard with favour or to confer benefits, as when God is said to bless his people. When we speak of our *blessing God*, it means to praise him or give thanks to him. When we speak of blessing *men*, it *unites* the two meanings, and signifies to confer favour, to thank, or to speak well of. ¶ *Despitefully use you.* The word thus translated means, first, to injure by prosecution in law; then, wantonly and unjustly to accuse, and to injure in any way. This seems to be its meaning here. ¶ *Persecute.* See Notes on ch. v. 10.

45. *That ye may be the children of your Father.* In Greek, the *sons* of your Father. The word son has a variety of significations. See Notes on Mat. i. 1. Christians are called the *sons* or *children* of God in several of these senses: as his offspring; as adopted; as his disciples; as imitators of him. In this passage the word is applied to them because, in doing good to enemies, they *resemble* God. *He* makes his sun to rise on the evil and good, and sends rain, without distinction, on the just and unjust. So his people should show that they *imitate* or resemble him, or that they possess his spirit, by doing good in a similar way.

46. *What reward have ye?* The word reward seems to be used in the sense of *deserving of praise.* If you only love those that love you, you are selfish; it is not genuine love for the *character*, but love for the *benefit*, and you deserve no commendation. The very *publicans* would do the same. ¶ *The publicans.* The publicans were tax-gatherers. Judea was a province of the Roman empire. The Jews bore this foreign yoke with great impatience, and paid their taxes with great reluctance. It happened, therefore, that those who were appointed to collect taxes were objects of great detestation. They were, besides, men who would be supposed to execute their office at all hazards; men who were willing to engage in an odious and hated employment; men often of abandoned character, oppressive in their exactions, and dissolute in their lives. By the Jews they were associated in character with thieves and adulterers; with the profane and the dissolute. Christ says that even these wretched men would love their benefactors.

47. *And if you salute your brethren,* &c. The word *salute* here means to show the customary tokens of civility, or to treat with the common marks of friendship. See Notes on Lu. x. 4. The Saviour says that the *worst* men, the very publicans, would do this. Christians should do more; they should show that they have a different spirit; they should treat their *enemies* as well as wicked men do their *friends.* This should be done: 1st. Because it is *right;* it is the only really amiable spirit; and, 2d. We should show that religion is not *selfish*, and is superior to all other principles of action.

48. *Be ye therefore perfect*, &c. The Saviour concludes this part of the discourse by commanding his disciples to be *perfect.* This word commonly means finished, complete, pure, holy. Origin-

ally it is applied to a piece of mechanism, as a machine that is complete in its parts. Applied to men, it refers to completeness of parts, or *perfection*, where no part is defective or wanting. Thus Job (i. 1) is said to be "perfect;" that is, not holy as God, or *sinless*—for fault is afterward found with him (Job ix. 20; xlii. 6); but his piety was *proportionate*—had a completeness of parts —was consistent and regular. He exhibited his religion as a prince, a father, an individual, a benefactor of the poor. He was not merely a pious man in one place, but uniformly. He was consistent everywhere. See Notes on that passage. This is the meaning in Matthew. Be not religious merely in loving your friends and neighbours, but let your piety be shown in loving your enemies; imitate God; let your piety be *complete*, *proportionate*, *regular*. This every Christian *may be;* this every Christian *must be.*

REMARKS ON CHAPTER V.

1st. The gospel pronounces blessings on things far different from what the world has thought to be a source of happiness. Men suppose that happiness is to be found in mirth, in wealth, in honour, in esteem, in freedom from persecution. Christ says that it is to be sought in the reverse. Often men are most happy in poverty, in sickness, in persecution, when supported by the presence and promises of a merciful God. And if God appoints our station there, we should submit to it, and learn therewith to be content.

2d. We may see the evil of anger. It is a species of murder. If secretly cherished, or exhibited by contempt and injury, it must bring down the displeasure of God. It is a source of misery. True enjoyment is found in meekness, peace, calmness, and benevolence. In such a firmness, and steadiness, and dependence on God as to keep the soul unruffled in the midst of provocation, is happiness. Such was Christ.

3d. We see the evil of indelicacy of feeling and sentiment, and the strictness and severity of the law respecting the intercourse of the sexes (ver. 28). And yet what law is more frequently violated? By obscene anecdotes and tales; by songs and gibes; by double meanings and innuendoes; by looks and gestures; by conversation, and obscene books and pictures, this law of our Saviour is perpetually violated. If there is any one sentiment of most value for the comfort, the character, the virtuous sociability of the young—one that will shed the greatest charm over society, and make it the most pure, it is that which inculcates *perfect delicacy* and *purity* in the intercourse of the sexes. Virtue of any kind never blooms where this is not cherished. Modesty and purity once gone, every flower that would diffuse its fragrance over life withers and dies with it. There is no one sin that so withers and blights *every* virtue, none that so enfeebles and prostrates every ennobling feeling of the soul, as the violation of the seventh commandment in spirit or in form, in thought or in act. How should purity dwell in the heart, breathe from the lips, kindle in the eye, live in the imagination, and dwell in the intercourse of all the young! An eternal, avenging God is near to every wanton thought, marks every eye that kindles with impure desire, rolls the thunder of justice over every polluted soul, and is preparing woe for every violator of the laws of purity and chastity, Pr. vii. 22, 23; v. 5; ii. 18.

4th. Revenge is equally forbidden. Persecution, slander, a spirit of litigation, anger, personal abuse, duelling, suicide, murder, are all violations of the law of God, and all must call down his vengeance.

5th. We are bound to love our enemies. This is a law of Christianity, original and peculiar. No system of religion but Christianity has required it, and no act of Christian piety is more difficult. None shows more the power of the grace of God; none is more ornamental to the character; none more like God; and none furnishes better evidence of piety. He that can meet a man kindly who is seeking his hurt; who can speak well of one that is perpetually slandering and cursing him; that can pray for a man that abuses, injures, and wounds him; and that can seek heaven for him that wishes *his* damnation, is in the way to life. This is religion, beautiful as its native skies; pure like its Source; kind like its Author; fresh like the dews of the morning; clear and diffusive like the beams of the rising sun; and holy like the feelings and words that come from the bosom of the Son of God. He that can do this need not doubt that he is a Christian. He has caught the very spirit of the Saviour, and he *must* inherit eternal life.

CHAPTER VI.

TAKE heed that ye do not your [1]alms before men, to be seen of them: otherwise ye have no reward [2]of your Father which is in heaven.

2 Therefore when thou doest *thine* alms, [3]do not sound a trumpet before thee, as the hypocrites do in the synagogues and in the streets, that they may have glory of men. Verily I say unto you, They have their reward.

3 But when thou doest alms, let not thy left hand know what thy right hand doeth:

4 That thine alms may be in secret; and thy Father, which seeth in secret, himself [a]shall reward thee openly.

1 or, *righteousness*, Ps.112.9.
2 or, *with*. 3 or, *cause not a trumpet to be sounded*.

a Lu.8.17; 14.14.

CHAPTER VI.

1. *Take heed that ye do not your alms.* The word *alms* here denotes liberality to the poor and needy. In the margin, as in the best editions of the Greek, it is *righteousness;* either referring to almsgiving as eminently a righteous act, or more probably including all that is specified in this and the following verses—almsgiving, prayer, fasting, ver. 2–18. Our Saviour here does not positively *command* his disciples to aid the poor, but supposes that they *would do* it of course, and gives them directions *how* to do it. It is the nature of religion to help those who are really needy; and a real Christian does not wait to be *commanded* to do it, but only asks for the opportunity. See Ga. ii. 10; Ja. i. 27; Lu. xix. 8. ¶ *Before men*, &c. Our Lord does not require us never to give alms before men, but only forbids our doing it *to be seen of them*, for the purposes of ostentation and to seek their praise. To a person who is disposed to do good from a right motive, it matters little whether it be in public or in private. The only thing that renders it even desirable that our good deeds should be seen is that God may be glorified. See ch. v. 16. ¶ *Otherwise.* If your only motive for doing it is to be seen of men, God will not reward you. Take heed, therefore, that you do not do it to be seen, *otherwise* God will not reward you.

2. *Do not sound a trumpet before thee, as the hypocrites do.* The word *hypocrite* is taken from *stage-players*, who act the part of others, or speak not their own sentiments, but the sentiments of others. It means here, and in the New Testament generally, those who *dissemble* or hide their real sentiments, and assume or express other feelings than their own—those who, for purposes of ostentation, gain, or applause, put on the appearance of religion. It is probable that such persons, when they were about to bestow alms, caused a trumpet to be sounded, *professedly* to call the poor together to receive it, but *really* to call the people to see the proofs of their liberality and piety; or perhaps it may mean that they should not make a great noise about it, *like* sounding a trumpet. ¶ *In the synagogues.* The word *synagogue* commonly means the place of assembling for religious worship known by that name. See Notes on Mat. iv. 23. It might mean, however, any *collection of people* assembled for any purpose, and it is not improbable that it has that meaning here. It does not appear that they made a noise in bestowing charity in the *synagogues*, or that charity was commonly bestowed there; but it was probably done on occasion of any great *assemblage*, in any place of concourse, and at the *corners of the streets*, where it could be seen by many. ¶ *They have their reward.* That is, they obtain the applause they seek—the reputation of being charitable; and as this applause was *all* they wished, there is, of course, no farther reward to be looked for or obtained.

3, 4. *Let not thy left hand know*, &c. This is a proverbial expression, signifying that the action should be done as secretly as possible. The Hebrews often attribute actions to *members* which properly belong to *persons*. The encouragement for performing our acts of charity in secret is that it will be pleasing to God; that he will see the act, however secret it may be, and will openly reward it. If the reward is not granted in *this* life, it will be in the life to come. In multitudes of cases, however, alms given to the poor are "lent to the Lord" (Pr. xix. 17), and will be repaid in this life. Rarely, perhaps never, has it been found that the man who is liberal to the poor has ever

5 And when thou prayest, thou shalt not be as the hypocrites *are:* for they love to pray standing in the synagogues and in the corners of the streets, that they may be seen of men. Verily I say unto you, [b]They have their reward.
6 But thou, when thou prayest,

b Pr.16.5; Ja.4.6.

suffered by it in his worldly circumstances.

5. *And when thou prayest*, &c. Hypocrites manifested the same spirit about prayer as almsgiving; it was done in public places. The word *synagogues*, here, clearly means, not the place of worship of that name, but places where many were accustomed to assemble—near the markets or courts, where they could be seen of many. Our Lord evidently could not mean to condemn prayers in the synagogues. It might be said that he condemned *ostentatious* prayer there, while they neglected *secret* prayer; but this does not appear to be his design. The Jews were much in the habit of praying in public places. At certain times of the day they always offered their prayers. Wherever they were, they suspended their employment and paid their devotions. This is also practised now everywhere by Mohammedans, and in many places by Roman Catholics. It seems, also, that they *sought* publicity, and regarded it as proof of great piety.

6. *Enter into thy closet.* Every Jewish house had a place for secret devotion. The roofs of their houses were *flat* places, well adapted for walking, conversation, and meditation. See Notes on Mat. ix. 2. Professor Hackett (*Illustrations of Scripture*, p. 82) says: "On the roof of the house in which I lodged at Damascus were chambers and rooms along the side and at the corners of the open space or terrace, which constitutes often a sort of upper story. I observed the same thing in connection with other houses." Over the *porch*, or entrance of the house, there was frequently a small room of the size of the porch, raised a story above the rest of the house, expressly appropriated for the place of retirement. Here, in secrecy and solitude, the pious Jew might offer his prayers, unseen by any but the Searcher of hearts. To this place, or to some similar place, our Saviour directed his disciples to repair when they wished to hold communion with God. This is the place commonly mentioned in the New Testament as the *upper room*, or the place for secret prayer. The meaning of the Saviour is, that there should be some place where we may be in secret—where we may be alone with God. There should be some *place* to which we may resort where no ear will hear us but *His* ear, and no eye can see us but *His* eye. Unless there is such a place, secret prayer will not be long or strictly maintained. It is often said that we have no such place, and can secure none. We are away from home; we are travelling; we are among strangers; we are in stages and steamboats, and how can we find such places of retirement? I answer, the *desire* to pray, and the love of prayer, will *create* such places in abundance. The Saviour had all the difficulties which we can have, but yet he lived in the practice of secret prayer. To be alone, he rose up "a great while before day," and went into a solitary place and prayed, Mar. i. 35. With him a grove, a mountain, a garden, furnished such a place, and, though a traveller, and among strangers, and without a house, he lived in the habit of secret prayer. What excuse can they have for not praying who have a home, and who spend the precious hours of the morning in sleep, and who will practise no self-denial that they may be alone with God? O Christian! thy Saviour would have broken in upon these hours, and would have trod his solitary way to the mountain or the grove that he might pray. He *did* do it. He did it to pray for thee, too indolent and too unconcerned about thy own salvation and that of the world to practise the least self-denial in order to commune with God! How can religion live thus? How can such a soul be saved?

The Saviour does not specify the *times* when we should pray in secret. He does not say how *often* it should be done. The reasons may have been: (1.) That he designed that his religion should be *voluntary*, and there is not a better *test* of true piety than a disposition to engage often in secret prayer. He intended to leave it to his people to show attachment to him by coming to God often, and as often as they chose. (2.) An attempt to specify the times when this should be done would tend to make religion formal and heartless.

enter into thy closet, and, when thou hast shut thy door, pray to thy Father which is in secret; and thy Father, which seeth in secret, [c]shall reward thee openly.

7 But when ye pray, [d]use not

c Ps.34.15; Is.65.24. d Ec.5.2.

Mohammed undertook to regulate this, and the consequence is a cold and formal prostration at the appointed hours of prayer all over the land where his religion has spread. (3.) The periods are so numerous, and the seasons for secret prayer vary so much, that it would not be easy to fix rules when this should be done. Yet without giving rules, where the Saviour has given none, we may suggest the following as times when secret prayer is proper: 1. In the morning. Nothing can be more appropriate when we have been preserved through the night, and when we are about to enter upon the duties and dangers of another day, than to render to our great Preserver thanks, and to commit ourselves to his fatherly care. 2. In the evening. When the day has closed, what more natural than to offer thanksgiving for the mercies of the day, and to implore forgiveness for what we have said or done amiss? and when about to lie down again to sleep, not knowing but it may be our *last* sleep and that we may awake in eternity, what more proper than to commend ourselves to the care of Him "who never slumbers nor sleeps?" 3. We should pray in times of embarrassment and perplexity. Such times occur in every man's life, and it is then a privilege and a duty to go to God and seek his direction. In the most difficult and embarrassed time of the American Revolution, Washington was seen to retire to a grove in the vicinity of the camp at Valley Forge. Curiosity led a man to observe him, and the father of his country was seen on his knees supplicating the God of hosts in prayer. Who can tell how much the liberty of this nation is owing to the answer to the secret prayer of Washington? 4. We should pray when we are beset with strong temptations. So the Saviour prayed in the garden of Gethsemane (comp. He. v. 7, 8), and so we should pray when we are tempted. 5. We should pray when the Spirit prompts us to pray; when we feel *just like praying;* when nothing can satisfy the soul but prayer. Such times occur in the life of every Christian, and they are "spring-times" of piety—favourable gales to waft us on to heaven. Prayer to the Christian, at such times, is just as congenial as conversation with a friend when the bosom is filled with love; as the society of father, mother, sister, child is, when the heart glows with attachment; as the strains of sweet music are to the ear best attuned to the love of harmony; as the most exquisite poetry is to the heart enamoured with the muses; and as the most delicious banquet is to the hungry. Prayer, then, is the element of being—the breath—the vital air; and, then, the Christian must and should pray. He is the most eminent Christian who is most favoured with such strong emotions urging him to prayer. The heart is then full; the soul is tender; the sun of glory shines with unusual splendour; no cloud intervenes; the Christian rises above the world, and pants for glory. *Then* we may go to be alone with God. We may enter the closet, and breathe forth our warm desires into his ever-open ear, and he who sees in secret will reward us openly. ¶ *In secret.* Who is unseen. ¶ *Who seeth in secret.* Who sees what the human eye cannot see; who sees the real designs and desires of the heart. Prayer should always be offered, remembering that God is acquainted with our *real desires;* and that it is those real desires, and not the *words* of prayer, that he will answer.

7. *Use not vain repetitions.* The original word here is supposed to be derived from the name of a Greek poet, who made long and weary verses, declaring by many forms and endless repetitions the same sentiment. Hence it means to repeat a thing often; to say the same thing in different words, or to repeat the same words, as though God did not *hear* at first. An example of this we have in 1 Ki. xviii. 26: "They called on Baal from morning until noon, saying, O Baal, hear us!"* It may serve to illustrate this passage, and to show how true is the description here of prevailing modes of prayer, to refer to the forms and modes of devotion still practised in Palestine by the Mohammedans. Dr. Thomson (*The Land and the Book*) gives

* The following is a *specimen* of the *vain repetitions* of the Romans: "Pious Antonine, the gods preserve thee. Gentle Antonine, the gods preserve thee. Gentle Antonine, the gods preserve thee."

vain repetitions, as the heathen
do: [e]for they think that they shall
be heard for their much speaking.
8 Be not ye therefore like unto
them: [f]for your Father knoweth
what things ye have need of before
ye ask him.
9 After this manner therefore

e 1 Ki.18.26,&c.

f Lu.12.30; Jn.16.23-27.

---

the following description of what actually occurs:—"See those men on that elevated terrace. One has spread his cloak, others their Persian rugs toward the south. They are Moslems, preparing to say prayers—*perform* them rather, in this most public place, and in the midst of all this noise and confusion.

"Let us stop and watch the ceremony as it goes on. That man next us raises his open hands till the thumbs touch the ears, exclaiming aloud, *Allah-hû-akbar*—'God is great.' After uttering mentally a few short petitions, the hands are brought down and folded together near the girdle, while he recites the first chapter of the Koran, and two or three other brief passages from the same book. And now he bends forward, rests his hands upon his knees, and repeats three times a formula of praise to 'God most great.' Then, standing erect, he cries *Allah-hû-akbar*, as at the beginning. Then see him drop upon his knees, and bend forward until his nose and forehead touch the ground directly between his expanded hands. This he repeats three times, muttering all the while the same short formulas of prayer and praise. The next move will bring him to his knees, and then, settling back upon his heels, he will mumble over various small petitions, with sundry grunts and exclamations, according to taste and habit. He has now gone through one regular Rek'āh; and, standing up as at the first, and on exactly the same spot, he will perform a second, and even a third, if specially devout, with precisely the same genuflections.

"They are obliged to repeat some expressions thirty times, others many hundred times. Would that these remarks did not apply to nominal Christians in this land as well as to Moslems!" ¶ *The heathen* do. The original word is that which is commonly translated *Gentile.* The world was divided into two parts, the Jews and the Gentiles; that is, in the original, the "*nations,*" the nations destitute of the true religion. Christ does not fix the *length* of our prayers. He says that we should not repeat the same thing, as though God did not hear; and it is not improbable that he intended to condemn the practice of long prayers. His own supplications were remarkably short.

9–13. This passage contains the Lord's prayer, a composition unequalled for comprehensiveness and for beauty. It is supposed that some of these petitions were taken from those in common use among the Jews. Indeed some of them are still to be found in Jewish writings, but they did not exist in this beautiful combination. This prayer is given as a *model.* It is designed to express the *manner* in which we are to pray, evidently not the precise words or petitions which we are to use. The substance of the prayer is recorded by Luke, ch. xi. 2, 3, 4. In Luke, however, it varies from the form given in Matthew, showing that he intended not to prescribe this as a *form* of prayer to be used always, but to express the *substance* of our petitions, or to show what petitions it would be proper to present to God. That he did not intend to prescribe this as a *form* to be invariably used is farther evident from the fact that there is no proof that either he or his disciples ever used exactly this form of prayer, but clear evidence that they prayed often in other language. See Mat. xxvi. 39–42, 44; Lu. xxii. 42; Jn. xvii.; Ac. i. 24.

9. *Our Father.* God is called a Father, 1st, as he is the Creator and the Great Parent of all; 2d, the Preserver of the human family and the Provider for their wants, ch. v. 45; vi. 32; 3d, in a peculiar sense he is the Father of those who are adopted into his family; who put confidence in him; who are the true followers of Christ, and made heirs of life, Ro. viii. 14–17. ¶ *Hallowed be thy name.* The word hallowed means to render or pronounce holy. God's name is essentially holy; and the meaning of this petition is, "Let thy name be celebrated, venerated, and *esteemed as holy* everywhere, and receive from all men proper honour." It is thus the expression of a *wish* or desire, on the part of the worshipper, that the name of God, or that God himself, should be held everywhere in proper veneration.

pray ye: [g]Our [h]Father which art
in[i] heaven, [k]Hallowed be thy name:
10 Thy [l]kingdom come. [m]Thy will
be done, in earth as *it is* in heaven:

11 Give us this day our [n]daily
bread:
12 And [o]forgive us our debts, as
we forgive our debtors:

g Lu.11.2,&c. *h* Ro.8.15. *i* Ps.115.3. *k* Ps.111.9; 139.20. *l* ch.16.28; Re.11.15. *m* Ps.103.20,21.

n Pr.30.8; Is.33.16. *o* ch.18.21-35; Lu.7.40-48.

10. *Thy kingdom come.* The word *kingdom* here means *reign.* Note, Mat. iii. 2. The petition is the expression of a wish that God may *reign* everywhere; that his laws may be obeyed; and especially that the gospel of Christ may be advanced everywhere, till the world shall be filled with his glory. ¶ *Thy will be done.* The will of God is, that men should obey his law, and be holy. The word *will*, here, has reference to his law, and to what would be *acceptable* to him. To pray, then, that his will may be done, on earth as in heaven, is to pray that his *law*, his *revealed will*, may be obeyed and loved. His law is perfectly obeyed in heaven, and his true children most ardently desire and pray that it may also be obeyed on the earth.

The object of these three *first* petitions, is, that God's name should be glorified and his kingdom established; and by being placed *first*, we learn that *his glory* and *kingdom* are of more consequence than *our* wants, and that these should be *first* in our hearts and petitions before a throne of grace.*

11. *Give us this day*, &c. The word bread, here, denotes doubtless everything necessary to sustain life. See Notes on Mat. iv. 4. Comp. De. viii. 3. This petition implies our dependence on God for the supply of our wants. As we are dependent on him one day as much as another, it was evidently the intention of the Saviour that prayer should be offered every day. The petition, moreover, is expressed in the plural number—give US—and it is evidently, therefore, intended to be used by more than one, or by some community of people. No community or congregation can meet every day for worship but families. It is therefore evident that this prayer contains a strong implied command for daily family prayer. It can nowhere else be used so as fully to come up to the meaning of the original intention; and nowhere else can it be breathed forth with so much propriety and beauty as from the lips of a father, the venerable priest of his household, and the pleader with God for those rich blessings which a parental bosom desires on his beloved offspring.

12. *And forgive us our debts*, &c. The word *debts* is here used figuratively. It does not mean *literally* that we are *debtors to God*, but that our sins have a resemblance to debts. Debtors are those who are bound to others for some claim in commercial transactions; for something which we have had, and for which we are bound to pay according to contract. *Literally* there can be no such transaction between God and us. It must be used figuratively. We have not met the claims of law. We have violated its obligations. We are exposed to its penalty. We are guilty, and God only can forgive, in the same way as none but a *creditor* can forgive a debtor. The word *debts* here, therefore, means *sins*, or offences against God—offences which none but God can forgive. In the parallel place in Lu. xi. 4, the word *sins* is used. The measure by which we may expect forgiveness is that which *we use* in reference to others. See Ps. xviii. 25, 26; Mat. xviii. 23; Mar. xi. 26; Lu. xi. 4. This is the invariable rule by which God dispenses pardon. He that comes before him unwilling to forgive, harbouring dark and revengeful thoughts, how can he expect that God will show him that mercy which he is unwilling to show to others? It is not, however, required that we should forgive *debts* in a pecuniary sense. To them we have a right, though they should not be pushed with an overbearing and oppressive spirit; not so as to

* Several of the petitions in this prayer are found in the writings of the Jews, and were doubtless familiar in the time of Christ. "That prayer," say the Rabbins, "in which there is no mention made of the kingdom of heaven, is *not* a prayer," "What," say they, "is a short prayer? *Answer.* Do thy will in heaven, and give rest to the spirits fearing thee below." "Give us this day," &c. The Jews had a prayer like this: "The necessities of thy people are many, and their knowledge small, so that they do not know how to make known their wants: let it be thy good pleasure to give to each one what is necessary for his sustenance," &c. "Deliver us from evil." The Jews prayed, "Be it thy good pleasure to free us from an evil man, and an evil event; from evil affections, from an evil companion and neighbour, from Satan," &c. The prayers of the Jews were generally closed with a doxology, or ascription of praise, not unlike this in the Lord's prayer. The people, at the close of the prayer, generally responded "Amen."

13 And [p]lead us not into temptation, but [q]deliver us from evil: for[r] thine is the kingdom, and the power, and the glory for ever. Amen.

14 For[s] if ye forgive men their

p ch.26.41; Lu.22.40,46. q Jn.17.15. r Re.5.12,13. s Ep.4.31.

sacrifice the feelings of mercy in order to secure the claims of justice. No man has a right to oppress; and when a debt cannot be paid, or when it would greatly distress a debtor's wife and children, or a widow and an orphan, or when calamity has put it out of the power of an honest man to pay the debt, the spirit of Christianity requires that it should be forgiven. To such cases this petition in the Lord's prayer doubtless extends. But it was probably intended to refer principally to injuries of character or person which we have received from others. If we cannot from the heart forgive *them*, we have the assurance that God will *never* forgive us.

13. *And lead us not into temptation.* A petition similar to this is offered by David, Ps. cxli. 4: "Incline not my heart to any evil thing, to practise wicked works with the workers of iniquity." God tempts no man. See Ja. i. 13. This phrase, then, must be used in the sense of *permitting*. Do not *suffer* us, or *permit* us, to be tempted to sin. In this it is implied that God has such control over the tempter as to save us from his power if we call upon him. The word *temptation*, however (see Note ch. iv. 1), means sometimes *trial, affliction*, anything that *tests* our virtue. If this be the meaning here, as it may be, then the import of the prayer is, "Do not afflict or try us." It is not wrong to pray that we may be saved from suffering if it be the will of God. See Lu. xxii. 42. ¶ *Deliver us from evil.* The original in this place has the article —deliver us from THE *evil*—that is, as has been supposed, the Evil One, or Satan. He is elsewhere called, by way of eminence, the *Evil One*, Mat. xiii. 19; 1 Jn. ii. 13, 14; iii. 12. The meaning here is, "deliver us from his power, his snares, his arts, his temptations." He is supposed to be the great parent of evil, and to be delivered from him is to be safe. Or it may mean, "deliver us from the various evils and trials which beset us, the heavy and oppressive calamities into which we are continually liable to fall." ¶ *Thine is the kingdom.* That is, thine is the *reign* or *dominion.* Thou hast control over all these things, and canst so order them as to answer these petitions. ¶ *Thine is the power.* Thou hast power to accomplish what we ask. *We* are weak, and cannot do it; but thou art Almighty, and all things are possible with thee. ¶ *Thine is the glory.* That is, thine is the honour or praise. Not for *our honour*, but that thy glory, thy goodness, may be displayed in providing for our wants; thy power exerted in defending us; thy praise be celebrated by causing thy kingdom to spread through the earth.

This *doxology*, or ascription of praise, is connected with the prayer by the word "*for*," to signify that all these things—the reign, power, and glory of God—will be manifested by granting these petitions. It is not because *we* are to be benefited, but that God's name and perfections may be manifested. *His* glory is, then, the first and principal thing which we are to seek when we approach him. We are to suffer *our* concerns to be lost sight of in the superior glory and honour of his name and dominion. We are to seek temporal and eternal life chiefly because the honour of our Maker will be promoted, and his name be more illustriously displayed to his creatures. He is to be "first, last, supremest, best," in our view; and all selfish and worldly views are to be absorbed in that one great desire of the soul that God may be "all in all." Approaching him with these feelings, our prayers will be answered; our devotions will ascend like incense, and the lifting up our hands will be like the evening sacrifice.

Amen. This is a word of Hebrew origin, from a verb signifying *to be firm, secure, to be true* and *faithful.* It is a word expressing consent or strong approbation; a word of strong asseveration. It means *verily, certainly, so be it.* It is probable that this word was used by the people in the synagogue to signify their assent to the prayer that was uttered by the minister, and, to some extent, it was probably so used in the Christian Church. See 1 Co. xiv. 16.

It may be proper to remark that this doxology, "for thine is the kingdom," &c., is wanting in many manuscripts, and that its authenticity is doubtful.

trespasses, your heavenly Father will also forgive you.

15 But[t] if ye forgive not men their trespasses, neither will your Father forgive your trespasses.

16 Moreover, [u]when ye fast, be
not, as the hypocrites, of a sad countenance: for they disfigure their faces, that they may appear unto men to fast. Verily I say unto you, They have their reward.

17 But thou, when thou fastest,

t Ja.2.13. u Is.58.3,5.

14, 15. *For if ye forgive men their trespasses.* If ye forgive others when they offend or injure you. ¶ *Your heavenly Father will also forgive you.* This is constantly required in the Bible. See Notes on ver. 12. Our Saviour says we should forgive even if the offence be committed seventy times seven times, Mat. xviii. 22. By this is meant, that when a man *asks* forgiveness, we are cordially and for ever to pardon the offence; we are to *declare* our willingness to forgive him. If he does not *ask* forgiveness, yet we are still to treat him kindly; not to harbour malice, not to speak ill of him, to be ready to do him good, and be always *prepared* to *declare* him forgiven when he asks it, and if we are not ready and willing to forgive him, we are assured that God will not forgive us.

16. *Moreover, when ye fast.* The word *fast* literally signifies to abstain from food and drink, whether from necessity or as a religious observance. It is, however, commonly applied in the Bible to the latter. It is, then, an expression of grief or sorrow. Such is the constitution of the body, that in a time of grief or sorrow we are not *disposed* to eat; or, we have no appetite. The grief of the *soul* is so absorbing as to destroy the natural appetites of the *body*. Men in deep affliction eat little, and often pine away and fall into sickness, because the *body* refuses, on account of the deep sorrow of the *mind*, to discharge the functions of health. *Fasting, then, is the natural expression of grief.* It is not arbitrary; it is what every person in sorrow naturally does. This is the foundation of its being applied to religion as a sacred rite. It is because the soul, when oppressed and burdened by a sense of sin, is so filled with grief that the body refuses food. It is, therefore, appropriate to scenes of penitence, of godly sorrow, of suffering, and to those facts connected with religion which are fitted to produce grief, as the prevalence of iniquity, or some dark impending calamity, or storm, or tempest, pestilence, plague, or famine. It is also useful to humble us, to bring us to reflection, to direct the thoughts away from the allurements of this world to the bliss of a better. It is not acceptable except it be the *real expression* of sorrow; the natural effect of the feeling that we are burdened with crime.

The Jews fasted often. They had four *annual fasts*—in commemoration of the capture of Jerusalem (Je. lii. 7), of the burning of the temple (Zec. vii. 3), of the death of Gedaliah (Je. xli. 4), and of the commencement of the attack on Jerusalem (Zec. viii. 19). In addition to these, they had a multitude of occasional fasts. It was customary, also, for the Pharisees to fast twice a week, Lu. xviii. 12. ¶ *Of a sad countenance.* That is, sour, morose; with assumed expressions of unfelt sorrow. ¶ *They disfigure their faces.* That is, they do not anoint and wash themselves as usual; they are uncombed, filthy, squalid, and haggard. It is said that they were often in the habit of throwing *ashes* on their heads and faces; and this, mixing with their tears, served still farther to disfigure their faces. So much pains will men take, and so much suffering will they undergo, and so much that is ridiculous will they assume, to impose on God and men. But they deceive neither. God sees through the flimsy veil. Human eyes can pierce a disguise so thin. Hypocrites overact their part. Not having the genuine principles of piety at heart, they know not what is its proper expression, and hence they appear supremely contemptible and abominable. Never should men exhibit outwardly more than they *feel;* and never should they attempt to *exhibit* anything for the mere sake of ostentation. ¶ *They have their reward.* They have all that they desired—the praise of men and *the pleasure of ostentation.* See Notes on ver. 2.

17, 18. *But thou when thou fastest, anoint,* &c. That is, appear as you do daily. Do not assume any new appearance, or change your visage or dress. The Jews and all neighbouring nations

anoint thine head, and wash thy face:

18 That thou appear not unto men to fast, but unto thy Father which is in secret: and thy Father, which seeth in secret, shall reward thee openly.

19 Lay[v] not up for yourselves treasures upon earth, where moth and rust doth corrupt, and where thieves break through and steal;

20 But[w] lay up for yourselves treasures in heaven, where neither moth nor rust doth corrupt, and where thieves do not break through nor steal:

21 For where your treasure is, there will your heart be also.

22 The[x] light of the body is the eye: If, therefore, thine eye be single, thy whole body shall be full of light:

23 But if thine eye be evil, thy whole body shall be full of dark-

v Pr.23.4; Lu.18.24,35; He.13.5.
w Is.33.6; Lu.12.33,34; 1 Ti.6.19.
x Lu.11.34,36.

were much in the habit of washing and anointing their bodies. This washing was performed at every meal; and where it could be effected, the head, or other parts of the body, was daily anointed with sweet or olive oil. In a warm climate, exposed to the great heat of the sun, this practice conduced much to health, preserved the skin smooth and tender, and afforded a most grateful sensation and odour. See Mar. vii. 2, 3; Ja. v. 14; Mar. xi. 13; Jn. xii. 3. The meaning of this whole commandment is, when you regard it to be your duty to fast, do it as a thing expressing deep feeling or sorrow for sin, not by assuming unfelt gravity and moroseness, but in your ordinary dress and appearance; not to attract attention, but as an expression of feeling towards God, and he will approve and reward it.

19. *Lay not up for yourselves treasures upon earth.* Treasures, or wealth, among the ancients, consisted in clothes or changes of raiment, as well as in gold, silver, gems, wine, lands, and oil. It meant an abundance of *anything* that was held to be conducive to the ornament or comfort of life. As the Orientals delighted much in display, in splendid equipage, and costly garments, their treasures, in fact, consisted much in beautiful and richly-ornamented articles of apparel. See Ge. xlv. 22, where Joseph gave to his brethren *changes of raiment;* Jos. vii. 21, where Achan coveted and secreted *a goodly Babylonish garment.* Compare also Ju. xiv. 12. This fact will account for the use of the word *moth.* When *we* speak of *wealth,* we think at once of gold, and silver, and lands, and houses. When a Hebrew or an Orientalist spoke of wealth, he thought first of what would make a *display;* and included, as an essential part, splendid articles of dress. The *moth* is a small insect that finds its way to clothes and garments, and destroys them. The *moth* would destroy their apparel, the *rust* their silver and gold; thus all their treasure would waste away. The word rendered *rust* signifies anything which *eats into,* and hence anything which would consume one's property, and may have a wider signification than mere *rust.* ¶ *And where thieves break through and steal.* The houses in the East were not unfrequently made of clay hardened in the sun, or of loose stones, and hence it was comparatively easy, as it was not uncommon, for thieves to *dig through* the wall, and effect an entrance in that way. See Notes on Job xxiv. 16.

20, 21. *Lay up for yourselves treasures in heaven.* That is, have provision made for your eternal felicity. Do not exhaust your strength and spend your days in providing for the life here, but let your *chief* anxiety be to be prepared for eternity. Comp. Notes on Is. lv. 2. In heaven nothing corrupts; nothing terminates; no enemies plunder or destroy. To have treasure in heaven is to possess evidence that its purity and joys will be ours. It is to be heirs of God, and joint-heirs with Christ, to an inheritance incorruptible, undefiled, and that fadeth not away, 1 Pe. i. 4. The *heart,* or affections, will of course be fixed on the treasure. To *regulate* the heart, it is therefore important that the treasure, or object of attachment, should be right.

22, 23. *The light of the body,* &c. The sentiment stated in the preceding verses —the duty of fixing the affections on heavenly things—Jesus proceeds to illustrate by a reference to the *eye.*

ness. If, therefore, the light that is in thee be darkness, how great *is* that darkness!

24 No[y] man can serve two masters: for either he will hate the one, and love the other; or else he will hold to the one, and despise the other. Ye[z] cannot serve God and Mammon.

25 Therefore I say unto you,

y Lu.16.13.

z Ga.1.10; 2 Ti.4.10; Ja.4.4.

When the eye is directed steadily toward an object, and is in health, *or is single*, everything is clear and plain. If it *vibrates*, flies to different objects, is fixed on no one singly, or is diseased, nothing is seen clearly. Everything is dim and confused. The man, therefore, is unsteady. The *eye* regulates the motion of the body. To have an object distinctly in view is necessary in order to correct and regulate action. Rope-dancers, that they may steady themselves, fix the eye on some object on the wall, and look steadily at that. If they should look *down* on the rope or the people, they might become dizzy, and fall. A man crossing a stream on a log, if he will look *across* at some object steadily, will be in little danger. If he looks down on the dashing and rolling waters, he will become dizzy, and fall. So Jesus says, in order that the *conduct* may be right, it is important to fix the affections on heaven. Having the affections there—having the eye of faith *single*, steady, unwavering—all the conduct will be correspondent. ¶ *Single.* Steady, directed to one object. Not confused, as persons' eyes are when they see *double.* ¶ *Thy body shall be full of light.* Your *conduct* will be regular and steady. All that is needful to direct the *body* is that the *eye* be fixed right. No other *light* is required. So all that is needful to direct the *soul* and the *conduct* is, that the eye of *faith* be fixed on heaven; that the affections be there. ¶ *If, therefore, the light that is in thee*, &c. The word *light*, here, signifies *the mind*, or principles of the soul. If this be dark, how great is that darkness! The meaning of this passage may be thus expressed: The light of the body, the guide and director, is the eye. All know how calamitous it is when that light is irregular or extinguished, as when the eye is diseased or lost. So the light that is in us is the soul. If that soul is debased by attending exclusively to earthly objects—if it is diseased, and not fixed on heaven—how much darker and more dreadful will it be than any darkness of the eye! Avarice darkens the mind, obscures the view, and brings in a dreadful and gloomy night over all the faculties.

24. *No man can serve two masters*, &c. Christ proceeds to illustrate the necessity of laying up treasures in heaven from a well-known fact, that a servant cannot serve two masters at the same time. His affections and obedience would be divided, and he would fail altogether in his duty to one or the other. One he would love, the other he would hate. To the interests of the one he would adhere, the interests of the other he would neglect. This is a law of human nature. The supreme affections can be fixed on only one object. So, says Jesus, the servant of God cannot at the same time obey *him* and be avaricious, or seek treasures supremely on earth. One interferes with the other, and one or the other *will* be, and *must* be, surrendered. ¶ *Mammon.* Mammon is a Syriac word, a name given to an idol worshipped as the god of riches. It has the same meaning as Plutus among the Greeks. It is not known that the Jews ever formally worshipped this idol, but they used the word to denote wealth. The meaning is, ye cannot serve the true God, and at the same time be supremely engaged in obtaining the riches of this world. One *must* interfere with the other. See Lu. xvi. 9–11.

25–34. *Therefore I say unto you, Take no thought*, &c. The general design of this paragraph, which closes the chapter, is to warn his disciples against avarice, and, at the same time, against anxiety about the supply of their wants. This he does by *four* arguments or considerations, expressing by unequalled beauty and force the duty of depending for the things which we need on the providence of God. The *first* is stated in the 25th verse: "Is not the life more than meat, and the body than raiment?" In the beginning of the verse he charged his disciples to take *no thought*—that is, not to be *anxious*—about the supply of their wants. In illustration of this he says

Take[a] no thought for your life,
what ye shall eat, or what ye shall
drink; nor yet for your body, what
ye shall put on. Is not the life
more than meat, and the body than
raiment?

26 Behold the fowls of the air:
for they sow not, neither do they
reap, nor gather into barns; [b]yet
your heavenly Father feedeth
them. Are ye not much better
than they?

27 Which of you, by taking

a 1 Co.7.32; Phi.4.6.

b Job 38.41; Lu.12.24,&c.

that God has given *life*, a far greater blessing than *meat;* that he has created the *body*, of far more consequence than raiment. Shall not he who has conferred the *greater* blessing be willing to confer the *less?* Shall not he who has formed the body so curiously, and made in its formation such a display of power and goodness, see that it is properly protected and clothed? He who has displayed *so great* goodness as to form the body, and breathe into it the breath of life, will surely *follow up* the blessing, and confer the *smaller* favour of providing that that body shall be clothed, and that life preserved. ¶ *No thought.* The word *thought*, when the Bible was translated, meant *anxiety*, and is so used frequently in old English authors. Thus Bacon says, "Haweis died with *thought* and anguish before his business came to an end." As such it is here used by our translators, and it answers exactly to the meaning of the original. Like many other words, it has since somewhat changed its signification, and would convey to most readers an improper idea. The word *anxiety* would now exactly express the sense, and is precisely the thing against which the Saviour would guard us. See Lu. viii. 14; xxi. 34; Phi. iv. 6. *Thought* about the future is right; *anxiety, solicitude, trouble* is wrong. There is a degree of *thinking* about the things of this life which is proper. See 1 Ti. v. 8; 2 Th. iii. 10; Ro. xii. 11. But it should not be our *supreme* concern; it should not lead to anxiety; it should not take time that ought to be devoted to religion. ¶ *For your life.* For what will *support* your life. ¶ *Meat.* This word here means *food* in general, as it does commonly in the Bible. *We* confine it now to animal food. When the Bible was translated, it denoted all kinds of food, and is so used in the old English writers. It is one of the words which has changed its meaning since the translation of the Bible was made. ¶ *Raiment.* Clothing.

26. *Behold the fowls of the air.* The second argument for confidence in the providence of God is derived from a beautiful reference to the fowls or feathered tribes. See, said the Saviour, see the fowls of the air: they have no anxiety about the supply of their wants; they do not sow or reap; they fill the grove with music, and meet the coming light of the morning with their songs, and pour their notes on the zephyrs of the evening, unanxious about the supply of their wants; yet how few die with hunger! how regularly are they fed from the hand of God! how he ministers to their unnumbered wants! how cheerfully and regularly are their necessities supplied! You, said the Saviour to his disciples, you are of more consequence than they are; and shall God feed *them* in such numbers, and suffer you to want? It cannot be. Put confidence, then, in that Universal Parent that feeds all the fowls of the air, and do not fear but that he will also supply *your* wants. ¶ *Better than they.* Of more consequence. Your lives are of more importance than theirs, and God will therefore provide for them.

27. *Which of you, by taking thought.* The third argument is taken from their extreme weakness and helplessness. With all your care you cannot increase your stature a single cubit. God has ordered your height. Beyond his appointment your powers are of no avail, and you can do nothing. So of raiment. He, by his providence, orders and arranges the circumstances of your life. *Beyond* that appointment of his providence, beyond *his* care for you, your efforts avail nothing. Seeing, then, that he alike orders your *growth* and the supply of your wants, how obvious is the duty of *depending* on him, and of beginning all your efforts, feeling that he only can grant you the means of preserving life. ¶ *One cubit.* The cubit was originally the length from the elbow to the end of the middle finger. The cubit of the Scriptures is not far from 22 inches. Terms of *length* are often applied to life, and it is

thought, can add one cubit unto his stature?

28 And why take ye thought for raiment? Consider the lilies of the field, how they grow; they toil not, neither do they spin:

29 And yet I say unto you, that even Solomon in all his glory was not arrayed like one of these.

30 Wherefore, if God so clothe the grass of the field, which to-day is, and to-morrow is cast into the oven, *shall he* not much more *clothe* you, O ye of little faith?

31 Therefore[c] take no thought, saying, What shall we eat? or, What shall we drink? or, Wherewithal shall we be clothed?

32 (For after all these things do the Gentiles seek:) for your heavenly Father knoweth that ye have need of all these things.

33 But [d]seek ye first the king-

c Ps.37.3; 55.22; 1 Pe.5.7. d 1 Ti.4.8.

---

thought by many to be so here. Thus it is said, "Thou hast made my days as a handbreadth" (Ps. xxxix. 5); "Teach me the MEASURE of my days" (Ps. xxxix. 4). In this place it is used to denote a *small length.* You cannot increase your stature even a cubit, or in the smallest degree. Comp. Lu. xii. 26. ¶ *Stature.* This word means *height.* The original word, however, means oftener *age*, Jn. ix. 21: "He is of *age;*" so also ver. 23. If this be its meaning here, as is probable (comp. Robinson, *Lex.*), it denotes that a man cannot increase the length of his life at all. The utmost anxiety will not prolong it one hour beyond the time appointed for death.

28, 29. ¶ *Consider the lilies of the field.* The fourth consideration is taken from the care which God bestows on lilies. Watch the growing of the lily. It toils not, and it spins not; yet night and day it grows. With a beauty with which the most splendid monarch of the East was never adorned, it expands its blossom and fills the air with fragrance. Yet this beauty is of short continuance. Soon it will fade, and the beautiful flower will be cut down and burned. God *so little* regards the bestowment of beauty and ornament as to give the highest adorning to this which is soon to perish. When he thus clothes a lily—a fair flower, soon to perish—will he be unmindful of his children? Shall *they*—dear to his heart and imbued with immortality—lack that which is proper for them, and shall *they* in vain trust the God that decks the lily of the valley? ¶ *Even Solomon in all his glory,* &c. The common dress of Eastern kings was purple, but they sometimes wore white robes. See Es. viii. 15; Da. vii. 9. It is to this that Christ refers. Solomon, says he, the richest and most magnificent king of Israel, was not clothed in a robe *of so pure a white* as the lily that grows wild in the field.

30. *Wherefore, if God so clothe the grass of the field.* What grows up in the field, or grows wild and without culture. The word *grass*, applied here to the lily, denotes merely that it is a vegetable production, or that it is among the things which grow wild, and which are used for fuel. ¶ *Which to-day is.* It lives to-day, or it lives for a day. It is short-lived, and seems to be a thing of no value, and is so treated. ¶ *Is cast into the oven.* The Jews had different modes of baking. In early times they frequently baked in the sand, warmed with the heat of the sun. They constructed, also, movable ovens made of clay, brick, or plates of iron. But the most common kind, and the one here probably referred to, was made by excavating the earth 2½ feet in diameter, and from 5 to 6 feet deep. This kind of oven still exists in Persia. The bottom was paved with stones. It was heated by putting wood or dry grass *into* the oven, and, when heated, the ashes were removed and the bread was placed on the heated stones. Frequently, however, the oven was an earthen vessel without a bottom, about 3 feet high, smeared outside and inside with clay, and placed upon a frame or support. Fire was made within or below it. When the sides were sufficiently heated, thin patches of dough were spread on the inside, and the top was covered, without removing the fire as in the other cases, and the bread was quickly baked.

32, 33. *For after all these things do the Gentiles seek.* That is, those destitute of the true doctrines of religion, and unacquainted with proper dependence on Divine Providence, make it their *chief anxiety* thus to seek food and rai-

dom of God, and his righteousness, and[e] all these things shall be added unto you.

34 Take, therefore, no thought for the morrow; for the morrow shall take [f]thought for the things of itself. Sufficient unto the day *is* the evil thereof.

e Le.25.20,21; 1 Ki.3.13; Ps.37.25; Mar.10.30.

f De.33.25; He.13.5,6.

---

ment. But *you*, who have a knowledge of your Father in heaven; who know that he will provide for your wants, should not be anxious. Seek first his kingdom; seek first to be righteous, and to become interested in his favour, and all necessary things will be added to you. He has control over all things, and he can give you that which you need. He *will* give you that which *he* deems best for you.

34. *Take therefore no thought*, &c. That is, no anxiety. Commit your way to God. The evil, the trouble, the anxiety of each day as it comes, is sufficient without perplexing the mind with restless cares about another day. It is wholly uncertain whether you live to see another day. If you do, it will bring its own trouble, and it will also bring the proper supply of your wants. God will be the same Father then as to-day, and will make then, as he does now, proper provision for your wants. ¶ *The morrow shall take thought.* The morrow will have anxieties and cares of its own, but it will also bring the proper provision for those cares. Though you will have *wants*, yet God will provide for them as they occur. Do not, therefore, increase the cares of *this day* by borrowing trouble from the future. Do your duty faithfully *now*, and depend on the mercy of God and his divine help for the troubles which are yet to come.

REMARKS ON CHAPTER VI.

1st. Christ has here forcibly taught the necessity of charity, of prayer, and of all religious duties.

2d. We see the necessity of sincerity and honesty in our religious duties. They are not to be done to be seen of men. If they are, they cannot be performed acceptably. God looks on the heart, nor is it possible to deceive him. And of what avail is it to deceive men? How poor and pitiable is the reward of a hypocrite! How contemptible the praise of men when God is displeased! How awful the condition of such a one beyond the grave!

3d. Christ has here, in a particular manner, urged the duty of prayer. He has given a model for prayer. Nothing can equal this composition in simplicity, beauty, and comprehensiveness. At the same time that it is so simple that it can be understood by a child, it contains the expression of all the wants of man at any age and in every rank of life.

The duty of prayer is urged by every consideration. None but God can provide for us; none but he can forgive, and guide, and support us; none but he can bring us into heaven. He is ever ready to hear us. The humble he sends not empty away. Those who ask receive, and they who seek find. How natural and proper, then, is prayer! How strange that any man can live, and not pour out his desires to God! How strange that anyone is willing to go to eternity with this sad reflection: "I have gone through this world, spent my probation, wasted my strength, and am dying, and have never prayed!" How awful will be the reflection of the soul through all eternity: "I was *offered* eternal life, but I never *asked* for it. I lived from day to day and from year to year in God's world, breathed his air, rioted on his beneficence, forgot his goodness, and never once asked him to save my soul!" Who will be to blame if the prayerless soul is lost?

Secret and family prayer should be daily. We daily have the same necessities, are exposed to the same dangers, tread on the borders of the same heaven or hell. How should the voice of praise and prayer go up as incense in the morning, and rise as a rich perfume in the shades of each evening! What more lovely object on earth is there than that of one in the bloom of health and the dew of youth, bending with reverence before the King of heaven, seeking forgiveness, peace, guidance, and salvation! And what a strange, misguided, and piteous object is a soul that never prays!

4th. Forgiveness is essential in prayer. If we come to God harbouring malice and unwilling to forgive, we have his solemn assurance that we shall not be ourselves forgiven.

5th. *Avarice* is alike foolish and an insult to God, ver. 19-24. It is the parent of many foolish and hurtful lusts. It alienates the affections from God; produces envy of another's prosperity; leads to fraud, deception, and crime to obtain wealth, and degrades the soul. Man is formed for nobler pursuits than the mere desire to be rich. He lives for eternity, where silver will not be needed and where gold will be of no value. That eternity is near; and though we have wealth like Solomon, and though we be adorned as the lily, yet like Solomon we must soon die, and like the lily our beauty will soon fade. Death will lay us alike low; the rich and the poor will sleep together; and the worm will feed no more sweetly on the unfed and unclothed son of poverty, than on the man clothed in fine linen, and the daughter of beauty and pride. As avarice is moreover the parent of discontent, he only that is contented with the allotments of Providence, and is not restless for a change, is happy. After all, this is the true source of enjoyment. Anxiety and care, perplexity and disappointment, find their way more readily to the mansions of the rich than to the cottages of the poor. It is the *mind*, not mansions, and gold, and adorning, that gives ease; and he that is content with his situation will "smile upon his stool, while Alexander weeps upon the throne of the world."

6th. We see how comparatively valueless is *beauty*. How little it is regarded by God! He gives it to the lily, and in a day it fades and is gone. He gives it to the wings of the butterfly, and soon it dies and its beauty is forgotten. He gives it to the flowers of the spring, soon to fall; to the leaves of the forest, soon to grow yellow and decay in the autumn. How many lilies and roses does he cause to blossom in solitude where no man is, where they "waste their sweetness on the desert air!" How many streams ripple in the wilderness, and how many cataracts, age after age, have poured their thunders on the air, unheard and unseen by mortals! So little does God think of beauty. So the human form and "face divine." How soon is all that beauty marred; and, as in the lily, how soon is its last trace obliterated! In the cold grave, among the undistinguished multitudes of the dead, who can tell which of all the mouldering host was blessed with a "lovely set of features or complexion?" Alas! all has faded like the morning flower. How vain, then, to set the affections on so frail a treasure!

7th. We see the duty and privilege of depending for our daily wants on the bounties of Providence. Satisfied with the troubles of to-day, let us not add to those troubles by anxieties about to-morrow. The heathen, and they who know not God, will be anxious about the future; but they who know him, and have caught the spirit of Jesus, may surely trust him for the supply of their wants. The young lions do roar, and seek their meat at the hand of God, Ps. civ. 21. The fowls of heaven are daily supplied. Shall man only, of all the creatures on earth, vex himself and be filled with anxious cares about the future? Rather, like the rest of the creation, let us depend on the aid of the universal Parent, and feel that HE who hears the young ravens which cry will also supply our necessities.

8th. Especially is the remark just made of value in reference to those in early life. Life is a stormy ocean. Over that ocean no being presides but God. He holds the winds in his hands, and can still their howlings, and calm the heaving billows. On that ocean the young have just launched their frail bark. Daily they will need protection; daily will they need supplies; daily will they be in danger, and exposed to the rolling of the billows that may ingulf them for ever. Ignorant, inexperienced, and in danger, how should they look to God to guide and aid them! Instead of vexing themselves with anxious cares about the future, how should they place humble reliance on God! Safe in his hand, we shall outride the storm and come to a haven of peace. *He* will supply our wants if we *trust* him, as he does those of the songsters of the grove. He will be the guide of our youth and the strength of our manhood. If we seek him, he will be found of us; if we forsake him, he will cast us off for ever, 1 Ch. xxviii. 9.

9th. From all this, how manifest is the propriety of seeking *first* the kingdom of God! First in our affections, first in the objects of pursuit, first in the feelings and associations of each morning, be the desire and the aim for heaven. Having this, we have assurance of all that we need. GOD, *our Father*, will then befriend us, and in life and death all will be well.

CHAPTER VII.

JUDGE[a] not, that ye be not judged.

2 For with what judgment ye judge, ye shall be judged; and with[b] what measure ye mete, it shall be measured to you again.

3 And why beholdest thou the mote that is in thy brother's eye, but considerest not the beam that is in thine own eye?

4 Or how wilt thou say to thy brother, Let me pull out the mote out of thine eye: and, behold, a beam *is* in thine own eye?

5 Thou hypocrite, [c]first cast out the beam out of thine own eye; and then shalt thou see clearly to cast out the mote out of thy brother's eye.

6 Give not that which is holy unto the dogs, neither [d]cast ye

a Lu.6.37; Ro.2.1; 1 Co.4.5. *b* Ju.1.7.

c Ga.6.1. *d* Pr.9.7,8; 23.9.

CHAPTER VII.

1. *Judge not*, &c. This command refers to rash, censorious, and unjust judgment. See Ro. ii. 1. Luke (vi. 37) explains it in the sense of *condemning.* Christ does not condemn judging as a magistrate, for that, when according to justice, is lawful and necessary. Nor does he condemn our *forming an opinion* of the conduct of others, for it is impossible *not* to form an opinion of conduct that we know to be evil. But what he refers to is a habit of forming a judgment hastily, harshly, and without an allowance for every palliating circumstance, and a habit of *expressing* such an opinion harshly and unnecessarily when formed. It rather refers to *private* judgment than *judicial*, and perhaps primarily to the customs of the scribes and Pharisees.

2. *With what judgment*, &c. This was a *proverb* among the Jews. It expressed a truth; and Christ did not hesitate to adopt it as conveying his own sentiments. It refers no less to the way in which *men* will judge of us, than to the rule by which God will judge us. See 2 Sa. xxii. 27; Mar. iv. 24; Ja. ii. 13. ¶ *Mete.* Measure. You shall be judged by the same rule which you apply to others.

3. *And why beholdest thou the mote*, &c. A mote signifies any *light substance*, as dry chaff, or fine spires of grass or grain. It probably most usually signified the small *spiculæ* or *beards* on a head of barley or wheat. It is thus placed in opposition to the word *beam.* ¶ *Beam.* The word here used signifies a large piece of squared timber. The one is an exceedingly small object, the other a large one. The meaning is, that *we are much more quick and acute to judge of small offences in others, than of much larger offences in ourselves.* Even a very *small* object in the eye of another we discern much more quickly than a much larger one in our own; a small fault in our neighbour we see much more readily than a large one in ourselves. This was also a proverb in frequent use among the Jews, and the same sentiment was common among the Greeks, and deserves to be expressed in every language.

5. *Thou hypocrite, first cast out,* &c. Christ directs us to the proper way of forming an opinion of others, and of reproving and correcting them. By first amending our own faults, or casting the beam out of our eye, we can *consistently* advance to correct the faults of others. There will then be no hypocrisy in our conduct. We shall also *see clearly* to do it. The beam, the thing that obscured our sight, will be removed, and we shall more clearly discern the *small* object that obscures the sight of our brother. The sentiment is, that the readiest way to judge of the imperfections of others is to be free from greater ones ourselves. This qualifies us for judging, makes us candid and consistent, and enables us to see things as they are, and to make proper allowances for frailty and imperfection.

6. *Give not that which is holy*, &c. By some the word *holy* has been supposed to mean *flesh offered in sacrifice*, made holy, or separated to a sacred use; but it probably means here *anything connected with religion*—admonition, precept, or doctrine. Pearls are precious stones found in shell-fish, chiefly in India, in the waters that surround Ceylon. They are used to denote anything peculiarly precious, Re. xvii. 4; xviii. 12–16; Mat. xiii. 45. In this place they are used to denote the doctrines of the gospel. *Dogs* signify men who spurn, oppose, and abuse that doctrine; men

your pearls before swine, lest they
trample them under their feet, and
turn again and rend you.
7 Ask,[e] and it shall be given
you; seek, and ye shall find; knock,
and it shall be opened unto you:
8 For [f]every one that asketh receiveth; [g]and he that seeketh findeth; and to him that knocketh it
shall be opened.
9 Or what man is there of you,
whom if his son ask bread, will he
give him a stone?
10 Or if he ask a fish, will he
give him a serpent?
11 If[h] ye then, being evil, know

e Is.55.6; Lu.18.1. f Ps.81.10,16; Jn.14.13,14; 16.23,24; 1 Jn.3.22; 5.14,15. g Pr.8.17; Je.29.12,13. h Lu.11.11,&c.

of peculiar sourness and malignity of temper, who meet it like growling and quarrelsome curs, Phi. iii. 2; 2 Pe. ii. 22; Re. xxii. 15. *Swine* denote those who would trample the precepts under feet; men of impurity of life; those who are corrupt, polluted, profane, obscene, and sensual; those who would not know the value of the gospel, and who would tread it down as swine would pearls, 2 Pe. ii. 22; Pr. xi. 22. The meaning of this proverb, then, is, do not offer your doctrine to those violent and abusive men who would growl and curse you; nor to those peculiarly debased and profligate who would not perceive its value, would trample it down, and would abuse you. This verse furnishes a beautiful instance of what has been called the *introverted parallelism*. The usual mode of poetry among the Hebrews, and a common mode of expression in proverbs and apothegms, was by the parallelism, where one member of a sentence answered to another, or expressed substantially the same sense with some addition or modification. See the Introduction to the Book of Job, vol. i. p. xxviii.-xxxix. Sometimes this was alternate, and sometimes it was introverted—where the first and fourth lines would correspond, and the second and third. This is the case here. The dogs would rend, and not the swine; the swine would trample the pearls under their feet, and not the dogs. It may be thus expressed:

Give not that which is holy unto the dogs,
Neither cast ye your pearls before swine,
Lest they [that is, the swine] trample them under their feet,
And turn again [that is, the dogs] and rend you.

7-11. *Ask, and it shall be given you*, &c. There are here three different forms presented of seeking the things which we need from God—*asking, seeking*, and *knocking*. The latter is taken from the act of knocking at a door for admittance. See Lu. xiii. 45; Re. iii. 20. The phrases signify to seek with earnestness, diligence, and perseverance.

The promise is, that what we seek shall be given us. It is of course implied that we seek with a proper spirit, with humility, sincerity, and perseverance. It is implied, also, that we ask the things which it may be consistent for God to give—that is, things which he has promised to give, and which would be best for us, and most for his own honour, 1 Jn. v. 14. Of that God is to be the judge. And here there is the utmost latitude which a creature can ask. God is willing to provide for us, to forgive our sins, to save our souls, to befriend us in trial, to comfort us in death, to extend the gospel through the world. Man *can* ask no higher things of God; and these he *may* ask, assured that he is willing to grant them.

Christ encourages us to do this by the conduct of parents. No parent turns away his child with that which would be injurious. He would not give him a stone instead of bread, or a serpent instead of a fish. God is better and kinder than the most tender earthly parents; and with what confidence, therefore, may we come as his children, and ask what we need! Parents, he says, are evil; that is, are imperfect, often partial, and not unfrequently passionate; but God is free from all this, and therefore is ready and willing to aid us. ¶ *Every one that asketh receiveth.* That is, every one that asks aright; that prays in faith, and in submission to the will of God. He does not always give the very thing which we ask, but he gives what would be better. A parent will not always confer the *very thing* which a child asks, but he will seek the welfare of the child, and give what *he* thinks will be most for its good. Paul asked that the thorn from his flesh might be removed. God did not *literally* grant the request, but told him that his *grace* should be *sufficient* for him. See Notes on 2 Co. xii. 7, 8, 9. ¶ *A fish.* A

how to give good gifts unto your children, how much more shall your Father which is in heaven give good things to them that ask him?

12 Therefore all things whatsoever ye would that men should do to you, do ye even so to them: [i]for this is the law and the prophets.

13 Enter[k] ye in at the strait gate: for wide *is* the gate, and broad *is* the way, that leadeth to destruction, and many there be which go in thereat:

14 Because[1] strait *is* the gate, and narrow *is* the way, which leadeth unto life; and [l]few there be that find it.

15 Beware[m] of false prophets, which come to you in sheep's clothing, but inwardly they are [n]ravening wolves:

i Le.19.18; Ro.13.8-10; Ga.5.14. *k* Lu.3.24.

1 or, *how*. *l* ch.20.16; 25.1-12; Ro.9.27,29. *m* De. 13.1-3; Je.23.13-16; 1 Jn.4.1. *n* Ac.20.29-31.

---

fish has some resemblance to a serpent; yet no parent would attempt to deceive his child in this. So God will not give to us that which might appear to be of use, but which would be injurious.

12. *All things whatsoever*, &c. This command has been usually called the *Saviour's golden rule*, a name given to it on account of its great value. All that you *expect* or *desire* of others in similar circumstances, do to them. Act not from selfishness or injustice, but put yourself in the place of the other, and ask what you would expect of him. This would make you impartial, candid, and just. It would destroy avarice, envy, treachery, unkindness, slander, theft, adultery, and murder. It has been well said that this law is what the balance-wheel is to machinery. It would prevent all irregularity of movement in the moral world, as that does in a steam-engine. It is easily applied, its justice is seen by all men, and all must acknowledge its force and value. ¶ *This is the law and the prophets.* That is, this is the sum or substance of the Old Testament. It is nowhere found in so many words, but it is a summary expression of all that the law required. The sentiment was in use among the Jews. Hillel, an ancient Rabbi, said to a man who wished to become a proselyte, and who asked him to teach him the whole law, "Whatever is hateful to you, do not do to another." Something of the same sentiment was found among the ancient Greeks and Romans, and is found in the writings of Confucius.

13, 14. *Enter ye in at the strait gate.* Christ here compares the way to life to an entrance through a gate. The words *straight* and *strait* have very different meanings. The former means *not crooked;* the latter, *pent up, narrow, difficult to be entered.* This is the word used here, and it means that the way to heaven is *pent up, narrow, close*, and not obviously entered. The way to death is open, broad, and thronged. The Saviour here referred probably to ancient cities. They were surrounded with walls and entered through gates. Some of those, connected with the great avenues to the city, were broad and admitted a throng; others, for more private purposes, were narrow, and few would be seen entering them. So, says Christ, is the path to heaven. It is narrow. It is not *the great highway* that men tread. Few go there. Here and there one may be seen—travelling in solitude and singularity. The way to death, on the other hand, is broad. Multitudes are in it. It is the great highway in which men go. They fall into it easily and without effort, and go without thought. If they wish to *leave that* and go by a narrow gate to the city, it would require effort and thought. So, says Christ, *diligence* is needed to enter life. See Lu. xiii. 24. None go of course. All must strive, to obtain it; and so narrow, unfrequented, and solitary is it, that few find it. This sentiment has been beautifully versified by Watts:

"Broad is the road that leads to death,
And thousands walk together there;
But wisdom shows a narrower path,
With here and there a traveller."

15. *False prophets.* The word prophet originally means one who foretells future events. As prophets, however, were commonly regarded as public instructors on the subject of religion, the word came to denote all who were religious teachers. See Notes on Ro. xii. 6. In this sense it is probably used here. A false prophet is a teacher of incorrect doctrine, or one falsely and unjustly laying claims to divine inspira-

16 Ye[o] shall know them by their fruits. Do men gather grapes of thorns, or figs of thistles?

17 Even so [p]every good tree bringeth forth good fruit; but a corrupt tree bringeth forth evil fruit.

18 A good tree cannot bring forth evil fruit, neither *can* a corrupt tree bring forth good fruit.

19 Every[q] tree that bringeth not forth good fruit, is hewn down, and cast into the fire.

o ch.12.33. *p* Lu.6.43,45. *q* ch.3.10; Jn.15.2,6.

20 Wherefore by their fruits ye shall know them.

21 Not every one that saith unto me, [r]Lord, Lord, shall enter into the kingdom of heaven; but he that doeth the will of my Father which is in heaven.

22 Many will say to me in that day, Lord, Lord, have we not [s]prophesied in thy name? and in thy name have cast out devils? and in thy name done many wonderful works?

r Is.48.1,2; ch.25.11,12; Lu.6.46; 13.25; Ro.2.13. *s* Nu.24.4; 1 Ki.22.11,&c.; Je.23.13,&c.; Ac.19.13-15; 1 Co.13.2.

---

tion. It probably had reference to the false teachers then among the Jews. ¶ *Who come in sheep's clothing.* The sheep is an emblem of innocence, sincerity, and harmlessness. To come in sheep's clothing is to assume the appearance of sanctity and innocence, when the heart is evil. ¶ *Ravening wolves.* Rapacious; voraciously devouring; hungry even to rage. Applied to the false teachers, it means that they assumed the appearance of holiness in order that they might the more readily get the *property* of the people. They were full of extortion and excess. See Mat. xxiii. 25.

16. *Ye shall know them by their fruits.* The Saviour gives the proper test of their character. Men do not judge of a tree by its leaves, or bark, or flowers, but by the fruit which it bears. The flowers may be beautiful and fragrant, the foliage thick and green; but these are merely ornamental. It is the *fruit* that is of chief service to man; and he forms his opinion of the nature and value of the tree by that fruit. So of pretensions to religion. The profession may be fair; but the *conduct*—the fruit—is to determine the nature of the principles.

17. *A corrupt tree.* The word corrupt here does not signify, as our translation would seem to indicate, that the tree *had been* good, but had become *vitiated;* but that it was a tree of a useless character, of a nature that produced nothing beneficial.

21. *Not every one that saith,* &c. The Saviour goes on to say that many, on the ground of a mere profession such as he had just referred to, would claim admittance into his kingdom. Many would plead that they had done miracles, and preached or prophesied much, and on the ground of that would demand an entrance into heaven. The power of working miracles had no necessary connection with piety. God may as well, if he chooses, give the power of raising the dead to a wicked man, as the skill of healing to a wicked physician. A miracle is a display *of his own power* through the medium of another. An act of healing the sick is also a display of *his power* through the agency of another. In neither of these cases is there any necessary connection with moral character. So of preaching or prophesying. God may use the agency of a man of talents, though not pious, to carry forward his purposes. Saving power on the mind is the work of God, and he may convey it by any agency which he chooses. Accordingly, many may be found in the day of judgment who may have been endowed with powers of prophecy or miracle, as Balaam or the magicians of Egypt; in the same way as many men of distinguished talents may be found, yet destitute of piety, and who will be shut out of his kingdom. See Mat. vii. 21; 1 Co. i. 26; xiii. 1–3. In this last place Paul says that, though he spoke with the tongue of angels, and had the gift of prophecy, and could remove mountains, and had not charity or love, all would be of no avail. See Notes on 1 Co. xiii. 1–3.

22. *In that day.* That is, in the last day, the day of judgment; the time when the principles of all pretenders to prophecy and piety shall be tried.

23. *Profess unto them.* Say unto them; plainly declare. ¶ *I never knew*

23 And then will I profess unto them, I never knew you: [t]depart from me, ye that work iniquity.

24 Therefore [u]whosoever heareth these sayings of mine, and doeth them, I will liken him unto a [v]wise man, which built his house upon a rock:

25 And the rain descended, and the floods came, and the winds blew, and beat upon that house; and it fell not: for it was [w]founded upon a rock.

26 And every one that heareth these sayings of mine, and doeth them not, shall be likened unto a [x]foolish man, which built his house upon the sand:

27 And the rain descended, and the floods came, and the winds

t Ps.5.5; ch.25.41; Re.22.15. *u* Lu.6.47,&c. *v* Ps.111.10; 119.99,130.

w Ps.92.13-15. *x* 1 Sa.2.30; Je.8.9.

you. That is, I never approved your conduct; never loved you; never regarded you as my friends. See Ps. i. 6; 2 Ti. ii. 19; 1 Co. viii. 3. This proves that, with all their pretensions, they had never been true followers of Christ. Jesus will not then say to false prophets and false professors of religion that he had once known them and then rejected them; that they had been once Christians and then had fallen away; that they had been pardoned and then had apostatized—but that he had *never known them*—THEY HAD NEVER BEEN TRUE CHRISTIANS. Whatever might have been their pretended joys, their raptures, their hopes, their self-confidence, their visions, their zeal, they had never been regarded by the Saviour as his true friends. I know not a more decided proof that Christians do not fall from grace than this text. It settles the question; and proves that whatever else such men had, they never had any true religion. See 1 Jn. ii. 19.

24–27. Jesus closes the sermon on the mount by a beautiful comparison, illustrating the benefit of attending to his words. It was not sufficient to *hear* them; they must be *obeyed*. He compares the man who should hear and obey him to a man who built his house on a rock. Palestine was to a considerable extent a land of hills and mountains. Like other countries of that description, it was subject to sudden and violent rains. The Jordan, the principal stream, was annually swollen to a great extent, and became rapid and furious in its course. The streams which ran among the hills, whose channels might have been dry during some months of the year, became suddenly swollen with the rain, and would pour down impetuously into the plains below. Everything in the way of these torrents would be swept off. Even houses, erected within the reach of these sudden inundations, and especially if founded on sand or on any unsolid basis, would not stand before them. The rising, bursting stream would shake it to its foundation; the rapid torrent would gradually wash away its base; it would totter and fall. Rocks in that country were common, and it was easy to secure for their houses a solid foundation. No comparison could, to a Jew, have been more striking.—So tempests, and storms of affliction and persecution, beat around the soul. Suddenly, when we think we are in safety, the heavens may be overcast, the storm may lower, and calamity may beat upon us. In a moment, health, friends, comforts may be gone. How desirable, then, to be possessed of something that the tempest cannot reach! Such is an interest in Christ, reliance on his promises, confidence in his protection, and a hope of heaven through his blood. Earthly calamities do not reach these; and, possessed of *religion*, all the storms and tempests of life may beat harmlessly around us.

There is another point in this comparison. The house built on the sand is beat upon by the floods and rains; its foundation gradually is worn away; it falls, and is borne down the stream and is destroyed. So falls the sinner. The floods are wearing away his sandy foundation; and soon one tremendous storm shall beat upon him, and he and his hopes shall fall, for ever fall. Out of Christ; perhaps having *heard* his words from very childhood; perhaps having taught them to others in the Sabbath-school; perhaps having been the means of laying the foundation on which others shall build for heaven, he has laid for himself no foundation, and soon an eternal tempest shall beat around his naked soul. How great will

blew, and [y]beat upon that house; and it fell: and [z]great was the fall of it.

28 And it came to pass, when Jesus had ended these sayings, the people were [a]astonished at his doctrine:

29 For he taught them as *one* having authority, and not as the scribes.

y 1 Co.3.13. z He.10.26,27. a Je.23.29; Mar.6.2.

be that fall! What will be his emotions when sinking for ever in the flood, and when he realizes that he is destined for ever to live and writhe in the peltings of that ceaseless storm that shall beat when "God shall rain snares, fire, and a horrible tempest" upon the wicked!

28, 29. *His doctrine.* His teaching. ¶ *As* one *having authority, and not as the scribes.* The scribes were the learned men and teachers of the Jewish nation, and were principally Pharisees. They taught chiefly the sentiments of their Rabbins, and the traditions which had been delivered; they consumed much of their time in useless disputes and "vain jangling." Jesus was open, plain, grave, useful, delivering truth as *became* the oracles of God; not spending his time in trifling disputes and debating questions of no importance, but confirming his doctrine by miracles and argument; teaching *as having power,* as it is in the original, and not in the vain and foolish manner of the Jewish doctors. He showed that he had authority to explain, to enforce, and to *change* the ceremonial laws of the Jews. He came with authority such as no *man* could have, and it is not remarkable that his explanations astonished them. From this chapter we may learn,

1st. The evil of censorious judging, ver. 1–5. We cannot see the heart. We have ourselves possibly greater faults than the persons that we condemn. They may possibly be of a different kind; but it is nevertheless not uncommon for persons to be very censorious toward faults in others, which they have to much greater extent themselves.

2d. We see how we are to treat men who are opposers of the gospel, ver. 6. We are *not* to present it to them when we know they will despise it and abuse us. We should, however, be cautious in forming that opinion of them. Many men may be far more ready to hear the gospel than we imagine, and a word seasonably and kindly spoken may be the means of saving them, Pr. xxv. 11; Ec. xi. 6. We should not meet violent and wicked opposers of the gospel with a harsh, overbearing, and lordly spirit—a spirit of dogmatizing and anger; nor should we violate the laws of social intercourse under the idea of *faithfulness.* Religion gains nothing by outraging the established laws of social life, 1 Pe. iii. 8. If men will not hear us when we speak to them kindly and respectfully, we may be sure they will not when we abuse them and become angry. We harden them against the truth, and confirm them in the opinion that religion is of no value. Our Saviour was always mild and kind, *and in not a single instance did he do violence to the laws of social intercourse, or fail in the respect due from one man to another.* When with harshness men speak to their superiors; when they abuse them with unkind words, coarse epithets, and unfeeling denunciations; when children and youth forget their station, and speak in harsh, authoritative tones to the aged, they are violating the very first principles of the gospel—meekness, respect, and love. Give honour to whom honour is due, and be *kind,* be *courteous.*

3d. Christ gives peculiar encouragement to prayer, ver. 7–11. Especially his remarks apply to the young. What child is there that would not go to his parent and ask him for things which were necessary? What child doubts the willingness of a kind parent to give what he thinks will be best for him? But God is more willing to give than the *best* parent. We need of *him* gifts of far more importance than we ever can of an earthly father. None but God can forgive, enlighten, sanctify, and save us. How strange that many ask favours of an *earthly* parent daily and hourly, and never ask of the Great Universal Father a single blessing for time or eternity!

4th. There is danger of losing the soul, ver. 13, 14. The way to ruin is broad, the path to heaven is narrow. Men naturally and readily go in the former; they never go in the latter without design. When we enter on the journey of life, we naturally fall into the broad and thronged way to ruin.

Our original propensity, our native depravity, our disinclination to God and religion, lead us to that, and we never leave it without effort. How much more natural to tread in a way in which multitudes go, than in one where there are few travellers, and which requires an effort to find it! And how much danger is there that we shall continue to walk in that way until it terminates in our ruin! No one is saved without effort. No one enters on the narrow way without design; no one by following his natural inclination and propensities. And yet how indisposed we are to effort! how unwilling to listen to the exhortations which would call us from the broad path to a narrower and less frequented course! How prone are men to feel that they are safe if they are with the many, and that the multitude that attend them constitute a safeguard from danger!

"Encompassed by a throng,
On *numbers* they depend;
They say so many can't be wrong,
And miss a happy end."

Yet did God ever spare a guilty city because it was large? Did he save the army of Sennacherib from the destroying angel because it was mighty? Does he hesitate to cut men down by the plague, the pestilence, and by famine, because they are numerous? Is he deterred from consigning men to the grave because they swarm upon the earth, and because a mighty throng is going to death? So in the way to hell. Not numbers, nor power, nor might, nor talent will make that way safe; nor will the path to heaven be a dangerous road because few are seen travelling there. The Saviour knew and *felt* that men are in danger; and hence, with much solemnity, he warned them when he lived, and now warns *us*, to strive to enter in at the strait gate.

5th. Sincerity is necessary in religion, ver. 15–23. Profession is of no value without it. God sees the heart, and the day is near when he will cut down and destroy all those who do not bring forth the fruits of righteousness in their lives. If in anything we should be honest and sincere, surely it should be in the things of religion. God is never deceived (Ga. vi. 7), and the things of eternity are of too much consequence to be lost by deluding ourselves or others. We may deceive our fellow-men, but we do not deceive our Maker; and soon he will strip off our thin covering, and show us as we are to the universe. If anything is of prominent value in religion, it is *honesty*—honesty to ourselves, to our fellow-men, and to God. Be willing to know the worst of your case. Be willing to be thought of, by God and men, *as you are.* Assume nothing which you do not possess, and pretend to nothing which you have not. Judge of yourselves as you do of others —not by words and promises, but by the *life.* Judge of yourselves as you do of trees; not by leaves and flowers, but by the *fruit.*

6th. We may learn the importance of building our hopes of heaven on a firm foundation, ver. 24–27. No other foundation can any man lay than that which is laid, which is Jesus Christ, 1 Co. iii. 11. He is the tried Corner Stone, 1 Pe. ii. 6; Ep. ii. 20. On an edifice raised on that foundation the storms of persecution and calamity will beat in vain. Hopes thus reared will sustain us in every adversity, will remain unshaken by the terrors of death, and will secure us from the tempests of wrath that shall beat upon the guilty. How awful, in the day of judgment, will it be to have been deceived! How dreadful the shock to find then that the house has been built on the sand! How dreadful the emotions, to see our hopes totter on the brink of ruin; to see sand after sand washed away, and the dwelling reel over the heaving deep, and fall into the abyss to rise no more! Ruin, awful and eternal ruin, awaits those who thus deceive themselves, and who trust to a name to live, while they are dead.

7th. Under what obligations are we for this *Sermon on the Mount!* In all languages there is not a discourse to be found that can be compared with it for purity, and truth, and beauty, and dignity. Were there no other evidence of the divine mission of Christ, this alone would be sufficient to prove that he was sent from God. Were these doctrines obeyed and loved, how pure and peaceful would be the world! How would hypocrisy be abashed and confounded! How would impurity hang its head! How would peace reign in every family and nation! How would anger and wrath flee! And how would the race—the lost and benighted tribes of men, the poor, and needy, and sorrowful—bend themselves before their common Father, and seek peace and eternal life at the hands of a merciful and faithful God!

CHAPTER VIII.

WHEN he was come down from the mountain, great multitudes followed him.

2 And, behold, [a]there came a leper and worshipped him, saying, Lord, if thou wilt, thou canst make me clean.

a Mar.1.40,&c.; Lu.5.12,&c.

CHAPTER VIII.

1. *When he was come down from the mountain.* That is, immediately on his descending from the mountain. His discourse had attracted great attention, and the fame of it drew together great multitudes, who were convinced that he had come from God. Then follows, in this chapter and the chapter succeeding, a succession of *miracles* not less remarkable than his teaching was; miracles that tended to confirm beyond a doubt the impression made by his sermon that he was sent from God. ¶ *Great multitudes followed him.* Great numbers of those who had been with him in the mountain, and great numbers of others who were attracted by the fame of that discourse.

2. *There came a leper.* No disease with which the human family has been afflicted has been more dreadful than that which is often mentioned in the Bible *as the leprosy.* It first exhibits itself on the surface of the skin. The appearance is not always the same, but it commonly resembles the spot made by the puncture of a pin or the pustules of a ringworm. The spots generally make their appearance very suddenly. Perhaps its appearance might be hastened by any sudden passion, as fear or anger. See Nu. xii. 10; 2 Ch. xxvi. 19. The spots commonly exhibit themselves at first on the face, about the nose and eyes, and increase in size a number of years, till they become as large as a pea or a bean.

There are three kinds of leprosy, distinguished by the appearance of the spots—the white, the black, and the red leprosy. These spots, though few at first, gradually spread till they cover the whole body.

But, though the *appearance* of the disease is at first in the skin, yet it is deeply seated in the bones, and marrow, and joints of the body. We have reason to suppose that in children it is concealed in the system for a number of years till they arrive at the age of puberty; and in adults for three or four years, till at last it gives fearful indications on the *skin* of its having gained a well-rooted and permanent existence. A leprous person may live twenty, or thirty, or even fifty years, if he received the disease at his birth, but they will be years of indescribable misery. The bones and marrow are pervaded with the disease. The malady advances from one stage to another with slow and certain ruin. "Life still lingers amid the desolation;" the joints, and hands, and feet lose their power; and the body *collapses*, or falls together in a form hideous and awful. There is a form of the disease in which it commences at the extremities: the joints separate; the fingers, toes, and other members one by one fall off; and the malady thus gradually approaches the seat of life. The wretched victim is thus doomed to see himself dying *piecemeal*, assured that no human power can arrest for a moment the silent and steady march of this foe to the seat of life.

This disease is contagious and hereditary. It is easily communicated from one to another, and is transmitted to the third and fourth generation. The last generation that is afflicted with it commonly exhibits the symptoms by decayed teeth, by a fetid breath, and by a diseased complexion.

Moses gave particular directions by which the real leprosy was to be distinguished from other diseases. See Le. xiii. The leprous person was, in order to avoid contagion, very properly separated from the congregation. The inspection of the disease was committed to the priest; and a declaration on his part that the person was healed, was sufficient evidence to restore the afflicted man to the congregation. It was required, also, that the leprous person should bring an offering to the priest of two birds, probably *sparrows* (see Le. xiv. 4, *margin*), one of which was slain and the other dismissed, Le. xiv. 5-7. In compliance with the laws of the land, Jesus directed the man that he had healed to make the customary offering, and to obtain the testimony of the priest that he was healed. The leprosy has once, and but once, appeared in America. This loathsome and most painful disease has in all other instances been confined to the

3 And Jesus put forth *his* hand,
and touched him, saying, I will;
be thou clean: and immediately his
leprosy was cleansed.
4 And Jesus saith unto him, [b]See
thou tell no man; but go thy way,
shew thyself to the priest, and
offer the gift that [c]Moses commanded, for a testimony unto them.
5 And when Jesus was entered
into Capernaum, there came unto
him a [d]centurion, beseeching him,

b ch.9.30; Mar.5.43. *c* Le.14.3,&c. *d* Lu.7.2,&c.

Old World, and chiefly to the Eastern nations. It is matter of profound gratitude to a benignant God that this scourge has been permitted *but* once to visit the New World. That awful calamity was in the island of Guadaloupe, in the West Indies, about the year 1730, and is thus described by an eye-witness:* "Its commencement is imperceptible. There appear only some few white spots on the skin. At first they are attended with no pain or inconvenience, but no means whatever will remove them. The disease imperceptibly increases for many years. The spots become larger, and spread over the whole body. When the disease advances, the upper part of the nose swells, the nostrils become enlarged, and the nose itself soft. Tumours appear on the jaws; the eye-brows swell; the ears become thick; the points of the fingers, as also the feet and the toes, swell; the nails become scaly; *the joints of the hands and feet separate and drop off.* In the last stage of the disease the patient becomes a hideous spectacle, *and falls to pieces.*" ¶ *Worshipped him.* Bowed down before him, to show him respect. See Notes on Mat. ii. 2. ¶ *If thou wilt.* This was an exhibition of great faith, and also an acknowledgment of his dependence on the *will* of Jesus, in order to be healed. So every sinner must come. He must feel that Jesus *can* save him. He must also feel that he has no claim on him; that it depends on his sovereign will; and must cast himself at his feet with the feelings of the leper:

"I can but perish if I go;
I am resolved to try;
For if I stay away, I know
I shall for ever die."

Happily, no one ever came to Jesus with this feeling who was not received and pardoned. ¶ *Make me clean.* Heal me. The leprosy was regarded as an unclean and disgusting disease. To be *healed*, therefore, was expressed by being *cleansed* from it.

* M. Peyssanel.

3. *And Jesus—touched him.* It was an offence to the Jews to *touch* a leprous person, and was regarded as making him who did it ceremonially impure, Le. xiii. 3. The act of putting forth his hand and *touching* him, therefore, expressed the intention of Jesus to cure him, and was a pledge that he *was*, in fact, already cured.

4. *See thou tell no man.* This command is to be understood as extending only to the time until he had made the proper representation to the priest. It was his duty to *hasten* to him immediately (Le. xiv. 2); not to delay by talking about it, but, as the *first* thing, to obey the laws of God, and make proper acknowledgments to him by an offering. The place where this cure was wrought was in Galilee, a distance of forty or fifty miles from Jerusalem; and it was his duty to make haste to the residence of the priest, and obtain his sanction to the reality of the cure. Perhaps, also, Christ was apprehensive that the report would go *before* the man if he delayed, and the priest, through opposition to Jesus, might pronounce it an imposition. ¶ *And offer the gift that Moses commanded.* That Moses directed to be offered by a leper when he was cured. That gift consisted of "two birds alive and clean, cedar-wood, scarlet, and hyssop," Le. xiv. 4. ¶ *For a testimony unto them.* Not to the *priest*, but to the people. Show thyself to the *priest*, and get his *testimony* to the reality of the cure, as a proof to the *people* that the healing is genuine. It was necessary that he should have that testimony before he could be received to the congregation or allowed to mingle with the people. Having this, he would be, of course, restored to the privileges of social and religious life, and the proof of the *miracle*, to the people, would be put beyond a doubt.

5. *Capernaum.* See Notes on chap. iv. 13. ¶ *There came unto him a centurion.* A centurion was the commander of a *hundred men* in the Roman armies. Judea was a Roman province, and gar-

6 And saying, Lord, my servant lieth at home sick of the palsy, grievously tormented.

7 And Jesus saith unto him, I will come and heal him.

8 The centurion answered and said, Lord, [e]I am not worthy that thou shouldst come under my roof: but [f]speak the word only, and my servant shall be healed.

9 For I am a man under authority, having soldiers under me: and I say to this *man*, Go, and he goeth; and to another, Come, and he cometh; and to my servant, Do this, and he doeth *it*.

10 When Jesus heard *it*, he marvelled, and said to them that followed, Verily I say unto you, I have not found so [g]great faith, no, not in Israel.

11 And I say unto you, That

e Ps.10.17; Lu.15.19,21. f Ps.33.9; 107.20. g ch.15.28.

---

risons were kept there to preserve the people in subjection. This man was probably by birth a Pagan. See verse 10.

6. *Sick of the palsy.* See Notes on ch. iv. 24. The particular form which the palsy assumed in this case is not mentioned. It seems it was a violent attack. Perhaps it was the painful form which produced violent *cramps*, and which immediately endangered his life.

8. *I am not worthy*, &c. This was an expression of great humility. It refers, doubtless, to his view of his *personal* unworthiness, and not merely to the fact that he was a *Gentile*. It was the expression of a conviction of the great dignity and power of the Saviour, and of a feeling that he was so unlike him that he was not fit that the Son of God should come into his dwelling. So every truly penitent sinner feels—a feeling which is appropriate when he comes to Christ.

9. *I am a man*, &c. He had full confidence in the ability of Jesus to heal his servant, and requested him simply to give the command. This request he presented in a manner appropriate to a soldier. I am a man, says he, under authority. That is, I am subject to the commands of others, and know how to obey. I have also under me soldiers who are accustomed to obedience. I say to one, Go, and he goes; and to another, Come, and he comes. I am *prepared*, therefore, to believe that your commands will be obeyed. As these obey me, so do diseases, storms, and seas obey you. If men obey me, who am an *inferior* officer, subject to another, how much more shall diseases obey you—the original source of power—having control over all things! He asked, therefore, simply that Christ would give commandment, and he felt assured he would be obeyed.

10. *When Jesus heard* it, *he marvelled.* He *wondered* at it, or *he deemed it remarkable.* ¶ *I have not found so great faith.* The word *faith*, here, means *confidence* or belief that Christ had power to heal his servant. It does not *of necessity* imply that he had saving faith; though, from the connection and the spirit manifested, it seems probable that he had. If this was so, then he was the first Gentile convert to Christianity, and was a very early illustration of what was more clearly revealed afterward—that the heathen were to be brought to the knowledge of the truth. ¶ *Not in Israel.* Israel was a name given to *Jacob* (Ge. xxxii. 28, 29), because, as a prince, he had power with God; because he persevered in wrestling with the angel that met him, and obtained the blessing. The name is derived from two Hebrew words signifying *Prince* and *God.* He was one of the patriarchs, a progenitor of the Jewish nation; and the names *Israel and Israelites* were given to them, as the name Romans to the Roman people was in honour of Romulus, and the name *American* to this continent from *Americus Vespuccius.* The name Israel was given to the whole nation till the time of Jeroboam, when only the ten tribes that revolted received the name, probably because they were a majority of the nation. After the captivity of Babylon it was given to *all* the Jews indiscriminately. See Mat. x. 6; Ac. vii. 42; He. viii. 8; Mar. xv. 32. It here means, "I have not found such an instance of *confidence* among the Jews."

11. *Many shall come from the east*, &c. Jesus takes occasion from the faith of a Roman centurion to state that this

many[h] shall come from the east and west, and shall sit down with Abraham, and Isaac, and Jacob, in the kingdom of heaven:

12 But the [i]children of the kingdom shall be cast out into outer darkness: [k]there shall be weeping and gnashing of teeth.

13 And Jesus said unto the centurion, Go thy way; and as thou

h Is.2.2,3; Lu.13.29; Ac.11.18; Ep.3.6; Re.7.9.
i ch.7.22,23.

k ch.13.42,50.

conversion would not be solitary; that *many* Pagans—many from the east and west—would be converted to the gospel, and be saved, as Abraham, Isaac, and Jacob were. The phrase "from the east and from the west," in the Scripture, is used to denote the *whole world*, Is. xlv. 6; lix. 19. The phrase, *shall sit down*, in the original, refers to the manner of sitting at meals (see Notes on Mat. xxiii. 6); and the enjoyments of heaven are described under the similitude of a feast or banquet—a very common manner of speaking of it, Mat. xxvi. 29; Lu. xiv. 15; xxii. 30. It is used here to denote *felicity*, *enjoyment*, or *honour*. To sit with those distinguished men was an honour, and would be expressive of great felicity.

12. *The children of the kingdom.* That is, the children, or the people, who *expected the kingdom*, or to whom it properly belonged; or, in other words, the Jews. *They* supposed themselves peculiarly the favourites of heaven. They thought that the Messiah would enlarge their nation and spread the triumphs of *their* kingdom. They called *themselves*, therefore, the children or the members of the kingdom of God, to the exclusion of the Gentiles. Our Saviour used the manner of speech to which they were accustomed, and said that *many of the Pagans would be saved, and many Jews lost.* ¶ *Shall be cast out into outer darkness*, &c. This is an image of future punishment. It is not improbable that the image was taken from Roman dungeons or prisons. They were commonly constructed under ground. They were shut out from the light of the sun. They were, of course, damp, dark, and unhealthy, and probably most filthy. Masters were in the habit of constructing such prisons for their slaves, where the unhappy prisoner, without light, or company, or comfort, spent his days and nights in weeping from grief, and in vainly gnashing his teeth from indignation. The image expresses the fact that the wicked who are lost will be shut out from the light of heaven, and from peace, and joy, and hope; will weep in hopeless grief, and will gnash their teeth in indignation against God, and murmur against his justice. What a striking image of future woe! Go to a damp, dark, solitary, and squalid dungeon; see a miserable and enraged victim; add to *his* sufferings the idea of eternity, and then remember that this, after all, is but an *image*, a faint image, of hell! Comp. Notes on Mat. xxii. 13.

13. *He was healed in that self-same hour.* This showed decisively the goodness and power of Jesus. No miracle could be more complete. There could be no imposition or deception.

This account, or one similar to this, is found in Lu. vii. 1–10. There has been a difference of opinion whether the account in Luke refers to the same case as that recorded in Matthew, or whether a *second* centurion, encouraged by the success of the first, applied to our Saviour in a similar case and manner, and obtained the same success. In support of the supposition that they are different narratives, it is said that they disagree so far that it is impossible to reconcile them, and that it is not *improbable* that a similar occurrence might take place, and be attended with similar results.

To a plain reader, however, the narratives appear to be the same. They agree in the character of the person, the place, and apparently the time; in the same substantial *structure* of the account; in the expression of similar feelings, the same answers, and the same result. It is very difficult to believe that all these circumstances would coincide in two different stories.

They differ, however. Matthew says that the centurion *came himself.* Luke says that he at first sent elders of the Jews, and then his particular friends. He also adds that he was friendly to the Jews, and had built them a synagogue. An infidel will ask whether there is not here a palpable contradiction. In explanation of this, let it be remarked: 1st. That the fact that the centurion came himself, supposing that to have

hast believed, *so* be it done unto thee. And his servant was healed in the self-same hour.

14 And when Jesus was come into Peter's house, he saw [l]his wife's mother laid, and sick of a fever.

15 And he touched her hand, and the fever left her: and she arose, and ministered unto them.

l Mar.1.30,31; Lu.4.38,39.

been the fact, is no evidence that others did not come also. It was *in* the city. The centurion was a great favourite, and had conferred on the Jews many favours, and they would be anxious that the favour which he desired of Jesus should be granted. At his suggestion, or of their own accord, his Jewish friends might apply to Jesus, and press the subject upon him, and be anxious to represent the case as favourably as possible. All this was probably done, as it would be in any other city, in considerable haste and apparent confusion; and one observer might fix his attention strongly on one circumstance, and another on another. It is not at all improbable that the *same* representation and request might have been made both by the centurion and his friends. Matthew might have fixed his eye very strongly on the fact that the centurion came *himself*, and been particularly *struck* with his deportment; and Luke on the remarkable zeal shown by the friends of a heathen, the interest they took in his welfare, and the circumstance that he had done much for them. Full of these interesting circumstances, he might comparatively have overlooked the centurion himself. But, 2d. It was a maxim among the Jews, as it is now in law, *that what a man does by another, he does himself*. So, in Mar. x. 35, James and John are represented as coming to the Saviour with a request: in Mat. xx. 20, it appears that they presented their request through their mother. In Jn. iv. 1, Jesus is said to baptize, when, in fact, he did not do it himself, but by his disciples. In Jn. xix. 1, Pilate is said to have scourged Jesus; but he certainly did not do it with his own hands. In the case of the centurion, Matthew narrates what occurred very briefly; Luke goes more into detail, and states more of the circumstances. Matthew was intent on the great leading facts of the cure. He was studious of brevity. He did not choose to explain the particular circumstances. He says that the centurion *made the application* and received the answer. He does not say whether by himself or by *an agent*. Luke explains particularly *how* it was done. There is no more contradiction, therefore, than there would be if it should be said of a man in a court of law that he came and made application for a new trial, when the application was really made by his lawyer. Two men, narrating the fact, might exhibit the same variety that Matthew and Luke have done, and both be true. It should never be forgotten that *the sacred narrative of an event is what it is stated to be by all the sacred writers; as the testimony in a court in which a case is decided is what is stated by all the credible witnesses, though one may have stated one circumstance and another another.*

One thing is most clearly shown by this narrative: that this account was not *invented* by the evangelists for the sake of imposition. If it had been, they would have *agreed in all the circumstances.*

14, 15. This account is contained also in Mar. i. 29-31, and Lu. iv. 38-41. Mark says that Simon and Andrew lived together, and that James and John went with them to the house. He adds, also, that *before* the miracle they spake to him about the sick person. The miracle was direct and complete. She that had been sick was so completely restored as to attend to them and minister to them. The mention of "*Peter's wife's mother*" proves that Peter either then was or had been married. The fair and obvious interpretation is, that his wife was then living. Comp. 1 Co. ix. 5, and see the Note on that place. Peter is claimed by the Roman Catholics to be the head of the church and the vicegerent of Christ. The Pope, according to their view, is the successor of this apostle. On what pretence do they maintain that it is wrong for *priests* to marry? Why did not Christ at once reject Peter from being an apostle for having a wife? How remarkable that *he* should be set up as the head of the church, and an example and a model to all who were to succeed him! But all this is human law, and is contrary to the New Testament.

16 When the even was come, they brought unto him [m]many that were possessed with devils: and he cast out the spirits with *his* word, and healed all that were sick:

17 That it might be fulfilled which was spoken by Esaias the prophet, saying, [n]Himself took our infirmities, and bare *our* sicknesses.

18 Now when Jesus saw great multitudes about him, he gave commandment to depart unto the other side.

19 And a certain scribe came, and said unto him, Master, [o]I will follow thee whithersoever thou goest.

20 And Jesus saith unto him, The foxes have holes, and the birds of the air *have* nests; but the Son of man hath not where to lay *his* head.

m Mar.1.32,&c. *n* Is.53.4; 1 Pe.2.24. *o* Lu.9.57,58.

Comp. 1 Ti. iii. 2, 4, 5. That Peter had a wife was no objection to his being an apostle, and marriage has been expressly declared to be "honourable in ALL," He. xiii. 4.

16. *When the even was come*, &c. The fame of the miracles of Jesus would probably draw together a crowd, and those who had friends that were afflicted would bring them. All that were brought to him he healed. This was proof of two things: first, of his great benevolence; and, secondly, of his divine mission. He might have established the latter by miracles that would do no good. None of his miracles were performed, however, merely to make a display of power, unless the cursing of the barren fig-tree be an exception. Comp. Mar. xi. 11–14. What is here recorded occurred on the evening of the Sabbath, Mar. i. 21–32. The Jews kept the Sabbath from evening to evening, Le. xxiii. 32. On the Sabbath they would not even bring their sick to be healed (Lu. xiii. 14); but as soon as it was closed, on the evening of the same day, they came in multitudes to be cured. ¶ *Possessed with devils.* See Notes on Mat. iv. 24. ¶ *With* his *word.* By his *command;* by a word.

17. *That it might be fulfilled*, &c. This passage is found in Is. liii. 4. Our English translation of that important passage is, "Surely he hath borne our griefs and carried our sorrows." The Greek in Matthew is an exact translation of the Hebrew, and the same translation should have been made in both places. In the fifty-third chapter, Isaiah fully states the doctrine of the atonement, or that the Messiah was to suffer for sin. In the verse quoted here, however, he states the very truth which Matthew declares. The word translated *griefs* in Isaiah, and *infirmities* in Matthew, means properly, in the Hebrew and Greek, *diseases of the body.* In neither does it refer to the disease of the mind, or to sin. To bear those griefs is clearly to bear them *away*, or to remove them. This was done by his miraculous power in healing the sick. The word rendered "sorrows" in Isaiah, and "sicknesses" in Matthew, means *pain, grief*, or *anguish of mind.* To *carry* these is to sympathize with the sufferers; to make provision for alleviating those sorrows, and to take them away. This he did by his precepts and by his example; and the *cause* of all sorrows—*sin*—he removed by the atonement. The passage in Isaiah and Matthew, therefore, mean precisely the same thing. See *Magee on Atonement*, and Notes on Isaiah, ch. liii.

18. *Unto the other side.* Jesus was now in Capernaum, a city at the north-west corner of the Sea of Tiberias, or Sea of Galilee. See Notes on Mat. iv. 18. The country to which he purposed to go was the region on the east of the Sea of Tiberias.

19, 20. *And a certain scribe came*, &c. It is not improbable that this man had seen the miracles of Jesus, and had formed an expectation that by following him he would obtain some considerable worldly advantage. Christ, in reply to his professed purpose to follow him, proclaimed his own poverty, and dashed the hopes of the avaricious scribe. The very foxes and birds, says he, have places of repose and shelter, but the Son of man has no home and no pillow. He is a stranger in his own world—a wanderer and an outcast from the abodes of men. Comp. Jn. i. 11. ¶ *Son of man.* This means, evidently, Jesus himself. No title is more frequently given to the Saviour than this, and yet there is much difficulty in ex-

21 And another of his disciples said unto him, [p]Lord, suffer me first to go and bury my father.

p 1 Ki.19.20.

22 But Jesus said unto him, Follow me; and let the dead bury their dead.

---

plaining it. The word *son* is used in a great variety of significations. See Notes on Mat. i. 1. The name *Son of man* is given to Jesus only three times in the New Testament (Ac. vii. 56; Re. i. 13; xiv. 14), except by himself. When he speaks of himself, this is the most common appellation by which he is known. The phrase *Son of God*, given to Christ, denotes a *peculiar* connection with God, Jn. x. 36. The name *Son of man* probably denotes a corresponding *peculiar* connection with man. Perhaps the Saviour used it to signify the interest he felt in man; his peculiar love and friendship for him; and his willingness to devote himself to the best interests of the race. It is sometimes, however, used as synonymous with *Messiah*, Mat. xvi. 28; Jn. i. 34; Ac. viii. 37; Jn. xii. 34.

21. *And another of his disciples*, &c. The word disciple properly signifies *learner*, and was given to the followers of Jesus because they received him as their teacher. See Notes on Mat. v. 1. It does not of necessity mean that a *disciple* was a pious man, but only one of the multitude, who, for various causes, might attend on his instructions. See Jn. vi. 66; ix. 28. ¶ *Suffer me first to go and bury my father.* This seemed to be a reasonable request, as respect for parents, living or dead, is one of the first duties of religion. But the Saviour saw that in his circumstances there might be danger, if he was thus permitted to go, that he would not return to him; and he commanded him, therefore, to perform the more important duty—the duty of attending to the salvation of his soul—even at the risk of the apparent neglect of another duty. The first duty of man is religion, and everything else should be made subordinate to that.

22. *Let the dead bury their dead.* The word dead is used in this passage in two different senses. It is apparently a paradox, but is fitted to convey the idea very distinctly to the mind. The Jews used the word *dead* often to express indifference toward a thing; or, rather, to show that that thing has no *influence* over us. Thus, to be dead to the world; to be dead to the law (Ro. vii. 4); to be dead to sin (Ro. vi. 11), means that the world, law, and sin have not influence or control over us; that we are free from them, and act *as though they were not.* A body in the grave is unaffected by the pomp and vanity, by the gaiety and revelry, by the ambition and splendour that may be near the tomb. So men of the world are dead to religion. They see not its beauty, hear not its voice, are not won by its loveliness. This is the class of men to which the Saviour refers here. Let men, says he, who are uninterested in my work, and who are *dead in sin* (Ep. ii. 1), take care of the dead. Your duty is now to follow me.

There may have been several reasons for this apparently harsh direction. One may have been to *test* the character and attachment of the man. If he had proper love for Christ, he would be willing to leave his friends, even in the most tender and trying circumstances. This is required, Mat. x. 27; Lu. xiv. 26. A second reason may have been, that if he returned *at that time*, his friends might ridicule or oppose him, or present plausible arguments, *in the afflictions of the family*, why he should not return to Christ. The thing to which he was called was moreover of more importance than any earthly consideration; and, for that time, Christ chose to require of the man a very extraordinary sacrifice, to show his sincere attachment to him. Or it may have been that the Saviour saw that the effect of visiting his home at that time might have been to drive away all his serious impressions, and that he would return to him no more. His impressions may not have been deep enough, and his purpose to follow the Saviour may not have been strong enough to bear the trial to which he would be subjected. Strange as it may seem, there are few scenes better fitted to drive away serious impressions than those connected with a funeral. We should have supposed it would be otherwise; but facts show it to be so, and demonstrate that if this was one of the reasons which influenced the Saviour, he had a thorough knowledge of human nature. The arrangements for the funeral, the preparation of mourning

23 And when he was entered into a ship, his disciples followed him.

24 And behold, [q]there arose a great tempest in the sea, insomuch that the ship was covered with the waves: but he was asleep.

25 And his disciples came to *him*, and awoke him, saying, Lord, save us: we perish.

26 And he saith unto them, Why are ye fearful, O ye of little faith? Then he arose, and [r]rebuked the winds and the sea; and there was a great calm.

27 But the men marvelled, say-

q Mar.4.37,&c.; Lu.8.23,&c.

r Job 38.11; Ps.89.9; 107.29.

---

apparel, and the depth of sorrow in such cases, divert the mind from its sins and its personal need of a Saviour; and hence few persons are awakened or converted as the result of death in a family. The case here was a *strong* one—it was as strong as can well be conceived; and the Saviour meant to teach by this that nothing is to be allowed to divert the mind from religion—nothing to be an excuse for not following him. Not even the death of a father, and the sorrows of an afflicted family, are to be suffered to lead a man to defer religion, or to put off the purpose to be a Christian. That is a fixed duty—a duty not to be deferred or neglected, whether in sickness or health, at home or abroad—whether surrounded by living and happy kindred, or whether a father, a mother, a child, or a sister lies in our house dead.

It is the *regular* duty of children to obey their parents, and to show them kindness in affliction, and to evince proper care and respect for them when dead. Nor did our Saviour show himself insensible to these duties. He taught here, however, as he always taught, that a regard to friends, and ease, and comfort, should be *subordinate to the gospel;* and that we should always be ready to sacrifice these when duty to God requires it.

23. *Into a ship.* This was on the Sea of Tiberias. The *ship* in which they sailed was probably a small open boat with sails, such as was commonly used for fishing on the lake. ¶ *His disciples.* Not merely the apostles, but probably many others. There were many other ships in company with him, Mar. iv. 36. This circumstance would render the miracle much more striking and impressive.

24. *A great tempest.* A violent storm; or a *wind* so strong as to endanger their lives. This lake was subject to sudden squalls. Dr. Thomson (*The Land and the Book*, vol. ii. p. 59) says: "Small as the lake is, and placid, in general, as a molten mirror, I have repeatedly seen it quiver, and leap, and boil like a caldron, when driven by fierce winds from the eastern mountains." ¶ *The ship was covered with the waves.* The billows dashed against the ship (Mar. iv. 37), so that it was fast filling and in danger of sinking. ¶ *He was asleep.* On the hinder part of the vessel, on a pillow, Mar. iv. 38. It was in the night, and Jesus had retired to rest. He was probably weary, and slept calmly and serenely. He apprehended no danger, and showed to his disciples how calmly one can sleep with a pure conscience, and who feels safe in the hands of God.

25. *Save us.* Save our lives. ¶ *We perish.* We are in danger of perishing. This showed great confidence in the Saviour. It shows, also, where sinners and Christians should always go who feel that they are in danger of perishing. There is none that can save from the storms of divine wrath but the Son of God.

26. *Why are ye fearful?* You should have remembered that the Son of God, the Messiah, was on board. You should not have forgotten that he had power to save, and that with him you are safe. So Christians should never fear danger, disease, or death. With Jesus they are safe. No enemy can reach *him;* and as *he* is safe, so they shall be also, Jn. xiv. 19. ¶ *Rebuked the winds.* Reproved them, or commanded them to be still. What a power was this! What irresistible proof that he was divine! His word awed the tempest and allayed the storm! There is not anywhere a sublimer description of a display of power. Nor could there be clearer proof that he was truly the Son of God. ¶ *A great calm.* The winds were still, and the sea ceased to dash against the vessel and to endanger their lives.

27. *The men marvelled.* Wondered,

ing, What manner of man is this, that even the winds and the sea obey him?

28 And[s] when he was come to the other side, into the country of the Gergesenes, there met him two

s Mar.5.1; Lu.8.26,&c.

or were amazed. ¶ *What manner of man.* What kind of a personage. How unlike other men! What a vast display of power! and how far exalted above mortals must he be!

Jesus spake to the winds; rebuked their raging, and the sea was suddenly calm. The storm subsided; the ship glided smoothly; danger fled; and in amazement they stood in the presence of him who controlled the tempests that God had raised; and they felt that *he* must be God himself, for none but God could calm the heaving billows and scatter the tempest. No scene could have been more grand than this display of the power of Jesus. The darkness; the dashing waves; the howling winds; the heaving and tossing ship; the fears and cries of the seamen, all by a single word hushed into calm repose, present an image of power and divinity irresistibly grand and awful. So the tempest rolls and thickens over the head of the awakened sinner. So he trembles over immediate and awful destruction. So, while the storm of wrath howls, and hell threatens to ingulf him, he comes trembling to the Saviour. He hears; he rebukes the storm, and the sinner is safe. An indescribable peace takes possession of the soul, and he glides on a tranquil sea to the haven of eternal rest. See Is. lvii. 20, 21; Ro. v. 1; Phi. iv. 7.

28-34. The same account of the demoniacs substantially is found in Mar. v. 1-20, and Lu. viii. 26-38.

28. *The other side.* The other side of the Sea of Tiberias. ¶ *Country of the Gergesenes.* Mark (v. 1) says that he came into the country of the *Gadarenes.* This difference is only apparent. *Gadara* was a city not far from the Lake Gennesareth, one of the ten cities that were called *Decapolis.* See Notes on Mat. iv. 25. *Gergesa* was a city about 12 miles to the south-east of Gadara, and about 20 miles to the east of the Jordan. There is no contradiction, therefore, in the evangelists. He came into the region in which the two cities were situated, and one evangelist mentioned one, and the other another. It shows that the writers had not *agreed* to impose on the world; for if they had, they would have mentioned the *same* city; and it shows, also, they were familiar with the country. No men would have written in this manner but those who were acquainted with the facts. Impostors do not mention *places* or *names* if they can avoid it. ¶ *There met him two.* Mark and Luke speak of only *one* that met him. "There met him out of the tombs *a man,*" Mar. v. 2. "There met him out of the tombs *a certain man,*" Lu. viii. 27. This difference of statement has given rise to considerable difficulty. It is to be observed, however, that neither Mark nor Luke say that there was *no more* than one. For particular reasons, they might have been led to fix their attention on the one that was more notorious, and furious, and difficult to be managed. Had they denied plainly that there was more than *one*, and had Matthew affirmed that there were *two*, there would have been an irreconcilable contradiction. As it is, they relate the affair as other men would. It shows that they were honest witnesses. Had they been impostors; had Matthew and Luke *agreed* to write books to deceive the world, they would have agreed exactly in a case so easy as this. They would have told the story with the same circumstances. Witnesses in courts of law often differ in unimportant matters; and, provided the *main* narrative coincides, their testimony is thought to be more valuable.

Luke has given us a hint why he recorded only the cure of *one* of them. He says there met him "*out of the city,*" a man, &c.; or, as it should be rendered, "*a man of the city,*" a *citizen.* Yet the man did not dwell in the city, for he adds in the same verse, "neither abode he in any house, but in the tombs." The truth of the case was, that he was born and educated in the city. He had probably been a man of wealth and eminence; he was well known, and the people felt a deep interest in the case. Luke was therefore particularly struck with his case; and as *his* cure fully established the power of Jesus, he recorded it. The other person that Matthew mentions was probably a stranger, or one less notorious as a maniac, and he felt less

possessed with devils, coming out of the tombs, exceeding fierce, so that no man might pass by that way.

29 And, behold, they cried out, saying, What have we to do with thee, Jesus, thou Son of God? art

---

interest in the cure. Let two persons go into a lunatic asylum and meet two insane persons, one of whom should be exceedingly fierce and ungovernable, and well known as having been a man of worth and standing; let them converse with them, and let the more violent one attract the principal attention, and they would very likely give the same account that Matthew and Luke do, and no one would doubt the statement was correct. ¶ *Possessed with devils.* See Notes on Mat. iv. 24. ¶ *Coming out of the tombs.* Mark and Luke say that they dwelt in the tombs. The sepulchres of the Jews were frequently *caves* beyond the walls of the cities in which they dwelt, or excavations made in the sides of hills, or sometimes in solid rocks. These caves or excavations were sometimes of great extent. They descended to them by flights of steps. These graves were not in the midst of cities, but in groves, and mountains, and solitudes. They afforded, therefore, to insane persons and demoniacs a place of retreat and shelter. They delighted in these gloomy and melancholy recesses, as being congenial to the wretched state of their minds. Josephus also states that these sepulchres were the haunts and lurking-places of those desperate bands of robbers that infested Judea. For further illustration of this subject see my Notes on Is. xiv. 9; xxii. 16; and lxv. 4. The ancient Gadara is commonly supposed to be the present Umkeis. "Near there Burckhardt reports that he found many sepulchres in the rocks, showing how naturally the conditions of the narrative respecting the demoniacs could have been fulfilled in that region. Reliable writers state that they have seen lunatics occupying such abodes of corruption and death."—Hackett's *Illustrations of Scripture*, p. 109. Dr. Thomson, however (*The Land and the Book*, vol. ii. p. 34–37), maintains that Gadara could not have been the place of the miracle, since that place is about "three hours" (some 10 or 12 miles) to the south of the extreme shore of the lake in that direction. He supposes that the miracle occurred at a place now called *Kerza* or *Gersa*, which he supposes was the ancient *Gergesa*. Of this place he says: "In this Gersa or Chersa we have a position which fulfils every requirement of the narratives, and with a name so near that in Matthew as to be in itself a strong corroboration of the truth of this identification. It is within a few rods of the shore, and an immense mountain rises directly above it, in which are ancient tombs, out of some of which the two men possessed of the devils may have issued to meet Jesus. The lake is so near the base of the mountain that the swine, rushing madly down it, could not stop, but would be hurried on into the water and drowned. The place is one which our Lord would be likely to visit, having Capernaum in full view to the north, and Galilee 'over against it,' as Luke says it was. The *name*, however, pronounced by Bedawin Arabs is so similar to Gergesa, that, to all my inquiries for this place, they invariably said it was at Chersa, and they insisted that they were identical, and I agree with them in this opinion."

29. *What have we to do with thee?* This might have been translated with great propriety, What hast thou to do with us? The meaning is "Why dost thou trouble or disturb us?" See 2 Sa. xvi. 10; 2 Ki. ix. 18; Ezr. iv. 3. ¶ *Son of God.* The title, *Son of God*, is often given to Christ. Men are sometimes called sons, or children of God, to denote their adoption into his family, 1 Jn. iii. 1. But the title given to Christ denotes his superiority to the prophets (He. i. 1); to Moses, the founder of the Jewish economy (He. iii. 6); it denotes his *peculiar* and near relation to the Father, as evinced by his resurrection (Ps. ii. 7; Ac. xiii. 33); it denotes his peculiar relation to God from his miraculous conception (Lu. i. 35); and is equivalent to a declaration that he is divine, or equal to the Father. See Notes on Jn. x. 36. ¶ *Art thou come hither to torment us?* &c. By *the time* here mentioned is meant the day of judgment. The Bible reveals the doctrine that evil spirits are not *now* bound as they will be after that day; that they are permitted to tempt and afflict men, but that in the day of judgment *they* also will be condemned to everlasting punishment with all the

thou come hither to torment us before the time?

30 And there was a good way off from them a herd of many swine, feeding.

31 So the devils besought him, saying, If thou cast us out, [t]suffer us to go away into the herd of swine.[u]

32 And he said unto them, Go. And when they were come out, they went into the herd of swine: and, behold, the whole herd of swine ran violently down a steep place into the sea, and perished in the waters.

33 And they that kept them fled, and went their ways into the city,

t Job 1.10-12; 2.3-6. *u* De.14.8; Is.65.3,4.

---

wicked, 2 Pe. ii. 4; Jude 6. These spirits seemed to be apprised of that, and were alarmed lest the day that they feared had come. They besought him, therefore, not to send them out of that country, not to consign them then to hell, but to put off the day of their final punishment.

Mark and Luke say that Jesus inquired the name of the principal demoniac, and that he called his name *Legion, for they were many.* The name legion was given to a division in the Roman army. It did not always denote the same number, but in the time of Christ it consisted of 6000—3000 foot and 3000 horsemen. It came, therefore, to signify *a large number*, without specifying the exact amount.

30. *A herd of many swine.* The word *herd*, here applied to swine, is now commonly given to *cattle.* Formerly it signified any collection of beasts, or even of men. The number that composed this *herd* was 2000, Mar. v. 13.

33. *They that kept them fled.* These swine were doubtless owned by the inhabitants of the country. Whether they were Jews or Gentiles is not certainly known. It was not properly in the territory of Judea; but, as it was on its borders, it is probable that the inhabitants were a mixture of Jews and Gentiles. Swine were to Jews unclean animals, and it was unlawful for them to eat them, Le. xi. 7. They were forbidden by their own laws to keep them, even for the purpose of traffic. Either, therefore, they had expressly violated the law, or these swine were owned by the Gentiles.

The keepers fled in consternation. They were amazed at the power of Jesus. Perhaps they feared a farther destruction of property; or, more likely, they were acquainted with the laws of the Jews, and regarded this as a judgment of heaven for keeping forbidden animals, and for tempting the Jews to violate the commands of God.

This is the only one of our Saviour's miracles, except the case of the fig-tree that he cursed (Mat. xxi. 18–20), in which he caused any destruction of property. It is a striking proof of his benevolence, that his miracles tended directly to the comfort of mankind. It was a proof of goodness *added* to the direct purpose for which his miracles were wrought. That purpose was to confirm his divine mission; and it might have been as fully done by splitting rocks, or removing mountains, or causing water to run up steep hills, as by any other display of power. He chose to exhibit the proof of his divine power, however, in such a way as to benefit mankind.

Infidels have objected to this whole narrative. They have said that this was a wanton and unauthorized violation of private rights in the destruction of property. They have said, also, that the account of devils going into swine, and destroying them, was ridiculous. In regard to these objections the narrative is easily vindicated. 1st. If Christ, as the Bible declares, is divine as well as human—God as well as man—then he had an original right to that and all other property, and might dispose of it as he pleased, Ps. l. 10–12. If God had destroyed the herd of swine by pestilence or by lightning, by an inundation or by an earthquake, neither the owners or anyone else would have had reason to complain. No one now feels that he has a right to murmur if God destroys a thousand times the amount of this property by overturning a city by an earthquake. Why, then, should complaints be brought against him if he should do the same thing in another way? 2d. If this property was held *by the Jews*, it was a violation of their law, and it was right that they should suffer the loss; if *by the Gentiles*, it was known also to be a violation of the law of the

and told every thing, and what was befallen to the possessed of the devils.

34 And, behold, the whole city came out to meet Jesus: and when they saw him, they besought *him* that he would [v]depart out of their coasts.

v Job 21.14; Lu.5.8; Ac.16.39.

people among whom they lived; a temptation and a snare to them; an abomination in their sight; and it was proper that the nuisance should be removed. 3d. The cure of two men, one of whom was probably a man of distinction and property, was of far more consequence than the amount of property destroyed. To restore a *deranged* man now would be an act for which *property* could not compensate, and which could not be measured in value by any pecuniary consideration. But, 4th. Jesus was not at all answerable for this destruction of property. He did not *command*, he only *suffered* or *permitted* the devils to go into the swine. He commanded them merely to *come out of the man*. *They* originated the purpose of destroying the property, doubtless for the sake of doing as much mischief as possible, and of destroying the effect of the miracle of Christ. In this they seem to have had most disastrous success, and they only are responsible. 5th. If it should be said that Christ *permitted* this, when he might have prevented it, it may be replied that the difficulty does not stop there. He *permits* all the evil that exists, when he might prevent it. He permits *men* to do much evil, when he might prevent it. He permits one bad man to injure the person and property of another bad man. He permits the bad to injure the good. He often permits a wicked man to fire a city, or to plunder a dwelling, or to rob a traveller, destroying property of many times the amount that was lost on this occasion. Why is it any more absurd to suffer a wicked spirit to do injury than a wicked man? or to suffer a *legion of devils* to destroy a herd of swine, than for *legions of men* to desolate nations, and cover fields and towns with ruin and slaughter?

34. *The whole city came out.* The people of the city probably came with a view of arresting him for the injury done to the property; but, seeing him, and being awed by his presence, they only besought him to leave them. ¶ *Out of their coasts.* Out of their country. This shows, 1st. That the design of Satan is to prejudice men against the Saviour, and even to make what Christ does an occasion why they should desire him to leave them. 2d. The power of avarice. These men preferred their property to the Saviour. They loved it so much that they were blind to the evidence of the miracle, and to the good he had done to the miserable men whom he had healed. It is no uncommon thing for men to love the world so much; to love property—even like that owned by the people of Gadara—so much as to see no beauty in religion and no excellence in the Saviour; and, rather than part with it, to beseech Jesus to withdraw from them. The most grovelling employment, the most abandoned sins, the most loathsome vices, are often loved more than the presence of Jesus, and more than all the blessings of his salvation.

REMARKS.

1st. The leprosy, the disease mentioned in this chapter, is a fit representation of the nature of sin. Like that, sin is loathsome; it is deep fixed in the frame; penetrating every part of the system; working its way to the surface imperceptibly, but surely; loosing the joints, and consuming the sinews of moral action; and adhering to the system till it terminates in eternal death. It goes down from age to age. It shuts out men from the society of the pure in heaven; nor can man be admitted there till God has cleansed the soul by his Spirit, and man is made pure and whole.

2d. The case of the centurion is a strong instance of the nature and value of humility, ver. 5–10. He sustained a fair character, and had done much for the Jews. Yet he had no exalted conception of himself. Compared with the Saviour, he felt that he was unworthy that he should come to his dwelling. So feels every humble soul. *Humility is an estimate of ourselves as we are.* It is a willingness to be known, and talked of, and treated just according to truth. It is a view of ourselves as lost, poor, and wandering creatures. Compared with other men—with angels, with Jesus, and with God—it is a feeling by which we regard ourselves as unworthy of notice. It is a readiness to occupy our appropriate station in the universe, and to put on humbleness of mind as our proper array, 1 Pe. v. 5.

3d. We have in the case of the centurion an equally beautiful exhibition of *faith*. He had unwavering confidence in the power of Jesus. He did not doubt at all that he was able to do for him just what he *needed*, *and what he wished him to do*. This is faith; and every man who has this *trust* or confidence in Christ for salvation, has *saving faith*.

4th. Humility and faith are always connected. The one prepares the mind for the other. Having a deep sense of our weakness and unworthiness, we are prepared to look to Him who *has* strength. Faith also produces humility. Jesus was humble; and believing on him, we catch his spirit and learn of him, Mat. xi. 28–30. Compared with him, we see our unworthiness. Seeing HIS *strength*, we see OUR *feebleness;* seeing *his* strength exerted to save creatures impure and ungrateful as we are, we sink away into an increased sense of our unfitness for his favour.

5th. We see the compassion and kindness of Jesus, ver. 16, 17. He has borne *our* heavy griefs. He provides comfort for us in sickness and sustains us in dying. But for his merciful arm, we should sink; and dying, we should die without hope. But

"Jesus can make a dying bed
Feel soft as downy pillows are;
While on his breast we lean our head,
And breathe our life out sweetly there."

6th. We are forcibly struck with his condescension, ver. 19, 20. Men of wickedness and crime dwell in splendid mansions, and stretch themselves on couches of ease; when afflicted, they recline on beds of down; but Jesus had no home and no pillow. The birds that fill the air with music and warble in the groves, nay, the very foxes, have homes and a shelter from the storms and elements; but He that made them, clothed in human flesh, was a wanderer, and had not where to lay his head. His sorrows he bore alone; his dwelling was in the mountains. In the palaces of the men for whom he toiled, and for whom he was about to bleed on a cross, he found no home and no sympathy. Surely this was compassion worthy of a God.

7th. It is no disgrace to be poor. The Son of God was poor, and it is no dishonour to be like him. If our Maker, then, has cast our lot in poverty; if he takes away by sickness or calamity the fruits of our toils; if he clothes us in homely and coarse apparel; if he bids the winds of heaven to howl around our open and lonely dwellings, let us remember that the Redeemer of mankind trod the same humble path, and that it can be no dishonour to be likened to him who was the beloved Son of God.

8th. We should be willing to embrace the gospel without hope of earthly reward, ver. 19–23. Religion promises no earthly honours or wealth. It bids its disciples to look beyond the grave for its highest rewards. It requires men to love religion *for its own sake;* to love the Saviour, even when poor, and cast out, and suffering, *because he is worthy of love;* and to be willing to forsake all the allurements which the world holds out to us for the sake of the purity and peace of the gospel.

9th. We learn the necessity of forsaking all for the sake of the gospel. Our *first* duty is to God, our Creator and Saviour; our second, to friends, to our relations, and to our country, ver. 22. When *God* commands we must follow him, nor should any consideration of ease, or safety, or imaginary duty deter us. To us it is of no consequence what men say or think of us. Let the will of God be prayerfully ascertained, and then let it be done though it carry us through ridicule and flames.

10th. Jesus can preserve us in the time of danger, ver. 23–27. He hushed the storm and his disciples were safe. *His* life was also in danger with *theirs*. Had the ship sunk, without a miracle he would have perished with them. So in every storm of trial or persecution, in every heaving sea of calamity, he is united to his followers. *His* interest and *theirs* is the same. He feels for them, he is touched with their infirmities, and he will sustain them. Because *I* live, says he, ye shall live also. Never, never, then, shall man or devil pluck one of his faithful followers from his hand, Jn. x. 27, 28.

11th. All that can disturb or injure us is under the control of the Christian's Friend, ver. 28–32. The very inhabitants of hell are bound, and beyond his permission they can never injure us. In spite, then, of all the malice of malignant beings, the friends of Jesus are safe.

12th. It is no uncommon thing for men to desire Jesus to depart from

CHAPTER IX.

AND he entered into a ship, and passed over, and came into his own city.

2 And,[a] behold, they brought to him a man sick of the palsy, lying on a bed: and Jesus, seeing

a Mar.2.3,&c.; Lu.5.18,&c.

---

them, ver. 34. Though he is ready to confer on them important favours, yet they hold *his* favours to be of far less consequence than some unimportant earthly possession. Sinners never love him, and always wish him away from their dwellings.

13th. It is no uncommon thing for Jesus to take men at their word, and leave them. He gives them over to worldly thoughts and pursuits; he suffers them to sink into crime, and they perish for ever. Alas! how many are there, like the dwellers in the country of the Gergesenes, that ask him to depart; that see him go without a sigh; and that never, never again behold him coming to bless them with salvation!

CHAPTER IX.

1. *And he entered into a ship*, &c. Jesus acceded to the request of the people of Gadara (ch. viii. 34), recrossed the Lake of Gennesareth, and returned to his own city. By *his own city* is meant Capernaum (Mar. ii. 1), the city which was at that time his home, or where he had his dwelling. See Notes on ch. iv. 13. This same account, with some additional circumstances, is contained in Mar. ii. 3-12, and Lu. v. 18-26.

2. *A man sick of the palsy.* See Notes on Mat. iv. 24. ¶ *Lying on a bed.* This was probably a mattress, or perhaps a mere blanket spread to lie on, so as to be easily borne. Being light, Jesus might with propriety command him to take it up and walk, ver. 6.

Mark says "*they uncovered the roof*," ch. ii. 4. Luke says "*they went upon the housetop, and let him down through the tiling*," ch. v. 19. To us it would appear that much injury must have been done to the house where Jesus was, and that they must be much incommoded by the removal of tiles and rafters, &c. An acquaintance, however, with the mode of building in the East removes every difficulty of this nature. Houses in Eastern countries are commonly square in their form, and of a single story. On approaching them from the street a single door is seen in the centre, and usually, directly above it, a single latticed window. This destitution of doors and lights from the streets, though it gives their dwellings a sombre appearance, is yet adapted to the habits of retirement and secrecy among the people of the East, where they are desirous of keeping their *females* from observation. See Notes on Mat. vi. 6. On entering the only door in front, the first room is a small square room, surrounded with benches, called the *porch*. In this room the master of the family commonly transacts business, and on private occasions receives visits. Passing through the porch, you enter a large square room directly in the centre of the building, called the *court*. Luke says that the *paralytic* was let down "*into the midst;*" not in the midst of the *people*, but of the *building*—the *middle place* of the house. This *court* is paved commonly with marble; and, if possible, a fountain of water is formed in the centre, to give it beauty, and to diffuse a grateful coolness. This room is surrounded by a gallery or covered walk on every side. From *that* covered walk doors open into the other apartments of the house.

This centre room, or court, is commonly uncovered or open above. In wet weather, however, and in times of great heat of the sun, it is covered with an awning or canvas, stretched on cords, and capable of being easily removed or rolled up. This is what Mark means when he says *they uncovered the roof*. They *rolled up* or removed this awning.

From the court to the roof the ascent is by flights of stairs, either in the covered walk or gallery or in the porch. The roof is nearly flat. It is made of earth; or, in houses of the rich, is a firmly constructed flooring, made of coals, chalk, gypsum, and ashes, made hard by repeated blows. On those roofs spears of grass, wheat, or barley sometimes spring up; but these are soon withered by the sun, Ps. cxxix. 6-8. The roof is a favourite place for walking, for repose in the cool of the day, for conversation, and for devotion. See Notes on Mat. vi. 6. On such a roof Rahab concealed the spies (Jos. ii. 6), Samuel talked with Saul (1 Sa. ix. 25), David walked at eventide (2 Sa. xi. 2),

their faith, said unto the sick of the palsy, [b]Son, be of good cheer; thy sins be forgiven thee.

b Mar.5.34.

3 And, behold, certain of the scribes said within themselves, This *man* blasphemeth.

---

and Peter went up to pray (Ac. x. 9). This roof was surrounded with a *balustrade*, or railing, breast-high, on the sides; but where a house was contiguous to another, and of the same height, the railing was lower, so as to walk from one roof to another. In cities where the houses were constructed in this manner, it was possible to walk through a considerable part of the city on the roofs. A breastwork or railing was of course built in the same manner around the *open space* in the centre, to prevent persons from falling *into* the court below. This railing, or breastwork, is what Luke (v. 19) says they let him down through. They removed it, probably, so that the couch could be conveniently let down with cords; and, standing on the roof *over* the Saviour, they let the man down directly before him. The perseverance they had manifested was the *evidence* of their faith or confidence in his power to heal the sick man.

The following cut exhibits the ground-plan of an Eastern dwelling, and illus-

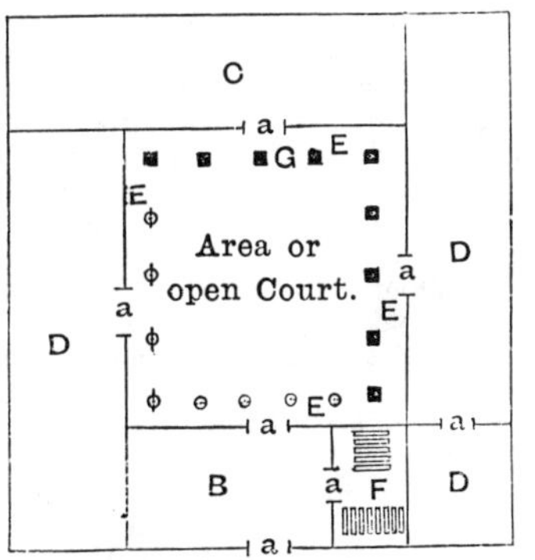

a Doors. B Porch.
C Harem, or room for women.
D Other rooms, for the family.
E Galleries, or walks between the court and rooms.
F Stairs to the second story, or to the roof.

trates the account of the cure of the sick man.

By looking at this it may be easily seen how the paralytic was presented to Jesus. Suppose the Saviour to be seated in the open court, say at G. The room was thronged. There was but one way of access, through *a*. It would be easy to ascend the stairs at F, and go round on the gallery till they came over Jesus, and remove a part of the balustrade or breastwork, and let him down directly before him. ¶ *Be of good cheer: thy sins be forgiven thee.* It may seem remarkable, since the man came only to be *healed*, that Jesus should have first declared his sins forgiven. For this the following reasons may be suggested: 1st. The man might have brought on this disease of the palsy by a long course of vicious indulgence. Conscious of guilt, he may have feared that he was so great a sinner that Christ would not regard him. He therefore assured him that his offences were pardoned, and that he might lay aside his fears. 2d. Jesus might be willing to show his power to forgive sins. Had he stated it without any miracle, the Jews would not have believed it, and even his disciples might have been staggered. In proof of it, he worked a miracle; and no one, therefore, could doubt that he had the power. The miracle was wrought in *express attestation* of the assertion that he had power to forgive sins. As God would not work a miracle to confirm a falsehood or to deceive men, the miracle was a solemn confirmation, on the part of God, that Jesus had the power to forgive sins. 3d. The Jews regarded disease as the effect of sin, Jn. ix. 2; Ja. v. 14, 15. There is a *real* connection between sin and suffering, as in the case of gluttony, intemperate drinking, lewdness, debauchery. Jesus might be willing to direct the minds of the spectators *to this fact;* and, by pointing them to a manifest instance of the effect of sin, to lead them to hate and forsake it. Diseases are sometimes the direct judgment of God for sin, 1 Co. v. 3-5; xi. 30; 2 Sa. xxiv. 10-14. This truth, also, Christ might have been desirous of impressing on the people.

3. *This* man *blasphemeth.* The word *blaspheme* originally means to speak evil of anyone; to injure by words; to blame unjustly. When applied to God, it means to speak of him unjustly; to ascribe to him acts and attributes which he does not possess; or to speak

4 And Jesus, [c]knowing their thoughts, said, Wherefore think ye evil in your hearts?
5 For whether is easier to say, *Thy* sins be forgiven thee; or to say, Arise, and walk?
6 But that ye may know that the Son of man hath power on earth to [d]forgive sins (then saith he to the sick of the palsy), Arise, take up thy bed, and go unto thine house.
7 And he arose, and departed to his house.
8 But when the multitude saw *it*, they marvelled, and [e]glorified God, which had given such power unto men.
9 And[f] as Jesus passed forth from thence, he saw a man, named

c Ps.139.2; Jn.2.24,25; He.4.12,13; Re.2.23. d Mi.7.18. e Ac.4.21; Ga.1.24. f Mar.2.14; Lu.5.27,&c.

---

impiously or profanely. It also means to say or do anything by which his name or honour is insulted, or which conveys an *impression* unfavourable to God. It means, also, to attempt to do, or say a thing, which belongs to him alone, or which he only can do. This is its meaning here. Christ was charged *with saying a thing in his own name, or attempting to do a thing, which properly belonged to God;* thus assuming the *place* of God, and doing him injury, as the scribes supposed, by an invasion of his prerogatives. "None," said they (see Mark and Luke), "can forgive sins but God only." In this they reasoned correctly. See Is. xliii. 25; xliv. 22. None of the prophets had this power; and by saying that *he forgave sins*, Jesus was understood to affirm that he was divine; and as he proved this by working a miracle *expressly* to confirm the claim, it follows that he is divine, or equal with the Father.

4. *Jesus, knowing their thoughts.* Mark says, "Jesus perceived *in his spirit* that they so reasoned." The power of searching the heart, and of knowing the thoughts of men, belongs only to God, 1 Ch. xxviii. 9; Ro. viii. 27; Re. ii. 23; Je. xvii. 10. In claiming this, as Jesus did here, and often elsewhere, he gave clear proofs of his omniscience, Jn. ii. 24, 25.

5. *For whether is easier to say,* Thy *sins be forgiven thee; or to say, Arise and walk?* The one involves divine *power*, the other divine *authority*, and neither can be done but by God. One is as easy as the other; and to be able to do the one, involves the right and the power to do the other.

6. *But that ye may know,* &c. That you may have full proof on that point; that you may see that I have power to forgive sin, I will perform an act which all must perceive and admit to require the power of God. ¶ *Arise, take up thy bed, and go unto thine own house.* The fact that the paralytic man could do this would *prove* that a miracle was wrought. He was healed by a word; it was done instantaneously; it was done in the most public manner. The fact that a man, just before perfectly helpless, could now take up and carry his own bed or couch, proved that a divine *power* had been exerted; and that fact proved that he who had performed the miracle *must* also have the *power* and the *authority* to forgive sin. It is proper to add, in illustrating this, that in the East a "*bed*" is often nothing more than a bolster and a blanket spread on the floor. "The bed provided for me," says Professor Hackett (*Illustrations of Scripture*, p. 112) "consisted merely of a bolster and a blanket spread on the floor. The latter could be drawn partially over the body if any one wished, though the expectation seemed to be that we should sleep in our ordinary dress, without any additional covering. Such a bed is obviously a portable one; it is easy to take it up, fold it together, and carry it from place to place, as convenience may require."

8. *They glorified God.* See Notes on Mat. v. 16. To *glorify* God, here, means to *praise him*, or to acknowledge his power. The expression, *which had given such power to men*, was a part of *their* praise. It expresses no sentiment of the evangelist about the nature of Christ, but is a record of *their* feelings and *their* praise.

9. *He saw a man, named Matthew, sitting at the receipt of custom.* That is, at the place where *custom*, or *tribute*, was received; or, in other words, he was a *publican* or tax-gatherer. See Notes on Mat. v. 47. This man was the writer of this gospel. The same

Matthew, sitting at the receipt of
custom: and he saith unto him,
Follow me. And he arose, and
followed him.

10 And it came to pass, as Jesus
sat at meat in the house, behold,
many publicans and sinners came
and sat down with him and his
disciples.

11 And when the Pharisees saw
it, they said unto his disciples,
Why eateth your Master with
[g]publicans and sinners?

12 But when Jesus heard *that*,
he said unto them, They that be
whole need not a physician, but
they that are sick.

13 But go ye and learn what

g ch.11.19; Lu.15.2; He.5.2.

account is found in Mar. ii. 14, and Lu. v. 27, 28. Both those evangelists call him *Levi*. That it was the same man is known by the circumstances in which he was called being the same in all the evangelists, and by their all concurring in the statement that the Saviour was present at a feast soon after he called him, and by the fact that *Levi* is not mentioned in the catalogue of the apostles. The Jews were in the habit of giving several names to the same person. Thus Peter was also called Simon and Cephas. It is worthy of remark that Luke has mentioned a circumstance favourable to Matthew, which Matthew himself has omitted. Luke says "*he left all.*" Had Matthew said this, it would have been a commendation of himself utterly unlike the evangelists. No men were ever farther from *praising themselves* than they were.

10. *And it came to pass, as Jesus sat at meat in the house.* This was at a feast given to him by *Levi* or *Matthew*, Lu. v. 29. This is another circumstance favourable to Matthew, but omitted by him, and recorded by Luke; showing also that the apostles were averse to praising themselves. To receive Christ hospitably and kindly was a commendable act, and it strongly evinces Matthew's freedom from ostentation that he has not himself mentioned the fact. It thus illustrates the command of the Saviour, as recorded by himself, Mat. vi. 1–4. ¶ *At meat.* At the table; at supper. ¶ *Many publicans and sinners came.* Probably the old friends of Matthew who had been invited by him. The character of a *publican*, or tax-gatherer, among the Jews was commonly not very respectable (see Notes on ch. v. 47; xviii. 17), and there is no improbability in supposing that Matthew, before his conversion, had sustained the general character of such men, and that his associations and friendships had been among those who were not remarkable for their morality.

11. *Why eateth and drinketh*, &c. To eat and drink with others denotes intimacy and familiarity. The Pharisees, by asking this question, accused him of seeking the society of such men, and of being the companion of the wicked. The inference which *they* would draw was, that he could not be himself righteous, since he delighted in the company of abandoned men.

12. *They that be whole*, &c. Jesus, in reply, said that the whole needed not a physician. Sick persons only needed his aid. A physician would not commonly be found with those that were in health. His proper place was among the sick. So, says he, "If you Pharisees are such as you think yourselves—already pure and holy—you do not need *my* aid. It would be of no use to you, and you would not thank me for it. With those persons who feel that they are sinners I may be useful, and there is my proper place." Or the expression may mean, "I came on purpose to save sinners: my business is with them. There are none righteous; and as a physician is in his proper place with the *sick*, so am I with guilty and miserable sinners."

13. *But go ye and learn*, &c. To reprove them, and to vindicate his own conduct, he appealed to a passage of Scripture with which they ought to have been acquainted: "I will have mercy, and not sacrifice," Ho. vi. 6. This is not a declaration on the part of God that he was opposed to *sacrifices* or *offerings for sin;* for he had appointed and commanded many, and had therefore expressed his approbation of them. It is a Hebrew mode of speaking, and means, *I prefer mercy to sacrifice;* or, *I am more pleased with acts of benevolence and kindness than with a mere external compliance with the duties of religion. Mercy* here means benevolence or kind-

that meaneth, [h]I will have mercy, and not sacrifice: for I am not come to call the righteous, [i]but sinners to repentance.

14 Then came to him the disciples of John, saying, Why do we and the Pharisees fast oft, but thy disciples fast not?

15 And Jesus said unto them, Can the children of the bride-chamber mourn as long as [k]the bridegroom is with them? but the days will come when the bridegroom shall be taken from them, and [l]then shall they fast.

16 No man putteth a piece of [1]new cloth unto an old garment; for that which is put in to fill it

h Pr.21.3; Ho.6.6; Mi.6.8; ch.12.7.
i Lu.24 47; Ac.5.31; 2 Pe.3.9.
k ch.25.1,10; Jn.3.29; Re.21.2.
l Is.22.12. 1 or, *raw*, or, *unwrought cloth*.

ness towards others. *Sacrifices* were offerings made to God on account of sin, or as an expression of thanksgiving. They were commonly bloody offerings, or animals slain; signifying that the sinner offering them deserved to die himself, and pointing to the great sacrifice or offering which Christ was to make for the sins of the world. *Sacrifices* were the principal part of the worship of the Jews, and hence came to signify *external worship in general.* This is the meaning of the word here. The sense in which our Saviour applies it is this: "You Pharisees are exceedingly tenacious of the *external* duties of religion; but God has declared that he prefers benevolence or mercy to those external duties. It is proper, therefore, that I should associate with sinners for the purpose of doing them good." ¶ *I came not to call the righteous*, &c. No human beings are by nature righteous, Ps. xiv. 3; Ro. i. 18–32; iii. 10–18. The Pharisees, however, *pretended* to be righteous. Christ might have meant by this answer that it was not the design of his coming to call such persons to repentance, knowing that they would spurn his efforts, and that to a great extent they would be vain; or, more probably, he meant to affirm that his proper and only business was to call to repentance such men as he was now with. He came to seek and save such, and it was his *proper business*, therefore, to associate with them. ¶ *Repentance.* See Notes on Mat. iii. 2.

14–17. *Then came the disciples of John*, &c. This narrative is found also in Mar. ii. 18–22; Lu. v. 33-39. The reference here is to John the Baptist. It is probable that they had understood that John was the forerunner of the Messiah; and if such was the case, they could not account for the fact that there was such a difference between them and the disciples of Jesus. The Pharisees fasted often—regularly twice a week, besides the great national days of fasting, Lu. xviii. 12. See Notes on Mat. vi. 16–18. This was the established custom of the land, and John did not feel himself authorized to make so great a change as to dispense with it. They were desirous of knowing, therefore, why Jesus had done it.

Besides, it is probable that this question was put to Jesus when John was in prison, and his disciples, involved in deep grief on account of it, observed days of fasting. Fasting was the natural expression of sorrow, and they wondered that the followers of Jesus did not join with them in lamenting the captivity of him who was the forerunner and baptizer of their Lord.

Christ, in reply to them, used three illustrations, all of them going to establish the same thing—that *we should observe a fitness and propriety in things.* The first is taken from a marriage. The children of the bride-chamber—that is, the bridemen, or *men who had the special care of the bridal chamber, and who were therefore his special friends*—do not think of fasting while he is with them. With them it is a time of festivity and rejoicing, and mourning would not be appropriate. When he is removed or taken away, then their festivity will be ended, and *then* will be the proper time for sorrow. So, says he, John, your friend and teacher, is in captivity. With you it is a time of deep grief, and it is fit that *you* should fast. I am *with* my disciples. It is with them a time of joy. It is not fit that they should use the tokens of grief, and fast now. When *I* am taken away, it will then be proper that they should fast. For an account of the ceremonies of an Eastern marriage, see Notes on Mat. xxv. 1–13.

16. *No man putteth a piece of new cloth*, &c. A second illustration was drawn

up taketh from the garment, and the rent is made worse.

17 Neither do men put new wine into old bottles; else [m]the bottles break, and the wine runneth out, and the bottles perish: but they put new wine into new bottles, and both are preserved.

18 While[n] he spake these things unto them, behold, there came a certain ruler and worshipped him, saying, My daughter is even now dead; but come and lay thy hand upon her, and [o]she shall live.

19 And Jesus arose and followed him, and *so did* his disciples.

m Job 32.19. *n* Mar.5.22; Lu.8.41,&c. *o* Jn.11.22,25.

---

from a well-known fact, showing also that there was *a propriety or fitness of things.* None of you, says he, in mending an old garment, would take a piece of entire new cloth. There would be a waste in it. An old piece, or a piece *like* the garment, would be better. The word here translated *new*, in the original means *rude, undressed, not fulled* by the cloth-dresser. In this state, if applied to an old garment, and if wet, it would *contract* and draw off a part of the garment to which it was attached, and thus make the rent worse than it was. So, says he, my *new* doctrines do not *match* with the old rites of the Pharisees. There is a fitness of things. Their doctrines require much fasting. In my system it would be incongruous; and if my *new* doctrines were to be attached to their old ones, it would only make the matter worse.

17. *Neither do men put new wine*, &c. The third illustration was taken from wine put into bottles. Bottles, in Eastern nations, were made, and are still made, of skins of beasts. Generally the skin was taken entire from a sheep or a goat, and, properly prepared, was filled with wine or water. Such bottles are still used, because, in crossing deserts of sand, they have no other conveyances but camels, or other beasts of burden. It would be difficult for them to carry glass bottles or kegs on them. They therefore fill two skins, and fasten them together and lay them across the back of a camel, and thus carry wine or water to a great distance. These bottles were, of course, of different sizes, as the skins of kids, goats, or oxen might be used. Bruce describes particularly a bottle which he saw in Arabia, made in this manner of an ox-skin, which would hold 60 gallons, and two of which were a load for a camel. By long usage, however, bottles of skins became tender and would be easily ruptured. New wine put into them would ferment, and swell and burst them open. New skins or bottles would *yield* to the fermenting wine, and be strong enough to hold it from bursting. So, says Christ, there is a *fitness* or propriety of things. It is not *fit* that my doctrine should be attached to or connected with the old and corrupt doctrines of the Pharisees. New things should be put together, and made to *match.*

This account of Eastern bottles may illustrate the following passages in the Bible: The Gibeonites took "wine-bottles, old, and rent, and bound up," Jos. ix. 4. "My belly is ready to burst, like new bottles," Job xxxii. 19. "I am become like a bottle in the smoke," Ps. cxix. 83; *i.e.* like a bottle of skin hung up in a tent filled with smoke.

18–26. The account contained in these verses is also recorded, with some additional circumstances, in Mar. v. 22–43, and Lu. viii. 41–56.

18. *There came a certain ruler.* Mark and Luke say that his name was Jairus, and that he was a *ruler of the synagogue;* that is, one of the elders to whom was committed the care of the synagogue. See Notes on Mat. iv. 23. ¶ *And worshipped him.* That is, fell down before him, or expressed his respect for him by a token of profound regard. See Notes on Mat. ii. 2. ¶ *My daughter is even now dead.* Luke says that this was his only daughter, and that she was twelve years of age. Mark and Luke say that she was *at the point of death,* and that information of her actual death was brought to him by one who was sent by the ruler of the synagogue, while Jesus was going. Matthew combined the two facts, and stated the representation which was made to Jesus, without stopping particularly to exhibit the *manner* in which it was done. In a summary way he says that the *ruler* communicated the information. Luke and Mark, dwelling more particularly on the circumstances, state at length the way in which it was done; that is, by himself stating, in a hurry, that she

20 And,[p] behold, a woman,
which was diseased with an issue
of blood twelve years, came behind
him, and touched the hem of his
garment:
21 For she said within herself,
If I may but touch [q]his garment,
I shall be whole.

22 But Jesus turned him about;
and when he saw her, he said,
Daughter, be of good comfort;
[r]thy faith hath made thee whole.
And the woman was made whole
[s]from that hour.
23 And[t] when Jesus came into
the ruler's house, and saw [u]the

p Mar.5.25; Lu.8.43. q Ac.19.12.

r Lu.7.50; 17.19; 18.42; Ac.14.9. s Jn.4.53.
t Mar.5.38; Lu.8.51. u 2 Ch.35.25.

was *about to die*, or *was dying*, and then in a few moments sending word that *she was dead*. The Greek word, rendered *is even now dead*, does not of necessity mean, as our translation would express, that she had actually expired, but only that she was *dying* or about to die. Comp. Ge. xlviii. 21. It is likely that a father, in these circumstances, would use a word as nearly expressing actual death as would be consistent with the fact that she was alive. The passage may be expressed thus: "My daughter was so sick that she must be by this time dead." ¶ *Come and lay thy hand upon her.* It was customary for the Jewish prophets, in conferring favours, to lay their hand on the person benefited. Jesus had probably done so also, and the ruler had probably witnessed the fact.

20. *And, behold, a woman*, &c. This disease was by the Jews reckoned unclean (Le. xv. 25), and the woman was therefore unwilling to make personal application to Jesus, or even to touch his person. The disease was regarded as incurable. She had expended all her property, and grew worse, Mar. v. 26. ¶ *Touched the hem of his garment.* This garment was probably the square garment which was thrown over the shoulders. See Notes on Mat. v. 40. This was surrounded by a border or *fringe;* and this *fringe*, or the loose threads hanging down, is what is meant by the *hem.* The Jews were commanded to wear this, in order to distinguish them from other nations. See Nu. xv. 38, 39; De. xxii. 12.

Mark says that *the woman, fearing and trembling*, came and told him all the truth. Perhaps she feared that, from the impure nature of her disease, he would be offended that she touched him.

22. *But Jesus turned him about, and when he saw her, he said, Daughter, be of good comfort.* Jesus silenced her fears, commended her faith, and sent her away in peace. He used an endearing appellation, calling her *daughter*, a word of tenderness and affection, and dismissed her who had been twelve long and tedious years labouring under a weakening and offensive disease, now in an instant made whole. Her faith, her strong confidence in Jesus, had been the means of her restoration. It was the *power* of Jesus that cured her; but that power would not have been exerted but in connection with faith. So in the salvation of a sinner. No one is saved who does not believe; but faith is the *instrument*, and not the *power*, that saves.

23. *And when Jesus came into the ruler's house*, &c. Jesus permitted only three of his disciples, Peter, James, and John the brother of James, and the father and mother of the damsel, to go in with him where the corpse lay, Mar. v. 37–40. It was important that there should be *witnesses* of the miracle, and he chose a sufficient number. *Five* witnesses were enough to establish the fact. The witnesses were impartial. The fact that she was dead was established beyond a doubt. Of this the mourners, the parents, the messengers, the people, were satisfied. If she was presented to the people *alive*, the proof of the miracle was complete. The presence of more than the *five* witnesses would have made the scene tumultuous, and have been less satisfactory evidence of the fact of the restoration of the child. Five sober witnesses are always better than the confused voices of a rabble. These were the same disciples that were with him in the mount of transfiguration and in the garden of Gethsemane, Mar. ix. 2, and xiv. 33; 2 Pe. i. 17, 18. ¶ *And saw the minstrels and the people making a noise. Minstrels* are persons who play on instruments of music. The people of the East used to bewail the dead by cutting the flesh, tearing the hair, and crying bitterly.

minstrels and the people making a noise,
24 He said unto them, Give place; [v]for the maid is not dead, but sleepeth. And they laughed him to scorn.

v Ac.20.10.

See Je. ix. 17; xvi. 6, 7; Eze. xxiv. 17. The expressions of grief at the death of a friend, in Eastern countries, are extreme. As soon as a person dies, all the females in the family set up a loud and doleful cry. They continue it as long as they can without taking breath, and the shriek of wailing dies away in a low sob. Nor do the relatives satisfy themselves with these expressions of violent grief. They hire persons of both sexes, whose employment it is to mourn for the dead in the like frantic manner. See Am. v. 16; Je. ix. 20. They sing the virtues of the deceased, recount his acts, dwell on his beauty, strength, or learning; on the comforts of his family and home, and in doleful strains ask him why he left his family and friends. To all this they add soft and melancholy music. They employ *minstrels* to aid their grief, and to increase the expressions of their sorrow. This violent grief continues, commonly, eight days. In the case of a king, or other very distinguished personage, it is prolonged through an entire month. This grief does not cease at the house; it is exhibited in the procession to the grave, and the air is rent with the wailings of real and of hired mourners. Professor Hackett (*Illustrations of Scripture*, p. 121, 122) says: "During my stay at Jerusalem I frequently heard a singular cry issuing from the houses in the neighbourhood of the place where I lodged, or from those on the streets through which I passed. It was to be heard at all hours—in the morning, at noonday, at evening, or in the deep silence of night. For some time I was at a loss to understand the cause of this strange interruption of the stillness which, for the most part, hangs so oppressively over the lonely city. Had it not been so irregular in its occurrence, I might have supposed it to indicate some festive occasion; for the tones of voice (yet hardly tones so much as shrieks) used for the expression of different feelings sound so much alike to the unpractised ear, that it is not easy always to distinguish the mournful and the joyous from each other. I ascertained, at length, that this peculiar cry was, no doubt, in most instances, the signal of the death of some person in the house from which it was heard. It is customary, when a member of the family is about to die, for the friends to assemble around him and watch the ebbing away of life, so as to remark the precise moment when he breathes his last, upon which they set up instantly a united outcry, attended with weeping, and often with beating upon the breast, and tearing out the hair of the head. This lamentation they repeat at other times, especially at the funeral, both during the procession to the grave and after the arrival there, as they commit the remains to their last resting-place."

The Jews were forbidden to tear their hair and cut their flesh. See Le. xix. 28; De. xiv. 1. They showed *their* grief by howling, by music, by concealing the chin with their garment, by rending the outer garment, by refusing to wash or anoint themselves, or to converse with people, by scattering ashes or dust in the air, or by lying down in them, Job i. 20; ii. 12; 2 Sa. i. 2–4; xiv. 2; xv. 30; Mar. xiv. 63. The expressions of grief, therefore, mentioned on this occasion, though excessive and foolish, were yet strictly in accordance with Eastern customs.

24. *The maid is not dead, but sleepeth.* It cannot be supposed that our Lord means *literally* to say that the child was not dead. Every possible evidence of her death had been given, and he acted on that himself, and conveyed to the people the idea that he raised her *from the dead.* He meant to speak in opposition to their opinions. It is not unlikely that Jairus and the people favoured the opinions of the Sadducees, and that *they* understood by her being dead that she had *ceased to be*, and that she would never be raised up again. In opposition to this, the Saviour used the expression *she sleepeth;* affirming mildly both that the *body* was dead, and *implying* that *her spirit* still lived, and that she would be raised up again. A similar mode of speaking occurs in Jn. xi. 11: "Our friend Lazarus *sleepeth.*" The sacred writers often spoke of the pious dead as *sleeping*, 2 Pe. iii. 4; Ac. vii. 60; 1 Co. xv. 6, 18; 1 Th. iv. 13–15. The meaning of this passage, then, is, the maid has not ceased to *exist;* but,

25 But[w] when the people were
put forth, he went in, and took
her by the hand, and the maid
arose.
26 And [2]the fame hereof went
abroad into all that land.
27 And when Jesus departed
thence, two blind men followed
him, crying, and saying, [x]*Thou*
Son of David, have mercy on us.
28 And when he was come into
the house, the blind men came to
him: and Jesus saith unto them,
Believe ye that I am able to do
this? They said unto him, Yea,
Lord.
29 Then touched he their eyes,
saying, According to your faith be
it unto you.
30 And their eyes were opened:
and Jesus straitly charged them,
saying, [y]See *that* no man know *it*.

w 2 Ki.4.33,&c. 2 or, *this fame.* x ch.15.22; 20.30,31.

y Is.42.2; 52.13; ch.12.16.

though her body is dead, yet her spirit lives, and she sleeps in the hope of the resurrection. ¶ *Laughed him to scorn.* Derided him; ridiculed him.

25. *He went in.* With the father, and mother, and three disciples, Mar. v. 37–40. ¶ *The maid arose.* She returned to life. There could be no deception here. *Parents* could not be imposed on in such a case, nor could such a multitude be deceived. The power of Jesus was undoubtedly shown to be sufficient to raise the dead.

27. *And when Jesus departed thence.* The scene of this miracle was near Capernaum. The blind men probably followed him with their cry for aid immediately on his leaving the house of Jairus. ¶ Thou *Son of David.* By the Son of David the Jews meant the Messiah. He was *the* descendant or Son of David by way of eminence, Is. ix. 7; Lu. i. 32; Re. xxii. 16. See Notes on Mat. i. 1. This was therefore a profession of belief, on the part of these blind men, of the Messiahship of Jesus, and, at the same time, the expression of a belief that, *being* the Messiah, he could heal them. ¶ *Have mercy on us.* That is, show compassion towards us in our affliction, and restore to us the blessing of sight.

28. *And when he was come into the house.* That is, either into the house which he usually occupied in Capernaum, or the house of some friend. They had followed him, but thus far he had not seemed to heed their cries, and he entered the house *as if* he did not intend to regard them—probably for the trial of their faith. ¶ *The blind men came to him.* That is, they followed him into the house. They showed a determination to persevere until they obtained what they asked. ¶ *Believe ye that I am able to do this?* To work such a miracle. Though they had followed him and cried after him, yet he required of them an open profession of their faith in regard to his power. ¶ *They said unto him, Yea, Lord.* We have no doubt of this. We came with that assurance; we have followed thee with that belief. It was on this simple profession of their faith that the miracle was wrought, as it is on the simple profession of *our* faith that our souls will be saved.

29. *Then touched he their eyes.* Simply to indicate that the power proceeded from him. Comp. ch. viii. 3. ¶ *According to your faith,* &c. That is, you have *believed* that you could be healed, be healed accordingly. Your faith covered the whole extent of the work respecting my power and the absolute restoration to sight, and that power is exerted accordingly, and your sight is restored. So with the sinner. If he has faith on the Son of God; if he believes that he is able and willing to save him; and if he earnestly desires to be saved, the power of Jesus will be put forth to the full extent of his faith.

30. *And their eyes were opened.* Immediately. That is, their sight was restored. ¶ *And Jesus straitly charged them.* He enjoined it on them in the most earnest and solemn manner. ¶ *See* that *no man know* it. That is, do not make proclamation of this; do not make it your business to tell every man of it; do not go forth as if *I* wished that you should proclaim this abroad. The injunction could not mean that they should screen the fact that no one *should* know it, for there were witnesses of it, and it would be made known; but they were not to make it a point to proclaim to the world what was done

31 But they, when they were departed, spread abroad his fame in all that country.

32 As they went out, behold, they brought to him [z]a dumb man possessed with a devil.

33 And when the devil was cast out, [a]the dumb spake: and the multitudes marvelled, saying, It was never so seen in Israel.

34 But the Pharisees said, [b]He casteth out devils through the prince of the devils.

35 And[c] Jesus went about all the cities and villages, teaching in their synagogues, and preaching the gospel of the kingdom, and healing every sickness and every disease among the people.

36 But when he saw the multi-

z ch.12.22; Lu.11.14. a Is.35.6. b ch.12.24; Mar.3.22; Lu.11.15. c ch.4.23.

---

to them. This was in accordance with the usual habit of the Saviour (ch. viii. 4; xii. 16), and also with his own precepts to others (ch. vi. 1–4).

31. *But they, when they were departed, spread abroad his fame.* The report of what he had done. This was not unnatural for them. They were so filled with joy that they could not repress their feelings. In this, however, they violated the express command of the Saviour; but he was not responsible for that.

32. *And as they went out, behold, they brought unto him.* That is, the friends of the dumb man brought him. This seems to have occurred as soon as the blind men which had been healed left him. Possibly it was from what they had observed of his power in healing them. ¶ *A dumb man possessed with a devil.* That is, the effect of the "possession," in his case, was to deprive him of speech. Those "possessed with devils" were affected in different ways (see Notes on ch. iv. 24), and there is no improbability in supposing that if other forms of disease occurred under demoniacal possessions, this form might occur also.

33. *And when the devil was cast out, the dumb spake.* The miracle is narrated in the briefest terms; but the effect was immediate and the restoration was complete. ¶ *It was never so seen in Israel.* Never was there in our land—among the Jews—such a succession of wonders, so striking, so marvellous, so full of the power of God. This was literally true.

34. *But the Pharisees said, He casteth out devils through the prince of the devils.* That is, Beelzebub. See Notes on Mat. xii. 24. They did not deny the reality of the miracle or the facts in the case, but they ascribed what was done to the power of the great leader of the fallen host, as if Jesus was in league with him. For the manner in which the Saviour met that reasoning, see Notes on Mat. xii. 25–28.

35. *And Jesus went about all the cities and villages,* &c. That is, in all parts of Galilee, for his labours were, as yet, confined to that part of Palestine. Comp. Notes on ch. iv. 24, 25.

36. *But when he saw the multitudes.* That followed him from place to place. When he saw their anxiety to be instructed and saved. ¶ *He was moved with compassion on them.* He pitied them. ¶ *Because they fainted.* The word used here refers to the weariness and fatigue which results from labour and being burdened. He saw the people *burdened* with the rites of religion and the doctrines of the Pharisees; sinking down under their ignorance and the weight of their traditions; neglected by those who *ought* to have been enlightened teachers; and *scattered* and driven out without care and attention. With great beauty he compares them to sheep wandering without a shepherd. Judea was a land of flocks and herds. The faithful shepherd, by day and night, was with his flock. He defended it, made it to lie down in green pastures, and led it beside the still waters, Ps. xxiii. 2. Without his care the sheep would stray away. They were in danger of wild beasts. They panted in the summer sun, and knew not where was the cooling shade and stream. So, said the Saviour, is it with this people. No wonder that the compassionate Redeemer was moved with pity.

37. *The harvest truly* is *plenteous,* &c. Another beautiful image. A waving field of golden grain invites many reapers and demands haste. By the reference to the harvest here, he meant that the multitude of people that flocked

tudes, he was moved with compassion on them, because they [3]fainted, and were scattered abroad, [d]as sheep having no shepherd.

37 Then saith he unto his disciples, [e]The harvest truly *is* plenteous, but the labourers *are* few:

38 Pray ye therefore the Lord of the harvest, that he will [f]send forth labourers into his harvest.

[3] or, *were tired and lay down.*
d Nu.27.17; 1 Ki.22.17; Eze.34.5; Zec.10.2.
e Lu.10.2; Jn.4.35.
f Ps.68.11.

---

to his ministry was great. The people expected the Messiah. They were prepared to receive the gospel; but the labourers were few. He directed them, therefore, to pray to the Lord of the harvest to send forth reapers. *God* is the proprietor of the great harvest of the world, and he only can send men to gather it in.

REMARKS.

1st. We are presented with an instance of proper perseverance in coming to Christ, ver. 1, 2. Nothing was suffered to prevent the purpose of presenting the helpless paralytic to the Saviour. So the poor helpless sinner should come. No obstacle should prevent him. He should lay himself at his feet, and feel that Jesus holds over him the power of life and death, and that no other being can save.

2d. Jesus has the power to forgive sins, ver. 6. He claimed it, and worked a miracle to prove it. If he had it then, he has it still. To him, then, the lost sinner may come with the assurance that as he freely *then* exerted that power, so he is ever the same, and will do it *now*.

3d. Jesus Christ is divine. Nothing could prove it more clearly than the power to pardon sinners. God only can pronounce what shall be done with transgressors of his law, Is. xliii. 25. He that claims this right must be either an impostor or God. But no impostor ever yet worked a real miracle. Jesus was therefore divine. He can save to the uttermost all that come to God through him.

4th. We see here the proper rule to be observed in mingling with the wicked, ver. 10–13. It should not be of choice or for pleasure. We should not enter into their follies or vices. We should not seek enjoyment in their society. We should mingle with them simply to transact necessary business and to do them good, *and no farther*, Ps. i. 1.

5th. In the case of the ruler and the woman that was diseased, we have a strong instance of the nature of faith. They came not doubting the power of Jesus—fully assured that he was able to heal. So all genuine believers come to him. They doubt not his power or willingness to save them. Poor, and lost, and ruined by sin, and in danger of eternal death, they come. His heart is open. He puts forth his power, and the soul is healed, and the sin and danger gone.

6th. The young must die, and may die in early life, ver. 18. Very short graves are in every burying-ground. Thousands and millions, not more than twelve years of age, have died. Thousands and millions, not more than twelve years of age, are yet to die. Many of these may be taken from Sunday-schools. Their class, their teacher—their parents, sisters, brothers—must be left, and the child be carried to the grave. Many children of that age that have been in Sunday-schools have died happy. They loved the Saviour, and they were ready to go to him. Jesus was near to them when they died, and they are now in heaven. Of every child we may ask, Are you ready also to go when God shall call you? Do you love the Lord Jesus, so as to be willing to leave all your friends here and go to him?

7th. Jesus can raise up the dead, and he will raise up all that love him, ver. 25. Many little children will be raised up to meet him in the last great day. He shall come in the clouds. The angel shall sound a trumpet, and all the dead shall hear. All shall be raised up and go to meet him. All that loved him here will go to heaven. All that were wicked, and did not love him here, will go to everlasting suffering.

8th. We see the duty of praying for the conversion of the world, ver. 37, 38. The harvest is as plenteous as it was in the time of Christ. More than six hundred millions are still without the gospel, and there are not yet many labourers to go into the harvest. The world is full of wickedness, and God only can qualify those who shall go and preach the gospel to the dark nations of the earth. Without ceasing we ought to

CHAPTER X.

AND when he had called unto
him his twelve disciples, [a]he
gave them power [1]*against* unclean
spirits, to cast them out, and to
heal all manner of sickness and
all manner of disease.
2 Now the [b]names of the twelve
apostles are these: The first, Simon, who is called Peter, and An-

a Mar.3.13,14; 6.7,&c.; Lu.9.1,&c. 1 or, *over*.

b Lu.6.13.

---

entreat of God to pity the nations, and to send to them faithful men who shall tell them of a dying Saviour.

CHAPTER X.

1. *And when he had called unto* him *his twelve disciples*, &c. This account of sending the apostles forth is recorded also in Mar. vi. 7–11, and Lu. ix. 1–6. Mark says that he sent them out two and two. This was a kind arrangement, that each one might have a companion, and that thus they might visit more places and accomplish more labour than if they were all together. These twelve were the original number of apostles. The word *apostle* means one that is *sent*, and was given to them because they were *sent forth* to preach the gospel. They were ambassadors of Christ. To this number Matthias was afterward added, to supply the place of Judas (Ac. i. 26), and Paul was specially called to be an apostle to the Gentiles, Ro. i. 1; 1 Co. xv. 8, 9; Ga. i. 1. In all, therefore, there were fourteen apostles.

In selecting *twelve* at first, it is probable that the Saviour was somewhat guided by the number of the tribes of Israel. Twelve was, with them, a well-known number, and it was natural that he should select one for every tribe. Their office was clearly made known. They were to heal the sick, cast out devils, raise the dead, preach the gospel. They were to be with him to receive his instructions, to learn the nature of his religion, be witnesses to his resurrection, and then to bear his gospel around the globe. The number twelve was the best number for these purposes that could be selected. It was sufficiently *large* to answer the purpose of testimony, and it was *so small* as not to tend to disorder, or that they could easily be divided into parties or factions. They were not *learned* men, and could not be supposed to spread their religion by art or talents. They were not men of wealth, and could not *bribe* men to follow them. They were not men of rank and office, and could not *compel* men to believe. They were just such men as are always found the best witnesses in courts of justice—plain men, of good sense, of fair character, of great honesty, and with favourable opportunities of ascertaining the facts to which they bore witness. Such men everybody believes, and especially when they are willing to lay down their lives to prove their sincerity.

It was important that the Saviour should choose them *early* in his ministry, in order that they might be fully acquainted with him; might treasure up his instructions, and observe his manner of life and his person, so that, by having been long acquainted with him, they might be able to testify to his identity and be competent witnesses of his resurrection. No witnesses were ever so well qualified to give testimony as they, and none ever gave so much evidence of their sincerity as they did. See Ac. i. 21, 22.

2. *Now the names of the twelve apostles.* The account of their being called is more fully given in Mar. iii. 13–18, and Lu. vi. 12–19. Each of those evangelists has recorded the circumstances of their appointment. They agree in saying it was done on a mountain; and, according to Luke, it was done *before* the sermon on the mount was delivered, perhaps on the same mountain, near Capernaum. Luke adds that the night previous had been spent *in prayer to God*. See Notes on Lu. vi. 12. ¶ *Simon, who is called Peter.* The word Peter means a rock. He was also called Cephas, Jn. i. 42; 1 Co. i. 12; iii. 22; xv. 5; Ga. ii. 9. This was a Syro-Chaldaic word signifying the same as Peter. This name was given probably in reference to the *resoluteness and firmness* which he *was* to exhibit in preaching the gospel. *Before* the Saviour's death he was rash, impetuous, and unstable. Afterward, as all history affirms, he was firm, zealous, steadfast, and immovable. The tradition is that he was at last crucified at Rome with his head downward, thinking it too great an honour to die as his Master did. See Notes on Jn. xxi. 18. There is no cer-

drew his brother; James *the son* of
Zebedee, and John his brother;
3 Philip, and Bartholomew;
Thomas, and Matthew the publican;
James *the son* of Alpheus;
and Lebbeus, whose surname was
Thaddeus;
4 Simon the Canaanite; and
Judas Iscariot, who also betrayed
him.
5 These twelve Jesus sent forth,
and commanded them, saying, Go
not into the way of the Gentiles,
and into *any* city of [c]the Samaritans
enter ye not:

c 2 Ki.17.24; Jn.4.5,9,20.

tain proof, however, that this occurred at Rome, and no absolute knowledge as to the place where he died. ¶ *James* the son *of Zebedee, and John his brother.* This James was slain by Herod in a persecution, Ac. xii. 2. The other James, the son of Alpheus, was stationed at Jerusalem, and was the author of the epistle that bears his name. See Ga. i. 19; ii. 9; Ac. xv. 13. A James is mentioned (Ga. i. 19) as *the Lord's brother.* It has not been easy to ascertain why he was thus called. He is here called the son of *Alpheus*, that is, of Cleophas, Jn. xix. 25. Alpheus and Cleophas were but different ways of writing and pronouncing the same name. This Mary, called the mother of James and Joses, is called the wife of Cleophas, Jn. xix. 25.

3. *Philip and Bartholomew.* These two were probably sent out together. Philip was a native of Bethsaida, the city of Andrew and Peter. He is not the same as Philip the evangelist, mentioned in Ac. vi. 5; xxi. 8. Bartholomew (literally *the son of Tolmai*). ¶ *Thomas.* Literally *a twin*, in reference to which he is also called *Didymus*, Jn. xi. 16. For his character, see Notes on Jn. xx. 25. ¶ *And Matthew the publican.* See Notes on ch. ix. 9. ¶ *James* the son *of Alpheus.* See Note above. ¶ *And Lebbeus, called Thaddeus.* These two words have the same signification in Hebrew. Luke calls him *Judas*, by a slight change from the name *Thaddeus.* Such changes are common in all writings.

4. *Simon the Canaanite.* Luke calls him Simon *Zelotes*, the zealous. It is probable that he was one of a small sect of the Jews called *Zealots*, on account of peculiar zeal in religion. His native place was probably *Cana.* Afterward he might with propriety be called by either title. ¶ *Judas Iscariot.* It is probable this name was given to him to designate his native place. *Carioth* was a small town in the tribe of Judah.

5. *Into the way of the Gentiles.* That is, *among* the Gentiles, or nowhere but among the Jews. The full time for preaching the gospel to the Gentiles was not come. It was proper that it should be *first* preached to the Jews, the ancient covenant people of God, and the people among whom the Messiah was born. He afterward gave them a charge to go into all the world, Mat. xxviii. 19. ¶ *And into* any *city of the Samaritans enter ye not.* The Samaritans occupied the country formerly belonging to the tribe of Ephraim and the half-tribe of Manasseh. This region was situated between Jerusalem and Galilee; so that in passing from the one to the other, it was a direct course to pass through Samaria. The capital of the country was Samaria, formerly a large and splendid city. It was situated about 15 miles to the north-west of the city of Shechem or Sychar (see Notes on Jn. iv. 5), and about 40 miles to the north of Jerusalem. For a description of this city, see Notes on Is. xxviii. 1. Sychar or Shechem was also a city within the limits of Samaria.

This people was formerly composed of a few of the ten tribes and a mixture of foreigners. When the ten tribes were carried away into captivity to Babylon, the King of Assyria sent people from Cutha, Ava, Hamath, and Sepharvaim to inhabit their country, 2 Ki. xvii. 24; Ezr. iv. 2–11. These people at first worshipped the idols of their own nations; but, being troubled with lions, which had increased greatly while the country remained uninhabited, they supposed it was because they had not honoured the *God of the country.* A Jewish priest was therefore sent to them from Babylon to instruct them in the Jewish religion. They were instructed partially from the books of Moses, but still retained many of their old rites and idolatrous customs, and embraced a religion made up of Judaism and idolatry, 2 Ki. xvii. 26–28.

The grounds of difference between the two nations were the following:—

6 But[d] go rather to the [e]lost
sheep of the house of Israel.
7 And as ye go, preach, saying,
The[f] kingdom of heaven is at
hand.
8 Heal the sick, cleanse the
lepers, raise the dead, cast out
devils: [g]freely ye have received,
freely give.
9 [2]Provide[h] neither gold, nor
silver, nor brass, in your purses:
10 Nor scrip for *your* journey,

d Ac.13.46. e Ps.119.176; Is.53.6; Je.50.6,17; Eze.34.5,6,8; 1 Pe.2.25. f ch.3.2; 4.17; Lu.9.2; 10.9.
g Ac.8.18,20. 2 or, *Get.* h Lu.22.35; 1 Co.9.7,&c.

1st. The Jews, after their return from Babylon, set about rebuilding their temple. The Samaritans offered to aid them. The Jews, however, perceiving that it was not from a love of true religion, but that they might obtain a part of the favours granted to the Jews by Cyrus, rejected their offer. The consequence was, that a state of long and bitter animosity arose between them and the Jews.

2d. While Nehemiah was engaged in building the walls of Jerusalem, the Samaritans used every art to thwart him in his undertaking, Ne. vi. 1–14.

3d. The Samaritans at length obtained leave of the Persian monarch to build a temple for themselves. This was erected on *Mount Gerizim*, and they strenuously contended that that was the place designated by Moses as the place where the nation should worship. Sanballat, the leader of the Samaritans, constituted his son-in-law, Manasses, high-priest. The religion of the Samaritans thus became perpetuated, and an irreconcilable hatred arose between them and the Jews. See Notes on Jn. iv. 20.

4th. Afterward Samaria became a place of resort for all the outlaws of Judea. They received willingly all the Jewish criminals and refugees from justice. The violators of the Jewish laws, and those who had been excommunicated, betook themselves for safety to Samaria, and greatly increased their numbers and the hatred which subsisted between the two nations.

5th. The Samaritans received only the five books of Moses, and rejected the writings of the prophets and all the Jewish traditions. From these causes arose an irreconcilable difference between them, so that the Jews regarded them as the worst of the human race (Jn. viii. 48), and had no dealings with them, Jn. iv. 9.

Our Saviour, however, preached the gospel to them afterward (Jn. iv. 6–26), and the apostles imitated his example, Ac. viii. 25. The gospel was, however, *first* preached to the Jews.

6. *But go rather to the lost sheep*, &c. That is, to the Jews. He regarded them as wandering and lost, like sheep straying without a shepherd. They had been the chosen people of God; they had long looked for the Messiah; and it was proper that the gospel should be first offered to them.

7. *The kingdom of heaven is at hand.* Or, more literally, the *reign* of heaven, or of God, draws near. See Notes on Mat. iii. 2.

8. *Freely ye have received, freely give.* That is, they were not to *sell* their favours of healing, preaching, &c. They were not to make a *money-making* business of it, to bargain specifically to heal for so much, and to cast out devils for so much. This, however, neither then nor afterward precluded them from receiving a competent support. See Lu. x. 7; 1 Co. ix. 8–14; 1 Ti. v. 18.

9–15. See also Mar. vi. 8–11, and Lu. ix. 3–5. In both these places the *substance* of this account is given, though not so particularly as in Matthew. The general subject is the instructions given to the apostles.

9. *Provide neither gold nor silver, nor brass.* This prohibition of gold, silver, and brass is designed to prevent their providing *money* for their journey. Pieces of money of *small value* were made of brass. ¶ *In your purses.* Literally in your *girdles*. See Notes on Mat. v. 38–41. A *girdle* or *sash* was an indispensable part of the dress. This girdle was made *hollow*, and answered the purpose of a purse. It was convenient, easily borne, and safe.

10. *Nor scrip.* That is, *knapsack.* This was made of skin or coarse cloth, to carry provisions in. It was commonly hung around the neck. ¶ *Neither two coats.* See Notes on Mat. v. 40. ¶ *Neither shoes.* The original is the word commonly rendered *sandals.* See Notes on Mat. iii. 11.

Mark says, in recording this discourse,

neither two coats, neither shoes, nor yet [3]staves: [i]for the workman is worthy of his meat.

11 And into whatsoever city or town ye shall enter, inquire who in it is worthy; and there abide till ye go thence.

12 And when ye come into an house, salute it.

13 And if the house be worthy,

[3] *a staff.* [i] Lu.10.7,&c.

"*but be shod with sandals.*" Between him and Matthew there is an apparent contradiction, but there is really no difference. According to Matthew, Jesus does not forbid their *wearing* the sandals which they probably had on, but only forbids their *supplying themselves with more*, or with *superfluous* ones. Instead of making provision for their feet when their *present* shoes were worn out, they were to trust to Providence to be supplied, and *go as they were.* The meaning of the two evangelists may be thus expressed: "Do not procure anything more for your journey than you have on. Go as you are, shod with sandals, without making any more preparation." ¶ *Nor yet staves.* In the margin, in all the ancient versions, and in the common Greek text, this is in the singular number—*nor yet* A STAFF. But Mark says that they might have a *staff:* "Jesus commanded them that they should take nothing for their journey, *save a staff only.*" To many this would appear to be a contradiction. Yet the *spirit* of the instruction, the main thing that the writers aim at, is the same. That was, that they were *to go just as they were*, to trust to Providence, and not to spend any time in making preparation for their journey. Some of them, probably, when he addressed them, *had staves*, and some had not. To those who *had*, he did not say that they should throw them away, as the instructions he was giving them might seem to require, but he suffered them to take them (Mark). To those who had not, he said they should not spend time in procuring them (Matthew), but *they were all to go just as they were.* ¶ *The workman is worthy of his meat.* This implies that they were to expect a proper supply for their wants from those who were benefited. They were not to make *bargain and sale* of the power of working miracles, but they were to expect competent support from preaching the gospel, and that not merely as a gift, but because they were *worthy* of it, and had a right to it.

11. *Who in it is worthy.* That is, who in it sustains such a character that he will be disposed to show you hospitality and to treat you kindly. This shows that they were not needlessly to throw themselves in the way of *insult.* ¶ *And there abide.* There remain; as Luke adds, "Go not from house to house." They were to content themselves with one house; not to wander about in the manner of vagrants and mendicants; not to appear to be men of idleness and fond of change; not to seem dissatisfied with the hospitality of the people; but to show that they had regular, important business; that they valued their time; that they were disposed to give themselves to labour, and were intent *only* on the business for which he had sent them. If ministers of the gospel are useful, it will be by not spending their time in idle chit-chat, and wandering about as if they had nothing to do, but in an honest and laborious improvement of their time in study, in prayer, in preaching, and in visiting their people.

12. *And when ye come into a house, salute it.* The word *house* here evidently means *family*, as it does in the following verse. See also Mat. xii. 25, and Jn. iv. 53: "And himself believed and *his whole house.*" The apostles were directed to *salute* the family—to show them the customary tokens of respect, and to treat them with civility. Religion never requires or permits its friends to outrage the common rules of social intercourse. It demands of them to exhibit to all the customary and proper tokens of respect, according to their age and station, 1 Pe. ii. 12–25; iii. 8–11; Phi. iv. 8. For the mode of salutation, see Notes on Lu. x. 4, 5.

13. *If the house be worthy.* That is, if the *family* be worthy, or be willing to receive you as my disciples. ¶ *Let your peace come upon it.* That is, let the *peace* or happiness which you seek or for which you pray in saluting it (see Lu. x. 5), come upon it; or seek *their* peace and happiness by prayer, instruction, by remaining with them, and imparting to them the blessings of the gospel. ¶ *But if it be not worthy*, &c. If the family be unwilling to receive

let your peace come upon it: but if it be not worthy, [k]let your peace return to you.

14 And whosoever shall not receive you, nor hear your words, when ye depart out of that house or city, [l]shake off the dust of your feet.

15 Verily I say unto you, [m]It shall be more tolerable for the land of Sodom and Gomorrah in the day of judgment than for that city.

16 Behold, I send you forth as sheep in the midst of wolves: [n]be ye therefore wise as serpents, and [4]harmless [o]as doves.

17 But[p] beware of men: [q]for they will deliver you up to the

k Ps.35.13. *l* Ne.5.13; Ac.13.51; 18.6. *m* ch.11.22,24.

n Ro.16.19; Ep.5.15. [4] or, *simple*. *o* Phi.2.15. *p* Phi.3.2. *q* ch.24.9; Mar.13.9.

you; if they show themselves unfriendly to you and your message. ¶ *Let your peace return to you.* This is a Hebrew mode of saying that your peace shall *not* come upon it, Ps. xxxv. 13. It is a mode of speaking derived from bestowing a gift. If people were willing to receive it, they derived the benefit from it; if not, then of course the present came back or remained in the hand of the giver. So Christ *figuratively* speaks of the peace which their labour would confer. If received kindly and hospitably by the people, they would confer on them most valuable blessings. If rejected and persecuted, the blessings which they sought for others would come upon themselves. *They* would reap the benefit of being cast out and persecuted for their Master's sake, Mat. v. 10.

14. *Shake off the dust of your feet.* The Jews taught uniformly that the dust of the Gentiles was impure, and was to be shaken off. To shake off the dust from the feet, therefore, was a significant act, denoting that they regarded them as impure, profane, and heathenish, and that they declined all farther connection with them. It is recorded that this was actually done by some of the apostles. See Ac. xiii. 51; xviii. 6.

15. *It shall be more tolerable for the land of Sodom,* &c. The cities here mentioned, together with Admah and Zeboim, were destroyed by fire and brimstone on account of their great wickedness. They occupied the place afterward covered by the Dead Sea, bounding Palestine on the south-east, Ge. xix. 24, 25. Christ said that *their* punishment will be more *tolerable*—that is, more easily borne—than that of the people who reject his gospel. The reason is, that they were not favoured with so much light and instruction. See Mat. xi. 23, 24; Lu. xii. 47, 48. Sodom and Gomorrah are often referred to as signal instances of divine vengeance, and as sure proofs that the wicked shall not go unpunished. See 2 Pe. ii. 6; Jude 7.

16. *As sheep in the midst of wolves.* That is, I send you, inoffensive and harmless, into a cold, unfriendly, and cruel world. Your innocence will not be a protection. ¶ *Be wise as serpents,* &c. Serpents have always been an emblem of wisdom and cunning, Ge. iii. 1. The Egyptians used the serpent in their hieroglyphics as a symbol of wisdom. Probably the thing in which Christ directed his followers to imitate the serpent was in its caution in avoiding danger. No animal equals them in the rapidity and skill which they evince in escaping danger. So said Christ to his disciples, You need caution and wisdom in the midst of a world that will seek your lives. He directs them, also, to be harmless, not to provoke danger, not to do injury, and thus make their fellow-men justly enraged against them. Doves are, and always have been, a striking emblem of innocence. Most men would foolishly destroy a serpent, be it ever so harmless, yet few are so hard-hearted as to kill a dove.

17. *But beware of men.* That is, be on your guard against men who are like wolves, ver. 16. Do not run unnecessarily into danger. Use suitable prudence and caution, and do not needlessly endanger your lives. ¶ *Councils.* The word here used commonly signifies the great council of the nation, *the Sanhedrim.* See Notes on Mat. v. 22. Here it seems to refer to any judicial tribunal, of which there were some in every village. ¶ *They will scourge you in their synagogues.* Scourging, or *whipping,* is often mentioned in the New Testament as a mode of punishment. The law of Moses directed that the number of stripes should not exceed forty, but might be any number less, at the dis-

councils, and [r]they will scourge you in their synagogues;

18 And[s] ye shall be brought before governors and kings for my sake, for a testimony against them and the Gentiles.

19 But[t] when they deliver you up, take no thought how or what ye shall speak; for it shall be given you in that same hour what ye shall speak.

20 For it is not ye that speak, but the Spirit of your Father which speaketh in you.

21 And the brother shall deliver up the brother to death, and the father the child: and the children

r Ac.5.40; 2 Co.11.24. s Ac.24. and 25. t Mar.13.11; Lu.12.11; 21.14,15.

---

cretion of the judge, De. xxv. 2, 3. The person who was sentenced to scourging was formerly laid upon the ground, and the blows inflicted on his back in the presence of the judge. In later times the criminal was tied to a low post. Scourging is still practised in the East, but the blows are commonly inflicted on the soles of the feet. It is called the *bastinado*.

The instrument formerly used was a *rod*. Afterward they employed thongs or lashes attached to the rod. To make the blows severe and more painful, they sometimes fastened sharp points of iron or pieces of lead in the thongs. These were called *scorpions*, 1 Ki. xii. 11. The law was express that the number of stripes should not exceed forty. The Jews, to secure greater accuracy in counting, used a scourge with three lashes, which inflicted three stripes at once. With this the criminal was struck thirteen times, making the number of blows thirty-nine. Paul was five times scourged in this way. See 2 Co. xi. 24.

The Romans did not feel themselves bound by the law of the Jews in regard to the *number* of stripes, but inflicted them at pleasure. Thus our Saviour was scourged till he was so weak as not to be able to bear his cross. This was often done in the *synagogue*. See Mat. xxiii. 34; Ac. xxii. 19; xxvi. 11.

18. *And ye shall be brought*, &c. This prediction was completely and abundantly fulfilled, Ac. v. 26; xii. 1-4; xxiii. 33; xxvi. 1, 28, 30. Peter is said to have been brought before Nero, and John before Domitian, Roman emperors; and others before Parthian, Scythian, and Indian kings. They were to stand there to bear a testimony *against* them; or, as it might be rendered, *to them*. That is, they were to be *witnesses to them* of the great facts and doctrines of the Christian religion; and if they rejected Christianity, they would be witnesses *against* them in the day of judgment. The fulfilment of this prophecy is a signal evidence that Christ possessed a knowledge of the future. Few things were more improbable when this was uttered than that the fishermen of Galilee would stand before the illustrious and mighty monarchs of the East and the West.

19, 20. *Take no thought*. That is, be not anxious or unduly solicitous. See Notes on Mat. vi. 25. This was a full promise that they should be inspired, and was a most seasonable consolation. Poor, and ignorant, and obscure fishermen would naturally be solicitous what they should *say* before the great men of the earth. Eastern people regarded kings as raised far above common mortals—as approaching to divinity. How consoling, then, the assurance that God would aid them and speak within them!

21. *And the brother shall deliver up the brother*, &c. Were there no evidence that this *had* been done, it would scarcely be *credible*. The ties which bind brothers and sisters, and parents and children together, are so strong that it could scarcely be believed that division of sentiment on religious subjects would cause them to forget these tender relations. Yet history assures us that this has been often done. If this be so, then how inexpressibly awful must be the malignity of the human heart by nature against religion! Nothing else but this dreadful opposition to God and his gospel ever *has* induced or ever *can* induce men to violate the most tender relations, and consign the best friends to torture, racks, and flames. It adds to the horrors of this, that those who were put to death in persecution were tormented in the most awful modes that human ingenuity could devise. They were crucified; were thrown into boiling oil; were burned at the stake; were roasted slowly over coals; were compelled to drink melted lead; were torn in pieces by beasts of prey; were covered with pitch and set

shall rise up against *their* parents,
and cause them to be put to death.
22 And ye shall be hated of all
men for my name's sake; but [u]he
that endureth to the end shall be
saved.
23 But when they persecute you
in this city, [v]flee ye into another:
for verily I say unto you, Ye shall
not [5]have gone over the cities of
Israel till the Son of Man be come.
24 The [w]disciple is not above *his*
master, nor the servant above his
lord.
25 It is enough for the disciple
that he be as his master, and the
servant as his lord. If [x]they have
called the master of the house
[6]Beelzebub, how much more *shall*
they call them of his household?
26 Fear them not therefore:
[y]for there is nothing covered that

u De.12.12,13; Re.2.10. *v* Ac.8.8.
5 or, *end*, or, *finish*.
w Lu.6.40; Jn.13.16;15.20. *x* Jn.8.48.
6 *Beelzebul*. *y* Mar.4.22; Lu.12.2,3; 1 Co.4.5.

---

on fire. Yet, dreadful as this prediction was, it was fulfilled; and, incredible as it seems, parents and children, husbands and wives, were found wicked enough to deliver up each other to these cruel modes of death on account of attachment to the gospel. Such is the opposition of the heart of man to the gospel! That hostility which will overcome the strong ties of natural affection, and which will be satisfied with nothing else to show its power, can be no slight opposition to the gospel of God.

22. *Ye shall be hated of all* men. That is, of *all kinds* of men. The human heart would be opposed to them, because it is opposed to Christ. ¶ *But he that endureth to the end*, &c. That is, to the end of life, be it longer or shorter. He that bears all these unspeakable sufferings, and who does not shrink and apostatize, will give decisive evidence of attachment to me, and shall enter into heaven. See Re. iii. 21, 22.

23. *When they persecute*, &c. The apostles were not permitted to *throw away* their lives. Where they could preserve them without denying their Lord, they were to do it. Yet all the commands of Christ, as well as their conduct, show that they were rather to lay down their lives than deny their Saviour. We are to preserve our lives by all proper means, but we are rather to *die* than save ourselves by doing anything wrong. ¶ *Ye shall not have gone over the cities of Israel*, &c. That is, in fleeing from persecutors from one city to another, you shall not have gone to every city in Judea till the end of the Jewish economy shall occur. See Notes on Mat. xxiv. 28-30. By *the coming of the Son of Man*, that is, of *Christ*, is probably meant the destruction of Jerusalem, which happened about thirty years after this was spoken. The words are often used in this sense. See Mat. xxiv. 30; Mar. xiii. 26; Lu. xxi. 27, 32.

24, 25. *The disciple is not above* his *master*, &c. That is, you must expect the same treatment which *I* have received. They have called me, your Master and Teacher, Beelzebub, the prince of the devils (see Mat. xii. 24; Lu. xi. 15; Jn. viii. 48), and you must expect that they will call all of the family by the same name. *Beelzebub* was a god of the Ekronites. See 2 Ki. i. 2. The word literally means *the god of flies*, so called because this idol was supposed to protect them from the numerous swarms of flies with which that country abounded. The correct reading here, as in Lu. xi. 15, 18, 19; Mar. iii. 22, is supposed to be, not *Beelzebub*, but *Beelzebul* (Griesbach, Hahn, Rob., *Lex.*) an Aramean form of the word meaning the *god of dung* or *filth*. The name, thus altered by the Jews by changing a single letter, was given to Satan to express supreme contempt and aversion. The Jews seem to have first given to Satan the name of a heathen god, and then, to express their sense of the character of Satan, to have changed that name by altering a single letter so as to express their aversion in the most emphatic manner. By giving the name to Christ, they poured upon him the greatest possible abuse and contempt.

26. *Fear them not*, &c. He encouraged them by the assurance that God would protect them, and that their truth and innocence should yet be vindicated. It is probable that the declaration, There is nothing covered, &c., was a proverb among the Jews. By it our Saviour meant that their *innocence*, their *principles*, and their *integrity*, though then

shall not be revealed; and hid, that shall not be known.

27 What I tell you in darkness, *that* speak ye in light: and what ye hear in the ear, *that* preach ye upon the house-tops.

28 And[z] fear not them which kill the body, but are not able to kill the soul: but rather fear him which is able to destroy both soul and body in hell.

z Is.8.12,13; 51.7,12; 1 Pe.3.14.

29 Are not two sparrows sold for a [7]farthing? and one of them shall not fall on the ground without your Father.

30 But[a] the very hairs of your head are all numbered.

31 Fear ye not therefore; ye are of more value than many sparrows.

32 Whosoever therefore shall confess me before men, [b]him will

7 In value, ***halfpenny farthing***, a 10th part of the Roman penny, ch.18.28. a Ac.27.34. b Re.3.5.

---

the world might not acknowledge them, in due time would be revealed, or God would vindicate them and the world would do them justice. They were, then, to be willing to be unknown, despised, persecuted for a time, with the assurance that their true characters would yet be understood and their sufferings appreciated.

27. *What I say to you in darkness*, &c. That is, *in secret*, in *private*, in *confidence*. The private instructions which I give you while with me do you proclaim publicly, on the *house-top*. The *house-top*, the flat roof, was a public, conspicuous place. See 2 Sa. xvi. 22. See also Notes on Mat. ix. 1-8.

28. *Them which kill the body*. That is, *men*, who have no power to injure the soul, the immortal part. The *body* is a small matter in comparison with the *soul*. Temporal death is a slight thing compared with eternal death. He directs them, therefore, not to be alarmed at the prospect of temporal death, but to fear *God*, who can destroy both soul and body for ever. This passage proves that the *bodies* of the wicked will be raised up to be punished for ever. ¶ *In hell*. See Notes on Mat. v. 22.

29-31. *Are not two sparrows*, &c. He encourages them not to fear by two striking considerations: first, that God takes care of sparrows, the smallest and least valuable of birds; and, secondly, by the fact that God numbers even the hairs of the head. The argument is, that if he takes care of *birds* of the least value, if he regards so small a thing as the hair of the head, and numbers it, he will certainly protect and provide for you. You need not, therefore, fear what man can do to you. ¶ *Sparrows*. The sparrows are well-known birds in Syria. They are small; they are found in great numbers; they are tame, intrusive, and nestle everywhere. "They are extremely pertinacious in asserting their right of possession, and have not the least reverence for any place or thing. David alludes to these characteristics of the sparrow in Ps. lxxxiv., when he complains that they had appropriated even the altars of God for their nests. Concerning himself, he says, I watch, and am as a sparrow upon the house-top, Ps. cii. 7. When one of them has lost its mate—a matter of everyday occurrence—he will sit on the house-top alone, and lament by the hour his sad bereavement. These birds are snared and caught in great numbers, but, as they are small, and not much relished for food, five sparrows may still be sold for two farthings; and when we see their countless numbers, and the eagerness with which they are destroyed as a worthless nuisance, we can better appreciate the assurance that our heavenly Father, who takes care of them, so that not one can fall to the ground without his notice, will surely take care of us, who are of more value than many sparrows."—*The Land and the Book* (Thomson), vol. i. p. 52, 53. ¶ *Farthing*. See Notes on Mat. v. 26. ¶ *Without your Father*. That is, God, your Father, guides and directs its fall. It falls only with *his* permission, and where *he* chooses.

30. *The very hairs of your head are all numbered*. That is, each one has exercised the care and attention of God. He has fixed the number; and, though of small importance, yet he does not think it beneath him to determine how few or how many they shall be. He will therefore take care of you.

32, 33. *Whosoever therefore shall confess me*, &c. The same word in the original is translated *confess* and *profess*, 1 Ti. vi.

I confess also before my Father which is in heaven.

33 But[c] whosoever shall deny me before men, him will I also deny before my Father which is in heaven.

34 Think not that I am come to send peace on earth: [d]I came not to send peace, but a sword.

35 For I am come to set a man at variance [e]against his father, and the daughter against her mother, and the daughter-in-law against her mother-in-law.

36 And[f] a man's foes *shall be* they of his own household.

37 He[g] that loveth father or mother more than me, is not worthy of me: and he that loveth son or daughter more than me, is not worthy of me.

38 And he that taketh not his cross, and followeth after me, is not worthy of me.

c 2 Ti.2.12. *d* Lu.12.49,53. *e* Mi.7.5,6. *f* Ps.41.9. *g* Lu.14.26.

12, 13; 2 Jn. 7; Ro. x. 10. It means to acknowledge the Lord Jesus Christ, and our dependence on him for salvation, and our attachment to him, *in every proper manner*. This profession may be made in uniting with a church, at the communion, in conversation, and in conduct. The Scriptures mean, by a profession of religion, an exhibition of it in every circumstance of the life and before all men. It is not merely in *one* act that we must do it, but in every act. We must be ashamed neither of the person, the character, the doctrines, nor the requirements of Christ. If we are; if we deny him in these things before men; if we are unwilling to express our attachment to him in every way possible, then it is *right* that he should *disown all connection with us*, or deny us before God, and he *will* do it.

34–36. *Think not that I am come*, &c. This is taken from Mi. vii. 6. Christ did not here mean to say that the *object* of his coming was to produce discord and contention, for he was the Prince of Peace, Is. ix. 6; xi. 6; Lu. ii. 14; but he means to say that such would be one of the *effects* of his coming. One part of a family that was opposed to *him* would set themselves against those who believed in him. The wickedness of men, and not the religion of the gospel, is the cause of this hostility. It is unnecessary to say that no prophecy has been more strikingly fulfilled; and it will *continue* to be fulfilled till all *unite* in obeying his commandments. Then his religion will produce universal peace. Comp. Notes on ver. 21. ¶ *But a sword.* The sword is an instrument of death, and *to send* a sword is the same as to produce hostility and war.

37. *He that loveth father or mother*, &c. The meaning of this is clear. Christ must be loved *supremely*, or he is not loved at all. If we are not willing to give up all earthly possessions, and forsake all earthly friends, and if we do not *obey* him rather than all others, we have no true attachment to him. ¶ *Is not worthy of me.* Is not fit to be regarded as a follower of me, or is not a Christian.

38. *And he that taketh not his cross*, &c. When persons were condemned to be crucified, a part of the sentence was that they should carry the *cross* on which they were to die to the place of execution. Thus Christ carried his, till he fainted from fatigue and exhaustion. See Notes on Mat. xxvii. 31. The cross was usually composed of two rough beams of wood, united in the form of this figure, †. It was an instrument of death. See Notes on ch. xxvii. 31, 32. To carry it was burdensome, was disgraceful, was trying to the feelings, was an addition to the punishment. So *to carry the cross* is a figurative expression, denoting that we must endure whatever is burdensome, or is trying, or is considered disgraceful, in following Christ. It consists simply in doing our duty, let the people of the world think of it or speak of it as they may. It does not consist in *making* trouble for ourselves, or doing things merely *to be opposed;* it is doing just what is *required* of us in the Scriptures, let it produce whatever shame, disgrace, or pain it may. This every follower of Jesus is required to do.

39. *He that findeth his life*, &c. The word *life* in this passage is used evidently in two senses. The meaning may be expressed thus: He that is anxious to save his *temporal* life, or his comfort and security here, shall lose *eternal* life, or shall fail of heaven. He that is

39 He[h] that findeth his life, shall lose it: and he that loseth his life for my sake, shall find it.

40 He[i] that receiveth you, receiveth me; and he that receiveth me, receiveth him that sent me.

41 He[k] that receiveth a prophet in the name of a prophet, shall receive a prophet's reward; and he that receiveth a righteous man in the name of a righteous man, shall receive a righteous man's reward.

42 And whosoever shall give to drink unto one of these little ones a cup of cold *water* only in the name of a disciple, verily I say unto you, he shall in no wise lose his reward.

h ch.16.25. *i* ch.18.5; 25.40,45; Jn.12.44. *k* 1 Ki.17.10; He.6.10.

---

willing to risk or lose his comfort and *life* here for my sake, shall find *life* everlasting, or shall be saved. The manner of speaking is similar to that where he said, "Let the dead bury their dead." See Notes on Mat. viii. 22.

40–42. *He that receiveth you,* &c. In all these three illustrations Christ meant to teach substantially the same thing—that he that would entertain kindly or treat with hospitality himself, his disciples, a prophet, or a righteous man, would show that he approved their character, and should not fail of proper reward. To receive in the *name of* a prophet is to receive *as* a prophet; to do proper honour to his character, and to evince attachment to the cause in which he was engaged.

42. *These little ones.* By *these little ones* are clearly meant his disciples. They are called *little ones* to denote their want of wealth, rank, learning, and whatever the world calls *great.* They were *little* in the estimation of the world and in their own estimation. They were *learners,* not yet *teachers;* and they made no pretensions to what attracts the admiration of mankind. ¶ *A cup of cold* water *only.* Few would refuse a cup of cold water to any man, if thirsty and weary, and yet not all men would give it to such a one *because he was a Christian,* or to express attachment to the Lord Jesus. In bestowing it on a man *because he was a Christian,* he would show love to the Saviour himself; in the other case he would give it from mere sympathy or kindness, evincing no regard for the Christian, the Christian's Master, or his cause. In one case he would show that he loved the cause of religion; in the other, not.

REMARKS.

1st. From the narrative in this chapter, in connection with that in Luke, we are permitted to see the Saviour's habits in regard to prayer. An important event was before him; an event on which, humanly speaking, depended the whole success of his religion—the choice of those who should be his messengers to mankind. He felt its importance; and even the Son of God sought the place of prayer, and during the night-watches asked the direction of his Father. His example shows that we, in great and trying circumstances, should seek particularly the direction of God.

2d. We see the *benevolence* of the gospel, ver. 7, 8. The apostles were to confer the highest favours on mankind without reward. Like air, and sunbeams, and water—gifts of God—they are without price. The poor are welcome; the rich, unaided by their wealth, are welcome also; the wide world may freely come and partake the rich blessings of the gospel of peace.

3d. Ministers of the gospel, and all the followers of Jesus, should depend on the providence of God for support and the supply of their wants, ver. 9, 10. He sent his apostles into a cold, unfriendly world, and he took care of them. So none that trust him shall want. The righteous shall not be forsaken. The God who has in his hand all the pearls of the ocean, the gold in the heart of the earth, and the cattle on a thousand hills, and that feeds the raven when it cries, will hear the cries of his children and supply their wants.

4th. We see the duty of treating kindly the messengers of salvation, ver. 11–13. Christ expected that in every city and town they would find some who would welcome them. He promised the reward of a prophet to those who should receive a prophet, and assured those of his favour who had nothing better to bestow than even a cup of cold water. The ministers of religion are sent to benefit the world.

CHAPTER XI.

AND it came to pass, when Jesus had made an end of commanding his twelve disciples, he departed thence, to teach and to preach in their cities.

2 Now[a] when John had heard in the prison the works of Christ, he sent two of his disciples,

3 And said unto him, Art thou he that should come, or do we look for another?

a Lu.7.18,&c.

It is but right that *in* that world they should be kindly received, and that their wants should be supplied.

5th. The guilt of rejecting the gospel, ver. 14, 15. It is not a small matter to reject an offer of heaven. A palace, a throne, a rich earthly inheritance, might be rejected, and, compared with rejecting the gospel, it would be a trifle. But life eternal is not like thrones, and gold, and palaces. This lost, all is lost. The gospel rejected, all is gone. Nor hope nor happiness awaits him that hath spurned this offer. God requires every one to believe the gospel; and woe, woe, a greater woe than befell guilty Sodom and Gomorrah, to him who rejects it.

6th. Judgment will certainly overtake the guilty, ver. 15. It fell on Sodom, and it will fall on all transgressors. None shall escape. Damnation may slumber long over the wicked, and they may long mock the God of truth, but in due time their feet will slide, and the whole creation shall not be able to save them from woe. How dangerous, how awful is the condition of an impenitent sinner!

7th. We are to take proper care of our lives, ver. 23. The apostles were to flee from danger, when they could do it without denying their Lord. So are we. He that throws away his life when it might have been, and ought to have been preserved, is a self-murderer. He that exposes himself when *duty* does not require it, and whose life pays the forfeit, goes before God "rushing unbidden into his Maker's presence," nor can he be held guiltless.

8th. We are to persevere *in our duty* through all trials, ver. 23. Neither the world, nor pain, nor poverty, nor persecution, nor death is to appal us. He that endures to the end shall be saved. We have but one thing to do—to do the will of God, to *be Christians everywhere*, and to leave the event with him.

9th. God exercises a particular providence, ver. 29, 30. He watches the falling sparrow, numbers the hairs of the head, and for the same reason he presides over all other things. The Lord reigneth, says the Psalmist, let the earth rejoice, Ps. xcvii. 1.

10th. The duty of making a profession of religion, ver. 32, 33. It must be done in a proper way, or Christ will disown us in the day of judgment. It is impossible to neglect it, and have evidence of piety. If ashamed of him, he will be ashamed of us.

11th. Religion is easy, and easily tested, ver. 40–42. What more easy than to give a cup of water to a stranger, and what more easy than to know from what motive we do it! Yet how many are there who, while they would do the thing, would yet *lose eternal life* rather than do it with a view of honouring Christ or showing attachment to him! How dreadful is the opposition of the human heart to religion! How amazing that man will not do the slightest act to secure an interest in the kingdom of God!

CHAPTER XI.

1. *And it came to pass*, &c. The directions to the apostles were given in the vicinity of Capernaum. The Saviour went from thence to preach in *their* cities; that is, in the cities in the vicinity of Capernaum, or in Galilee. He did not yet go into Judea.

2. The account contained in this chapter of Matthew, to the 19th verse, is found, with no material variation, in Lu. vii. 18–35. John was in prison. Herod had thrown him into confinement on account of his faithfulness in reproving him for marrying his brother Philip's wife. See Mat. xiv. 3, 4.

It is not certainly known why John sent to Jesus. It might have been to satisfy his disciples that he was the Messiah; or he might have been desirous of ascertaining for himself whether this person, of whom he heard so much, was the same one whom he had baptized, and whom he knew to be the Messiah. See Jn. i. 29.

3. *Art thou he that should come?* That is, Art thou the Messiah, or the Christ?

4 Jesus answered and said unto
them, Go and show John again
those things which ye do hear and
see:
5 The blind receive their sight,
and the lame walk, the lepers are
cleansed, and the deaf hear, the
dead are raised up, and the poor
have the gospel preached to them.
6 And blessed is *he*, whosoever
shall not [b]be offended in me.
7 And as they departed, Jesus
began to say unto the multitudes
concerning John, [c]What went ye

b Is.8.14,15; 1 Co.1.22,23; 1 Pe.2.8. *c* Lu.7.24-30.

The Jews expected a Saviour. His coming had been long foretold, Ge. xlix. 10; Is. ix. 1-6; xi. 1-5; xxxv. 4-6; liii.; Da. ix. 24-27. See also Jn. vi. 14. Comp. De. xviii. 18, 19. In common language, therefore, he was familiarly described as *he that was to come*. Luke adds here (ch. vii. 21), that at the time when the messengers came to him, Jesus "cured many of their infirmities, and plagues, and of evil spirits." An answer was therefore ready to the inquiries of John.

4, 5. *Go and show John again*, &c. Jesus referred them for an answer to these miracles. They were proof that he was the Messiah. Prophets had indeed wrought miracles, but no prophet had wrought so many, or any so important. Jesus, moreover, wrought them *in his own name* and by his own power. Prophets had done it by the power of God. Jesus, therefore, performed the works which none but the Messiah could do, and John might easily *infer* that he was the Christ. ¶ *The poor have the gospel preached to them.* It was predicted of the Messiah that he would preach good tidings to the meek (Is. lxi. 1); or, as it is rendered in the New Testament, "He hath anointed me to preach the gospel to the poor," Lu. iv. 18. By this, therefore, also, John might infer that he was truly the Messiah. It adds to the force of this testimony that the *poor* have always been overlooked by Pharisees and philosophers. No sect of philosophers had condescended to notice them before Christ, and no system of religion had attempted to instruct them before the Christian religion. In all other schemes the poor have been passed by as unworthy of notice.

6. *And blessed is* he, &c. The word *offence* means a *stumbling-block*. See Notes on Mat. v. 29. This verse might be rendered, "Happy is he to whom I shall not prove a stumbling-block." That is, happy is he who shall not take offence at my poverty and lowliness of life, so as to reject me and my doctrine. Happy is he who can, notwithstanding that poverty and obscurity, see the evidence that I am the Messiah, and follow me. It is not improbable that John wished Jesus publicly to proclaim himself as the Christ, instead of seeking retirement. Jesus replied that he gave sufficient evidence of that by his works; that a man might discover it if he chose; and that he was blessed or happy who should appreciate that evidence and embrace him as the Christ, in spite of his humble manner of life.

7. *And as they departed*, &c. Jesus took occasion, from the inquiries made by John's disciples, to instruct the people respecting the true character of John. Multitudes had gone out to hear him when he preached in the desert (Mat. iii.), and it is probable that many had been attracted by the novelty of his appearance or doctrines, or had gone simply to see and hear a man of singular habits and opinions. Probably many who followed Christ had been of that number. He took occasion, therefore, by some striking questions, to examine the motives by which they had been drawn to his ministry. ¶ *A reed shaken with the wind?* The region of country in which John preached, being overflowed annually by the Jordan, produced great quantities of *reeds* or *canes*, of a light fragile nature, easily shaken by the wind. They were therefore an image of a light, changing, inconstant man. John's sending to Christ to inquire his character might have led some to suppose that he was changing and inconstant, like a reed. He had once acknowledged him to be the Messiah, and now, being in prison and sending to him to inquire into the fact, they might have supposed he had no firmness or fixed principles. Jesus, by asking this question, declared that, notwithstanding this appearance, this was not the character of John.

8. *Clothed in soft raiment.* The kind of raiment here denoted was the light, thin clothing worn by effeminate per-

out into the wilderness to see? [d]a
reed shaken with the wind?
8 But what went ye out for to
see? a man clothed in soft raiment? Behold, they that wear
soft *clothing* are in kings' houses.
9 But what went ye out for to
see? a prophet? yea, I say unto
you, and more than a prophet.
10 For this is *he* of whom it is
written, [e]Behold, I send my messenger before thy face, which shall
prepare thy way before thee.
11 Verily I say unto you, [f]Among
them that are born of women
there hath not risen a greater
than John the Baptist: notwithstanding, [g]he that is least in the
kingdom of heaven is greater
than he.
12 And from the days of John
the Baptist until now the kingdom

d Ep.4.14; Ja.1.6. *e* Is.40.3; Mal.3.1; Lu.1.76. *f* Jn.5.35. *g* Jn.1.15,27; 3.30.

---

sons. It was made commonly of fine linen, and was worn chiefly for ornament. Christ asks them whether they were attracted by anything like that. He says that the desert was not the place to expect it. In the palaces of kings, in the court of Herod, it might be expected, but not in the place where John was. This kind of clothing was an emblem of riches, splendour, effeminacy, feebleness of character. He meant to say that John was a man of a different stamp—coarse in his exterior, hardy in his character, firm in his virtue, fitted to endure trials and privations, and thus qualified to be the forerunner of the toiling and suffering Messiah.

9. *A prophet?* He next asks whether they went to see a prophet. They *had* regarded him as such, and Jesus tells them that in this their apprehensions of him were correct. ¶ *More than a prophet.* Sustaining a character more elevated and sacred than the most distinguished of the ancient prophets. Those had been regarded as the most eminent of the prophets who had most clearly predicted the Messiah. Isaiah had been distinguished above all others for the sublimity of his writings, and the clearness with which he had foretold the coming of Christ. Yet John surpassed even him. He lived in the time of the Messiah himself. He predicted his coming with still more clearness. He was the instrument of introducing him to the nation. He was, therefore, first among the prophets.

10. *For this is* he, &c. The passage of Scripture here quoted is found in Mal. iii. 1. The substance of it is contained also in Is. xl. 3. ¶ *Prepare thy way.* That is, to prepare *the people;* to make them ready, by proper instructions, to receive the Messiah.

11. *Among them that are born of women.* This is an emphatic way of saying that there *had never* been a greater *man* than John. See Job xiv. 1. ¶ *He that is least in the kingdom of heaven is greater than he.* The phrase "kingdom of heaven" is used in many senses. See Notes on Mat. iii. 2. It here probably means, *in preaching the kingdom of God*, or the gospel. It could hardly be affirmed of the obscurest and most ignorant Christian that he had clearer views than Isaiah or John; but of the apostles of the Saviour, of the first preachers who were with him and who heard his instructions, it might be said that they had more correct apprehensions than any of the ancient prophets, or than John.

12. *And from the days of John*, &c. That is, from the days when John began to preach. It is not known how long this was, but it was not probably more than a year. Our Saviour here simply states a fact. He says there was a great *rush* or a *crowd* pressing to hear John. Multitudes went out to hear him, as if they were about to take the kingdom of heaven by force. See Mat. iii. 5. So, says he, it has continued. Since *the kingdom of heaven*, or *the gospel*, has been preached, there has been a *rush* to it. Men have been *earnest* about it; they have come *pressing* to obtain the blessing, as if they would take it by violence. There is allusion here to the manner in which cities were taken. Besiegers *pressed* upon them with violence and demolished the walls. With such *earnestness* and *violence*, he says, men had pressed around him and John since they began to preach. There is no allusion here to the manner in which individual sinners seek salvation, but it is a simple record of the fact that multitudes had thronged around him and John to hear the gospel.

of heaven [1]suffereth violence, and the violent [h]take it by force.

13 For all the prophets and the law prophesied until John.

14 And if ye will receive *it*, this is [i]Elias which was for to come.

15 He[k] that hath ears to hear, let him hear.

16 But[l] whereunto shall I liken this generation? It is like unto children sitting in the markets, and calling unto their fellows,

17 And saying, We have piped unto you, and ye have not danced; we have mourned unto you, and ye have not lamented.

18 For John came neither eating nor drinking; and they say, [m]He hath a devil.

19 The Son of man came [n]eat-

1 or, *is gotten by force, and they that thrust men, take it*, &c. *h* Lu.16.16; Ep.6.11-13. *i* Mal.4.5; ch.17.12. *k* Re.2.7,&c. *l* Lu.7.31.

m ch.10.25; Jn.7.20. *n* ch.9.10; Jn.2.2.

13. *All the prophets*, &c. It is meant by this verse that John introduced a new dispensation; and that the *old* one, under which the prophets and the law of Moses were the guide, was closed when he preached that the kingdom of heaven was at hand. By the *law* is meant here the five books of Moses; by the prophets, the remainder of the books of the Old Testament.

14. *If ye will receive* it. This is a mode of speaking implying that the doctrine which he was about to state was different from their common views; that he was about to state something which varied from the common expectation, and which therefore they might be disposed to reject. ¶ *This is Elias*, &c. That is, *Elijah*. Elias is the *Greek* mode of writing the Hebrew word *Elijah*. An account of him is found in the first and second books of Kings. He was a distinguished prophet, and was taken up to heaven in a chariot of fire, 2 Ki. ii. 11. The prophet Malachi (ch. iv. 5, 6) predicted that *Elijah* would be sent before the coming of the Messiah to prepare the way for him. By this was evidently meant, not that he should appear *in person*, but that one should appear with a striking resemblance to him; or, as Luke (ch. i. 17) expresses it, "in the spirit and power of Elijah." But the Jews understood it differently. They supposed that Elijah would appear in person. They also supposed that Jeremiah and some other of the prophets would appear also to usher in the promised Messiah and to grace his advent. See Mat. xvi. 14; xvii. 10; Jn. i. 21. This prevalent belief was the reason why he used the words *if ye will receive it*, implying that the affirmation that *John* was the promised Elijah was a doctrine contrary to their expectation.

15. *He that hath ears*, &c. This expression is frequently used by Christ. It is a proverbial expression, implying that the highest attention should be given to what was spoken. The doctrine about John he regarded as of the greatest importance. He among you, says he, that has the faculty of understanding this, or that will believe that this is the Elijah spoken of, let him attend to it and remember it.

16–19. *But whereunto shall I liken*, &c. Christ proceeds to reprove the inconsistency and fickleness of that age of men. He says they were like children—nothing pleased them. He refers here to the *plays* or *sports* of children. Instrumental music, or piping and dancing, were used in marriages and festivals as a sign of joy. See Notes on Is. v. 11, 12. Comp. Job xxi. 11; 2 Sa. vi. 14; Ju. xi. 34; Lu. xv. 25. Children imitate their parents and others, and *act over* in play what they see done by others. Among their childish sports, therefore, was probably an imitation of a wedding or festal occasion. We have seen also (Notes on Mat. ix. 23) that funerals were attended with mournful music, and lamentation, and howling. It is not improbable that children also, in play, imitated a mournful funeral procession. One part are represented as sullen and dissatisfied. They would not enter into the play: nothing pleased them. The others complained of it. We have, said they, taken all pains to please you. We have piped to you, have played lively tunes, and have engaged in cheerful sports, but you would not join with us; and then we have played different games, and imitated the mourning at funerals, and you are equally sullen; *you have not lamented;* you have not joined with us. Nothing pleases you. So, said Christ, is this generation of men. *John* came one

ing and drinking; and they say,
Behold a man gluttonous, and a
wine-bibber, a friend of [o]publicans
and sinners. But [p]wisdom is justified of her children.
20 Then[q] began he to upbraid
the cities wherein most of his
mighty works were done, because
they repented not:
21 Woe unto thee, Chorazin!
woe unto thee, [r]Bethsaida! for
if the mighty works which were

o Lu.15.2; 19.7. p Ps.92.5,6; Pr.17.24. q Lu.10.13,&c. r Jn.12.21.

---

way, *neither eating nor drinking*, abstaining as a Nazarite, and you were not pleased with him. I, the Son of man, have come in a different manner, *eating and drinking;* not practising any austerity, but living like other men, and you are equally dissatisfied—nay, you are less pleased. You calumniate him, and abuse me for not doing the very thing which displeased you in John. Nothing pleases you. You are fickle, changeable, inconstant, and abusive. ¶ *Markets.* Places to sell provisions; places of concourse, where also children flocked together for play. ¶ *We have piped.* We have played on musical instruments. A *pipe* was a wind instrument of music often used by shepherds. ¶ *Neither eating nor drinking.* That is, abstaining from some kinds of food and wine, as a Nazarite. It does not mean that he did not eat at all, but that he was remarkable for abstinence. ¶ *He hath a devil.* He is actuated by a bad spirit. He is irregular, strange, and cannot be a good man. ¶ *The Son of man came eating and drinking.* That is, living as others do; not practising austerity; and they accuse him of being *fond* of excess, and seeking the society of the wicked. ¶ *Gluttonous.* One given to excessive *eating.* ¶ *Wine-bibber.* One who drinks much wine. Jesus undoubtedly lived according to the general customs of the people of his time. He did not affect singularity; he did not separate himself as a Nazarite; he did not practise severe austerities. He ate that which was common and drank that which was common. As wine was a common article of beverage among the people, he drank it. It was the pure juice of the grape, and for anything that can be proved, it was without fermentation. In regard to the kind of wine which was used, see Notes on Jn. ii. 10. No one should plead the example, at anyrate, in favour of making use of the wines that are commonly used in this country—wines, many of which are manufactured here, and without a particle of the pure juice of the grape, and most of which are mixed with noxious drugs to give them colour and flavour. ¶ *Wisdom is justified of her children.* The children of wisdom are *the wise*—those who understand. The Saviour means that though that generation of Pharisees and fault-finders did not appreciate the conduct of John and himself, yet the *wise*, the candid—those who understood the reasons of their conduct—would approve of and do justice to it.

20. *Then began he to upbraid*, &c. That is, to reprove, to rebuke, to denounce heavy judgment.

21. *Chorazin and Bethsaida.* These were towns not far from Capernaum, but the precise situation is unknown. See *The Land and the Book* (Thomson), vol. ii. p. 8, 9. Bethsaida means literally a *house of hunting* or *of game*, and it was probably situated on the banks of the Sea of Galilee, and supported itself by hunting or fishing. It was the residence of Philip, Andrew, and Peter, Jn. i. 44. It was enlarged by Philip the Tetrarch, and called *Julia*, after the emperor's daughter. ¶ *Tyre and Sidon.* These were cities of Phœnicia, formerly very opulent, and distinguished for merchandise. They were situated on the shore of the Mediterranean Sea, and were in the western part of Judea. They were therefore well known to the Jews. Tyre is frequently mentioned in the Old Testament as being the place through which Solomon derived many of the materials for building the temple, 2 Ch. ii. 11–16. It was also a place against which one of the most important and pointed prophecies of Isaiah was directed. See Notes on Is. xxiii. Comp. Eze. xxvi. 4–14. Both these cities were very ancient. Sidon was situated within the bounds of the tribe of Asher (Jos. xix. 28), but this tribe could never get possession of it, Ju. i. 31. It was famous for its great trade and navigation. Its inhabitants were the first remarkable merchants in the world, and were much celebrated for

done in you had been done in Tyre and Sidon, they would have repented long ago in sackcloth and ashes.

22 But I say unto you, [s]It shall be more tolerable for Tyre and Sidon at the day of judgment than for you.

23 And thou, Capernaum, [t]which art exalted unto heaven, shalt be

s ch.10.15.

t Is.14.13-15; La.2.1.

their luxury. In the time of our Saviour it was probably a city of much splendour and extensive commerce. It is now called Seide, or Saide, and is far less populous and splendid than it was in the time of Christ. It was subdued successively by the Babylonians, Egyptians, and Romans, the latter of whom deprived it of its freedom.

Messrs. Fisk and King, American missionaries, passed through Sidon in the summer of 1823, and estimated the population, as others have estimated it, at 8000 or 10,000; but Mr. Goodell, another American missionary, took up his residence there in June, 1824, for the purpose of studying the Armenian language with a bishop of the Armenian Church who lives there, and of course had far better opportunities to know the statistics of the place. He tells us there are six Mohammedan mosques, a Jewish synagogue, a Maronite, Latin, and Greek church. Dr. Thomson (*The Land and the Book*, vol. i. p. 164) supposes that the population may now be about 10,000 — about 6800 Moslems, 850 Greek Catholics, 750 Maronites, 150 Greeks, and 300 Jews. It exports tobacco, oil, fruit, and silk, but the amount of exports is small.

Tyre was situated about twenty miles south of Sidon. It was built partly on a small island about seventy paces from the shore, and partly on the mainland. It was a city of great extent and splendour, and extensive commerce. It abounded in luxury and wickedness. It was often besieged. It held out against Shalmaneser five years, and was taken by Nebuchadnezzar after a siege of *thirteen* years. It was afterward rebuilt, and was at length taken by Alexander the Great, after a most obstinate siege of five months. There are no signs now of the ancient city. It is the residence only of a few miserable fishermen, and contains, amid the ruins of its former magnificence, only a few huts. Thus was fulfilled the prophecy of Ezekiel: *Thou shalt be built no more; though thou be sought for, yet shalt thou never be found again* (xxvi. 21). For a description of Tyre as it was formerly and as it is now, see Notes on Is. xxiii. ¶ *In sackcloth and ashes.* Sackcloth was a coarse cloth, like canvas, used for the dress of the poor, and for the more common articles of domestic economy. It was worn also as a sign of mourning. The Jews also frequently threw ashes on their heads as expressive of grief, Job i. 21; ii. 12; Jer. vi. 26. The meaning is, that they would have repented *with expressions of deep sorrow.* Like Nineveh, they would have seen their guilt and danger, and would have turned from their iniquities. *Heathen* cities would have received him better than the cities of the Jews, his native land.

23. *And thou, Capernaum.* See Notes on Mat. iv. 13. ¶ *Which art exalted to heaven.* This is an expression used to denote great privileges. He meant that they were peculiarly favoured with instruction. The city was prosperous. It was signally favoured by its wealth. Most of all, it was signally favoured by the presence, the preaching, and the miracles of the Lord Jesus Christ. Here he spent a large portion of his time in the early part of his ministry, and in Capernaum and its neighbourhood he performed his chief miracles. ¶ *Shalt be brought down to hell.* This does not mean that all the *people* would go to hell, but that the city which had flourished so prosperously would lose its prosperity, and occupy the *lowest place* among cities. The word *hell* is used here, not to denote a place of punishment in the future world, but a state of *desolation and destruction.* It stands in contrast with the word *heaven.* As their being exalted *to heaven* did not mean that the *people* would all be saved or dwell in heaven, so their being brought down to *hell* refers to the desolation of the *city.* Their privileges, honours, wealth, &c., would be taken away, and they would sink *as low* among cities as they had been before exalted. This has been strictly fulfilled. In the wars between the Jews and the Romans, Chorazin, Bethsaida, Capernaum, &c.,

brought down to hell: for if the mighty works which have been done in thee had been done in Sodom, it would have remained until this day.

24 But I say unto you, [u]That it shall be more tolerable for the land of Sodom in the day of judgment than for thee.

25 At[v] that time Jesus answered and said, I thank thee, O Father, Lord of heaven and earth, because [w]thou hast hid these things from the wise and prudent, and hast revealed them unto babes.

26 Even so, Father: for so it seemed good in thy sight.

27 All[x] things are delivered unto me of my Father: and no man knoweth the Son but the Father; [y]neither knoweth any man the Father save the Son, and *he* to whomsoever the Son will reveal *him*.

u ver.22. *v* Lu.10.21,&c.

w Ps.8.2; Je.1.7,8; 1 Co.1.27. *x* ch.28.18; Lu.10 22; Jn.3.35; 17.2; 1 Co.15.27. *y* Jn.1.18; 1 Jn.5.20.

---

were so completely desolated that it is difficult to determine their former situation. See Notes on ch. iv. 13. It is not to be denied, also, that he threatened future punishment on those who rejected him. The truth inculcated is, that those who are peculiarly favoured will be punished accordingly if they abuse their privileges. ¶ *If the mighty works—had been done in Sodom.* See Notes on Mat. x. 15. Sodom was destroyed on account of its great wickedness. Christ says if his miracles had been performed *there*, they would have repented, and consequently the city would not have been destroyed. As it was, it would be better for Sodom in the day of judgment than for Capernaum, for its inhabitants would not be called to answer for the abuse of so great privileges.

25, 26. *From the wise and prudent.* That is, from those who *thought* themselves wise—*wise* according to the world's estimation of wisdom, 1 Co. i. 26, 27. ¶ *Hast revealed them unto babes.* To the poor, the ignorant, and the obscure; the teachable, the simple, the humble. By the wise and prudent here he had reference probably to the proud and haughty scribes and Pharisees in Capernaum. They rejected his gospel, but it was the pleasure of God to reveal it to obscure and more humble men. The reason given, the only satisfactory reason, is, that it so seemed good in the sight of God. In this the Saviour acquiesced, saying, *Even so, Father;* and in the dealings of God it is fit that all should acquiesce. *Such is the will of God* is often the only explanation which can be offered in regard to the various events which happen to us on earth. *Such is the will of God* is the only account which can be given of the reason of the dispensations of his grace. Our understanding is often confounded. We are unsuccessful in all our efforts at explanation. Our philosophy fails, and all that we can say is, "Even so, Father; for so it seems good to thee." And this is enough. That GOD does a thing, is, after all, the best reason which we *can* have that it is right. It is a *security* that nothing wrong is done; and though now mysterious, yet light will hereafter shine upon it like the light of noonday. I have more certainty that a thing is right if I can say that I know such is the will of God, than I could have by depending on my own reason. In the one case I confide in the infallible and most perfect God; in the other I rely on the reason of a frail and erring man. God never errs; but nothing is more common than for men to err.

27. *All things are delivered*, &c. The same doctrine is clearly taught often in the New Testament. See Jn. iii. 35; vi. 46; x. 15; Col. i. 16, 17. It means that Christ has control over all things for the good of his church; that the government of the universe is committed to him *as Mediator*, that he may redeem his people and guide them to glory, Ep. i. 20–22. ¶ *No man knoweth the Son.* That is, such is the nature of the Son of God, such the mystery of the union between the divine and human nature, such his exalted character as *divine*, that no mortal can fully comprehend him. None but God *fully* knows him. Had he been a mere man, this language surely would not have been used of him. ¶ *Neither knoweth any man the Father*, &c. In the original this is, neither knoweth *any one* the Father except the Son. That is, no man or angel clearly and fully com-

28 Come unto me, [z]all *ye* that labour and are heavy laden, and I will give you rest.

29 Take my yoke upon you, and [a]learn of me; for I am meek and [b]lowly in heart: and [c]ye shall find rest unto your souls.

30 For[d] my yoke *is* easy, and my burden is light.

z Is.53.2,3. a Phi.2.5-8; 1 Pe.2.21. b Zec.9.9. c Je.6.16. d 1 Jn.5.3.

prehends the character of the infinite God; none but the Son—the Lord Jesus—and he to whom he makes him known, have any just apprehensions of his being and perfections.

28. *All* ye *that labour and are heavy laden.* The Saviour here, perhaps, refers primarily to the Jews, who groaned under the weight of their ceremonial laws and the traditions of the elders, Ac. xv. 10. He tells them that by coming to him, and embracing the new system of religion, they would be freed from these burdensome rites and ceremonies. There can be no doubt, however, that he meant here chiefly to address the poor, lost, ruined sinner: the man *burdened* with a consciousness of his transgressions, trembling at his danger, and seeking deliverance. For such there *is* relief. Christ tells them to come to him, to believe in him, and to *trust* him, and him only, for salvation. Doing this, he will give them rest—rest from their sins, from the alarms of conscience, from the terrors of the law, and from the fears of eternal death.

29. *Take my yoke.* This is a figure taken from the use of oxen, and hence signifying to labour for one, or in the service of anyone. The *yoke* is used in the Bible as an emblem (1.) of bondage or slavery, Le. xxvi. 13; De. xxviii. 38. (2.) Of afflictions or crosses, La. iii. 27. (3.) Of the punishment of sin, La. i. 14. (4.) Of the commandments of God. (5.) Of legal ceremonies, Ac. xv. 10; Ga. v. 1. It refers here to the religion of the Redeemer; and the idea is, that they should embrace his system of religion and obey him. All virtue and all religion imply *restraint*—the restraint of our bad passions and inclinations—and subjection to laws; and the Saviour here means to say that the restraints and laws of his religion are mild, and gentle, and easy. Let anyone compare them with the burdensome and expensive ceremonies of the Jews (see Ac. xv. 10), or with the religious rites of the heathen everywhere, or with the requirements of the Popish system, and he will see how true it is that *his* yoke is easy. And let his laws and requirements be compared with the laws which *sin* imposes on its votaries—the laws of fashion, and honour, and sensuality—and he will feel that religion is "freedom," Jn. viii. 36. "He is a freeman whom the truth makes free, and all are slaves besides." It is *easier* to be a Christian than a sinner; and of all the *yokes* ever imposed on men, that of the Redeemer is the lightest. ¶ *For I am meek,* &c. See Notes on Mat. v. 5. This was eminently Christ's personal character. But this is not its meaning here. He is giving a reason why they should embrace his religion. That was, that he was not harsh, overbearing, and oppressive, like the Pharisees, but meek, mild, and gentle in his government. His laws were reasonable and tender, and it would be easy to obey him.

30. *My yoke* is *easy,* &c. That is, the services that I shall require are easily rendered. They are not burdensome, like all other systems of religion. So the Christian always finds them. In coming to him there is *a peace which passeth all understanding*; in believing in him, *joy;* in following him *through evil and good report,* a comfort *which the world giveth not;* in bearing trials and in persecution, *the hope of glory;* and in keeping his commandments, *great reward.*

REMARKS.

1st. A spirit of inquiry about the person and works of Christ is peculiarly proper, ver. 2, 3. John was solicitous to ascertain his true character, and nothing is of more importance for all than to understand his true character. On him depends all the hope that man has of happiness beyond the grave. He saves, or man must perish. *He* will save, or we must die for ever. With what earnestness, therefore, should the old and the young inquire into his character. Our eternal all demands it; and while *this* is delayed, we are endangering our everlasting felicity.

2d. Clear proof has been furnished that Jesus is the Christ and can save us, ver. 4, 5. If his miracles did not prove that he came from God, nothing can prove it. If he could open the eyes of the blind, then he can enlighten the sinner; if he could unstop the ears of the deaf, then he can cause us to hear and live; if he could heal the sick, and make the lame walk, then he can heal *our* spiritual maladies, and make us walk in the way of life; if he could raise the dead, then he can raise those dead in sin, and breathe into us the breath of eternal life. If he was willing to do all this for the *body* which is soon to perish, then he will be much more willing to do it for the *soul*, that never dies. Then the poor, lost sinner may come and live.

3d. We see in this chapter Christ's manner of praising or complimenting men, ver. 7-15. He gave, in no measured terms, his exalted opinion of John—gave him praise which had been bestowed on no other mortal—ranked him far above the purest and sublimest of the prophets. But this was not done in the presence of John, *nor was it done in the presence of those who would inform John of it.* It was when the disciples of John had "*departed*," and his commendation of John was spoken to "the multitude," ver. 7. He waited till his disciples were gone, apprehending, doubtless, that *they* would be likely to report what he said in praise of their master, and *then* expressed his high opinion of his character. The practice of the *world* is to praise others to their faces, or in the presence of those who will be sure to inform them of it, and to speak evil of them when absent. Jesus delivered his unfavourable opinions of others to the men themselves; their excellences he took pains to commend where they would not be likely to hear of them. He did good to both, and in both prevented the existence of pride.

4th. The wicked take much pains, and are often fickle and inconsistent, for the sake of abusing and calumniating religious men, ver. 18, 19. They found much fault with the Saviour for doing the very same thing which they blamed John for *not* doing. So it is commonly with men who slander professors of religion. They risk their own characters, to prove that others are hypocrites or sinners. The object is not truth, but calumny and opposition to religion; and hitherto no means have been too base or too wicked to pour contempt on the followers of Christ.

5th. The purest characters may expect the shaft of calumny and malice, and often in proportion to their purity, ver. 19. Even the Saviour of the world was accused of being intemperate and a glutton. If the only perfectly pure being that ever trod the earth was thus accused, let not his followers think that any strange thing has happened to them if *they* are falsely accused.

6th. Judgments will overtake guilty men, and cities, and nations, ver. 21, 22. They fell on Sodom, Tyre, Sidon, and Capernaum. They may long linger; but in due time the hand of God will fall on the wicked, and they will die—for ever die.

7th. The wicked will suffer in proportion to their privileges, ver. 23, 24. So it was with Capernaum. And if they of ancient days suffered thus; if more tremendous judgments fell on them than even on guilty Sodom, what shall be the doom of those who go down to hell from this day of light? The Saviour was indeed there a few days; he worked a few miracles; but they had not, as *we* have, all his instructions; they had not Sabbath-schools, and Bible-classes, and the stated preaching of the gospel, nor was the world blessed then, as now, with extensive and powerful revivals of religion. How awful must be the doom of those who are educated in the ways of religion—who are instructed from Sabbath to Sabbath—who grow up amid the means of grace—and then are lost!

8th. The poor and needy; the weary and heavy-laden; the soul sick of sin and of the world; the sinner conscious of guilt and afraid to die, may come to Jesus Christ and live, ver. 28-30. The invitation is wide as the world. The child and the old man may seek and find salvation at the feet of the same Saviour. No child is too young; no man is too old; no one is too great a sinner. Christ is *full* of mercy, and all who come shall find peace. O how should we, in this sinful and miserable world, borne down with sin, and exposed each moment to death—how should we come and find the peace which he has promised to all, and take the yoke which all have found to be light!

CHAPTER XII.

1-8. The account contained in these verses is also recorded in Mar. ii. 23-28, and Lu. vi. 1-5.

1. *At that time.* Luke (chap. vi. 1) fixes the time more particularly. He says that it was *the second Sabbath after*

CHAPTER XII.

AT that time [a]Jesus went on the Sabbath day through the corn; and his disciples were an hungered, and began to [b]pluck the ears of corn, and to eat.

2 But when the Pharisees saw *it*, they said unto him, Behold, thy disciples do that which is [c]not lawful to do upon the Sabbath day.

3 But he said unto them, Have ye not read [d]what David did when he was an hungered, and they that were with him;

4 How he entered into the house of God, and did eat [e]the shew-bread, which was not lawful for him to eat, neither for them which were with him, [f]but only for the priests?

a Mar.2.23,&c.; Lu.6.1,&c. *b* De.23.25. *c* Ex.31.15. *d* 1 Sa.21.6. *e* Ex.25.30. *f* Ex.29.32,33.

the first. To understand this, it is proper to remark that the *Passover* was observed during the month *Abib*, or Nisan, answering to the latter part of March and the first of April. The feast was held seven days, commencing on the fourteenth day of the month (Ex. xii. 1–28; xxiii. 15), on the *second* day of the paschal week. The law required that a sheaf of *barley* should be offered up as the first-fruits of the harvest, Le. xxiii. 10, 11. From this day was reckoned seven weeks to the feast of *Pentecost* (Le. xxiii. 15, 16), called also the feast of *weeks* (De. xvi. 10), and the feast of the harvest, Ex. xxiii. 16. This second day in the feast of the Passover, or of unleavened bread, was the *beginning*, therefore, from which they reckoned *toward* the Pentecost. The Sabbath in the week following would be the *second Sabbath* after this first one in the reckoning, and this was doubtless the time mentioned when Christ went through the fields. It should be farther mentioned, that in Judea the barley harvest commences about the beginning of May, and both that and the wheat harvest are over by the twentieth. Barley is in full ear in the beginning of April. There is no improbability, therefore, in this narrative on account of the season of the year. This feast was always held at Jerusalem. ¶ *Through the corn.* Through the *barley*, or *wheat*. The word *corn*, as used in our translation of the Bible, has no reference to *maize*, or *Indian corn*, as it has with us. Indian corn was unknown till the discovery of America, and it is scarcely probable that the translators knew anything of it. The word was applied, as it is still in England, to wheat, rye, oats, and barley. This explains the circumstance that they *rubbed it in their hands* (Lu. vi. 1) to separate the grain from the chaff.

2. *Upon the Sabbath day.* The Pharisees, doubtless desirous of finding fault with Christ, said that in plucking the grain on the *Sabbath day* they had violated the commandment. Moses had commanded the Hebrews to abstain from all servile work on the Sabbath, Ex. xx. 10; xxxv. 2, 3; Nu. xv. 32–36. On any other day this would have been clearly lawful, for it was permitted, De. xxiii. 25.

3. *But he said unto them*, &c. To vindicate his disciples, he referred them to a similar case, recorded in the Old Testament, and therefore one with which they *ought* to have been acquainted. This was the case of David. The law commanded that twelve loaves of bread should be laid on the table in the holy place in the tabernacle, to remain a week, and then to be eaten by the *priests only*. Their place was then supplied by *fresh bread*. This was called the *shew-bread*, Le. xxiv. 5–9. David, fleeing before Saul, weary and hungry, had come to Ahimelech the priest; had found only this bread; had asked it of him, and had eaten it contrary to the *letter* of the law, 1 Sa. xxi. 1–7. David, among the Jews, had high authority. This act had passed uncondemned. It proved that in *cases of necessity the laws did not bind a man*—a principle which all laws admit. So the *necessity* of the disciples justified them in doing on the Sabbath what would have been otherwise unlawful.

4, 5. *How he entered into the house of God.* That is, the *tabernacle*, the temple not being then built. ¶ *Have ye not read in the law?* In the law, or in the books of Moses. ¶ *Profane the Sabbath.* He referred them to the conduct of the priests also. On the Sabbath days they were engaged, as well as on other days, in killing beasts for sacrifice, Nu. xxviii. 9, 10. Two lambs were killed on the

5 Or have ye not read in [g]the law how that on the Sabbath days the[h] priests in the temple profane the Sabbath, and are blameless?

6 But I say unto you, That in this place is [i]*one* greater than the temple.

7 But if ye had known what *this* meaneth, [k]I will have mercy, and not sacrifice, ye would not have condemned the guiltless.

8 For the Son of man is Lord even of the Sabbath day.

g Nu.28.9. *h* Jn.7.22,23.
i 2 Ch.6.18; Mal.3.1; ch.23.17-21. *k* Ho.6.6.

9 And[l] when he was departed thence, he went into their synagogue:

10 And, behold, there was a man which had his hand withered. And they asked him, saying, [m]Is it lawful to heal on the Sabbath days? that they might accuse him.

11 And he said unto them, What man shall there be among you that shall have one sheep, and [n]if it fall into a pit on the Sabbath day, will he not lay hold on it, and lift *it* out?

l Mar.3.1,&c.; Lu.6.6,&c. *m* Lu.14.3. *n* De.22.4

Sabbath, in addition to the *daily* sacrifice. The priests must be engaged in slaying them, and making fires to burn them in sacrifice, whereas to kindle a fire was expressly forbidden the Jews on the Sabbath, Ex. xxxv. 3. They did that which, for other persons to do, would have been *profaning* the Sabbath. Yet they were blameless. They did what was necessary and commanded. This was done in the *very temple*, too, the place of holiness, where the law should be most strictly observed.

6, 7. One *greater than the temple.* Here the Saviour refers to himself, and to his own dignity and power. "I have power over the laws; I can grant to my disciples a dispensation from those laws. An act which *I* command or permit them to do is therefore right." This proves that he was divine. None but God can authorize men to do a thing contrary to the divine laws. He refers them again (ver. 7) to a passage he had before quoted (See Notes on Mat. ix. 13), showing that God preferred acts of righteousness, rather than a precise observance of a ceremonial law.

Mark adds (ii. 27) "the Sabbath was made for man, and not man for the Sabbath." That is, the Sabbath was intended for the welfare of man; it was designed to promote his happiness, and not to produce misery by harsh, unfeeling requirements. It is not to be so interpreted as to produce suffering by making the necessary supply of wants unlawful. Man was not made for the Sabbath.. Man was created first, and then the Sabbath was appointed for his happiness, Ge. ii. 1–3. His *necessities*, his *real* comforts and wants, are not to be made to bend to that which was made *for him*. The laws are to be interpreted favourably to his *real* wants and comforts. This authorizes works only of *real* necessity, not of imaginary wants, or amusements, or common business and worldly employments.

8. *For the Son of man is Lord even of the Sabbath day.* To crown all, Christ says that he was Lord of the Sabbath. He had a right to direct the manner of its observance—undoubted proof that he is divine.

9–13. The account contained in these verses is recorded also in Mar. iii. 1–5, and Lu. vi. 6–10.

10. *A man which had his hand withered.* This was probably one form of the palsy. See Notes on Mat. iv. 24.

Mark and Luke have mentioned some circumstances omitted by Matthew. They say that Jesus first addressed the man, and told him to stand forth in the midst. He then addressed the people. He asked them if it was lawful to do *good* on the Sabbath day. This was admitted by all their teachers, and it could not be denied. They were therefore silent. He then appealed to *them*, and drew an argument from their own conduct. A man that had a sheep that should fall into a pit on the Sabbath day would exercise the common offices of humanity and draw it out. If it was lawful to save the life of a *sheep*, was it not proper to save the life of a man? By a reference to their own conduct he silenced them.

Mark adds that he looked on them *with anger*—that is, with strong disapprobation of their conduct. Their envy and malignity excited feelings of holy indignation. See Notes on Mar. iii. 5.

12. *How much, then, is a man better*

12 How much, then, is a man
better than a sheep? Wherefore
it is lawful to do well on the
Sabbath days.
13 Then saith he to the man,
Stretch forth thine hand. And
he stretched *it* forth; and it was
restored whole, like as the other.
14 Then the Pharisees went out,
and [1]held a council against him,
how they might destroy him.
15 But when Jesus knew *it*, he

[1] or, *took counsel*.

than a sheep? Of more consequence or value. If you would show an act of kindness to a brute beast on the Sabbath, how much more important is it to evince similar kindness to one made in the image of God! ¶ *It is lawful to do well on the Sabbath days.* This was universally allowed by the Jews in the abstract; and Jesus only showed them that the *principle* on which they acted in other things applied with *more force* to the case before him, and that the act which he was about to perform was, by their own confession, lawful.

13. *Then saith he to the man, Stretch forth thine hand.* This was a remarkable commandment. The man *might* have said that he had no strength—that it was a thing which he could not do. Yet, *being commanded*, it was his duty to obey. He did so, and was healed. So the sinner. It is his duty to obey whatever God commands. He will *give* strength to those who endeavour to do his will. It is not right to plead, when God commands us to do a thing, that we have no strength. He will give us strength, if there is a disposition to obey. At the same time, however, this passage should not be applied to the sinner as if it proved that he has no more strength or ability than the man who had the withered hand. It proves no such thing: it has no reference to any such case. It may be used to prove that man should *instantly obey* the commands of God, without pausing to examine the question about his ability, and especially without saying *that he can do nothing.* What would the Saviour have said to this man if he had objected that he *could not* stretch out his hand? ¶ *It was restored whole.* Christ had before *claimed* divine authority and power (ver. 6–9), he now showed that he *possessed* it. By his *own power* he healed him, thus evincing by a miracle that his claim of being Lord of the Sabbath was well founded.

These two cases determine what may be done on the Sabbath. The one was a case of *necessity*, the other of *mercy*. The example of the Saviour, and his explanations, show that these are a part of the proper duties of that holy day. Beyond an *honest* and *conscientious* discharge of these two duties, men may not devote the Sabbath to any secular purpose. If they do, they do it at their peril. They go beyond what *his* authority authorizes them to do. They do what *he* claimed the special right of doing, as being Lord of the Sabbath. They usurp *his* place, and act and legislate where God only has a right to act and legislate. Men may as well trample down any other law of the Bible as that respecting the Sabbath.

14–21. This account is found also in Mar. iii. 6–12.

14. *The Pharisees—held a council*, &c. Mark adds that the *Herodians* also took a part in this plot. They were probably a *political* party attached firmly to Herod Antipas, son of Herod the Great, tetrarch of Galilee. He was the same man who had imprisoned and beheaded John the Baptist, and to whom the Saviour, when arraigned, was sent by Pilate. See Notes on Lu. iii. 1. He was under Roman authority, and was a strong advocate of Roman power. All the friends of the family of Herod were opposed to Christ, and ever ready to join any plot against his life. They remembered, doubtless, the attempts of Herod the Great against him when he was the babe of Bethelem, and they were stung with the memory of the escape of Jesus from his bloody hands. The attempt against him now, on the part of the Pharisees, was the effect of *envy.* They hated his popularity, they were losing their influence, and they therefore resolved to take him out of the way.

15. *But when Jesus knew* it, *he withdrew himself*, &c. He knew of the plot which they had formed against his life; but his hour was not yet come, and he therefore sought security. By remaining, his presence would only have provoked them farther and endangered his own life. He acted, therefore, the part of prudence and withdrew. Comp. Notes on Mat. x. 23.

withdrew himself from thence: and great multitudes followed him, and he healed them all;
16 And charged them that they should not make him known:
17 That it might be fulfilled which was spoken by Esaias the prophet, saying,
18 Behold[o] my servant, whom I have chosen; my beloved, in whom my soul is well pleased: I will put my spirit upon him, and he shall show judgment to the Gentiles.
19 He shall not strive, nor cry; neither shall any man hear his voice in the streets.
20 A bruised reed shall he not break, and smoking flax shall he

o Is.42.1.

Mark adds that he withdrew *to the sea;* that is, to the Sea of Galilee, or Tiberias. He states also (ch. iii. 7, 8) that "*a great multitude* from Galilee followed him, and from Judea, and from Jerusalem, and from Idumea, and from beyond Jordan; and they about Tyre and Sidon, a great multitude, when they heard what great things he did, came unto him." As some of these places were without the limits of Judea or inhabited by *Gentiles*, this statement of Mark throws light on the passage quoted by Matthew (ver. 21), "In his name shall the *Gentiles* trust."

Pressed by the crowd (Mar. iii. 9), Jesus went aboard a *small vessel*, or *boat*, called by Mark a *ship*. This he did for the convenience of being separated from them and more easily addressing them. We are to suppose the lake still and calm; the multitudes, most of whom were sick and diseased, on the shore and pressing to the water's edge; and Jesus thus healing their diseases, and preaching to them the good news of salvation. No scene could be more sublime than this.

16. *And he charged them*, &c. He was *at this time* desirous of concealment. He wished to avoid their plots and to save his life.

17. *That it might be fulfilled*, &c. Matthew here quotes a passage from Is. xlii. 1–4, to show the *reason why he thus retired from his enemies and sought concealment.* The Jews, and the disciples also at first, expected that the Messiah would be a conqueror, and vindicate himself from all his enemies. When they saw him retiring before them, and, instead of subduing them by force, seeking a place of concealment, it was contrary to all their previous notions of the Messiah. Matthew by this quotation shows that *their* conceptions of him had been wrong. Instead of a warrior and an earthly conqueror, he was *predicted* under a totally different character. Instead of shouting for battle, lifting up his voice in the streets, oppressing the feeble—*breaking bruised reeds and quenching smoking flax, as a conqueror*—he would be peaceful, retiring; would strengthen the feeble, and would cherish the faintest desires of holiness. This appears to be the *general* meaning of this quotation here. Comp. Notes on Is. xlii. 1–4.

18. *My servant.* That is, the Messiah, the Lord Jesus; called a servant from his taking the *form* of a *servant*, or his being born in a humble condition (Phi. ii. 7), and from his obeying or *serving* God. See He. x. 9. ¶ *Shall show judgment to the Gentiles.* The word *judgment* means, in the Hebrew, *law, commands*, &c., Ps. xix. 9; cxix. 29, 30. It means the *whole system of truth;* the law of God in general; the purpose, plan, or *judgment* of God about human duty and conduct. Here it means, evidently, the system of *gospel truth*, the *Christian scheme.* ¶ *Gentiles.* All who were not Jews. This prophecy was fulfilled by the multitudes coming to him from Idumea and beyond Jordan, and from Tyre and Sidon, as recorded by Mar. iii. 7, 8.

19. *He shall not strive*, &c. He shall not shout as a warrior. He shall be meek, retiring, and peaceful. Streets were places of concourse. The meaning is, that he should not seek publicity and popularity.

20. *A bruised reed*, &c. The reed is an emblem of feebleness, as well as of fickleness or want of stability, Mat. xi. 7. A bruised, broken reed is an emblem of the poor and oppressed. It means that he would not oppress the feeble and poor, as victorious warriors and conquerors did. It is also an expressive emblem of the soul broken and contrite on account of sin; weeping and mourning for transgression. He will not break it; that is, he will not be severe, unforgiving, and cruel. He will heal it, pardon it, and give it

not quench, till he send forth judgment unto victory.

21 And in his name shall the Gentiles trust.

22 Then[p] was brought unto him one possessed with a devil, blind and dumb: and he healed him, insomuch that the blind and dumb both spake and saw.

23 And all the people were amazed; and said, Is not this the Son of David?

24 But when the Pharisees heard *it*, they said, This *fellow* doth not cast out devils, but by [2]Beelzebub the prince of the devils.

25 And Jesus [q]knew their thoughts, and said unto them,

p Mar.3.11; Lu.11.14.

2 *Beelzebul.* q Ps.139.2; Jn.2.24,25.

---

strength. ¶ *Smoking flax.* This refers to the *wick* of a lamp when the oil is exhausted—the dying, flickering flame and smoke that hang over it. It is an emblem, also, of feebleness and infirmity. He would not farther oppress those who had a little strength; he would not put out hope and life when it seemed to be almost extinct. He would not be like the Pharisees, proud and overbearing, and trampling down the poor. It is expressive, also, of the languishing graces of the people of God. He will not treat them harshly or unkindly, but will cherish the feeble flame, minister the *oil* of grace, and kindle it into a blaze. ¶ *Till he send forth judgment unto victory. Judgment* here means *truth*—the truth of God, the gospel. It shall be victorious—it shall not be vanquished. Though the Messiah is not *such* a conqueror as the Jews expected, yet he *shall* conquer. Though mild and retiring, yet he will be victorious.

21. *And in his name,* &c. The Hebrew in Isaiah is, "And the isles shall wait for his law." The idea is, however, the same. The *isles* denote the Gentiles, or a part of the Gentiles—those out of Judea. The meaning is, that the gospel should be preached to the Gentiles, and that they should receive it. See Notes on Is. xli. 1 for an explanation of the word *islands*, as it is used in the Bible.

22–30. *Then was brought unto him one possessed with a devil.* See Notes on Mat. iv. 24. The same account, substantially, is found in Mar. iii. 22–27, and Lu. xi. 14–26.

23. *Is not this the Son of David?* That is, Is not this the promised *descendant* of David, the Messiah? They were acquainted with the prophecy in Is. xxxv. 5, "Then the eyes of the blind shall be opened, and the ears of the deaf shall be unstopped," and they inferred that he must be the promised Messiah who was able to do this. This inference was drawn by the common people, and not by the proud and haughty Pharisees. It is not uncommon that men of plain common sense, though unlearned, see the true meaning of the Bible, while those who are filled with pride and science, falsely so called, are blinded.

24. *But when the Pharisees heard* it, &c. It was necessary for the Pharisees, who had determined to reject Jesus of Nazareth, to account in *some* way for the miracles he had wrought. Here was a manifest miracle, an exertion of power unquestionably superior to what *men* could put forth. The common people were fast drawing the proper inference from it, and coming into the belief that this was the Messiah. The authority and power of the Pharisees were declining. Unless, therefore, some way should be devised of accounting for these facts, their influence would be at an end. Whatever way of accounting for them was adopted, it was necessary that they should acknowledge that there was *superhuman power*. The people were fully persuaded of this, and no man could deny it. They therefore ascribed it to the prince of the devils—to Beelzebub. In this they had *two* objects: 1st. To concede to the people that here was a *miracle*, or a work above mere human power. 2d. To throw all possible contempt on Jesus. Beelzebub, or Beelzebul, as it is in the Greek, and correctly rendered in the margin, was an opprobrious name given to the leader of the devils as an expression of supreme contempt. See Notes on Mat. x. 25.

25, 26. *And Jesus knew their thoughts,* &c. To know the thoughts of the heart belongs only to God, Ps. cxxxix. 2; Je. xvii. 10. ¶ *Every kingdom,* &c. Their subtle and cunning device was completely foiled, and Jesus made their argument recoil on their own heads.

Every kingdom divided against itself is brought to desolation; and every city or house divided against itself shall not stand:

26 And if Satan cast out Satan, he is divided against himself; how shall then his kingdom stand?

27 And if I [r]by Beelzebub cast out devils, by whom do your children cast *them* out? Therefore they shall be your judges.

28 But if I cast out devils by the Spirit of God, then [s]the kingdom of God is come unto you.

29 Or else how can one enter into a strong man's house, [t]and spoil his goods, except he first bind the strong man? and then he will spoil his house.

30 He[u] that is not with me, is against me; and he that gathereth not with me, scattereth abroad.

31 Wherefore I say unto you, [v]All manner of sin and blasphemy shall be forgiven unto men; [w]but the blasphemy *against* the *Holy* Ghost shall not be forgiven unto men.

r ver.24.
s Da.2.44; ch.6.33; Lu.11.20; 17.21; Ro.14.17.
t Is.49.24; 53.12; Re.12.7-10; 20.2,3. *u* 1 Jn.2.19.
v Mar.3.28; Lu.12.10. *w* He.10.29; 1 Jn.5.16.

A kingdom or a family can prosper only by living in harmony. The different parts and members must unite in promoting the same objects. If divided—if one part *undoes* what the other *does*—it must fall. So with the kingdom of Satan. It is your doctrine that Satan has *possessed* these whom *I have cured*. It is also your doctrine that *he* has *helped me* to cure them. If so, then he has helped me to undo what he had done. He has aided me to cast himself out—that is, to oppose and discomfit himself. At this rate, how can there be any stability in his kingdom? It must fall, and Satan must have less than human prudence.

27. *By whom do your children cast* them *out?* Your disciples; your followers. See Notes on Mat. i. 1. Christ was not satisfied by showing them the intrinsic absurdity of their argument. He showed them that it might as well be applied to them as to him. *Your* disciples, taught by you and encouraged by you, pretend to cast out devils. If your argument be true that a man who casts out devils must be in league with the devil, then *your disciples* have made a covenant with him also. You must therefore either give up this argument, or admit that the working of miracles is proof of the assistance of God. ¶ *Therefore they shall be your judges.* They condemn you and your argument. They are conclusive witnesses against the force of your reasoning.

28. *But if I cast out devils by the Spirit of God*, &c. The Spirit of God, here, means the *power* of God—in Luke, by the *finger* of God. Comp. Ex. viii. 19; Ps. viii. 3. If this work is not by the aid of Satan, then it is by the aid of God. Then his kingdom, or *reign*, is come, Mat. iii. 2. The *reign* of Satan over men, and the *reign* of God are in opposition. If God *expels* Satan from his dominion over men, then *his* reign has come.

29. *Or else*, &c. The Saviour makes use of a new illustration to confute the Pharisees, drawn from breaking into a house. A man could not break into the house of a strong man and take his property unless he had rendered the man himself helpless. If he had taken his goods, it would therefore be sufficient proof that he had bound the man. So I, says he, have taken this *property—this possessed person*—from the dominion of Satan. It is clear proof that I have subdued *Satan himself*, the *strong* being that had him in possession. The words *or else* mean *or how:* "*How*, or *in what way*, can one," &c. ¶ *Spoil his goods.* The word *spoil* commonly means, now, to corrupt, injure, or destroy. Here it means *to plunder*, to take with violence, as it commonly does in the Bible. See Col. ii. 8, 15; Ex. iii. 22.

30. *He that is not with me*, &c. In addition to his other arguments, Jesus urges this general principle, that there can be but two parties in the universe. If anyone did not act *with* him, he was against him. If he gathered not with him, he scattered. This is taken from the practice of persons in harvest. He that did not gather with him, or *aid* him, scattered abroad, or opposed him. The application of this was, "As I have not united with Satan, but opposed him, there can be no league between us." The charge, therefore, is a false one.

32 And whosoever [x]speaketh a word against the Son of man, it shall be forgiven him: but whosoever speaketh against the Holy Ghost, it shall not be forgiven him, neither in this world, neither in the *world* to come.

x Lu.7.34; Jn.7.12; 1 Ti.1.13.

33 Either make the tree good, and his fruit good; or else make the tree corrupt, and his fruit cor-

31, 32. In this place, and in Mar. iii. 28–30, Jesus states the awful nature of the sin of which they had been guilty. That sin was the sin against the Holy Ghost. It consisted in charging him with being in league with the devil, or accusing him of working his miracles, not by the *spirit* or *power* of God, but by the aid of the prince of the devils. It was therefore a direct insult, abuse, or evil speaking against the Holy Ghost—the spirit by which Jesus worked his miracles. That this was what he intended by this sin, at that time, is clear from Mar. iii. 30, "BECAUSE they said he had an unclean spirit." All other sins—all speaking against the Saviour himself—might be remitted. But this sin was clearly against the Holy One; it was alleging that the highest displays of God's mercy and power were the work of the devil; and it argued, therefore, the deepest depravity of mind. The sin of which he speaks is therefore clearly stated. It was accusing him of working miracles by the aid of the devil, thus dishonouring the Holy Ghost. ¶ *All manner of sin and blasphemy shall be forgiven.* That is, only on condition that men repent and believe. If they *continue* in this sin they cannot be forgiven, Mar. xvi. 16; Ro. ii. 6–9. ¶ *Blasphemy.* Injurious or evil speaking of God. See Notes on Mat. ix. 3. ¶ *A word against the Son of man.* The Jews were offended at the humble life and appearance of the Saviour. They reproached him as being a Nazarene—sprung from Nazareth, a place from which no good was expected to proceed; with being a Galilean, from Galilee, a place from which no prophet came, Jn. vii. 52. Jesus says that reproaches of this kind could be pardoned. Reflections on his poverty, on his humble birth, and on the lowliness of his human nature might be forgiven; but for those which affected his divine nature, accusing him of being in league with the devil, denying his divinity, and attributing the power which manifestly *implied* divinity to the prince of fallen spirits, there could be no pardon. This sin was a very different thing from what is now often supposed to be the sin against the Holy Ghost. It was a wanton and blasphemous attack on the divine power and nature of Christ. Such a sin God would not forgive. ¶ *Speaketh against the Holy Ghost.* The word *ghost* means *spirit*, and probably refers here to the *divine nature* of Christ—the power by which he wrought his miracles. There is no evidence that it refers to the third person of the Trinity; and the meaning of the whole passage may be: "He that speaks against me as a man of Nazareth—that speaks contemptuously of my humble birth, &c., may be pardoned; but he that reproaches my divine nature, charging me with being in league with Satan, and blaspheming the power of God manifestly displayed *by me*, can never obtain forgiveness." ¶ *Neither in this world, nor in that which is to come.* That is, as Mark expresses it, *hath never forgiveness, but is in danger of eternal damnation.* This fixes the meaning of the phrase. It means, then, not the future age or dispensation, known among the Jews as the world to come, but it means that the guilt will be unpardoned for ever; that such is the purpose of God that he *will* not forgive a sin so direct, presumptuous, and awful. It cannot be inferred from this that any sins will be forgiven in hell. The Saviour meant simply to say that there were *no possible circumstances* in which the offender could obtain forgiveness. He certainly did *not* say that any sin unpardoned here would be pardoned hereafter.

33. *Either make*, &c. The fact asserted in this verse is, that a tree is known, not by its leaves, or bark, or form, but by its fruit. The application to the argument is this: "You are to judge of man's being in league with Satan by his works. If my doctrines and works be properly the works of Satan, then *I* am corrupt; if not, then your charge is blasphemy. So, on the other hand, if, notwithstanding *your* professions, your works are the works of the devil, and your doctrines are

rupt: [y]for the tree is known by *his* fruit.

34 O[z] generation of vipers! how can ye, being evil, speak good things? [a]for out of the abundance of the heart the mouth speaketh.

35 A good man out of the good treasure of the heart bringeth forth good things; and an evil man, out of the evil treasure, bringeth forth evil things.

36 But I say unto you, that every idle word that men shall speak, [b]they shall give account thereof in the day of judgment:

37 For[c] by thy words thou shalt be justified, and by thy words thou shalt be condemned.

38 Then certain of the scribes

y ch.7.16,17. z ch.3.7. a Lu.6.45. b Ec.12.14; Ep.5.4,6; Jude 15. c Pr.13.3.

---

such as *he* would teach, it would prove respecting you that which you charge on me." In this indirect but powerful manner he advances to the charge against them, which he urges in the following verses.

34, 35. *O generation of vipers!* Christ here applies the argument which he had suggested in the previous verse. They were a wicked race; like poisonous reptiles, with a corrupt and evil nature. They could not be *expected* to speak good things—that is, to speak favourably of *him* and his works. As the bad fruit of a tree was the proper effect of its *nature*, so were their *words* about him and his works the proper effect of *their* nature. The *abundance* or fulness of the *heart* produced the words of the lips. *Vipers* are a poisonous kind of serpents, not often a yard long, and about an inch thick, having a flat head. The males have two large teeth, through which a most deadly poison is thrown into the wound made by the bite. They are an emblem of malignity and mischief. These were strong expressions to be used by the *meek and lowly Jesus;* but they were not the effect of anger and malice; they were a declaration of the true character of the men with whom he was conversing—a declaration most justly deserved. See Notes on Mat. iii. 7.

36. *But I say unto you,* &c. Christ closes this address to his malignant and wicked hearers by a solemn declaration that for these things God would bring them into judgment. *They,* therefore, who had spoken so malignantly against him, could not escape. ¶ *Idle word.* This literally means a vain, thoughtless, useless word; a word that accomplishes no good. Here it means, evidently, *wicked, injurious, false, malicious,* for *such* were the words which they had spoken.

37. *By thy words thou shalt be justified,* &c. That is, *words* are the indication of the true principles of the heart; by *words* the heart shall be known, as the tree is by its fruit. If they are true, proper, chaste, instructive, pious, they will prove that the heart is right. If false, envious, malignant, and impious, they will prove that the heart is *wrong,* and will therefore be among the causes of condemnation. It is not meant that words will be the *only* thing that will condemn man, but that they will be an important *part* of the things for which he shall be condemned. See Ja. iii. 3–12.

38–42. *We would see a sign from thee.* See Lu. xi. 16, 29–32. A *sign* commonly signifies a miracle—that is, a *sign* that God was with the person or had sent him. Comp. Notes on Is. vii. 11. Luke adds that this was done *tempting him;* that is, trying him, doubting if he had the power to do it. If these persons had been present with him for any considerable time, they had already seen sufficient proofs that he was what he claimed to be. They might have been, however, those who had recently come, and then the emphasis must be laid on "*we*"—*we,* as well as the others, would see a proof that thou art the Christ. In either case it was a temptation. If they had not *seen* him work a miracle, yet they should have believed it by testimony. Comp. Jn. xx. 29. Perhaps, however, the emphasis is to be laid on the words *from heaven.* They might profess not to doubt that his miracles were real, but they were not quite satisfactory. They were desirous of seeing something, therefore, that should clear up their doubts—where there could be no opportunity for dispute. A comet, or lightning, or thunder, or sudden darkness, or the gift of food raining upon them,

and of the Pharisees answered, saying, [d]Master, we would see a sign from thee.

39 But he answered and said unto them, An evil and [e]adulterous generation seeketh after a sign; and there shall no sign be given to it but the sign of the prophet Jonas;

40 For[f] as Jonas was three days and three nights in the whale's belly, so shall the Son of man be three days and three nights in the heart of the earth.

41 The men of Nineveh shall rise in judgment with this generation, and [g]shall condemn it: [h]because they repented at the preaching

d ch.16.1; 1 Co.1.22. e Is.57.3. f Jonah 1.17. g Ro.2.27. h Jonah 3.5.

they supposed would be decisive. Possibly they referred in this to Moses. *He* had been with God amid thunders and lightnings, and *he* had given them manna — *bread from heaven* — to eat. They wished Jesus to show some miracle equally undoubted.

39. *An evil and adulterous generation.* The relation of the Jews to God was often represented as a marriage contract—God as the husband, and the Jewish people as the wife. See Is. lvii. 3; Ho. iii. 1; Eze. xvi. 15. Hence their apostasy and idolatry are often represented as adultery. This is the meaning, probably, here. They were *evil*, and unfaithful to the covenant or to the commandments of God — an apostate and corrupt people. There is, however, evidence that they were literally an adulterous people. ¶ *There shall no sign be given to it*, &c. They sought some direct miracle *from heaven*. Jesus replied that no *such* miracle should be given. He did not mean to say that he would work no more miracles, or give no more evidence that he was the Christ, but he would give *no such miracle* as they required. *He would give one that ought to be as satisfactory evidence to them that he was from God, as the miraculous preservation of Jonah was to the Ninevites that he was divinely commissioned.* As Jonah was preserved three days by miracle and then restored *alive*, so he would be raised from the dead after three days. As on the ground of this preservation the Ninevites believed Jonah and repented, so, on the ground of his resurrection, the men of an adulterous and wicked generation ought to repent, and believe that he was from God. "The sign of the prophet Jonas" means the *sign or evidence* which was given to the people of Nineveh that he was from God—to wit, that he had been miraculously preserved, and was therefore divinely commissioned. The word *Jonas* is the Greek way of writing the Hebrew word *Jonah*, as *Elias* is for *Elijah*.

40. *For as Jonas was three days*, &c. See Jonah i. 17. This event took place in the Mediterranean Sea, somewhere between Joppa and Tarshish, when he was fleeing *from* Nineveh. It is said that the *whale* seldom passes into that sea, and that its throat is too small to admit a man. It is probable, therefore, that a fish of the *shark kind* is intended. Sharks have been known often to swallow a man entire. The fish in the book of Jonah is described merely as a *great fish*, without specifying the kind. It is well known that the Greek word translated *whale*, in the New Testament, does not of necessity mean a whale, but may denote a large fish or sea-monster of any kind.—Robinson, *Lex.*

40. *Three days and three nights.* It will be seen in the account of the resurrection of Christ that he was in the grave but two nights and a part of three days. See Mat. xviii. 6. This computation is, however, strictly in accordance with the Jewish mode of reckoning. If it had *not* been, the Jews would have understood it, and would have charged our Saviour as being a false prophet, for it was well known to them that he had spoken this prophecy, Mat. xxvii. 63. Such a charge, however, was never made; and it is plain, therefore, that what was *meant* by the prediction was accomplished. It was a maxim, also, among the Jews, in computing time, that a part of a day was to be received as the whole. Many instances of this kind occur in both sacred and profane history. See 2 Ch. x. 5, 12; Ge. xlii. 17, 18. Comp. Es. iv. 16 with v. 1. ¶ *In the heart of the earth.* The Jews used the word *heart* to denote the *interior* of a thing, or to speak of being *in* a thing. It means, here, to be in the grave or sepulchre.

of Jonas; and, behold, a greater than Jonas *is* here.

42 The [i]queen of the south shall rise up in the judgment with this generation, and shall condemn it: for [k]she came from the uttermost parts of the earth to hear the wisdom of Solomon; and, behold, a greater than Solomon *is* here.

43 When[l] the unclean spirit is

i Lu.11.31,&c. *k* 2 Ch.9.1. *l* Lu.11.24.

---

41. *The men of Nineveh.* Nineveh was the capital of the Assyrian empire. It was founded by Asshur, Ge. x. 11. It was situated on the banks of the river Tigris, to the north-east of Babylon. It was a city of vast extent, and of corresponding wickedness. It was 48 miles in circuit; its walls were 100 feet high and 10 thick, and were defended by fifteen hundred towers, each 200 feet in height. It contained in the time of Jonah, it is supposed, six hundred thousand inhabitants. The destruction of Nineveh, threatened by Jonah in forty days, was suspended, by their repentance, two hundred years. It was then overthrown by the Babylonians about six hundred years before Christ. During the siege a mighty inundation of the river Tigris took place, which threw down a part of the walls, through which the enemy entered, and sacked and destroyed the city. This destruction had been foretold one hundred and fifteen years before by Nahum (ch. i. 8): "But with an overwhelming flood he will make an utter end of the place thereof;" and ii. 6: "The gates of the river shall be opened, and the palace shall be dissolved." Its ruins have been lately discovered by Layard, and have contributed much to the establishment of the truth of Scripture history. Those remains are on the east side of the river Tigris, nearly opposite to the city of Mosul. ¶ *Shall condemn it.* That is, their conduct, in repenting under the preaching of Jonah, shall condemn this generation. They, ignorant and wicked heathen, repented when threatened with *temporal* judgment by a mere man—Jonah; you, Jews, professing to be enlightened, though threatened for your great wickedness with eternal punishment *by the Son of God*—a far greater being than Jonah—repent not, and must therefore meet with a far heavier condemnation.

42. *The queen of the south.* That is, the Queen of Sheba, 1 Ki. x. 1. Sheba was probably a city of Arabia, situated to the south of Judea. Comp. Notes on Is. lx. 6. ¶ *From the uttermost parts of the earth.* This means simply from the most distant parts of the habitable world *then known.* See a similar expression in De. xxviii. 49. As the knowledge of geography was limited, the place was, *in fact*, by no means in the extreme parts of the earth. It means that she came from a remote country; and she would condemn that generation, for she came *a great distance* to hear the wisdom of Solomon, but the Jews of that age would not listen to the wisdom of one *much greater* than Solomon, *though present with them.*

43–45. *When the unclean spirit*, &c. The *general sentiment* which our Saviour here teaches is much more easily understood than the illustration which he uses. The Jews had asked a sign *from heaven* that should decisively prove that he was the Messiah, and satisfy their unbelief. He replies that, though he should give them such a sign—a proof conclusive and satisfactory, and though for a time they should profess to believe and apparently reform, yet such was the obstinacy of their unbelief and wickedness, that they would soon return to their former course, and become worse and worse. Infidelity and wickedness, like an evil spirit in a possessed man, were appropriately *at home* in them. If driven out, they would find no other place so comfortable and undisturbed as their bosoms. Everywhere they would be, comparatively, like an evil spirit going through deserts and lonely places, and finding no place of rest. They would return, therefore, and dwell with them. ¶ *He walketh through dry places.* That is, through *deserts*—regions of country unwatered, sandy, barren, desolate. That our Saviour here speaks according to the ancient belief of the Jews that evil spirits had their abodes in those desolate, uninhabited regions, there can be no doubt; nor can there be any doubt that the Bible gives countenance to the opinion. Thus Re. xviii. 2: "Babylon—is become the habitation *of devils* and the hold of *every foul spirit;* that is, has become *desolate*

gone out of a man, [m]he walketh through dry places, seeking rest, and findeth none.

44 Then he saith, I will return into my house, from whence I came out; and when he is come, he findeth *it* empty, swept, and garnished.

45 Then goeth he and taketh with himself seven other spirits more wicked than himself, and they enter in and dwell there: and the last *state* of that man is [n]worse than the first. Even so shall it be also unto this wicked generation.

46 While he yet talked to the people, behold, [o]*his* mother and [p]his brethren stood without, desiring to speak with him.

47 Then one said unto him, Behold, thy mother and thy brethren stand without, desiring to speak with thee.

m Job 1.7; 1 Pe.5.8.

n He.6.4; 10.26; 2 Pe.2.20,22. o Mar.3.31,&c.; Lu.8.19,&c. p ch.13.55.

—a place where evil spirits appropriately dwell. So Is. xiii. 21: "And *satyrs* shall dance there;" *i.e.* according to the ancient Greek translation, "*devils* or *demons* shall dance there." See also Je. l. 39. Comp. Notes on Is. xxxiv. 14. De. xxxii. 17. ¶ *Seeking rest, and findeth none.* These desolate and dry regions are represented as uncomfortable habitations; so much so, that the dissatisfied spirit, better pleased with a dwelling in the bosoms of men, as affording an opportunity of doing evil, seeks a return there.

44. *Then he saith, I will return into my house*, &c. The *man* is called his *house*, because the spirit had dwelt in him. ¶ *He findeth* it *empty*, &c. There is here a continuance of the reference to the dwelling of the spirit in men. The man was called his *house.* By the absence of the evil spirit the house is represented as unoccupied, or *empty*, *swept*, and *garnished;* that is, while the evil spirit was away, the man was restored to his right mind, or was freed from the influence of the evil spirit. ¶ *Garnished.* Adorned, put in order, furnished. Applied to the *man*, it means that his mind was sane and regular when the evil spirit was gone, or he had a *lucid interval.*

45. *Then goeth he*, &c. Seeing the state of the man; dissatisfied with a lonely dwelling in the desert where he could do no evil; envious of the happiness of the individual, and supremely bent on wickedness, he resolved to increase his power of malignant influences and to return. He is therefore represented as taking seven other spirits still worse than himself, and returning to his former habitation. Seven denotes a large but indefinite number. It was a favourite number with the Jews, and was used to denote *completeness* or *perfection*, or any *finished* or *complete* number. See 1 Sa. ii. 5. Comp. Rev. i. 4. Here it means a sufficient number completely to occupy and harass his soul. ¶ *Even so shall it be with this generation.* This shows the scope and design of this illustration. The state of that man was a representation of that generation of men. Much might be done to cure their unbelief, much to reform them externally; but such was the firm hold which the principles of infidelity and wickedness had taken of their minds *as their proper habitation*, that they would return, after all the means used to reform them, and they would be worse and worse. And this was literally accomplished. After all the instructions and miracles of the Saviour and his apostles; after all that had been done for them by holy men and prophets, and by the judgments and mercies of God; and after all their external temporary reformations—like the temporary departure of an evil spirit from a man possessed—yet such was their love of wickedness that the nation became worse and worse. They increased in crime, like the seven-fold misery and wretchedness of the man into whose bosom the seven additional evil spirits came. They rejected God's messengers, abused his mercies, crucified his Son, and God gave their temple, and capital, and nation into the hands of the Romans, and thousands of the people to destruction.

It is not *proved* by this passage that evil spirits actually *dwell* in deserts. It is proved only that such was the opinion of the Jews; that that opinion was drawn from some expressions in the Bible; and that *such expressions were sufficiently clear to justify the Saviour in*

48 But he answered and said unto him that told him, Who is my mother? and who are my brethren?

49 And he stretched forth his hand toward his disciples, and said, Behold my mother, and my brethren!

50 For[q] whosoever shall do the will of my father which is in heaven, the same is my brother, and sister, and mother.

q ch.7.20; Jn.15.14; Ga.5.6; He.2.11; 1 Jn.2.17.

---

drawing an argument from them to confound those who firmly believed that such was the case. Nor is there any absurdity in the opinion; for, 1st. There are evil spirits. See Notes on ch. viii. 33. 2d. They must exist in *some place.* 3d. There is as much propriety that they should be located about our earth as anywhere. 4th. The clear doctrine of the Bible is, that many of them have much to do with our world. 5th. It is as reasonable that they should dwell commonly in desolate and uninhabited regions as anywhere else.

46-50. See also Mar. iii. 31-35; Lu. viii. 19-21. ¶ *His brethren.* There has been some difference of opinion about the persons who are referred to here, some supposing that they were children of Mary his mother, others that they were the children of Mary, the wife of Cleophas or Alpheus, his *cousins*, and called *brethren* according to the customs of the Jews. The natural and obvious meaning is, however, that they were the children of Mary his mother. See also Mar. vi. 3. To this opinion, moreover, there can be no valid objection.

48. *Who is my mother?* &c. There was no want of affection or respect in Jesus toward his mother, as is proved by his whole life. See especially Lu. ii. 51, and Jn. xix. 25-27. This question was asked merely *to fix the attention* of the hearers and to prepare them for the answer—that is, to show them who sustained toward him the nearest and most tender relation. To do this he pointed to his disciples. Dear and tender as were the ties which bound him to his mother and brethren, yet those which bound him to his disciples were more tender and sacred. How great was his love for his disciples, when it was more than even that for his mother! And what a bright illustration of his own doctrine, that we ought to forsake father, and mother and friends, and houses, and lands, to be his followers!

REMARKS.

1st. Our Saviour has taught us the right use of the Sabbath, ver. 1-13. His conduct was an explanation of the meaning of the fourth commandment. By his example we may learn what may be done. He himself performed only those works on the Sabbath which were strictly necessary for life, and those which tended to benefit the poor, the afflicted, and needy. Whatever work is done on the Sabbath that is not for these ends must be wrong. All labour that can as well be done on another day—all which is not for the support of life, or to aid the ignorant, poor, and sick, must be wrong. This example justifies teaching the ignorant, supplying the wants of the poor, instructing children in the precepts of religion, teaching those to read in Sabbath-schools who have no other opportunity for learning, and visiting the sick, when we go not for formality, or *to save time on some other day*, but to do them good.

2d. The Sabbath is of vast service to mankind. It was made for man—not for man to violate or profane, or to be a day of mere idleness, but to improve to his spiritual and eternal good. Where men are employed through *six* days in worldly occupations, it is kind toward *them* to give them *one* day particularly to prepare for eternity. Where there is no Sabbath there is no religion. This truth, from the history of the world, will bear to be recorded in letters of gold—*that true religion will exist among men only when they strictly observe the Sabbath.* They, therefore, who do most to promote the observance of the Sabbath, are doing most for religion and the welfare of man. In this respect Sunday-school teachers may do more, perhaps, than all the world besides for the best interests of the world.

3d. In the conduct of Christ (ver. 14, 15) we have an illustration of the nature of Christian prudence. He did not throw himself needlessly into danger. He did not remain to provoke opposition. He felt that his time was not come, and that his life, by a prudent course, should be preserved. He therefore withdrew. Religion requires us to sacrifice our lives rather than deny the Saviour. To throw our lives away when, with good conscience, they might be preserved, is self-murder.

4th. The rejection of the gospel in one place is often the occasion of its being received elsewhere, ver. 15. Men may reject it to their own destruction; but somewhere it *will* be preached, and will be the power of God unto salvation. The wicked cannot drive it out of the world. They only secure their own ruin, and, against their will, benefit and save others. To reject it is like turning a beautiful and fertilizing stream from a man's own land. He does not, he cannot dry it up. *It will flow somewhere else.* He injures himself and perhaps benefits multitudes. Men never commit so great foolishness and wickedness, and so completely fail in what they aim at, as in rejecting the gospel. A man, hating the light of the sun, might get into a cave or dungeon, and be in total darkness; but the sun will continue to shine, and millions, in spite of him, will be benefited by it. So it is with the gospel.

5th. Christ was mild, quiet, retiring—not clamorous or noisy, ver. 19. So is all religion. There is no piety in noise; if there was, then thunder and artillery would be piety. Confusion and discord are not religion. Loud words and shouting are not religion. Religion is love, reverence, fear, holiness, a deep and awful regard for the presence of God, profound apprehensions of the solemnities of eternity, imitation of the Saviour. It is still. It is full of awe — an awe too great to strive, or cry, or lift up the voice in the streets. If men ever should be overawed and filled with emotions *repressing* noise and clamour, it should be when they approach *the great God.*

6th. The feeble may trust to Jesus, ver. 20. A child of any age, an ignorant person, the poorest man, may come, and he shall in nowise be cast out. It is a sense of our weakness that Jesus seeks. Where that is *he* will strengthen us, and we shall not fail.

7th. Grace will not be extinguished, ver. 20. Jesus, where he finds it in the feeblest degree, will not destroy it. He will cherish it. He will kindle it to a flame. It will burn brighter and brighter, till it "glows like that of the pure spirits above."

8th. Men are greatly prone to ascribe all religion to the devil, ver. 24. Anything that is unusual, anything that confounds them, anything that troubles their consciences, they ascribe to fanaticism, overheated zeal, and Satan. It has always been so. It is sometimes an easy way to stifle their own convictions, and to bring religion into contempt. *Somehow or other*, like the Pharisees, infidels must account for revivals of religion, for striking instances of conversion, and for the great and undeniable effects which the gospel produces. How easy to *say* that it is *delusion*, and that it is the work of the devil! How easy to show at once the terrible opposition of their own hearts to God, and to boast themselves in their own wisdom, in having found a *cause* so simple for all the effects which religion produces in the world! How much pains, also, men will take to secure their own perdition, rather than to admit it to be *possible* that Christianity is true!

9th. We see the danger of blasphemy—the danger of trifling with the influences of the Holy Spirit, ver. 31, 32. Even if we do not commit the unpardonable sin, yet we see that *all* trifling with the Holy Ghost is a sin very near to God, and attended with infinite danger. He that *laughs away* the thoughts of death and eternity; he that seeks the society of the gay and trifling, or of the sensual and profane, for the *express* purpose of driving away these thoughts; and he that struggles directly against his convictions, and is resolved that he *will not* submit to God, may be, for aught he knows, making his damnation sure. Why should God *ever* return when a man has *once* rejected the gospel? Who would be to blame if the sinner is then lost? Assuredly not God. None but himself. Children sometimes do this. Then is the time, the very time, when they should begin to love God and Jesus Christ. Then the Spirit also strives. Many *have then* given their hearts to him and become Christians. Many more *might* have done so, if they had not grieved away the Spirit of God.

10th. We see the danger of rejecting Christ, ver. 38-42. All past ages, all the wicked and the good, the foolish and the wise, will rise up in the day of judgment, and condemn us, if we do not believe the gospel. No people, heretofore, have seen so much light as we do in this age. And no people can be so awfully condemned as those who,

CHAPTER XIII.

THE same day went Jesus out of the house, and sat by the sea-side.

2 And great multitudes were gathered together unto him, so that [a]he went into a ship, and sat; and the whole multitude stood on the shore.

a Lu.5.3.

---

in a land of light, of Sabbaths and Sabbath-schools, reject Christ and go to hell. Among the hundred and twenty thousand children of Nineveh (Jonah iv. 11) there was not one single Sunday-school. There was no one to tell them of God and the Saviour. They have died and gone to judgment. Children now living will die also, and go to meet them in the day of judgment. How will they condemn the children of this age, if they do not love the Lord Jesus Christ!

11th. Sinners, when awakened, if they grieve away the Spirit of God, become worse than before, ver. 43-45. They are never as they were before. Their hearts are harder, their consciences are more seared, they have a more bitter hatred of religious men, and they plunge deeper and deeper into sin. Seven devils often dwell where one did, and God gives the man over to blindness of mind and hardness of heart. This shows, also, the great guilt and danger of grieving the Holy Ghost.

12th. We see the love of Christ for his followers, ver. 46-50. Much as he loved his mother, yet he loved his disciples more. He still loves them. He will always love them. His heart is full of affection for them. And though poor, and despised, and unknown to the rich and mighty, yet to Jesus they are dearer than mother, and sisters, and brothers.

CHAPTER XIII.

1, 2. *The sea-side.* This was the Sea of Tiberias. The multitude stood on the shore near to him, so that he could be easily heard. He went into a ship—that is, a boat, and sat down to address them. Few spectacles could be more interesting than a vast crowd on the banks of a smooth and tranquil sea—an emblem of his instructions—and the Son of God addressing them on the great interests of eternity.

3-9. *In parables.* The word *parable* is derived from a Greek word signifying *to compare together*, and denotes a similitude taken from a natural object to illustrate a spiritual or moral subject. It is a narrative of some fictitious or real event, in order to illustrate more clearly some truth that the speaker wished to communicate. In early ages it was much used. Heathen writers, as Æsop, often employed it. In the time of Christ it was in common use. The prophets had used it, and Christ employed it often in teaching his disciples. It is not necessary to suppose that the narratives were strictly true. The main thing—*the inculcation of spiritual truth*—was gained equally, whether it was true or was only a supposed case. Nor was there any dishonesty in this. It was well understood—no person was deceived. The speaker was not *understood* to affirm the thing *literally narrated*, but only to fix the attention more firmly on the moral truth that he presented. The *design* of speaking in parables was the following: 1st. To convey truth in a more interesting manner to the mind, adding to the truth conveyed the beauty of a lovely image or narrative. 2d. To teach spiritual truth so as to arrest the attention of ignorant people, making an appeal to them through the *senses.* 3d. To convey some offensive truth, some pointed personal rebuke, in such a way as to bring it *home* to the conscience. Of this kind was the parable which Nathan delivered to David (2 Sa. xii. 1-7), and many of our Saviour's parables addressed to the Jews. 4th. To *conceal* from one part of his audience truths which he intended others should understand. Thus Christ often, by this means, delivered truths to his disciples in the presence of the Jews, which he well knew the Jews would not understand; truths pertaining to them particularly, and which he was under no obligations to explain to the Jews. See Mar. iv. 33; Mat. xiii. 13-16.

Our Saviour's parables are distinguished above all others for clearness, purity, chasteness, importance of instruction, and simplicity. They are taken mostly from the affairs of common life, and intelligible, therefore, to all men. They contain much of *himself*—his doctrine, life, design in coming, and claims, and are therefore of import-

3 And he spake many things
unto them in parables, saying,
Behold,[b] a sower went forth to
sow:
4 And when he sowed, some
seeds fell by the way-side, and
the fowls came and devoured
them up.
5 Some fell upon stony places,
where they had not much earth;
and forthwith they sprung up,
because they had no deepness of
earth:
6 And when the sun was up,
they were scorched: and because
they had no root, they withered
away.
7 And some fell among thorns,
and the thorns sprung up, and
choked them.
8 But other fell into good
ground, and brought forth fruit,
some an hundred-fold, some sixty-
fold, some thirty-fold.
9 Who[c] hath ears to hear, let
him hear.
10 And the disciples came, and
said unto him, Why speakest thou
unto them in parables?
11 He answered and said unto

b Mar.4.2; Lu.8.5,&c.

c ch.11.15.

---

ance to all men; and they are told in a style of simplicity intelligible to the child, yet instructive to men of every rank and age. In his parables, as in all his instructions, he excelled all men in the purity, importance, and sublimity of his doctrine.

3. *A sower went forth to sow.* The image here is taken from an employment known to all men, and therefore intelligible to all. Nor can there be a more striking illustration of preaching the gospel than placing the seed in the ground, to spring up hereafter and bear fruit. ¶ *Sower.* One who sows or scatters seed—a farmer. It is not improbable that one was near the Saviour when he spoke this parable.

4. *Some* seeds *fell by the way-side.* That is, the hard *path* or headland, which the plough had not touched, and where there was no opportunity for it to sink into the earth.

5. *Stony places.* Where there was little earth, but where it was hard and rocky, so that the roots could not strike down into the earth for sufficient moisture to support the plant. When the sun became hot they of course withered away. They sprang up the sooner because there was little earth to cover them. ¶ *Forthwith.* Immediately. Not that they sprouted and grew any quicker or faster than the others, but they were not so long in reaching the surface. Having little root, they soon withered away.

7. *Among thorns.* That is, in a part of the field where the thorns and shrubs had been imperfectly cleared away and not destroyed. They grew with the grain, crowded it, shaded it, exhausted the earth, and thus choked it.

8. *Into good ground.* The fertile and rich soil. In sowing, by far the largest proportion of seed will fall into the good soil; but Christ did not intend to teach that these proportions would be exactly the same among those who heard the gospel. Parables are designed to teach some *general* truth, and the *circumstances* should not be pressed too much in explaining them. ¶ *An hundred-fold,* &c. That is, a hundred, sixty, or thirty *grains* for each one that was sowed—an increase by no means uncommon. Some grains of wheat will produce twelve or fifteen hundred grains. The usual proportion on a field sown, however, is not more than twenty, fifty, or sixty bushels for one.

9. *Who hath ears,* &c. This is a proverbial expression, implying that it was every man's duty to pay attention to what was spoken, Mat. xi. 15.

10–17. Christ, in these verses, gives a *reason* why he used this manner of instruction. See also Mar. iv. 10–12; Lu. viii. 9, 10.

11. *The mysteries of the kingdom.* The word *mystery,* in the Bible, properly means a thing that is *concealed,* or that *has been concealed.* It does not mean that the thing was *incomprehensible,* or even difficult to be understood. The thing might be *plain* enough if revealed, but it means simply that it *had* not been before made known. Thus the *mysteries of the kingdom* do not mean any doctrines incomprehensible in themselves considered, but simply doctrines about the preaching of the gospel and

them, Because it is given unto
you [d]to know the mysteries of the
kingdom of heaven, but to them
it is not given.
12 For[e] whosoever hath, to him
shall be given, and he shall have
more abundance: but whosoever
hath not, from him shall be taken
away even that he hath.
13 Therefore speak I to them
in parables: because they seeing,
see not; and hearing, they hear
not, neither do they understand.
14 And in them is fulfilled the
prophecy of [f]Esaias, which saith,
[g]By hearing ye shall hear, and
shall not understand; and seeing
ye shall see, and shall not perceive:
15 For this people's heart is
waxed gross, and *their* ears are
[h]dull of hearing, and their eyes
they have closed; lest at any time

d ch.11.25; Mar.4.11; 1 Co.2.10,14; Ep.1.9,18; 3.9; Col.1.26,27; 1 Jn.2.27. *e* ch.25,29; Lu.19.26.
f Is.6.9. *g* Eze.12.2; Jn.12.40; Ac.28.26,27; Ro.11.8; 2 Co.3.14,15. *h* He.5.11.

the establishment of the new kingdom of the Messiah, which *had not* been understood, and which were *as yet* concealed from the great body of the Jews. See Ro. xvi. 25; xi. 25; Ep. iii. 3, 4, 9. Of this nature was the truth that the gospel was to be preached to the Gentiles; that the Jewish polity was to cease; that the Messiah was to die, &c. To the disciples it was given to know these truths. This was important for them, as they were to carry the gospel around the globe. To the others it was not *then* given. They were too gross, too earthly; they had too grovelling conceptions of the Messiah's kingdom to understand these truths, even if communicated to them. They were not to preach the gospel, and hence our Saviour was at particular pains to instruct his apostles in the system which they were to preach. The Pharisees, and Jews generally, were not prepared to receive the system, and would not have believed it, and therefore he purposely employed a kind of teaching which was intended for his apostles only.

12. *Whosoever hath*, &c. This is a proverbial method of speaking. It means that a man who improves what light, grace, and opportunities he has, shall have them increased. From him that improves them not, it is proper that they should be taken away. The Jews had many opportunities of learning the truth, and some light still lingered among them; but they were gross and sensual, and misimproved them, and it was a just judgment that they should be deprived of them. Superior knowledge was given to the disciples of Christ: they improved it, however slowly, and the promise was that it should be greatly increased.

13. *Because they seeing, see not.* Mark (iv. 12) and Luke (viii. 10) say, "That seeing, they may not see," &c.; but there is no difference. Matthew simply states the *fact*, that though they saw the *natural* meaning of the story—though they literally understood the parable—yet they did not understand its *spiritual* signification. Mark and Luke do not state the *fact*, but affirm that he spoke with this *intention*—implying that such *was* the result. Nor was there any dishonesty in this, or any unfair disguise. He had truths to state which he wished his *disciples particularly* to understand. They were of great importance to their ministry. Had he clearly and fully stated them to the Jews, they would have taken his life long before they did. He therefore chose to state the doctrines so that if their *hearts* had been right, and if they had not been malignant and blind, *they might have understood them.* His doctrines he stated in the best possible way, and it was not *his* fault if they did not understand him. By little and little, in this way, he prepared many even of the Jews to receive the truth, by the only possible way of ever gaining access to their minds. It was, moreover, entirely proper and right to impart instruction to his disciples which he did not *intend* for others.

14. *And in them is fulfilled*, &c. This place is quoted substantially from Is. vi. 9, 10. It was literally fulfilled in the time of Isaiah. In the time of Christ the people had the same character. Like them, they closed their eyes upon the truth, and rejected the divine teaching. The words of Isaiah were therefore *as well fitted* to express the character of the people in the time of Christ as in that of the prophet. In this sense they were *fulfilled*, or *filled up;* that is, *a case occurred that corresponded to their*

they should see with *their* eyes, and hear with *their* ears, and should understand with *their* heart, and should be converted, and I should heal them.

16 But[i] blessed *are* your eyes, for they see; and your ears, for they hear.

17 For verily I say unto you, That[k] many prophets and righteous *men* have desired to see *those things* which ye see, and have not seen *them;* and to hear *those things* which ye hear, and have not heard *them.*

18 Hear[l] ye therefore the parable of the sower.

19 When any one heareth [m]the word of the kingdom, and understandeth *it* not, then cometh [n]the wicked *one*, and catcheth away that which was sown in his heart. This is he which received seed by the way-side.

20 But he that received the seed into stony places, the same

i ch.16.17; Lu.10.23,24; Jn.20.29; 2 Co.4.6. *k* Ep.3.5,6; He.11.13; 1 Pe.1.10,11.

l Mar.4.14,&c.; Lu.8.11,&c. *m* ch.4.23. *n* 1 Jn.2.13,14; 3.12.

---

meaning. See Notes on Mat. i. 22. It is not by any means intended that Isaiah, when he spoke these words, had any reference to the time of Christ. The meaning in both places is, that the people were so gross, sensual, and prejudiced, that they *would* not see the truth, or understand anything that was contrary to their grovelling opinions and sensual desires; a case by no means uncommon in the world. See the passage more fully explained in my Notes on Is. vi. ¶ *Waxed gross.* Literally, *has become fat.* This language is commonly applied to *the body*, but is also used to denote one who is stupid and foolish in mind. Here it means that the people were so sensual and corrupt that they did not see or understand the pure spiritual principles of the gospel. ¶ *Lest they should see*, &c. Lest they should see their lost condition as sinners, and turn and live. The reason given here why they did not hear and understand the gospel is, that their *heart* was *wrong.* They *would* not attend to the things that belonged to their peace. ¶ *I should heal them.* Should pardon, sanctify, and save them. Sin is often represented as a disease, and the pardon and recovery of the soul from sin as *healing.*

16. *Blessed* are *your eyes*, &c. That is, you are happy that you are permitted to see *truth* which they *will* not see. You are permitted to understand the spiritual meaning of the parables, and in some degree the plan of salvation.

17. *Many prophets and righteous* men, &c. They wished to see the times of the Messiah. They looked to it as a time when the hopes of the world would be fulfilled, and when the righteous would be happy, Jn. viii. 56. "Abraham rejoiced to see my day, and he saw it and was glad." Comp. also 1 Pe. i. 10–12; He. xi. 13. So Isaiah and the prophets looked forward to the coming of the Messiah as the consummation of their wishes and the end of the prophecies, Re. xix. 10. The object always dearest to the hearts of all righteous men is to witness the coming and advancement of the kingdom of Christ. Comp. Re. xxii. 20.

18–23. See also Mar. iv. 13–20; Lu. viii. 11–15. *Hear ye, therefore, the parable of the sower.* That is, hear the *explanation* or the *spiritual meaning* of the narrative given before. Mark adds (iv. 13), "Know ye not this parable? And how, then, shall ye know all parables?" By which it seems that the Saviour regarded this as one of the simplest and plainest of the parables, and gave an explanation of it that they might understand the general principles of interpreting others.

19. *When any one heareth*, &c. The seed represents the word of God communicated in any manner to the minds of men—by the Scriptures, by preaching, by acts of Providence, or by the direct influences of the Holy Spirit. ¶ *Then cometh the wicked* one. That is, Satan (Mar. iv. 15), or the devil (Lu. viii. 12)—the one eminently *wicked*, the accuser, the tempter. He is represented by the fowls that came and picked up the seed by the way-side. The gospel is preached to men hardened in sin. It makes no impression. It lies like seed on the *hard path;* it is easily taken away, and never suffered to take root.

20, 21. *But he that received the seed into stony places.* Jesus explains this as de-

is he that heareth the word, and
anon [o]with joy receiveth it:
21 Yet hath he not root in himself, but dureth for a while; for when tribulation or persecution ariseth because of the word, by and by [p]he is offended.
22 He also that received seed
among the thorns is he that heareth the word; and the [q]care of this world and the [r]deceitfulness of riches choke the word, and he becometh unfruitful.
23 But he that received seed into the good ground is he that heareth the word, and understandeth

o Is.58.2; Eze.33.31,32; Jn.5.35; Ga.4.15. *p* ch.24.10; 26.31; 2 Ti.4.16.
q Lu.14.16-24. *r* Mar.10.23; 1 Ti.6.9; 2 Ti.4.10.

noting those who hear the gospel; who are caught with it as something new or pleasing; who profess to be greatly delighted with it, and who are full of zeal for it. Yet they have no root in themselves. They are not true Christians. Their hearts are not changed. They have not seen their guilt and danger, and the true excellency of Christ. They are not *really* attached to the gospel; and when they are tried and persecution comes, they *fall*—as the rootless grain withers before the scorching rays of the noonday sun. ¶ *Anon. Quickly*, or *readily*. ¶ *With joy receiveth it.* They are under deep distress for sin; they are apprehensive of danger; they hear the offer of mercy, and they *seem* to themselves to embrace the gospel. It offers them peace, pardon, salvation, and religion assumes for a time a lovely aspect. They *imagine* that they are pardoned, and they have a temporary peace and joy. Their anxieties subside. Their fears are gone. They are for a time happy. *The mere subsiding of anxious feeling from any cause will make the mind for a time happy.* They have only to imagine, therefore, that their sins are forgiven, to produce a certain kind of peace and joy. But there is no ground of permanent joy, as there is in true pardon, and soon their joy subsides, and all evidence of piety disappears. There is no strength of *principle* to resist temptation; there is no real love of the Saviour; and in times of trial and persecution they show that they have no true religion, and fall away. ¶ *By and by.* Mark, *Immediately.* That is, it soon occurs, or this is an effect which may be expected *soon* to follow. ¶ *Is offended.* Stumbles or falls, for this is the meaning of the word *offend* in the New Testament. See Notes on ch. v. 29. Persecution and trial are placed in his path, and he falls as he would over a *stumbling-block*. He has no strength of principle—no real confidence in God—no true religion. Mere excited animal feeling is all that he ever had, and that is not sufficient to sustain him when the trial comes.

22. *He also that received seed among the thorns.* These represent the cares, the anxieties, and the deceitful lure of riches, or the way in which a *desire* to be rich deceives men. They take the time and attention. They do not leave opportunity to examine the state of the soul. Besides, riches allure, and promise what they do not yield. They promise to make us happy; but, when gained, they do not do it. The soul is not satisfied. There is the same desire to possess more wealth. And to this there is no end *but death.* In doing it there is every temptation to be dishonest, to cheat, to take advantage of others, to oppress others, and to wring their hard earnings from the poor. Every evil passion is therefore cherished by the love of gain; and it is no wonder that the word is choked, and every good feeling destroyed, by this "execrable love of gold." See Notes on 1 Ti. vi. 7-11. How many, O how many, thus foolishly drown themselves in destruction and perdition! How many more *might* reach heaven, if it were not for this deep-seated love of that which fills the mind with care, deceives the soul, and finally leaves it naked, and guilty, and lost!

23. *Into good ground.* Those whose hearts are prepared by grace to receive it honestly, and to give it full opportunity to grow. In a rich and mellow soil—in a heart that submits itself to the full influence of truth, unchecked by cares and anxieties; under the showers and summer suns of divine grace; with the heart spread open, like a broad, luxuriant field, to the rays of the morning and to evening dews, the gospel takes deep root and grows; it has full room, and then and there only shows *what it is.*

24-30. *The kingdom of heaven is*

it; which also [s]beareth fruit, and bringeth forth, some an hundredfold, some sixty, some thirty.
24 Another[t] parable put he forth unto them, saying, The kingdom of heaven is likened unto a man
which sowed [u]good seed in his field:
25 But while men slept, his enemy came and sowed tares among the wheat, and went his way.

s Jn.15.5. *t* Is.28.10,13. *u* 1 Pe.1.23.

---

likened, &c. That is, the *gospel resembles*. The kingdom of heaven (see Notes on Mat. iii. 2) means here the effect of the gospel by its being preached. The meaning of this parable is plain. The field represents the *world*, in which the gospel is preached. The *good seed*, the truths preached by Christ and his apostles.

25. *While men slept, his enemy came*, &c. That is, *in the night*, when it could be done without being seen, an enemy came and scattered bad seed on the new-ploughed field, perhaps before the good seed had been harrowed in. Satan thus sows false doctrine in darkness. In the very place where the truth is preached, and while the hearts of people are open to receive it, by false but plausible teachers he takes care to inculcate false sentiments. Often it is one of his arts, in a revival of religion, to spread secretly dangerous notions of piety. Multitudes are persuaded that they are Christians who are deceived. They are awakened, convicted, and alarmed. They take this for conversion. Or they find their burden gone; they fancy that they hear a voice; or a text of Scripture is *brought* to them, saying that their sins are forgiven; or they *see* Christ hanging on the cross in a vision; or they dream that their sins are pardoned, and they suppose they are Christians. But they are deceived. None of these things are any conclusive evidence of piety. All these *may* exist, and still there be no true love to God or Christ, and no real hatred of sin and change of heart. An enemy may do it to deceive them, and to bring dishonour on religion. ¶ *Sowed tares.* By *tares* is probably meant a degenerate kind of wheat, or the darnel-grass growing in Palestine. In its growth and form it has a strong resemblance to genuine wheat; but it either produces no grain, or that of a very inferior and hurtful kind. Probably it comes near to what we mean by *chess*. It was extremely difficult to separate it from the genuine wheat, on account of its similarity while growing. "The tare abounds all over the East, and is a great nuisance to the farmer. It resembles the American *cheat* [*chess*], but the *head* does not droop like cheat, nor does it branch out like oats. The grain, also, is smaller, and is arranged along the upper part of the stalk, which stands perfectly erect. The *taste* is bitter, and when eaten separately, or even when diffused in ordinary bread, it causes dizziness, and often acts as a violent emetic. Barn-door fowls also become dizzy from eating it. In short, it is a strong soporific poison, and must be carefully winnowed, and picked out of the wheat grain by grain, before grinding, or the flour is not healthy. Even the farmers, who in this country generally *weed* their fields, do not attempt to separate the one from the other. They would not only mistake good grain for them, but very commonly the roots of the two are so intertwined that it is impossible to separate them without plucking up both. Both, therefore, must be left to *grow together* until the time of harvest."—(Thomson) *The Land and the Book*, vol. ii. p. 111, 112. Thus *tares* aptly represented hypocrites in the church. Strongly resembling Christians in their experience, and, in some respects, their lives, it is impossible to distinguish them from genuine Christians, nor can they be separated until it is done by the Great Searcher of hearts at the day of judgment. An enemy—the devil—hath done it. And nowhere has he shown profounder cunning, or done more to adulterate the purity of the gospel. ¶ *And went his way.* There is something very expressive in this. He knew the soil; he knew how the seed would take root and grow. He had only to sow the seed and let it alone. So Satan knows the soil in which he sows his doctrine. He knows that in the human heart it will take deep and rapid root. It needs but little culture. Grace needs constant attendance and care. Error, and sin, and hypocrisy are the native products of the human heart, and, when left alone, start up with deadly luxuriancy.

26 But when the blade was
sprung up, and brought forth fruit,
then appeared the tares also.
27 So the servants of the householder came and said unto him,
Sir, didst not thou sow good seed
in thy field? from whence, then,
hath it tares?
28 He said unto them, An enemy
hath done this. The servants said
unto him, Wilt thou, then, that we
go and gather them up?
29 But he said, Nay; lest while
ye gather up the tares, ye root up
also the wheat with them.
30 Let both grow together until
the harvest: and in [v]the time of
harvest I will say to the reapers,
Gather ye together first the tares,
and bind them in bundles [w]to
burn them; but [x]gather the wheat
into my barn.
31 Another parable put he forth
unto them, saying, The kingdom
of heaven is like to [y]a grain of
mustard-seed, which a man took
and sowed in his field:
32 Which indeed is the least of
all seeds; but when it is grown,
it is the greatest among herbs,

v 1 Ti.5.24. *w* Mal.4.1. *x* Lu.3.17. *y* Mar.4.30.

26. *Then appeared the tares also.* That is, then the tares were *first discovered.* They had grown with the wheat, but were so much like it as not to be noticed till the wheat began to ripen. So true piety and false hopes are not known by professions, by "blades," and leaves, and flowers, but *by the fruit.*

29. *Ye root up also the wheat.* They so much resembled the true wheat that even then it would be difficult to separate them. By gathering them, they would tread down the wheat, loosen and disturb the earth, and greatly injure the crop. In the harvest it could be done without injury.

30. *Let both grow together.* They would not spoil the true wheat, and in time of harvest it would be easy to separate them. Our Saviour teaches us here—1st. That hypocrites and deceived persons must be expected in the church. 2d. That this is the work of the enemy of man. They are not the work of Christianity any more than traitors are of patriotism, or counterfeiters are of the proper effect of legislating about money. They belong to the world, and hypocrisy is only one form of sin. The Christian religion never *made* a hypocrite, nor is there a hypocrite on the earth whose principles and practice it does not condemn. 3d. That all hope of removing them entirely would be vain. 4th. That an *attempt* to remove them altogether would injure real Christianity, by causing excitements, discord, and hard feelings even among Christians. 5th. That Christ will himself separate them at the proper time. There is no doubt that it is the duty of the church to keep itself pure, and to cut off gross and manifest offenders, 1 Co. v. 4, 5; but the Saviour refers here to those who may be *suspected* of hypocrisy, but against whom it cannot be proved; to those who so successfully imitate Christians as to make it difficult or impossible for man to distinguish them.

31, 32. See also Mar. iv. 30–32. *The kingdom of heaven.* See Notes on Mat. iii. 2. It means here either piety in a renewed heart or the church. In either case the commencement is small. In the heart it is at first feeble, easily injured, and much exposed. In the church there were few at first, ignorant, unknown, and unhonoured; yet soon it was to spread through the world. ¶ *Grain of mustard-seed.* The plant here described was very different from that which is known among us. It was several years before it bore fruit and became properly a tree. Mustard, with us, is an annual plant: it is always small, and is properly an herb. The Hebrew writers speak of the mustard-tree as one on which they could *climb,* as on a fig-tree. Its size was much owing to the climate. All plants of that nature grow much larger in a warm climate, like that of Palestine, than in colder regions. The seeds of this tree were remarkably small, so that they, with the great size of the plant, were an apt illustration of the progress of the church and of the nature of faith, Mat. xvii. 20. "I have seen," says Dr. Thomson, "this plant on the rich plain of Akkar as tall as the horse and his rider. It has occurred to me on former visits that

and [z]becometh a tree, so that the
birds of the air come and lodge in
the branches thereof.
33 Another parable spake he
unto them: The kingdom of
heaven is like unto leaven, which
a woman took, and hid in three
measures[1] of meal, till the whole
was leavened.
34 All these things spake Jesus
unto the multitude [a]in parables;
and without a parable spake he
not unto them;

z Eze.17.23.
1 The Greek word signifies *a measure about a peck and a half, wanting a little more than a pint.*
a Mar.4.33.

35 That it might be fulfilled
which was spoken by the prophet,
saying, [b]I will open my mouth in
parables; I will utter things which
have been [c]kept secret from the
foundation of the world.
36 Then Jesus sent the multitude away, and went into the
house; and his disciples came
unto him, saying, Declare unto
us the parable of the tares of the
field.
37 He answered and said unto

b Ps.78.2. *c* Lu.10.14; Ro.16.25,26; Col.1.26.

the mustard-tree of the parable probably grew at this spot, or possibly at Tabiga, near Capernaum, for the water in both is somewhat similar, and so are the vegetable productions. To furnish an adequate basis for the proverb, it is necessary to suppose that a variety of it was cultivated in the time of our Saviour, which grew to an enormous size, and shot forth large branches, so that the fowls of the air could lodge in the branches of it. It may have been perennial, and have grown to a considerable tree; and there are traditions in the country of such so large that a man could climb into them; and after having seen *red pepper* bushes grow on year after year, into tall shrubs, and the *castor-bean* line the brooks about Damascus like the willows and the poplars, I can readily credit the existence of mustard-trees large enough to meet all the demands of our Lord's parable." — *The Land and the Book*, vol. ii. p. 101.

Young converts often suppose they have much religion. It is not so. They are, indeed, in a new world. Their hearts glow with new affections. They have an elevation, an ecstasy of emotion, which they may not have afterward—like a blind man suddenly restored to sight. The sensation is new and peculiarly vivid, yet little is seen distinctly. His impressions are indeed more vivid and cheering than those of him who has long seen and to whom objects are familiar. In a little time, too, the young convert will see more distinctly, will judge more intelligently, will love more strongly, though not with so much *new emotion*, and will be prepared to make more sacrifices for the cause of Christ.

33. *The kingdom of heaven.* The meaning here is the same as in the last parable; perhaps, however, intending to denote more properly the secret and hidden nature of piety in the soul. The other parable declared the *fact* that the gospel would greatly spread, and that piety in the heart would greatly increase. This states the *way* or *mode* in which it would be done. It is secret, silent, steady; pervading all the faculties of the soul and all the kingdoms of the world, as leaven, or yeast, though hidden in the flour, and though deposited only in one place, works silently till *all* the mass is brought under its influence. ¶ *Three measures.* These were small measures (see the margin); but the particular amount is of no consequence to the story; nor is anything to be inferred from the fact that *three* are mentioned. That number is mentioned as a circumstance giving interest to the parable, but designed to convey no spiritual instruction. The *measure* mentioned here probably contained about a peck and a half.

34, 35. *That it might be fulfilled.* This is taken from Ps. lxxviii. 2, 3. The *sense*, and not the very words of the Psalm, are given. Christ taught, as did that prophet—Asaph—in parables. The words of Asaph described the manner in which Christ taught, and in this sense it could be said that they were fulfilled. See Notes on Mat. i. 22, 23.

36–43. *Declare unto us.* That is, explain the meaning of the parable. This was done in so plain a manner as to render comment unnecessary. The Son of man, the Lord Jesus, sows the good seed — that is, preaches the gospel.

them, He that soweth the good
seed is the Son of man:
38 The field is [d]the world: the
good seed are [e]the children of the
kingdom; but the tares are [f]the
children of the wicked *one*.
39 The enemy that sowed them
is the devil: [g]the harvest is the
end of the world; and [h]the reapers
are the angels.
40 As, therefore, [i]the tares are
gathered and burned in the fire,
so shall it be in the end of this
world.
41 The Son of man shall send
forth his angels, and they shall
gather out of his kingdom all
[2]things that offend, [k]and them
which do iniquity;
42 And[l] shall cast them into a
furnace of fire: [m]there shall be
wailing and gnashing of teeth.
43 Then shall the righteous
[n]shine forth as the sun, in the
kingdom of their Father. Who
hath ears to hear, let him hear.
44 Again, the kingdom of
heaven is like unto [o]treasure
hid in a field; the which when
a man hath found, he hideth,

d Ro.10.18; Col.1.6. *e* 1 Pe.1.23. *f* Jn.8.44; Ac.13.10; 1 Jn.3.8. *g* Joel 3.13; Re.14.15. *h* Re.14.15-19. *i* ver.30.

2 or, *scandals*. *k* Lu.13.27. *l* ch.3.12; Re.19.20; 20.10. *m* ver.50; ch.8.12. *n* Da.12.3; 1 Co.15.49. *o* Pr.2.4,5.

This he did personally, and does now by his ministers, his providence, and his Spirit, by all the means of conveying *truth* to the mind. This seed was, by various means, to be carried over all the world. It was to be confined to no particular nation or people. The good seed was the children of the kingdom; that is, of the kingdom of God, or Christians. For these the Saviour toiled and died. They are the fruit of his labours. Yet amid them were wicked men; and all hypocrites and unbelievers in the church are the work of Satan. Yet they must remain together till the end, when they shall be separated, and the righteous saved and the wicked lost. The one shall shine clear as the sun, the other be cast into a furnace of fire—a most expressive image of suffering. We have no idea of more acute suffering than to be thrown into the fire, and to have our bodies made capable of bearing the burning heat, and living on in this burning heat for ever and for ever. It is not certain that our Saviour meant to teach here that hell is made up of *material* fire; but it *is* certain that he meant to teach that this would be a proper *representation* of the sufferings of the lost. We may be farther assured that the Redeemer would not deceive us, or use words to torment and tantalize us. He would not talk of hell-fire which had no existence, nor would the Saviour of men hold out frightful images merely to terrify mankind. If *he* has spoken of hell, then there *is* a hell. If *he* meant to say that the wicked shall suffer, then they *will* suffer. If he did not mean to deceive mankind, then there *is* a hell, and then the wicked *will* be punished. The impenitent, therefore, should be alarmed. And the righteous, however much wickedness they may see, and however many hypocrites there may be in the church, should be cheered with the prospect that soon the just will be separated from the unjust, and that *they* shall shine as the sun in the kingdom of their Father.

44. *The kingdom of heaven.* The gospel. The new dispensation. The offer of eternal life. See Notes on Mat. iii. 2. The Saviour in this parable compares that kingdom to treasure hid in a field; that is, to money concealed; or more likely to a mine of silver or gold that was unknown to the owner of the field. ¶ *He hideth.* That is, he conceals the fact that he has found it; he does not tell of it. With a view of obtaining this, Jesus says that a man would go and sell his property and buy the field. The conduct of the man would be *dishonest*. It would be his duty to inform the owner of the field of the discovery. He would be really endeavouring to gain property belonging to another at far less than its real value, and the principle of real integrity would require him to inform the owner of the discovery. But Christ does not intend to vindicate his conduct. He merely states the way in which men do *actually* manage to obtain wealth. He states a case where a man *would* actually *sacrifice his property*, and practise diligence and watchfulness to obtain the wealth which

and for joy thereof goeth and
selleth[p] all that he hath, and
buyeth[q] that field.
45 Again, the kingdom of
heaven is like unto a merchantman seeking goodly pearls;
46 Who, when he had found
one [r]pearl of great price, went
and sold all that he had, and
bought it.
47 Again, the kingdom of
heaven is like unto a net, that
was cast into the sea, and [s]gath-
ered of every kind:
48 Which, when it was full,
they drew to shore, and sat down,
and gathered the good into vessels,
but cast the bad away.
49 So shall it be at the end of
the world: the angels shall come
forth, and [t]sever the wicked from
among the just;
50 And[u] shall cast them into
the furnace of fire: there shall be
wailing and gnashing of teeth.
51 Jesus saith unto them, Have
ye understood all these things?
They say unto him, Yea, Lord.
52 Then said he unto them,
Therefore every scribe *which is*

p Phi.3.7,8. *q* Is.55.1; Re.3.18. *r* Pr.3.14,15; 8.11. *s* ch.22.10.

t ch.25.32. *u* ver.42.

he had discovered. The *point* of the parable lies in his *earnestness*, his anxiety, his care, and his actually obtaining it. The gospel is more valuable than such a treasure, Ps. xix. 10; Pr. iii. 13–15. From most men it is hid. When a man sees it and hears it, it is his duty to sacrifice all that hinders his obtaining it, and to seek it with the earnestness with which other men seek for gold. The truth often lies buried; it is like rich veins of ore in the sacred Scriptures; it must be searched out with diligence, and its discovery will repay a man for all his sacrifices, Lu. xiv. 33; Phi. iii. 8.

45, 46. *The kingdom of heaven is like unto a merchantman.* The meaning is, that the proper seeking for salvation, or the proper conduct in reference to religion, is like the conduct of a *merchantman.* In his searches he found *one* pearl of great value, and sold all his possessions to obtain it. So, says the Saviour, men seeking for happiness and finding the gospel—the pearl of great price—should be willing to sacrifice all other things for this. Pearls are precious stones found in the shells of oysters, chiefly in the East Indies. See Notes on Mat. vii. 6. They are valuable on account of their beauty and because they are rare. The value of them is greatly increased by their size. The meaning of this parable is nearly the same as the other. It is designed to represent the gospel as of more value than all other things, and to impress on us the duty of sacrificing *all* that we possess in order to obtain it.

47–50. *The kingdom of heaven is like unto a net,* &c. This parable does not differ in meaning from that of the tares. The gospel is compared to a net dragging along on the bottom of a lake, and collecting all—good and bad. The gospel may be expected to do the same; but in the end of the world, when the net *is drawn in,* the bad will be separated from the good; the one will be cast away, and the other saved. Our Saviour never fails to keep before our minds the great truth that there is to be a day of judgment, and that there will be a separation of the good and the evil. He came to preach salvation; and it is a remarkable fact, also, that the most fearful accounts of hell and of the sufferings of the damned, in the Scriptures, are from his lips. How does this agree with the representations of those who say that all will be saved?

51–53. Jesus kindly asked them whether they had understood these things. If not, he was still willing to teach them. He enjoined on them their duty to make a proper use of this knowledge by speaking another parable. ¶ *Every scribe* which is *instructed unto the kingdom of heaven.* That is, every man that is acquainted with the gospel or with the truth. As the disciples had said that *they* had understood the truth, he says that it should not be unemployed. They should bring it forth in due time, like a householder bringing out of his treasury, or place of deposit, what had been laid up there at any time, as it was needed. ¶ *Bringeth forth.* As occasion demands; as sickness, or calamity, or the wants of his family, or the poor require. ¶ *Treasure.* The word *treasure* here means a place of

instructed unto the kingdom of heaven is like unto a man that *is* an householder, which [v]bringeth forth out of his treasure [w]*things* new and old.

53 And it came to pass, *that* when Jesus had finished these parables, he departed thence.

54 And[x] when he was come into his own country, he taught them in their synagogue, insomuch that they were astonished, and said, Whence hath this *man* this wisdom, and these mighty works?

55 Is not this the carpenter's son? is not his mother called Mary? and his brethren, James, and Joses, and Simon, and Judas?

56 And his sisters, are they not all with us? Whence, then, hath this *man* all these things?

v Pr.10.21; 15.7; 18.4. w Ca.7.13.
x Mar.6.1,&c.; Lu.4.16,&c.

---

deposit, not for money merely, but for anything necessary for the comfort of a family. It is the same as *treasury* or a place of *deposit.* ¶ *New and old.* Things lately acquired, or things that had been laid up for a long time. *So,* said Christ, you, my disciples, are to be. The truth, new or old, which you have gained, keep it not laid up and hid, but bring it forth, in due season and on proper occasions, to benefit others. Every preacher should be properly instructed. Christ for three years gave instructions to the apostles; and they who preach should be able to understand the gospel, to defend it, and to communicate it to others. Human learning alone is indeed of no value to a minister; but all learning that will enable a man better to understand the Bible and communicate its truths *is* valuable, and should, if possible, be gained. A minister should be like the father of a family—distributing to the church as it needs; and out of his treasures bringing forth truth to confirm the feeble, to enlighten the ignorant, and to recover and guide those who are in danger of straying away.

54. *Into his own country.* That is, into Nazareth. Mark, who has also recorded this (ch. vi. 1-6), says that it took place on the Sabbath. It was common for our Saviour to speak in the synagogues. Any Jew had a right to address the people, if called on by the minister; and our Saviour often availed himself of the right to instruct the people and declare his doctrines. See Mat. iv. 23.

55, 56. *Is not this the carpenter's son?* Mark says, "Is not this the *carpenter*, the son of Mary?" Both these expressions would probably be used in the course of the conversation, and Matthew has recorded one and Mark the other. The expression recorded by Mark is a strong, perhaps decisive proof that he had himself worked at the business till he was thirty years of age. The people in the neighbourhood would understand well the nature of his early employments. It is therefore almost certain that this had been his manner of life. A useful employment is always honourable. Idleness is the parent of mischief. Our Saviour, therefore, spent the greatest part of his life in honest, useful industry. Till the age of thirty he did not choose to enter on his great work; and it was proper before that time that he should set an example to the world of honourable though humble industry. Life is not wasted in such employments. They are appointed as the lot of man; and in the faithful discharge of duties in the relations of life, though obscure; in honest industry, however humble; in patient labour, if connected with a life of religion, we may be sure that God will approve our conduct. It was, moreover, the custom of the Jews—even those of wealth and learning—to train all their children to some *trade* or manual occupation. Thus Paul was a tent-maker. Comp. Ac. xviii. 3.

This was, on the part of the Saviour, an example of great condescension and humility. It staggers the faith of many that the Son of God should labour in an occupation so obscure and lowly. The infidel sneers at the idea that *He that made the worlds* should live thirty years in humble life as a poor and unknown mechanic. Yet the same infidel will loudly praise Peter the Great of Russia because he laid aside his imperial dignity and entered the British service as a *ship-carpenter*, that he might learn the art of building a navy. Was the purpose of *Peter* of more importance

57 And they [y]were offended in
him. But Jesus said unto them,
A prophet is not without honour
save in his own country and in his
own house.
58 And he did not many mighty
works there, because of their unbelief.

y Is.49.7; 53.3; Jn.6.42.

CHAPTER XIV.

AT that time [a]Herod the tetrarch
heard of the fame of Jesus;
2 And said unto his servants,

a Mar.6.14; Lu.9.7,&c.

than that of the Son of God? If Peter, the heir to the throne of the Czars, might leave his elevated rank and descend to a humble employment, and secure by it the applause of the world, why might not the King of kings evince a similar character for an infinitely higher object? ¶ *His brethren, James,* &c. The fair interpretation of this passage is, that these were the sons and daughters of Joseph and Mary. The people in the neighbourhood thought so, and spoke of them as such.

57. *And they were offended in him.* That is, they took offence at his humble birth, and at the indigent circumstances of his family. They were too proud to be taught by one who, in family connections, they took to be their equal or inferior. Men always look with envy on those of their own rank who advance pretensions to uncommon wisdom or superior power. ¶ *A prophet is not without honour,* &c. This seems to be a proverbial expression. Jesus advances it as a *general* truth. There *might be* some exceptions to it, but *he* was not an exception. Everywhere else he had been more honoured than at home. There they knew his family. They had seen his humble life. They had been his companions. They were envious of his wisdom, and were too proud to be taught by him. A case remarkably similar to this occurs in the history of the discovery of America. Columbus, a native of Genoa, had by patient study conceived the idea that there was a vast continent which might be reached by sailing to the west. Of this his countrymen had no belief. Learned men had long studied the science of geography, and they had never imagined that such a continent could exist; and they were indignant that *he*, an obscure man, should suppose that he "possessed wisdom superior to all the rest of mankind united." It was accordingly a fact that he was obliged to seek for patrons of his undertaking out of his own country; that there he received his first honours; and that to other kingdoms the discoveries of the obscure Genoese gave their chief wealth and highest splendour.

58. *Did not many mighty works.* Miracles. This implies that he performed *some* miracles. Mark tells us what they were: "He laid his hands upon a few sick folk and healed them," Mar. vi. 5. ¶ *Because of their unbelief.* That is, it would have been useless to the great purposes of his mission to have worked miracles there. We are not to suppose that his *power* was limited by the belief or unbelief of men; but they were so *prejudiced*, so set against him, that they were not in a condition to *judge of evidence* and to be convinced. They would have charged it to derangement, or sorcery, or the agency of the devil. Comp. Jn. x. 20. It would have been of no use, therefore, in proving *to them* that he was from God, to have worked miracles. He did, therefore, only those things which were the proper work of benevolence, and which could not easily be charged on the devil. He gave *sufficient* proof of his mission, and left them in their chosen unbelief without excuse. It is also true, in spiritual things, that the unbelief of a people prevents the influences of the Holy Spirit from being sent down to bless them. God requires faith. He hears only the prayers of faith. And when there is little true belief, and prayer is cold and formal, there the people sleep in spiritual death and are unblessed.

CHAPTER XIV.

1. *Herod the tetrarch.* See also Mar. vi. 14–16; Lu. ix. 7–9. This was a son of Herod the Great. Herod the Great died probably in the first year after the birth of Christ, and left his kingdom to his three sons, of whom this *Herod Antipas* was one. He ruled over Galilee and Perea. See Notes on Mat. ii. 15. The title *tetrarch* literally denotes one who rules over a *fourth* part of any country. It came, however, to signify the governor or ruler of any province subject to the Roman emperor.—Robinson, *Lex.*

This is John the Baptist: he is risen from the dead; and therefore mighty works [1]do show forth themselves in him.

3 For Herod had laid hold on John, and bound him, and put *him* in prison for Herodias' sake, his brother Philip's wife.

4 For John said unto him, It[b] is not lawful for thee to have her.

5 And when he would have put him to death, he feared the multitude, because [c]they counted him as a prophet.

6 But when Herod's birthday was kept, the daughter of Herodias danced [2]before them, and pleased Herod.

7 Whereupon he promised with an oath to give her whatsoever she would ask.

1 or, *are wrought by him.* b Le.18.16; 20.21.

c ch.21.26; Lu.20.6. 2 *in the midst.*

¶ *Heard of the fame of Jesus.* Jesus had been a considerable time engaged in the work of the ministry, and it may seem remarkable that he had not before heard of him. Herod might, however, have been absent on some expedition to a remote part of the country. It is to be remembered, also, that he was a man of much dissoluteness of morals, and that he paid little attention to the affairs of the people. He might have *heard* of Jesus before, but it had not arrested his attention. He did not think it a matter worthy of much regard.

2. *This is John the Baptist.* Herod feared John. His conscience smote him for his crimes. He remembered that he had wickedly put him to death. He knew him to be a distinguished prophet; and he concluded that no other one was capable of working such miracles but he who had been so eminent a servant of God in his life, and who, he supposed, had again risen from the dead and entered the dominions of his murderer. The alarm in his court, it seems, was general. Herod's *conscience* told him that this was John. Others thought that it might be the expected Elijah or one of the old prophets, Mar. vi. 15.

3–5. *For Herod had laid hold on John,* &c. See Mar. vi. 17–20; Lu. iii. 19, 20. This Herodias was a granddaughter of Herod the Great. She was first married to Herod Philip, by whom she had a daughter, Salome, probably the one that danced and pleased Herod. Josephus says that this marriage of Herod Antipas with Herodias took place while he was on a journey to Rome. He stopped at his brother's; fell in love with his wife; agreed to put away his own wife, the daughter of Aretas, King of Petræa; and Herodias agreed to leave her own husband and live with him. They were living, therefore, in adultery; and John, in faithfulness, though at the risk of his life, had reproved them for their crimes. Herod was guilty of two crimes in this act: 1st. Of *adultery*, as she was the wife of another man. 2d. Of *incest*, as she was a near relation, and such marriages were expressly forbidden, Le. xviii. 16.

6–13. See also Mar. vi. 21–29. *But when Herod's birthday was come.* Kings were accustomed to observe the day of their birth with much pomp, and commonly, also, by giving a *feast* to their principal nobility. See Ge. xl. 20. Mark adds that this birthday was kept by making a supper to his "lords, high captains, and chief estates in Galilee;" that is, to the chief men in office. *High captains* means, in the original, commanders of *thousands*, or of a division of a thousand men. ¶ *The daughter of Herodias;* that is, *Salome*, her daughter by her former husband. This was a violation of all the rules of modesty and propriety. One great principle of all eastern nations is to keep their females from public view. For this purpose they are confined in a particular part of the house, called the *harem*. See Notes on Mat. ix. 1–8. If they appear in public, it is always with a veil, so closely drawn that their faces cannot be seen. No modest woman would have appeared in this manner before the court, and it is probable, therefore, that she partook of the dissolute principles of her mother. It is also probable that the *dance* was one well known in Greece—the lascivious and wanton dance of the *Ionics*.

7. *He promised with an oath.* This was a foolish and wicked oath. To please a wanton girl, the monarch called the eternal God to witness his willingness to give her half his kingdom,

8 And she, being before instructed of her mother, said, [d]Give
me here John Baptist's head in
a charger.
9 And[e] the king was sorry:
nevertheless, [f]for the oath's sake,
and them which sat with him
at meat, he commanded *it* to be
given *her*.
10 And he sent and beheaded
John in the prison.
11 And his head was brought

d Pr.29.10. *e* Ju.11.31,35; Da.6.14-16. *f* Ju.21.1; 1 Sa.14.28; 25.22; Ec.5.2.

Mar. vi. 23. It seems, also, that he was willing to shed the holiest blood it contained. An oath like this it was not lawful to make, and it should have been broken. See ver. 9.

8. *Being before instructed of her mother.* Not before she danced, but afterward, and before she made the request of Herod. See Mar. vi. 24. The only *appearance* of what was right in the whole transaction was her *honouring* her mother by consulting her, but in this she only intended to accomplish the purposes of wickedness more effectually. ¶ *In a charger.* The original word means a large *platter* on which food is placed. We should have supposed that she would have been struck with abhorrence at such a direction from her mother; but she seems to have been gratified. John, by his faithfulness, had offended the whole family, and here was ample opportunity for an adulterous mother and her dissolute child to gratify their resentment. It was customary for princes to require the *heads* of persons ordered for execution to be brought to them. For this there were two reasons: 1st. To gratify their resentment—to feast their eyes on the proof that their enemy was dead; and, 2d. To ascertain the fact that the sentence had been executed. There is a similar instance in Roman history of a *woman* requiring the head of an enemy to be brought to her. Agrippina, the mother of Nero, who was afterward emperor, sent an officer to put to death Lollia Paulina, who had been her rival for the imperial dignity. When Lollia's head was brought to her, not knowing it at first, she examined it with her own hands till she perceived some particular feature by which the lady was distinguished.*

9. *And the king was sorry.* There might have been several reasons for this. 1st. Herod had a high respect for John, and feared him. He knew that he was a holy man, and had "*observed* him," Mar. vi. 20. In the margin (Mark) this is *kept him*, or *saved him*. In fact, he had interposed and saved John from being put to death by Herodias, who had had a quarrel with John, and would have killed him but for Herod, Mar. vi. 19. Herod, though a bad man, had a respect and veneration for John as a holy and just man, as wicked men often will have. 2d. John was in high repute among the people, and Herod might have been afraid that his murder might excite commotion. 3d. Herod, though a wicked man, does not appear to have been insensible to some of the common principles of human nature. Here was a great and most manifest crime proposed—no less than the *murder* of an acknowledged prophet of the Lord. It was deliberate. It was to gratify the malice of a wicked woman. It was the price of a few moments' entertainment. His *conscience*, though in feeble and dying accents, checked him. He would have preferred a request not so manifestly wicked, and that would not have involved him in so much difficulty. ¶ *For the oath's sake.* Herod felt that he was bound by this oath; but he was not. The oath should not have been taken; but, *being* taken, he could not be bound by it. No oath could justify a man in committing murder. The true principle is, that Herod was bound by a prior obligation—by the law of God—*not* to commit murder; and no act of his, be it an *oath* or anything else, could free him from that obligation. ¶ *And them which sat with him at meat.* This was the strongest reason why Herod murdered John. He had not firmness enough to obey the law of God and to follow the dictates of conscience against the opinions of wicked men. He was afraid of the charge of cowardice and want of spirit; afraid of ridicule and the contempt of the wicked. This is the principle of *the laws of honour;* this the foundation of *duelling.* It is not so much *for his own sake* that one man murders another in a duel, for the offence is often a mere trifle—it is a *word*, or *look*, that never would injure

* Lardner's *Credibility*, part i. book i. ch. i.

in a charger, and given to the
damsel: and she brought *it* to her
mother.
12 And his disciples came and
took up the body, and [g]buried it,
and went and told Jesus.
13 When Jesus heard *of it*,
[h]he departed thence by ship into
a desert place apart: and when
the people had heard *thereof*, they
followed him on foot out of the
cities.
14 And Jesus went forth, [i]and
saw a great multitude, and was

g Ac.8.2.

h ch.10.23; 12.15; Mar.6.32,&c.; Lu.9.10,&c.; Jn.6.1,2,&c. i ch.9.36; 15.32,&c.

him. It is because the *men of honour*, as they call themselves, his companions, would consider him a coward and would laugh at him. Those companions may be unprincipled contemners of the laws of God and man; and yet the duellist, against his own conscience, against the laws of God, against the good opinion of the virtuous part of the world, and against the laws of his country, seeks by deadly aim to *murder* another merely to gratify his dissolute companions. And this is the law of honour! This is the secret of duelling! This the source of that remorse that settles in awful blackness, and that thunders damnation around the duellist in his dying hours! It should be added, this is the course of all *youthful* guilt. Young men are led along by others. They have not firmness enough to follow the teachings of a father and of the law of God. They are afraid of being called *mean* and *cowardly* by the wicked; and they often sink low in vice and crime, never to rise again. ¶ *At meat;* that is, at supper. The word *meat*, at the time the Bible was translated, meant provisions of all kinds. It is now restricted to *flesh*, and does not convey a full idea of the original.

11. *And his head was brought in a charger*, &c. For the sake of these wicked men, the bloody offering—the head of the slaughtered prophet—was brought and given as the reward to the daughter and mother. What an offering to a woman! Josephus says of Herodias that "she was a woman full of ambition and envy, having a mighty influence on Herod, *and able to persuade him to things he was not at all inclined to.*" This is one of the many proofs that we have that the evangelists drew characters according to truth.

12. *And his disciples*, &c. The *head* was with Herodias. The body, with pious care, they buried. ¶ *And went and told Jesus.* This was done, probably, for the following reasons: 1st. It was an important event, and one particularly connected with the work of Jesus. John was his forerunner, and it was important that he should be made acquainted with his death. 2d. It is not unreasonable to suppose that in their affliction they came to him for consolation; nor is it improper in *our* affliction to follow their example, *and go and tell Jesus.* 3d. *Their* master had been slain by a cruel king. Jesus was engaged in the same cause, and they probably supposed that *he* was in danger. They therefore came to warn him of it, and he (ver. 13) sought a place of safety.

13–21. A full narrative of the feeding the five thousand is given in each of the other evangelists: in Mar. vi. 32–44; in Lu. ix. 10–17; in Jn. vi. 1–14.

13. *And when Jesus heard* of it, *he departed.* He went to a place of safety. He never threw himself unnecessarily into danger. It was proper that he should secure his life till the appointed time had come for him to die. ¶ *By a ship into a desert place.* That is, he crossed the Sea of Galilee. He went to the country *east* of the sea, into a place little inhabited. Luke says (ix. 10) he went to a place called Bethsaida. See Notes on Mat. xi. 21. *A desert place* means a place little cultivated, where there were few or no inhabitants. On the east of the Sea of Galilee there was a large tract of country of this description—rough, uncultivated, and chiefly used to pasture flocks.

14. *Was moved with compassion.* That is, pitied them. Mark (vi. 34) says he was moved with compassion because they were as sheep having no shepherd. A shepherd is one who takes care of a flock. It was his duty to feed it; to defend it from wolves and other wild beasts; to take care of the young and feeble; to lead it by green pastures and still waters, Ps. xxiii. In Eastern countries this was a principal employment of the inhabitants. When Christ says the people were as sheep without a shepherd, he means that they had no

moved with [k]compassion toward them, and he healed their sick.

15 And when it was evening his disciples came to him, saying, This is a desert place, and the time is now past; send the multitude away, that they may go into the villages and buy themselves victuals.

16 But Jesus said unto them, They need not depart; give ye them to eat.

17 And they say unto him, We have here but five loaves and two fishes.

18 He said, Bring them hither to me.

19 And he commanded the multitude to sit down on the grass; and took the five loaves and the

k He.4.15.

teachers and *guides* who cared for them and took pains to instruct them. The scribes and Pharisees were haughty and proud, and cared little for the common people; and when they *did* attempt to teach them, they led them astray. They therefore came in great multitudes to him who preached the gospel to the poor (Mat. xi. 5), and who was thus the good shepherd, Jn. x. 14.

15. *The time is now past.* That is, the day is passing away; it is near night, and it is proper to make some provision for the temporal wants of so many. Perhaps it may mean it was past the usual time for refreshment.

16. *Jesus said—They need not depart; give ye them to eat.* John adds (ch. vi. 5, 6) that previous to this Jesus had addressed Philip, and asked, Whence shall we buy bread that these may eat? and that he "said this to prove him; for he himself knew what he would do;" that is, he said this to try his *faith;* to *test* the confidence of Philip in himself. Philip, it seems, had not the *kind* of confidence which he ought to have had. He immediately began to think of their ability to *purchase* food for them. Two hundred pennyworth of bread, said he, would not be enough, Jn. vi. 7. In the original it is two hundred *denarii.* These were Roman coins amounting to about fourteen cents (7*d.*) each. The whole two hundred, therefore, would have been equal to about twenty-eight dollars. In the view of Philip this was a great sum—a sum which twelve poor fishermen were by no means able to provide. It was this fact, and not any unwillingness to provide for them, which led the disciples to request that they should be sent into the villages around in order to obtain food. Jesus knew how much they had, and he required of them, as he does of all, implicit faith, and told them to give them to eat. He requires us to do what he commands, and we need not doubt that he will give us strength to accomplish it.

17. *We have here but five loaves,* &c. These loaves were in the possession of a *lad,* or young man, who was with them, and were made of barley, Jn. vi. 9. It is possible that this lad was one in attendance on the apostles to carry their food, but it is most probable he was one who had provision to sell among the multitude. Barley was a cheap kind of food, scarcely one-third the value of wheat, and was much used by poor people. A considerable part of the food of the people in that region was probably fish, as they lived on the borders of a lake that abounded in fish.

19. *And he commanded the multitude to sit down.* In the original it is *to recline* on the grass, or to lie as they did at their meals. The Jews never *sat,* as we do, at meals, but *reclined* or lay at length. See Notes on Mat. xxiii. 6. Mark and Luke add that they reclined in companies, by hundreds and by fifties. ¶ *And looking up to heaven, he blessed.* Luke adds, he blessed *them;* that is, the loaves. The word *to bless* means, often, to give thanks; sometimes to pray for a blessing; that is, to pray for the divine favour and friendship; to pray that what we do may meet his approbation. In seeking a blessing on our food, it means that we pray that it may be made nourishing to our bodies; that we may have proper gratitude to God, the giver, for providing for our wants; and that we may remember the Creator while we partake the bounties of his providence. Our Saviour *always* sought a blessing on his food. In this he was an example for us. What he did we should do. It is right thus to seek the blessing of God. He provides for us; he daily opens his hand and satisfies our wants, and it is proper that we should render suitable acknowledgments for his goodness.

The custom among the Jews was

two fishes, and, looking up to heaven, he blessed, and brake; and gave the loaves to *his* disciples, and the disciples to the multitude.

20 And they did all eat and were filled: and they [l]took up of the fragments that remained twelve baskets full.

21 And they that had eaten were about five thousand men, beside women and children.

22 And straightway Jesus constrained his disciples to get into a ship, and to go before him unto the other side, while he sent the multitudes away.

23 And when he had sent the multitudes away, [m]he went up into a mountain apart to pray:

l 2 Ki.4.1-7.

m Mar.6.46.

---

universal. The form of prayer which they used in the time of Christ has been preserved by their writers, the Talmudists. It is this: "Blessed be thou, O Lord our God, the King of the world, who hast produced this food and this drink from the earth and the vine." ¶ *And brake.* The loaves of bread, among the Jews, were made *thin* and *brittle*, and were therefore broken and not cut.

20. *And they did all eat, and were filled.* This was an undoubted *miracle.* The quantity *must* have been greatly increased to have supplied so many. He that could *increase* that small quantity so much had the power of *creation;* and he that could do that could create the world out of nothing, and had no less than divine power. ¶ *Twelve baskets full.* The size of these *baskets* is unknown. They were probably such as travellers carried their provisions in. They were used commonly by the Jews in their journeys. In travelling among the Gentiles or Samaritans, a *Jew* could expect little hospitality. There were not, as now, public houses for the entertainment of strangers. At great distances there were *caravansaries*, but they were intended chiefly as lodging-places for the night, and not to provide *food* for travellers. Hence, in journeying among strangers or in deserts, they carried *baskets* of provisions, and this is the reason why they were furnished with them here. It is probable that each of the apostles had *one*, and they were all filled. John (vi. 12) says that Jesus *directed* them to gather up these fragments, that nothing might be lost—an example of economy. God *creates* all food; it has, therefore, a kind of sacredness; it is all *needed* by some person or other, and none should be lost.

21. *Five thousand men, besides*, &c. Probably the whole number might have been ten thousand. To feed so many was an act of great benevolence and a stupendous miracle.

22, 23. *And straightway Jesus constrained*, &c. See Mar. vi. 45–56; Jn. vi. 15–21. The word *straightway* means immediately; that is, as soon as the fragments were gathered up. To *constrain* usually means to *compel.* It here means to *command.* There was no need of *compulsion.* They were at this time on the east side of the Lake of Gennesareth. He directed them to get into a ship and cross over to the other side; that is, to Capernaum. Mark adds that he sent them to *Bethsaida* (vi. 45). Bethsaida was situated at the place where the Jordan empties into the lake on the east side of the river. Comp. Notes on ch. xi. 21. It is probable that he directed them to go in a ship or boat to *Bethsaida*, and remain there till he should dismiss the people, and that he would meet them there, and with them cross the lake. The effect of the miracle on the multitude was so great (Jn. vi. 14) that they believed him to be that prophet which should come into the world; that is, the *Messiah*, the *king* that they had expected, and they were about to take him *by force* and make him a king, Jn. vi. 15. To avoid this, Jesus got away from them as privately as possible. He went into a solitary mountain alone. In view of the temptation—when human honours were offered to him and almost *forced* upon him—he retired for private prayer; an example for all who are tempted with human honours and applause. Nothing is better to keep the mind humble and unambitious than to seek some lonely place; to shut out the world with all its honours; to realize that the great God, before whom all creatures and all honours sink to nothing, is round about us; and to ask

and when the evening was come,
he was there alone.
24 But the ship was now in the
midst of the sea, tossed with waves;
for the wind was contrary.
25 And in the fourth watch of
the night Jesus went unto them,
walking on the sea.
26 And[n] when the disciples saw
him walking on the sea, [o]they
were troubled, saying, It is a
spirit; and they cried out for fear.
27 But straightway Jesus spake
unto them, saying, [p]Be of good
cheer; it is I; be not afraid.
28 And Peter answered him and
said, [q]Lord, if it be thou, bid me
come unto thee on the water.
29 And he said, Come. And when
Peter was come down out of the
ship, he walked on the water to
go to Jesus.
30 But when he saw the wind
[3]boisterous, he was afraid; and
beginning to sink, he cried, saying,
[r]Lord, save me!
31 And immediately [s]Jesus
stretched forth *his* hand, and
caught him, and said unto him,
O thou of little faith, [t]wherefore
didst thou doubt?

n Job 9.8; Jn.6.19. *o* Lu.24.37. *p* Ac.23.11.

q Phi.4.13. 3 or, *strong*. *r* Ps.69.1,2; La.3.57. *s* Is.63.12. *t* Ja.1.6.

---

him to keep us from pride and vain-glory.

24. *But the ship was now in the midst of the sea.* John says they had sailed about 25 or 30 furlongs. About 7½ Jewish furlongs made a mile; so that the distance they had sailed was not more than about 4 miles. At no place is the Sea of Tiberias much more than 10 miles in breadth, so that they were literally in the midst of the sea.

25. *And in the fourth watch of the night.* The Jews anciently divided the night into three parts of four hours each, usually called *watches.* The *first* of these watches is mentioned in La. ii. 19, the *middle watch* in Ju. vii. 19, and the *morning watch* in Ex. xiv. 24. In the time of our Saviour they divided the night into four watches, the fourth having been introduced by the Romans. These watches consisted of three hours each. The first commenced at six and continued till nine; the second from nine to twelve; the third from twelve to three; and the fourth from three to six. The first was called evening; the second midnight; the third cock-crowing; the fourth morning, Mar. xiii. 35. It is probable that the term *watch* was given to each of these divisions from the practice of placing sentinels around the camp in time of war, or in cities, to *watch* or *guard* the camp or city; and that they were at first relieved *three* times in the night, but under the Romans *four* times. It was in the last of these watches, or between three and six in the morning, that Jesus appeared to the disciples, so that he had spent most of the night alone on the mountain in prayer. ¶ *Walking on the sea.* A manifest and wonderful miracle. It was a boisterous sea. It was in a dark night. The little boat was 4 or 5 miles from the shore, tossed by the billows.

26. *They were troubled.* They were afraid. The sight was remarkable. It was sufficient to awe them. In the dark night, amid the tumultuous billows appeared the form of a man. They thought it was a spirit—an apparition. It was a common belief among the ancients that the spirits of men after death frequently appeared to the living.

28-31. *And Peter answered*, &c. Here is an instance of the characteristic ardour and rashness of Peter. He had less *real* faith than he supposed, and more ardour than his faith would justify. He was rash, headlong, incautious, really attached to Jesus, but still easily daunted and prone to fall. He was afraid, therefore, when in danger, and, sinking, cried again for help. Thus he was suffered to learn his own character, and his dependence on Jesus; a lesson which all Christians are permitted sooner or later to learn by dear-bought experience.

32. *And when they were come into the ship the wind ceased.* Here was a new proof of the power of Jesus. He that has power over winds and waves has all power. John adds (vi. 21) that the ship was immediately at the land whither they went; another proof, amid this collection of wonders, that the Son of God was with them. They came, therefore, and worshipped him,

32 And when they were come into the ship [u]the wind ceased.

33 Then they that were in the ship came and worshipped him, saying, Of a truth thou art [v]the Son of God.

34 And[w] when they were gone over, they came into the land of Gennesaret.

35 And when the men of that place had knowledge of him, they sent out into all that country round about, and brought unto him all that were diseased;

36 And besought him that they might only touch [x]the hem of his garment: and [y]as many as touched were made perfectly whole.

u Ps.107.29. *v* Da.3.25; Lu.4.41; Jn.1.49; 6 69; 11.27; Ac.8.37; Ro.1.4. *w* Mar.6 53. *x* Nu.15.38; ch.9.20; Mar.3.10; Lu.6.19; Ac.19.12. *y* Jn.6.37.

---

acknowledging him to be the Son of God. That is, they gave him homage, or honoured him as the Son of God.

34–36. *Land of Gennesaret.* This region was in Galilee, on the west side of the Sea of Tiberias; and *in* this land was situated Capernaum, to which he had directed his disciples to go. ¶ *The hem of his garment.* That is, the fringe or border on the outer garment. See Notes on Mat. ix. 20.

REMARKS.

1st. We learn from this chapter the power of conscience, ver. 1–4. Herod's guilt was the only reason why he thought John the Baptist had risen. At another time he would altogether have disbelieved it. Consciousness of guilt will at some period infallibly torment a man.

2d. The duty of faithfulness, ver. 4. John reproved Herod at the hazard of his life, and he died for it; but he had the approbation of conscience and of God. So will all who do their duty. Here was an example of fidelity to all ministers of religion. They are not to fear the face of man, however rich, or mighty, or wicked.

3d. The righteous will *command* the respect of the wicked. Herod was a wicked man, but he respected John and feared him, Mar. vi. 20. The wicked profess to despise religion, and many really do; but their consciences tell them that religion is a good thing. In times of trial they will sooner trust Christians than others. In sickness and death they are often glad to see them and hear them pray, and desire the comfort which *they* have; and, like Balaam, say, "Let me die the death of the righteous," Nu. xxiii. 10. No person, young or old, is ever the less really esteemed for being a Christian.

4th. Men are often restrained from great sins by mere selfish motives, as Herod was by the love of popularity, ver. 5. Herod would have put John to death long before had it not been that he feared the people. His constantly desiring to do it was a kind of *prolonged murder.* God will hold men guilty for *desiring* to do evil; and will not justify them if they are restrained, *not* by the fear of him, but by the fear of men.

5th. We see the effect of what is called the principle *of honour*, ver. 9. It was in obedience to this that Herod committed murder. This is the principle of duelling and war. No principle is so foolish and wicked. The great mass of men disapprove of it. The wise and good have always disapproved of it. This principle of honour is usually the mere love of revenge. It is often the fear of being laughed at. It produces evil. God cannot and will not love it. The way to prevent duels and murders is to restrain the passions and cultivate a spirit of meekness and forgiveness when young; that is, to come early under the full influence of the gospel.

6th. Men should be cautious about promises, and especially about oaths. Herod made a foolish promise, and confirmed it by a wicked oath, ver. 9. Promises should not be made without *knowing* what is promised, and without *knowing* that it will be *right* to perform them. Oaths are always wicked except when made before a magistrate, and on occasions of real magnitude. The practice of profane and common swearing, like that of Herod, is always foolish and wicked, and sooner or later will bring men into difficulty.

7th. Amusements are often attended with evil consequences, ver. 6–11. The dancing of a gay and profligate girl was the means of the death of one of the holiest of men. Dancing, balls, splendid parties, and theatres are by many thought innocent; but they are a profitless waste of time. They lead to forgetfulness of God. They nourish passion and sensual desires. They often lead to the seduction and ruin of the innocent. They are *unfit* for dying creatures. From the very midst of such scenes the gay may go to the bar of God. How poor a preparation to die! How dreadful the judgment-seat to such!

8th. Jesus will take care of the poor, ver. 14–21. He regarded the *temporal* as well as the spiritual wants of the people. Rather than see them suffer, he worked a miracle to feed them. So, rather than see *us* suffer, God is daily doing what man *cannot do*. He causes the grain to grow; he fills the land, and seas, and air with living creatures; nay, he provides in desert places for the support of man. How soon would all men and beasts die if he did not put forth continued power and goodness for the supply of our wants!

9th. It is the duty of Christians to be solicitous about the temporal wants of the poor, ver. 15. They are with us. By regarding them, and providing for them, we have an opportunity of showing our attachment to Christ, and our resemblance to God, who continually does good.

10th. A blessing should be sought on our enjoyments, ver. 19. It is always right to imitate Christ. It is right to acknowledge our dependence on God, and in the midst of mercies to pray that we may not forget the Giver.

11th. We see the duty of economy. The Saviour, who had power to create worlds by a word, yet commanded to take up the fragments, that nothing might be lost, Jn. vi. 12. Nothing that *God* has created and given to us should be *wasted*.

12th. It is proper to *make preparation* for private prayer. Jesus sent the people away that he might be alone, ver. 22, 23. So Christians should *take pains* that they may have times and places for retirement. A grove or a mountain was the place where our Saviour sought to pray, and there, too, may *we* find and worship God.

13th. In time of temptation, of prosperity, and honour, it is right to devote much time to secret prayer. Jesus, when the people were about to make him a king, retired to the mountain, and continued there till the early morning in prayer, Jn. vi. 15.

14th. When Christ commands us to do a thing we should do it, ver. 22. Even if it should expose us to danger, it should be done.

15th. In times of danger and distress, Jesus will see us and will come to our relief, ver. 25, 26. Even in the tempest that howls, or on the waves of affliction that beat around us, he will come, and we shall be safe.

16th. We should never be afraid of him. We should always have *good cheer* when we see him, ver. 27. When he says, "It is I," he also says, "be not afraid." He can still the waves, and conduct us safely to the port which we seek.

17th. Nothing is too difficult for us when we act under the command of Christ. Peter at his command leaves the ship and walks on the billows, ver. 29.

18th. Christ sometimes leaves his people to see their weakness and their need of strength. Without his continued aid they would sink. Peter had no strength of his own to walk on the deep, and Christ suffered him to see his dependence, ver. 30.

19th. The eye, in difficulty, should be fixed on Christ. As soon as Peter began to look at the waves and winds, rather than Christ, he began to sink, ver. 30. True courage in difficulties consists not in confidence in ourselves, but in confidence in Jesus, the Almighty Saviour and Friend.

20th. Prayer may be instantly answered. When we are in immediate danger, and offer a prayer of faith, we may expect immediate aid, ver. 31.

21st. Pride comes before a fall. Peter was self-confident and proud, and he fell. His confidence and rashness were the very means of showing the weakness of his faith, ver. 31.

22d. It is proper to render homage to Jesus, and to worship him as the Son of God, ver. 33.

23d. We should be desirous that all about us should partake of the benefits that Christ confers. When we *know* him and have tested his goodness, we should take pains that all around us may also be brought to him and be saved, ver. 35.

24th. Jesus only can make us perfectly whole. No other being can save us. He that could heal the *body* can save the soul. A word can save us. With what earnestness ought we to plead with him that we may obtain his saving grace! ver. 36.

CHAPTER XV.

THEN[a] came to Jesus scribes
and Pharisees, which were of
Jerusalem, saying,
2 Why do thy disciples transgress the tradition of the elders?
for they wash not their hands
when they eat bread.
3 But he answered and said unto
them, [b]Why do ye also transgress
the commandment of God by your
tradition?
4 For God commanded, saying,
[c]Honour thy father and mother:
and, [d]He that curseth father or
mother, let him die the death.
5 But ye say, Whosoever shall
say to *his* father or *his* mother, *It is* a

a Mar.7.1,&c.

b Col.2.8,23; Tit.1.14. c Ex.20.12; De.5.16. d Ex.21.17; Le.20.9.

CHAPTER XV.

1-9. See also Mar. vii. 1-9. ¶ *Then came to Jesus*, &c. Mark says that they *saw* the disciples of Jesus eating with hands unwashed.

2. *Transgress the tradition of the elders.* The world *elders* means literally *old men.* It here means the *ancients*, or their *ancestors.* The *tradition of the elders* meant something handed down from one to another by memory; some precept or custom not commanded in the *written law*, but which scribes and Pharisees held themselves bound to observe. They supposed that when Moses was on Mount Sinai two sets of laws were delivered to him: one, they said, was recorded, and is that contained in the Old Testament; the other was handed down from father to son, and kept uncorrupted to their day. They believed that Moses, before he died, delivered this law to Joshua; he to the Judges; they to the prophets; so that it was kept pure till it was recorded in the Talmuds. In these books these pretended laws are now contained. They are exceedingly numerous and very trifling. They are, however, regarded by the Jews as more important than either Moses or the prophets. One point in which the Pharisees differed from the Sadducees was in holding to these traditions. It seems, however, that in the particular traditions here mentioned all the Jews were united; for Mark adds (ch. vii. 3) that "the Pharisees and *all the Jews*, except they wash their hands oft, eat not, *holding the tradition of the elders.*" Mark has also added that this custom of washing extended not merely to their hands before eating, but in coming from the market; and also to cups, and pots, and brazen vessels, and tables, Mar. vii. 3, 4. They did this professedly for the sake of *cleanliness.* So far it was well. But they made it also a matter of superstition. They regarded *external* purity as of much more importance than the purity of the heart. They had many foolish rules about it respecting the quantity of water that was to be used, the way in which it should be applied, the number of times it should be changed, the number of those that might wash at a time, &c. These rules our Saviour did not think it proper to regard, and this was the reason why they found fault with him.

3. *But he answered*, &c. They accused him of violating their traditions, as though they were obligatory. In his answer he *implied* that his disciples were not bound to obey their traditions—they were invented by men. He said, also, that those traditions *could not* be binding, as they violated the commandments of God. He proceeds to specify *a case* in which their tradition made void one of the plain laws of God; and if that was their character, then they could not blame him for not regarding them.

4. *For God commanded*, &c. That is, in the fifth commandment (Ex. xx. 12), and in Ex. xxi. 17. To *honour* is to obey, to reverence, to speak kindly *to*, to speak and think well *of.* To *curse* is to disobey, to treat with irreverence, *to swear at*, to speak ill of, to think evil of in the heart, to meditate or do *any* evil to a parent. All this is included in the original word. ¶ *Let him die the death.* This is a Hebrew phrase, the same as saying, *let him surely die.* The Jewish law punished this crime with death. This duty of honouring and obeying a parent was what Christ said they had violated by their traditions. He proceeds to state the way in which it was done.

5. It is *a gift.* In Mark it is *corban.* The word *corban* is a Hebrew word denoting *a gift.* It here means a thing *dedicated to the service of God, and therefore not to be appropriated to any other use.* The Jews were in the habit of

gift, by whatsoever thou mightest be profited by me;

6 And[e] honour not his father or his mother, *he shall be free.* Thus have ye made the commandment of God of none effect by your tradition.

7 *Ye* hypocrites! well did Esaias prophesy of you, saying,

8 This[f] people draweth nigh unto

e De.27.16.

f Is.29.13.

making such dedications. They devoted their property to him for sacred uses, as they pleased. In doing this they used the word *corban*, or some similar word, saying, this thing is *corban*, *i.e.* it is a gift to God, or is sacred to him. The law required that when a dedication of this kind was made it should be fulfilled. "Vow and pay unto the Lord your God," Ps. lxxvi. 11. See De. xxiii. 21. The law of God required that a son should *honour* his parent; *i.e.* among other things, that he should provide for his wants when he was old and in distress. Yet the Jewish teachers said that it was more important for a man *to dedicate his property to God* than to *provide for the wants of his parent.* If he had *once* devoted his property—once *said* it was *corban*, or a gift to God—it could not be appropriated even to the support of a parent. If a parent was needy and poor, and if he should apply to a son for assistance, and the son should reply, though in in anger, "It is devoted to God; this property which you need, *and by which you might be profited by me, is corban—I have given it to God;*" the Jews said the property could not be recalled, and the son was not under obligation to aid a parent with it. He had done a more important thing in giving it to God. The son was free. He could not be required to do anything for his father after that. Thus he might *in a moment* free himself from the obligation to obey his father or mother. In a sense somewhat similar to this, the chiefs and priests of the Sandwich Islands had the power of devoting anything to the service of the gods by saying that it was *taboo*, or *tabooed;* that is, it became consecrated to the service of religion; and, no matter who had been the owner, it could then be appropriated to no other use. In this way they had complete power over all the possessions of the people, and could appropriate them to their own use under the pretence of devoting them to religion. They thus deprived the *people* of their property under the plea that it was consecrated to the gods. The Jewish son deprived his *parents* of a support under the plea that the property was devoted to the service of religion. The principle was the same, and both systems were equally a violation of the rights of others.

Besides, the law said that a man should die that *cursed* his father, *i.e.* that refused to obey him, or to provide for him, or spoke in anger to him. Yet the *Jews* said that though in *anger*, and in real *spite* and *hatred*, a son said to his father, "All that I have which could profit *you* I have given to God," he should be free from blame. Thus the whole law was made void, or of no use, by what *appeared* to have the appearance of piety. *No man, according to their views, was bound to obey the fifth commandment and support an aged and needy parent, if, either from superstition or spite, he chose to give his property to God, that is, to devote it to some religious use.*

Our Saviour did not mean to condemn the practice of giving to God, or to religious and charitable objects. This the law and the gospel equally required. He commended even a poor widow that gave all her living, Mar. xii. 44. But he meant to condemn the practice of giving to God where it interfered with our duty to parents and relations; where it was done to *get rid* of the duty of aiding them; and where it was done out of a malignant and rebellious spirit, with the *semblance* of piety, to get clear of doing to earthly parents what God required.

7. Ye *hypocrites!* See Notes on Mat. vii. 5. Hypocrisy is the concealment of some base principle under the pretence of religion. Never was there a clearer instance of it than this—*an attempt to get rid of the duty of providing for needy parents under an appearance of piety towards God.* ¶ *Esaias.* That is, *Isaiah.* This prophecy is found in Is. xxix. 13. ¶ *Prophesy of you.* That is, he spoke of the people of his day—of the Jews, *as* Jews—in terms that apply to the whole people. He properly *characterized the nation* in calling

me with their mouth, and honoureth
me with *their* lips; but their heart
is far from me.
9 But in vain they do worship
me, [g]teaching *for* doctrines the
commandments of men.
10 And he called the multitude,
and said unto them, Hear, and understand:
11 Not[h] that which goeth into the
mouth defileth a man; but that
which cometh out of the mouth,
this defileth a man.
12 Then came his disciples, and
said unto him, Knowest thou that
the Pharisees were offended after
they heard this saying?
13 But he answered and said,
[i]Every plant which my heavenly
Father hath not planted shall be
rooted up.
14 Let them alone: [k]they be

g Col.2.22. h Ac.10.15; Ro.14.14,20; 1 Ti.4.4; Tit.1.15. i Jn.15.2,6. k ch.23.16; Lu.6.39.

---

them hypocrites. The words are applicable to the nation at all times, and they apply, therefore, to *you*. He did not mean particularly to speak of the nation in the time of Christ, but he spoke of them as having a national character of hypocrisy. Comp. Notes on ch. i. 22, 23.

8. *Draweth nigh unto me with their mouth*, &c. That is, they are regular in the *forms* of worship; they are strict in ceremonial observances, and keep the law outwardly; but God requires the heart, and *that* they have not rendered.

9. *In vain do they worship me.* That is, their attempts to worship are *vain*, or are not real worship — they are mere *forms*. ¶ *Teaching* for *doctrines*, &c. The word *doctrines*, here, means the requirements of religion—things to be believed and practised in religion. God only has a right to declare what shall be done in his service; but they held their traditions to be superior to the written word of God, and taught them as *doctrines* binding the conscience. See Notes on Is. xxix. 13.

10–14. See also Mar. vii. 15–17. *And he called the multitude.* In opposition to the doctrines of the Pharisees, the Saviour took occasion to show them that the great source of pollution was the *heart*. *They* supposed that external things chiefly defiled a man. On this all their doctrines about purification were founded. This opinion of the Jews it was of great importance to correct. The Saviour took occasion, therefore, to direct the people to the true source of defilement—their own hearts. He particularly directed them to it as of importance—*Hear and understand.*

11. *Not that which goeth into the mouth*, &c. The disciples were charged with being sinners for transgressing the tradition of the elders in eating with unwashed hands. Christ replies that what they should *eat* could not render them sinners. The *man*, the moral agent, the soul, could not be polluted by anything that was eaten. What proceeds from the man himself, from his *heart*, would defile him. ¶ *Defileth.* Pollutes, corrupts, or renders sinful.

12. *The Pharisees were offended.* They were so zealous of their traditions that they could not endure that their absurdities should be exposed.

13. *Every plant*, &c. Religious *doctrine* is not inaptly compared to a plant. See 1 Co. iii. 6–8. It is *planted* in the mind for the purpose of producing fruit in the life, or *right conduct*. Jesus here says that all those doctrines of which his Father was not the author must be *rooted up* or corrected. The false doctrines of the Pharisees, therefore, must be attacked, and it was no wonder if they were indignant. It could not be helped. It was his duty to attack them. He was not surprised that they were enraged; but, notwithstanding their opposition, their doctrine should be destroyed.

14. *Let them alone.* That is, do not be troubled at their rage. Be not anxious about it. This result is to be expected. They are greatly attached to their traditions, and you are not to wonder that they are indignant. They lead, also, the blind. They have a vast influence over the multitude, and it is to be expected that they will be enraged at any doctrines that go to lessen their authority or influence. By commanding them *to let them alone*, Christ does not mean that they were to be suffered to remain in error without any attempt to refute or correct them, for this *he* was doing then; but he meant to charge his disciples not *to mind them* or to regard their opposition—it was to

blind leaders of the blind. And
if the blind lead the blind, both
shall fall into the ditch.
15 Then answered Peter, and said
unto him, Declare unto us this
parable.
16 And Jesus said, Are ye also
yet without understanding?
17 Do ye not yet understand that
whatsoever entereth in at the mouth
goeth into the belly, and is cast out
into the draught?
18 But those things which [l]proceed
out of the mouth come forth
from the heart, and they defile the
man.
19 For[m] out of the heart proceed
evil thoughts, murders, adulteries,

[l] Lu.6.45; Ja.3.6. [m] Ge.6.5; 8.21; Pr.6.14; 24.9; Je.17.9; Ro.3.10-19; Ga.5.19-21; Ep.2.3; Tit.3.3.

be expected. ¶ *If the blind lead the blind*, &c. This was a plain proposition. A blind man, attempting to conduct blind men, would fall into every ditch that was in the way. So with religious teachers. If these Pharisees, themselves ignorant and blind, should be suffered to lead the ignorant multitude, both would be destroyed. This was another reason for confuting their errors, or for rooting up the plants which God had not planted. He wished, by doing it, to save the deluded multitude.

God often suffers one man to lead many to ruin. A rich and profligate man, an infidel, a man of learning, a politician, or a teacher, is allowed to sweep multitudes to ruin. This is not unjust, for those who are led are not *compelled* to follow such men. They are *free* in choosing such leaders, and they are answerable for *being led* to ruin.

15–20. See also Mar. vii. 17–23. *Then answered Peter, and said unto him, Declare unto us this parable.* See Notes on Mat. xiii. 3. The word *parable* sometimes means a *dark* or *obscure saying*, Ps. lxxviii. 2. Peter meant, "Explain to us more fully this obscure and novel doctrine." To us, now, it is plain; to the disciples, just coming out of Judaism, the doctrine of Jesus was obscure. Mark says that the *disciples* asked him. There is no contradiction. The question was put by Peter *in the name* of the disciples; or several of them put the question, though Matthew has mentioned only one. An omission is not a contradiction.

16. *Are ye also yet without understanding?* Jesus appeals, in explaining this, to their *common sense;* and he wonders that they had not yet learned to judge the foolish traditions of the Jews by the decisions of common sense and by his own instructions.

17. *Do ye not understand*, &c. The meaning of this may be thus expressed: The food which is eaten does not affect the *mind*, and therefore cannot pollute it. The doctrine of the Pharisees, that neglect of washing and of similar observances defiles a man, cannot be true. Those things pertain to the *body* as much as food does, and they cannot affect the soul. That must be purified by something else than external washing, and it is polluted by other things than a neglect of mere outward ceremonies. The seat of corruption is *within*—it is the heart itself; and if men would be made pure, this must be cleansed. If that is corrupt, the whole man is corrupt.

18–20. Christ proceeds to state what *does* defile the man, or render him a sinner: 1st. *Evil thoughts.* These are the first things—these are the fountains of all others. Thought precedes action. Thought, or purpose, or motive, gives its *character* to conduct. All evil thoughts are here intended. Though we labour to suppress them, yet they defile us. They leave pollution behind them. 2d. *Murders.* Taking the life of others *with malice*. The *malice* has its seat in the *heart*, and the murder therefore proceeds from the heart, 1 Jn. iii. 15. 3d. *Adulteries, fornication.* See Mat. v. 28. 4th. *Thefts.* Theft is the taking and carrying away the goods of others without their knowledge or consent. Thefts are caused by *coveting* the property of others. They proceed, therefore, from the heart, and violate at the same time two commandments—the *tenth* in thought and the *eighth* in act. 5th. *False witness.* Giving wrong testimony. *Concealing* the truth, or stating what we know to be false—a violation of the ninth commandment. It proceeds from a desire to injure others, to take away their character or property, or to do them injustice. It proceeds thus from the heart. 6th. *Blasphemies.* See Notes on Mat. ix. 3. Blasphemy proceeds from opposition to God, hatred of his character (Ro. viii. 7), and from

fornications, thefts, false witness,
blasphemies:
20 These are *the things* which
defile a man; but to eat with unwashen hands defileth not a man.
21 Then[n] Jesus went thence, and
departed into the coasts of Tyre
and Sidon.
22 And behold, a woman of
Canaan came out of the same
coasts, and cried unto him, saying, Have mercy on me, O Lord,
[o]*thou* son of David! my daughter
is grievously vexed with a devil.
23 But he [p]answered her not a
word. And his disciples came and
besought him, saying, Send her
away; for she crieth after us.
24 But he answered and said,
[q]I am not sent but unto the lost
sheep of the house of Israel.
25 Then came she, and wor-

n Mar.7.24.

o Lu.18.38,39. *p* Ps.28.1; La.3.8. *q* ch.10.5,6; Ac.3.26.

---

a *desire* that there should be no God. It proceeds from the heart. See Ps. xiv. 1. Mark adds several things to those enumerated by Matthew: (*a*) *Covetousness.* This always proceeds from the heart—the unlawful desire of what others possess. (*b*) *Wickedness.* The original here means *malice*, or a *desire of injuring others*, Ro. i. 29. (*c*) *Deceit*, *i.e.* fraud, concealment, cheating in trade. This proceeds from a desire to benefit ourselves by doing injustice to others, and thus proceeds from the heart. (*d*) *Lasciviousness.* Lust, obscenity, unbridled passion—a strong, evil desire of the heart. (*e*) *An evil eye.* That is, an eye sour, malignant, proud; or an eye of lust and passion. See Mat. v. 28; xx. 15; 2 Pe. ii. 14. "Having eyes full of adultery, that cannot cease from sin." (*f*) *Pride.* An improper estimate of our own importance; thinking that we are of much more consequence than we really are—always the work of an evil heart. (*g*) *Foolishness.* Not want of intellect—man is not to blame for that; but *moral folly*, consisting in choosing bad ends, and bad means of gaining them; or, in other words, sin and wickedness. All sin is folly. It is foolish for a man to disobey God, and foolish for anyone to go to hell.

20. *These are* the things *which defile a man.* These are the true sources of pollution in man. These are what corrupt and degrade. It is not the neglect of washing the *body* which defiles; it is the deep, inward corruption of the heart. And what a fountain of pollution is the human soul! What an array of crimes to proceed from the heart of man! What a proof of guilt! What strictness is there in the law of God! How universal is depravity!

21–28. This narrative is also found in Mar. vii. 24–30. ¶ *The coasts of Tyre and Sidon.* These cities were on the *sea-coast* or shore of the Mediterranean. See Notes on Mat. xi. 21. Jesus went there for the purpose of concealment (Mar. vii. 24), perhaps still to avoid Herod.

22. *A woman of Canaan.* This woman is called, also, a Greek, a Syro-Phœnician by birth, Mar. vii. 26. Anciently the whole land, including Tyre and Sidon, was in the possession of the Canaanites, and called Canaan. The Phœnicians were descended from the Canaanites. The country, including Tyre and Sidon, was called Phœnicia, or Syro-Phœnicia. That country was taken by the Greeks under Alexander the Great, and those cities, in the time of Christ, were Greek cities. This woman was therefore a Gentile, living under the Greek government, and probably speaking the Greek language. She was by birth a Syro-Phœnician, born in that country, and descended, therefore, from the ancient Canaanites. All these names might with propriety be given to her. ¶ *Coasts.* Regions or countries. ¶ Thou *son of David.* Descendant of David. See Notes on Mat. i. 1. The phrase here means the Messiah. ¶ *Is grievously vexed with a devil.* See Notes on Mat. iv. 24. The woman showed great earnestness. She *cried* unto him, and fell at his feet, Mar. vii. 25.

23. *But he answered her not a word.* This was done to test her faith, and that there might be exhibited to the apostles an example of the effect of persevering supplication. The result shows that it was not unwillingness to aid her, or neglect of her. It was proper that the strength of her faith should be fully tried.

24. *But he answered and said, I am not sent*, &c. This answer was made to

shipped him, saying, Lord, help
me!

26 But he answered and said, It
is not meet to take the children's
bread, and to [r]cast *it* to dogs.

27 And she said, Truth, Lord:
yet the dogs eat of the crumbs
which fall from their masters'
table.

28 Then[s] Jesus answered and
said unto her, O woman, great *is*
thy faith: [t]be it unto thee even
as thou wilt. And her daughter
was made whole [u]from that very
hour.

29 And[v] Jesus departed from
thence, and came nigh unto the
sea of Galilee; and went up into
a mountain, and sat down there.

30 And great multitudes came
unto him, having with them *those
that were* lame, blind, dumb,
maimed, and many others, and
cast them down at Jesus' feet;
[w]and he healed them;

31 Insomuch that the multitude

r ch.7.6; Re.22.15.
s Job 13.15; 23.10; La.3.32.
t Ps.145.19.
u Jn.4.50-53.
v Mar.7.31.
w Ps.103.3; Is.35.5,6.

---

the *woman*, not to the disciples. *The lost sheep of the house of Israel* were the Jews. He came first to them. He came as their expected Messiah. He came to preach the gospel himself to the Jews only. Afterward it was preached to the Gentiles, but the ministry of Jesus was confined almost entirely to the Jews.

25. *She came and worshipped.* That is, bowed down to him or did him reverence. See Notes on Mat. viii. 2. ¶ *Lord, help me!* A proper cry for a poor sinner, who needs the help of the Lord Jesus.

26. *But he answered and said, It is not meet*, &c. That is, it is not *fit or proper*. ¶ *Children's bread.* The Jews considered themselves as the peculiar children of God. To all other nations they were accustomed to apply terms of contempt, of which *dogs* was the most common. The Mohammedans still apply the term *dogs* to Christians, and Christians and Jews to each other. The term is designed as an expression of the highest contempt. The Saviour means to say that he was sent to the Jews. The woman was a Gentile. He meant merely—using a term in common use, and designed to test her faith in the strongest manner—that it did not comport with the design of his personal ministry to apply benefits intended for the Jews to others. Evidently he cannot be understood as intending to justify or sanction the use of such terms, or *calling names.* He meant to try her faith. As if he had said, "You are a Gentile; I am a Jew. The Jews call themselves children of God. You they vilify and abuse, calling you *a dog.* Are you willing to receive of *a Jew*, then, a favour? Are you willing to submit to these appellations to receive a favour of one of that nation, and to acknowledge your dependence on a people that so despise you?" It was, therefore, a trial of her faith, and was not a lending of his sanction to the propriety of the abusive term. *He* regarded her with a different feeling.

27. *And she said, Truth, Lord*, &c. "What you say is true. Let it be that the *best* food should be given to the children—let the *Jews* have the chief benefit of thy ministry; but the dogs beneath the table eat the crumbs. So let me be regarded as a dog, a heathen, as unworthy of everything. Yet grant *one* exertion of that almighty power displayed so signally among the Jews, and heal the despised daughter of a despised heathen mother."

28. *Great is thy faith.* That is, thy trust, confidence. The word here seems to include, also, the humility and perseverance manifested in pressing her suit. The daughter was healed then. Going home, she found her well and composed, Mar. vii. 30.

29–31. *Sea of Galilee.* That is, the Lake of Gennesaret. For an account of the principal diseases mentioned here, see Notes on Mat. iv. 24. ¶ *Maimed.* Those to whom a hand or foot was wanting. See Mat. xviii. 8. To cure them—that is, to *restore* a hand or foot—was a direct act of *creative* power. It is no wonder, therefore, that the people wondered. ¶ *And they glorified the God of Israel.* To glorify here means to *praise;* to acknowledge his power and goodness. The God of Israel was the God that the Israelites or Jews worshipped.

32–39. The miracle recorded here—

wondered, when they saw the dumb to speak, the maimed to be whole, the lame to walk, and the blind to see: and they glorified the God of Israel.

32 Then[x] Jesus called his disciples *unto him*, and said, I have compassion on the multitude, because they continue with me now three days, and have nothing to eat: and I will not send them away fasting, lest they faint in the way.

33 And[y] his disciples say unto him, Whence should we have so much bread in the wilderness as to fill so great a multitude?

34 And Jesus saith unto them, How many loaves have ye? And they said, Seven, and a few little fishes.

35 And[z] he commanded the multitude to sit down on the ground.

36 And he took the seven loaves and the fishes, and [a]gave thanks, and brake *them*, and gave to his disciples, and the disciples to the multitude.

37 And they did all eat, and were filled: and they took up of the broken *meat* that was left seven baskets full.

38 And they that did eat were four thousand men, beside women and children.

39 And he sent away the multitude, and took ship, and [b]came into the coasts of Măgdala.

x Mar.8.1,&c. *y* 2 Ki.4.43,44.

z ch.14.19,&c. *a* 1 Sa.9.13; Lu.22.19; 24.30. *b* Mar.8.10.

---

the feeding of the four thousand—took place on a mountain near the Sea of Galilee. The same account is recorded in Mar. viii. 1–10. The circumstances of the miracle are so similar to the one recorded in Mat. xiv. 14–21, as to need little additional explanation.

32. *Three days, and have nothing to eat.* This is not, perhaps, to be taken literally, but only that during that time they had been deprived of their ordinary or regular food. They had had only a very scanty supply, and on the third day even that began to fail.

39. *Coasts of Magdala.* Mark says, "*The parts of Dalmanutha.*" Magdala was probably the same place which was formerly called *Migdol*, Jos. xix. 38. It is now called Mejdel, and is situated a few miles north of the city of Tiberias, in the land of Gennesaret, on the western side of the Sea of Tiberias, and directly east of Cana of Galilee. "It is a wretched hamlet of a dozen low huts huddled into one, and the whole ready to tumble into a dismal heap of black basaltic rubbish."—*The Land and the Book* (Thomson), vol. ii. p. 108. This was the birthplace of Mary Magdalene, out of whom the Saviour cast seven devils, Mar. xvi. 9. Dalmanutha was probably a small village near to Magdala, of which no remains have been discovered. There is no contradiction in the statements of the two evangelists here, for they do not say that Jesus went to *either* of these towns, but only to the *coasts* or *parts* where they were situated.

REMARKS.

We learn from this chapter,

1st. That men are often far more attached to traditions and the commandments of men than to the law of God, ver. 1–6.

2d. That men are strongly disposed to *explain away* the law of God, if possible. It is too strict for them, and too spiritual. They dare not often attack it directly, but they will *explain* it and *dilute* it so as to make it mean nothing. Wicked men do not love God's law, ver. 4–6.

3d. Men are prone to introduce foolish *rites* into religion. They do not love what God has commanded, and they attempt to compensate for not loving *his* doctrines by being great sticklers for their own, ver. 2; Mar. vii. 3, 4.

4th. All addition to the law of God is evil, ver. 3. All ceremonies in religion which are not authorized by the New Testament are wrong. Man has no right to ordain rites to bind the conscience where God has commanded none, Col. ii. 23. Men come the nearest to that which is right when they live nearest to just what God has commanded in the Bible.

5th. Hypocrites should be unmasked and detected, ver. 7. He does a great service to men who detects their hypocrisy. That close and faithful preaching which lays open the heart, and shows men what they are, is that which comes nearest to the example of Christ. It may pain them, but the wounds of a friend are faithful (Pr. xxvii. 6); and we should honour and love the man that, by the grace of God, can show us our own hearts. We always honour most the physician of the body that is most skilled in detecting and curing disease, and so should we the physician of the soul.

6th. We should be exceedingly cautious in avoiding *formality* in worship, ver. 8, 9. It is hypocrisy. God requires the heart. To render to him only the service of the lips is to mock him. Nothing can be acceptable but true piety, genuine love, and hearty obedience; nothing more *hateful* than an appearance of worshipping God, while the *heart* is in sin and the world.

7th. The duty of honouring parents, ver. 4–6. Nothing can explain away this duty. It is binding on all. Parents should be obeyed, loved, respected. God requires it and we cannot be free from the duty. *Under age*, a child is bound always to obey a parent where the parent does not command anything contrary to the Bible; but when the parent commands anything contrary to the Bible, the child is not bound to obey, Ac. v. 29. *After* the child is of age, he is to respect, love, and honour the parent; and, if poor and needy, to provide for his wants till he dies. It is certainly proper that we should do all that we can to comfort those in old age who did so much for us in childhood. A child can never repay a parent for his kindness to him.

8th. We are not at liberty to give to anything else—not even to religious uses—what is *necessary* to render our parents comfortable, ver. 4–6. They have the first claim on us. And though it is our duty to do *much* in the cause of benevolence, yet our first duty should be to see that our parents do not suffer.

9th. Men easily take offence when they are faithfully reproved, and especially when their hypocrisy is exposed; and especially if this exposure is about some *small matter* on which they have greatly set their hearts—some ceremony in worship or some foolish rite, ver. 12.

10th. Every false doctrine is to be opposed and should be rooted up, ver. 13. It is to be opposed by arguments and candid investigation, and not by abuse and misrepresentation. Christ never *misrepresented* any man's doctrine. He always stated it just as it was—just as *they* held it; and then, by *argument* and the word of God, he showed it was wrong. This is the proper way to manage all controversies.

11th. It is of great importance to search the *heart*, ver. 19, 20. It is a fountain of evil. It is the source of all crime. External conduct is comparatively of little importance. In the sight of God the *heart* is of more importance; and if that were pure, all would be well.

12th. The doctrine of man's depravity is true, ver. 19. If the *heart* produces those things which are specified by the Saviour it cannot be pure. And yet who is there from whose heart, at some time, these things have not proceeded? Alas! the world is *full* of instances that prove that the human heart may produce *all* these things.

13th. In our distress, and the distress of our children and friends, we should go to Jesus. We should, indeed, use all proper means to restore our friends when they are sick; but we should feel that God only can grant returning health and life, ver. 22.

14th. We should not be discouraged that our prayers are not immediately answered. God knows the proper time to answer them, and it may be of great importance to *us* that the answer should be deferred, ver. 23.

15th. We should still persevere, ver. 24–27. We should not be discouraged. We should not be disheartened even by the appearance of neglect or unkind treatment.

16th. Our prayers will be answered if we persevere, ver. 28. They that seek shall find. In due time—in the *best* and most proper time—a gracious God will lend an ear to our request, and grant the thing we need.

17th. We should come with humility and faith, ver. 27. We can never think too little of ourselves, or too much of the mercy and faithfulness of Christ. Prayers of humility and faith only are answered.

18th. Christ will take care of his poor and needy followers. We may be assured that he has *power* to give us all we need, and that in times of necessity he will supply our wants, ver. 32–38.

19th. The great number of poor in the world is no reason why he should not supply them, ver. 38. He daily supplies the wants of nine hundred millions of

CHAPTER XVI.

THE Pharisees also, with the Sadducees, came, and, tempting, [a]desired him that he would show them a sign from heaven.

2 He answered and said unto them, When it is evening, ye say, *It will be* fair weather; for the sky is red:

3 And in the morning, *It will be* foul weather to-day; for the sky is red and lowering. O *ye* hypocrites! ye can discern the face of the sky, but can ye not *discern* the signs of the times?

4 A wicked and adulterous generation seeketh after a sign; and there shall no sign be given unto it but the sign of the prophet [b]Jonas. And he left them, and departed.

5 And when his disciples were come to the other side, they had forgotten to take bread.

6 Then Jesus said unto them, [c]Take heed, and beware of [d]the leaven of the Pharisees and of the Sadducees.

7 And they reasoned among themselves, saying, *It is* because we have taken no bread.

a ch.12.38,&c.; Mar.8.11,&c.; Lu.11.16; 12.54-56; 1 Co.1.22.

b Jonah 1.17. *c* Lu.12.1. *d* 1 Co.5.6-8; Ga.5.9; 2 Ti.2.16,17.

---

human beings, besides countless numbers of the beasts of the field, of the fowls of heaven, and the fishes of the sea. It is a small thing to supply the wants of the few poor on the earth, and He who feeds the world will take care of *us* in the time of want.

20th. We should be grateful to God for our daily food. We should render to him proper thanksgiving, ver. 36.

CHAPTER XVI.

1-4. See also Mar. viii. 11, 12. *The Pharisees also, and the Sadducees.* See Notes on Mat. iii. 7. ¶ *Tempting.* That is, *trying him*—feigning a desire to see evidence that he was the Messiah, but with a real desire to see him make the attempt to work a miracle and fail, that they might betray and ruin him. ¶ *A sign from heaven.* Some miraculous appearance in the sky. Such appearances had been given by the prophets; and they supposed, if he was the Messiah, that his miracles would not all be confined *to the earth*, but that he was able to give some signal miracle from heaven. Samuel had caused it to thunder (1 Sa. xii. 16-18); Isaiah had caused the shadow to go back ten degrees on the dial of Ahaz (Is. xxxviii. 8); and Moses had sent manna from heaven, Ex. xvi. 4; Jn. vi. 31. It is proper to say, that though Christ did not choose *then* to show such wonders, yet far more stupendous *signs from heaven* than these were exhibited at his death.

2, 3. *He answered*, &c. The meaning of this answer is, There are certain indications by which you judge about the weather. In the evening you think you can predict the weather tomorrow. You have evidence in the redness of the sky by which you judge. So there are sufficient indications on which you should judge concerning *me* and these times. My miracles, and the state of affairs in Judea, are an indication by which you should judge. ¶ *Is red.* Almost all nations have observed this as an indication of fair weather. ¶ *In the morning—the sky is red and lowering.* That is, there are threatening clouds in the sky, which are made red by the rays of the rising sun. This, in Judea, was a sign of a tempest. In other places, however, the signs of a storm may be different. ¶ *The face of the sky.* The *appearance* of the sky.

4. *A wicked and adulterous generation*, &c. See Notes on Mat. xii. 38-40. Mark adds (viii. 12) *that he sighed deeply in spirit.* He did not say this without feeling; he was greatly affected with their perverseness and obstinacy.

5-12. The account in these verses is also recorded in Mar. viii. 13-21.

5. *And when his disciples were come to the other side.* That is, to the other side of the Sea of Galilee. Mark says that he entered into a ship again, and departed to the other side. The conversation with the Pharisees and Sadducees had been on the western side of the Sea of Galilee. See Notes on ch. xv. 39. They crossed from that side again to the east. ¶ *Had forgotten to take bread.* That is, had forgotten to *lay in* a sufficient supply. They had, it seems, not more than one loaf, Mar. viii. 14.

8 *Which* when Jesus perceived,
he said unto them, [e]O ye of little faith, why reason ye among yourselves because ye have brought no bread?
9 Do ye not yet understand,
neither remember the [f]five loaves of the five thousand, and how many baskets ye took up?
10 Neither the [g]seven loaves of
the four thousand, and how many baskets ye took up?
11 How is it that ye do not
understand that I spake *it* not to you concerning bread, that ye should beware of the leaven of the Pharisees and of the Sadducees?
12 Then understood they how
that he bade *them* not beware of the leaven of bread, but of [h]the doctrine of the Pharisees and of the Sadducees.
13 When Jesus came into the
coasts of Cesarea Philippi, he

e ch.6.30; 8.26; 14.31. f ch.14.19,&c. g ch.15.34,&c. h ch.15.1-9.

6-11. *Take heed*, &c. That is, be cautious, be on your guard. ¶ *The leaven of the Pharisees and Sadducees.* Leaven is used in making bread. It passes secretly, silently, but certainly through the mass of dough. See Notes on ch. xiii. 33. None can see its progress. So it was with the doctrines of the Pharisees. They were insinuating, artful, plausible. They *concealed* the real tendency of their doctrines; they instilled them secretly into the mind, until they pervaded all the faculties like leaven. ¶ *They reasoned*, &c. The disciples did not understand him as referring to the doctrine of the Pharisees and Sadducees, because the word *leaven* was not often used among the Jews to denote *doctrines*, no other instance of this use of the word occurring in the Scriptures. Besides, the Jews had many particular rules about the *leaven* which might be used in making bread. Many held that it was not lawful to eat bread made by the Gentiles; and the disciples, perhaps, supposed that he was cautioning them not to procure a supply from the Pharisees and Sadducees. ¶ *O ye of little faith!* Jesus, in reply, said that they should not be so anxious about the supply of their temporal wants. *They should not have supposed, after the miracles that he had wrought in feeding so many*, that HE would caution them to be *anxious* about procuring *bread* for their necessities. It was improper, then, for them to reason about a thing like that, but they should have supposed that he referred to something more important. The miracles had been full proof that he could supply all their wants without such anxiety.

12. *Then understood they*, &c. After this explanation they immediately saw that he referred to the *doctrines* of the Pharisees and Sadducees. Erroneous doctrines are like *leaven* in the following respects: 1st. They are at first slight and unimportant in appearance, as leaven is small in quantity as compared with the mass that is to be leavened. 2d. They are insinuated into the soul unawares and silently, and are difficult of detection. 3d. They act gradually. 4th. They act most certainly. 5th. They will pervade all the soul, and bring all the faculties under their control.

13-20. See also Mar. viii. 27-29, and Lu. ix. 18-20. ¶ *Cesarea Philippi.* There were two cities in Judea called Cesarea. One was situated on the borders of the Mediterranean (See Notes on Ac. viii. 40), and the other was the one mentioned here. This city was greatly enlarged and ornamented by Philip the tetrarch, son of Herod, and called Cesarea in honour of the Roman emperor, Tiberius Cæsar. To distinguish it from the other Cesarea the name of Philip was added to it, and it was called *Cesarea Philippi*, or *Cesarea of Philip*. It was situated in the boundaries of the tribe of Naphtali, at the foot of Mount Hermon. It is now called *Panias* or *Banias*, and contains about 200 houses, and is inhabited chiefly by Turks. The word *coasts* here—now usually applied to land in the vicinity of the sea—means *borders* or *regions*. He came into the part of the country which *appertained* to Cesarea Philippi. He was passing *northward* from the region of Bethsaida, on the coasts of Magdala (ch. xv. 39), where the transactions recorded in the previous verses had occurred. ¶ *When Jesus came.* The original is, *when Jesus was coming*. Mark says (viii. 27) that

asked his disciples, saying, [i]Whom
do men say that I, the Son of
man, am?
14 And they said, [k]Some *say
that thou art* John the Baptist;
some, Elias; and others, Jeremias,
or one of the prophets.
15 He saith unto them, But
whom say ye that I am?
16 And Simon Peter answered
and said, [l]Thou art the Christ,
the Son of the living God.
17 And Jesus answered and said
unto him, Blessed art thou, Simon
Bar-jona; [m]for flesh and blood
hath not revealed *it* unto thee,
[n]but my Father which is in heaven.
18 And I say also unto thee,

i Mar.8.27; Lu.9.18,&c. k ch.14.2; Lu.9.7-9.

l Ps.2.7; ch.14.33; Jn.1.49; Ac.9.20; He.1.2,5. m 1 Co.2.10; Ga.1.16; Ep.2.8. n 1 Jn.4.15; 5.20.

this conversation took place when they were *in the way*, and this idea should have been retained in translating Matthew. While in the way, Jesus took occasion to call their attention *to the truth that he was the Messiah.* This truth it was of much consequence that they should fully believe and understand; and it was important, therefore, that he should often learn their views, to establish them if right, and correct them if wrong. He began, therefore, by inquiring what was the common report respecting him. ¶ *Whom do men say*, &c. This passage has been variously rendered. Some have translated it, "Whom do men say that I am? the Son of man?" Others, "Whom do men say that I am—*I*, who am the Son of man—*i.e.* the Messiah?" The meaning is nearly the same. He wished to obtain the sentiments of the people respecting himself.

14. *And they said*, &c. See Notes on Mat. xi. 14. They supposed that he might be John the Baptist, as Herod did, risen from the dead. See Mat. xiv. 2. He performed many miracles, and strongly resembled John in his manner of life, and in the doctrines which he taught.

16. *And Simon Peter answered*, &c. Peter, expressing the views of the apostles, with characteristic forwardness answered the question proposed to them by Jesus: "Thou art the Christ, the Son of the living God." ¶ *The Christ.* The Messiah, the *Anointed* of God. See Notes on Mat. i. 1. ¶ *The Son.* That is, the Son by way of eminence—in a peculiar sense. See Notes on Mat. i. 17. This appellation was understood as implying divinity, Jn. x. 29-36. ¶ *Of the living God.* The term *living* was given to the true God to distinguish him from *idols*, that are dead, or lifeless—blocks and stones. He is also the Source of life, temporal, spiritual, and eternal. The term *living* is often given to him in the Old Testament, Jos. iii. 10; 1 Sa. xvii. 26, 36; Je. x. 9, 10, &c. In this noble confession Peter expressed the full belief of himself and of his brethren that he was the long-expected Messiah. Other men had very different opinions of him, but *they* were satisfied, and were not ashamed to confess it.

17. *And Jesus answered—Blessed art thou*, &c. Simon Bar-jona is the same as Simon *son of* Jona. *Bar* is a Syriac word signifying *son.* The father of Peter, therefore, was Jona, or Jonas, Jn. i. 42; xxi. 16, 17. ¶ *Blessed.* That is, happy, honoured, evincing a proper spirit, and entitled to the approbation of God. ¶ *For flesh and blood.* This phrase usually signifies *man* (see Ga. i. 16; Ep. vi. 12), and it has been commonly supposed that Jesus meant to say that *man* had not revealed it, but he seems rather to have referred to *himself.* "This truth you have not learned from my lowly appearance, from my human nature, from my apparent rank and standing in the world. You, Jews, were expecting to know the Messiah by his external splendour; his pomp and power *as a man;* but you have not learned me in this manner. I have shown no *such* indication of my Messiahship. Flesh and blood have not shown it. In spite of my appearance—my lowly state—my want of resemblance to what you have expected, you have learned it as of God." This they had been taught by his miracles, his instructions, and by the direct teachings of God on their minds. To *reveal* is to make known, or communicate something that was unknown or secret.

18. *And I say also unto thee, That thou art Peter.* The word *Peter*, in Greek, means a rock. It was given to Simon by Christ when he called him to be a disciple, Jn. i. 42. *Cephas* is a Syriac word, meaning the same as Peter—a

That thou art [o]Peter; and [p]upon this rock I will build my church; and [q]the gates of hell [r]shall not prevail against it.

o Jn.1.42. p Ep.2.20; Re.21.14. q Ps.9.13. r Is.54.17.

rock, or stone. The meaning of this phrase may be thus expressed: "Thou, in saying that I am the Son of God, hast called me by a name expressive of my true character. I, also, have given to *thee* a name expressive of your character. I have called you *Peter*, *a rock*, denoting firmness, solidity, stability, and your confession has shown that the name is appropriate. I see that you are worthy of the name, and will be a distinguished support of my religion." ¶ *And upon this rock*, &c. This passage has given rise to many different interpretations. Some have supposed that the word ROCK refers to Peter's *confession*, and that Jesus meant to say, upon this rock—this *truth* that thou hast confessed, that I am the Messiah—and upon confessions of this from all believers, I will build my church. Confessions like this shall be the test of piety, and in such confessions shall my church stand amid the flames of persecution, the fury *of the gates of hell*. Others have thought that Jesus referred to himself. Christ is called a *rock*, Is. xxviii. 16; 1 Pe. ii. 8. And it has been thought that he turned from Peter to himself, and said, "Upon this rock, this truth that I am the Messiah—*upon myself* as the Messiah, I will build my church." Both these interpretations, though plausible, seem forced upon the passage to avoid the main difficulty in it. Another interpretation is, that the word *rock* refers to *Peter himself*. This is the obvious meaning of the passage; and had it not been that the Church of Rome has abused it, and applied it to what was never intended, no other would have been sought for. "Thou art a rock. Thou hast shown thyself firm, and fit for the work of laying the foundation of the church. Upon thee will I build it. Thou shalt be highly honoured; thou shalt be *first* in making known the gospel to both Jews and Gentiles." This was accomplished. See Ac. ii. 14–36, where he *first* preached to the Jews, and Ac. x., where he preached the gospel to Cornelius and his neighbours, who were Gentiles. Peter had thus the honour of laying the foundation of the church among the Jews and Gentiles; and this is the plain meaning of this passage. See also Ga. ii. 9. But Christ did *not* mean, as the Roman Catholics say he did, to exalt Peter to supreme authority above all the other apostles, or to say that he was the *only one* on whom he would rear his church. See Ac. xv., where the advice of *James*, and not of *Peter*, was followed. See also Ga. ii. 11, where Paul withstood Peter to his face, because he was to be blamed—a thing which could not have happened if Christ, as the Roman Catholics say, meant that Peter should be absolute and infallible. More than all, it is not said here, or anywhere else in the Bible, that Peter should have infallible successors who would be the vicegerents of Christ and the head of the church. The whole meaning of the passage is this: "I will make you the honoured instrument of making known my gospel first to Jews and Gentiles, and will make you a firm and distinguished preacher in building my church." ¶ *Will build my church*. This refers to the custom of building in Judea on a *rock* or other very firm foundation. See Notes on Mat. vii. 24. The word *church* means literally those *called out*, and often means *an assembly* or *congregation*. See Ac. xix. 32, Gr.; Ac. vii. 38. It is applied to Christians as being *called out* from the world. It means sometimes the whole body of believers, Ep. i. 22; 1 Co. x. 32. This is its meaning in this place. It means, also, a particular society of believers worshipping in one place, Ac. viii. 1; ix. 31; 1 Co. i. 2, &c.; sometimes, also, a society in a single house, as Ro. xvi. 5. In common language it means the church *visible*—*i.e.* all who *profess* religion; or *invisible*, *i.e.* all who are real Christians, professors or not. ¶ *And the gates of hell*, &c. Ancient cities were surrounded by walls. In the *gates* by which they were entered were the principal places for holding courts, transacting business, and *deliberating* on public matters. See Notes on Mat. vii. 13. Comp. Notes on Job xxix. 7. See also De. xxii. 4; 1 Sa. iv. 18; Je. xxxvi. 10; Ge. xix. 1; Ps. lxix. 12; ix. 14; Pr. i. 21. The word *gates*, therefore, is used for *counsels*, *designs*, *machinations*, *evil purposes*. ¶ *Hell* means, here, the place of departed spirits, particularly *evil spirits;* and the meaning of the passage is, that all the

19 And I will give unto thee the keys of the kingdom of heaven: and [s]whatsoever thou shalt bind on earth shall be bound in heaven, and whatsoever thou shalt loose on earth shall be loosed in heaven.

20 Then [t]charged he his disciples that they should tell no man that he was Jesus the Christ.

21 From[u] that time forth began Jesus to show unto his disciples how that he must go unto Jeru-

s ch.18.18. t Mar.8.30. u Lu.9.22; 18.31; 24.6,7; 1 Co.15.3,4.

plots, *stratagems*, and *machinations* of the enemies of the church would not be able to overcome it—a promise that has been remarkably fulfilled.

19. *And I will give unto thee*, &c. A *key* is an instrument for opening a door. He that is in possession of it has the power of access, and has a general *care* of a house. Hence, in the Bible, a *key* is used as a symbol of superintendence—an emblem of power and authority. See Notes on Is. xxii. 22; Re. i. 18; iii. 7. The kingdom of heaven here means, doubtless, the church on earth. See Notes on Mat. iii. 2. When the Saviour says, therefore, he will give to Peter the keys of the kingdom of heaven, he means that he will make him *the instrument of opening the door of faith to the world*—the *first* to preach the gospel to both Jews and Gentiles. This was done, Ac. ii. 14-36, and x. The "power of the keys" was given, on this occasion, to Peter alone, *solely for this reason;* the power of "*binding* and loosing" on earth was given to the other apostles *with him*. See Mat. xviii. 18. The only pre-eminence, then, that Peter had was the honour of *first* opening the doors of the gospel to the world. ¶ *Whatsoever thou shalt bind*, &c. The phrase *to bind* and *to loose* was often used by the Jews. It meant *to prohibit* and *to permit*. To *bind* a thing was to forbid it; to *loose* it, to allow it to be done. Thus they said about gathering wood on the Sabbath day, "The school of Shammei *binds it*"—*i.e. forbids it;* "the school of Hillel *looses it*"—*i.e. allows it*. When Jesus gave this power to the apostles, he meant that whatsoever they *forbade* in the church should *have divine authority;* whatever they *permitted*, or commanded, should *also have divine authority*—that is, should be bound or loosed in heaven, or *meet the approbation of God*. They were to be guided infallibly in the organization of the church, 1st, by the teaching of Christ, and, 2d, by the teaching of the Holy Spirit.

This does not refer to *persons*, but to *things*—"*whatsoever*," not *whosoever*. It refers to rites and ceremonies in the church. Such of the Jewish customs as they should forbid were to be forbidden, and such as they thought proper to permit were to be allowed. Such rites as *they* should appoint in the church were to have the force of divine authority. Accordingly, they commanded the Gentile converts to "abstain from pollutions of idols, and from fornication, and from things strangled, and from blood" (Ac. xv. 20); and, in general, they organized the church, and directed what was to be observed and what was to be avoided. The rules laid down by them in the Acts of the Apostles and in the Epistles, in connection with the teachings of the Saviour as recorded in the evangelists, constitute the *only* law binding on Christians in regard to the order of the church, and the rites and ceremonies to be observed in it.

20. *Then charged*, &c. That is, he *commanded* them. Mark (viii. 30) and Luke (ix. 21) say (Greek) that he *strictly* or *severely* charged them. He laid emphasis on it, as a matter of much importance. The reason of this seems to be that his time had not fully come; that he was not willing to rouse the Jewish malice, and to endanger his life, by having it proclaimed that he was the Messiah. The word *Jesus* is wanting in many manuscripts, and should probably be omitted: "Then he charged them strictly to tell no man that he was *the Christ* or *Messiah*."

21-23. See also Mar. vii. 31-33; Lu. ix. 22. *From that time forth*. This was the first intimation that he gave that he was to die in this cruel manner. He had taken much pains to convince them that he was the Messiah; he saw by the confession of Peter that they *were* convinced, and he *then* began to prepare their minds for the awful event which was before him. Had he declared this when he first called them they would never have followed him. Their minds were not prepared for it. They expected a temporal, triumphant prince as the Messiah. He *first*, therefore, con-

salem, and suffer many things of the elders, and chief priests, and scribes, and be killed, and be raised again the third day.

22 Then Peter took him, and began to rebuke him, saying, [1]Be it far from thee, Lord: this shall not be unto thee.

23 But he turned and said unto Peter, Get thee behind me, [v]Satan; thou art [w]an offence unto me: for thou savourest not the things that be of God, but those that be of men.

24 Then said Jesus unto his disciples, [x]If any *man* will come after me, let him deny himself, and take up his cross, and follow me.

25 For[y] whosoever will save his life shall lose it, and whosoever will lose his life for my sake shall find it.

26 For what is a man profited if

1 *Pity thyself.*
v 2 Sa.19.22. w Ro.14 13.

x ch.10.38; Mar.8.34; Lu.9.23; 14.27; Ac.14.22; 1 Th.3.3. y Jn.12.25; Es.4.14.

---

vinced them that he was the Christ, and then, with great prudence, began to correct their apprehensions of the proper character of the Messiah. ¶ *Elders.* The men of the great council or Sanhedrim. See Notes on Mat. v. 7. ¶ *Chief priests and scribes.* See Notes on Mat. iii. 7.

22. *Then Peter took him.* This may mean either that he interrupted him, or that he took him aside, or that he *took him by the hand* as a friend. This latter is probably the true meaning. Peter was strongly attached to him. He could not bear to think of his death. He expected, moreover, that he would be the triumphant Messiah. In his ardour, and confidence, and strong attachment, he seized him by the hand as a friend, and said, "Be it *far* from thee." This phrase might have been translated, "God be merciful to thee; this shall not be unto thee." It expressed Peter's strong desire that it *might* not be. The word *rebuke* here means to *admonish* or *earnestly to entreat*, as in Lu. xvii. 3. It does not mean that Peter assumed *authority* over Christ, but that *he earnestly expressed his wish that it might not be so.* Even this was improper. He should have been submissive, and not have interfered.

23. *Get thee behind me, Satan.* The word Satan means literally an *adversary*, or one that opposes us in the accomplishment of our designs. It is applied to the devil commonly, as the *opposer* or *adversary* of man; but there is no evidence that the Lord Jesus meant to apply this term to Peter, as signifying that *he* was Satan or the devil, or that he used the term in anger. He may have used it in the *general* sense which the word bore as an *adversary* or *opposer;* and the meaning may be, that such sentiments as Peter expressed then were *opposed* to him and his plans. His interference was improper. His views and feelings stood in the way of the accomplishment of the Saviour's designs. There was, undoubtedly, a *rebuke* in this language, for the conduct of Peter was improper; but the idea which is commonly attached to it, and which, perhaps, our translation conveys, implies a more severe and harsh rebuke than the Saviour intended, and than the language which he used would express. ¶ *Thou art an offence.* That is, a stumbling-block. Your advice and wishes are *in my way.* If followed, they would *prevent* the very thing for which I came. ¶ *Thou savourest not.* Literally, *thou thinkest not upon;* or your language and spirit are not such as spring from a supreme regard to the will of God, or from proper views of him, but such as spring from the common views entertained by men. *You* think that those things should *not* be done which *God* wishes to be done. You judge of this matter as *men* do who are desirous of honour; and not as *God*, who sees it best that I should die, to promote the great interests of mankind.

24–28. This discourse is also recorded in Mar. viii. 34–38; ix. 1; and Lu. ix. 23–27. ¶ *Let him deny himself.* That is, let him surrender to God his will, his affections, his body, and his soul. Let him not seek his own happiness as the supreme object, but be willing to renounce all, and lay down his *life* also, if required. ¶ *Take up his cross.* See Notes on Mat. x. 38.

25. *Whosoever will save his life,* &c. See Notes on Mat. x. 39.

26. *For what is a man profited,* &c.

he shall gain the whole world and lose his own soul? or [z]what shall a man give in exchange for his soul?

27 For[a] the Son of man shall come in the glory of his Father, with his angels, and [b]then he shall reward every man according to his works.

28 Verily I say unto you, [c]There be some standing here which shall not [d]taste of death till they see the Son of man coming in his kingdom.

z Ps.49.7,8. a Da.7.9,10; Zec.14.5; Jude 14. b Re.22.12.

c Mar.9.1. d He.2.9.

To gain the whole world means to possess it as our own—all its riches, its honours, and its pleasures. *To lose his own soul* means to be cast away, to be shut out from heaven, to be sent to hell. Two things are implied by Christ in these questions: 1st. That they who are striving to gain the world, and are unwilling to give it up for the sake of religion, will lose their souls; and, 2d. That if the soul *is* lost, nothing can be given in exchange for it, or that it can never afterward be saved. There is no redemption in hell.

27. *For the Son of man*, &c. That is, he will return to judge the world. He will come in glory—the glory of his Father—the majesty with which God is accustomed to appear, and which befits God. He will be attended by angels. He will judge all men. ¶ *Reward.* The word *reward* means recompense. He will deal with them according to their character. The righteous he will reward in heaven with glory and happiness. The wicked he will send to hell, as a *reward* or recompense for their evil works. This fact, *that he will come to judgment*, he gives as a reason why we should be willing to deny ourselves and follow him. Even though it should be *now* attended with contempt and suffering, yet *then* he will *reward* his followers for all their shame and sorrow, and receive them to his kingdom. He adds (Mar. viii. 38), that if we are ashamed of him here, he will be ashamed of us there. That is, if we reject and disown *him* here, he will reject and disown *us* there.

28. *Verily I say unto you*, &c. To encourage them, he assured them that, though his kingdom was now obscure and despised—though he was cast out and little known—yet the time was near when *he* would be regarded in a different manner, and his kingdom be established with great power. This cannot refer to the end of the world, and there is no need of referring it to the destruction of Jerusalem. ¶ *Taste of death.* That is, *die.* Before they die they shall see this. ¶ *Son of man coming in his kingdom.* Mark and Luke have explained this: Mar. ix. 1, "Until they have seen the kingdom of God come with power;" Lu. ix. 27, "Till they see the kingdom of God." The meaning evidently is, till they shall see my kingdom, *i.e.* my church, now small, feeble, and despised, greatly enlarged, established, and spreading with great rapidity and extent. All this was accomplished. All these apostles, except Judas, lived to see the wonders of the day of Pentecost; some of them, John particularly, saw the Jewish nation scattered, the temple destroyed, the gospel established in Asia, Rome, Greece, and in a large part of the known world.

REMARKS.

1st. Men will often judge far more correctly about natural than about spiritual things, ver. 1–3. In respect to natural objects they are watchful. In them they feel a deep interest, and they watch for every *sign* that may affect their interest. They are too much concerned to judge falsely. But they feel no such interest in religious things. Hence it happens that men who have good sense and much wisdom in regard to worldly concerns, are often exceedingly foolish in regard to religion. They believe reports respecting religion, revivals, and missions, which they would despise on any other subject. They read and believe newspapers and other publications, which they would hold in contempt on any other topic but religion. They give a degree of weight to arguments *against* the Bible, and *against* the doctrines of the gospel, to which they would attach little or no importance on any other subject. They sustain themselves in infidelity by arguments which they would regard as of no force if the same kind of reasoning was urged in defence of anything else.

2d. It is of importance to watch the

signs of the times, ver. 3. In the days of Christ it was the duty of the people to look at the evidence that he was the Messiah. The proofs were clear that he was the Messiah. It is also important to look at the signs of the times in which we live. They are clear also. Much is doing; and the diffusion of the Bible, the labours among the heathen, the distribution of tracts, and perhaps, above all, the institution of Sabbath-schools, betoken an eventful age, and are an indication that brighter days are about to dawn on the world. We should watch these signs that we may rejoice; that we may pray with more fervour, and that we may do *our* part to advance the kingdom of God. Little children should grow up believing that they live in an important age; that they enjoy many peculiar privileges, and that they *may* and *must* do much to spread the gospel through the earth. Even *when* children, they should pray, and they should give to benefit others; and, most of all, they should give *themselves* to Christ, that they may benefit others with a right spirit.

3d. Sinners should be addressed with deep feeling and faithfulness, Mar. viii. 12. Jesus *sighed deeply*. So should we. We should not be harsh, or sour, or cold and unfeeling when we address our fellow-men about eternity. We should weep over them, and pray for them, and speak to them, not as if we were better than they, but with an earnest desire for their salvation. Comp. Ac. xx. 31; Phi. iii. 18.

4th. Men easily mistake plain instruction, ver. 7. And especially is this the case where there is any chance of giving a worldly turn to the instruction. If men's thoughts—even those of Christians—were more off from the world, and they thought less of the supply of their temporal wants, they would understand the truths of religion much better than they do. No man can understand the doctrines of religion aright whose principal concern is what he shall eat, and drink, and wear. Hence even Christians are often strangely ignorant of the plainest truths of religion; and hence the importance of teaching those truths to children before their thoughts become engrossed by the world; and hence, too, the importance of Sabbath-schools.

5th. We should not have undue anxiety about the supply of our wants. Christ supplied many thousands by a word, and he can easily supply us, ver. 9–12.

6th. We should learn, from his past goodness, to trust him for the future, ver. 9–12.

7th. We should be on our guard against error, ver. 11. It is sly, artful, plausible, working secretly, but effectually. We should always be cautious of what we believe, and examine it by the word of God. False doctrines are often made as much *like* the truth as possible, for the very purpose of deceiving. "Satan himself is transformed into an angel of light," 2 Cor. xi. 14.

8th. It is important to ascertain our views of Christ, ver. 13–15. Our all depends on this. If we do not think and feel right respecting him we cannot be safe. We should often, then, ask ourselves—we should ask one another—what we think of Christ.

9th. It is our duty to profess attachment to Christ. It should be done boldly, and always, ver. 16. We should never be ashamed of him. And to do this, we should always, *in our own hearts*, believe that he *is* the Christ, the Son of the living God.

10th. We should esteem it a great happiness and honour to be enabled thus to show our attachment to him. The world may not honour us, but God will, and will pronounce us blessed, ver. 17.

11th. God only reveals to men right views of Christ, ver. 17. This he does by his word and Spirit. We should, then, search the Bible; and we should pray much that God would *reveal his Son in us*, and enable us boldly to confess him before men.

12th. The church is safe, ver. 18. It may be small—it may be feeble—it may weep much—it may be much opposed and ridiculed—it may have mighty enemies—the rich and the great may set themselves against it—but it is safe. It is founded on a rock. Its enemies shall never be able to overcome it. Jesus has promised it, and in all ages he has shown that he has remembered his promise. It has not been suffered to become extinct. It has been persecuted, opposed, ridiculed, and almost driven from the world; but *a few* have been found who have loved the Lord; and soon the flame has kindled, and the church has shone forth "fair as the sun, clear as the moon, and terrible as an army with banners." So it is still. Feeble churches may mourn

CHAPTER XVII.

AND[a] after six days Jesus taketh Peter, James, and John his brother, and bringeth them up into a high mountain apart,

2 And was transfigured before

a Mar.9.2,&c.; Lu.9.28,&c.

much—iniquity may abound—the few pious people may weep in secret places; but Jesus hears their groans and counts their tears, and they and the church *are safe*. *He* is their friend, and all the powers of hell shall not prevail against his church.

13th. The importance of prudence in delivering truth, ver. 21. It should be well-timed—it should be when people are prepared to receive it. Especially is this true of young converts. They have need of milk, and not of strong meat. They should not be surprised that many doctrines of the Bible are mysterious now; but they may fully comprehend them hereafter. Peter, a young convert, did not understand the plain doctrine that Jesus must die for sin; yet it was afterward clear to him, and most cordially he loved it.

14th. It is highly wicked and improper to attempt to counsel God, or to think that we understand things better than he does, ver. 22, 23. His plan is the best plan; and though it does not fall in with *our* views of wisdom, yet we should be still. It is all wise. What he does we know not now, yet we shall know hereafter.

15th. We see what religion requires, ver. 24. We must deny ourselves. We must submit to trials. We must do our duty. We must welcome persecution, Mat. v. 10. We must be, in all places, among all men, and in every employment, *Christians*, no matter what may happen. Come poverty, disease, persecution, death, it is ours to take up the cross and do our duty. So apostles, and martyrs, and the Saviour himself have gone before us, and *we* must follow in their steps.

"Shall I be carried to the skies
On flowery beds of ease,
While others fought to win the prize,
And sailed through bloody seas?

"Sure I must fight if I would reign;
Increase my courage, Lord,
To bear the cross, endure the shame,
Supported by thy word."

16th. How foolish are the men o. this world! ver. 26. In a little time how worthless will be all their wealth! It is gained by anxiety, and toil, and tears. It never satisfies. It harasses them with constant care. It smooths no wrinkles on their brow, alleviates no pain when they are sick, saves no friend from death, gives no consolation in regard to the future, and may be left at any moment. Others will soon possess, and perhaps scatter in dissipation, what they have obtained by so much toil. See Ps. xxxix. 6. And while they scatter or enjoy it, where shall the soul of him be who spent all his probation to obtain it? Alas! lost, lost, lost—for ever lost! and no wealth, no man, no devil, no angel, can redeem him, or be given *for* his soul. The harvest will be past, the summer ended, and he not saved. In *gaining* the world he made two things certain—disappointment and trouble here, and an eternity of woe hereafter. How foolish and wicked is man!

17th. The righteous should rejoice that Jesus will come again to our world. He will reward them, ver. 27. He will come as their friend, and they shall ascend with him to heaven.

18th. The wicked should weep and wail that Jesus will come again to our world. He will punish them for their crimes, ver. 27. They cannot escape. See Re. i. 7.

19th. It will not be long before he will come, ver. 28. At anyrate, it will not be long before *we* shall meet him. Death is near; and then we must stand before him, and give an account of the deeds done in the body.

CHAPTER XVII.

1-9. See also Mar. ix. 2-10; Lu. ix. 28-36.

1. *And after six days.* That is, six days from the conversation recorded in the last chapter. Luke (ix. 28) says, about an eight days after. Matthew mentions the six days that intervened between the day of the conversation and the transfiguration. Luke *includes* both those days, and thus reckons eight. Besides, Luke does not pretend to fix the precise time. He says, "*about* an eight days after." ¶ *Taketh Peter, and James, and John.* These three disciples were with him, also, in the garden of Gethsemane, Mar. xiv. 33. He designed to fit them in an eminent degree for the work of the gospel ministry by the previous manifestations of his glory, and of his

them: and [b]his face did shine as the sun, and his raiment was white as the light.

3 And, behold, there appeared unto them Moses and Elias, talking with him.

4 Then answered Peter, and said unto Jesus, Lord, it is good

b Re.1.16.

patience in suffering. ¶ *Into a high mountain apart.* That is, *apart* from the other disciples. It is commonly supposed that this was Mount Tabor, a high mountain in Galilee. The name of the mountain is not, however, mentioned in the New Testament. Luke adds (ix. 28) that he went up there *to pray.* Our Saviour prayed much. When he did it he chose to be alone. For this purpose he often ascended mountains or went into the deserts. There is something in the solitude and deep and awful stillness of a lofty mountain favourable to devotion.

2. *And was transfigured before them.* The word *transfigure* means *to change the appearance or form.* It does not denote the change of the *substance* of a thing, but simply of its *appearance.* It puts on a new aspect. What this change was we are expressly told. 1st. His face shone as the sun; that is, with a peculiar brightness. A similar appearance is described respecting Moses when he came down from the mount, Ex. xxxiv. 29, 30. See also He. i. 3, where Christ is called the brightness of the glory of God; in the original, the *splendour* or *shining*, like the brightness of the sun. 2d. The second change was that of his garments. They were white as the light. Mark says, "exceeding white as snow; so as no fuller on earth could white them." The word "fuller" means, commonly, one who dresses cloth or *fulls* it, so as to make it more thick and strong. Here it means one who *bleaches* cloth or makes it white; one who cleanses garments when by wearing they become soiled. Among the Greeks that was a distinct trade. Luke says, "white *and* glistering;" that is, resplendent, shining, or a very bright white. There is no evidence here that what is commonly said of him is true, that his *body* was so changed as to show what his glorified body is. His body, so far as the sacred writers inform us, underwent no change. All this splendour and glory was a change *in appearance* only. The Scriptures should be taken *just as they are*, without any attempt to affix a meaning to them which the sacred writers did not intend. ¶ *Raiment.* Clothing. John may refer to this transfiguration in ch. i. 14, as Peter does in his second epistle, i. 16, 17.

3. *And behold there appeared unto them Moses and Elias.* Moses, a distinguished servant of God, by whom the *law* was given, and whose institutions typified the Messiah. It was particularly proper that *he* should appear, when his prophecies and types were about to be fulfilled, and the rites which he had instituted were about to be done away. Elias, or Elijah, a distinguished prophet, taken to heaven without seeing death. See 2 Ki. ii. 11. Elijah had been honoured eminently by being thus translated, and still more by being made the *model* of the forerunner of the Messiah, Mal. iv. 5; Lu. i. 17; Mat. xi. 14. They appeared "in glory" (Lu. ix. 31); *i.e.* as they are *in heaven*—with the glory which the redeemed have there. ¶ *Talking with him.* Luke (ix. 31) informs us that they conversed about "his decease which he should accomplish at Jerusalem." To redeemed spirits that death was an object of intense interest. By faith in that death they had been saved; and now that the Redeemer of mankind was about to die, it is no wonder that this was the burden of his and their thoughts.

Luke adds (ix. 32) that "Peter and they that were with him were heavy with sleep." It is not improbable that this was in the night; that Jesus was engaged in prayer; and that he had *permitted* his weary followers to compose themselves to rest. It was after they were awaked that they saw this vision. Probably the sudden splendour, the bright shining aroused them from sleep.

4. *Let us make here three tabernacles.* A tabernacle is a *tent.* It was made, commonly, by fixing posts into the ground, and stretching on them cloth fastened by cords. See Notes on Is. xxxiii. 20. In some instances they were made of branches of trees—a temporary shelter from the sun and rain, not a permanent dwelling. Peter was rejoiced at the vision and desirous of continuing it. He proposed, therefore, that they should prolong this interview and dwell

for us to be here: if thou wilt,
let us make here three tabernacles;
one for thee, and one for Moses,
and one for Elias.
5 While he yet spake, behold, a
bright cloud overshadowed them:
and behold [c]a voice out of the
cloud, which said, This is my beloved Son, [d]in whom I am well
pleased; [e]hear ye him.
6 And when the disciples heard
it, they fell on their face, and were
sore afraid.
7 And Jesus came and [f]touched
them, and said, Arise, and be not
afraid.
8 And when they had lifted up
their eyes, they saw no man, save
Jesus only.
9 And as they came down from
the mountain, Jesus charged them,
saying, Tell the vision to no man

c ch.3.17; Mar.1.11; Lu.3.22; 2 Pe.1.17. *d* Is.42.1,21. *e* De.18.15,19; Ac.3.22,23; He.1.1,2; 2.1-3.

f Da.10.10,18; Re.1.17.

there. Mark adds, "For he wist not [that is, knew not] what to say, for they were sore afraid." They were frightened, amazed, and rejoiced; and, in the ecstasy of the moment, Peter proposed to remain there.

5. *A bright cloud overshadowed them.* The word *overshadow* here means, rather, to *be diffused* or *spread* over them. It does not mean that it made *a shade.* A cloud was the symbol of the divine presence. Thus God went before the Israelites in a cloudy pillar—dark by day and bright by night (Ex. xiv. 19, 20); he appeared on Mount Sinai in a cloud bright by fire (Ex. xxiv. 15–17); and a *cloud*, the symbol of the divine presence—called the *Shechinah*—dwelt continually in the most holy place in the temple, 1 Ki. viii. 10, 11; Eze. i. 4; x. 4. When, therefore, the disciples saw this cloud, they were prepared to hear the word of the Lord. ¶ *This is my beloved Son.* This was the voice of God. This was the second time that, in a remarkable manner, God had declared this. See Mat. iii. 17. This was spoken to confirm the disciples; to make known to them that it was their duty to hear Christ rather than any other, and to honour *him* more than Moses and Elijah; and to strengthen their faith in him when they should go forth to preach the gospel after he was shamefully put to death. After this, it was impossible for them to doubt that he was truly the Son of God. See 2 Pe. i. 17, 18.

6. *They fell on their face.* They entered into the cloud, or the cloud enveloped them, Lu. ix. 34. They were therefore afraid. They were awed at the presence of God, and prostrated themselves in solemn adoration on the ground, and their fears were removed only by the voice of their beloved Master. No man can see God and live; and it is only the glory of God, as it shines in the face of Christ (see 2 Co. iv. 6), that mortals can bear.

9. *Tell the vision to no man.* This vision was designed particularly to confirm them in the truth that he was the Messiah. While he was with them it was unnecessary that they should relate what they had seen. When he was crucified they would need this evidence that he was the Christ. Then they were to use it. There were three witnesses of it—as many as the law required (De. xvii. 6; He. x. 28), and the proof that he was the Messiah was clear. Besides, if they had told it then, it would have provoked the Jews and endangered his life. His time was not yet come. ¶ *Vision.* Sight; appearance. What they had seen on the mount. ¶ *Charged them.* Gave them a commandment.

The *sole* design of this transfiguration was to convince them that he was the Christ; that he was greater than the greatest of the prophets; that he was the Son of God.

Mark adds (ix. 10), "they kept that saying with themselves, questioning one with another what the rising from the dead should mean." The Pharisees believed that the dead would rise, and there is no doubt that the disciples believed it; but their views were not clear, and, in particular, they did not understand what he meant by *his* rising from the dead. They do not appear to have understood, though he had told them (ch. xii. 40) that he would rise after three days.

10–13. See also Mar. ix. 11–13. *Why then say the scribes*, &c. The disciples appear to have been satisfied now that he was the Messiah. The *transfigura-*

until the Son of man be risen again from the dead.

10 And his disciples asked him, saying, [g]Why then say the scribes that Elias must first come?

11 And Jesus answered and said unto them, Elias truly shall first come, and restore all things.

12 But I say unto you, That Elias is come already, and they knew him not, but have done unto him whatsoever they listed. Likewise [h]shall also the Son of man suffer of them.

13 Then the disciples understood that he spake unto them of John the Baptist.

14 And[i] when they were come

g Mal.4.5,6; ch.11.14. h ch.16.21. i Mar.9.14,&c.; Lu.9.37,&c.

tion had taken away all their doubts, but they recollected that it was a common doctrine among the Jews that *Elijah* would appear before the Messiah came, and they did not then recollect that he had appeared. To this difficulty the word *then* refers. "We are satisfied that thou art the Christ, but Elijah has not yet come, as was expected; what, then, is the meaning of the common opinions of our learned men, the scribes? Were they right or wrong in their expectation of Elijah?" See Notes on Mat. xi. 14.

11. *Elias truly shall first come, and restore all things.* He did not mean by this that Elijah *was yet* to come, for he tells them immediately (ver. 12) that he *had* come; but he meant to affirm that it was *a true doctrine* which the scribes taught, that Elijah *would* appear before the coming of the Messiah. *To restore* means to put into the former situation. See Mat. xii. 13. Hence it means *to heal, to correct, to put in proper order.* Here it means that Elijah would put things in a proper state; he would be the instrument of *reforming* the people, or of *restoring* them, in some measure, to proper notions about the Messiah and preparing them for his coming. Before the coming of John their views were erroneous, their expectations worldly, and their conduct exceedingly depraved. He corrected many of their notions about the Messiah (see Mat. iii.), and was the instrument of an extensive reformation, and thus *restored* them, in some degree, to correct views of their own economy and of the Messiah, and to a preparation for his advent.

12. *Elias is come already.* That is, John the Baptist has come, in the spirit and power of Elias. See Lu. i. 17. ¶ *They have done unto him whatsoever they listed.* The word *list* is an old English word, signifying *to choose,* to desire, to be inclined. See Jn. iii. 8. It means, here, that they had done to John as they pleased; that is, they had put him to death, Mat. xiv. 10.

Mark adds (ix. 12) that Jesus told them that it was "written of the Son of man that he must suffer many things, and be set at naught." This was written of him particularly in Is. liii. To be set at naught is to be esteemed as worthless or as nothing; to be cast out and despised. No prophecy was ever more strikingly fulfilled. See Lu. xxiii. 11.

14–21. This narrative, with some additions, is found in Mar. ix. 14–29, and Lu. ix. 37–43.

14. *And when they were come to the multitude.* This took place on the day following the transfiguration, Lu. ix. 37. This multitude was probably composed of persons who had attended on his ministry, many of whom were his real disciples. *With them,* as Mark (ix. 15) informs us, were "scribes questioning with them." That is, they were probably *professedly* making inquiries about the Saviour, but *really* attempting to introduce their own sentiments, and to draw them off from him. They probably artfully asked them many questions about his birth, his family, his appearance, his manner of life, and his instructions, all which were contrary to the general expectation respecting the Messiah, and they intended, therefore, to insinuate that *such* a person could not be the Christ. The people were persuaded that he was the Messiah, and it would not have done to have attacked their opinions openly, but they attempted to gain the same point by sly insinuations. Error is always subtle, and often puts on the appearance of calm and honest inquiry. Well had he compared them to *leaven*, Mat. xvi. 11, 12. The multitude, seeing Jesus coming down, left the scribes, and ran to meet him (Mark). They were *amazed*, probably because they had not expected to see him there. In their joy at meeting him in this unexpected manner,

to the multitude, there came to him a *certain* man kneeling down to him, and saying,

15 Lord, have mercy on my son; for he is lunatic, and sore vexed; for ofttimes he falleth into the fire, and oft into the water.

16 And I brought him to thy disciples, and they could not cure him.

17 Then Jesus answered and said, O faithless and perverse generation! how long shall I be with

---

they *saluted* him (Mark); that is, probably they prostrated themselves before him after the manner of salutation in Eastern countries. See Notes on Lu. x. 4. Jesus, seeing the scribes and their artful design, reproved them by asking them *why* they questioned thus with his disciples, Mar. ix. 16. Conscious of their guilt and their base purpose, they returned no answer. ¶ *A* certain *man kneeling down to him.* That is, *saluting* him, or showing high regard for him. See Notes on Lu. x. 4. It did not imply religious homage, but merely high respect and earnest entreaty.

15. *Lord, have mercy.* The word Lord here means *Sir*, a title of civility, not implying divinity. ¶ *My son.* This was an only son (Luke). He was possessed with a devil. This calamity was attended with the following symptoms: he was *lunatic* (see Notes on Mat. iv. 24); he was sore vexed; that is, he suffered greatly, or was greatly afflicted; he fell often suddenly, in the manner of persons having epileptic fits; he was dumb—that is, he was dumb except when the fit was *coming on him*, for Luke says that when the spirit took him he cried suddenly out; he foamed and gnashed with his teeth, and wasted away, or became poor and emaciated. Luke (ix. 39) adds of the evil spirit, "it teareth him that he foameth again, and, bruising him, hardly departeth from him;" that is, scarcely departed from him, or he had only short intervals of reason, for so the passage in Luke, "bruising him, hardly departeth from him," should be translated.

16. *And I brought him to thy disciples,* &c. That is, not to the apostles, for they had power over unclean spirits (Mat. x. 8), but to others of his followers who attempted to work miracles. It is probable that many of his disciples attempted this who were not personal attendants on his ministry, Mar. ix. 38.

17. *Then Jesus answered and said, O faithless and perverse generation! Perverse* means that which is *twisted* or *turned* from the proper direction; and is often used of the *eyes*, when one or both are turned from their natural position. Applied to a *generation* or *race* of men, it means that they hold opinions *turned* or *perverted* from the truth, and that they were wicked in their conduct. Jesus applied this, probably, to the Jews, and not to his real disciples. ¶ *How long shall I suffer you?* That is, how long shall I bear with you? How long is it necessary to show such patience and forbearance with your unbelief and perversity? This was not so much an expression of impatience or complaint as a reproof for their being so slow to believe that he was the Messiah, notwithstanding his miracles.

Mark adds (ix. 20–22) that when he that was possessed was brought, the spirit, by a last desperate struggle, threw him down and tore him, and left him apparently dead. He adds farther, that the case had existed during the whole life of his son, from a child. This was a case of uncommon obstinacy. The affliction was fixed and lasting. The disciples, seeing the obstinacy of the case—seeing him dumb, wasted away, torn, and foaming—despaired of being able to cure him. They lacked the *faith* which was necessary; *doubted* whether they could cure him, and *therefore* could not.

The father of the child said (Mar. ix. 22), "*If thou canst do anything*, have compassion on us and help us;" an expression implying a weak faith, a lingering doubt whether he *could* restore him. Jesus replied to this, "*If thou canst* BELIEVE, all things are possible to him that believeth" (Mar. ix. 23); implying that the difficulty in the case was *not* that he could not heal him, but that he had not the proper kind and degree of faith with which to come to him. That is, this cure shall be effected if you have faith. Not that *his* faith would give Jesus the *power* to heal him, but it *would render it proper* that he should exert that power in his favour. In this way, and in this only, are all things possible to believers.

you? how long shall I suffer you?
Bring him hither to me.
18 And Jesus rebuked the devil,
and he departed out of him: and
the child was cured from that very
hour.
19 Then came the disciples to
Jesus apart, and said, Why could
not we cast him out?
20 And Jesus said unto them,
Because [k] of your unbelief: for
verily I say unto you, [l]If ye have
faith as a grain of mustard-seed,
ye shall say unto this mountain,
Remove hence to yonder place,
and it shall remove; and nothing
shall be impossible unto you.
21 Howbeit, this kind goeth not
out but by prayer and fasting.
22 And [m]while they abode in
Galilee, Jesus said unto them, The
Son of man shall be betrayed into
the hands of men;
23 And they shall kill him, and

k He.3.19.
l ch.21.21; Mar.11.23; Lu.17.6; 1 Co.13.2.
m ch.16.21; 20.17; Mar.8.31; 9.30,31; 10.33; Lu.9.22,44; 18.31; 24.6,26,46.

The man had faith, Mar. ix. 24. The father came, as a father *should* do, weeping, and praying that his faith might be increased, so as to make it *proper* that Jesus should interpose in his behalf, and save his child.

Help my unbelief, Mar. ix. 24. This was an expression of humility. If my faith is defective, supply what is lacking. Help me to overcome my unbelief. Let not the defect of my faith be in the way of this blessing.

18. *And Jesus rebuked the devil.* The word *rebuke* has the combined force of *reproving* and *commanding*. He *reproved* him for having afflicted the child, and he *commanded* him to come out of him. Mark (ix. 25) has recorded the words which he used—words implying reproof and command: "Thou dumb and deaf spirit, I charge thee come out of him, and enter no more into him." And the spirit cried, and with a mighty convulsion came out, leaving the child apparently dead. Jesus lifted him up by the hand (Mark), and gave him to his father (Luke).

19. *Then came the disciples*, &c. This inquiry was made in some house to which they retired near the place where the miracle was performed (Mark). Jesus told them, in reply, that it was because of their unbelief that they had not been able to cast him out. They were appalled by the difficulty of the case and the obstinacy of the disease. Their *faith* would not have made it more easy for God to work this miracle, but such was his *will*—such the way in which he worked miracles, that he required faith in those who were the instruments.

20. *As a grain of mustard-seed.* See Notes on Mat. xiii. 31, 32. The mustard-seed was the smallest of all seeds. It has been supposed by some, therefore, that he meant to say, If you have the smallest or feeblest faith that is genuine, you can do all things. The mustard-seed produced the largest of all herbs. It has been supposed by others, therefore, to mean, If you have increasing, expanding, enlarged faith, growing and strengthening from small beginnings, you can perform the most difficult undertaking. There is a principle of vitality in the grain of seed stretching forward to great results, which illustrates the nature of faith. Your faith should be *like* that. This is probably the true meaning. ¶ *Ye shall say unto this mountain*, &c. Probably he pointed to a mountain near, to assure them that if they had such faith they might accomplish the most difficult undertakings—things that at first would appear impossible.

21. *Howbeit, this kind*, &c. This *kind* means this kind of devils—this species of possession. Where they have had long possession—where they produce such painful, fixed, and alarming effects, they can be expelled only in connection with prayer and fasting. ¶ *Goeth not out but by prayer and fasting.* That is, in order to work miracles of this kind—to cast out devils in cases so obstinate and dreadful as this, *faith of the highest kind is necessary.* That faith is produced and kept vigorous only by much prayer, and by such abstinence from food as fits the mind for the highest exercises of religion, and leaves it free to hold communion with God.

22, 23. See also Mar. ix. 30-33; Lu. ix. 43-45. *And while they abode in Galilee.* Galilee, the northern part of Palestine. See Notes on Mat. ii. 22. ¶ *The Son of man shall be betrayed*, &c.

the third day he shall be raised again. And they were exceeding sorry.

24 And when they were come to Capernaum, they that received tribute-*money*[1] came to Peter, and said, Doth not your master pay tribute?

25 He saith, Yes. And when he was come into the house, Jesus prevented him, saying, What thinkest thou, Simon? of whom do the kings of the earth take custom or tribute? of their own children, or of strangers?

26 Peter saith unto him, Of strangers. Jesus saith unto him, Then are the children free.

1 *didrachma*, in value 15*d.*, Ex.38.26.

To betray means to deliver up in a treacherous manner. This was done by Judas Iscariot, called for that act the traitor, Mat. xxvi. 14-16, 47-50. A traitor, or betrayer, is one who makes use of confidence reposed in him for the purpose of delivering him up who puts that confidence in him to the hands of enemies.

23. *And they shall kill him, and the third day he shall be raised again.* See Mat. xii. 40. Mark and Luke add that they understood not that saying, and it was hid from them, and they were afraid to ask him. The reasons of this may have been, 1st. They were strongly attached to him, and were *exceedingly sorry* (Matthew) at any intimation that he was soon to leave them. They learned with great slowness and reluctance, therefore, that he was to be treated in this manner. 2d. They were not *willing* to believe it. They knew that he was the Messiah, but they supposed that he was to be a distinguished prince, and was to restore the kingdom to Israel, Ac. i. 6. But to be betrayed into the hands of his enemies, and be put to death, appeared to them to be frustrating all these expectations. 3d. Though what he said was plain enough, yet they did not understand it; they *could not see* how he could be the Messiah, and yet be put to death in this manner; nor did they understand it fully till after the resurrection.

24-27. *And when they were come to Capernaum.* See Notes on Mat. iv. 13. ¶ *They that received tribute.* In the original this is, they who received *the didrachma*, or *double drachma*. The *drachma* was a Grecian coin worth about fifteen cents (7½*d.*) of our money. The didrachma, or double drachma, was a silver coin equal to the Attic drachma, and, in the time of Josephus, equal to the Jewish half shekel, that is, about thirty cents of our money. This *tribute*, consisting of the didrachma or double drachma, was not paid to the Roman government, but to the Jewish collectors for the use of the temple service. It was permitted in the law of Moses (see Ex. xxx. 11-16) that in numbering the people half a shekel should be received of each man for the services of religion. This was in addition to the *tithes* paid by the whole nation, and seems to have been considered as a voluntary offering. It was devoted to the purchase of animals for the daily sacrifice, wood, flour, salt, incense, &c., for the use of the temple. ¶ *Doth not your master pay tribute?* This tribute was voluntary, and they therefore asked him whether he was in the habit of paying taxes for the support of the temple. Peter replied that it was his custom to pay all the usual taxes of the nation.

25. *Jesus prevented him.* That is, Jesus *commenced speaking before Peter*, or spoke before Peter had told him what he had said. This implies that, though not present with Peter when he gave the answer, yet Jesus was acquainted with what he had said. ¶ *Prevent.* To go before, or precede. It did not mean, as it now does with us, *to hinder* or obstruct. See the same use of the word in Ps. lix. 10; lxxix. 8; lxxxviii. 13; 1 Th. iv. 15; Ps. cxix. 148. ¶ *Of whom do the kings of the earth*, &c. That is, earthly kings. ¶ *Their own children.* Their sons; the members of their own family. ¶ *Or of strangers?* The word strangers does not mean foreigners, but those that were not their own sons or members of their family. Peter replied that tribute was collected of those *out of* their own family. Jesus answered, Then are the children, or *sons* of the kings, *free;* that is, taxes are not required of them. The meaning of this may be thus expressed: "Kings do not tax their own sons. This tribute-money is taken up for the temple service; that is, the service of *my* Father. I, therefore, being *the Son of God*, for whom this is taken up, cannot be law-

27 Notwithstanding, lest we should [n]offend them, go thou to the sea, and cast a hook, and take up the fish that first cometh up; and when thou hast opened his mouth, thou shalt find [2]a piece of money: that take, and give unto them, for me and thee.

n Ro.14.21; 15.1-3; 2 Co.6.3.

2 *a stater*, which was half an ounce of silver.

---

fully *required* to pay this tribute." This argument is based on the supposition that this was a *religious*, and not a *civil* tax. If it had been the latter, the illustration would not have been pertinent.

27. *Notwithstanding, lest we should offend them.* That is, lest they should think that we despise the temple and its service, and thus provoke needless opposition; though we are not under *obligation* to pay it, yet it is best to pay it to them. ¶ *Go to the sea.* This was at Capernaum, on the shore of the Sea of Tiberias. ¶ *Thou shalt find a piece of money.* In the original, thou shalt find a *stater*, a Roman silver coin of the value of four drachmas, or *one* shekel, and of course sufficient to pay the tribute for two—himself and Peter. In whatever way this is regarded, it is proof that Jesus was possessed of divine attributes. If he *knew* that the first fish that came up would have such a coin in his mouth, it was proof of *omniscience*. If he *created* the coin for the occasion and placed it there, then it was proof of divine power. The former is the most probable supposition. It is by no means absurd that a *fish* should have swallowed a silver coin. Many of them *bite* eagerly at anything bright, and would not hesitate, therefore, at swallowing a piece of money.

REMARKS.

1st. It is proper to withdraw from those around us that we may engage in secret prayer; and it is desirable for every one to have a place where he may be alone with God, ver. 1. Christ often went into deserts and on mountains that he might be by himself. This should be done—1. To avoid the appearance of ostentation. 2. Pride is easily excited when we know that others hear us pray. Every one should have some place—some closet—to which he may retire at any time, with the assurance that none sees him but God. See Notes on ch. vi. 6.

2d. In such seasons we shall meet God, ver. 2. It was in such a season that the divine favour was peculiarly shown to Christ. Then the *transfiguration* took place—the brightest manifestation of his glory that ever occurred on earth. So the clearest and most precious manifestations of the love and glory of God will be made to *us* in prayer.

3d. We see the great glory of Christ, ver. 2. No such favour had been granted to any prophet before him. We see the regard in which he was held by Moses and Elias—among the greatest of the prophets. We see the honour which God put on him, exalting him far above them both, ver. 5. The glory of heaven encompasses the Lord Jesus, and all its redeemed pay him reverence. In him the divine nature shines illustriously; and of him and to him the divinity speaks in glory as the only begotten Son of God.

4th. It is right to have particular affection for some Christians more than others, at the same time that we should love them all. Christ loved *all* his disciples, but he admitted some to peculiar friendship and favours, ver. 1. Some Christians may be more *congenial* to us in feeling, age, and education than others; and it is proper, and may be greatly to our advantage, to admit them among our peculiar friends.

5th. The death of Jesus is an object of great interest to the redeemed. Moses and Elias talked of it, Lu. ix. 31. Angels also desire to look into this great subject, 1 Pe. i. 12. By that death all the redeemed are saved, and *in* that death the angels see the most signal display of the justice and love of God.

6th. Christians should delight to be where God has manifested his glory. The feeling of Peter was natural, ver. 4. His love of the glorious presence of Christ and the redeemed was right. He erred only in the *manner* of manifesting that love. *We* should always love the house of prayer—the sanctuary—the place where Christ has manifested himself as peculiarly glorious and precious to our souls, or as peculiarly our Friend and Deliverer.

7th. We need not be afraid of the most awful displays of deity if Christ be with us, ver. 7. Were we *alone* we *should* fear. None could see God and live, for he is a consuming fire, He. xii. 29. But with Jesus for our friend we may go confidently down to death; we may meet him at his awful bar; we may dwell in the full splendours of his presence to all eternity.

8th. Saints at death are taken to happiness and live now in glory, ver. 3. Moses and Elias were not *created anew*, but went to heaven as they were. They came from heaven and returned thither. The spirits of all men live, therefore, in happiness or woe after the body is dead.

9th. It is not unreasonable to suppose that saints may have *some* knowledge of what is done here on earth. Moses and Elias appear to have been acquainted with the fact that Jesus was about to die at Jerusalem.

10th. The Scriptures will be fulfilled. The fulfilment may take place when we little know it, or in events that we should not suppose were intended for a fulfilment, ver. 12.

11th. Erroneous teachers will endeavour to draw us away from the truth, Mar. ix. 14. They will do it by art, and caution, and the appearance of calm inquiry. We should always be on our guard against any teachers *appearing* to call in question what Christ has plainly taught us.

12th. Christ, in his word and by his Spirit, is a safe teacher, Mar. ix. 15. When men are suggesting plausible doubts about doctrine, or attempting to unsettle our minds by cavils and inquiry, we should leave them, and apply by prayer, and by searching the Bible, to Christ, the great Prophet, who is the way, the *truth*, and the life.

13th. Parents should be earnest for the welfare of their children, ver. 15. It is right for them to pray to God, in times of sickness, that he would heal them. Miracles are not to be expected, but God only can bless the means which parents use for their sick and afflicted children.

14th. Parents may do much by faith and prayer for their children. Here the faith of the parent was the means of saving the life of the child, ver. 14–18. So the faith of parents—a faith producing diligent instruction, a holy example, and much prayer, may be the means of saving their souls. God will not, indeed, save them *on account* of the faith of the parent, but the holy life of a father and mother may be the means of training up their children for heaven.

15th. It is proper to pray to Jesus to increase our faith, Mar. ix. 24. We may be sensible of our unbelief—may feel that we deserve condemnation, and that we deserve no favour that is usually bestowed on faith; but we may come to him and implore of him an increase of faith, and thus obtain the object of our desires.

16th. Our unbelief hinders our doing much that we *might* do, ver. 20. We shrink from great difficulties, we fail in great duties, because we do not put confidence in God, who is able to help us. The proper way to live a life of religion and peace is to do *just what God requires of us*, depending on his grace to aid us.

17th. We see the proper way of increasing our faith, ver. 21. It is by much prayer, self-denial, and fasting. Faith is a plant that never grows in an uncultivated soil, and is never luxuriant unless it is often exposed to the beams of the Sun of Righteousness.

18th. It is right to weep and mourn over the death of Jesus, ver. 23. It was a cruel death, and we should mourn that our *best Friend* passed through such sufferings. Yet we should rather mourn that *our sins* were the cause of such bitter sorrows; and that, but for our sins, and the sins of the rest of mankind, he might have been always happy.

"'Twas you, my sins, my cruel sins,
His chief tormentors were;
Each of my crimes became a nail,
And unbelief the spear.

"'Twas you that pulled the vengeance down
Upon his guiltless head.
Break, break, my heart! O burst, mine eyes!
And let my sorrows bleed."

19th. At the same time, we should rejoice that God made his death the source of the richest blessings that ever descended on mankind. He rose and brought life and immortality to light, ver. 23.

20th. We should comply with all the requirements of the laws of the land, if not contrary to the law of God. It is important that governments should be supported, ver. 25. See also Ro. xiii. 1–7.

21st. We should also be willing to contribute our just proportion to the support of the institutions of religion. The *tribute* which Jesus paid here by a miracle was for the support of religion in the temple, ver. 24–27. He under-

CHAPTER XVIII.

AT[a] the same time came the disciples unto Jesus, saying, Who is the greatest in the kingdom of heaven?

2 And Jesus called a little child unto him, and set him in the midst of them,

3 And said, Verily I say unto you, [b]Except ye be converted, and

a Mar.9.33,&c.; Lu.9.46,&c.; 22.24,&c.

b Ps.51.10-13; Jn.3.3.

---

stood of how much value are the institutions of religion to the welfare of man. He worked a miracle, therefore, to make a *voluntary offering* to support it. Religion promotes the purity, peace, intelligence, and order of the community, and every man is therefore under obligation to do his part toward its support. If any man doubts this, he has only to go to the places where there is no religion—among scoffers, and thieves, and adulterers, and prostitutes, and pickpockets, and drunkards. No money is ever lost that goes in any way to suppress these vices and to make men better.

CHAPTER XVIII.

1-6. See also Mar. ix. 33–41; Lu. ix. 46-50. *Who is the greatest in the kingdom of heaven?* By the kingdom of heaven they meant the kingdom which they supposed he was about to set up—his kingdom as the Messiah. They asked the question because they supposed, in accordance with the common expectation of the Jews, that he was about to set up a temporal kingdom of great splendour, and they wished to know who should have the principal offices, and posts of honour and profit. This was among them a frequent subject of inquiry and controversy. Mark (ix. 34) informs us that they had had a dispute on this subject in the way. Jesus, he says, inquired of them what they had been disputing about. Luke (ix. 47) says that Jesus perceived the thought of their heart—an act implying omniscience, for none can search the heart but God, Je. xvii. 10. The disciples, conscious that the subject of their dispute was known, requested Jesus to decide it, Mat. xviii. 1. *They* were at first *silent* through shame (Mark), but, perceiving that the subject of their dispute was known, they came, as Matthew states, and referred the matter to him for his opinion.

2, 3. *Except ye be converted.* The word "converted" means *changed* or turned. The verb means to change or turn from one habit of life or set of opinions to another, Ja. v. 19; Lu. xxii. 32. See also Mat. vii. 6; xvi. 23; Lu. vii. 9, &c., where the same word is used in the original. It sometimes refers to that great change called the new birth or regeneration (Ps. li. 13; Is. lx. 5; Ac. iii. 19), but not always. It is a *general* word, meaning *any* change. The word *regeneration* denotes a particular change—the beginning to live a spiritual life. The phrase, "Except ye be converted," does not imply, of necessity, that they were not Christians *before*, or had not been born again. It means that their opinions and feelings about the kingdom of the Messiah must be *changed.* They had supposed that he was to be a temporal prince. They expected he would reign as other kings did. They supposed he would have his great officers of state, as other monarchs had, and they were ambitiously inquiring who should hold the highest offices. Jesus told them that they were wrong in their views and expectations. No such things would take place. From these notions they must be *turned*, *changed*, or *converted*, or they could have no part in his kingdom. These ideas did not fit at all *the nature* of his kingdom. ¶ *And become as little children.* Children are, to a great extent, destitute of ambition, pride, and haughtiness. They are characteristically humble and teachable. By requiring his disciples to be *like them*, he did not intend to express any opinion about the native moral character of children, but simply that *in these respects* they must become like them. They must lay aside their ambitious views and their pride, and be willing to occupy their proper station—a very lowly one. Mark says (ix. 35) that Jesus, *before* he placed the little child in the midst of them, told them that "if any man desire to be first, the same shall be last of all and servant of all." That is, he shall be the most distinguished Christian who is the most humble, and who is willing to be esteemed *least* and last of all. To esteem ourselves as *God* esteems us is humility, and it cannot be degrading to think of ourselves *as*

become[c] as little children, ye shall not enter into the kingdom of heaven.

4 Whosoever therefore shall humble[d] himself as this little child, the same is greatest in the kingdom of heaven.

5 And whoso shall [e]receive one such little child in my name, receiveth me.

6 But whoso shall [f]offend one of these little ones which believe in me, it were better for him that a millstone were hanged about his neck, and *that* he were drowned in the depth of the sea.

7 Woe unto the world because of offences! [g]for it must needs be that offences come; but [h]woe to that man by whom the offence cometh!

8 Wherefore, [i]if thy hand or

c 1 Co.14.20; 1 Pe.2.2. d Lu.14.11; Ja.4.10. e ch.10.42. f Mar.9.42; Lu.17.1,2.

g 1 Co.11.19; Jude 4. h Jude 11. i ch.5.29,30; Mar.9.43,45.

---

we are; but pride, or an attempt to be thought of more importance than we are, is foolish, wicked, and degrading.

4. *The greatest,* &c. That is, shall be the most eminent Christian—shall have most of the *true spirit* of religion.

5. *And whoso shall receive one such little child.* That is, whoso shall receive and love one with a spirit like this child —one who is humble, meek, and unambitious — that is, a real Christian. ¶ *In my name.* As a follower of me, or because he is attached to me. Whoso receives one possessed of my spirit, or who loves him *because* he has that spirit, loves me also. The word "receive" means to approve, love, or treat with kindness; to aid in the time of need. See Mat. xxv. 35-40.

Mark (ix. 38) and Luke (ix. 49) add a conversation that took place on this occasion, which has been omitted by Matthew. John told him that they had seen one casting out devils in his name, and they forbade him, because he followed not with them. Jesus replied that he should not have been forbidden, for there was no one who could work a miracle in his name that could lightly speak evil of him. That is, though he did not attend them—though he had not joined himself to their society, yet he could not *really* be opposed to him. Indeed, they should have remembered that the power to work a miracle must always come from the same source, that is, God; and that he who had the ability given him to work a miracle, and who did it in the name of Christ, must be a real friend to him. It is probable, from this, that the power of working miracles in the name of Christ was given to many who did not attend on his ministry.

6. *Whoso shall offend.* That is, cause to fall, or to sin; or who should place anything in their way to hinder their piety or happiness. See Notes on Mat. v. 29. ¶ *These little ones.* That is, Christians manifesting the spirit of little children, 1 Jn. ii. 1, 12, 18, 28. ¶ *It were better for him that a millstone,* &c. Mills, anciently, were either turned by hand (see Notes on Mat. xxiv. 41), or by beasts, chiefly by *mules.* These last were of the larger kind, and the *original* words denote that it was this kind that was intended. This was one mode of capital punishment practised by the Greeks, Syrians, Romans, and by some other nations. The meaning is, it would be better for him to have died before he had committed the sin. To injure, or to cause to sin, the feeblest Christian, will be regarded by Christ as a most serious offence, and will be punished accordingly.

7. *Woe unto the world because of offences.* That is, offences will be the cause of woe or of suffering. *Offences,* here, mean things that will produce sin; that will cause *us* to sin, or temptations to induce others to sin. See Notes on Mat. v. 29. ¶ *It must needs be,* &c. That is, such is the depravity of man that there *will* be always some who are attempting to make others sin; some men of wickedness endeavouring to lead Christians astray, and rejoicing when they have succeeded in causing them to fall. Such, also, is the strength of our native corruption and the force of passion, that *our besetting sins* will lead us astray. ¶ *Woe to that man by whom the offence cometh.* He who leads others into sin is awfully guilty — no man can be more guilty. No wickedness can be more deeply seated in the heart than that which attempts to mar the peace, defile the purity, and destroy the souls of others; and yet in all ages there have been multitudes who, by

thy foot offend thee, cut them off, and cast *them* from thee: it is better for thee to enter into life halt or maimed, rather than, having two hands or two feet, to be cast into everlasting fire.

9 And if thine eye offend thee, pluck it out and cast *it* from thee: it is better for thee to [k]enter into life with one eye, rather than, [l]having two eyes, to be cast into hell fire.

10 Take heed that ye despise not one of these little ones; for I say unto you, that in heaven [m]their angels do always [n]behold the face of my Father which is in heaven.

11 For the Son of man is come to [o]save that which was lost.

12 How think ye? [p]if a man

k He.4.11.

l Lu.9.25. *m* Ac.12.15. *n* Ps.17.15. *o* ch.1.21; Lu.9.56; 19.10; Jn.3.17; 10.10; 12.47; 1 Ti.1.15. *p* Lu.15.4,&c.

---

persecution, threats, arts, allurements, and persuasion, have endeavoured to seduce Christians from the faith and to lead them into sin.

8, 9. *If thy hand*, &c. See Notes on Mat. v. 29, 30. The sense in all these instances is the same. Worldly attachments, friendships, and employments of any kind, that cannot be pursued without leading us into sin, be they ever so dear to us, must be abandoned, or the soul will be lost. ¶ *It is better for thee to enter into life halt or maimed*, &c. It is not meant, by this, that when the body shall be raised it will be maimed and disfigured in this manner. It will be perfect. See 1 Co. xv. 42–44. But these things are said for the purpose of carrying out or making complete *the figure* or the representation of cutting off the hands, &c. The meaning is, it is better to go to heaven *without enjoying* the things that caused us to sin, than to enjoy them *here* and then be lost. ¶ *Halt*. Lame. *Maimed*. With a loss of limbs. ¶ *Into hell fire*. It is implied, in all this, that if their sins, however dear to them, were not abandoned, the soul must go into everlasting fire. This is conclusive proof that the sufferings of the wicked will be eternal. See Notes on Mar. ix. 44, 46, 48.

10. *Take heed that ye despise not one of these little ones*, &c. That is, one who has become like a little child, or a Christian. ¶ *For I say unto you*, &c. Jesus then proceeds to state the reason why we should not despise his feeblest and obscurest follower. That reason is drawn from the *care* which God exercises over them. The first instance of that *care* is, that *in heaven their angels do always behold his face*. He does not mean, I suppose, to state that every good man has his guardian angel, as many of the Jews believed; but that the angels were, *in general*, the guards of his followers, and aided them and watched over them. See Notes on He. i. 14. ¶ *Do always behold the face of God*. This is taken from the practice of earthly courts. To be admitted to the presence of a king; to be allowed to see his face continually; to have free access to him at all times, was deemed a mark of peculiar favour (1 Ki. x. 8; Es. i. 14), and was esteemed a security for his protection. So, says our Saviour, we should not despise the obscurest Christian, for he is ministered to by the highest and noblest of beings—by beings who are always enjoying the favour and friendship of God.

11. *For the Son of man*, &c. This is a second reason why we should not despise Christians. That reason is, that the Son of man came to seek and save them. He came in search of them when lost; he found them; he redeemed them. It was the great object of his life; and, though they may be obscure and little in the eye of the world, yet that cannot be an object of contempt which the Son of God sought by his toils and his death. ¶ *Son of man*. See Notes on Mat. viii. 19, 20. ¶ *That which was lost*. Property is *lost* when it is consumed, mislaid, wasted, sunk in the ocean, &c.—when *we* have no longer the use of it. Friends are lost when they die—we enjoy their society no longer. A wicked and profligate man is said to be *lost* to virtue and happiness. He is useless to society. So all men are *lost*. They are wicked, miserable wanderers from God. They are lost to piety, to happiness, to heaven. These Jesus came to save by giving his own life a ransom, and shedding his own blood that they might be recovered and saved.

12–14. To show still further the reason why we should not despise Christians, he introduced a parable showing the

have a hundred sheep, and one of
them be gone astray, doth he not
leave the ninety and nine, and goeth
into the mountains and seeketh that
which is gone astray?
13 And if so be that he find it,
verily I say unto you, he rejoiceth
more of that *sheep*, than of the
ninety and nine which went not
astray.
14 Even so it is not the will of
your Father which is in heaven
[q]that one of these little ones should
perish.
15 Moreover, [r]if thy brother
shall trespass against thee, go and
tell him his fault between thee
and him alone: [s]if he shall hear
thee, thou hast gained thy brother.
16 But if he will not hear *thee*,
then take with thee one or two
more, that in [t]the mouth of two
or three witnesses every word may
be established.

q 2 Pe.3.9. *r* Le.19.17; Lu.17.3. *s* Ja.5.20. *t* De.19.15.

joy felt when a thing lost is found. A shepherd rejoices over the recovery of one of his flock that had wandered more than over all that remained; so God rejoices that man is restored; so he seeks his salvation, and wills that not one thus found should perish. If *God* thus loves and preserves the redeemed, then surely *man* should not despise them. See this passage farther explained in Lu. xv. 4–10.

15. *Moreover, if thy brother.* The word *brother*, here, evidently means a fellow-professor of religion. Christians are called *brethren* because they belong to the same redeemed family, having a common Father—God; and because they are united in the same feelings, objects, and destiny. ¶ *Trespass against thee.* That is, *injure* thee in any way, by words or conduct. The original word means *sin* against thee. This may be done by injuring the character, person, or property. ¶ *Go and tell him his fault between thee and him alone.* This was required under the *law*, Le. xix. 17. In the original it is "go and *reprove* him." Seek an explanation of his conduct, and if he has done wrong, administer a friendly and brotherly reproof. This is required to be done *alone:* 1st. That he may have an opportunity of explaining his conduct. In nine cases out of ten, where one supposes that he has been injured, a little friendly conversation would set the matter right and prevent difficulty. 2d. That he may have an opportunity of acknowledging his offence or making reparation, if he has done wrong. Many would be *glad* of such an opportunity, and it is our duty to furnish it by calling on them. 3d. That we may admonish them of their error if they have done an injury to the cause of religion. This should not be blazoned abroad. It can do no good—it does injury; it is what the enemies of religion wish. Christ is often wounded in the house of his friends; and religion, as well as an injured brother, often suffers by spreading such faults before the world. ¶ *Thou hast gained thy brother.* To *gain* means, sometimes, to *preserve* or to save, 1 Co. ix. 19. Here it means thou hast *preserved* him, or *restored* him, to be a consistent Christian. Perhaps it may include the idea, also, thou hast reconciled him to thyself—thou hast gained him as a Christian brother.

16. *But if he will not hear* thee, &c. That is, if he spurns or abuses you, or will not be entreated by you, and will not reform. ¶ *Take with thee one or two more.* The design of taking them seems to be, 1st. That he might be induced to listen to *them*, ver. 17. They should be persons of influence or authority; his personal friends, or those in whom he could put confidence. 2d. That they might be witnesses of his conduct before the church, ver. 17. The law of Moses required two or three witnesses, De. xix. 15; 2 Co. xiii. 1; Jn. viii. 17.

17. *Tell it to the church.* See Notes on Mat. xvi. 18. The church may here mean the whole assembly of believers, or it may mean those who are authorized to try such cases—the representatives of the church, or those who act for the church. In the Jewish synagogue there was a bench of elders before whom trials of this kind were brought. It was to be brought to the church in order that he might be admonished, entreated, and, if possible, reformed. This was, and is always to be, the first business in disciplining an offending brother. ¶ *But if he neglect to hear the church, let him be*, &c. The Jews gave

17 And if he shall neglect to hear them, tell *it* unto the church: but if he neglect to hear the church, [u]let him be unto thee as an heathen man and a publican.

18 Verily I say unto you, [v]Whatsoever ye shall bind on earth shall be bound in heaven; and whatsoever ye shall loose on earth shall be loosed in heaven.

19 Again I say unto you, That if two of you shall agree on earth as touching any thing that they shall ask, [w]it shall be done for them of my Father which is in heaven.

20 For where two or three are [x]gathered together in my name, there am I in the midst of them.

21 Then came Peter to him, and said, Lord, how oft shall my

u Ro.16.17; 1 Co.5.3-5; 2 Th.3.6,14.
v ch.16.19; Jn.20.23; Ac.15.23-31; 2 Co.2.10.
w Mar.11.24; Jn.16.24; 1 Jn.5.14.
x Jn.20.19; 1 Co.5.4.

the name *heathen* or *Gentile* to all other nations but themselves. With them they had no *religious* intercourse or communion. ¶ *Publican.* See Notes on Mat. v. 47. Publicans were men of abandoned character, and the Jews would have no intercourse with them. The meaning of this is, cease to have *religious* intercourse with him, or to acknowledge him as a Christian brother. It does not mean that we should cease to show kindness to him and aid him in affliction or trial, for *that* is required toward all men; but it means that we should *disown* him as a *Christian brother*, and treat him as we do other men not connected with the church. This should not be done till *all* these steps are taken. This is the only way of kindness. This is the only way to preserve peace and purity in the church.

18. *Whatsoever ye shall bind*, &c. See Notes on Mat. xvi. 19. These words were spoken to the apostles. Jesus had before addressed the same words to Peter, ch. xvi. 19. He employs them here to signify that they *all had the same power;* that in ordering the affairs of the church he did not intend to give *Peter* any supremacy or any exclusive right to regulate it. The meaning of this verse is, whatever you shall do in the discipline of the church shall be approved by God or bound in heaven. This promise, therefore, cannot be understood as extending to all Christians or ministers, for all others but the apostles may err.

19. *Again I say unto you, That if two of you*, &c. This is connected with the previous verses. The connection is this: The obstinate man is to be excluded from the church, ver. 17. The care of the church—the power of admitting or excluding members—of organizing and establishing it—is committed to you, the apostles, ver. 18. Yet there is not need of *the whole* to give validity to the transaction. When two of you agree, or have the same mind, feelings, and opinion, about the arrangement of affairs in the church, or about things desired for its welfare, and shall ask of God, it shall be done for them. See Ac. i. 14–26; xv. 1–29. The promise *here* has respect to the apostles in organizing the church. It cannot with any propriety be applied to the ordinary prayers of believers. Other promises are made to them, and it is true that the prayer of faith will be answered, *but that is not the truth taught here.*

20. *For where two or three*, &c. This is a *general* assertion made to support the *particular* promise made (ver. 19) to his apostles. He affirms that *wherever* two or three are assembled together in his name, he is in the midst of them. ¶ *In my name.* That is, 1st. By *my authority*, acting *for me* in my church. See Jn. x. 25; xvi. 23. 2d. It may mean for my service; in the place of prayer and praise, assembled in obedience to my command, and with a desire to promote my glory. ¶ *There am I in the midst of them.* Nothing could more clearly prove that Jesus must be omnipresent, and, of course, be God. Every day, perhaps every hour, two or three, or many more, may be assembled in every city or village in the United States, in England, in Greenland, in Africa, in Ceylon, in the Sandwich Islands, in Russia, and in Judea—in almost every part of the world—and in the midst *of them all* is Jesus the Saviour. Millions thus at the same time, in every quarter of the globe, worship in his name, and experience the truth of the promise that he is present with them. It is impossible that he should be in all these places and not be God.

21. *Then came Peter*, &c. The men-

brother sin against me, and I [y]for-
give him? till seven times?
22 Jesus saith unto him, I say
not unto thee, Until seven times;
but, Until seventy times seven.
23 Therefore is the kingdom of
heaven likened unto a certain king
which would [z]take account of his
servants.
24 And when he had begun to
reckon, one was brought unto him
which owed him ten thousand
[1]talents:
25 But forasmuch as he had not
to pay, his lord commanded him
[a]to be sold, and his wife and children, and all that he had, and payment to be made.
26 The servant therefore fell
down, and [2]worshipped him, say-

y Mar.11.25; Lu.17.4; Col.3.13. z Ro.14.12.

1 *A talent is* 750 *ounces of silver, which, at* 5s. *the ounce, is* £187, 10s. a 2 Ki.4.1; Is.50.1. 2 or, *besought him.*

tion of the duty (ver. 15) of *seeing* a brother when he had offended us, *implying* that it was a duty to forgive him, led Peter to ask *how often* this was to be done. ¶ *Forgive him.* To forgive is to treat as though the offence was not committed—to *declare* that we will not harbour malice or treat unkindly, but that the matter shall be buried and forgotten. ¶ *Till seven times?* The Jews taught that a man was to forgive another *three* times, but not the *fourth.* Peter more than doubled this, and asked whether forgiveness was to be exercised to so great an extent. ¶ *I say not unto thee, Until seven times, but, Until seventy times seven.* The meaning is, that we are not to limit our forgiveness *to any fixed number of times.* See Ge. iv. 24. As often as a brother injures us and asks forgiveness, we are to forgive him. It is, indeed, his duty to *ask* forgiveness, Lu. xvii. 4. If he does this, it is our duty to *declare* that we forgive him, and to treat him accordingly. If he does not *ask* us to forgive him, yet we are not at liberty to follow him with revenge and malice, but are still to treat him kindly and to do him good, Lu. x. 30–37.

23. *Therefore is the kingdom of heaven likened,* &c. The phrase, "the kingdom of heaven," here has reference to the church, or to the way in which God will deal with his people. "It shall be in my church as it was with a certain king; or *God* will deal with the members of his church as a certain king did with his servants." See Notes on Mat. iii. 2. This *parable* (see Mat. xiii. 3) is related to show the duty of forgiving others. It is not necessary to suppose that it was a *true* narrative, but only that it *illustrated* the truth which he was teaching. At the same time it *may* be true that such an occurrence really took place. ¶ *Would take account of his servants.* To take account means to reckon, to settle up affairs. The word *servants* here means, probably, *petty princes,* or, more likely, *collectors of the revenue* or *taxes.* Among the ancients kings often *farmed out,* or sold for a certain sum, the taxes of a particular district or province. Thus, when Judea was subject to Egypt or Rome, the kings frequently *sold* to the high-priest the taxes to be raised from Judea on condition of a much smaller sum being paid to them. This *secured* to them a *certain sum,* but it gave occasion to much oppression in the collection of the taxes. It is probable that some such persons are intended by the word servants.

24. *Ten thousand talents.* A *talent* was a sum of money, or *weight* of silver or gold amounting to three thousand shekels. A silver *shekel* was worth, after the captivity, not far from half a dollar of our money. A talent of *silver* was worth $1519, 23 cts. = £342, 3*s.* 9*d.*; of gold, $243,098, 88 cts. = £5475. If these were *silver* talents, as is probable, then the sum owed by the servant was fifteen millions one hundred and eighty thousand dollars, or about £3,421,875 sterling, a sum which proves that he was not a domestic, but some tributary prince. The sum is used to show that the debt was immensely large, and that our *sins* are so great that they cannot be estimated or numbered. Comp. Job xxii. 5.

25. *His lord commanded him to be sold,* &c. By the laws of the Hebrews they were permitted to sell debtors, with their wives and children, into servitude for a time sufficient to pay a debt. See 2 Ki. iv. 1; Le. xxv. 39-46; Am. viii. 6.

26. *The servant therefore fell down, and worshipped him.* This does not

ing, Lord, have patience with me, and I will pay thee all.

27 Then the Lord of that servant was [b]moved with compassion, and loosed him, and forgave him the debt.

28 But the same servant went out, and found one of his fellow-servants which owed him an hundred [3]pence; and he laid hands on him, and took *him* by the throat, saying, Pay me that thou owest.

29 And his fellow-servant fell down at his feet, and besought him, saying, [c]Have patience with me, and I will pay thee all.

30 And he would not; but went and cast him into prison till he should pay the debt.

31 So when his fellow-servants saw what was done, they were very sorry, and came and told unto their lord all that was done.

32 Then his lord, after that he had called him, said unto him, O thou [d]wicked servant, I forgave

b Ps.78.38.
[3] *The Roman penny is the 8th part of an ounce, which, at 5s. the ounce, is 7d. halfpenny,* ch.20.2.

c ver.26. *d* Lu.19.22.

mean that he paid him *religious* homage, but that in a humble, reverent, and earnest manner he entreated him to have patience with him. He prostrated himself before his lord, as is customary in all Eastern nations when *subjects* are in the presence of their king. See Notes on Mat. ii. 2.

27. *The lord of that servant was moved with compassion,* &c. He had pity on him. He saw his distressed condition. He pitied his family. He forgave him the whole debt. This represents the mercy of God to men. They have sinned. They owe to God more than can be paid. They are about to be cast off; but God has mercy on them, and, in connection with their prayers, forgives them. We are not to interpret the circumstances of a parable too strictly. The illustration taken from selling the wife and children (ver. 25) is not to be taken literally, as if *God* would punish a man for the sins of his father; but it is a circumstance thrown in *to keep up the story*—to make it consistent—to explain the reason *why* the servant was so anxious to obtain a *delay* of the time of payment.

28, 29. *But the same servant went out, and found one of his fellow-servants which owed him an hundred pence.* Greek, *denarion;* Latin, *denarius;* a Roman silver coin in common use. When Greece became subject to the Romans, and especially under the emperors, the denarius was regarded as of equal value with the Attic drachma—about $7\frac{1}{2}d.$ sterling, or fifteen cents; consequently this debt was about fifteen dollars—a very small sum compared with what had been forgiven to the first servant. Perhaps our Saviour, by this, meant to teach that the offences which our fellow-men commit against us are very small and insignificant compared with our offences against God. Since God has forgiven us *so much,* we ought to forgive each other the *small* offences which are committed. ¶ *Took* him *by the throat.* Took him in a violent and rough manner—half choked or *throttled* him. This was the more criminal and base, as he had himself been so kindly treated and dealt so mildly with by his lord. ¶ *Besought.* Entreated, pled with him.

31. *So when his fellow-servants,* &c. This is a mere circumstance thrown into the story for the sake of *keeping,* or making a consistent narrative. It *cannot* be intended to teach that other Christians should go and tell God what a brother has done; for God well knows all the actions of his children, and does not need us surely to *inform* him of what is done. It is abusing the Bible, and departing from the *design* of parables, to press every circumstance, and to endeavour to extract from it some spiritual meaning. Our Saviour, in this parable, designed most clearly to exhibit only *one great truth*—the duty of forgiving our brethren, and the great evil of *not* forgiving a brother when he offends us. The circumstances of the parable are intended only to make the story *consistent* with itself, and thus to impress the general truth more fully on the mind.

34. *Delivered him to the tormentors.* The word *tormentors* here probably means *keepers of the prison.* Torments were inflicted on *criminals,* not on debtors. They were inflicted by stretching the limbs, or pinching the flesh, or putting out the eyes, or taking off the

thee all that debt, because thou
desiredst me:
33 Shouldest not thou also have
had compassion on thy fellow-servant, even as I had pity on thee?
34 And his lord was wroth, and
delivered him to the tormentors till
he should pay all that was due
unto him.
35 So [e]likewise shall my heavenly Father do also unto you, if
ye from your hearts forgive not
every one his brother their trespasses.

e Pr.21.13; ch.6.12; Ja.2.13.

---

skin while alive, &c. It is not probable that anything of this kind is intended, but only that the servant was punished by imprisonment till the debt should be paid.

35. *So likewise*, &c. This verse contains the sum or *moral* of the parable. When Christ has explained one of his own parables, we are to receive it *just* as he has explained it, and not attempt to draw spiritual instruction from any parts or circumstances which he has not explained. The following seems to be the particulars of the general truth which he meant to teach: 1st. That our sins are great. 2d. That God freely forgives them. 3d. That the offences committed against us by our brethren are comparatively small. 4th. That we should therefore most freely forgive them. 5th. That if we do not, God will be justly angry with us, and punish us. ¶ *From your hearts.* That is, not merely in words, but really and truly to feel and act toward him as if he had not offended us. ¶ *Trespasses.* Offences, injuries. Words and actions designed to do us wrong.

REMARKS.

1st. We see that it is possible to make a profession of religion an occasion of ambition, ver. 1. The apostles at first sought honour, and expected office as a consequence of following Christ. So thousands have done since. Religion, notwithstanding all the opposition it has met with, *really* commands the confidence of mankind. To make a profession of it may be a way of access to that confidence. Thousands, it is to be feared, even yet enter the church merely to obtain some worldly benefit. Especially does this danger beset ministers of the gospel. There are few paths to the confidence of mankind so easily trod as to enter the ministry. Every minister, of course, if at all worthy of his office, has access to the confidence of multitudes, and is never despised but by the worst and lowest of mankind. No way is so easy to step at once to public confidence. Other men toil long to establish influence by personal character. The minister has it by virtue of his office. Those who now enter the ministry are tempted far more in this respect than were the apostles; and how should they search their own hearts, to see that no such abominable motive has induced them to seek that office!

2d. It is consummate wickedness thus to prostitute the most sacred of all offices to the worst of purposes. The apostles at this time were ignorant. They expected a kingdom in which it would be right to seek distinction. But we labour under no such ignorance. We *know* that the kingdom of Christ is not of this world, and woe to the man that acts *as though* it were. Deep and awful must be the doom of him who thus seeks the honours of the world while he is professedly following the meek and lowly Jesus!

3d. Humility is indispensable to religion, ver. 3. No man who is not humble can possibly be a Christian. He must be willing to esteem himself *as he is*, and to have others esteem him so also. This is humility, and humility is lovely. It is not meanness—it is not cowardice—it is not want of proper self-esteem; it is a view of ourselves *just as we are*, and a willingness that God and all creatures should so esteem us. What can be more lovely than such an estimation of ourselves! and how foolish and wicked is it to be proud—that is, to think more of ourselves, and wish others to think so, than we really deserve! To put on appearances, and to magnify our own importance, and to think that the affairs of the universe could not go on without us, and to be indignant when all the world does not bow down to do us homage—this is hypocrisy as well as wickedness; and there *may be*, therefore, hypocrites *out of the church* as well as *in it*.

4th. Humility is the best evidence of piety, ver. 4. The most humble man is the most eminent Christian. He is *greatest* in the kingdom of heaven. The effect of sin is to produce pride. Religion overcomes it by producing a just sense of ourselves, of other men, of angels, and of God. We may therefore measure the advance of piety in our own souls by the increase of humility.

5th. We see the danger of despising and doing injury to real Christians, and more especially the guilt of attempting to draw them into sin, ver. 6. God watches over them. He loves them. In the eye of the world they may be of little importance, but not so with God. The most obscure follower of Christ is dear, infinitely dear, to him, and he will take care of him. He that attempts to injure a Christian, attempts to injure God; for God has redeemed him, and loves him.

6th. Men will do much to lead others into sin, ver. 7. In all communities there are some who seem to *live* for this. They have often much wealth, or learning, or accomplishment, or address, or professional influence, and they employ it for the sake of seducing the unwary and leading them into ruin. Hence offences come, and many of the young and thoughtless are led astray. But He who has all power has pronounced *woe* upon them, and judgment will not always linger. No class of men have a more fearful account to render to God than they who thus lead others into vice and infidelity.

7th. We must forsake our dearest sins, ver. 8, 9. We must do this, or go to hell-fire. There is no way of avoiding it. We cannot love and cherish those sins and be saved.

8th. The wicked—they who will *not* forsake their sins—must certainly go to eternal punishment, ver. 8, 9. So said the compassionate Saviour. The fair and obvious meaning of his words is that the sufferings of hell are eternal, and Christ did not use words without meaning. He did not mean to frighten us by bugbears or to hold up imaginary fears. If *Christ* speaks of hell, then there is a hell. If he says it is eternal, then it is so. Of this we may be sure, that EVERY WORD *which the God of mercy has spoken about the punishment of the wicked is* FULL OF MEANING.

9th. Christians are protected, ver. 10. Angels are appointed as their friends and guardians. *Those friends* are very near to God. They enjoy his favour, and his children shall be safe.

10th. Christians are safe, ver. 11–14. Jesus came to save them. He left the heavens for this end. God rejoices in their salvation. He secures it at great sacrifices, and none can pluck them out of his hand. After the coming of Jesus to save them—after all that he has done for that, and that only—after the joy of God and of angels at their recovery, it is *impossible* that they should be wrested from him and destroyed. See Jn. x. 27, 28.

11th. It is our duty to admonish our brethren when they injure us, ver. 15. We have no right to speak of the offence to anyone else, not even to our best friends, until we have given them an opportunity to explain.

12th. The way to treat offending brethren is clearly pointed out, ver. 15–17. Nor have we a right to take any other course. Infinite Wisdom—the *Prince of Peace*—has declared that this is the way to treat our brethren. No other can be right; and no other, therefore, can be so well adapted to promote the peace of the church. And yet how different from this is the course commonly pursued! How few go honestly to an offending brother and tell him his fault! Instead of this, every breeze bears the report—it is magnified—mole-hills swell to mountains, and a quarrel of years often succeeds what *might* have been settled at once. No robber is so cruel as he who steals away the *character* of another. Nothing can compensate for the loss of this. Wealth, health, mansions, equipage, all are trifles compared with this. Especially is this true of a *Christian*. His reputation gone, he has lost his power of doing good; he has brought dishonour on the cause he most loved; he has lost his peace, and worlds cannot repay him.

"Who steals my purse, steals trash: 'tis something, nothing:
'Twas mine, 'tis his, and has been slave to thousands.
But he that filches from me my good name
Robs me of that which not enriches him,
And makes me poor indeed."

13th. We have every encouragement to pray, ver. 20. We are poor, and sinful, and dying, and none can comfort us but God. At his throne we may find all that we want. We know not which is most wonderful—that God deigns to hear our prayers, or that men are so unwilling to use so simple and easy a way of obtaining what they so much need.

14th. We should never be weary of forgiving our brethren, ver. 22. We

CHAPTER XIX.

AND it came to pass, *that* when Jesus had finished these sayings, [a] he departed from Galilee, and came into the coasts of Judea beyond Jordan:

2 And great multitudes followed him, and he healed them there.

a Mar.10.1; Jn.10.40.

should do it cheerfully. We should do it always. We are never better employed than when we are doing good to those who have injured us. Thus doing, we are most like God.

15th. There will be a day in which we must give up our account, ver. 23. It may tarry long; but God will *reckon* with us, and everything shall be brought into judgment.

16th. We are greatly indebted to God—far, far beyond what we are able to pay, ver. 24. We have sinned, and *in no way* can *we* make atonement for past sins; but Jesus the Saviour *has* made an atonement and paid our debt, and we may be free.

17th. It is right to pray to God when we feel that we have sinned, and are unable to pay the debt, ver. 26. We have no other way. Poor, and needy, and wretched, we *must* cast ourselves upon his mercy or *die*—die for ever.

18th. God will have compassion on those who do this, ver. 27. At *his* feet, in the attitude of prayer, the burdened sinner finds peace. We have nowhere else to go but to the very Being that we have offended. None but he can save us from death.

19th. From the kindness of God to us we should learn *not* to oppress others, ver. 28.

20th. It is our true *interest*, as well as duty, to forgive those that offend us, ver. 34. God will take vengeance, and in due time we *must* suffer if we do not forgive others.

21st. Christians are often great sufferers for harbouring malice. As a punishment, God withdraws the light of his countenance; they walk in darkness; they cannot enjoy religion; their conscience smites them, and they are wretched. No man ever did or ever can enjoy religion who did not from his heart forgive his brother his trespasses.

22d. One reason why Christians ever walk in darkness is, that there is some such duty neglected. They think they have been injured, and very possibly they may have been; they think they are in the right, and possibly they are so; but mingled with a consciousness of this is an unforgiving spirit, and they cannot enjoy religion till that is subdued.

23d. Forgiveness must not be in word merely, but from the heart, ver. 35. No other can be genuine. No other is like God.

CHAPTER XIX.

1-12. See also Mar. x. 1-12.

1. *Coasts of Judea beyond Jordan.* The narrative here refers to the last journey of the Saviour from Galilee to Jerusalem, to attend the last Passover which he celebrated. A considerable lapse of time occurred between his last discourse in the preceding chapter and what is recorded here, and several important events have been recorded by Luke and John which occurred in the interval, as the sending out of the seventy disciples (Lu. x. 1-16); the Saviour's going up to the feast of Tabernacles, and his final departure from Galilee, passing through Samaria (Lu. ix. 51-56; Jn. vii. 2-10); the healing of the ten lepers (Lu. xvii. 11-19); the public teaching of Jesus at the feast of Tabernacles (Jn. vii. 11-53); the account of the woman taken in adultery (Jn. viii. 1); the reproof of the unbelieving Jews, and the escape of the Saviour from their hands (Jn. viii. 12-59); the instruction of the lawyer, and the parable of the good Samaritan (Lu. x. 28-37); the incidents in the house of Martha and Mary (Lu. x. 38-42); the return of the seventy (Lu. x. 17-24); the healing of the blind man on the Sabbath (Jn. ix. 1-41); the festival of the Dedication (Jn. x. 22-42); the raising of Lazarus (Jn. xi. 1-46); and the counsel of Caiaphas against Jesus, and the retiring of Jesus from Jerusalem (Jn. xi. 47-54). See Robinson's *Harmony*. Matthew and Mark now resume the narrative by relating that after Jesus had left Galilee he approached Jerusalem by passing through the country beyond Jordan. The country was, in general, called *Perea*, and appertained to *Judea*, being the region formerly occupied by the tribes of Reuben, Gad, and Manasseh. The word *coasts* means *regions* or *parts*. See Notes on Mat. ii. 16.

3. *The Pharisees came.* See Notes on Mat. iii. 7. ¶ *Tempting him.* This

3 The Pharisees also came unto
him, tempting him, and saying unto
him, Is it lawful for a man to put
away his wife for every cause?
4 And he answered and said unto
them, Have ye not read, that [b]he
which made *them* at the beginning
made them male and female,
5 And said, [c]For this cause shall a
man leave father and mother, and
shall cleave to his wife; and they
twain shall be one flesh?
6 Wherefore they are no more
twain, but one flesh. What [d]there-
fore God hath joined together, let
not man put asunder.
7 They say unto him, [e]Why did
Moses then command to give a
writing of divorcement, and to put
her away?

b Ge.1.27; 5.2; Mal.2.15. *c* Ge.2.24; Ep.5.31. *d* 1 Co.7.10. *e* De.24.1; Is.50.1.

---

means, to get him, if possible, to express an opinion that should involve him in difficulty. ¶ *Is it lawful*, &c. There was the more art in the captious question which they proposed, as at that time the people were very much divided on the subject. A part, following the opinions of *Hillel*, said that a man might divorce his wife for any offence, or any dislike he might have of her. See Notes on Mat. v. 31. Others, of the school of *Shammai*, maintained that divorce was unlawful except in case of adultery. Whatever opinion, therefore, Christ expressed, they expected that he would involve himself in difficulty with one of their parties.

4–6. *And he answered and said*, &c. Instead of referring to the opinions of either party, Jesus called their attention to the original design of marriage, to the authority of *Moses*—an authority acknowledged by them both. ¶ *Have ye not read?* Ge. i. 27; ii. 21, 22. ¶ *And said, For this cause*, &c., Ge. ii. 24. That is, *God*, at the beginning, made but *one* man and *one* woman: their posterity should learn that the original intention of marriage was that a man should have but one wife. ¶ *Shall leave his father and mother.* This means, shall bind himself more strongly to his wife than he was to his father or mother. The marriage connection is the most tender and endearing of all human relations—more tender than even that bond which unites us to a parent. ¶ *And shall cleave unto his wife.* The word *cleave* denotes a union of the firmest kind. It is in the original taken from *gluing*, and means so firmly to *adhere* together that nothing can separate them. ¶ *They twain shall be one flesh.* That is, they *two*, or they that *were* two, shall be united as one—one in law, in feeling, in interest, in affection. They shall no longer have separate interests, but shall act in all things *as if* they were *one*—animated by one soul and one wish. The argument of Jesus here is, that since they are so intimately united as to be one, and since in the beginning God made but one woman for one man, it follows that they cannot be separated but by the authority of God. Man may *not* put away his wife for every cause. What *God* has joined together *man* may not put asunder. In this decision he *really* decided in favour of one of the parties; and it shows that when it was proper, Jesus answered questions without regard to consequences, from whatever cause they might have been proposed, and however much difficulty it might involve him in. Our Lord, in this, also showed consummate wisdom. He answered the question, not from Hillel or Shammai, their teachers, but from *Moses*, and thus defeated their malice.

7. *Why did Moses*, &c. To this they objected that *Moses* had allowed such divorces (De. xxiv. 1); and if *he* had allowed them, they inferred that they could not be unlawful. See Notes on Mat. v. 31.

8. *He saith unto them*, &c. Jesus *admits* that this was allowed, but still he contends that this was not the *original design* of marriage. It was only a *temporary* expedient growing out of a peculiar state of things, and not designed to be perpetual. It was on account *of the hardness of their hearts.* Moses found the custom in use. He found a hard-hearted and rebellious people. In this state of things he did not deem it prudent to forbid a practice so universal; but it might be regulated; and, instead of suffering the husband to divorce his wife *in a passion*, he required him, in order that he might take time to *consider* the matter, and thus make it probable that divorces

8 He saith unto them, Moses, because of the hardness of your hearts, suffered you to put away your wives; but from the beginning it was not so.

9 And I say unto you, [f]Whosoever shall put away his wife, except *it be* for fornication, and shall marry another, committeth adultery; and whoso marrieth her which is put away doth commit adultery.

10 His disciples say unto him, [g]If the case of the man be so with *his* wife, it is not good to marry.

11 But he said unto them, All *men* cannot receive this saying, save *they* to whom it is given.

12 For there are some eunuchs which were so born from *their* mothers' womb; and there are some eunuchs which were made eunuchs of men; and [h]there be eunuchs which have made them-

f ch.5.32; Lu.16.18. g Pr.19.13; 21.9,19. h 1 Co.7.32.

would be less frequent, to give her a writing; to sit down deliberately to look at the matter, and probably, also, to bring the case before some *scribe* or learned man, to write a divorce in the legal form. Thus doing, there might be an opportunity for the matter to be reconciled, and the man to be persuaded *not* to divorce his wife. This, says our Saviour, was a permission growing out of a particular state of things, and designed to remedy a prevailing evil; but at first it was not so. God intended that marriage should be between one man and one woman, and that they were only to be separated, in the case specified, by him who had formed the union. ¶ *Hardness of your hearts.* He speaks here of his hearers as a part of the nation. The hardness of *you Jews;* as when we say, *we* fought with England and gained our independence; that is, we, the American people, though it was done by our fathers. He does not mean to say, therefore, that this was done on account of the people whom he addressed, but of the *national* hardness of heart—the stubbornness of the Jewish people as a people.

9. *And I say unto you.* Emphasis should be laid here on the word *I.* This was the opinion of Jesus—this he proclaimed to be the law of his kingdom—this the command of God ever afterward. Indulgence had been given by the laws of Moses; but that indulgence was to cease, and the marriage relation *to be brought back to its original intention.* Only *one* offence was to make divorce lawful. This is the law of God; and by the same law, all marriages which take place after divorce, where adultery is not the cause of divorce, are adulterous. Legislatures have no right to say that men may put away their wives for any other cause; and where they do, and where there is marriage afterward, by the law of God such marriages are adulterous.

10. *His disciples say*, &c. The disciples were full of Jewish notions. They thought that the privilege of divorcing a wife when there was a quarrelsome disposition, or anything else that rendered the marriage unhappy, was a great privilege; and that in such cases to be always *bound* to live with a wife was a great calamity. They said, therefore, that if such *was the case*—such the condition on which men married—it was better not to marry.

11. *All* men *cannot receive this saying.* The minds of men are not prepared for this. *This saying* evidently means what the disciples had just said—that it was *good for a man not to marry.* It might be good in certain circumstances—in times of persecution and trial, or for the sake of labouring in the cause of religion without the care and burden of a family. It might be good for many to live, as some of the apostles did, without marriage, but it was not *given* to all men, 1 Co. vii. 1, 7, 9. To be married, or unmarried, might be lawful, according to circumstances, 1 Co. vii. 26.

12. *For there are some eunuchs*, &c. Jesus proceeds to state that there *were* some who were able to receive that saying and to remain in an unmarried state. Some were so born; some were made such by the cruelty of men; and there were some who voluntarily abstained from marriage *for the kingdom of heaven's sake*—that is, that they might devote themselves entirely to the proper business of religion. Perhaps he refers here to the ESSENES, a sect of the Jews (see Notes on Mat. iii. 7), who held that

selves eunuchs for the kingdom of heaven's sake. He that is able to receive *it*, let him receive *it*.

13 Then were there brought unto
him little children, that he should put *his* hands on them and pray: and the disciples rebuked them.

14 But Jesus said, [i]Suffer little children, and forbid them not, to come unto me; for of [k]such is the kingdom of heaven.

15 And he laid *his* hands on them, and departed thence.

16 And behold, one came and

i Mar.10.14; Lu.18.16,&c. *k* ch.18.3.

marriage was unsuitable to their condition; who had no children of their own, but perpetuated their sect by adopting the poor children of others. *Eunuchs* were employed chiefly in attending on the females or in the harem. They rose often to distinction, and held important offices in the state. Hence the *word* is sometimes used with reference to such an officer of state, Ac. viii. 27.

13. *Then were brought little children.* See also Mar. x. 13–16; Lu. xviii. 15–17. Probably these were brought by some of his followers, who desired not only to devote *themselves* to Jesus, but all that they had—their *children* as well as themselves. All the Jews were accustomed to devote their children to God by circumcision. It was natural, therefore, under the new dispensation, that it should be done. Luke says they were *infants*. They were undoubtedly those who were not old enough to come by choice, but their coming was *an act of the parents*. ¶ *Put* his *hands on them and pray.* It was customary among the Jews, when blessings were sought for others in prayer, to lay the hands on the head of the person prayed for, implying a kind of consecration to God. See Ge. xlviii. 14; Mat. ix. 18. They had also much confidence in the prayers of pious men, believing that those blessed by a saint or a prophet would be happy. See Nu. xxii. 6; Lu. ii. 28. ¶ *The disciples rebuked them.* That is, *reproved* them, or told them it was improper. This they did, probably, either, 1st, because they thought that they were too young; or, 2d, because they thought that they would be troublesome to their Master.

14. *Jesus said, Suffer little children*, &c. Mark adds, *he was much displeased* at what the disciples said. It was a thing highly gratifying to him, and which he earnestly sought, that children should be brought to him, and a case where it was very improper that they should interfere. ¶ *Of such is the kingdom of heaven.* The kingdom of heaven evidently means here *the church*. See Notes on Mat. iii. 2. In Mark and Luke it is said he immediately added, "Whosoever shall not receive the kingdom of God as a little child shall not enter therein." Whosoever shall not be humble, unambitious, and docile, shall not be a true follower of Christ or a member of his kingdom. *Of such as these*—that is, of persons with such tempers as these—is the church to be composed. He does not say *of those infants*, but of such persons as *resemble* them, or are *like* them in temper, is the kingdom of heaven made up. As emblematic, therefore, of what his own followers were to be, and as having traits of character so strongly resembling what he required in his followers, it was proper that they should be brought to him. At the same time, it was proper on their own account that they should be brought to him, and that his blessing should be sought on them. All are fallen; all have a tendency to sin, and none but Jesus can save them. Little children, too, are in a world of sickness and death, and in the beginning of life it is proper to invoke on them the blessing of the Saviour. They are to live for ever beyond the grave; and as they have just entered on a career of existence which *can never terminate*, it is an appropriate act to seek the blessing of that Saviour who only can make them happy for ever, as they enter on their career of existence. No act, therefore, can be more proper than that by which parents, in a solemn ordinance of religion, give them up to God in baptism, consecrating them to his service, and seeking for them the blessing of the Saviour. It is probable—it is greatly to be hoped—that all infants will be saved. No contrary doctrine is taught in the sacred Scriptures. But it does not appear to be the design of *this* passage to teach that all infants will be saved. It means simply that they should be suffered to be brought to Christ as amiable, lovely, and uncorrupted by

said unto him, [l]Good Master, what good thing shall I do, that I may have eternal life?

17 And he said unto him, Why callest thou me good? *there is* none good but one, *that is* God: but if thou wilt enter into life, keep the commandments.

l Mar.10.17; Lu.10.25; 18.18.

the world; as having traits of mind *resembling* those among real Christians; and as themselves needing his blessing.

15. *He laid* his *hands on them.* Mark says *he blessed them.* That is, he pronounced or sought a blessing on them.

16-30. This account is found also in Mar. x. 17-31; Lu. xviii. 18-30.

16. *One came.* This was a *young* man, ver. 20. He was a *ruler* (Luke); probably a ruler in a synagogue, or of the great council of the nation; a place to which he was chosen on account of his unblemished character and promising talents. He came *running* (Mark); evincing great earnestness and anxiety, He fell upon his knees (Mark); not to worship him, but to pay the customary repectful salutation; exhibiting the highest regard for Jesus as an extraordinary religious teacher. ¶ *Good Master.* The word *good* here means, doubtless, *most excellent;* referring not so much to the MORAL *character* of Jesus as to his *character as a religious teacher.* It was probably a title which the Jews were in the habit of applying to their religious teachers. The word *Master* here means *teacher.* ¶ *What good thing shall I do?* He had attempted to keep all the commandments. He had been taught by his Jewish teachers that men were to be saved by *doing* something—that is, by their works; and he supposed that this was to be the way under every system of religion. He had lived externally a blameless life, but yet he was not at peace; he was anxious, and he came to ascertain what, in the view of Jesus, was to be *done*, that his righteousness might be complete. To *have eternal life* means to be saved. The happiness of *heaven* is called *life*, in opposition to the pains of hell, called *death*, or an eternal *dying*, Re. ii. 2; xx. 14. The one is real *life*, answering the purposes of *living*—living to the honour of God and in eternal happiness; the other is a failure of the great ends of existence—prolonged, eternal suffering, of which temporal *death* is but the feeble image.

17. *Why callest thou me good?* Why do you give to me a title that belongs only to God? *You* suppose me to be only a man, yet you give me an appellation that belongs only to God. It is improper to use titles in this manner. As you Jews use them they are unmeaning; and though the title may apply to me, yet you did not *intend* to use it in the sense in which it is proper, as denoting infinite perfection or divinity; but you *intended* to use it as a complimentary or a flattering title, applied to me as if I were a mere man—a title which belongs only to God. The *intention*, the *habit* of using mere titles, and applying *as a compliment* terms belonging only to God, is wrong. Christ did not intend here to disclaim divinity, or to say anything about *his own character*, but simply to reprove the intention and habit of the young man—a most severe reproof of a foolish habit of compliment and flattery, and seeking pompous titles. ¶ *Keep the commandments.* That is, *do* what God has commanded. He in the next verses informs him what he meant by the commandments. Jesus said this, doubtless, to try him, and to *convince him* that he had by no means kept the commandments, and that in supposing he *had* he was altogether deceived. The young man *thought* he had kept them, and was relying on them for salvation. It was of great importance, therefore, to convince him that he was, after all, a sinner. Christ did not mean to say that any man *would* be saved by the works of the law, for the Bible teaches plainly that such *will not* be the case, Ro. iii. 20, 28; iv. 6; Ga. ii. 16; Ep. ii. 9; 2 Ti. i. 9. At the same time, however, it is true that if a man perfectly complied with the requirements of the law he would be saved, for there would be no reason why he should be condemned. Jesus, therefore, since he saw he was *depending* on his works, told him that if he would enter into life—that is, into heaven—he *must* keep the commandments; if he was *depending* on them he must keep them *perfectly*, and if this was done he would be saved. The reasons why Christ gave him this direction were, probably, 1st. Because it was his duty to keep them. 2d. Because the young man *depended* on them, and he ought to understand what was required if he did—that they should be

18 He saith unto him, Which? Jesus said, [m]Thou shalt do no murder, Thou shalt not commit adultery, Thou shalt not steal, Thou shalt not bear false witness;
19 Honour thy father and *thy* mother; and, [n]Thou shalt love thy neighbour as thyself.
20 The young man saith unto him, All these things have I kept from my youth up; what lack I yet?
21 Jesus said unto him, If thou

m Ex.20.13; De.5.17,&c.
n Le.19.18.

---

kept perfectly, or that they were not kept at all. 3d. Because he wanted to *test* him, to show him that he did *not* keep them, and thus to show him his need of a Saviour.

18, 19. *He saith unto him, Which?* In reply to the inquiry of the young man, Jesus directed him to the sixth, seventh, eighth, ninth, and fifth (Ex. xx. 12–16), as containing the *substance* of the whole—as containing *particularly* what he intended to show him that he had not kept. See Notes on Mat. v. 21, 27. ¶ *Jesus said, Thou shalt do no murder.* See Notes on Mat. v. 21–26. ¶ *Thou shalt not commit adultery.* See Notes on Mat. v. 27–32. ¶ *Thou shalt not steal.* To *steal* is to take the property of another without his knowledge or consent. ¶ *Thou shalt not bear false witness.* Give testimony contrary to *truth*. This may be done in a court of justice, or by private or public slander. It means to say things of another which are not true. ¶ *Honour thy father*, &c. That is, 1st. *Obey them*, keep their commands, Col. iii. 20; Ep. vi. 1-3. 2d. *Respect them*, show them reverence. 3d. Treat their *opinions* with respect—do not despise them or ridicule them. 4th. Treat their *habits* with respect. Those habits may be different from ours; they may be antiquated, and to us strange, odd, or whimsical; but they are the habits of a *parent*, and they are not to be ridiculed. 5th. Provide for them when sick, weary, old, and infirm. Bear with their weakness, comply with their wishes, speak to them kindly, and deny yourselves of rest, and sleep, and ease, to promote their welfare. To this he added another—the duty of loving our neighbour, Le. xix. 18. This Christ declared to be the *second* great commandment of the law, Mat. xxii. 39. *A neighbour* means, 1st. Any person who lives near to us. 2d. Any person with whom we have dealings. 3d. A friend or relative, Mat. v. 43. 4th. Any person—friend, relative, countryman, or foe, Mar. xii. 31. 5th. Any person who does us good or confers a favour on us, Lu. x. 27-37. This commandment means, evidently, 1st. That we should not *injure* our neighbour in his person, property, or character. 2d. That we should not be selfish, but should seek to do him good. 3d. That in a case of debt, difference, or debate, we should do what is *right*, regarding his interest *as much* as our own. 4th. That we should treat *his* character, property, &c., as we do our own, according to what is *right*. 5th. That, in order to benefit him, we should practise self-denial, or do as we would wish him to do to us, Mat. vii. 12. It does *not* mean, 1st. That the love of ourselves, *according to what we are*, or according to *truth*, is improper. The happiness of *myself* is of as much importance as that of any other man, and it is *as* proper that it should be sought. 2d. It does not mean that I am to neglect *my own business* to take care of my neighbour's. *My* happiness, salvation, health, and family are committed peculiarly to myself; and, provided I do not interfere with my neighbour's rights or violate my obligations to him, it is my duty to seek the welfare of my own as my first duty, 1 Ti. v. 8, 13; Tit. ii. 5. Mark adds to these commandments, "Defraud not;" by which he meant, doubtless, to express the substance of this—to love our neighbour as ourselves. It means, literally, to take away the property of another by violence or by deceiving him, thus showing that he is not loved as we love ourselves.

20. *All these things have I kept from my youth up.* I have made them the rule of my life. I have endeavoured to obey them. Is there anything that I lack—are there any new commandments to be kept? Do you, the Messiah, teach any command besides those which I have learned from the law and from the Jewish teachers, which it is necessary for me to obey in order to be saved?

21. *If thou wilt be perfect.* The word *perfect* means *complete* in all its parts, *finished*, having no part wanting. Thus

wilt be perfect, [o]go *and* sell that thou hast and give to the poor, and thou shalt have treasure in heaven; and come *and* [p]follow me.
22 But when the young man heard that saying, he went away sorrowful, for he had great possessions.
23 Then said Jesus unto his disciples, Verily I say unto you, [q]That a rich man shall hardly enter into the kingdom of heaven.

o Lu.12.33; 16.9; Ac.2.45; 4.34,35; 1 Ti.6.18,19. p Jn.12.26.

q 1 Ti.6.9,10.

a *watch* is perfect or complete when it has all its proper wheels, and hands, and casements in order. Job was said to be perfect (see Notes on Job i. 1), not that he was sinless, for he is afterward reproved by God himself (Job xxxviii., xxxix., xl. 4); but because his piety was properly proportioned, or had a completeness of parts. He was a pious father, a pious magistrate, a pious neighbour, a pious citizen. His religion was not confined to *one* thing, but it extended to all. *Perfect* means, sometimes, the *filling up*, or the *carrying out*, or the *expression* of a principle of action. Thus, 1 Jn. ii. 5: "Whoso keepeth his word, in him verily is the love of God *perfected*." That is, the keeping of the commandments of God is the proper *expression, carrying out*, or *completion* of the love of God. This is its meaning here. If thou wilt be *perfect, complete, finished*—if thou wilt show the *proper expression* of this keeping of the commandments, go, &c. Make the obedience *complete*.

Mark says (x. 21), *Jesus, beholding him, loved him*. He was pleased with his amiableness, his correct character, his frankness, his ingenuousness. Jesus, as a man, was capable of all the emotions of most tender friendship. As a man, we may suppose that his disposition was tender and affectionate, mild and calm. Hence he loved with peculiar affection the disciple John, eminently endowed with these qualities; and hence he *was pleased* with the same traits in this young man. Still, with all this amiableness, there is reason to think he was not a Christian, and that the love of *mere amiable qualities* was all the affection that was ever bestowed on him by the Saviour.

One thing, adds Mark, *thou lackest*. There is one thing wanting. You are not *complete*. This done, you would show that your obedience lacked no essential part, but was *complete, finished, proportionate, perfect*. ¶ *Go and sell that thou hast*, &c. The young man declared that he had kept the law. That law required, among other things, that he should love his neighbour as himself. It required, also, that he should love the Lord his God supremely; that is, more than all other objects. If he *had* that true love to God and man—if he loved his Maker and fellow-creatures more than he did his property, he would be willing to give up his wealth to the service of God and of man. Jesus commanded him to do this, therefore, to *test* his character, and to show him that he had *not* kept the law as he pretended, and thus to show him that he needed a better righteousness than his own. ¶ *Treasure in heaven*. See Notes on Mat. vi. 20. ¶ *Follow me*. To follow Jesus *then* meant to be a personal attendant on his ministry; to go about with him from place to place, as well as to imitate and obey him. *Now* it means, 1st. To obey his commandments. 2d. To imitate his example, and to live like him.

22. *He had great possessions*. He was very rich. He made an *idol* of his wealth. He loved it more than God. *He had* NOT *kept the commandments from his youth up*, nor had he kept them at all; and rather than do good with his treasures, and seek his salvation by obeying God, he chose to turn away from the Saviour and give over his inquiry about eternal life. He probably returned no more. Alas! how many lovely and amiable young persons follow his example!

23. *A rich man shall hardly enter into the kingdom of heaven*. Shall *with difficulty* be saved. He has much to struggle with, and it will require the greatest of human efforts to break away from his temptations and idols, and to secure his salvation. Comp. Notes on 1 Ti. vi. 9, 10.

24. *It is easier for a camel*, &c. This was a *proverb* in common use among the Jews, and is still common among the Arabians. To denote that a thing was *impossible* or *exceedingly difficult*, they said that a *camel* or an *elephant* might as soon walk through a needle's

24 And again I say unto you, It is easier for a camel to go through the eye of a needle, than for a rich man to enter into the kingdom of God.

25 When his disciples heard *it*, they were exceedingly amazed, saying, Who then can be saved?

26 But Jesus beheld *them*, and said unto them, With men this is impossible; but [r]with God all things are possible.

27 Then[s] answered Peter and said unto him, Behold, [t]we have forsaken all and followed thee: what shall we have, therefore?

28 And Jesus said unto them, Verily I say unto you, that ye which have followed me, in the regeneration, when the Son of man shall sit

r Ps.3.8; 62.11; Zec.8.6.
s Mar.10.28; Lu.18.28. *t* Phi.3.8.

---

eye. In the use of such proverbs it is not necessary to understand them *literally*. They merely denote the extreme difficulty of the case. ¶ *A camel.* A beast of burden much used in Eastern countries. It is about the size of the largest ox, with one or two bunches on his back, with long neck and legs, no horns, and with feet adapted to the hot and dry sand. They are capable of carrying heavy burdens, will travel sometimes faster than the fleetest horse, and are provided with a stomach which they fill with water, by means of which they can live four or five days without drink. They are very mild and tame, and kneel down to receive and unload their burden. They are chiefly used in deserts and hot climates, where other beasts of burden are with difficulty kept alive. ¶ *A rich man.* This rather means one who *loves* his riches and makes an idol of them, or one who *supremely* desires to be rich. Mark says (x. 24) "How hard is it for them that trust in riches." While a man has this feeling—relying on his wealth alone—it is literally *impossible* that he should be a Christian; for religion is a love of God rather than the world—the love of Jesus and his cause more than gold. Still a man may have much *property*, and not have this feeling. He *may* have great wealth, and love God more; as a poor man may have little, and love that little more than God. The difficulties in the way of the salvation of a rich man are—1st. That riches engross the affections. 2d. That men consider wealth as the *chief good*, and when this is obtained they think they have gained all. 3d. That they are proud of their wealth, and unwilling to be numbered with the poor and despised followers of Jesus. 4th. That riches engross the *time*, and fill the mind with cares and anxieties, and leave little for God. 5th. That they often produce luxury, dissipation, and vice. 6th. That it is difficult to obtain wealth without sin, without avarice, without covetousness, fraud, and oppression, 1 Ti. vi. 9, 10, 17; Ja. v. 1–5; Lu. xii. 16–21; xvi. 19–31. Still, Jesus says (ver. 26), all these *may* be overcome. God can give grace to do it. Though to *men* it may appear impossible, yet it is easy for God.

27. *We have forsaken all.* Probably nothing but their fishing-nets, small boats, and cottages. But they were their *all*—their *living*, their *home;* and, forsaking *them*, they had as really shown their sincerity as though they had possessed the gold of Ophir and dwelt in the palaces of kings. ¶ *What shall we have, therefore?* We have *done* as thou didst command this young man to do. What reward may we expect for it?

28. *Verily I say unto you.* Jesus in this verse declares the reward which they would have. They were not to look for it *now*, but in a future period. ¶ *That ye which have followed me, in the regeneration.* This word occurs but once elsewhere in the New Testament, Tit. iii. 5. It literally means a new birth, or being born again. Applied to man, it denotes the great change when the heart is renewed, or when the sinner begins to be a Christian. This is its meaning, clearly, in the passage referred to in *Titus;* but this meaning cannot be applied here. Christ was not born again, and in no proper sense could it be said that they *had followed him in the new birth;* but the word also means any great change, or a restoration of things to a former state or *to a better state.* In this sense it is probably used here. It refers to that great revolution—that restoration of order in the universe—that universal *new birth* which will occur when the dead shall

in the throne of his glory, [u]ye also shall sit upon twelve thrones, judging the twelve tribes of Israel.

29 And[v] every one that hath forsaken houses, or brethren, or sisters, or father, or mother, or wife, or children, or lands, for my name's sake, shall receive an hundred-fold, and shall inherit everlasting life.

30 But[w] many *that are* first shall be last, and the last *shall be* first.

u ch.20.21; Lu.22.28-30; 1 Co.6.2,3; Re.2.26.
v Mar.10.29,30; Lu.18.29,30; 1 Co.2.9.
w ch.20.16; 21.31,32; Mar.10.31; Lu.13.30; Ga.5.7; He.4 1.

---

rise, and all human things shall be changed, and a new order of things shall start up out of the ruins of the old, when the Son of man shall come to judgment. The passage, then, should be read, "Ye which have followed me shall, as a reward in the great day of the resurrection of the dead, and of forming the new and eternal order of things—the day of judgment, the *regeneration*—be signally honoured and blessed." ¶ *When the Son of man shall sit in the throne of his glory.* That is, to judge the world. *Throne of glory* means *glorious throne* or a splendid throne. It is not to be taken literally, but is used to denote his character as a *king and judge*, and to signify the great dignity and majesty which will be displayed by him. See Mat. xxiv. 30; xxvi. 64; Ac. i. 11; xvii. 31. ¶ *Sit upon twelve thrones.* This is figurative. To sit on a throne denotes power and honour, and means here that they would be distinguished above others, and be more highly honoured and rewarded. ¶ *Judging the twelve tribes of Israel.* Jesus will be the Judge of quick and dead. He only is qualified for it, and the Father hath given all judgment to the Son, Jn. v. 22. To be a *judge* denotes rank, authority, power. The ancient *judges* of Israel were men of distinguished courage, patriotism, honour, and valour. Hence the word comes to denote *not so much an actual exercise of the power of passing judgment*, as the *honour* attached to the office; and as earthly kings have those around them dignified with honours and office—counsellors and judges, so Christ says that his apostles will occupy the same *relative* station in the great day. They will be honoured by him, and by all, *as* apostles, as having, in the face of persecution, left all; as having laid the foundations of his church, and endured all the persecutions of the world. ¶ *The twelve tribes of Israel.* This was the number of the ancient tribes. By *this name* the people of God were denoted. By this name Jesus here denotes *his redeemed people.* See also Ja. i. 1, where *Christians* are called the twelve tribes. Here it means also, not the *Jews*, not the *world*, not the *wicked*, not that the apostles are to pronounce sentence on the enemies of God, but *the people of God*, the redeemed. Among them Jesus says his apostles will be *honoured* in the day of judgment, as earthly kings place in posts of office and honour those who have signally served them. Comp. Notes on 1 Co. vi. 2.

29. *And every one that hath forsaken houses*, &c. In the days of Jesus, those who followed him were *obliged*, generally, to forsake houses and home, and to attend him. In our time it is not often required that we should *literally leave* them, except when the life is devoted to him among the heathen; but it is always required that we love them *less* than we do him, that we give up all that is inconsistent with religion, and that we be *ready* to give up all when he demands it. ¶ *For my name's sake.* From attachment to me. Mark adds, "and for the gospel's;" that is, from obedience to the requirements of the gospel, and love for the service of the gospel. ¶ *Shall receive a hundred-fold.* Mark says "a hundred-fold now in this time, houses, and brethren, and sisters," &c. *A hundred-fold* means a hundred times as much. This is not to be understood *literally*, but that he will give what will *be worth* a hundred times as much in the peace, and joy, and rewards of religion. It is also literally true that no man's *temporal interest* is injured by the love of God. Mark adds, "*with persecutions.*" These are not promised as a part of the *reward;* but *amid* their trials and persecutions they should find reward and peace.

30. This verse should have been connected with the following chapter. The parable there spoken is expressly to illustrate this sentiment. See it explained in the Notes on ch. xx. 16.

REMARKS.

1st. We should not throw ourselves *unnecessarily* in the way of the enemies of religion, ver. 1. Jesus, to avoid the dangers to which he was exposed, left Jerusalem, and passed over to the other side of the Jordan. If *duty* calls us to remain in the presence of our enemies and the enemies of religion, we should do it. If we can do them good, we should do it. If our presence will only provoke them to anger and bitterness, then we should turn aside. Comp. Notes on ch. x. 23.

2d. Men will seek every occasion to *ensnare* Christians, ver. 3. Questions will be proposed with great art, and with an appearance of sincerity, only for the purpose of leading them into difficulty. Cunning men know *well* how to propose such questions, and triumph much when they have perplexed believers. This is often the boast of men of some standing, who think they accomplish the great purposes of their existence if they can confound other men, and think it signal triumph if they can make others as miserable as themselves.

3d. We should not refuse to answer such persons with mildness, when the Bible has settled the question, ver. 4-6. Jesus answered a captious question, proposed on purpose to ensnare him. We may often do much to confound the enemies of religion, and to recommend it, when without passion we hear their inquiries, and deliberately inform them that the question has been settled by God. We had better, however, far better, say nothing in reply, than to answer in anger or to show that we are irritated. All the object of the enemy is gained if he can *make us angry*.

4th. Men will search and pervert the Bible for authority to indulge their sins and to perplex Christians, ver. 7. No device is more common than to produce a passage of Scripture *known* to be misquoted or perverted, yet plausible, for the purpose of perplexing Christians. In such cases, the best way, often, is to say nothing. If unanswered, men will be ashamed of it; if answered, they gain their point, and are ready for debate and abuse.

5th. We learn from this chapter that there is no union so intimate as the marriage connection, ver. 6. Nothing is so tender and endearing as this union appointed by God for the welfare of man.

6th. This union should not be entered into slightly or rashly. It involves *all* the happiness of this life and *much* of that to come. The union demands—1st, congeniality of feeling and disposition; 2d, of rank or standing in life; 3d, of temper; 4th, similarity of acquirements; 5th, of age; 6th, of talent; 7th, intimate acquaintance. It should also be a union on religious feelings and opinions: 1st, because religion is more important than anything else; 2d, because it will give more happiness in the married life than anything else; 3d, because where *one* only is pious, there is danger that the religion of the other will be obscured and blighted; 4th, because no prospect is so painful as that of eternal separation; 5th, because it is heathenish, brutal, and mad, to partake the gifts of God in a family and offer no thanksgiving; inexpressibly wicked to live from day to day as if there were no God, no heaven, no hell; 6th, because death is near, and nothing will soothe the pangs of parting but the hope of meeting in the resurrection of the just.

7th. No human legislature has a right to declare divorces except in one single case, ver. 9. If they do, they are accessories to the crime that may follow, and presume to legislate where *God* has legislated before them.

8th. Those *thus* divorced, or pretended to be divorced, and marrying again, are, by the declaration of Jesus Christ, living in adultery, ver. 9. It is no excuse to say that the law of the land divorced them. The law had no such right. If all the legislatures of the world were to say that it was lawful for a man to steal or to commit murder, it would not make it so, and, in spite of human permission, God would hold a man answerable for theft and murder. So, also, of adultery.

9th. The marriage union demands *kindness* and *love*, ver. 6. The husband and the wife are *one*. Love to each other is love to a second self. Hatred, and anger, and quarrels are against *ourselves*. The evils and quarrels in married life will descend on ourselves, and be gall and wormwood in our own cup.

10th. Infants may be brought to Jesus to receive his blessing, ver. 12-15. While on earth, he admitted them to his presence and blessed them with his prayers. If they might be brought *then*, they may be brought *now*. Their souls are as precious; their dangers are as great; their salvation is as important. A parent should require the most indubitable evidence that Jesus will *not* receive his offspring, and will be *displeased* if the offering is made, to deter him from this inestimable privilege.

11th. If children *may* be brought, they *should* be brought. It is the solemn duty of a parent to seize upon all possible means of benefiting his children, and of presenting them to God to implore his blessing. In family prayer, in the sanctuary, and in the ordinance of baptism, the blessing of the Redeemer should be sought early and constantly on their precious and immortal souls.

12th. Earnestness and deep anxiety are proper in seeking salvation, ver. 16. The young man came running; he kneeled. It was not form and ceremony; it was life and reality. Religion is a great subject. Salvation is important beyond the power of language to express. Eternity is near, and damnation thunders along the path of the guilty. The sinner *must* be saved soon, or die for ever. He cannot be too earnest. He cannot press with too great haste to Jesus. He should come running, and kneeling, and humbled, and lifting the agonizing cry, "What must I do to be saved?"

13th. We should come young, ver. 20. No one can come *too young*. God has the *first* claim on our affections. He made us, he keeps us, he provides for us, and it is right that we should give our first affections to him. No one who has become a Christian ever yet felt that he had become one too young. No young person that has given his heart to the Redeemer ever yet regretted it. They may give up the gay world to do it; they may leave the circles of the dance and the song; they may be exposed to contempt and persecution, but no matter. He who becomes a true Christian, no matter of what age or rank, blesses God that he was inclined to do it, and the time never *can* come when for one moment he will regret it. Why, then, will not the young give their hearts to the Saviour, and do that which they know they never can for one moment regret?

14th. It is no dishonour for those who hold *offices*, and who are men of rank, to inquire on the subject of religion, Lu. xviii. 18. Men of rank often suppose that it is only the *weak*, the *credulous*, and the *ignorant* that ever feel any anxiety about religion. Never was a greater mistake. It has been only profligate, and weak, and ignorant men that have been thoughtless. Two-thirds of all the profound investigations of the world have been on this very subject. The wisest and best of the heathens have devoted their lives to inquire about God and their own destiny. So in Christian lands. Were Bacon, Newton, Locke, Milton, Hale, and Boerhaave men of weak minds? Yet their deepest thoughts and most anxious inquiries were on this very subject. So in our own land. Were Washington, Ames, Henry, Jay, and Rush men of weak minds? Yet they were professed believers in revelation. And yet young men of rank, and wealth, and learning often think that they show great independence in refusing to *think* of what occupied the profound attention of these men, and fancy they are great only by refusing to tread in their steps. Never was a greater or more foolish mistake. If anything demands attention, it is, surely, the inquiry whether we are to be happy for ever, or wretched; whether there is a God and Saviour; or whether we are "in a forsaken and fatherless world."

15th. It is as important for the *rich* to seek religion as the poor, ver. 22. They will as certainly die; they as much need religion. Without it they *cannot* be happy. Riches will drive away no pain on a death-bed—will not go with us when we die—will not save us.

16th. It is of *special* importance that wealthy young persons should be Christians. They are exposed to many dangers. The world—the gay and flattering world—will lead them astray. Fond of fashion, dress, and amusement, as many of them are, they are exposed to a thousand follies and dangers, from which nothing but religion can *secure* them. Besides, they may do much good; and God will hold them answerable for all the good they *might* have done with their wealth.

17th. The amiable, the lovely, the moral, need also an interest in Christ, Mar. x. 21. If amiable, we should suppose they would be ready to embrace the Saviour. None was ever so moral, so lovely, so pure as he. If we really *loved* amiableness, then we should come to him—we should love him. But, alas! how many amiable young persons turn

CHAPTER XX.

FOR the kingdom of heaven is like unto a man *that is* an householder, [a]which went out early in the morning to hire labourers into his vineyard.

a Ca.8.11,12.

away from him, and refuse to follow him! Can they be really lovers of that which is pure and lovely? If so, then why turn away from the Lamb of God?

18th. The amiable and the lovely need a better righteousness than their own. With all this, they may make an idol of the world; they may be proud, sensual, selfish, prayerless, and thoughtless about dying. Externally they appear lovely; but oh, how far is the heart from God!

19th. Inquirers about religion usually depend on their own works, ver. 16. They are not willing to trust to Jesus for salvation, and they ask what they shall *do;* and it is only when they find that they can do nothing—that they are poor, and helpless, and wretched—that they cast themselves on the mercy of God and find peace.

20th. Compliments and flattering titles are evil, ver. 17. They ascribe something to others which we know they do not possess. Often beauty is praised where we know there is no beauty—accomplishment where there is no accomplishment—talent where there is no talent. Such praises are *falsehood.* We know them to be such. We intend to to deceive by them, and we know that they will produce pride and vanity. Often they they are used for the purpose of destruction. If a man praises us too much, we should look to our purse or our virtue. We should feel that we are in danger, and the next thing will be a dreadful blow—the heavier for all this flattery. They that use compliments much, expect them from others; are galled and vexed when they are *not* obtained; and are in danger when they are.

21st. If we are to be saved, we must do just what God commands us, ver. 17, 18. This is *all* we have to do. We are not to *invent* anything of our own. God has marked out the course, and we must follow it.

22d. We are easily deceived about keeping the law, ver. 17. We often *think* we observe it, when it is only the *outward* form that we have kept. The law is spiritual, and God requires the heart.

23d. Riches are a blessing if used aright; if not, they are deceitful, dangerous, ruinous, ver. 23, 24. Thousands have lost their souls by the love of riches. None have ever been saved by it.

24th. It is our duty to forsake all for Christ, ver. 27-29. Be it little or much, it is all the same to him. It is the *heart* that he looks at; and we may as really show our love by giving up a fishing-boat and net, as by giving up a palace or a crown. If done in either case, it will be accepted.

25th. Religion has its own rewards, ver. 28, 29. It gives more than it takes. It more than compensates for all that we surrender. It gives peace, joy, comfort in trial and in death, and heaven beyond. This is the testimony of all Christians of all denominations—of all that *have* lived, and of all that *do* live—that they never knew true peace till they found it in the gospel. The testimony of so many must be true. They have tried the world in all its forms of gaiety, folly, and vice, and they come and say with one voice, Here only is true peace. On any other subject they would be believed. Their testimony here *must* be true.

26th. Those eminent for usefulness here will be received to distinguished honours and rewards in heaven, ver. 28. They that turn many to righteousness shall shine as stars in the firmament for ever. See Notes on Da. xii. 3.

CHAPTER XX.

1. *For the kingdom of heaven,* &c. The word "for" shows that this chapter should have been connected with the preceding. The parable was spoken expressly to illustrate the sentiment in the last verse of that chapter: "Many that are first shall be last, and the last shall be first." The kingdom of heaven means here the church, including, perhaps, its state here and hereafter. See Notes on Mat. iii. 2. It has reference to *rewards,* and the meaning may be thus expressed: "Rewards shall be bestowed in my kingdom, or on my followers, in the same manner as they were by a certain householder—in such a way that the last shall be equal to the first, and the first last." ¶ *A householder.* A master of a family. One at the head of family affairs. ¶ *His vineyard.* No

2 And when he had agreed with the labourers for a [b]penny a day, he sent them into his vineyard.

3 And he went out about the third hour, and saw others standing idle in the market-place,

4 And said unto them, Go ye also into the vineyard, and whatsoever is right, I will give you. And they went their way.

5 Again he went out about the sixth and ninth hour, and did likewise.

6 And about the eleventh hour he went out and found others standing idle, and saith unto them, [c]Why stand ye here all the day idle?

7 They say unto him, Because no man hath hired us. He saith unto them, [d]Go ye also into the vineyard; and whatsoever is right, *that* shall ye receive.

b ch.18.28.

c Pr.19.15; Eze.16.49; Ac.17.21; He.6.12.
d Ec.9.10; Jn.9.4.

inconsiderable part of Judea was employed in the culture of the grape. *Vineyards* are often used, therefore, to represent a fertile or well-cultivated place, and hence the church, denoting the care and culture that God has bestowed on it. See Notes on Is. v. 7. Comp. Je. xii. 10. For the manner of their construction, see Notes on Mat. xxi. 33.

2. *A penny a day.* The coin here referred to was a Roman coin, equal in value, at different periods, to fifteen or seventeen cents ($7\frac{1}{2}d.$ to $8\frac{1}{2}d.$) of our money. The original denotes the Roman denarius (δηνάριον), a silver coin, which was originally equivalent to *ten ases* (a brass Roman coin), whence its name. The consular denarius bore on one side a head of Rome, and an X or a star, to denote the value in *ases*, and a chariot with either two or four horses. At a later period the casts of different deities were on the obverse, and these were finally superseded by the heads of the Cæsars. Many specimens of this coin have been preserved. The following cut shows their usual appearance.

Denarius of Tiberius.

It was probably at that time the price of a day's labour. See Tobit v. 14. This was the common wages of a Roman soldier. In England, before the discovery of the mines of gold and silver in South America, and consequently before money was plenty, the price of labour was about in proportion. In 1351 the price of labour was regulated by law, and was a *penny* a day; but provisions were of course proportionally cheap, and the avails of a man's labour in articles of food were nearly as much as they are now.

3. *About the third hour.* The Jews divided their days into *twelve* equal parts, or hours, beginning at sunrise and ending at sunset. This was, therefore, about nine o'clock in the morning. ¶ *Standing idle in the market-place.* A place where provisions are sold in towns. Of course, many resort to such places, and it would be the readiest place to meet persons and find employers. They were not, therefore, *disposed* to be idle, but were waiting in the proper place to find employers.

4. *Whatsoever is right.* Whatsoever it shall appear you can earn. The contract with the first was definite; with this one it depended on the judgment of the employer.

5. *The sixth and ninth hour.* That is, about twelve and three o'clock.

6. *The eleventh hour.* About five o'clock in the afternoon, or when there was but one working hour of the day left.

8. *When even was come.* That is, when the twelfth hour was come; the day was ended, and the time of payment was come. ¶ *The steward.* A *steward* is one who transacts business in the place of another. He was one who had the administration of affairs in the absence of the householder, who provided for the family, and who was intrusted with the payment of labourers and servants. He was commonly the most trusty and faithful of the servants, raised to that station as a reward for his fidelity. ¶ *Beginning from the last unto the first.* It was immaterial where he *began* to pay, provided he dealt justly by them. In the parable this order is mentioned

8 So when even was come, the lord of the vineyard saith unto his steward, Call the labourers, and give[e] them *their* hire, beginning from the last unto the first.

9 And when they came that *were hired* about the [f]eleventh hour, they received every man a penny.

10 But when the first came, they supposed that they should have received more; and they likewise received every man a penny.

11 And when they had received *it*, they [g]murmured against the goodman of the house,

12 Saying, These last [1]have wrought *but* one hour, and thou hast made them equal unto us, which have borne the burden and the heat of the day.

13 But he answered one of them, and said, [h]Friend, I do thee no wrong: didst not thou agree with me for a penny?

14 Take *that* thine *is*, and go thy way: [i]I will give unto this last even as unto thee.

15 Is[k] it not lawful for me to do what I will with mine own? Is[l] thine eye evil because I am good?

16 So[m] the last shall be first,

e Lu.10.7. f Lu.23.40-43. g Lu.15.29,30.
1 or, *have continued one hour only*.

h ch.22.12. i Jn.17.2. k Ro.9.15-24; Ja.1.18.
l De.15.9; ch.6.23. m ch.19.30.

to give opportunity for the remarks which follow. Had those first hired been first paid, they would have departed satisfied, and the *point* of the parable would have been lost.

9. *They received every man a penny.* There was no agreement how much they should receive, but merely that justice should be done, ver. 4, 5, 7. The householder supposed they had earned it, or chose to make a present to them to compensate for the loss of the first part of the day, when they were willing to work, but could not find employment.

10. *They supposed that they should have received more.* They had worked longer—they had been in the heat; they supposed that it was his intention to pay them, not according to *contract*, but according to the time of the labour.

11. *Murmured.* Complained; found fault with. ¶ *The goodman of the house.* The original here is the same word which in ver. 1 is translated *householder*, and should have been so translated here. It is the old English way of denoting the father of a family. It expresses no *moral* quality.

12. *The burden and heat of the day.* The *burden* means the heavy labour, the severe toil. We have *continued* at that toil in the heat of the day. The others had worked only a little while, and that in the cool of the evening, and when it was far more pleasant and much less fatiguing.

13. *Friend, I do thee no wrong.* I have fully complied with the contract. We had an agreement: I have paid all that I promised. If I choose to *give* a penny to another man if he labours little or not at all—if I should choose to give *all* my property away to others, it would not affect this contract with *you:* it is fully met; and with my own—with that on which *you* have no farther claim—I may do as I please. So, if Christians are *just*, and pay their lawful debts, and injure no one, the world has no right to complain if they give the rest of their property to the poor, or devote it to send the gospel to the heathen, or to release the prisoner or the captive. It is their *own*. They have a right to do with it as they please. They are answerable, not to men, but to God, and infidels, and worldly men, and cold professors in the church have no right to interfere.

14. *Take* that *thine* is. Take what is justly *due* to you—what is properly your own.

15. *Is thine eye evil because I am good?* The Hebrews used the word *evil*, when applied to the eye, to denote one *envious* and *malicious*, De. xv. 9; Pr. xxiii. 6. The eye is called *evil* in such cases, because envy and malice show themselves directly in the eye. No passions are so fully expressed by the eye as these. "Does *envy* show itself in the eye? is thine eye so soon turned to express envy and malice because I have chosen to do good?"

16. *So the last shall be first*, &c. This is the *moral* or *scope* of the parable. To teach this it was spoken. Many that, in the *order of time*, are brought last into the kingdom, shall be first in the re-

and the first last: for [n]many be called, but few chosen.

17 And[o] Jesus, going up to Jerusalem, took the twelve disciples apart in the way, and said unto them,

18 Behold, we go up to Jerusalem; and the Son of man shall be betrayed unto the chief priests and unto the scribes, and they shall condemn him to death,

19 And[p] shall deliver him to the

n ch.22.14; 2 Th.2.13; Ja.1.23-25.
o ch.16.21,&c.; Mar.10.32,&c.; Lu.18.31,&c.; Jn. 12.12,&c.
p ch.27.2,&c.; Mar.15.1,16,&c.; Lu.23.1,&c.; Jn.18. 28,&c.; Ac.3.13; 1 Co.15.3-7.

---

wards. Higher *proportionate* rewards shall be given to them than to others. To *all* justice shall be done. To all to whom the rewards of heaven are *promised* they shall be given. Nothing shall be withheld that was promised. If, among this number who are called into the kingdom, I choose to raise some to stations of distinguished usefulness, and to confer on them peculiar talents and higher rewards, I injure no other one. They shall enter heaven, as was promised. If, amid the multitude of Christians, I choose to signalize such men as Paul, and Martyn, and Brainerd, and Spencer, and Summerfield—to appoint some of them to short labour but to wide usefulness, and raise them to signal rewards, I injure not the great multitude of others who live long lives less useful and less rewarded. All shall reach heaven, and all shall receive what I promise to the faithful. ¶ *Many be called, but few chosen.* The meaning of this, in this connection, I take to be simply this: "Many are called into my kingdom; they come and labour as I command them; many of them are comparatively unknown and obscure; yet they are real Christians, and shall all receive the proper reward. A few I have chosen for higher stations in the church. I have endowed them with apostolic gifts or with superior talents, and fitted them for wider usefulness. They may not be as long in the vineyard as others; their race may be sooner run; but I have chosen to honour them in this manner, and I have a right to do it. I injure no one, and have a right to do what I will with my own." Thus explained, this parable has no reference to the call of the Gentiles, nor to the call of aged sinners, nor to the call of sinners out of the church at all. It is simply designed to teach that *in* the church, among the multitudes who will be saved, Christ makes a difference. He makes some more useful than others, without regard to the *time* which they serve, and he will reward them accordingly. The parable teaches *one* truth, and *but* one; and where Jesus has explained it, we have no right to add to it, and say that it teaches anything else. It adds to the reason for this interpretation, that Christ was conversing about the rewards that should be given to his followers, and not about the numbers that should be called, or about the doctrine of election. See ch. xix. 27–29.

17–19. See also Mar. x. 32–34; Lu. xviii. 31–34. *And Jesus, going up to Jerusalem.* That is, doubtless, to the Passover. This journey was from the east side of Jordan. See Notes on ch. xix. 1. At this time he was on this journey to Jerusalem, probably not far from Jericho. This was his last journey to Jerusalem. He was going up to die for the sins of the world. ¶ *Took the twelve disciples apart.* All the *males* of the Jews were required to be at this feast, Ex. xxiii. 17. The roads, therefore, on such occasions, would probably be thronged. It is probable, also, that they would travel in companies, or that whole neighbourhoods would go together. See Lu. ii. 44. By his *taking them apart* is meant his taking them aside from the company. He had something to communicate which he did not wish the others to hear. Mark adds: "And Jesus went before them, and they were amazed; and as they followed they were sore afraid." He led the way. He had told them before (ch. xvii. 22) that he should be betrayed into the hands of men and be put to death. They began now to be afraid that this would happen, and to be solicitous for his life and for their own safety, and they were "amazed" at his boldness and calmness, and at his fixed determination to go up to Jerusalem in these circumstances.

18, 19. *Behold, we go up to Jerusalem.* Jesus assured them that what they feared would come to pass, but he had, in some measure, prepared their minds for this state of suffering by the promises which he had made to them, ch.

Gentiles, to mock, and to [q]scourge, and to crucify *him:* and the third day he shall rise again.

20 Then[r] came to him the mother of Zebedee's children, with her sons, worshipping *him*, and desiring a certain thing of him.

21 And he said unto her, What wilt thou? She saith unto him, Grant that these my two sons may sit, the one on thy right hand, and the other on the left, in thy kingdom.

22 But Jesus answered and said, Ye know not what ye ask. Are ye able to drink of the cup that I shall drink of, and to be baptized with [s]the baptism that I am baptized

q Is.53.5. r Mar.10.35. s Lu.12.50.

---

xix. 27–30; xx. 1–16. In all their sufferings they might be assured that eternal rewards were before them. ¶ *Shall be betrayed.* See ch. xvii. 22. ¶ *Unto the chief priests and scribes.* The high-priest, and the learned men who composed the Sanhedrim or Great Council of the nation. He *was* thus betrayed by Judas, Mat. xxvi. 15. He *was* delivered to the chief priests and scribes, Mat. xxvi. 57. ¶ *And they shall condemn him to death.* They had not power to *inflict* death, as that power had been taken away by the Romans; but they had the power of *expressing an opinion*, and of delivering him to the Romans to be put to death. This they did, Mat. xxvi. 66; xxvii. 2. ¶ *Shall deliver him to the Gentiles.* That is, because they have not the right of inflicting capital punishment, they will deliver him to those who have—to the Roman authorities. *The Gentiles* here means Pontius Pilate and the Roman soldiers. See Mat. xxvii. 2, 27–30. ¶ *To mock.* See Notes on Mat. ii. 16. ¶ *To scourge.* That is, to *whip.* This was done with thongs, or a whip made for the purpose, and this punishment was commonly inflicted upon criminals before crucifixion. See Notes on ch. x. 17. ¶ *To crucify* him. That is, to put him to death on a cross—the common punishment of slaves. See Notes on Mat. xxvii. 31, 32. ¶ *The third day*, &c. For the evidence that this was fulfilled, see Notes on Mat. xxviii. 15. Mark and Luke say that he would be spit upon. *Spitting* on another has always been considered an expression of the deepest contempt. Luke says (xviii. 31), "All things that are written by the prophets concerning the Son of man shall be accomplished." Among other things, he says he shall be "spitefully entreated;" that is, treated with *spite* or malice; malice, implying contempt. These sufferings of our Saviour, and this treatment, and his death, had been predicted in many places. See Is. liii.; Da. ix. 26, 27.

20–28. See also Mar. x. 35–45.

20. *Then came to him the mother of Zebedee's children*, &c. This was probably Salome, Mar. xv. 40; xvi. 1. ¶ *With her sons.* The names of these sons were James and John, Mar. x. 35. Mark says *they* came and made the request. That is, they made it, as appears from Matthew, through the medium of their mother; they requested *her* to ask it for them. It is not improbable that she was an ambitious woman, and was desirous to see her sons honoured. ¶ *Worshipping* him. Showing him respect; respectfully saluting him. In the original, *kneeling.* See Notes on Mat. viii. 2.

21. *Grant that these my two sons may sit*, &c. They were still looking for a temporal kingdom. They expected that he would reign on the earth with great pomp and glory. They anticipated that he would conquer as a prince and a warrior. They wished to be distinguished in the day of his triumph. To sit on the right and left hand of a prince was a token of confidence, and the highest honour granted to his friends, 1 Ki. ii. 19; Ps. cx. 1; 1 Sa. xx. 25. The disciples, here, had no reference to the kingdom of heaven, but only to the kingdom which they supposed he was about to set up on the earth.

22. *Ye know not what ye ask.* You do not know the nature of your request, nor what would be involved in it. You suppose that it would be attended only with honour and happiness if the request was granted, whereas it would require much suffering and trial. ¶ *Are ye able to drink of the cup*, &c. To drink of a cup, in the Scriptures, often signifies *to be afflicted, or to be punished*, Mat. xxvi. 39; Is. li. 17, 22; Ps. lxxiii. 10; lxxv. 8; Jer. xxv. 15; Re. xvi. 9. The figure is taken from *a feast*, where the master of a feast ex-

with? They say unto him, We are able.

23 And he saith unto them, Ye[t] shall drink indeed of my cup, and be baptized with the baptism that I am baptized with; but to sit on my right hand, and on my left, is not mine to give, but *it shall be given to them* for whom it is prepared of my Father.

24 And when the ten heard *it*, they were moved with indignation against the two brethren.

25 But Jesus called them *unto him*, and said, [u]Ye know that the princes of the Gentiles exercise dominion over them, and they that are great exercise authority upon them.

26 But[v] it shall not be so among you: but [w]whosoever will be great among you, let him be your minister;

27 And whosoever will be chief among you, let him be your servant:

t Ac.12.2; Ro.8.17; 2 Co.1.7; Re.1.9.

u Lu.22.25,26. *v* 1 Pe.5.3. *w* ch.23.11; Mar.9.35; 10.43.

---

tends a cup to those present. Thus God is represented as extending to his Son a cup filled with a bitter mixture—one causing deep sufferings, Jn. xviii. 11. This was the cup to which he referred. ¶ *The baptism that I am baptized with.* This is evidently a phrase denoting the same thing. Are ye able *to suffer* with me—to endure the *trials* and *pains* which shall come upon you and me in endeavouring to build up my kingdom? Are you able to bear it when sorrows shall cover you like water, and you shall be sunk beneath calamities as floods, in the work of religion? Afflictions are often expressed by being sunk in the floods and plunged in deep waters, Ps. lxix. 2; Is. xliii. 2; Ps. cxxiv. 4, 5; La. iii. 54.

23. *Ye shall indeed drink of my cup,* &c. You will follow me, and you will partake of my afflictions, and will suffer as *I* shall. This was fulfilled. James was slain with the sword by Herod, Ac. xii. 2. John lived many years; but he attended the Saviour through his sufferings, and was himself banished to Patmos, a solitary island, for the testimony of Jesus Christ—a companion of others *in tribulation*, Re. i. 9. ¶ *Is not mine to give,* &c. The translation of this place evidently does not express the sense of the original. The translation expresses the idea that Jesus has nothing to do in bestowing rewards on his followers. This is at variance with the uniform testimony of the Scriptures, Mat. xxv. 31-40; Jn. v. 22-30. The correct translation of the passage would be, "To sit on my right hand and on my left is not mine to give, *except to those* for whom it is prepared by my Father." The passage thus declares that *Christ* would give rewards to his followers, but only to such as should be entitled to them according to the *purpose of his Father.* Much as he might be attached to these two disciples, yet he could not bestow any such signal favours on them out of the regular course of things. Rewards were prepared for his followers, and in due time they should be bestowed. *He* would bestow them according as they had been provided from eternity by God the Father, Mat. xxv. 34. The correct sense is seen by leaving out that part of the verse *in italics*, and this is one of the places in the Bible where the sense has been obscured by the introduction of words which have nothing to correspond with them in the original. See a similar instance in 1 Jn. ii. 23.

24. *The ten heard* it. That is, the ten other apostles. ¶ *They were moved with indignation.* They were offended at their ambition, and at their desire to be exalted above their brethren. The word "*it*" refers not to what Jesus said, but to their request. When the ten heard *the request* which they had made they were indignant.

25–27. *But Jesus called them* unto him. That is, he called *all* the apostles to him, and stated the principles on which they were to act. ¶ *The princes of the Gentiles exercise dominion over them.* That is, over *their subjects.* "You know that such honours are customary among nations. The kings of the earth raise their favourites to posts of trust and power—they give *authority* to some over others; but my kingdom is established in a different manner. All are to be on a level. The rich, the poor, the learned, the unlearned, the bond, the free, are to be equal. He will be the

28 Even as the Son of man came not to be ministered unto, but [x] to minister, and [y] to give his life a ransom for many.

x Lu.22.27; Jn.13.4,14; Phi.2.7.
y Is.53.5,8,11; Da.9.24,26; 1 Ti.2.6; Tit.2.14; He.9.28; 1 Pe.1.18,19; Re.1.5.

29 And as they departed from Jericho a great multitude followed him.

30 And,[z] behold, two blind men,

z ch.9.27; Mar.10.46; Lu.18.35.

most distinguished that shows most humility, the deepest sense of his unworthiness, and the most earnest desire to promote the welfare of his brethren." ¶ *Gentiles.* All who were not Jews—used here to denote the manner in which human governments are constituted. ¶ *Minister.* A servant. The original word is *deacon*—a word meaning a servant of any kind; one especially who served at the table, and, in the New Testament, one who *serves* the church, Ac. vi. 1–4; 1 Ti. iii. 8. Preachers of the gospel are called *ministers* because they are the servants of God and of the church (1 Co. iii. 5; iv. 1; 2 Co. iii. 6; vi. 4; Ep. iv. 12); an office, therefore, which forbids them to lord it over God's heritage, which is the very opposite of a station of superiority, and which demands the very lowest degree of humility.

28. *Even as the Son of man*, &c. See Notes on Mat. viii. 20. Jesus points them to his own example. He was in the form of God in heaven, Phi. ii. 6. He came to men in the form of a servant, Phi. ii. 7. He came not with pomp and glory, but as a man in humble life; and since he came he had not required them to minister to him. He laboured *for* them. He strove to do them good. He provided for their wants; fared as poorly as they did; went before them in dangers and sufferings; practised self-denial on their account, and for them was about to lay down his life. See Jn. xiii. 4, 5. ¶ *To give his life a ransom for many.* The word *ransom* means literally a price paid for the redemption of captives. In war, when prisoners are taken by an enemy, the money demanded for their release is called a ransom; that is, it is the *means* by which they are set at liberty. So anything that releases anyone from a state of punishment, or suffering, or sin, is called a ransom. Men are by nature captives to sin. They are sold under it. They are under condemnation, Ep. ii. 3; Ro. iii. 9–20, 23; 1 Jn. v. 19. They are under a curse, Ga. iii. 10. They are in love with sin. They are under its withering dominion, and are exposed to death eternal, Eze. xviii. 4; Ps. ix. 17; xi. 6; lxviii. 2; cxxxix. 19; Mat. xxv. 46; Ro. ii. 6–9. They must have perished unless there had been some way by which they could be rescued. This was done by *the death* of Jesus—by giving his life a ransom. The meaning is, that he died *in the place* of sinners, and that God was willing to *accept* the pains of *his death* in the place of the eternal suffering of the redeemed. The reasons why such a ransom was necessary are—1st. That God had declared that the sinner shall die; that is, that he would punish, or show his hatred to, all sin. 2d. That all men had sinned, and, if justice was to take its regular course, all must perish. 3d. That man could make no atonement for his own sins. All that he could do, were he holy, would be only to do his duty, and would make no amends for the past. Repentance and future obedience would not blot away one sin. 4th. No man was pure, and no angel could make atonement. God was pleased, therefore, to appoint his only-begotten Son to make such a ransom. See Jn. iii. 16; 1 Jn. iv. 10; 1 Pe. i. 18, 19; Re. xiii. 8; Jn. i. 29; Ep. v. 2; He. viii. 27; Is. liii. This is commonly called *the atonement.* See Notes on Ro. v. 2. ¶ *For many.* See also Mat. xxvi. 28; Jn. x. 15; 1 Ti. ii. 6; 1 Jn. ii. 2; 2 Co. v. 14, 15; He. ii. 9.

29–34. See Mar. x. 46–52, and Lu. xviii. 35–43; xix. 1, where this account of his restoring to sight two blind men is also recorded. *And as they departed from Jericho.* This was a large town about eight miles west of the Jordan, and about nineteen miles north-east from Jerusalem. Near to this city the Israelites crossed the Jordan when they entered into the land of Canaan, Jos. iii. 16. It was the first city taken by Joshua, who destroyed it to the foundation, and pronounced a curse on him who should rebuild it, Jos. vi. 20, 21, 26. This curse was literally fulfilled in the days of Ahab, nearly five hundred years after, 1 Ki. xvi. 34. It afterward became the place of the school of the prophets, 2 Ki. ii. 5. In this place Elisha

sitting by the way-side, when they heard that Jesus passed by, cried out, saying, Have mercy on us, O Lord, *thou* son of David!

---

worked a signal miracle, greatly to the advantage of the inhabitants, by rendering the waters near it, that were before bitter, sweet and wholesome, 2 Ki. ii. 21. In point of size it was second only to Jerusalem. It was sometimes called the city of palm-trees, from the fact that there were many palms in the vicinity. A few of them are still remaining, 2 Ch. xxviii. 15; Ju. i. 16; iii. 13. At this place died Herod the Great, of a most wretched and foul disease. See Notes on Mat. ii. 19. It is now a small village, wretched in its appearance, and inhabited by a very few persons, and called *Riha*, or *Rah*, situated on the ruins of the ancient city (or, as some think, three or four miles east of it), which a modern traveller describes as a poor, dirty village of the Arabs. There are perhaps fifty houses, of rough stone, with roofs of bushes and mud, and the population, two or three hundred in number, is entirely Mohammedan. Dr. Thomson (*The Land and the Book*, vol. ii. p. 443) says of this village, that there "are some forty or fifty of the most forlorn habitations that I have seen. And this is Jericho! These houses, or rather huts, are surrounded by a peculiar kind of fortification, made of nubk, a species of bush very abundant in this plain. Its thorns are so sharp and the branches are so plaited together that neither horse nor man will attack it." The road from Jerusalem to Jericho lies through what is called the *wilderness of Jericho*, and is described by modern travellers as the most dangerous and forbidding about Palestine. As lately as 1820, an English traveller, Sir Frederick Henniker, was attacked on this road by the Arabs with firearms, who left him naked and severely wounded. See Notes on Lu. x. 30. Jesus was going to Jerusalem from the east side of the Jordan (ch. xix. 1); his regular journey was therefore through Jericho. ¶ *As they departed from Jericho.* Luke says, "*As he was come nigh unto Jericho.*" The original word used in Luke, translated *was come nigh*, commonly expresses *approach to* a place, but it does not of necessity mean that always. It may denote *nearness* to a place, whether going to it or from it. It would be here rendered correctly, "*when they were near to Jericho*," or when they were in the *vicinity* of it, without saying whether they were going *to* it or *from* it. Matthew and Mark say they were going from it. The passage in Lu. xix. 1—*and Jesus entered and passed through Jericho*—which seems to be mentioned as having taken place *after* the cure of the blind man, does not necessarily suppose that. That passage might be intended to be connected with the account of Zaccheus, and not to denote *the order of time* in which these events took place; but simply that as he was passing through Jericho, Zaccheus sought to see him, and invited him to his house. Historians vary in the circumstances and order of events. The *main facts* of the narrative are observed; and such variations of circumstances and order, where there is no palpable contradiction, show the *honesty* of the writers—show that they did not *conspire together* to deceive, and are in courts of justice considered as confirmations of the truth of the testimony.

30. *Two blind men.* Mark and Luke mention but one. They do not say, however, that there was no more than one. They mention one because he was probably well known; perhaps the son of a distinguished citizen reduced to poverty. His name was Bartimeus. *Bar* is a Syraic word, meaning *son;* and the name means, therefore, "the son of Timeus." Probably *Timeus* was a man of distinction; and as the case of his son attracted most attention, Mark and Luke recorded it particularly. Had they said there was *only* one healed, there would have been a contradiction. As it is, there is no more contradiction or difficulty than there is in the fact that the evangelists, like all other historians, often omit many facts which they do not choose to record. ¶ *Heard that Jesus passed by.* They learned who he was by inquiring. They heard a noise, and asked who it was (Luke). They had doubtless heard much of his fame, but had never before been where he was, and probably would not be again. They were therefore more earnest in calling upon him. ¶ *Son of David.* That is, *Messiah*, or *Christ.* This was the name by which the Messiah was commonly known. He was the illustrious *descendant* of David in whom the pro-

31 And the multitude rebuked them, because they should hold their peace: but they cried the more, saying, Have mercy on us, O Lord, *thou* son of David!
32 And Jesus stood still, and called them, and said, What will ye that I shall do unto you?
33 They say unto him, Lord, that our eyes may be opened.
34 So Jesus had compassion *on them*, and touched their eyes: and immediately their eyes received sight, and they followed him.

---

mises especially centred, Ps. cxxxii. 11, 12; lxxxix. 3, 4. It was the universal opinion of the Jews that the Messiah was to be the descendant of David. See ch. xxii. 42. On the use of the word *son*, see Notes on Mat. i. 1.

31. *And the multitude rebuked them because*, &c. They chid or reproved them, and in a threatening manner told them to be silent. ¶ *They cried the more.* Jesus, standing still, ordered them to be brought to him (Mark). His friends *then* addressed the blind men and told them that Jesus called (Mark). Mark adds that Bartimeus cast away his garment, and rose and came to Jesus. *The garment* was not his only raiment, but was the *outer* garment, thrown loosely over him, and commonly laid aside when persons laboured or ran. See Notes on Mat. v. 40. His doing it denoted haste and earnestness in order to come to Jesus.

34. *And touched their eyes.* Mark and Luke say he added, *Thy faith hath saved thee.* Thy *confidence*, or *belief* that I could cure, has been the means of obtaining this blessing. Faith had no power to open the eyes, but it led the blind men to Jesus; it showed that they had just views of his power; it was connected with the cure. So *faith* has no power to save from sin, but it leads the poor, lost, blind sinner to him who *has* power, and in this sense it is said we are saved by faith. His *touching* their eyes was merely *a sign* that the power of healing proceeded from him.

Here was an undoubted miracle. 1st. These blind men were well known. One, at least, had been long blind. 2d. They were strangers to Jesus. They could not have, therefore, *feigned* themselves blind, or done this by any *collusion* or *agreement* between him and themselves in order to impose on the multitude. 3d. The miracle was in the presence of multitudes who took a deep interest in it, and who could easily have detected the imposition if there had been any. 4th. The men followed him. They praised or *glorified* God (Mark and Luke). The people gave praise to God also (Luke). They were all satisfied that a *real* miracle was performed.

REMARKS.

1st. From the parable at the beginning of this chapter (ver. 1–16) we learn that it is not so much the *time* that we serve Christ as the *manner*, that is to entitle us to high rewards in heaven. Some may be in the church many years, yet accomplish little. Others in a few years may be more distinguished in the success of their labours and in their rewards.

2d. God will do justice to all, ver. 13. He will give to every one of his followers all that he promised to give. To him entitled to the least he will give everything which he has promised, and to each one infinitely more than he has deserved.

3d. On some he will bestow higher rewards than on others, ver. 16. There is no reason to think that the condition of men in heaven will be *equal*, any more than it is on earth. Difference of rank may run through all God's government, and still no one be degraded or be deprived of his rights.

4th. God does as he pleases with his own, ver. 15. It is his right to do so—a right which *men* claim, and which God may claim. If he does injustice to *no one*, he has a right to bestow what favours on others he pleases. In doing good to another man he does no injury to me. He violated none of *my* rights by bestowing great talents on Newton or great wealth on Solomon. He did not injure *me* by making Paul a man of distinguished talents and piety, or John a man of much meekness and love. What he gives me I should be thankful for and improve; nor should I be envious or malignant that he has given to others more than he has to me. Nay, I should rejoice that he has bestowed such favours on undeserving men at all; that *the race* is in possession of such talents and rewards, to whomsoever given; and should believe that in the hands of God such favours will be well bestowed. God is a sovereign, and the Judge of all the earth will do that which is right.

5th. It is our duty to go into the vineyard and labour faithfully whenever the Lord Jesus calls us, and till he calls us to receive our reward, ver. 1–16. He has a right to call us, and there are none who are not invited to labour for him.

6th. Rewards are offered to all who will serve him, ver. 4. It is not that we *deserve* any favour, or that we shall not say at the end of life that we have been *unprofitable* servants, but he graciously promises that our rewards shall be measured by our faithfulness in his cause. *He* will have the glory of bringing us into his kingdom and saving us, while he will bestow rewards on us according as we have been faithful in his service.

7th. Men may be saved in old age, ver. 6. Old men are sometimes brought into the kingdom of Christ and made holy, but it is rare. Few aged men are converted—they drop into the grave as they lived; and to a man who wastes his youth and his middle life in sin, and goes down into the vale of years a rebel against God, there is a dreadful probability that he will die as he lived. It will be found to be true, probably, that by far more than half who are saved are converted before they reach the age of twenty. Besides, it is foolish as well as wicked to spend the *best* of our days in the service of Satan, and to give to God only the poor remnant of our lives that we can no longer use in the cause of wickedness. God should have our *first* and *best* days.

8th. Neither this parable nor any part of the Bible should be so abused as to lead us to put off the time of repentance to old age. It is *possible*, though not *probable*, that *we* shall live to be old. Few, few, of all the world, live to old age. Thousands die in childhood. The time, the accepted time to serve God, is in early life; and God will require it at the hands of parents and teachers if they do not train up the children committed to them to love and obey him.

9th. One reason why we do not understand the plain doctrines of the Bible is our prejudice, ver. 17–19. Our Saviour plainly told his disciples that he must die. He stated the manner of his death, and the principal circumstances. To us, all this is plain, but *they* did not understand it (Luke). They had filled their heads with notions about his earthly glory and honour, and they were not *willing* to see the truth as he stated it. Never was there a juster proverb than that "none are so blind as those who *will* not see." So to us the Bible might be plain enough. The doctrines of truth are revealed as clear as a sunbeam, but we are filled with previous notions—we are determined to think differently; and the easiest way to gratify this is to say we do not *see* it so. The only correct principle of interpretation is, that the Bible is to be taken *just as it is*. The meaning that the sacred writers intended to teach is to be sought honestly; and when found, that, and that only, is religious truth.

10th. Mothers should be cautious about seeking places of honour for their sons, ver. 20–22. Doing this, they seldom know what they ask. They may be seeking the ruin of their children. It is not in posts of honour that happiness or salvation are certainly secured. Contentment and peace are found oftenest in the humble vale of honest and sober industry—in attempting to fill up our days with usefulness in the situation where God has placed us. As the purest and loveliest streams often flow in the retired grove, far from the thundering cataract or the stormy ocean, so is the sweet peace of the soul; it dwells oftenest far from the bustle of public life, and the storms and tempests of ambition.

11th. Ambition in the church is exceedingly improper, ver. 22–28. It is not the nature of religion to produce it. It is opposed to all the modest, retiring, and pure virtues that Christianity produces. An ambitious man will be destitute of religion just in proportion to his ambition, and piety may always be measured by humility. He that has the most lowly views of himself, and the highest of God—that is willing to stoop the lowest to aid his fellow-creatures and to honour God—has the most genuine piety. Such was the example of our Saviour, and it can never be any dishonour to imitate the Son of God.

12th. The case of the blind men is an expressive representation of the condition of the sinner, ver. 30–34. 1st. Men

CHAPTER XXI.

AND[a] when they drew nigh unto Jerusalem, and were come to Bethphage, unto the mount of Olives, then sent Jesus two disciples,

a Mar.11.1; Lu.19.29.

---

are blinded by sin. They do not by nature see the truth of religion. 2d. It is proper in this state of *blindness* to call upon Jesus to open our eyes. If we ever *see*, it will be by the grace of God. God is the fountain of light, and those in darkness should seek him. 3d. Present opportunities should be improved. This was the first time that Jesus had been in Jericho. It was the last time he would be there. He was passing *through it* on his way to Jerusalem. So he passes among us by his ordinances. So it may be the *last time* that we shall have an opportunity to call upon him. While he is near we should seek him. 4th. When people rebuke us and laugh at us, it should not deter us from calling on the Saviour. There is danger that they will *laugh* us out of our purpose to seek him, and we should cry the more earnestly to him. We should feel that our eternal all depends on our being heard. 5th. The persevering cry of those who seek the Saviour aright will not be in vain. They who cry to him, sensible of their blindness, and sensible that he only can open their eyes, will be heard. He turns none away who thus call upon him. 6th. Sinners must "rise" and come to Jesus. They must cast away everything that hinders their coming. As the blind Bartimeus threw off his "garments," so sinners should throw away everything that hinders their going to him—everything that obstructs their progress—and cast themselves at his feet. No man will be saved while *sitting still.* The command is, "Strive to enter in;" and the promise is made to those only who "ask," and "seek," and "knock." 7th. *Faith* is the only channel through which we shall receive mercy. According to our *faith*—that is, our *confidence* in Jesus, our trust and reliance on him—so will it be to us. Without that, we shall perish. 8th. They who apply to Jesus thus will receive sight. Their eyes will be opened and they will see clearly. 9th. They who are thus restored to sight should follow Jesus. They should follow him wherever he leads; they should follow him always; they should follow none else but him. He that can give sight to the blind cannot lead us astray. He that can shed light in the *beginning* of our faith, can enlighten our goings through all our pilgrimage, and even down through the dark valley of the shadow of death.

CHAPTER XXI.

1-16. See also Mar. xi. 1-11; Lu. xix. 29-44.

1. *And when they drew nigh unto Jerusalem.* They were going up now from Jericho, ch. xx. 29. The distance was about nineteen miles. The most of the way was a desert, or filled with caves, and rocks, and woods—a fit place for robbers. See Lu. x. 30. The Mount of Olives, or *Olivet*, is on the east of Jerusalem. Between this and Jerusalem there runs a small stream called the brook Kidron, or Cedron. It is dry in the hot seasons of the year, but swells to a considerable size in time of heavy rains. See Notes on Jn. xviii. 1. The Mount of Olives was so called from its producing in abundance the olive. It was from Jerusalem about a Sabbath-day's journey. See Notes on Ac. i. 12. On the *west* side of the mountain was the garden of Gethsemane, Lu. xxii. 39; Mar. xiv. 32. On the eastern declivity of the mountain were the villages of Bethphage and Bethany. Mark and Luke say that he came near to both those places. He appears to have come first to Bethany, where he passed the night (Jn. xii. 1, 9-11), and in the morning sent over to the adjacent village Bethphage. Bethany was the place where Lazarus dwelt, whom he raised from the dead (Jn. xi.); where Martha and Mary dwelt; and where Mary anointed him with ointment against the day of his burying, Jn. xii. 1-7. The Mount of Olives is about a mile in length and about 700 feet in height, and overlooks Jerusalem, so that from its summit almost every part of the city can be seen. The mountain is composed of three peaks or summits. The *olive* is a fruit well known among us as an article of commerce. The tree blooms in June, and bears white flowers. The fruit is small. It is first green, then whitish, and, when fully ripe, black. It incloses a hard stone in which are the seeds. The *wild olive* was common, and

2 Saying unto them, Go into
the village over against you, and
straightway ye shall find an ass
tied, and a colt with her: loose
them, and bring *them* unto me.
3 And if any *man* say aught unto
you, ye shall say, The Lord hath
need of them; and straightway he
will send them.
4 All this was done, that it might
be fulfilled which was spoken by
the [b]prophet, saying,

[b] Zec.9.9.

5 Tell[c] ye the daughter of Sion,
Behold, thy King cometh unto
thee, meek, and sitting upon an
ass, and a colt the foal of an ass.
6 And the disciples went, and
did as Jesus commanded them,
7 And brought the ass, and the
colt, and put on them their clothes,
and they set *him* thereon.
8 And a very great multitude
spread their garments in the way:
others cut down branches from

[c] Is.62.11; Mar.11 4,&c.; Jn.12.15.

---

differed from the other only in being of a smaller size. There are two roads from Jerusalem to Bethany; one around the southern end of the Mount of Olives, and the other across the summit. The latter is considerably shorter, but more difficult, and it was probably along this road that the Saviour went.

2. *Go into the village over against you.* That is, to Bethphage. See Notes on ver. 1. ¶ *Ye shall find an ass tied*, &c. In Judea there were few horses, and those were chiefly used in war. Men seldom employed them in common life and in ordinary journeys. The ass, the mule, and the camel are still most used in Eastern countries. To ride on a horse was sometimes an emblem of war; on a mule and an ass, the emblem of peace. Kings and princes commonly rode on them in times of peace, and it is mentioned as a mark of rank and dignity to ride in that manner, Ju. x. 4; xii. 14; 1 Sa. xxv. 20. So Solomon, when he was inaugurated as king, rode on a *mule*, 1 Ki. i. 33. Riding in this manner, then, denoted neither poverty nor degradation, but was the appropriate way in which a king should ride, and in which, therefore, the King of Zion should enter into his capital, the city of Jerusalem.

Mark and Luke say that he told them they should find "a colt tied." This they were directed to bring. They mention only the *colt*, because it was this on which he rode.

3. *The Lord hath need of them.* This means no more than the *master* has need of them. The word *Lord* often means no more than *master* as opposed to *servant*, Mat. x. 24; Ep. vi. 5; 1 Pe. iii. 5, 6. The word is sometimes used in the Bible as applied to God, or as a translation of the name JEHOVAH. Its common use is a mere title of respect given by an inferior to a superior, by a servant to a master, by a disciple to a teacher. As a title of *high respect* it was given to Christ, or the Messiah. The persons to whom these disciples were sent were probably acquainted with the miracles of Jesus and favourably disposed toward him. He had attracted great notice in that region, particularly by raising Lazarus from the dead, and most of the people regarded him as the Messiah.

4, 5. *All this was done*, &c. The prophecy here quoted is found in Zec. ix. 9. It was always, by the Jews, applied to the Messiah. ¶ *Daughter of Zion.* That is, *Jerusalem. Zion* was one of the hills on which the city of Jerusalem was built. On this stood the city of David and some strong fortresses. The names *daughter* and *virgin* were given to it often, in accordance with the Oriental figurative manner of expression. See Notes on Is. i. 8. Comp. Am. v. 2; Ps. xlv. 13; cxxxvii. 8; Is. xlvii. 1. It was given to them as an expression of their beauty or comeliness. ¶ *Meek.* See Notes on Mat. v. 5. The expression here rather denotes *peaceful*, not *warlike;* not with pomp, and state, and the ensigns of ambition. He came in the manner in which kings were accustomed to ride, but with none of their pride and ambitious feeling. ¶ *Sitting upon an ass*, &c. He rode on the colt (Mark and Luke). This expression in Matthew is one which is common with all writers. See Ge. xix. 29; Ju. xii. 7.

7. *And put on them their clothes.* This was done as a token of respect, 2 Ki. ix. 13.

8. *And a very great multitude*, &c. Others showed the same respect by throwing their garments before him;

the trees, and strewed *them* in the way.
9 And the multitudes that went
before, and that followed, cried, saying, Hosanna to the son of David! Blessed[d] is he that cometh

d Ps.118.26; ch.23.39.

others by cutting down branches of trees and casting them in the way. This was the way in which conquerors and princes were often honoured. To cast flowers, or garlands, or evergreens before a warrior returning from victory, or a king entering into his kingdom, was a common way of testifying joyful and triumphant feeling. Thus Josephus says that Alexander and Agrippa were received at Jerusalem. So in our own land some of the most acceptable tokens of rejoicing ever bestowed upon Washington were garlands of roses scattered in his path by children. So the path of Lafayette was often strewed with flowers, as a mark of respect and of a nation's gratitude. John says (xii. 13) that these branches were branches of the *palm-tree*. The *palm* was an emblem of *joy* and *victory*. It was used by the Roman soldiers, as well as the Jews, as a symbol of peace. See 1 Mac. xiii. 51; 2 Mac. x. 6, 7; Re. vii. 9.

The *palm-tree* is common in warm climates, and was abundant in Palestine. The finest grew about Jericho and Engedi. Hence Jericho was called the city of *palm-trees*. The palm has a long and straight body, a spreading top, and an appearance of very great beauty. It produces an agreeable fruit, a pleasant shade, a kind of *honey* little inferior to the honey of bees, and from it was drawn a pleasant *wine* much used in the East. On ancient coins the palm-tree is often a symbol of Judea. On coins made after Jerusalem was taken, Judea is represented by a female sitting and weeping under a palm-tree. A reference to the palm-tree occurs often in the Bible, and its general form and uses are familiar to most readers.

Strictly speaking, the palm has no branches, but at the summit from forty to eighty twigs or leaf-stalks spring forth. These are referred to in Ne. viii. 15. The leaves are set around the trunk in circles of about six. The lower row is of great length, and the vast leaves bend themselves in a curve toward the earth: as the circles ascend, the leaves are shorter. In the month of February, there sprout from between the junctures of the lower stalks and the trunk little scales, which develop a kind of bud, the germ of the coming fruit. These germs are contained in a thick and tough skin, not unlike leather. According to the account of a modern traveller, a single tree in Barbary and Egypt bears from fifteen to twenty large clusters of dates, weighing from 15 to 20 lbs. each. The palm-tree lives more than 200 years, and is most productive from the thirtieth until the eightieth year. The Arabs speak of 260 uses to which the different parts of the palm-tree are applied.

The inhabitants of Egypt, Arabia, and Persia depend much on the fruit of the palm-tree for their subsistence. Camels feed on the seed, and the leaves, branches, fibres, and sap are all very valuable.

The "branches" referred to by John (xii. 13) are the long *leaves* which shoot out from the top of the tree, and which were often carried about as the symbol of victory. Comp. Notes on Is. iii. 26.

9. *Hosanna to the son of David*, &c. The word *hosanna* means "save now," or "save, I beseech thee." It is a Syriac word, and was a form of acclamation used among the Jews. It was probably used in the celebration of their great festivals. During those festivals they sang the 115th, 116th, 117th, and 118th Psalms. In the chanting or singing of those psalms, the Jewish writers inform us that the people responded frequently *hallelujah*, or *hosanna*. Their use of it on this occasion was a joyful acclamation, and an invocation of a divine blessing by the *Messiah*. ¶ *Son of David*. The Messiah. ¶ *Blessed be he*, &c. That is, blessed be the *Messiah*. This passage is taken from Ps. cxviii. 25, 26. To come *in the name of the Lord* here means to come *by the authority* of the Lord, or to come *commissioned* by him to reveal his will. The Jews had commonly applied this to the Messiah. ¶ *Hosanna in the highest*. This may mean either "Hosanna in the highest, loftiest strains," or it may be for a prayer to God—"Save now, O thou that dwellest in the highest heaven, or among the highest angels." Perhaps the whole song of hosanna may be a prayer to the Supreme God, as well as a note of

in the name of the Lord; [e]Hosanna
in the highest!
10 And when he was come into
Jerusalem, all the city was moved,
saying, Who is this?

11 And the multitude said, This
is Jesus, the prophet of Nazareth
of Galilee.
12 And[f] Jesus went into the
temple of God, and cast out all

e Lu.2.14.

f Mar.11.11; Lu.19.45,&c.; Jn.2.15,&c.

---

triumphant acclamation: "Save now, O thou supremely great and glorious God; save by the Messiah that comes in thy name."

Mark adds that they shouted, "Blessed be the kingdom of our father David, that cometh in the name of the Lord." That is, the kingdom *promised* to David, 1 Ki. ii. 4; viii. 25. *Coming in the name of the Lord* here evidently means coming according to the *promise* of the Lord. The sense may be thus expressed: "Prosperity to the reign of our father David, advancing now according to the promise made to him, and about to be established by the long predicted Messiah, his descendant."

Luke adds (xix. 38) that they said, "Peace in heaven and glory in the highest." The word *peace* is used here as significant of joy, triumph, exultation at this event. There will be increased peace and rejoicing in heaven from the accession of the redeemed: there will be augmented glory—new songs of praise *among the highest angels.*

There is no contradiction here among the evangelists. Among such a multitude, the shouts of exultation and triumph would by no means be confined to the same words. Some would say one thing and some another; and one evangelist recorded what was said by a part of the multitude, and another what was said by another part.

10. *And when he was come into Jerusalem, all the city was moved.* There was great excitement. The sight of such a multitude, the shouts of the people, and the triumphant procession through the city, excited much attention and inquiry.

12–22. This paragraph contains the account of the barren fig-tree, and of the cleansing of the temple. See also Mar. xi. 12–19; Lu. xix. 45–48.

12. *And Jesus went into the temple of God*, &c. From Mar. xi. 11–15, it is probable that this cleansing of the temple did not take place on the day that he entered Jerusalem in triumph, but on the day following. He came and looked round upon all things, Mark says, and went out to Bethany with the twelve. On the day following, returning from Bethany, he saw the fig-tree. Entering into the temple, he purified it *on that day;* or perhaps he *finished* the work of purifying it on that day, which he commenced the day before. Matthew has mentioned the purifying of the temple, which was performed, probably, on two successive days, or has stated the *fact*, without being particular as to the order of events. Mark has stated the order more particularly, and has *divided* what Matthew mentions together.

The "temple of God," that is, the temple dedicated and devoted to the service of God, was built on Mount Moriah. The first temple was built by Solomon, about 1005 years before Christ, 1 Ki. vi. He was seven years in building it, 1 Ki. vi. 38. David, his father, had contemplated the design of building it, and had prepared many materials for it, but was prevented because he had been a man of war, 1 Ch. xxii. 1–9; 1 Ki. v. 5. This temple, erected with great magnificence, remained till it was destroyed by the Babylonians under Nebuchadnezzar, 584 years before Christ, 2 Ch. xxxvi. 6, 7, 19.

After the Babylonish captivity the temple was rebuilt by Zerubbabel, but with vastly inferior and diminished splendour. The aged men wept when they compared it with the glory of the former temple, Ezr. iii. 8, 12. This was called the *second* temple. This temple was often defiled in the wars before the time of Christ. It had become much decayed and impaired. Herod the Great, being exceedingly unpopular among the Jews on account of his cruelties (see Notes on Mat. ii.), was desirous of doing something to obtain the favour of the people, and accordingly, about sixteen years before Christ, and in the eighteenth year of his reign, he commenced the work of repairing it. This he did, not by taking it down entirely at once, but by removing one part after another, till it had become, in fact, a new temple, greatly surpassing the for-

them that sold and bought in the temple, and overthrew the tables of the money-changers, and the seats of them that sold doves;

---

mer in magnificence. It was still called by the Jews the *second* temple; and by Christ's coming to this temple thus repaired, was fulfilled the prophecy in Hag. ii. 9. On this building Herod employed eighteen thousand men, and completed it so as to be fit for use in nine years, or about eight years before Christ. But additions continued to be made to it, and it continued increasing in splendour and magnificence till A.D. 64. John says (ii. 20), forty and six years was this temple in building. Christ was then thirty years of age, which, added to the sixteen years occupied in repairing it before his birth, makes forty-six years.

The word *temple* was given not merely to the sacred edifice or house itself, but to all the numerous chambers, courts, and rooms connected with it on the top of Mount Moriah. The temple itself was a small edifice, and was surrounded by courts and chambers half a mile in circumference. Into the sacred edifice itself our Saviour never went. The high-priest only went into the holy of holies, and that but once a year, and none but priests were permitted to enter the holy place. Our Saviour was neither. He was of the tribe of *Judah*, and he consequently was allowed to enter no farther than the other Israelites into the temple. The works that he is said to have performed in the temple, therefore, are to be understood as having been performed in the *courts* surrounding the sacred edifice. These courts will now be described.

The temple was erected on Mount Moriah. The space on the summit of the mount was not, however, large enough for the buildings necessary to be erected. It was therefore enlarged by building high walls from the valley below and filling up the space within. One of these walls was 600 feet in height. The ascent to the temple was by high flights of steps. The entrance to the temple, or to the *courts* on the top of the mount, was by nine gates, all of them extremely splendid. On every side they were thickly coated with gold and silver. But there was one gate of peculiar magnificence: this was called *the Beautiful* gate, Ac. iii. 2. It was on the east side, and was made of Corinthian brass, one of the most precious metals in ancient times. See the Introduction to 1 Corinthians, § 1. This gate was 50 cubits, or 75 feet, in height.

The whole temple, with all its courts, was surrounded by a wall about 25 feet in height. This was built on the wall raised from the base to the top of the mountain, so that from the top of it to the bottom, in a perpendicular descent, was in some places not far from 600 feet. This was particularly the case on the south-east corner; and it was here, probably, that Satan wished our Saviour to cast himself down. See Notes on Mat. iv. 6.

On the inside of this wall, between the gates, were piazzas or covered porches. On the eastern, northern, and western sides there were two rows of these porches; on the south, three. These porches were covered walks, about 20 feet in width, paved with marble of different colours, with a flat roof of costly cedar, which was supported by pillars of solid marble, so large that three men could scarcely stretch their arms so as to meet around them. These walks or porches afforded a grateful shade and protection to the people in hot or stormy weather. The one on the east side was distinguished for its beauty, and was called Solomon's porch, Jn. x. 23; Ac. iii. 11. It stood over the vast terrace or wall which he had raised from the valley beneath, and which was the only thing of his work that remained in the second temple.

When a person entered any of the gates into this space within the wall he saw the temple rising before him with great magnificence; but the space was not clear all the way up to it. Going forward, he came to another wall, inclosing considerable ground, considered more holy than the rest of the hill. The space between this first and second wall was called *the court of the Gentiles.* It was so called because Gentiles might come into it; but they could proceed no farther. On the second wall and on the gates were inscriptions in Hebrew, Greek, and Latin, forbidding any Gentile or unclean person from proceeding farther on pain of death. This *court* was not of equal dimensions all the way round the temple. On the east, north, and west it was quite narrow. On the south it was wide, occupying nearly half of the whole surface of the hill. In this court the Gentiles might come. Here was the place where much secular business was transacted. This was the place occupied by the buyers and sellers, and by the money-changers, and which Jesus purified by casting them out.

The inclosure within the second wall was nearly twice as long from east to west as from north to south. This inclosure was also divided. The eastern part of it was called *the court of the women;* so called because women might advance thus far, but no farther. This court was square. It was entered by three gates; one on the north, one on the east directly opposite to the Beautiful gate, and one on the south. In passing from the court of the Gentiles to that of the women, it was necessary to ascend about 9 feet by steps. This court of the women was inclosed with a double wall, with a space between the walls about 15 feet in width, paved with marble. The inner of these two walls was much higher than the one outside. The court of the women was paved with marble. In the corners of that court were different structures for the various uses of the temple. It was in *this* court that the Jews commonly worshipped. Here, probably, Peter and John, with others, went up to pray, Ac. iii. 1. Here, too, the Pharisee and publican prayed—the Pharisee near the gate that led forward to the temple; the publican standing far off, on the other side of the court, Lu. xviii. 9–14. Paul also was seized here, and charged with defiling the temple by bringing the Gentiles into that holy place, Ac. xxi. 26–30.

A high wall on the west side of the court of the women divided it from the court of the Israelites, so called because all the *males* of the Jews might advance there. To this court there was an ascent of fifteen steps. These steps were in the form of a half circle. The great gate to which these steps led was called the gate *Nicanor*. Besides this, there were three gates on each side, leading from the court of the women to the court of the Israelites.

Within the court of the *Israelites* was the court of the *priests*, separated by a wall about 1½ foot in height. Within that court was the altar of burnt-offering and the laver standing in front of it. Here the priests performed the daily service of the temple. In this place, also, were accommodations for the *priests* when not engaged in conducting the service of the temple, and for the Levites who conducted the *music* of the sanctuary.

The temple, properly so called, stood within this court. It surpassed in splendour all the other buildings of the holy city; perhaps in magnificence it was unequalled in the world. It fronted the east, looking down through the gates Nicanor and the Beautiful gate, and onward to the Mount of Olives. From the Mount of Olives on the east there was a beautiful and commanding view of the whole sacred edifice. It was there that our Saviour sat when the disciples directed his attention to the goodly stones with which the temple was built, Mar. xiii. 1. The entrance into the temple itself was from the *court of the priests*, by an ascent of twelve steps. The *porch* in front of the temple was 150 feet high and as many broad. The open space in this porch through which the temple was entered was 115 feet high and 37 broad, without doors of any sort. The appearance of this, built, as it was, with white marble, and decorated with plates of silver, from the Mount of Olives was exceedingly dazzling and splendid. Josephus says that in the rising of the sun it reflected so strong and dazzling an effulgence that the eye of the spectator was obliged to turn away. To strangers at a distance, it appeared like a mountain covered with snow, for where it was not decorated with plates of gold it was extremely white and glistening.

The temple itself was divided into two parts. The first, called the *sanctuary* or holy place, was 60 feet in length 60 feet in height, and 30 feet in width. In this was the golden candlestick, the table of shew-bread, and the altar of incense. The *holy of holies* or the *most holy place*, was 30 feet each way. In the first temple this contained the ark of the covenant, the tables of the law, and over the ark was the mercy-seat and the cherubim. Into this place no person entered but the high-priest, and he but once in the year. These two apartments were separated only by a vail, very costly and curiously wrought. It was this vail which was rent from the top to the bottom when the Saviour died, Mat. xxvii. 51. Around the walls of the *temple*, properly so called, was a structure three stories high, containing chambers for the use of the officers of the temple. The temple was wholly razed to the ground by the Romans under Titus and Vespasian, and was effectually destroyed, according to the predictions of the Saviour. See Notes on ch. xxiv. 2. The site of it was made like a ploughed field. Julian the apostate attempted to rebuild it, but the workmen, according to his own historian, Ammianus Marcellinus, were prevented by balls of fire breaking out from the ground. See Warburton's *Divine Legation of Moses.* Its site is now occupied by the Mosque of Omar, one of the most splendid specimens of Saracenic architecture in the world.

The following is a view of the temple and its courts, as just described:—

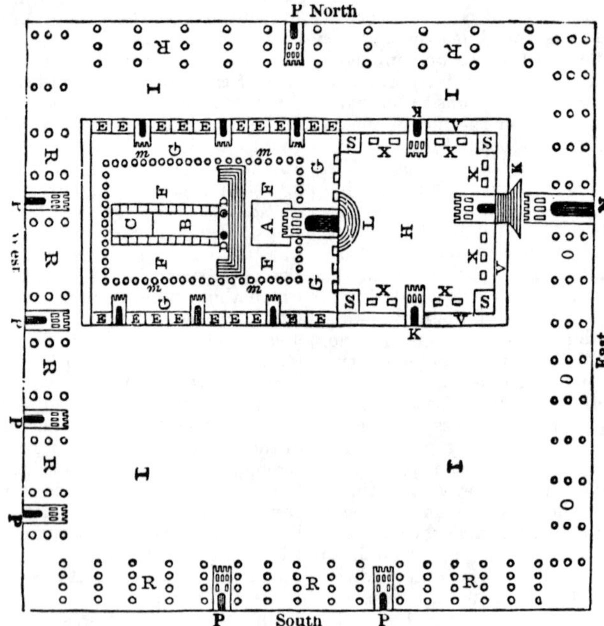

Explanation.

A Altar of burnt offerings. B Holy place.
C Holy of holies. D D Pillars of Jachin and Boaz.
E E E, &c. Rooms for the use of the Levites: for wood, instruments, beds, &c.
F F F F Court of the priests. G G G G Court of the Israelites.
H Court of the women. I I I I Court of the Gentiles.
K K K Gates from the court of the Gentiles to the court of the women.
L Ascent from the court of the women to the court of the Israelites.
M M M, &c. Inclosure between the court of the Israelites and that of the priests.
N The Beautiful gate of the temple. O O O Solomon's porch. P P P, &c. Gates of the temple.
R R R, &c. Porches or covered walks, supported by marble pillars.
X X X X X Boxes to receive money: the treasury, Mar. xi. 41.
S S S S Small rooms for various uses in the temple.
V V V V Space 15 feet wide between the court of the women and the Gentiles.

12. *And cast out all them that sold and bought in the temple.* The place where this was done was not the temple itself, but the outer court, or *the court of the Gentiles.* This was esteemed the least sacred part of the temple; and the Jews, it seems, did not consider it profanation to appropriate this to any business in any way connected with the temple service. The things which they bought and sold were at first those pertaining to the sacrifices. It is not improbable, however, that the traffic afterward extended to all kinds of merchandise. It gave rise to much confusion, noise, contention, and fraud, and was exceedingly improper in the temple of the Lord. ¶ *The tables of the money-changers.* Judea was subject to the Romans. The money in current use was Roman coin; yet the Jewish law required that every man should pay a tribute to the ser-

13 And said unto them, It is written, [g]My house shall be called the house of prayer; but ye have made it [h]a den of thieves.

14 And the blind and the lame came to him in the temple; and he[i] healed them.

15 And when the chief priests and scribes saw the wonderful things that he did, and the children crying in the temple, and saying, [k]Hosanna to the son of David! they were sore displeased,

16 And said unto him, Hearest thou what these say? And Jesus saith unto them, Yea: have ye

g Is.56.7. h Je.7.11. i Is.35.6. k ver.9.

---

vice of the sanctuary of *half a shekel*, Ex. xxx. 11–16. This was a Jewish coin, and the tribute was required to be paid in that coin. It became, therefore, a matter of convenience to have a place where the *Roman* coin might be exchanged for the Jewish half shekel. This was the *professed* business of these men. Of course, they would demand a small sum for the exchange; and, among so many thousands as came up to the great feasts, it would be a very profitable employment, and one easily giving rise to much fraud and oppression. ¶ *The seats of them that sold doves.* Doves were required to be offered in sacrifice—Le. xiv. 22; Lu. ii. 24—yet it was difficult to bring them from the distant parts of Judea. It was found much easier to purchase them in Jerusalem. Hence it became a business to keep them to sell to those who were required to offer them.

Mark adds (xi. 16) that he "would not suffer that any man should carry any vessel through the temple." That is, probably, any of the vessels or implements connected with the traffic in oil, incense, wine, &c., that were kept for sale in the temple.

13. *And said—It is written*, &c. This is written in Is. lvi. 7. The first part of this verse only is quoted from Isaiah. The rest—"but ye have made it a den of thieves"—was added by Jesus, denoting their abuse of the temple. Thieves and robbers live in dens and caves. Judea was then much infested with them. In their dens thieves devise and practise iniquity. These buyers and sellers imitated them. They made the temple a place of gain; they cheated and defrauded; they took advantage of the poor, and, by their being under a necessity of purchasing these articles for sacrifice, they *robbed* them by selling what they had at an enormous price.

The following reasons may be given why this company of buyers and sellers obeyed Christ: 1st. They were overawed by his authority, and struck with the consciousness that he had a right to command. 2d. Their own consciences reproved them; they knew they were guilty, and they dared make no resistance. 3d. The people generally were then on the side of Jesus, believing him to be the Messiah. 4th. It had always been the belief of the Jews that a *prophet* had a right to change, regulate, and order the various affairs relating to external worship. They supposed Jesus to be such, and they did not dare to resist him.

Mark and Luke add, that in consequence of this, the scribes and chief priests attempted to put him to death, Mar. xi. 18, 19; Lu. xix. 47, 48. This they did from *envy*, Mat. xxvii. 18. He drew off the people from them, and they envied and hated him. They were *restrained*, then, for the fear of the people; and this was the reason why they plotted *secretly* to put him to death, and why they afterward so gladly heard the proposals of the traitor, Mat. xxvi. 14, 15.

15, 16. *When the chief priests*, &c. The chief men of the nation were envious of his popularity. They could not prevent it; but, being determined to find fault, they took occasion to do so from the shouts of the children. Men often are offended that *children* have anything to do with religion, and deem it very improper that *they* should rejoice that the Saviour has come. Our Lord Jesus viewed this subject differently. He saw that it was proper that they should rejoice. *They* are interested in the concerns of religion, and before evil principles get fast hold of their minds is a proper time for them to love and obey him. The Lord Jesus silenced those who made the objection by appealing to a text of their own Scriptures. This text is found in Ps. viii. 2. The quotation is not made directly from the Hebrew, but from the Greek translation. This, however, should create no

never read, [l]Out of the mouth of babes and sucklings thou hast perfected praise?

17 And he left them, and went out of the city into Bethany; and he lodged there.

18 Now in the morning, as he returned into the city, he hungered.

19 And[m] when he saw [1]a fig-tree in the way, he came to it, and found nothing thereon but leaves only, and said unto it, Let no fruit

l Ps.8.2.

m Mar.11.13. 1 *one fig-tree.*

---

difficulty. The *point* of the quotation was to prove that *children* might offer praise to God. This is expressed in both the Hebrew and the Greek.

17. *Bethany.* See Notes on Mat. xxi. 1.

19. *And when he saw a fig-tree in the way*, &c. This tree was standing in the public road. It was therefore common property and anyone might lawfully use its fruit. Mark says (xi. 13), "Seeing a fig-tree afar off, having leaves, he came," &c. Not far off *from the road*, but at a considerable distance from the place where he was. Having leaves, and appearing healthy and luxuriant, they presumed that there would be fruit on it. Mark says (xi. 13), "he came, if haply he might find anything thereon." That is, judging from the *appearance* of the tree, it was *probable* that there would be fruit on it. We are not to suppose that our Lord was ignorant of the true condition of the tree, but he acted according to the appearance of things; being a man as well as divine, he acted, of course, as men *do act* in such circumstances. ¶ *And found nothing thereon but leaves only.* Mark (xi. 13) gives as a reason for this that "the time of figs was not yet." That is, the time *of gathering* the figs was not yet, or had not passed. It was a time when figs were ripe or fit to eat, or he would not have gone to it, expecting to find them; but the time *of gathering* them had not passed, and it was to be presumed that they were still on the tree. This took place on the week of the Passover, or in the beginning of April. Figs, in Palestine, are commonly ripe at the Passover. The summer in Palestine begins in March, and it is no uncommon thing that figs should be eatable in April. It is said that they sometimes produce fruit the year round.

Mark (xi. 12, 13) says that this took place on the morning of the day on which he purified the temple. Matthew would lead us to suppose that it was on the day following. Matthew records *briefly* what Mark records more *fully*. Matthew states the fact that the fig-tree was barren and withered away, without regarding minutely the order or the circumstances in which the event took place. There is no contradiction, for Matthew does not *affirm* that this took place on the morning *after* the temple was cleansed, though he places it in that order; nor does he say that a day did *not* elapse after the fig-tree was cursed before the disciples discovered that it was withered, though he does not affirm that it *was* so. Such circumstantial variations, where there is no *positive* contradiction, go greatly to confirm the truth of a narrative. They show that the writers were honest men, and did not *conspire* to deceive the world. ¶ *And said unto it, Let no fruit grow on thee*, &c. Mark calls this *cursing* the tree (ch. xi. 21). The word *curse*, as used by him, does not imply *anger*, or disappointment, or malice. It means only *devoting it to destruction*, or causing it to wither away. All the *curse* that was pronounced was in the words *that no fruit should grow on it.* The Jews used the word *curse* not as always implying *wrath* or *anger*, but to devote to *death*, or to any kind of destruction, He. vi. 8. It has been commonly thought that the Saviour wrought this miracle to denote the sudden *withering away* or destruction of the Jewish people. They, like the fig-tree, promised fair. That was full of leaves, and they full of professions. Yet both were equally barren; and as that was destroyed, so they were soon to be. It was certain that this would be a good *illustration* of the destruction of the Jewish people, but there is no evidence that Jesus *intended* it as such, and without such evidence we have no right to say that was its meaning. ¶ *And presently the fig-tree withered away.* That is, *before* another day. See Mark. It is probable that they were passing directly onward, and did not stop then to consider it. Matthew does not affirm that it withered away *in their presence*,

grow on thee henceforward for
ever. And presently the fig-tree
withered[n] away.
20 And when the disciples saw
it, they marvelled, saying, How
soon is the fig-tree withered away!
21 Jesus answered and said unto
them, Verily I say unto you, [o]If ye
have faith, and doubt not, ye shall
not only do this *which is done* to the
fig-tree, but also if ye shall say unto
this mountain, [p]Be thou removed,
and be thou cast into the sea, it
shall be done.
22 And [q]all things whatsoever
ye shall ask in prayer, believing,
ye shall receive.
23 And[r] when he was come into
the temple, the chief priests and
the elders of the people came unto
him as he was teaching, and said,
[s]By what authority doest thou
these things? and who gave thee
this authority?
24 And Jesus answered and said
unto them, I also will ask you one
thing, which if ye tell me, I in like
wise will tell you by what authority
I do these things.
25 The baptism of John, whence

n Jude 12. *o* ch.17.20; Lu.17.6; Ja.1.6. *p* 1 Co.13.2. *q* ch.7.7; Mar.11.24; Ja.5.16; 1 Jn.3.22; 5.14.

r Mar.11.27; Lu.20.1. *s* Ex.2.14.

and Mark affirms that they made the discovery on the morning after it was "cursed."

20. *And when the disciples saw* it. That is, on the morning following that on which it was cursed, Mar. xi. 20. ¶ *They marvelled, saying*, &c. Peter said this, Mar. xi. 21. Matthew means only to say that this was said to him; Mark tells us which one of them said it.

21. *Jesus answered and said*, &c. Jesus took occasion from this to establish their faith in God, Mar. xi. 22. He told them that any difficulty could be overcome by faith. To remove a mountain denotes the power of surmounting or removing any difficulty. The phrase was so used by the Jews. There is no doubt that this was *literally* true—that if *they* had *the faith of miracles*, they could remove the mountain before them—the Mount of Olives—for this was as easy for God to do by them as to heal the sick or raise the dead. But the Saviour rather referred, probably, to the difficulties and trials which they would be called to endure in preaching the gospel.

22. *And all things*, &c. He adds an encouragement for them to pray, assuring them that they should have *all* things which they asked. This promise was evidently a *special* one, given to them in regard to working miracles. To them it was true, but it is manifest that we have no right to apply *this* promise to ourselves. It was designed specially for the apostles; nor have we a right to turn it from its original meaning. There are other promises in abundance on which we *may* rely in prayer, with confident assurance that our prayers will be heard. Comp. Notes on Mat. vii. 7–11.

23–27. See also Mar. xi. 27–33; Lu. xx. 1–9.

23. *When he was come into the temple*. That is, probably, into the inner court—the court of the Israelites. They took this opportunity of questioning him on this subject when he was not surrounded by the multitude. ¶ *By what authority*, &c. There was a *show* of propriety in this question. He was making great changes in the affairs of the temple, and they claimed the right to know why this was done, contrary to their permission. He was not a *priest;* he had no civil or ecclesiastical authority as a Jew. It was *sufficient* authority, indeed, that he came as a prophet and worked miracles. But they professed not to be satisfied with that. ¶ *These things*. The things which he had just done, in overturning the seats of those that were engaged in traffic, ver. 12.

24, 25. *And Jesus answered*, &c. Jesus was under no obligation to give them an answer. They well knew by what authority he did this. He had not concealed his power in working miracles, and had not kept back the knowledge that he was the Messiah. He therefore referred them to a similar case—that of John the Baptist. He knew the estimation in which John was held by the people, and he took the wise in their own craftiness. Whatever answer they gave, he knew they would convict themselves, and so they saw when they looked

was it? from heaven or of men?
And they reasoned with themselves, saying, If we shall say,
From heaven; he will say unto us,
Why did ye not then believe him?
26 But if we shall say, Of men;
we fear the people; for [t]all hold
John as a prophet.
27 And they answered Jesus, and
said, We cannot tell. And he said
unto them, Neither tell I you by
what authority I do these things.
28 But what think ye? A [u]*certain*
man had two sons: and he came
to the first, and said, Son, go work
to-day in my vineyard.
29 He answered and said, I will
not; but [v]afterward he repented,
and went.
30 And he came to the second, and
said likewise. And he answered
and said, I *go*, sir; and went not.
31 Whether of them twain did the
will of his father? They say unto
him, The first. Jesus saith unto
them, Verily I say unto you, that

t ch.14.5. *u* Lu.15.11,&c. *v* 2 Ch.33.12,13; 1 Co.6.11; Ep.2.1-13.

---

at the question. They reasoned correctly. If they should say that John received authority to baptize from God or from heaven, he would directly ask why they did not believe him. They professed to hear all the prophets. If they said, "*Of men*," they would be in danger, for all the people believed that John was a prophet. ¶ *The baptism of John.* For an account of this, see Mat. iii. The word *baptism* here probably includes all his work. This was his principal employment; and hence he was called the Baptist, or the *Baptizer.* But our Saviour's question refers *to his whole ministry.* "The *ministry of John*—his baptism, preaching, prophecies—was it from God, or not?" If it *was*, then the inference was clear that Jesus was the Messiah, and then they might easily know by what authority he did those things. ¶ *From heaven.* By divine authority, or by the command of God. ¶ *From men.* By human authority.

26. *We fear the people.* They feared that the people would stone them (Luke). Such an unpopular sentiment as to profess that all that *John* did was *imposture*, would have probably ended in tumult, perhaps in their death.

27. *We cannot tell.* This was a direct falsehood. They *could* have told; and the answer should have been, "We *will* not tell." There was no reason but that why they did not tell. The reason, probably, why they would not acknowledge that John was a prophet, was that, if they did, they saw he could easily show them by *what authority* he did those things; that is, by his authority as Messiah. John came as his forerunner, pointed him out to the people, baptized him, and bore his public and solemn testimony to the fact that he was the Messiah, Mat. iii. 13–15; Jn. i. 29–34. If they acknowledged one, they must the other. In this way our Saviour was about to lead these crafty men to answer their own question, to their own confusion, about his authority. They saw this; and, having given them a *sufficient* answer, there was no need of stating anything farther.

28–32. *But what think ye?* A way of speaking designed to direct them particularly to what he was saying, that they might be self-convicted. ¶ *Two sons.* By those two sons our Lord intends to represent the conduct of the Jews, and that of the publicans and sinners. ¶ *In my vineyard.* See Notes on ver. 33. To work in the vineyard here represents the work which God requires man to do. ¶ *I will not.* This *had* been the language of the publicans and wicked men. They refused at first, and did not *profess* to be willing to go. ¶ *Repented.* Changed his mind. Afterward, at the preaching of John and Christ, the publicans—the wicked—repented and obeyed. ¶ *The second—said, I go sir; and went not.* This represented the conduct of the scribes and Pharisees—*professing* to obey God, observing the external rites of religion, but opposed *really* to the kingdom of God, and about to put his Son to death. ¶ *Whether of them twain*, &c. Which of the two. ¶ *They say unto him, The first.* This answer was correct; but it is strange that they did not perceive that it condemned themselves. ¶ *Go into the kingdom of God.* Become Christians, or more readily follow the Saviour. See Notes on Mat. iii. 2. ¶ *Before you.* Rather than you. They are more *likely* to do it than you. You are self-righteous, self-willed and obstinate. ¶ *John*

the publicans and the harlots go into
the kingdom of God before you.
32 For John came unto you in
the way of righteousness, and ye
believed him not; but the [w]pub-
licans and the [x]harlots believed
him: and ye, when ye had seen *it*,
[y]repented not afterward, that ye
might believe him.
33 Hear another parable: There
was a certain householder, which
[z]planted a vineyard, and hedged
it round about, and digged a wine-
press in it, and built a tower, and

w Lu.3.12. x Lu.7.37,&c.

y Re.2.21. z Ps.80.8-16; Ca.8.11,12; Is.5.1-7; Je.2.21; Mar.12.1; Lu.20.9,&c.

came in the way of righteousness. Many of them have believed, but you have not. That is, in the right way, or *teaching* the way to be righteous; to wit, by repentance. Publicans and harlots heard him and *became* righteous, but *they* did not. They *saw* it, but, as in a thousand other cases, it did not produce the proper effect on them, and they would not repent.

33–46. *The parable of the vineyard.* This is also recorded in Mar. xii. 1-12; Lu. xx. 9–19.

33. *Hear another parable.* See Notes on Mat. xiii. 3. ¶ *A certain householder.* See Notes on Mat. xx. 1. ¶ *Planted a vineyard.* A place for the cultivation of grapes. It is often used to represent the church of God, as a place *cultivated* and *valuable*. Judea was favourable to vines, and the figure is frequently used, therefore, in the sacred writers. See Mat. xx. 1. It is used here to represent the *Jewish people*—the people chosen of the Lord, cultivated with care, and signally favoured; or perhaps more definitely, *the city of Jerusalem.* ¶ *Hedged it round about.* This means he *inclosed it*, either with a fence of wood or stone, or more probably with *thorns*, thick set and growing—a common way of inclosing fields in Judea, as it is in England. ¶ *And digged a wine-press in it.* Mark says, *digged a place for the wine-fat.* This should have been so rendered in Matthew. The original word does not mean the *press* in which the grapes were trodden, but the *vat* or *large cistern* into which the wine ran. This was commonly made by digging into the side of a hill. The *wine-press* was made of two receptacles. The upper one, in Persia at present, is about 8 feet square and 4 feet high. In this the grapes are thrown and *trodden* by men, and the juice runs into the large receptacle or cistern below. See Notes on Is. lxiii. 2, 3. ¶ *And built a tower.* See also Notes on Is. v. 2. In Eastern countries at present, these towers are often 80 feet high and 30 feet square. They were for the keepers, who defended the vineyards from thieves and animals, especially from foxes, Ca. i. 6; ii. 15. Professor Hackett (*Illustrations of Scripture*, p. 171, 172) says of such towers: "They caught my attention first as I was approaching Bethlehem from the south-east. They appeared in almost every field within sight from that direction. They were circular in shape, 15 or 20 feet high, and, being built of stones, looked, at a distance, like a little forest of obelisks. I was perplexed for some time to decide what they were; my travelling companions were equally at fault. Suddenly, in a lucky moment, the words crossed my mind, 'A certain man planted a vineyard, and set a hedge about it, and built a tower, and let it out to husbandmen, and went into a far country,' Mar. xii. 1. This recollection cleared up the mystery. There, before my eyes, stood the towers of which I had so often read and thought; such as stood there when David led forth his flocks to the neighbouring pastures; such as furnished to the sacred writers and the Saviour himself so many illustrations for enforcing what they taught.

"These towers are said to be sometimes square in form as well as round, and as high as 40 or 50 feet. Those which I examined had a small door near the ground, and a level space on the top, where a man could sit and command a view of the plantation. I afterwards saw a great many of these structures near Hebron, where the vine still flourishes in its ancient home; for there, probably, was Eshcol, whence the Hebrew spies returned to Joshua with the clusters of grapes which they had gathered as evidence of the fertility of the land. Some of the towers here are so built as to serve as houses; and during the vintage, it is said that the inhabitants of Hebron take up their abode in them in such numbers as to leave the

let it out to husbandmen, and went into a far country:

34 And when the time of the fruit drew near, he [a]sent his servants to the husbandmen, that they might receive the fruits of it.

35 And[b] the husbandmen took his servants, and beat one, and killed another, and stoned another.

36 Again, he sent other servants more than the first: and they did unto them likewise.

37 But, last of all, he sent unto them his son, saying, They will reverence my son.

38 But when the husbandmen saw the son, they said among themselves, [c]This is the heir; come, let

a 2 Ki.17.13,&c.
b 2 Ch.36.16; Ne.9.26; Je.25.3-7; ch.5.12; 23.34-37; Ac.7.52; 1 Th.2.15; He.11.36,37; Re.6.9.
c He.1.1,2.

town almost deserted." ¶ *And let it out*, &c. This was not an uncommon thing. Vineyards were often planted to be let out for profit. ¶ *Into a far country*. This means, in the original, only that he departed from them. It does not mean that he went out of the *land*. Luke adds, "for a long time." That is, as appears, till the time of the fruit; perhaps for a year. This vineyard denotes, doubtless, the Jewish people, or Jerusalem. But these circumstances are not to be particularly explained. They serve to *keep up* the story. They denote *in general* that God had taken proper care of his vineyard—that is, of his people; but beyond that we cannot affirm that these *circumstances* of building the tower, &c., mean any particular thing, for he has not told us that they do, and where he has not explained them we have no right to attempt it.

34. *And when the time of the fruit drew near*, &c. The time of gathering the fruit. The vineyard was let out, probably, for a part of the fruit, and the owner sent to receive the part that was his. ¶ *Sent his servants*. These, doubtless, represent the prophets sent to the Jewish people.

35. *And beat one*. The word here translated *beat* properly means to *flay* or to take off the skin; hence to beat or to whip so that the skin in many places is taken off. ¶ *And killed another*. Isaiah is said to have been put to death by sawing him asunder. Many other of the prophets were also put to death. See Lu. xiii. 34; He. xi. 37; 1 Sa. xxii. 18; 1 Ki. xix. 10. ¶ *And stoned another*. This was among the Jews a common mode of punishment, De. xiii. 10; xvii. 7; Jos. vii. 25. Especially was this the case in times of popular tumult, and of sudden indignation among the people, Ac. vii. 58; xiv. 19; Jn. viii. 59; x. 31. This does not imply, of necessity, that those who were stoned *died*, but they might be only severely wounded. Mark says, "At him they cast stones and wounded him in the head, and sent him away," &c.

There is a little variation in the circumstances as mentioned by Matthew, and by Mark and Luke, but the substance is the same. Mark and Luke are more particular, and state the *order* in which the servants were sent one after another. They all denote the dealing of the people of Israel towards the prophets. All these things had been done to them. See He. xi. 37; Je. xliv. 4-6; 2 Ch. xxxvi. 16; Ne. ix. 26; 2 Ch. xxiv. 20, 21.

37. *Last of all*, &c. Mark adds that this was an only son, greatly beloved. This beautifully and most tenderly exhibits the love of God in sending his only Son, Jesus Christ, into the world to die for men. Long had he sent the prophets, and they had been persecuted and slain. There was no use in sending any more prophets to the people. They had done all that they could do. God had one only-begotten and well-beloved Son, whom he might send, and whom the world *ought* to reverence even as they should the Father, Jn. v. 23. God is often represented in the Bible as giving his Son, his only-begotten and well-beloved Son, for a lost world, Jn. iii. 16, 17; 1 Jn. iv. 9, 14; Ro. viii. 3, 32; Ga. iv. 4. ¶ *Saying, They will reverence my son*. To *reverence* means to honour, to esteem, to show deference to. It is that feeling which we have in the presence of one who is greatly our superior. It means to give to such a person, in our feelings and our deportment, the honour which is due to his rank and character.

38. *But when the husbandmen*, &c. They determined to kill him, and as he was the only son, they supposed they could easily seize on the property. It

us kill him, and let us seize on his
inheritance.
39 And [d]they caught him, and
cast *him* out of the vineyard, and
slew *him*.
40 When the lord, therefore, of
the vineyard cometh, what will he
do unto those husbandmen?
41 They say unto him, [e]He will
miserably destroy those wicked
men, and [f]let out *his* vineyard
unto other husbandmen, which
shall render him the fruits in their
seasons.
42 Jesus saith unto them, Did
ye never read in the scriptures,
[g]The stone which the builders
rejected, the same is become the
head of the corner: this is the
Lord's doing, and it is marvellous
in our eyes?
43 Therefore I say unto you,

d Ac.2.23; 4.25-27. *e* Ps.2.4,5,9; Zec.12.2. *f* Lu.21.24; Ro.9.26; 11.11.
g Ps.118.22; Is.28 16; 1 Pe.2.6,7.

was rented to them; was in their possession; and they resolved to keep it. This circumstance has probably no reference to any particular conduct of the Jews, but is thrown in to keep up the story and fill up the narrative. An *heir* is one who succeeds to an estate, commonly a son; an *inheritance* is what an heir receives.

39. *And they caught him*, &c. This refers to the conduct of the Jews in putting the Saviour to death. So they understood it, ver. 45. The Jews put him to death after they had persecuted and slain the prophets. This was done by giving him into the hands of the Romans and seeking his crucifixion, Mat. xxvii. 20–25; Ac. ii. 23; vii. 51, 52. ¶ *And cast* him *out of the vineyard.* The vineyard in this parable may represent Jerusalem. Jesus was crucified *out* of Jerusalem, on Mount Calvary, Lu. xxiii. 23. See Notes on He. xiii. 12.

40. *When the lord, therefore,* &c. Jesus then asked them a question about the proper way of dealing with those men. The *design* of asking them this question was that they might condemn themselves, and admit the justice of the punishment that was soon to come upon them.

41. *They say,* &c. They answered according as they knew men would act, and would act justly in doing it. He would take away their privileges and confer them on others. This was the answer which Jesus wished. The case was so clear that they could not answer otherwise. He wished to show them the justice of taking away their national privileges, and punishing them in the destruction of their city and nation. Had he stated this at first they would not have heard him. He, however, by a parable, led them along to *state themselves* the very truth which he wished to communicate, and they had then nothing to answer. They did not, however, yet see the bearing of what they had admitted.

42, 43. *Jesus saith,* &c. Jesus, having led them to admit the justice of the great *principle* on which God was about to act towards *them* proceeds to apply it by a text of Scripture, declaring that this very thing which they admitted to be proper in the case of the *husbandmen* had been predicted respecting *themselves.* This passage is found in Ps. cxviii. 22, 23. It was first applicable to David, but no less to Jesus. ¶ *The stone.* The figure is taken from building a house. The principal stone for size and beauty is that commonly laid as the corner-stone. ¶ *Which the builders rejected.* On account of its want of beauty or size it was laid aside, or deemed unfit to be a corner-stone. This represents the Lord Jesus, proposed to the Jews as the foundation or corner-stone on which to build the church, but rejected by them—the builders—on account of his want of comeliness or beauty; that is, of what *they* esteemed to be comely or desirable, Is. liii. 2, 3. ¶ *The same is become,* &c. Though rejected by *them*, yet God chose him, and made him the foundation of the church. Christ is often compared to a stone, a corner-stone, a *tried*, that is, a *sure*, firm foundation—all in allusion to the custom of building, Ac. iv. 11; Ro. ix. 33; Ep. ii. 20; 1 Pe. ii. 7. ¶ *Lord's doing.* The appointment of Jesus of Nazareth to be the foundation of the church is *proved* by miracle and prophecy to be the work of God. ¶ *Marvellous in our eyes.* Wonderful in the sight of his people. That he should select his only Son—that he should stoop so low, be despised, rejected, and put to death—

The[h] kingdom of God shall be taken from you, and given to [i]a nation bringing forth the fruits thereof.

44 And whosoever [k]shall fall on this stone shall be broken; but on whomsoever it shall fall, [l]it will grind him to powder.

45 And when the chief priests and Pharisees had heard his parables, they perceived that he spake of them.

46 But when they sought to lay hands on him, they feared the multitude, because [m]they took him for a prophet.

h ch.8.12. *i* Is.26.2. *k* Is.8.14,15. *l* He.2.2,3.

m Lu.7.16; Jn.7.40.

that God should raise him up, and build a church on this foundation, embracing the Gentile as well as the Jew, and spreading through all the world, is a subject of wonder and praise to all the redeemed.

43. *The kingdom of God*, &c. Jesus applies the parable to *them*—the Jews. They *had* been the children of the kingdom, or under the *reign* of God; having his law and acknowledging him as King. They *had* been his chosen and peculiar people, but he says that now this privilege would be taken away; that they would cease to be the peculiar people of God, and that the blessing would be given to a nation who would bring forth the fruits thereof, or *be righteous*—that is, to the Gentiles, Ac. xxviii. 28.

44. *Whosoever shall fall*, &c. There is a reference here, doubtless, to Is. viii. 14, 15. Having made an allusion to himself *as a stone*, or a rock (ver. 42), he proceeds to state the consequences of coming in contact with it. He that falls upon it shall be broken; he that *runs against it*—a corner-stone, standing *out* from the other parts of the foundation—shall be injured, or broken in his limbs or body. He that is offended with *my* being the foundation, or that opposes me, shall by the act injure himself, or make himself miserable *by so doing*, even were there nothing farther. But there *is* something farther. ¶ *On whomsoever it shall fall, it will grind him to powder.* That is, in the original, will reduce him to dust, so that it may be scattered by the winds. There is an allusion here, doubtless, to the custom of stoning as a punishment among the Jews. A scaffold was erected twice the height of the man to be stoned. Standing on its edge, he was violently struck off by one of the witnesses: if he died by the blow and the fall, nothing farther was done; if not, a heavy stone was thrown down on him, which at once killed him. So the Saviour speaks of the *falling* of the stone on his enemies. They who oppose him, who reject him, and who continue impenitent, shall be *crushed* by him in the day of judgment, and perish for ever.

45, 46. They *at last* perceived that he spoke of them, and would have gratified their malice at once, but they feared the people.

REMARKS.

1st. Jesus is omniscient, and sees and knows all things, ver. 2.

2d. It is our duty to obey the Lord Jesus, and to do it at once, ver. 3. When *he* commands there should be no delay. What he orders is right, and we should not hesitate or deliberate about it.

3d. Especially is this the case where *he* is to be honoured, as he was on this occasion, ver. 3, 8. If it was for *our* interest or honour only that we obeyed him, it would be of less consequence; but *our* obedience will honour *him*, and we should seek that honour by any sacrifice or self-denial.

4th. We should be willing to give up our property to honour the Lord Jesus, ver. 3. He has a right to it. If given to spread the gospel, it goes, as this did, to increase "the triumphs of our King." We should be willing to give our wealth that he might "gird on his sword," and "ride prosperously among the heathen." Every one that is saved among the heathen by sending the gospel to them will be for the honour of Jesus. They will go to swell his train when he shall enter triumphantly into his kingdom at the day of judgment.

5th. It is our duty to *honour* him, ver. 7–9. He is King of Zion. He is Lord of all. He reigns, and shall always reign.

"Sinners! whose love can ne'er forget
The wormwood and the gall,
Go spread your trophies at his feet,
And crown him Lord of all.

"Ye chosen seed of Israel's race;
Ye ransomed from the fall;

Hail him who saves you by his grace,
And crown him Lord of all.

"Let every kindred, every tribe,
On this terrestrial ball,
To him all majesty ascribe,
And crown him Lord of all."

6th. *Children* should also honour him and shout *hosanna* to him, ver. 15. The chief priests and scribes, in the time of our Saviour, were displeased that they did it; and many of the great, and many formal professors since, have been displeased that *children* should profess to love and honour Jesus. They have opposed Sunday-schools, and opposed the praying of children, and opposed their singing to his praise, and opposed their *giving* their money to spread his gospel; but Jesus loves such praise and such service. The mouths of babes and sucklings should be taught to speak his name; and whatever the world may say, whatever the proud, the rich, or the formal may say, children should seek him early and give their first years to him. He loves their praises. Perhaps few of all the songs of thanksgiving are so pleasant to his ears as the *hosannas* of a Sabbath-school.

7th. We have here a view of the glory of Jesus, ver. 9-11. Though humble, yet he was King. Though most of his life *unhonoured*, yet once he had the honours of his station rendered to him, and entered the city of his father David as a triumphant King of Zion. He will be yet *more* honoured. He will come with all his saints, with the glory of his Father, and with the holy angels. There *we* shall be; and we should be prepared to join with the vast host in shouting hosanna to the returning King of Zion.

8th. Yet, amid all these honours, he was meek and lowly, ver. 5. Others would have been proud and lifted up, but he was always meek; his heart was not proud. He is the only one of kings that could bear triumph and honours without being lifted up by it and made proud.

9th. Yet amid all his triumphs he wept over Jerusalem (Luke). No king, no conqueror, ever before showed compassion like this. Men weep when *they* are afflicted, or are poor and needy; but what prince has ever, in the moment of his triumph, *wept* over the miseries and dangers of his subjects? Not an instance can be found in all history where an earthly conqueror ever showed compassion like this. So Jesus has still compassion over blind, ruined, wretched man. Amid all the triumphs of the gospel, he does not forget those who are yet in their sins, but stretches out his arms to welcome them to his embrace.

10th. Prophecy will be certainly and exactly fulfilled (Luke). That respecting Jerusalem was literally accomplished; and in like manner will *all* that is predicted of *all* sinners assuredly come to pass. If Jerusalem had repented it would have been saved; so if sinners repent they will be saved. If not, like Jerusalem, in due time they will perish.

11th. Jesus purified the temple, ver. 12. It was the house of God. So *our hearts* should be the dwelling-place of the Holy Spirit; so, also, they should be pure. All worldly cares, and traffic, and business, that would interfere with the dwelling of the Spirit there, and all wickedness, oppression, extortion, cheating, and pollution should be banished. God dwells not in such polluted temples; and unless we *are pure in heart*, he will not be with us, and we shall not see his face in peace. Comp. Notes on 1 Co. iii. 16, 17.

12th. Jesus only can purify our hearts. He does it by his blood and Spirit. Over all our sins he holds the same *power* as he did over the traffickers in the temple. At his command they will flee, and we shall be pure. If our hearts are ever purified, therefore, it will be by the power of Jesus. Nor should we wait in sin for him to do it. We should come to him, and beseech him to have mercy, and to save us from our pollutions.

13th. Envy and hatred will take hold of very small matters, to show itself against the good and even the prudent, ver. 15. When the enemies of Jesus could find nothing else to blame, they chose to find fault with the shouting of children. So always in a revival of religion, or any great work of the Lord, it is some small matter that is seized upon—something not exactly to the view of wicked objectors—that is made the occasion of reproach and opposition.

14th. We must produce *fruit* in our lives as well as *flowers*, ver. 19. A profession of religion is like the flowers of spring. A *revival* is like fragrant blossoms. They are beautiful, and promise much fruit; but how many wither, and droop, and fall useless to the ground! How few of all the blossoms of the spring produce ripe and mellow fruit in

CHAPTER XXII.

AND Jesus answered and spake unto them again in parables, and said,

2 The[a] kingdom of heaven is like unto a certain king, which made [b]a marriage for his son,

3 And [c]sent forth his servants

a Lu.14.16. b Re.19.7,9. c Ps.68.11; Je.25.4; 35.15; Re.22.17.

autumn! So, alas! it is often with those who appear well in revivals of religion.

15th. If we make a profession and do not produce fruit, Jesus will curse us, and we shall soon wither away, ver. 19, 20. He will suffer none to enter into his kingdom on the ground of profession only. If we bear fruit and live lives of piety, we are Christians; if not, all our professions are like the blossoms of spring or the leaves of the tree. They will not save us from the withering frown of Jesus.

16th. Men will do almost anything—right or wrong, and as often wrong as right—to court popularity, ver. 24. It is generally not asked by such men what is *right* or what is *true*, but what will secure popularity. If they have that, they are satisfied.

17th. Men often tell a direct falsehood rather than acknowledge the truth, ver. 27. Especially is this the case when the truth makes against them.

18th. Double-dealing and an attempt to evade the truth commonly lead into difficulty. If these men had been honest, they would have had far less trouble, ver. 27.

19th. A state of gross and open sin is often more *hopeful* than one of hypocrisy, pride, and self-conceit, together with external conformity to religion, ver. 28. Multitudes of profane and licentious people may be saved, while the proud and self-righteous will be cut off. The reasons are, 1st. That the wicked, the gross, have no righteousness on which they can pretend to rely. 2d. Nothing so effectually prevents religion as pride and self-confidence. 3d. There is often really more ingenuousness and candour, and less of malignity against the gospel, among the openly wicked, than among those who are outwardly righteous, but who are inwardly like whited sepulchres, full of dead men's bones and all uncleanness.

20th. Multitudes of people profess to go, and go not, ver. 30. They profess to love God, and love themselves better. They profess to obey him, and yet obey their lusts. They are hypocrites, and destruction must come upon them.

21st. Sinners, when they see the effect of truth on others, should repent, ver. 32. It is proof of the truth of religion, and they, as much as others, need it.

22d. We see the goodness of God in sending his messengers to a lost world, ver. 33–38. His prophets he sent one after another, and they were put to death. His well-beloved Son he sent, and *he* also was put to death. Nor is his mercy yet stayed. He still sends his message to sinners. Thousands have died, as his Son did, in attempting to spread the gospel, but still he sends it. We have often, often rejected it, yet still he sends it. What earthly monarch would be treated in this manner? What earthly parent would be so patient and so kind?

23d. If we improve not our privileges they will be taken away from us, ver. 43. The gospel will be sent to many of the heathen, and they will be saved, but woe to those who have had it all their lives and are not saved.

24th. All who reject the Saviour must perish, ver. 44.

CHAPTER XXII.

1. *And Jesus answered and spake unto them again in parables.* See Notes on Mat. xiii. 3. That is, he answered or made reply to the Pharisees, who had been enraged at him for what he had already spoken to them, ch. xxi. 45, 46. He made a still farther statement, to show how the gospel would be received and treated by them. The real *answer* here, as is frequently the case in the New Testament, refers to what was passing in the mind, or to the conduct of those who were addressed, not to what they *said*.

2. *The kingdom of heaven.* See Notes on Mat. iii. 2. The idea here is, "God deals with man in his kingdom, or in regard to the dispensation of the gospel, as a certain king did," &c. This parable refers, undoubtedly, to the rejection of the Jews and to the calling of the Gentiles. The gospel, with all its privileges, was offered to the Jewish people; but through their wickedness and pride

to call them that were bidden to
the wedding: and they would not
come.
4 Again, he sent forth other
servants, saying, Tell them which
are bidden, Behold, I have prepared my dinner; my oxen and
my fatlings *are* killed, and all
things *are* ready: come unto the
marriage.
5 But they [d]made light of *it*, and
went their ways, one to his farm,
and another to his merchandise:

d Ps.106.24,25; Pr.1.24,25; Ac.24.25; Ro.2.4.

6 And the remnant took his servants, and [e]entreated *them* spitefully, and slew *them*.
7 But when the king heard
thereof, he was wroth: and he sent
forth his armies, and [f]destroyed
those murderers, and burnt up
their city.
8 Then saith he to his servants,
The wedding is ready, but they
which were bidden were not
[g]worthy.
9 Go ye therefore into the high-

e 1 Th.2.15. *f* Da.9.26; Lu.19.27. *g* ch.10.11,13; Ac.13.46; Re.3.4; 22.14.

they rejected it, and all its blessings were offered to the Gentiles and accepted. This is the *general* truth. Many circumstances are thrown in to fill out the narrative which cannot be particularly explained. ¶ *A marriage for his son.* Rather a *marriage-feast*, or a feast on the occasion of the marriage of his son. The king here doubtless represents *God* providing for the salvation of the world.

3. *And sent forth his servants.* These represent the messengers that God has sent to invite men to his kingdom. ¶ *To call them that were bidden.* That is, to give notice to those who had before been invited that the feast was ready. It appears that there were two invitations—one considerably previous to the time of the feast, that they might have opportunity to prepare for it, and the other to give notice of the precise time when they were expected. ¶ *The wedding.* The marriage-feast. The same word in the original as in ver. 2. ¶ *They would not come.* They *might* have come if they had chosen, but they would not. So all the difficulty that sinners ever labour under in regard to salvation is in the *will*. It is a fixed determination *not* to come and be saved. See Notes on Jn. v. 45.

4. *Other servants.* Who might *press* it on their attention. So God repeats his message to sinners when they reject it. ¶ *My dinner.* This word literally denotes the meal taken about noon. It is also taken for a meal in general. As marriages were, among Eastern nations, in the evening, it refers here to a meal taken at that time. ¶ *Fatlings.* This word does not refer to any particular species of animals. It denotes any fat animals. As *oxen* are also mentioned, however, it refers here, probably, to lambs or calves, 2 Sa. vi. 13; 1 Ch. xv. 26.

5. *But they made light of* it. Treated it with contempt, as a thing of no consequence—an exact representation of the conduct of sinners in regard to the gospel. ¶ *One to his farm.* So men are engaged so much in their worldly employment that they pretend they have no time to attend to religion. The world is, in their view, of more value than God. ¶ *Merchandise.* Traffic; trading.

6. *And the remnant*, &c. That is, *a part* made light of it; treated it with silent contempt, and coolly went about their business. The others were not satisfied with that, but showed positive malignity. Some sinners seem to be well satisfied by merely neglecting religion; others proceed against it with open violence and bitter malice. ¶ *Entreated* them *spitefully.* Used harsh and opprobrious words. Reviled and abused them. This was done because they hated and despised the king. So sinners often abuse and calumniate ministers of religion because they themselves hate God, and can in no way else show their hatred so well.

7. *But when the king heard*, &c. This doubtless refers to the Jews and to Jerusalem. They were murderers, having slain the prophets; and God was about to send forth the armies of the Romans under his providential direction, and to burn up their city. See Notes on Mat. xxiv. ¶ *Wroth.* Angry; displeased.

9. *The highways.* Literally, the *exit* or *going out* of the *paths* or *roads.* It means the square or principal street, into which a number of smaller streets

ways; and as many as ye shall find, bid to the marriage.

10 So those servants went out into the highways, and [h]gathered together all, as many as they found, both bad and good: and the wedding was furnished with guests.

11 And when the king came in to[i] see the guests, he saw there a man which had not on a [k]wedding garment:

12 And he saith unto him, Friend, how camest thou in hither, not having a wedding garment? And he [l]was speechless.

13 Then said the king to the servants, Bind him hand and foot, and [m]take him away, and [n]cast *him* into outer darkness: there shall be weeping and gnashing of teeth.

14 For[o] many are called, but few *are* chosen.

h ch.13.47. *i* Zep.1.12. *k* Ps.45.14; Is.61.10; 2 Co.5.3; Ep.4.24; Re.16.15; 19.8.

l Je.2.26. *m* Is.52.1; Re.21.27. *n* ch.8.12. *o* ch.7.14; 20.16; Lu.13.23,24.

---

enter; a place, therefore, of confluence, where many persons would be seen, and persons of all descriptions. By this is represented the offering of the gospel to the Gentiles. They were commonly regarded among the Jews as living in highways and hedges—cast out and despised.

10. *Bad and good.* All descriptions of people. None are good by nature; if they were they would not need the gospel; but some are worse than others, and they have special need of it. None can be saved without it.

11. *A man which had not on a wedding garment.* Anciently kings and princes were accustomed to make presents of changes of raiment to their friends and favourites, to refuse to receive which was an expression of highest contempt, Ge. xlv. 22; 2 Ki. x. 22; Es. vi. 8; viii. 15. It was, of course, expected that such garments would be worn when they came into the presence of the benefactor. The garments worn on festival occasions were chiefly long white robes, and it was the custom of the person who made the feast to prepare such robes to be worn by the guests. This renders the conduct of this man more inexcusable. He came in his common and ordinary dress, as he was taken from the highway; and though he had not a garment of his own suitable for the occasion, yet one had been provided for him, if he had applied for it. His not doing it was expressive of the highest disrespect for the king. This beautifully represents the conduct of the hypocrite in the church. A garment of salvation might be his, wrought by the hands of the Saviour, and dyed in his blood; but the hypocrite chooses the filthy rags of his own righteousness, and thus offers the highest contempt for that provided in the gospel. He is to blame, not for being invited—not for coming, if he would come, for he is freely invited—but for offering the highest contempt to the King of Zion in presenting himself with all his filth and rags, and in refusing to be saved in the way provided in the gospel.

12. *Friend.* Rather, *companion.* The word does not imply friendship. ¶ *He was speechless.* He had no excuse. So it will be with all hypocrites.

13. *Cast* him *into outer darkness.* See Notes on Mat. viii. 12. This, without doubt, refers to the future punishment of the hypocrite, Mat. xxiii. 23-33; xxiv. 51.

14. *Many are called, but few* are *chosen.* Our Saviour often uses this expression. It was probably proverbial. The Jews had been called, but few of them had been chosen to life. The great mass of the nation was wicked, and they showed by their lives that they were not chosen to salvation. The Gentiles also were invited to be saved, Is. xlv. 22. Nation after nation has been called; but few, few have yet showed that they were real Christians, the elect of God. It is also true that many who are in the church may prove to be without the wedding garment, and show at last that they were not the chosen of God. This remark in the 14th verse is the inference from the *whole parable*, and not of the part about the man without the wedding garment. It does not mean, therefore, that the great mass in the church are simply called and not chosen, or are hypocrites; but the great mass in *the human family*, in the time of Christ, who had been *called*, had rejected the mercy of God.

15 Then[p] went the Pharisees and took counsel how they might entangle him in *his* talk.

16 And they sent out unto him their disciples, with the Herodians, saying, Master, we know that thou art true, and teachest the way of God in truth, neither carest thou for any *man:* for thou regardest not the person of men.

17 Tell us therefore, What thinkest thou? Is it lawful to give tribute unto Cæsar, or not?

18 But Jesus perceived their

p Mar.12.13,&c.; Lu.20.20,&c.

15–22. *The Pharisees and Herodians endeavour to entangle Jesus.* This narrative is also found in Mar. xii. 12–17; Lu. xx. 20–26.

15. *Then went the Pharisees.* See Notes on Mat. iii. 7. ¶ *How they might entangle him.* To *entangle* means to *ensnare,* as birds are taken by a net. This is done secretly, by leading them within the compass of the net and then suddenly springing it over them. So to entangle is artfully to lay a plan for enticing; to beguile by proposing a question, and by leading, if possible, to an incautious answer. This was what the Pharisees and Herodians endeavoured to do in regard to Jesus. ¶ *In* his *talk.* The word *his* is supplied by the translators, perhaps improperly. It means *in conversation,* or by *talking* with him; not alluding to anything that he had before said.

16. *The Herodians.* It is not certainly known who these were. It is probable that they took their name from Herod the Great. Perhaps they were first a political party, and were then distinguished for holding some of the peculiar opinions of Herod. Dr. Prideaux thinks that those opinions referred to two things. The first respected subjection to a foreign power. The law of Moses was, that a *stranger should not be set over the Jews as a king,* De. xvii. 15. Herod, who had received the kingdom of Judea by appointment of the Romans, maintained that the law of Moses referred only to a voluntary choice of a king, and did not refer to a necessary submission where they had been overpowered by force. His followers supposed, therefore, that it was lawful in such cases to pay tribute to a foreign prince. This opinion was, however, extensively unpopular among the Jews, and particularly the Pharisees, who looked upon it as a violation of their law, and regarded all the acts growing out of it as oppressive. Hence the difficulty of the question proposed by them. Whatever way he decided, they supposed he would be involved in difficulty. If he should say it was not lawful, the Herodians were ready to accuse him as being an enemy of Cæsar; if he said it was lawful, the Pharisees were ready to accuse him to the people of holding an opinion extremely unpopular among them, and as being an enemy of their rights. The other opinion of Herod, which they seem to have followed, was, that when a people were subjugated by a foreign force, it was right to adopt the rites and customs of their religion. This was what was meant by the *leaven of Herod,* Mar. viii. 15. The Herodians and Sadducees seem on most questions to have been united. Comp. Mat. xvi. 6; Mar. viii. 15. ¶ *We know that thou art true.* A hypocritical compliment, not believed by them, but artfully said, as compliments often are, to conceal their true design. ¶ *Neither carest thou for any* man. That is, thou art an independent teacher, delivering your sentiments without regard to the fear or favour of man. This was true, and probably they believed this. Whatever else they might believe about him, they had no reason to doubt that he delivered his sentiments openly and freely. ¶ *For thou regardest not the person of men.* Thou art not *partial.* Thou wilt decide according to truth, and not from any bias toward either party. To regard the person, or to respect the person, is in the Bible uniformly used to denote *partiality,* or being influenced in a decision, not by truth, but by previous attachment to a *person,* or to one of the parties—by friendship, or bias, or prejudice, Le. xix. 15; Jude 16; De. xvi. 19; 2 Sa. xiv. 14; Ac. x. 34; Ja. ii. 1, 3, 9; 1 Pe. i. 17.

17. *Is it lawful to give tribute unto Cæsar?* Tribute was the tax paid to the Roman government. ¶ *Cæsar.* The Roman emperor. The name *Cæsar,* after the time of Julius Cæsar, became common to all the emperors, as *Pharaoh* was the common name of all the kings of Egypt. *The Cæsar* that reigned at this time was *Tiberius*—a man distin-

wickedness, and said, Why tempt
ye me, *ye* hypocrites?
19 Show me the tribute-money.
And they brought unto him [1]a
penny.
20 And he saith unto them, Whose
is this image and [2]superscription?
21 They say unto him, Cæsar's.
Then saith he unto them, [q]Render
therefore unto Cæsar the things
which are Cæsar's, and [r]unto God
the things that are God's.

1 in value 7 pence halfpenny. 2 or, *inscription*. *q* ch.17.25,27; Ro.13.7. *r* Mal.1.6-8; 3.8-10.

22 When they had heard *these*
words, they marvelled, and left
him, and went their way.
23 The[s] same day came to him
the Sadducees, [t]which say that there
is no resurrection, and asked him,
24 Saying, Master, Moses said,
[u]If a man die, having no children,
his brother shall marry his wife,
and raise up seed unto his brother.
25 Now there were with us seven
brethren: and the first, when he

s Mar.12.18,&c.; Lu.20.27,&c. *t* Ac.23.8. *u* De.25.5; Ru.1.11.

guished for the grossest vices and most disgusting and debasing sensuality.

18. *Jesus perceived their wickedness.* This must have been done by his power of searching the heart, and proves that he was omniscient. No mere man has the power of discerning the motives of others. ¶ *Tempt ye me.* Try me, or endeavour to lead me into difficulty by an insidious question. ¶ *Hypocrites.* Dissemblers. Professing to be candid inquirers, when their only object was to lead into difficulty. See Notes on Mat. vi. 2.

19. *The tribute-money.* The money in which the tribute was paid. This was a Roman coin. The tribute for the temple service was paid in the Jewish shekel; that for the Roman government in foreign coin. Their having that coin about them, and using it, was proof that they themselves held it lawful to pay the tribute; and their pretensions, therefore, were mere hypocrisy. ¶ *A penny.* A Roman denarius, worth about fourteen cents = 7*d*.

20. *This image.* The likeness of the reigning prince was usually struck on the coins. ¶ *Superscription.* The name and titles of the emperor.

21. *Render, therefore, to Cæsar,* &c. Cæsar's image and name on the coin proved that it was his. It was proper, therefore, to give it back to him when he called for it. But while this was done, Jesus took occasion to charge them, also, to give to God what he claimed. This may mean either, 1st. The annual tribute due to the temple service, implying that paying tribute to Cæsar did not free them from the obligation to do that; or, 2d. That they should give their hearts, lives, property, and influence all to God, as his due.

22. *They marvelled.* They had been foiled in their attempt. Though he had apparently decided in favour of the Herodians, yet his answer confounded both parties, and wholly prevented the use which they intended to make of it. It was so wise; it so clearly detected their wickedness and foiled their aim, that they were confounded, and retired covered with shame.

23-33. *Conversation of Jesus with the Sadducees respecting the resurrection.* See also Mar. xii. 18-27; Lu. xx. 27-38.

23. *The same day came the Sadducees.* For an account of the Sadducees, see Notes on Mat. iii. 7. ¶ *No resurrection.* The word *resurrection* usually means the raising up the *body* to life after it is dead, Jn. xi. 24; v. 29; 1 Co. xv. 22. But the Sadducees not only denied this, but also a future state, and the separate existence of the soul after death altogether, as well as the existence of angels and spirits, Ac. xxiii. 8. Both these doctrines have commonly stood or fallen together, and the answer of our Saviour respects both, though it more distinctly refers *to the separate existence of the soul, and to a future state of rewards and punishments*, than to the resurrection of the body.

24. *Saying, Master, Moses said,* &c., De. xxv. 5, 6. This law was given by Moses in order to keep the families and tribes of the Israelites distinct, and to perpetuate them. ¶ *Raise up seed unto his brother.* That is, the children shall be reckoned in the genealogy of the deceased brother; or, to all civil purposes, shall be considered as his.

25-28. *There were with us seven brethren.* It is probable that they stated a case as difficult as possible; and though no such case might have occurred, yet it was

had married a wife, deceased, and,
having no issue, left his wife unto
his brother:
26 Likewise the second also, and
the third, unto the [3]seventh.
27 And last of all the woman
died also.
28 Therefore, in the resurrection,
whose wife shall she be of the seven?
for they all had her.
29 Jesus answered and said unto
them, Ye do err, [v]not knowing the
scriptures, nor the power of God.
30 For in the resurrection they
neither marry, nor are given in
marriage, but are as [w]the angels
of God in heaven.
31 But as touching the resurrection of the dead, have ye not read
that which was spoken unto you
by God, saying,
32 I[x] am the God of Abraham,

3 *seven.*

v Jn.20.9. w ch.18.10; 1 Jn.3.2. x Ex.3.6,15,16; He.11.16.

supposable, and in their view it presented a real difficulty. The difficulty arose from the fact, that they supposed that, substantially, the same state of things must take place in the other world as here; that if there is such a world, husbands and wives must be there reunited; and they professed not to be able to see how *one* woman could be the wife of seven men.

29. *Ye do err, not knowing*, &c. They had taken a wrong view of the doctrine of the resurrection. It was not taught that men would marry there. The *Scriptures*, here, mean the books of the Old Testament. By appealing to them, Jesus showed that the doctrine of the future state was there, and that the Sadducees should have believed it as it was, and not have added the absurd doctrine to it that men must live there as they do here. The way in which the enemies of the truth often attempt to make a doctrine of the Bible ridiculous is by adding to it, and then calling it absurd. The reason why the Saviour produced a passage from the books of Moses (ver. 32) was that they had also appealed to his writings, ver. 24. Other places of the Old Testament, in fact, asserted the doctrine more clearly (Da. xii. 2; Is. xxvi. 19), but he wished to meet them on their own ground. None of those scriptures asserted that men would live there as they do here, and therefore their reasoning was false. ¶ *Nor the power of God.* They probably denied, as many have done since, that God could gather the scattered dust of the dead and remould it into a body. On this ground they affirmed that the doctrine could not be true—opposing reason to revelation, and supposing that infinite power could not reorganize a body that it had at first organized, and raise a body from its own dust which it had at first raised from nothing.

30. *Neither marry*, &c. This was a full answer to the objections of the Sadducees. ¶ *But are as the angels of God.* That is, in the manner of their intercourse; in regard to marriage and the mode of their existence. Luke adds that they shall be *equal with the angels.* That is, they shall be elevated above the circumstances of mortality, and live in a manner and in a kind of intercourse similar to that of the angels. It does not imply that they shall be equal in intellect, but only *in the circumstances of their existence*, as that is distinguished from the way in which mortals live. He also adds, "Neither do they die any more, but are the children of God, being the children of the resurrection," or being accounted worthy to be raised up to life, and therefore *sons of God raised up to him.*

31, 32. *As touching*, &c. That is, in proof that the dead are raised. The passage which he quotes is recorded in Ex. iii. 6, 15. This was at the burning bush (Mark and Luke). Abraham, Isaac, and Jacob had been long dead when Moses spoke this—Abraham 329 years, Isaac 224, and Jacob 198—yet God spake then as being still *their God.* They must, therefore, be still somewhere living, for God is not the God of the dead; that is, it is absurd to say that God rules over those who are *extinct* or *annihilated*, but he is the God only of those who have an existence. Luke adds, *all live unto him.* That is, all the righteous dead, all of whom he can be properly called their God, live unto his glory. This passage does not prove *directly* that the dead *body* would be raised, but only by consequence. It proves that Abraham, Isaac, and Jacob had an existence then, or that their

and the God of Isaac, and the God of Jacob? God is not the God of the dead, but of the living.

33 And when the multitude heard *this*, they were [y]astonished at his doctrine.

34 But when the Pharisees had heard that he had put the Sadducees to silence, they were gathered together.

35 Then[z] one of them, *which was* a lawyer, asked *him a question*, tempting him, and saying,

36 Master, which *is* the great commandment in the law?

37 Jesus said unto him, [a]Thou

y ch.7.28; Mar.12.17. z Lu.10.25,&c. a De.6.5; 10.12.

---

souls were alive. This the Sadducees denied (Ac. xxiii. 8), and this was the main point in dispute. If this was admitted—if there was a state of rewards and punishments—then it would easily follow that the bodies of the dead would be raised.

34-40. *Jesus converses with a Pharisee respecting the law.* See also Mar. xii. 28-34.

34. *The Pharisees—were gathered together.* That is, either to rejoice that their great rivals, the Sadducees, had been so completely silenced, or to lay a new plan for ensnaring him, or perhaps both. They would rejoice that the Sadducees had been confounded, but they would not be the less desirous to involve Jesus in difficulty. They therefore endeavoured, probably, to find the most difficult question in dispute among themselves, and proposed it to him to perplex him.

35. *A lawyer.* This does not mean one that *practised* law, as among us, but one learned or skilled in the law of Moses. Mark calls him *one of the scribes.* This means the same thing. The scribes were men of learning—particularly men skilled in the law of Moses. This lawyer had heard Jesus reasoning with the Sadducees, and perceived that he had put them to silence. He was evidently supposed by the Pharisees to be better qualified to hold a debate with him than the Sadducees were, and they had therefore put him forward for that purpose. This man was probably of a candid turn of mind; perhaps willing to know the truth, and not entering very fully into their malicious intentions, but acting as their agent, Mar. xii. 34. ¶ *Tempting him.* Trying him. Proposing a question to test his knowledge of the law.

36. *Which is the great commandment?* That is, the *greatest* commandment, or the one most important. The Jews are said to have divided the law into *greater* and *smaller* commandments. Which was of the greatest importance they had not determined. Some held that it was the law respecting sacrifice; others, that respecting circumcision; others, that pertaining to washings and purifying, &c. ¶ *The law.* The word *law* has a great variety of significations; it means, commonly, in the Bible, as it does here, *the law given by Moses,* recorded in the first five books of the Bible.

37. *Jesus said unto him,* &c. Mark says that he introduced this by referring to the doctrine of the unity of God—"Hear, O Israel! the Lord thy God is one Lord"—taken from De. vi. 4. This was said, probably, because all true obedience depends on the correct knowledge of God. None can keep his commandments who are not acquainted with his nature, his perfections, and his right to command. ¶ *Thou shalt love the Lord thy God with all thy heart.* The meaning of this is, thou shalt love him with all thy faculties or powers. Thou shalt love him supremely, more than all other beings and things, and with all the ardour possible. To love him with all the heart is to fix the affections supremely on him, more strongly than on anything else, and to be willing to give up all that we hold dear at his command. ¶ *With all thy soul.* Or, with all thy *life.* This means, to be willing to give up the life to him, and to devote it all to his service; to live to him, and to be willing to die at his command. ¶ *With all thy mind.* To submit the *intellect* to his will. To love his law and gospel more than we do the decisions of our own minds. To be willing to submit all our faculties to his teaching and guidance, and to devote to him all our intellectual attainments and all the results of our intellectual efforts. ¶ *With all thy strength* (Mark). With all the faculties of soul and body. To labour and toil for his glory, and to make that the great object of all our efforts.

shalt love the Lord thy God with
all thy heart, and with all thy
soul, and with all thy mind.
38 This is the first and great
commandment.
39 And the second *is* like unto
it, [b]Thou shalt love thy neighbour
as thyself.
40 On [c]these two command-

b Le.19.18. c Ro.13.9; Ja.2.8.

ments hang all the law and the
prophets.
41 While the Pharisees were
gathered together, Jesus asked
them,
42 Saying, [d]What think ye of
Christ? whose son is he? They
say unto him, *The son* of David.
43 He saith unto them, How

d Mar.12.35,&c.; Lu.20.41,&c.

38. *This the first and great commandment.* This commandment is found in De. vi. 5. It is the first and greatest of all; *first*, not in *order of time*, but of *importance; greatest* in dignity, in excellence, in extent, and duration. It is the fountain of all others. All beings are to be loved according to their excellence. As God is the most excellent and glorious of all beings, he is to be loved supremely. If he is loved aright, then our affections will be directed toward all created objects in a right manner.

39. *The second* is *like unto it.* Le. xix. 18. That is, it resembles it in importance, dignity, purity, and usefulness. This had not been asked by the lawyer, but Jesus took occasion to acquaint him with the substance of the whole law. For its meaning, see Notes on Mat. xix. 19. Comp. Ro. xiii. 9. Mark adds, *there is none other commandment greater than these.* None respecting circumcision or sacrifice is greater. They are the fountain of all.

40. *On these two commandments hang*, &c. That is, these comprehend the substance of what Moses in the law and what the prophets have spoken. What they have said has been to endeavour to win men to love God and to love each other. Love to God and man comprehends the whole of religion, and to produce this has been the design of Moses, the prophets, the Saviour, and the apostles.

Mark (xii. 32–34) adds that the scribe said, "Well, Master, thou hast said the truth;" and that he assented to what Jesus had said, and admitted that to love God and man in this manner was more than all burnt-offerings and sacrifices; that is, was of more value or importance. Jesus, in reply, told him that he was "not far from the kingdom of heaven;" in other words, by his reply he had shown that he was almost prepared to receive the doctrines of the gospel. He had evinced such an acquaintance with the law as to prove that he was nearly prepared to receive the teachings of Jesus. See Notes on Mat. iii. 2.

Mark and Luke say that this had such an effect that no man after that durst ask him any question, Lu. xx. 40; Mar. xii. 34. This does not mean that none of his disciples durst ask him any question, but none of the Jews. He had confounded all their sects—the Herodians (Mat. xxii. 15–22); the Sadducees (23–33); and, last, the Pharisees (34–40). All, finding themselves unable to confound him, at last gave up the attempt.

41–46. *Jesus proposes a question concerning the Messiah.* See also Mar. xii. 35–37; Lu. xx. 41–44.

41. *While the Pharisees*, &c. Jesus, having confounded the great sects of the Jews, proceeds, in his turn, to propose to them a question for their solution. This was done, not for the purpose of vain parade and triumph, but, 1st. To show them how ignorant they were of their prophecies. 2d. To humble them in view of their ignorance. 3d. To bring to their attention the true doctrine respecting the Messiah—his being possessed of a character superior to that of David, the most mighty king of Israel—being his Lord, at the same time that he was his descendant.

42. *What think ye of Christ?* What are your views respecting THE MESSIAH, or *the Christ*, especially respecting his *genealogy?* He did not ask them their views respecting him in general, but only respecting his ancestry. The article should have been retained in the translation—*the* Christ or *the* Messiah. He did not ask them their opinion respecting himself, his person, and work, as would seem in our translation, but their views respecting the Messiah whom they expected. ¶ *Whose son is he?* Whose *descendant?* See the Notes on

then doth David in spirit [e] call him Lord? saying,

44 The LORD said unto my Lord, Sit thou on my right hand, till I make thine enemies thy footstool.

45 If David then call him Lord, how is he his son?

46 And [f] no man was able to answer him a word; [g] neither durst any *man*, from that day forth, ask him any more *questions*.

e Ps.110.1; Ac.2.34,35; He.1.13; 10.12,13. f Lu.14 6. g Mar.12.34; Lu.20.40.

Mat. i. 1. ¶ The son *of David.* The descendant of David, according to the promise.

43. *How then,* &c. How is this doctrine that he is *descended* from David consistent with what David says when he calls him *lord?* How can your opinion be reconciled with that? That declaration of David is recorded in Ps. cx. 1. A *lord* or master is a superior. The word here does not necessarily imply divinity, but only superiority. David calls him his superior, his lord, his master, his lawgiver, and expresses his willingness to obey him. If the Messiah was to be merely a descendant of David, as other men descended from parents—if he was to have a human nature only—if he did not exist when David wrote—with what propriety could he, then, call him his lord? ¶ *In spirit.* By the inspiration of the Holy Spirit. As a prophet, Ac. ii. 30; i. 16; 2 Sa. xxiii. 2.

44. *The* LORD *said,* &c. This is the language of David. "Jehovah said to *my* lord—*the Messiah*—sit thou," &c. This was a prediction respecting the exaltation of Christ. To be raised to the right hand of a king was significant of favour, trust, and power. See Notes on Mat. xx. 21. This was done respecting Christ, Mar. xvi. 19; Ac. vii. 55; Ro. viii. 34; Ep. i. 20; He. i. 3; viii. 1; x. 12. *Thine enemies thy footstool.* A footstool is that which is under the feet when we are sitting—implying that we have it under subjection, or at our control. So Christ shall put all enemies under his feet—all his spiritual foes—all that rise up against him, Ps. ii. 9, 12; He. x. 13; 1 Co. xv. 25.

45. *If David,* &c. If he was then David's lord—if he was his superior—if he had an existence at that time—how could he be descended from him? They could not answer him. Nor is there any way of answering the question but by the admission that the Messiah was divine as well as human; that he had an existence at the time of David, and was his lord and master, his God and king, and that as man he was descended from him.

REMARKS.

1st. Multitudes of men, who are invited to be saved, reject the gospel and perish in their sins, ver. 3.

2d. If they perish, they only will be to blame. The offer was freely made, the salvation was provided, and the only reason why they were not saved was that they would not come, ver. 3.

3d. Attention to the affairs of this life, the love of the world, will shut many out of the kingdom of heaven, ver. 5. Some attention to those things is necessary; but such a devotion to these things as to lead to the loss of the soul never can be right.

4th. It is treating God ungratefully to reject his gospel, ver. 3–5. He has sent his Son to die for us; he has entreated us to be saved; he has followed us with mercies; and to reject all these, and refuse to be saved, is to treat him with contempt, as well as to overwhelm ourselves in condemnation. *Man has no right to be damned.* He is under the most solemn obligations to be *saved;* and after what God has done for us, deep and dreadful woe will await us if we are so foolish and wicked as to be lost.

5th. Many of the poor and needy will be saved, while the haughty and rich will perish for ever, ver. 9, 10.

6th. Let those who make a profession of religion look often to the great day when Christ will search them, ver. 11. There is a day coming that will try us. His eye will be upon us. He will read our hearts, and see whether we are clothed in his righteousness, or only the filthy rags of our own.

7th. A profession of religion will not save us, ver. 11–13. It is foolish to deceive ourselves. Nothing but genuine piety, true faith in Jesus, and a holy life, will save us. God asks not profession merely, but the heart. He asks not mockery, but sincerity; not pretension, but reality.

8th. The hypocrite must perish, ver. 13. It is right that he should perish. He knew his Master's will and would not do it. He must perish with an awful condemnation. No man sins amid so much light, none with so high a hand. No sin is so awful as to attempt to deceive God, and to palm pretensions on him for reality.

9th. Pretended friends are sometimes more dangerous than avowed enemies, ver. 16. Pretended friendship is often for the purpose of decoying us into evil. It throws us off our guard, and we are more easily taken.

10th. The truth is often admitted by wicked men from mere hypocrisy, ver. 16. It is only for the purpose of deceiving others and leading them into sin.

11th. Wicked men can decide correctly on the character of a public preacher, ver. 16. They often admit his claim in words, but for an evil purpose.

12th. It may be right for us sometimes to attend to artful and captious questions, ver. 18. It may afford opportunity to do good; to confound the wicked and to inculcate truth.

13th. No cunning can overreach God, ver. 18. He knows the heart, and he perceives the wickedness of all who attempt to deceive him.

14th. It is right, and it is our duty to obey the law of the land, when it does not contravene the law of God, ver. 21. *Conscientious Christians make the best citizens.* Comp. Notes on Ro. xiii. 1-7.

15th. We should give honour to civil rulers, ver. 21. We should pay respect to the *office*, whatever may be the character of the ruler. We should speak well of it, not abuse it; yield proper obedience to its requirements, and not rebel against it. Men may be wicked who hold an office, but the office is ordained by God (Ro. xiii. 1, 2); and for the sake of the office we must be patient, meek, submissive, and obedient, Mat. xxiii. 3.

16th. Yet we are to obey civil rulers no farther than their commands are consistent with the law of God, ver. 21. God is to be obeyed rather than man; and when a civil ruler commands a thing contrary to the laws of the Bible and the dictates of our consciences, we may, we must resist it, Ac. v. 29.

17th. The objections of men to the doctrines of the Bible are often founded on ignorance of what those doctrines are, and distrust of the power of God, ver. 29. Men often set up a notion which they call a doctrine of the Bible, and then fight a shadow, and think they have confuted the truth of God, while that truth was, in fact, untouched. It is a totally different thing from what they supposed.

18th. When men attack a doctrine they should be certain that they understand it, ver. 29. The Sadducees did not understand the true doctrine of the resurrection. The inquiry which they should have made was whether they had correct views of it. This is the inquiry which men ought always first to make when they approach a doctrine of the Bible.

19th. We learn the glory and happiness of the state after the resurrection, ver. 30 (Luke). We shall be in some respects equal to the angels. Like them we shall be free from sin, suffering, and death. Like them we shall be complete in knowledge and felicity. Like them we shall be secure of eternal joy. Happy are those—the good of all the earth—who shall have part in that resurrection of the just!

20th. The dead shall be raised, ver. 31, 32. There is a state of happiness hereafter. This the gospel has revealed; and it is the most consoling and cheering truth that has ever beamed upon the heart of man.

21st. Our pious friends that have died are now happy, ver. 31, 32. They are with God. God is still their God. A father, or mother, or sister, or friend that may have left us is there—there in perfect felicity. We should rejoice at that, nor should we wish them back to the poor comforts and the many sufferings of this world.

22d. It is our duty to love God with all the heart, ver. 37. No half, formal, cold, and selfish affection comes up to the requirement. It must be full, entire, absolute. It must be pleasure in *all* his attributes — his justice, his power, his purposes, as well as his mercy and his goodness. God is to be loved just as he is. If man is not pleased with his whole character he is not pleased with him at all.

23d. God is worthy of love. He is perfect. He should be *early* loved. Children should love him more than they do father, or mother, or friends. Their first affections should be fixed on God, and fixed on him supremely, till they die.

24th. We must love our neighbour, ver. 39. We must do to all as we would have them do to us. This is the law and

CHAPTER XXIII.

THEN spake Jesus to the multitude, and to his disciples,
2 Saying, [a]The scribes and the Pharisees sit in Moses' seat:
3 All, therefore, whatsoever they bid you observe, *that* observe and do; but do not ye after their works; for [b]they say, and do not.
4 For they bind [c]heavy burdens, and grievous to be borne, and lay *them* on men's shoulders; but they *themselves* will not move them with one of their fingers.

a Mal.2.7. b Ro.2.21-23. c Ac.15.10.

---

the prophets: this is the way of justice, of peace, of kindness, of charity, of benevolence. If all men obeyed these laws, the earth would be a paradise, and man would taste the bliss of heaven here below.

25th. We may ask here of each one, What think you of Christ? ver. 42. What think you of the necessity of a Saviour? What think you of his nature? Is he God as well as man, or do you regard him only as a man? What think you of his character? Do you see him to be lovely and pure, and is he such as to draw forth the warm affections of your heart? What think you of salvation by him? Do you depend on him, and trust in him, and expect heaven only on the ground of his merits? or do you reject and despise him, and would you have joined in putting him to death? Nothing more certainly tests the character, and shows what the feelings are, than the views which we entertain of Christ. Error here is fatal error; but he who has just views of the Redeemer, and right feelings toward him, is SURE OF SALVATION.

26th. We have in this chapter an illustrious specimen of the wisdom of Jesus. He successfully met the snares of his mighty and crafty foes, and with infinite ease confounded them. No art of man could confound him. Never was wisdom more clear, never more triumphant.

CHAPTER XXIII.

2. *Scribes and Pharisees.* See Notes on Mat. iii. 7. ¶ *Moses' seat.* Moses was the great legislator of the Jews. By him the law was given. The office of explaining that law among the Jews devolved on the scribes and Pharisees. In the synagogues they sat while expounding the law, and rose when they read it. By *sitting in the seat of Moses* we are to understand authority to teach the law; or, as he taught the nation by giving the law, so they taught it by explaining it.

3. *All, therefore, whatsoever,* &c. That is, all that they teach that is consistent with the law of Moses—all the commands of Moses which they read to you and properly explain. The word *all* could not be taken without such a restriction, for Christ himself accuses them of teaching many things contrary to that law, and of making it void by their traditions, Mat. xv. 1-6. ¶ *They say, and do not.* The interpretation which they give to the law is in the main correct, but their lives do not correspond with their teaching. It is not the duty of men to imitate their teachers unless their lives are pure; they are to obey the law of God, and not to frame their lives by the example of evil men.

4. *They bind heavy burdens,* &c. This phrase is derived from the custom of loading animals. The load or burden is bound up and then laid on the beast. So the Pharisees appointed weighty burdens, or grievous and heavy precepts, and insisted that the people should obey them, though they lent no assistance. The *heavy burdens* refer not here to the traditions and foolish customs of the Pharisees, for Jesus would not command the people to observe them; but they clearly mean the ceremonies and rights appointed by Moses, which Peter says neither *they nor their fathers were able to bear,* Ac. xv. 10. Those rites were numerous, expensive, requiring much time, much property, and laborious. The Pharisees were rigid in requiring that all the people should pay the taxes, give of their property, comply with every part of the law with the utmost rigour, yet they indulged themselves, and bore as little of the expense and trouble as possible; so that, where they could avoid it, they would not lend the least aid to the people in the toils and expense of their religious rites. ¶ *With one of their fingers.* In the least degree. They will not render the least aid.

5. *Their phylacteries.* The word *phy-*

5 But [d]all their works they do for to be seen of men: they make broad their [e]phylacteries, and enlarge the borders of their garments,

6 And [f]love the uppermost rooms at feasts, and the chief seats in the synagogues,

7 And greetings in the markets,

d ch.6.1-16. *e* Nu.15.38. *f* Mar.12.38,&c.; Lu.11.43,&c.

lactery comes from a word signifying to keep, preserve, or guard. The name was given because phylacteries were worn as amulets or charms, and were supposed to defend or preserve those who wore them from evil. They were small slips of parchment or vellum, on which were written certain portions of the Old Testament. The practice of using phylacteries was founded on a literal interpretation of that passage where God commands the Hebrews to have the law as a sign on their foreheads, and as frontlets between their eyes, Ex. xiii. 16; comp. Pr. iii. 1, 3; vi. 21. One kind of phylactery was called a *frontlet*, and was composed of four pieces of parchment, on the first of which was written Ex. xii. 2–10; on the second, Ex. xiii. 11–21; on the third, De. vi. 4–9; and on the fourth, De. xi. 18–21. These pieces of parchment, thus inscribed, they inclosed in a piece of tough skin, making a square, on one side of which is placed the Hebrew letter *shin*, ש, and bound them round their foreheads with a thong or ribbon when they went to the synagogue. Some wore them evening and morning; others only at the morning prayer.

As the token upon the hand was required, as well as the frontlets between the eyes (Ex. xiii. 16), the Jews made two rolls of parchment, written in square letters, with an ink made on purpose, and with much care. They were rolled up to a point, and inclosed in a sort of case of black calf-skin. They were put upon a square bit of the same leather, whence hung a thong of the same, of about a finger in breadth, and about 2 feet long. These rolls were placed at the bending of the left arm, and after one end of the thong had been made into a little knot in the form of the Hebrew letter *yod*, י, it was wound about the arm in a spiral line, which ended at the top of the middle finger. The Pharisees enlarged them, or made them wider than other people, either that they might make the letters larger or write more on them, to show, as they supposed, that they had peculiar reverence for the law. ¶ *Enlarge the borders of their garments.* This refers to the loose threads which were attached to the borders of the outer garment as a fringe. This fringe was commanded in order to distinguish them from other nations, and that they might remember to keep the commandments of God, Nu. xv. 38–40; De. xxii. 12. The Pharisees made them broader than other people wore them, to show that they had peculiar respect for the law.

6. *The uppermost rooms at feasts.* The word *rooms*, here, by no means expresses the meaning of the original. It would be correctly rendered the uppermost *places* or *couches* at feasts. To understand this, it is necessary to remark that the custom among the Jews was not to eat sitting, as we do, but reclining on couches. The table was made by *three* tables, raised like ours and placed so as to form a square, with a clear space in the midst, and one end quite open. Around these tables were placed cushions capable of containing three or more persons. On these the guests reclined, leaning on their left side, with their feet extended from the table, and so lying that the head of one naturally reclined on the bosom of another. To recline near to one in this manner denoted intimacy, and was what was meant by lying *in the bosom* of another, Jn. xiii. 23; Lu. xvi. 22, 23. As the feet were extended *from* the table, and as they reclined instead of sitting, it was easy to approach the feet behind, and even unperceived. Thus, in Lu. vii. 37, 38, while Jesus reclined in this manner, a woman that had been a sinner came to his feet *behind him*, and washed them with her tears, and wiped them with the hairs of her head. She stood on the outside of the couches. So our Saviour washed the feet of his disciples as they reclined on a couch in this manner, Jn. xiii. 4–12. Whenever we read in the New Testament of *sitting* at meals, it always means reclining in this manner, and never sitting as we do. The chief seat, or the *uppermost* one, was the middle couch at the upper end of the table. This the Pharisees loved, as a post of honour or distinction.

Chief seats in the synagogues. The

and to be called of men, Rabbi,
Rabbi.
8 But[g] be not ye called Rabbi:
for one is your Master, *even* Christ;
and all ye are brethren.
9 And call no *man* your Father
upon the earth: for one is your
[h]Father, which is in heaven.
10 Neither be ye called masters:
for one is your Master, *even* Christ.

g Ja.3.1.

h ch.6.9.

seats usually occupied by the elders of the synagogue, near the pulpit. The meaning is, they love a place of distinction. See Notes on Mat. iv. 23.

7. *Greetings in the markets.* Markets were places where multitudes of people were assembled together. They were pleased with special attention in public places, and desired that all should show them particular respect. ¶ *Greetings.* Salutations. See Notes on Lu. x. 4. ¶ *To be called Rabbi, Rabbi.* This word literally signifies *great.* It was a title given to eminent teachers of the law among the Jews; a title of honour and dignity, denoting authority and ability to teach. They were gratified with such titles, and wished it given to themselves as denoting superiority. Every time it was given to them it implied their superiority to the persons who used it, and they were fond, therefore, of hearing it often applied to them. There were three titles in use among the Jews—Rab, Rabbi, and Rabban—denoting different degrees of learning and ability, as literary degrees do among us.

8. *Be not ye,* &c. Jesus forbade his disciples to seek such titles of distinction. The reason which he gave was that he was himself their Master and Teacher. They were on a level; they were to be equal in authority; they were brethren; and they should neither covet nor receive a title which implied either an elevation of one above another, or which appeared to infringe on the absolute right of the Saviour to be their only Teacher and Master. The direction here is an express command to his disciples not to *receive* such a title of distinction. They were not to covet it; they were not to seek it; they were not to do anything that implied a wish or a willingness that it should be appended to their names. Everything which would tend to make a distinction among them or destroy their parity—everything which would lead the world to suppose that there were ranks and grades among them as ministers, they were to avoid. It is to be observed that the command is that they were not to *receive* the title—"*Be not ye called Rabbi.*" The Saviour did not forbid them giving the title to others when it was customary or not regarded as improper (comp. Ac. xxvi. 25), but *they* were not to receive it. It was to be unknown among them. This title corresponds with the title "*Doctor of Divinity*" as applied to ministers of the gospel; and, so far as I can see, the spirit of the Saviour's command is violated by the reception of such a title, as really as it would have been by their being called Rabbi. It makes a distinction among ministers. It tends to engender pride and a sense of superiority in those who obtain it, and envy and a sense of inferiority in those who do not; and the whole spirit and tendency of it is contrary to the "simplicity that is in Christ."

9. *And call no* man *your Father,* &c. This does not, of course, forbid us to apply the term to our real father. Religion requires all proper honour to be shown to him, Ex. xx. 12; Mat. xv. 4; Ep. vi. 1-3. But the word *father* also denotes *authority, eminence, superiority, a right to command,* and *a claim to particular respect.* In this sense it is used here. In this sense it belongs eminently to God, and it is not right to give it to men. Christian brethren are equal. God only has supreme authority. He only has a right to give laws; to declare doctrines that shall bind the conscience; to punish disobedience. The Jewish teachers affected that title because they seem to have supposed that a teacher formed the man, or gave him real life, and sought, therefore, to be called father. Christ taught them that the source of all life and truth was God, and they ought not to seek or receive a title which properly belongs to him.

10. *Neither be ye called masters.* That is, *leaders, guides,* for this is the literal meaning of the word. It refers to those who go before others; who claim, therefore, the right to direct and control others. This was also a title conferred on Jewish teachers.

Neither of these commands forbids

11 But[i] he that is greatest among
you shall be your servant.
12 And[k] whosoever shall exalt
himself shall be abased; and he
that shall humble himself shall be
exalted.
13 But woe unto you, scribes and
Pharisees, hypocrites! for ye shut
up the kingdom of heaven against
men: for ye neither go in *yourselves*, neither suffer ye them that
are entering to go in.
14 Woe unto you, scribes and
Pharisees, hypocrites! [l]for ye devour widows' houses, and for a
pretence make long prayer: there-

i ch.20.26,27. *k* Pr.15.33; Ja.4.6. *l* 2 Ti.3.6; Tit.1.11.

---

us to give proper titles of civil office to men, or to render them the honour belonging to their station, Mat. xxii. 21; Ro. xiii. 7; 1 Pe. ii. 17. They prohibit the disciples of Jesus from seeking or receiving mere empty titles, producing distinctions among themselves, implying authority to control the opinions and conduct of others, and claiming that others should acknowledge them to be superior to them.

11, 12. See Notes on Mat. xx. 26. *He that shall humble himself*, &c. God will exalt or honour him that is humble, and that seeks a lowly place among men. That is true religion, and God will reward it.

13. *Woe unto you.* You are guilty, and punishment will come upon you. Jesus proceeds to state wherein they were guilty. This most eloquent, most appalling, and most terrible of all discourses ever delivered to mortals was pronounced in the temple, in the presence of multitudes. Never was there more faithful dealing, more terrible reproof, more profound knowledge of the workings of hypocrisy, or more skill in detecting the concealments of sin. This was the last of the Saviour's public discourses; and it is a most impressive summary of all that he had ever said, or that he had to say, of a wicked and hypocritical generation. ¶ *Scribes and Pharisees.* See Notes on Mat. iii. 7. ¶ *Hypocrites.* Note, Mat. vi. 2. ¶ *Ye shut up the kingdom of heaven.* Note, Mat. iii. 2. They shut it up by teaching false doctrines respecting the Messiah; by binding the people to an observance of their traditions; by opposing Jesus, and attempting to convince the people that he was an impostor, thus preventing many from becoming his followers. Many were ready to embrace him as the Messiah, and were about entering into the kingdom of heaven—that is, the church—but they prevented it. Luke says (xi. 52) they had taken away the key of knowledge, and thus prevented their entering in—that is, they had taken away the right interpretation of the ancient prophecies respecting the Messiah, and thus had done all that they could to prevent the people from receiving Jesus as their Redeemer.

14. *Devour widows' houses.* The word *houses* is here used to denote *property* or possessions of any kind. You take away or get possession of the property of widows by improper arts and pretences. This was done in two ways: 1st. They claimed a very exact knowledge of the law and a perfect observance of it. They pretended to extraordinary justice toward the poor, friendship for the distressed, and willingness to aid those who were in embarrassed circumstances. They thus induced *widows* and poor people to commit the management of their property to them as guardians and executors, and then took advantage of them and defrauded them. 2d. They put on the appearance of great sanctity, and induced many conscientious but credulous women to give them much, under pretence of devoting it to religious purposes. ¶ *Long prayer.* Their prayers are said to have been often three hours in length. One rule among them, says Lightfoot, was to meditate an hour, then pray an hour, and then meditate another hour—all of which was included in their *long prayers* or *devotions.* ¶ *Damnation.* Condemnation. The word here probably refers to future punishment. It does not always, however. It means, frequently, no more than *condemnation*, or the divine disapprobation of a certain course of conduct, as in 1 Co. xi. 29: "He that eateth and drinketh unworthily, eateth and drinketh *damnation* to himself;" that is, he that eateth and drinketh in an unworthy manner—disorderly, not with reverence—is guilty, and his conduct will be disapproved or condemned by God—referring solely to the impropriety of the manner of partaking of the Lord's supper, and not at

fore ye shall receive the greater damnation.

15 Woe unto you, scribes and Pharisees, hypocrites! for ye compass sea and land to make one proselyte; and when he is made, ye make him twofold more [m]the child of hell than yourselves.

16 Woe unto you, *ye* [n]blind guides, which say, Whosoever shall swear by the temple, it is nothing; but whosoever shall swear by the gold of the temple, he is a debtor.

17 *Ye*[o] fools, and blind! for whether is greater, the gold, or the temple that sanctifieth the gold?

18 And, Whosoever shall swear by the altar, it is nothing; but whosoever sweareth by the gift that is upon it, he is [1]guilty.

19 *Ye* fools, and blind! for whe-

m Jn.8.44; Ac.13.10; Ep.2.3. *n* ch.15.14. *o* Ps.94.8. 1 or, *debtor*, or, *bound*.

---

all to the worthiness or unworthiness of the person. See Notes on that place. Comp. Ro. xiv. 23. ¶ *For a pretence.* For appearance or show; in order that they might the better defraud poor people. They would not be condemned for *making* long prayers, but because they did it with an evil design. Public prayers should, however, be short, and always to the point. A man praying in a Sunday-school should pray for the school, and, usually, not for everything else.

15. *Ye compass sea and land.* You take every means, spare no pains, to gain proselytes. ¶ *Proselyte.* One that comes over from a foreign nation, religion, or sect to us—a convert. Among the Jews there were two kinds of proselytes: 1st. *Proselytes of righteousness*, or those who wholly and fully embraced the Jewish religion, who were baptized, who were circumcised, and who conformed to all the rites of the Mosaic institutions. 2d. *Proselytes of the gate*, or those who approved of the Jewish religion, renounced the Pagan superstitions, and conformed to some of the rites of the Jews, but were not circumcised or baptized. ¶ *Twofold more the child of hell.* That is, twice as bad. To be a child of hell was a Hebrew phrase, signifying to be deserving of hell, to be awfully wicked. Comp. Notes on Mat. i. 1. The Jewish writers themselves say that the proselytes were "scabs of Israel," and "hindered the coming of the Messiah" by their great wickedness. The Pharisees gained them either to swell their own numbers, or to make gain by extorting their money under various pretences; and when they had accomplished that, they took no pains to instruct them or to restrain them. They had renounced their superstition which had before somewhat restrained them, but the Pharisees had given them no religion in its place to restrain them, and they were consequently left to the full indulgence of their vices.

16. *Whosoever shall swear*, &c. See Notes on Mat. v. 33–37. ¶ *The temple.* See Notes on Mat. xxi. 12. ¶ *It is nothing.* It amounts to nothing—it is not binding. ¶ *The gold of the temple.* Either the golden vessels in the temple—the candlestick, &c.; or the gold with which the doors and other parts of the temple were covered; or the gold in the treasury. This, it seems, they considered far more sacred than any other part of the temple, but it is not known why. ¶ *He is a debtor.* He is bound to keep his oath. He is guilty if he violates it.

17. *The temple that sanctifieth the gold.* To sanctify is to make holy. The gold had no holiness but what it derived from the temple. If in any other place, it would be no more holy than any other gold. It was foolish, then, to suppose that that was more holy than the temple, from which it received all the sanctity which it possessed.

18. *The altar.* The altar of burnt-offerings, in the court of the priests. See Notes on Mat. xxi. 12. It was made of brass, about 30 feet in length and breadth, and 15 feet in height, 2 Ch. iv. 1. On this altar were offered all the beasts and bloody oblations of the temple. ¶ *The gift that is upon it.* The gift or offering made to God, so called because it was devoted or *given* to him. The gift upon this altar was always beasts and birds.

19. *The altar that sanctifieth the gift.* The altar, dedicated to God, gave all the value or holiness to the offering, and must therefore be the greatest or of the most importance. If, therefore, either bound to the fulfilment of an oath, it must be the altar.

ther *is* greater, the gift, or [p]the altar
that sanctifieth the gift?
20 Whoso therefore shall swear
by the altar, sweareth by it, and
by all things thereon.
21 And whoso shall swear by the
temple, sweareth by it, and by [q]him
that dwelleth therein.
22 And he that shall swear by
heaven, sweareth by [r]the throne
of God, and by him that sitteth
thereon.
23 Woe unto you, scribes and
Pharisees, hypocrites! [s]for ye pay
tithe of mint, and [2]anise, and
cummin, and [t]have omitted the
weightier *matters* of the law, judgment, mercy, and faith: these ought
ye to have done, and not to leave
the other undone.

p Ex.29.37; 30.29. q 2 Ch.6.2; Ps.26.8. r Ps.11.4; Is.66.1; ch.5.34.

s Lu.11.42. 2 *dill.* t 1 Sa.15.22; Je.22.15,16; Ho.6.6; Mi.6.8; ch.9.13.

---

21. *Him that dwelleth therein.* That is, God. The temple was his house, his dwelling. In the first, or Solomon's temple, he dwelt between the cherubims in the most holy place. He manifested himself there by a visible symbol, in the form of a cloud resting on the mercy-seat, 1 Ki. viii. 10, 13; Ps. lxxx. 1.

22. *The throne of God.* Heaven is his throne, Mat. v. 34. It is so called as being the place where he sits in glory. Jesus says, here, that all who swear at all do, in fact, swear by God, or the oath is good for nothing. To swear by an altar, a gift, or a temple is of no force unless it be meant to appeal to God himself. The essential thing in an oath is calling God to witness our sincerity. If a real oath is taken, therefore, God is appealed to. If not it is foolish and wicked to swear by anything else.

23. *Ye pay tithe.* A tenth part. The law required the Jews to devote a tenth part of all their property to the support of the Levites, Nu. xviii. 20–24. Another tenth part they paid for the service of the sanctuary, commonly in cattle or grain, but where they lived far from the place of worship they changed it to money, De. xiv. 22–24. Besides these, there was to be every third year a tenth part given to the poor, to be eaten at their own dwellings (De. xiv. 28, 29); so that nearly one-third of the property of the Jews was devoted to religious services by law. This was besides the voluntary offerings which they made. How much more mild and gentle are the laws of Christianity under which we live! ¶ *Mint.* A garden herb, in the original so called from its agreeable flavour. It was used to sprinkle the floors of their houses and synagogues to produce a pleasant fragrance. ¶ *Anise.* Known commonly among us as *dill.* It has a fine aromatic smell, and is used by confectioners and perfumers. ¶ *Cummin.* A plant of the same genus, like *fennel*, and used for similar purposes. These were all herbs of little value. The law of Moses said that they should pay tithes of the *fruits of the earth*, De. xiv. 22. It said nothing, however, about herbs. It was a question whether these should be tithed. The Pharisees maintained, in their extraordinary strictness, that they ought. Our Saviour says that they were precise in doing small matters which the law had not expressly commanded, while they omitted the greater things which it had enjoined. ¶ *Judgment.* Justice to others, as magistrates, neighbours, citizens. Giving to all their just dues. ¶ *Mercy.* Compassion and kindness to the poor and miserable. ¶ *Faith.* Piety toward God; confidence in him. Faith in God here means that we are to give to him what is his due; as mercy and justice mean to do to MEN, in all circumstances, what is right toward them. ¶ *These ought ye to have done.* Attention to even the smallest points of the law of God is proper, but it should not interfere with the *higher* and more important parts of that law.

24. *Which strain at a gnat*, &c. This is a proverb. There is, however, a mistranslation or misprint here, which makes the verse unmeaning. *To strain* AT *a gnat* conveys no sense. It should have been to strain OUT a gnat; and so it is printed in some of the earlier versions, and so it was undoubtedly rendered by the translators. The common reading is a *misprint*, and should be corrected. The Greek means to *strain out* by a cloth or sieve. ¶ *A gnat.* The gnat has its origin in the water; not in great rivers, but in pools and marshes. In the stagnant waters they appear in the form of small *grubs* or

24 *Ye* blind guides! which strain
at a gnat, and swallow a camel.
25 Woe unto you, scribes and
Pharisees, hypocrites! [u]for ye make
clean the outside of the cup and of
the platter, but within they are
full of extortion and excess.
26 *Thou* blind Pharisee! cleanse
first that *which is* within the cup
and platter, that the outside of
them may be clean also.
27 Woe unto you, scribes and
Pharisees, hypocrites! [v]for ye are
like unto whited sepulchres, which
indeed appear beautiful outward,
but are within full of dead *men's*
bones, and of all uncleanness.
28 Even so ye also outwardly
appear righteous unto men, but
within ye are full of hypocrisy and
iniquity.
29 Woe unto you, scribes and

u Mar.7.4,&c.

v Lu.11.44; Ac.23.3.

---

larvæ. These larvæ retain their form about three weeks, after which they turn to chrysalids, and after three or four days they pass to the form of gnats. They are then distinguished by their well-known sharp sting. It is probable that the Saviour here refers to the insect as it exists in its *grub* or *larva* form, before it appears in the form of a gnat. Water is then its element, and those who were nice in their drink would take pains to strain it out. Hence the proverb. See Calmet's *Dict.*, art. "Gnat." It is here used to denote a very small matter, as a camel is to denote a large object. "You Jews take great pains to avoid offence in very small matters, superstitiously observing the smallest points of the law, like a man carefully straining out the animalculæ from what he drinks, while you are at no pains to avoid great sins—hypocrisy, deceit, oppression, and lust—like a man who should swallow a camel." The Arabians have a similar proverb: "He eats an elephant, and is suffocated with a gnat." He is troubled with little things, but pays no attention to great matters.

25. *The cup and the platter.* The drinking-cup and the dish containing food. The Pharisees were diligent in observing all the washings and obligations required by their traditions. See Notes on Mar. vii. 4. ¶ *Full of extortion and excess.* The outside appeared well; the inside was filled with the fruit of extortion, oppression, and wickedness. The meaning is, that though they took much pains to appear well, yet they obtained a living by extortion and crime. Their cups, neat as they appeared outward, were filled, not with the fruits of honest industry, but with that which had been extorted from the poor by wicked arts. Instead of *excess,* many manuscripts and editions of the Greek Testament read *wickedness.*

26. *Cleanse first that* which is *within the cup and the platter.* Let them be filled with the fruits of honest industry, and then the outside and the inside will be really *clean.* By this allusion to the cup and platter he taught them that it was necessary to cleanse the heart first, that the external conduct might be really pure and holy.

27. *Like unto whited sepulchres.* For the construction of sepulchres, see Notes on Mat. viii. 28. Those tombs were annually whitewashed to prevent the people from accidentally coming in contact with them as they went up to Jerusalem. This custom is still continued. Dr. Thomson (*The Land and the Book*, vol. i. p. 148) says, "I have been in places where this is repeated very often. The graves are kept clean and white as snow, a very striking emblem of those painted hypocrites, the Pharisees, beautiful without, but full of dead men's bones and of all uncleanness within." The law considered those persons unclean who had touched anything belonging to the dead, Nu. xix. 16. Sepulchres were therefore often whitewashed, that they might be distinctly seen. Thus "whited," they appeared beautiful; but within they contained the bones and corrupting bodies of the dead. So the Pharisees. Their outward conduct appeared well, but their hearts were full of hypocrisy, envy, pride, lust, and malice—fitly represented by the corruption within a whited tomb.

29. *Ye build the tombs of the prophets.* That is, you build sepulchres or tombs over the prophets that have been slain. This they did professedly from veneration and respect for their character. This is often done at the East at the

Pharisees, hypocrites! because ye build the tombs of the prophets, and garnish the sepulchres of the righteous,

30 And say, If we had been in the days of our fathers, we would not have been partakers with them in the blood of the prophets.

31 Wherefore ye be witnesses unto yourselves that ye are the children of them which [w]killed the prophets.

32 Fill[x] ye up, then, the measure of your fathers.

33 *Ye* serpents, *ye* [y]generation of vipers! how can ye escape the damnation of hell?

34 Wherefore, behold, I send

w Ac.7.52; 1 Th.2.15.
x Ge.15.16; 1 Th.2.16. y ch.3.7.

present day, and indeed elsewhere. Among the Mohammedans it is a common way of showing respect for any distinguished man to build a tomb for him. By doing this, they profess respect for his character and veneration for his memory. So the Pharisees, by building tombs in this manner, professedly approved of the character and conduct of the prophets, and disapproved of the conduct of their fathers in killing them. ¶ *And garnish*, &c. That is, adorn or ornament. This was done by rebuilding them with more taste, decorating them, and keeping them neat and clean. The original word means, also, to show any proper honour to the memory of the dead, as by speaking well of them, praying near them, or rearing synagogues near them in honour of their memory.

30. *And say*, &c. This they professed to say by rebuilding their tombs. They also, probably, publicly expressed their disapprobation of the conduct of their fathers. All this, in building and ornamenting tombs, was a profession of extraordinary piety. Our Lord showed them it was mere pretence.

31. *Ye be witnesses unto yourselves.* The emphasis, here, lies in the words "*to yourselves.*" It is an appeal to their conscience. It was not by their building the tombs that they were witnesses that they were the children of those who slew the prophets; but that, in spite of all this pretence of piety, under all this cloak of profession, they knew in their consciences, and were witnesses to themselves, that it was mere hypocrisy, and that they really approved the conduct of those who slew the prophets. ¶ *Children of them*, &c. Resembling them; approving their conduct; inheriting their feelings. See Notes on Mat. i. 1. They not only showed that they were descended from them, but that they possessed their spirit, and that, in similar circumstances, they would have done as they did.

32. *Fill ye up, then*, &c. This is a prediction of what they were about to do. He would have them act out their true spirit, and show what they were, and evince to all that they had the spirit of their fathers. Comp. Notes on Jn. xiii. 27. This was done be putting him to death, and persecuting the apostles. ¶ *The measure.* The full amount, so as to make it complete. By your slaying me, fill up what is lacking of the iniquity of your fathers till the measure is full; till the national iniquity is complete; till as much has been committed as God can possibly bear, and then shall come upon you all this blood, and you shall be destroyed, ver. 34, 35.

33. Ye *serpents.* This name is given to them on account of their pretending to be pious, and very much devoted to God, but being secretly evil. At the heart, with all their pretensions, they were filled with evil designs, as the serpent was, Ge. iii. 1–5. ¶ *Generation of vipers.* See Notes on Mat. xii. 34. ¶ *Damnation of hell.* This refers, beyond all question, to future punishment. So great was their wickedness and hypocrisy, that, if they persevered in this course, it was impossible to escape the damnation that should come on the guilty. This is the sternest language that Jesus ever used to wicked men. But it by no means authorizes ministers to use such language to sinners now. Christ knew that this was true of them. He had an authority which none now have. It is not the province of ministers to denounce judgment, or to use severe names, least of all to do it on pretence of imitating Christ. He knew the hearts of men. We know them not. He had authority to declare certainly that those whom he addressed would be lost. We have no such authority. He addressed persons; we address characters.

unto you prophets, and wise men, and scribes: and [z]*some* of them ye shall kill and crucify; and [a]*some* of them shall ye scourge in your synagogues, and [b]persecute *them* from city to city:
35 That[c] upon you may come all the righteous blood shed upon the earth, [d]from the blood of righteous Abel unto [e]the blood of Zacharias, son of Barachias, whom ye slew between the temple and the altar.
36 Verily I say unto you, All these things shall come upon this generation.
37 O[f] Jerusalem, Jerusalem, *thou*

z Ac.7.59. a Ac.5.40; 2 Co.11.24,25. b He.11.37. c Re.18.24.

d Ge.4.8. e 2 Ch.24.20,21. f Lu.13.34.

34. *I send unto you prophets*, &c. Jesus doubtless refers here to the apostles, and other teachers of religion. Prophets, wise men, and scribes were the names by which the teachers of religion were known among the Jews, and he therefore used the same terms when speaking of the messengers which he would send. *I send* has the force of the future, I *will* send. ¶ Some *of them ye shall kill.* As in the case of Stephen (Ac. vii. 59) and James (Ac. xii. 1, 2). ¶ *Crucify.* Punish with death on the cross. There are no cases of this mentioned; but few historical records of this age have come down to us. The Jews had not the power of crucifying, but they had power to deliver those whom they condemned to death into the hands of the Romans to do it. ¶ *Shall scourge.* See Notes on Mat. x. 17. This was done, Ac. xxii. 19–24; 2 Co. xi. 24, 25. *Persecute*, &c. See Notes on Mat. v. 10. This was fulfilled in the case of nearly all the apostles.

35. *That upon you may come*, &c. That is, the nation is guilty. Your fathers were guilty. You have shown yourselves to be like them. You are about, by slaying the Messiah and his messengers, to fill up the iniquity of the land. The patience of God is nearly exhausted, and the nation is about to be visited with signal vengeance. These national crimes deserve national judgments; and the proper judgment for all these crimes are about to come upon you in the destruction of your temple and city. ¶ *All the righteous blood.* That is, all the judgments due for shedding that blood. God did not hold them guilty for what their fathers had done; but temporal judgments descend on children in consequence of the wickedness of parents, as in the case of drunken and profligate parents. A drunken father wastes the property that his children might have possessed. A gambler reduces his children to poverty and want. An imprudent and foolish parent is the occasion of leading his sons into places of poverty, ignorance, and crime, materially affecting their character and destiny. See Notes on Ro. v. 12–19. So of the Jews. The appropriate effects of their fathers' crimes were coming on the nation, and they would suffer. ¶ *Upon the earth.* Upon the land of *Judea.* The word is often used with this limitation. See Mat. iv. 8. ¶ *Righteous Abel.* Slain by Cain, his brother, Ge. iv. 8. ¶ *Zacharias, son of Barachias.* It is not certainly known who this was. Some have thought that it was the Zecharias whose death is recorded in 2 Ch. xxiv. 20, 21. He is there called the son of Jehoiada; but it is known that it was common among the Jews to have two names, as Matthew is called Levi; Lebbeus, Thaddeus; and Simon, Cephas. Others have thought that Jesus referred to Zecharias the prophet, who might have been massacred by the Jews, though no account of his death is recorded. It might have been known by tradition. ¶ *Whom ye slew.* Whom you, Jews, slew. Whom your nation killed. ¶ *Between the temple and the altar.* Between the temple, properly so called, and the altar of burnt-offering in the court of the priests. See the plan of the temple, Mat. xxi. 12.

36. *Upon this generation.* The destruction of Jerusalem took place about forty years after this was spoken. See the next chapter.

37. *O Jerusalem*, &c. See Notes on Lu. xix. 41, 42. ¶ *Would I have gathered.* Would have protected and saved. ¶ *Thy children.* Thy people.

38. *Your house.* The temple. The house of worship of the Jews. The chief ornament of Jerusalem. ¶ *Desolate.* About to be desolate or destroyed. To be forsaken as a place of worship, and delivered into the hands of the Ro-

that killest the prophets, and stonest them which are sent unto thee, how often would [g]I have gathered thy children together, even as a hen gathereth her chickens under *her* wings, and ye would not!

38 Behold,[h] your house is left unto you desolate.

39 For I say unto you, Ye shall not see me henceforth till ye shall say, [i]Blessed *is* he that cometh in the name of the Lord.

g De.32.11,12; Ps.91.4. *h* Zec.11.6. *i* Ps.118.26; ch.21.9.

---

mans, and destroyed. See Notes on ch. xxiv.

39. *Ye shall not see me*, &c. The day of your mercy is gone by. I have offered you protection and salvation, and you have rejected it. You are about to crucify me, and your temple to be destroyed, and you, as a nation, to be given up to long and dreadful suffering. You will not see me as a merciful Saviour, offering you redemption any more, till you have borne these heavy judgments. They must come upon you, and be borne, until you would be glad to hail a deliverer, and say, Blessed is he that cometh in the name of the Lord. Blessed be he that comes as the Messiah, to bring deliverance. This has not been yet accomplished, but the days will come when the Jews, long cast out and rejected, will hail Jesus as the Messiah, and receive him whom their fathers slew as the merciful Saviour, Ro. xi. 25–32.

REMARKS.

1st. Proper respect should always be shown to teachers and rulers, ver. 3.

2d. We are not to copy the *example* of wicked men, though they *are* our teachers or rulers, ver. 3. We are to frame our conduct by the law of God, and not by the example of *men*.

3d. Men are often very rigid in exacting of others what they fail altogether of performing themselves, ver. 4.

4th. We are not to seek human honours (ver. 8), nor to *give* flattering titles to others, nor to allow others to give them to us (ver. 9). Our highest honour is in humility, and he is most exalted who is most lowly, ver. 11, 12.

5th. In the descriptions of the scribes and Pharisees in this chapter, we have a full-length portrait of a hypocrite. 1st. They shut up the kingdom of heaven against others, ver. 13. They made great pretensions to knowledge, but they neither entered in themselves, nor suffered others. 2d. They committed the grossest iniquity under a cloak of religion, ver. 14. They cheated widows out of their property, and made long prayers to hide their villainy. 3d. They showed great zeal in making proselytes, yet did it only for gain, and made them more wicked, ver. 15. 4th. They taught false doctrine, and they resorted to artful contrivances to destroy the force of oaths, and to shut out the Creator from their view, ver. 16–22. 5th. They were superstitious, ver. 23. Small matters they were exact in; matters of real importance they cared little about. 6th. They took great pains to *appear* well, while they themselves knew that it was all deceit and falsehood, ver. 25–28. 7th. They professed great veneration for the memory of the pious dead, while at the same time they were conscious that they really approved the conduct of those that killed them, ver. 29–31. Never, perhaps, was there a combination of more wicked feelings and hypocritical actions than among them; and never was there more profound knowledge of the human heart, and more faithfulness, than in him who tore off the mask, and showed them what they were.

6th. It is amazing with what power and authority our blessed Lord reproves this wicked people. It is wonderful that they ever waited for a mock trial, and did not kill him at once. But his time was not come, and they were restrained, and not suffered to act out the fury of their mad passions.

7th. Jesus pities dying sinners, ver. 37. He seeks their salvation. He pleads with them to be saved. He would gather them to him, if they would come. The most hardened, even like the sinners of Jerusalem, he would save if they would come to him. But they will not. They turn from him, and tread the road to death.

8th. The reason why the wicked are not saved is their own obstinacy. They choose not to be saved, and they die. If they will not come to Christ, it is right that they should die. If they do not come, they must die.

9th. The sinner will be destroyed, ver.

CHAPTER XXIV.

AND[a] Jesus went out, and departed from the temple; and his disciples came to *him* for to show him the buildings of the temple.

2 And Jesus said unto them, See ye not all these things? Verily I say unto you, [b]There shall not be left here one stone upon another, that shall not be thrown down.

3 And as he sat upon the Mount

a Mar.13.1; Lu.21.5.

b 1 Ki.9.7; Je.26.18; Lu.19.44.

---

38. The day will come when the mercy of God will be clean gone for ever, and the forbearance of God exhausted, and then the sinner must perish. When once God has given him over, he must die. No man, no parent, no minister, no friend, no angel, no archangel, can then save. Salvation is lost, for ever lost. Oh how amazing is the folly of the wicked, that they weary out the forbearance of God, and perish in their sins!

CHAPTER XXIV.

Jesus foretells the destruction of the temple as he takes his final leave of it, and teaches what were the signs of his coming. These predictions are also recorded in Mar. xiii.; Lu. xxi. 5–38.

1. *And Jesus went out.* He was going over to the Mount of Olives, ver. 3. ¶ *The buildings of the temple.* The temple itself, with the surrounding courts, porches, and other edifices. See Notes on Mat. xxi. 12. Mark says that they particularly pointed out the *stones* of the temple, as well as the buildings. "In that temple," says Josephus, the Jewish historian, "were several stones which were 45 cubits in length, 5 in height, and 6 in breadth;" that is, more than 70 feet long, 10 wide, and 8 high. These stones, of such enormous size, were principally used in building the high wall on the east side, from the base to the top of the mountain. They were also, it is said, beautifully painted with variegated colours.

2. *There shall not be left here one stone upon another.* At the time this was spoken, no event was more improbable than this. The temple was vast, rich, splendid. It was the pride of the nation, and the nation was at peace. Yet in the short space of forty years all this was exactly accomplished. Jerusalem was taken by the Roman armies, under the command of Titus, A.D. 70. The account of the siege and destruction of the city is left us by Josephus, a historian of undoubted veracity and singular fidelity. He was a Jewish priest. In the wars of which he gives an account, he fell into the hands of the Romans, and remained with them during the siege and destruction of the city. Being a Jew, he would of course say nothing designed to confirm the prophecies of Jesus Christ; yet his whole history appears almost like a running commentary on these predictions respecting the destruction of the temple. The following particulars are given on his authority:—

After the city was taken, Josephus says that Titus "gave orders that they should now *demolish the whole city and temple*, except three towers, which he reserved standing. But for the rest of the wall, it was laid so completely even with the ground by those who *dug it up from the foundation*, that there was nothing left to make those believe who came hither that it had ever been inhabited." Maimonides, a Jewish writer, has also recorded that "Terentius Rufus, an officer in the army of Titus, with a ploughshare tore up the foundations of the temple, that the prophecy might be fulfilled, 'Zion shall be plowed as a field,'" Mi. iii. 12. This was all done by the direction of divine Providence. Titus was desirous of preserving the temple, and frequently sent Josephus to the Jews to induce them to surrender and save the temple and city. But the prediction of the Saviour had gone forth, and, notwithstanding the wish of the Roman general, the temple was to be destroyed. The Jews themselves first set fire to the porticoes of the temple. One of the Roman soldiers, without any command, threw a burning firebrand into the golden window, and soon the temple was in flames. Titus gave orders to extinguish the fire; but, amid the tumult, none of his orders were obeyed. The soldiers pressed to the temple, and neither fear nor entreaties, nor stripes could restrain them. Their hatred of the Jews urged them on to the work of destruction, and thus, says Josephus, the temple was burned against the will of Cæsar.—*Jewish Wars*, b. vi. ch. 4, § 5–7.

of Olives, the disciples came unto
him privately, saying, Tell us, when
shall these things be? and [c]what
shall be the sign of thy coming, and
of the end of the world?
4 And Jesus answered and said
unto them, [d]Take heed that no
man deceive you.
5 For[e] many shall come in my
name, saying, I am Christ; and
shall deceive many.
6 And ye [f]shall hear of wars,

c 1 Th.5.1,&c. d Col.2.8; 2 Th.2.3. e Je.14.14. f Da.11.1,&c.

---

3. *He sat upon the Mount of Olives.* See Notes on Mat. xxi. 1. From that mount there was a magnificent view of the whole city. ¶ *The disciples came unto him privately.* Not all of them, but Peter, James, John, and Andrew, Mar. xiii. 3. The prediction that the temple would be destroyed (ver. 2) had been made in the presence of all the apostles. *A part* now came privately to know more particularly when this would be. ¶ *When shall these things be?* There are three questions here. 1st. When those things should take place. 2d. What should be the signs of his own coming. 3d. What should be the signs that the end of the world was near. To these questions he replies in this and the following chapters. This he does, not by noticing them distinctly, but by intermingling the descriptions of the destruction of Jerusalem and of the end of the world, so that it is sometimes difficult to tell to what particular subject his remarks apply. The *principle* on which this combined description of two events was spoken appears to be, that *they could be described in the same words*, and therefore the accounts are intermingled. A similar use of language is found in some parts of Isaiah, where the same language will describe the return from the Babylonish captivity, and deliverance by the Messiah. See Introduction to Isaiah, § 7. ¶ *Sign of thy coming.* Evidence that thou art coming. By what token shall we know that thou art coming?

4, 5. *Take heed,* &c. Jesus, in reply to their question, first gives them a caution to beware of deception. They were to be constantly on their guard, because many would arise to deceive the people. ¶ *Many shall come in my name.* Not in the name or by the authority of Jesus, or claiming to be *his* followers, and to be sent by *him*, but in the name of the *Messiah*, or claiming to be the Messiah. ¶ *I am Christ.* I am the Messiah. See Notes on Mat. i. 1. The Messiah was expected at that time, Mat. ii. 1, 2. Many would lay claims to being the Messiah, and, as he was universally expected, multitudes would easily be led to believe in them. There is abundant evidence that this was fully accomplished. Josephus informs us that there were many who pretended to divine inspiration; who deceived the people, leading out numbers of them into the desert. "The land," says he "was overrun with magicians, seducers, and impostors, who drew the people after them in multitudes into solitudes and deserts, to see the signs and miracles which they promised to show by the power of God." Among these are mentioned particularly Dositheus, the Samaritan, who affirmed that he was Christ; Simon Magus, who said he appeared among the Jews as the Son of God; and Theudas, who persuaded many to go with him to the river Jordan, to see the waters divided. The names of *twenty-four* false Messiahs are recorded as having appeared between the time of the Emperor Adrian and the year 1682.

6. *And ye shall hear of wars,* &c. It is recorded in the history of Rome that violent agitations prevailed in the Roman empire previous to the destruction of Jerusalem. Four emperors, Nero, Galba, Otho, and Vitellius, suffered violent deaths in the short space of eighteen months. In consequence of these changes in the government, there were commotions throughout the empire. Parties were formed, and bloody and violent wars were the consequence of attachment to particular emperors. This is the more remarkable, as at the time that the prophecy was made, the empire was in a state of peace. ¶ *Rumours of wars.* Wars declared or threatened, but not carried into execution. Josephus says that Bardanes, and after him Vologeses, declared war against the Jews, but it was not carried into execution, *Antiq.* xx. 34. He also says that Vitellius, governor of Syria, declared war against Aretas, king of Arabia, and wished to lead his army through Palestine, but the death of

and rumours of wars: see that ye
be not troubled: for all *these things*
must come to pass, but the end is
not yet.
7 For[g] nation shall rise against
nation, and kingdom against king-

g Hag.2.21,22.

dom: and there shall be famines,
and pestilences, and earthquakes,
in divers places.
8 All these *are* the beginning of
sorrows.
9 Then[h] shall they deliver you

h Lu.21.12.

Tiberius prevented the war, *Antiq.* xviii. 5. 3. ¶ *The end is not yet.* The end of the Jewish economy; the destruction of Jerusalem will not *immediately* follow. Be not, therefore, alarmed when you hear of those commotions. Other signs will warn you when to be alarmed and seek security.

7. *Nation shall rise against nation, and kingdom against kingdom.* At Cæsarea the Jews and Syrians contended about the right to the city, and twenty thousand of the Jews were slain. At this blow the whole nation of the Jews was exasperated, and carried war and desolation through the Syrian cities and villages. Sedition and civil war spread throughout Judea; Italy was also thrown into civil war by the contests between Otho and Vitellius for the crown. ¶ *And there shall be famines.* There was a famine foretold by Agabus (Ac. xi. 28), which is mentioned by Tacitus, Suetonius, and Eusebius, and which was so severe in Jerusalem, Josephus says, that many people perished for want of food, *Antiq.* xx. 2. Four times in the reign of Claudius (A.D. 41–54) famine prevailed in Rome, Palestine, and Greece. ¶ *Pestilences.* Raging epidemic diseases; the plague, sweeping off multitudes of people at once. It is commonly the attendant of famine, and often produced by it. A pestilence is recorded as raging in Babylonia, A.D. 40 (Joseph. *Antiq.* xviii. 9. 8); in Italy, A.D. 66 (Tacit. 16. 13). Both of these took place before the destruction of Jerusalem. ¶ *Earthquakes.* In prophetic language, earthquakes sometimes mean political commotions. Literally they are tremors or shakings of the earth, often shaking cities and towns to ruin. The earth opens, and houses and people sink indiscriminately to destruction. Many of these are mentioned as preceding the destruction of Jerusalem. Tacitus mentions one in the reign of Claudius, at Rome, and says that in the reign of Nero the cities of Laodicea, Hierapolis, and Colosse were overthrown, and the celebrated Pompeii was overwhelmed and almost destroyed by an earthquake, *Annales,* 15. 22. Others are mentioned as occurring at Smyrna, Miletus, Chios, and Samos. Luke adds, "*And fearful sights and great signs shall there be from heaven,*" xxi. 11. Josephus, who had probably never heard of this prophecy, and who certainly would have done nothing designedly to show its fulfilment, records the prodigies and signs which he says preceded the destruction of the city. A star, says he, resembling a sword, stood over the city, and a comet that continued a whole year. At the feast of unleavened bread, during the night, a bright light shone round the altar and the temple, so that it seemed to be bright day, for half an hour. The eastern gate of the temple, of solid brass, fastened with strong bolts and bars, and which had been shut with difficulty by twenty men, opened in the night of its own accord. A few days after that feast, he says, "Before sunsetting, chariots and troops of soldiers in their armour were seen running about among the clouds, and surrounding of cities." A great noise, as of the sound of a multitude, was heard in the temple, saying, "LET US REMOVE HENCE." Four years before the war began, Jesus, the son of Ananus, a plebeian and a husbandman, came to the feast of the tabernacles when the city was in peace and prosperity, and began to cry aloud, "A voice from the east, a voice from the west, a voice from the four winds, a voice against Jerusalem and the holy house, a voice against the bridegroom and the brides, and a voice against this whole people!" He was scourged, and at every stroke of the whip he cried, "Woe, woe to Jerusalem!" This cry, Josephus says, was continued every day for more than seven years, till he was killed in the siege of the city, exclaiming, "Woe, woe to myself also!"—*Jewish Wars,* b. vi. ch. 9, § 3.

8. *The beginning of sorrows.* Far heavier calamities are yet to come before the end.

up to be afflicted, and [i]shall kill you: and ye shall be hated of all nations for my name's sake.

10 And then shall many be [k]offended, and shall betray one another, and shall hate one another.

11 And[l] many false prophets shall rise, and shall [m]deceive many.

i Jn.16.2; Ac.7.59. *k* ch.13.21. *l* 2 Pe.2.1; 1 Jn.4.3. *m* 1 Ti.4.1.

---

9. *To be afflicted.* By persecution, imprisonment, scourging, &c. ¶ *They shall deliver you up to councils* (Mark). To the great council, or Sanhedrim—for this is the word in the original. See Notes on Mat. v. 22. This was fulfilled when Peter and John were brought before the council, Ac. iv. 5-7. Mark farther adds (xiii. 9) that they should be delivered to synagogues and to prisons to be beaten, and should be brought before rulers and kings for his name's sake. All this was remarkably fulfilled. Peter and John were imprisoned (Ac. iv. 3); Paul and Silas were imprisoned (Ac. xvi. 24), and also beaten (Ac. xvi. 23); Paul was brought before Gallio (Ac. xviii. 12), before Felix (Ac. xxiv. 24), and before Agrippa (Ac. xxv. 23). ¶ *And shall kill you.* That is, shall kill some of you. Stephen was stoned (Ac. vii. 59); James was killed by Herod (Ac. xii. 2); and, in addition to all that the sacred writers have told us, the persecution under Nero took place before the destruction of Jerusalem, in which were put to death, with many others, Peter and Paul. Most of the apostles, it is believed, died by persecution.

When they were delivered up, Jesus told them not to premeditate what they should say, for he would give them a mouth and wisdom which all their adversaries would not be able to gainsay or resist, Lu. xxi. 14, 15. The fulfilment of this is recorded in the case of Stephen (Ac. vi. 10), and of Paul, who made Felix *tremble*, Ac. xxiv. 25. ¶ *Ye shall be hated of all nations.* This was fulfilled then, and has been in all ages. It was judged to be a crime to be a Christian. Multitudes for this, and for nothing else, were put to death. ¶ *For my name's sake.* On account of attachment to me, or because you bear my *name* as *Christians.*

10. *Many shall be offended.* See Notes on Mat. v. 29. Many shall stumble, fall, apostatize from a profession of religion. Many who *professed* to love me will then show that they had no *real* attachment to me; and in those trying times it will be seen that they knew nothing of genuine Christian love. See 1 Jn. ii. 19. ¶ *Shall betray one another.* Those who thus apostatize from professed attachment to me will betray others who really love me. This they would do to secure their own safety, by revealing the names, habitations, or places of concealment of others. ¶ *Shall hate one another.* Not that real Christians would do this, but those who had *professed* to be such would then show that they were not his true followers, and would hate one another. Luke adds that they should be betrayed *by parents, and brethren, and kinsfolks, and friends*, Lu. xxi. 16. They would break over the most tender ties to surrender Christians to punishment. So great would be their hatred of Christianity, that it would overcome all the natural endearments of kindred and home. This, in the persecutions of Christians, has often occurred, and nothing shows more fully the deep and deadly hatred of the human heart to the gospel. Comp. Notes on ch. x. 21.

11. *And many false prophets.* Many men pretending to be prophets or foretellers of future events. This refers not to the false *Messiahs* of which he had spoken (ver. 5), but to prophets who should appear during the *siege* of the city. Of them Josephus says: "The tyrannical zealots who ruled the city suborned *many false prophets* to declare that aid would be given to the people from heaven. This was done to prevent them from attempting to desert, and to inspire confidence in God."—*Jewish Wars*, b. vi. ch. 5, § 2, 3.

12. *And because iniquity*, &c. The word *iniquity* here seems to include the cruelty of the Jews and Romans in their persecutions; the betraying of Christians by those who professed to be such; and the pernicious errors of false prophets and others. The effect of all this would be, that the ardour of feeling of many Christians would be lessened. The word *wax* means to *become.* It is an old Saxon word, not used now in this sense except in the Bible. The fear of death, and the deluding influence of false teachers, would lessen the

12 And because iniquity shall abound, [n]the love of many shall wax cold.
13 But[o] he that shall endure unto the end, the same shall be saved.
14 And[p] this gospel of the kingdom shall be preached in all the world for a witness unto all nations; and then shall the end come.
15 When ye, therefore, shall see the abomination of desolation spoken of by [q]Daniel the prophet,

n Re.3.15,16. o Re.2.10. p ch.28.19; Ro.10.18; Re.14.6.

q Da.9.27; 12.11.

zeal of many timid and weak professors; perhaps, also, of many real but feeble Christians.

13. *He that shall endure unto the end, the same shall be saved.* The word "end," here, has by some been thought to mean the destruction of Jerusalem, or the *end* of the Jewish economy, and the meaning has been supposed to be "he that perseveres in bearing these persecutions to the end of the wars shall be safe. God will protect his people from harm, so that not a hair of the head shall perish." Others, with more probability, have referred this to final salvation, and refer the "end" to the close of life. "He that bears afflictions and persecutions faithfully—that constantly adheres to his religion, and does not shrink till death—shall be saved, or shall enter heaven." So Luke (xxi. 18) says, *there shall not an hair of your head perish*—that is, they would be saved. *An hair of the head*, or the smallest part or portion, is a proverbial expression, denoting the *certainty* and *completeness* of their salvation. Luke (xxi. 19) farther adds, *In your patience possess ye your souls*—that is, keep your souls *patient;* keep proper possession of patience as your own. It is a part of religion to teach it, and in these trying times let it not depart from you.

14. *And this gospel of the kingdom shall be preached in all the world.* The evidence that this was done is to be chiefly derived from the New Testament, and there it is clear. Thus Paul declares that it was preached to every creature under heaven (Col. i. 6, 23); that the faith of the Romans was spoken of throughout the whole world (Ro. i. 8); that he preached in Arabia (Ga. i. 17), and at Jerusalem, and round about unto Illyricum (Ro. xv. 19). We know also that he travelled through Asia Minor, Greece, and Crete; that he was in Italy, and probably in Spain and Gaul, Ro. xv. 24–28. At the same time, the other apostles were not idle; and there is full proof that within thirty years after this prophecy was spoken, churches were established in all these regions. ¶ *For a witness unto all nations.* This preaching the gospel indiscriminately to *all* the Gentiles shall be a *proof* to them, or a witness, that the division between the Jews and Gentiles was about to be broken down. Hitherto the blessings of revelation had been confined to the Jews. They were the peculiar people of God. His messages had been sent to them only. When, therefore, God sent the gospel to *all* other people, it was proof, or *a witness unto them*, that the peculiar Jewish economy was at an end. ¶ *Then shall the end come.* The end of the Jewish economy; the destruction of the temple and city.

15. *The abomination of desolation.* This is a Hebrew expression, meaning an abominable or hateful destroyer. The Gentiles were all held in abomination by the Jews, Ac. x. 28. The abomination of desolation means the Roman army, and is so explained by Lu. xxi. 20. The Roman army is farther called the *abomination* on account of the images of the emperor, and the eagles, carried in front of the legions, and regarded by the Romans with divine honours. ¶ *Spoken of by Daniel the prophet.* Da. ix. 26, 27; xi. 31; xii. 11. See Notes on those passages. ¶ *Standing in the holy place.* Mark says, *standing where it ought not*, meaning the same thing. All Jerusalem was esteemed *holy*, Mat. iv. 5. The meaning of this is, when you see the Roman armies standing in the holy city or encamped around the temple, or the Roman ensigns or standards in the temple. Josephus relates that when the city was taken, the Romans brought their idols into the temple, and placed them over the eastern gate, and sacrificed to them there, *Jewish Wars*, b. vi. ch. 6, § 1. *Whoso readeth*, &c. This seems to be a remark made by the evangelist to direct the attention of the reader particularly to the meaning of the prophecy by Daniel.

16. *Then let them*, &c. Then Chris-

stand in the holy place, (whoso
readeth, let him understand:)
16 Then let them which be in
Judea flee into the mountains:
17 Let him which is on the
house-top not come down to take
any thing out of his house:
18 Neither let him which is in
the field return back to take his
clothes.
19 And[r] woe unto them that are
with child, and to them that give
suck in those days.
20 But pray ye that your flight
be not in the winter, neither on
the sabbath-day;

r Lu.23.29.

tians may know that the end is come, and should seek a place of safety. Destruction would not only visit the *city*, but would extend to the surrounding part of Judea. ¶ *The mountains.* The mountains of Palestine abound in caves, a safe retreat for those who are pursued. In all ages these caves have been the favourite places of robbers, and they were also resorted to by those in danger, 1 Sa. xiii. 6; xxii. 1; 2 Sa. xxiii. 13; Jos. x. 16. In those mountains they would be safe.

17. *Him which is on the house-top.* The roofs of the houses in Eastern countries were made flat, so that they were favourable places for walking and retirement. See Notes on Mat. ix. 1–8. The meaning here is, that he who should be on the house-top when this calamity came upon the city *should flee without delay;* he should not even take time to secure any article of apparel from his house. So sudden would be the calamity, that by attempting to do this he would endanger his life.

18. *Return back to take his clothes.* His clothes which, in *working*, he had laid aside, or which, in fleeing, he should throw off as an encumbrance. *Clothes* here means the *outer* garment, commonly laid aside when men worked or ran. See Notes on Mat. v. 40.

These directions were followed. It is said that the Christians, warned by these predictions, fled from Jerusalem to Pella, and other places beyond the Jordan; so that there is not evidence that a single *Christian* perished in Jerusalem.—Euseb. *Hist. Eccl.*, lib. iii. ch. 6.

20. *But pray ye*, &c. The destruction was certainly coming. It could not be prevented; yet it was right to pray for a mitigation of the circumstances, that it might be as mild as possible. So we know that calamity is before us; sickness, pain, bereavement, and death are in our path; yet, though we know that these things *must* come upon us, it is right to pray that they may come in as mild a manner as may be consistent with the will of God. We *must die*, but it is right to pray that the pains of our dying may be neither long nor severe. ¶ *In the winter.* On account of the cold, storms, &c. To be turned then from home, and compelled to take up an abode in caverns, would be a double calamity. ¶ *Neither on the sabbath-day.* Long journeys were prohibited by the law on the Sabbath, Ex. xvi. 29. The law of Moses did not mention the distance to which persons *might* go on the Sabbath, but most of the Jews maintained that it should not be more than 2000 cubits. Some supposed that it was 7 furlongs, or nearly a mile. This distance was allowed in order that they might go to their places of worship. Most of them held that it was not lawful to go farther, under any circumstances of war or affliction. Jesus teaches his disciples to pray that their flight might not be on the Sabbath, because, if they should *not* go farther than a Sabbath-day's journey, they would not be beyond the reach of danger, and if they did, they would be exposed to the charge of violating the law. It should be added that it was almost impracticable to travel in Judea on that day, as the gates of the cities were usually closed, Ne. xiii. 19–22.

21. *There shall be great tribulation.* The word tribulation means *calamity* or *suffering.* Luke (xxi. 24) has specified in what this tribulation would consist: "They shall fall by the edge of the sword, and shall be led away captive into all nations, and Jerusalem shall be trodden down of the Gentiles, until the times of the Gentiles shall be fulfilled." That is, until the time allotted for the Gentiles *to do it* shall be fully accomplished, or as long as God is pleased to suffer them to do it.

The first thing mentioned by Luke is, that they should fall *by the edge of the sword*—that is, would be slain in war, as the sword was then principally used

21 For[s] then shall be great tribulation, such as was not since the beginning of the world to this time, no, nor ever shall be.

s Da.12.1.

22 And except those days should be shortened, there should no flesh be saved: [t]but for the elect's sake those days shall be shortened.

t Is.65.8,9.

---

in war. This was most strikingly fulfilled. Josephus, in describing it, uses almost the very words of our Saviour. *All the calamities*, says he, *which had befallen any nation from the beginning of the world* were but small in comparison with those of the Jews.—*Jewish Wars*, b. i. preface, § 4.

He has given the following account of one part of the massacre when the city was taken: "And now, rushing into the city, they slew whomsoever they found, without distinction, and burned the houses and all the people who had fled into them; and when they entered for the sake of plunder, they found whole families of dead persons, and houses full of carcasses destroyed by famine, then they came out with their hands empty. And though they thus pitied the dead, they had not the same emotion for the living, but killed all they met, whereby they filled the lanes with dead bodies. *The whole city ran with blood*, insomuch that many things which were burning were extinguished by the blood."—*Jewish Wars*, b. vi. ch. 8, § 5; ch. 9, § 2, 3. He adds that in the siege of Jerusalem not fewer than *eleven hundred thousand* perished (*Jewish Wars*, b. vi. ch. 9, § 3)—a number almost half as great as are in the whole city of London. In the adjacent provinces no fewer than *two hundred and fifty thousand* are reckoned to have been slain; making in all whose deaths were ascertained the almost incredible number of *one million three hundred and fifty thousand* who were put to death. These were not, indeed, all slain with the sword. Many were crucified. "Many hundreds," says Josephus (*Jewish Wars*, b. v. ch. 11, § 1), "were first whipped, then tormented with various kinds of tortures, and finally crucified; the Roman soldiers nailing them (out of the wrath and hatred they bore to the Jews), one after one way and another after another, to crosses, *by way of jest*, until at length the multitude became so great that room was wanting for crosses, and crosses for the bodies." So terribly was their imprecation fulfilled—*his blood be on us and on our children*, Mat. xxvii. 25. If it be asked how it was possible for so many people to be slain in a single city, it is to be remembered that the siege of Jerusalem commenced during the time of the Passover, when all the males of the Jews were required to be there, and when it is estimated that more than *three millions* were usually assembled. See Josephus, *Jewish Wars*, b. vi. ch. 9, § 3, 4.

A horrible instance of the distress of Jerusalem is related by Josephus. The famine during the siege became so great that they ate what the most sordid animals refused to touch. A woman of distinguished rank, having been plundered by the soldiers, in hunger, rage, and despair, killed and roasted her own babe, and had eaten one half of it before the deed was discovered.—*Jewish Wars*, b. vi. ch. 3, § 3, 4. This cruel and dreadful act was also in fulfilment of prophecy, De. xxviii. 53, 56, 57.

Another thing added by Luke (ch. xxi. 24), was, that *they should be led away captive into all nations*. Josephus informs us that the captives taken during the whole war amounted to *ninety-seven thousand*. The tall and handsome young men Titus reserved for triumph; of the rest, many were distributed through the Roman provinces to be destroyed by wild beasts in theatres; many were sent to the works in Egypt; many, especially those under seventeen years of age, were sold for slaves.—*Jewish Wars*, b. vi. ch. 9, § 2, 3.

22. *Except those days should be shortened*. If the calamities of the siege should be lengthened out. If famine and war should be suffered to rage. ¶ *No flesh be saved*. None of the nation would be preserved alive. All the inhabitants of Judea would perish. The war, famine, and pestilence would entirely destroy them. ¶ *But for the elect's sake*. The *elect* here doubtless means *Christians*. See 1 Pe. i. 2; Ro. i. 7; Ep. i. 4; 1 Th. i. 4. The word *elect* means *to choose*. It is given to Christians because they are *chosen to salvation through sanctification of the Spirit and belief of the truth*, 1 Pe. i. 2. It is probable that in Jerusalem and the adjacent parts of

23 Then[u] if any man shall say
unto you, Lo, here *is* Christ, or
there; believe *it* not.
24 For[v] there shall arise false
Christs, and false prophets, [w]and
shall show great signs and wonders; insomuch that, [x]if *it were*
possible, they shall deceive the
very elect.
25 Behold, I have told you before.
26 Wherefore if they shall say

u De.13.1-3. *v* ver.5,11. *w* 2 Th.2.9-11; Re.13.13. *x* Jn.10.28,29.

Judea there were many who were true followers of Christ. On *their* account—to preserve them alive, and to make them the instruments of spreading the gospel — Jesus said that those days should not be lengthened out so as to produce their destruction. It is related by Josephus (*Jewish Wars*, b. i. ch. 12, § 1) that Titus at first resolved to reduce the city by famine. He therefore built a wall around it to keep any provisions from being carried in, and any of the people from going out. The Jews, however, drew up their army near the walls, engaged in battle, and the Romans pursued them, provoked by their attempts, and broke into the city. The affairs of Rome, also, at that time demanded the presence of Titus there; and, contrary to his original intention, he pressed the siege and took the city by storm, thus *shortening* the time that *would* have been occupied in reducing it by famine. This was for the benefit of the "elect." So the designs of wicked men, intended *by them* for the destruction of the people of God, are intended by God for the good of his chosen people. See Notes on Is. x. 7.

23. *Lo, here* is *Christ.* The Messiah. The Jews expected the Messiah to deliver them from Roman oppression. In the time of these great calamities they would anxiously look for him. Many would claim *to be* the Messiah. Many would follow those who set up that claim. Many would rejoice to believe that he was come, and would call on others, Christians with the rest, to follow them. ¶ *Believe* it *not.* You have evidence that the Messiah *has* come, and you are not to be deceived by the plausible pretensions of others.

24. *False Christs.* Persons claiming to be the Messiah. ¶ *False prophets.* Persons claiming to be *the prophet* spoken of by Moses (De. xviii. 15); or persons pretending to declare the way of deliverance from the Romans, and calling the people to follow them. See ver. 5. ¶ *Shall show great signs and wonders.* That is, shall pretend to work miracles. They will so *nearly* resemble prophets in their miraculous power as to render it difficult to detect the imposture. Josephus represents the false Christs and prophets that appeared as *magicians* and *sorcerers.* He says they led the people out into the deserts, and promised to work miracles to deliver them, *Antiq.* b. xx. ch. 8, § 6. ¶ *If* it were *possible, they shall deceive the very elect.* So nearly would their pretended miracles resemble true miracles as to render it difficult to detect the imposture; so much so, that if it were possible they would persuade even true Christians that they were the Messiah. But that was not possible. His real friends would be too firmly established in the belief that he was the Christ to be wholly led away by others. Christians may be sometimes led far astray; they may be in doubt about some great doctrines of religion; they may be perplexed by the cavils and cunning craftiness of those who do not love the truth, but they cannot be *wholly* deceived and seduced from the Saviour. Our Saviour says that if this *were possible,* it would be done then; but it was not possible. Comp. Notes on Jn. x. 28, 29.

25. *Behold, I have told you before.* Mark adds (ch. xiii. 23), *take ye heed.* The reason why he told them before was that they might be on their guard, and be prepared for those calamities.

26. *Behold, he is in the desert.* The Jews had formed the expectation that the Messiah would appear suddenly from some unexpected quarter; hence many would be looking to desert places, expecting that he would come from them. Accordingly, most of the impostors and pretended prophets led their people into the deserts. ¶ *Go not forth.* Do not follow them; they will only deceive you. ¶ *In secret chambers.* Concealed in some house, or some retired part of the city. Many would, doubtless, pretend that the Messiah was *concealed* there, and, either for the purpose of encouraging or deceiving the

unto you, Behold, he is in the
desert; go not forth: Behold, *he is*
in the secret chambers; believe *it*
not.
27 For as [y]the lightning cometh
out of the east, and shineth even
unto the west, so shall also the
coming of the Son of man be.
28 For[z] wheresoever the carcase
is, there will the eagles be gathered
together.
29 Immediately after the tribu-

y Zec.9.14; Lu.17.24,&c.

z Job 39.30.

---

people, would pretend that they had discovered him.

27. *For as the lightning cometh out of the east*, &c. This is not designed to denote the *quarter* from which he would come, but the *manner*. He does not mean to affirm that the *Son of man* will come from the *east*, but that he will come in a rapid and unexpected manner, like the lightning. Many would be looking for him in the desert, many in secret places; but he said it would be useless to be looking in that manner; it was useless to look to any particular part of the heavens to know where the lightning would next flash. In a moment it would blaze in an unexpected part of the heavens, and shine at once to the other part. So rapidly, so unexpectedly, in so unlooked-for a quarter, would be his coming. See Lu. x. 18; Zec. ix. 14. ¶ *The coming of the Son of man.* It has been doubted whether this refers to the destruction of Jerusalem, or to the coming at the day of judgment. For the solution of this doubt let it be remarked—1st. That those two events are the principal scenes in which our Lord said he would come, either in person or in judgment. 2d. That the destruction of Jerusalem is described as *his* coming, *his* act. 3d. That these events—the judgment of Jerusalem and the final judgment—in many respects greatly resemble each other. 4th. That they *will bear*, therefore, to be described in the same language; and, 5th, therefore, that the same words often include *both* events, as properly described by them. The words had, doubtless, a primary reference to the destruction of Jerusalem, but they had, at the same time, such an amplitude of meaning as also to express his coming to judgment. See Introduction to Isaiah, § 7, (3).

28. *Wheresoever*, &c. The words in this verse are proverbial. Vultures and eagles easily ascertain where dead bodies are, and hasten to devour them. So with the Roman army. Jerusalem is like a dead and putrid corpse. Its life is gone, and it is ready to be devoured. The Roman armies will find it out, as the vultures do a dead carcass, and will come around it to devour it. This proverb also teaches a universal truth. Wherever wicked men are, there will be assembled the instruments of their chastisement. The providence of God will direct them there, as the eagles are directed to a dead carcass.

This verse is connected with the preceding by the word "for," implying that this is a reason for what is said there—that the Son of man would *certainly* come to destroy the city, and that he would come *suddenly*. The meaning is that he would come, by means of the Roman armies, as certainly, as suddenly, and as unexpectedly as whole flocks of vultures and eagles, though unseen before, see their prey at a great distance and suddenly gather in multitudes around it. Travellers in the deserts of Arabia tell us that they sometimes witness a speck in the distant sky which for a long time is scarcely visible. At length it grows larger, it comes nearer, and they at last find that it is a vulture that has from an immense distance seen a carcass lying on the sand. So keen is their vision as aptly to represent the Roman armies, though at an immense distance, spying, as it were, Jerusalem, a putrid carcass, and hastening in multitudes to destroy it.

29. *Immediately after the tribulation of those days.* That is, immediately after these tribulations, events will occur that *may be properly represented* by the darkening of the sun and moon, and by the stars falling from heaven. The word rendered *immediately*—εὐθέως—means, properly, *straightway*, *forthwith*, Mat. viii. 3; xiii. 5; Mar. i. 31; Ac. xii. 10; then *shortly*, 3 Jn. 14. This is the meaning here. Such events would *shortly* or *soon* occur. In the fulfilment of the predictions they would be *the next in order*, and would occur *before long*. The term here requires us to admit that, in order to the fulfilment

lation of those days [a]shall the sun
be darkened, and the moon shall
not give her light, and the stars
shall fall from heaven, and the
[b]powers of the heavens shall be
shaken.
30 And then shall appear the
sign of [c]the Son of man in heaven:

a Is.13.10; Eze.32.7; Am.5.20; Ac.2.20; Re.6.12.
b 2 Pe.3.10. *c* Da.7.13; Re.1.7.

of the prophecy, it can be shown, or it actually happened, that things *did* soon occur "after the tribulation of those days" which would be *properly represented* or *described* by the images which the Saviour employs. It is not necessary to show that there could not have been *a more remote* reference to events lying far in the future, in which there would be a more complete fulfilment or *filling up* of the meaning of the words (comp. Notes on Mat. i. 22, 23); but it *is* necessary that there should have been events which would be *properly expressed* by the language which the Saviour uses, or which would have been in some proper sense *fulfilled*, even if there had not been reference to more remote events. It will be seen in the exposition that this was actually the case, and that therefore there was a propriety in saying that these events would occur *immediately*—that is, *soon*, or *the next in order*. Comp. Notes on Re. i. 1. ¶ *Shall the sun be darkened*, &c. The images here used are not to be taken literally. They are often employed by the sacred writers to denote *any great calamities*. As the darkening of the sun and moon, and the falling of the stars, would be an inexpressible calamity, so any great catastrophe—any overturning of kingdoms or cities, or dethroning of kings and princes—is represented by the darkening of the sun and moon, and by some terrible convulsion in the elements. Thus the destruction of Babylon is foretold in similar terms (Is. xiii. 10), and of Tyre (Is. xxiv. 23). The slaughter in Bozrah and Idumea is predicted in the same language, Is. xxxiv. 4. See also Is. l. 3; lx. 19, 20; Eze. xxxii. 7; Joel iii. 15. To the description in Matthew, Luke has added (ch. xxi. 25, 26), "And upon the earth distress of nations, with perplexity; the sea and the waves roaring; men's hearts failing them for fear, and for looking after those things which are coming on the earth." All these are figures of great and terrible calamities. The roaring of the waves of the sea denotes great tumult and affliction among the people. *Perplexity* means doubt, anxiety; not knowing what to do to escape. *Men's hearts should fail them for fear*, or by reason of *fear*. Their fears would be so great as to take away their courage and strength.

30. *The sign of the Son of man.* The *evidence* that he is coming to destroy the city of Jerusalem. It is not to be denied, however, that this description is applicable also to his coming at the day of judgment. The disciples had asked him (ver. 3) what should be the sign of his coming, and *of the end of the world*. In his answer he has reference to both events, and his language may be regarded as descriptive of both. At the destruction of Jerusalem, the *sign* or *evidence* of his coming was found in the fulfilment of these predictions. At the end of the world, the sign of his coming will be his personal approach with the glory of his Father and the holy angels, 1 Th. iv. 16; Lu. xxi. 27; Mat. xxvi. 64; Ac. i. 11. ¶ *All the tribes of the earth mourn.* That is, either all the *tribes* or *people* of the land of Judea shall mourn at the great calamities coming upon them, or all the nations of the world shall wail when he comes to judgment. All the wicked shall mourn at the prospect of their doom, Re. i. 7. The *cause* of their wailing at the day of judgment will be chiefly that they have pierced, killed, rejected the Saviour, and that they *deserve* the condemnation that is coming upon them, Jn. xix. 37; Zec. xii. 12. ¶ *And they shall see the Son of man.* The Lord Jesus coming to judgment. Probably this refers more directly to his coming at the last day, though it may also mean that the *evidence* of his coming to destroy Jerusalem will then be seen. ¶ *In the clouds of heaven.* He ascended in a cloud, Ac. i. 9. He shall return in like manner, Ac. i. 11. *The clouds of heaven* denote not the clouds *in* heaven, but the clouds that *appear* to shut heaven, or the sky, from our view. ¶ *With power.* Power, manifest in the destruction of Jerusalem, by the wonders that preceded it, and by the overturning of the temple and city. In the day of judgment, power manifest by consuming the material world (2 Pe. iii. 7, 10, 12); by raising the dead (Jn.

and then shall all the tribes of the earth mourn, and [d]they shall see the Son of man coming in the clouds of heaven, with power and great glory.

d ch.16.27; Mar.13.26; Lu.22.69.

31 And he shall send his angels [1]with a [e]great sound of a trumpet; and they shall [f]gather together his elect from the four winds, from one end of heaven to the other.

1 or, *with a trumpet and a great voice.*
e 1 Th.4.16. *f* Zec.14.5.

v. 29, 30; 1 Co. xv. 52); by changing those who may be alive when he shall come—that is, making their bodies like those who have died, and who have been raised up (1 Th. iv. 17; 1 Co. xv. 52); by bringing the affairs of the world to a close, receiving the righteous to heaven (Mat. xxv. 34; 1 Co. xv. 57), and sending the wicked, however numerous or however strong, down to hell, Mat. xxv. 41, 46; Jn. v. 29. ¶ *Great glory.* The word *glory* here means the visible display of honour and majesty. This glory will be manifested by the manner of his coming (Mat. xxvi. 64), by the presence of the angels (Mat. xxv. 31), and by the wonders that shall attend him down the sky.

31. *And he shall send his angels. Angels* signify, literally, *messengers*, Lu. vii. 24; ix. 52. The word is often applied to *inanimate* objects, or to anything that God employs to rescue his people from danger (Ps. civ. 4); but it most commonly refers to the race of intelligent beings more exalted than man, who are employed often in the work of man's rescue from ruin, and aiding his salvation, He. i. 14. In either of these senses it *might* here refer to deliverance granted to his people in the calamities of Jerusalem. It is said that there is reason to believe that not *one* Christian perished in the destruction of that city, God having in various ways secured their escape, so that they fled to Pella, where they dwelt when the city was destroyed. But the language seems to refer rather to the end of the world, and, no doubt, its *principal* application was intended to be to the gathering of his elect at the day of judgment. ¶ *With a great sound of a trumpet.* The Jewish assemblies used to be called together by the sound of a trumpet, as ours are by bells, Le. xxv. 9; Nu. x. 2; Ju. iii. 27. Hence, when they spoke of convening an assembly, they spoke also of doing it by sounding a trumpet. Our Saviour, speaking to Jews, used language to which they were accustomed, and described the *assembling* of the people at the last day in language which they were accustomed to use in calling assemblies together. It is not certain, however, that he meant that this would be *literally* so, but it may be designed only to denote the certainty that the *world would be assembled together.* Similar language is often used when speaking of the judgment, 1 Th. iv. 16; 1 Co. xv. 52. A *trump*, or *trumpet*, was a wind instrument, made at first of the horns of oxen, and afterward of rams' horns, cut off at the smaller extremity. In some instances it was made of brass, in the form of a horn. The common trumpet was straight, made of brass or silver, a cubit in length, the larger extremity shaped so as to resemble a small bell. In times of peace, in assembling the people, this was sounded softly. In times of calamity, or war, or any great commotion, it was sounded *loud.* Perhaps this was referred to when our Saviour said, with a *great* sound of a trumpet. ¶ *They shall gather together his elect.* Elect. See Notes on ver. 22. The word means *Christians* —the chosen of God. If this refers to the destruction of Jerusalem, it means, "God shall send forth his messengers —whatever he may choose to employ for that purpose: signs, wonders, human messengers, or the angels themselves— and gather Christians into a place of safety, so that they shall not be destroyed with the Jews." If it refers to the last judgment, as it doubtless in a primary or secondary sense does, then it means that he will send his angels to gather his chosen, his elect, together from all places, Mat. xiii. 39, 41-43. This shall be done before the living shall be changed, 1 Co. xv. 51, 52; 1 Th. iv. 16, 17. ¶ *From the four winds.* That is, from the four quarters of the globe— east, west, north, and south. The Jews expressed those quarters by the *winds* blowing from them. See Eze. xxxvii. 9. See also Is. xliii. 5, 6. ¶ *From one end of heaven*, &c. Mark says (xiii. 27), from the uttermost part of the earth to the uttermost part of heaven. The expression denotes that they shall be gathered from all parts of the earth where they

32 Now[g] learn a parable of the fig-tree: When his branch is yet tender, and putteth forth leaves, ye know that summer *is* nigh:
33 So likewise ye, when ye shall see all these things, know that [2]it is near, [h]*even* at the doors.
34 Verily I say unto you, This generation shall not pass till all these things be fulfilled.
35 Heaven[i] and earth shall pass away, but my words shall not pass away.
36 But[k] of that day and hour knoweth no *man*, no, not the angels of heaven, but my Father only.
37 But as the days of Noe *were*, so shall also the coming of the Son of man be.
38 For as in the days that were before the flood they were eating and drinking, marrying and giv-

g Lu.21.29. [2]or, *He.* *h* Ja.5.9. *i* Ps.102.26; Is.51.6.

k Zec.14.7; 1 Th.5.2.

are scattered. The word *heaven* is here used to denote the *visible* heavens or the sky, meaning that through *the whole world* he would gather them. See Ps. xix. 1–7; De. iv. 32.

32. *Now learn a parable.* See Notes on Mat. xiii. 3. The word here means, rather, *an illustration*—make a *comparison*, or judge of this as you do respecting a fig-tree. ¶ *Fig-tree.* This was spoken on the Mount of Olives, which produced not only olives, but figs. Possibly one was near when he spoke this. ¶ *When his branch,* &c. When the juices return from the roots into the branches, and the buds swell and burst, *as if tender*, and too feeble to contain the pressing and expanding leaves—when you see that, you judge that spring and summer are near.

33. *So likewise ye,* &c. In the same manner, when you see what I have predicted—the *signs* around Jerusalem—then know that its destruction is at hand. ¶ *Is near.* Luke says (xxi. 28), *your redemption draweth nigh*, and (xxi. 31) *the kingdom of God is nigh at hand.* Your deliverance from the dangers that threaten the city approaches, and the kingdom of God will be set up in the earth; or your everlasting redemption from sin and death will come at the day of judgment, and his eternal kingdom will be established in the heavens.

34. *This generation,* &c. This age; this race of men. A generation is about thirty or forty years. The destruction of Jerusalem took place about forty years after this was spoken. See Notes on Mat. xvi. 28. ¶ *Till all these things,* &c. Till these things shall be accomplished. Till events shall take place which shall be a fulfilment of these words, if there were nothing farther intended. He does not mean to *exclude* the reference to the judgment, but to say that the destruction of Jerusalem would be such as to make *appropriate* the words of the prediction, were there nothing beyond. Comp. Notes on Mat. i. 22, 23. So when *death* was threatened to Adam, the propriety of the threatening would have been seen, and the threatening would have been fulfilled, had men suffered only *temporal death.* At the same time the threatening had *a fulness of meaning* that would cover also, and justify, eternal death. Thus the words of Christ describing the destruction of Jerusalem had a fulness of signification that would meet also the events of the judgment, and whose meaning would not be *entirely filled up* till the world was closed.

35. *Heaven and earth shall pass away,* &c. You may sooner expect to see the heaven and earth pass away and return to nothing, than my words to fail.

36. *But of that day and hour.* Of the precise time of the fulfilment. The *general signs* of its approach have been given, as the budding of the fig-tree is a *certain* indication that summer is near; but *the precise time* is not indicated by these things. One part of their inquiry was (ver. 3) *when* those things should be. He now replies to them by saying that the *precise* time would not be foretold. Comp. Notes on Ac. i. 7. ¶ *Knoweth no* man, *no, not the angels.* See Notes on Mar. xiii. 32.

37. *Noe.* The Greek way of writing *Noah.* See Ge. vi., vii., viii., ix. The coming of the Son of man would be as it was in the days of Noah—1st. In its being sudden and unexpected, the *precise time* not being made known, though the *general* indications had been given. 2d. The world would be found as it was then.

38. *For as in the days,* &c. The things mentioned here denote attention to the

ing in marriage, [l]until the day that Noe entered into the ark,

39 And knew not, until the flood came and took them all away; so shall also the coming of the Son of man be.

40 Then shall two be in the field; the one shall be taken, and the other left.

41 Two *women shall be* grinding at the mill; the one shall be taken, and the other left.

42 Watch,[m] therefore; for ye know not what hour your Lord doth come.

43 But know this, that if the goodman of the house had known in what watch the thief would come, he would have watched, and would not have suffered his house to be broken up.

44 Therefore be ye also ready; for in such an hour as ye think not, the Son of man cometh.

45 Who, then, is a faithful and wise servant, whom his lord hath

l Ge.6.2. m Lu.12.39,40; Re.3.3; 16.15.

affairs of this life rather than to what was coming on them. It does not mean that these things were wrong, but only that such was their actual employment, and that they were regardless of what was coming upon them.

39. *They knew not.* That is, they knew not the exact time until it came upon them. *So*, says he, it shall be when the Son of man shall come. They shall not know *the precise time* until he comes, and then they will be found engaged in the ordinary business of life unconcerned.

40. *Then shall two be in the field*, &c. The calamity will come suddenly. There will be no escape for those whom it overtakes. ¶ *One shall be taken.* The word *taken* may mean either to be taken away from the danger—that is, rescued, as Lot was (Lu. xvii. 28, 29), or to be taken away *by death.* Probably the latter is the meaning.

41. *Two* women, &c. Grinding in the East was performed, as it is now, chiefly by hand. The millstones were about 2 feet in diameter and ½ foot in thickness. The lower one was fixed, and the upper one was turned by a handle or crank. This was done by two persons, who sat opposite to each other. One took hold of the mill-handle and turned it half-way round; the other then seized it and completed the revolution. This was done by women—by servants of the lowest order—and was a very laborious employment. See Ex. xi. 5; Job xxxi. 10; Is. xlvii. 2; Ju. xvi. 21. The meaning of this verse is similar to the former. Of two persons sitting *near* to each other, one shall be taken and the other left. The calamity would be sudden, and would come upon them before they were aware.

42. *Watch.* Be looking for his coming. Be expecting it as near; as a great event; as coming in an unexpected manner. Watch the signs of his coming, and be ready.

43. *But know this*, &c. If a man knew the hour, or *about the hour*, when a robber would come, he would be ready for him. So you know not the exact hour, but you know it is near, when the Son of man will come. He will come suddenly, as a thief comes, without giving previous warning, 1 Th. v. 2; 2 Pe. iii. 10; Re. iii. 3; xvi. 15. ¶ *Goodman.* See Notes on Mat. xx. 11. ¶ *Thief.* A robber. A thief, with us, means one who takes goods without doing violence—secretly, silently. The original word means one who does it by housebreaking, or by highway violence, Lu. x. 30. ¶ *Broken up.* Broken into—either by the doors or windows. See Notes on ch. vi. 19. ¶ *In what watch.* In which of the four quarters of the night. See Notes on Mat. xiv. 25.

44. *Be ye also ready.* Luke (xxi. 36) says that he charged them to pray always, that they might be accounted worthy to escape those things—the judgments coming upon the wicked—and to stand before the Son of man—that is, to stand there *approved* by him, or to be admitted to his favour. He also charged them (Lu. xxi. 34) to take heed and not to suffer their hearts to be overcharged with surfeiting, or too much eating, or drunkenness, or the cares of this life, lest that day should come upon them unawares; things improper if there were no judgment—peculiarly mad and wicked when the judgment is near.

45-51. This passage is, in fact, a *parable*, though it is not expressly so called. The design is to show that his disciples should act *as if* they were each mo-

made [n]ruler over his household, [o]to give them meat in due season?

46 Blessed *is* that servant, whom his lord, when he cometh, shall find so doing.

47 Verily I say unto you, that he shall [p]make him ruler over all his goods.

48 But and if that evil servant shall say in his heart, My lord delayeth his coming;

49 And shall begin to smite *his* fellow-servants, and to eat and drink with the drunken;

50 The lord of that servant [q]shall come in a day when he looketh not for *him*, and in an hour that he is not aware of,

51 And shall [3]cut him asunder, and appoint *him* his portion with the hypocrites: [r]there shall be weeping and gnashing of teeth.

n Je.3.15. *o* ch.13.52. *p* ch.25.21.

q 1 Th.5.3; Re.3.3. 3 or, *cut him off*. *r* ch.25.30.

ment expecting his return. This he illustrates by the conduct of a servant who did not expect his master soon to return, who acted with great impropriety, and who was accordingly punished.

45. *Who, then, is a faithful and wise servant*, &c. By the conduct of a faithful and wise servant Jesus intends to denote a faithful Christian, a servant of God, or a teacher of religion. ¶ *Whom his lord.* His master. The word here has no reference to God. It means the *lord* or master of the servant. Applied to Christian teachers, in the spiritual meaning of the parable, it refers to *Christ*, who has appointed them as teachers, and who is their Lord and Master, Jn. xiii. 13, 14. ¶ *Over his household.* His family. Christian ministers are the servants of God appointed over the church, the family of Christ, 1 Th. v. 12, 13; 1 Co. iii. 5; iv. 1, 2; xii. 28. ¶ *Meat in due season.* The word *meat* here means food of all kinds. When the Bible was translated into English, the word included, as the original does, all kinds of provisions requisite to support and nourish life. ¶ *In due season.* As they need it, or in the accustomed times. This was the office of a steward. Among the ancients this office was often filled by *a slave*—one who had shown himself trusty and faithful. The duty was to have a general superintendence over the affairs of the family. Applied to Christian ministers, it means that they are to feed the flock of God, to *minister* to their wants, and to do it as they need it, Jn. xxi. 15-17; Ac. xx. 28; 1 Co. iv. 1, 2.

47. *Shall make him ruler*, &c. Shall confirm his appointment over his household, and, as a reward, shall place him over *all* his property. This does not mean that ministers will have a higher rank or office, but is a circumstance *of the parable* or story, designed to show the effect of faithfulness. Faithful servants of Christ shall be rewarded. This will be done by *his* approbation, and by the rewards of the heavenly world.

48. *That evil servant.* If that servant, so appointed, having this office, should be evil or wicked. ¶ *Say in his heart.* Secretly suppose. ¶ *Delayeth his coming.* Will not return in a long time; or does not return as soon as was expected, and perhaps may not at all.

49. *Smite* his *fellow-servants*, &c. This is the conduct of a wicked servant, who, supposing he would not be called to account, and abusing his authority, gave himself up to oppression, carousing, and debauchery. It is designed to represent the conduct of ministers who are unfaithful and overbearing, and who abuse their trust in the church.

51. *Shall cut him asunder.* This kind of punishment was anciently practised. Sometimes it was done by the sword, sometimes by saws. It was practised among the Chaldeans (Da. ii. 5; iii. 29), and among the Hebrews, 2 Sa. xii. 31; 1 Sa. xv. 33; 1 Ki. iii. 25; He. xi. 37. It was also practised by the Egyptians and Romans. It is not, perhaps, here to be taken *literally*, but signifies that the wicked servant should be severely punished. ¶ *Hypocrites.* See Notes on Mat. vi. 2. They are spoken of here as the worst of men. ¶ *Weeping and gnashing of teeth.* See Notes on Mat. viii. 12, 13. The unfaithful and wicked minister of God, who lives without expectation or fear of judgment, shall suffer the severest punishment inflicted on sinners in the world of woe.

CHAPTER XXV.

1. *Then shall the kingdom of heaven.* See Notes on Mat. iii. 2. The phrase

CHAPTER XXV.

THEN shall the kingdom of heaven be likened unto ten virgins,[a] which took their lamps, and went forth to meet [b]the bridegroom.

2 And [c]five of them were wise, and five *were* foolish.

a Ps.45.14; Ca.6.8,9; 2 Co.11.2. b Jn.3.29. c Je.24.2-9; ch.22.10.

---

here refers to his coming in the day of judgment. ¶ *Shall be likened.* Or shall resemble. The meaning is, "When the Son of man returns to judgment, it will be as it was in the case of ten virgins in a marriage ceremony." The coming of Christ to receive his people to himself is often represented under the similitude of a marriage, the church being represented as his spouse or bride. The marriage relation is the most tender, firm, and endearing of any known on earth, and on this account it fitly represents the union of believers to Christ. See Mat. ix. 15; Jn. iii. 29; Re. xix. 7; xxi. 9; Ep. v. 25-32. ¶ *Ten virgins.* These virgins, doubtless, represent the church—a name given to it because it is pure and holy. See 2 Co. xi. 2; La. i. 15; ii. 13. ¶ *Which took their lamps, and went forth to meet the bridegroom.* The *lamps* used on such occasions were rather *torches* or *flambeaux*. They were made by winding rags around pieces of iron or earthenware, sometimes hollowed so as to contain oil, and fastened to handles of wood. These torches were dipped in oil, and gave a large light. Marriage ceremonies in the East were conducted with great pomp and solemnity. The *ceremony* of marriage was performed commonly in the open air, on the banks of a stream. Both the bridegroom and bride were attended by friends. They were escorted in a *palanquin*, carried by four or more persons. After the ceremony of marriage succeeded a feast of seven days if the bride was a virgin, or three days if she was a widow. This feast was celebrated in her father's house. At the end of that time the bridegroom conducted the bride with great pomp and splendour to his own home. This was done in the evening, or at night, Je. vii. 34; xxv. 10; xxxiii. 11. Many friends and relations attended them; and besides those who went with them from the house of the bride, there was another company that came out from the house of the bridegroom to meet them and welcome them. These were probably female friends and relatives of the bridegroom, who went out to welcome him and his new companion to their home. These are the virgins mentioned in this parable. Not knowing *precisely* the time when the procession would come, they probably went out early, and waited till they should see indications of its approach. In the celebration of marriage in the East at the present day, many of the peculiar customs of ancient times are observed. "At a Hindoo marriage," says a modern missionary, "the procession of which I saw some years ago, the bridegroom came from a distance, and the bride lived at Serampore, to which place the bridegroom was to come by water. After waiting two or three hours, at length, near midnight, it was announced, in the very words of Scripture, '*Behold the bridegroom cometh; go ye out to meet him.*' All the persons employed now lighted their lamps, and ran with them in their hands to fill up their stations in the procession. Some of them had lost their lights and were unprepared, but it was then too late to seek them, and the cavalcade moved forward to the house of the bride, at which place the company entered a large and splendidly illuminated area before the house, covered with an awning, where a great multitude of friends, dressed in their best apparel, were seated upon mats. The bridegroom was carried in the arms of a friend, and placed in a superb seat in the midst of the company, where he sat a short time, and then went into the house, the door of which was immediately shut and guarded by sepoys. I and others expostulated with the doorkeepers, but in vain. Never was I so struck with our Lord's beautiful parable as at this moment—*And the door was shut.*"

The journal of one of the American missionaries in Greece contains an account of an Armenian wedding which she attended; and, after describing the dresses and previous ceremonies, she says that at twelve o'clock at night precisely the cry was made by some of the attendants, *Behold, the bridegroom cometh;* and immediately five or six men set off to meet him. ¶ *Bridegroom.* A man newly married.

2, 3, 4. *And five of them were wise.*

3 They that *were* foolish took
their lamps, and took [d]no oil with
them:
4 But the wise [e]took oil in their
vessels with their lamps.
5 While the bridegroom tarried,
they all [f]slumbered and slept.
6 And at [g]midnight there was a
cry[h] made, Behold, the bridegroom
cometh; [i]go ye out to meet him.

d Is.48.1. e 1 Jn.2.20. f 1 Th.5.6. g Re.16.15. h 1 Th.4.16. i Am.4.12.

7 Then all those virgins arose,
and trimmed their lamps.
8 And the foolish said unto the
wise, Give us of your oil; [k]for our
lamps are [1]gone out.
9 But the wise answered, saying,
Not so; lest there be not enough
for us and you: but [l]go ye rather
to them that sell, and buy for yourselves.

k Lu.12.35. 1 or, *going out.* l Is.55.1,6.

The words *wise* and *foolish*, here, refer only to their conduct in regard to the oil. The one part was *wise* in taking oil, the other *foolish* in neglecting it. The conduct of those who were *wise* refers to those who are *prepared* for the coming of Christ—prepared by possessing *real* piety, and not being merely his professed followers. The conduct of those *without* oil expresses the conduct of those who *profess* to love him, but are destitute of true grace, and are therefore unprepared to meet him. Nothing can be argued from the *number* here in regard to the proportion of sincere Christians among professors. *Circumstances* in parables are not to be pressed literally. They are necessary to keep up the story, and we must look chiefly or entirely to the *scope* or *design* of the parable to understand its meaning. In this parable the scope is to teach us to *watch* or be ready, ver. 13. It is *not* to teach us the relative *number* of those who shall be saved and who shall not. In teaching us to *watch* and *to be ready*, our Lord gives great additional interest by the circumstances of this narrative; but there is no authority for saying that he meant to teach that *just half* of professing Christians would be deceived. The moral certainty is that *nothing like* that number will be found to have been hypocrites. ¶ *Oil in their vessels.* The five foolish virgins probably expected that the bridegroom would come immediately; they therefore made no provision for any delay. The wise virgins knew that the time of his coming was uncertain, and they therefore furnished themselves with oil. This was carried in vessels, so that it could be poured on the torches when it was necessary. ¶ *Vessels.* Cups, cans, or anything to hold oil.

5. *The bridegroom tarried.* That is, while they waited for him. It was uncertain at what time he would come. He delayed longer than they expected. ¶ *All slumbered and slept.* Waiting till near midnight, they fell into repose. This circumstance is not to be pressed to prove that all *Christians* will be asleep, or cold and careless, when the Lord Jesus shall come. *Many* may be so, but many, also, will be looking for his coming. This circumstance is designed simply to show more clearly the *duty of being ready*, ver. 13. It does not mean to affirm it as *a fact* that none will be ready.

6. *At midnight.* Later than was the usual custom, and hence they had fallen asleep. ¶ *A cry made.* Of those who were coming with the bridegroom.

7. *Trimmed their lamps.* Burning till midnight, the oil was exhausted: they gave a dim and obscure light. They trimmed them by removing the burnt parts of the *linen* or the torch, so that they would burn clear. It was needful, also, to dip them again in oil, or to pour oil upon them. This strikingly represents the conduct of most men at the approach of death. They *then* begin to make ready. They are alarmed, anxious, and trembling, and then they ask the aid of others, but often when it is for ever too late.

10. *Went in with him to the marriage.* The *marriage-feast.* The marriage *ceremony* took place before the bride left her father's house, but a feast was given at the house of her husband, which was also called the *marriage*, or a part of the marriage solemnities. This part of the parable doubtless represents the entrance of those who *are ready*, or prepared, into the kingdom of God, when the Son of man shall come. They will be *ready* who have repented of their sins; who truly believe on the Lord Jesus; who live a holy life; and who wait for his coming. See Mar. xvi. 16; Jn. v. 24; Ac. iii. 19; Re. xxiii.

10 And [m]while they went to buy, the bridegroom came; and they that were ready went in with him to the marriage: [n]and the door was shut.

11 Afterward came also the other virgins, saying, [o]Lord, Lord, open to us.

12 But he answered and said, Verily I say unto you, [p]I know you not.

13 Watch,[q] therefore, for ye know neither the day nor the hour wherein the Son of man cometh.

14 For[r] *the kingdom of heaven is* as a man travelling into a far

m Am.8.12,13. *n* He.3.18,19; Re.22.11. *o* ch.7.21-23; He.12.17.

p Hab.1.13. *q* ch.24.42,44; Mar.13.33,35; Lu.21.36. *r* Lu.19.12,&c.

11; 2 Pe. iii. 11, 12; 1 Ti. vi. 17-19; 2 Ti. iv. 6-8. ¶ *The door was shut.* No more could be admitted to the marriage-feast. So, when the truly righteous shall all be received into heaven, the door will be closed against all others. There will be no room for preparation afterward, Re. xxii. 11; Ec. xi. 3; ix. 10; Mat. xxv. 46.

11. *Open unto us.* This is not to be understood as implying that any will come after the righteous shall be admitted into the kingdom, and claim admission then. It is a part of the *parable* to illustrate the general truth inculcated, or to prepare the way for what is afterwards said, and to keep up the narrative and make it consistent.

12. *I know you not.* You were not in the company of those who attended me to the marriage-feast, and are unknown to me. Applied to professing Christians, having *only* a profession of religion, but no real piety, it means, I do not know or *acknowledge* you as Christians. I do not approve of you, or delight in you, or admit that you are my friends. The word *know* is often used in the sense of approving, loving, acknowledging as real friends and followers. See Mat. vii. 23; Ps. i. 6; 2 Ti. ii. 19; 1 Th. v. 12.

13. *Watch, therefore,* &c. This is the scope or design of the whole parable. This is the great truth that Christ wished to inculcate, and all parts of the parable are to be interpreted in reference to this admonition. Like the virgins, many are professedly going to meet the Bridegroom—the Lord Jesus Christ. Like the coming of the bridegroom, his advent will be sudden. It will be to many at an unexpected time. Many, even professing Christians, will be engaged in the business of the world; thoughtless about eternity; not expecting his approach, and not prepared. They will only *profess* to know him, but in *works* they will deny him. So death will come. All approaches of the Son of God to judge men are *sudden,* and to many unexpected. So many, when they shall see him coming, at death or the judgment, will begin, like the foolish virgins, to be active, and to prepare to die; but it will be too late. They that are ready will enter in, and heaven will be closed for ever against all others. The *coming* of the Saviour is certain. The precise time *when* he will come is not certain. As the virgins should all have watched and been ready, so should we. They who are Christians should be ever watchful; and they who are not should lose no time to be ready, for in such an hour as they think not the Son of man shall come. ¶ *The Son of man cometh.* This refers, doubtless, to his coming in the day of judgment. The circumstances of the parable do not seem at all to apply to his coming to destroy Jerusalem, but are aptly expressive of his advent to judge the world.

14. *For* the kingdom of heaven, &c. The *parable of the talents* was spoken still farther to illustrate the manner in which he would deal with men at his return to judgment. The words *the kingdom of heaven* are not in the original, but are very properly inserted by the translators. The design of the parable is to teach that those who improve their talents or faculties in the cause of religion—who improve them to their own salvation and in doing good to others—shall be proportionally rewarded; but they who neglect their talents, and who neither secure their own salvation nor do good to others, will be punished. The kingdom of heaven is like such a man—that is, *God deals with men in his government as such a man did.* ¶ *His own servants.* That is, such of them as he judged to be worthy of such a trust. These represent the apostles, Christian ministers, professing Christians, and perhaps all men. The going into a far country

country, *who* called his own servants, and delivered unto them his goods.

15 And unto one he gave five talents,[2] to another two, and to another one; [s]to every man according to his several ability; and straightway took his journey.

16 Then he that had received the five talents went and traded with the same, and made *them* other five talents.

17 And likewise he that *had received* two, he also gained other two.

18 But he that had received one went and digged in the earth, and hid his lord's money.

19 After a [t]long time, the lord of those servants cometh, and [u]reckoneth with them.

20 And so he that had received five talents came, and brought other five talents, saying, Lord, thou deliveredst unto me five talents; behold, I have gained beside them five talents more.

21 His lord said unto him, Well done, *thou* good and faithful servant: thou hast been faithful over a

2 A talent is £187, 10s., ch.18.24.
s Ro.12.6; 1 Co.12.4,&c.; Ep.4.11.
t ch.24.48. *u* ch.18.23,24.

---

may represent the Lord Jesus going into heaven. He has given to all talents to improve, Ep. iv. 8; ii. 12. ¶ *His goods.* His property—representing the offices, abilities, and opportunities for doing good, which he has given to his professed followers.

15. *Five talents.* See Notes on Mat. xviii. 24. The word *talents* here is used to denote indefinitely *a large sum*, and is designed to refer to the endowments conferred on men. We have retained in our language the word *talent* as referring to the abilities or gifts of men. ¶ *According to his several ability.* According to the ability of each one. According as he saw each one was adapted to improve it. So in the church and the world. God gives men stations which he judges them adapted to fill, and requires them to fill them. He makes *distinctions* among men in regard to abilities, and in the powers and opportunities of usefulness, requiring them only to occupy those stations, and to discharge their duties there, 1 Co. iv. 7.

16, 17. The two who had received most employed their money in trade, and by honest industry doubled it before their master returned, representing the conduct of those who make a good improvement of their abilities, and employ them in doing good.

18. *Digged in the earth*, &c. This represents the conduct of those who neglect the abilities that God has given, and fail to do what he has required. This is done often: 1st. On the plea that they do not occupy a high station. 2d. That they have slender abilities, and can do little good. 3d. As it was in this case, that God had not given them as much as he did others, and they will therefore do nothing. These pleas are without foundation; for, First. God does not require us to do as much as those who have greater abilities; but this is not a reason why we should do nothing, 2 Co. viii. 12. Second. Any situation is honourable, and may be useful, where God has placed us; and though humble, yet in that we may do much good, 1 Co. xii. 11–31. Third. Men of slender abilities may often do more good in the world than men of much greater talents. It is rather a *warm heart* than a *strong head* which is required to do good. A humble Christian, by his life, example, and conversation, may often do much more good than *is* done by those in more elevated stations and with far greater gifts.

We are not to suppose by this, however, that our Saviour meant to teach that only those of *feeble* talents neglected their duty. The parable does not require us to do this; and the *fact* is, perhaps, that those most highly endowed are the farthest from properly improving their talents.

19. *After a long time*, &c. By the return of the lord of those servants to reckon with them is denoted the return of Christ to call men to an account for the manner in which they have improved their talents. See Ro. xiv. 12; 2 Co. v. 10; 1 Th. iv. 16; Ac. i. 11; xvii. 31. ¶ *Reckon with them.* To reckon is to settle accounts. Here it means to inquire into their faithfulness, and to reward or punish them accordingly.

few things, I will make thee [v]ruler over many things: enter thou into the joy of thy lord.

22 He also that had received two talents came, and said, Lord, thou deliveredst unto me two talents: behold, I have gained two other talents beside them.

23 His lord said unto him, Well done, good and faithful servant: thou hast been faithful over a few things, I will make thee ruler over many things: enter thou into the joy of thy lord.

24 Then he which had received the one talent came, and said, Lord, I knew thee that thou art [w]an hard man, [x]reaping where thou hast not sown, and gathering where thou hast not strawed:

25 And I was [y]afraid, and went and hid thy talent in the earth: lo, *there* thou hast *that is* thine.

26 His lord answered and said unto him, [z]*Thou* wicked and slothful servant, thou knewest that I reap where I sowed not, and gather where I have not strawed:

v Lu.12.44; 22.29; Re.3.21.

w Job 21.15. *x* Je.2.31. *y* Pr.26.13; Re.21.8. *z* Job 15.5,6; ch.18.32; Lu.19.22; Jude 15.

---

20. *I have gained.* Gained by trading or by honest industry, ver. 16.

21. *Ruler over many things.* I will promote thee to greater honours and to more important trusts. ¶ *Joy of thy lord.* In the meantime share the pleasures and enjoyments of his palace; be his companion, and receive the rewards which he has promised thee. *The joy of his lord* may mean either the festivals and rejoicings at his return, or the rewards which his lord had prepared for his faithful servants. Applied to Christians, it means that they who rightly improve their talents will, at the return of Christ, be promoted to great honours in heaven, and be partakers of the joys of their Lord in the world of glory. See ver. 34; also 1 Jn. ii. 28.

24. *The one talent.* The design of this part of the parable is to show that no one is excused for neglecting his duty because he has few talents. God will require of him only according to his ability, 1 Co. iv. 2; Lu. xii. 48; 2 Co. viii. 12. ¶ *A hard man.* Of a sordid, griping disposition; taking advantage of the poor, and oppressing them. ¶ *Reaping,* &c. This is indicative of an avaricious and overbearing disposition; compelling the poor to sow for him, and reaping all the benefit himself. ¶ *Hast not strawed.* The word *straw* means to *scatter*—as men scatter seed in sowing it. It may mean, also, to *ventilate,* or to *fan* by *ventilating* or winnowing. As *sowing* the seed is mentioned just before, it may be that this refers to gathering grain fanned or winnowed by others, while he did nothing—indicating, also, a hard or sordid disposition.

25. *I was afraid.* I feared lest, by some accident, thy talent would be lost if I put it out to trade, and that I should be severely punished by a hard master. I therefore kept it laid up safely, and hid it where it could not be lost. ¶ That is *thine.* There is what properly belongs to thee. There is the original talent that thou gavest me, and that is all that can be reasonably required. Observe here—1st. That this expresses exactly the feelings of all sinners. God, in their view, is hard, cruel, unjust. 2d. All the excuses of sinners are excuses for indolence and sin, and the effect is to cheat themselves out of heaven. The effect of this excuse was that the reward was lost, and such will always be the result of the excuses of sinners for not doing their duty. 3d. Sinners grudge everything to God. They are never willing to be liberal toward him, but are stinted and close; and if they give, they do it with hard feelings, and say that *that* is all that he can claim.

26. *Slothful.* Indolent, lazy, who had done nothing. God will judge men not merely for doing wrong, but for *not doing* right. See ver. 45. That servant was *wicked,* because he had such an opinion of his master; he had shown that he was slothful by not making good use of the talent, ver. 27. ¶ *Thou knewest,* &c. This should be understood, and might have been translated, as a question. If you knew that I was such a man you ought to have acted accordingly, so as to have escaped punishment. Didst thou know that I reap, &c.? Then thou shouldst have given my money to the exchangers, &c. This is not in-

27 Thou oughtest therefore to
have put my money to the exchangers, and *then* at my coming
I should have received mine own
with usury.
28 Take, therefore, the talent
from him, and give *it* unto him
which hath ten talents.
29 For[a] unto every one that hath
shall be given, and he shall have
abundance; but from him that hath
not shall be [b]taken away even that
which he hath.
30 And cast ye the unprofitable
servant into [c]outer darkness: there
shall be weeping and gnashing of
teeth.
31 When[d] the Son of man shall

a ch.13.12; Mar.4.25; Lu.8.18; 19.26.

b Lu.10.42. c ch.8.12.
d Da.7.13; Zec.14.5; ch.16.27; 19.28; Mar.8.38; Ac. 1.11; 1 Th.4.16; 2 Th.1.7; Jude 14; Re.1.7.

tended to *admit* that he was such a man, but to convict the slothful servant of guilt and folly in not having been prepared to meet him.

27. *The exchangers.* The *exchangers* were persons who were in the habit of borrowing money, or receiving it on deposit at a low rate of interest, to be loaned to others at higher interest. They commonly sat by *tables* in the temple, with money ready to exchange or loan. See Mat. xxi. 12. This money was left with the servant, not to exchange, nor to increase it by any such idle means, but by honest industry and merchandise; but since he was too indolent for that, he ought at least to have loaned it to the exchangers, that his master might have received some benefit from it. ¶ *With usury.* With interest, increase, or gain. The word *usury*, in our language, has a bad signification, meaning unlawful or exorbitant interest. This was contrary to the law, Ex. xxii. 25; Le. xxv. 36. The original means *gain*, increase, or lawful interest.

29. *For unto every one that hath shall be given.* See Notes on Mat. xiii. 12. This seems to be a proverbial expression. It means, whosoever rightly improves what is committed to him shall receive more, or shall be rewarded; but he that misimproves what is committed to him shall *not* be rewarded. In pecuniary matters—in the *literal* sense of this parable—they who improve their money by industry or merchandise increase it. They who do not—who are indolent or vicious—lose what they did possess, and it goes into the hands of the faithful and industrious. In the spiritual sense of the parable it means that they who are faithful shall be rewarded—not, however, that anything shall be taken from the unfaithful and given to them; and it means also that the unfaithful and indolent shall be taken away from their privileges and punished.

30. *And cast*, &c. See Notes on Mat. viii. 12. The spiritual meaning of the parable may be thus summed up: 1st. The servants of God are not all endowed with equal gifts and talents. 2d. All, whatever may be their ability, are bound to employ their talents in promoting his honour, and in a proper improvement of them. 3d. By employing their talents in a proper manner, they improve and strengthen them. 4th. They will be judged according to the improvements which they have made. 5th. All sinners look on God as a hard master, and as unreasonable and tyrannical. 6th. Men will be judged not merely for *doing wrong*, but for *neglecting to do right.* 7th. If the servant who kept the talent entire without injuring it, and who returned it to his master as he received it, was nevertheless judged, condemned, and cast away, what must they expect who abuse their talents, destroy by drunkenness and lust the noble faculties conferred on them, and squander the property that might be employed in advancing the interests of morals and religion!

31. *When the Son of man*, &c. This is in answer to the question which the disciples proposed to Jesus respecting the end of the world, ch. xxiv. 3. That this refers to the last judgment, and not, as some have supposed, to the destruction of Jerusalem, appears—1st. From the fact that it was in answer to an express inquiry respecting *the end* of the world. 2d. *All nations* were to be assembled, which did not take place at the destruction of Jerusalem. 3d. A separation was to take place between the righteous and the wicked, which was not done at Jerusalem. 4th. The rewards and punishments are declared to be *eternal.* None of these things took place at the destruction of Jerusalem. ¶ *In his glory.* In his own

come in his glory, and all the holy
angels with him, then shall he sit
upon the throne of his glory:
32 And[e] before him shall be
gathered all nations; and he[f] shall
separate them one from another,
as a [g]shepherd divideth *his* sheep
from the goats:
33 And he shall set the sheep
on his [h]right hand, but the goats
on the left.
34 Then shall the King say unto
them on his right hand, Come, [i]ye
blessed of my Father, [k]inherit the
[l]kingdom [m]prepared for you from
the foundation of the world:

e Ro.14.10; 2 Co.5.10; Re.20.12.
f Eze.20.38; ch.13.49. *g* Ps.78.52; Jn.10.14,27.
h He.1.3. *i* Ps.115.15.
k Ro.8.17; 1 Pe.1.4. *l* 1 Th.2.12; Re.5.10.
m 1 Co.2.9; He.11.16.

---

proper honour. With his glorified body, and as the head and king of the universe, Ac. i. 11; Ep. i. 20–22; 1 Th. iv. 16; 1 Co. xv. 24, 25, 52. ¶ *The throne of his glory.* This means, in the language of the Hebrews, his glorious or splendid throne. It is not to be taken literally, as if there would be a material throne or seat for the King of Zion. It expresses the idea that he will come *as a king and judge* to assemble his subjects before him, and to appoint them their rewards.

32. *And before him*, &c. At his coming to judgment the world will be burned up, 2 Pe. iii. 10, 12; Re. xx. 11. The dead in Christ—that is, all true Christians—will be raised up from their graves, 1 Th. iv. 16. The living will be changed—*i.e.* will be made like the glorified bodies of those that are raised from the dead, 1 Co. xv. 52–54; 1 Th. iv. 17. All the wicked will rise and come forth to judgment, Jn. v. 28, 29; Da. xii. 2; Mat. xiii. 41, 42; Re. xx. 13. Then shall the world be judged, the righteous saved, and the wicked punished. ¶ *And he shall separate,* &c. Shall determine respecting their character, and shall appoint them their doom accordingly.

33. *Shall set the sheep*, &c. By *the sheep* are denoted, here, the righteous. The name is given to them because the sheep is an emblem of innocence and harmlessness. See Jn. x. 7, 14, 15, 16, 27; Ps. c. 3; lxxiv. 1; xxiii. ¶ *On the right hand.* The right hand is the place of honour, and denotes the situation of those who *are* honoured, or those who are virtuous. See Ec. x. 2; Ep. i. 20; Ps. cx. 1; Ac. ii. 25, 33. ¶ *The goats.* The wicked. See Eze. xxxiv. 17. ¶ *The left.* That is, the left hand. This was the place of dishonour, denoting condemnation. See Ec. x. 2.

34. *The King.* That is, the Lord Jesus, the King of Zion and of the universe, now acting as Judge, Lu. xix. 38; Jn. xviii. 37; Re. xvii. 14; xix. 16. ¶ *Blessed of my Father.* Made happy or raised to felicity by my Father. See Notes on Mat. v. 3. ¶ *Inherit the kingdom.* Receive *as heirs* the kingdom, or be received there as the sons of God. Christians are often called heirs of God, Ro. viii. 17; Ga. iv. 6, 7; He. i. 14; 1 Jn. iii. 2. ¶ *Prepared for you*, &c. That is, *designed* for you, or appointed for you. The phrase *from the foundation of the world* is used to denote that this was appointed for them in the beginning; that God has no new plan; that the rewards which he will now confer on them he always *intended* to confer. Christ says to the righteous that the kingdom was prepared for *them.* Of course, God meant to confer it on *them.* They were individuals, and it follows that he intended to bestow his salvation on them *as* individuals. Accordingly, the salvation of his people is universally represented as the result of the free gift of God, according to his own pleasure, bestowed on individuals, and by a plan which is eternal, Ro. viii. 29, 30; Ep. i. 4, 5, 11, 12; 2 Th. ii. 13; 1 Pe. i. 2; Jn. vi. 37. This is right and consistent with justice; for, 1st. All men are by nature equally undeserving. 2d. Bestowing favours on one does not do injustice to another, where neither deserves favour. Pardoning one criminal is not injuring another. Bestowing great talents on Locke, Newton, or Paul did not injure me. 3d. If it is right for God to *give* eternal life to his people, or to *admit* them to heaven, it was right to *determine* to do it, which is but another way of saying that God resolved from all eternity to *do right.* 4th. Those who perish *choose* the paths which lead to death, and *will* not be saved by the merits of Jesus. No blame can be charged on God if he does not save them against their will, Jn. v. 40; Mar. xvi. 15, 16.

35 For[n] I was an hungered, and
ye gave me meat: I was thirsty,
and ye gave me drink: I was [o]a
stranger, and ye took me in:
36 Naked,[p] and ye clothed me: I
was sick, and [q]ye visited me: I was
in[r] prison, and ye came unto me.
37 Then shall the righteous
answer him, saying, Lord, when
saw we thee an hungered, and fed
thee? or thirsty, and gave *thee*
drink?
38 When saw we thee a stranger,
and took *thee* in? or naked, and
clothed *thee?*
39 Or when saw we thee sick, or
in prison, and came unto thee?
40 And the King shall answer
and say unto them, Verily I say
unto you, [s]Inasmuch as ye have
done *it* unto one of the least of
these my brethren, ye have done
it unto me.
41 Then shall he say also unto

n Is.58.7; Eze.18.7. *o* 1 Pe.4.9; 3 Jn.5. *p* Ja.2.15,16. *q* Ja.1.27. *r* 2 Ti.1.16; He.13.2.

s Pr.19.17; Mar.9.41; He.6.10.

35, 36. *I was an hungered.* The union between Christ and his people is the most tender and endearing of all connections. It is represented by the closest unions of which we have knowledge, Jn. xv. 4–6; Ep. v. 23–32; 1 Co. vi. 15. This is a union—not physical, but moral; a union of feelings, interests, plans, destiny; or, in other words, he and his people have similar feelings, love the same objects, share the same trials, and inherit the same blessedness, Jn. xiv. 19; Re. iii. 5, 21; Ro. viii. 17. Hence he considers favours shown to his people as shown to himself, and will reward them accordingly, Mat. x. 40, 42. They show attachment to him, and love to his cause. By showing kindness to the poor, the needy, and the sick, they show that they possess *his* spirit, for he did it when on earth; they evince attachment to him, for *he* was poor and needy; and they show that they have the proper spirit to fit them for heaven, 1 Jn. iii. 14, 17; Ja. ii. 1–5; Mar. ix. 41. ¶ *Was a stranger.* The word *stranger* means a *foreigner* or traveller; in our language, one unknown to us. To receive such to the rites of hospitality was, in Eastern countries, where there were few or no public houses, a great virtue. See Ge. xviii. 1–8; He. xiii. 2. ¶ *Took me in.* Into your house. Received me kindly. ¶ *Naked.* Poorly clothed. Among the Jews they were called *naked* who were clad in poor raiment, or who had on only the *tunic* or inner garment, without any outer garment. See Notes on Mat. v. 40; also Ac. xix. 16; Mar. xiv. 51, 52; Job xxii. 6; Is. lviii. 7.

37–39. *Then shall the righteous,* &c. This answer is indicative of humility—a deep sense of their being unworthy such commendation. They will feel that their poor acts of kindness have come so far short of what they *should* have been, that they have no claim to praise or reward. It is not, however, to be supposed that in the day of judgment this will be actually *said* by the righteous, but that this would be a proper expression of their feelings.

40. *One of the least of these.* One of the obscurest, the least known, the poorest, the most despised and afflicted. ¶ *My brethren.* Either those who are Christians, whom he condescends to call brethren, or those who are afflicted, poor, and persecuted, who are his brethren and companions in suffering, and who suffer as he did on earth. See He. ii. 11; Mat. xii. 50. How great is the condescension and kindness of the Judge of the world, thus to reward our actions, and to consider what *we* have done to the poor as done to him!

41. *On the left hand.* The wicked. ¶ *Ye cursed.* That is, you who are devoted to destruction, whose characters deserve everlasting punishment, and who are about to enter into it. *To curse* is the opposite of *to bless.* It implies a negation of all the blessings of heaven, and a positive infliction of eternal sufferings. ¶ *Everlasting fire. Fire,* here, is used to denote punishment. The image is employed to express extreme suffering, as a death by burning is one of the most horrible that can be conceived. The image was taken, probably, from the *fires* burning in the Valley of Hinnom. See Notes on Mat. v. 22. It has been asked whether the wicked will be burned in literal fire, and the common impression has been that they will be. Respecting that, however, it is to be observed—1st. That the *main truth* intended to be taught refers not to the

them on the left hand, [t]Depart from me, ye cursed, into [u]everlasting fire, [v]prepared for the devil and his angels:

42 For I was an hungered, and ye gave me no meat: I was thirsty, and ye gave me no drink:

43 I was a stranger, and ye took me not in: naked, and ye clothed me not: sick, and in prison, and ye visited me not.

44 Then shall they also answer him, saying, Lord, when saw we thee an hungered, or athirst, or a stranger, or naked, or sick, or in prison, and did not minister unto thee?

45 Then shall he answer them, saying, Verily I say unto you, [w]Inasmuch as ye did *it* not to one of the least of these, ye did *it* not to me.

t Lu.13.27. *u* ch.13.40,42; Re.14.11. *v* Jude 6; Re.20.10.

w Zec.2.8; Ac.9.5.

manner of suffering, but to the *certainty* and *intensity* of it. 2d. That the design, therefore, was to present an image of terrific and appalling suffering--an image well represented by fire. 3d. That this image was well known to the Jews (Is. lxvi. 24), and therefore expressed the idea in a very strong manner. 4th. That all the *truth* that Christ intended to convey appears to be expressed in the certainty, intensity, and eternity of future torment. 5th. That there is no distinct affirmation respecting the *mode* of that punishment, where the *mode* was the subject of discourse. 6th. That to us it is a subject of comparatively little consequence what will be the *mode* of punishment. The fact that the wicked will be eternally punished, cursed of God, should awe every spirit, and lead every man to strive most earnestly to secure his salvation. As, however, the *body* will be raised, it is not unreasonable to suppose that a mode of punishment will be adopted suited to the body—perhaps bearing some analogy to suffering here, in its various forms of flames, and racks, and cold, and heat, and disease, and ungratified desire, and remorse—perhaps the concentration of all earthly woes, all that makes man miserable here, poured upon the naked body and spirit of the wicked in hell for ever and ever. ¶ *Prepared for the devil.* The devil is the prince of evil spirits. This place of punishment was fitted up for *him* when he rebelled against God, Jude 6; Re. xii. 8, 9. ¶ *His angels.* His messengers, his servants, or those angels that he drew off from heaven by his rebellion, and whom he has employed as his *messengers* to do evil. The word *may* extend also to *all* his followers—fallen angels or men. There is a remarkable difference between the manner in which the righteous will be addressed, and the wicked. Christ will say to the one that the kingdom was prepared for *them;* to the other, that the fire was not prepared for *them,* but for another race of beings. *They* will inherit it because they have the same character *as the devil*, and are therefore fitted to the same place—not because it was originally *prepared for them.*

45. *Inasmuch as ye did it not*, &c. By not doing good to the *followers* of Christ, they showed that they had no real love to *him.* By not doing good to the poor and needy, to the stranger and the prisoner, they showed that they had not his spirit, and were not like him, and were unfit for his kingdom. Let it be observed here that the public ground of their condemnation is the *neglect* of duty, or because *they did it not.* We are not to suppose that they will not also be condemned for their open and positive sins. See Ro. ii. 9; Ep. v. 5; Col. iii. 5, 6; 1 Co. vi. 9, 10; Re. xxi. 8; Ps. ix. 17. But their neglect of doing good to him and his people may be the *public* reason of condemning them: 1st. Because he wished to give *pre-eminence* to those virtues, to excite his followers to do them. 2d. Men should be punished for *neglect* as well as for positive sin. Sin is a violation of the law, or *refusing* to do what God commands. 3d. Nothing better shows the true state of the *heart* than the proper performance of those duties, and the true character can be as well tested by neglecting them as by open crimes.

If it be asked how the heathen who never heard of the name of Christ can be justly condemned in this manner, it may be answered—1st. That Christ acknowledges all the poor, and needy, and strangers of every land, as his brethren. See ver. 40. 2d. That by ne-

46 And[x] these shall go away into everlasting punishment; but the righteous into life eternal.

x Da.12.2; Jn.5.29.

glecting the duties of charity they show that they have not his spirit—are not like him. 3d. That these duties are clearly made known by conscience and by the light of nature, as well as by revelation, and men may therefore be condemned for the neglect of them. 4th. That they are not condemned for not believing in Christ, of whom they have not heard, but for a wrong spirit, neglect of duty, open crime; for being *unlike Christ*, and therefore *unfit* for heaven. ¶ *One of the least of these.* These on my right hand. My brethren. Those who are saved.

46. *And these shall go away.* These *persons.* Many, holding the doctrine of universal salvation have contended that God would punish *sin* only. Christ says that *those on his left hand*, shall go away—not *sins*, but *sinners.* Besides, *sin*, as an abstract thing, cannot be punished. Sin is nothing but an *act*—the act of a transgressor, and, to be reached at all, it must be reached by punishing the offender himself. ¶ *Into everlasting punishment.* The original word here translated *punishment* means torment, or suffering inflicted for crime. The noun is used but in one other place in the New Testament—1 Jn. iv. 18: "Fear hath *torment.*" The verb from which the noun is derived is twice used—Ac. iv. 21; 2 Pe. ii. 9. In all these places it denotes anguish, suffering, punishment. It does not mean simply a *state* or *condition*, but absolute, positive suffering; and if this word does not teach it, no word *could* express the idea that the wicked would suffer. It has been contended that the sufferings of the wicked will not be *eternal* or *without end.* It is not the purpose of these *Notes* to enter into debates of that kind farther than to ascertain the meaning of the language used by the sacred writers. In regard to the meaning of the word *everlasting* in this place, it is to be observed—1st. That the *literal* meaning of the word expresses absolute eternity—*always being*, Mat. xviii. 8; xix. 16; Mar. iii. 29; Ro. ii. 7; He. v. 9. 2d. That the obvious and plain interpretation of the word demands this signification in this place. The original word—*aionion*—is employed in the New Testament sixty-six times. Of these, in fifty-one instances it is used of the happiness of the righteous; in two, of God's existence; in six, of the church and the Messiah's kingdom; and in the remaining seven, of the future punishment of the wicked. If in these seven instances we attach to the word the idea of limited duration, consistency requires that the same idea of limited duration should be given it in the fifty-one cases of its application to the future glory of the righteous, and the two instances of its application to God's existence, and the six cases of its appropriation to the future reign of the Messiah and the glory and perpetuity of the church. But no one will presume to deny that in these instances it denotes unlimited duration, and therefore, in accordance with the sound laws of interpretation and of language itself, the same sense of unlimited duration must be given it when used of future punishment.—Owen, *in loc.* 3d. That, admitting that it was the Saviour's design *ever* to teach this doctrine, this would be *the very word* to express it; and if this does not teach it, it *could not* be taught. 4th. That it is not taught in any plainer manner in any confession of faith on the globe; and if this may be explained away, all those may be. 5th. That our Saviour knew that this would be so understood by nine-tenths of the world; and if he did *not* mean to teach it, he has knowingly led them into error, and his honesty cannot be vindicated. 6th. That he knew that the doctrine was calculated to produce *fear* and *terror;* and if he was benevolent, and actually used language calculated to produce this fear and terror, his conduct cannot be vindicated in exciting unnecessary alarms. 7th. *That the word used here is the same in the original as that used to express the eternal life of the righteous;* if one can be proved to be limited in duration, the other can by the *same arguments. The proof that the righteous will be happy for ever is precisely the same, and no other, than that the wicked will, be miserable for ever.* 8th. That it is confirmed by many other passages of Scripture, 2 Th. i. 7-9; Lu. xvi. 26; Re. xiv. 11; Ps. ix. 17; Is. xxxiii. 14; Mar. xvi. 16; Jn. iii. 36. ¶ *Life eternal.* Man by sin has plunged himself into death, temporal, spiritual, eternal. Christ, by coming and dying, has abolished death,

CHAPTER XXVI.

AND it came to pass, when Jesus had finished all these sayings, he said unto his disciples,

2 Ye[a] know that after two days is *the feast of the* passover, and the Son of man is betrayed to be crucified.

a Mar.14.1,&c.; Lu.22.1,&c.; Jn.13.1,&c.

---

and brought life and immortality to light, 2 Ti. i. 10. *Life* is the opposite of death. It denotes, here, freedom from death, and positive holiness and happiness for ever.

CHAPTER XXVI.

1–16. See also Mar. xiv. 1–11; Lu. xxii. 1–6; Jn. xii. 1–7.

2. *After two days is* the feast of the *passover*. See Notes on Mat. xii. 1–8. The festival of the Passover was designed to preserve among the Jews the memory of their liberation from Egyptian servitude, and of the safety of their first-born in that night when the first-born of the Egyptians perished, Ex. xii. The name *Passover* was given to the feast because the Lord *passed over* the houses of the Israelites without slaying their first-born, while the Egyptians were cut off, Ex. xii. 13. It was celebrated seven days, viz. from the 15th to the 21st of the month ABIB or NISAN (April), Ex. xii. 15–20; xxiii. 15. During all this period the people ate unleavened bread, and hence the festival was sometimes called *the feast of unleavened bread*, Ex. xii. 18; Le. xxiii. 6. On the evening of the fourteenth day, all the leaven or yeast in the family was removed with great care, as it is to the present time—a circumstance to which the apostle alludes in 1 Co. v. 7. On the tenth day of the month the master of a family separated a lamb or a goat of a year old from the flock (Ex. xii. 1–6), which he slew on the fourteenth day before the altar, De. xvi. 2, 5, 6. The lamb was commonly slain at about 3 o'clock P.M. The blood of the paschal lamb was, in Egypt, sprinkled on the door-posts of the houses; afterward it was poured by the priests at the foot of the altar, Ex. xii. 7. The lamb thus slain was roasted whole, with two spits thrust through it—one lengthwise and one transversely—crossing each other near the forelegs, so that the animal was in a manner, crucified. Not a bone of it might be broken—a circumstance strongly representing the sufferings of our Lord Jesus, the Passover slain for us, Jn. xix. 36; 1 Co. v. 7. Thus roasted, the lamb was served up with wild and bitter herbs. Not fewer than ten, nor more than twenty persons, were admitted to these sacred feasts. At first it was observed with their loins girt about, with sandals on their feet, and with all the preparations for an immediate journey. This, in Egypt, was significant of the haste with which they were about to depart from the land of bondage. The custom was afterward retained.

The order of the celebration of this feast was as follows:—The ceremony commenced with drinking a cup of wine mingled with water, after having given thanks to God for it. This was the *first cup*. Then followed the *washing of hands*, with another short form of thanksgiving to God. The table was then supplied with the provisions, viz. the bitter salad, the unleavened bread, the lamb, and a thick sauce composed of dates, figs, raisins, vinegar, &c. They then took a small quantity of salad, with another thanksgiving, and ate it; after which, all the dishes were removed from the table, and a second cup of wine was set before each guest, as at first. The dishes were removed, it is said, to excite the curiosity of children, and to lead them to make inquiry into the cause of this observance. See Ex. xii. 26, 27. The leading person at the feast then began and rehearsed the history of the servitude of the Jews in Egypt, the manner of their deliverance, and the reason of instituting the Passover. The dishes were then returned to the table, and he said, "*This is the Passover which we eat, because that the Lord passed over the houses of our fathers in Egypt;*" and then, holding up the salad and the unleavened bread, he stated the *design*, viz. that the one represented the *bitterness* of the Egyptian bondage, and the other the *suddenness* of their deliverance. This done, he repeated the 113th and 114th Psalms, offered a short prayer, and all the company drank the wine that had been standing some time before them. This was the *second cup*. The hands were then again washed, and the meal then eaten with the usual forms and solemnities; after which they washed the hands again, and then drank another cup of

3 Then assembled together the chief priests, and the scribes, and the elders of the people, unto the palace of the high-priest, who was called Caiaphas,

4 And[b] consulted that they might take Jesus by subtilty and kill *him*.

5 But they said, Not on the feast-*day*, lest there be an uproar among the people.

b Ps.2.2.

wine, called *the cup of blessing*, because the leader was accustomed in a particular manner, over that cup, to offer thanks to God for his goodness. This is the cup which our Saviour is supposed to have taken when he instituted the Lord's Supper, called by Paul *the cup of blessing*, 1 Co. x. 16. There was still another cup, which was drunk when they were about to separate, called the Hallel, because in connection with it they were accustomed to repeat the lesser *Hallel*, or the 115th, 116th, 117th, 118th Psalms. In accordance with this, our Saviour and his disciples sang a hymn as they were about to go to the Mount of Olives, ver. 30. It is probable that our Saviour complied with these rites according to the custom of the Jews. While doing it, he signified that the *typical* reference of the Passover was about to be accomplished, and he instituted in place of it *the supper*—the communion—and, of course, the obligation to keep the Passover then ceased. ¶ *The Son of man is betrayed.* Will be betrayed. He did not mean to say that they then knew that he would be betrayed, for it does not appear that they had been informed of the precise time; but they knew that the Passover was at hand, and *he then* informed them that he would be betrayed. ¶ *To be crucified.* To be put to death on the cross. See Notes on Mat. xxvii. 35.

3. *Then assembled*, &c. This was a meeting of the great council or Sanhedrim. See Notes on Mat. v. 22. ¶ *The palace.* The original word properly denotes the *hall* or large area in the centre of the dwelling, called the court. See Notes on Mat. ix. 1–8. It may be understood, however, as referring to the palace itself. ¶ *The high-priest.* Holding the office that was first conferred on Aaron, Ex. xxviii. The office was at first hereditary, descending on the oldest son, Nu. iii. 10. Antiochus Epiphanes (B.C. 160), when he had possession of Judea, sold the office to the highest bidder. In the year 152 B.C., Alexander, King of Syria, conferred the office on JONATHAN (1 Mac. x. 18–20), whose brother Simon was afterward created by the Jews both prince and high-priest, 1 Mac. xiv. 35–47. His posterity, who at the same time sustained the office of kings, occupied the station of high-priest till the time of Herod, who changed the incumbents of the office at pleasure—a liberty which the Romans ever afterward exercised without any restraint. The office was never more fluctuating than in the time of our Saviour. Hence it is said that *Caiaphas* was high-priest *for that year*, Jn. xi. 51. Persons who *had been* high-priests, and had been removed from office, still retained the name. Hence more than one high-priest is sometimes mentioned, though strictly there was but one who held the office.

4. *By subtilty.* By guile, deceit, or in some secret manner, so that the people would not know it. Jesus was regarded by the people as a distinguished prophet, and by most of them, probably, as the Messiah; and the Sanhedrim did not dare to take him away openly, lest the people should rise and rescue him. They were probably aware that he had gone out to Bethany, or to some place adjacent to the city; and as he passed his nights there and not in the city, there was need of guile to ascertain the place to which he had retired, and to take him.

5. *Not on the feast*-day. Not during the *feast.* The feast lasted seven days. A vast multitude attended from all parts of Judea. Jerusalem is said to have contained at such times *three millions of people.* Amid such a multitude there were frequent tumults and seditions, and the Sanhedrim was justly apprehensive there *would* be now, if, in open day and in the temple, they took away a teacher so popular as Jesus, and put him to death. They therefore sought how they might do it secretly and by guile.

6. *In Bethany.* See Notes on ch. xxi. 1. ¶ *Simon the leper.* Simon, who *had been* a leper. ¶ *Leper.* See Notes on Mat. viii. 1. It was *unlawful* to eat with persons that *had* the leprosy, and it is more than probable, therefore,

6 Now when Jesus was in Bethany, in the house of Simon the leper,
7 There[c] came unto him a woman having an alabaster box of very precious ointment, and poured it on his head as he sat *at meat.*

c Jn.11.1,2; 12.3.

---

that this Simon had been healed—perhaps by our Lord himself. John (xii. 1) says that this was the house where Lazarus was, who had been raised from the dead. Probably Lazarus was a relative of Simon's, and was living with him. He farther says that they made Jesus a supper, and that Martha served. He says that this was six days before the Passover. From the order in which Matthew and Mark mention it, it would have been supposed that it was but *two days* before the Passover, and *after* the cleansing of the temple; but it is to be observed, 1st. That Matthew and Mark often neglect the exact order of the events that they record. 2d. That they do not *affirm* at what time this was. They leave it indefinite, saying that *while* Jesus was in Bethany he was anointed by Mary. 3d. That Matthew introduced it here for the purpose of giving a *connected* account of the conduct of *Judas. Judas* murmured at the waste of the ointment (Jn. xii. 4), and one of the *effects* of his indignation, it seems, was to betray his Lord.

7. *There came to him a woman.* This woman was *Mary*, the sister of Lazarus and Martha, Jn. xii. 3. ¶ *Having an alabaster box.* The *alabaster* is a species of marble, distinguished for being light, and of a beautiful white colour, almost transparent. It was much used by the ancients for the purpose of preserving various kinds of ointment in. ¶ *Of very precious ointment.* That is, of ointment *of great value;* that was rare and difficult to be obtained. Mark (xiv. 3) and John (xii. 3) say that it was ointment of spikenard. In the original it is *nard.* It was procured from an herb growing in the Indies, chiefly obtained from the root, though sometimes also from the bark. It was liquid, so as easily to flow when the box or vial was open, and was distinguished particularly for an agreeable smell. See Ca. i. 12. The ancients were much in the habit of *anointing* or *perfuming* their bodies, and the *nard* was esteemed one of the most precious perfumes. John says there was a *pound* of this, ch. xii. 3. The *pound* in use among the Jews was the Roman, of twelve ounces, answering to our troy weight. That there was a large quantity is farther evident from the fact that Judas says it might have been sold for three hundred pence (about £9), and that the *house* was filled with the odour of the ointment (John). ¶ *And poured it on his head.* They were accustomed chiefly to anoint the head or hair. John says (xii. 3) that she poured it on the *feet* of Jesus, and wiped them with her hair. There is, however, no contradiction. She probably poured it *both* on his head and his feet. Matthew and Mark having recorded the former, John, who wrote his gospel in part to record events omitted by them, completes the account by saying that the ointment was also poured on the feet of the Saviour. To pour ointment on the *head* was common. To pour it on the *feet* was an act of distinguished *humility* and of attachment to the Saviour, and therefore deserved to be particularly recorded. ¶ *As he sat* at meat. That is, at supper. In the original, as he *reclined* at supper. The ancients did not *sit* at their meals, but *reclined* at length on couches. See Notes on Mat. xxiii. 6. She came up, therefore, *behind him* as he lay reclined at the table, and, bending down over the couch, poured the ointment on his head and his feet, and, probably kneeling at his feet, wiped them with her hair.

8. *They had indignation.* John says that *Judas expressed* indignation. Probably some of the others *felt* indignation, but Judas only gave vent to his feelings. The reason why Judas was indignant was, that he had the *bag* (Jn. xii. 6)—that is, the *purse*, or repository of articles *given* to the disciples and to the Saviour. He was a thief, and was in the habit, it seems, of taking out and appropriating to his own use what was put in for them in common. The leading trait of Judas's character was *avarice*, and no opportunity was suffered to pass without attempting by base and wicked means to make money. In his example an avaricious man may learn the true nature and the effect of that grovelling and wicked passion. It led him to commit the enormous crime of betraying his Lord to death, and it will always lead its possessor to guilt. No small part of the sins of the world can be traced to avarice, and many and many

8 But when his disciples saw *it*, they had indignation, saying, To what purpose *is* this waste?

9 For this ointment might have been sold for much, and given to the poor.

10 When Jesus understood *it*, he said unto them, Why trouble ye the woman? for she hath wrought a good work upon me.

11 For[d] ye have the poor always with you; [e]but me ye have not always.

12 For in that she hath poured this ointment on my body, she did *it* for my burial.

13 Verily I say unto you, Wheresoever this gospel shall be preached in the whole world, *there* shall also this, that this woman hath done, be told for a memorial of her.

14 Then [f]one of the twelve, called

d De.15.11. e Jn.14.19; 17.11. f ch.10.4.

---

a time since the days of Judas has the Lord Jesus been betrayed among his professed friends by the same base propensity. ¶ Is *this waste.* This *loss* or *destruction* of property. They could see no use in it, and they therefore supposed it was lost.

9. *Sold for much.* Mark and John say for three hundred pence—that is, for about £9. This, to them, was a large sum. Mark says they murmured against her. There was also an *implied* murmuring against the Saviour for suffering it to be done. The murmuring was, however, without cause. It was the *property* of Mary. She had a right to dispose of it as she pleased, answerable not to *them*, but *to God.* *They* had no right over it, and no cause of complaint if it *had* been wasted. So Christians now are at liberty to dispose of their property as they please, either in distributing the Bible, in supporting the gospel, in sending it to heathen nations, or in aiding the poor. The men of the world, like Judas, regard it as *wasted.* Like Judas, they are indignant. They say it might be disposed of in a better way. Yet, like Judas, they are interfering in that which concerns them not. Like other men, Christians have a right to dispose of their property as they please, answerable only to God. And though an avaricious world esteems it to be *wasted*, yet, if their Lord commands it, it will be found to be the *only way* in which it was *right* for them to dispose of that property, and will be found not to have been in vain.

10. *Trouble ye the woman.* That is, disturb her mind by insinuations, as if she had done wrong. ¶ *A good work on me.* She has done it with a mind grateful, and full of love to me. The work was *good*, also, as it was preparative for his death, ver. 12.

11. *For ye have the poor*, &c. Mark adds, "Whensoever ye will, ye may do them good." It was right that they should regard the poor. It was a plain precept of religion (see Ps. xli. 1; Pr. xiv. 21; xxix. 7; Ga. ii. 10), and our Saviour would not prohibit it, but do all that was possible to excite his followers to the duty. But every duty should be done in its place, and the duty *then* incumbent was that which Mary had performed. They would afterward have abundant occasion to show their regard for the poor. ¶ *Me ye have not always.* He alludes here to his dying, and his going away to heaven. He would still be their friend and their Saviour, but would not be *bodily* present with them always, so that they could show kindness *in this way* to him.

12. *She did* it *for my burial.* It is not to be supposed that Mary understood clearly that he was *then* about to die—for the apostles, it seems, did not fully comprehend it, or that she *intended* it for his burial; but she had done it as an act of kindness and love, to show her regard for her Lord. *He* said that it was a *proper preparation* for his burial. Anciently, bodies were anointed and embalmed for the purpose of the sepulchre. Jesus said that this was *really* a preparation for that burial; a fitting him in a proper manner for the tomb.

13. *A memorial.* Anything to produce *remembrance.* This would be told to her honour and credit, as a memorial of her piety and self-denial; and it is right that the good deeds of the pious should be recorded and had in recollection.

14. *Then one of the twelve*, &c. Luke says that Satan entered into Judas. That is, Satan *tempted* or instigated him to do it. Probably he tempted Judas by appealing to his avarice, his ruling passion, and by suggesting that now

Judas Iscariot, went unto the chief priests,

15 And said *unto them*, What will ye give me, and I will deliver him unto you? And they [g]covenanted with him for thirty pieces of silver.

16 And from that time he sought opportunity to betray him.

17 Now[h] the first *day* of the *feast of* unleavened bread, the disciples came to Jesus, saying unto him, Where wilt thou that we prepare for thee to eat the passover?

g Zec.11.12,13; ch.27.3.

h Ex.12.6,18.

---

was a favourable opportunity to make money rapidly by selling his Lord. ¶ *Judas Iscariot.* See Notes on Mat. x. 4. ¶ *Unto the chief priests.* The high-priest, and those who *had* been high-priests. The ruling men of the Sanhedrim. Luke adds that he went also to *the captains* (xxii. 4). It was necessary, on account of the great wealth deposited there, and its great sacredness, to *guard* the temple by night. Accordingly, men were stationed around it, whose leaders or commanders were called *captains*, Ac. iv. 1. These men were commonly of the tribe of Levi, were closely connected with the priests, were men of influence, and Judas went to them, therefore, as well as to the priests, to offer his services in accomplishing what they so much desired to secure. Probably his object was to get as much money as possible, and he might therefore have attempted to make a bargain with several of them apart from each other.

15. *And they covenanted with him.* Made a bargain with him. Agreed to give him. Mark says they *promised* to give him money. They did not pay it to him *then*, lest he should deceive them. When the deed was done, and before he was made sensible of its guilt, they paid him. See Mat. xxvii. 3; Ac. i. 18. ¶ *Thirty pieces of silver.* Mark and Luke do not mention the sum. They say that they promised him *money*—in the original, *silver.* In Matthew, in the original, it is thirty *silvers*, or *silverlings.* This was the price *of a slave* (see Ex. xxi. 32), and it is not unlikely that this sum was fixed on by them to show their *contempt* of Jesus, and that they regarded him as of little value. There is no doubt, also, that they understood that such was the anxiety of Judas to obtain money, that he would betray his Lord for *any* sum. The money usually denoted by *pieces* of silver, when the precise sum is not mentioned, is a *shekel*—a silver Jewish coin amounting to about 50 cents, or 2*s.* 3*d.* The whole sum, therefore, for which Judas committed this crime was $15, or £3, 7*s.* 6*d.*

16. *Sought opportunity to betray him.* Luke adds, "in the absence of the multitude." This was the chief difficulty—to deliver him into the hands of the priests so as not to have it known by the people, or so as not to excite tumult. The *opportunity* which he sought, therefore, was one in which the multitude *would* not see him, or *could* not rescue the Saviour. ¶ *To betray him.* The word *betray* commonly means to deliver into the hands of an enemy by treachery or breach of trust; to do it while friendship or faithfulness is *professed.* All this took place in the case of Judas. But the word in the original does not necessarily imply this. It means simply to *deliver up*, or to give into their hands. He sought opportunity *how he might deliver him up to them*, agreeably to the contract.

17–19. See also Mar. xiv. 12–16; Lu. xxii. 7–13.

17. *The first* day, &c. The feast continued *eight* days, including the day on which the paschal lamb was killed and eaten, Ex. xii. 15. That was the fourteenth day of the month Abib, answering to parts of our March and April. ¶ Of *unleavened bread.* Called so because during those eight days no bread made with yeast or leaven was allowed to be eaten. Luke says, "in which the passover must be killed"—that is, in which the *paschal lamb*, or the lamb eaten on the occasion, was killed. The word in the original, translated *Passover*, commonly means, not the *feast* itself, but the *lamb* that was killed on the occasion, Ex. xii. 43; Nu. ix. 11; Jn. xviii. 28. See also 1 Co. v. 7, where Christ, *our Passover*, is said to be slain for us; that is, our paschal lamb, so called on account of his innocence, and his being offered as a victim or *sacrifice* for our sins.

18. *Go into the city to such a man.* That is, Jerusalem, called *the* city by way of eminence. Luke says that the

18 And he said, Go into the city to such a man, and say unto him, The Master saith, My time is at hand: I will keep the passover at thy house with my disciples.
19 And the disciples did as Jesus

---

disciples whom he sent were Peter and John. The man to whom they were to go he did not mention by name, but he told them that when they came into the city, a man would meet them bearing a pitcher of water. See Mark and Luke. Him they were to follow, and in the house which he entered they would find a room prepared. The *name* of the man was not mentioned. The *house* in which they were to keep the Passover was not mentioned. The reason of this probably was, that Christ was desirous of concealing from *Judas* the place where they would keep the Passover. He was acquainted with the design of Judas to betray him. He knew that if Judas was acquainted with the place *beforehand*, he could easily give information to the chief priests, and it would give them a favourable opportunity to surprise them, and apprehend *him* without making a tumult. Though it was certain that he would not be delivered up before the time appointed by the Father, yet it was proper *to use the means* to prevent it. There can be little doubt that Jesus was acquainted with this man, and that he was a disciple. The direction which he gave his disciples most clearly proves that he was omniscient. Amid so great a multitude going at that time into the city, it was impossible to know that *a particular man would be met*—a man bearing a pitcher of water—unless Jesus had all knowledge, and was therefore divine. ¶ *The Master saith.* This was the name by which Jesus was probably known among the disciples, and one which he directed them to give him. See Mat. xxiii. 8, 10. It means, literally, *the teacher*, as opposed to *the disciple*, or learner; not the *master*, as opposed to the *servant* or *slave.* The fact that they used this name *as if* the man would know whom they meant, and the fact that the man understood them and made no further inquiries, shows that he was acquainted with Jesus, and was probably himself a disciple. ¶ *My time is at hand.* That is, *is near.* By *his time*, here, may be meant either his time to eat the Passover, or the time of his death. It has been supposed by many that Jesus, in accordance with a part of the Jews who rejected traditions, anticipated the usual observance of the Passover, or kept it one day sooner. The Pharisees had devised many forms of ascertaining when the month commenced. They placed witnesses around the heights of the temple to observe the first appearance of the new moon; they examined the witnesses with much formality, and endeavoured also to obtain the exact time by astronomical calculations. Others held that the month properly commenced when the moon was *visible.* Thus it is said a difference arose between them about the time of the Passover, and that Jesus kept it one day sooner than most of the people. The foundation of the opinion that he anticipated the usual time of keeping the Passover is the following: 1st. In Jn. xviii. 28, it is said that on the day on which our Lord was crucified, and of course the *day after* he had eaten the Passover, the chief priests would not go into the judgment-hall lest they should be defiled, *but that they might eat the passover*, evidently meaning that it was to be eaten that day. 2d. In Jn. xix. 14, the day on which he was crucified is called *the preparation of the passover*—that is, the day on which it was prepared to be eaten in the evening. 3d. In Jn. xix. 31, the day in which our Lord lay in the grave was called the great day of the Sabbath—"a high day;" that is, the day after the Passover was killed, the Sabbath occurring on the first day of the feast properly, and therefore a day of peculiar solemnity; yet our Saviour had partaken of it *two* days before, and therefore the *day before* the body of the people. If this opinion be true, then the phrase "my time is at hand" means *my* time for keeping the Passover is near. Whether this opinion be true or not, there may be a reference also *to his death.* The man with whom they were to go was probably a disciple of his, though perhaps a secret one. Jesus might purpose to keep the Passover at his house, that he might inform him more particularly respecting his death, and prepare him for it. He sent, therefore, to him and said, "I will keep the passover *at thy house.*"

Mark and Luke add that he would

had appointed them; and they made
ready the passover.
20 Now when the even was come,
he sat down with the twelve.
21 And as they did eat, he said,
Verily I say unto you, that one of
you shall betray me.
22 And they were exceeding

---

show them "a large upper room, furnished and prepared." Ancient writers remark that, at the time of the great feasts, the houses in Jerusalem were all open to receive guests—that they were in a manner common to the people of Judea; and there is no doubt, therefore, that the master of a house would have it ready on such occasions for company. It is possible, also, that there might have been an agreement between this man and our Lord that he would prepare his house for him, though this was unknown to the disciples. The word rendered *furnished* means, literally, *spread;* that is, *spread* with carpets, and with *couches* on which to recline at the table, after the manner of the East. See Notes on Mat. xxiii. 6.

19. *They made ready the passover.* That is, they procured a *lamb*, multitudes of which were kept for sale in the temple; they had it killed and flayed by the priests, and the blood poured by the altar; they roasted the lamb, and prepared the bitter herbs, the sauce, and the unleavened bread. This was done, it seems, while our Lord was absent, by the two disciples.

20. *When the even was come.* The lamb was killed *between the evenings*, Ex. xii. 6 (Hebrew)—that is between three o'clock, P.M., and nine in the evening. The Jews reckoned two evenings—one from three o'clock P.M. to sunset, the other from sunset to the close of the first watch in the night, or nine o'clock. The paschal supper was commonly eaten *after* the setting of the sun, and often in the night, Ex. xii. 8. ¶ *He sat down.* At first the supper was eaten standing, with their loins girded and their staff in their hand, denoting the haste with which they were about to flee from Egypt. Afterward, however, they introduced the practice, it seems, of partaking of this as they did of their ordinary meals. The original word is, *he reclined*—that is, he placed himself on the couch in a reclining posture, in the usual manner in which they partook of their meals. See Notes on Mat. xxiii. 6. While reclining there at the supper, the disciples had a dispute which should be the greatest. See Notes on Lu. xxii. 24-30. At this time, also, before the institution of the Lord's supper, Jesus washed the feet of his disciples, to teach them humility. See Notes on Jn. xiii. 1-20.

21-24. *As they did eat*, &c. The account contained in these verses is also recorded in Mar. xiv. 18-21; Lu. xxii. 21-23; Jn. xiii. 21, 22. John says that before Jesus declared that one of them should betray him, *he was troubled in spirit, and testified;* that is, he *felt deeply* in view of the greatness of the crime that Judas was about to commit, and the sufferings that he was to endure, and *testified*, or gave utterance to his inward feelings of sorrow.

22. *They were exceeding sorrowful.* John says (ch. xiii. 22) "they looked one on another, doubting of whom he spake"—that is, they anxiously looked one at another, conscious each one, except Judas, of no such intention, and each one beginning to examine himself to find whether he was the person intended. This showed their innocence, and their attachment to Jesus. It showed how *sensitive* they were to the least suspicion of the kind. It showed that they were willing to know themselves, thus evincing the spirit of the true Christian. Judas only was silent, and was the last to make the inquiry, and that after he had been plainly pointed out (ver. 25), thus showing, 1st, that guilt is slow to suspect itself; 2d, that it shrinks from the light; 3d, that it was his purpose to conceal his intention; and, 4th, that nothing but the consciousness that his Lord *knew his design* could induce him to make inquiry. The guilty would, if possible, always conceal their crimes. The innocent are ready to suspect that they *may* have done wrong. Their feelings are tender, and they inquire with solicitude whether there may not be something in their bosoms, unknown to themselves, that may be a departure from right feeling.

23. *He that dippeth* his *hand with me in the dish.* The Jews, at the observance of this ordinance, used a bitter *sauce*, made of bunches of raisins, mixed with vinegar and other seasoning of the like kind, which they said represented the *clay* which their fathers were com-

sorrowful, and began every one of them to say unto him, Lord, is it I?

23 And he answered and said, He[i] that dippeth *his* hand with me in the dish, the same shall betray me.

24 The Son of man goeth [k]as *it* is written of him: but woe unto that man by whom the Son of

i Ps.41.9; 55.12-15.

k Ps.22.; Is.53.

---

pelled to use in Egypt in making brick, thus reminding them of their bitter bondage there. This was probably the *dish* to which reference is made here. It is not improbable that Judas reclined near to our Saviour at the feast, and by his saying it was one that dipped *with him* in the dish, he meant one that was near to him, designating him more particularly than he had done before. John adds (xiii. 23–30; see Notes on that place), that "there was leaning on Jesus' bosom one of his disciples whom Jesus loved"—referring to himself; that Simon Peter beckoned to him to ask Jesus more particularly who it was; that Jesus signified who it was by giving *Judas* a *sop*—that is, a piece of *bread* or *meat* dipped in the thick sauce; and that Judas, having received it, went out to accomplish his wicked design of betraying him. Judas was not, therefore, present at the institution of the Lord's supper.

24. *The Son of man goeth.* That is, the Messiah—the Christ. See Notes on Mat. viii. 20. ¶ *Goeth.* Dies, or will die. The Hebrews often spoke in this manner of death, Ps. xxxix. 13; Ge. xv. 2. ¶ *As* it *is written of him.* That is, as it is *written* or prophesied of him in the Old Testament. Comp. Ps. xli. 9 with Jn. xiii. 18. See also Da. ix. 26, 27; Is. liii. 4–9. Luke (xxii. 22) says, *as it was determined.* In the Greek, as it was *marked out by a boundary*—that is, in the divine purpose. It was the previous *intention* of God to give him up to die for sin, or it could not have been certainly predicted. It is also declared to have been by his *determinate counsel and foreknowledge.* See Notes on Ac. ii. 23. ¶ *Woe unto that man,* &c. The crime is great and awful, and he will be punished accordingly. He states the greatness of his misery or "*woe*" in the phrase following. ¶ *It had been good,* &c. That is, it would have been better for him if he had not been born; or it would be better *now* for him if he was to be as *if* he had not been born, or if he was annihilated. This was a proverbial mode of speaking among the Jews in frequent use. In relation to *Judas,* it *proves* the following things: 1st, that the crime which he was about to commit was exceedingly great; 2d, that the misery or punishment *due to it* would *certainly* come upon him; 3d, that he would certainly *deserve* that misery, or it would not have been threatened or inflicted; and, 4th, that his punishment would be *eternal.* If there should be any *period* when the sufferings of Judas should *end,* and he be restored and raised to heaven, the blessings of that *happiness without end* would infinitely overbalance all the sufferings he could endure in a limited time, and consequently it would *not* be true that it would have been better for him not to have been born. Existence, to him, would, on the whole, be an infinite blessing. This passage proves farther that, in relation to *one* wicked man, the sufferings of hell will be eternal. If of *one,* then it is equally certain and proper that *all* the wicked will perish for ever.

If it be asked how this crime of Judas could be so great, or could be a crime at all, when it was determined beforehand that the Saviour should be betrayed and die in this manner, it may be answered—1st. That the crime was what it was *in itself,* apart from any determination of God. It was a violation of all the duties he owed to God and to the Lord Jesus—awful ingratitude, detestable covetousness, and most base treachery. As such it *deserved* to be punished. 2d. The previous purpose of God did not *force* Judas to do this. In it he acted freely. He did just what his wicked heart prompted him to do. 3d. A previous *knowledge* of a thing, or a previous *purpose* to permit a thing, does not alter *its nature,* or cause it to be a different thing from what it is. 4th. God, who is the best judge of the nature of crime, holds all that was done in crucifying the Saviour, though it was by his determinate counsel and foreknowledge, *to be by wicked hands,* Ac. ii. 23. This punishment of Judas proves, also, that sinners cannot take shelter for their sins in the decrees of God, or

man is betrayed! it had been
good for that man if he had not
been born.
25 Then Judas, which betrayed
him, answered and said, Master,
is it I? He said unto him, Thou
hast said.
26 And [l] as they were eating,
Jesus took bread, and [1]blessed *it*,
and brake *it*, and gave *it* to the

[l] 1 Co.11.23,&c.
[1] Many Greek copies have, *gave thanks*.

plead them as an excuse. God will punish crimes for what they *are in themselves*. His own deep and inscrutable purposes in regard to human actions will not change *the nature* of those actions, or screen the sinner from the punishment which he deserves.

25. *Thou hast said.* That is, thou hast said the truth. It is so. Thou art the man. Comp. ver. 64 of this chapter with Mar. xiv. 62.

26–30. See also Mar. xiv. 22–26; Lu. xxii. 15–20; 1 Co. xi. 23–25.

26. *As they were eating.* As they were eating the paschal supper, near the close of the meal. Luke adds that he said, just before instituting the sacramental supper, "With desire have I desired to eat this passover with you before I suffer." This is a Hebrew manner of expression, signifying *I have greatly desired.* He had desired it, doubtless, (1), that he might institute the Supper, to be a perpetual memorial of him; (2), that he might strengthen them for their approaching trials; (3), that he might explain to them the true nature of the Passover; and, (4), that he might spend another season with them in the duties of religion. Every *Christian* about to die will also seek opportunities of drawing specially near to God, and of holding communion with him and with his people. ¶ *Jesus took bread.* That is, the unleavened bread which they used at the celebration of the Passover, made into thin cakes, easily broken and distributed. ¶ *And blessed* it. Or sought a blessing on it; or *gave thanks* to God for it. The word rendered *blessed* not unfrequently means *to give thanks.* Comp. Lu. ix. 16 and Jn. vi. 11. It is also to be remarked that some manuscripts have the word rendered *gave thanks*, instead of the one translated *blessed.* It appears from the writings of Philo and the Rabbins that the Jews were never accustomed to eat without giving thanks to God and seeking his blessing. This was especially the case in both the bread and the wine used at the Passover. ¶ *And brake* it. This *breaking* of the bread represented the sufferings of Jesus about to take place—his body *broken* or wounded for sin. Hence Paul (1 Co. xi. 24) adds, "This is my body which is *broken* for you;" that is, which is *about to be* broken for you by death, or wounded, pierced, bruised, to make atonement for your sins. ¶ *This is my body.* This *represents* my body. This broken bread shows the manner in which my body will be broken; or this will serve to recall my dying sufferings to your remembrance. It is not meant that his body would be literally *broken* as the bread was, but that the bread would be a significant emblem or symbol to recall to their recollection his sufferings. It is not improbable that our Lord pointed to the broken bread, or laid his hands on it, as if he had said, "Lo, my body!" or, "Behold my body!—that which *represents* my broken body to you." This *could not* be intended to mean that that bread was literally his body. It was not. His body was then before them *living.* And there is no greater absurdity than to imagine his *living body* there changed at once to *a dead body*, and then the *bread* to be changed *into* that dead body, and that all the while the *living* body of Jesus was before them. Yet this is the absurd and impossible doctrine of the Roman Catholics, holding that the *bread* and *wine* were literally changed into the *body* and *blood* of our Lord. The language employed by the Saviour was in accordance with a common mode of speaking among the Jews, and exactly similar to that used by Moses at the institution of the Passover (Ex. xii. 11): "It"—that is, the lamb—"*is* the Lord's passover." That is, the lamb and the feast *represent* the Lord's *passing over* the houses of the Israelites. It serves to *remind* you of it. It surely cannot be meant that that lamb was the literal *passing over* their houses—a palpable absurdity—but that it *represented* it. So Paul and Luke say of the bread, "This is my body broken for you: *this do* IN REMEMBRANCE *of me.*" This expresses the whole design of the sacramental bread. It is to call *to remembrance*, in a vivid manner, the dying

disciples, and said, Take, eat; this
is my body.
27 And he took the cup, and
gave thanks, and gave *it* to them,
saying, Drink ye all of it;
28 For this is my blood of the
[m]new testament, which is shed for
many for the remission of sins.
29 But I say unto you, I will
not drink henceforth of this fruit

m Je.31.31.

---

sufferings of our Lord. The sacred writers, moreover, often denote that one thing is *represented* by another by using the word *is*. See Mat. xiii. 37: "He that soweth the good seed IS the Son of man"—that is, represents the Son of man. Ge. xli. 26: "The seven good kine ARE seven years"—that is, *represent* or signify seven years. See also Jn. xv. 1, 5; Ge. xvii. 10. The meaning of this important passage may be thus expressed: "As I give this broken bread to you to eat, *so* will I deliver my body to be afflicted and slain for your sins."

27. *And he took the cup.* That is, the cup of wine which was used at the feast of the Passover, called the cup of *Hallel*, or praise, because they commenced then repeating the *Psalms* with which they closed the Passover. See ver. 30. This cup, Luke says, he took *after supper*—that is, after they had finished the ordinary celebration of *eating* the Passover. The *bread* was taken *while* they were eating, the cup after they had done eating. ¶ *And gave thanks.* See Notes on ver. 26. ¶ *Drink ye all of it.* That is, "all of you, disciples, drink of it;" not, "drink *all* the wine."

28. *For this is my blood.* This *represents* my blood, as the bread does my body. Luke and Paul vary the expression, adding what Matthew and Mark have omitted. "This cup is the new testament in my blood." By this *cup* he meant the wine *in* the cup, and not the cup itself. Pointing to it, probably, he said, "This—*wine*—represents my blood about to be shed." The phrase "new testament" should have been rendered *new covenant*, referring to the *covenant* or *compact* that God was about to make with men through a Redeemer. The *old* covenant was that which was made with the Jews by the sprinkling of the blood of sacrifices. See Ex. xxiv. 8: "And Moses took the blood and sprinkled it on the people, and said, Behold the blood of the covenant which the Lord hath made with you," &c. In allusion to that, Jesus says, this cup is the NEW *covenant* in my blood; that is, which is *ratified, sealed,* or *sanctioned by my blood.* Anciently, covenants or contracts were ratified by slaying an animal; by the shedding of its blood, imprecating similar vengeance if either party failed in the compact. See Notes on He. ix. 16. So Jesus says the covenant which God is about to form with men—the new covenant, or the gospel economy—is sealed or ratified with *my* blood. ¶ *Which is shed for many for the remission of sins.* In order that sins may be remitted, or forgiven. That is, this is the appointed way by which God will pardon transgressions. That blood is efficacious for the pardon of sin—1st. Because it is *the life* of Jesus, the *blood* being used by the sacred writers as representing *life itself*, or as containing the elements of life, Ge. ix. 4; Le. xvii. 14. It was forbidden, therefore, to eat blood, because it contained the life, or was the life, of the animal. When, therefore, Jesus says that his blood was shed for many, it is the same as saying that *his life* was given for many. See Notes on Ro. iii. 25. 2d. His life was given for sinners, or he died in the place of sinners as their substitute. By his death on the cross, the death or punishment due to them in hell may be removed and their souls be saved. He endured *so much* suffering, bore *so much* agony, that God was pleased to accept it in the place of the eternal torments of all the redeemed. The interests of justice, the honour and stability of his government, would be as secure in saving them in this manner as if the suffering were inflicted on them personally in hell. God, by giving his Son to die for sinners, has shown his infinite abhorrence of sin; since, according to his view, and therefore according to *truth*, nothing else would show its evil nature but the awful sufferings of his own Son. That he died *in the stead* or *place* of sinners is abundantly clear from the following passages of Scripture: Jn. i. 29; Ep. v. 2; He. vii. 27; 1 Jn. ii. 2; iv. 10; Is. liii. 10; Ro. viii. 32; 2 Co. v. 15.

of the vine, until [n]that day when
I drink it new with you in my
Father's kingdom.
30 And when they had sung an
hymn,[2] they went out into the
mount of Olives.
31 Then saith Jesus unto them,
All ye shall be offended because of
me this night: for it is written,
[o]I will smite the Shepherd, and
the sheep of the flock shall be
scattered abroad.
32 But after I am risen again,
[p]I will go before you into Galilee.

n Is.25.6. 2 or, *psalm*. o Zec.13.7. p ch.28.7,10,16.

29. *But I say unto you*, &c. That is, the observance of the Passover, and of the rites shadowing forth future things, here end. I am about to die. The design of all these types and shadows is about to be accomplished. This is the last time that I shall partake of them with you. Hereafter, when my Father's kingdom is established in heaven, we will partake together of the thing represented by these *types* and *ceremonial observances*—the blessings and triumphs of redemption. ¶ *Fruit of the vine.* *Wine*, the *fruit* or *produce* of the vine—made of the grapes of the vine. ¶ *Until that day.* Probably the time when they should be received to heaven. It does not mean here on earth, farther than that they would partake with him in the happiness of spreading the gospel and the triumphs of his kingdom. ¶ *When I drink it new with you.* Not that he would partake with them of *literal* wine there, but in the thing represented by it. Wine was an important part of the feast of the Passover, and of all feasts. The kingdom of heaven is often represented under the image of a feast. It means that he will partake of joy with them in heaven; that they will share together the honours and happiness of the heavenly world. ¶ *New.* In a new manner, or perhaps *afresh.* ¶ *In my Father's kingdom.* In heaven. The place where God shall reign in a kingdom fully established and pure.

30. *And when they had sung a hymn.* The Passover was observed by the Jews by singing or *chanting* the 113th, 114th, 115th, 116th, 117th, and 118th Psalms. These they divided into two parts. The 113th and 114th Psalms they sung during the observance of the Passover, and the others at the close. There can be no doubt that our Saviour, and the apostles also, used the same psalms in their observance of the Passover. The word rendered *sung a hymn* is a participle, literally meaning *hymning*—not confined to a single hymn, but admitting many. ¶ *Mount of Olives.* See Notes on Mat. xx. 1.

31–35. *Jesus foretells the fall of Peter.* This is also recorded in Mar. xiv. 27–31; Lu. xxii. 31–34; Jn. xiii. 34–38.

31. *Then saith Jesus unto them.* The *occasion* of his saying this was Peter's bold affirmation that he was ready to *die* with him, Jn. xiii. 36. Jesus had told them that he was going away—that is, was about to die. Peter asked him whither he was going. Jesus replied that he could not follow him then, but should afterward. Peter, not satisfied with that, said that he was ready to lay down his life for him. Jesus then distinctly informed them that all of them would forsake him that very night. ¶ *All ye shall be offended because of me.* See Notes on Mat. v. 29. This language means, here, you will all *stumble* at my being taken, abused, and set at naught; you will be *ashamed* to own me as a teacher, and to acknowledge yourselves as my disciples; or, my being betrayed will prove a snare to you all, so that you will be guilty of the sin of forsaking me, and, by your conduct, of denying me. ¶ *For it is written*, &c. See Zec. xiii. 7. This is affirmed here to have reference to the Saviour, and to be fulfilled in him. ¶ *I will smite.* This is the language of God the Father. *I* will smite means either that I will give him up to be smitten (comp. Ex. iv. 21 with viii. 15, &c.), or that *I* will do it myself. Both of these things were done. God gave him up to the Jews and Romans, to be smitten for the sins of the world (Ro. viii. 32); and he himself *left* him to deep and awful sorrows—to bear "the burden of the world's atonement" alone. See Mar. xv. 34. ¶ *The Shepherd.* The Lord Jesus—the Shepherd of his people, Jn. x. 11, 14. Comp. Notes on Is. xl. 11. ¶ *The sheep.* This means *here* particularly *the apostles.* It also refers sometimes to all the followers of Jesus, the friends of God, Jn. x. 16; Ps. c. 3. ¶ *Shall be scattered abroad.* This refers

33 Peter answered and said unto him, Though all *men* shall be offended because of thee, *yet* will I never be offended.

34 Jesus said unto him, Verily I say unto thee, That this night, before the cock crow, thou shalt deny me thrice.

35 Peter said unto him, Though I should die with thee, yet will I

---

to their *fleeing*, and was fulfilled in that. See ver. 56 of this chapter.

32. *But after I am risen*, &c. This promise was given them to encourage and support them, and also to give them an indication where he might be found. He did not deny that he would first appear to a part of them before he met them all together (comp. Lu. xxiv. 13–31, 34; 1 Co. xv. 5), but that he would meet them *all* in Galilee. This was done. See Mar. xvi. 7; Mat. xxviii. 16. ¶ *Galilee.* See Notes on Mat. ii. 22.

33. *Peter answered—Though all* men, &c. The word *men* is improperly inserted here by the translators. Peter meant only to affirm this of *the disciples.* This confidence of Peter was entirely characteristic. He was ardent, sincere, and really attached to his Master. Yet this declaration was made evidently, 1st. From true love to Jesus. 2d. From too much reliance on his own strength. 3d. From ignorance of himself, and of the trials which he was soon to pass through. And it most impressively teaches us, 1st. That no strength of attachment to Jesus can justify such confident promises of fidelity, made without dependence on him. 2d. That all promises to adhere to him should be made relying on him for aid. 3d. That we little know how feeble we are till we are tried. 4th. That Christians *may be left* to great and disgraceful sins to show them their weakness.

Luke adds that Jesus said to Peter that Satan had desired to have him, that he might sift him as wheat—that is, that he might thoroughly *try* him. But Jesus says that he had prayed for him that his faith should not fail, and charged him when he was *converted*—that is, when he was *turned* from this sin—to strengthen his brethren; to wit, by teaching them to take warning by his example. See Notes on Lu. xxii. 31–33.

34. *This night.* This was in the *evening* when this was spoken, after the observance of the Passover, and, we may suppose, near nine o'clock. ¶ *Before the cock crow.* Mark and Luke add, before the cock crow *twice.* The cock is accustomed to crow twice—once at midnight, and once in the morning at break of day. The latter was commonly called cock-crowing. See Mar. xiii. 35. This was the time familiarly known as the cock-crowing, and of this Matthew and John speak, without referring to the other. Mark and Luke speak of the *second* crowing, and mean the same time, so that there is no contradiction between them. ¶ *Deny me thrice.* That is, as Luke adds, deny that *thou knowest* me. See ver. 74.

35. *Will I not deny thee.* Will not deny my connection with thee, or that I knew thee. *All* the disciples said the same thing, and all fled at the approach of danger, *forsaking* their Master and Friend, and practically denying that they knew him, ver. 56.

36–45. *Jesus's agony in Gethsemane.* This account is also recorded in Mar. xiv. 32–42; Lu. xxii. 39–46; Jn. xviii. 1.

36. *Then cometh*, &c. After the institution of the Supper, in the early part of the night, he went out to the Mount of Olives. In his journey he passed over the brook Cedron (Jn. xviii. 1), which bounded Jerusalem on the east. ¶ *Unto a place.* John calls this *a garden.* This garden was on the western side of the Mount of Olives, and a short distance from Jerusalem. The word used by John means not properly a garden for the cultivation of *vegetables*, but a place planted with the olive and other trees, perhaps with a fountain of water, and with walks and groves; a proper place of refreshment in a hot climate, and of retirement from the noise of the adjacent city. Such places were doubtless common in the vicinity of Jerusalem. Messrs. Fisk and King, American missionaries, were at the place which is commonly supposed to have been the garden of Gethsemane in 1823. They tell us that the garden is about a stone's cast from the brook of Cedron; that it now contains eight large and venerable-looking olives, whose trunks show their great antiquity. The spot is sandy and barren, and appears like a forsaken place. A low broken wall surrounds it. Mr.

not deny thee. Likewise also said all the disciples.

36 Then[q] cometh Jesus with them unto a place called Gethsemane, and saith unto the disciples, Sit ye here, while I go and pray yonder.

37 And he took with him Peter and the two sons of Zebedee, and began to be sorrowful and very heavy.

38 Then saith he unto them, [r]My soul is exceeding sorrowful, even unto death: tarry ye here, and watch with me.

39 And he went a little farther,

q Mar.14.32,&c.; Lu.22.39,&c.; Jn.18.1,&c.

r Ps.116.3; Is.53.3,10; Jn.12.27.

King sat down beneath one of the trees and read Is. liii., and also the gospel history of our Redeemer's sorrow during that memorable night in which he was there betrayed; and the interest of the association was heightened by the passing through the place of a party of Bedouins, armed with spears and swords. A recent traveller says of this place that it "is a field or garden about fifty paces square, with a few shrubs growing in it, and eight olive-trees of great antiquity, the whole inclosed with a stone wall." The place was probably fixed upon, as Dr. Robinson supposes, during the visit of Helena to Jerusalem, A.D. 326, when the places of the crucifixion and resurrection were believed to be identified. There is, however, no absolute certainty respecting the places. Dr. Thomson (*The Land and the Book*, vol. ii. p. 484) supposes it most probable that the real "Garden of Gethsemane" was several hundred yards to the north-west of the present Gethsemane, in a place much more secluded than the one usually regarded as that where the agony of the Saviour occurred, and therefore more likely to have been the place of his retirement. Nothing, however, that is of importance depends on ascertaining the exact spot.

Luke says that Jesus "went as he was wont"—that is, accustomed—"to the Mount of Olives." Probably he had been in the habit of retiring from Jerusalem to that place for meditation and prayer, thus enforcing by his example what he had so often done by his precepts—the duty of retiring from the noise and bustle of the world to hold communion with God. ¶ *Gethsemane.* This word is made up either of two Hebrew words, signifying *valley of fatness*—that is, a fertile valley; or of two words, signifying *an olive-press*, given to it, probably, because the place was filled with olives. ¶ *Sit ye here.* That is, in one part of the garden to which they first came. ¶ *While I go and pray yonder.* That is, at the distance of a stone's cast, Lu. xxii. 41. Luke adds that when he came to the garden he charged them to pray that they might not enter into temptation—that is, into deep *trials* and *afflictions*, or, more probably, into scenes and dangers that would tempt them to deny him.

37. *And he took with him Peter and the two sons of Zebedee.* That is, James and John, Mat. x. 2. On two other occasions he had favoured these disciples in a particular manner, suffering them to go with him to witness his power and glory, viz. at the healing of the ruler's daughter (Lu. viii. 51), and at his transfiguration on the mount, Mat. xvii. 1. ¶ *Sorrowful.* Affected with grief. ¶ *Very heavy.* The word in the original is much stronger than the one translated *sorrowful.* It means, to be pressed down or overwhelmed with great anguish. This was produced, doubtless, by a foresight of his great sufferings on the cross in making an atonement for the sins of men.

38. *My soul is exceeding sorrowful.* His human nature—his soul—was much and deeply affected and pressed down. ¶ *Even unto death.* This denotes extreme sorrow and agony. The sufferings of death are the greatest of which we have any knowledge; they are the most feared and dreaded by man; and those sufferings are therefore put for extreme and indescribable anguish. The meaning may be thus expressed: My sorrows are so great that under their burden I am ready to die; such is the anxiety of mind, that I seem to bear the pains of death! ¶ *Tarry ye here and watch with me.* The word rendered *watch* means, literally, to abstain from sleep; then to be vigilant, or to guard against danger. Here it seems to mean to sympathize with him, to unite with him in seeking divine support, and to prepare themselves for approaching dangers.

and fell on his face, and [s]prayed, saying, O my Father, if it be possible, let [t]this cup pass from me! nevertheless, [u]not as I will, but as thou *wilt*.

40 And he cometh unto the disciples, and findeth them asleep, and saith unto Peter, What! could ye not watch with me one hour?

41 Watch,[v] and pray, that [w]ye

s He.5.7. *t* ch.20.22. *u* Jn.5.30; 6.38; Ro.15.3; Phi.2.8.

v Mar.13.33; 14.38; Lu.22.40; Ep.6.18; Re.16.15. *w* Pr.4.14,15.

39. *And he went a little farther.* That is, at the distance that a man could conveniently cast a stone (Luke). ¶ *Fell on his face.* Luke says "he kneeled down." He did both. He *first* kneeled, and then, in the fervency of his prayer and the depth of his sorrow, he fell with his face on the ground, denoting the deepest anguish and the most earnest entreaty. This was the usual posture of prayer in times of great earnestness. See Nu. xvi. 22; 2 Ch. xx. 18; Ne. viii. 6. ¶ *If it be possible.* That is, if the world can be redeemed—if it be consistent with justice, and with maintaining the government of the universe, that men should be saved *without* this extremity of sorrow, let it be done. There is no doubt that if it had been possible it would have been done; and the fact that these sufferings were *not* removed, and that the Saviour went forward and bore them without mitigation, shows that it was *not* consistent with the justice of God and with the welfare of the universe that men should be saved without the awful sufferings of *such an atonement.* ¶ *Let this cup.* These bitter sufferings. These approaching trials. The word *cup* is often used in this sense, denoting sufferings. See Notes on Mat. xx. 22. ¶ *Not as I will, but as thou* wilt. As Jesus was man as well as God, there is nothing inconsistent in supposing that, *as* man, he was deeply affected in view of these sorrows. When he speaks of *his* will, he expresses what *human nature*, in view of such great sufferings, would desire. It naturally shrunk from them and sought deliverance. Yet he sought to do the will of God. He chose rather that the high purpose of God should be done, than that *that* purpose should be abandoned from regard to the fears of his human nature. In this he has left a model of prayer in all times of affliction. It is *right*, in times of calamity, to seek deliverance. Like the Saviour, also, in such seasons we *should*, we *must* submit cheerfully to the will of God, confident that in all these trials he is wise, and merciful, and good.

40. *And findeth them asleep.* It may seem remarkable that in such circumstances, with a suffering, pleading Redeemer near, surrounded by danger, and having received a special charge to *watch*—that is, not to sleep—they should so soon have fallen asleep. It is frequently supposed that this was proof of wonderful stupidity, and indifference to their Lord's sufferings. The truth is, however, that it was just the reverse; *it was proof of their great attachment, and their deep sympathy in his sorrows.* Luke has added that *he found them sleeping* FOR SORROW—that is, *on account* of their sorrow; or their grief was so great that they naturally fell asleep. Multitudes of facts might be brought to show that this is in accordance with the regular effects of grief. Dr. Rush says: "There is another symptom of grief, which is not often noticed, and that is *profound sleep.* I have often witnessed it even in mothers, immediately after the death of a child. Criminals, we are told by Mr. Akerman, the keeper of Newgate, in London, often sleep soundly the night before their execution. The son of General Custine slept nine hours the night before he was led to the guillotine in Paris."—*Diseases of the Mind*, p. 319. ¶ *Saith unto Peter*, &c. This earnest appeal was addressed to Peter particularly on account of his warm professions, his rash zeal, and his self-confidence. If he could not keep awake and watch with the Saviour for one hour, how little probability was there that he would adhere to him in the trials through which he was soon to pass!

41. *Watch.* See ver. 38. Greater trials are coming on. It is necessary, therefore, still to be on your guard. ¶ *And pray.* Seek aid from God by supplication, in view of the thickening calamities. ¶ *That ye enter not into temptation.* That ye be not *overcome* and *oppressed* with these trials of your faith so as to deny me. The word *temptation* here properly means what would *try* their faith in the approaching calamities—in his rejection and death. It

enter not into [x]temptation: [y]the spirit indeed *is* willing, but the flesh *is* weak.

42 He went away again the second time, and prayed, saying, O my Father, if this cup may not pass away from me, except I drink it, thy will be done.

x Re.3.10. y Is.26.8,9; Ro.7.18-25; Ga.5.17.

would *try* their faith, because, though they believed that he was the Messiah, they were not very clearly aware of the necessity of his death, and they did not fully understand that he was to rise again. They had cherished the belief that he was to establish a kingdom *while he lived*. When they should see him, therefore, rejected, tried, crucified, dead—when they should see him submit to all this *as if* he had not power to deliver himself—*then* would be the trial of their faith; and, in view of that, he exhorted them to pray that they might not *so* enter temptation as to be overcome by it and fall. ¶ *The spirit indeed* is *willing*, &c. The mind, the heart is ready and disposed to bear these trials, but the *flesh*, the natural feelings, through the fear of danger, is weak, and will be likely to lead you astray when the trial comes. Though you may have strong faith, and believe now that you will not deny me, yet human nature is weak, and shrinks at trials, and you should therefore seek strength from on high. This was intended to excite them, notwithstanding he knew that they loved him, to be on their guard, lest the weakness of human nature should be insufficient to sustain them in the hour of their temptation.

42–44. It is probable that our Lord spent considerable time in prayer, and that the evangelists have recorded rather *the substance* of his petitions than the very *words*. He returned repeatedly to his disciples, doubtless to caution them against danger, to show the deep interest which he had in their welfare, and to show them the extent of his sufferings on their behalf. Each time that he returned these sorrows deepened. Again he sought the place of prayer, and as his approaching sufferings overwhelmed him, this was the burden of his prayer, and he prayed the same words. Luke adds that amid his agonies an angel appeared from heaven strengthening him. His human nature began to sink, as unequal to his sufferings, and a messenger from heaven appeared, to support him in these heavy trials. It may seem strange that, since Jesus was divine (Jn. i. 1), the *divine nature* did not minister strength to the human, and that he that was *God* should receive strength from an *angel*. But it should be remembered that Jesus came in his human nature not only to make an atonement, but to be a perfect example of a holy man; that, as such, it was necessary to submit to the *common conditions* of humanity—that he should live as other men, be sustained as other men, suffer as other men, and be strengthened as other men; that he should, so to speak, take no advantage in favour of his piety, from his divinity, but submit in all things to the common lot of pious men. Hence he supplied his wants, not by his being divine, but in the ordinary way of human life; he preserved himself from danger, not *as God*, but by seeking the usual ways of human prudence and precaution; he met trials as a man; he received comfort as a man; and there is no absurdity in supposing that, in accordance with the condition of his people, his human nature should be strengthened, *as they are*, by those who are sent forth to be ministering spirits to the heirs of salvation, He. i. 14.

Luke farther adds (xxii. 44) that, being in an agony, he prayed more earnestly, and his sweat was as it were great drops of blood falling down to the ground. The word *agony* is taken from the anxiety, effort, and strong emotion of the *wrestlers* in the Greek games about to engage in a mighty struggle. Here it denotes the extreme anguish of mind, the strong conflict produced in sinking human nature from the prospect of deep and overwhelming calamities. ¶ *Great drops of blood*, Lu. xxii. 44. The word here rendered *great drops* does not mean drops gently falling on the ground, but rather thick and clammy masses of gore, pressed by inward agony through the skin, and, mixing with the sweat, falling thus to the ground. It has been doubted by some whether the sacred writer meant to say that there was actually *blood* in this sweat, or only that the sweat was *in the form* of great drops. The natural meaning is, doubtless, that the blood was mingled with his sweat; that it fell profusely—falling masses of gore; that it was pressed out by his inward anguish; and that this was caused

43 And he came and found them asleep again; for their eyes were heavy.

44 And he left them, and went away again, and prayed the [z]third time, saying the same words.

45 Then cometh he to his disciples, and saith unto them, Sleep on now and take *your* rest; behold, the hour is at hand, and the Son of man is betrayed into the hands of sinners.

z 2 Co.12.8.

in some way in view of his approaching death. This effect of extreme sufferings, of mental anguish, has been known in several other instances. Bloody sweats have been mentioned by many writers as caused by extreme suffering. Dr. Doddridge says (Note on Lu. xxii. 44) that "Aristotle and Diodorus Siculus both mention bloody sweats as attending some extraordinary agony of mind; and I find Loti, in his *Life of Pope Sextus V.*, and Sir John Chardin, in his *History of Persia*, mentioning a like phenomenon, to which Dr. Jackson adds another from Thuanus." It has been objected to this account that it is improbable, and that such an event could not occur. The instances, however, which are referred to by Doddridge and others show sufficiently that the objection is unfounded. In addition to these, I may observe that Voltaire has himself narrated a fact which ought for ever to stop the mouths of infidels. Speaking of Charles IX. of France, in his *Universal History*, he says: "He died in his thirty-fifth year. His disorder was of a very remarkable kind; the blood oozed out of all his pores. This malady, of which there have been other instances, was owing to either excessive fear, or violent agitation, or to a feverish and melancholy temperament."

Various opinions have been given of the probable causes of these sorrows of the Saviour. Some have thought it was a strong shrinking from the manner of dying on the cross, or from an apprehension of being *forsaken* there by the Father; others, that Satan was permitted in a peculiar manner to try him, and to fill his mind with horrors, having departed from him at the beginning of his ministry for a season (Lu. iv. 13), only to renew his temptations in a more dreadful manner now; and others that these sufferings were sent upon him as the wrath of God manifested against sin—that God *inflicted* them directly upon him by his own hand, to show his abhorrence of the sins of men for which he was about to die. Where the Scriptures are silent about *the cause*, it does not become us confidently to express an opinion. We may suppose, perhaps, without presumption, that a part or all these things were *combined* to produce this awful suffering. There is no need of supposing that there was a *single* thing that produced it; but it is rather probable that this was a *rush* of feeling from every quarter—his situation, his approaching death, the temptations of the enemy, the awful suffering on account of men's sins, and God's hatred of it about to be manifested in his own death—all coming upon his soul at once—sorrow flowing in from every quarter—the *concentration* of the sufferings of the atonement pouring together upon him and filling him with unspeakable anguish.

45. *Sleep on now and take* your *rest.* Most interpreters have supposed that this should be translated as a *question* rather than a command. "Do you sleep *now* and take your rest? Is this a time, amid so much danger and so many enemies, to give yourselves to sleep?" This construction is strongly countenanced by Lu. xxii. 46, where the expression, Why sleep ye? evidently refers to the same point of time. There is no doubt that the Greek will bear this construction, and in this way the apparent inconsistency will be removed between this command *to sleep*, and that in the next verse, *to rise* and be going. Others suppose that, his agony being over, and the necessity of watching *with him* being now past, he kindly *permitted* them to seek repose till they should be roused by the coming of the traitor; that while they slept Jesus continued still awake; that some considerable time elapsed between what was spoken here and in the next verse; and that Jesus suffered them to sleep until he saw Judas coming, and then aroused them. This is the most probable opinion. Others have supposed that he spoke this in irony: "Sleep on now, if you can; take rest, if possible, in such dangers and at such a time." But this supposition is un-

46 Rise, let us be going: behold, he is at hand that doth betray me.
47 And while he yet spake, lo, [a]Judas, one of the twelve, came, and with him a great multitude, with swords and staves, from the chief priests and elders of the people.
48 Now he that betrayed him gave them [b]a sign, saying, Whomsoever I shall kiss, that same is he: hold him fast.

a Ac.1.16.

b Ps.38.12.

---

worthy the Saviour and the occasion. Mark adds, "It is enough." That is, sufficient time has been given to sleep. It is time to arise and be going. ¶ *The hour is at hand.* The *time* when the Son of man is to be betrayed is near. ¶ *Sinners.* Judas, the Roman soldiers, and the Jews.

46. *Rise, let us be going.* That is, probably, *with them.* Let us go wheresoever they shall lead us. The time when *I must die* is come. It is no longer proper to attempt an escape, and no more time can be given to repose.

47–57. The account of Jesus's being betrayed by Judas is recorded by all the evangelists. See Mar. xiv. 43–52; Lu. xxii. 47–53; Jn. xviii. 2–12.

47. *Judas, one of the twelve, came.* This was done while Jesus was addressing his disciples. John informs us that Judas knew the place, because Jesus was in the habit of going there with his disciples. Judas had passed the time, after he left Jesus and the other disciples at the Passover, in arranging matters with the Jews, collecting the band, and preparing to go. Perhaps, also, on this occasion they *gave* him the money which they had promised. ¶ *A great multitude with swords and staves.* John says that he had *received a band of men and officers from the chief priests and Pharisees.* Josephus says (*Antiq.* b. xx. ch. iv.) that at the festival of the Passover, when a great multitude of people came to observe the feast, lest there should be any disorder, a band of men was commanded to keep watch at the porches of the temple, to repress a tumult if any should be excited. This *band,* or guard, was at the disposal of the chief priests, Mat. xxvii. 65. It was composed of Roman soldiers, and was stationed chiefly at the tower of Antonia, at the north-west side of the temple. In addition to this, they had *constant* guards stationed around the temple, composed of Levites. The Roman soldiers were armed with *swords.* The other persons that went out carried, probably, whatever was accessible as a weapon. These were the persons *sent* by the priests to apprehend Jesus. Perhaps other desperate men might have joined them. ¶ *Staves.* In the original, "*wood;*" used here in the plural number. It means rather *clubs* or *sticks* than spears. It does not mean *staves.* Probably it means any weapon at hand, such as a mob could conveniently collect. John says that they had *lanterns* and *torches.* The Passover was celebrated at the *full moon;* but this night might have been cloudy. The place to which they were going was also shaded with trees, and lights, therefore, might be necessary.

48. *Gave them a sign.* That is, told them of a way by which they might know whom to apprehend—to wit, by his kissing him. It was night. Jesus was, besides, probably personally unknown to the *Romans*—perhaps to the others also. Judas, therefore, being well acquainted with him, to prevent the possibility of mistake, agreed to designate him by one of the tokens of friendship.

John tells us that Jesus, knowing all things that should come upon him, when they approached him, asked them whom they sought, and that they replied, Jesus of Nazareth. He then informed them that he was the person they sought. They, when they heard it, overawed by his presence and smitten with the consciousness of guilt, went backward and fell to the ground. He again asked them whom they sought. They made the same declaration—Jesus of Nazareth. Jesus then, since they *professed* to seek only *him,* claimed the right that his disciples should be suffered to escape, "that the saying might be fulfilled which he spake (Jn. xviii. 9): Of them which thou gavest me have I lost none."

49. *Hail, Master.* The word translated *hail,* here, means to *rejoice,* to have joy, and also to have *cause* of joy. It thus expresses the *joy* which one friend has when he meets another,

49 And forthwith he came to Jesus, and said, Hail, Master; and [c]kissed him.

50 And Jesus said unto him, Friend,[d] wherefore art thou come? Then came they and laid hands on Jesus, and took him.

51 And, behold, one of them which were with Jesus stretched out *his* hand and drew his sword, and struck a servant of the high-priest, and smote off his ear.

52 Then said Jesus unto him, Put up again thy sword into his place; [e]for all they that take the sword shall perish with the sword.

53 Thinkest thou that I cannot now pray to my Father, and he

c 2 Sa.3.27; 20.9; Ps.28.3. d Ps.41.9; 55.13. e Ge.9.6; Eze.35.5,6; Re.13.10.

especially after an absence. It was used by the Jews and Greeks as a mode of salutation among friends. It would here seem to express the *joy* of Judas at finding his Master and again being *with him*. ¶ *Master.* In the original, *Rabbi.* See Notes on Mat. xxiii. 7. ¶ *Kissed him.* Gave him the common salutation of friends when meeting after absence. This mode of salutation was more common among Eastern nations than with us.

50. *And Jesus said unto him, Friend.* It seems strange to us that Jesus should give the endeared name *friend* to a man that he knew was his enemy, and that was about to betray him. It should be remarked, however, that this is the fault of *our language*, not of the original. In the Greek there are two words which our translators have rendered *friend*—one implying *affection* and *regard*, the other not. One is properly rendered *friend;* the other expresses more nearly what we mean by *companion.* It is this *latter* word which is given to the disaffected labourer in the vineyard: "*Friend*, I do thee no wrong" (Mat. xx. 13); to the guest which had not on the wedding-garment, in the parable of the marriage feast (Mat. xxii. 12); and to *Judas* in this place. ¶ *Wherefore art thou come?* This was said, not because he was ignorant why he had come, but probably to fill the mind of Judas with the consciousness of his crime, and by a striking question to *compel* him *to think* of what he was doing.

51. *One of them which were with Jesus.* John informs us that this was *Peter.* The other evangelists concealed the name, probably because they wrote while Peter was living, and it might have endangered Peter to have it known. ¶ *And drew his sword.* The apostles were not commonly armed. On this occasion they had provided *two swords*, Lu. xxii. 38. In seasons of danger, when travelling, they were under a necessity of providing means of defending themselves against the robbers that infested the country. This will account for their having *any* swords in their possession. See Notes on Lu. x. 30. Josephus informs us that the people were accustomed to carry swords under their garments as they went up to Jerusalem. ¶ *A servant of the high-priest.* His name, John informs us, was *Malchus.* Luke adds that Jesus touched the ear and healed it, thus showing his benevolence to his foes when they sought his life, and giving them proof that they were attacking him that was sent from heaven.

52. *Thy sword into his place.* Into the sheath. ¶ *For all they that take the sword*, &c. This passage is capable of different significations. 1st. They who resist by the sword the civil magistrate shall be punished; and it is dangerous, therefore, to oppose those who come with the authority of the civil ruler. 2d. These men, Jews and Romans, who have taken the sword against the innocent, shall perish by the sword. God will take vengeance on them. But, 3d. The most satisfactory interpretation is that which regards it as a *caution* to Peter. Peter was rash. Alone he had attacked the whole band. Jesus told him that his unseasonable and imprudent defence might be the occasion of his own destruction. In doing it he would endanger his life, for they who took the sword perished by it. This was probably a proverb, denoting that they who engaged in wars commonly perished there.

53. *Thinkest thou*, &c. Jesus says that not only would Peter endanger himself, but his resistance implied a distrust of the protection of God, and was an improper resistance of his will. If it had been proper that they should be rescued, God could easily have furnished far more efficient aid than that of Peter—a mighty host of angels. ¶ *Twelve*

shall presently give me [f]more than twelve legions of angels?

54 But how then shall the scriptures be fulfilled, that [g]thus it must be?

55 In that same hour said Jesus to the multitudes, Are ye come out, as against a thief, with swords and staves for to take me? I sat daily with you teaching in the temple, and ye laid no hold on me.

56 But all this was done that the [h]scriptures of the prophets might be fulfilled. Then all the disciples forsook him, and fled.

57 And[i] they that had laid hold on Jesus led *him* away to Caiaphas

f 2 Ki.6.17; Da.7.10; ch.4.11. *g* Lu.24.26,46.

h Ge.3.15; Ps.22.; 69.; Is.53.; La.4.20; Da.9.24,26; Zec.13.7; Ac.1.16.
i Mar.14.53,&c.; Lu.22.54,&c.; Jn.18.12,&c.

legions. A legion was a division of the Roman army amounting to more than six thousand men. See Notes on Mat. viii. 29. The number *twelve* was mentioned, perhaps, in reference to the number of his apostles and himself. Judas being away, but eleven disciples remained. God could guard *him*, and each disciple, with a legion of angels: that is, God could easily protect him, if he should pray to him, and if it was his will.

54. *But how then shall the scriptures be fulfilled*, &c. That is, the Scriptures which foretold of his dying for the world. In *some way* that must be accomplished, and the time had come when, having finished the work which the Father gave him to do, it was proper that he should submit to death. This was said, doubtless, to comfort his disciples; to show them that his death was not a matter of surprise or disappointment to him; and that *they*, therefore, should not be offended and forsake him.

55. *Against a thief.* Rather a *robber.* This was the *manner* in which they would have sought to take a highwayman of desperate character, and armed to defend his life. It adds not a little to the depth of his humiliation that he consented to be *hunted down* thus by wicked men, and to be treated as if he had been the worst of mankind. ¶ *Daily with you teaching in the temple.* For many days before the Passover, as recorded in the previous chapter.

56. *Scriptures of the prophets.* The *writings* of the prophets, for that is the meaning of the word *scriptures.* He alludes to those parts of the prophetic writings which foretold his sufferings and death. ¶ *Then all the disciples*, &c. Overcome with fear when they saw their Master actually taken; alarmed with the terrific appearance of armed men and torches in a dark night, and forgetting their promises *not* to forsake him, they all left their Saviour to go *alone* to trial and to death! Alas! how many, when attachment to Christ would lead them to danger, leave him and flee! Mark adds that after the disciples had fled, a young man, having a linen cloth cast about his naked body, attempted to follow him. It is not known who he was, but not improbably he may have been the *owner* of the garden and a friend of Jesus. Aroused by the noise from his repose, he came to defend, or at least to follow the Saviour. He cast, in his hurry, such a covering as was at hand around his body, and came to him. The young men among the Romans and Jews attempted to seize him also, and he only secured his safety by leaving in their hands the covering that he had hastily thrown around him. It is not known *why* this circumstance was recorded by Mark, but it would seem to be probable that it was to mention him with honour, as showing his interest in the Saviour, and his willingness to aid him. See Notes on Mar. xiv. 50, 51. This circumstance *may* have been recorded for the purpose of honouring him by placing his conduct in strong contrast with that of the apostles, who had all forsaken the Saviour and fled.

57–75. The trial of our Lord before the council, and the denial of Peter happening at the same time, might be related one before the other, according to the evangelists' pleasure. Accordingly, Matthew and Mark relate the *trial* first, and Peter's denial afterward; Luke mentions the denial first, and John has probably observed the natural order. The parallel places are recorded in Mar. xiv. 53–72; Lu. xxii. 54–71; and Jn. xviii. 13–27.

57. *To Caiaphas.* John says that they led him first to Annas, the father-in-law of Caiaphas. This was done, probably as a mark of respect, he having

the high-priest, where the scribes and the elders were assembled.

58 But Peter followed him afar off, unto the high-priest's palace, and went in, and sat with the servants, to see the end.

59 Now the chief priests and elders, and all the council, sought

---

been high-priest, and perhaps distinguished for prudence, and capable of *advising* his son-in-law in a difficult case. The Saviour was *detained* there, probably, until the chief priests and elders were assembled. ¶ *The high-priest.* Note, Mat. xxvi. 3. John says he was high-priest for that year. Annas had been high-priest some years before. In the time of our Saviour the office was frequently changed by the civil ruler. This Caiaphas had prophesied that it was expedient that one should die for the people. See Notes on Jn. xi. 49, 50. ¶ *The scribes and elders.* The men composing the great council of the nation, or Sanhedrim, Mat. v. 22. It is not probable that they could be immediately assembled, and some part of the transaction respecting the denial of Peter probably took place while they were collecting.

58. *Peter followed afar off.* By this he evinced two things: 1st. Real attachment to his Master; a desire to be near him and to witness his trial. 2d. Fear respecting his personal safety. He therefore kept so far off as to be out of danger, and yet so near as that he might witness the transactions respecting his Master. Perhaps he expected to be lost and unobserved in the crowd. Many, in this, imitate Peter. They are afraid to follow the Saviour closely. They fear danger, ridicule, or persecution. They *follow him*, but it is at a great distance—*so far* that it is difficult to discern that they are in the train, and are his friends at all. Religion requires us to be near to Christ. We may measure our piety by our desire to be with him, to be like him, and by our willingness to follow him always—through trials, contempt, persecution, and death. Comp. Notes on Phi. iii. 10. John says that another disciple went with Peter. By that other disciple it is commonly supposed, as he did not mention his name, that he meant himself. He was acquainted with the high-priest, and went immediately into the hall. ¶ *Unto the high-priest's palace.* The word rendered *palace* means, rather, the *hall*, or middle court, or *area* of his house. It was situated in the centre of the palace, and was commonly uncovered. See Notes and plan of a house in Mat. ix. 1–8. ¶ *And went in.* John informs us that he did not go immediately in; but the other disciple, being known to the high-priest, went in first, while Peter remained at the *gate* or entrance. The other disciple then went out and brought in Peter. Matthew, Mark, and Luke have omitted this circumstance. John recorded it, probably, *because* they had omitted it, and because *he* was the "other disciple" concerned in it. ¶ *Sat with the servants to see the end.* That is, the end of the trial, or to see how it would go with his Master. The other evangelists say that he stood with the servants warming himself. John says, it being cold, they had made a fire of coals and warmed themselves. It was then, probably, not far from midnight. The place where they were was uncovered; and travellers say that, though the *days* are warm in Judea at that season of the year, yet that the nights are often uncomfortably cold. This fire was made *in the hall* (Luke). The fire was not in *a fireplace*, as we commonly suppose, but was probably made of *coals* laid on the pavement. At this place and time was Peter's first *denial* of his Lord, as is recorded afterward. See ver. 69.

59. *False witness.* That is, they sought for witnesses who would accuse him of crime—of violation of the laws of the land or of God. We are not to suppose that *they wished* them to be *false* witnesses. They were indifferent, probably, whether they were true or false, if they could succeed in condemning him. *The evangelist* calls it false testimony. Before these witnesses were sought, we learn from John (xviii. 19–23) that the high-priest asked Jesus of his disciples and his doctrine. Jesus replied that he had taught openly in the temple, and in secret had said nothing; that is, he had no *secret doctrines* which he had not been willing openly to teach, and he referred the high-priest to those who had heard him. In a firm, dignified manner he put himself on trial, and insisted on his rights. "If I have spoken evil, bear witness of the evil; but if well, why smitest thou me?" Jn. xviii. 23.

false witness against Jesus, to put him to death;

60 But found none; yea, though many false witnesses came, *yet* found they none. At the last came [k]two false witnesses,

61 And said, This *fellow* said, I[l] am able to destroy the temple of God, and to build it in three days.

62 And the high-priest arose, and said unto him, Answerest thou nothing? What *is it which* these witness against thee?

63 But [m]Jesus held his peace. And the high-priest answered and said unto him, I [n]adjure thee by the living God that thou tell us whether thou be [o]the Christ, the Son of God.

k Ps.27.12; 35.11. l Jn.2.19,21.

m Is.53.7; ch.27.12,14.
n 1 Sa.14.26,28; 1 Ki.22.16. o ch.16.16; Jn.1.34.

This conversation took place, probably, before the council was assembled, and during this time the denials by Peter occurred. Luke informs us (xxii. 66) that the council came together as soon as it was day; that is, probably, near the morning, or not far from the break of day—after Peter had denied him and gone out.

60. *Found none.* That is, they found none on whose testimony they could with any show of reason convict him. The reason was, as Mark says (xiv. 56), that "their witnesses agreed not together." They differed about facts, times, and circumstances, as all false witnesses do. Two witnesses were required by their law, and they did not *dare* to condemn him without conforming, *in appearance* at least, to the requirements of the law.

61. *And said, This* fellow *said*, &c. Mark has recorded this testimony differently. According to him, they said, "We heard him say, I will destroy this temple that is made with hands, and within three days I will build another made without hands." Probably both forms of giving in the testimony were used on the trial, and Matthew has recorded it as it was given at one time and Mark at another, so that there is no contradiction. Mark adds, "But neither so did their witnesses agree together." That which they *attempted* to accuse him of is what he had said respecting his body and their destroying it, Jn. ii. 19: "Destroy this temple, and in three days I will raise it up." This he spoke of his body; they perverted it, endeavouring to show that he meant the temple at Jerusalem. They neither stated it as it was, nor did they state correctly its meaning, nor did they agree about the *words* used. It was therefore very little to their purpose.

62, 63. *Jesus held his peace.* Was silent. He knew that the evidence did not even *appear* to amount to anything worth a reply. He knew that they were aware of that, and that feeling that, the high-priest attempted to draw something from him on which they could condemn him. ¶ *I adjure thee by the living God.* I put thee upon thy oath before God. This was the usual form of putting an oath among the Jews. It implies calling God to witness the truth of what was said. The law respecting witnesses also made it a violation of an oath to *conceal* any part of the truth; and though our Saviour might have felt that such a question, put in such a manner, was very improper or was unlawful, yet he also knew that to be silent would be construed into a denial of his being the Christ. The question was probably put in anger. They had utterly failed in their proof. They had no way left to accomplish their purpose of condemning him but to draw it from his own lips. This cunning question was therefore proposed. The difficulty of the question consisted in this: If he *confessed* that he was the Son of God, they stood ready to condemn him for *blasphemy;* if he *denied it*, they were prepared to condemn him for being an *impostor*, and for deluding the people under the pretence of being the Messiah. ¶ *The living God.* Jehovah is called the *living* God in opposition to *idols*, which were without life. ¶ *The Christ.* The Messiah, the Anointed. See Notes on Mat. i. 1. ¶ *The Son of God.* The Jews uniformly expected that the Messiah would be the Son of God. In their view it denoted, also, that he would be *divine*, or equal to the Father, Jn. x. 31–36. To claim that title was therefore, in their view, *blasphemy;* and as they had determined beforehand in their own minds that he was *not* the Messiah, they were ready at once to accuse him of blasphemy.

64 Jesus saith unto him, Thou hast said: nevertheless I say unto you, [p]Hereafter shall ye see the Son of man sitting on the [q]right hand of power, and coming in the clouds of heaven.

65 Then the high-priest rent his clothes, saying, He hath spoken blasphemy; what further need have we of witnesses? behold, now ye have heard his blasphemy.

66 What think ye? They answered and said, [r]He is guilty of death.

67 Then[s] did they spit in his face, and buffeted him; and others

p Da.7.13; Jn.1.51; 1 Th.4.16; Re.1.7. q Ps.110.1; Ac.7.55.

r Le.24.16; Jn.19.7. s Is.50.6.

---

64. *Thou hast said.* This is a form of *assenting* or affirming. Thou hast said the *truth;* or, as Luke (xxii. 70) has it, "Ye say that I am." This was not, however, said *immediately*. Before Jesus acknowledged himself to be the Messiah, he said to them (Lu. xxii. 67, 68), "*If I tell you ye will not believe, and if I also ask you*"—that is, propose the proofs of my mission, and require you to give your opinion of them—"*ye will not answer me, nor let me go.*" ¶ *Nevertheless.* This word should have been translated *moreover* or *furthermore*. What follows is designed to explain and give confirmation to what he had said. ¶ *Sitting on the right hand of power.* That is, of God, called here *the Power*—equivalent to *the Mighty*, or *the Almighty*. It denotes dignity and majesty; for to sit at the right hand of a prince was the chief place of honour. See Notes on Mat. xx. 21. ¶ *Coming in the clouds of heaven.* See Notes on Mat. xxiv., xxv. The meaning of this is, You shall see *the sign from heaven* which you have so often demanded; even the Messiah returning himself *as the sign*, with great glory, to destroy your city and to judge the world.

65. *Then the high-priest rent his clothes.* The Jews were accustomed to rend their clothes as a token of grief. This was done often as a matter of form, and consisted in tearing a particular part of the garment reserved for this purpose. It was not lawful for the high-priest to rend his clothes, Le. x. 6; xxi. 10. By that was probably intended the robes of his priestly office. The garment which he *now* rent was probably his ordinary garment, or the garments which he wore as president of the Sanhedrim—not those in which he officiated as high-priest in the things of religion. This was done on this occasion to denote the *great grief* of the high-priest that so great a sin as blasphemy had been committed in his presence. ¶ *He hath spoken blasphemy.* That is, he has, under oath, arrogated to himself what belongs to God. In asserting that he is the Son of God, and therefore equal in dignity with the Father, and that he would yet sit at his right hand, he has claimed what belongs to no *man*, and what is therefore an invasion of the divine prerogative. If he had not been the *Messiah*, the charge would have been true; but the question was whether he had not given evidence that he *was* the Messiah, and that therefore his claims were just. This point—the only *proper* point of inquiry—they never examined. They *assumed* that he was an *impostor*, and that point being assumed, everything like a pretension to being the Messiah was, in their view, proof that he deserved to die.

66. *What think ye?* What is your *opinion?* What *sentence* do you pronounce? As president of the Sanhedrim he demanded their judgment. ¶ *He is guilty of death.* This was the form which was used when a criminal was condemned to die. The meaning is, he is guilty of a crime to which the law annexes death. This sentence was used before the Jews became subject to the Romans, when they had the power of inflicting death. After they were subject to the Romans, though the power of *inflicting* capital punishment was taken away, yet they retained the *form* when they expressed their opinion of the guilt of an offender. The law under which they condemned him was that recorded in Le. xxiv. 10–16, which sentenced him that was guilty of blasphemy to death by *stoning*. The chief priests, however, were unwilling to excite a popular tumult by stoning him, and they therefore consulted to deliver him to the Romans to be crucified, *under the authority of the Roman name*, and thus to prevent any excitement among the people.

67. *Then did they spit in his face.* This, among the Jews, as among us,

smote *him* with [3]the palms of their hands,

68 Saying, Prophesy unto us, thou Christ, who is he that smote thee?

69 Now[t] Peter sat without in the palace: and a damsel came unto him, saying, Thou also wast with Jesus of Galilee.

70 But he denied before *them* all, saying, I know not what thou sayest.

71 And when he was gone out into the porch, another *maid* saw

[3] or, *rods*.
t Mar.14.66,&c.; Lu.22.55,&c.; Jn.18.16,&c.

was significant of the highest contempt and insult, Nu. xii. 14; Isa. l. 6; Job xxx. 10. ¶ *And buffeted him.* That is, they struck him with their hands closed, or with the *fist.* ¶ *Others smote* him *with the palms of their hands.* The word used in the original here means literally to strike with *rods.* It also means to strike *the mouth* with the open hand, as if to prevent a person's speaking, or to evince abhorrence of what he had spoken.

68. *Saying, Prophesy unto us,* &c. Mark informs us that before they said this they had blindfolded him. Having prevented his seeing, they ridiculed his pretensions of being the Messiah. If he was the Christ, they supposed he could tell who smote him. As he bore it patiently and did not answer, they doubtless supposed that they had discovered another reason to think he was an impostor. The word *prophesy* does not mean only to foretell future events, although that is the proper meaning of the word, but also to declare anything that is unknown, or anything which cannot be known by natural knowledge or without revelation. Luke adds, "And many other things blasphemously spake they against him." There is something very remarkable in this expression. They had charged *him* with *blasphemy* in claiming to be the Son of God. This charge they were not able to prove; but the evangelist *fixes* the charge of *blasphemy* on them, because he really *was* the Son of God, and they denied it.

69. *Now Peter sat without in the palace.* Mark says the first denial took place while Peter was "beneath in the palace." This *palace* was the large *hall* or court belonging to the residence of the high-priest. The part of it where Jesus and the council were was *elevated*, probably above the rest for a tribunal. Peter was *beneath*, or in the *lower part* of the hall, with the servants at the fire. Yet, as Matthew says, he sat *without* in the palace—that is, *out of* the palace where they were trying Jesus—to wit, in the lower part of the hall with the servants; both narratives are therefore consistent. ¶ *And a damsel came unto him.* John (xviii. 17) says that this damsel was one that kept the door. ¶ *Thou also wast with Jesus of Galilee.* Probably she suspected him from his being in company with John. This was in the early part of the trial of Jesus.

70. *But he denied before* them *all*, &c. He denied that he was a disciple; he denied that he knew Jesus; he denied (Mark) that he *understood* what was meant—that is, he did not see any reason why this question was asked. All this was palpable falsehood, and Peter must have known that it was such. This is remarkable, because Peter had just before been so confident. It is more remarkable, because the edge of the charge was taken off by the insinuation that *John* was known to be a disciple—thou *also* wast with Jesus of Galilee.

71. *When he was gone out into the porch.* The *entrance*, or the small apartment between the outer door and the large hall in the centre of the building. See plan of a house, Notes, Mat. ix. 1–8. Peter was embarrassed and confused by the question, and to save his confusion from attracting notice, he went away from the fire into the porch, where he expected to be unobserved—yet in vain. By the very movement to avoid detection, he came into contact with another who knew him and repeated the charge. How clearly does it prove that our Lord was omniscient, that all these things were foreseen! ¶ *Another* maid *saw him.* Mark simply says that *a maid* saw him. From Luke it would appear that *a man* spoke to him, Lu. xxii. 58. The truth probably is that both were done. When he first went out, *a maid* charged him with being a follower of Jesus. He was probably there a considerable time. To this charge he might have been silent, thinking, perhaps, that he was con-

him, and said unto them that were
there, This *fellow* was also with
Jesus of Nazareth.
72 And again he denied with
an oath, I do not know the man.
73 And after a while came unto
him they that stood by, and said
to Peter, Surely thou also art *one*
of them, for thy speech bewrayeth
thee.
74 Then began he to curse and
to swear, *saying*, I know not the
man. And immediately the cock
crew.
75 And Peter remembered [u]the
word of Jesus, which said unto

u ver.34; Lu.22.31-34.

cealed, and there was no need of denying Jesus then. Yet it is very likely that the charge would be repeated. A *man*, also, might have repeated it; and Peter, irritated, provoked, perhaps thinking that he was in danger, *then* denied his Master the second time. This denial was in a stronger manner and with an oath. While in the porch, Mark says, the cock crew—that is, the first crowing, or not far from midnight.

73. *And after a while.* That is, about an hour after (Luke). Peter by this time had returned into the palace or hall, and stood warming himself by the fire, Jn. xviii. 25. ¶ *Thy speech bewrayeth thee.* Your language makes it manifest that you are of his company. That is, as Mark adds, he was *a Galilean*, and in this way his speech betrayed him. It is probable that the Galileans were distinguished for some peculiarity of pronunciation, perhaps some peculiar rusticity or coarseness in their manner of speaking, that distinguished them from the refinement of the capital, Jerusalem. This charge, John says (xviii. 26), was supported by the express affirmation of a kinsman of Malchus, the servant of the high-priest, that he had seen him in the garden.

74. *Then began he to curse*, &c. Peter was now irritated beyond endurance. He could no longer resist the evidence that he was known. It had been repeatedly charged on him. His language had betrayed him, and there was a positive witness who had seen him. He felt it necessary, therefore, to be still more decided, and he accordingly added to the sin of denying his Lord the deep aggravation of profane cursing and swearing, affirming what he must have known was false, that he knew not the man. Immediately then the cock crew—that is, the second crowing, or not far from three in the morning.

75. *And Peter remembered the word of Jesus*, &c. Luke has mentioned a beautiful and touching circumstance omitted by the other evangelists, that when the cock crew, *Jesus turned and looked upon Peter*, and that then he remembered his words. They were in the same room—Jesus at the upper end of the hall, elevated for a tribunal and Peter below with the servants, so that Jesus could look down upon Peter standing near the fire. By a tender and compassionate look—a single glance of his eye—the injured Saviour brought to remembrance all Peter's promises, his own predictions, and the great guilt of the disciple; he overwhelmed him with the remembrance of his sin, and pierced his heart through with many sorrows. The consciousness of deep and awful guilt rushed over Peter's soul; he flew from the palace, he went where he might be alone in the darkness of the night, and *wept bitterly*.

The fall of Peter is one of the most melancholy instances of depravity ever committed in our world. But a little while before so confident; seated at the table of the Lord; distinguished throughout the ministry of Christ with peculiar favours; cautioned against this very thing; yet so soon denying him, forgetting his promises, and profanely calling on God to witness what he knew to be false—that he did not *know* him! Had it been but *once*, it would have been awful guilt—guilt deeply piercing the Redeemer's soul in the day of trial; but it was three times repeated, and at last with profane cursing and swearing. Yet, while we weep over Peter's fall, and seek not to palliate his crime, we should draw from it important practical uses: 1st. The danger of self-confidence. He that thinketh he standeth should take heed lest he fall. True Christian confidence is that which relies on God for strength, and feels safety only in the belief that *He* is able and willing to keep from temptation. 2d. The highest favours, the most exalted privileges, do not secure us from the danger of falling

him, Before the cock crow, thou shalt deny me thrice. And he went out and wept bitterly.

CHAPTER XXVII.

WHEN the morning was come, all the chief priests and

---

into sin. Few men were ever so highly favoured as Peter; few ever so dreadfully departed from the Saviour, and brought so deep a scandal on religion. 3d. When a man *begins* to sin, his fall from one act to another is easy—perhaps almost certain. At first Peter's sin was only simple denial; then it increased to more violent affirmation, and ended with open profaneness. So the downward road of crime is easy. When sin is *once* indulged, the way is open for a whole deluge of crime, nor is the course easily stayed till the soul is overwhelmed in awful guilt. 4th. True repentance is deep, thorough, bitter. Peter wept bitterly. It was sincere sorrow — sorrow proportioned to the nature of the offence he had committed. 5th. A look from Jesus—a look of mingled affection, pity, and reproof—produces bitter sorrow for sin. *Him* we injure by our crimes; and *his* tender look, when we err, pierces the soul through with many sorrows, opens fountains of tears in the bosom, and leads us to weep with bitterness over our transgressions. 6th. When we sin —when we fall into temptation—let us retire from the world, seek the place of solitude, and pour out our sorrows before God. He will mark our groans; he will hear our sighs; he will behold our tears; and he will receive us to his arms again. 7th. Real Christians may be suffered to go far astray. To show them their weakness, to check self-confidence, and to produce dependence on Jesus Christ, they may be permitted to show how weak, and feeble, and rash they are. Peter was a real believer. Jesus had prayed for him *that his faith should fail not*, Lu. xxii. 32. Jesus was *always* heard in his prayer, Jn. xi. 42. He was heard, therefore, then. Peter's *faith* did not fail—that is, his *belief* in Jesus, his real piety, his *true* attachment to the Saviour. He *knew* during the whole transaction that Jesus was the Messiah, and that *he himself* was well acquainted with him; but he was suffered to declare that which he knew was not true, and in *this* consisted his sin. Yet, 8th. Though a Christian *may* be suffered to go astray—*may* fall into sin—yet he who should, from this example of Peter, think that he might lawfully do it, or who should *resolve* to do it, thinking that he might, like Peter, weep and repent, would give evidence that he knew nothing of the grace of God. He that *resolves* to sin under the expectation of repenting hereafter *cannot be a Christian.*

It is worthy of further remark, that the fact that the fall of Peter is recorded by *all* the evangelists is high proof of their *honesty*. They were willing to tell the truth as it was; to conceal no fact, even if it made much against themselves, and to make mention of their *own* faults without attempting to *appear* to be better than they were. And it is worthy of special observation that *Mark* has recorded this with *all* the circumstances of aggravation, perhaps even more so than the others. Yet, by the universal belief of antiquity, the Gospel of *Mark* was written under *Peter's* direction, and every part of it submitted to him for examination. Higher proof of the *honesty* and *candour* of the evangelists could not be demanded.

CHAPTER XXVII.

1, 2. *Jesus is brought before Pilate.* See also Mar. xvi. 1; Lu. xxiii. 1; Jn. xviii. 28.

1. *When the morning was come.* This was not long after Jesus had been condemned by the Sanhedrim. Peter's last denial was probably not far from three o'clock, or near the break of day. As soon as it was light, the Jews consulted together for the purpose of taking his life. The sun rose at that season of the year in Judea not far from five o'clock, and the time when they assembled, therefore, was not long after Peter's denial. ¶ *The chief priests and elders of the people took counsel.* They had on his trial (ch. xxvi. 65, 66) agreed that he deserved to die, *on a charge of blasphemy;* yet they did not *dare* to put him to death by stoning, as they did afterward Stephen (Ac. vii.), and as the law commanded in case of blasphemy, for they feared the people. They therefore *consulted*, or took counsel together, to determine on what pretence they could deliver him to the Roman emperor, or to fix some charge of a civil nature by which Pilate might be in-

elders of the people [a]took counsel
against Jesus to put him to death.
2 And when they had bound
him, they led *him* away, and [b]de-
livered him to Pontius Pilate the
governor.
3 Then Judas, which had be-

a Ps.2.2. *b* ch.20.19.

trayed him, when he saw that
he was condemned, repented himself, and brought again the thirty
pieces of silver to the chief priests
and elders,
4 Saying, I have sinned, in
that I have betrayed the [c]innocent

c 2 Ki.24.4.

---

duced to condemn him. The charge which they fixed on was not that on which *they* had tried him, and on which they had determined he ought to die, but *that of perverting the nation, and of forbidding to give tribute to Cæsar*, Lu. xxiii. 2. On *this* accusation, if made out, they supposed Pilate could be induced to condemn Jesus. On a charge of *blasphemy* they knew he could not, as that was not an offence against the Roman laws, and over which, therefore, Pilate claimed no jurisdiction. ¶ *To put him to death.* To devise some way by which he might be put to death under the authority of the Roman governor.

2. *And when they had bound him.* He was *bound* when they took him in the garden, Jn. xviii. 12. Probably when he was tried before the Sanhedrim in the palace of Caiaphas, he had been loosed from his bonds, being there surrounded by multitudes, and supposed to be safe. As they were about to lead him to another part of the city now, they again bound him. The binding consisted, probably, in nothing more than tying his hands. ¶ *Pontius Pilate, the governor.* The governor appointed by the Romans over Judea. The governor commonly resided at *Cesarea;* but he came up to Jerusalem usually at the great feasts, when great numbers of the Jews were assembled, to administer justice, and to suppress tumults if any should arise. The *title* which Pilate received was that of *governor* or *procurator.* The duties of the office were, chiefly, to collect the revenues due to the Roman emperor, and in certain cases to administer justice. Pilate was appointed governor of Judea by Tiberius, then Emperor of Rome. John says (xviii. 28) that they led Jesus from Caiaphas to the hall of judgment—that is, to the part of the *prætorium*, or governor's palace, where justice was administered. The Jews did not, however, enter in themselves, lest they should be defiled, but that they might eat the Passover. In Nu. xix. 22 it is said that whosoever touched an unclean thing should be unclean. For this reason they would not enter into the house of a *heathen*, lest they should contract some defilement that would render them unfit to keep the Passover.

3. *Then Judas, when he saw that he was condemned, repented himself.* This shows that Judas did not suppose that the affair would have resulted in this calamitous manner. He probably expected that Jesus would work a miracle to deliver himself, and not suffer this condemnation to come upon him. When he saw him taken, bound, tried, and condemned—when he saw that all probability that he would deliver himself was taken away—he was overwhelmed with disappointment, sorrow, and remorse. The word rendered *repented himself*, it has been observed, does not of necessity denote a change *for the better*, but *any* change of views and feelings. Here it evidently means no other change than that produced by the horrors of a guilty conscience, and by deep remorse for crime at its unexpected results. It was not saving repentance. That leads to a holy life—this led to an increase of crime in his own death. True repentence leads the sinner to the Saviour. This led *away* from the Saviour to the gallows. Judas, if he had been a true penitent, would have come *then* to Jesus; would have confessed his crime at his feet, and sought for pardon there. But, overwhelmed with remorse and the conviction of vast guilt, he was not willing to come into his presence, and added to the crime of *treason* that of *self-murder*. Assuredly such a man could not be a true penitent.

4. *I have sinned.* I have been guilty. I have done wrong. ¶ *In that I have betrayed the innocent blood.* That is, in betraying an innocent being to death. *Blood* is put here for *life*, or for the *man*. The meaning is, that he knew and felt that Jesus was innocent. This

blood. And they said, What *is*
that to us? See thou *to that*.
5 And he cast down the pieces of
silver in the temple, and departed,
and went and [d]hanged himself.
6 And the chief priests took the

d Ps.55.23; 2 Sa.17.23; Ac.1.18.

confession is a remarkable proof that Jesus *was* innocent. Judas had been with him three years. He had seen him in public and private; he had heard his public teaching and his private views; he had seen him in all circumstances; and if he *had* done anything evil, or advanced anything against the Roman emperor, Judas was competent to testify it. Had he *known* any such thing he would have stated it. *His* testimony, being a disciple of Jesus, would have been to the chief priests far more valuable than that of any other man; and he might not only have escaped the horrors of a troubled conscience and an awful death, but have looked for an ample reward. That he did *not* make such a charge—that he fully and frankly confessed that Jesus *was* innocent—and that he gave up the ill-gotten price of *treason*, is full proof that, in the belief of Judas, the Saviour was free from crime, and even the *suspicion of crime*. ¶ *What* is that *to us?* This form of speaking denoted that they had nothing to do with his remorse of conscience, and his belief that Jesus was innocent. *They* had secured what they wanted—the person of Jesus—and they cared little now for the feelings of the traitor. So all wicked men who make use of the agency of others for the accomplishment of crime or the gratification of passion care little for the effect on the instrument. They will soon cast him off and despise him, and in thousands of instances the instruments of villainy and the panders to the pleasures of others are abandoned to remorse, wretchedness, crime, and death.

5. *And he cast down*, &c. This was an evidence of his remorse of conscience for his crime. His ill-gotten gain now did him no good. It would not produce relief to his agonized mind. He *attempted*, therefore, to obtain relief by throwing back the price of treason; but he attempted it in vain. The consciousness of guilt was fastened to his soul; and Judas found, as all will find, that to cast away or abandon ill-gotten wealth will not alleviate a guilty conscience. ¶ *In the temple.* It is not quite certain what part of the temple is here meant. Some have thought that it was the place where the Sanhedrim were accustomed to sit; others, the treasury; others, the part where the priests offered sacrifice. It is probable that Judas cared little or thought little to what particular part of the temple he went. In his deep remorse he hurried to the temple, and probably cast the money down in the most convenient spot, and fled to some place where he might take his life. ¶ *And went and hanged himself.* The word used in the original, here, has given rise to much discussion, whether it means that he was suffocated or strangled by his great grief, or whether he took his life by suspending himself. It is acknowledged on all hands, however, that the latter is its most usual meaning, and it is certainly the most obvious meaning. Peter says, in giving an account of the death of Jesus (Ac. i. 18), that Judas, "falling headlong, burst asunder in the midst, and all his bowels gushed out." There has been supposed to be some difficulty in reconciling these two accounts, but there is really no necessary difference. Both accounts are true. Matthew records the *mode* in which Judas *attempted* his death by hanging. Peter speaks of *the result*. Judas probably passed out of the temple in great haste and perturbation of mind. He sought a place where he might perpetrate this crime. He would not, probably, be very careful about the fitness of the means he used. In his anguish, his haste, his desire to die, he seized upon a rope and suspended himself; and it is not at all remarkable, or indeed unusual, that the rope might prove too weak and break. Falling headlong—that is, on his face—he burst asunder, and in awful horrors died—a double death, with double pains and double horrors—the reward of his aggravated guilt. The explanation here suggested will be rendered more probable if it be supposed that he hung himself near some precipitous valley. "Interpreters have suggested," says Professor Hackett (*Illustrations of Scripture*, p. 275, 276), "that Judas may have hung himself on a tree near a precipice over the valley of Hinnom, and that, the limb or rope breaking, he fell to the bottom, and was

silver pieces, and said, It is not lawful for to put them into the treasury, because it is the price of blood.

7 And they took counsel, and bought with them the potter's field, to bury strangers in.

8 Wherefore that field was called, The field of blood, unto this day.

---

dashed to pieces by the fall. For myself, I felt, as I stood in this valley and looked up to the rocky terraces which hang over it, that the proposed explanation was a perfectly natural one. I was more than ever satisfied with it. I measured the precipitous, almost perpendicular walls in different places, and found the height to be, variously, 40, 36, 33, 30, and 25 feet. Trees still grow quite near the edge of these rocks, and, no doubt, in former times were still more numerous in the same place. A rocky pavement exists, also, at the bottom of the ledges, and hence on that account, too, a person who should fall from above would be liable to be crushed and mangled as well as killed. The traitor may have struck, in his fall, upon some pointed rock, which entered the body and caused 'his bowels to gush out.'"

6. *It is not lawful*, &c. It was forbidden (De. xxiii. 18) to take what was esteemed as an abomination and to offer it to God. The price of blood—that is, of the life of a man—they justly considered as an improper and unlawful offering. ¶ *The treasury.* The *treasury* was kept in the court of the women. See plan of the temple, Mat. xxi. 12. It was composed of a number of small *chests* placed in different parts of the *courts* to receive the voluntary offerings of the people, as well as the half shekel required of every Jew. The original word here rendered *treasury* contains the notion of an *offering to God.* What was given there was considered as an offering made to him. ¶ *The price of blood.* The life is in the blood. See Notes on Ro. iii. 25. The word *blood* here means the same as *life.* The price of blood means the price by which the life of a man has been purchased. This was an acknowledgment that in their view Jesus was innocent. They had *bought* him, not condemned him justly. It is remarkable that they were so scrupulous now about so small a matter, comparatively, as putting this money in the treasury, when they had no remorse about *murdering an innocent man*, and crucifying him who had given full evidence that he was the Messiah. Men are often very scrupulous in *small* matters, who stick not at great crimes.

7. *And they took counsel*, &c. They consulted among themselves about the proper way to dispose of this money. ¶ *And bought with them.* In Ac. i. 18 it is said of Judas that "*he* purchased a field with the reward of his iniquity." By the passage in the Acts is meant no more than that he *furnished the means* or *was the occasion* of purchasing the field. It is not of necessity implied that *Judas* actually made the contract and paid down the money to buy a field to bury strangers in—a thing which would be in itself very improbable, but that it was *by his means* that the field was purchased. It is very frequent in the Scriptures, as well as in other writings, to represent a man as doing that which he is only the cause or occasion of another's doing. See Ac. ii. 23; Jn. xix. 1; Mat. xxviii. 59, 60. ¶ *The potter's field.* Probably this was some field well known by that name, which was used for the purpose of making earthen vessels. The price paid for a field so near Jerusalem may appear to be very small; but it is not improbable that it had been worked till the clay was exhausted, and was neither fit for that business nor for tillage, and was therefore considered as of little value. ¶ *To bury strangers in. Jews*, who came up from other parts of the world to attend the great feasts at Jerusalem. The high-priests, who regarded the *Gentiles* as abominable, would not be inclined to provide a burial-place for *them.*

8. *The field of blood.* The field purchased by the price of blood. The name by which this field was called was *Aceldama*, Ac. i. 19. It was just without the walls of Jerusalem, on the south of Mount Zion. It is now used as a burying-place by the Armenian Christians in Jerusalem, who have a magnificent convent on Mount Zion.—*Missionary Herald*, 1824, p. 66. See Plan of Jerusalem. ¶ *To this day.* That is, to the day when Matthew wrote this gospel, about thirty years after the field was purchased.

9. *Spoken by Jeremy the prophet.* The

9 (Then was fulfilled that which was spoken by Jeremy the prophet, saying, [e]And they took the thirty pieces of silver, the price of him that was valued, [1]whom they of the children of Israel did value;

10 And gave them for the potter's field, as the Lord appointed me.)

e Zec.11.12,13.

1 or, *whom they bought of the children of Israel.*

---

words quoted here are not to be found in the prophecy of Jeremiah. Words similar to these are recorded in Zec. xi. 12, 13, and from that place this quotation has been doubtless made. Much difficulty has been experienced in explaining this quotation. Anciently, according to the Jewish writers, *Jeremiah* was reckoned the first of the prophets, and was placed first in the Book of the Prophets, thus: Jeremiah, Ezekiel, Isaiah, and the twelve minor prophets. Some have thought that Matthew, quoting this place, quoted the *Book of the Prophets* under the name of that which had the *first* place in the book, that is, Jeremiah; and though the words are those of Zechariah, yet they are quoted correctly as the words of the Book of the Prophets, the first of which was Jeremiah. Others have thought that there was a mistake made by ancient transcribers, writing the name Jeremiah instead of Zechariah; and it is observed that this might be done by the change of only a single letter. It was often the custom to *abridge* words in writing them. Thus, instead of writing the name of Jeremiah in full, it would be written in Greek, *Iriou.* So Zechariah would be written *Zriou.* By the mere change of *Z* into *I*, therefore, the mistake might easily be made. Probably this is the correct explanation. Others have supposed that the words were *spoken* by *Jeremiah*, and that *Zechariah* recorded them, and that Matthew quoted them as they *were*—the words of Jeremiah. The passage is not quoted literally; and by its being *fulfilled* is meant, probably, that the language used by Zechariah on a similar occasion would *express* also this event. See Notes on Mat. i. 22, 23. It was language appropriate to this occasion. ¶ *The price of him that was valued.* That is, the price of him on whom a value was set. The word rendered "valued," here, does not, as often in our language, mean to *esteem*, but to *estimate;* not to love, approve, or regard, but to fix a *price on*, to *estimate the value of.* This they considered to be thirty pieces of silver, *the common price of a slave.* ¶ *They of the children of Israel did value.* Some of the Jews, the leaders or priests, acting in the name of the nation. ¶ *Did value.* Did estimate, or fix a price on.

10. *And gave them.* In Zechariah it is, *I* gave them. Here it is represented as being given by the priests. The meaning is not, however, different. It is, that this price *was given* for the potter's field. ¶ *As the Lord appointed me.* That is, *commanded* me. The meaning of the place in Zechariah is this: He was directed to go to the Jews as a prophet—a pastor of the people. They treated him, as they had done others, with great contempt. He asks them to give him *his price*—that is, the price which they thought he and his pastoral labours were worth, or to show *their* estimate of his office. If they thought it of value, they were to pay him accordingly; if not, they were to "forbear"—that is, to give nothing. To show their *great contempt* of him and his office, and of God who had sent him, they gave him thirty pieces of silver—*the price of a slave.* This God commanded or *appointed him* to give to the potter, or to throw into the pottery—to throw away. So in the time of Jesus the same thing was substantially repeated. Jesus came as the Messiah. They hated and rejected him. To show their contempt of him and his cause, they *valued* him *at the price of a slave.* This was thrown down in the temple, taken by the priests, and appropriated to the purchase of a field owned by a *potter*—worn-out land of little or no value; *all* showing at how low a price, through the whole transaction, the Son of God was estimated. Though the *words* quoted here are not *precisely* like those in Zechariah, yet the *sense* and *general structure* are the same.

11. *And Jesus stood before the governor.* Many things are omitted by Matthew, in the account of this trial, which are recorded by the other evangelists. A much more full account is found in Jn. xviii. 28-40. ¶ *And the governor asked him*, &c. This question was asked on account of the *charge* which the Jews brought against Jesus, *of perverting the nation, and forbidding to give tribute to Cæsar*, Lu. xxiii. 2. It was on *this*

11 And Jesus stood before the
governor: and the governor asked
him, saying, Art thou the King of
the Jews? And Jesus said unto
him, Thou sayest.
12 And when he was accused of
the chief priests and elders, he
[f]answered nothing.
13 Then saith Pilate unto him,
Hearest thou not how many things
they witness against thee?
14 And he answered him to never

f ch.26.63.

charge that, after consultation, they had agreed to arraign him before Pilate. See Notes on ver. 1. *They* had condemned him for *blasphemy*, but they well knew that Pilate would altogether disregard an accusation of that kind. They therefore attempted to substitute a totally different accusation from that on which they had professed to find him guilty, to excite the jealousy of the Roman governor, and to procure his death on a charge of treason against the Roman emperor. ¶ *Thou sayest.* That is, thou sayest right, or thou sayest the truth. We may wonder why the Jews, if they heard this confession, did not press it upon the attention of Pilate as a full confession of his guilt. It was what they had accused him of. But it might be doubtful whether, in the confusion, they heard the confession; or, if they did, Jesus took away all occasion of triumph by explaining to Pilate the *nature* of his kingdom, Jn. xviii. 36. Though he acknowledged that he was a king, yet he stated fully that *his kingdom was not of this world*, and that therefore it could not be alleged against him as treason against the Roman emperor. This was done *in the palace*, apart from the Jews, and fully satisfied Pilate of his innocence, Jn. xviii. 23.

12. *When he was accused*, &c. To wit, of perverting the nation, and of forbidding to give tribute to Cæsar, Lu. xxiii. 2, 5. Probably this was done in a tumultuous manner and in every variety of form. ¶ *He answered nothing.* He was conscious of his innocence. He knew that they could not *prove* these charges. They offered no testimony to prove them, and, in conscious innocence, he was silent.

13. *They witness against thee.* This means, rather, that they *accused* him. They were not *witnesses*, but accusers. These accusations were repeated and pressed. They charged him with exciting the people, teaching throughout all Judea from Galilee to Jerusalem, and exciting the nation to sedition, Lu. xxiii. 5.

14. *To never a word.* That is, not at all. He said nothing. This is, an *emphatic* way of saying that he answered nothing. There was no *need* of his replying. He was innocent, and they offered no proof of guilt. Besides, his *appearance* was full evidence in his favour. He was poor, unarmed, without powerful friends, and alone. His life had been public, and his sentiments were well known, and the charge had on the face of it the aspect of absurdity. It deserved, therefore, no answer. ¶ *Marvelled greatly.* Wondered exceedingly, or was much surprised. He was probably more surprised that he bore this *so meekly*, and did not return railing for railing, than that he did not set up a defence. The latter was unnecessary—the former was unusual. The governor was not accustomed to see it, and was therefore greatly amazed.

It was at this time that Pilate, having heard them speak of Galilee (Lu. xxiii. 5), asked if he was a Galilean. Having ascertained that he was, and being probably desirous of freeing himself from any farther trouble in the affair, under pretence that he belonged to Herod's jurisdiction, he sent Jesus to Herod, who was then at Jerusalem attending the feast of the Passover, Lu. xxiii. 6–12. Herod, having examined him, and finding no cause of death in him, sent him back to Pilate. Pleased with the respect which had been shown him, Herod laid aside his enmity against Pilate, and they became friends. The cause of their friendship does not appear to be at all that they were united in opposing the claims of Jesus to be the Messiah, but the respect which Pilate had shown in sending Jesus to him.

15–23. See also the parallel places in Mar. xv. 6–14; Lu. xxiii. 17–23; Jn. xviii. 39, 40.

15. *At* that *feast.* The feast of the Passover. ¶ *The governor was wont to release*, &c. Was *accustomed* to release. From what this custom arose, or by whom it was introduced, is not known.

a word; insomuch that the governor marvelled greatly.
15 Now[g] at *that* feast the governor
was wont to release unto the people
a prisoner, whom they would.
16 And they had then a notable
prisoner, called Barabbas.

g Mar.15.6,&c.; Lu.23.17,&c.; Jn.18.39,&c.

17 Therefore, when they were
gathered together, Pilate said unto
them, Whom will ye that I release
unto you? Barabbas, or Jesus,
which is called Christ?
18 For he knew that [h]for envy
they had delivered him.

h Pr.27.4; Ec.4.4.

It was probably adopted to secure popularity among the Jews, and to render the government of the Romans less odious. Any little indulgence granted to the Jews during the heavy oppression of the Romans would serve to conciliate their favour, and to keep the nation from sedition. It might happen often that when persons were arraigned before the Romans on charge of sedition, some peculiar favourite of the people, or some leader, might be among the number. It is evident that if they had the privilege of recovering such a person, it would serve much to allay their feelings, and make tolerable the yoke under which they groaned.

16. *A notable prisoner.* The word *notable* means one that is *distinguished* in any way either for great virtues or great crimes. In this place it evidently means the latter. He was perhaps the leader of a band who had been guilty of sedition, and had committed murder in an insurrection, Lu. xxiii. 19.

17. *Whom will ye that I release,* &c. Pilate was satisfied of the innocence of Jesus, Lu. xxiii. 13–16. He was therefore desirous of releasing him. He expected to release one to the people. He knew that Jesus, though condemned by the chief priests, was yet popular among the *people.* He therefore attempted in this manner to rescue him from the hands of the priests, and expected that the *people* would prefer *him* to an odious and infamous robber and murderer. Had the people been left to themselves it would probably have been done. ¶ *Jesus, which is called Christ.* That is, Jesus, who claims to be the Messiah. Pilate probably did not believe it, or care much for it. He used the name which Jesus had acquired among the people. Perhaps, also, he thought that they would be more likely to ask him to be released if he was presented to them as the Messiah. Mark (xv. 9) adds that he asked them whether they would that he should release *the King of the Jews?* It is probable that he asked the question in both ways. Perhaps it was several times repeated, and Matthew has recorded one way in which it was asked, and Mark another. He asked them whether they would demand him who *was called the Christ,* expecting that they would be moved by the claims of the Messiah—claims which, when he entered Jerusalem in triumph, and in the temple, they had acknowledged. He asked them whether they would have the *King of the Jews*—probably to ridicule the priests who had delivered him on that charge. He did it to show the *people* how absurd the accusation was. There Jesus stood, apparently a poor, inoffensive, unarmed, and despised man. Herod had set him at naught and scourged him, and sent him back. The charge, therefore, of the priests, that he was a *king* opposed to the Roman emperor, was *supremely ridiculous;* and Pilate, expecting that the people would see it so, hoped also that they would ask that he might be released.

18. *For he knew that for envy,* &c. This was envy at his popularity. He drew away the people from them. This Pilate understood, probably, from his knowledge of the pride and ambition of the rulers, and from the fact that no danger *could* arise from a person that appeared like Jesus. If Pilate *knew* this, he was bound to release him himself. As a governor and judge, he was under obligation to protect the innocent, and should, in spite of all the opposition of the Jews, at once have set him at liberty. But the Scriptures could not then have been fulfilled. It was necessary, in order that an atonement should be made, that Jesus should be condemned to die. At the same time, it shows the wisdom of the overruling providence of God, that he was condemned by a man who was satisfied of his innocence, and who proclaimed before his accusers his *full belief* that there was no fault in him.

19. *When he was set down on the judgment-seat.* Literally, *While he was sit-*

19 When he was set down on the
judgment-seat, his wife sent unto
him, saying, Have thou nothing to
do with [i]that just man; for I have
suffered many things this day in a
dream because of him.
20 But the chief priests and elders
persuaded the multitude that they
should [k]ask Barabbas, and destroy
Jesus.
21 The governor answered and
said unto them, Whether of the
twain will ye that I release unto
you? They said, Barabbas.
22 Pilate saith unto them, What
shall I do, then, with Jesus, which
is called Christ? *They* all say unto
him, Let him be crucified.
23 And the governor said, Why,
what evil hath he done? But they
cried out the more, saying, [l]Let him
be crucified.
24 When Pilate saw that he could
prevail nothing, but *that* rather a

i Is.53.11; Zec.9.9; Lu.23.47; 1 Pe.2.22; 1 Jn.2.1. *k* Ac.3.14.

l ch.21.38,39.

ting. This message was probably received when he had resumed his place on the judgment-seat, after Jesus had been sent to Herod. See Notes on ver. 14. ¶ *His wife sent unto him.* The reason why she sent to him is immediately stated—that she had a *dream* respecting him. We know nothing more of her. We do not know whether she had ever seen the Saviour herself, but it would seem that she was apprised of what was taking place, and probably anticipated that the affair would involve her husband in trouble. ¶ *Have thou nothing to do,* &c. That is, do not condemn him. Perhaps she was afraid that the vengeance of heaven would follow her husband and family if he condemned the innocent. ¶ *That just man.* The word *just,* here, has the sense of *innocent,* or not guilty. She might have been satisfied of his innocence from other sources as well as from the dream. ¶ *I have suffered many things,* &c. Dreams were considered as indications of the divine will, and among the Romans and Greeks, as well as the Jews, great reliance was placed on them. Her mind was probably agitated with the subject. She was satisfied of the innocence of Jesus; and, knowing that the Jews would make every effort to secure his condemnation, it was not unnatural that her mind should be excited during her sleep, perhaps with a frightful prospect of the judgments that would descend on the family of Pilate if Jesus was condemned. She therefore sent to him to secure, if possible, his release. ¶ *This day.* It was now early in the morning. The Jewish *day* began at sunset, and she employed the usual language of the Jews respecting time. The dream was, in fact, in the night.

20. *Persuaded the multitude.* The release of a prisoner was to be to the *people,* not to the *rulers.* The rulers, therefore, in order to secure the condemnation of Jesus, urged on the people to demand Barabbas. The people were greatly under the influence of the priests. Galileans among the citizens of Jerusalem were held in contempt. The priests turned the pretensions of Jesus into ridicule. Hence, in a popular tumult, among a flexible and changing multitude, they easily excited those who, but a little before, had cried Hosanna, to cry, Crucify him.

21. *Whether of the twain?* Which of the two, Jesus or Barabbas?

23. *And the governor said, Why?* Luke informs us that Pilate put this question to them *three times,* so anxious was he to release him. He affirmed that he had found no cause of death in him. He said, therefore, that he would chastise him and let him go. He expected, probably, by causing him to be publicly whipped, to excite their compassion, to satisfy *them,* and thus to evade the demands of the priests, and to set him at liberty with the consent of the people. So weak and irresolute was this Roman governor! Satisfied of his innocence, he should at once have preferred *justice* to *popularity,* and acted as became a magistrate in acquitting the innocent. ¶ *Let him be crucified.* See Notes on ver. 39. Luke says they were *instant* with loud voices demanding this. They *urged* it. They demanded it with a popular clamour.

24. *He took water,* &c. The Jews were accustomed to wash their hands when they wished to show that they were innocent of a crime committed by others. See De. xxi. 6; Ps. xxvi. 6. Pilate, in doing this, meant to denote that they

tumult was made, he [m]took water, and washed *his* hands before the multitude, saying, I am innocent of the blood of this just person: see ye *to it*.

25 Then answered all the people, and said, [n]His blood *be* on us, and on our children.

26 Then released he Barabbas unto them: and when he had [o]scourged Jesus, he delivered *him* to be crucified.

27 Then the soldiers of the governor took Jesus into the [2]common hall, and gathered unto him the whole band *of soldiers*.

m De.21.6.
n De.19.10; Jos.2.19; ch.21.44; Ac.5.28.
o Is.53.5; Lu.18.33. 2 or, *governor's house*.

were guilty of his death, but that he was innocent. But the mere washing of his hands did not free him from guilt. He was *bound* as a magistrate to free an innocent man; and whatever might be the clamour of the Jews, *he* was guilty at the bar of God for suffering the holy Saviour to be led to execution, in order to gratify the malice of enraged priests and the clamours of a tumultuous populace. ¶ *See ye* to it. That is, take it upon yourselves. You are responsible for it, if you put him to death.

25. *His blood* be *on us*, &c. That is, let the guilt of putting him to death, if there be any, be on us and our children. We will be answerable for it, and will consent to bear the punishment for it. It is remarked by writers that, among the Athenians, if anyone accused another of a capital crime, he devoted himself and children to the same punishment if the accused was afterward found innocent. So in all countries the conduct of the parent involves the children in the consequences of his conduct. The Jews had no *right* to call down this vengeance on their children, but, in the righteous judgment of God, it has come upon them. In less than forty years their city and temple were overthrown and destroyed. More than a million of people perished in the siege. Thousands died by famine; thousands by disease; thousands by the sword; and their blood ran down the streets like water, so that, Josephus says, it extinguished things that were burning in the city. Thousands were *crucified*—suffering the same punishment that they had inflicted on the Messiah. So great was the number of those who were crucified, that, Josephus says, they were obliged to cease from it, "room being wanted for the crosses, and crosses for the men." See Notes on ch. xxiv. To this day, also, the curse has remained. They have been a nation scattered and peeled; persecuted almost everywhere, and a hissing and a byword among men. No single nation, probably, has suffered so much; and yet they have been preserved. All classes of men, all the governments of the earth, have conspired to overwhelm them with calamity, and yet they still live as monuments of the justice of God, and as proofs, going down from age to age, that the Christian religion is true—standing demonstrations of the crime of their fathers in putting the Messiah to death, and in calling down vengeance on their heads.

26. *And when he had scourged Jesus.* See Notes on Mat. x. 17. Among the Romans it was customary to scourge or whip *a slave* before he was crucified. This was done to inflict greater suffering than crucifixion would be alone, and to add to the horrors of the punishment. Our Lord, being about to be put to death after the manner of a *slave*, was also treated as a slave—as one of the lowest and most despised of mankind. ¶ *He delivered* him *to be crucified.* Not merely gave him up to *them* to crucify him, as if *they* only were answerable, but he gave him up *as a judge*, when he ought to have saved his life and might have done it. Crucifixion was a Roman punishment; it was performed by Roman soldiers; Pilate pronounced the sentence from a Roman tribunal, and Pilate affixed the title to the cross. Pilate, therefore, as well as the Jews, was answerable to God for the death of the Saviour of the world.

27–31. See also Mar. xv. 15–20; Jn. xix. 1–3.

27. *Into the common hall.* The original word here means, rather, the governor's palace or dwelling. The trial of Jesus had taken place outside of the palace. The Jews would not enter in (Jn. xviii. 28), and it is probable that courts were held often in a larger and more public place than would be a room in his dwelling. Jesus,

28 And they stripped him, and put on him a scarlet robe.

29 And when they had platted a crown of thorns, they put *it* upon his head, and a reed in his right hand: and they bowed the knee before him, and [p] mocked him, saying, Hail, King of the Jews!

p Ps.69.19,20.

being condemned, was led by the soldiers away from the Jews *within* the palace, and subjected there to their profane mockery and sport. ¶ *The whole band.* The *band* or cohort was a tenth part of a Roman legion, and consisted of from 400 to 600 men, according to the size of the legion. Comp. Notes on ch. viii. 29.

28. *And they stripped him.* That is, they either took off all his upper garments or removed all his clothing, probably the former. ¶ *A scarlet robe.* Mark says they clothed him in *purple.* The *scarlet* colour was obtained from a species of fruit; *purple* from shell-fish. See Notes on Is. i. 18. The ancients gave the name *purple* to any colour that had a mixture of *red* in it, and consequently these different colours might be sometimes called by the same name. The *robe* here used was the same kind worn by Roman generals and other distinguished officers of the Roman army, and also by the Roman governors. It was made so as to be placed on the shoulders, and was bound around the body so as to leave the right arm at liberty. As we cannot suppose that Pilate would array him in a new and splendid robe, we must suppose that this was one which had been worn and cast off as useless, and was now used to array the Son of God as an object of ridicule and scorn.

29. *Had platted.* The word *platted* here means *woven together.* They made a *wreath* of a thorn-bush. ¶ *A crown.* Or perhaps, rather, a *wreath.* A crown was worn by kings, commonly made of gold and precious stones. To ridicule the pretensions of Jesus that he was a king, they probably plucked up a thorn-bush growing near, made it into something resembling in shape a royal crown, so as to correspond with the old purple robe, and to complete the mockery. ¶ *Of thorns.* What was the precise species of shrub denoted here is not certainly known. It was, however, doubtless, one of that species that has sharp points of very hard wood. They could therefore be easily pressed into the skin and cause considerable pain. Probably they seized upon the first thing in their way that could be made into a crown, and this happened to be a *thorn*, thus increasing the sufferings of the Redeemer. Palestine abounds with thorny shrubs and plants. "The traveller finds them in his path, go where he may. Many of them are small, but some grow as high as a man's head. The Rabbinical writers say that there are no less than twenty-two words in the Hebrew Bible denoting thorny and prickly plants."—Professor's Hackett's *Illustrations of Scripture*, p. 135. Comp. Pr. xxiv. 30, 31; xv. 19; Je. iv. 3. ¶ *And a reed in his right hand.* A *reed* is a straight, slender herb, growing in marshy places, and abundant on the banks of the Jordan. It was often used for the purpose of making *staves* for walking, and it is not improbable that this was such a staff in the possession of some person present. The word is several times thus used. See 2 Ki. xviii. 21; Is. xxxvi. 6; Eze. xxix. 6. Kings commonly carried a *sceptre*, made of ivory or gold, as a sign of their office or rank, Es. iv. 11; viii. 4. This *reed* or *staff* they put in his hand, in imitation of a *sceptre*, to deride, also, his pretensions of being a king. ¶ *And they bowed the knee.* This was done for mockery. It was an act of pretended homage. It was to ridicule his saying that he was a king. The common mode of showing respect or homage for kings was by kneeling or prostration. It shows amazing forbearance on the part of Jesus that he thus consented to be ridiculed and set at naught. No mere *human* being would have borne it. None but he who loved us unto death, and who saw the grand results that would come from this scene of sufferings, could have endured such mockery. ¶ *Hail, King of the Jews!* The term *hail* was a common mode of salutation to a king, or even to a friend. It implies, commonly, the highest respect for office as well as the person, and is an invocation of blessings. Here it was used to carry on what they thought to be the *farce* of his being a king; to ridicule in every possible way the pretensions of a poor, unattended, unarmed man of Nazareth, as if he was a weak impostor or was deranged.

30. *And they spit upon him.* This was

30 And they [q]spit upon him, and took the reed, and smote him on the head.

31 And after that they had mocked him, they took the robe off from him, and put his own raiment on him, and [r]led him away to crucify *him*.

32 And as they came out, they found a man of Cyrene, Simon by name: him they compelled to bear his cross.

33 And when they were come unto a place called Golgotha, that is to say, A place of a skull,

q Is.49.7; 50.6; 53.3,7.
r Nu.15.35; 1 Ki.21.10,13; Ac.7.58; He.13.12.

a token of the deepest contempt and insult. See Notes on Mat. xxvi. 67. ¶ *And took the reed.* The cane, probably so large as to inflict a heavy blow. ¶ *And smote him on the head.* Not merely to injure him by the force of the blow, but to press the *thorns* into his head, and thus to add cruelty to insult.

31, 32. *As they came out.* That is, either out of the governor's palace where he had been treated with such cruelty and contempt, or out of the gates of the city, to crucify him. ¶ *A man of Cyrene.* Cyrene was a city of Libya, in Africa, lying west of Egypt. There were many Jews there, and they were in the habit, like others, of going frequently to Jerusalem. ¶ *Him they compelled to bear his cross.* John says (xix. 17) that Jesus went forth *bearing his cross.* Luke says (xxiii. 26) that they laid the cross on Simon, that he might bear it after Jesus. There is no contradiction in these accounts. It was a part of the usual punishment of those who were crucified that they should bear their own cross to the place of execution. It was accordingly laid at first on Jesus, and he went forth, as John says, bearing it. Weak, however, and exhausted by suffering and watchfulness, he probably sunk under the heavy burden, and they laid hold of Simon that he might bear *one end* of the cross, as Luke says, *after Jesus.* The cross was composed of two pieces of wood, one of which was placed upright in the earth, and the other crossed it after the form of the figure †. The upright part was commonly so high that the feet of the person crucified were 2 or 3 feet from the ground. On the middle of that upright part there was usually a projection or seat on which the person crucified sat, or, as it were, *rode.* This was necessary, as the hands were not alone strong enough to bear the weight of the body; as the body was left exposed often many days, and not unfrequently suffered to remain till the flesh had been devoured by vultures or putrefied in the sun. The feet were fastened to this upright piece either by nailing them with large spikes driven through the tender part, or by being lashed by cords. To the cross-piece at the top, the hands, being extended, were also fastened, either by spikes or by cords, or perhaps, in some cases, by both. The hands and feet of our Saviour were both fastened by spikes. Crosses were also sometimes made in the form of the letter X, the limbs of the person crucified being extended to the four parts, and he suffered to die a lingering death in this cruel manner. The cross used in the crucifixion of Christ appears to have been the former. The mention of the cross often occurs in the New Testament. It was the instrument on which the Saviour made atonement for the sins of the world. The whole of the Christian's hope of heaven, and all his peace and consolation in trial and in death, depend on the sacrifice there made for sin, and on just views and feelings in regard to the fact and the design of the Redeemer's death. See Notes on Jn. xxi. 18.

33. *Golgotha.* This is a Hebrew word, signifying the place of a skull. This is the word which in Luke is called *Calvary.* The original Greek, there, also means *a skull.* The word *calvary* is a *Latin* word meaning *skull,* or place of *skulls.* It is not known certainly why this name was given to this place. Some have supposed that it was because the mount resembled in shape a human skull. The most probable opinion, however, is that it was a place of execution; that malefactors were beheaded there or otherwise put to death, and that their bones remained unburied or unburned. Golgotha, or Calvary, was probably a small eminence on the northwest of Jerusalem, without the walls of the city, but at a short distance. Jesus was put to death *out* of the city, because capital punishments were not allowed within the walls. See Nu. xv. 35; 1 Ki.

34 They[s] gave him vinegar to drink, mingled with gall: and when he had tasted *thereof*, he would not drink.

s Ps.69.21.

35 And[t] they crucified him, and parted his garments, casting lots; that it might be fulfilled which was spoken by the prophet, [u]They

t Ps.22.16; Mar.15.24,&c.; Lu.23.34,&c.; Jn.19.24,&c. *u* Ps.22.18.

xxi. 13. This was a law among the Romans as well as the Jews. He also died there, because the bodies of the beasts slain in sacrifice as typical of him were *burned without the camp*. He also, as the antitype, suffered *without the gate*, He. xiii. 11, 12. The place which is shown as Calvary now is within the city, and must also have been within the ancient walls, and there is no reason to suppose that it is the place where the Saviour was put to death.

34. *They gave him vinegar*, &c. Mark says that, "*they gave him to drink wine mingled with myrrh*." The two evangelists mean the same thing. Vinegar was made of light wine rendered acid, and was the common drink of the Roman soldiers, and this might be called either vinegar or wine in common language. *Myrrh* is a bitter substance produced in Arabia, but is used often to denote anything bitter. The meaning of the name is *bitterness*. See Notes on Mat. ii. 11. *Gall* is properly a bitter secretion from the liver, but the word is also used to denote anything exceedingly *bitter*, as wormwood, &c. The drink, therefore, was vinegar or sour wine, rendered *bitter* by the infusion of wormwood or some other very bitter substance. The effect of this, it is said, was to stupefy the senses. It was often given to those who were crucified, to render them insensible to the pains of death. Our Lord, knowing this, when he had tasted it refused to drink. He was unwilling to blunt the pains of dying. The *cup* which his *Father* gave him he rather chose to drink. He came to suffer. His sorrows were necessary for the work of the atonement, and he gave himself up to the unmitigated sufferings of the cross. This was presented to him in the early part of his sufferings, or when he was about to be suspended on the cross. *Afterward*, when he was on the cross and just before his death, vinegar was offered to him *without the myrrh*—the vinegar which the soldiers usually drank—and of this he drank. See ver. 49, and Jn. xix. 28–30. When Matthew and Mark say that he "would not drink," they refer to a different thing and a different time from John, and there is no contradiction.

35. *And they crucified him*. To *crucify* means to put to death on a cross. The *cross* has been described at ver. 32. The usual *manner* of the crucifixion was as follows: After the criminal had carried the cross, attended with every possible gibe and insult, to the place of execution, a hole was dug in the earth to receive the foot of it. The cross was laid on the ground; the person condemned to suffer was stripped and was extended on it, and the soldiers fastened the hands and feet either by nails or thongs. After they had driven the nails deeply in the wood, they elevated the cross with the agonizing sufferer on it, and, in order to fix it more firmly in the earth, they let it fall violently into the hole which they had dug to receive it. This sudden fall gave to the person that was nailed to it a violent and convulsive shock, and greatly increased his sufferings. The crucified person was then suffered to hang, commonly, till pain, exhaustion, thirst, and hunger ended his life. Sometimes the sufferings continued for days; and when friendly death terminated the life, the body was often suffered to remain—a loathsome object, putrefying in the sun or devoured by birds.

This punishment was deemed the most disgraceful and ignominious that was practised among the Romans. It was the way in which slaves, robbers, and the most notorious and abandoned wretches were commonly put to death. It was this, among other things, that exposed those who preached the gospel to so much shame and contempt among the Greeks and Romans. They despised everything that was connected with the death of one who had been put to death as a slave and an outlaw.

As it was the most ignominious punishment known, so it was the most painful. The following circumstances made it a death of peculiar pain: 1st. The position of the arms and the body was unnatural, the arms being extended back and almost immovable. The least motion gave violent pain in the hands

parted my garments among them, and upon my vesture did they cast lots.

36 And sitting down, they watched him there;

37 And set up over his head his accusation written, THIS IS JESUS, THE KING OF THE JEWS.

38 Then were there two [v]thieves crucified with him; one on the right hand, and another on the left.

39 And they that passed by reviled him, [w]wagging their heads,

v Is.53.12. w Ps.22.7; 109.25.

and feet, and in the back, which was lacerated with stripes. 2d. The nails, being driven through the parts of the hands and feet which abound with *nerves*, created the most exquisite anguish. 3d. The exposure of so many wounds to the air brought on a violent inflammation, which greatly increased the poignancy of the suffering. 4th. The free circulation of the blood was prevented. More blood was carried out in the *arteries* than could be returned by the *veins*. The consequence was, that there was a great increase of blood in the veins of the head, producing an intense pressure and violent pain. The same was true of other parts of the body. This intense pressure in the blood-vessels was the source of inexpressible misery. 5th. The pain gradually increased. There was no relaxation and no rest. There was no prospect but death. The sufferer was commonly able to endure it till the third, and sometimes even to the seventh day. The intense sufferings of the Saviour, however, were sooner terminated. This was caused, perhaps, in some measure, by his previous fatigue and exhaustion, but still more by the intense sufferings of his soul in bearing *our* griefs and carrying *our* sorrows—in making an atonement for the sins of the world. See Notes on Mat. xv. 44. ¶ *And parted his garments.* It was customary to crucify a person naked. The clothes of the sufferer belonged to those who were executioners. John says (xix. 23) that they divided his garments into four parts, to each soldier a part, but for his coat they cast lots. See Notes on the place. When Matthew says, therefore, that they parted his garments, casting lots, it is to be understood that they *divided* one part of them, and for the other part of them they cast lots. ¶ *That it might be fulfilled,* &c. The words here quoted are found in Ps. xxii. 18. The whole psalm is usually referred to Christ, and is a most striking description of his sufferings and death.

36. *They watched him there.* That is, the four soldiers who had crucified him. They watched him lest his friends should come and release him.

37. *And set up over his head.* John says (xix. 19) that Pilate wrote the title and put it upon the cross. Probably Pilate wrote it or caused it to be written, and directed the soldiers to set it up. A man is often said to do what he directs others to do. It was customary to set up over the heads of persons crucified the crime for which they suffered, and the name of the sufferer. The accusation on which Jesus had been condemned by Pilate was his claiming to be the King of the Jews. ¶ *This is Jesus, the King of the Jews.* The evangelists differ in the account of this title. Mark (xv. 26) says it was, "The King of the Jews." Luke (xxiii. 38), "This is the King of the Jews." John (xix. 19), "Jesus of Nazareth, the King of the Jews." But the difficulty may be easily removed. John says that the title was written in Hebrew, Greek, and Latin. It is not at all improbable that the inscription *varied* in these languages. One evangelist may have translated it from the Hebrew, another from the Greek, a third from the Latin, and a fourth may have translated one of the inscriptions a little differently from another. Besides, the evangelists all agree in the main point of the inscription, viz. that he was the King of the Jews.

38. *Two thieves crucified,* &c. Rather two *robbers.* Pilate did not reside in Jerusalem. When he came there on the great feasts, or at other times, it was, in part, to hold courts for the trial of criminals. These robbers had been probably condemned at that time; and to show greater contempt for Jesus, he was crucified between men of that abandoned character, and on a cross that *should* have been occupied by their companion and leader, *Barabbas.*

39. *Wagging their heads.* In token of derision and insult. See Job xvi. 4; Ps. cix. 25.

40 And saying, Thou that destroyest the temple, and buildest
it in three days, save thyself. If
thou be the Son of God, come
down from the cross.
41 Likewise, also, the chief priests,
mocking[x] *him*, with the scribes and
elders, said,
42 He saved others, himself he
cannot save. If he be the King of
Israel, let him now come down from
the cross, and we will believe him.
43 He trusted in God; [y]let him
deliver him now, if he will have
him: for he said, [z]I am the Son
of God.
44 The thieves also, which were
crucified with him, cast the same in
his teeth.
45 Now from the sixth hour

x Job 13.9; Ps.35.16; Is.28.22; Lu.18.32.

y Ps.3.2; 22.8; 42.10; 71.11. z Jn.5.17,18; 10.30,36.

---

40. *Thou that destroyest the temple*, &c. Meaning, Thou that didst boast that thou couldst do it. This was one of the things that had been falsely charged on him. It was intended for painful sarcasm and derision. If he could destroy the *temple*, they thought he might easily come down from the cross.

42, 43. *He saved others.* It does not seem probable that they meant to admit that he had actually saved others, but only that he *pretended* to save them from death by miracles, or that he claimed to be the Messiah, and thus affirmed that he *could* save them. This is, therefore, cutting irony. ¶ *If he be the King of Israel*, &c. It may seem strange to some that Jesus did not vindicate by a miracle his claims to be the Messiah, and come down from the cross. But the time had come for him to make an atonement. He *had* given full and sufficient proof that he was the Christ. Those who had rejected him, and who mocked and taunted him, would have been little likely to admit his claims if he *had* come down from the cross, since they had set at naught all his other miracles. They said this for the purpose of insult; and Jesus chose rather to suffer, though his character was assailed, than to work a new miracle for their gratification. He had foretold his death, and the time had come; and now, amid revilings, and gibes, and curses, and the severe sarcasms of an angry and apparently triumphant priesthood, he chose to die for the sins of the world. To this they added *insult* to God, profanely calling upon him to interpose by miracle and save him, if he was his friend; and all this when their prophets had foretold this very scene, and when they were fulfilling the predictions of their own Scriptures. See Notes on Is. liii., and Da. ix. 24-27. So wonderful is the way by which God causes his word to be fulfilled.

44. *The thieves also.* The robbers, or highwaymen. Luke says (xxiii. 39) that one of them did it, and that the other reproved him and was penitent. The account in Luke may, however, easily be reconciled with that in Matthew by supposing that *at first both* of them reviled the Saviour, and that it is of this fact that Matthew speaks. Afterward one of them relented and became penitent—perhaps from witnessing the patient sufferings of Christ. It is of this one particularly that Luke speaks. Or it may be that what is true of one of the malefactors is by Matthew attributed to both. The evangelists, when for the sake of brevity they avoid particularizing, often attribute to many what is said or done by single persons, meaning no more than that it was done by some one or more of them, without specifying the one. Comp. Mar. vii. 17 with Mat. xv. 15; Mar. v. 31 with Lu. viii. 45; Lu. ix. 13 with Jn. vi. 8, 9. ¶ *Cast the same in his teeth.* This is a most unhappy translation. It means in the original simply, they upbraided him or reproached him in the same manner.

45. *Now from the sixth hour.* That is, from our twelve o'clock. The Jews divided their day into twelve hours, beginning to count at sunrise. ¶ *There was darkness.* This could not have been an eclipse of the sun, for the Passover was celebrated at the time of the full moon, when the moon is opposite to the sun. Luke says (xxiii. 45) that *the sun was darkened*, but it was not by an eclipse. The only cause of this was the interposing power of God—furnishing testimony to the dignity of the sufferer, and causing the elements to sympathize with the pains of his dying Son. It was also peculiarly proper to furnish this testimony when the *Sun of righte-*

there was [a]darkness over all the land unto the ninth hour.

46 And about the ninth hour Jesus cried with a loud voice, saying, Eli, Eli, lama sabachthani? that is to say, [b]My God, my God, why hast thou forsaken me?

47 Some of them that stood

a Am.8.9.

b Ps.22.1; Is.53.10; La.1.12.

ousness was withdrawing his beams for a time, and the Redeemer of men was expiring. A thick darkness, shutting out the light of day, and clothing every object with the gloom of midnight, was the appropriate drapery with which the world should be clad when the Son of God expired. This darkness was noticed by one at least of the Pagan writers. *Phlegon*, a Roman astronomer, speaking of the fourteenth year of the reign of Tiberius, which is supposed to be that in which our Saviour died, says "that the greatest eclipse of the sun that was ever known happened then, for the day was so turned into night that the stars appeared." ¶ *Over all the land.* That is, probably, over the whole land of Judea, and perhaps some of the adjacent countries. The extent of the darkness is not known. ¶ *The ninth hour.* Till about three o'clock in the afternoon, at which time the Saviour is supposed to have died.

46. *Eli, Eli,* &c. This language is not pure Hebrew nor Syriac, but a mixture of both, called commonly *Syro-Chaldaic.* This was probably the language which the Saviour commonly spoke. The words are taken from Ps. xxii. 1. ¶ *My God, my God,* &c. This expression is one denoting intense suffering. It has been difficult to understand in what sense Jesus was *forsaken by God.* It is certain that God *approved* his work. It is certain that he was innocent. He had done nothing to forfeit the favour of God. As his own Son—holy, harmless, undefiled, and obedient—God still loved him. In either of these senses God could not have forsaken him. But the expression was probably used in reference to the following circumstances, viz.: 1st. His great bodily sufferings on the cross, greatly aggravated by his previous scourging, and by the want of sympathy, and by the revilings of his enemies on the cross. A person suffering thus might address God as if he was forsaken, or given up to extreme anguish. 2d. He himself said that this was "the power of darkness," Lu. xxii. 53. It was the time when his enemies, including the Jews and Satan, were suffered to do *their utmost.* It was said of the serpent that he should bruise the heel of the seed of the woman, Ge. iii. 15. By that has been commonly understood to be meant that, though the Messiah would finally crush and destroy the power of Satan, yet he should himself suffer *through the power of the devil.* When he was tempted (Lu. iv.), it was said that the tempter *departed from him for a season.* There is no improbability in supposing that he might be permitted to return at the time of his death, and exercise his power in increasing the sufferings of the Lord Jesus. In what way this might be done can be only conjectured. It might be by horrid thoughts; by temptation to despair, or to distrust God, who thus permitted his innocent Son to suffer; or by an increased horror of the pains of dying. 3d. There might have been *withheld* from the Saviour those strong religious consolations, those clear views of the justice and goodness of God, which would have blunted his pains and soothed his agonies. Martyrs, under the influence of strong religious feeling, have gone triumphantly to the stake, but it is possible that those views might have been withheld from the Redeemer when he came to die. His sufferings were accumulated sufferings, and the design of the atonement seemed to require that he should suffer all that human nature *could be made to endure* in so short a time. Yet, 4th. We have reason to think that there was still something more than all this that produced this exclamation. Had there been no deeper and more awful sufferings, it would be difficult to see why Jesus should have shrunk from these sorrows and used such a remarkable expression. Isaiah tells us (liii. 4, 5) that *he bore our griefs and carried our sorrows; that he was wounded for our transgressions, and bruised for our iniquities; that the chastisement of our peace was laid upon him; that by his stripes we are healed.* He hath redeemed us from the curse of the law, being made a curse for us (Ga. iii. 13); he was made a sin-offering (2 Co. v. 21); he died *in our place,* on *our* account, that he might

there, when they heard *that,* said,
This *man* calleth for Elias.
48 And straightway one of them
ran, and took a sponge, and [c]filled
it with vinegar, and put *it* on a
reed, and gave him to drink.
49 The rest said, Let be; let us
see whether Elias will come to
save him.
50 Jesus, when he had cried
again with a loud voice, yielded
up the ghost.
51 And, behold, [d]the vail of the
temple was [e]rent in twain, from

c Ps.69.21.

d Ex.26.31; Le.16.2,15; 21.23; 2 Ch.3.14. *e* Is.25.7.

---

bring us near to God. It was this, doubtless, which caused his intense sufferings. It was the manifestation of God's hatred of sin, in some way which he has not explained, that he experienced in that dread hour. It was suffering endured by *him* that was due to *us*, and suffering by which, and by which alone, we can be saved from eternal death.

47. *This* man *calleth for Elias.* This was done purposely to deride him and his pretensions to be the Messiah. The words Eli, Eli, they might easily pretend that they understood to mean Elias, or so pervert them. The taunt would be more cutting, because it was the universal belief of the Jews, as well as the doctrine of Christ, that *Elias* would come before the Messiah. They derided him now, as calling upon *Elias* when *God* would not help him; still keeping up the pretensions to being the Messiah, and invoking *Elijah* to come from the dead to aid him. Or it is possible that this might have been said by some by-standers who did not understand the language in which he spoke, or who might not have been near enough to hear him distinctly.

48. *One of them ran.* John (xix. 28) says that this was in consequence of Jesus' saying "I thirst." One of the effects of crucifixion was excessive thirst. ¶ *Took a sponge.* A sponge is a well-known porous substance that easily absorbs water. It was used in this case because, Jesus being elevated, it was difficult to convey a cup to his lips. ¶ *Filled* it *with vinegar.* This was the common drink of Roman soldiers. It was a light wine, turned sour and mixed with water. John says (xix. 29) there was a vessel set full of vinegar, probably for the use of the soldiers who watched his crucifixion. ¶ *And put* it *on a reed.* John says it was put upon *hyssop.* The *hyssop* was a *shrub*, growing so large sometimes as to be called a *tree*, 1 Ki. iv. 33. The *stalk* of this was what Matthew calls a *reed.* The sponge fastened to this could easily be *extended* to reach the mouth of *Jesus.* This vinegar Jesus drank, for it was not intended to *stupefy* him or blunt his sense of pain, like the *wine and myrrh.*

49. *The rest said,* &c. Still deriding his sufferings, and refusing to allow even the poor consolation of a drink, to assuage the thirst of the Saviour of the world in his dying agonies.

50. *Cried again with a loud voice.* He cried, "It is finished," Jn. xix. 30. It was in the height of his agony, probably attended with deep groaning, and uttered amid sorrows which were never else experienced in our world. It finished the work of atonement, made the way of salvation possible, rolled away the curse from guilty men, and opened the kingdom of heaven to all true believers. ¶ *Yielded up the ghost.* This, though a literal translation, is unhappy. It means resigned his spirit, or *expired.* The same phrase is used by the LXX. in describing the death of Rachel, Ge. xxxv. 18.

51. *The vail of the temple.* This was doubtless the vail, curiously wrought, which separated the holy from the most holy place, dividing the temple into two apartments, Ex. xxvi. 31–33. ¶ *In twain.* In two pieces or parts. This was the time of day when the priest was burning incense in the holy place, and it is probable that he witnessed it. The most holy place has been usually considered as a type of heaven, and the rending of the vail to signify that the way to heaven was now open to all —the great High-priest, the Lord Jesus, being about to enter in as the forerunner of his people. However, about the *design* of the rending of the vail, the Scriptures are silent, and conjecture is useless. ¶ *And the earth did quake.* Or shook. Earthquakes are violent convulsions of the ground, caused commonly by confined and rarefied air. This was probably, however, a miraculous convulsion of the earth, in attes-

the top to the bottom; and the earth did quake, and the rocks rent;

52 And[f] the graves were opened, and [g]many bodies of the saints which slept arose,

53 And [h]came out of the graves after his resurrection, and went into the holy city, and appeared unto many.

54 Now[i] when the centurion, and they that were with him watching Jesus, saw the earthquake, and those things that were done, they feared greatly, saying, Truly this was the Son of God.

55 And many women were there beholding afar off, [k]which followed Jesus from Galilee, ministering unto him;

f Is.25.8; 26.19; Ho.13.14; Jn.5.25,28. *g* Da.12.2; 1 Th.4.14. *h* 1 Co.15.20.

i Mar.15.39; Lu.23.47,&c. *k* Lu.8.2,3.

tation of the truth that the sufferer was the Messiah, the Son of God, and as an exhibition of *wrath* at the crimes of those who put him to death. It was not confined to Judea, but was felt in other countries. It is mentioned by Roman writers. ¶ *The rocks rent.* That is, were torn asunder. Rocks are still seen at Mount Calvary thus rent asunder, which are *said* to be the ones that were convulsed when the Saviour died.

52. *And the graves were opened. Graves* or sepulchres were most commonly made, among the Jews, in solid rocks or in caves of rocks. The rending of the rocks, therefore, would lay them open. The graves were *opened* by this earthquake, but the dead in them did not rise till after his resurrection. ¶ *And many bodies of the saints arose.* Of course, it is not known who these were, nor what became of them. It is probable that they were persons who had recently died, and they appear to have been known in Jerusalem; at least, had the ancient saints risen, they would not have been known, and would not so soon have been credited as those who had recently died. ¶ *Which slept.* Which had died. The death of saints is often called *sleep*, Da. xii. 2; 1 Co. xv. 18; 1 Th. iv. 15.

53. *And came out of the graves after his resurrection.* The narrative of Matthew does not determine whether they came to life *before* Jesus rose, and remained in the tombs, or came to life *after* he died. The latter is probably the correct opinion. There is nothing said of the *reason* why they were raised. It is not improbable to suppose that it was, amid the other wonders attending the death of Jesus, to convince the Jews that he was the Messiah. Perhaps some who had been his open friends were raised up now as an attestation that he in whom they had believed was the Christ. What became of them after they had entered into the city—whether they again died or ascended to heaven, is not revealed, and conjecture is vain. ¶ *The holy city.* Jerusalem, called holy because the temple was there, because it was devoted to God, and because it was the place of religious solemnities.

54. *Now when the centurion,* &c. Centurion, a captain of a hundred soldiers. He was here placed over the band that attended the crucifixion. ¶ *They feared greatly.* They regarded these things as proof that God was angry, and they were terrified at the prospect that vengeance was coming on them. ¶ *Truly this was the Son of God.* They had heard, probably, that Jesus professed to be the Son of God. Seeing these wonders, they believed that God was now attesting the truth of his professions. The centurion was a heathen, and had probably no very distinct notions of the phrase *the Son of God*—perhaps understanding by it only that he was like the heathen heroes who had been deified; but he certainly regarded these wonders as proof that he was *what he professed to be.* In the original it is "a son of a god;" an expression perfectly suitable to a polytheist, who believed in the existence of many gods. Mark (xv. 39) says that they affirmed that "this man was the Son of God." Luke (xxiii. 47), that they said, "Certainly this was a righteous man." These things were said by *different persons*, or at different periods of his sufferings—one evangelist having recorded one saying, and another another.

55. *Beholding afar off.* These women were probably not suffered to come near the cross because it was surrounded by soldiers. They witnessed with intense feelings his sufferings from some con-

56 Among which was Mary Magdalene, and Mary the mother of James and Joses, and the mother of Zebedee's children.

57 When[l] the even was come, there came a rich man of Arimathea, named Joseph, who also himself was Jesus' disciple:

l Mar.15.42; Lu.23.50; Jn.19.38.

58 He went to Pilate, and begged the body of Jesus. Then Pilate commanded the body to be delivered.

59 And when Joseph had taken the body, he wrapped it in a clean linen cloth,

60 And[m] laid it in his own new tomb, which he had hewn out in

m Is.53.9.

---

venient place as near as they could approach. ¶ *Ministering unto him.* Attending him and providing for his wants. While multitudes of *men* joined in the cry Crucify him! and forsook him in his trying moments, it does not appear that any of his *female* followers were thus unfaithful. In the midst of all his trials, and all the contempt poured upon him, they adhered to their Redeemer. Never did female constancy shine more brightly, and never was a happier example set for all who should afterward believe on him.

56. *Mary Magdalene.* Mary of Magdala. She had peculiar cause of attachment to the Saviour, having been relieved by him of a most dreadful calamity and restored to her right mind, after being possessed by seven devils. See Notes on Lu. viii. 2. ¶ *And the mother of Zebedee's children.* That is, of James and John, Mat. x. 2. Her name was Salome, Mar. xv. 40.

57. *When the even was come.* That is, some time after three o'clock in the afternoon. Before this, the Jews had besought Pilate that the legs of those who were crucified might be broken and the bodies be taken down, that they might not remain on the cross during the Sabbath. The soldiers, coming to Jesus for that purpose, found that he was already dead, contrary to their expectation. A soldier, however, thrust a spear into his side, and there was furnished the fullest proof that he had expired. See Notes on Jn. xix. 31-37. ¶ *A rich man of Arimathea.* It is uncertain where Arimathea was. There were several cities of that name in Judea. It is commonly supposed to be the same as Rama. See Notes on ch. ii. 17. Luke says that this was a *city of the Jews*, and it is probable, therefore, that it was in the tribe of Benjamin, and but a short distance from Jerusalem. This man sustained a high character. He was an "honourable counsellor, who also waited for the kingdom of God" (Mar. xv. 43); he was "a good man and a just" (Lu. xxiii. 50); he had nobly set himself against the wicked purposes of the Sanhedrim (Lu. xxiii. 51); he was a disciple of Jesus, though he was not openly his follower, because he feared the Jews, Jn. xix. 38.

58. *He went to Pilate.* Because no one had a right to remove the body but by authority of the magistrate. Jesus was condemned to be crucified, usually a long and most bitter death, and in common cases it would have been unlawful to have removed the body so soon.

59. *He wrapped it in a clean linen cloth.* John adds that this was done *with spices* (xix. 40). The Jews were accustomed to use myrrh, aloes, and other aromatics in large quantities when they buried their dead. When they were not regularly embalmed, which was a long and tedious process, they inclosed the spices in the folds of the linen, or wrapped the body in it. Spices were sometimes used in such quantities as to form a *heap* or *bed*, on which the dead body was laid. Thus it is said of Asa (2 Ch. xvi. 14), "they laid him in the bed which was filled with sweet odours and spices," &c. There not being time properly to embalm the body of Jesus, he was buried in this manner. The women who attended him, either not being aware of this, or desirous of showing a farther regard for him, returned from the sepulchre and prepared other spices with which to embalm him on the first day of the week, Lu. xxiii. 56; xxiv. 1.

60. *In his own new tomb.* John says (xix. 41) that this was in a garden that was *in* or *near* the place where he was crucified. This tomb Joseph had prepared for himself, as was not uncommon among the Jews. Comp. Notes on Isa. xxii. 16. In this tomb Luke and John inform us that no man had been laid. This was so ordered, in the pro-

the rock: and he rolled a great
stone to the door of the sepulchre,
and departed.
61 And there was Mary Magdalene, and the other Mary, sitting
over against the sepulchre.
62 Now the next day, that followed the day of the preparation,
the chief priests and Pharisees
came together unto Pilate,
63 Saying, Sir, we remember that
that [n]deceiver said, while he was yet
alive, [o]After three days I will rise
again.
64 Command, therefore, that the
sepulchre be made sure until the
third day, lest his disciples [p]come
by night and steal him away, and
say unto the people, He is risen
from the dead: so the last error
shall be worse than the first.
65 Pilate said unto them, Ye
have a watch: go your way, make
it as sure as you can.

n Jn.7.12,47; 2 Co.6.8.

o ch.16.21; 17.23; 20.19; Lu.24.6,7; Jn.2.19.
p ch.28.13.

---

vidence of God, doubtless, that there might be no suspicion about his identity when he rose; that it might not be alleged that another person had risen, or that he was raised by touching the bones of some prophet, as happened to the corpse that touched the bones of Elisha, 2 Ki. xiii. 21. Farther, by being buried here an important prophecy was remarkably fulfilled (Is. liii. 9): *He made his grave—with the rich in his death.* The fulfilment of this is the more remarkable, because during his life he associated with the poor and was himself poor. See Notes on Is. liii. 9. ¶ *Which he had hewn out in the rock.* This was a common way of constructing tombs in Judea. See Notes on Mat. viii. 28. Being cut out of a rock, there was no way by which the disciples could have access to it but by the entrance, at which the guard was placed, and consequently it was impossible for them to steal him away. The sepulchre, thus secure, was rendered more so by rolling a great stone at its entrance; all possible precautions thus being used, in the providence of God, against imposition and deceit.

62. *Now the next day, that followed the day of the preparation.* The first day of the feast of the Passover was called the day of *preparation*, because all things were on that day got in readiness for the observances of the paschal week. The Jewish day closed at sunset, and the Sabbath at that time commenced. The *next day* mentioned here does not mean the following day in *our* acceptation of the word, or the following *morning*, but the next day in the Jewish way of speaking—that is, after the next day had commenced, or after sundown. To suppose them to have waited till the next morning would be absurd, as the disciples would be as likely to steal him away the first night as the second.

63. *We remember.* They had either heard him say this, or, more probably, had understood that this was one of his doctrines. ¶ *That deceiver.* One of the charges against him was that he deceived the people, Jn. vii. 12. By this title they still chose to designate him, thinking that his death had fully confirmed the truth of the charges against him.

64. *Until the third day.* That is, during two nights and the intervening day. This proves that when the Jews spoke of *three days*, they did not of necessity mean three *whole days*, but *parts* of three days, as was the case in our Saviour's lying in the grave. See Notes on ch. xii. 40. ¶ *The last error shall be worse than the first.* That is, the last *deception*, or the taking him from the tomb, pretending that he rose, will have a wider influence among the people than the *first*, or his pretending to be the Messiah.

65. *Ye have a watch.* The Jews had a guard of Roman soldiers, who kept watch in the tower of Antonia, on the north-west of the temple. Pilate either referred to these, or to the *watch* that attended the crucifixion—the whole *band* that had been appointed for that. As the torments of crucifixion sometimes lasted many days, the band had been probably granted to them during that time, and they were therefore still at the direction of the chief priests.

66. *Sealing the stone.* The sepulchre was made sure by affixing the large stone to the entrance in such a way that it could not be removed without detection. It was sealed. In what way this

66 So they went, and made the sepulchre sure, [q]sealing the stone, and setting a watch.

q Da.6.17.

CHAPTER XXVIII.

IN[a] the end of the sabbath, as it began to dawn toward the first

a Mar.16.1; Lu.24.1,&c.; Jn.20.1,&c.

was done cannot now be certainly told. The cave in which Daniel was cast was fastened in the same manner, and sealed with the king's signet (Da. vi. 17), perhaps by fastening the stone in its place with cords, and bringing them together and uniting them with wax, and impressing on that the seal of the king. In this way letters and books were anciently sealed. Possibly on the sepulchre of Jesus was impressed in this manner the seal of Pilate—the seal of office—making it doubly sure; or it may be that the stone was fitted into the tomb with clay or cement, and on that was impressed the seal of Pilate. ¶ *Setting a watch.* That is, as large a number of soldiers as they judged necessary to secure the tomb.

We cannot but be struck with the wisdom of God in ordering the circumstances of the Saviour's burial in such a manner as to avoid the possibility of deception. Had all this been done by his *friends*, it might have been said that they only pretended to secure the tomb, and only pretended that he was dead. But he was adjudged to be dead *by the Jews themselves;* Pilate was satisfied that that was the fact; they had their own way about his burial; he was buried alone; the place of his sepulchre was made sure, *expressly to prevent his being removed;* and they placed around him a guard, in their own judgment large enough to prevent his being taken away by force or strength. His very enemies, therefore, took every possible precaution to place his resurrection beyond the possibility of suspicion of fraud and imposture, and those precautions were the very means of furnishing the most striking proof that his death, burial, and resurrection were not impositions, but most affecting, awful, and yet cheering realities.

CHAPTER XXVIII.

1. *In the end of the sabbath.* The word *end* here means the same as *after* the Sabbath—that is, after the Sabbath was fully completed or finished, and may be expressed in this manner: "In the night following the Sabbath, for the Sabbath closed at sunset, as it began to dawn," &c. ¶ *As it began to dawn toward the first* day *of the week.* The word *dawn* is not of necessity in the original. The word there properly means as the first day *approached*, or drew on, without specifying the precise time. Mark says (xvi. 1, 2) that it was after "the sabbath was past, and very early in the morning, at the rising of the sun"—that is, not that the sun *was risen*, but that it was *about to rise*, or at the early break of day. Luke says (xxiv. 1) that it was "very early in the morning;" in the Greek, *deep twilight*, or when there was scarcely any light. John (xx. 1) says it was "very early, while it was yet dark"—that is, it was not yet full daylight, or the sun had not yet risen. The time when they came, therefore, was at the break of day, when the sun was about to rise, but while it was yet so dark as to render objects obscure, or not distinctly visible. ¶ *The first* day *of the week.* The day which is observed by Christians as the Sabbath. The Jews observed the seventh day of the week, or our Saturday. During that day our Saviour was in the grave. As he rose on the morning of the first day, that day has always been observed in commemoration of so glorious an event. ¶ *Came Mary Magdalene and the other Mary.* From Mary Magdalene Christ had cast out seven devils. Grateful for his great mercy, she was one of his firmest and most faithful followers, and was first at the sepulchre, and was first permitted to see her risen Lord. The *other Mary* was not the mother of Jesus, but the mother of James and Joses (Mark). Mark says that *Salome* attended them. Salome was the wife of Zebedee, and the mother of James and John. From Luke (xxiv. 10) it appears that Joanna, wife of Chusa, Herod's steward (see Lu. viii. 3), was with them. These four women, Mark says (ch. xvi. 1), having bought sweet spices, came to anoint him. They had prepared a part of them on the evening before the Sabbath, Lu. xxiii. 56. They now, according to Mark, *completed* the preparation and bought more; or the meaning in Mark may be merely that, *having bought* sweet spices, without specifying the time *when*, they came now to embalm him. John men-

day of the week, came [b]Mary Magdalene, and the other Mary, to see the sepulchre.

2 And, behold, there [1]was a great earthquake; for the angel of the Lord descended from heaven, and came and rolled back the stone from the door, and sat upon it.

3 His[c] countenance was like lightning, and his raiment white as snow:

4 And for fear of him the keepers did shake, and became as dead *men*.

5 And[d] the angel answered and said unto the women, Fear not ye; for[e] I know that ye seek Jesus, which was crucified.

b ch.27.56. 1 or, *had been*.

c Ps.104.4; Eze.1.4-14; Da.10.6; Re.1.14-16. *d* He.1.14. *e* Ps.105.3,4.

tions only Mary Magdalene. He does this, probably, because his object was to give a particular account of her interview with the risen Saviour. There is no contradiction among the evangelists; for while one mentions only the names of a part of those who were there, he does not deny that *others* were present also. It is an old maxim, that "he who mentions a few does not deny that there are more." ¶ *To see the sepulchre.* To see whether it was as it had been left on the evening when he was laid there. To see if the stone was still there, by which they would know that he had not been removed. Mark and Luke say that the design of their coming was to anoint him with the sweet spices which they had prepared. Matthew does not mention that, but he does not *deny* that that was the ultimate design of their coming. It is not improbable that they might have known the manner in which he was buried, with a large quantity of myrrh and aloes; but that was done in in haste—it was done by depositing the myrrh and aloes, without mixture or preparation, in the grave-clothes. *They* came that they might embalm his body more deliberately, or at least that they might *anoint the bandages* and complete the work of embalming.

2. *There was a great earthquake.* Rather there *had been.* It does not mean that this was while they were there, or while they were going, but that there *had been* so violent a commotion as to remove the stone. The word here rendered *earthquake* does not of necessity mean that the convulsion extended to the earth, but only that there had been such a concussion as to remove the stone. ¶ *And sat upon it.* Sat upon it when the keepers saw him, ver. 4. It is not said that he was sitting when he appeared to the women. From Luke it would rather appear that he was standing.

3. *His countenance.* In our language the word *countenance* refers to the *face only;* in the original it refers to his *whole person.* His *general aspect*, or *the appearance of the angel himself*, was, &c. ¶ *Like lightning.* Peculiarly bright and shining. ¶ *His raiment white as snow.* Celestial beings are usually represented as clothed in white, Ac. i. 10; Da. vii. 9; Re. iii. 4, 5; iv. 4; vii. 13, 14. *White*, among the Jews, was the symbol of *purity* or *innocence*.

4. *The keepers did shake.* It was night. The appearance was sudden and unexpected, and to them terrific. The stone was probably suddenly removed. At the noise, the light, the suddenness of the appearance, they were affrighted. ¶ *And became as dead* men. Probably by terror they fainted, or were thrown into a swoon. At this time it is probable that the Lord Jesus arose, and hence he was not seen by them when he came forth. At what *precise time* of the night this was we are not certainly informed. The narrative, however, leads us to suppose that it was not long before the women came to the sepulchre, or near the break of day.

5. *And the angel answered and said*, &c. This was not on the *outside* of the tomb, for Matthew does not say that the angel appeared to the *women* there, but only to the keepers. Mark says, "entering into the sepulchre, they saw a young man sitting on the right side, clothed in a long white garment" (xvi.5). Luke says (xxiv. 3), "they entered in, and found not the body of the Lord Jesus; and as they were much perplexed thereabout, behold, two men stood by them in shining garments." Seeing the stone rolled away and the sepulchre open, they of course anxiously entered into it, to see if the body was there. They did not find it, and *there* they saw the vision of the angels, who gave them information respecting his resurrection. Infidels have objected that there are three inconsistencies in the accounts by Mark and Luke: 1st.

6 He is not here; for he is risen,
as[f] he said. Come, see the place
where the Lord lay.
7 And go quickly, and tell his
disciples that [g]he is risen from the
dead; and, behold, he goeth before
you into Galilee; [h]there shall ye
see him: lo, I have told you.
8 And they departed quickly
from the sepulchre, with fear and
great joy, and did run to bring his
disciples word.
9 And as they went to tell his
disciples, behold, Jesus met them,
saying, [i]All hail. And they came
and held him by the feet, and worshipped him.
10 Then said Jesus unto them,

f ch.27.63. *g* Lu.24.34; 1 Co.15.4. *h* ver.16,17.

i Jn.20.19.

That Mark says the angel was sitting, and Luke says they were standing. *Answer.* The word in Luke does not of necessity mean that they *stood*, but only that they were *present.* Or it may be that the one that *Mark* mentions was sitting when they entered, and then arose. 2d. It is objected that Luke mentions *two*, but Mark and Matthew *one*. *Answer.* Mark mentions the one who spoke; for it cannot be supposed they both spake the same thing. He does not *deny* that another was present with him. Luke affirms that there was. This way of speaking is not unfrequent. Thus Mark and Luke mention only one demoniac who was cured at Gadara. Matthew mentions two. In like manner Mark and Luke speak of only one blind man who was cured at Jericho, while from Matthew it is certain that two were. The fact that but one is mentioned, where it is not *denied* that there were others, does not prove that there could not be others. 3d. Matthew calls this an *angel*. Mark and Luke *a man*. *Answer.* Angels, in the Scriptures, from *appearing* in the form of men, are often called as they *appear*, and are mentioned as men. See Ge. xviii. 2, 16, 22; xix. 1, 5. ¶ *Fear not ye.* That is, "Be not agitated, or troubled, that you do not find the body of the Saviour. I know that ye seek him, and are troubled that he is removed; but you need not *fear* that he has been stolen. You will see him again in Galilee."

6. *He has risen, as he said.* Jesus had often predicted that he would rise, but the disciples did not understand it, and consequently did not expect it, Mat. xvi. 21; xx. 19. ¶ *The place where the Lord lay.* The place where a body was deposited in a sepulchre was commonly a *niche* cut in the wall of the sepulchre. The sepulchre was usually large; that of David was more than 100 feet in length, cut out of solid rock under ground, and separated into various apartments. All round the sides of those apartments were *niches* for the dead; or they were ranged around the sides, in places cut in the solid rock just large enough to contain the body. In such a place, probably, our Lord lay.

7. *Tell his disciples.* Mark adds particularly, "tell Peter." This was a kind message to Peter, who had so recently denied his Lord. It would serve to cheer him in his despondency, and to assure him that his sin had been forgiven; and it shows the tender love and remembrance of Jesus, even for his unfaithful friends.

8. *And they departed quickly.* Joyful at the *news*, and wishing to impart it to all, they fled to find the disciples, and to tell them that the Lord was risen. ¶ *With fear and great joy.* Fear, 1st, at the wonderful scenes which they had witnessed—the stone rolled away, and the presence of an angel; 2d, a confused state of mind, apprehensive, perhaps, that it might not, after all, be true. The news was too good to be credited at once, yet they had sufficient faith in it to fill them with great and unexpected joy. Perhaps no language could better express the state of their minds —the mingled awe and rejoicing—than that which is here used. ¶ *And did run*, &c. They ran to announce what they had seen to the disciples. The city, where the disciples were, was half a mile or more from the place.

9. *And as they went—Jesus met them.* This was when they left the sepulchre the *second* time. Jesus *first* appeared to Mary Magdalene when alone, Jn. xx. 14. *Afterward* he appeared to the other women, as related by Matthew. See the accounts of the resurrection harmonized at the end of this chapter. ¶ *All hail.* This is a term of salutation. The word "all" has been supplied by the translators. It is not in the original. The meaning of the word "hail," here,

Be not afraid: go tell [k]my brethren
that they go into Galilee, and there
shall they see me.
11 Now when they were going,
behold, some of the watch came
into the city, and showed unto the
chief priests all the things that
were done.

k He.2.11.

12 And when they were assembled with the elders, and had taken
counsel, they gave large money unto
the soldiers,
13 Saying, Say ye, [l]His disciples
came by night, and stole him *away*
while we slept.
14 And if this come to the gov-

l ch.27.64.

---

is *rejoice;* a term of salutation connected with the idea of joy—joy at his resurrection, and at meeting them again. ¶ *Held him by the feet.* Or threw themselves prostrate before him. This was the usual posture of supplication. See 2 Ki. iv. 37. It does not mean that they took hold of his feet, but only that they cast themselves down before him. ¶ *And worshipped him.* See Notes on Mat. viii. 2. In this place the word *worship* seems to denote the homage due to the Messiah risen from the dead; regarded by *them* now in a proper light, and entitled to the honour which was due to God, agreeably to Jn. v. 23.

10. *Be not afraid.* The ancients, when in the presence of a heavenly being—an angel, or one who was supposed to be possessed of divine power—were commonly struck with great *fear*, as well as a great sense of their unworthiness. See Lu. v. 8; Ju. vi. 22, 23; xiii. 21, 22. These women were in like manner alarmed when they saw Jesus, believing him now peculiarly to be a divine being; seeing him returning from the regions of the dead, and doubtless impressed with a new consciousness that they were unworthy of being in his presence. Jesus comforted them. He was the *same Jesus* with whom they had been before his death, and they had no reason now to fear him. ¶ *Go tell my brethren.* There is something exceedingly tender in the appellation here used—"my brethren." Though he was risen from the dead, though about to be exalted to heaven, yet he did not disdain to call his disciples his brethren. This was calculated still farther to silence the fears of the women and to inspire them with confidence. ¶ *Into Galilee.* Galilee was the northern part of the land. There the Saviour commenced his ministry; and there, away from the noise and confusion of the city, he purposed again to meet them, in retirement and quietness, to satisfy them of his resurrection, and to commission them to go forth and preach the everlasting gospel.

11. *When they were going.* Or when they had gone from the tomb. ¶ *Some of the watch.* Some of the guard that had been set around the tomb to keep it safe. Probably the leaders or officers came to give a true account of what had happened. ¶ *Showed unto the chief priests.* To Annas and Caiaphas.

12. *And when they were assembled,* &c. They deemed the matter of so much importance as to justify the calling together of the great council of the nation. Notwithstanding all their caution, it was plain that the body of Jesus was gone. It was farther plain that the disciples would affirm that he was restored to life again. It was not improbable that Jesus would himself appear, and convince multitudes that he was the Messiah, and that the guilt of putting him to death would, after all their caution and cunning, be charged on them. They had been at great pains to procure his death. They had convinced Pilate that he was dead. They had placed a guard for the express purpose of preventing his being taken away. It would be in vain, after this, to *pretend* that he was not dead; that he was in a swoon; that he died in appearance only. They had shut themselves out from this, which would have been the most plausible plea, and, whatever course they might now adopt, they were *obliged* to proceed on the admission that he had been *really dead*, and that all proper measures had been taken to prevent his being stolen. They concluded, after consultation, that but one way was left—to bribe the soldiers—to induce them to tell a falsehood—and to attempt to convince the world that Jesus, in spite of themselves, and in the face of all probability, had been really stolen. ¶ *Large money.* Much money. This was given to bribe them; to induce them to conceal the truth, and to affirm what they knew was false.

ernor's ears, we will persuade him, and secure you.

15 So they took the money, and did as they were taught: and

14. *The governor's ears.* To Pilate. If it is reported to him that Jesus was stolen while you slept. ¶ *We will persuade him.* We will convince or satisfy him, so that he shall not punish you. This they might promise with safety; for, 1st. They knew from the character of Pilate that he could be easily bribed. 2d. Pilate, after the feast of the Passover, was accustomed to return to Cesarea. 3d. He had not been inclined at all to interfere in anything concerning the Saviour until it was urged upon him by the Jews. He would not be disposed, *of himself*, to take any farther trouble about the matter. He would feel that all that could be demanded of him had been done, and would not be disposed farther to interfere, unless the Sanhedrim should demand it. This, of course, they would not do.

15. *This saying is commonly reported.* This account of the disappearance of the body of Jesus from the sepulchre is commonly given. ¶ *Until this day.* The time when Matthew wrote this gospel—that is, about thirty years after the resurrection.

The *resurrection* of the Lord Jesus, of which an account is given in this chapter, is one of the most important doctrines of the Christian religion, and is attested by the strongest evidence that can be adduced in favour of any ancient fact. Let it be considered—1st. That he had often foretold his own death and resurrection. See Mat. xii. 40; xvi. 21; xx. 19. 2d. There was no doubt that he was really dead. Of this the Jews, the Romans, and the disciples were all equally well satisfied. 3d. Every proper precaution was taken to prevent his removal by stealth. A guard, usually consisting of sixty men, was placed there for the express purpose of keeping him, and the sepulchre was secured by a large stone and by a seal. 4th. On the third day the body was missing. In this all were agreed. The high-priests did not dare to call that in question. They laboured, therefore, to account for it. The disciples affirmed that he was alive. The Jews hired the Roman soldiers to affirm that he was stolen while they slept, and succeeded in making many of the people believe it. This account of the Jews is attended with the following difficulties and absurdities: 1st. The Roman guard was composed usually of sixty men, and they were stationed there for the express purpose of guarding the body of Jesus. 2d. The punishment of *sleeping* while on guard in the Roman army was *death*, and it is perfectly incredible that those soldiers should expose themselves in this manner to death. 3d. The disciples were few in number, unarmed, weak, and timid. They had just fled before those who took Jesus in the garden, and how can it be believed that in so short a time they would dare to *attempt* to take away from a Roman guard of armed men what they were expressly set to defend? 4th. How could the disciples *presume* that they would find the Roman soldiers asleep? or, if they should, how was it possible to remove the stone and the body without awaking even *one* of their number? 5th. The *regularity* and *order* of the grave-clothes (Jn. xx. 6, 7) show that the body had not been stolen. When men rob graves of the bodies of the dead, they do not wait coolly to fold up the grave-clothes and lay them carefully by themselves. 6th. If the soldiers were *asleep*, how did they, or how could they know that the disciples stole the body away? If they were *awake*, why did they suffer it? The whole account, therefore, was intrinsically absurd. On the other hand, the account given by the disciples is perfectly natural and credible. 1st. They account for the reason why the soldiers did not see the Saviour when he rose. Terrified at the vision of an angel, they became as dead men. 2d. They affirmed that they saw him. All the apostles affirmed this, and many others. 3d. They affirmed it in Jerusalem, in the presence of the Jews, before the high-priests and the people. See the Acts of the Apostles. If the Jews really *believed* the account which they themselves had given, why did they not apprehend the apostles, and *prove* them guilty of the theft and of falsehood?—things which they never attempted, and which show, therefore, that they did not credit their own report. 4th. In regard to the Saviour they could not be deceived. They had been with him three years. They knew him as a friend. They again ate and drank with him; they put their fingers

this saying is commonly reported among the Jews until this day.

16 Then[m] the eleven disciples went away into Galilee, into a mountain where Jesus had appointed them.

17 And when they [n]saw him, they worshipped him: but some doubted.

18 And Jesus came and spake unto them, saying, [o]All power is given unto me in heaven and in earth.

m ch.26.32. *n* ch.16.28.

o Ps.2.6; 89.19; 110.1-3; Is.9.6,7; Da.7.14; ch.11.27; Lu.1.32; Jn.17.2; Ro.14.9; Ep.1.20,21; He.2.8; 1 Pe. 3.22; Re.11.15.

into his hands and side; they conversed with him; they were with him forty days. There were *enough* of them to bear witness. Law commonly requires not more than one or two competent witnesses, but here were *eleven* plain, honest men, who affirmed in all places and at all times that they had seen him. Can it be possible that they could be deceived? Then all faith in testimony must be given up. 5th. They gave every possible evidence of their sincerity. They were persecuted, ridiculed, scourged, and put to death for affirming this. Yet not one of them ever expressed the least doubt of its truth. They bore everything rather than to deny that they had seen him. They had no motive in doing this but the love of truth. They obtained no wealth by it, no honour, no pleasure. They gave themselves up to great and unparalleled sufferings—going from land to land; crossing almost every sea; enduring the dangers, toils, and privations of almost every clime—for the simple object of affirming everywhere that a Saviour died and rose. If they knew this was an imposition—and if it *had been* they would have known it—in what way is this remarkable conduct to be accounted for? Do men conduct in this way for nought? and especially in a *plain case*, where all that can be required is the testimony of the senses? 6th. The world believed them. Three thousand of the Jews themselves believed in the risen Saviour on the day of Pentecost, but fifty days after his resurrection, Ac. ii. 41. Multitudes of other Jews believed during the lives of the apostles. Thousands of Gentiles believed also, and in three hundred years the belief that Jesus rose had spread over and changed the whole Roman empire. *Had* the apostles been deceivers, that was the age in which they could most easily have been detected. Yet *that* was the age when converts were most rapidly multiplied, and God affixed his seal to their testimony that it was true.

16. *Then the eleven disciples.* Judas was dead, leaving but eleven of the original number of the apostles. ¶ *Into a mountain where Jesus had appointed them.* This *appointment* is recorded in Mat. xxvi. 32. On what particular mountain this was is not known. It is probable that Jesus, when he made the appointment, specified the place, which has been omitted by the evangelists. Matthew has omitted many appearances which Jesus made to his disciples which have been recorded by Luke, John, and Paul. See the harmony of the resurrection at the end of the chapter.

17. *They worshipped him.* Paid him honour as the Messiah. ¶ *But some doubted.* As, for example, Thomas, Jn. xx. 25. The disciples had not expected his resurrection; they were therefore slow to believe. The mention of their doubting shows that they were honest men—that they were not easily imposed on—that they had not previously *agreed* to affirm that he had risen—that they were convinced only by the strength of the evidence. Their caution in examining the evidence; their slowness to believe; their firm conviction after all their doubts; and their willingness to show their conviction even by their *death*, is most conclusive proof that they were *not* deceived in regard to the fact of his resurrection.

18. *All power is given unto me in heaven and in earth.* The *Son of God*, as *Creator*, had an original right to all things, to control them and dispose of them. See Jn. i. 3; Col. i. 16, 17; He. i. 8. But the universe is put under him more particularly as Mediator, that he might redeem his people; that he might gather a church; that he might defend his chosen; that he might subdue all their enemies, and bring them off conquerors and more than conquerors, Ep. i. 20-23; 1 Co. xv. 25-27; Jn. v. 22, 23; Phi. ii. 6-11. It is in reference to *this*, doubtless, that he speaks here—power or *authority* committed to him over all things, that he might redeem, defend,

19 Go[p] ye, therefore, [q]and [2]teach all nations, baptizing them in the name of the Father, and of the Son, and of the Holy Ghost;

p Mar.16.15. q Is.52.10; Ro.10.18.
2 or, *make disciples*, or, *Christians, of all nations.*

and save the church purchased with his own blood. His mediatorial government extends, therefore, over the material world, over angels, over devils, over wicked men, and over his own people.

19. *Go ye therefore. Because* all power is mine, go. I can defend you. The world is placed under my control. It is redeemed. It is given me in promise by my Father, as the purchase of my death. Though you are weak, yet I am strong. Though you will encounter many troubles and dangers, yet I can defend you. Though *you* die, yet *I* live, and the work shall be accomplished. ¶ *Teach all nations.* The word rendered *teach*, here, is not the one that is usually so translated in the New Testament. This word properly means *disciple*, or *make disciples of.* This was to be done, however, by teaching, and by administering the rite of baptism. ¶ *All nations.* This gracious commission was the foundation of their authority to go to the Gentiles. The Jews had expected that the offers of life under the Messiah would be confined to their own nation. Jesus broke down the partition wall, and commissioned his disciples to go everywhere, and bring the *world* to the knowledge of himself. ¶ *Baptizing them.* Applying to them water, as an emblem of the purifying influences of the Christian religion through the Holy Spirit, and solemnly devoting them to God. ¶ *In the name*, &c. This phrase does not mean, here, *by the authority* of the Father, &c. To be baptized *in* the name of the Father, &c., is the same as to be baptized *unto* the Father; as to believe on the *name* of Christ is the same as to believe *on Christ*, Jn. i. 12; ii. 23; iii. 18; 1 Co. i. 13. To be baptized *unto* anyone is publicly to receive and adopt him as a religious teacher or lawgiver; to receive his system of religion. Thus the Jews were baptized *unto Moses*, 1 Co. x. 2. That is, they received the system that he taught; they acknowledged him as their lawgiver and teacher. So Paul asks (1 Co. i. 13), "Were ye baptized in the name of Paul?"—that is, Were you devoted to Paul by this rite? Did you bind yourselves to *him*, and give yourselves away to *him*, or to God? So to be baptized in the name of the Father, or unto the Father, means publicly, by a significant rite, to receive his system of religion; to bind the soul to obey his laws; to be devoted to him; to receive, as the guide and comforter of the life, his instructions, and to trust to his promises. To be baptized unto the Son, in like manner, is to receive him as the Messiah—our Prophet, Priest, and King—to submit to his laws, and to receive him as a Saviour. To be baptized unto the Holy Ghost is to receive him publicly as the Sanctifier, Comforter, and Guide of the soul. The meaning, then, may be thus expressed: Baptizing them unto the Father, Son, and Holy Ghost by a solemn profession of the only true religion, and by a solemn consecration to the service of the sacred Trinity.

The union of these three names in the form of baptism proves that the Son and Holy Ghost are *equal* with the Father. Nothing would be more absurd or blasphemous than to unite the name of a creature—a man or an angel—with the name of the ever-living God in this solemn rite. If Jesus was a mere man or an angel, as is held by many who deny his divinity, and if the Holy Ghost was a mere *attribute* of God, then it would have been the height of absurdity to use a form like this, or to direct the apostles to baptize men under them. How absurd would be the direction—nay, how blasphemous—to have said, "Baptize them unto God, and unto Paul, and unto the *wisdom* or *power* of God!" Can we believe that our Saviour would have given a direction so absurd as this? Yet, unless he himself is divine, and the Holy Spirit is divine, Jesus gave a direction substantially the same as this. The form of baptism, therefore, has been always regarded as an irrefragable argument for the doctrine of the Trinity, or that the Son and Holy Spirit are equal with the Father.

20. *Lo, I am with you.* That is, by my Spirit, my providence, my attending counsel and guidance. I will strengthen, assist, and direct you. This also proves that Christ is divine. If he is a mere man, or a creature, though of the highest order, how could he promise to be *with* his disciples *always*, or

20 Teaching[r] them to observe all things whatsoever I have commanded you: and, lo, [s]I am with you alway, *even* unto the end of the world. Amen.

r Ac.2.42; 1 Co.11.2.

s ch.18.20; Re.1.18.

at all? They would be scattered far and wide. His disciples would greatly increase. If he was *with them* always, he was God; for no finite creature could thus be present with many men scattered in different parts of the world. ¶ *Unto the end of the world.* The word rendered *world*, here, sometimes means *age* or *state;* and by some it has been supposed to mean, I will be with you until the end of this *age*, or during the continuance of the Jewish state, to the destruction of Jerusalem. But as the presence of Christ was no less necessary *after* that than before, there seems to be no propriety in limiting the promise to his own age. It may therefore be considered as a gracious assurance that he would aid, strengthen, guide, and defend all his disciples, but more especially his ministers, to the end of time.

HARMONY OF THE ACCOUNTS

OF THE

RESURRECTION, APPEARANCES, AND ASCENSION OF CHRIST.

I. THE RESURRECTION.

As much difficulty has been felt in reconciling the accounts of the different evangelists respecting the resurrection of Christ, and as infidels have maintained that they are utterly irreconcilable, it may be proper, in closing the Notes on Matthew, to give these accounts at *one view*. One thing should always be borne in mind by all who read the Gospels, viz. *that the sacred narrative of an event is what it is declared to be by* ALL *the evangelists.* That a thing is omitted by *one* does not prove that another is false because he has recorded it, for the very object of the different Gospels was to give the testimony of independent witnesses to the great facts of the life and death of Jesus. Nor does it prove that there is a contradiction because one relates facts in a different *order* from another, for neither of them professes to relate facts in the *precise order* in which they occurred. The object was to relate the *facts themselves.* With these principles in view, which are conceded to *profane* historians always, let us look at the accounts which are presented in the *sacred narrative* respecting the resurrection, appearance, and ascension of Christ.

1. Jesus was laid in the tomb on Friday evening, having been wrapped in linen with myrrh and aloes in a hurried manner, Jn. xix. 39, 40. The *women*, not apprised of that, or desiring also to testify their regard for him, prepared spices on the same evening to embalm him, Lu. xxiii. 56. As it was too late that night to complete the preparation, they deferred it till the first day of the week, resting on the Sabbath, Lu. xxiii. 56.

2. On the first day of the week, early, the women completed their preparation, purchased more spices, and properly mixed them to make an *unguent* to anoint the bandages in which the body was rolled, Mar. xvi. 1. Or this *may* refer to the purchase which is mentioned by Luke, meaning that they *had* bought them—that is, on Friday evening.

3. They came to the sepulchre just as the day began to dawn, or just as the light appeared in the east, yet so *dark* as to render objects indistinct. It was "in the end of the Sabbath, as it began to dawn toward the first day of the week," Mat. xxviii. 1. "Very early in the morning, at the rising of the sun," or as the sun was *about* to rise, Mar. xvi. 2. "Very early in the morning," Lu. xxiv. 1. "Early, while it was yet dark," Jn. xx. 1.

4. Those who came were Mary Magdalene, Mat. xxviii. 1, Jn. xx. 1; Mary the mother of James and Joses, Mat. xxviii. 1, Lu. xxiv. 10, Mar. xv. 40; Salome, the wife of Zebedee, and mother of James and John, comp. Mat. xxvii. 56, Mar. xv. 40; Joanna, the wife of Chuza, Herod's steward, comp. Lu. xxiv. 10, viii. 3; and certain others not specified, Lu. xxiv. 1, 10.

5. The objects of their coming were, 1st. To see the sepulchre, Mat. xxviii. 1. 2d. To embalm him, or to *finish* embalming him, Mar. xvi. 1, Lu. xxiv. 1.

6. While on the way they inquired who should roll away the stone for them, that they might have access to the body of Jesus, Mar. xvi. 3.

7. When they arrived they found that there *had been* an earthquake or shaking of the tomb, so that the stone was rolled away, Mat. xxviii. 2; Mar. xvi. 4.

8. The angel who rolled the stone away *had* sat down on it, and had appeared to the *keepers* and frightened them; though he did not appear in this place to the *women*, but only to the *keepers*, Mat. xxviii. 2–4. At that time probably our Saviour had risen—how long before the women came is not known and cannot be ascertained.

9. When they came there, *Mary Magdalene*, greatly agitated with the appearance of things, and probably supposing that the body had been stolen, left the other women, and ran to the city, at the distance of half a mile, to inform the disciples, Jn. xx. 2.

10. While Mary was gone the others probably looked round the garden in search of the body, and then came and examined the sepulchre to see if it was not there. The tomb was large, and they entered *into* it. *There* "the angel spake unto them," Mat. xxviii. 5. "They saw a young man"—that is, an angel in the appearance of a young man—"sitting on the right side," Mar. xvi. 5. When they entered he was *sitting;* as they entered he *rose* and stood, Lu. xxiv. 4. Luke adds that there was another with him, xxiv. 4; this *other one* was not seen when they entered into the sepulchre at the time mentioned by *Mark*, but was seen when they had fully entered in, as mentioned by Luke.

11. The angel charged them to go and tell the disciples and Peter, Mat. xxviii. 7, Mar. xvi. 7; and to assure them that he would see them in Galilee. He also reminded them of what Jesus had said when they were in Galilee, Lu. xxiv. 6, 7.

12. They went immediately toward the city, yet taking a different way from the one that Mary had taken, or going in such a way that they did not meet her when she was returning from the city with Peter and John, Mat. xxviii. 8, Mar. xvi. 8. "They said nothing to any man," Lu. xxiv. 9, 10. In Lu. xxiv. 10 it is said that it was Mary Magdalene, and Joanna, and Mary the mother of James, that told these things to the disciples. Not that Luke affirms that they were *together* when they told them, but that the information was given *by them*, though perhaps at different times.

13. While they were gone Mary Magdalene returned to the sepulchre, following Peter and John, who came running, Jn. xx. 2–9. They examined the sepulchre, and found that the body was really gone, but as yet they did not know the reason, not having seen the other women to whom the angel had told the cause, and Mary Magdalene having left the women before the angel had spoken to them. As yet, therefore, *she* was ignorant of the reason of his removal.

14. Peter and John then left the sepulchre, returned to the city, and left Mary alone, Jn. xx. 10.

15. While Mary was there alone she looked into the sepulchre, and saw two angels, probably the same that had appeared to the other women, Jn. xx. 11–13.

16. Jesus appeared to Mary while she sat alone at the sepulchre, Jn. xx. 14–18. Thus, according to Mark (xvi. 9), he appeared to Mary Magdalene "*first.*"

17. Mary then went to tell the disciples that she had seen him, but they did not fully believe her, Jn. xx. 18; Mar. xvi. 10, 11.

18. *Afterward* Jesus appeared to the other women, Mat. xxviii. 9: "As they went to tell his disciples, behold, Jesus met them, saying, All hail." This would *seem*, in Matthew, to be immediately after they left the sepulchre the first time; but many critics observe that the words "to tell his disciples" are wanting in many manuscripts, and of doubtful authority. It may be far-

ther said that the words "as they were going" might have been rendered "*after* they were gone." They do not imply of necessity that the appearance took place *immediately*, but only *after* they were gone, without specifying the time. Probably it was not long after he had appeared to Mary Magdalene. They would naturally return to the garden after they had informed the disciples, and linger around there, that they might ascertain what had become of him, or learn whether he had been seen by anyone. It was, then, probably *after* they had been away and returned, and *after* he had been seen by Mary, that they saw him.

II. APPEARANCES OF JESUS AFTER THE RESURRECTION.

1. To Mary Magdalene, Jn. xx. 14; Mar. xvi. 9.
2. To the other women, Mat. xxviii. 9.
3. To Peter, 1 Co. xv. 5; Lu. xxiv. 34.
4. To two disciples as they were going to Emmaus, Mar. xvi. 12, 13; Lu. xxiv. 13–32.
5. The same day, at evening, to the apostles, in the absence of Thomas, 1 Co. xv. 5; Mar. xvi. 14; Lu. xxiv. 36; Jn. xx. 19, 24.
6. To the apostles when Thomas was present, Jn. xx. 24–29.
7. In Galilee, at the Sea of Tiberias, to Peter, Thomas, Nathaniel, James and John, and two others, Jn. xxi. 1–14. This is said to be *the third time* that he showed himself to the disciples—that is, *to the apostles when they were assembled together*, Jn. xxi. 14.
8. To the disciples on a mountain in Galilee, Mat. xxviii. 16.
9. To more than five hundred brethren at once, 1 Co. xv. 6.
10. To James, one of the apostles, 1 Co. xv. 7.
11. To all the apostles assembled together, 1 Co. xv. 7. He was seen by them forty days after he rose—probably conversing with them familiarly.
12. To the apostles at his ascension, Lu. xxiv. 50, 51; Ac. i. 9, 10.
13. To Paul, 1 Co. xv. 8; Ac. ix. 3–5; xxii. 6–10.

III. THE ASCENSION.

1. It was forty days after his resurrection, Ac. i. 3.
2. He ascended from the Mount of Olives, near Bethany, Lu. xxiv. 50; Ac. i. 12.
3. It was in the presence of all the apostles, Lu. xxiv. 50; Ac. i. 9, 10.
4. He was received into a cloud, and ascended to heaven, Ac. i. 9, 11; Lu. xxiv. 51; Ep. i. 20–22.

PREFACE

TO THE GOSPEL ACCORDING TO MARK

Of Mark, the writer of this Gospel, little is certainly known. He is commonly supposed to be the same that is several times mentioned in the New Testament. He was not an apostle, or companion of the Lord Jesus, during his ministry, though some of the fathers affirm that he was one of the seventy disciples. This is improbable, as he is mentioned by Peter (1 Pe. v. 13) as *his son;* from which it is supposed that he was converted by the instrumentality of Peter.

From the New Testament we learn that he was sister's son to Barnabas (Col. iv. 10); and that his mother's name was Mary, a pious woman in Jerusalem, at whose house the apostles and primitive Christians often assembled, Ac. xii. 12.

His Hebrew name was John (Ac. xii. 12), and it is probable that he adopted a name better known or more familiar when he visited the Gentiles, a practice not uncommon in that age. He was at first the companion of Paul and Barnabas in their journeys to propagate Christianity, Ac. xii. 25; xiii. 5; xv. 37. He chose not to attend them through their whole journey, but left them in Pamphylia, and probably returned to Jerusalem, Ac. xv. 38. Probably at this time he was the companion of Peter, and travelled with him to Babylon, 1 Pe. vi. 13. Afterward he went with Barnabas to Cyprus, Ac. xv. 39. Subsequently he went to Rome, at the express desire of Paul, in company with Timothy, 2 Ti. iv. 11. He remained at Rome while Paul was a captive there, but how long is uncertain, Col. iv. 10; Phile. 24. From Eusebius, Epiphanius, and Jerome we hear that Mark went from Rome to Alexandria, in Egypt, where he planted a church, and died in the eighth year of the reign of Nero, A.D. 64.

The time when this Gospel was written is not certainly known. It is supposed to have been between the years 56 and 63. It is allowed by all that it was written at Rome; of course it was during the latter years of his life, after the apostles had left Judea, Mar. xvi. 20. Mark was for a considerable time the companion of Peter. Though he had not himself been with the Saviour in his ministry, yet, from his long acquaintance with *Peter,* he was familiar with the events of his life, and with his instructions. The uniform testimony of the fathers is that he was the *interpreter* of Peter, and that he wrote this Gospel under the eye of Peter and with his approbation. It has come down to us, therefore, with the sanction of Peter's authority. Its right to a place among the inspired books has never been questioned. That it was written by Mark, that it was with Peter's approbation, that it was a record of the *facts* which Peter stated in his ministry, and that it was therefore an inspired book, has never been questioned.

THE
GOSPEL ACCORDING TO MARK

CHAPTER I.

THE beginning of the gospel
of Jesus Christ, the [a]Son of
God;
2 As it is written in the prophets, [b]Behold, I send my messenger
before thy face, which shall prepare
thy way before thee.
3 The[c] voice of one crying in the
wilderness, Prepare ye the way of
the Lord, make his paths straight.
4 John[d] did baptize in the wilderness, and preach the baptism of
repentance, [1]for the [e]remission of
sins.
5 And there went out unto him
all the land of Judea, and they of
Jerusalem, and were all baptized
of him in the river of Jordan, [f]con-
fessing their sins.
6 And John was clothed with
camel's hair, and with a girdle of
a skin about his loins; and he did
eat [g]locusts and wild honey;
7 And preached, saying, [h]There
cometh one mightier than I after
me, the latchet of whose shoes I
am not worthy to stoop down and
unloose.
8 I indeed have baptized you
with water; but [i]he shall baptize
you with the Holy Ghost.
9 And it came to pass in those
days that Jesus came from Nazareth of Galilee, and [k]was baptized
of John in Jordan.
10 And straightway coming
up out of the water, he saw the
heavens [2]opened, and [l]the Spirit,
like a dove, descending upon him:
11 And there came a voice from
heaven, *saying*, [m]Thou art my
beloved Son, in whom I am well
pleased.
12 And immediately the Spirit
driveth him into the wilderness.
13 And[n] he was there in the
wilderness forty days, tempted of

a He.1.1,2. *b* Mal.3.1. *c* Is.40.3.
d Mat.3.1; Lu.3.3; Jn.3.23. [1] or, *unto*. *e* Ac.22.16.
f Le.26.40-42; Ps.32.5; Pr.28.13; 1 Jn.1.8-10.
g Le.11.22.
h Mat.3.11; Jn.1.27; Ac.13.25.
i Joel 2.28; Ac.1.5; 2.4; 10.45; 11.15,16; 1 Co.12.13.
k Mat.3.13; Lu.3.21. [2] or, *cloven*, or, *rent*.
l Is.42.1; Jn.1.32. *m* Ps.2.7.
n Mat.4.1,&c.; Lu.4.1,&c.

---

1. *The beginning of the gospel.* The word *gospel* literally signifies good tidings, and particularly the good tidings respecting the way of salvation by the Lord Jesus Christ. Some have understood the word *gospel* here to mean *history* or *life—the beginning of the history*, &c.; but Mark says nothing of the early life of the Saviour. The word *gospel* here has reference rather to the preaching of John, an account of which immediately follows, and means the beginning of the good news, or annunciation respecting the Messiah. It was very customary thus to prefix a title to a book. ¶ *The Son of God.* This title was used here to attract attention, and secure the respect of those who should read the gospel. It is no common history. It does not recount the deeds of man—of a hero or a philosopher—but the doctrines and doings of THE SON OF GOD. The history, therefore, *commands* respect.

2, 3. *As it is written in the prophets.* Mark mentions *prophets* here without specifying which. The places are found in Mal. iii. 1, and in Is. xli. 3. See Notes on Mat. iii. 3.

4-8. See Notes on Mat. iii. 3, 5, 6, 11.

9-11. See Notes on Mat. iii. 13-17.

12, 13. Mark here relates concisely what Matthew has recorded more at length in ch. iv. ¶ *The Spirit driveth.* The word *driveth* does not mean that he was compelled forcibly against his will to go there, but that he was inclined to go there by the Spirit, or was led there. The Spirit of God, for important purposes, *caused* him to go. Comp. Mat. ix. 25, where the same word is

Satan; and was with the wild
beasts; and the angels ministered
unto him.
14 Now after that John was
put in prison, [o]Jesus came into
Galilee, preaching the [p]gospel of
the kingdom of God,
15 And saying, [q]The time is
fulfilled, and the kingdom of God
is at hand: [r]repent ye, and [s]believe
the gospel.
16 Now[t] as he walked by the
sea of Galilee, he saw Simon, and
Andrew his brother, casting a net
into the sea: (for they were
fishers.)
17 And Jesus said unto them,
Come ye after me, and I will make
you to become fishers of men.
18 And straightway they forsook
their nets and followed him.

o Mat.4.23. p Lu.8.1.
q Da.2.44; 9.25; Ga.4.4; Ep.1.10. r Ac.2.38.
s Ro.16.26. t Mat.4.18,&c.; Lu.5.4,&c.

19 And when he had gone a
little further thence, he saw James
the *son* of Zebedee, and John his
brother, who also were in the ship
mending their nets.
20 And straightway he called
them: and they left their father
Zebedee in the ship with the hired
servants, and went after him.
21 And they went into Capernaum: and straightway on the
sabbath-day he entered into the
synagogue and taught.
22 And[u] they were astonished
at his doctrine: for he taught them
as one that had authority, and not
as the scribes.
23 And[v] there was in their synagogue a man with an unclean spirit;
and he cried out,
24 Saying, Let *us* alone; what

u Mat.7.28. v Lu.4.33,&c.

---

used in the original: "And when they were all *put forth*"—in Greek, *all driven out.* ¶ *And was with the wild beasts.* This is added to show the desolation and danger of his dwelling there. In this place, surrounded by such dangers, the temptations offered by Satan were the stronger. Amid want and perils, Satan might suppose that he would be more easily seduced from God. But he trusted in his Father, and was alike delivered from dangers, from the wild beasts, and from the power of temptation, thus teaching *us* what to do in the day of danger and trial. ¶ *And the angels ministered unto him.* From Lu. iv. 2 we learn that in those days he did eat nothing. When Mark says, therefore, that the angels ministered to him, it means *after* the days of temptation had expired, as is said by Mat. iv. 11.

14. *Now after that John was put in prison.* John was imprisoned by Herod, Mat. xiv. 3. ¶ *Jesus came into Galilee.* He left Judea and went into the more retired country of Galilee. He supposed that if he remained in Judea, Herod would also persecute him and attempt to take his life. His time of death had not come, and he therefore prudently sought safety in retirement. Hence we may learn that when we have great duties to perform for the church of God we are not wantonly to endanger our lives. When we can secure them without a sacrifice of *principle*, we are to do it. See Mat. xxiv. 16.

15. *The time is fulfilled.* That is, the time for the appearance of the Messiah, the time so long foretold, has come. ¶ *The kingdom of God is at hand.* See Notes on Mat. iii. 2. ¶ *Repent ye.* Exercise sorrow for sins, and turn from them. ¶ *And believe the gospel.* Literally, trust in the gospel, or believe the good tidings—to wit, respecting salvation. See Notes on Mat. iv. 17.

16–20. See Notes on Mat. iv. 18–22.

21–27. See also Lu. iv. 31–37.

21. *And they went into Capernaum.* For the situation of Capernaum see Notes on Mat. iv. 13. ¶ *Straightway.* Immediately. On the following Sabbath. ¶ *The synagogue.* See Notes on Mat. iv. 23. ¶ *And taught.* In the synagogue, the presiding elder, after reading the Scriptures, invited any who chose to address the people, Ac. xiii. 15. Though our Saviour was not a *priest* of the Levitical order or an *officer* of the synagogue, yet we find him often availing himself of this privilege, and delivering his doctrines to the Jews.

22. *He taught them as one that had authority*, &c. See Notes on Mat. vii. 29.

23. *A man with an unclean spirit.*

have we to do with thee, thou Jesus of Nazareth? art thou come to destroy us? I know thee who thou art, the Holy One of God.

25 And Jesus rebuked him, saying, Hold thy peace, and come out of him.

26 And when the unclean spirit had torn him, and cried with a loud voice, he came out of him.

27 And they were all amazed, insomuch that they questioned among themselves, saying, What thing is this? what new doctrine *is* this? for with authority commandeth he even the unclean spirits, and they do obey him.

28 And immediately his fame spread abroad throughout all the region round about Galilee.

See Mat. iv. 24. It is probable that this man had lucid intervals, or he would not have been admitted into the synagogue. When there, one of his fits came on, and he suddenly cried out.

24. *Let* us *alone.* Though but *one* impure spirit is mentioned as possessing this man, yet that spirit speaks also in the name of others. They were leagued together in the work of evil, and this one knew that if *he* was punished, others would also share the same fate. ¶ *What have we to do with thee?* See Notes on Mat. viii. 29. By this the spirit meant to say that if Jesus cast him out he would use an improper interference. But this was untrue. The possession of the man was a direct assault on God and his works. Jesus came to destroy the works of the devil, and he had a right, therefore, to liberate the captive, and to punish him who had possessed him. So Satan still considers it an infringement of his rights when God frees a *sinner* from bondage and destroys his influence over the soul. So he still asks to be let alone, and to be suffered to lead men captive at his will. ¶ *Art thou come to destroy us?* Implying that this could not be the intention of the *benevolent* Messiah; that to be cast out of that man would, in fact, be his destruction, and that therefore he might be suffered still to remain. Or it may imply, as in Mat. viii. 29, that the time of their destruction had not come, and that he ought not to destroy them before that. ¶ *I know thee who thou art.* Evil spirits seem to have been acquainted at once with the Messiah. Besides, they had learned from his miracles that he was the Messiah, and had power over them. ¶ *The Holy One of God.* The Messiah. See Da. ix. 24. He is called the Holy One of God because—1st. He was eminently pure. 2d. Because he was the only begotten Son of God—equal with the Father. And, 3d. Because he was anointed or set apart to the work of the Messiah, the mediator between God and man.

25. *And Jesus rebuked him.* Chid him, or commanded him, with a threatening. This was not the *man* that he rebuked, but the *spirit*, for he instantly commanded the same being to come out of the man. In all this Jesus did not once *address the man.* His conversation was with the *evil spirit*, proving conclusively that it was not a mere disease or mental derangement—for how could the Son of God hold converse with *disease* or *insanity?*—but that he conversed with a *being* who also conversed, reasoned, cavilled, felt, resisted, and knew him. There *are*, therefore, evil spirits, and those spirits *have* taken possession of men. ¶ *Hold thy peace.* Greek, *Be muzzled.* Restrain thyself. Cease from complaints, and come out of the man. This was a very signal proof of the power of Jesus, to be able by a word to silence an evil angel, and, against his will, to compel him to leave a man whom he delighted to torment.

26. *And when the unclean spirit*, &c. Still malignant, though doomed to obey—submitting because he was obliged to, not because he chose—he exerted his last power, inflicted all the pain he could, and then bowed to the Son of God and came out. This is the nature of an evil disposition. Though compelled to obey, though prevented by the command and providence of God from doing what it *would*, yet, in seeming to obey, it does all the ill it can, and makes even the appearance of obedience the occasion for increased crime and mischief.

27, 28. *And they were all amazed*, &c. The power of casting out devils was to them new. It was done by a word. Jesus did it in his own name and by his own authority. This proved that he was *superior* to all the unclean spirits. In consequence, his fame spread throughout all the country, and the

29 And[w] forthwith, when they were come out of the synagogue, they entered into the house of Simon and Andrew, with James and John.

30 But Simon's wife's mother lay sick of a fever; and anon they tell him of her.

31 And he came, and took her by the hand, and lifted her up; and immediately the fever left her, and she ministered unto them.

32 And at even, when the sun did set, they brought unto him all that were diseased, and them that were possessed with devils.

33 And all the city was gathered together at the door.

34 And he healed many that were sick of divers diseases, and cast out many devils; and suffered not the devils [3]to speak, because they knew him.

35 And in the morning, rising up a great while before day, he went out, and departed into a solitary place, and there prayed.

36 And Simon, and they that were with him, followed after him.

37 And when they had found him, they said unto him, All *men* seek for thee.

w Mat.8.14; Lu.4.38.

3 or, *to say that they knew him.*

---

impression became prevalent that he was the Messiah.

29–31. See Notes on Mat. viii. 14, 15.

32–34. See Notes on Mat. viii. 16, 17. ¶ *And at even, when the sun did set.* See Notes on Mat. viii. 16.

33. *All the city.* A great part of the city. A great multitude from the city.

34. *And suffered not the devils to speak, because they knew him.* They knew that he was the Messiah. If they had spoken, they would have made that known to the people. Jesus was not desirous at that time that that should be publicly known, or that his name should be blazoned abroad. The time had not come when he wished it to be promulgated that he was the Messiah, and he therefore imposed silence on the evil spirits.

35–37. *And in the morning, rising up a great while before day.* Luke says (iv. 42), *when it was day.* The passage in Mark means, in the original, not literally *a great while before day*, but very early, or while there was yet *much appearance of night.* The place in Luke means *at daybreak*, at the beginning of day. Then, also, there is much appearance of night; and Luke and Mark therefore refer to the same time—before it was fully light, or just at daybreak. ¶ *And departed into a solitary place, and there prayed.* Here observe, 1st. That the Saviour, though perfectly holy, regarded the duty of secret prayer as of great importance. 2d. That he sought a solitary place for it—far away from the world and even from his disciples. 3d. That it was early in the morning—always the *best* time, and a time when it should not be omitted. 4th. If Jesus prayed, how much more important is it for us! If *he* did it in the morning, how much more important is it for *us*, before the world gets possession of our thoughts; before Satan fills us with unholy feelings; when we rise fresh from beds of repose, and while the world around us is still! David also thus prayed, Ps. v. 3; cxix. 147. He that wishes to enjoy religion will seek a place of secret prayer in the morning. If that is omitted, all will go wrong, our piety will wither. The world will fill our thoughts. Temptations will be strong. Through the day we shall find it impossible to raise our feelings to a state of proper devotion. It will be found to be true universally, *that the religious enjoyment through the day will be according to the state of the heart in the morning, and can therefore be measured by our faithfulness in early secret prayer.* How different, too, was the conduct of the Saviour from those who spend the precious hours of the morning in sleep! He knew the value of the morning hours; he rose while the world was still; he saw the light as it spread abroad in the east with fresh tokens of his Father's presence, and joined with the universal creation in offering praise to the everywhere present God.

36. *And Simon.* Simon Peter. ¶ *They that were with him.* The other apostles.

37. *All* men *seek for thee.* That is, many men, or multitudes. The inquiry after him was general. They told him this, evidently, with a view to induce

38 And he said unto them, Let us go into the next towns, that I may preach there also; for [x]therefore came I forth.

39 And he preached in their synagogues throughout all Galilee, and cast out devils.

40 And[y] there came a leper to him, beseeching him, and kneeling down to him, and saying unto him, If thou wilt, thou canst make me clean.

41 And Jesus, moved with compassion, put forth *his* hand, and touched him, and saith unto him, I will; be thou clean.

42 And as soon as he had spoken, [z]immediately the leprosy departed from him, and he was cleansed.

43 And he straitly charged him, and forthwith sent him away;

44 And saith unto him, See thou say nothing to any man; but go thy way, show thyself to the priest,

x Is.61.1,2; Jn.17.8. y Mat.8.2; Lu.5.12. z Ps.33.9; Jn.15.3.

---

him to leave his place of retirement, and to prevail upon him to appear publicly to instruct the multitudes.

38. *And he said unto them*, &c. This was said in answer to their *implied* request that he would go and meet the multitudes. "Since the anxiety to hear the truth is so great, since such multitudes are waiting to hear the word, let us go into the next towns," &c. ¶ *Next towns.* Towns in the neighbourhood or vicinity of Capernaum. He proposed to carry the gospel to them, rather than that multitudes should leave their homes and attend him in his ministry. The word here rendered *towns* denotes places in size between *cities* and *villages*, or large places, but without walls. ¶ *For therefore came I forth.* That is, came forth from God, or was sent by God. Luke says (iv. 43), "for therefore am I sent." Comp. Jn. xvi. 28: "I came forth from the Father, and am come into the world." The meaning of this verse therefore is, "Since multitudes press to hear the word, let us not remain here, but go into the neighbouring towns also; for I was sent by God not to preach at Capernaum only, but *throughout Judea*, and it is therefore improper to confine my labours to this place."

39. *And he preached in their synagogues.* See Mat. iv. 23. ¶ *All Galilee.* See Mat. i. 22. ¶ *And cast out devils.* See Mat. iv. 24.

40–45. *And there came a leper*, &c. See Notes on Mat. viii. 1–4. ¶ *Kneeling down to him.* He kneeled and inclined his face to the ground, in token of deep humiliation and earnest entreaty. Comp. Lu. v. 12. ¶ *If thou wilt.* This was an acknowledgment of the almighty power of Jesus, and an appeal to his benevolence. ¶ *Make me clean.* Canst heal me of this loathsome and offensive disease, in the eye of the law justly regarded as *unclean*, and render me *legally* clean, and restore me to the privileges of the congregation. ¶ *And Jesus—touched him.* It was by the law considered as unclean to touch a leprous man. See Nu. v. 2. The fact that Jesus *touched* him was evidence that the requisite power had been already put forth to heal him; that Jesus regarded him as already clean. ¶ *I will.* Here was a most manifest proof of his divine power. None but God can work a miracle; yet Jesus does it by his *own will*—by an exertion of his own power. He is therefore divine. ¶ *See thou say nothing to any man.* The law of Moses required that a man who was healed of the leprosy should be pronounced clean by the priest before he could be admitted again to the privileges of the congregation, Le. xiv. Christ, though *he* had cleansed him, yet required him to be obedient to the law of the land—to go at once to the priest, and not to make delay by stopping to converse about his being healed. It was also possible that, if he did not go at once, evil-minded men would go before him and prejudice the priest, and prevent his declaring the healing to be thorough because it was done by Jesus. It was farther of importance that *the priest* should pronounce it to be a genuine cure, that there might be no cavils among the Jews against its being a real miracle. ¶ *Offer for thy cleansing those things*, &c. Two birds, and cedar-wood, and scarlet, and hyssop; and after eight days, two he-lambs, without blemish, and one ewe-lamb, and fine flour, and oil, Le. xiv. 4, 10. ¶ *For a testimony unto them.* Not to the *priest*, but to the *people*, that they may have evidence

and offer for thy cleansing [a]those
things which Moses commanded,
for a [b]testimony unto them.
45 But he went out, and began
to [c]publish *it* much, and to blaze
abroad the matter, insomuch that
Jesus could no more openly enter
into the city, but was without in
desert places: and [d]they came to
him from every quarter.

CHAPTER II.

AND again he entered into
Capernaum after *some* days;
and it was noised that he was in
the house.
2 And straightway many were
gathered together, insomuch that
there was no room to receive *them*,
no, not so much as about the door:
and he [a]preached the word unto
them.
3 And[b] they come unto him,
bringing one sick of the palsy,
which was borne of four.
4 And when they could not come
nigh unto him for the press, they
uncovered the roof where he was:
and when they had broken *it* up,
they let down the bed wherein the
sick of the palsy lay.
5 When Jesus [c]saw their faith,
he said unto the sick of the palsy,
Son, thy sins be forgiven thee.

a Le.14.2-32. *b* Ro.15.4; 1 Co.10.11. *c* Ps.77.11,12; Tit.1.10. *d* ch.2.13.

a Ps.40.9. *b* Mat.9.1,&c.; Lu.5.18,&c. *c* Ac.14.9; Ep.2.8.

---

that it is a real cure. The testimony of the priest on the subject would be decisive.

45. *Began to publish* it *much.* That is, he made known his own cure. He was so deeply affected with it, and so much rejoiced, that he followed the natural dictates of his own feelings rather than the command of the Saviour. ¶ *Jesus could no more enter openly into the city.* The word *could*, here, does not refer to any natural inability, or to any physical obstacle in his way, but only denotes that there was difficulty, inconvenience, or impropriety in his doing it then; that he judged it best *not* then to enter into the city. The difficulty was, probably, that his being in the city drew such crowds of people as rendered it difficult to accommodate them, or so as to excite the opposition of civil rulers. ¶ *The city.* The city or large town where the leper was cured. The same reason for not entering that city applied also to others, so that he remained in the deserts, where the multitudes could come to him without any difficulty or opposition.

CHAPTER II.

1. *Into Capernaum.* See Notes on Mat. iv. 13. ¶ *After* some *days.* The number of days is not known. Probably he remained long enough in the desert to heal the sick that were brought to him, and to give instructions to the multitudes that attended his preaching. Capernaum was not *the city* mentioned in ch. i. 45, and it is probable that there was no difficulty in his remaining there and preaching. ¶ *And it was noised,* &c. He entered the city, doubtless, privately; but his being there was soon known, and so great had his popularity become that multitudes pressed to hear him.

2. *So much as about the door.* In the *court* or *yard* before the door. They could not get near enough to hear him. ¶ *Preached the word unto them.* The word of God; the revelation or doctrine which he came to deliver, called *the Word*, and *the Word of God*, because it was spoken or revealed by God. Comp. Ac. vi. 2–7.

3–12. See this miracle explained in Mat. ix. 2–8. ¶ *Palsy.* See Notes on Mat. iv. 24. ¶ *Borne of four.* Borne on a couch (Mat. ix. 2) by four men.

4. *The press.* The crowd, the multitude of people. Jesus was probably in the large open area or hall in the centre of the house. See Notes on Mat. ix. 2. The people pressed into the area, and blocked up the door so that they could not have access to him. ¶ *They uncovered the roof where he was.* See Notes on Mat. ix. 2. ¶ *When they had broken it up.* When they had removed the awning or covering, so that they could let the man down. See Notes on Mat. ix. 2.

5. *Their faith.* Their confidence or belief that he could heal them. ¶ *Son.* Literally *child.* The Hebrews used the

6 But there were certain of the
scribes sitting there, and reasoning
in their hearts,
7 Why doth this *man* thus speak
blasphemies? Who can [d]forgive
sins but God only?
8 And immediately, when Jesus
perceived in his spirit that they
so reasoned within themselves, he
said unto them, Why reason ye
these things in your hearts?
9 Whether is it easier to say to
the sick of the palsy, *Thy* sins be
forgiven thee; or to say, Arise,
and take up thy bed, and walk?
10 But that ye may know that
the Son of man hath [e]power on
earth to forgive sins, (he saith to
the sick of the palsy,)
11 I say unto thee, Arise, and
take up thy bed, and go thy way
into thine house.
12 And immediately he arose,
took up the bed, and went forth
before them all; insomuch that
they were all amazed, and glorified
God, saying, [f]We never saw it on
this fashion.
13 And he went forth again by
the sea-side; and all the multitude
resorted unto him, and he taught
them.
14 And[g] as he passed by, he saw
Levi, the son of Alpheus, sitting
[1]at the receipt of custom, and said
unto him, Follow me. And he
arose and followed him.
15 And[h] it came to pass, that, as
Jesus sat at meat in his house,
many [i]publicans and sinners sat
also together with Jesus and his
disciples: for there were many,
and they followed him.
16 And when the scribes and
Pharisees saw him eat with publicans and sinners, they said unto his
disciples, How is it that he eateth
and drinketh with publicans and
sinners?
17 When Jesus heard *it*, he saith

d Is.43.25; Da.9.9. *e* Ac.5.31.

f Jn.7.31; 9.32. *g* Mat.9.9; Lu.5.27.
1 or, *at the place where the custom was received.*
h Mat.9.10,&c. *i* Lu.15.1-5.

words *son* and *child* with a great latitude of signification. They were applied to children, to grandchildren, to adopted children, to any descendants, to disciples, followers, young people, and to dependants. See Notes on Mat. i. 1. In this place it denotes affection or kindness. It was a word of consolation—an endearing appellation, applied by the Saviour to the sick man to show his *compassion*, to inspire confidence, and to assure him that he would heal him.

12. *We never saw it on this fashion.* Literally, "We never saw it so." We never saw anything like this.

13. *By the sea-side.* That is, by the Sea of Tiberias, on the shore of which Capernaum was situated. See Notes on Mat. iv. 13.

14. *Levi, the son of Alpheus.* The same, undoubtedly, as *Matthew*, the writer of the gospel which bears his name. It was not uncommon among the Jews to have two names. ¶ *The receipt of custom.* See Notes on Mat. ix. 9.

15. *Sat at meat in the house.* The words "at meat" are not in the original. The phrase means "as he reclined at his meal," or "as he was eating." This feast was made by Matthew in honour of the Saviour. See Lu. v. 29. ¶ *Publicans.* See Notes on Mat. v. 47. ¶ *Sinners.* Sinners of abandoned character—of the same character that publicans commonly sustained—fit companions of publicans—great sinners. ¶ *There were many.* That is, many *disciples.* Their following him, leaving their homes, and going with him from place to place, was proof of their attachment to him. There is no doubt that our Saviour, in the early part of his ministry, was extremely popular. Multitudes of the common people attended him, and gave conclusive evidence that they were his real disciples, and it was only after much opposition from the rich and the great that he ever became unpopular among the people. Perhaps no preacher has ever attracted so universal attention, and produced so decisive effects on mankind, as our Lord did in his personal ministry.

16, 17. See Notes on Mat. ix. 12, 13.

unto them, [k]They that are whole have no need of the physician, but they that are sick: I came not to call the righteous, [l]but sinners to repentance.

18 And the disciples of John and of the Pharisees used to fast: and they come and say unto him, Why do the disciples of John and of the Pharisees fast, but thy disciples fast not?

19 And Jesus said unto them, Can the children of the bride-chamber fast while the [m]bridegroom is with them? As long as they have the bridegroom with them, they cannot fast.

20 But the days will come when the bridegroom shall be taken away from them, and [n]then shall they fast in those days.

21 No man also seweth a piece of [2]new cloth on an old garment; else the new piece that filled it up taketh away from the old, and the rent is made worse.

22 And no man putteth new wine into old bottles; else the new wine doth burst the bottles, and the wine is spilled, and [o]the bottles will be marred: but new wine must be put into new bottles.

23 And[p] it came to pass, that he went through the corn-fields on the sabbath-day; and his disciples began, as they went, to [q]pluck the ears of corn.

24 And the Pharisees said unto him, Behold, why do they on the sabbath-day that which is not lawful?

25 And he said unto them, Have ye never read [r]what David did, when he had need, and was an hungered, he, and they that were with him?

26 How he went into the house of God in the days of Abiathar the

k Mat.9.12,13; Lu.5.31,32.
l Is.1.18; 55.7; Mat.18.11; Lu.19.10; 1 Co.6.9-11; 1 Ti.1.15. *m* Mat.25.1. *n* Ac.13.2.
2 or, *raw*, or, *unwrought*.

o Job 32.19; Ps.119.80,83.
p Mat.12.1,&c.; Lu.6.1,&c. *q* De.23.25. *r* 1 Sa.21.6.

18. *And the disciples of John and of the Pharisees used to fast.* Were accustomed often to fast. Comp. Lu. v. 33; xviii. 12. ¶ *And they come and say.* The disciples of John come, Mat. ix. 4.

19–22. See Notes on Mat. ix. 15–17.

23–28. See Mat. xii. 1–8. ¶ *The corn-fields.* The fields sown with wheat or barley. The word *corn*, in the Bible, refers only to grain of that kind, and never to *maize* or *Indian corn.* ¶ *To pluck the ears of corn.* They were hungry, Mat. xii. 1. They therefore gathered the wheat or barley as they walked, and rubbed it in their hands to shell it, and thus to satisfy their appetite. Though our Lord was with them, and though he had all things at his control, yet he suffered them to resort to this method of supplying their wants. When Jesus, thus *with* his disciples, suffered them to be *poor*, we may learn that poverty is not disgraceful; that God often suffers it for the good of his people; and that he will take care, in some way, that their wants shall be supplied. It was *lawful* for them thus to supply their wants. Though the property belonged to another, yet the law of Moses allowed the poor to satisfy their wants when hungry. See De. xxiii. 25.

24. *That which is not lawful.* That is, that which they esteemed to be unlawful on the *Sabbath-day.* It was made lawful by Moses, without any distinction of days, but *they* had denied its lawfulness on the Sabbath. Christ shows them from their own law that it was *not* unlawful.

25. *Have ye never read*, &c. See Notes on Mat. xii. 3.

26. *Abiathar the priest.* From 1 Sa. xxi. 1, it appears that *Ahimelech* was high-priest at the time here referred to. And from 1 Sa. xxiii. 6, it appears that *Abiathar* was the son of *Ahimelech.* Some difficulty has been felt in reconciling these accounts. The probable reason why Mark says it was in the days of *Abiathar* is that Abiathar was better known than Ahimelech. The son of the high-priest was regarded as his successor, and was often associated with him in the duties of his office. It was not improper, therefore, to designate him as high-priest even during the life of his father, especially as that was the name by which he was afterward known.

high-priest, and did eat the [s]shew-bread, which is not lawful to eat but for the priests, and gave also to them which were with him?

27 And he said unto them, [t]The sabbath was made for man, and not[u] man for the sabbath:

28 Therefore [v]the Son of man is Lord also of the sabbath.

CHAPTER III.

AND[a] he entered again into the synagogue; and there was a man there which had a withered hand.

s Ex.29.32,33; Le.24.9.
t Ne.9.14; Is.58.13; Eze.20.12,20.
u Col.2.16.
v Jn.9.14; Ep.1.22; Re.1.10.
a Mat.12.9,&c.; Lu.6.6,&c.

Abiathar, moreover, in the calamitous times when David came to the throne, left the interest of Saul and fled to David, bringing with him the ephod, one of the peculiar garments of the high-priest. For a long time, during David's reign, he was high-priest, and it became natural, therefore, to associate *his* name with that of David; to speak of David as king, and Abiathar the high-priest of his time. This will account for the fact that he was spoken of rather than his father. At the same time this was strictly true, that this was done in the days of *Abiathar*, who was afterward high-priest, and was familiarly spoken of as such; as we say that *General* Washington was present at the defeat of Braddock and saved his army, though the title of *General* did not belong to him till many years afterward. Comp. Notes on Lu. ii. 2. ¶ *Shew-bread.* See Notes on Mat. xii. 4.

27. *The sabbath was made for man.* For his rest from toil, his rest from the cares and anxieties of the world, to give him an opportunity to call off his attention from earthly concerns and to direct it to the affairs of eternity. It was a kind provision for man that he might refresh his body by relaxing his labours; that he might have undisturbed time to seek the consolations of religion to cheer him in the anxieties and sorrows of a troubled world; and that he might render to God that homage which is most justly due to him as the Creator, Preserver, Benefactor, and Redeemer of the world. And it is easily capable of proof that no institution has been more signally blessed to man's welfare than the Sabbath. To that we owe, more than to anything else, the peace and order of a civilized community. Where there is no Sabbath there is ignorance, vice, disorder, and crime. On that holy day the poor and the ignorant, as well as the learned, have undisturbed time to learn the requirements of religion, the nature of morals, the law of God, and the way of salvation. On that day man may offer his praises to the Great Giver of all good, and in the sanctuary seek the blessing of him whose favour is life. Where that day is observed in any manner as it should be, order prevails, morals are promoted, the poor are elevated in their condition, vice flies away, and the cmomunity puts on the appearance of neatness, industry, morality, and religion. The Sabbath was therefore pre-eminently intended for man's welfare, and the best interests of mankind demand that it should be sacredly regarded as an appointment of merciful heaven intended for our best good, and, where improved aright, infallibly resulting in our temporal and eternal peace. ¶ *Not man for the sabbath.* Man was made *first*, and then the Sabbath was appointed for his welfare, Ge. ii. 1–3. The Sabbath was not *first* made or contemplated, and then the man made with reference to that. Since, therefore, the Sabbath was intended for man's *good*, the law respecting it must not be interpreted so as to oppose his real welfare. It must be explained in consistency with a proper attention to the duties of mercy to the poor and the sick, and to those in peril. It must be, however, in accordance with man's *real good on the whole*, and with the law of God. The law of God contemplates man's *real good on the whole;* and we have no right, under the plea that the Sabbath was made for man, to do anything contrary to what the law of God admits. It would not be for our *real good,* but for our real and eternal injury, to devote the Sabbath to vice, to labour, or to amusement.

28. *Therefore the Son of man*, &c. See Notes on Mat. xii. 8.

CHAPTER III.

1–5. See this explained in Mat. xii. 9–13.

4. *Or to do evil? to save life, or to kill?*

2 And they [b]watched him whether he would heal him on the sabbath-day, that they might accuse him.

3 And he saith unto the man which had the withered hand, Stand[1] forth.

4 And he saith unto them, Is it lawful to do good on the sabbath-days, or to do evil? [c]to save life, or to kill? But they held their peace.

5 And when he had looked round about on them with anger, being grieved for the [2]hardness of their hearts, he saith unto the man, Stretch forth thine hand. And he stretched *it* out; and his hand was restored whole as the other.

6 And the Pharisees went forth, and straightway took counsel with the [d]Herodians against him, how they might destroy him.

b Lu.14.1. 1 *Arise in the midst.* *c* Ho.6.6. 2 or, *blindness.* *d* Mat.22.16.

It seems to have been a maxim with the Jews that *not* to do good when we have an opportunity is to do evil; *not* to save life is to kill or to be guilty of murder. If a man has an opportunity of saving a man's life when he is in danger, and does not do it, he is evidently guilty of his death. On this principle our Saviour puts this question to the Jews—whether it was better for him, having the *power* to heal this man, to do it, or to suffer him to remain in this suffering condition; and he illustrates it by an example, showing that in a manner of much less importance—that respecting their cattle—they would do on the Sabbath just as *he* would if he should heal this man. The same remark may apply to all opportunities of doing good. "The ability to do good imposes an *obligation* to do it" (Cotton Mather). He that has the means of feeding the hungry, and clothing the naked, and instructing the ignorant, and sending the gospel to the destitute, and that does it not, is guilty, for he is practically doing evil; he is suffering evils to exist which he might remove. So the wicked will be condemned in the day of judgment because *they did it not*, Mat. xxv. 45. If this be true, what an obligation rests on the rich to do good!

5. *With anger.* With a severe and stern countenance; with indignation at their hypocrisy and hardness of heart. This was not, however, a spiteful or revengeful passion; it was caused by excessive *grief* at their state: "being *grieved* for the hardness of their hearts." It was not hatred of the *men* whose hearts were so hard; it was hatred of the *sin* which they exhibited, joined with the extreme grief that neither his teaching nor the law of God, nor any means which could be used, overcame their confirmed wickedness. Such anger is not unlawful, Ep. iv. 26. But in this instance our Lord has taught us that anger is never lawful except when it is tempered with grief or compassion for those who have offended. ¶ *Hardness of their hearts.* The heart, figuratively the seat of feeling or affection, is said to be tender when it is easily affected by the sufferings of others—by our own sin and danger—by the love and commands of God; when we are easily made to *feel* on the great subjects pertaining to our interest, Eze. xi. 19, 20. It is hard when nothing moves it; when a man is alike insensible to the sufferings of others, to the dangers of his own condition, and to the commands, the love, and the threatenings of God. It is most tender in youth, or when we have committed fewest crimes. It is *made* hard by indulgence in sin, by long resisting the offers of salvation, or by opposing any great and affecting appeals which God may make to us by his Spirit or providence, by affliction, or by a revival of religion. Hence it is that the most favourable period for securing an interest in Christ, or for becoming a Christian, is in youth—the first, the tenderest, and the best days of life. Nay, in the days of childhood, in the Sabbath-school, God may be found, and the soul prepared to die.

6. *Straightway.* Immediately, or as soon as possible. ¶ *Took counsel.* Laid a plan. Consulted with them. Literally, "made a consultation." ¶ *The Herodians.* See Notes on Mat. xxii. 16. ¶ *How they might destroy him.* They hated him, he was so holy; because he reproved them; because he laid open their hypocrisy; and because he won the hearts of the people and lessened their influence. They therefore determined to remove him, if possible, and thus avoid his reproofs.

7 But Jesus withdrew himself with his disciples to the sea: and a great[e] multitude from Galilee followed him, and from Judea,

8 And from Jerusalem, and from Idumea, and *from* beyond Jordan; and they about Tyre and Sidon, a great multitude, when they had heard what great things he did, came unto him.

9 And he spake to his disciples, that a small ship should wait on him because of the multitude, lest they should throng him.

10 For he had [f]healed many; insomuch that they [3]pressed upon him for to touch him, as many as had plagues.

11 And[g] unclean spirits, when they saw him, fell down before him, and cried, saying, Thou art the Son of God.

e Lu.6.17.

f Mat.12.15; 14.14. 3 or, *rushed.* g ch.1.24; Mat.14.33; Lu.4.41; Ja.2.19.

Sinners would often rather put to death the man that reproves them than forsake their sins. The Pharisees had rather commit any crime, even to the murder of the Messiah, than forsake the sins for which he rebuked them.

7, 8. *To the sea.* The Sea of Galilee, or to the lonely regions which surrounded the sea, where he might be in obscurity, and avoid their designs against his life. His time had not yet come, and he prudently took care of his life, thus showing that we are not needlessly to throw ourselves into danger. ¶ *Galilee.* See Notes on Mat. ii. 22. ¶ *Judea.* The southern division of the land of Palestine. ¶ *Jerusalem.* Jerusalem was *in* Judea. It is mentioned particularly to show that not only the people of the surrounding *country* came, but also many from the capital, the place of wealth, and honour, and power. ¶ *Idumea.* The country formerly inhabited by the *Edomites.* In the time of the Saviour it was embraced in the country belonging to the Jews. It was south of Judea proper. The word *Idumea* is a Greek word made from the Hebrew *Edom.* It signifies the land of Edom, a name given to Esau, one of the sons of Isaac, Ge. xxv. 30. The word signifies *red,* and the name was given to him, because he sought of Jacob red pottage as the price of his birthright. He settled in Mount Seir (De. ii. 5), on the south of the land of Canaan, and the country of Idumea was bounded by Palestine on the north. During the Babylonish captivity the Edomites spread themselves into the country of Judea, and occupied a considerable part of the south of Palestine. They had, however, submitted to the rite of circumcision, and were incorporated with the Jews. From them sprang Herod the Great. ¶ From *beyond Jordan.* From the region lying *east* of the river Jordan. The sacred writers lived on the *west* side of Jordan, and by the country *beyond Jordan* they meant that on the *east* side. ¶ *Tyre and Sidon.* See Notes on Mat. xi. 21.

9. *A small ship.* Rather a *boat.* There were properly speaking, no *ships* on the Sea of Tiberias. This was probably a small boat that belonged to the disciples, in which he could draw off from the shore, and teach the people without being pressed by them. ¶ *Lest they should throng him.* They pressed upon him in great numbers. He had healed many, and those who were still diseased pressed or crowded on him, so that his labours were interrupted and embarrassed. He therefore withdrew from the multitude, and sought a situation where he might address them to greater advantage. ¶ *As many as had plagues.* As many as had diseases or maladies of body or mind. The word *plague,* now confined to the pestilence, does not express the meaning of the original, and tends to mislead.

11, 12. *Unclean spirits.* Persons who were possessed of evil spirits. ¶ *Thou art the Son of God.* The Son of God, by way of eminence. In this place it is equivalent to the Messiah, who was, among the Jews, called the Son of God. Hence they were charged not to make him known, because he was not desirous that it should be blazoned abroad that he claimed to be the Messiah. He had not yet done what he wished in order to establish his claims to the Messiahship. He was poor and unhonoured, and the claim would be treated as that of an impostor. *For the present,* therefore, he did not wish that it should be proclaimed abroad that he was the Messiah.

The circumstance here referred to

12 And[h] he straitly charged them
that they should not make him
known.
13 And[i] he goeth up into a
mountain, and calleth *unto him*
whom[k] he would; and they came
unto him.
14 And he ordained twelve, that
they should be with him, and
that he might send them forth to
preach,
15 And to have power to heal
sicknesses, and to cast out devils:
16 And [l] Simon he surnamed
Peter;
17 And James the *son* of Zebedee, and John the brother of James,
and he surnamed them Boanerges,
which is, [m]The sons of thunder;
18 And Andrew, and Philip, and
Bartholomew, and Matthew, and
Thomas, and James the *son* of Alpheus, and Thaddeus, and Simon
the Canaanite,
19 And Judas Iscariot, which also
betrayed him: and they went [4] into
an house.
20 And the multitude cometh
together again, [n]so that they could
not so much as eat bread.
21 And when his [5]friends heard
of it, they went out to lay hold on

h ch.1.25,34. *i* Mat.10.1. *k* Jn.15.16. *l* Jn.1.42.

m Is.58.1; Je.23.29. *n* ch.6.31.

4 or, *home*. 5 or, *kinsmen*.

demonstrates the existence of evil spirits. If these were merely diseased or deranged persons, then it is strange that they should be endowed with knowledge so much superior to those in health. If they were under the influence of an order of spirits superior to man — whose appropriate habitation was in another world—then it is not strange that they should know him, even in the midst of his poverty, to be the Messiah, the Son of God.

13–19. For an account of the appointment of the apostles, see Notes on Mat. x. 1–4. ¶ *And calleth* unto him *whom he would.* Those whom he chose; whom he was about to appoint to the apostleship. See Notes on Jn. xv. 16.

14. *He ordained twelve.* The word rendered *ordained* here does not express our notion of ordination to the ministry. It means, literally, "he made"—that is, he *appointed* twelve to be with him. ¶ *Twelve.* The reason why *twelve* were chosen was, probably, that such a number would be deemed competent witnesses of what they saw; that they could not be easily charged with being excited by sympathy, or being deluded, as a multitude might; and that, being destined to go into all the world, a considerable number seemed indispensable. Perhaps, also, there was some reference to the fact that *twelve* was the number of the twelve tribes of Israel.

17. *Boanerges.* This word is made up of two Hebrew words signifying *sons of thunder*, meaning that they, on some accounts, *resembled* thunder. See Notes on Mat. i. 1. It is not known why this name was given to James and John. They are nowhere else called by it. Some suppose it was because they wished to call down fire from heaven and consume a certain village of the Samaritans, Lu. ix. 54. It is, however, more probable that it was on account of something fervid, and glowing, and powerful in their genius and eloquence.

20. *They could not so much as eat bread.* Their time and attention were so occupied that they were obliged to forego their regular meals. The affairs of religion *may* so occupy the attention of ministers and others as to prevent their engaging in their customary pursuits. Religion is all-important—far more important than the ordinary business of this life; and there is nothing unreasonable if our *temporal* affairs sometimes give way to the higher interests of our own souls and the souls of others. At the same time, it is true that religion is ordinarily consistent with a close attention to worldly business. It promotes industry, economy, order, neatness, and punctuality—all indispensable to worldly prosperity. Of these there has been no more illustrious example than that of our Saviour himself.

21. *When his friends.* Greek, "they who were of him." Not the apostles, but his relatives, his friends, who were in the place of his nativity. ¶ *Heard* of it. Heard of his conduct; his preaching; his appointing the apostles; his drawing such a multitude to his preaching. This shows that by "his friends" were not meant the apostles, but his

him: for they said, [o]He is beside
himself.
22 And the scribes which came
down from Jerusalem said, [p]He
hath Beelzebub, and by the prince
of the devils casteth he out devils.
23 And he called them *unto him*,
and said unto them in parables,
How can Satan cast out Satan?
24 And if a kingdom be divided
against itself, that kingdom cannot stand.
25 And if a house be divided
against itself, that house cannot
stand.
26 And if Satan rise up against
himself, and be divided, he cannot stand, but hath an end.
27 No[q] man can enter into a
strong man's house, and spoil his
goods, except he will first bind the
strong man; and then he will spoil
his house.
28 Verily I say unto you, [r]All

o Ho.9.7; Jn.10.20.
p Mat.9.34; 10.25; 12.24; Lu.11.15; Jn.7.20; 8.48,52.
q Is.49.24,26; 61.1; Mat.12.29.
r Mat.12.31; Lu.12.10.

sins shall be forgiven unto the sons
of men, and blasphemies wherewith
soever they shall blaspheme:
29 But he that shall [s]blaspheme
against the Holy Ghost hath never
forgiveness, but is in danger of
eternal damnation:
30 Because they said, He hath an
unclean spirit.
31 There[t] came then his brethren
and his mother, and, standing without, sent unto him, calling him.
32 And the multitude sat about
him; and they said unto him, Behold, thy mother and thy brethren
without seek for thee.
33 And he answered them, saying, Who is my mother, or my
brethren?
34 And he looked round about
on them which sat about him, and
said, Behold my mother and my
brethren!
35 For whosoever shall [u]do the

s He.10.29. *t* Mat.12.46-48; Lu.8.19-21.
u Ja.1.25; 1 Jn.2.17.

neighbours and others who *heard* of his conduct. ¶ *They went out to lay hold on him.* To take him away from the multitude, and to remove him to his home, that he might be treated as a maniac, so that, by absence from the *causes* of excitement, he might be restored to his right mind. ¶ *They said.* That is, common report said; or his friends and relatives said, for they did not believe on him, Jn. vii. 5. Probably the enemies of Jesus raised the report, and his relatives were persuaded to believe it to be true. ¶ *He is beside himself.* He is delirious or deranged. The reason why this report gained any belief was, probably, that he had lived among them as a carpenter; that he was poor and unknown; and that now, at thirty years of age, he broke off from his occupations, abandoned his common employment, spent much time in the deserts, denied himself the common comforts of life, and set up his claims to be the Messiah who was expected by all the people to come with great pomp and splendour. The charge of *derangement* on account of attention to religion has not been confined to the Saviour. Let a man be made deeply sensible of his sins, and spend much of his time in prayer, and have no relish for the ordinary amusements or business of life; or let a Christian be much impressed with his obligation to devote himself to God, and *act* as if he believed there was an *eternity*, and warn his neighbours of their danger; or let a minister show uncommon zeal and spend his strength in the service of his Master, and the world is not slow to call it derangement. And none will be more ready to originate or believe the charge than an ungodly and infidel parent or brother, a self-righteous Pharisee or professor in the church. At the same time, men may endanger themselves on the bosom of the deep or in the bowels of the earth for wealth; or may plunge into the vortex of fashion, folly, and vice, and break in upon the hours of repose, and neglect their duties to their family and the demands of business, and in the view of the world it is wisdom and proof of a sane mind! Such is the consistency of boasted reason; such the wisdom and prudence of worldly men!

22-30. *And the scribes,* &c. See Notes

will of God, the same is my brother, and my sister, and my mother.

CHAPTER IV.

AND[a] he began again to teach by the sea-side: and there was gathered unto him a great multitude, so that he entered into a ship, and sat in the sea; and the whole multitude was by the sea on the land.

2 And he taught them many things by [b]parables, and said unto them in his doctrine,

3 Hearken:[c] Behold, there went out a sower to sow:

4 And it came to pass, as he sowed, some fell by the way-side, and [d]the fowls of the air came and devoured it up.

5 And some fell on [e]stony ground, where it had not much earth; and immediately it sprang up, because it had no depth of earth:

6 But when the sun was up, it was scorched; and [f]because it had no root, it withered away.

7 And some fell [g]among thorns; and the thorns grew up, and choked it, and it yielded no fruit.

8 And other fell on [h]good ground, and did [i]yield fruit that sprang up and increased, and brought forth, some thirty, and some sixty, and some an hundred.

9 And he said unto them, He that hath ears to hear, let him hear.

10 And[k] when he was alone, they that were about him with the twelve asked of him the parable.

11 And he said unto them, [l]Unto you it is given to know the mystery of the kingdom of God; but unto [m]them that are without, all *these* things are done in parables:

12 That[n] seeing they may see, and not perceive; and hearing they may hear, and not understand; lest at any time they should be converted, and *their* sins should be forgiven them.

13 And he said unto them, Know ye not this parable? and how then will ye know all parables?

14 The sower [o]soweth the word.

15 And these are they by the way-side, where the word is sown; but when they have heard, [p]Satan cometh immediately, and [q]taketh away the word that was sown in their hearts.

16 And these are they likewise which are sown on stony ground; who, when they have heard the word, immediately receive it with gladness;

17 And have [r]no root in themselves, and so endure [s]but for a

a Mat.13.1,&c.; Lu.8.4,&c. *b* Ps.78.2; ver.34. *c* ver.9,23; ch.7.16. *d* Ge.15.11. *e* Eze.11.19; 36.26. *f* Ps.1.4; Ja.1.11. *g* Je.4.3. *h* He.6.7,8. *i* Col.1.6.

k Mat.13.10,&c. *l* Ep.1.9. *m* Col.4.5; 1 Th.4.12; 1 Ti.3.7. *n* Is.6.9,10; Jn.12.40; Ac.28.26,27; Ro.11.8. *o* Is.32.20; 1 Pe.1.25. *p* 1 Pe.5.8; Re.12.9. *q* He.2.1. *r* Job 19.28. *s* Job 27.10.

---

on Mat. xii. 24–32. The occasion of their saying this was, that he had healed a man possessed with a devil. The scribes, who came from Jerusalem to watch his conduct, charged him with having made a compact or agreement with the prince of the devils.

31–35. See Notes on Mat. xii. 46–50.

CHAPTER IV.

1–9. See the parable of the sower explained in the Notes on Mat. xiii. 1–9.

10–13. See Notes on Mat. xiii. 10–17. On ver. 12, see Notes on Jn. xii. 39, 40.

¶ *When he was alone.* That is, separate from the multitude. When he withdrew from the multitude a few followed him for the purpose of farther instruction.

13. *Know ye not this parable?* This which is so plain and obvious. ¶ *How then will ye know all parables?* Those which are more difficult and obscure. As they were themselves to be *teachers*, it was important that they should be acquainted with the whole system of religion—of much more importance for them at that time than for the mass of the people.

time: afterward, when affliction or
persecution ariseth for the word's
sake, [t]immediately they are offended.
18 And these are they which are
sown among thorns; such as hear
the word,
19 And the [u]cares of this world,
and the [v]deceitfulness of riches,
and the [w]lusts of other things entering in, choke the word, and [x]it
becometh unfruitful.
20 And these are they which are
sown on good ground; such as
hear the word, and receive *it*, and
bring[y] forth fruit, some thirty-fold,
some sixty, and some an hundred.
21 And he said unto them, Is a
candle brought to be put under a
[1]bushel, or under a bed, and not
to be set on a candlestick?
22 For[z] there is nothing hid
which shall not be manifested,
neither was any thing kept secret
but that it should come abroad.
23 If any man have ears to
hear, let him hear.
24 And he saith unto them, Take
heed [a]what ye hear: [b]with what
measure ye mete, it shall be measured to you; and unto you that
hear shall more be given.
25 For he that hath, to him shall
be given; and he that hath not,
[c]from him shall be taken even that
which he hath.

t 2 Ti.1.15. u Lu.14.18-20; 1 Ti.6.9,17; 2 Ti.4.10. v Pr.23.5. w 1 Jn.2.16,17. x Is.5.2,4. y Ro.7.4; Col.1.10; 2 Pe.1.8.

1 See on Mat.5.15. z Ec.12.14; Mat.10.26; Lu.12.2; 1 Co.4.5. a 1 Pe.2.2. b Mat.7.2. c Lu.8.18.

14–20. See Notes on Mat. xiii. 18–23.

21. *Is a candle brought*, &c. A candle is not lit up to be put immediately under a measure or a bed, where it can give no light. Its design is to give light. So my preaching by parables is not designed to obscure the truth, but to throw light on it. You should understand those parables, and, understanding them, should impart the truth to others also, as a candle throws its beams upon a dark world. ¶ *Bushel.* The word here used in the original means a measure for grain containing about 12 quarts. ¶ *Bed.* A couch, either to sleep on at night or to recline on at their meals. Probably the latter is here meant, and is equivalent to our saying a candle is not brought to be put *under* the table, but *on* it. See Notes on Mat. xxiii. 6.

22. *There is nothing hid*, &c. See Notes on Mat. x. 26.

24. *Take heed what ye hear.* Or, consider well what you hear. Make a good improvement of it. ¶ *With what measure ye mete*, &c. You shall be treated according to the use you make of your opportunities of learning. If you consider it well, and make a good improvement of what you hear, you shall be well rewarded. If not, your reward shall be small. This is a proverbial expression. See it explained in the Notes on Mat. vii. 1, 2. ¶ *Mete.* Measure. With what measure ye measure. ¶ *Unto you that hear.* To you who are *attentive*, and who improve what you hear.

25. *For he that hath*, &c. See Notes on Mat. xiii. 12. The meaning here seems to be, he that diligently attends to my words shall increase more and more in the knowledge of the truth; but he that neglects them and is inattentive shall become more ignorant; the few things which he had learned he will forget, and his trifling knowledge will be diminished. ¶ *Hath not.* Does not improve what he possessed, or does not make proper use of his means of learning. ¶ *That which he hath.* That which he had already learned. By this we are taught the indispensable necessity of giving attention to the means of instruction. The attention must be *continued*. It is not sufficient that we have learned some things, or appear to have learned much. All will be in vain unless we go forward, and improve every opportunity of learning the will of God and the way of salvation. So what children are taught will be of little use unless they follow it up and endeavour to improve themselves.

26. *So is the kingdom of God.* The gospel, or religion in the soul, may be compared to this. See Notes on Mat. iii. 2. This parable is recorded only by Mark.

27. *And should sleep, and rise night and day.* Should sleep in the night and rise by day, for so the expression is to

26 And he said, [d]So is the kingdom of God, as if a man should cast seed into the ground;
27 And should sleep, and rise night and day, and the seed should spring and grow up, he knoweth not how.
28 For[e] the earth bringeth forth fruit of herself; [f]first the blade, then the ear; after that, the full corn in the ear.
29 But when the fruit is [2]brought forth, immediately [g]he putteth in the sickle, because the harvest is come.
30 And he said, Whereunto shall

d Mat.13.24. e Ge.1.11,12. f Ec.3.1,11. 2 or, *ripe*, Job 5.26. g Re.14.15.

be understood. That is, should live in his usual way, without exerting any influence over the growing grain. By this we are not to infer that men are to use no diligence in the obtaining and in the growth of piety; but the illustration shows only that as we cannot tell *how* grain grows, so we cannot tell the *mode* in which piety increases in the heart. ¶ *He knoweth not how.* This is still true. After all the researches of philosophers, no one has been able to tell the way in which grain grows. They can observe one fact after another; they can see the changes; they can see the necessity of rains and suns, of care and shelter, but beyond this they cannot go. So in religion. We can mark the change; we can see the need of prayer, and self-examination, and searching the Scriptures, and the ordinances of religion, but we cannot tell *in what way* the religious principle is developed and strengthened. As God unseen, yet by the use of proper means, makes the grass to flourish, so God unseen, but by proper means, nourishes the soul, and the plants of piety spring up, and bloom, and bear fruit. Comp. Notes on Jn. iii. 8.

28. *For the earth bringeth forth fruit of herself.* That is, it is done without the power of man. It is done while man is engaged in other things. The scope of this passage does not require us to suppose that our Saviour meant to say that the earth had any productive power *of itself*, but only that it produced its fruits not by the *power of man.* God gives it its power. It has no power of its own. So religion in the heart is not by the *power* of man. It grows he cannot tell how, and of course he cannot, without divine aid, control it. It is by the power of God. At the same time, as without industry man would have no harvest, so without active effort he would have no religion. Both are connected with his effort; both are to be measured commonly by his effort (Phi. ii. 12); both grow he cannot tell how; both increase when the proper means are used, and both depend on God for increase. ¶ *First the blade.* The green, tender shoot, that first starts out of the earth before the stalk is formed. ¶ *Then the ear.* The original means the *stalk* or *spire* of wheat or barley, as well as the ear. ¶ *The full corn.* The ripe wheat. The grain swollen to its proper size. By this is denoted, undoubtedly, that grace or religion in the heart is of gradual growth. It is at first tender, feeble, perhaps almost imperceptible, like the first shootings of the grain in the earth. Perhaps also, like grain, it often lies long in the earth before there are signs of life. Like the tender grain, also, it needs care, kindness, and culture. A frost, a cold storm, or a burning sun alike injure it. So tender piety in the heart needs care, kindness, culture. It needs shelter from the frosts and storms of a cold, unfeeling world. It needs the genial dews and mild suns of heaven; in other words, it needs instruction, prayer, and friendly counsel from parents, teachers, ministers, and experienced Christians, that it may grow, and bring forth the full fruits of holiness. Like the grain, also, in due time it will grow strong; it will produce its appropriate fruit—a full and rich harvest—to the praise of God.

29. *Immediately he putteth in the sickle.* This is the way with the husbandman. As soon as the grain is ripe it is cut down. So it is often with the Christian. As soon as he is prepared for heaven he is taken there. But we are not to press this part of the parable, as if it meant that *all* are removed as soon as they are fit for heaven. Every parable contains circumstances thrown in to fill up the story, which cannot be literally interpreted. In this, the circumstance of *sleeping* and *rising* cannot be applied to Christ; and in like manner, the harvest, I suppose, is not to be literally in-

we liken the kingdom of God?
or with what comparison shall we
compare it?
31 *It*[h] *is* like a grain of mustard-
seed, which, when it is sown in
the earth, is less than all the seeds
that be in the earth:
32 But when it is sown, it grow-
eth up, and becometh [i]greater than
all herbs, and shooteth out great
branches; so that the fowls of the
air may lodge under the shadow
of it.
33 And with many such parables
spake he the word unto them, [k]as
they were able to hear *it*.
34 But without a parable spake
he not unto them: and when they
were alone he expounded all things
to his disciples.
35 And the same day, when the
even was come, he saith unto them,
Let us pass over unto the other
side.
36 And when they had sent away
the multitude, they took him even

h Mat.13.31,32; Lu.13.18,19.
i Pr.4.18; Is.11.9; Da.2.44; Mal.1.11.
k Jn.16.12.

terpreted. Perhaps the whole parable may be differently interpreted. The seed sown may mean the gospel which he was preaching. In Judea its beginnings were small; yet he would leave it, commit it to his disciples, and return to his Father. The gospel, in the meantime, left by him, would take root, spring up, and produce an abundant harvest. In due time he would return, send forth the angels, and gather in the harvest, and save his people for ever. Comp. Notes on Mat. xiii. 31–33.

30. *Whereunto shall we liken*, &c. This shows the great solicitude which Jesus had to adapt his instructions to the capacity of his disciples. He sought out the most plain and striking illustrations—an example which should be followed by all the ministers of the gospel. At the same time that the instructions of the pulpit should be dignified—as our Saviour's always were—they should be adapted to the capacity of the audience and easily understood. To do this the following things are necessary in a minister: 1st. *Humility*. A freedom from a desire to shine, and to astonish the world by the splendour of his talents, and by his learning and eloquence. 2d. *Good sense*. A satisfaction in being understood. 3d. Acquaintance with the habits of thought and manner of speaking among the people. To do this, frequent intercourse with them is necessary. 4th. *A good sound education*. It is the men of ignorance, with some smattering of learning, and with a desire to confound and astonish men by the use of unintelligible words, and by the introduction of matter that is wholly unconnected with the subject, that most often shoot over the heads of the people. Preachers of humility, good sense, and education are content with being understood, and free from the affectation of saying things to amaze and confound their auditors. ¶ *The kingdom of God*. See Notes on Mat. iii. 2.

31, 32. See Notes on Mat. xiii. 31, 32.

33. *Spake he the word*. The word of God. The doctrines of his gospel. ¶ *As they were able to hear* it. As they could comprehend it. They were like children; and he was obliged to lead them along cautiously and by degrees to a full understanding of the plan of salvation.

34. *Without a parable spake he not unto them*. That is, the things pertaining to his kingdom. On other subjects he spake without parables. On these, such was their prejudice, so many notions had they contrary to the nature of his kingdom, and so liable would plain instructions have been to give offence, that he employed this method to *insinuate* truth gradually into their minds, and to prepare them fully to understand the nature of his kingdom. ¶ *They were alone*. His disciples. ¶ *He expounded*. Explained. Showed them more at length the spiritual meaning of the parables.

35–41. See Notes on Mat. viii. 18–27.

36. *Even as he was in the ship*. They took him without making any preparation for the voyage; without providing any food or raiment. He was sitting in a ship, or boat, instructing the people. In the same boat, probably ill fitted to encounter a storm on the lake, they sailed. This would render their danger more imminent and the miracle more striking. ¶ *There were with him other little ships*. Belonging probably to the people, who, seeing him sail, resolved to follow him.

as he was in the ship: and there
were also with him other little
ships.
37 And[l] there arose a great
storm of wind, and the waves beat
into the ship, so that it was now
full.
38 And he was in the hinder part
of the ship, asleep on a pillow: and
they awake him, and say unto him,
Master,[m] carest thou not that we
perish?
39 And he arose, and rebuked the
wind, and said unto the sea, Peace,
be still. And[n] the wind ceased,
and there was a great calm.
40 And he said unto them, [o]Why
are ye so fearful? how is it that
ye have no faith?
41 And they [p]feared exceedingly,
and said one to another, What
manner of man is this, that even
the wind and the [q]sea obey him?

CHAPTER V.

AND[a] they came over unto the
other side of the sea, into the
country of the Gadarenes,

l Mat.8.24; Lu.8.23. *m* Ps.10.1; Is.40.27; La.3.8.

n Ps.89.9; La.3.31,32. *o* Ps.46.1,2; Is.43.2. *p* Jonah 1.10,16. *q* Job 38.11. *a* Mat.8.28,&c.; Lu.8.26,&c.

---

39. *Peace, be still.* There is something exceedingly authoritative and majestic in this command of our Lord. Standing amid the howling tempest, on the heaving sea, and in the darkness of night, by his own power he stills the waves and bids the storm subside. None but the *God* of the storms and the billows could awe by a word the troubled elements, and send a universal peace and stillness among the winds and waves. He *must*, therefore, be divine. The following remarks by Dr. Thomson, long a resident in Syria, and familiar with the scenes which occur there, will farther illustrate this passage, and the parallel account in Mat. viii. 18–27, and also the passage in Mat. xiv. 23–32. The extract which follows is taken from *The Land and the Book*, vol. ii. p. 32, 33:—"To understand the causes of these sudden and violent tempests, we must remember that the lake lies low—600 feet lower than the ocean; that the vast and naked plateaus of the Jaulan rise to a great height, spreading backward to the wilds of the Hauran and upward to snowy Hermon; that the water-courses have cut out profound ravines and wild gorges, converging to the head of this lake, and that these act like gigantic *funnels* to draw down the cold winds from the mountains. On the occasion referred to we subsequently pitched our tents at the shore, and remained for three days and nights exposed to this tremendous wind. We had to double-pin all the tent-ropes, and frequently were obliged to hang with our whole weight upon them to keep the quivering tabernacle from being carried up bodily into the air. No wonder the disciples toiled and rowed hard all that night; and how natural their amazement and terror at the sight of Jesus walking on the waves! The faith of Peter in desiring and *daring* to set foot on such a sea is most striking and impressive; more so, indeed, than its failure after he made the attempt. The whole lake, as we had it, was lashed into fury; the waves repeatedly rolled up to our tent door, tumbling over the ropes with such violence as to carry away the tent-pins. And moreover, those winds are not only violent, but they come done suddenly, and often when the sky is perfectly clear. I once went in to swim near the hot baths, and, before I was aware, a wind came rushing over the cliffs with such force that it was with great difficulty I could regain the shore. Some such sudden wind it was, I suppose, that filled the ship with waves 'so that it was now full,' while Jesus was asleep on a pillow in the hinder part of the ship; nor is it strange that the disciples aroused him with the cry of Master! Master! carest thou not that we perish!"

CHAPTER V.

1–20. See this account of the demoniacs fully explained in the Notes on Mat. viii. 28–34.

4. *He had been often bound with fetters and chains.* Efforts had been made to confine him, but his great strength—his strength increased by his malady—had prevented it. There often appears to be a great increase of strength produced by insanity, and what is here stated in regard to this maniac often

2 And when he was come out of
the ship, immediately there met
him out of the tombs a man with
an unclean spirit,
3 Who[b] had *his* dwelling among
the tombs; and no man could bind
him, no, not with chains:
4 Because that he had been often
bound with fetters and chains, and
the chains had been plucked asunder by him, and the fetters broken
in pieces: neither could any *man*
tame him.
5 And always, night and day, he
was in the mountains, and in the
tombs, crying, and cutting himself
with stones.
6 But when he saw Jesus afar
off, he ran and [c]worshipped him,
7 And cried with a loud voice,
and said, What have I to do with
thee, Jesus, *thou* Son of the most
high God? I adjure thee by God
that thou torment me not.
8 (For he said unto him, [d]Come
out of the man, *thou* unclean
spirit.)
9 And he asked him, What *is* thy
name? And he answered, saying,
My name *is* Legion; [e]for we are
many.
10 And he besought him much
that he would not send them away
out of the country.
11 Now there was there, nigh
unto the mountains, a great herd
of [f]swine feeding.
12 And all the devils [g]besought
him, saying, Send us into the
swine, that we may enter into
them.
13 And forthwith [h]Jesus gave
them leave. And the unclean
spirits went out, and entered into
the swine; and the herd ran violently down a steep place into the
sea, (they were about two thousand,) and were choked in the sea.
14 And they that fed the swine
fled, and told *it* in the city, and
in the country. And they went
out to see what it was that was
done.
15 And they came to Jesus, and
see him that was possessed with
the devil, and [i]had the legion, sit-

b Is.65.4. *c* Ps.72.9. *d* Ac.16.18; He.2.14; 1 Jn.3.8.
e Mat.12.45. *f* Le.11.7,8; De.14.8. *g* Job 1.10,12; 2.5,6. *h* Re.13.7; 1 Pe.3.22. *i* Is.49.25; Col.1.13.

occurs in Palestine and elsewhere now. Dr. Thomson (*The Land and the Book*, vol. i. p. 213) says respecting this case: "There are some very similar at the present day—furious and dangerous maniacs, who wander about the mountains, and sleep in tombs and caves. In their worst paroxysms they are quite unmanageable and prodigiously strong." Luke (ch. viii. 27) says of him that "he wore no clothes," or that he was naked, which is also implied in the account in Mark, who tells us that after he was healed he was found "*clothed* and in his right mind," ver. 15. This is often a striking characteristic of insanity. Dr. Pritchard (on *Insanity*, p. 26) quotes from an Italian physician's description of raving madness or mania: "A striking and characteristic circumstance is the propensity to go quite naked. The patient tears his clothes to tatters." So Dr. Thomson (*The Land and the Book*, vol. i. p. 213) says: "It is one of the most common traits in this madness that the victims refuse to wear clothes. I have often seen them absolutely naked in the crowded streets of Beirut and Sidon. There are also cases in which they run wildly about the country and frighten the whole neighbourhood. These poor wretches are held in the greatest reverence by Moslems, who, through some monstrous perversion of ideas, believe them to be inspired and peculiarly holy."

5. *Cutting himself with stones.* These are all marks of a *madman*—a man bereft of reason, a wretched outcast, strong and dangerous. The inspired penman says that this madness was caused by an unclean spirit, or by his being under the influence of a devil. That this account is not irrational, see Notes on Mat. iv. 24.

6. *Worshipped him.* Bowed down before him; rendered him homage. This was an acknowledgment of his power, and of his control over fallen spirits.

9. *My name* is *Legion.* See Notes on Mat. viii. 29.

ting, and clothed, and in his right
mind: and [k]they were afraid.
16 And they that saw *it* told
them how it befell to him that
was possessed with the devil, and
also concerning the swine.
17 And they began to pray him
to [l]depart out of their coasts.
18 And when he was come into
the ship, he that had been possessed with the devil prayed him
that he might be with him.
19 Howbeit, Jesus suffered him
not, but saith unto him, Go home
to thy friends, and [m]tell them how
great things the Lord hath done
for thee, and hath had compassion
on thee.
20 And he departed, and began
to publish in Decapolis how great
things Jesus had done for him:
and all *men* did marvel.
21 And when Jesus was passed
over again by ship unto the other
side, much people gathered unto

k Job 13.11; Ps.14.5; 2 Ti.1.7.
l Job 21.14; Lu.5.8; Ac.16.39.
m Ps.66.16; Is.38.19.

him; and he was nigh unto the
sea.
22 And,[n] behold, there cometh
one of the rulers of the synagogue,
Jairus by name; and when he saw
him, he fell at his feet,
23 And besought him greatly,
saying, My little daughter lieth at
the [o]point of death: *I pray thee*
come and lay thy hands on her,
that she may be healed; and she
shall live.
24 And *Jesus* went with him;
and much people followed him,
and thronged him.
25 And a certain woman, which
had an [p]issue of blood twelve
years,
26 And had suffered many things
of many physicians, and had spent
all that she had, and was [q]nothing
bettered, but rather grew worse,
27 When she had heard of Jesus, came in the press behind and
[r]touched his garment:

n Mat.9.18,&c.; Lu.8.41,&c. o Ps.107.18.
p Le.15.19,&c. q Job 13.4; Ps.108.12; Je.30.12,13.
r 2 Ki.13.21; Mat.14.36; Ac.5.15; 19.12.

---

15. *Sitting, and clothed, and in his right mind.* There could be no doubt of the reality of this miracle. The man had been well known. He had long dwelt among the tombs, an object of terror and alarm. To see him all at once peaceful, calm, and rational, was proof that it was the power of God only that had done it. ¶ *They were afraid.* They were *awed*, as in the presence of God. The word does not mean here that they feared that any *evil* would happen to them, but that they were affected with *awe;* they felt that God was there; they were struck with astonishment at what Jesus had done.

19. *Jesus suffered him not.* Various reasons have been conjectured why Jesus did not suffer this man to go with him. It might have been that he wished to leave him among the people as a conclusive evidence of his power to work miracles. Or it might have been that the man feared that if Jesus left him the devils would return, and that Jesus told him to remain to show to him that the cure was complete, and that he had power over the devils when absent as well as when present. But the probable reason is, that he desired to restore him to his family and friends. Jesus was unwilling to delay the joy of his friends, and to prolong their anxiety by suffering him to remain away from them.

20. *In Decapolis.* See Notes on Mat. iv. 25. ¶ *How great things*, &c. This was the natural expression of right feeling at being cured of such a calamity. So the desire of sinners freed from sin is to honour Jesus, and to invite the world to participate in the same salvation, and to join them in doing honour to the Son of God. Comp. Ps. lxvi. 16.

22–43. See the account of the raising of Jairus's daughter, and the healing of the woman with an issue of blood, fully explained in the Notes on Mat. ix. 18–26.

23. *Lieth at the point of death.* Is dying; in the last agonies.

26. *Had suffered many things.* Had resorted to many things painful, by the direction of the physicians, in order to be healed.

28 For she said, If I may touch
but his clothes, I shall be whole.
29 And straightway the fountain
of her blood was dried up, and she
felt in *her* body that she was healed
of that plague.
30 And Jesus, immediately knowing in himself that [s]virtue had
gone out of him, turned him about
in the press, and said, Who touched
my clothes?
31 And his disciples said unto
him, Thou seest the multitude
thronging thee, and sayest thou,
Who touched me?
32 And he looked round about
to see her that had done this
thing.
33 But the woman, fearing and
trembling, knowing what was
done in her, came and fell down
before him, and [t]told him all the
truth.
34 And he said unto her, Daughter, [u]thy faith hath made thee
whole: [v]go in peace, and be whole
of thy plague.
35 While he yet spake, there
came from the ruler of the synagogue's *house certain* which said,
[w]Thy daughter is dead: why
troublest thou the Master any
further?
36 As soon as Jesus heard the
word that was spoken, he saith
unto the ruler of the synagogue,
Be not afraid, [x]only believe.
37 And he suffered no man to
follow him, [y]save Peter, and James,
and John the brother of James.
38 And he cometh to the house
of the ruler of the synagogue, and
seeth the tumult, and them that
wept and wailed greatly.
39 And when he was come in,
he saith unto them, Why make ye
this ado and weep? the damsel is
not dead, but [z]sleepeth.
40 And they laughed him to
scorn. But when he had put them
all out, he taketh the father and
the mother of the damsel, and
them that were with him, and entereth in where the damsel was
lying.
41 And he took the damsel by the

s Lu.6.19. *t* Ps.30.2. *u* ch.10.52; Ac.14.9. *v* 1 Sa.1.17; 20.42; 2 Ki.5.19.

w Jn.5.25; 11.25. *x* 2 Ch.20.20; Jn.11.40. *y* ch.9.2; 14.33. *z* Jn.11.11-13.

27. *Came in the press behind.* In the crowd that pressed upon him. This was done to avoid being noticed. It was an act of faith. She was full of confidence that Jesus was *able* to heal, but she trembled on account of her conscious unworthiness, thus illustrating the humility and confidence of a sinner coming to God for pardon and life.

30. *Virtue had gone out of him.* Power to heal. The word in the original means *power.* ¶ *Who touched my clothes?* This he said, not to obtain information, for he had healed her, and must have known on whom the blessing was conferred; but he did it that the woman might herself make a confession of the whole matter, so that the power of her faith and the greatness of the miracle might be manifested to the praise of God.

34. *Daughter.* A word of kindness, tending to inspire confidence and to dissipate her fears. ¶ *Be whole.* That is, *continue* to be whole, for she was already cured. ¶ *Of thy plague.* Thy disease; literally, thy *scourge.* So a word from Jesus heals the moral malady of the sinner.

35, 36. *Why troublest thou,* &c. It seems that the people had not yet confidence that Jesus could raise the dead. He had not yet done it; and as the child was now dead, and as they supposed that his power over her was at an end, they wished no farther to trouble him. Jesus kindly set the fears of the ruler at rest, and assured him that he had equal power over the dead and the living, and could as easily raise those who had expired as those who were expiring.

38. *The tumult.* The confusion and weeping of the assembled people. ¶ *Wailed.* Making inarticulate, mournful sounds; howling for the dead.

39. *This ado.* This tumult, this bustle or confusion. ¶ *And weep.* Weep in this inordinate and improper manner. See Notes on Mat. ix. 23. ¶ *But sleepeth.* See Notes on Mat. ix. 24.

hand, and said unto her, Talitha
cumi; which is, being interpreted,
Damsel, (I say unto thee,) [y]arise.
42 And straightway the damsel
arose and walked; for she was *of*
the age of twelve years. And they
were astonished with a great astonishment.
43 And he [z]charged them straitly
that no man should know it; and
commanded that something should
be given her to eat.

CHAPTER VI.

AND he went out from thence,
and came into his own country; and his disciples follow him.
2 And[a] when the sabbath-day
was come, he began to teach in
the synagogue: and many, hearing *him*, were astonished, saying,
From[b] whence hath this man these
things? and what wisdom *is* this
which is given unto him, that even
such mighty works are wrought
by his hands?
3 Is not this the carpenter, the
son of Mary, the brother of [c]James,
and Joses, and of Juda, and Simon? and are not his sisters here
with us? And they were [d]offended
at him.
4 But Jesus said unto them, [e]A
prophet is not without honour,
but in his own country, and among
his own kin, and in his own house.
5 And he [f]could there do no
mighty work, save that he laid his
hand upon a few sick folk and
healed *them*.
6 And he [g]marvelled because
of their unbelief. And [h]he went
round about the villages, teaching.
7 And[i] he called *unto him* the
twelve, and began to send them
forth by two and two, and gave
them power over unclean spirits;
8 And commanded them that
they should take nothing for *their*
journey save a staff only; no scrip,
no bread, no [1]money in *their* purse;
9 But *be* [k]shod with [l]sandals;
and not put on two coats.
10 And he said unto them, In
what place soever ye enter into an
house, there abide till ye depart
from that place.
11 And whosoever shall not re-

y Ac.9.40. *z* Mat.8.4; 12.16-18; ch.3.12; Lu.5.14.
a Mat.13.54,&c.; Lu.4.16,&c. *b* Jn.6.42. *c* Ga.1.19.
d Mat.11.6. *e* Mat.13.57; Jn.4.44.
f Ge.19.22; ch.9.23. *g* Is.59.16; Je.2.12.
h Mat.9.35; Lu.13.22; Ac.10.38.
i Mat.10.1,&c.; ch.3.13,&c.; Lu.9.1,&c.; 10.3,&c.
1 The word signifies a piece of brass money, in value somewhat less than a farthing, Mat.10.9, but here it is taken in general for money: Lu.9.3.
k Ep.6.15. *l* Ac.12.8.

41. *Talitha cumi.* This is the language which our Saviour commonly spoke. It is a mixture of Syriac and Chaldee, called Syro-Chaldaic. The proper translation is given by the evangelist—"Damsel, arise."

43. *Something should be given her to eat.* "He had raised her by *extraordinary* power, but he willed that she should be sustained by *ordinary* means." He also in this gave full evidence that she was really restored to life and health. The changes were great, sudden, and certain. There could be no illusion. So, when the Saviour had risen, he gave evidence of his own resurrection by eating with his disciples, Jn. xxi. 1-13.

CHAPTER VI.

1-6. See this passage explained in the Notes on Mat. xiii. 54-58.

7. *And he called* unto him *the twelve.* See Notes on Mat. x. 1. ¶ *And began to send them forth by two and two.* In order that they might *support* and *encourage* each other in their work. Amid the trials and opposition with which they would meet, mutual counsel and aid would greatly lighten their burdens and alleviate their calamities. Mutual counsel might also contribute to their success, and lead to *united* plans to advance the kingdom of the Redeemer. Jesus here, as in all the work of religion, consulted at the same time the *happiness* and the *usefulness* of his disciples; nor are they ever separated. Whatever contributes to the *usefulness* of his people produces also their happiness; or, in other words, the secret of being happy is to be *useful*.

8-11. See these verses fully explained in the Notes on Mat. x. 9-15. In Mat.

ceive you, nor hear you, when ye depart thence, [m]shake off the dust under your feet for a testimony against them. Verily I say unto you, It shall be more tolerable for Sodom [2]and Gomorrah in the day of judgment than for that city.

12 And they went out, and preached[n] that men should repent.

13 And they [o]cast out many devils, and [p]anointed with oil many that were sick, and healed *them.*

14 And[q] king Herod heard *of him;* (for his name was spread abroad;) and he said, That John the Baptist was risen from the dead, and therefore mighty works do show forth themselves in him.

15 Others[r] said, That it is Elias. And others said, That it is a prophet, or as one of the prophets.

16 But when Herod heard *thereof,* he said, It is John, whom I beheaded: he is risen from the dead.

17 For Herod himself had sent forth, and laid hold upon John, and bound him in prison, for Herodias' sake, his brother Philip's wife: for he had married her.

18 For John had said unto Herod, [s]It is not lawful for thee to have thy brother's wife.

19 Therefore Herodias had [3]a quarrel against him, and would have killed him; but she could not.

20 For [t]Herod feared John, knowing that he was a just man and an holy, and [4]observed him; and when he heard him, he did many things, and heard him gladly.

m Ne.5.13; Ac.13.51. 2 *or.* *n* Lu.24.47; Ac.2.38; 3.19. *o* Lu.10.17. *p* Ja.5.14. *q* Mat.14.1,&c.; Lu.9.7,&c. *r* Mat.16.14; ch.8.28.

s Le.18.16. 3 or, *an inward grudge.* *t* Ex.11.3; Eze.2.5-7. 4 or, *kept him,* or, *saved him.*

---

x. 5 they were commanded not to go among the Gentiles or Samaritans. Mark omits that direction, perhaps, because he was writing for the *Gentiles,* and the direction might create unnecessary difficulty or offence. Perhaps he omits it also because the command was given for a temporary purpose, and was not in force at the time of his writing.

12. *Preached that men should repent.* See the nature of repentance explained in Notes on Mat. iii. 2. They were now called upon to repent and reform their lives because sin was evil, because the Messiah had come to preach forgiveness to the penitent, and because at *his* presence it was fit that the nation should turn from its sins and prepare to receive him.

13. *Cast out many devils.* See Notes on Mat. iv. 24. ¶ *And anointed with oil,* &c. Anointing with oil was in common use among the Jews in cases of sickness. It was supposed to have a mild, soothing, and alleviating effect on the body. In Ja. v. 14, the elders of the church, in connection with prayer, were directed also to anoint the sick with oil. See Notes on that passage. It was also used in wounds. See Notes on Is. i. 6. The good Samaritan poured *oil* and wine into the wounds of the waylaid Jew, Lu. x. 34. Josephus says that in the last sickness of Herod his physicians commanded him to be anointed with oil. It need not be supposed, however, that the apostles used oil for mere *medical* purposes. It was used, probably, like the imposition of hands, or like our Saviour's anointing the eyes of the blind with clay; also as a sign, in expectation of imparting that aid and comfort from God which was sought, and which was *represented* by the soothing and gentle effect of oil.

14–20. See this account of the death of John the Baptist fully explained in the Notes on Mat. xiv. 1–12.

20. *For Herod feared John.* That is, he stood in awe of him on account of his sanctity, and his boldness and fearlessness in reproving sin. ¶ *Knowing that he was a just man and an holy.* A holy, pious, upright, *honest* man—a man who would not be afraid of him, or afraid to speak his real sentiments. ¶ *And observed him*—marg. "*kept him,* or *saved him.*" This does not mean that he "observed" or obeyed his teachings, but that he kept him in safe custody in order to preserve him from the machinations of Herodias. He was willing to show his respect for John, and to secure him from danger, and even to do "many things" which might indicate respect for him—at least, to do

21 And when a convenient day was come, that Herod on [u]his birthday made a supper to his lords, high captains, and chief *estates* of Galilee;

22 And when the daughter of the said Herodias came in, and danced,[v] and pleased Herod and them that sat with him, the king said unto the damsel, Ask of me whatsoever thou wilt, and I will give *it* thee.

23 And he sware unto her, Whatsoever[w] thou shalt ask of me, I will give *it* thee, unto the half of my kingdom.

24 And she went forth, and said unto her mother, What shall I ask? And she said, The head of John the Baptist.

25 And she came in straightway with haste unto the king, and asked, saying, I will that thou give me by and by, in a charger, [x]the head of John the Baptist.

26 And the king was exceeding sorry; *yet* for his oath's sake, and for their sakes which sat with him, he would not reject her.

27 And immediately the king sent [5]an executioner, and commanded his head to be brought; and he went and beheaded him in the prison,

28 And brought his head in a charger, and gave it to the damsel: and the damsel gave it to her mother.

29 And when his disciples heard *of it*, [y]they came and took up his corpse, and laid it in a tomb.

30 And[z] the apostles gathered themselves together unto Jesus, and told him all things, both what they had done, and what they had taught.

31 And he said unto them, Come ye yourselves apart into a desert place and rest a while: for there were many coming and going, and they had no leisure so much as to eat.

32 And they departed into a desert place by ship privately.

u Ge.40.20. *v* Is.3.16. *w* Es.5.3,6; 7.2. *x* Ps.37.12,14.

5 or, *one of his guard*. *y* Ac.8.2. *z* Lu.9.10.

---

so much as to guard him from his enemies. ¶ *And did many things.* But he did not do the thing which was demanded of him—to break off from his sins. He attempted to make a compromise with his conscience. He still loved his sins, and did *other* things which he supposed might be accepted in the place of putting away, as he ought, the wife of his brother—the polluted and adulterous woman with whom he lived. Perhaps he treated John kindly, or spoke well of him, or aided him in his wants, and attempted in this way to silence his rebukes and destroy his faithfulness. This was probably before John was imprisoned. So sinners often treat ministers kindly, and do much to make them comfortable, and hear them gladly, while they are still unwilling to do *the thing* which is demanded of them—to repent and believe the gospel. They expect that their kind attentions will be accepted in the place of what God demands—repentance and the forsaking of their sins.

30. *And the apostles gathered themselves together.* That is, those whom he had sent out two and two, ver. 7. Having travelled around the country, they returned and met the Saviour at Capernaum.

31. *A desert place.* A retired place, across the sea from Capernaum, where they would be free from interruption. ¶ *There were many coming and going.* Coming to be healed and retiring, or coming to hear him preach. It means that they were *thronged*, or that there was a vast multitude attending his preaching.

32–44. See this narrative explained in the Notes on Mat. xiv. 13–21.

32. *By ship.* By a boat or a small vessel. ¶ *Privately.* Without making their plan known. They *intended* to go privately. It appears, however, that their intention became known, and multitudes followed them.

33. *Afoot thither.* On foot to the place where they saw them going. ¶ *Out of all cities.* All cities or large towns in the neighbourhood.

33 And the people saw them departing, and many knew him, and ran afoot thither out of all cities, and outwent them, and came together unto him.

34 And Jesus, when he came out, saw much people, and was moved with compassion toward them, because [a]they were as sheep not having a shepherd: and he began to teach them many things.

35 And[b] when the day was now far spent, his disciples came unto him and said, This is a desert place, and now the time *is* far passed:

36 Send them away, that they may go into the country round about, and into the villages, and buy themselves bread; for they have nothing to eat.

37 He answered and said unto them, Give ye them to eat. And they say unto him, [c]Shall we go and buy two hundred [6]pennyworth of bread, and give them to eat?

38 He saith unto them, How many loaves have ye? go and see. And when they knew, they say, Five, and two fishes.

39 And[d] he commanded them to make all sit down by companies upon the green grass.

40 And they sat down in ranks, by hundreds and by fifties.

41 And when he had taken the five loaves and the two fishes, he looked up to heaven, and [e]blessed and brake the loaves, and gave *them* to his disciples to set before them; and the two fishes divided he among them all.

42 And[f] they did all eat, and were filled.

43 And they took up twelve baskets full of the fragments, and of the fishes.

44 And they that did eat of the loaves were about five thousand men.

45 And[g] straightway he constrained his disciples to get into the ship, and to go to the other side before [7]unto Bethsaida, while he sent away the people.

46 And when he had sent them

a 1 Ki.22.17. *b* Mat.14.15,&c.; Lu.9.12,&c.; Jn.6.5,&c. *c* Nu.11.13,22; 2 Ki.4.43. [6] See on Mat.18.28.

d Mat.15.35; ch.8.6. *e* 1 Sa.9.13; Mat.26.26; Lu.24.30. *f* De.8.3. *g* Mat.14.22,&c.; Jn.6.17,&c. [7] or, *over against Bethsaida.*

34. *Much people—as sheep*, &c. They had no one to teach them and guide them. The priests and scribes were proud and corrupt; they despised the common people and neglected them.

35. *The time* is *far passed.* The day is almost gone. It is drawing near night.

37. *Two hundred pennyworth of bread.* About twenty-eight dollars, or £6. See Notes on Mat. xiv. 16. As the disciples had a common purse in which they carried their little property, consisting of the donations of their friends and money to be given to the poor (comp. Jn. xii. 6; Mat. xxvi. 8, 9; Lu. viii. 3), it is not improbable that they had at this time about this sum in their possession. Philip—for it was he who asked the question (Jn. vi. 7)—asked, with a mixture of wonder and agitation, whether they should take *all* their little property and spend it on a single meal? And even if we should, said he, it would not be sufficient to satisfy such a multitude. It was implied in this that, in *his* view, they could not provide for them if they wished to, and that it would be better to send them away than to attempt it.

40. *In ranks.* Literally, in the form of square beds in a garden. By regularly formed companies. ¶ *By hundreds and by fifties.* Some companies had a hundred in, and some fifty. We need not suppose that these were *exactly* formed or arranged, but that this was *about* the number. The expression indicates a *multitude.* There were so many that they sat down, by *hundreds* and by *fifties*, in separate companies, on the green grass.

43. *Twelve baskets.* Baskets belonging to the disciples, in which they carried their provisions, or, perhaps, belonging to some of the multitude. ¶ *Fragments.* Broken pieces of the bread that remained.

45-56. See this passage explained in the Notes on Mat. xiv. 22-36.

away, [h]he departed into a mountain to pray.

47 And when even was come, the ship was in the midst of the sea, and he alone on the land.

48 And he saw them [i]toiling in rowing; for the wind was contrary unto them: and about the fourth watch of the night he cometh unto them, walking upon the sea, and [k]would have passed by them.

49 But when they saw him walking[l] upon the sea, [m]they supposed it had been a spirit, and cried out:

50 (For they all saw him, and were troubled:) and immediately he talked with them, and saith unto them, [n]Be of good cheer: it is I; be not afraid.

51 And he went up unto them into the ship; and [o]the wind ceased; and they were sore amazed in themselves beyond measure, and wondered.

52 For they considered not *the miracle* of the loaves; for [p]their heart was hardened.

53 And[q] when they had passed over, they came into the land of Gennesaret, and drew to the shore.

54 And when they were come out of the ship, straightway they knew him,

55 And[r] ran through that whole region round about, and began to carry about in beds those that were sick, where they heard he was.

56 And whithersoever he entered, into villages, or cities, or country, they laid the sick in the streets, and besought him that they might [s]touch if it were but the [t]border of his garment: and as many as touched [8]him were made whole.

CHAPTER VII.

THEN[a] came together unto him the Pharisees, and certain of the scribes, which came from Jerusalem.

2 And when they saw some of his disciples eat bread with [1]defiled (that is to say, with unwashen) hands, they found fault.

3 For the Pharisees, and all the

h Mat.6.6; ch.1.35; Lu.6.12. *i* Jonah 1.13. *k* Lu.24.28. *l* Job 9.8. *m* Lu.24.37. *n* Is.43.2. *o* Ps.93.3,4. *p* Is.63.17.

q Mat.14.34. *r* Mat.4.24; ch.2.1-3. *s* Mat.9.20; ch.5.27,28; Ac.19.12. *t* Nu.15.38,39. [8] or, *it*. *a* Mat.15.1,&c. [1] or, *common*.

52. *They considered not* the miracle *of the loaves.* They did not remember or call to mind the *power* which Jesus had shown in feeding the five thousand by a miracle, and that, having done that, he had power also to save them from the storm. ¶ *Their heart was hardened.* Their *mind* was dull to perceive it. This does not mean that they were *opposed* to Jesus, or that they had what we denominate *hardness of heart*, but simply that they were slow to perceive his power. They did not quickly learn, as they ought to have done, that he had *all* power, and could therefore allay the storm. The word *heart* is frequently used in this sense. See Ep. i. 18, in Greek; Ro. i. 21; ii. 15; 2 Co. iv. 6.

54. *They knew him.* They *recollected* him, for he had been there before and worked miracles.

56. *The border of his garment.* Comp. Notes on Mat. ix. 20.

CHAPTER VII.

1–23. See this passage explained in the Notes on Mat. xv. 1–20.

1. *Came from Jerusalem.* Probably to observe his conduct, and to find matter of accusation against him.

2. *Defiled hands.* The hands were considered defiled or polluted unless they were washed previous to every meal.

3. *Except they wash their hands oft.* Our word *oft* means frequently, often. The Greek word translated *oft* has been rendered various ways. Some have said that it means "*up to the wrist*"—unless they wash their hands up to the wrist. Others have said "up to the elbow." There is evidence that the Pharisees had some such foolish rule as this about washing, and it is likely that they practised it faithfully. But the Greek word πυγμῇ—*pugmē*—means properly the *fist*, and the meaning here

Jews, except they wash *their* hands
oft,[2] eat not, holding the [b]tradition
of the elders.
4 And *when they come* from the
market, except they [c]wash, they
eat not. And many other things
there be which they have received
to hold, *as* the washing of cups,
and [3]pots, brazen vessels, and of
tables.[4]
5 Then the Pharisees and scribes
asked him, Why walk not thy disciples according to the tradition
of the elders, but eat bread with
unwashen hands?

2 or, *diligently:* Gr. *with the fist:* Theophylact, *up to the elbow.*
b Ga.1.14; Col.2.8,22,23. *c* Job 9.30,31.
3 Sextarius is about a pint and a half. 4 or, *beds.*

6 He answered and said unto
them, Well hath [d]Esaias prophesied
of you hypocrites, as it is written,
This people honoureth me with
their lips, but their heart is far
from me.
7 Howbeit, in vain do they
worship me, teaching *for* doctrines
the commandments of men.
8 For [e]laying aside the commandment of God, ye hold the
tradition of men, *as* the washing
of pots and cups: and many other
such like things ye do.
9 And he said unto them, Full

d Is.29.13. *e* Is.1.12.

is, "Unless they wash their hands (rubbing them) *with the fist*"—that is, not merely dipping the finger or hands in water as a sign of ablution, but rubbing the hands together as a ball or fist, in the usual Oriental manner when water is poured over them. Hence the phrase comes to mean *diligently, carefully, sedulously.*—Robinson, *Lex.* The idea is, unless they pay the utmost attention to it, and do it carefully and according to rule. ¶ *The tradition.* What had been handed down; not what was delivered *by writing* in the law of Moses, but what had been communicated from father to son as being proper and binding. ¶ *The elders.* The ancients; not the old men *then living,* but those who had lived formerly.

4. *Market.* This word means either the place where provisions were sold, or the place where men were convened for any purpose. Here it probably means the former. ¶ *Except they wash.* In the original, "Except they *baptize.*" In this place it does not mean to immerse the whole body, but the hands only. There is no evidence that the Jews washed their *whole bodies* every time they came from market. It is probable that they often washed with the use of a very small quantity of water. ¶ *The washing of cups.* In the Greek, the *baptism of cups.* ¶ *Cups.* Drinking vessels. Those used at their meals. ¶ *Pots.* Measures of *liquids.* Vessels made of wood, used to hold wine, vinegar, &c. ¶ *Brazen vessels.* Vessels made of brass, used in cooking or otherwise. These, if much polluted, were commonly passed through the fire; if slightly polluted they were washed. Earthen vessels, if defiled, were usually broken. ¶ *Tables.* This word means, in the original, *beds* or *couches.* It refers not to the *tables* on which they ate, but to the *couches* on which they reclined at their meals. See Notes on Mat. xxiii. 6. These were supposed to be defiled when any unclean or polluted person had reclined on them, and they deemed it necessary to purify them with water. The word *baptism* is here used—in the original, *the baptism of tables;* but as it cannot be supposed that *couches* were entirely *immersed* in water, the word *baptism* here must denote some other application of water, by sprinkling or otherwise, and shows that the term is used in the sense of washing in any way. If the word is used *here,* as is clear it is, to denote anything except entire immersion, it may be elsewhere, and baptism is lawfully performed, therefore, without immersing the whole body in water.

7. For *doctrines.* For commands of God binding on the conscience. Imposing *your* traditions as equal in authority to the laws of God.

8. *Laying aside.* Rejecting, or making it give place to traditions; considering the traditions as superior in authority to the divine law. This was the uniform doctrine of the Pharisees. See Notes on Mat. xv. 1–9. ¶ *The tradition of men.* What has been handed down by men, or what rests solely on their authority.

9. *Full well.* These words are capable of different interpretations. Some read them as a question: "Do ye do *well* in

well ye [5]reject the commandment of God, that ye may keep your own tradition.

10 For Moses said, [f]Honour thy father and thy mother; and, Whoso[g] curseth father or mother, let him die the death.

11 But ye say, If a man shall say to his father or mother, *It is* Corban,[h] that is to say, a gift, by whatsoever thou mightest be profited by me, *he shall be free.*

12 And ye suffer him no more to do aught for his father or his mother;

13 Making the word of God of none effect through your tradition, which ye have delivered: and many such like things do ye.

14 And when he had called all the people *unto him,* he said unto them, [i]Hearken unto me every one *of you,* and understand:

15 There is nothing from without a man that, entering into him, can defile him; but the things which come out of him, those are they that defile the man.

16 If[k] any man have ears to hear, let him hear.

17 And[l] when he was entered into the house from the people, his disciples asked him concerning the parable.

18 And he saith unto them, Are ye so without understanding also? Do ye not perceive, that whatsoever thing from without entereth into the man, *it* cannot defile him;

19 Because it entereth not into

5 or, *frustrate,* ver.13. *f* Ex.20.12; De.5.16. *g* Ex.21.17; Le.20.9; Pr.20.20. *h* Mat.15.5; 23.18.

i Pr.8.5; Is.6.9; Ac.8.30. *k* Mat.11.15. *l* Mat.15.15,&c.

rejecting?" &c. Others suppose they mean *skilfully, cunningly.* "You show great cunning, or art, in laying aside God's commands and substituting in their place those of men." Others suppose them to be ironical. "How nobly you act! From conscientious attachment to your traditions you have made void the law of God;" meaning to intimate by it that they had acted wickedly and basely.

17. *The parable.* The *obscure* and difficult remarks which he had made in ver. 15. The word *parable,* here, means *obscure* and *difficult saying.* They could not understand it. They had probably imbibed many of the popular notions of the Pharisees, and they could not understand why a man was not defiled by external things. It was, moreover, a doctrine of the law that men were ceremonially polluted by contact with dead bodies, &c., and they could not understand how it could be otherwise.

18. *Cannot defile him.* Cannot render his *soul* polluted; cannot make him a *sinner* so as to need this purifying as a *religious* observance.

19. *Entereth not into his heart.* Does not reach or affect the *mind,* the *soul,* and consequently cannot pollute it. Even if it should affect the *body,* yet it cannot the *soul,* and consequently cannot need to be cleansed by a religious ordinance. The notions of the Pharisees, therefore, are not founded in *reason,* but are mere *superstition.* ¶ *The draught.* The sink, the vault. ¶ *Purging all meats.* The word *purging,* here, means to purify, to cleanse. What is thrown out of the body is the innutritious part of the food taken into the stomach, and leaving only that which is proper for the support of life; and it cannot, therefore, defile the soul. ¶ *All meats.* All food; all that is taken into the body to support life. The meaning is, that the economy or process by which life is supported *purifies* or *renders nutritious* all kinds of food. The unwholesome or innutritious parts are separated, and the wholesome only are taken into the system. This agrees with all that has since been discovered of the process of digestion and of the support of life. The food taken into the stomach is by the gastric juice converted into a thick pulp called chyme. The nutritious part of this is conveyed into small vessels, and changed into a milky substance called *chyle.* This is poured by the thoracic duct into the left subclavian vein, and mingles with the blood, and conveys nutriment and support to all parts of the system. The useless parts of the food are thrown off.

20. *That which cometh out of the man.* His words; the expression of his thoughts and feelings; his conduct, as the development of inward malice, anger,

his heart, but [m]into the belly, and
goeth out into the draught, purging all meats?
20 And he said, That which
cometh out of the man, that defileth the man.
21 For[n] from within, out of the
heart of men, proceed evil thoughts,
adulteries, fornications, murders,
22 Thefts, [6]covetousness, wickedness, deceit, lasciviousness, an evil
eye, blasphemy, pride, foolishness:
23 All these evil things come
from within, and defile the man.
24 And[o] from thence he arose,
and went into the borders of Tyre
and Sidon, and entered into an
house, and would have no man
know *it:* but [p]he could not be hid.
25 For a *certain* woman, whose
young daughter had an unclean
spirit, heard of him, and came and
fell at his feet:
26 The woman was a [7]Greek, a
Syrophenician by nation: and she
besought him that he would cast
forth the devil out of her daughter.

m 1 Co.6.13. *n* Ge.6.5; Ps.14.1,3; 53.1,3; Je.17.9. 6 *covetousnesses, wickednesses.* *o* Mat.15.21,&c. *p* ch.2.1. 7 or, *Gentile,* Is.49.12.

27 But Jesus said unto her, Let
the children first be filled: for [q]it
is not meet to take the children's
bread, and to cast *it* unto the dogs.
28 And she answered and said
unto him, Yes, Lord; yet [r]the dogs
under the table eat of the children's crumbs.
29 And he said unto her, [s]For
this saying go thy way; the devil
is gone out of thy daughter.
30 And when she was come to
her house, she found [t]the devil
gone out, and her daughter laid
upon the bed.
31 And[u] again, departing from
the coasts of Tyre and Sidon, he
came unto the sea of Galilee,
through the midst of the coasts
of Decapolis.
32 And they bring unto him one
that was deaf, and had an impediment in his speech; and they beseech him to put his hand upon
him.
33 And he took him aside from
the multitude, and put his fingers

q Mat.7.6; 10.5,6. *r* Ro.15.8,9; Ep.2.12-14. *s* Is.66.2. *t* 1 Jn.3.8. *u* Mat.15.29,&c.

---

covetousness, lust, &c. ¶ *Defileth the man.* Makes him *really* polluted or offensive in the sight of God. This renders the soul corrupt and abominable in his sight. See Mat. xv. 18–20.

24–30. See this miracle explained in the Notes on Mat. xv. 21–28.

24. *Would have no man know* it. To avoid the designs of the Pharisees he wished to be retired.

26. *A Greek.* The Jews called all persons *Greeks* who were not of their nation. Comp. Ro. i. 14. The whole world was considered as divided into Jews and Greeks. Though she might not have been strictly a *Greek*, yet she came under this general appellation as a foreigner.

31. *Departing from the coasts.* The country or regions of Tyre. ¶ *Came unto the sea of Galilee.* The Sea of Tiberias. See Notes on Mat. iv. 18. ¶ *Decapolis.* See Notes on Mat. iv. 25. He did not go immediately into Capernaum, or any city where he was known, but into the retired regions around the Sea of Galilee. This was done to avoid the designs of the Pharisees, who sought his life.

32. *They bring.* That is, his friends brought, or the people brought. ¶ *One that was deaf, and had an impediment in his speech.* Not entirely dumb, but who spoke indistinctly or with difficulty. His deafness might not have been of long standing, and his speech, therefore, not entirely ruined. ¶ *To put his hand upon him.* That is, to cure him. Blessings were commonly imparted by laying on the hands.

33. *And he took him aside from the multitude.* Why this was done we have no means of information. It might have been to conceal from the multitude everything respecting the *manner* of cure, in order that none might attempt to cure in a similar way. ¶ *And he put his fingers into his ears,* &c. Why this was done it has been found exceedingly difficult to explain. Jesus had power at once to open his ears and loose his tongue, but for some cause he

into his ears, and [u]he spit, and touched his tongue;

34 And [v]looking up to heaven, he [w]sighed, and saith unto him, Ephphatha, that is, Be opened.

35 And[x] straightway his ears were opened, and the string of his tongue was loosed, and he spake plain.

36 And he charged them that they should tell no man: but the more he charged them, so much the more a great deal they published *it;*

37 And were beyond measure astonished, saying, [y]He hath done all things well: [z]he maketh both the deaf to hear and the dumb to speak.

CHAPTER VIII.

IN[a] those days, the multitude being very great, and having nothing to eat, Jesus called his disciples *unto him,* and saith unto them,

2 I have [b]compassion on the multitude, because they have now been with me three days, and have nothing to eat:

3 And if I send them away fasting to their own houses, they will faint by the way: for divers of them came from far.

4 And his disciples answered him, [c]From whence can a man satisfy these *men* with bread here in the wilderness?

5 And he asked them, How many loaves have ye? And they said, Seven.

6 And he commanded the people to sit down on the ground: and he took the seven loaves, and gave thanks, and brake, and gave to his disciples to set before *them;* and they did set *them* before the people.

7 And they had a few small fishes: and [d]he blessed, and commanded to set them also before *them.*

8 So they did eat, and [e]were filled: and [f]they took up of the broken *meat* that was left seven baskets.

9 And they that had eaten were

u ch.8.23; Jn.9.6. *v* ch.6.41; Jn.11.41; 17.1. *w* Jn.11.33,38. *x* Is.35.5,6; Mat.11.5. *y* Ps.139.14; Ac.14.11. *z* Ex.4.10,11. *a* Mat.15.32,&c. *b* Ps.145.8,15; He.5.2.

c ch.6.36,37,&c. *d* Mat.14.19. *e* Ps.107.5,6; 145.16. *f* 1 Ki.17.14-16; 2 Ki.4.2-7,42-44.

---

chose to accompany it with a sign. This was intended, probably, simply to denote that the power of healing came from him; to satisfy the man by the touch that he had this power, and that it could come from no other quarter. Our Saviour often used signs in this way to denote his power to heal. See Mar. viii. 23; Jn. ix. 6.

34. *Looked up to heaven.* To lift up the eyes to heaven is an act imploring aid from God, and is an attitude of prayer, Ps. cxxi. 1, 2; Mar. vi. 41; Jn. xi. 41. ¶ *He sighed.* Pitying the sufferings of the man who stood before him. ¶ *Ephphatha.* This word is *Syriac,* the language which our Lord used in addressing the man, and means "Be opened."

35. *The string of his tongue was loosed.* The difficulty in his speaking was removed.

36. *Tell no man.* Do not noise it abroad. He was not ambitious of being known, and he knew that if much was said of his cures, it would excite the jealousy of the Pharisees and endanger his life.

37. *Beyond measure.* Exceedingly; very much. In the Greek, "Very abundantly." ¶ *He hath done all things well.* All things in a remarkable manner; or, he has perfectly effected the cure of the deaf and the dumb.

CHAPTER VIII.

1–9. See this passage explained in the Notes on Mat. xv. 32–39.

1. *In those days.* While in the wilderness, where he had cured the deaf and dumb man. ¶ *Having nothing to eat.* Having come unprovided, or having consumed what they had brought.

2. *I have compassion.* I pity their condition. I am disposed to relieve them.

9. *Four thousand.* Four thousand *men,* besides women and children. See Mat. xv. 38.

about four thousand; and he sent them away.

10 And[g] straightway he entered into a ship with his disciples, and came into the parts of Dalmanutha.

11 And[h] the Pharisees came forth, and began to question with him, seeking of him a sign from heaven, tempting him.

12 And he sighed deeply in his spirit, and saith, Why doth this generation seek after a sign? Verily I say unto you, There shall no sign be given unto this generation.

13 And he left them, and, entering into the ship again, departed to the other side.

14 Now *the disciples* had forgotten to take bread, neither had they in the ship with them more than one loaf.

15 And he charged them, saying, Take heed, [i]beware of the leaven[k] of the Pharisees, and *of* the leaven of Herod.

16 And they reasoned among themselves, saying, *It is* because we have no bread.

17 And when Jesus knew *it*, he saith unto them, Why reason ye, because ye have no bread? [l]perceive ye not yet, neither understand? have ye your [m]heart yet hardened?

18 Having[n] eyes, see ye not? and having ears, hear ye not? and [o]do ye not remember?

19 When I brake the [p]five loaves among five thousand, how many baskets full of fragments took ye up? They say unto him, Twelve.

20 And when the [q]seven among four thousand, how many baskets full of fragments took ye up? And they said, Seven.

21 And he said unto them, How is it that ye do not understand?

22 And he cometh to Bethsaida; and they bring a blind man unto him, and besought him to [r]touch him.

23 And he took the blind man by the hand, and led him out of

g Mat.15.39. h Mat.12.38; 16.1,&c.; Jn 6.30. i Pr.19.27; Lu.12.1. k Ex.12.20; Le.2.11; 1 Co.5.6-8.

l ch.6 52. m ch.3.5; 16.14. n Is.44.18. o 2 Pe.1.12. p ch.6.38,44; Mat.14.17-21; Lu.9.12-17; Jn 6.5-13. q ver.1-9; Mat.15.34-38. r Mat.8.3,15.

10. *Dalmanutha.* In Mat. xv. 39 it is said that he came into the coasts of *Magdala.* See Note on the place.

11–21. See this passage explained in Mat. xvi. 1–12.

12. *Sighed deeply in his spirit.* His heart was deeply affected at their wickedness and hypocrisy. The word *spirit* here is taken as the seat of the emotions, passions, affections. He drew groans deeply from his breast. ¶ *No sign be given.* That is, no such sign as they asked, to wit, a sign *from heaven.* He said a sign should be given, the same as was furnished by Jonas, Mat. xvi. 4. But this was not what they *asked*, nor would it be given *because* they asked it.

15. *Beware of the leaven of the Pharisees.* See Mat. xvi. 6. ¶ *Of Herod.* Of the Herodians—of Herod and his followers. Matthew, instead of "Herod," has "the Sadducees." It is not improbable that he cautioned them against them all. The Pharisees sought his life, and were exceedingly corrupt in their doctrine and practice; the Sadducees denied some of the essential doctrines of religion, and the Herodians probably were distinguished for irreligion, sensuality, and corrupt living. They were united, therefore, with the Pharisees and Sadducees in opposing the claims of Jesus. Matthew has recorded his caution to avoid the Pharisees and Sadducees, and Mark has added, what Matthew had omitted, the caution likewise to beware of the Herodians. Thus the evangelists speak the same thing.

22. *To Bethsaida.* See Notes on Mat. xi. 21. ¶ *And they bring a blind man unto him.* The healing of the blind man of Bethsaida is recorded only by Mark. ¶ *Besought him to touch him.* That is, to *heal* him, for they believed that his touch would restore his sight.

23. *Led him out of the town.* Why this was done the sacred writers have not told us. It *might* have been to avoid the collecting of a multitude, and thus to have escaped the designs

the town; and when he had [s]spit
on his eyes, and put his hands
upon him, he asked him if he saw
aught.
24 And he looked up, and said,
I[t] see men, as trees, walking.
25 After that, he put *his* hands
again upon his eyes, and made him
look up: and he was restored, [u]and
saw every man clearly.
26 And he sent him away to his
house, saying, Neither go into the
town, nor tell *it* to any in the town.
27 And[v] Jesus went out, and his
disciples, into the towns of Cesarea
Philippi: and by the way he asked
his disciples, saying unto them,
Whom do men say that I am?
28 And they answered, [w]John
the Baptist: but some *say* Elias;
and others, One of the prophets.
29 And he saith unto them, But
whom say ye that I am? And
Peter answereth and saith unto
him, [x]Thou art the Christ.
30 And he charged them that
they should tell no man.
31 And he began to teach them,

s ch.7.33. *t* Ju.9.36; Is.29.18; 1 Co.13.11,12. *u* Pr.4.18; Is.32.3; 1 Pe.2.9. *v* Mat.16.13,&c.; Lu.9.18,&c.
w Mat.14.2. *x* Jn.1.41-49; 6.69; 11.27; Ac.8.37; 1 Jn.5.1.

of the Pharisees' who were attempting to take his life, and chiefly on a charge of sedition and of exciting the people. On this account Jesus chose to perform the miracle alone, thus showing that while he did good, he desired to do it in such a way as to avoid the *appearance* of evil, and to prevent, at the same time, ostentation and the malice of his enemies. ¶ *Spit on his eyes.* Why this was done is not known. It was evidently not intended to perform the cure by any natural effect of the spittle. It was to the man a *sign*, an evidence that it was the power of Jesus. The eyes were probably closed. They were perhaps "gummed" or united together by a secretion that had become hard. To apply spittle to them—to wet them—would be a *sign*, a natural expression of removing the obstruction and opening them. The power was not in the spittle, but it attended the application of it. ¶ *Saw aught.* Saw anything.

24. *I see men, as trees, walking.* I see men walking, but see them so indistinctly that, but for their *motion*, I could not distinguish them from trees. I cannot distinctly see their shapes and features. Probably our Lord did not *at once* restore him fully to sight, that he might strengthen his faith. Seeing that Jesus had *partially* restored him, it was evidence that he could *wholly*, and it led him to exercise faith anew in him, and to feel more strikingly his dependence on him.

25. *Every man clearly.* Could see their form and features. His sight was completely restored. Though our Lord did not by this, probably, *intend* to teach any lesson in regard to the way in which the mind of a sinner is enlightened, yet it affords a striking illustration of it. Sinners are by nature blind, 2 Co. iv. 4; 1 Jn. ii. 11; Jn. ix. 39. The effect of religion, or of the influence of the Holy Spirit, is to open the eyes, to show the sinner his condition and his danger, and to lead him to *look* on him as a Saviour. Yet at first he sees indistinctly. He does not soon learn to distinguish objects. When converted he is in a new world. Light is shed on every object, and he sees the Scriptures, the Saviour, and the works of creation, the sun, the stars, the hills, the vales, in a new light. He sees the beauty of the plan of salvation, and wonders that he has not seen it before. Yet he sees at first indistinctly. It is only by repeated applications to the Source of light that he sees all things clearly. At first religion appears full of mysteries. Doctrines and facts are brought before his mind that he cannot fully comprehend. He is still perplexed, and he may doubt whether he has ever seen anything aright, or has been ever renewed. Yet let him not despair. Light, in due time, will be shed on these obscure and mysterious truths. Faithful and repeated application to the Father of lights in prayer, and in searching the Scriptures, and in the ordinances of religion, will dissipate these doubts, and he will see all things clearly, and the universe will appear to be filled with one broad flood of light.

26. *The town.* The town of Bethsaida. ¶ *Nor tell* it, &c. Lest it excite the

that the Son of man must suffer
many things; and be rejected of
the elders, and *of* the chief priests
and scribes, and be killed; and
after three days rise again.
32 And he spake that saying
openly. And Peter took him, and
began to rebuke him.
33 But when he had turned
about, and looked on his disciples,
he [y]rebuked Peter, saying, Get
thee behind me, [z]Satan; for thou
savourest not the things that be
of God, but the things that be
of men.
34 And when he had called the
people *unto him*, with his disciples
also, he said unto them, [a]Whoso-
ever will come after me, let him
deny himself, and take up his cross,
and follow me.
35 For [b]whosoever will save his
life shall lose it; but whosoever
shall lose his life for my sake or
the gospel's, the same shall save it.
36 For what shall it profit a man
if he shall gain the whole world
and lose his own soul?
37 Or what shall a man give in
exchange for his soul?
38 Whosoever,[a] therefore, shall
be ashamed of me, and of my
words, in this adulterous and sinful generation, of him also shall
the Son of man be ashamed, when
he cometh in the glory of his
Father, with the holy angels.

CHAPTER IX.

AND he said unto them, [b]Verily
I say unto you, that there be
some of them that stand here
which shall not [c]taste of death till
they have seen the kingdom of
God come with power.
2 And[d] after six days Jesus taketh
with him Peter, and James, and
John, and leadeth them up into
an high mountain apart by themselves: and he was transfigured
before them.
3 And his raiment became shining, exceeding [e]white as snow;
so as no fuller on earth can white
them.
4 And there appeared unto them

y Re.3.19. *z* 1 Co.5.5.
a Mat.10.38; 16.24; Lu.9.23; 14.27; Tit.2.12.
b Es.4.14; Mat.10.39; 16.25; Lu.9.24; 17.33; Jn.12.25; 2 Ti.2.11; 4.6,8; Re.2.10; 7.14-17.

a Lu.12.9; 2 Ti.1.8.
b Mat.16.28; Lu.9.27. *c* Jn.8.52; He.2.9.
d Mat.17.1,&c.; Lu.9.28,&c. *e* Da.7.9; Mat.28.3.

jealousy of the Pharisees, and produce commotion and danger.

27-38. See this passage illustrated in the Notes on Mat. xvi. 13-28.

32. *He spake that saying openly.* With boldness or confidence, or without parables or figures, so that there could be no possibility of misunderstanding him.

38. *Ashamed of me.* Ashamed to own attachment to me on account of my lowly appearance and my poverty. ¶ *And of my words.* My doctrines, my instructions. ¶ *This adulterous and sinful generation.* This age given to wickedness, particularly to adultery. ¶ *In the glory of his Father.* In the day of judgment. See Notes on Mat. xxvi. 64. The meaning of this verse is, Whosoever shall refuse, through pride or wickedness, to acknowledge and serve Christ here, shall be excluded from his kingdom hereafter. He was lowly, meek, and despised; yet there was an inimitable beauty in his character even then. But he will come again in awful grandeur; not as the babe of Bethlehem, not as the man of Nazareth, but as the Son of God, in majesty and glory. They that would not acknowledge him *here* must be rejected by him *there;* they that would not serve him on earth will not enjoy his favour in heaven; they that would cast *him* out and despise him must be cast out *by* him, and consigned to eternal, hopeless sorrow.

CHAPTER IX.

1. *Verily I say,* &c. See Notes on Mat. xvi. 28. This verse properly belongs to the preceding chapter and the preceding discourse.

2-10. *And after six days,* &c. See this passage explained in the Notes on Mat. xvii. 1-9.

3. *No fuller.* Rather, no *scourer.* The office of the person here mentioned was to *scour* or *whiten* cloth; not to *full* it, or to render it thicker.

Elias, with Moses; and they were talking with Jesus.

5 And Peter answered and said to Jesus, Master, it is [e]good for us to be here: and let us make three tabernacles; one for thee, and one for Moses, and one for Elias.

6 For he [f]wist not what to say; for they were sore afraid.

7 And there was a cloud that overshadowed them; and a voice came out of the cloud, saying, This[g] is my beloved Son; [h]hear him.

8 And suddenly, when they had looked round about, they saw no man any more, save Jesus only with themselves.

9 And as they came down from the mountain, he charged them that they should tell no man what things they had seen till the Son of man were risen from the dead.

10 And they kept that saying with themselves, questioning one with another [i]what the rising from the dead should mean.

11 And they asked him, saying, Why say the scribes that [k]Elias must first come?

12 And he answered and told them, Elias verily cometh first, and restoreth all things; and how it is [l]written of the Son of man that he must suffer many things, and [m]be set at nought.

13 But I say unto you, [n]That Elias is indeed come, and they have done unto him whatsoever they listed, as it is written of him.

14 And when he came to *his* disciples, he saw a great multitude about them, and the scribes questioning with them.

15 And straightway all the people, when they beheld him, were greatly amazed; and running to *him*, saluted him.

16 And he asked the scribes, What question ye [1]with them?

17 And one of the multitude answered and said, Master, I have brought unto thee my son, which hath a [o]dumb spirit:

18 And wheresoever he taketh him, he [2]teareth him; and he [p]foameth, and gnasheth with his teeth, and pineth away: and I spake to thy disciples, that they should cast him out; and they could not.

19 He answereth him, and saith,

e Ps.63.2; 84.10. *f* Da.10.15; Re.1.17. *g* Ps.2.7; Mat.3.17; 2 Pe.1.17. *h* De.18.15. *i* Ac.17.18. *k* Mal.4.5.

l Ps.22.; Is.53.; Da.9.26; Zec.13.7. *m* Ps.74.22; Lu.23.11; Phi.2.7. *n* Mat.11.14; Lu.1.17. 1 or, *among yourselves*. *o* Mat.12.22; Lu.11.14. 2 or, *dasheth him*. *p* Jude 13.

6. *He wist not.* He *knew* not. He was desirous of saying something, and he knew not what would be proper.

11–13. *Why say the scribes,* &c. See Notes on Mat. xvii. 10–13.

14–29. See this passage explained in the Notes on Mat. xvii. 14–21.

14. *Questioning with them.* Debating with the disciples, and attempting to confound them. This he saw as he came down from the mount. In his absence they had taken occasion to attempt to perplex and confound his followers.

15. *Were greatly amazed.* Were astonished and surprised at his sudden appearance among them. ¶ *Saluted him.* Received him with the customary marks of affection and respect. It is probable that this was not by any *formal* manner of salutation, but by the *rush* of the multitude, and by hailing him as the Messiah.

16. *What question ye?* What is the subject of your inquiry or debate with the disciples?

17. *A dumb spirit.* A spirit which deprived his son of the power of speaking.

18. *And wheresoever.* In whatever place —at home or abroad, alone or in public. ¶ *He teareth him.* He rends, distracts, or throws him into convulsions. ¶ *He foameth.* At the mouth, like a mad animal. Among us these would all be considered as marks of violent derangement or madness. ¶ *And pineth away.* Becomes thin, haggard, and emaciated. This was the effect of the violence of his struggles, and perhaps of the want of food.

O [q]faithless generation! how long shall I be with you? how long shall I suffer you? Bring him unto me.

20 And they brought him unto him: and when he saw him, straightway the spirit tare him; and he fell on the ground, and wallowed foaming.

21 And he asked his father, How long is it ago since this came unto him? And he said, [r]Of a child:

22 And ofttimes it hath cast him into the fire, and into the waters, to destroy him; but if thou canst do any thing, have compassion on us and help us.

23 Jesus said unto him, [s]If thou canst believe, all things *are* possible to him that believeth.

24 And straightway the father of the child cried out, and said [t]with tears, Lord, I believe; [u]help thou mine unbelief.

25 When Jesus saw that the people came running together, he rebuked the foul spirit, saying unto him, *Thou* dumb and deaf spirit, I charge thee, come out of him, and enter no more into him.

26 And *the spirit* cried, and [v]rent him sore, and came out of him; and he was as one dead, insomuch that many said, He is dead.

27 But Jesus [w]took him by the hand, and lifted him up, and he arose.

28 And when he was come into the house, his disciples asked him privately, Why could not we cast him out?

29 And he said unto them, This

q De.32.20; Ps.78.8; He.3.10. *r* Job 5.7; Ps.51.5. *s* 2 Ch.20.20; Mat.17.20; ch.11.23; Lu.17.6; Jn.11.40; He.11.6.

t Ps.126.5. *u* He.12.2. *v* Re.12.12. *w* Is.41.13.

---

22. *If thou canst do any thing.* I have brought him to the disciples, and they could not help him. If THOU canst do anything, have compassion.

23. *If thou canst believe.* This was an answer to the request, and there was a reference in the answer to the *doubt* in the man's mind about the power of Jesus. *I* can help him. If THOU *canst believe*, it shall be done. Jesus here demanded *faith* or confidence in his power of healing. His design here is to show the man that the difficulty in the case was not in the want of *power* on his part, but in the want of *faith* in the man; in other words, to rebuke him for having *doubted* at all whether he *could* heal him. So he demands faith of every sinner that comes to him, and none that come without *confidence* in him can obtain the blessing. ¶ *All things* are *possible to him that believeth.* All things can be effected or accomplished—to wit, by God—in favour of him that believes, and if thou canst believe, this will be done. God will do nothing in our favour without faith. It is right that we should have confidence in him; and if we *have* confidence, it is easy for him to help us, and he willingly does it. In our weakness, then, we should go to God our Saviour; and though we have no strength, yet *he* can aid us, and he will make all things easy for us.

24. *Said with tears.* The man felt the implied rebuke in the Saviour's language; and feeling grieved that he should be thought to be destitute of faith, and feeling deeply for the welfare of his afflicted son, he wept. Nothing can be more touching or natural than this. An anxious father, distressed at the condition of his son, having applied to the disciples in vain, now coming to the Saviour; and not having full confidence that he had the proper qualification to be aided, he wept. Any man would have wept in his condition, nor would the Saviour turn the weeping suppliant away. ¶ *I believe.* I have faith. I do put confidence in thee, though I know that my faith is not as strong as it should be. ¶ *Lord.* This word here signifies merely *master*, or *sir*, as it does often in the New Testament. We have no evidence that he had any knowledge of the divine nature of the Saviour, and he applied the word, probably, as he would have done to any other teacher or worker of miracles. ¶ *Help thou mine unbelief.* Supply thou the defects of my faith. Give me strength and grace to put *entire* confidence in thee. Everyone who comes to the Saviour for help has need of offering this prayer. In our unbelief

kind can come forth by nothing
but by [x]prayer and [y]fasting.
30 And they departed thence,
and passed through Galilee; and
he would not that any man should
know *it*.
31 For he taught his disciples,
and said unto them, The Son of
man is delivered into the hands of
men, and they shall kill him; and
after that he is killed, he shall rise
the third day.
32 But they understood not that
saying, and were afraid to [z]ask
him.
33 And[a] he came to Capernaum:
and being in the house, he asked
them, What was it that ye disputed
among yourselves by the way?
34 But they held their peace:
for by the way they had disputed
among themselves who *should be*
the greatest.
35 And he sat down, and called
the twelve, and saith unto them,
[b]If any man desire to be first, *the*
same shall be last of all, and servant of all.
36 And he took a child, and set
him in the midst of them: and
when he had taken him in his
arms, he said unto them,
37 Whosoever[c] shall receive one
of such children in my name, receiveth me; and whosoever shall
receive me, receiveth not me, but
him that sent me.
38 And John answered him, saying, [d]Master, we saw one casting
out devils in thy name, and he
followeth not us; and we forbad
him, because he followeth not us.
39 But Jesus said, Forbid him
not; [e]for there is no man which
shall do a miracle in my name
that can lightly speak evil of me.
40 For[f] he that is not against us
is on our part.

x Ep.6.18. *y* 1 Co.9.27. *z* Jn.16.19. *a* Mat.18.1,&c.; Lu.9.46,&c.; 22.24,&c.
b Mat.20.26,27; ch.10.43. *c* Lu.9.48. *d* Nu.11.26-28. *e* 1 Co.12.3. *f* Mat.12.30.

---

and our doubts we need his aid, nor shall we ever put sufficient reliance on him without his gracious help.

30–33. See Notes on Mat. xvii. 22, 23.

31. *Is delivered.* Is given to men to make an atonement by his sufferings and death, and will in due time be taken and killed.

33–37. See Notes on Mat. xviii. 1–5.

38. *We saw one*, &c. There is no improbability in supposing that this might have been one of the disciples of John, or one of the seventy whom Jesus had sent out, and who, though he did not *personally* attend on Jesus, yet had the power of working miracles. There is no evidence that he was merely an *exorcist*, or that he used the name of Jesus merely as a pretence.

39. *Forbid him not.* Do not prevent his doing good. If he can work a miracle in my name, it is sufficient proof of attachment to me, and he should not be prevented. ¶ *Can lightly speak evil of me.* The word here rendered *lightly* means *quickly* or *immediately*. The meaning of the passage is, that he to whom God gave the power of working a miracle, by that gave evidence that he could not be found among the enemies of Jesus. He ought not, therefore, to be prevented from doing it. There is no reason to think here that John had any improper designs in opposing the man. He thought that it was evidence that he could not be right, because he did not join them and follow the Saviour. Our Lord taught him differently. He opposed no one who gave evidence that he loved him. Wherever he might be or whatever his work, yet, if he did it in the name of Jesus and with the approbation of God, it was evidence sufficient that he was right. Christians should rejoice in good done by their brethren of any denomination. There are men calling themselves Christians who seem to look with doubt and suspicion on all that is done by those who do not walk with them. They undervalue their labours, and attempt to lessen the evidences of their success and to diminish their influence. True likeness to the Saviour would lead us to rejoice in *all* the good accomplished, by whomsoever it may be done—to rejoice that the kingdom of Christ is advanced, whether by a Presbyterian, an Episcopalian, a Baptist, or a Methodist. Comp. Phi. i. 18.

41 For[g] whosoever shall give you a cup of water to drink in my name, because ye belong to Christ, verily I say unto you, he shall not lose his reward.

42 And whosoever shall [h]offend one of *these* little ones that believe in me, it is better for him that a millstone were hanged about his neck, and he were cast into the sea.

43 And[i] if thy hand [3]offend thee, cut it off: it is better for thee to enter into life maimed, than, having two hands, to go into hell, into the fire that never shall be quenched;

44 Where[k] their worm dieth not, and the fire is not quenched.

45 And if thy foot [4]offend thee, cut it off: it is better for thee to enter halt into life, than, having two feet, to be cast into hell, into the fire that never shall be quenched;

46 Where their worm dieth not, and the fire is not quenched.

47 And if thine eye [5]offend thee, pluck it out: it is better for thee to enter into the kingdom of God with one eye, than, having two eyes, to be cast into hell-fire;

48 Where their worm dieth not, and the [l]fire is not quenched.

49 For every one shall be salted

g Mat.10.42; 25.40.
h Mat.18.6; Lu.17.1,2. *i* De.13.6; Mat.5.29.
3 or, *cause thee to offend;* and so ver. 45 and 47.

k Is.66.24; Re.14.11. 4 See ver.43.
5 See ver.43. *l* ver.44,46; Lu.16.24.

---

41. *Whosoever shall give you a cup*, &c. How easy it is to be a Christian! What is easier than to give a cup of cold water to a thirsty disciple of Jesus! But it must be in his name—that is, because he *is* a Christian, and therefore from love *to the Saviour*. This is very different from giving it from a mere motive of common kindness. If done from love to Christ, it *will* be rewarded; and hence we learn that the humblest acts of Christians—the lowest service that is rendered—will be graciously noticed by Jesus and rewarded. None are so humble in his kingdom as not to be able to do good, and none so poor that he may not show attachment to him. The feeblest service will be accepted, and acts of love that may be forgotten by *man*, will be remembered by *him*, and rewarded in heaven.

42–50. See Notes on Mat. xviii. 7–9. *Millstone.* See Mat. xviii. 6.

44–46. *Their worm.* This figure is taken from Is. lxvi. 24. See Notes on that passage. In describing the great prosperity of the kingdom of the Messiah, Isaiah says that the people of God "shall go forth, and look upon the carcases of the men who have transgressed against God." Their enemies would be overcome. They would be slain. The people of God would triumph. The figure is taken from heaps of the dead slain in battle; and the prophet says that the number would be so great that their worm—the worm feeding on the dead—would not die, would live long—as long as there were carcasses to be devoured; and that the fire which was used to burn the bodies of the dead would continue long to burn, and would not be extinguished till they were consumed. The figure, therefore, denotes great misery, and certain and terrible destruction. In these verses it is applied to the state beyond the grave, and is intended to denote that the destruction of the wicked will be awful, wide-spread, and eternal. It is not to be supposed that there will be any *real* worm in hell—perhaps no *material* fire; nor can it be told what was particularly intended by the undying worm. There is no authority for applying it, as is often done, to remorse of conscience, any more than to any other of the pains and reflections of hell. It is a mere image of loathsome, dreadful, and *eternal* suffering. In what that suffering will consist it is probably beyond the power of any living mortal to imagine. The word "their," in the phrase "their worm," is used merely to keep up the *image* or *figure*. Dead bodies putrefying in that valley would be overrun with worms, while the *fire* would not be confined to them, but would spread to other objects kindled by combustibles through all the valley. It is *not* meant, therefore, that every particular sufferer has a peculiar worm, or has particular sins that cause remorse of conscience. That is a truth, but it does not appear that it is intended to be taught here.

49. *Every one shall be salted with fire.*

with fire, and [m]every sacrifice shall be salted with salt.

50 Salt *is* good; [n]but if the salt have lost his saltness, wherewith will ye season it? Have [o]salt in yourselves, and [p]have peace one with another.

CHAPTER X.

AND[a] he arose from thence, and cometh into the coasts of Judea, by the farther side of Jordan: and the people resort unto him again; and, as he was wont, he taught them again.

2 And the Pharisees came to him, and asked him, Is it lawful for a man to put away *his* wife? tempting him.

3 And he answered and said unto them, What did Moses command you?

4 And they said, [b]Moses suffered to write a bill of divorcement, and to put *her* away.

5 And Jesus answered and said

m Le.2.13; Eze.43.24. *n* Mat.5.13; Lu.14.34. *o* Col.4.6. *p* Ps.34.14; 2 Co.13.11; He.12.14. *a* Mat.19.1,&c.; Jn.10.40.

b De.24.1; Mat.5.31.

Perhaps no passage in the New Testament has given more perplexity to commentators than this, and it may be impossible now to fix its precise meaning. The common idea affixed to it has been, that as salt preserves from putrefaction, so fire, applied to the wicked in hell, will have the property of preserving them in existence, or they will *be* preserved amid the sprinkling of fire, to be continually in their sufferings a sacrifice to the justice of God; but this meaning is not quite satisfactory. Another opinion has been, that as salt was sprinkled on the victim preparatory to its being devoted to God (see Le. ii. 13), so would *the apostles*, by trials, calamities, &c., represented here by *fire*, be prepared as a sacrifice and offering to God. Probably the passage has not reference at all to future punishment; and the difficulty of interpreting it has arisen from supposing it to be connected with the 48th verse, or given as a *reason* for what is said in *that* verse, rather than considering it as designed to illustrate the *general design* of the passage. The main scope of the passage was not to discourse of future punishment; that is brought in incidentally. The chief object of the passage was—1st. To teach the apostles that *other men*, not *with them*, might be true Christians, ver. 38, 39. 2d. That they ought to be disposed to look favourably upon the slightest evidence that they *might be true believers*, ver. 41. 3d. That they ought to avoid giving *offence* to such feeble and obscure Christians, ver. 42. 4th. That *everything* calculated to give offence, or to dishonour religion, should be removed, ver. 43. And 5th. That everything which would endanger their salvation should be sacrificed; that they should *deny* themselves in every way in order to obtain eternal life. In this way they would be *preserved* to eternal life. The word "fire," here, therefore denotes self-denials, sacrifices, trials, in keeping ourselves from the gratification of the flesh. As if he had said, "Look at the sacrifice on the altar. It is an offering to God, about to be presented to him. It is sprinkled with *salt, emblematic of* PURITY, *of* PRESERVATION, *and of fitting it, therefore, for a sacrifice.* So *you* are devoted to God. You are sacrifices, victims, offerings to him in his service. To make you *acceptable* offerings, everything must be done to *preserve* you from sin and to *purify* you. Self-denials, subduing the lusts, enduring trials, removing offences, are the proper *preservatives* in the service of God. Doing this, you will be acceptable offerings and be saved; without this, you will be *unfit* for his eternal service and will be lost."

50. *Lost its saltness*, &c. See Notes on Mat. v. 13. ¶ *Have salt in yourselves.* Have the preserving, purifying principle always; the principles of denying yourselves, of suppressing pride, ambition, contention, &c., and thus you will be an acceptable offering to God. ¶ *Have peace.* Avoid contention and quarrelling, struggling for places, honours, and office, and seek each other's welfare, and religion will be honoured and preserved in the world.

CHAPTER X.

1-12. See this question about divorce explained in the Notes on Mat. xix. 1-12.

12. *And if a woman shall put away her husband.* It would seem, from this, that

unto them, For the hardness of your heart he wrote you this precept:

6 But from the beginning of the creation [c]God made them male and female.

7 For[d] this cause shall a man leave his father and mother, and cleave to his wife;

8 And they twain shall be [e]one flesh: so then they are no more twain, but one flesh.

9 What therefore God hath joined together, let not man put asunder.

10 And in the house his disciples asked him again of the same *matter*.

11 And he saith unto them, Whosoever[f] shall put away his wife, and marry another, committeth adultery against her.

12 And if a woman shall put away her husband, and be married to another, she committeth adultery.

13 And[g] they brought young children to him, that he should touch them; and *his* disciples rebuked those that brought *them*.

14 But when Jesus saw *it* he was [h]much displeased, and said unto them, Suffer the little children to come unto me, and forbid them not; [i]for of such is the kingdom of God.

15 Verily I say unto you, Whosoever shall not receive the kingdom of God as a little child, he shall not enter therein.

c Ge.1.27; 5.2; Mal.2.15. d Ge.2.24.
e 1 Co.6.16; Ep.5.31.
f Mat.5.32; 19.9; Lu.16.18; Ro.7.3; 1 Co.7.10,11.
g Mat.19.13; Lu.18.15. h Ep.4.26.
i Mat.18.10; 1 Co.14.20; 1 Pe.2.2; Re.14.5.

a woman, among the Jews, had the power of separating herself from her husband, yet this right is not given her by the law of Moses. There is not, however, any positive evidence that females often claimed or exercised this right. Cases had occurred, indeed, in which it had been done. The wife of Herod had rejected her former husband and married Herod. And though instances of this kind *might* have been attempted to be defended by the example of Pagans, yet our Saviour was desirous of showing them that it did not free them from the charge of adultery. The apostles were going forth to teach Pagan nations, and it was proper for Christ to teach them how to act in such cases, and to show them that they were cases of real adultery.

13-16. See Notes on Mat. xix. 13-15.

13. *Should touch them.* That is, should lay his hands on them, and pray for them, and bless them. Comp. Mat. xix. 13. It was common to lay the hands on the head of a person for whom a blessing was asked. See the case of Jacob, Ge. xlviii. 14.

14. *Saw* it. Saw the conduct of his disciples. ¶ *Was much displeased.* Because, first, it was a pleasure *to him* to receive and bless little children; and, secondly, they were doing what they were not commanded to do—interfering in a case where it was evidently improper.

15. *Whosoever shall not receive.* Whosoever shall not manifest the spirit of a little child. ¶ *The kingdom of God.* The gospel. The new dispensation by the Messiah, *or the reign of God through a Mediator.* See Notes on Mat. iii. 2. ¶ *As a little child.* With the temper and spirit of a child—teachable, mild, humble, and free from prejudice and obstinacy. ¶ *Shall not enter therein.* Shall not be a Christian; shall not be a *real* member of the family of Christ on earth, though he may be a *professor*, and shall never enter heaven.

16. *Took them up in his arms.* These were small children. ¶ *Blessed them.* Prayed for them, sought a blessing on them, or gave them the assurance of his favour as the Messiah.

How happy would it be if *all* parents thus felt it to be their privilege to present their children to Christ! The question with a parent should be, not whether he *ought* to present them by prayer, but whether he *may* do it. And so, too, the question respecting infant baptism is not so much whether a parent OUGHT to devote his children to God in this ordinance, as whether he MAY do it. It is an inestimable privilege to do it; it is not a matter of mere stern and iron-handed duty; and a parent with right feelings will come to God with his

16 And he took them up in his
arms, put *his* hands upon them,
and blessed them.

17 And[k] when he was gone forth
into the way, there came one running, and kneeled to him, and
asked him, Good Master, what
shall I do that I may inherit eternal life?

18 And Jesus said unto him, Why
callest thou me good? *There is*
none good [l]but one, *that is* God.

19 Thou knowest [m]the commandments, Do not commit adultery, Do not kill, Do not steal, Do
not bear false witness, Defraud not,
Honour thy father and mother.

20 And he answered and said
unto him, Master, [n]all these have
I observed from my youth.

21 Then Jesus beholding him,
loved him, and said unto him, [o]One
thing thou lackest: go thy way,
sell whatsoever thou hast, and give

k Mat.19.16,&c.; Lu.18.18,&c. *l* Ps.86.5; 119.68.

m Ex.20.; Ro.13.9.
n Is.58.2; Eze.33.31,32; Mal.3.8; Ro.7.9; Phi.3.6.
o Ja.2.10.

children *in every way*, and seek his blessing on them in the beginning of their journey of life. Our children are given to us but for a little time. They are in a world of danger, sin, and woe. They are exposed to temptation on every hand. If God be not their friend, they *have* no friend that can aid them in the day of adversity, or keep them from the snares of the destroyer. If *he* is their friend they have nothing to fear. The *proper expression, then, of parental feeling*, is to come and offer them early to God. A parent should ask only the *privilege* of doing it. He should seek *God's* favour as the best inheritance of his children; and if a parent *may* devote his offspring to God—if he *may* daily seek his blessing on them by prayer—it is all that he should ask. With proper feelings he will rush to the throne of grace, and daily seek the protection and guidance of God for his children amid the temptations and snares of an ungodly world, and implore *him* to be their guide when the parent shall be laid in the silent grave.

So children who have been devoted to God—who have been the daily objects of a father's prayers and a mother's tears—who have been again and again presented to Jesus in infancy and childhood—are under the most sacred obligations to live to God. They should never forget that a parent sought the favour of God as the chief blessing; and, having been offered to *Jesus* by prayer and baptism in their first days on earth, they should make it their great aim to be prepared to meet *him* when he shall come in the clouds of heaven.

17-31. See this passage illustrated in the Notes on Mat. xix. 16-30.

17. *Gone forth.* From the place where he had been teaching. ¶ *Into the way.* Into the road or path on his journey. ¶ *Running.* Thus showing the intensity with which he desired to know the way of life. Zeal to know the way to be saved is proper, nor is it possible that it should be too intense if well directed. Nothing else is so important, and nothing demands, therefore, so much effort and haste.

19. *Defraud not.* Do not take away your neighbour's property by fraud or dishonesty. To *cheat* or *defraud*, supposes a covetous desire of a neighbour's property, and is usually attended with *falsehood* or *false witness* against a neighbour in obtaining it. It is thus a violation of the ninth and tenth commandments; and our Saviour very properly, therefore, *condensed* the two, and expressed their substance in this—not to defraud. It is, besides, expressly forbidden in Le. xix. 13: "Thou shalt not defraud thy neighbour."

21. *Jesus beholding him, loved him.* What occurred afterward showed that the young man did not love the Saviour, or was not a true disciple; so that this expression denotes simply natural affection, or means that Jesus was pleased with his amiableness, his morality, and his *external* regard for the law of God. At the same time, this was entirely consistent with deep sorrow that he would not give his heart to God, and with deep abhorrence of such a love of the world as to blind the mind to the beauty of true religion, and to lead to the rejection of the Messiah and the destruction of the soul. ¶ *One thing thou lackest.* When the young man came to Jesus he asked him, "What lack I yet?" Mat. xix. 20. This *question*

to the poor, and thou shalt have
treasure[p] in heaven; and come,
take up the cross and follow me.
22 And he was sad at that saying, and went away grieved; for he
had great possessions.
23 And Jesus looked round
about, and saith unto his disciples, How hardly shall they that
have riches enter into the kingdom
of God!
24 And the disciples were astonished at his words. But Jesus
answereth again, and saith unto
them, Children, how hard is it for
them that [q]trust in riches to enter
into the kingdom of God!
25 It is easier for a camel to go
through the eye of a needle, than
for a rich man to enter into the
kingdom of God.
26 And they were astonished out
of measure, saying among themselves, Who then can be saved?
27 And Jesus looking upon them,
saith, With men *it is* impossible,
but not with God; for [r]with God
all things are possible.
28 Then Peter began to say unto
him, Lo, we have left all, and have
followed thee.
29 And Jesus answered and said,
Verily I say unto you, there is no
man that hath left house, or brethren, or sisters, or father, or mother,
or wife, or children, or lands, for
my sake, and the gospel's,
30 But he shall receive an hun-

p Mat.6.19,20; Lu.12.33; 16.9.
q Job 31.24; Ps.52.7; 62.10; Hab.2.9; 1 Ti.6.17; Re.3.17.
r Ge.18.14; Job 42.2; Je.32.17; Lu.1.37.

Mark has omitted, but he has retained the *answer*. The answer means, there is *one thing* yet wanting. Though all that you have said should be *true*, yet, to make the system complete, or to show that you *really* are disposed to keep the commands of God, go and sell your property. See whether you love *God* more than you do your *wealth*. By doing that you will show that your love of God is supreme; that your obedience is not merely *external* and *formal*, but *sincere* and *real;* the thing now *lacking* will be made up.

24. *Children.* An expression of affection, perhaps also implying a reproof that their slowness of understanding was like that of children. When they should have seen at once the truth of what he said, they were slow to learn it. It became necessary, therefore, to *repeat* what he had said. ¶ *How hard.* With how much difficulty.

26. *Out of measure.* Very much, or exceedingly. The Greek means no more than this.

30. *An hundred-fold.* A hundred times as much. ¶ *In this time.* In this life. In the *time* that he forsakes all. ¶ *Houses,* &c. This cannot be taken literally, as promising a hundred times as many *mothers, sisters,* &c. It means, evidently, that the loss shall be a hundred times *compensated* or made up; or that, in the possession of religion, we have a hundred times the *value* of all we forsake. This consists in the pardon of sin, in the favour of God, in peace of conscience, in support in trials and in death, and in raising up *friends* in the place of those who are left—*spiritual brethren, and sisters, and mothers,* &c. And this corresponds to the experience of all who ever became Christians. At the same time, it is true that godliness is profitable *for all things,* having the promise of the life that is, as well as of that which is to come. See Notes on 1 Ti. iv. 8. *The favour of God* is the security for every blessing. Obedience to his law secures industry, temperance, chastity, economy, prudence, health, and the confidence of the world—all indispensable to success in life, and all connected, commonly, with success. Though the wicked *sometimes* prosper, yet the *surest* way of prosperity is to fear God and keep his commandments. Thus will all *needed* blessings descend on us *here,* and *eternal* blessings *hereafter.* ¶ *With persecutions.* Persecutions, or the contempt of the world, and bodily sufferings on account of their religion, they *must* meet. Jesus did not conceal this; but he consoled them. He assured them that *amid* these, or perhaps it should be rendered "*after*" these, they should find friends and comfort. It is well to bear trial if *God* be our Friend. With the promises of the Bible in our hand, we may hail

dred-fold now in this time, houses, and brethren, and sisters, and mothers, and children, and lands, with persecutions; and in the world to come eternal life.

31 But[s] many *that are* first shall be last, and the last first.

32 And[t] they were in the way going up to Jerusalem; and Jesus went before them: and they were amazed; and as they followed, they were afraid. And he took again the twelve, and began to tell them what things should happen unto him,

33 *Saying*, Behold, [u]we go up to Jerusalem; and the Son of man shall be delivered unto the chief priests, and unto the scribes; and they shall condemn him to death, and shall deliver him to the Gentiles;

34 And[v] they shall mock him, and shall scourge him, and shall spit upon him, and shall kill him; and the third day he shall rise again.

35 And James and John, the sons of Zebedee, come unto him, saying, Master, we would that thou shouldest do for us whatsoever we shall desire.

36 And he said unto them, What would ye that I should do for you?

37 They said unto him, Grant unto us that we may sit, one on thy right hand, and the other on thy left hand, in thy glory.

38 But Jesus said unto them, [w]Ye know not what ye ask. Can ye drink of the cup that I drink of? and be baptized with [x]the baptism that I am baptized with?

39 And they say unto him, We can. And Jesus said unto them, [y]Ye shall indeed drink of the [z]cup that I drink of, and with the baptism that I am baptized withal shall ye be baptized:

40 But to sit on my right hand and on my left hand is not mine to give; but *it shall be given to them* [a]for whom it is prepared.

41 And when the ten heard *it*, they began to be much displeased with James and John.

42 But Jesus called them *to him*, and saith unto them, [b]Ye know that they which [1]are accounted to rule over the Gentiles exercise lordship over them; and their great ones exercise authority upon them.

43 But so shall it not be among you; [c]but whosoever will be great among you shall be your minister,

44 And whosoever of you will be the chiefest, shall be servant of all.

45 For even the Son of man came not to be ministered unto, but [d]to minister, and [e]to give his life a ransom for many.

46 And[f] they came to Jericho,

s Mat.20.16; Lu.13.30. t Mat.20.17,&c.; Lu.18.31,&c.
u Ac.20.22. v Ps.22.6,7,13.

w Ja.4.3. x Lu.12.50.
y Mat.10.25; Jn.17.14. z ch.14.36.
a Mat.25.34; He.11.16. b Lu.22.25.
1 or, *think good*. c Mat.20.26,28; ch.9.35; Lu.9.48.
d Jn.13.14; Phi.2.7.
e Is.53.11,12; Da.9.26; 2 Co.5.21; Ga.3.13; 1 Ti.2.6; Tit.2.14. f Mat.20.29,&c.; Lu.18.35,&c.

persecutions, and thank God that, amid so many sorrows, he has furnished such abundant consolations.

32–34. See Notes on Mat. xx. 17–19.

32. *Jesus went before him.* In the manner of an intrepid, fearless leader and guide, exposing *himself* to danger and death rather than his followers. ¶ *And they were amazed*, &c. They were afraid that evil would befall him in the city; that the scribes and Pharisees, who had so often sought to kill him, would then do it. Their fear and amazement were increased when he told them what would befall him there. They were *amazed* that, when he knew so well what would happen, he should still persevere in going up to the city.

35–45. See Notes on Mat. xx. 20–28.

35. *And James and John—came unto him.* They did this through the instrumentality of their mother. They did not come in *person*, but they got their mother to make the request for them. Comp. Notes on Mat. xx. 20.

46–52. See this passage explained in the Notes on Mat. xx. 29–34.

46. *Blind Bartimeus.* Matthew says

and as he went out of Jericho, with
his disciples and a great number
of people, blind Bartimeus, the son
of Timeus, sat by the highway side
begging.
47 And when he heard that it
was Jesus of Nazareth, he began
to cry out, and say, Jesus, *thou*
son of David, have mercy on me.
48 And many charged him that
he should hold his peace; but he
cried[g] the more a great deal, *Thou*
son of David, [h]have mercy on me.
49 And Jesus stood still and commanded him to be called. And
they called the blind man, saying
unto him, Be of good comfort, rise;
he[i] calleth thee.
50 And he, [k]casting away his
garment, rose and came to Jesus.
51 And Jesus answered and said
unto him, What wilt thou that I
should do unto thee? The blind
man said unto him, Lord, that I
might receive my sight.
52 And Jesus said unto him, Go
thy way: [l]thy faith hath [2]made
thee whole. And immediately he
received his sight, and followed
Jesus in the way.

CHAPTER XI.

AND[a] when they came nigh to
Jerusalem, unto Bethphage,
and Bethany, at the mount of
Olives, he sendeth forth two of
his disciples,
2 And saith unto them, Go your
way into the village over against
you; and as soon as ye be entered
into it ye shall find a colt tied,
whereon never man sat; loose him
and bring *him*.
3 And if any man say unto you,
Why do ye this? say ye that the
[b]Lord hath need of him; and
straightway he will send him
hither.
4 And they went their way, and
found the colt tied by the door
without, in a place where two ways
met, and they loose him.
5 And certain of them that stood
there said unto them, What do ye
loosing the colt?
6 And they said unto them even
as Jesus had commanded; and
they let them go.
7 And they brought the colt to
Jesus, and cast their garments on
him, and [c]he sat upon him.
8 And many spread their garments in the way; and others cut
down branches off the trees and
strawed *them* in the way.
9 And they that went before, and
they that followed, cried, saying,
[d]Hosanna, Blessed *is* he that cometh
in the name of the Lord:
10 Blessed *be* the [e]kingdom of

g Je.29.13. *h* Ps.62.12. *i* Jn.11.28.
k Phi.3.7-9. *l* Mat.9.22; ch.5.34. 2 or, *saved thee.*
a Mat.21.1,&c.; Lu.19.29,&c.; Jn.12.14,&c.

b Ac.17.25. *c* Zec.9.9.
d Ps.118.26. *e* Is.9.7; Je.33.15.

there were two. Mark mentions but one, though he does not deny that there was another. He mentions this man because he was well known—Bartimeus, THE *blind man.*

50. *Casting away his garment.* That is, his *outer* garment—the one that was thrown loosely over him. See Notes on Mat. v. 40. He threw it off, full of joy at the prospect of being healed, and that he might run without impediment to Jesus. This may be used to illustrate—though it had no such original reference—the manner in which a sinner should come to Jesus. He should throw away the garments of his own righteousness—he should rise speedily—should run with joy—should have full faith in the power of Jesus, and cast himself entirely upon his mercy.

CHAPTER XI.

1–11. See this passage illustrated in the Notes on Mat. xxi. 1–16.

4. *Two ways met.* Cross-roads. A public place, probably near the centre of the village.

5. *What do ye, loosing the colt?* Or, why do ye do this? What authority have you for doing it?

11–26. See this passage explained in the Notes on Mat. xxi. 18–22.

11. *Into the temple.* Not into the

our father David, that cometh in
the name of the Lord: Hosanna
in[f] the highest.

11 And Jesus entered into Jerusalem, and into the temple: and
when[g] he had looked round about
upon all things, and now the eventide was come, he went out unto
Bethany with the twelve.

12 And[h] on the morrow, when
they were come from Bethany, he
was hungry:

13 And seeing a fig-tree afar off,
having leaves, he came, if haply
he might find anything thereon:
and when he came to it [i]he found
nothing but leaves; for the time
of figs was not *yet*.

14 And Jesus answered and said
unto it, No man eat fruit of thee
hereafter for ever. And his disciples heard *it*.

15 And[k] they come to Jerusalem:
and Jesus went into the temple,
and began to cast out them that
sold and bought in the temple,
and overthrew the tables of the
money-changers,[l] and the seats of
them that sold doves;

16 And would not suffer that
any man should carry *any* vessel
through the temple.

17 And he taught, saying unto
them, Is it not written, [m]My house
shall be called [1]of all nations the
house of prayer? but ye have
made it a [n]den of thieves.

18 And the scribes and chief
priests heard *it*, and sought how
they might destroy him; for they
feared him, because all the people
was [o]astonished at his doctrine.

19 And when even was come, he
went out of the city.

20 And in the morning, as they
passed by, they saw the fig-tree
dried up from the roots.

21 And Peter, calling to remembrance, saith unto him, Master,
behold, the fig-tree which thou
cursedst is withered away!

22 And Jesus, answering, saith
unto them, [2]Have faith in God.

23 For verily I say unto you,
That [p]whosoever shall say unto
this mountain, Be thou removed,
and be thou cast into the sea, and
shall not doubt in his heart, but

f Ps.148.1. *g* Zep.1.12; Eze.8.9. *h* Mat.21.18,&c. *i* Is.5.7. *k* Mat.21.12,&c.; Lu.19.45,&c.; Jn.2.14,&c. *l* De.14.25,26.

m Is.56.7. 1 or, *an house of prayer for all nations.* *n* Je.7.11. *o* Mat.7.28; ch.1.22; Lu.4.32. 2 or, *Have the faith of God.* *p* Mat.17.20; Lu.17.6.

---

edifice properly called *the temple*, but into the *courts* which surrounded the principal edifice. Our Saviour, not being of the tribe of Levi, was not permitted to enter into the holy or most holy place; and when, therefore, it is said that he went into the *temple*, it is always to be understood of the *courts* surrounding the temple. See Notes on Mat. xxi. 12. ¶ *And when he had looked round about upon all things.* Having seen or examined everything. He saw the abominations and abuses which he afterward corrected. It may be a matter of wonder that he did not *at once* correct them, instead of waiting to another day; but it may be observed that God is slow to anger; that he does not *at once* smite the guilty, but waits patiently before he rebukes and chastises. ¶ *The eventide.* The evening; the time after three o'clock P.M. It is very probable that this was before sunset. The religious services of the temple closed at the offering of the evening sacrifice, at three o'clock, and Jesus probably soon left the city.

13, 14. *Afar off.* See Notes on Mat. xxi. 19.

15–24. See Notes on Mat. xxi. 12–22.

16. Any *vessel.* Any vessel used in cooking, or connected with the sale of their articles of merchandise.

18. *All the people were astonished.* He became popular among them. The Pharisees saw that their authority was lessened or destroyed. They were therefore envious of him, and sought his life. ¶ *His doctrine.* His teaching. He taught with power and authority so great that the multitudes were awed, and were constrained to obey.

21. *Thou cursedst.* To curse means to devote to destruction. This is its meaning here. It does not in this place imply blame, but simply that it should be destroyed.

22. *Have faith in God.* Literally,

shall believe that those things
which he saith shall come to pass,
he shall have whatsoever he saith.
24 Therefore I say unto you,
What[q] things soever ye desire
when ye pray, believe that ye receive *them*, and ye shall have *them*.
25 And when ye stand praying,
forgive,[r] if ye have aught against
any; that your Father also which
is in heaven may forgive you your
trespasses.
26 But [s]if ye do not forgive,
neither will your father which is
in heaven forgive your trespasses.
27 And they come again to Jerusalem: [t]and as he was walking in
the temple, there come to him the
chief priests, and the scribes, and
the elders,
28 And say unto him, [u]By what
authority doest thou these things?
and who gave thee this authority
to do these things?
29 And Jesus answered and said
unto them, I will also ask of you
one [3]question, and answer me, and
I will tell you by what authority I
do these things.
30 The baptism of John, was *it*
from heaven or of men? Answer me.
31 And they reasoned with themselves, saying, If we shall say,

q Mat.7.7; Lu.11.9; 18.1; Jn.14.13; 15.7; 16.24; Ja. 1.5,6. r Mat.6.14; Col.3.13. s Mat.18.35. t Mat.21.23,&c.; Lu.20.1,&c. u Nu.16.3. [3] or, *thing*.

From heaven, he will say, Why
then did ye not believe him?
32 But if we shall say, Of men,
they feared the people; [v]for all
men counted John that he was a
prophet indeed.
33 And they answered and said
unto Jesus, [w]We cannot tell. And
Jesus answering, saith unto them,
Neither do [x]I tell you by what
authority I do these things.

CHAPTER XII.

AND he began to speak unto
them by parables. A[a] *certain*
man planted a vineyard, and set
an hedge about *it*, and digged *a*
place for the wine-fat, and built
a tower, and let it out to husbandmen, and went into a far
country.
2 And at the season he sent to
the husbandmen a servant, that he
might receive from the husbandmen of the [b]fruit of the vineyard.
3 And they caught *him*, and beat
him, and sent *him* away empty.
4 And again he sent unto them
another servant; and at him they
[c]cast stones, and wounded *him* in
the head, and sent *him* away shamefully handled.
5 And again he sent another,

v Mat.3.5,6; 14.5; ch.6.20. w Is.1.3; 29.14; Je.8.7; Ho.4.6. x Lu.10.21,22. a Mat.21.33; Lu.20.9,&c. b Ca.8.11; Mi.7.1; Lu.12.48; Jn.15.1-8. c He.11.37.

"Have the faith of God." This may mean, have strong faith, or have confidence in God; a strong belief that he is able to accomplish things that appear most difficult with infinite ease, as the fig-tree was made to wither away by a word.

25. *And when ye stand praying.* When ye pray. It seems that the posture in prayer was sometimes standing and sometimes kneeling. God looks upon *the heart* rather than upon our position in worship; and if the heart be right, any posture may be proper. It cannot be doubted, however, that in private, in the family, and wherever it can be conveniently done, the kneeling posture is more proper, as expressing more humility and reverence, and more in accordance with Scripture examples. Comp. Ps. xcv. 6; 2 Ch. vi. 13; Da. vi. 10; Lu. xxii. 41; Ac. vii. 60; ix. 40. Yet a subject like this may be made of too much consequence, and we should be careful that anxiety about a mere *form* should not exclude anxiety about a far more important matter—the state of the soul. ¶ *Forgive*, &c. See Notes on Mat. vi. 12, 15.

27–33. See Notes on Mat. xx. 23–27.

CHAPTER XII.

1–12. See this parable explained in the Notes on Mat. xxi. 33–46.

13–17. See Notes on Mat. xxii. 15–22.

18–27. See this passage fully ex-

and him they killed; [d]and many others, beating some and [e]killing some.

6 Having yet, therefore, one son, his well-beloved, [f]he sent him also last unto them, saying, They will reverence my son.

7 But those husbandmen said among themselves, This is the heir; come, let us kill him, and the inheritance shall be ours.

8 And they took him, and killed *him*, and cast *him* [g]out of the vineyard.

9 What shall therefore the lord of the vineyard do? He will [h]come and destroy the husbandmen, and will [i]give the vineyard unto others.

10 And have ye not read this scripture? [k]The stone which the builders rejected is become the head of the corner:

11 This was the Lord's doing, and it is marvellous in our eyes.

12 And[l] they sought to lay hold on him, but feared the people; for they knew that he had spoken the parable against them: and they left him and went their way.

13 And [m]they sent unto him certain of the Pharisees, and of the Herodians, to catch him in *his* words.

14 And when they were come, they say unto him, Master, we know that thou art true, and carest for no man; for thou regardest not the person of men, but teachest the way of God in truth: Is it lawful to give tribute to Cæsar, or not?

15 Shall we give, or shall we not give? But he, knowing their hypocrisy, said unto them, Why tempt ye me? Bring me a [1]penny, that I may see *it*.

16 And they brought *it*. And he saith unto them, Whose *is* this image and superscription? And they said unto him, Cæsar's.

17 And Jesus, answering, said unto them, [n]Render to Cæsar the things that are Cæsar's, and [o]to God the things that are God's. And they marvelled at him.

18 Then[p] come unto him the Sadducees, [q]which say there is no resurrection; and they asked him, saying,

19 Master, [r]Moses wrote unto us, If a man's brother die, and leave *his* wife *behind him*, and leave no children, that [s]his brother should take his wife and raise up seed unto his brother.

20 Now there were seven brethren: and the first took a wife, and dying, left no seed.

21 And the second took her, and died, neither left he any seed; and the third likewise.

22 And the seven had her, and left no seed: last of all the woman died also.

23 In the resurrection, therefore, when they shall rise, whose wife shall she be of them? for the seven had her to wife.

24 And Jesus, answering, said unto them, Do ye not therefore err because ye know not the scriptures, neither the power of God?

25 For when they shall rise from the dead, they neither marry nor are given in marriage, [t]but are as the angels which are in heaven.

d Ne.9.30; Je.7.25,&c. *e* Mat.23.37. *f* He.1.1,2. *g* He.13.12. *h* Pr.1.24-31; Is.5.5-7; Da.9.26. *i* Je.17.3. *k* Ps.118.22. *l* ch.11.18; Jn.7.30. *m* Mat.22.15; Lu.20.20,&c.

1 Valuing of our money seven pence halfpenny, as Mat.22.19. *n* Mat.17.25-27; Ro.13.7; 1 Pe.2.17. *o* Ec.5.4,5; Mal.1.6. *p* Mat.22.23; Lu.20.27,&c. *q* Ac.23.8. *r* De.25.5. *s* Ru.1.11,13. *t* 1 Co.15.42-53.

---

plained in the Notes on Mat. xxii. 23–33.

25. *Are as the angels.* That is, as the angels in respect to connections and relations. What those connections and relations may be we know not, but this passage teaches that the peculiar relation of *marriage* will not exist. It does not affirm, however, that there will be no recollection of former marriages, or

26 And as touching the dead,
that they rise; have ye not read
in the book of Moses how in the
bush God spake unto him, saying,
I[u] *am* the God of Abraham, and
the God of Isaac, and the God of
Jacob?
27 He is not the God of the
dead, but the God of the living:
ye[v] therefore do greatly err.
28 And[w] one of the scribes came,
and having heard them reasoning
together, and perceiving that he
had answered them well, asked
him, Which is the first commandment of all?
29 And Jesus answered him, The
first of all the commandments *is*,
Hear,[x] O Israel; the Lord our God
is one Lord:
30 And thou shalt love the Lord
thy God with all thy heart, and
with all thy soul, and with all thy
mind, and with all thy strength.
This *is* the first commandment.
31 And the second *is* like, *namely*
this, [y]Thou shalt love thy neighbour as thyself. There is none other
commandment greater than these.
32 And the scribe said unto him,
Well, Master, thou hast said the
truth; for there is one God, [z]and
there is none other but he:
33 And to love him with all the
heart, and with all the understanding, and with all the soul, and with
all the strength, and to love *his*
neighbour as himself, is [a]more than
all whole burnt-offerings and sacrifices.
34 And when Jesus saw that he
answered discreetly, he said unto
him, Thou art not far from the
kingdom of God. And no man
after that durst [b]ask him *any
question*.

u Ex.3.6. *v* ver.24. *w* Mat.22.35. *x* De.6.4,5; Lu.10.27.
y Le.19.18; Mat.22.39; Ro.13.9. *z* De.4.39; Is.45.5,6,14; 46.9. *a* 1 Sa.15.22; Ho.6.6; Mi.6.6–8. *b* Mat.22.46.

---

no recognition of each other as having existed in this tender relation.

26. *How in the bush.* At the burning bush. See Ex. iii. 16. The meaning is, "in that part of the *book* of Exodus which contains the account of the burning bush." When there were no chapters and verses, it was the easiest way of quoting a book of the Old Testament *by the subject*, and in this way it was often done by the Jews.

28–34. See Notes on Mat. xxii. 34–40.

28. *Perceiving that he answered them well.* That is, with wisdom, and with a proper understanding of the law. In this case the opinion of the Saviour corresponded with that of the Pharisees; and the question which this scribe put to him now seems to have been one of the very few candid inquiries of him by the Jews for the purpose of obtaining information. Jesus answered it in the spirit of kindness, and commended the conduct of the man.

29. *Hear, O Israel!* This was said to call the attention of the Jews to the great importance of the truth about to be proclaimed. See De. vi. 4, 5. ¶ *The Lord our God*, &c. Literally, "Jehovah, our God, is one Jehovah." The other nations worshipped many gods, but the God of the Jews was one, and one only. Jehovah was undivided; and this great truth it was the design of the separation of the Jewish people from other nations to keep in mind. This was the *peculiar* truth which was communicated to the Jews, and this they were required to keep and remember for ever.

30. *And thou shalt love*, &c. If Jehovah was the *only* God, then they ought not to love any other being supremely—then they might not bow down before any idol. They were required to love God above all other beings or things, and with all the faculties of their minds. See Notes on Mat. xxii. 37.

32–34. This answer of the scribe is not found in Matthew. ¶ *Is more than all.* Is of more importance and value. ¶ *Discreetly.* Wisely, according to truth. ¶ *Not far from the kingdom of God.* Thou who dost prefer the *internal* to the *external* worship of God—who hast so just a view of the requirements of the law—canst easily become a follower of me, and art almost fit to be numbered among my disciples. This shows that a proper understanding of the Old Testament, of its laws and requirements, would prepare the mind for

35 And[c] Jesus answered and said, while he taught in the temple, How say the scribes that Christ is the son of David?

36 For David himself said [d]by the Holy Ghost, [e]The Lord said to my Lord, Sit thou on my right hand, till I make thine enemies thy footstool.

37 David therefore himself calleth him Lord; and whence is he *then* his son? And the common people heard him gladly.

38 And he [f]said unto them in his doctrine, [g]Beware of the scribes, which love to go in long clothing, and *love* salutations in the market-places,

39 And [h]the chief seats in the synagogues, and the uppermost rooms at feasts;

40 Which [i]devour widows' houses, and for a pretence make long prayers: these shall receive greater damnation.

41 And[k] Jesus sat over against the treasury, and beheld how the people cast [2]money into the treasury; and many that were rich cast in much.

c Mat.22.41; Lu.20.41,&c. d 2 Sa.23.2; 2 Ti.3.16. e Ps.110.1. f ch.4.2. g Mat.23.1; Lu.20.46,&c.

h Lu.11.43. i 2 Ti.3.6. k Lu.21.1,&c. 2 *a piece of brass money;* see Mat.10.9.

Christianity, and fit a man at once to embrace it when presented. One system is grafted on the other, agreeably to Ga. iii. 24. ¶ *And no man after that durst ask him* any question. That is, no one of the scribes, the Pharisees, or the Sadducees durst ask him a question for the purpose of *tempting* him or entangling him. He had completely silenced them. It does not appear, however, but that his *disciples* dared to ask him questions for the purpose of information.

35-37. See Notes on Mat. xxii. 41-46.

37. *The common people heard him gladly.* The success of the Saviour in his preaching was chiefly among the common or the poorer class of people. The rich and the mighty were too proud to listen to his instructions. So it is still. The main success of the gospel is there, and there it pours down its chief blessings. This is not the fault of *the gospel.* It would bless the rich and the mighty as well as the poor, if they came with like humble hearts. God knows no distinctions of men in conferring his favours; and wherever there is a poor, contrite, and humble spirit—be it clothed in rags or in purple—be it on a throne or on a dunghill—there he confers the blessings of salvation.

38. *In his doctrine.* In his *teaching,* for so it should be rendered. ¶ *Beware of the scribes.* Be on your guard. Be cautious about hearing them or following them. ¶ *Scribes.* The learned men of the Jewish nation. ¶ *Which love to go in long clothing.* In long, flowing robes, as significant of their consequence, leisure, and learning. ¶ *Salutations,* &c. See Notes on Mat. xxiii. 6, 7.

40. *Which devour widows' houses.* Which devour the families of widows, or the means of supporting their families. This they did under pretence of counselling them in the knowledge of the law and in the management of their estates. They took advantage of their ignorance and their unprotected state, and either extorted large sums for their counsel, or perverted the property to their own use.

No wonder that our Saviour denounced them! If there is any sin of peculiar enormity, it is that of taking advantage of the circumstances of the poor, the needy, and the helpless, to wrong them out of the pittance on which they depend for the support of their families; and as God is the friend of the widow and the fatherless, it may be expected that such will be visited with heavy condemnation. ¶ *For a pretence.* For show, or *pretending* great devotion.

41. *Sat over against.* Opposite to, in full sight of. ¶ *The treasury.* This was in the court of the women. See Notes on Mat. xxi. 12. In that court there were fixed a number of places or coffers, made with a large open mouth in the shape of a trumpet, for the purpose of receiving the offerings of the people; and the money thus contributed was devoted to the service of the temple—to incense, sacrifices, &c.

42. *Two mites.* The word translated *mite* denotes a small coin made of brass—the smallest in use among the Jews. The precise value cannot now be easily estimated. It was much less than any

42 And there came a certain
poor widow, and she threw in two
mites,[3] which make a farthing.
43 And he called *unto him* his
disciples, and saith unto them,
Verily I say unto you, [l]That this
poor widow hath cast more in than
all they which have cast into the
treasury:
44 For all *they* did cast in [m]of
their abundance; but she of her
want did cast in all that she had,
even [n]all her living.

[3] 7th part of that piece of brass money.
l 2 Co.8.2,12. m 1 Ch.29.3,17; 2 Ch.24.10. n De.24.6.

CHAPTER XIII.

AND[a] as he went out of the
temple, one of his disciples
saith unto him, Master, see what
manner of stones and what buildings *are here!*
2 And Jesus, answering, said
unto him, Seest thou these great
buildings? [b]there shall not be left
one stone upon another that shall
not be thrown down.
3 And as he sat upon the mount
of Olives, over against the temple,

a Mat.24.1,&c.; Lu.21.5,&c. b Lu.19.44.

coin we have, as the *farthing* was less than an English farthing. It was in value about three mills and a half, or one-third of a cent.

43. *This poor widow hath cast more in,* &c. That is, more in proportion to her means, and therefore more that was acceptable to God. He does not mean that this was more in value than all which the others had put in, but it showed more love to the sacred cause, more self-denial, and, of course, more sincerity in what she did. This is the rule by which God will reward us. Comp. 2 Co. viii. 12.

44. *Of their abundance.* Of their superfluous store. They have given what they did not *need.* They could afford it as well as not, and in doing it they have shown no self-denial. ¶ *She of her want.* Of her poverty. ¶ *All her living.* All that she had to live on. She trusted in God to supply her wants, and devoted her little property entirely to him.

From this passage we may learn—1st. That God is pleased with offerings made to him and his cause. 2d. That it is our duty to devote our property to God. We received it from him, and we shall not employ it in a proper manner unless we feel that we are stewards, and ask of him what we shall do with it. Jesus approved the conduct of all who had given money to the treasury. 3d. That the highest evidence of love to the cause of religion is not the *amount* given, but the amount compared with our means. 4th. That it *may be* proper to give *all* our property to God, and to depend on his providence for the supply of our wants. 5th. That God does not despise the humblest offering, if made in sincerity. He loves a cheerful giver. 6th. That there are none who may not in this way show their love to the cause of religion. There are few, very few scholars in Sabbath-schools who may not give as much to the cause of religion as this poor widow; and Jesus would be as ready to approve their offerings as he was hers; and the time to *begin* to be benevolent and to do good is in early life, in childhood. 7th. That it is every man's duty to inquire, not how *much* he gives, but how much compared with what he *has;* how much self-denial he practises, and what is the *motive* with which it is done. 8th. We may remark that few practise self-denial for the purpose of charity. Most give of their abundance—that is, what they can spare without feeling it, and many feel that this is the same as throwing it away. Among all the thousands who give to these objects, how few deny themselves of *one* comfort, even the least, that they may advance the kingdom of Christ!

CHAPTER XIII.

The principal things in this chapter are fully explained in Mat. xxiv.

1. *What manner of stones.* The stones here referred to were those used in the building of the temple, and the walls on the sides of Mount Moriah, on which the temple stood. The temple was constructed of white marble, and the blocks were of a prodigious size. Josephus says that these stones were, some of them, 50 feet long, 24 broad, and 16 in thickness.

3. *On the mount of Olives, over against the temple.* The Mount of Olives was

Peter, and James, and John, and
Andrew asked him privately,
4 Tell us, when shall these things
be? and what *shall be* the sign
when all these things shall be fulfilled?
5 And Jesus, answering them,
began to say, [c]Take heed lest any
man deceive you:
6 For many shall [d]come in my
name, saying, I am *Christ*, and
shall deceive many.
7 And when ye shall hear of
wars and rumours of wars, [e]be ye
not troubled; for *such things* must
needs be; but the end *shall* not *be*
yet.
8 For nation shall rise against
nation, and kingdom against kingdom; and there shall be earthquakes in divers places, and there
shall be famines and troubles:
these *are* the beginnings of [1]sor-
rows.
9 But take heed to yourselves;
for they [f]shall deliver you up to
councils; and in the synagogues
ye shall be beaten; and ye shall
be brought before rulers and kings
for my sake, for a testimony against
them.
10 And[g] the gospel must first be
published among all nations.
11 But when they shall lead
you, and deliver you up, take no
thought beforehand what ye shall
speak, neither do ye premeditate;
but whatsoever shall be given you
in that hour, that speak ye; for it
is not ye that speak, but [h]the Holy
Ghost.
12 Now the [i]brother shall betray
the brother to death, and the father
the son; and children shall rise
up against *their* parents, and shall
cause them to be put to death.
13 And ye shall be [k]hated of all
men for my name's sake; but [l]he
that shall endure unto the end, the
same shall be saved.

c Je.29.8; Ep.5.6; 2 Th.2.3; Re.20.7,8.
d Ac.5.36-39; 1 Jn.4.1.
e Ps.27.3; 46.1,2; Pr.3.25; Jn.14.1,27.
1 The word in the original importeth *the pains of a woman in travail.*

f Mat.10.17,&c.; Re.2.10. g Mat.28.19; Re.14.6.
h Ac.2.4; 4.8,31; 6.10. i Mi.7.6.
k Lu.6.22; Jn.17.14. l Da.12.12; Re.2.10.

directly east of Jerusalem, and from it there was a fine view of the temple.

9. *Take heed to yourselves.* Be cautious that no man deceive you; or, take care of your lives, not to run into unnecessary danger. ¶ *To councils.* The higher ecclesiastical courts of the Jews, including the Sanhedrim, or great council of the nation. ¶ *Rulers and kings.* Referring to Roman officers. ¶ *For a testimony against them.* Rather to bear testimony *to* them, or to be witnesses *before them* of the truth. This was *for the sake* of Jesus, or because they were attached to him; and God would overrule it so that at the same time they should bear witness *to* the rulers of the truth, as was the case with Peter and John, Ac. iv.; with Stephen, Ac. vi. vii.; and with Paul, Ac. xxiii.; xxiv. 24, 25.

11. *Neither do ye premeditate.* Do not think beforehand, or *prepare* an answer. You know not what the accusations will be, and God will furnish you with a reply that shall be adapted to the occasion. ¶ *Not ye that speak, but the Holy Ghost.* This is a full promise that they should be inspired, and consequently their defences recorded in the Acts of the Apostles are the words of the Holy Ghost. There could be no more explicit promise that they should be under an infallible guidance, and we are not left to doubt that they were taught of God. At the same time, this was a most desirable and gracious aid. They were illiterate, unknown, without power. They were unfit of themselves to make the important statements of religion which were requisite, but God gave them power, and they spake with a wisdom, fearlessness, pungency, and ability which no other men have ever manifested—full proof that these illiterate fishermen were under the influence of the Holy Ghost.

12. *The brother shall betray*, &c. The brother shall give up in a treacherous manner his brother to be put to death, on account of his attachment to Jesus. Through fear, or from the hope of reward and from the hatred of the gospel, he will overcome all the natural ties of brotherhood, and give up his own kindred to be burnt or crucified.

14 But when ye shall see the abomination of desolation, spoken of by [m]Daniel the prophet, standing where it ought not, (let him that readeth understand,) then let them that be in Judea flee to the mountains;

15 And let him that is on the house-top not go down into the house, neither enter *therein* to take any thing out of his house.

16 And let him that is in the field not turn back again for to take up his garment.

17 But woe to them that are with child, and to them that give suck in those days!

18 And pray ye that your flight be not in the winter.

19 For[n] *in* those days shall be affliction, such as was not from the beginning of the creation which God created unto this time, neither shall be.

20 And except that the Lord had shortened those days, no flesh should be saved: but for the elect's sake, whom he hath chosen, he hath shortened the days.

21 And then if any man shall say to you, [o]Lo, here *is* Christ, or, Lo, *he is* there, believe *him* not;

22 For false Christs and false prophets shall rise, and shall show signs and wonders, to seduce, if *it were* possible, even the elect.

23 But[p] take ye heed: behold, I have foretold you all things.

24 But in those days, after [q]that tribulation, the sun shall be darkened, and the moon shall not give her light;

25 And[r] the stars of heaven shall fall, and the powers that are in heaven shall be shaken.

26 And[s] then shall they see the Son of man coming in the clouds, with great power and glory.

27 And then shall he send his angels, and shall gather together his elect from the four winds, from the uttermost part of the earth to the uttermost part of heaven.

28 Now learn a parable of the fig-tree: When her branch is yet tender, and putteth forth leaves, ye know that summer is near:

29 So ye in like manner, when ye shall see these things come to pass, know that it is nigh, *even* at the doors.

30 Verily I say unto you, that this generation shall not pass till all these things be done.

31 Heaven and earth shall pass away, but [t]my words shall not pass away.

32 But of that day and *that* hour

m Da.9.27. *n* Da.12.1; Joel 2.2. *o* Lu.17.23.

p 2 Pe.3.17. *q* Da.12.1; Zep.1.15-17. *r* Is.13.10; 24.20,23; Je.4.28; 2 Pe.3.10,12; Re.6.12-14; 20.11. *s* Da.7.9-14; Mat.16.27; 24.30; ch.14.62; Ac.1.11; 1 Th.4.16; 2 Th.1.7,10; Re.1.7. *t* Is.40.8.

Perhaps nothing could more clearly show the dreadful evil of those times, as well as the natural opposition of the heart to the religion of Christ.

15. *On the house-top.* See Notes on Mat. ix. 1–8.

32. *Neither the Son.* This text has always presented serious difficulties. It has been asked, If Jesus had a divine nature, how could he say that he knew not the day and hour of a future event? In reply, it has been said that the passage was wanting, according to Ambrose, in some Greek manuscripts; but it is now found in all, and there can be little doubt that the passage is genuine. Others have said that the verb rendered "knoweth" means sometimes to *make* known or to reveal, and that the passage means, "that day and hour none makes known, neither the angels, nor the Son, but the Father." It is true that the word has sometimes that meaning, as in 1 Cor. ii. 2, but then it is natural to ask where has *the Father* made it known? In what place did he reveal it? After all, the passage has no more difficulty than that in Lu. ii. 52, where it is said that Jesus increased in wisdom and stature. He had a human nature. He grew as a man in knowledge. As a man his knowledge must be finite, for the faculties of the human soul are not infinite. As a man he often spoke, reasoned,

knoweth no man, no, not the angels which are in heaven, neither the Son, but the Father.

33 Take[u] ye heed, watch and pray; for ye know not when the time is.

34 *For the Son of man is* as a man taking a far journey, who left his house, and gave authority to his servants, and to every man his work, and commanded the porter to watch.

35 Watch ye, therefore; for ye know not when the master of the house cometh, at even, or at midnight, or at the cock-crowing, or in the morning;

36 Lest, coming suddenly, [v]he find you sleeping.

37 And what I say unto you, I say unto all, [w]Watch.

CHAPTER XIV.

AFTER two days was *the feast of* the passover, and of unleavened bread; and the chief priests and the scribes sought how they might take him by craft and put *him* to death.

2 But they said, Not on the feast-*day*, lest there be an uproar of the people.

3 And[a] being in Bethany, in the house of Simon the leper, as he sat

u Mat.24.42; 25.13; Lu.12.40; 21.34; Ro.13.11,12; 1 Th.5.6; Re.16.15.
v Mat.25.5. w ver.33,35.
a Mat.26.6,&c.; Lu.7.37; Jn.12.1,&c.

---

inquired, felt, feared, read, learned, ate, drank, and walked. Why are not all these, which imply that he was a *man*—that, *as a man*, he was not infinite—why are not these as difficult as the want of knowledge respecting the particular *time* of a future event, especially when that time must be made known by God, and when he chose that the man Christ Jesus should grow, and think, and speak *as a man?*

34. *Who left his house.* The word *house* often means family. Our Saviour here represents himself as going away, leaving his household the church, assigning to the apostles and all his servants their duty, and leaving it uncertain when he would return. As his return was a matter of vast consequence, and as the affairs of his kingdom were intrusted to them, just as the affairs of a house are to servants when the master is absent, so it was of vast importance that they should be faithful at their post, that they should defend the house from danger, and be ready for his return. ¶ *The porter.* The doorkeeper. To the janitor or doorkeeper was intrusted particularly the care of the house, whose duty it was to attend faithfully on those who came and those who left the house.

35. *Watch ye.* Be diligent, faithful, and waiting for the return of your Lord, who will come at an unexpected hour. ¶ *Master of the house.* Denoting here the Lord Jesus. ¶ *At even, or at midnight, or,* &c. This refers to the four divisions into which the Jews divided the night.

36. *Find you sleeping.* Inattentive to your post, neglecting your duty, and unprepared for his coming.

37. *I say unto all, Watch.* This command was proper, not only for those who were expecting the calamities that were soon to come upon the Jews, but for all who are soon to die and to go to the judgment. We know not the time of our death. We know not how soon we shall be called to the judgment. The Son of man may come at any moment, and we should therefore be ready. If we are his friends; if we have been renewed and pardoned; if we have repented of our sins, and have believed on him, and are leading a holy life, we *are* ready. If not, we are unprepared, and soon—probably while we are not expecting it—the cold hand of death will be laid on us, and we shall be hurried to the place where is weeping, and wailing, and gnashing of teeth. Oh how important it is to be ready, and to escape the awful sufferings of an ETERNAL HELL!

CHAPTER XIV.

1–11. See this passage explained in the Notes on Mat. xxvi. 1–16.

1. *And of unleavened bread.* So called because at that feast no other bread was used but that which had been made without leaven or yeast. ¶ *By craft.* By subtilty (Matthew); that is, by some secret plan that would secure possession

at meat, there came a woman having an alabaster-box of ointment
of [1]spikenard, very precious; and
she brake the box, and poured *it*
on his head.
4 And there were some that had
indignation within themselves, and
said, Why was this waste of the
ointment made?
5 For it might have been sold
for more than three hundred
pence,[2] and have been given to the
poor. And they murmured against
her.
6 And Jesus said, Let her alone;
why trouble ye her? She hath
wrought a good work on me.
7 For[b] ye have the poor with
you always, and whensoever ye
will ye may do them good; but
me ye have not always.
8 She hath done what she could:
she is come aforehand to anoint
my body to the burying.

1 or, *pure nard;* or, *liquid nard.*
2 See Mat.18.28. b De.15.11.

9 Verily I say unto you, Wheresoever this gospel shall be preached
throughout the whole world, *this*
also that she hath done shall be
spoken of for a memorial of her.
10 And[c] Judas Iscariot, one of
the twelve, went unto the chief
priests, to [d]betray him unto them.
11 And when they heard *it* they
were glad, and promised to [e]give
him money. And he sought how
he might conveniently betray him.
12 And the first day of [f]unlea-
vened bread, when they [3]killed the
passover, his disciples said unto
him, Where wilt thou that we go
and prepare, that thou mayest eat
the passover?
13 And he sendeth forth two of
his disciples, and saith unto them,
[g]Go ye into the city, and there shall
meet you a man bearing a pitcher
of water: follow him,
14 And wheresoever he shall go

c Mat.26.14,&c.; Lu.22.3,&c. d Jn.13.2.
e 1 Ki.21.20; Pr.1.10-16. f Ex.12.8,&c.
3 or, *sacrificed.* g ch.11.2,3; He.4.13.

---

of him without exciting the opposition of the people.

3. *Ointment.* This word does not convey quite the proper meaning. This was a perfume. It was used only to give a pleasant odour, and was liquid. ¶ *Of spikenard.* The *nard,* from which this perfume was made, is a plant of the East Indies, with a small, slender stalk, and a heavy, thick root. The best perfume is obtained from the root, though the stalk and fruit are used for that purpose. ¶ *And she brake the box.* This may mean no more than that she broke the *seal* of the box, so that it could be poured out. Boxes of perfumes are often sealed or made fast with wax, to prevent the perfume from escaping. It was not likely that she would break the box itself when it was unnecessary, and when the unguent, being liquid, would have been wasted; nor from a broken box or vial could she easily have *poured it* on his head.

5. *Three hundred pence.* About forty dollars (or £9). See Notes on Mat. xxvi. 7.

8. *She hath done what she could.* She has showed the highest attachment in her power; and it was, as it is now, a sufficient argument against there being any *real* waste, that it was done for the honour of Christ.

12–16. See Notes on Mat. xxvi. 17–19.

12. *They killed the passover.* The *paschal lamb,* which was slain in keeping the Passover. ¶ *Go and prepare.* Go and provide a lamb, have it roasted, and properly prepared with the usual things to eat with it.

13. *The city.* The city of Jerusalem. They were now in Bethany, about 2 miles from the city. ¶ *A man bearing a pitcher of water.* This could have been known only by the infinite knowledge of Christ. Such a thing could not have been conjectured, nor was there any concert between him and the man that *at that time* he should be in a particular place to meet them, for the disciples themselves proposed the inquiry. If Jesus knew a circumstance like that, then he in the same way must have known all things; then he sees *all* the actions of men—hears every word, and marks every thought; then the righteous are under his care, and the wicked, much as they may wish to be unseen, cannot escape the notice of his eye.

in, say ye to the goodman of the house, The [h]Master saith, Where is the guest-chamber, where I shall eat[i] the passover with my disciples?

15 And he will show you a large upper room furnished *and* prepared: there make ready for us.

16 And his disciples went forth, and came into the city, and [k]found as he had said unto them: and they made ready the passover.

17 And in the evening he cometh with the twelve.

18 And as they sat and did eat, Jesus said, Verily I say unto you, One[l] of you which eateth with me shall betray me.

19 And they began to be sorrowful, and to say unto him one by one, *Is* it I? and another *said, Is* it I?

20 And he answered and said unto them, *It is* one of the twelve, that dippeth with me in the dish.

21 The Son of man indeed goeth, as it is written of him; but woe to that man by whom the Son of man is betrayed! [m]good were it for that man if he had never been born.

22 And[n] as they did eat, Jesus took bread, and blessed, and brake *it*, and gave to them, and said, Take,[o] eat; this is my body.

23 And he took the cup; and when he had given thanks he gave *it* to them: and they all drank of it.

24 And he said unto them, [p]This

h Jn.11.28; 13.13. *i* Re.3.20.
k Jn.16.4. *l* Ps.41.9; 55.13,14. *m* Mat.18.6,7.
n Mat.26.26,&c.; Lu.22.19; 1 Co.11.23,&c.
o Jn.6.48-58. *p* 1 Co.10.16; Jn.6.53.

is my blood of the new testament, which is shed for many.

25 Verily I say unto you, I will drink no more of the fruit of the vine, until that day that I [q]drink it new in the kingdom of God.

26 And when they had sung an [4]hymn, they went out into the mount of Olives.

27 And Jesus saith unto them, All ye shall be offended because of me this night; for it is written, [r]I will smite the shepherd, and the sheep shall be scattered.

28 But[s] after that I am risen, I will go before you into Galilee.

29 But[t] Peter said unto him, Although all shall be offended, yet *will* not I.

30 And Jesus saith unto him, Verily I say unto thee, That this day, *even* in this night, before the cock crow twice, thou shalt deny me thrice.

31 But he spake the more vehemently, If I should die with thee, I will not deny thee in any wise. Likewise also said they all.

32 And[u] they came to a place which was named Gethsemane; and he saith to his disciples, Sit ye here, while I shall pray.

33 And he taketh with him Peter, and James, and John, and began to be sore amazed, and to be very heavy;

34 And saith unto them, [v]My soul is exceeding sorrowful unto death: tarry ye here, and watch.

35 And he went forward a little,

q Joel 3.18; Am.9.13,14. [4] or, *psalm.* *r* Zec.13.7.
s ch.16.7. *t* Mat.26.33,34; Lu.22.33,34; Jn.13.37,38.
u Mat.26.36,&c.; Lu.22.39,&c.; Jn.18.1,&c.
v Jn.12.27.

14. *The goodman of the house.* This signifies simply the *master* of the house. The original word expresses nothing respecting his character, whether it was good or bad. ¶ *The guest-chamber.* A chamber for guests or friends—an unoccupied room.

15. *A large upper room.* The word used here denotes the upper room devoted to purposes of prayer, repose, and often of eating. See Notes on Mat. ix. 1-8. ¶ *Furnished* and *prepared.* Literally *spread* and *ready.* Spread with a carpet, or with *couches* such as were used in eating. See Notes on Mat. xxiii. 6.

17-31. See this passage explained in the Notes on Mat. xxvi. 20-35.

31. *More vehemently.* More earnestly, more confidently.

and fell on the ground, and [w]prayed
that, if it were possible, the hour
might pass from him.
36 And he said, [x]Abba, Father,
all things *are* possible unto thee;
take away this cup from me: nevertheless, [y]not what I will, but what
thou wilt.
37 And he cometh, and findeth
them sleeping, and saith unto Peter, Simon, sleepest thou? couldst
not thou watch one hour?
38 Watch ye, and pray, lest ye
enter into temptation. The [z]spirit
truly *is* ready, but the flesh *is*
weak.
39 And again he went away, and
prayed, and spake the same words.
40 And when he returned, he
found them asleep again, (for their
eyes were heavy,) neither wist they
what to answer him.
41 And he cometh the third time,
and saith unto them, Sleep on now,
and take *your* rest: it is enough,
the [a]hour is come: behold, the Son
of man is betrayed into the hands
of sinners.
42 Rise up, let us go; lo, he that
betrayeth me is at hand.
43 And[b] immediately, while he
yet spake, cometh Judas, one of
the twelve, and with him a [c]great
multitude with swords and staves,
from the [d]chief priests, and the
scribes, and the elders.
44 And he that betrayed him
had given them a token, saying,
Whomsoever I shall [e]kiss, that
same is he: take him and lead *him*
away safely.
45 And as soon as he was come,
he goeth straightway to him, and
saith, [f]Master, master; and kissed
him.
46 And they laid their hands on
him, and took him.
47 And one of them that stood
by drew a sword, and smote a servant of the high-priest, and cut off
his ear.
48 And Jesus answered and said
unto them, Are ye come out, as
against a thief, with swords and
with staves to take me?
49 I was daily with you in the
temple, teaching, and ye took me
not: but the [g]scriptures must be
fulfilled.
50 And[h] they all forsook him
and fled.
51 And there followed him a certain young man, having a linen
cloth cast about *his* naked *body*,

w He.5.7. *x* Ro.8.15; Ga.4.6.
y Ps.40.8; Jn.4.34; 5.30; 6.38,39; 18.11; Phi.2.8.
z Ro.7.18–25; Ga.5.17. *a* Jn.7.30; 8.20; 13.1.
b Mat.26.47; Lu.22.47,&c.; Jn.18.3,&c.

c Ps.3.1,2. *d* Ps.2.2. *e* 2 Sa.20.9; Ps.55.21; Pr.27.6.
f Lu.6.46. *g* Ps.22.; Is.53.; Lu.24.44.
h Ps.88.8; Is.63.3; ver.27.

32–42. See Notes on Mat. xxvi. 36–46.

36. *Abba.* This word denotes *father.* It is a Syriac word, and is used by the Saviour as a word denoting filial affection and tenderness. Comp. Ro. viii. 15.

40. *Neither wist they,* &c. Neither *knew* they. They were so conscious of the impropriety of sleeping at that time, that they could not find any answer to give to the inquiry why they had done it.

41. *It is enough.* There has been much difficulty in determining the meaning of this phrase. Campbell translates it, "all is over"—that is, the time when you could have been of service to me is gone by. They *might* have aided him by watching for him when they were sleeping, but now the time was past, and he was already, as it were, in the hands of his enemies. It is not improbable, however, that *after* his agony some time elapsed before Judas came. He had required them to watch—that is, to keep awake during that season of agony. After that they might have been suffered to sleep, while Jesus watched alone. As he saw Judas approach he probably roused them, saying, It is sufficient—as much repose has been taken as is allowable—the enemy is near, and the Son of man is about to be betrayed.

43–52. See Notes on Mat. xxvi. 47–57.

45. *Master, master.* As if expressing great joy that he had found him again.

51. *A certain young man.* Who this was we have no means of determining,

and the young men laid hold on him;

52 And he [i]left the linen cloth, and fled from them naked.

53 And[k] they led Jesus away to the high-priest: and with him were assembled all the chief priests, and the elders, and the scribes.

54 And Peter followed him afar off, even into the palace of the high-priest: and he sat with the servants, and warmed himself at the fire.

55 And the chief priests and all the council sought for witness against Jesus to put him to death, and found none.

56 For[l] many bare false witness against him, but their witness agreed not together.

57 And there arose certain, and bare false witness against him, saying,

58 We heard him say, I will destroy[m] this temple that is made with hands, and within three days I will build another made without hands.

59 But neither so did their witness agree together.

60 And[n] the high-priest stood up in the midst, and asked Jesus, saying, Answerest thou nothing? What *is it which* these witness against thee?

61 But he [o]held his peace and answered nothing. Again the high-priest asked him, and said unto him, Art thou the Christ, the Son of the Blessed?

62 And Jesus said, I am; and [p]ye shall see the Son of man sitting on the right hand of power, and coming in the clouds of heaven.

63 Then the high-priest [q]rent his clothes, and saith, What need we any further witnesses?

64 Ye have heard the blasphemy; what think ye? And they all condemned him to be guilty of death.

65 And some began to [r]spit on him, and to cover his face, and to buffet him, and to say unto him, Prophesy: and the servants did strike him with the palms of their hands.

66 And[s] as Peter was beneath in the palace, there cometh one of the maids of the high-priest.

67 And when she saw Peter warming himself, she looked upon him and said, And thou also wast with Jesus of Nazareth.

68 But he [t]denied, saying, I know not, neither understand I what thou sayest. And he went out into the porch; and the cock crew.

69 And a maid saw him again, and began to say to them that stood by, This is *one* of them.

i ch.13.16.
k Mat.26.57,&c.; Lu.22.54,&c.; Jn.18.13,&c.
l Ps.35.11. *m* ch.15.29; Jn.2.19.
n Mat.26.62,&c. *o* Ps.39.9; Is.53.7; 1 Pe.2.23.

p Da.7.13; Mat.24.30; 26.64; Lu.22.69; Re.1.7.
q Is.37.1. *r* Is.50.6; ch.15.19.
s Mat.26.69,&c.; Lu.22.55,&c.; Jn.18.16,&c.
t 2 Ti.2.12,13.

but it seems not improbable that he may have been the owner of the garden, and that he may have had an understanding with Jesus that he should visit it for retirement when he withdrew from the city. That he was not one of the apostles is clear. It is probable that he was roused from sleep by the noise made by the rabble, and came to render any aid in his power in quelling the disturbance. It is not known why this circumstance is recorded by Mark. It is omitted by all the other evangelists. It may have been recorded to show that the conspirators had instructions to take the *apostles* as well as Jesus, and supposing *him* to be one of them, they laid hold of him to take him before the high-priest; or it *may* have been recorded in order to place his conduct in strong and honourable contrast with the timidity and fear of the disciples, who had all fled. Comp. Notes on Mat. xxvi. 56. ¶ *A linen cloth cast about* his *naked* body. He was roused from sleep, and probably threw around him, in his haste, what was most convenient. It was common to sleep in linen bed-

70 And he denied it again. And a little after, they that stood by said again to Peter, Surely thou art *one* of them; for thou art a Galilean,[u] and thy speech agreeth *thereto*.

71 But he began to curse and to swear, *saying*, I know not this man of whom ye speak.

72 And the second time the cock crew. And Peter called to mind the word that Jesus said unto him, Before the cock crow twice thou shalt deny me thrice. And [5]when he thought thereon, he [v]wept.

CHAPTER XV.

AND straightway in the morning the [a]chief priests held a consultation with the elders and scribes and the whole council, and bound Jesus, and carried *him* away, and delivered *him* to Pilate.

2 And Pilate asked him, Art thou the King of the Jews? And he, answering, said unto him, Thou sayest *it*.

3 And the chief priests accused him of many things, but he answered nothing.

4 And Pilate asked him again, saying, Answerest thou nothing? behold how many things they witness against thee.

5 But[b] Jesus yet answered nothing; so that Pilate marvelled.

6 Now[c] at *that* feast he released unto them one prisoner, whomsoever they desired.

7 And there was *one* named Barabbas, *which lay* bound with them that had made insurrection with him, who had committed murder in the insurrection.

8 And the multitude, crying aloud, began to desire *him to do* as he had ever done unto them.

9 But Pilate answered them, saying, Will ye that I release unto you the King of the Jews?

10 (For he knew that the chief priests had delivered him [d]for envy.)

11 But the chief priests moved the people that he should rather release [e]Barabbas unto them.

12 And Pilate answered, and said again unto them, What will ye, then, that I shall do *unto him* whom ye call the [f]King of the Jews?

13 And they cried out again, Crucify him.

14 Then Pilate said unto them, Why, [g]what evil hath he done? And they cried out the more exceedingly, Crucify him.

15 And *so* Pilate, willing to content the people, released Barabbas unto them, and delivered Jesus, when he had scourged *him*, to be crucified.

16 And[h] the soldiers led him away into the hall called Pretorium; and they call together the whole band.

17 And they clothed him with purple, and platted a crown of thorns, and put it about his *head*;

u Ac.2.7.
[5] or, *he wept abundantly;* or, *he began to weep.*
v 2 Co.7.10.
a Ps.2.2; Mat.27.1,&c.; Lu.23.1,&c.; Jn.18.28,&c.; Ac.3.13; 4.26.
b Is.53.7; Jn.19.9. *c* Mat.27.15; Lu.23.17; Jn.18.39.
d Pr.27.4; Ec.4.4; Ac.13.45; Tit.3.3. *e* Ac.3.14.
f Ps.2.6; Je.23.5; Ac.5.31. *g* Is.53.9.
h Mat.27.27; Jn.18.28,33; 19.9.

---

clothes, and he seized a part of the clothes and hastily threw it round him. ¶ *The young men.* The Roman soldiers. They were called *young men* because they were made up chiefly of youth. This was a Jewish mode of speaking. See Ge. xiv. 24; 2 Sa. ii. 14; Is. xiii. 18. ¶ *Laid hold on him.* Supposing him to be one of the apostles.

53–72. See this fully explained in the Notes on Mat. xxvi. 57–75.

CHAPTER XV.

See the principal events in this chapter explained in the Notes on Mat. xxvii.

16. *Called Pretorium.* The hall of the *prætor*, or Roman governor, where he sat to administer justice. ¶ *Whole band.* See Notes on Mat. xxvii. 27.

18 And began to salute him,
Hail, King of the Jews!
19 And they smote him on the
head with a reed, and did [i]spit
upon him, and, bowing *their* knees,
worshipped him.
20 And when they had [k]mocked
him, they took off the purple from
him, and put his own clothes on
him, and led him out to crucify
him.
21 And they compel one Simon,
a Cyrenian, who passed by, coming
out of the country, the father of
Alexander and Rufus, to bear his
cross.
22 And[l] they bring him unto the
place Golgotha, which is, being interpreted,
The place of a skull.
23 And they gave him to drink
wine mingled with myrrh; but he
received *it* not.
24 And when they had crucified
him, [m]they parted his garments,
casting lots upon them, what every
man should take.
25 And it was the third hour;
and they crucified him.

i ch.14.65. *k* Job 13.9; Ps.35.16; Mat.20.19; ch.10.34; Lu.22.63; 23.11,36.
l Mat.27.33,&c.; Lu.23.33,&c.; Jn.19.17,&c.
m Ps.22.18.

17. *With purple.* Matthew says *scarlet.* See Notes on Mat. xxvii. 28. ¶ *About his* head. In the form of a garland or diadem. The whole head was not covered, but it was placed in a circle round the temples.

19. *Worshipped him.* Mocked him with the *appearance* of homage. The word *worship* here denotes only the respect and honour shown to princes and kings. It does not refer to any *religious* homage. They regarded him as foolishly and madly claiming to be *a king* —not as claiming to be *divine.*

23. *Wine mingled,* &c. Matthew says *vinegar.* It was probably *wine soured,* so that it might be called either. This was the common drink of the Roman soldiers. ¶ *Myrrh.* See Notes on Mat. xxvii. 34.

25. *And it was the third hour,* &c. In Jn. xix. 14 it is said, "And it was the preparation of the passover, and about the sixth hour," &c. Much difficulty has been felt in reconciling these passages, and infidels have usually adduced them to prove that the evangelists have contradicted themselves. In reconciling them the following remarks may perhaps make the matter clear: (1.) The Jews divided both the night and the day into four equal parts of three hours each. See Notes on Mat. xiv. 25. The first division of the day commenced at six o'clock in the morning, and ended at nine; the second commenced at nine and ended at twelve, &c. The *third* hour mentioned by Mark would therefore correspond with our nine o'clock; the *sixth* hour mentioned by John would correspond with our twelve, or noon. (2.) Mark professes to give the time accurately; John does not. He says "it was *about* the sixth hour," without affirming that this was exactly the time. (3.) A mistake in *numbers* is easily made; and if it should be admitted that such an error had crept into the text here, it would be nothing more than has occurred in many ancient writings. It has been proved, moreover, that it was common not to write the *words* indicating numbers *at length,* but to use *letters.* The Greeks designated numbers by the letters of the alphabet, and this mode of computation is found in ancient manuscripts. For example, the Cambridge MS. of the New Testament has in this very place in Mark, not the word *third* written at length, but the letter γ, gamma, the usual notation for third. Now it is well known that it would be easy to mistake this for the mark denoting *six,* ϛ. An error of this kind in an early MS. might be extensively propagated, and might have led to the present reading of the text. Such an error is actually known to exist in the *Chronicon* of Paschal, where Otho is said to have reigned ϛ (six) months, whereas it is known that he reigned but three, and in this place, therefore, the γ, three, was mistaken for ϛ, six. (4.) There is some external authority for reading "third" in Jn. xix. 14. The Cambridge MS. has this reading. Nonnus, who lived in the fifth century, says that this was the true reading (Wetstein). Peter of Alexandria, in a fragment concerning the Passover, as quoted by Usher, says, "It was the preparation of the Passover, and about the *third* hour, as," he adds, "the most accurate copies of the Bible have it;

26 And the superscription of his accusation was written over, THE KING OF THE JEWS.

27 And with him they crucify two thieves; the one on his right hand, and the other on his left.

28 And the scripture was fulfilled which saith, [n]And he was numbered with the transgressors.

29 And [o] they that passed by railed on him, wagging their heads, and saying, Ah, thou that [p]de-

n Is.53.12. o Ps.22.7. p ch.14.58; Jn.2.19.

---

and this was the handwriting of the evangelist (John), which is kept, by the grace of God, in his most holy church at Ephesus" (Mill). It is to be admitted, however, that no great reliance is to be placed on this account. That a mistake *might* have occurred in the early MSS. is not improbable. No man can *prove* that it did *not* so occur, and so long as this cannot be proved, the passages should not be adduced as conclusive proof of contradiction.

After all, perhaps, without the supposition that there is any error in the text, the whole difficulty may be removed by the following statements: (1.) Calvary was *without* the walls of Jerusalem. It was a considerable distance from the place where Jesus was tried and condemned. Some time, more or less, would be occupied in going there, and in the preparatory measures for crucifying him. (2.) It is not necessary to understand *Mark* as saying that it was precisely nine o'clock, according to our expression. With the Jews it was six until seven; it was the third hour until the fourth commenced; it was the ninth until it was the tenth. They *included* in the *third* hour the whole time from the third to the fourth. The same mode they adopted in regard to their days. See Notes on Mat. xii. 40. (3.) It is not unduly pressing the matter to suppose that Mark spoke of the time when the process for crucifixion commenced—that is, when he was condemned—when they entered upon it—when they made the preparation. Between that and the time when he was taken *out* of Jerusalem to Mount Calvary, and when he was actually nailed to the tree, there is no improbability in supposing that there might have been an interval of more than an hour. Indeed, the presumption is that considerably more time than that would elapse. (4.) John does not profess, as has been remarked, to be strictly accurate. He says "it was *about* the sixth hour," &c. (5.) Now suppose that John meant to indicate the time when he was *actually* suspended on the cross—that he spoke of the *crucifixion* denoting the *act of suspension*, as it struck *him*—and there is no difficulty. Any other two men—any witnesses—might give just such an account now. One man would speak of the time when the process for an execution commenced; another, perhaps, of the very *act* of the execution, and would *both* speak of it in general terms, and say that a man was executed at such a time; and the circumstantial variation would *prove* that there was no collusion, no agreement to *impose* on a court—that they were honest witnesses. That is *proved* here. (6.) That this is the true account of the matter is clear from the evangelists themselves, and *especially* from *Mark*. The three first evangelists concur in stating that there was a remarkable *darkness* over the whole land from the *sixth* to the *ninth* hour, Mat. xxvii. 45; *Mar. xv. 33;* Lu. xxiii. 44. This fact—in which *Mark* concurs—would seem to indicate that *the actual crucifixion* continued only during that time—that he was, in fact, *suspended* at about the sixth hour, though the preparations for crucifying him had been going on (Mark) for two hours before. The fact that *Mark* (xv. 33) mentions this darkness as commencing at the *sixth* and not at the *third* hour, is one of the circumstances undesignedly occurring that seems to signify that the crucifixion then had *actually* taken place, though the various arrangements for it (ver. 25) had been going on from the *third* hour.

One thing is conclusively proved by this—that the evangelists did not *conspire together* to impose on the world. They are independent witnesses, and they were honest men; and the circumstance adverted to here is one that is allowed to be of great value in testimony in courts of justice—*circumstantial variation with essential agreement.*

26. *The superscription.* The writing over his head on the cross. ¶ *The King of the Jews.* See Notes on Mat. xxvii. 37.

28. *And the scripture was fulfilled,* &c.

stroyest the temple, and buildest *it* in three days,

30 Save thyself, and come down from the cross.

31 Likewise also the chief priests, mocking, said among themselves with the scribes, He saved others; himself he cannot save.

32 Let Christ the King of Israel descend now from the cross, that we may [q]see, and believe. And they that were crucified with him reviled him.

33 And[r] when the sixth hour was come, there was darkness over the whole land until the ninth hour.

34 And at the ninth hour Jesus cried with a loud voice, saying, Eloi,[s] Eloi, lama sabachthani? which is, being interpreted, My God, my God, why hast thou [t]forsaken me?

35 And some of them that stood by, when they heard *it*, said, Behold, he calleth Elias.

36 And one ran and filled a spunge full of vinegar, and put *it* on a reed, and [u]gave him to drink, saying, Let alone; Let us see whether Elias will come to take him down.

37 And[v] Jesus cried with a loud voice, and gave up the ghost.

38 And the vail of the temple was rent in twain, from the top to the bottom.

39 And when the centurion, which stood over against him, saw that he so cried out, and gave up the ghost, he said, Truly this man was the Son of God.

40 There were also women looking on [w]afar off; among whom was Mary Magdalene, and Mary the mother of James the less, and of Joses, and Salome;

41 (Who also, when he was in Galilee, followed him, and [x]ministered unto him;) and many other women which came up with him unto Jerusalem.

42 And now when the even was come, because it was the Preparation, that is, the day before the sabbath,

43 Joseph of Arimathea, an honourable counsellor, which also [y]waited for the kingdom of God,

q Ro.3.3; 2 Ti.2.13.
r Mat.27.45; Lu.23.44.
s Ps.22.1.
t Ps.42.9; 71.11; La.1.12.
u Ps.69.21.
v Mat.27.50; Lu.23.46; Jn.19.30.
w Ps.38.11.
x Lu.8.2,3.
y Lu.2.25,38.

This passage of Scripture is found in Is. liii. 12. This does not mean that he *was* a transgressor, but simply that in dying he *had a place with* transgressors. Nor does it mean that GOD regarded him as a sinner; but that at his death, in popular estimation, or by the sentence of the judge, he was *regarded as* a transgressor, and was treated in the same manner as the others who were put to death for their transgressions. Jesus died, the *just* for the *unjust*, and in his death, as well as in his life, he was *holy, harmless, undefiled.*

42. *The even.* The time after three o'clock in the afternoon. ¶ *The Preparation,* &c. The following day was to be a day of peculiar solemnity, called the *great day* of the feast. More than ordinary preparation was therefore made for *that* Sabbath on the day before. Hence the day was known as a day of preparation. This consisted in the preparation of food, &c., to be used on the Sabbath.

43. *Joseph, an honourable counsellor.* A distinguished man, who probably held a high office among the Jews, as one of their great council, or a Jewish senator. The word *honourable*, here, is not a mere title of *office*, but is given in reference to his personal character, as being a man of integrity and blameless life. ¶ *Waited for the kingdom of God.* Waited for, or expected, the coming of the Messiah. But this expression means more than an *indefinite* expectation that the Messiah *would* come, for all the Jews expected that. It implies that he believed *Jesus* to be the Messiah, and that he had *waited* for *him* to build up the kingdom of God; and this agrees with what John says (xix. 38), that he was a disciple of Jesus, but secretly, for fear of the Jews. He had retained his *secret* belief, in the hope that Jesus would be proclaimed and treated as the

came, and went in boldly unto Pilate, and craved the body of Jesus.

44 And Pilate marvelled if he were already dead: and calling *unto him* the centurion, he asked him whether he had been any while dead.

45 And when he knew *it* of the centurion, he gave the body to Joseph.

46 And he bought fine linen, and took him down, and wrapped him in the linen, and laid him in a sepulchre which was hewn out of a rock, and [z]rolled a stone unto the door of the sepulchre.

47 And Mary Magdalene and Mary *the mother* of Joses beheld where he was laid.

z ch.16.3,4.

Messiah, and then he probably proposed openly to acknowledge his attachment to him. But God called him to a public profession of attachment in a different manner, and gave this distinguished man grace to evince it. So men often delay a profession of attachment to Christ. They cherish a secret love, they indulge a hope in the mercy of God, but they conceal it for fear of man; whereas God requires that the attachment should be made known. "Whosoever is ashamed of me," said the Saviour, "and of my words, of him also shall the Son of man be ashamed when he cometh in the glory of his Father and with the holy angels," Mar. viii. 38. Those who love the Saviour have no right to hide their light under a bushel. As soon as they have evidence satisfactory to their own mind that they are Christians, or have a *prevalent* belief, after faithful examination, that they truly love God, and that they depend on the Lord Jesus for salvation, so soon are they bound to profess Christ before men. This is the command of God, and this is the way of peace. None have the prospect of *comfort* in religion who do not have respect to *all* of the commandments of God. ¶ *Went in boldly unto Pilate.* God had raised up this distinguished counsellor and secret disciple for a special and most important occasion. The disciples of Jesus had fled, and if they had not, they had no influence with Pilate. Unless there had been a special application to Pilate in behalf of Jesus, his body would have been buried *that night* in the same grave with the malefactors, for it was a law of the Jews that the body of an executed man should not remain on the cross on the Sabbath. At this critical juncture God called forward this secret disciple—this friend of Jesus, though unknown as such to the world—and gave him confidence. He dared to express sympathy for the Saviour; he went in boldly and begged the body of Jesus. It needed no small measure of courage to do this. Jesus had just been condemned, mocked, spit on, crucified—the death of a slave or of the most guilty wretch. To avow attachment for him *now* was proof of sincere affection; and the Holy Spirit has thought this worthy of special notice, and has set down this bold attachment of a senator for Jesus for our imitation. ¶ *Craved the body.* Begged, or asked.

44. *And Pilate marvelled if.* Wondered if he was dead, or wondered that he was so soon dead. It was not common for persons crucified to expire under two or three days, sometimes not until the sixth or seventh. Joseph had asked for the *body*, implying that he was dead. That he *was*, had been ascertained by the soldiers. See Jn. xix. 33.

45. *When he knew* it *of the centurion.* Being informed by the centurion of the fact that he was dead. The centurion had charge of the soldiers who watched him, and could therefore give correct information.

47. *Beheld where he was laid.* The affection of these pious females never forsook them, in all the trials and sufferings of their Lord. With true love they followed him to the cross; they came as near to him as they were permitted to come in his last moments; they followed him when taken down and laid in the tomb. The strong, the mighty, the youthful, had fled; but female love never forsook him, even in his deepest humiliation. This is the nature of true love; it is strongest in such scenes. While *professed* attachment will abound in prosperity a d live most in sunshine, it is only genuine love that will go into the dark shades of adversity and flourish there. In

CHAPTER XVI.

AND[a] when the sabbath was
past, Mary Magdalene, and
Mary the *mother* of James, and
Salome, had bought [b]sweet spices,
that they might come and anoint
him.

2 And very early in the morning,
the first *day* of the week, they came
unto the sepulchre at the rising of
the sun.

3 And they said among themselves, Who shall roll us away the
stone from the door of the sepulchre?

4 (And when they looked, they
saw that the stone was rolled
away:) for it was very great.

5 And entering into the sepulchre, they saw a young man sitting
on the right side, clothed in a long
white garment; and they were
affrighted.

a Mat.28.1,&c.; Lu.24.1,&c.; Jn.20.1,&c.
b Lu.23.56.

6 And he saith unto them, Be
not affrighted: Ye seek Jesus of
Nazareth, which was crucified:
[c]he is risen; he is not here; behold
the place where they laid him.

7 But go your way, tell his
disciples and Peter that he goeth
before you into Galilee; there shall
ye see him, as he said unto you.

8 And they went out quickly,
and fled from the sepulchre; for
they trembled and were amazed:
neither said they any thing to any
man; for they were afraid.

9 Now when *Jesus* was risen
early the first *day* of the week, he
appeared first to Mary Magdalene,
out of whom he had cast seven
devils.

10 *And* she went and told them
that had been with him, as they
mourned and wept.

11 And they, when they had

c Ps.71.20.

---

scenes of poverty, want, affliction, and death, it shows its genuineness. That which lives there is genuine. That which turns away from such scenes is spurious.

CHAPTER XVI.

1–8. See this passage explained in the Notes on Mat. xxviii. 1–8.

1. *Sweet spices. Aromatics.* Substances used in embalming. The idea of sweetness is not, however, implied in the original. Many of the substances used for embalming were *bitter* — as, *e.g.* myrrh — and none of them, perhaps, could properly be called *sweet.* The word *spices* expresses all that there is in the original. ¶ *Anoint him.* Embalm him, or apply these spices to his body to keep it from putrefaction. This is proof that they did not suppose he would rise again; and the fact that they did not *expect* he would rise, gives more strength to the evidence for his resurrection.

4. *It was very great.* These words belong to the third verse: "Who shall roll us away the stone from the door of the sepulchre?" for, the evangelist adds, it was very great.

5. *Sitting on the right side.* As they entered. The sepulchre was large enough to admit persons to go into it; not unlike, in that respect, our vaults.

7. *Tell his disciples and Peter.* It is remarkable that Peter is singled out for special notice. It was proof of the kindness and mercy of the Lord Jesus. Peter, just before the death of Jesus, had denied him. He had brought dishonour on his profession of attachment to him. It would have been right if the Lord Jesus had from that moment cast him off and noticed him no more. But he loved him still. Having loved him once, he loved unto the end, Jn. xiii. 1. As a proof that he forgave him and still loved him, he sent him this *special* message — the assurance that though he had denied him, and had done much to aggravate his sufferings, yet he had risen, and was still his Lord and Redeemer. We are not to infer, because the angel said, "Tell his disciples *and* Peter," that Peter was not still a disciple. The meaning is, "Tell his disciples, and especially Peter," sending to him a particular message. Peter was still a disciple. Before his fall, Jesus had prayed for him that his faith should not fail (Lu. xxii. 32); and as the prayer of Jesus was *always* heard (Jn. xi. 42), so it follows that

heard that he was alive, and had
been seen of her, believed not.
12 After that he appeared in
another form unto [d]two of them,
as they walked, and went into the
country.
13 And they went and told *it*
unto the residue; neither believed
they them.
14 Afterward[e] he appeared unto
the eleven as they sat [1]at meat,
and [f]upbraided them with their
unbelief and hardness of heart,
because they believed not them
which had seen him after he was
risen.
15 And he said unto them, [g]Go
ye into all the world, and preach
the gospel [h]to every creature.
16 He[i] that believeth, and is

d Lu.24.13. *e* Lu.24.36; 1 Co.15.5.

1 or, *together*. *f* Lu.24.25.
g Mat.28.19; Jn.20.21. *h* Ro.10.18; Col.1.23.
i Jn.3.18,36; Ac.16.31-33; Ro.10.9; 1 Pe.3.21.

Peter still retained faith sufficient to be a disciple, though he was suffered to fall into sin.

11. *Believed not.* This is proof that they did not *expect* his resurrection; proof that they were not easily deceived, and that nothing but the clearest evidence could undeceive them.

12. *He appeared in another form.* In a form unlike his ordinary appearance—so much so that they did not at first know him. See Notes on Lu. xxiv. 13–31. ¶ *As they walked and went into the country.* To Emmaus, Lu. xxiv. 13.

13. *The residue.* The remainder. Those who remained at Jerusalem.

14. *Afterward he appeared unto the eleven.* Judas was dead, and the apostles were then called "*the eleven.*" This was done even when one of them was absent, as Thomas was on this occasion. See the "Harmony of the Accounts of the Resurrection, Appearances, and Ascension of Christ," ii. 5, at the close of the Notes on Matthew. ¶ *As they sat at meat.* The word *meat* here means food, or meals. As they were reclining at their meals. ¶ *And upbraided them,* &c. Rebuked them, or reproached them. This was done because, after all the evidence they had had of his resurrection, still they did not believe. This is a most important circumstance in the history of our Lord's resurrection. Never were men more difficult to be convinced of anything than *they* were of that fact. And this shows conclusively that they had not conspired to impose on the world; that they had given up all for lost when he died; that they did not expect his resurrection; and all this is the strongest proof that he truly rose. *They* were not convinced until it was impossible for them longer to deny it. Had they expected it, they would have caught easily at the slightest evidence, and would have turned every circumstance in favour of such an event. It may be added that it was impossible that eleven men of good natural understanding should have been deceived in so plain a case. They had been with Jesus three years; they perfectly knew his features, voice, manner; and it is not credible that they should have been deceived by anyone who might have *pretended* to have been the Lord Jesus.

15. *Into all the world.* To the Gentiles as well as the Jews. It was contrary to the opinions of the Jews that the Gentiles should be admitted to the privileges of the Messiah's kingdom, or that the partition wall between them should be broken down. See Ac. xxii. 21, 22. It was long before the disciples could be trained to the belief that the gospel was to be preached to all men; and it was only by special revelation, even *after* this command, that Peter preached to the Gentile centurion, Ac. x. Jesus has graciously ordered that the preaching of the gospel shall be stopped by no barriers. Wherever there is man, there it is to be proclaimed. To every sinner he offers life, and all the world is included in the message of mercy, and every child of Adam is offered eternal salvation. ¶ *Preach.* Proclaim; make known; offer. To do this to every creature is to offer pardon and eternal life to him on the terms of the plan of mercy—through repentance, and faith in the Lord Jesus. ¶ *The gospel.* The good news. The tidings of salvation. The assurance that the Messiah has come, and that sin may be forgiven and the soul saved. ¶ *To every creature.* That is, to every human being. Man has no right to limit this offer to any class of men. God commands his servants to offer the salva-

baptized, shall be saved; but
he[k] that believeth not, shall be
damned.
17 And these signs shall follow
them that believe: In [l]my name
shall they cast out devils; they
shall [m]speak with new tongues;
18 They shall [n]take up serpents;

k Jn.12.48; 2 Th.2.12.

l Lu.10.17; Ac.5.16; 8.7; 16.18; 19.12.
m Ac.2.4; 10.46; 1 Co.10.12,28. n Lu.10.19; Ac.28.5.

tion to *all men*. If *they* reject, it is at their peril. God is not to blame if they do not choose to be saved. His mercy is manifest; his grace is boundless in offering life to a creature so guilty as man.

16. *He that believeth.* That is, believeth the gospel. *He who credits it to be true, and acts as if it were true.* This is the whole of faith. Man is a sinner. He should act on the belief of this truth and repent. There is a God. Man should believe it, and fear and love him, and seek his favour. The Lord Jesus died to save him. To have faith in him is to believe that this is true, and to *act* accordingly; that is, to trust him, to rely on him, to love him, to feel that we have no merit, and to cast our all upon him. There is a heaven and a hell. To *believe* this is to credit the account and act as if it were true—to seek the one and avoid the other. We are to die. To believe this is to act as if this were so; to be in readiness for it, and to expect it daily and hourly. In one word, faith is feeling and acting as if there were a God, a Saviour, a heaven, a hell; as if we were sinners and must die; as if we deserved eternal death and were in danger of it; and, in view of all, casting our eternal interests on the mercy of God in Christ Jesus. To do this is to be a Christian: not to do it is to be an infidel. ¶ *Is baptized.* Is initiated into the church by the application of water, as significant that he is a sinner, and needs the purifying influences of the Holy Ghost. It is worthy of remark that Jesus has made *baptism* of so much importance. He did not say, indeed, that a man *could not* be saved without baptism, but he has strongly implied that where this is neglected *knowing it to be a command of the Saviour*, it endangers the salvation of the soul. *Faith* and *baptism* are the beginnings of a Christian life: the one the beginning of piety *in the soul*, the other of its manifestation *before men*, or of a *profession* of religion. Every man endangers his eternal interest by being ashamed of Christ before men. See Mar. viii. 38. ¶ *Shall be saved.* Saved from sin (Mat. i. 21) and from eternal death (Jn. v. 24; iii. 36), and raised to eternal life in heaven, Jn. v. 28; xvii. 2, 24. ¶ *Shall be damned.* That is, condemned by God and cast off from his presence, 2 Th. i. 6–9. It implies that they will be adjudged to be guilty by God in the day of judgment (Ro. ii. 12, 16; Mat. xxv. 41); that they will deserve to die for ever (Ro. ii. 6, 8), and that they will be cast out into a place of woe to all eternity, Mat. xxv. 46. It may be asked how it can be *just* in God to condemn men for ever for not believing the gospel? I answer—1st. God has a right to appoint his own terms of mercy. 2d. Man has no claim on him for heaven. 3d. The sinner rejects the terms of salvation, knowingly, deliberately, and perseveringly. 4th. He has a special disregard and contempt for the gospel. 5th. His unbelief is produced by the love of sin. 6th. He shows by this that he has no love for God, and his law, and for eternity. 7th. He slights the objects dearest to God and most like him; and, 8th. He *must* be miserable. A creature who has *no confidence* in God; who does not believe that he is *true* or worthy of his regard, and who never seeks his favour, *must* be wretched. He rejects God, and he must go into eternity without a Father and without a God. He has no source of comfort in himself, and *must* die for ever. There is no being in eternity *but* God that can make man happy, and without his favour the sinner *must* be wretched.

17. *And these signs.* These miracles. These evidences that they are sent from God. ¶ *Them that believe.* The apostles, and those in the primitive age who were endowed with like power. This promise was fulfilled if it can be shown that these signs followed in the case of *any* who believed, and it is not necessary to suppose that they would follow in the case of *all*. The meaning is, that they would be the result of *faith*, or of the belief of the gospel. It is true that they were. These signs were shown in the case of the apostles and early Chris-

and if they drink any deadly thing, it shall not hurt them; they shall lay[o] hands on the sick, and they shall recover.

o Ac.5.15,16; 28.8; Ja.5.14,15.

19 So then [p]after the Lord had spoken unto them, he was received up into heaven, and [q]sat on the right hand of God.

p Ac.1.2,3; Lu.24.51.
q Ps.110.1; 1 Pe.3.22; Re.3.21.

tians. The infidel cannot say that the promise has not been fulfilled unless he can show that this *never* occurred; the Christian should be satisfied that the promise was fulfilled if these miracles were *ever* actually wrought, though they do not occur now; and the believer now should not expect a miracle in his case. Miracles were necessary for the establishment of religion in the world; they are not necessary for its continuance now. ¶ *In my name.* By my authority, and using the power that I would in such cases, if bodily present. This was done; and in this they differed essentially from the manner in which Jesus himself wrought miracles. He did it in *his own name*, and as possessing original, underived authority. See the account of his stilling the sea (Mat. viii. 26, &c.); of his healing the sick (Mat. ix. 5, 6); of his raising Lazarus, Jn. xi. The prophets spoke *in the name of the Lord.* The apostles did likewise, Ac. iii. 6, &c. There was, therefore, an important difference between Jesus and all the other messengers that God has sent into the world. He acted in his own name; they in the name of another. He wielded *his own* power; they were the *instruments* by which God put forth the omnipotence of his arm to save. *He* was therefore God; *they* were men, of like passions as other men, Ac. xiv. 15. ¶ *Shall they cast out devils.* See Notes on Mat. iv. 24. Comp. Ac. xvi. 16–18. ¶ *Shall speak with new tongues.* Shall speak other languages than their native language. This was remarkably fulfilled on the day of Pentecost, Ac. ii. 4–11. It existed, also, in other places. See 1 Co. xii. 10.

18. *They shall take up serpents.* When it is necessary for the sake of establishing religion, they shall handle poisonous reptiles without injury, thus showing that *God* was with them to keep them from harm. This was literally fulfilled when Paul shook the viper from his hand. See Ac. xxviii. 5, 6. ¶ *Any deadly thing.* Any poison usually causing death. ¶ *Shall not hurt them.* There is a similar promise in Is. xliii. 2. ¶ *They shall lay hands on the sick*, &c. See instances of this in the Acts of the Apostles, ch. iii. 6, 7; v. 15, &c.

19. *He was received up into heaven.* In a cloud from the Mount of Olives. See Ac. i. 9. ¶ *The right hand of God.* We are not to suppose that God has *hands*, or that Jesus sits in any particular *direction* from God. This phrase is taken from the manner of speaking among men, and means that he was exalted to honour and power in the heavens. It was esteemed the place of the *highest* honour to be seated at the right hand of a prince. So, to be seated at the right hand of God, means that Jesus is exalted to the highest honour of the universe. Comp. Ep. i. 20–22.

20. *They went forth.* The apostles. ¶ *Every where.* In all parts of the world. See the account in the Acts and the Epistles. ¶ *The Lord working with them.* By miracles; by removing obstacles; by supporting them; and by giving the gospel success and making it effectual to saving men. ¶ *Confirming the word.* Showing it to be the word of God or a revelation from heaven. ¶ *By signs following.* By attending miracles. By raising the dead, healing the sick, &c., as *signs* that God was with them, and had sent them forth to preach. ¶ *Amen.* Truly, verily. So be it. This word here, however, is of no authority. There is no reason to think that it was added by Mark.

Mark is more concise than either of the other evangelists. In most instances he coincides with Matthew, though he has added some circumstances which Matthew had omitted. There is no evidence, however, that he copied from Matthew. The last chapter in Mark contains some things omitted in Matthew, and some things of fearful import. We learn from it that the gospel is to be preached to all mankind. Every man is to be offered eternal life, and he rejects it at his peril. The condition of the man who *will* not believe is fearfully awful. The Son of God has solemnly declared that he shall be damned. *He* will judge the world, and there is none that can deliver out of his hand. No excuse will be allowed for

20 And they went forth, and preached every where, [r] the Lord working with *them*, and confirming the word with signs following. Amen.

r Ac 5.12; 14.3; He.2.4.

---

not believing. Unless a man has faith he *must* be lost for ever. This is the solemn assurance of the Bible; and in view of this awful declaration of the *merciful* Redeemer, how sad is the condition of him who has no confidence in Jesus, and who has never looked to him for eternal life! And how important that without delay he should make his peace with God, and possess that faith which is connected with everlasting salvation!

SCRIPTURE WEIGHTS, MEASURES, AND MONEY

I.—Scriptural Measures of Length, reduced to English Measure.

								Feet.	Inches.
A Digit,								0	0·912
4	A Palm,							0	3·648
12	3	A Span,						0	10·944
24	6	3	A Cubit,					1	9·888
96	24	6	2	A Fathom,				7	3·552
144	36	12	6	1·5	Ezekiel's Reed,			10	11·328
192	48	16	8	2	1·3	An Arabian Pole,		14	7·104
1920	480	160	80	20	13·3	10	A *Schœnus*, or Measuring Line,	145	11·04

II.—The Long Scripture Measures.

						Miles.	Paces.	Feet.
A Cubit,						0	0	1·824
400	A Stadium, or Furlong,					0	145	4·6
2000	5	A Sabbath Day's Journey,				0	729	3
4000	10	2	An Eastern Mile,			1	403	1
12000	30	6	3	A Parasang,		4	153	3
96000	240	48	24	8	A Day's Journey,	33	172	4

III.—Jewish Money reduced to our Standard.

					£	s.	d.
A Gerah,					0	0	1·2687
10	A Bekah,				0	1	1·6875
20	2	A Shekel,			0	2	3·375
1200	120	50	A Maneh, or Mina,		5	14	0·75
60000	6000	3000	60	A Talent of Silver,	342	3	9
A gold Shekel was worth					1	16	6
A Talent of gold was worth					5475	0	0

IV.—Roman Money, mentioned in the New Testament, reduced to our Standard.

A Mite, about three-eighths of a farthing.
A Farthing, about three-fourths of a farthing.
A Penny or Denarius, sevenpence three farthings.
A Pound or Mina, three pounds two shillings and sixpence.

INDEX

TO THE NOTES ON THE GOSPELS BY MATTHEW AND MARK

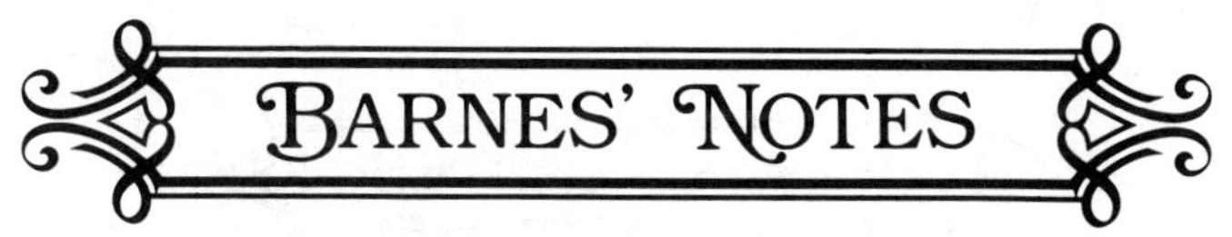

Notes on the New Testament

Albert Barnes

Edited by

Robert Frew

LUKE AND JOHN

Heritage Edition

Fourteen Volumes 0834-4

1. Genesis (Murphy)	0835-2	8. Minor Prophets (Pusey)	0842-5
2. Exodus to Esther (Cook)	0836-0	9. The Gospels	0843-3
3. Job	0837 9	10. Acts and Romans	0844-1
4. Psalms	0838-7	11. I Corinthians to Galatians	0846-8
5. Proverbs to Ezekiel (Cook)	0839-5	12. Ephesians to Philemon	0847-6
6. Isaiah	0840-9	13. Hebrews to Jude	0848-4
7. Daniel	0841-7	14. Revelation	0849-2

When ordering by ISBN (International Standard Book Number), numbers listed above should be preceded by 0-8010-.

Reprinted from the 1847 edition published
by Blackie & Son, London

Reprinted 2005 by Baker Books
a division of Baker Book House Company
P.O. Box 6287, Grand Rapids, MI 49516-6287

Printed in the United States of America

PREFACE

TO THE GOSPEL ACCORDING TO LUKE.

LITTLE is *certainly* known concerning the time and place of writing this Gospel, or concerning the author. The first time we have any mention of the author is in his own history, Ac. xvi. 10, 11. He was then the companion of Paul in his travels, and it is evident that he often attended Paul in his journeys, comp. Ac. xvi. 11–17; xxi. 1–6. In each of these places the author of "the Acts" speaks of *his* being in company with Paul. That the same person was the writer of this Gospel is also clear from Ac. i. 1.

From this circumstance the ancients regarded this Gospel as in fact the Gospel which Paul had preached. They affirm that Luke recorded what the apostle preached. Thus Irenæus says, "Luke, the companion of Paul, put down in a book the gospel preached by him." He also says, "Luke was not only a companion, but also a fellow-labourer of the apostles, especially of Paul." Origen, speaking of the Gospels, says, "The third is that according to Luke, the gospel commended by Paul, published for the sake of the Gentile converts." The testimony of the fathers is uniform that it was written by Luke, the companion of Paul, and was therefore regarded by them as really the gospel which Paul preached.

It is not known *where* it was written. Jerome says it was composed in Achaia. There seems to be some probability that it was written to persons that were well acquainted with Jewish manners, as the author does not stop to explain the peculiar customs of the Jews, as some of the other evangelists have done. Respecting the *time* when it was written nothing very definite is known. All that can with certainty be ascertained is that it was written before the death of Paul (A.D. 65), for it was written before the Acts (Ac. i. 1), and that book only brings down the life of Paul to his imprisonment at Rome, and previous to his going into Spain.

It has been made a matter of inquiry whether Luke was a Gentile or a Jew. On this subject there is no positive testimony. Jerome and others of the fathers say that he was a Syrian, and born at Antioch. The most probable opinion seems to be that he was a proselyte to the Jewish religion, though descended from Gentile parents. For this opinion two reasons may be assigned of some weight. 1st. He was intimately acquainted, as appears by the Gospel and the Acts, with the Jewish rites, customs, opinions, and prejudices; and he wrote in their *dialect*, that is, with much of the Hebrew phraseology, in a style similar to the other evangelists, from which it appears that he was accustomed to the Jewish religion, and was, therefore, probably a proselyte. Yet the *preface* to his Gospel, as critics have remarked, is pure classic Greek, unlike the Greek that was used by native Jews; from which it seems not improbable that he was by birth and education a Gentile. 2d. In Acts xxi. 27, it is said that the Asiatic Jews excited the multitude against Paul because he had introduced *Gentiles* into the temple, thus defiling it. In ver. 28 it is said that the Gentile to whom they had reference was *Trophimus*, an Ephesian. Yet *Luke* was also at that time with Paul. If *he* had been regarded as *a Gentile* it is probable that they would have made complaint respecting *him* as well as *Trophimus;* from which it is supposed that he was a Jewish proselyte.

But again, in the Epistle to the Colossians, ch. iv. 9–11, we find Paul saying that Aristarchus, and Marcus, and Barnabas, and Justus saluted them, "who are," he adds, "*of the circumcision*," that is, Jews by birth. In ver. 14 he says that *Luke*, the beloved physician, and Demas also saluted them; from which it is inferred that they were *not of the circumcision*, but were by birth Gentiles.

Most writers suppose that Luke, the writer of this Gospel, was intended in the above place in Colossians. If so, his profession was that of *a physician;* and it has been remarked that his descriptions of diseases are more accurate and circumstantial, and have more of *technical* correctness than those of the other evangelists.

Luke does not profess to have been an eye-witness of what he recorded. See ch. i. 2, 3. It is clear, therefore, that he was not one of the seventy disciples, nor one of the two who went to Emmaus, as has been sometimes supposed. Nor was he an apostle. By the fathers he is uniformly called the *companion* of the apostles, and especially of Paul.

If he was not one of the apostles, and if he was not one of those expressly commissioned by our Lord to whom the promise of the infallible teaching of the Holy Ghost was given, the question arises by what authority his Gospel and the Acts have a place in the sacred canon, or what evidence is there that he was divinely inspired?

In regard to this question the following considerations may give satisfaction: 1st. They were received by all the churches on the same footing as the first three Gospels. There is not a dissenting voice in regard to their authenticity and authority. The value of this argument is this—that if they had been spurious, or without authority, the fathers were the proper persons to know it. 2d. They were published during the lives of the apostles Peter, Paul, and John, and were received *during* their lives as books of sacred authority. If the writings of Luke were not inspired, and had no authority, those apostles could easily have destroyed their credit, and we have reason to think it would have been done. 3d. It is the united testimony of the fathers that this Gospel was submitted to Paul, and received his express approbation. It was regarded as the substance of his preaching, and if it received his approbation it comes to *us* on the authority of his name. Indeed, if this be the case, it rests on the same authority as the epistles of Paul himself. 4th. It bears the same marks of inspiration as the other books. It is simple, pure, yet sublime; there is nothing unworthy of God; and it is elevated far above the writings of any uninspired man. 5th. If he was *not* inspired—if, as we suppose, he was a Gentile by birth—and if, as is most clear, he was not an eye-witness of what he records, it is inconceivable that he did not contradict the other evangelists. That he did not *borrow* from them is clear. Nor is it possible to conceive that he could write a book varying in the order of its *arrangement* so much, and adding so many new facts, and repeating so many recorded also by the others, without *often* having contradicted what was written by them. Let any man compare this Gospel with the spurious gospels of the following centuries, and he will be struck with the force of this remark. 6th. If it be objected that, not being an apostle, he did not come within the *promise* of inspiration (Jn. xiv. 26; xvi. 13, 14) made to the apostles, it may be replied that this was also the case with Paul; yet no small part of the New Testament is composed of his writings. The evidence of the inspiration of the writings of Luke and Paul is to be judged, not only by that *promise*, but by the early reception of the churches; by the testimony of the fathers as to the judgment of *inspired men* when living, and by the internal character of the works. Luke has all these equally with the other evangelists.

THE
GOSPEL ACCORDING TO LUKE

CHAPTER I.

FORASMUCH as many have
taken in hand to set forth in
order a declaration of those things
which are most surely believed
among us,
2 Even as they delivered them
unto us, which [a]from the beginning
were eye-witnesses and [b]ministers
of the word;
3 It seemed good to me also,
having had perfect understanding

a Jn.15.27; He.2.3; 1 Pe.5.1; 2 Pe.1.16; 1 Jn.1.1.
b Ro.15.16; Ep.3.7; 4.11,12.

---

1. *Forasmuch as many.* It has been doubted who are referred to here by the word *many.* It seems clear that it could not be the other evangelists, for the gospel by *John* was not yet written, and the word *many* denotes clearly more than *two.* Besides, it is said that they undertook to record what the *eye-witnesses* had delivered to them, so that the writers did not pretend to be eye-witnesses themselves. It is clear, therefore, that other writings are meant than the gospels which we now have, but what they were is a matter of conjecture. What are now known as spurious gospels were written long after Luke wrote his. It is probable that Luke refers to *fragments* of history, or to narratives of *detached* sayings, acts, or parables of our Lord, which had been made and circulated among the disciples and others. His doctrines were original, bold, pure, and authoritative. His miracles had been extraordinary, clear, and awful. His life and death had been peculiar; and it is not improbable—indeed it is highly probable—that such broken accounts and narratives of detached facts would be preserved. That this is what Luke means appears farther from ver. 3, where *he* professes to give a regular, full, and systematic account from the very beginning—"having had perfect understanding of *all things from the very first.*" The records of the others—the "many"—were broken and incomplete. His were to be regular and full. ¶ *Taken in hand.* Undertaken, attempted. ¶ *To set forth in order.* To compose a narrative. It does not refer to the *order* or *arrangement,* but means simply to give a narrative. The word rendered here *in order* is different from that in the third verse, which *has* reference *to order,* or to a full and fair *arrangement* of the principal facts, &c., in the history of our Lord. ¶ *A declaration.* A narrative—an account of. ¶ *Which are most surely believed among us.* Among Christians—among *all* the Christians then living. Here we may remark—1st. That Christians of *that* day had the best of all opportunities for knowing whether those things were true. Many had seen them, and all others had had the account from those who had witnessed them. 2d. That infidels now cannot *possibly* be as good judges in the matter as those who lived at the time, and who were thus competent to determine whether these things were true or false. 3d. That all Christians do *most surely believe* the truth of the gospel. It is their life, their hope, their all. Nor can they doubt that their Saviour lived, bled, died, rose, and still lives; that he was their atoning sacrifice, and that he is God over all, blessed for ever.

2. *As they delivered them.* As they *narrated* them. As they gave an account of them. ¶ *From the beginning.* From the commencement of these things—that is, from the birth of John, or perhaps from the beginning of the ministry of Jesus. ¶ *Eye-witnesses.* Who had seen those things themselves, and who were therefore proper witnesses. ¶ *Ministers of the word.* The term *word* here means the *gospel.* Luke never uses it, as *John* does, to denote the second person of the Trinity. These eye-witnesses and ministers refer, doubtless, to the seventy disciples, to the apostles, and perhaps to other preachers who had gone forth to proclaim the same things.

of all things from the very first, to write unto thee [c]in order, most excellent [d]Theophilus,

4 That thou mightest [e]know the certainty of those things wherein thou hast been instructed.

5 THERE was, [f]in the days of Herod the king of Judea, a certain priest named Zacharias, of the course of [g]Abia: and his wife *was* of the daughters of Aaron, and her name *was* Elisabeth.

c Ac.11.4. d Ac.1.1. e Jn.20.31.

f Mat.2.1. g 1 Ch.24.10; Ne.12.4,17.

3. *It seemed good.* I thought it best; or, I have also determined. It seemed *to be called for* that there should be a full, authentic, and accurate account of these matters. ¶ *Having had perfect understanding*, &c. The literal translation of the original here would be, "having exactly traced everything from the first;" or, "having, by diligent and careful investigation, *followed up* everything to the *source*, to obtain an accurate account of the matter." This much better expresses the idea. Luke did not profess to have *seen* these things, and this expression is designed to show how he acquired his information. It was by *tracing up* every account till he became satisfied of its truth. Here observe, 1st. That in religion God does not set aside our natural faculties. He calls us to look at evidence; to examine accounts; to make up our own minds. Nor will any man be convinced of the truth of religion who does *not* make investigation and set himself seriously to the task. 2d. We see the nature of Luke's inspiration. It was consistent with his using his natural faculties or his own powers of mind in investigating the truth. God, by his Holy Spirit, presided *over* his faculties, directed them, and kept him from error. ¶ *In order.* This word does not indicate that the exact order of *time* would be observed, for that is *not* the way in which he writes; but it means *distinctly*, *particularly*, in opposition to the confused and broken accounts to which he had referred before. ¶ *Most excellent Theophilus.* The word Theophilus means *a friend of God*, or a pious man; and it has been supposed by some that Luke did not refer to any particular *individual*, but to any man that loved God; but there is no reason for this opinion. Significant names were very common, and there is no good reason to doubt that this was some individual known to Luke. The application of the title "*most excellent*" farther proves it. It would not be given to an unknown man. The title *most excellent* has by some been supposed to be given to express his *character*, but it is rather to be considered as denoting *rank* or *office*. It occurs only in three other places in the New Testament, and is there given to men *in office*—to Felix and Festus, Ac. xxiii. 26; xxiv. 3; xxvi. 25. These titles express no quality of the *men*, but belong to the *office;* and we may hence learn that it is not improper for Christians, in giving honour to whom honour is due, to address men in office by their customary titles, even if their moral character be altogether unworthy of it. Who *Theophilus* was is unknown. It is probable that he was some distinguished Roman or Greek who had been converted, who was a friend of Luke, and who had requested an account of these things. It is possible that this *preface* might have been sent to him as a *private* letter *with* the gospel, and Theophilus chose to have them published together.

4. *The certainty.* Have full evidence or proof of. ¶ *Been instructed.* By the preachers of the gospel. The original word is the one from which is derived our word *catechism—been catechised;* but it does not here denote the *manner* in which the instruction was imparted, as it does with us, but simply the *fact* that he had been *taught* those things.

5. *In the days of Herod.* See Notes on Mat. ii. 1. ¶ *Of the course of Abia.* When the priests became so numerous that they could not at once minister at the altar, David divided them into twenty-four classes or *courses*, each one of which officiated for a week, 1 Ch. xxiv. The class or course of Abia was the *eighth* in order, 1 Ch. xxiv. 10. Comp. 2 Ch. viii. 14. The word *course* means the same as *class*, or order. The *Greek* word *Abia* is the same as the *Hebrew* word *Abijah.* ¶ *His wife was of the daughters of Aaron.* A descendant of Aaron, the first high-priest of the Jews; so that *John the Baptist* was descended, on the father's and the mother's side, from priests. Our Saviour was not on either side. John would have been *legally* entitled to a place among the

6 And they were both [h]righteous before God, walking in all the commandments and [i]ordinances of the Lord blameless.

7 And they had no child, because that Elisabeth was barren, and they both were *now* well stricken in years.

8 And it came to pass, that while he executed the priest's office before God in the order of his course,

9 According to the custom of the priest's office, his lot was to [k]burn incense when he went into the temple of the Lord.

10 And the whole multitude of the people were praying [l]without, at the time of incense.

11 And there appeared unto him an angel of the Lord standing on the right side of the [m]altar of incense.

h Ge.7.1; 1 Ki.9.4; 2 Ki.20.3. *i* 1 Co.11.2; Phi.3.6. *k* Ex.30.7,8. *l* Le.16.17. *m* Ex.30.1; Re.8.3,4.

---

priests; our Saviour, being of the tribe of *Judah*, would not.

6. *Both righteous.* Both *just* or holy. This means here more than external conformity to the law. It is an honourable testimonial of their *piety* toward God. ¶ *Walking in*, &c. *Keeping* the commandments. To *walk* in the way that God commands is *to obey.* ¶ *Ordinances.* Rites and customs which God had *ordained* or appointed. These words refer to all the duties of religion which were made known to them. ¶ *Blameless.* That is, no fault or deficiency could be found in them. They were strict, exact, punctual. Yet this, if it had been mere *external* observance, might have been no proof of piety. Paul, before his conversion, also kept the law *externally* blameless, Phi. iii. 6. But in the case of Zachariah and Elisabeth it was real love to God and sincere regard for his law.

7. *Well stricken in years.* Old or advanced in life, so as to render the prospect of having children hopeless.

8. *Before God.* In the temple, where God dwelt by the symbols of his presence. The temple was regarded by the Jews as the *house* or dwelling of God; and in the *first* temple there was, in the most holy place, a *cloud* called the Shechinah, or a visible sign of the presence of God. It was thus *before God* that Zachariah offered incense.

9. *According to the custom of the priest's office, his lot was.* The Jewish writers inform us that it was customary for the priests to divide their daily task by *lot.* ¶ *To burn incense.* Incense is an aromatic or white rosin procured from trees, chiefly in Arabia. It is obtained by making incisions in the tree, and the gum flows out. It is distinguished for a peculiarly pleasant *smell* when burned, and was therefore used in ancient worship. It was burned by the priest twice a day (Ex. xxx. 7), and it seems to have been emblematic of prayer and praise, or of the grateful offerings of the heart wafted toward heaven. The incense used in the temple was made of stacte, onycha, and galbanum (Ex. xxx. 34), with pure frankincense, and it was not lawful for this compound to be used elsewhere than in the house of God. ¶ *Into the temple.* See Notes on Mat. xxi. 12. The *part* of the temple where incense was burned was the *holy place.*

10. *The whole multitude.* This was the regular time of evening prayer, and multitudes came up to the temple to worship. ¶ *Praying without.* That is, in the *courts* around the temple, particularly in the court of the women.

11. *An angel.* An *angel* is a messenger sent from God. See Notes on Mat. i. 20. It had now been about four hundred years since the time of *Malachi*, and since there had been any divine revelation. During that time the nation was looking for the Messiah, but still with nothing more than the ancient prophecies to direct them. Now that he was about to appear, God sent his messenger to announce his coming, to encourage the hearts of his people, and to prepare them to receive him. ¶ *On the right side*, &c. The altar of incense stood close by the veil which divided the holy place from the most holy. On the north stood the table of shew-bread; on the south the golden candlestick. As Zacharias entered, therefore, with his face to the west, the angel would stand on the north, or near the table of shew-bread. That table was 18 inches square and 3 feet high. The top, as well as the sides and horns, was overlaid with pure gold, and it was finished around the upper surface with a crown

12 And when Zacharias saw *him*, he was [n]troubled, and fear fell upon him.

13 But the angel said unto him, Fear not, Zacharias; for thy prayer is heard; and thy wife Elisabeth shall bear thee a son, and thou shalt call his name [o]John.

14 And thou shalt have joy and gladness; and many shall [p]rejoice at his birth.

15 For he shall be [q]great in the sight of the Lord, and shall [r]drink neither wine nor strong drink; and he shall be filled with the Holy Ghost, even [s]from his mother's womb.

n Ju.13.22; ver.29. *o* ver.60,63.

p ver.58. *q* ch.7.28. *r* Nu.6.3. *s* Je.1.5.

or border of gold. Just below this border, four golden rings were attached to each side of the altar, one near each corner. The staves or rods for bearing the altar passed through these rings, and were made of the same wood with the altar itself, and richly overlaid with the same precious metal. Upon this altar incense was burned every morning and every evening, so that it was literally perpetual, Ex. xxx. 8. Neither burnt-sacrifice, nor meat-offering, nor drink-offering was permitted upon this altar; nor was it ever stained with blood except once annually, when the priest made atonement, Le. xvi. 18, 19.

12. *He was troubled.* He was alone, in the presence of God. The appearance of the angel was sudden, unexpected, and therefore fearful.

13. *Thy prayer is heard.* That is, thy prayer for offspring. This, among the Jews, was an object of intense desire. No prospect was more gloomy to them than that of dying childless, so that their *name should perish.* Special pains, therefore, had been taken in the law to keep up the names of families by requiring a man to marry his brother's wife, De. xxv. 5.

14. *Many shall rejoice at his birth.* This does not refer so much to the *time* of his birth as to the subsequent rejoicing. Such will be his *character*, that he will be an honour to the family, and many will rejoice that he lived; or, in other words, he will be a blessing to mankind.

15. *Shall be great.* Shall be eminent, or distinguished as a preacher. ¶ *In the sight of the Lord.* Greek, *before the Lord.* That is, shall be *really* or *truly* great. God shall regard him as such. ¶ *Shall drink neither wine.* The kind of wine commonly used in Judea was a light wine, often not stronger than cider in this country. It was the common drink of all classes of the people. See Notes on Jn. ii. 11. The use of wine was forbidden only to the Nazarite, Nu. vi. 3. It was because John sustained this character that he abstained from the use of wine. ¶ *Strong drink.* It is not easy to ascertain precisely what is meant by this word, but we are certain that it does not mean strong drink in *our* sense of the term. Distilled spirits were not then known. The art of distilling was discovered by an Arabian chemist in the ninth or tenth century; but distilled liquors are not used by Arabians. They banished them at once, as if sensible of their pernicious influence; nor are they used in Eastern nations at all. Europe and America have been the places where this poison has been most extensively used, and there it has beggared and ruined millions, and is yearly sweeping thousands unprepared into a wretched eternity. The *strong drink* among the Jews was probably nothing more than fermented liquors, or a drink obtained from fermented dates, figs, and the juice of the palm, or the lees of wine, mingled with sugar, and having the property of producing intoxication. Many of the Jewish writers say that by the word here translated *strong drink* was meant nothing more than *old wine*, which probably had the power of producing intoxication. See Notes on Is. v. 11. ¶ *Shall be filled with the Holy Ghost*, &c. Shall be divinely designated or appointed to this office, and qualified for it by all needful communications of the Holy Spirit. To be *filled* with the Holy Spirit is to be illuminated, sanctified, and guided by his influence. In this place it refers—1st. To the divine *intention* that he should be set apart to this work, as God designed that Paul should be an apostle from his mother's womb, Ga. i. 15. 2d. It refers to an actual fitting for the work from the birth by the influence of the Holy Spirit, as was the case with Jeremiah (Je. i. 5), and with the Messiah himself, Ps. xxii. 9, 10.

16 And many of the children of Israel shall he turn to the Lord their God.

17 And[t] he shall go before him in the spirit and power of Elias, to turn the hearts of the fathers to the children, and the disobedient [1]to the [u]wisdom of the just; to make ready a [v]people prepared for the Lord.

18 And Zacharias said unto the angel, Whereby shall I know this? for [w]I am an old man, and my wife well stricken in years.

19 And the angel answering, said unto him, I am [x]Gabriel, that stand

t Mal.4.5,6; Mat.11.14; Mar.9.12,13. [1] or, *by*. *u* Ps.111.10.

v 1 Pe.2.9. *w* Ge.17.17. *x* Da.8.16; ver.26.

16. *Children of Israel.* Jews. Descendants of Israel or Jacob. ¶ *Shall he turn.* By repentance. He shall call them from their sins, and persuade them to forsake them, and to seek the Lord their God.

17. *Shall go before him.* Before the Messiah. The connection here leads us to suppose that the word *him* refers to the "Lord their God" in the previous verse. If so, then it will follow that the Messiah was the Lord God of Israel—a character abundantly given him in other parts of the New Testament. ¶ *In the spirit and power of Elias.* See Notes on Mat. xi. 14. ¶ *To turn the hearts of the fathers to the children.* In the time of John the Jews were divided into a number of different sects. See Notes on Mat. iii. 7. They were opposed violently to each other, and pursued their opposition with great animosity. It was impossible but that this opposition should find its way into *families*, and divide parents and children from each other. John came that he might allay these animosities and produce better feeling. By directing them *all* to *one Master*, the Messiah, he would divert their attention from the causes of their difference and bring them to union. He would restore peace to their families, and reconcile those parents and children who had chosen different sects, and who had suffered their attachment *to sect* to interrupt the harmony of their households. The effect of true religion on a family will always be to produce harmony. It attaches all the family to *one* great Master, and by attachment to *him* all minor causes of difference are forgotten. ¶ *And the disobedient to the wisdom of the just.* The *disobedient* here are the unbelieving, and hence the impious, the wicked. These he would turn to the wisdom of the just, or to such wisdom as the *just* or pious manifest—that is, to true wisdom. ¶ *To make ready a people*, &c. To prepare them for his coming by announcing that the Messiah was about to appear, and by calling them to repentance. God has always required men to be pure in a special manner when he was about to appear among them. Thus the Israelites were required to purify themselves for three days when he was about to come down on Mount Sinai, Ex. xix. 14, 15. And so, when God the Son was about to appear as the Redeemer, he required that men should *prepare* themselves for his coming. So in view of the future judgment—the second coming of the Son of man—he requires that men should repent, believe, and be pure, 1 Pe. iv. 7; 2 Pe. iii. 11, 12.

18. *Whereby shall I know this?* The thing was improbable, and he desired *evidence* that it would take place. The testimony of an *angel*, and in such *a place*, should have been proof enough; but men are slow to believe the testimony of heavenly messengers. As a consequence of not believing, he was struck dumb.

19. *I am Gabriel.* The word *Gabriel* is made up of two Hebrew words, and signifies *man of God.* This angel is mentioned as having been deputed to inform *Daniel* that his prayers were heard. See Notes on Da. viii. 16; ix. 21. ¶ *That stand in the presence of God.* To stand in the presence of one is a phrase denoting *honour* or *favour.* To be admitted to the presence of a king, or to be with him, was a token of favour. So to stand before God signifies merely that he was honoured or favoured by God. He was permitted to come near him, and to see much of his glory. Comp. 1 Ki. x. 8; xii. 6; xvii. 1; Pr. xxii. 29. ¶ *And am sent*, &c. The angels are "*ministering spirits* sent forth to minister for them who shall be heirs of salvation," He. i. 7, 14. They delight to do the will of God, and one way of doing that will is by aiding his children here, by succouring the afflicted, and by defending those who are in danger.

in the presence of God; and am [y]sent to speak unto thee, and to show thee these glad tidings.

20 And, behold, thou [z]shalt be dumb, and not able to speak, until the day that these things shall be performed, because thou believest not my words, which shall be fulfilled in their season.

21 And the people waited for Zacharias, and marvelled that he tarried so long in the temple.

22 And when he came out he could not speak unto them; and they perceived that he had seen a vision in the temple; for he beckoned unto them, and remained speechless.

23 And it came to pass that, as soon as the days of his ministration were accomplished, he departed to his own house.

24 And after those days his wife Elisabeth conceived, and hid herself five months, saying,

25 Thus hath the Lord dealt

y He.1.14. *z* Eze.3.26.

There is no more absurdity or impropriety in supposing that *angels* may render such aid, than there is in supposing that good men may assist one another; and there can be no doubt that it affords high pleasure to the angels of God to be *permitted* to aid those who are treading the dangerous and trying path which leads to eternity. Holiness is the same as benevolence, and holy beings seek and love opportunities to do good to their fellow-creatures. In the eye of holy beings all God's creatures are parts of one great family, and whenever they can do them good they rejoice in the opportunity, at any sacrifice. ¶ *These glad tidings.* This good news respecting the birth of a son.

20. *Because thou believest not*, &c. This was both a sign and a judgment—a sign that he had come from God, and that the thing would be fulfilled; and a judgment for not giving credit to what he had said. There is no sin in the sight of God more aggravated than unbelief. When GOD speaks, man should believe; nor can he that *will not* believe escape punishment. God speaks only truth, and we should believe him. God speaks only what is for our good, and it is right that we should suffer if we do not credit what he says.

21. *The people waited.* That is, beyond the usual time. ¶ *Marvelled.* Wondered. The priest, it is said, was not accustomed to remain in the temple more than half an hour commonly. Having remained on this occasion a longer time, the people became apprehensive of his safety, and wondered what had happened to him.

22. *Had seen a vision.* The word *vision* means *sight*, *appearance*, or *spectre*, and is commonly applied to spirits, or to beings from another world. When he came out of the temple, it is probable that they *suspected* that something of this nature had detained him there, and that, on inquiry of him, he signified by a nod that this was the case. He was unable to speak, and they had no way of "*perceiving*" it but by such a sign. On the word *vision*, see Notes on Is. i. 1. ¶ *For he beckoned unto them.* That is, by beckoning unto them, or by a sign, he informed them of what he had seen.

23. *As soon as the days of his ministration*, &c. As soon as he had fulfilled the duties of the week. It might have been supposed that the extraordinary occurrence in the temple, together with his own calamity, would have induced him at once to leave this place and return home; but his duty was in the temple. His piety prompted him to remain there in the service of God. He was not unfitted for burning incense by his dumbness, and it was not proper for him to leave his post. It is the duty of ministers of religion to remain at their work until they are unfitted for it, and unable to serve God in their profession. Then they *must* retire. But until that time, he that for trifling causes forsakes his post is guilty of unfaithfulness to his Master.

24. *Hid herself.* Did not go forth into public, and concealed her condition. This might have been done that she might spend her time more entirely in giving praise to God for his mercies, and that she might have the fullest proof of the accomplishment of the promise before she appeared in public or spoke of the mercies of God.

25. *Thus.* In this merciful manner. ¶ *To take away my reproach.* Among

with me in the days wherein he
looked on *me*, to [a]take away my
reproach among men.
26 And in the sixth month the
angel Gabriel was sent from God
unto a city of Galilee named Nazareth,
27 To a [b]virgin espoused to a
man whose name was Joseph, of
the house of David; and the virgin's name *was* Mary.
28 And the angel came in unto
her, and said, Hail, [c]*thou that art*
highly[2] favoured, [d]the Lord *is*
with thee: blessed *art* thou among
women.

a Ge.30.23; 1 Sa.1.6; Is.54.1,4.
b Mat.1.18. *c* Da.9.23.
2 or, *graciously accepted;* or, *much graced.*
d Ju.6.12.

29 And when she saw *him*, she
was troubled at his saying, and
cast in her mind what manner of
salutation this should be.
30 And the angel said unto her,
Fear not, Mary; for thou hast
found favour with God.
31 And, behold, [e]thou shalt conceive in thy womb, and bring forth
a son, and shalt call his name
JESUS.
32 He shall be [f]great, and shall
be called the [g]Son of the Highest:
and the Lord God shall give unto
him the [h]throne of his father
David:

e Is.7.14; Mat.1.21. *f* Mat.12.42. *g* He.1.2-8.
h 2 Sa.7.11,12; Is.9.6,7.

the Jews, a family of children was counted a signal blessing, an evidence of the favour of God, Ps. cxiii. 9; cxxviii. 3; Is. iv. 1; xliv. 3, 4; Le. xxvi. 9. To be *barren*, therefore, or to be destitute of children, was considered a *reproach* or a *disgrace*, 1 Sa. i. 6.

26. *In the sixth month.* The sixth month after Elisabeth's conception. ¶ *A city of Galilee, named Nazareth.* See Notes on Mat. ii. 22, 23.

27. *To a virgin espoused*, &c. See Notes on Mat. i. 18, 19. Comp. Notes on Is. vii. 14. ¶ *House of David.* Family of David, or descendants of David.

28. *Hail.* This word of salutation is equivalent to *Peace be with thee*, or *Joy be with thee;* a form of speech implying that she was signally favoured, and expressing joy at meeting her. ¶ *Highly favoured.* By being the mother of the long-expected Messiah—the mother of the Redeemer of mankind. Long had he been predicted; long had the eyes of the nation been turned to him, and long had his coming been an object of intense desire. To be reckoned among his *ancestors* was accounted sufficient honour for even Abraham and David. But now the happy *individual* was designated who was to be his mother; and on Mary, a poor virgin of Nazareth, was to come this honour, which would have rendered infinitely illustrious any of the daughters of Adam—the honour of giving birth to the world's Redeemer and the Son of God. ¶ *The Lord is with thee.* The word *is* is not in the original, and the passage may be rendered either "the Lord *is* with thee," or "the Lord *be* with thee," implying the prayer of the angel that all blessings from God might descend and rest upon her. ¶ *Blessed art thou among women.* This passage is equivalent to saying "thou art the most happy of women."

29. *Troubled at his saying.* Disturbed or perplexed at what he said. It was so unexpected, so sudden, so extraordinary, and was so high an honour, that she was filled with anxious thoughts, and did not know what to make of it. ¶ *Cast in her mind.* Thought, or revolved in her mind. ¶ *What manner of salutation.* What this salutation could mean.

30. *Fear not, Mary.* Do not be alarmed at this appearance of an angel. He only comes to announce to you good tidings. Similar language was addressed by an angel to Joseph. See Notes on Mat. i. 20. ¶ *Thou hast found favour with God.* Eminent favour or mercy in being selected to be the mother of the Messiah.

31. *And, behold, thou shalt conceive in thy womb.* See Notes on Is. vii. 14. ¶ *And shalt call his name Jesus.* A Saviour. See Notes on Mat. i. 21. All this was announced, also, by an angel to Joseph, *after* this visitation to Mary. See Notes on Mat. i. 20, 21.

32. *He shall be great.* There is undoubted reference in this passage to Is. ix. 6, 7. By his being *great* is meant he shall be distinguished or illustrious; great in power, in wisdom, in dominion, on earth and in heaven. ¶ *Shall be*

33 And he shall reign over the
house of Jacob for ever; and [i]of
his kingdom there shall be no end.
34 Then said Mary unto the
angel, How shall this be, seeing I
know not a man?
35 And the angel answered and
said unto her, The Holy Ghost
shall come upon thee, and the
power of the Highest shall overshadow thee; therefore also that
holy thing which shall be born of
thee shall be called [k]the Son of
God.

i Da.7.14,27; Mi.4.7. *k* Mar.1.1; Jn.1.34.

36 And, behold, thy cousin Elisabeth, she hath also conceived a
son in her old age: and this is the
sixth month with her who was
called barren.
37 For[l] with God nothing shall
be impossible.
38 And Mary said, Behold the
[m]handmaid of the Lord; be it unto
me [n]according to thy word. And
the angel departed from her.
39 And Mary arose in those days,
and went into the hill country with
haste, into a [o]city of Juda;

l Mat.19.26; Ro.4.21. *m* Ps.116.16. *n* Ps.119.38. *o* Jos.21.9-11.

---

called. This is the same as to say he *shall be* the Son, &c. The Hebrews often used this form of speech. See Mat. xxi. 13. ¶ *The Highest.* God, who is infinitely exalted; called *the* Highest, because he is exalted over all his creatures on earth and in heaven. See Mar. v. 7. ¶ *The throne.* The kingdom; or shall appoint him as the lineal successor of David in the kingdom. ¶ *His father David.* David is called his *father* because Jesus was lineally descended from him. See Mat. i. 1. The promise to David was, that there should *not fail a man to sit on his throne*, or that his throne should be perpetual (1 Ki. ii. 4; viii. 25; ix. 5; 2 Ch. vi. 16), and the promise was fulfilled by exalting Jesus to be a Prince and a Saviour, and the perpetual King of his people.

33. *Over the house of Jacob.* The *house* of Jacob means the same thing as the *family* of Jacob, or the descendants of Jacob—that is, the children of Israel. This was the name by which the ancient people of God were known, and it is the same as saying that he would reign over his own church and people for ever. This he does by giving them laws, by defending them, and by guiding them; and this he will do for ever in the kingdom of his glory. ¶ *Of his kingdom there shall be no end.* He shall reign among his people on earth until the end of time, and be their king for ever in heaven. *His* is the only kingdom that shall never have an end; *He* the only King that shall never lay aside his diadem and robes, and that shall never die. *He* the only King that can defend us from all our enemies, sustain us in death, and reward us in eternity. O how important, then, to have an interest in his kingdom! and how unimportant, compared with *his* favour, is the favour of all earthly monarchs!

35. *The Holy Ghost shall come upon thee.* See Mat. i. 20. ¶ *The power of the Highest*, &c. This evidently means that the body of Jesus would be created by the direct power of God. It was not by ordinary generation; but, as the Messiah came to redeem sinners—to make atonement for *others*, and not for himself—it was necessary that his human nature should be pure, and free from the corruption of the fall. God therefore prepared him a body by direct creation that should be pure and holy. See He. x. 5. ¶ *That holy thing*, &c. That holy progeny or child. ¶ *Shall be called the Son of God.* This is spoken in reference to the human nature of Christ, and this passage proves, beyond controversy, that *one* reason why Jesus was called the Son of God was because he was begotten in a supernatural manner. He is also called the *Son of God* on account of his resurrection, Ro. i. 4; Ac. xiii. 33, compared with Ps. ii. 7.

36, 37. *Thy cousin Elisabeth*, &c. The case of Elisabeth is mentioned to inspire Mary with confidence, and to assure her that what was now promised would be fulfilled. It was almost as improbable that Elisabeth should have a child at her time of life, as it was that Mary should under the circumstances promised..

38. *And Mary said, Behold the handmaid*, &c. This was an expression of resignation to the will of God, and of faith in the promise. To be the *handmaid of the Lord* is to be submissive and obedient, and is the same as saying, "I fully credit all that is said, and am per-

40 And entered into the house of
Zacharias, and saluted Elisabeth.
41 And it came to pass, that,
when Elisabeth heard the salutation of Mary, the babe leaped in
her womb; and Elisabeth was
filled with the Holy Ghost:
42 And she spake out with a
loud voice; and said, [p] Blessed *art*
thou among women; and blessed
is the fruit of thy womb.
43 And whence *is* this to me,
that the mother of my [q] Lord
should come to me?
44 For lo, as soon as the voice
of thy salutation sounded in mine
ears, the babe leaped in my womb
for joy.
45 And blessed *is* she [3] that
believed: for there shall be a performance of those things which
were told her from the Lord.
46 And Mary said, [r] My soul
doth magnify the Lord,

p Ju.5.24; ver.28.

q Jn.13.13.
3 or, *which believed that there shall be.*
r 1 Sa.2.1; Ps.34.2,3.

fectly ready to obey all the commands of the Lord."

39. *And Mary arose.* The word *arose* here is equivalent to *setting out*, or starting on a journey. ¶ *The hill country.* The region in the vicinity of Jerusalem, commonly called the hill country of Judea. ¶ *City of Juda.* What city is meant is not known. Some have supposed it to be Jerusalem, others Hebron; but all is conjecture. It was probably a Levitical city, and the residence of Zacharias when he was not employed in the temple.

40. *Saluted Elisabeth.* Expressed great joy and gratification at seeing her, and used the customary tokens of affectionate salutation.

41. *Elisabeth was filled with the Holy Ghost.* The meaning of this seems to be that she was filled with joy; with a disposition to praise God; with a prophetic spirit, or a knowledge of the character of the child that should be born of her. All these were produced by the Holy Ghost.

42. *Blessed* art *thou among women.* She here repeated nearly the words of the angel to Mary, esteeming it to be the highest honour among mothers to be the mother of the Messiah. See Notes on ver. 28.

43. *And whence is this to me?* An expression of humility. Why is it that the mother of my Lord should come to *me*, as if to honour me? ¶ *Mother of my Lord.* The word *Lord* sometimes denotes *divinity*, and sometimes superior, master, teacher, or governor. It was given by the Jews to their expected Messiah; but whether they understood it as denoting divinity cannot now be ascertained. It is clear only that Elisabeth used it as denoting great dignity and honour.

45. *Blessed* is *she that believed.* That is, *Mary*, who believed what the angel spoke to her. She was blessed not only in the *act* of believing, but because the thing promised would certainly be fulfilled.

From these expressions of Elisabeth we may learn—1st. That the spirit of prophecy had not entirely ceased among the Jews. 2d. That the Holy Ghost is the source of light, comfort, and joy. 3d. That everything about the birth of Jesus was remarkable, and that he must have been more than a mere man. 4th. That the prospect of the coming of the Messiah was one of great joy and rejoicing to ancient saints; and, 5th. That it was a high honour to be *the mother* of him that should redeem mankind. It is from *that honour* that the Roman Catholics have determined that it is right to worship the Virgin Mary and to offer prayers to her—an act of worship as idolatrous as any that could be offered to a creature. For—1st. It is not anywhere commanded in the Bible. 2d. It is expressly forbidden to worship any being but God, Ex. xxxiv. 14; xx. 4, 5; De. vi. 13, 14; Is. xlv. 20. 3d. It is idolatry to worship or pray to a creature. 4th. It is absurd to suppose that the Virgin Mary can be in all places at the same time to hear the prayers of thousands at once, or to aid them. There is no idolatry more gross, and of course more wicked, than to worship *the creature* more than *the Creator*, Ro. i. 25.

46. *My soul doth magnify the Lord.* To *magnify* means to *make great*, and then to *extol*, to *praise*, to *celebrate*. It does not mean here strictly to *make great*, but to increase *in our estimation*

47 And my spirit hath [s]rejoiced
in God my Saviour.
48 For he hath regarded the
low[t] estate of his handmaiden;
for, behold, from henceforth all
generations shall [u]call me blessed.
49 For he that is [v]mighty hath
done to me [w]great things; and
[x]holy is his name.
50 And[y] his mercy *is* on them
that fear him, from generation to
generation.
51 He[z] hath showed strength
with his arm; he hath [a]scattered

s Ps.35.9; Hab.3.18. t Ps.136.23.
u Mal.3.12; ch.11.27. v Ge.17.1.

w Ps.71.21; 126.2,3; Ep.3.20. x Ps.111.9.
y Ge.17.17; Ex.20.6; Ps.103.17.
z Ps.98.1; Is.51.9; 52.10; 63.5. a 1 Sa.2.9; Da.4.37.

—that is, to praise or extol. See Ps. xxxiv. 3; 2 Sa. vii. 26.

47. *In God my Saviour.* God is called *Saviour*, as he saves people from sin and death. He was *Mary's* Saviour, as he had redeemed her soul and given her a title to eternal life; and she rejoiced for that, and especially for his mercy in honouring her by her being made the mother of the Messiah.

48. *He hath regarded the low estate of his handmaid.* Literally, he has looked upon the low or humble condition of his handmaid. That is, notwithstanding her humble rank and poverty, he has shown her favour. And this example abundantly teaches what is elsewhere fully taught in the Bible, that God is not a respecter of persons; that he is not influenced, in conferring favours, by wealth, honour, or office, Ro. ii. 11; x. 11, 12. He seeks the humble and the contrite; he imparts his rich blessings to those who feel that they need them, and who will bless him for them, Ps. cxxxviii. 6; Is. lvii. 15. ¶ *From henceforth.* Hereafter, or in consequence of this. ¶ *All generations.* All men. All posterity. ¶ *Call me blessed.* Pronounce me highly favoured or happy in being the mother of the Messiah. It is therefore right to consider her as highly favoured or happy; but this certainly does not warrant us to worship her or to pray to her. Abraham was blessed in being the father of the faithful; Paul in being the apostle to the Gentiles; Peter in first preaching the gospel to them; but who would think of worshipping or praying to Abraham, Paul, or Peter?

49. *He that is mighty.* God. ¶ *Hath done to me great things.* Hath conferred on me great favours and distinguished mercies. ¶ *And holy is his name.* This is an expression of Mary's feelings, desiring to bestow on God all honour and praise. As the highest honour, she declared that his *name* was *holy*—that is, that God was free from sin, injustice, and impurity. The "*name*" of God is often put for God himself. The proper name of God is *Jehovah*, a word expressive of his *essential being*, derived from the word *to be*, Ex. iii. 14; vi. 3; Ps. lxxxiii. 18. That name is holy; is to be regarded as holy; and to make a common or profane use of it is solemnly forbidden, Ex. xx. 7.

50. *His mercy.* Favour shown to the miserable and the guilty. ¶ Is *on them.* Is *shown* or manifested to them. ¶ *That fear him.* That *reverence* or honour him. One kind of fear is that which a servant has of a cruel master, or which a man has of a precipice, the plague, or death. This is not the *fear* which we ought to have toward God. It is the fear which a dutiful child has of a kind and virtuous father—a fear of injuring his feelings; of dishonouring him by our life; of doing anything which he would disapprove. It is on those who have *such* fear of God that his mercy descends. This is the fear of the Lord which is the beginning of wisdom, Ps. cxi. 10; Job xxviii. 28. ¶ *From generation to generation.* From one age to another —that is, it is unceasing; it continues and abounds. But it means also more than this. It means that God's mercy will descend on the children and children's children of those that fear him and keep his commandments, Ex. xx. 6. In this respect it is an unspeakable privilege to be descended from pious parents; to have been the subject of their prayers, and to have received their blessing. It is also a matter of vast guilt *not* to copy their example and to walk in their steps. If God is *disposed* to show mercy to thousands of generations, how heavy will be the condemnation if the children of pious parents do not avail themselves of it and early seek his favour!

51. *Hath showed strength with his arm.* The *arm* is the symbol of strength. The expression in this and the subsequent verses has no particular reference to his

the proud in the imagination of
their hearts.
52 He[b] hath put down the
mighty from *their* seats, and exalted them of low degree.
53 He[c] hath filled the hungry
with good things, and the rich he
hath sent empty away.
54 He hath holpen his servant
Israel, [d] in remembrance of *his*
mercy;
55 As he [e]spake to our fathers,

b Job 5.11; ch.18.14. *c* 1 Sa.2.5. *d* Ps.98.3. *e* Ge.17.19; Ps.132.11.

---

mercy to *Mary*. From a contemplation of his goodness to *her*, she enlarges her views to a contemplation of his goodness and power *in general*, and to a celebration of the praises of God for *all* that he has done to all men. This is the nature of true piety. It does not terminate in thinking of God's mercy toward *ourselves*. It thinks of *others*, and praises God that *others* also are made partakers of his mercy, and that his goodness is manifested to all his works. ¶ *He scattereth the proud.* He hath often done it in time of battle and war. When the proud Assyrian, Egyptian, or Babylonian had come against the people of God, he had often scattered them and driven away their armies. ¶ *In the imagination of their hearts.* Those who were lifted up or exalted in their own view. Those who *thought themselves* to be superior to other men.

52. *Hath put down the mighty.* The *mighty* here denotes princes, kings, or conquerors. See Is. xiv. 12–14. ¶ Their *seats.* Their *thrones*, or the places where they sat in pomp and power. ¶ *Exalted them.* Raised them up, or placed them in the seats of those who had been removed. ¶ *Low degree.* Low or humble birth and condition in life. This probably has reference to the case of her ancestor David. Mary was celebrating the mercies of God to *herself*, to her *family*, and of course to her ancestors. It was natural to allude to that great event in their history when Saul was overcome in battle, and when *David* was taken from the sheepfold and placed on the throne. The origin of illustrious families is often obscure. Men are often raised by industry, talent, and the favour of God, from very humble stations —from the farm or mechanic's shop— to places of great trust in the church and state. They who are thus elevated, if imbued with right feelings, will not despise their former employments nor their former companions, nor will they esteem their parents or friends the less *because* they still remain in the same rank in life. No conduct is more odious and unchristian than to be ashamed of our birth or the humble circumstances of our friends.

53. *He hath filled the hungry with good things.* This is a celebration of the general mercy of God. He hath daily fed the poor, the needy, and those who came to him with humble hearts. ¶ *The rich he hath sent*, &c. While the poor come to him for a supply of their daily wants, the rich come not that their necessities should be supplied, but come with lofty hearts, and insatiable desires that their riches may be increased. When this is the case, God not unfrequently not only *withholds* what they ask, but he takes their riches away by fire, or flood, or disappointments, and sends them away empty, Pr. xxiii. 5. It is better to be poor and go to God for our daily bread, than to be rich and forget our dependence on him, and to seek only a great increase of our property.

54. *Hath holpen.* Hath *helped* or assisted. The word rendered "holpen" denotes properly, *to take hold of one, to help him up when he is in danger of falling*, and here means that God had succoured his people when they were feeble, and were in danger of falling or being overthrown. ¶ *His servant Israel.* His people the Israelites, or those who truly feared him and kept his commandments. See Is. xli. 8, 9; Ho. xi. 1. ¶ *In remembrance of* his *mercy.* Or that his mercy *may* be remembered.

55. *As he spake to our fathers*, &c. That is, he has dealt mercifully with the children of Israel, according as he promised Abraham, Isaac, and Jacob. The promise *particularly* here referred to is that respecting the *Messiah* which was now about to be fulfilled; but there is no doubt that there was also included the promises respecting all the other mercies which had been conferred on the children of Israel. See Ge. xxii. 17, 18. ¶ *For ever.* These words are to be referred to the preceding verse— "in remembrance of his mercy *for ever*,

to Abraham, and to his seed for ever.

56 And Mary abode with her about three months, and returned to her own house.

57 Now Elisabeth's full time came that she should be delivered; and she brought forth a son.

58 And her neighbours and her cousins heard how the Lord had showed great mercy upon her; and they[f] rejoiced with her.

59 And it came to pass, that on the eighth day they came to circumcise the child; and they called him Zacharias, after the name of his father.

60 And his mother answered and said, Not *so;* but he shall be called John.

61 And they said unto her, There is none of thy kindred that is called by this name.

62 And they made signs to his father how he would have him called.

63 And he asked for a writing table, and wrote, saying, His name is [g]John. And they marvelled all.

64 And his [h]mouth was opened immediately, and his tongue *loosed,* and he spake, and praised God.

65 And fear came on all that dwelt round about them: and all these [4]sayings were noised abroad throughout all the hill country of Judea;

66 And all they that heard *them* [i]laid *them* up in their hearts, saying,

f ver.14.

g ver.13. *h* ver.20. [4] or, *things.* *i* ch.2.19,51.

as he spake," &c. They denote that the *mercy of God* manifested to his people should be had in everlasting remembrance.

There is a striking similarity between this song of praise by Mary and that spoken by *Hannah,* 1 Sa. ii. 2–10. There are few pieces of *poetry*—for this is poetry, and almost the only poetry in the New Testament—more beautiful than this. It is the language of a humble, thankful, pious, female heart praising God—1st. For his mercy to her, ver. 46–49; 2d. For his mercy to all men—his *general* goodness, ver. 50–53; and, 3d. His special goodness to his people, ver. 54, 55.

59. *On the eighth day.* This was the day on which it was required to circumcise children, Ge. xxi. 4. ¶ *And they called him Zacharias.* The *name* of the child was commonly given at the time of the circumcision, Ge. xxi. 3, 4. The name *commonly* given to the eldest son was that of the father.

60. *Shall be called John.* This was the name which the angel had said should be given to him, of which Zacharias had probably informed Elisabeth by writing.

61. *There is none of thy kindred,* &c. The Jewish tribes and families were kept distinct. To do this, and to avoid confusion in their genealogical tables, they probably gave only those names which were found among their ancestors. Another reason for this, common to all people, is the respect which is felt for honoured parents and ancestors.

63. *He asked.* That is, by signs. ¶ *A writing table.* The table denoted by this word was usually made of wood and covered with wax. The ancients used to write on such tables, as they had not the use of paper. The instrument used for writing was an iron pen or *style,* by which they *marked* on the wax which covered the table. Sometimes the writing-table was made entirely of lead.

64. *His mouth was opened,* &c. That is, he was enabled to speak. For nine months he had been dumb, and it is probable that they supposed that he had been afflicted with a paralytic affection, and that he would not recover. Hence their amazement when he spoke. For one act of disbelief all this calamity had come upon him, and it had not come without effect. With true gratitude he offered praise to God for the birth of a son, and for his restoration to the blessings of speech.

65. *And fear came,* &c. The word fear often denotes *religious reverence.* The remarkable circumstances attending the birth of John, and the fact that Zacharias was suddenly restored to speech, convinced them that *God* was there, and filled their minds with awe and veneration.

What manner of child shall this be? And the [k]hand of the Lord was with him.

67 And his father Zacharias was filled with the Holy Ghost, and prophesied, saying,

68 Blessed[l] *be* the Lord God of Israel; for he hath visited and redeemed his people,

69 And hath raised up an horn of [m]salvation for us in the house of his servant David;

k Ps.80.17. *l* Ps.72.18. *m* Ps.111.9.

66. *What manner of child*, &c. Such were the remarkable circumstances of his birth that they apprehended that he would be distinguished as a prophet, or that great events would result from his life. ¶ *The hand of the Lord was with him.* The word *hand* is used to denote *aid, protection, favour.* We stretch out the hand to aid those whom we wish to help. The expression here means that God *aided* him, *protected* him, or showed him favour. Some think that these words are a part of the speech of the neighbours—"What manner of child shall this be? God is so evidently with him!"

67. *Filled with the Holy Ghost.* See ver. 15. ¶ *And prophesied.* The word *prophesy* means—1st. To foretell future events. 2d. To celebrate the praises of God (see 1 Sa. x. 5, 6; 1 Ki. xviii. 29); then to, 3d. Teach or preach the gospel, &c. See Notes on Ro. xii. 6. This song of Zacharias partakes of all. It is principally employed in the praises of God, but it also predicts the future character and preaching of John.

68. *Blessed.* See Notes on Mat. v. 3. ¶ *Hath visited.* The word here rendered *visited* means properly *to look upon;* then to look upon in order *to know the state of anyone;* then to visit for the purpose of *aiding those who need aid*, or alleviating misery. Comp. Mat. xxv. 43. In this sense it is used here. God *looked upon* the world—he saw it miserable—he came to relieve it, and brought salvation. ¶ *And redeemed.* That is, was *about to redeem*, or had given the pledge that he *would redeem.* This was spoken under the belief that the Messiah, *the Redeemer*, was about to appear, and would certainly accomplish his work. The literal translation of this passage is, "He hath made a *ransom* for his people. A *ransom* was the *price* paid to deliver a captive taken in war. A is a prisoner taken in war by B. B has a right to detain him as a prisoner by the laws of war, but C offers B a *price* if he will release A and suffer him to go at liberty. The price which he pays, and which must be *satisfactory* to B—that is, be a *reason* to B why he should release him—is called *a price or ransom.* Men are sinners. They are bound over to just punishment by the law. The law is holy, and God, as a just governor, must see that the law is honoured and the wicked punished; but if anything can be done which will have the same *good effect* as the punishment of the sinner, or which will be an *equivalent* for it—that is, be of equal value to the universe—God may consistently release him. If he can show the same hatred of sin, and deter others from sinning, and secure the purity of the sinner, the sinner may be released. Whatever will accomplish *this* is called a *ransom*, because it is, in the eye of God, a sufficient *reason* why the sinner should not be punished; it is an *equivalent* for his sufferings, and God is satisfied. The *blood of Jesus*—that is, his *death* in the place of sinners—constitutes such a ransom. It is in their stead. It is for them. It is equivalent to their punishment. It is not itself a *punishment*, for that always supposes *personal crime*, but it is what God is pleased *to accept* in the place of the eternal sufferings of the sinner. The king of the *Locrians* made a law that an adulterer should be punished with the loss of his eyes. His *son* was the first offender, and the father decreed that his son should lose *one* eye, and *he himself* one also. This was the *ransom.* He showed his *love*, his regard for the honour of his law, and the determination that the guilty should not escape. So God gave his Son *a ransom* to show his love, his regard to justice, and his willingness to save men; and his Son, in his death, was a ransom. He is often so called in the New Testament, Mat. xx. 28; Mar. x. 45; Tit. ii. 14; He. ix. 12. For a fuller view of the nature of a *ransom*, see Notes on Ro. iii. 24, 25.

69. *And hath raised up a horn.* A *horn* is a symbol of *strength.* The figure is taken from the fact that in horned animals the strength lies in the *horn.*

70 As he [n]spake by the mouth
of his holy prophets, which have
been since the world began:
71 That we should be [o]saved
from our enemies, and from the
hand of all that hate us;
72 To perform the mercy *promised*
to our fathers, and to [p]remember his
holy covenant,

n Je.23 5 6; Da.9.24. *o* Is.54.7-17; Je.30.10,11.
p Le.26.42; Ps.105.8-10; Eze.16.60.

73 The [q]oath which he sware to
our father Abraham,
74 That he would grant unto us,
that we, being delivered out of the
hand of our enemies, might [r]serve
him without fear,
75 In [s]holiness and righteousness
before him, [t]all the days of our life.
76 And thou, child, shalt be called

q Ge.22.16,17. *r* Ro.6.22.
s Tit.2.11,12; 1 Pe.1.14,15. *t* Re.2.10.

Particularly, the great power of the rhinoceros or unicorn is manifested by the use of a single horn of great strength, placed on the head near the end of the nose. When the sacred writers, therefore, speak of great *strength* they often use the word *horn*, Ps. cxlviii. 14; De. xxxiii. 17; Da. vii. 7, 8; viii. 21. The word *salvation*, connected here with the word *horn*, means that this *strength*, or this mighty Redeemer, was able to save. It is possible that this whole figure may be taken from the Jewish *altar*. On each of the four corners of the altar there was an eminence or small projection called a *horn*. To this persons might flee for safety when in danger, and be safe, 1 Ki. i. 50; ii. 28. Comp. Notes on ch. i. 11. So the Redeemer *may be* called the "horn of salvation," because those who flee to him are safe. ¶ *In the house.* In the *family*, or among the *descendants* of David.

70. *His holy prophets*, &c. All the prophets are said to have referred to the Messiah, from the beginning of the world. The most striking of these were Jacob (Ge. xlix. 10); Moses (De. xviii. 15); Isaiah (ix. 6, 7; liii.). ¶ *Since the world began.* This is not to be taken *literally*, for there were no prophets *immediately* after the creation. It is merely a *general* expression, designed to denote that *all* the prophets had predicted the coming of the Messiah. Comp. Notes on Lu. xxiv. 27; Re. xix. 10.

71. *Saved from our enemies.* The enemies of *man* are his sins, his carnal propensities, his lusts, and the great adversary Satan and his angels, who continually seek to destroy him. From *these* the Messiah came to save us. Comp. Ge. iii. 15; Mat. i. 21. ¶ *The hand.* The power; or to save us from *them*.

72. *To perform the mercy.* To show the mercy promised. The expression in the *original* is, "To make mercy with our fathers"—that is, to show kindness to our fathers; and the propriety of it is founded on the fact that mercy to *children* is regarded as kindness to the *parent*. Blessing the *children* was blessing the *nation;* was fulfilling the promises made to the fathers, and *showing* that he regarded them in mercy. ¶ *His holy covenant.* The word *covenant* means compact or agreement. This is in use among men. It implies equality in the parties; freedom from constraint; freedom from previous obligation to do the thing now covenanted; and freedom from obligation to enter into a compact, unless a man chooses so to do. Such a transaction evidently can never take place between man and God, for they are not equal. Man is not at liberty to *decline* what God proposes, and he is under obligation to do *all* that God commands. When the word *covenant*, therefore, is used in the Bible, it means sometimes a *command;* sometimes a *promise;* sometimes a *regular law*—as *the covenant of the day and night;* and sometimes the way in which God dispenses mercy—that is, by the old and new covenants. In the place before us it means *the promise* made to Abraham, as the following verses clearly show.

73. *The oath.* This oath is recorded in Ge. xxii. 16, 17. It was an oath in which God swore by himself (because he could swear by no greater, He. vi. 13, 14) that he would surely bless Abraham and his posterity. That promise was now to be entirely fulfilled by the coming of the Messiah.

74. *Might serve him.* Might obey, honour, and worship him. This was regarded as a *favour*. This was what was promised, and for this Zacharias praised God. ¶ *Without fear.* Fear of death, of spiritual enemies, or of ex-

the Prophet of the Highest, for thou
shalt [u]go before the face of the Lord,
to prepare his ways;
77 To give knowledge of salvation
unto his people [5]by the [v]remission
of their sins,
78 Through the [6]tender mercy of
our God; whereby the [7]dayspring
from on high hath visited us.

u Mal.3.1. [5] or, *for.* *v* Ac.5.31.
[6] or, *bowels of the mercy.* [7] or, *sunrising;* or, *branch,* Is.11.1; Zec.3.8; 6.12.

79 To[w] give light to them that
sit in darkness and *in* the shadow
of death, to guide our feet into the
way of peace.
80 And the child grew, and
waxed strong in spirit, and was in
the deserts till the day of his showing unto Israel.

w Is.9.2; 49.9.

---

ternal foes. In the sure hope of God's *eternal* favour beyond the grave.

75. *In holiness,* &c. In piety and strict justice. ¶ *Before him.* In the presence of God. Performed as in his presence, and with the full consciousness that he sees the heart. The *holiness* was not to be merely *external,* but spiritual, internal, pure, such as *God* would see and approve. ¶ *All the days of our life.* To death. True religion increases and expands till death.

76. *And thou, child,* &c. Zacharias predicts in this and the following verses the dignity, the employment, and the success of John. He declares what would be the subject of his preaching, and what his success. ¶ *Prophet of the Highest.* Prophet of God; a prophet *appointed by God* to declare his will, and to prepare the way for the coming of the Messiah. ¶ *The face of the Lord.* The Lord Jesus, the Messiah, that was about to appear. To go before *the face of one* is the same as to go *immediately* before one, or to be *immediately* followed by another. ¶ *To prepare his ways.* This is taken from Is. xl. 3. See Notes on Mat. iii. 3, and on Is. xl. 3.

77. *To give knowledge of salvation.* Knowledge of the *way* of salvation; that it was provided, and that the author of salvation was about to appear. ¶ *By the remission of their sins.* The word remission means pardon or forgiveness. It implies that God will treat the sinner *as if* he had not committed the sin. The idea here is, that the *salvation* about to be offered was that which was connected with the pardon of sin. There can be no other. God cannot treat men as his friends unless they come to him by repentance and obtain forgiveness. When that is obtained, which he is always disposed to grant, they can be treated with kindness and mercy.

78. *Whereby the dayspring,* &c. The word *dayspring* means the morning light, the aurora, the rising of the sun. It is called the dayspring *from on high* because the light of the gospel shines forth from heaven. God is its author, and through his mercy it shines on men. There is here, doubtless, a reference to Is. lx. 1, 2; indeed, almost the very words of that place are quoted. Comp. also Re. xxii. 16.

79. *To give light,* &c. See Notes on Mat. iv. 16. ¶ *To guide our feet,* &c. The figure in these verses is taken from travellers, who, being overtaken by night, know not what to do, and who wait patiently for the morning light, that they may know which way to go. So man wandered. So he became benighted. So he sat in the shadow of death. So he knew not which way to go until the Sun of righteousness arose, and *then* the light shone brightly on his way, and the road was open to the promised land of rest—to heaven.

This song of Zacharias is exceedingly beautiful. It expresses with elegance the great points of the plan of redemption, and the mercy of God in providing that plan. That mercy *is great.* It is worthy of praise—of our highest, loftiest songs of thanksgiving; for we were in the shadow of death—sinful, wretched, wandering—and the light arose, the gospel came, and men may rejoice in hope of eternal life.

80. *Waxed strong in spirit.* That is, in courage, understanding, and purposes of good, fitting him for his future work. The word *wax* means to *increase, to grow,* from an old Saxon word. ¶ *In the deserts.* In Hebron, and in the hill country where his father resided. He dwelt in obscurity, and was not known publicly by the people. ¶ *Until the day of his showing.* Until he entered on his public ministry, as recorded in Mat. iii.—that is, probably, until he was about thirty years of age. See Lu. iii.

CHAPTER II.

AND it came to pass in those days that there went out a decree from Cæsar Augustus that all the world should be [1]taxed.

2 (*And* this taxing was first made when Cyrenius was governor of Syria.)

3 And all went to be taxed, every one into his own city.

[1] or, *inrolled*.

CHAPTER II.

1. *In those days.* About the time of the birth of John and of Christ. ¶ *A decree.* A law commanding a thing to be done. ¶ *Cæsar Augustus.* This was the Roman emperor. His first name was Octavianus. He was the nephew of Julius Cæsar, and obtained the empire after his death. He took the name *Augustus—i.e. august*, or honourable—as a compliment to his own greatness; and from him the month *August*, which was before called *Sextilis*, received its name. ¶ *That all the world.* There has been much difficulty respecting this passage, from the fact that no such taxing *of all the world* is mentioned by ancient writers. It should have been rendered *the whole land*—that is, the whole land of Palestine. The *whole land* is mentioned to show that it was not *Judea* only, but that it included also *Galilee*, the place where Joseph and Mary dwelt. That the passage refers only to the land of Palestine, and not to the whole world, or to all the Roman empire, is clear from the following considerations: 1st. The fact that no such taxing is mentioned as pertaining to any other country. 2d. The account of Luke demands only that it should be understood of Palestine, or the country where the Saviour was born. 3d. The words *world* and *whole world* are not unfrequently used in this limited sense as confined to a single country. See Mat. iv. 8, where Satan is said to have shown to Christ all the kingdoms *of the world*, that is, of the land of Judea. See also Jos. ii. 3; Lu. iv. 25 (Greek); Lu. xxi. 26; Ac. xi. 28. ¶ *Should be taxed.* Our word *tax* means to levy and raise money for the use of the government. This is not the meaning of the original word here. It means rather to *enroll*, or take a *list* of the citizens, with their employments, the amount of their property, &c., equivalent to what was meant by *census.* Judea was at that time tributary to Rome. It paid taxes to the Roman emperor; and, though Herod was *king*, yet he held his appointment under the Roman emperor, and was subject in most matters to him. Farther, as this *enrolment* was merely to ascertain the numbers and property of the Jews, it is probable that they were very willing to be enrolled in this manner; and hence we hear that they went willingly, without tumult—contrary to the common way when they were *to be taxed*.

2. And *this taxing was first made*, &c. This verse has given as much perplexity, perhaps, as any one in the New Testament. The difficulty consists in the fact that *Cyrenius*, or *Quirinius*, was not governor of Syria until twelve or fifteen years after the birth of Jesus. Jesus was born during the reign of Herod. At that time *Varus* was president of Syria. Herod was succeeded by *Archelaus*, who reigned eight or nine years; and *after* he was removed, Judea was annexed to the province of Syria, and Cyrenius was sent as the governor (Josephus, *Ant.*, b. xvii. § 5). The difficulty has been to reconcile this account with that in Luke. Various attempts have been made to do this. The one that seems most satisfactory is that proposed by Dr. Lardner. According to his view, the passage here means, "This was the *first* census of Cyrenius, governor of Syria." It is called the *first* to distinguish it from one *afterward* taken by Cyrenius, Ac. v. 37. It is said to be the census taken by *Cyrenius, governor of Syria;* not that he was *then* governor, but that it was taken by him who was *afterward* familiarly known as governor. *Cyrenius, governor of Syria*, was the name by which the man was known when Luke wrote his gospel, and it was not improper to say that the taxing was made by *Cyrenius, the governor of Syria*, though he might not have been actually governor for many years afterward. Thus Herodian says that "to Marcus *the emperor* were born several daughters and two sons," though several of those children were born to him *before* he was emperor. Thus it is not improper to say that General Washington saved Braddock's army, or was engaged in the old French war, though he was not actually made *general* till

4 And Joseph also went up from Galilee, out of the city of Nazareth, into Judea, unto the city of David, which is called Bethlehem, (because he was of the house and lineage of David,)

5 To be taxed with Mary, his espoused wife, being great with child.

6 And so it was that while they were there the days were accomplished that she should be delivered.

---

many years afterward. According to this Augustus sent Cyrenius, an active, enterprising man, to take the census. At that time he was a Roman senator. Afterward he was made governor of the same country, and received the title which Luke gives him. ¶ *Syria.* The region of country north of Palestine, and lying between the Mediterranean and the Euphrates. *Syria*, called in the Hebrew *Aram*, from a son of Shem (Ge. x. 22), in its largest acceptation extended from the Mediterranean and the river Cydnus to the Euphrates, and from Mount Taurus on the north to Arabia and the border of Egypt on the south. It was divided into *Syria Palestina*, including Canaan and Phœnicia; *Cœle-Syria,* the tract of country lying between two ridges of Mount Lebanon and *Upper Syria.* The last was known as *Syria* in the restricted sense, or as the term was commonly used.

The leading features in the physical aspect of Syria consist of the great mountainous chains of Lebanon, or Libanus and Anti-Libanus, extending from north to south, and the great desert lying on the south-east and east. The valleys are of great fertility, and yield abundance of grain, vines, mulberries, tobacco, olives, excellent fruits, as oranges, figs, pistachios, &c. The climate in the inhabited parts is exceedingly fine. Syria is inhabited by various descriptions of people, but Turks and Greeks form the basis of the population in the cities. The only tribes that can be considered as peculiar to Syria are the tenants of the heights of Lebanon. The most remarkable of these are the Druses and Maronites. The general language is Arabic; the soldiers and officers of government speak Turkish. Of the old Syriac language no traces now exist.

4. *The city of David.* Bethlehem, called the city of David because it was the place of his birth. See Notes on Mat. ii. 1. ¶ *Because he was of the house.* Of the family. ¶ *And lineage.* The *lineage* denotes that he was descended from David as his father or ancestor. In taking a Jewish census, families were kept distinct; hence all went to the *place* where their family had resided. Joseph was of the *family* of David, and hence he went up to the city of David. It is not improbable that he might also have had a small paternal estate in Bethlehem that rendered his presence there more desirable.

7. *Her first-born son.* Whether Mary had any other children or not has been a matter of controversy. The obvious meaning of the Bible is that she had; and if this be the case, the word *first-born* is here to be taken in its common signification. ¶ *Swaddling clothes.* When a child among the Hebrews was born, it was washed in water, rubbed in salt, and then wrapped in swaddling clothes; that is, not garments regularly made, as with us, but bands or blankets that confined the limbs closely, Eze. xvi. 4. There was nothing peculiar in the manner in which the infant Jesus was treated. ¶ *Laid him in a manger.* The word rendered "inn" in this verse means simply a place of halting, a lodging-place; in modern terms, a khan or caravanserai (Robinson's *Bib. Res. in Palest.*, iii. 431). The word rendered "manger" means simply a crib or place where cattle were fed. "Inns," in our sense of the term, were anciently unknown in the East, and now they are not common. Hospitality was generally practised, so that a traveller had little difficulty in obtaining shelter and food when necessary. As travelling became more frequent, however, khans or caravanserais were erected for public use—large structures where the traveller might freely repair and find lodging for himself and his beast, he himself providing food and forage. Many such khans were placed at regular intervals in Persia. To such a place it was, though already crowded, that Joseph and Mary resorted at Bethlehem. Instead of finding a place in the "inn," or the part of the caravanserai where the travellers themselves found a place of repose, they were obliged to be contented in one of the stalls or re-

7 And she [a]brought forth her first-born son, and wrapped him in swaddling clothes, and laid him in a manger; because there was no room for them in the inn.

8 And there were in the same

[a] Mat.1.25.

cesses appropriated to the beasts on which they rode.

The following description of an Eastern inn or caravanserai, by Dr. Kitto, will well illustrate this passage: "It presents an external appearance which suggests to a European traveller the idea of a fortress, being an extensive square pile of strong and lofty walls, mostly of brick upon a basement of stone, with a grand archway entrance. This leads . . . to a large open area, with a well in the middle, and surrounded on three or four sides with a kind of piazza raised upon a platform 3 or 4 feet high, in the wall behind which are small doors leading to the cells or oblong chambers which form the lodgings. The cell, with the space on the platform in front of it, forms the domain of each individual traveller, where he is completely secluded, as the apparent piazza is not open, but is composed of the front arches of each compartment. There is, however, in the centre of one or more of the sides a large arched hall quite open in front. . . . The cells are completely unfurnished, and have generally no light but from the door, and the traveller is generally seen in the recess in front of his apartment except during the heat of the day. . . . Many of these caravanserais have no stables, the cattle of the travellers being accommodated in the open area; but in the more complete establishments . . . there are . . . spacious stables, formed of covered avenues extending between the back wall of the lodging apartments and the outer wall of the whole building, the entrance being at one or more of the corners of the inner quadrangle. The stable is on the same level with the court, and thus below the level of the tenements which stand on the raised platform. Nevertheless, this platform is allowed to project behind into the stable, so as to form a bench. . . . It also often happens that not only this bench exists in the stable, forming a more or less narrow platform along its extent, but also recesses corresponding to these *in front* of the cells toward the open area, and formed, in fact, by the side-walls of these cells being allowed to project behind to the boundary of the platform. These, though small and shallow, form convenient retreats for servants and muleteers in bad weather. . . . Such a recess we conceive that Joseph and Mary occupied, with their ass or mule—if they had one, as they perhaps had—tethered in front. . . . It might be rendered quite private by a cloth being stretched across the lower part."

It may be remarked that the fact that Joseph and Mary were in that place, and under a necessity of taking up their lodgings there, was in itself no proof of poverty; it was a simple matter of necessity—there was *no room* at the inn. Yet it is worthy of our consideration that Jesus was born *poor*. He did not inherit a princely estate. He was not cradled, as many are, in a palace. He had no rich friends. He had virtuous, pious parents, of more value to a child than many riches. And in this we are shown that it is no dishonour to be poor. Happy is that child who, whether his parents be rich or poor, has a *pious* father and mother. It is no matter if he has not as much wealth, as fine clothes, or as splendid a house as another. It is enough for him to be as *Jesus* was, and God will bless him. ¶ *No room at the inn.* Many people assembled to be *enrolled*, and the tavern was filled before Joseph and Mary arrived.

8. *The same country.* Round about Bethlehem. ¶ *Shepherds.* Men who tended flocks of sheep. ¶ *Abiding in the field.* Remaining out of doors, under the open sky, with their flocks. This was commonly done. The climate was mild, and, to keep their flocks from straying, they spent the night with them. It is also a fact that the Jews sent out their flocks into the mountainous and desert regions during the summer months, and took them up in the latter part of October or the first of November, when the cold weather commenced. While away in these deserts and mountainous regions, it was proper that there should be some one to attend them to keep them from straying, and from the ravages of wolves and other wild beasts. It is probable from this that our Saviour was born before the 25th of December, or before

country shepherds abiding in the
field, keeping [2]watch over their
flock by night.
9 And, lo, the angel of the Lord
came upon them, and the glory of
the Lord shone round about them;
and they were sore afraid.
10 And the angel said unto them,
Fear not: for, behold, I bring you
good tidings of great joy, which
shall be to all people.
11 For [b]unto you is born this
day, in the city of David, a
Saviour, which is Christ the Lord.
12 And this *shall be* a sign

[2] or, *the night-watches*. [b] Is.9.6.

unto you: Ye shall find the babe
wrapped in swaddling clothes,
lying in a manger.
13 And suddenly there was
[c]with the angel a multitude of
the heavenly host, praising God,
and saying,
14 Glory to God in the highest,
and on earth [d]peace, good will
toward men.
15 And it came to pass, as the
angels were gone away from them
into heaven, [3]the shepherds said
one to another, Let us now go even
unto Bethlehem, and see this thing

[c] Ps.103.20,21; 1 Pe.1.12. [d] Is.57.19.
[3] *the men, the shepherds.*

---

what we call *Christmas*. At that time it is cold, and especially in the high and mountainous regions about Bethlehem. But the exact time of his birth is unknown; there is no way to ascertain it. By different learned men it has been fixed at each month in the year. Nor is it of consequence to *know* the time; if it were, God would have preserved the record of it. Matters of moment are clearly revealed; those which *he* regards as of no importance are concealed. ¶ *Keeping watch*, &c. More literally, "tending their flocks *by turns* through the night watches."

9. *The glory of the Lord.* This is the same as a *great* glory—that is, a splendid appearance or *light*. The word *glory* is often the same as light, 1 Co. xv. 41; Lu. ix. 31; Ac. xxii. 11. The words *Lord* and *God* are often used to denote *greatness* or *intensity*. Thus, *trees of God* mean great trees; *hills of God*, high or lofty hills, &c. So *the glory of the Lord* here means an exceedingly great or bright luminous appearance—perhaps not unlike what Paul saw on the way to Damascus.

12. *This* shall be *a sign*, &c. The evidence by which you shall know the child is that you will find him wrapped in swaddling clothes and lying in a manger.

14. *Glory to God.* Praise be to God, or honour be to God. That is, the praise of redeeming man is due to God. The plan of redemption will bring glory to God, and is designed to express his glory. This it does by evincing his love to men, his mercy, his condescension, and his regard to the honour of his law and the stability of his own government. It is the highest expression of his love and mercy. Nowhere, so far as *we* can see, could his glory be more strikingly exhibited than in giving his only-begotten Son to die for men. ¶ *In the highest.* This is capable of several meanings: 1st. In the highest *strains*, or in the highest possible manner. 2d. *Among* the highest—that is, among the angels of God; indicating that *they* felt a deep interest in this work, and were called on to praise God for the redemption of man. 3d. In the highest *heavens*—indicating that the praise of redemption should not be confined to the *earth*, but should spread throughout the universe. 4th. The words "God in the highest" may be equivalent to *the most high God*, and be the same as saying, "Let the most high God be praised for his love and mercy to men." Which of these meanings is the true one it is difficult to determine; but in this they all agree, that high praise is to be given to God for his love in redeeming men. O that not only *angels*, but *men*, would join universally in this song of praise! ¶ *On earth peace.* That is, the gospel will bring peace. The Saviour was predicted as the Prince of peace, Is. ix. 6. The world is at war with God; sinners are at enmity against their Maker and against each other. There is no peace to the wicked. But Jesus came to make peace; and this he did, 1st. By reconciling the world to God by his atonement. 2d. By bringing the sinner to a state of peace with his Maker; inducing him to lay down the weapons of rebellion and to submit his soul to God, thus giving him the peace which passeth all

which is to come to pass, which the Lord hath made known unto us.

16 And they came with haste, and found Mary and Joseph, and the babe lying in a manger.

17 And when they had seen *it*, they made known abroad the saying which was told them concerning this child.

18 And all they that heard *it* wondered at those things which were told them by the shepherds.

19 But Mary kept all these things, and pondered *them* in her heart.

---

understanding. 3d. By diffusing in the heart universal good-will to men—*disposing* men to lay aside their differences, to love one another, to seek each other's welfare, and to banish envy, malice, pride, lust, passion, and covetousness—in all ages the most fruitful causes of difference among men. And, 4th. By diffusing the principles of universal peace among nations. If the gospel of Jesus should universally prevail, there would be an end of war. In the days of the millennium there will be universal peace; all the causes of war will have ceased; men will love each other and do justly; all nations will be brought under the influence of the gospel. O how should each one toil and pray that the great object of the gospel should be universally accomplished, and the world be filled with peace! ¶ *Good will toward men.* The gift of the Saviour is an expression of good-will or *love* to men, and therefore God is to be praised. The work of redemption is uniformly represented as the fruit of the *love of God*, Jn. iii. 16; Ep. v. 2; 1 Jn. iv. 10; Re. i. 5. No words can express the greatness of that love. It can only be measured by the *misery*, *helplessness*, and *danger* of man; by the extent of his sufferings here and in the world of woe if he had not been saved; by the condescension, sufferings, and death of Jesus; and by the eternal honour and happiness to which he will raise his people. All these are beyond our full comprehension. Yet how little does man feel it! and how many turn away from the highest love of God, and treat the expression of that love with contempt! Surely, if God so loved us *first*, we ought also to love him, 1 Jn. iv. 19.

16. *Unto Bethlehem.* The city of David, where the angel had told them they would find the Saviour. These shepherds appear to have been pious men. They were waiting for the coming of the Messiah. On the first intimation that he had actually appeared they went with haste to find him. So all men should without delay seek the Saviour. When told of him by the servants of God, they should, like these shepherds, forsake all, and give no rest to their eyes until they have found him. We may *always* find him. We need not travel to Bethlehem. We have only to cast our eyes to heaven; to look to him and to believe on him, and we shall find him ever near to us, and for ever *our* Saviour and friend.

17. *When they had seen* it. When they had satisfied themselves of the truth of the coming of the Messiah, and had ascertained that they could not have been mistaken in the appearance of the angels. There was evidence enough to satisfy *them* that what the angels said was true, or they would not have gone to Bethlehem. Having seen the child themselves, they had now evidence that would satisfy others; and accordingly they became the first preachers of the *gospel*, and went and proclaimed to others that the Messiah had come. One of the first duties of those who are newly converted to God, and a duty in which they delight, is to proclaim to others what they have seen and felt. It should be done in a proper way and at the proper time; but nothing can or should prevent a Christian recently converted from telling his feelings and views to others—to his friends, to his parents, to his brothers, and to his old companions. And it may be remarked that often more good may be done then than during any other period of their life. Entreaties then make an impression; nor can a sinner well resist the appeals made to him by one who was just now with him in the way to ruin, but who now treads the way to heaven.

19. *Mary kept all these things.* All that happened, and all that was said respecting her child. She *remembered* what the angel had said to *her;* what had happened to Elisabeth and to the shepherds—all the extraordinary circumstances which had attended the birth of her son. Here is a delicate and beautiful expression of the feelings

20 And the shepherds returned, glorifying and praising God for all the things that they had heard and seen, as it was told unto them.

21 And when [e]eight days were accomplished for the circumcising of the child, his name was called JESUS, which was so named of the angel[f] before he was conceived in the womb.

22 And when [g]the days of her purification, according to the law of Moses, were accomplished, they brought him to Jerusalem, to present *him* to the Lord;

23 (As it is written in the law of the Lord, [h]Every male that openeth the womb shall be called holy to the Lord;)

24 And to offer a sacrifice accord-

e Le.12.3. f Mat.1.21; ch.1.31. g Le.12.2,&c. h Ex.13.12; 22.29; Nu.8.17.

---

of a mother. A *mother* forgets none of those things which occur respecting her children. Everything they do or suffer — everything that is said of them, is treasured up in her mind; and often, often, she thinks of those things, and anxiously seeks what they may indicate respecting the future character and welfare of her child. ¶ *Pondered.* Weighed. This is the original meaning of the word *weighed.* She kept them; she revolved them; she *weighed* them in her mind, giving to each circumstance its just importance, and anxiously seeking what it might indicate respecting her child. ¶ *In her heart.* In her mind. She *thought* of these things often and anxiously.

20. *The shepherds returned.* To their flocks. ¶ *Glorifying,* &c. Giving honour to God, and celebrating his praises.

21. *Eight days,* &c. This was the regular time for performing the rite of circumcision, Ge. xvii. 12. ¶ *Called Jesus.* See Notes on Mat. i. 21.

22. *Days of her purification.* Among the Hebrews a mother was required to remain at home for about forty days after the birth of a male child and about eighty for a female, and during that time she was reckoned as *impure* —that is, she was not permitted to go to the temple or to engage in religious services with the congregation, Le. xii. 3, 4. ¶ *To Jerusalem.* The place where the temple was, and where the ordinances of religion were celebrated. ¶ *To present* him *to the Lord.* Every first-born male child among the Jews was regarded as *holy* to the Lord, Ex. xiii. 2. By their being *holy unto the Lord* was meant that unto them belonged the office of *priests.* It was theirs to be set apart to the service of God—to offer sacrifice, and to perform the duties of religion. It is probable that at first the duties of religion devolved on the *father*, and that, when he became infirm or died, that duty devolved on the eldest son; and it is still manifestly proper that where the father is infirm or has deceased, the duty of conducting family worship should be performed by the eldest son. Afterward God chose *the tribe of Levi in the place* of the eldest sons, to serve him in the sanctuary, Nu. viii. 13–18. Yet still it was proper to present the child to God, and it was required that it should be done with an offering.

23. *As it is written,* &c., Ex. xiii. 2.

24. *And to offer a sacrifice,* &c. Those who were able on such an occasion were required to offer a lamb for a burnt-offering, and a pigeon or a turtle-dove for a sin-offering. If not able to bring a *lamb*, then they were permitted to bring two turtle-doves or two young pigeons, Le. xii. 6, 8. ¶ *Turtle-doves.* Doves distinguished for having a plaintive and tender voice. By Mary's making this offering she showed her poverty; and our Saviour, by coming in a state of poverty, has shown that it is not dishonourable to be poor. No station is dishonourable where *God* places us. He knows what is best for us, and he often makes a state of poverty an occasion of the highest blessings. If *with* poverty he grants us, as is often the case, peace, contentment, and religion, it is worth far more than all the jewels of Golconda or the gold of Mexico. If it be asked why, since the Saviour was pure from any moral defilement in his conception and birth, it was necessary to offer such a sacrifice; why was it necessary that he should be circumcised, since he had no sin, it may be answered—1st. That it was proper to fulfil all righteousness, and to show obedience to the law, Mat. iii. 15. 2d. It was necessary for the future usefulness of Christ. Unless he had been circumcised, he could not

ing to that which is said in the law
of the Lord, A pair of turtle-doves,
or two young pigeons.
25 And, behold, there was a
man in Jerusalem whose name
was Simeon; and the same man
was just and [i]devout, waiting for
the [k]consolation of Israel: and the
Holy Ghost was upon him.
26 And it was revealed unto him

i Mar.15.43; ver.38. k Is.40.1.

by the Holy Ghost that he should
not [l]see death before he had seen
the Lord's Christ.
27 And he came by the Spirit into
the temple: and when the parents
brought in the child Jesus, to do for
him after the custom of the law,
28 Then took he him up in his
arms, and blessed God, and said,
29 Lord, [m]now lettest thou thy

l Ps.89.48; He.11.5. m Ge.46.30.

---

have been admitted to any synagogue or to the temple. He would have had no access to the people, and *could* not have been regarded as the Messiah. Both he and Mary, therefore, yielded obedience to the laws of the land, and thus set us an example that we should walk in their steps. Comp. Notes on on Mat. iii. 15.

25. *Whose name* was *Simeon*. Some have supposed that this Simeon was a son of the famous *Hillel*, a distinguished teacher in Jerusalem, and president of the Sanhedrim; but nothing is certainly known of him but what is here related. He was an aged man, of distinguished piety and reputation, and was anxiously expecting the coming of the Messiah. Such an *old age* is peculiarly honourable. No spectacle is more sublime than an old man of piety and high character looking for the appearing of the Lord, and patiently waiting for the time to come when he may be blessed with the sight of his Redeemer. ¶ *Just*. Righteous before God and man; approved by God as a righteous man, and discharging faithfully his duty to man. ¶ *Devout*. This word means *a religious man*, or a *pious* man. The original expresses the idea of *good reputation*, *well received*, or of high standing among the people. ¶ *Waiting for the consolation of Israel*. That is, waiting for the *Messiah*, who is called *the consolation of Israel* because he would give comfort to them by his appearing. This term was often applied to the Messiah before he actually appeared. It was common to swear, also, by "the consolation of Israel"—that is, by the Messiah about to come. See Lightfoot on this place. ¶ *The Holy Ghost*, &c. He was a holy man, and was *divinely inspired* respecting the Messiah about to appear.

26. *And it was revealed unto him*. In what way this was done we are not informed. Sometimes a revelation was made by a dream, at others by a voice, and at others by silent suggestion. All we know of this is that it was by the Holy Ghost. ¶ *Not see death*. Should not die. To *see* death and to *taste* of death, was a common way among the Hebrews of expressing death itself. Comp. Ps. lxxxix. 48. ¶ *The Lord's Christ*. Rather *the Lord's Anointed*. The word *Christ* means *anointed*, and it would have been better to use that word here. To an aged man who had been long waiting for the Messiah, how grateful must have been this revelation—this solemn assurance that the Messiah was near! But this revelation is now given to every man, that he need not taste of death till, by the eye of faith, he may see the Christ of God. He is offered freely. He has come. He waits to manifest himself to the world, and he is not willing that any should die for ever. To us also it will be as great a privilege in our dying hours to have seen Christ by faith as it was to Simeon. It will be the only thing that can support us then—the only thing that will enable us to depart in peace.

27. *By the Spirit*. By the *direction* of the Spirit. ¶ *Into the temple*. Into that part of the temple where the public worship was chiefly performed—into the court of the women. See Notes on Mat. xxi. 12. ¶ *The custom of the law*. That is, to make an offering for purification, and to present him to God.

28. *Blessed God*. Thanked or praised God.

29. *Now lettest*. Now thou *dost* let or permit. This word is in the indicative mood, and signifies that God *was permitting* him to die in peace, by having relieved his anxieties, allayed his

servant depart in [n]peace, according to thy word;

30 For mine eyes have [o]seen thy salvation,

31 Which thou hast prepared before the face of all people:

32 A light to lighten the [p]Gentiles, and the glory of thy people Israel.

33 And Joseph and his mother marvelled at those things which were spoken of him.

n Is.57.2; Re.14.13. *o* Is.52.10; ch.3.6; Ac.4.12. *p* Is.42.6; 49.6; 60.3; Ac.13.47,48.

---

fears, fulfilled the promises, and having, by the appearing of the Messiah, removed every reason why he should live any longer, and every wish to live. ¶ *Depart.* Die. ¶ *According to thy word.* Thy promise made by revelation. God never disappoints. To many it might have appeared improbable, when such a promise was made to an old man, that it should be fulfilled. But God fulfils all his word, keeps all his promises, and NEVER disappoints those who trust in him.

30. *Thy salvation.* Him who is to procure salvation for his people; or, the Saviour.

31. *Before the face of all people.* Whom thou hast provided *for* all people, or whom thou dost design *to reveal to* all people.

32. *A light to lighten the Gentiles.* This is in accordance with the prophecies in the Old Testament, Is. xlix.; ix. 6, 7; Ps. xcviii. 3; Mal. iv. 2. The Gentiles are represented as sitting in darkness—that is, in ignorance and sin. Christ is *a light* to them, as by him they will be made acquainted with the character of the true God, his law, and the plan of redemption. As the darkness rolls away when the sun arises, so ignorance and error flee away when Jesus gives light to the mind. Nations shall come to his light, and kings to the brightness of his rising, Is. lx. 3. ¶ *And the glory*, &c. The first offer of salvation was made to the Jews, Jn. iv. 22; Lu. xxiv. 47. Jesus was born among the Jews; to them had been given the prophecies respecting him, and his first ministry was among them. Hence he was their glory, their honour, their light. But it is a subject of special gratitude to us that the Saviour was given also for the Gentiles; for, 1. We are Gentiles, and if *he* had not come we should have been shut out from the blessings of redemption. 2. It is he only that now

> "Can make our dying bed
> Feel soft as downy pillows are,
> While on his breast we lean our head,
> And breathe our life out sweetly there."

Thus our departure may be like that of Simeon. Thus we may die in peace. Thus it will be a blessing to die. But, 3. In order to do this, our life must be like that of Simeon. We must *wait* for the consolation of Israel. We must look for his coming. We must be holy, harmless, undefiled, *loving* the Saviour. Then death to us, like death to Simeon, will have no terror; we shall depart in peace, and in heaven see the salvation of God, 2 Pe. iii. 11, 12. But, 4. Children, as well as the hoary-headed Simeon, may look for the coming of Christ. They too must die; and *their* death will be happy only as they depend on the Lord Jesus, and are prepared to meet him.

34. *Simeon blessed them.* Joseph and Mary. On them he sought the blessing of God. ¶ *Is set.* Is appointed or constituted for that, or such will be the effect of his coming. ¶ *The fall.* The word *fall* here denotes *misery, suffering, disappointment,* or *ruin.* There is a plain reference to the passage where it is said that he should be *a stone of stumbling and a rock of offence*, Is. viii. 14, 15. Many expected a *temporal* prince, and in this they were disappointed. They loved darkness rather than light, and rejected him, and *fell* unto destruction. Many that were proud were brought low by his preaching. They *fell* from the vain and giddy height of their own self-righteousness, and were humbled before God, and then, through him, rose again to a better righteousness and to better hopes. The nation also rejected him and put him to death, and, as a judgment, *fell* into the hands of the Romans. Thousands were led into captivity, and thousands perished. The nation rushed into ruin, the temple was destroyed, and the people were scattered into all the nations. See Ro. ix. 32, 33; 1 Pe. ii. 8; 1 Co. i. 23, 24. ¶ *And rising again.* The word "again" is not expressed in the Greek. It seems to be supposed, in our translation, that the *same persons* would fall and rise again; but this is not the meaning of the passage. It denotes that many would be

34 And Simeon blessed them,
and said unto Mary his mother,
Behold, this *child* is set for the
fall[q] and rising again of many in
Israel; and for a sign which shall
be [r]spoken against;
35 (Yea, a [s]sword shall pierce
through thy own soul also;) that
the[t] thoughts of many hearts may
be revealed.
36 And there was one Anna,
a prophetess, the daughter of
Phanuel, of the tribe of Aser;
she was of a great age, and had
lived with an husband seven years
from her virginity;
37 And she *was* a widow of
about fourscore and four years,
which departed not from the
temple, but served *God* with fastings and [u]prayers night and day.
38 And she, coming in that
instant, gave thanks likewise unto
the Lord, and spake of him to all
them that looked for redemption
in [4]Jerusalem.
39 And when they had per-
formed all things according to the

q Is.8.14; Ro.9.32,33; 1 Co.1.23,24; 2 Co.2.16; 1 Pe. 2.7,8. *r* Ac.28.22. *s* Jn.19.25. *t* Ju.5.15,16; 1 Co.11.19.

u Ac.26.7; 1 Ti.5.5. *v* ver.25. 4 or, *Israel.*

ruined by his coming, and that many *others* would be made happy or be saved. Many of the poor and humble, that were *willing* to receive him, would obtain pardon of sin and peace—would *rise* from their sins and sorrows here, and finally ascend to eternal life. ¶ *And for a sign*, &c. The word *sign* here denotes a conspicuous or distinguished object, and the Lord Jesus was such an object of contempt and rejection by all the people. He was despised, and his religion has been the common *mark* or *sign* for all the wicked, the profligate, and the profane, to curse, and ridicule, and oppose. Comp. Is. viii. 18, and Ac. xxviii. 22. Never was a prophecy more exactly fulfilled than this. Thousands have rejected the gospel and fallen into ruin; thousands are still falling of those who are ashamed of Jesus; thousands blaspheme him, deny him, speak all manner of evil against him, and would crucify him again if he were in their hands; but thousands also *by* him are renewed, justified, and raised up to life and peace.

35. *Yea, a sword*, &c. The sufferings and death of thy Son shall deeply afflict thy soul. And if Mary had not been thus forewarned and sustained by strong faith, she could not have borne the trials which came upon her Son; but God prepared her for it, and the holy mother of the dying Saviour was sustained. ¶ *That the thoughts*, &c. This is connected with the preceding verse: "He shall be a sign, a conspicuous object to be spoken against, that the thoughts of many hearts may be made manifest"—that is, that they *might show* how much they hated holiness. Nothing so *brings out* the feelings of sinners as to tell them of Jesus Christ. Many treat him with silent contempt; many are ready to gnash their teeth; many curse him; all show how much by nature the heart is opposed to religion, and thus are really, in spite of themselves, fulfilling the Scriptures and the prophecies. So true is it that "none can say that Jesus is Lord but by the Holy Ghost," 1 Co. xii. 3.

36. *Of the tribe of Aser.* The tribe of Aser, or Asher, dwelt in the northern part of the land of Canaan. Why Anna was called a prophetess is not known. It might be because she had been the wife of a prophet, or because she was employed in celebrating the praises of God (comp. 1 Ch. xxv. 1, 2, 4; 1 Sa. x. 5), or because she herself had foretold future events, being inspired.

37. *And she* was *a widow of about fourscore and four years.* That is, she was about eighty-four years *of age.* It does not mean that she had been a *widow* for that long time. ¶ *Fastings and prayers.* Constant religious service. Spending her time in prayer, and in all the ordinances of religion. ¶ *Night and day.* Continually—that is, at the usual times of public worship and in private. When it is said that she departed not from the temple, it is meant that she was *constant* and *regular* in all the public services at the temple, or was never absent from those services. God blesses those who wait at his temple gates.

39. *They returned into Galilee.* Not immediately, but after a time. Luke has omitted the flight into Egypt recorded by Matthew; but he has not denied it, nor are his words to be pressed

law of the Lord, they returned into Galilee, to their own city Nazareth.

40 And the child grew, and waxed strong in spirit, [w]filled with wisdom; and the grace of God was upon him.

41 Now his parents went to Jerusalem [x]every year at the feast of the passover.

42 And when he was twelve years old, they went up to Jerusalem, after the custom of the feast.

43 And when they had fulfilled the days, as they returned, the child Jesus tarried behind in Jerusalem; and Joseph and his mother knew not *of it*.

44 But they, supposing him to have been in the company, went

w Is.11.2,3; ver.52. *x* Ex.23.15; De.16.1.

---

as if he meant to affirm that they went *immediately* to Nazareth. A parallel case we have in the life of Paul. When he was converted it is said that he came to Jerusalem, as if he had gone there immediately after his conversion (Ac. ix. 26); yet we learn in another place that this was after an interval of three years, Ga. i. 17, 18. In the case before us there is no improbability in supposing that they returned to Bethlehem, then went to Egypt, and then to Galilee.

40. *Strong in spirit.* In mind, intellect, understanding. Jesus had a human soul, and *that* soul was subject to all the proper laws of a human spirit. It therefore increased in knowledge, strength, and character. Nor is it any more inconsistent with his being God to say that his soul expanded, than to say that his body grew. ¶ *Filled with wisdom.* Eminent for wisdom when a child—that is, exhibiting an extraordinary understanding, and *wise* to flee from everything sinful and evil. ¶ *And the grace of God*, &c. The word *grace* in the New Testament commonly means unmerited favour shown *to sinners*. Here it means no more than *favour*. God showed him *favour*, or was pleased with him and blessed him.

It is remarkable that this is all that is recorded of the infancy of Jesus; and this, with the short account that follows of his going to Jerusalem, is all that we know of him for thirty years of his life. The design of the evangelists was to give an account of his *public ministry*, and not his private life. Hence they say little of him in regard to his first years. What they *do* say, however, corresponds entirely with what we might expect. He was wise, pure, pleasing God, and deeply skilled in the knowledge of the divine law. He set a lovely example for all children; was subject to his parents, and increased in favour with God and man.

42. *Twelve years old.* All males among the Hebrews were required to appear three times a year before God, to attend on the ordinances of religion in the temple, and it is probable that this was the age at which they first went up to Jerusalem, Ex. xxiii. 14–17; De. xvi. 16. ¶ *To Jerusalem.* Where the feasts of the Jews were all held. This was a journey from Nazareth of about 70 miles. ¶ *After the custom of the feast.* According to the usual manner of the feast.

43. *Had fulfilled the days.* The days of the Passover. These were eight days in all—one day for killing the paschal lamb, and seven days for the observance of the feast of unleavened bread, Ex. xii. 15; Le. xxiii. 5, 6.

44. *Supposing him to have been in the company.* It may seem very remarkable that parents should not have been more attentive to their only son, and that they should not have been assured of his presence with them when they left Jerusalem; but the difficulty may be explained by the following considerations: 1. In going to these great feasts, families and neighbours would join together, and form a large collection. 2. It is not improbable that Jesus was *with* them when they were about to start from Jerusalem and were making preparations. Seeing him then, they might have been certain as to his presence. 3. A part of the company might have left before the others, and Joseph and Mary may have supposed that he was with them, until they overtook them at night and ascertained their mistake. ¶ *Kinsfolk.* Relatives. ¶ *Acquaintances.* Neighbours who had gone up with them in the same company to Jerusalem.

46. *After three days.* This means, probably, *on the third day* after they had left Jerusalem—that is, the first day they went toward Galilee, on the second

a day's journey; and they sought
him among *their* kinsfolk and
among their acquaintance.
45 And when they found him
not, they turned back again to
Jerusalem, seeking him.
46 And it came to pass, that
after three days they found him in
the temple, sitting in the midst of
the doctors, both hearing them and
asking them questions.
47 And all that heard him were
astonished at his [y]understanding
and answers.

y Ps.119.99; Mat.7.28; Mar.1.22; ch.4.22,32; Jn.7.15,46.

48 And when they saw him,
they were amazed: and his mother
said unto him, Son, why hast thou
thus dealt with us? behold, thy
father and I have sought thee
sorrowing.
49 And he said unto them,
How is it that ye sought me?
wist ye not that [z]I must be about
my Father's business?
50 And they understood not the
saying which he spake unto them.
51 And he went down with
them and came to Nazareth, and

z Jn.5.17; 9.4.

---

they returned to Jerusalem, and on the third they found him. Comp. Mat. xxvii. 63; Mar. viii. 31. ¶ *In the temple.* In the *court* of the temple, for Jesus, not being a Levitical priest, could not enter into the temple itself. See Mat. xxi. 12. ¶ *In the midst of the doctors.* The *teachers*, the *Rabbins*, who were the instructors of the people in matters of religion. ¶ *Asking them questions.* Proposing questions to them respecting the law and the prophets. There is no reason to suppose that this was for the purpose of perplexing or confounding them. The questions were doubtless proposed in a respectful manner, and the answers listened to with proper deference to their age and rank. Jesus was a child, and religion does not teach a child to be rude or uncivil, even though he may really know much more than more aged persons. Religion teaches all, and especially the young, to treat others with respect, to show them the honour that is due, to venerate age, and to speak kindly to all, 1 Pe. ii. 17; iii. 8, 9; Ex. xx. 12; Mat. xxiii. 3; Ro. xiii. 7.

48. *Why hast thou thus dealt with us?* Why hast thou given us all this trouble and anxiety, in going so far and returning with so much solicitude? ¶ *Thy father.* Joseph was not the *real* father of Jesus, but he was *legally* so; and as the secret of his birth was not commonly known, he was called his father. Mary, in accordance with that usage, also called him so. ¶ *Sorrowing.* Anxious, lest in the multitude he might not be found, or lest some accident might have happened to him.

49. *How is it*, &c. *Why* have ye sought me with so much anxiety? *Mary* should have known that the Son of God was safe; that his heavenly Father would take care of him, and that he *could* do nothing amiss. ¶ *Wist ye not.* *Know* ye not. You had reason to know. You knew my design in coming into the world, and that design was *superior* to the duty of obeying earthly parents, and *they* should be willing always to give me up to the proper business for which I live. ¶ *My Father's business.* Some think that this should be translated "in my Father's house"—that is, in the temple. Jesus reminded them here that he came down from heaven; that he had a higher Father than an earthly parent; and that, even in early life, it was proper that he should be engaged in the work for which he came. He did not enter, indeed, upon his *public* work for eighteen years after this; yet still the work of God was *his* work, and always, even in childhood, it was proper for him to be engaged in the great business for which he came down from heaven.

50. *They understood not*, &c. It is remarkable that they did not understand Jesus in this, but it shows how slow persons are to believe. Even his parents, after all that had taken place, did not seem to comprehend that *he* was to be the Saviour of men, or if they did, they understood it in a very imperfect manner.

51. *Went down with them.* Down from Jerusalem, which was in a high, mountainous region. ¶ *Was subject unto them.* Performed the duty of a faithful and obedient child, and not improbably was engaged in the trade of Joseph—that of a carpenter. Every Jew was required

was subject unto them: but his mother [a]kept all these sayings in her heart.

52 And Jesus [b]increased in wisdom and [5]stature, and in favour with God and man.

a Da.7.28; ver.19. *b* 1 Sa.2.26; ver.40. [5] or, *age.*

CHAPTER III.

NOW in the fifteenth year of the reign of Tiberius Cæsar, Pontius Pilate being governor of Judea, and Herod being tetrarch of Galilee, and his brother Philip

---

to learn some trade, and there is every reason to think that our Saviour followed that of his reputed father. And from this we learn—1. That obedience to parents is a duty. Jesus has set an example in this that all children should follow. Though he was the Son of God, and on proper occasions was engaged in the great work of redemption, yet he was also the *son of Mary*, and he loved and obeyed his mother, and was *subject* to her. 2. It is no dishonour to be a mechanic, or to be brought up in an obscure employment. Jesus has conferred honour on virtuous industry, and no man should be ashamed of industrious parents, though poor, or of a condition of life that is far from ease and affluence. Industry is honourable, and virtuous poverty should not be regarded as a matter of reproach. The only thing to be ashamed of, in regard to this matter, is when men are idle, or when children are too proud to hear or speak of the occupation of their parents, or to *follow* the same occupation.

52. *In favour with God.* That is, in proportion to his advance in wisdom. This does not imply that he ever *lacked* the favour of God, but that God regarded him with favour *in proportion* as he showed an understanding and spirit like his own. Happy are those children who imitate the example of Jesus—who are obedient to parents—who increase in wisdom—who are sober, temperate, and industrious, and who thus increase in favour with God and men.

CHAPTER III.

1. *Now in the fifteenth year.* This was the *thirteenth* year of his being sole emperor. He was *two* years joint emperor with Augustus, and Luke reckons from the time when he was admitted to share the empire with Augustus Cæsar. See Lardner's *Credibility*, vol. i. ¶ *Tiberius Cæsar.* Tiberius succeeded Augustus in the empire, and began his *sole* reign Aug. 19, A.D. 14. He was a most infamous character—a scourge to the Roman people. He reigned twenty-three years, and was succeeded by *Caius Caligula*, whom he appointed his successor on account of his notorious wickedness, and that he might be, as he expressed it, a *serpent* to the Romans. ¶ *Pontius Pilate.* Herod the Great left his kingdom to three sons. See Notes on Mat. ii. 22. To *Archelaus* he left *Judea.* Archelaus reigned *nine* years, when, on account of his crimes, he was banished into Vienne, and Judea was made a Roman province, and placed entirely under Roman governors or *procurators*, and became completely tributary to Rome. Pontius Pilate was the *fifth* governor that had been sent, and of course had been in Judea but a short time. See the chronological table at the end of the volume. ¶ *Herod being tetrarch of Galilee.* This was *Herod Antipas*, son of Herod the Great, to whom Galilee had been left as his part of his father's kingdom. The word *tetrarch* properly denotes one who presides over a *fourth part* of a country or province; but it also came to be a general title, denoting one who reigned over any part—a third, a half, &c. In this case Herod had a *third* of the dominions of his father, but he was called tetrarch. It was this Herod who imprisoned John the Baptist, and to whom our Saviour, when arraigned, was sent by Pilate. ¶ *And his brother Philip tetrarch of Iturea. Iturea* was so called from *Jetur*, one of the sons of Ishmael, Ge. xxv. 15; 1 Ch. i. 31. It was situated on the east side of the Jordan, and was taken from the descendants of Jetur by the tribes of Reuben and Gad and the half tribe of Manasseh, 1 Ch. v. 19. ¶ *Region of Trachonitis.* This region was also on the east of the Jordan, and extended northward to the district of Damascus and eastward to the deserts of Arabia. It was bounded on the west by Gaulonitis and south by the city of Bostra. Philip had obtained this region from the Romans on condition that he would extirpate the robbers. ¶ *Lysanias the tetrarch of Abilene.* Abilene was so called from *Abila*, its chief city. It was situated in Syria, north-west of

tetrarch of Iturea, and of the
region of Trachonitis, and Lysanias
the tetrarch of Abilene,
2 Annas[a] and Caiaphas being
the high-priests, the word of God
came unto John, the son of Zacharias,
in the wilderness.
3 And[b] he came into all the
country about Jordan, preaching
the[c] baptism of repentance for the
remission of sins;
4 As it is written in the book of
the words of Esaias the prophet,
saying, [d]The voice of one crying
in the wilderness, Prepare ye the
way of the Lord, make his paths
straight.
5 Every valley shall be filled,
and every mountain and hill shall
be brought low; and the crooked
shall be made straight, and the
rough ways *shall be* made smooth;
6 And[e] all flesh shall see the
salvation of God.
7 Then said he to the multitude
that came forth to be baptized of
him, [f]O generation of vipers! who
hath warned you to flee from the
wrath to come?
8 Bring forth, therefore, fruits
[1]worthy of repentance; and begin
not to say within yourselves, We
have Abraham to *our* father: for I
say unto you, that God is able of
these stones to raise up children
unto Abraham.
9 And now also the axe is laid
unto the root of the trees: [g]every
tree, therefore, which bringeth not
forth good fruit is hewn down and
cast into the fire.
10 And the people asked him,
saying, What shall we do, then?
11 He answereth and saith unto

a Jn.11.49,51; 18.13; Ac.4.6. *b* Mat.3.1; Mar.1.4. *c* ch.1.77. *d* Is.40.3.
e Ps.98.2; Is.40.5; 49.6; 52.10; Ro.10.12,18. *f* Mat.3.7. [1] or, *meet for*. *g* Mat.7.19; ch.13.7,9.

Damascus and south-east of Mount Lebanon, and was adjacent to Galilee.

2. *Annas and Caiaphas being high-priests.* There was, properly speaking, but *one* high-priest of the Jews; yet the *name* of high-priest continued to be given to those who had been in that office, and especially when they still possessed some civil office after they had left the high-priesthood. In this case it appears that *Caiaphas* was high-priest, and Annas *had been*, but had been dismissed from the office. It is highly probable that he still held an office under the Romans, and was perhaps president of the Sanhedrim. He is mentioned *before* Caiaphas because he was father-in-law to Caiaphas, and probably was the eldest, and had been longest in office. Instances similar to this may be found in Josephus.

There is one remark to be made here about the manner in which the gospels are written. They have every mark of openness and honesty. An impostor does not mention names, and times, and places particularly. If he did, it would be easy to ascertain that he *was* an impostor. But the sacred writers describe objects and men as if they were perfectly familiar with them. They never appear to be *guarding* themselves. They speak of things most minutely. If, therefore, they had been impostors, it would have been easy to detect them. If, for example, John did *not* begin to preach in the fifteenth year of Tiberius—if Philip was *not* tetrarch of Iturea—if Pontius Pilate was *not* governor of Judea, how easy would it have been to detect them in falsehood! Yet it was never done. Nay, we have evidence of that age, in Josephus, that these descriptions are strictly true; and, consequently, the gospels must have been written by men who were personally acquainted with what they wrote, who were not impostors, and who were *honest* men. If they were *honest*, then the Christian religion is true.

3-9. On the baptism of John, see Notes on Mat. iii.

10. *What shall we do, then?* John had told them to bring forth fruits appropriate to repentance, or to lead a life which showed that their repentance was genuine. They very properly, therefore, asked how it should be done, or what *would be* such a life.

11. *He that hath two coats,* &c. Or, in other words, aid the poor according to your ability; be benevolent, and you will thus show that your repentance is

them, [h]He that hath two coats, let him impart to him that hath none; and he that hath meat, let him do likewise.

12 Then came also [i]publicans to be baptized, and said unto him, Master, what shall we do?

13 And he said unto them, [k]Exact no more than that which is appointed you.

14 And the soldiers likewise demanded of him, saying, And what shall we do? And he said unto them, [2]Do violence to no man,

h ch.11.41; 2 Co.8.14; 1 Jn.3.17. *i* Mat.21.32; ch.7.29.

k ch.19.8; 1 Co.6.10. 2 or, *Put no man in fear.*

genuine. It is remarkable that one of the *first* demands of religion is to do good, and it is in *this* way that it may be shown that the repentance is not feigned. For 1st. The *nature* of religion is to do good. 2d. This requires self-denial, and none will deny themselves who are not attached to God. And 3d. This is to imitate Jesus Christ, who, though he was rich, yet for our sakes became poor. ¶ *Coats.* See Notes on Mat. v. 40. ¶ *Meat.* Provision of any kind.

12. *The publicans.* See Notes on Mat. v. 47. There is reason to think that the *publicans* or *tax-gatherers* were peculiarly oppressive and hard in their dealings with the people; and that, as they had every opportunity of exacting more than they ought, so they often did it, and thus enriched themselves. The evidence of repentance in them would be to break off their sins in this respect, and to deal justly.

13. *Exact.* Demand, or take, no more. ¶ *Than that which is appointed.* That is, by the government. John does not condemn the office, or say that the employment should be forsaken. Though it was hated by the people—though often abused and therefore unpopular —yet *the office itself* was not dishonourable. If there is a government, it must be supported; and of course there must be men whose duty it is to collect taxes, as the means of the proper support of the government; and as such a support of the government is necessary, so the people should pay cheerfully the just apportionment of their rulers, and regard favourably those who are authorized to collect it. See Ro. xiii. 1-6.

14. *The soldiers likewise.* It seems that *they* also came to his baptism. Whether these were Jews or Romans cannot be ascertained. It is not improbable that, as Judea was a Roman province, they were Jews or Jewish proselytes in the service of Herod Antipas or Philip, and so were really in the Roman service. ¶ *Do violence*, &c. Do not take the property of any by unlawful force, or do not use unjust force against the person or property of any individual. It is probable that many of them were oppressive, or prone to violence, rapine, or theft, and burdensome even in times of peace to the inhabitants. ¶ *Neither accuse* any *falsely.* It is probable that when they wished the property of others and could not obtain it by violence, or when there was no pretext for violence, they often attempted the same thing in another way, and falsely accused the persons of crime. The word rendered *falsely accused* is the one from which our word *sycophant* is derived. The proper meaning of the word *sycophant* was this: There was a law in Athens which prohibited the importation of *figs.* The *sycophant* (literally *the man who made figs to appear*, or who showed them) was one who made complaint to the magistrate of persons who had imported figs contrary to law, or who was an *informer;* and then the word came to be used in a general sense to denote *any* complainer—a calumniator—an accuser —an informer. As such persons were usually cringing and fawning, and looked for a reward, the word came to be used also to denote a fawner or flatterer. It is always used in a bad sense. It is correctly rendered here, "do not accuse any falsely." ¶ *Be content*, &c. Do not murmur or complain, or take unlawful means to increase your wages. ¶ *Wages.* This word means not only the *money* which was paid them, but also their *rations* or daily allowance of food. By this they were to show that their repentance was genuine; that it had a practical influence; that it produced a *real* reformation of life; and it is clear that *no other* repentance would be genuine. Every profession of repentance which is not attended with a change of life is mere hypocrisy. It may farther be remarked that John

neither [l]accuse *any* falsely; and be content[m] with your [3]wages.

15 And as the people were [4]in expectation, and all men [5]mused in their hearts of John, whether he were the Christ or not;

16 John answered, saying unto *them* all, I indeed baptize you with water; but one mightier than I cometh, the latchet of whose shoes I am not worthy to unloose: he shall baptize you with the Holy Ghost, and with fire:

17 Whose [n]fan *is* in his hand, and he will thoroughly purge his floor, and [o]will gather the wheat into his garner; but the [p]chaff he will [q]burn with fire unquenchable.

18 And many other things, in his exhortation, preached he unto the people.

19 But[r] Herod the tetrarch, being reproved by him for Herodias his brother Philip's wife, and for all the evils which Herod had done,

20 Added yet this above all, that he shut up John in prison.

21 Now when all the people were baptized, [s]it came to pass, that Jesus also being baptized, and praying, the heaven was opened,

22 And the Holy Ghost descended in a bodily shape like a dove upon him; and a voice came from heaven, which said, Thou art my beloved Son; in thee I am well pleased.

l Ex.23.1; Le.19.11. *m* 1 Ti.6.8. [3] or, *allowance.* [4] or, *in suspense.* [5] or, *reasoned;* or, *debated.* *n* Je.15.7. *o* Mi.4.12; Mat.13.30. *p* Ps.1.4. *q* Ps.21.9; Mar.9.44,48.

r Mat.14.3; Mar.6.17. *s* Mat.3.13,&c.; Jn.1.32,&c.

---

did not condemn their profession, or say that it was unlawful to be a soldier, or that they must abandon the business in order to be true penitents. It was possible to be a good man and yet a soldier. What was required was that in their profession they should show that they were really upright, and did not commit the crimes which were often practised in that calling. It is lawful to defend one's self, one's family, or one's country, and hence it is lawful to be a soldier. Man everywhere, in all professions, should be a Christian, and then he will do honour to his profession, and his profession, if it is not a direct violation of the law of God, will be honourable.

15. *In expectation.* Expecting the Messiah. Marg. *suspense.* That is, they were not certain whether John was not himself the Messiah. They confidently *expected* his appearing, and there minds were in *suspense*, or they were in a state of doubt whether he had not already come, and whether John was not the Messiah. ¶ *Mused in their hearts of John.* Thought of his character, his preaching, and his success, and anxiously inquired whether he did not do the things which were expected of the Messiah.

16–18. See Notes on Mat. iii. 11, 12.

19, 20. See Notes on Mat. xiv. 1–13. *Added this above all.* To all his former crimes he added this; not implying that this was the *worst* of his acts, but that this was *one* of his deeds, of like character as the others. The event here mentioned did not take place until some time after this, but it is mentioned here to show what was the end of John's preaching, or to *fill out* the account concerning him.

21, 22. See Notes on Mat. iii. 13–17. *Jesus being baptized;* or, Jesus *having been* baptized. This took place *after* the baptism, and not *during* its administration, Mat. iii. 16. ¶ *Praying.* This circumstance is omitted by the other evangelists; and it shows, 1st. That Jesus was in the habit of prayer. 2d. That it is proper to offer up special prayer at the administration of the ordinances of religion. 3d. That it is possible to pray in the midst of a great multitude, yet in secret. The prayer consisted, doubtless, in lifting up the heart silently to God. So *we* may do it anywhere—about our daily toil—in the midst of multitudes, and thus may pray *always*.

22. *In a bodily shape.* This was a real visible appearance, and was doubtless seen by the people. The dove is an emblem of purity and harmlessness, and the form of the dove was assumed on this occasion to signify, probably, that the spirit with which Jesus would be endowed would be one of purity and innocence. The *Holy Spirit*, when he assumes a visible form, assumes that

23 And Jesus himself began to
be about thirty years of age, being
(as was supposed) the [t]son of Joseph, which was *the son* of Heli,
24 Which was *the son* of Matthat,
which was *the son* of Levi, which
was *the son* of Melchi, which was
the son of Janna, which was *the son*
of Joseph,
25 Which was *the son* of Mattathias, which was *the son* of Amos,
which was *the son* of Naum, which
was *the son* of Esli, which was *the
son* of Nagge,
26 Which was *the son* of Maath,
which was *the son* of Mattathias,
which was *the son* of Semei, which
was *the son* of Joseph, which was
the son of Juda,
27 Which was *the son* of Joanna,
which was *the son* of Rhesa, which
was *the son* of Zorobabel, which
was *the son* of Salathiel, which was
the son of Neri,
28 Which was *the son* of Melchi,
which was *the son* of Addi, which
was *the son* of Cosam, which was
the son of Elmodam, which was *the
son* of Er,
29 Which was *the son* of Jose,
which was *the son* of Eliezer, which
was *the son* of Jorim, which was
the son of Matthat, which was *the
son* of Levi,
30 Which was *the son* of Simeon,
which was *the son* of Juda, which
was *the son* of Joseph, which was
the son of Jonan, which was *the son*
of Eliakim,

t Mat.13.55; Jn.6.42.

31 Which was *the son* of Melea,
which was *the son* of Menan, which
was *the son* of Mattatha, which was
the son of [u]Nathan, which was *the
son* of David,
32 Which was *the son* of [v]Jesse,
which was *the son* of Obed, which
was *the son* of Booz, which was *the
son* of Salmon, which was *the son*
of Naasson,
33 Which was *the son* of Aminadab, which was *the son* of Aram,
which was *the son* of Esrom, which
was *the son* of Phares, which was
the son of Juda,
34 Which was *the son* of Jacob,
which was *the son* of Isaac, which
was *the son* of [w]Abraham, which
was *the son* of Thara, which was
the son of Nachor,
35 Which was *the son* of Saruch,
which was *the son* of Ragau, which
was *the son* of Phalec, which was
the son of Heber, which was *the son*
of Sala,
36 Which was *the son* of Cainan,
which was *the son* of [x]Arphaxad,
which was *the son* of Sem, which
was *the son* of Noe, which was *the
son* of [y]Lamech,
37 Which was *the son* of Mathu-
sala, which was *the son* of Enoch,
which was *the son* of Jared, which
was *the son* of Maleleel, which was
the son of Cainan,
38 Which was *the son* of Enos,
which was *the son* of Seth, which
was *the son* of Adam, which was
the [z]*son* of God.

u Zec.12.12; 2 Sa.5.14. *v* Ru.4.18,22.
w Ge.11.24-26. *x* Ge.11.12. *y* Ge.5.25.
z Ge.1.26; 2.7; Is.64.8; 1 Co.15.45,47.

---

which will be emblematic of the thing to be represented. Thus he assumed the form of *tongues*, to signify the miraculous powers of language with which the apostles would be endowed; the appearance of *fire*, to denote their power, &c., Ac. ii. 3.

23. *Jesus began to be*, &c. This was the age at which the priests entered on their office, Nu. iv. 3, 47; but it is not evident that Jesus had any reference to that in delaying his work to his thirtieth year. He was not subjected to the Levitical law in regard to the priesthood, and it does not appear that prophets and teachers did not commence their work before that age. ¶ *As was supposed.* As was commonly thought, or perhaps being *legally* reckoned as his son.

24–38. See, on this genealogy, the Notes on Mat. i. 1–16.

CHAPTER IV.

1–14. On the temptation of Jesus, see Notes on Mat. iv. 1–11.

CHAPTER IV.

AND[a] Jesus, being full of the Holy Ghost, returned from Jordan, and was led by the Spirit into the wilderness,

2 Being forty days tempted of the devil. And [b]in those days he did eat nothing: and when they were ended he afterward hungered.

3 And the devil said unto him, If thou be the Son of God, command this stone that it be made bread.

4 And Jesus answered him, saying, [c]It is written, that man shall not live by bread alone, but by every word of God.

5 And the devil, taking him up into a high mountain, showed unto him all the kingdoms of the world in a moment of time.

6 And the devil said unto him, All this power will I give thee, and the glory of them: [d]for that is delivered unto me; and to whomsoever I will I give it.

7 If thou, therefore, wilt [1]worship me, all shall be thine.

8 And Jesus answered and said unto him, Get thee behind me, Satan: for it is written, [e]Thou shalt worship the Lord thy God, and him only shalt thou serve.

9 And he brought him to Jerusalem, and set him on a pinnacle of the temple, and said unto him, If thou be the Son of God, cast thyself down from hence:

10 For it is written, [f]He shall give his angels charge over thee, to keep thee;

11 And in *their* hands they shall bear thee up, lest at any time thou dash thy foot against a stone.

12 And Jesus, answering, said unto him, It is said, [g]Thou shalt not tempt the Lord thy God.

13 And when the devil had ended [h]all the temptation, he departed from him for a season.

14 And Jesus [i]returned in the power of the Spirit into Galilee: and there went out a fame of him through all the region round about.

15 And he taught in their synagogues, being glorified of all.

16 And he came to [k]Nazareth, where he had been brought up:

a Mat.4.1,&c.; Mar.1.12,&c.; ver.14.
b Ex.34.28; 1 Ki.19.8.
c De.8.3. *d* Jn.12.31; 14.30; Ep.2.2; Re.13.2,7.
1 or, *fall down before me.*
e De.6.13; 10.20. *f* Ps.91.11. *g* De.6.16.
h He.4.15. *i* Jn.4.43; Ac.10.37. *k* Mat.2.23.

---

2. *Being forty days tempted.* That is, through forty days he was *tried* in various ways by the devil. The temptations, however, which are recorded by Matthew and Luke did not take place until the forty days were *finished.* See Mat. iv. 2, 3. ¶ *He did eat nothing.* He was sustained by the power of God during this season of extraordinary fasting.

13. *Departed for a season.* For a time. From this it appears that our Saviour was *afterward* subjected to temptations by Satan, but no *particular* temptations are recorded after this. From Jn. xiv. 30, it seems that the devil tried or tempted him in the agony in Gethsemane. Comp. Notes on He. xii. 4. It is more than probable, also, that Satan did much to excite the Pharisees and Sadducees to endeavour to *entangle him,* and the priests and rulers to oppose him; yet out of all his temptations God delivered him; and so he will make a way to escape for *all* that are tempted, and will not suffer them to be tempted above that which they are able to bear, 1 Co. x. 13.

14. *In the power of the Spirit.* By the *influence* or direction of the Spirit. ¶ *A fame.* A report. See Matthew iv. 24.

15. *Glorified of all.* Praised by all; or, all were pleased with his instructions, and admired his wisdom.

16. *And, as his custom was, he went,* &c. From this it appears that the Saviour regularly attended the service of the synagogue. In that service the Scriptures of the Old Testament were read, prayers were offered, and the Word of God was explained. See Notes on Mat. iv. 23. There was great corruption in doctrine and practice at that time, but Christ did not on that account

and, as his custom was, [l]he went into the synagogue on the sabbath-day, and stood up for to read.

17 And there was delivered unto him the book of the prophet Esaias. And when he had opened the book, he found the place where it was written,

18 The[m] Spirit of the Lord *is* upon me, because he hath anointed

l Mat.13.54; Jn.18.20; Ac.13.14; 17.2. *m* Is.61.1.

keep away from the place of public worship. From this we may learn—1st. That it is our duty *regularly* to attend public worship. 2d. That it is better to attend a place of worship which is not entirely pure, or where just such doctrines are not delivered as we would wish, than not attend at all. It is of vast importance that the public worship of God should be maintained; and it is *our* duty to assist in maintaining it, to show by our example that we love it, and to win others also to love it. See He. x. 25. At the same time, this remark should not be construed as enjoining it as our duty to attend where the *true* God is not worshipped, or where he is worshipped by pagan rites and pagan prayers. If, therefore, the Unitarian does not worship the true God, and if the Roman Catholic worships God in a manner forbidden, and offers homage to the *creatures* of God, thus being guilty of idolatry, it cannot be a duty to attend on such a place of worship. ¶ *The synagogue.* See Mat. iv. 23. ¶ *Stood up for to read.* The books of Moses were so divided that they could be read through in the synagogues once in a year. To these were added portions out of the prophets, so that no small part of them was read also once a year. It is not known whether our Saviour read the lesson which was the regular one for that day, though it might seem *probable* that he would not depart from the usual custom. Yet, as the eyes of all were fixed on him; as he deliberately looked out a place; and as the people were evidently surprised at what he did, it seems to be intimated that he selected a lesson which was *not* the regular one for that day. The same ceremonies in regard to conducting public worship which are here described are observed at Jerusalem by the Jews at the present time. Professor Hackett (*Illustrations of Scripture*, p. 232) says: "I attended the Jewish worship at Jerusalem, and was struck with the accordance of the ceremonies with those mentioned in the New Testament. The sacred roll was brought from the chest or closet where it was kept; it was handed by an attendant to the reader; a portion of it was rehearsed; the congregation rose and stood while it was read, whereas the speaker, as well as the others present, sat during the delivery of the address which formed a part of the service."

17. *There was delivered unto him.* By the minister of the synagogue, or the keeper of the sacred books. They were kept in an *ark* or chest, not far from the pulpit, and the minister gave them to whomsoever he chose, to read them publicly. ¶ *The book.* The volume contained the prophecy of Isaiah. It would seem, from this, that the books were kept separate, and not united into one as with us. ¶ *When he had opened the book.* Literally, when he had *unrolled* the book. Books, among the ancients, were written on parchments or vellum that is, skins of beasts, and were *rolled* together on two rollers, beginning at each end, so that while reading they rolled *off* from one to the other. Different forms of books were indeed used, but this was the most common. When used the reader unrolled the MS. as far as the place which he wished to find, and kept before him just so much as he would read. When the roller was done with, it was carefully deposited in a case. ¶ *The place where it was written.* Is. lxi. 1, 2.

18. *The Spirit of the Lord* is *upon me.* Or, I speak by divine appointment. I am divinely inspired to speak. There can be no doubt that the passage in Isaiah had a principal reference to the Messiah. Our Saviour directly applies it to himself, and it is not easily applicable to any other prophet. Its *first* application might have been to the restoration of the Jews from Babylon; but the language of prophecy is often applicable to two similar events, and the secondary event is often the most important. In this case the prophet uses most striking poetic images to depict the return from Babylon, but the same images also describe the appro-

me to preach the gospel to the poor;
he hath sent me to [n]heal the broken-
hearted, to preach deliverance to
the captives, and [o]recovering of
sight to the blind, to set at liberty
[p]them that are bruised,
19 To preach the [q]acceptable
year of the Lord.

n 2 Ch.34.27; Ps.34.18; 51.17; 147.3; Is.57.15. *o* Ps.146.8; Is.29.18.

p Is.42.3; Mat.12.20. *q* Is.61.2; 63.4.

priate work of the Son of God. ¶ *Hath anointed me.* Anciently kings and prophets and the high-priest were set apart to their work by anointing with oil, 1 Ki. xix. 15, 16; Ex. xxix. 7; 1 Sa. ix. 16, &c. This oil or ointment was made of various substances, and it was forbidden to imitate it, Ex. xxx. 34–38. Hence those who were set apart to the work of God as king, prophet, or priest, were called the Lord's anointed, 1 Sa. xvi. 6; Ps. lxxxiv. 9; Is. xlv. 1. Hence the Son of God is called the *Messiah*, a Hebrew word signifying the *Anointed*, or the *Christ*, a Greek word signifying the same thing. And by his being *anointed* is not meant that he was *literally* anointed, for he was never set apart in that manner, but that *God had set him apart* for this work; that *he* had constituted or appointed him to be the prophet, priest, and king of his people. See Notes on Mat. i. 1. ¶ *To preach the gospel to the poor.* The English word *gospel* is derived from two words—*God* or *good*, and *spell*, an old Saxon word meaning *history*, *relation*, *narration*, *word*, or *speech*, and the word therefore means *a good communication* or *message.* This corresponds exactly with the meaning of the Greek word—*a good* or *joyful message—glad tidings.* By the *poor* are meant all those who are destitute of the comforts of this life, and who therefore may be more readily disposed to seek treasures in heaven; all those who are sensible of their sins, or are poor in spirit (Mat. v. 3); and all the *miserable* and the afflicted, Is. lviii. 7. Our Saviour gave it as one proof that he was the Messiah, or was from God, that he preached to *the poor*, Mat. xi. 5. The Pharisees and Sadducees despised the poor; ancient philosophers neglected them; but the gospel seeks to bless them—to give comfort where it is felt to be needed, and where it will be received with gratitude. Riches fill the mind with pride, with self-complacency, and with a feeling that the gospel is not needed. The poor *feel* their need of some sources of comfort that the world cannot give, and accordingly our Saviour met with his greatest success among the poor; and there also, *since*, the gospel has shed its richest blessings and its purest joys. It is also one proof that the gospel is true. If it had been of *men*, it would have sought the rich and mighty; but it pours contempt on all human greatness, and seeks, like God, to do good to those whom the world overlooks or despises. See Notes on 1 Co. i. 26. ¶ *To heal the broken-hearted.* To console those who are deeply afflicted, or whose hearts are *broken* by external calamities or by a sense of their sinfulness. ¶ *Deliverance to the captives.* This is a figure originally applicable to those who were in captivity in Babylon. They were miserable. To grant deliverance to *them* and restore them to their country—to grant deliverance to those who are in prison and restore them to their families—to give liberty to the slave and restore him to freedom, was to confer the highest benefit and impart the richest favour. In this manner the gospel imparts favour. It does not, indeed, *literally* open the doors of prisons, but it releases the *mind* captive under sin; it gives comfort to the prisoner, and it will finally open all prison doors and break off all the chains of slavery, and, by preventing *crime*, prevent also the sufferings that are the consequence of crime. ¶ *Sight to the blind.* This was often literally fulfilled, Mat. xi. 5; Jn. ix. 11; Mat. ix. 30, &c. ¶ *To set at liberty them that are bruised.* The word *bruised*, here, evidently has the same *general* signification as *broken-hearted* or the contrite. It means those who are *pressed down* by great calamity, or whose hearts are *pressed* or *bruised* by the consciousness of sin. To set them *at liberty* is the same as to free them from this pressure, or to give them consolation.

19. *To preach the acceptable year of the Lord.* The time when God is willing to accept of men, or to receive sinners coming to him. The gospel assures us that the guilty *may* return, and that God will graciously receive them. There is, perhaps, here, an allusion to the year of jubilee—the fiftieth year, when the trumpet was blown, and through the whole land proclama-

20 And he closed the book, and he gave *it* again to the minister, and sat down. And the eyes of all them that were in the synagogue were fastened on him.

21 And he began to say unto them, This day is this scripture fulfilled in your ears.

22 And all bare him witness, and wondered at the [r]gracious words which proceeded out of his mouth. And they said, [s]Is not this Joseph's son?

23 And he said unto them, Ye will surely say unto me this proverb, Physician, heal thyself: what-

r Ps.45.2; Is.50.4; Mat.13.54; Mar.6.2; ch.2.47.
s Jn.6.42.

tion was made of the liberty of Hebrew slaves, of the remission of debts, and of the restoration of possessions to their original families, Le. xxv. 8–13. The phrase "the acceptable year" means the time when it would be acceptable to God to proclaim such a message, or *agreeable* to him—to wit, under the gospel.

20. *And he closed the book.* That is, he rolled it up again. See Notes on ver. 17. ¶ *And he gave* it *again to the minister.* That is, to the one in the synagogue who had charge of the books. The word means *servant*, and the office was not much unlike that of a sexton now. It was his duty, among other things, to take charge of the books, to hand them to the reader of the law, and then return them to their place. ¶ *And sat down.* This was usual in speaking in their synagogues. See Notes on Mat. v. 1. ¶ *Were fastened on him.* Were intently fixed on him, waiting to see what explanation he would give of the words.

21. *This scripture.* This *writing*, or this *part* of the Scriptures. ¶ *Fulfilled.* It is coming to pass; the thing originally intended by it is about to be accomplished. ¶ *In your ears.* In your *hearing;* or you *hear*, in my preaching, the fulfilment of this prophecy. It is probable that he said much *more* than is here recorded, but Luke has preserved only the *substance* of his discourse. This was the *amount* or *sum* of his sermon, or his explanation of the passage, that it was now receiving its accomplishment.

22. *All bare him witness.* All were witnesses of the power and truth of what he said. Their reason and conscience approved of it, and they were constrained to admit the force and propriety of it, and on this account they wondered. ¶ *They wondered.* They were struck with the truth and force of his words; and especially when they remembered that he was a native of their own place, and that they had been long acquainted with him, and that he should *now* claim to be the Messiah, and give so much evidence that he *was* the Christ. ¶ *The gracious words.* The words of grace or favour; the kind, affectionate, and tender exposition of the words, and explanation of the design of his coming, and the nature of the plan of redemption. It was so different from the harsh and unfeeling mode of the Pharisees; so different from all their expectations respecting the Messiah, who they supposed to be a prince and a bloody conqueror, that they were filled with astonishment and awe.

23. *Physician, heal thyself.* This proverb was probably in common use at that time. The meaning is this: Suppose that a man should attempt to heal another when he was himself diseased in the same manner; it would be natural to ask him *first* to cure himself, and thus to render it manifest that he was worthy of confidence. The connection of this proverb, here, is this: "You profess to be the Messiah. You have wrought miracles at Capernaum. You profess to be able to deliver us from our maladies, our sins, our afflictions. Show that you have the power, that you are worthy of our confidence, by working miracles *here*, as you profess to have done at Capernaum." It does not refer, therefore, to any purification of his own, or imply any reflection on him for setting up to teach them. It was only a demand that he would show the proper evidence *by miracles* why they should trust in him, and he proceeds to show them why he would not give them this evidence. ¶ *Whatsoever we have heard done.* Whatsoever we have heard that thou hast done. It would seem, from this, that Christ had *before* this wrought miracles in Capernaum, though the evangelist has not recorded them. ¶ *In Capernaum.* Capernaum was on the north-west corner of the Sea of Tiberias, and was not far from Nazareth.

soever we have heard [t]done in
Capernaum, do also here in thy
country.
24 And he said, Verily I say unto
you, [u]No prophet is accepted in
his own country.
25 But I tell you of a truth,
Many[v] widows were in Israel in the
days of Elias, when [w]the heaven
was shut up three years and six
months, when great famine was
throughout all the land;

t Mat.4.13; 11.23,&c. u Mat.13.57; Jn.4.44.
v 1 Ki.17.9. w Ja.5.17.

26 But unto none of them was
Elias sent, save unto Sarepta, *a city*
of Sidon, unto a woman *that was*
a widow.
27 And[x] many lepers were in
Israel in the time of Eliseus the
prophet, and none of them was
cleansed saving Naaman the Syrian.
28 And all they in the synagogue, when they heard these
things, were filled with wrath,

x 2 Ki.5.14.

It is not improbable that some of those who then heard him might have been present and witnessed some of his miracles at Capernaum. See Notes on Mat. iv. 13.

24. *No prophet is accepted.* Has honour, or is acknowledged as a prophet. See Notes on Mat. xiii. 57.

25. *Of a truth.* Truly, and therefore worthy of your credit. He calls attention to two cases where *acknowledged* prophets had so little honour in their own nation that they bestowed their favours on foreigners. So, says he, such is the want of faith in my own country, that I shall work no miracles here, but shall give the evidence of my divine mission to others. ¶ *In Israel.* In the land of Israel, or Judea. It was therefore the more remarkable, since there were so many in his own country whom he *might* have helped, that the prophet should have gone to a heathen city and aided a poor widow there. ¶ *The days of Elias.* The days of Elijah. See the account of this in 1 Ki. xvii. 8–24. ¶ *Three years and six months.* From 1 Ki. xviii. 1, 45, it would seem that the rain fell on the *third year*—that is, at the *end* of the third year after the rain had ceased to fall at the usual time. There were two seasons of the year when rains fell in Judea—in October and April, called the *early* and *latter* rain; consequently there was an interval between them of six months. To the three years, therefore, when rain was withheld *at the usual times*, are to be added the previous six months, when no rain fell as a matter of course, and consequently three years *and six months* elapsed without rain. ¶ *A great famine.* A great want of food, from long-continued and distressing drought.

26. *Save unto Sarepta.* Sarepta was a town between Tyre and Sidon, near the Mediterranean Sea. It was not a *Jewish* city, but a Sidonian, and therefore a *Gentile* town. The word "save" in this verse does not express the meaning of the original. It would seem to imply that the city was Jewish. The meaning of the verse is this: "He was sent to none of the widows in Israel. He was not sent except to Sarepta, to a woman that was a *Sidonian.*" Dr. Thomson (*The Land and the Book*, vol. i. p. 232–236) regards Sarepta as the modern Sarafend. He says that the ruins have been frequently dug over for stone to build the barracks at Beirout, and that the broken columns, marble slabs, sarcophagi, and other ruins indicate that it was once a flourishing city. A large town was built there in the time of the Crusades.

27. *Many lepers.* For an account of the leprosy see Notes on Mat. viii. 1. ¶ *Time of Eliseus.* Time of *Elisha.* The word *Eliseus* is the Greek way of writing the word Elisha, as Elias is of Elijah. ¶ *Saving Naaman the Syrian.* The account of his cure is contained in 2 Ki. v.

28. *Filled with wrath.* They were enraged, probably, for the following reasons: 1st. They saw that the cases applied to themselves, because they would not receive the miraculous evidences of his mission. 2d. That he would direct his attention to others, and not to them. 3d. That the *Gentiles* were objects of compassion with God, and that God often showed more favour to a *single* Gentile than to multitudes of Jews in the same circumstances. 4th. That they might be *worse* than the Gentiles. And, 5th. That it was a part of his design to preach the gospel to the

29 And rose up, and thrust him out of the city, and led him unto the [2]brow of the hill whereon their city was built, [y]that they might cast him down headlong.

30 But he, [z]passing through the midst of them, went his way,

31 And came down to Capernaum, a city of Galilee, and taught them on the sabbath-days.

32 And they were astonished at his doctrine; [a]for his word was with power.

33 And[b] in the synagogue there was a man which had a spirit of an unclean devil, and cried out with a loud voice,

34 Saying, [3]Let *us* alone; [c]what have we to do with thee, *thou* Jesus of Nazareth? art thou come to destroy us? [d]I know thee who thou art; [e]the Holy One of God.

35 And Jesus rebuked him, saying, Hold thy peace, and come out of him. And when the devil had thrown him in the midst, he came out of him, and hurt him not.

36 And they were all amazed, and spake among themselves, saying, What a word *is* this! for with authority and power he commandeth the unclean spirits, [f]and they come out.

37 And the fame of him went out into every place of the country round about.

38 And he arose out of the synagogue, and entered into Simon's house. And[g] Simon's wife's mother was taken with a great fever; and they besought him for her.

39 And he stood over her, and rebuked the fever, and it left her; and immediately she arose and ministered unto them.

40 Now when the sun was setting, all they that had any sick with divers diseases brought them unto him; and he laid his hands on every one of them, and healed them.

41 And devils also came out of many, crying out, and saying, Thou art Christ the Son of God. And he, rebuking *them*, suffered them not [4]to speak; for they knew that he was Christ.

2 or, *edge*. *y* Ps.37.14,32,33. *z* Jn.8.59; 10.39. *a* Je.23.29; Mat.7.28,29; Tit.2.15; He.4.12. *b* Mar.1.23. 3 or, *Away*. *c* Ja.2.19. *d* ver.41. *e* Ps.16.10; Da.9.24; ch.1.35; Ac.3.14.

f 1 Pe.3.22. *g* Mat.8.14,&c.; Mar.1.29,&c. 4 or, *to say that they knew him to be Christ*.

Gentiles, and not confine his labours to them only. On these accounts their favour was soon turned to wrath, and the whole transaction shows us—1st. That popular applause is of little value. 2d. That the slightest circumstances may soon turn the warmest professed friendship to hatred. And, 3d. That men are exceedingly unreasonable in being unwilling to hear the truth and profit by it.

29. *The brow of the hill whereon*, &c. The region in which Nazareth was is hilly, though Nazareth was situated *between* two hills, or in a vale among mountains. The place to which they led the Saviour is still shown, and is called the *Mount of Precipitation*. It is at a short distance to the *south* of Nazareth. See Notes on Mat. ii. 23. ¶ *Cast him down*. This was the effect of a popular tumult. They had no legal right to take life on any occasion, and least of all in this furious and irregular manner. The whole transaction shows—1st. That the character given of the Galileans elsewhere as being peculiarly wicked was a just one. 2d. To what extremities the wickedness of the heart will lead men when it is acted out. And, 3d. That men are opposed to the truth, and that they would do *anything*, if not restrained, to manifest their opposition.

30. *Passing through the midst of them, went his way*. This escape was very remarkable. It is remarkable that he should escape out of their hands when their very object was to destroy him, and that he should escape in so peaceful a manner, without violence or conflict. A similar case is recorded in Jn. viii. 59. There are but two ways of accounting for this: 1st. That *other Nazarenes*, who had not been present in the synagogue, heard what was doing and came to rescue him, and in the contest that rose between the two par-

42 And when it was day, he departed, and went into a desert place: and the people sought him, and came unto him, and stayed him, that he should not depart from them.

43 And he said unto them, I must preach the kingdom of God to other cities also; for [h]therefore am I sent.

44 And he preached in the synagogues of Galilee.

CHAPTER V.

AND[a] it came to pass, that, as the people pressed upon him to hear the word of God, he stood by the lake of Gennesaret,

2 And saw two ships standing by the lake; but the fishermen

h Mar.1.38.

a Mat.4.18,&c.; Mar.1.16,&c.

ties Jesus silently escaped. 2d. More probably that Jesus by divine power, by the force of a word or look, stilled their passions, arrested their purposes, and passed silently through them. That he *had* such a power over the spirits of men we learn from the occurrence in Gethsemane, when he said, "I am he; and they went backward and fell to the ground," Jn. xviii. 6.

31–44. See this explained in the Notes on Mar. i. 21–39.

CHAPTER V.

1. *The people pressed upon him.* Multitudes came to hear. There were times in the life of our Saviour when thousands were anxious to hear him, and when many, as we have no reason to doubt, became his true followers. Indeed, it is not possible to tell what *might* have been his success, had not the Pharisees and scribes, and those who were in office, opposed him, and taken measures to draw the people away from his ministry; *for the common people heard him gladly*, Mar. xii. 37. ¶ *The Lake of Gennesaret.* Called also the Sea of Galilee and the Sea of Tiberias. "Gennesaret was the more ancient name of the lake, taken from a small territory or plain of that name on its western borders. See Nu. xxxiv. 11; Jos. xix. 35, where, after the Hebrew orthography, it is called Chinnereth" (Owen). The plain lying between Capernaum and Tiberias is said by Dr. Thomson (*The Land and the Book*, vol. i. p. 536) to be a little longer than thirty, and not quite twenty furlongs in breadth. It is described by Josephus as being, in his time, universally fertile. "Its nature is wonderful as well as its beauty. Its soil is so fruitful that all sorts of trees can grow upon it, and the inhabitants accordingly plant all sorts of trees there; for the temperature of the air is so well mixed that it agrees very well with those several sorts; particularly walnuts, which require the coldest air, flourish there in vast plenty. One may call this the ambition of Nature, where it forces those plants which are naturally enemies to one another to agree together. It is a happy conjunction of the seasons, as if every one laid claim to this country; for it not only nourishes different sorts of autumnal fruits beyond men's expectations, but preserves them a great while. It supplies men with the principal fruits; with grapes and figs continually during ten months of the year, and the rest of the fruits, as they become ripe, through the whole year; for, besides the good temperature of the air, it is also watered from a most fertile fountain." Dr. Thomson describes it now as "pre-eminently fruitful in thorns." This was the region of the early toils of our Redeemer. Here he performed some of his first and most amazing miracles; here he selected his disciples; and here, on the shores of this little and retired lake, among people of poverty and inured to the privations of fishermen, he laid the foundation of a religion which is yet to spread through all the world, and which *has* already blessed millions of guilty and miserable men, and translated them to heaven.

2. *Two ships.* The *ships* used on so small a lake were probably no more than fishing-boats without decks, and easily drawn up on the beach. Josephus says there were 230 of them on the lake, attended by four or five men each. That they were small is also clear from the account commonly given of them. A single large draught of fishes endangered them and came near sinking them. ¶ *Standing by the lake.* Anchored by the lake, or drawn up upon the beach.

3. *Which was Simon's.* Simon Peter's. ¶ *Prayed him.* Asked him. ¶ *He sat*

were gone out of them, and were
washing *their* nets.
3 And he entered into one of
the ships, which was Simon's, and
prayed him that he would thrust
out a little from the land. And he
sat down, and taught the people
out of the ship.
4 Now when he had left speaking, he said unto Simon, [b]Launch
out into the deep, and let down
your nets for a draught.
5 And Simon, answering, said
unto him, [c]Master, we have toiled
all the night and have taken nothing: nevertheless, at thy word I
will let down the net.
6 And[d] when they had this done,
they inclosed a great multitude of
fishes: and their net brake.
7 And they beckoned unto *their*
partners, which were in the other
ship, that they should come and
[e]help them. And they came, and

b Jn.21.6.

c Ps.127.1,2; Eze.37.11,12. *d* Ec.11.6; Ga.6.9. *e* Ex.23.5; Ga.6.2; Pr.18.24.

down. This was the common posture of Jewish teachers. They seldom or never spoke to the people *standing.* Comp. Mat. v. 1. It may be somewhat difficult to conceive why Jesus should go into a boat and put off from the shore in order to speak to the multitude; but it is probable that this was a small bay or cove, and that when he was *in* the boat, the people on the shore stood round him in the form of an amphitheatre. It is not improbable that the lake was still; that scarcely a breeze passed over it; that all was silence on the shore, and that there was nothing to disturb his voice. In such a situation he could be heard by multitudes; and no spectacle could be more sublime than that of the Son of God—the Redeemer of the world—thus speaking from the bosom of a placid lake—the emblem of the peaceful influence of his own doctrines—to the poor, the ignorant, and the attentive multitudes assembled on the shore. Oh how much *more* effect may we suppose the gospel would have in such circumstances, than when proclaimed among the proud, the gay, the honoured, even when assembled in the most splendid edifice that wealth and art could finish!

4. *Launch out.* Go out with your vessels. ¶ *Into the deep.* Into the sea; at a distance from the shore. ¶ *For a draught.* A draught of fish; or let down your nets for the *taking* of fish.

5. *Master.* This is the first time that the word here translated *Master* occurs in the New Testament, and it is used only by Luke. The other evangelists call him Rabbi, or Lord. The word here used means a *prefect*, or one placed *over* others, and hence it comes to mean *teacher* or *guide.* ¶ *At thy word.* At thy command. Though it seemed so improbable that they would take anything after having in vain toiled all night, yet he was willing to trust the *word* of Jesus and make the trial. This was a remarkable instance of *faith.* Peter, as it appears, knew little then of Jesus. He was not then a chosen apostle. Jesus came to these fishermen almost a stranger and unknown, and yet at his command Peter resolved to make another trial, and go once more out into the deep. Oh, if *all* would as readily obey him, all would be in like manner blessed. If sinners would thus obey him, they would find *all* his promises sure. He never disappoints. He asks only that we have *confidence* in him, and he will give to us every needful blessing.

6. *Their net brake.* Or their net *began* to break, or was *about* to break. This is all that is implied in the Greek word. If their nets had actually *broken*, as our English word seems to suppose, the fish would have escaped; but no more is meant than that there was such a multitude of fishes that their net was *on the point* of being rent asunder.

7. *They beckoned.* They gave signs. Perhaps they were at a considerable distance, so that they could not be easily heard. ¶ Their *partners.* James and John. See ver. 10. The following remarks of Dr. Thomson (*The Land and the Book*, vol. ii. p. 80, 81) will furnish a good illustration of this passage. After describing the mode of fishing with the "hand-net" and the "drag-net," he adds: "Again, there is the bag-net and basket-net, of various kinds, which are so constructed and worked as to inclose the fish out in deep water. I have seen them of almost every conceivable size and pattern. It was with some one of this sort,

filled both the ships, so that they
began to sink.
8 When Simon Peter saw *it*, [f]he
fell down at Jesus' knees, saying,
Depart from me; for I am a sinful
man, O Lord.
9 For he was astonished, and
all that were with him, at the
draught of the [g]fishes which they
had taken;
10 And so *was* also James and
John, the sons of Zebedee, which
were partners with Simon. And
Jesus said unto Simon, Fear not;
from henceforth thou shalt catch
men.
11 And when they had brought
their ships to land, they [h]forsook
all and followed him.
12 And[i] it came to pass, when

f Ju.13.22; 2 Sa.6.9; 1 Ki.17.18; Is.6.5. *g* Ps.8.6,8.
h Mat.4.20; 19.27; Phi.3.7,8.
i Mat.8.2,&c.; Mar.1.40,&c.

I suppose, that Simon had toiled all night without catching anything, but which, when let down at the command of Jesus, inclosed so great a multitude that the net brake, and they filled two ships with the fish until they began to sink. Peter here speaks of toiling all night; and there are certain kinds of fishing always carried on at night. It is a beautiful sight. With blazing torch the boat glides over the flashing sea, and the men stand gazing keenly into it until their prey is sighted, when, quick as lightning, they fling their net or fly their spear; and often you see the tired fishermen come sullenly into harbour in the morning, having toiled all night in vain. Indeed, every kind of fishing is uncertain. A dozen times the angler jerks out a naked hook; the hand-net closes down on nothing; the drag-net brings in only weeds; the bag comes up empty. And then again, every throw is successful—every net is full; and frequently without any other apparent reason than that of throwing it on the right side of the ship instead of the left, as it happened to the disciples here at Tiberias."

8. *When Simon Peter saw* it. Saw the great amount of fishes; the remarkable success of letting down the net. ¶ *He fell down at Jesus' knees.* This was a common posture of *supplication.* He had no doubt now of the power and knowledge of Jesus. In amazement, wonder, and gratitude, and not doubting that he was in the presence of some divine being, he prostrated himself to the earth, trembling and afraid. So should sinful men *always* throw themselves at the feet of Jesus at the proofs of his power; so should they humble themselves before him at the manifestations of his goodness. ¶ *Depart from me.* This is an expression of Peter's humility, and of his consciousness of his unworthiness. It was not from want of love to Jesus; it did not show that he would not be pleased with his favour and presence; but it was the result of being convinced that Jesus was a messenger from God—a high and holy being; and he felt that *he* was unworthy to be in his presence. In his deep consciousness of sin, therefore, he requested that Jesus would depart from him and his little vessel. Peter's feeling was not unnatural, though it was not proper to request Jesus to leave him. It was an involuntary, sudden request, and arose from ignorance of the character of Jesus. We *are* not worthy to be with him, to be reckoned among his friends, or to dwell in heaven with him; but he came to seek the lost and to save the impure. He graciously condescends to dwell with those who are humble and contrite, though they are conscious that they are not worthy of his presence; and we may therefore come boldly to him, and ask him to receive us to his home—to an eternal dwelling with him in the heavens.

10. *Fear not.* He calmed their fears. With mildness and tenderness he stilled all their troubled feelings, and to their surprise announced that henceforward they should be appointed as heralds of salvation. ¶ *From henceforth.* Hereafter. ¶ *Shalt catch men.* Thou shalt be a minister of the gospel, and thy business shall be to win men to the truth that they may be saved.

11. *Forsook all.* It was not *much* that they left—a couple of small boats and their nets; but it was all they had, even all their living. But this showed their love of Jesus, and their willingness to deny themselves, as *really* as if they had forsaken palaces and gold. All that Jesus asks is that we should leave *all* we have for him; that we should love him *more* than we do whatever friends

he was in a certain city, behold, a man full of leprosy; who, seeing Jesus, fell on *his* face, and besought him, saying, Lord, if thou wilt, thou canst make me clean.

13 And he put forth *his* hand, and touched him, saying, [k]I will; be thou clean. And immediately the leprosy departed from him.

14 And he charged him to tell no man; but go and show thyself to the priest, and offer for thy cleansing, according as [l]Moses commanded, for a testimony unto them.

15 But so much the more went there a fame abroad of him: [m]and great multitudes came together, to hear, and to be healed by him of their infirmities.

16 And[n] he withdrew himself into the wilderness and prayed.

17 And it came to pass on a certain day, as he was teaching, [o]that there were Pharisees and doctors of the law sitting by, which were come out of every town of Galilee, and Judea, and Jerusalem; and the power of the Lord was *present* to heal them.

18 And,[p] behold, men brought in a bed a man which was taken with a palsy; and they sought *means* to bring him in, and to lay *him* before him.

19 And when they could not find by what *way* they might bring him in because of the multitude, they went upon the house-top, and let him down through the tiling, with *his* couch, into the midst before Jesus.

20 And when he saw their faith, he said unto him, Man, thy sins are forgiven thee.

21 And the scribes and the Pharisees began to reason, saying, Who is this which speaketh blasphemies? Who can [q]forgive sins but God alone?

22 But when Jesus perceived their thoughts, he, answering, said unto them, What reason ye in your hearts?

23 Whether is easier to say, Thy sins be forgiven thee, or to say, Rise up and walk?

24 But that ye may know that the Son of man hath power upon earth to forgive sins, (he said unto the sick of the palsy,) I say unto thee, Arise, and [r]take up thy couch, and go unto thine house.

25 And immediately he rose up before them, and took up that whereon he lay, and departed to his own house, glorifying God.

26 And they were all amazed, and [s]they glorified God, and [t]were filled with fear, saying, We have seen strange things to-day.

27 And[u] after these things he went forth, and saw a publican, named Levi, sitting at the receipt of custom: and he said unto him, Follow me.

28 And he left all, rose up, and followed him.

29 And Levi made him a great feast in his own house: and [v]there

k 2 Ki.5.10,14. *l* Le.14.4,&c.
m Mat.4.25; Mar.3.7; Jn.6.2.
n Mat.14.23; Mar.6.46. *o* Jn.3.21.
p Mat.9.2,&c.; Mar.2.3,&c.

q Ps.32.5; 103.3; 130.4; Is.1.18; 43.25.
r Jn.5.8,12. *s* Ac.4.21; Ga.1.24. *t* ver.8.
u Mat.9.9,&c.; Mar.2.13. *v* ch.15.1,&c.

---

or property we may possess, and be willing to give them all up when he requires it.

12–16. See Notes on Mat. viii. 2–4.

17–26. See this passage explained in the Notes on Mat. ix. 1–7.

17. *On a certain day.* The time and place are not particularly mentioned here, but from Mat. ix. 1 it seems it was at Capernaum.

19. *The tiling.* See Notes on Mat. ix. 1–7.

27–32. See Notes on Mat. ix. 9–13.

29. *Made him a great feast.* This circumstance *Matthew*, or *Levi* as he is here called, has omitted in his own gospel. This fact shows how little inclined the evangelists are to say anything in favour of themselves or to praise themselves. True religion does

was a great company of publicans and of others that sat down with them.

30 But their scribes and Pharisees murmured against his disciples, saying, Why do ye eat and drink with publicans and sinners?

31 And Jesus, answering, said unto them, They that are whole need not a [w]physician; but they that are sick.

32 I came not to call the righteous but [x]sinners to repentance.

33 And they said unto him, Why do the disciples of John fast often, and make prayers, and likewise *the disciples* of the Pharisees; [y]but thine eat and drink?

34 And he said unto them, Can ye make the children of the bride-

w Je.8.22.
x Lu.15.7,10; 1 Co.6.9-11; 1 Ti.1.15; 2 Pe.3.9.
y ch.7.34,35.

chamber fast while the bridegroom is with them?

35 But the days will come when the bridegroom shall be taken away from them, and then shall they [z]fast in those days.

36 And[a] he spake also a parable unto them: No man putteth a piece of a new garment upon an old; if otherwise, then both the new maketh a rent, and the piece that was *taken* out of the new [b]agreeth not with the old.

37 And no man putteth new wine into old bottles; else the new wine will burst the bottles and be spilled, and the bottles shall perish.

38 But new wine must be put into new bottles, and both are preserved.

z Is.22.12. *a* Mat.9.16,17; Mar.2.21,22.
b Le.19.19; De.22.11; 2 Co.6.16.

---

not seek to commend itself, or to speak of what it does, even when it is done for the Son of God. It seeks retirement; it delights rather in the *consciousness* of doing well than in its being known; and it leaves its good deeds to be spoken of, if spoken of at all, by others. This is agreeable to the direction of Solomon (Pr. xxvii. 2): "Let another man praise thee, and not thine own mouth." This feast was made expressly for our Lord, and was attended by many publicans, probably men of wicked character; and it is not improbable that Matthew got them together for the purpose of bringing them into contact with our Lord to do them good. Our Saviour did not refuse to go, and to go, too, at the risk of being accused of being a gluttonous man and a winebibber, a friend of publicans and sinners, Mat. xi. 19. But his motives were pure. In the thing itself there was no harm. It afforded an opportunity of doing good, and we have no reason to doubt that the opportunity was improved by the Lord Jesus. Happy would it be if all the *great feasts* that are made were made in honour of our Lord; happy if *he* would be a welcome guest there; and happy if ministers and pious people who attend them demeaned themselves as the Lord Jesus did, and they were always made the means of advancing his kingdom. But, alas! there are few places where our Lord would be *so unwelcome* as at great feasts, and few places that serve so much to render the mind gross, dissipated, and irreligious.

33–39. See this passage illustrated in the Notes on Mat. ix. 14–17.

39. *Having drunk old* wine, &c. Wine increases its strength and flavour, and its mildness and mellowness, by age, and the old is therefore preferable. They who had tasted such mild and mellow wine would not readily drink the comparatively sour and astringent juice of the grape as it came from the press. The meaning of this proverb in this place seems to be this: You Pharisees wish to draw my disciples to the *austere* and *rigid* duties of the ceremonial law—to fasting and painful rites; but they have come under a milder system. They have tasted the gentle and tender blessings of the gospel; they have no *relish* for your stern and harsh requirements. To insist *now* on their observing them would be like telling a man who had tasted of good, ripe, and mild wine to partake of that which is sour and unpalatable. At the proper time all the sterner duties of religion will be properly regarded; but *at present*, to teach them to fast when they see *no occasion* for it—when they are full of joy at the presence of their

39 No man, also, having drunk old *wine*, straightway desireth new; for he saith, [z]The old is better.

CHAPTER VI.

AND[a] it came to pass on the second sabbath after the first, that he went through the corn-fields, and his disciples plucked the ears of corn, and did eat, rubbing *them* in *their* hands.

2 And certain of the Pharisees said unto them, Why do ye [b]that which is not lawful to do on the sabbath-days?

3 And Jesus answering them, said, Have ye not read so much as this, [c]what David did when himself was an hungered, and they which were with him;

4 How he went into the house of God, and did take and eat the shew-bread, and gave also to them that were with him; [d]which it is not lawful to eat, but for the priests alone?

5 And he said unto them, That the Son of man is Lord also of the sabbath.

6 And[e] it came to pass also on another sabbath, that he entered into the synagogue and taught; and there was a man whose right hand was withered.

7 And the scribes and Pharisees watched him, whether he would

z Je.6.16. a Mat.12.1,&c.; Mar.2.23,&c. b Ex.20.10; Is.58.13. c 1 Sa.21.6.

d Le.24.9.
e Mat.12.10,&c.; Mar.3.1,&c.; ch.13.14; 14.3.

Master—would be like putting a piece of new cloth on an old garment, or new wine into old bottles, or drinking unpleasant wine after one had tasted that which was pleasanter. It would be ill-timed, inappropriate, and incongruous.

CHAPTER VI.

1-11. See this passage explained in the Notes on Mat. xii. 1-13.

1. *Second sabbath after the first.* See Notes on Mat. xii. 1. This phrase has given great perplexity to commentators. A *literal* translation would be, "on the Sabbath called *second first*," or second first Sabbath. The word occurs nowhere else. It is therefore exceedingly difficult of interpretation. The most natural and easy explanation is that proposed by Scaliger. The *second* day of the Passover was a great festival, on which the wave-sheaf was offered, Le. xxiii. 11. From *that day* they reckoned *seven weeks*, or seven *Sabbaths*, to the day of Pentecost. The *first* Sabbath after that *second day* was called the *second first*, or the *first* from the second day of the feast. The *second* Sabbath was called the *second second*, or the second Sabbath from the second day of the feast; the third the *third second*, &c. *This* day, therefore, on which the Saviour went through the fields, was the first Sabbath that occurred after the second day of the feast. ¶ *Rubbing* them *in* their *hands.* The word *corn* here means wheat or barley, and not maize, as in America. They *rubbed* it in their hands to separate the grain from the chaff. This was common and allowable. Dr. Thomson (*The Land and the Book*, vol. ii. p. 510, 511) says: "I have often seen my muleteers, as we passed along the wheat-fields, pluck off ears, rub them in their hands, and eat the grains, unroasted, just as the apostles are said to have done. This also is allowable. The Pharisees did not object to the thing itself, only to the time when it was done. They said it was not lawful to do this on the Sabbath-day. It was work forbidden by those who, through their traditions, had made man for the Sabbath, not the Sabbath for man." So Professor Hackett (*Illustrations of Scripture*, p. 176, 177) says: "The incident of plucking the ears of wheat, rubbing out the kernels in their hands, and eating them (Lu. vi. 1), is one which the traveller sees often at present who is in Palestine at the time of the gathering of the harvest. Dr. Robinson relates the following case: 'Our Arabs were an hungered, and, going into the fields, they plucked the ears of corn and did eat, rubbing them in their hands. On being questioned, they said this was an old custom, and no one would speak against it; they were supposed to be hungry, and it was allowed as a charity.'* The Pharisees complained of the disciples for violat-

* *Biblical Researches*, vol. ii. p. 192.

heal [f]on the sabbath-day, that they might find an accusation against him.

8 But he [g]knew their thoughts, and said to the man which had the withered hand, Rise up, and stand forth in the midst. And he arose, and stood forth.

9 Then Jesus said unto them, I will ask you one thing: [h]Is it lawful on the sabbath-days to do good, or to do evil? to save life, or to destroy *it?*

10 And[i] looking round about upon them all, he said unto the man, Stretch forth thy hand. And he did so; and his hand was restored whole as the other.

11 And they were filled with madness; and [k]communed one with another what they might do to Jesus.

12 And[l] it came to pass in those days, that he went out [m]into a mountain to pray, and continued all night in prayer to God.

f Jn.9.16. *g* Job 42.2. *h* Ex.20.10; ch.14.3. *i* Mar.3.5. *k* Ps.2.1,2. *l* Mat.14.23. *m* Mat.6.6.

---

ing the Sabbath, and not any rights of property."

8. *But he knew their thoughts.* He knew their thoughts—their dark, malicious designs—by the *question* which they proposed to him, whether it was lawful to heal on the Sabbath-days (Matthew). In *reply* to their question, Jesus asked them whether they would not release a *sheep* on the Sabbath-day if it was fallen into a pit, and also asked *them* whether it was better to do good than to do evil on that day, implying that to *omit* to do *good* was, in fact, doing *evil.*

11. *Were filled with madness.* Probably—1st. Because he had shown his *power* to work a miracle. 2d. Because he had shown his power to do it *contrary* to what *they* thought was right. 3d. Because by doing it he had shown that he was from *God*, and that *they* were therefore *wrong* in their views of the Sabbath. And, 4th. Because he had shown no respect to *their views* of what the law of God demanded. Pride, obstinacy, malice, and disappointed self-confidence were *all* combined, therefore, in producing madness. Nor were they alone. Men are often enraged because others do good in a way which *they* do not approve of. God gives success to others; and because he has not accommodated himself to *their* views of what is right, and done it in the way which *they* would have prescribed, they are enraged, and filled with envy at men more successful than themselves. ¶ *Communed one with another.* Spoke together, or laid a plan.

12. *And it came to pass in those days.* The designation of the time here is very general. It means *about* the time when the events occurred which had been just narrated. ¶ *He went out into a mountain.* Jesus was accustomed to resort to such places to hold communion with God, Mar. vi. 46. He did it because it was retired, free from interruption, and fitted by impressiveness and grandeur to raise the thoughts to the God that had formed the high hills and the deep-shaded groves. ¶ *And continued all night in prayer to God.* There has been a difference of opinion about this passage, whether it means that he spent the night in the act of *praying* to God, or in a *place of* prayer. The Jews had places of prayer, called *oratories*, built *out* of their cities or towns, where they could retire from the bustle of a city and hold communion with God. They were built on the banks of rivers (comp. Ac. xvi. 13), in groves, or on hills. They were rude inclosures, made by building a rough wall of stone around a level piece of ground, and capable of accommodating a small number who might resort thither to pray. But the more probable opinion is that he spent the whole night in supplication; for—1st. This is the obvious meaning of the passage. 2d. The object for which he went out was *to pray.* 3d. It was an occasion of great importance. He was about to send out his apostles—to lay the foundation of his religion—and he therefore set apart this time specially to seek the divine blessing. 4th. It was no unusual thing for Jesus to spend much time in prayer, and we are not to wonder that he passed an entire night in supplication. If it be asked why Jesus should pray *at all* if he was divine, it may be replied that he was also *a man*—a man subject to the same sufferings as others, and, *as a man,*

13 And when it was day, he called *unto him* his disciples; and of them he [n]chose twelve, whom also he named apostles;
14 Simon, (whom he [o]also named Peter,) and Andrew his brother, James and John, Philip and Bartholomew,
15 Matthew and Thomas, James the *son* of Alpheus, and Simon called Zelotes,
16 And [p]Judas *the brother* of James, and Judas Iscariot, which also was the traitor.
17 And he came down with them, and stood in the plain, and the company of his disciples, and a [q]great multitude of people out of all Judea and Jerusalem, and from the sea-coast of Tyre and Sidon, which came to hear him, and [r]to be healed of their diseases;
18 And they that were vexed with unclean spirits, and they were healed.
19 And the whole multitude sought to [s]touch him; for [t]there went virtue out of him, and healed *them* all.
20 And[u] he lifted up his eyes on

n Mat.10.1,&c.; Mar.3.13; 6.7. *o* Jn.1.42. *p* Jude 1.
q Mat.4.25,&c.; Mar.3.7,&c. *r* Ps.103.3; 107.17-20. *s* Nu.21.8,9; Mat.14.36; Jn.3.14,15. *t* Mar.5.30; ch.8.46. *u* Mat.5.2,&c.

needing the divine blessing. There was no more inconsistency in his *praying* than there was in his *eating*. Both were *means* employed for an end, and both were equally consistent with his being divine. But Jesus was also *Mediator*, and as such it was proper to seek the divine direction and blessing. In *this* case he has set us an example that we should follow. In great emergencies, when we have important duties, or are about to encounter special difficulties, we should seek the divine blessing and direction by *prayer*. We should set apart an unusual portion of time for supplication. Nay, if we pass the *whole night* in prayer, it should not be charged as enthusiasm. Our Saviour did it. Men of the world often pass whole nights in plans of gain or in dissipation, and shall it be esteemed strange that Christians should spend an equal portion of time in the far more important business of religion?

13-16. See Notes on Mat. x. 1-4.

17. *And stood in the plain.* It is not affirmed, however, that he stood in the plain when he delivered the following discourse. There has been some doubt whether the following discourse is the same as that recorded in the 5th, 6th, and 7th chapters of Matthew, or whether the Saviour *repeated* the substance of that discourse, and that Luke recorded it as he repeated it. The reasons which have led many to suppose that they refer to the same are—1st. That the beginning and the close are alike. 2d. That the *substance* of each is the same. And, 3d. That *after* the discourse was delivered, both affirm that Jesus went to Capernaum and healed the servant of the centurion, Mat. viii. 5-13; Lu. vii. 1-10. On the other hand, *Matthew* says that the sermon was delivered on the *mountain* (Mat. v. 1); it is thought to be implied that *Luke* affirms that it was in the *plain*. Matthew says that he *sat;* Luke, that he *stood*. Yet there is no reason to suppose that there is a difference in the evangelists. Jesus spent the night on the mountain in prayer. In the morning he descended into the open plain and healed many. While there, as Luke says, he "*stood*" and received those who came to him, and healed their diseases. There is no impropriety in supposing that, being pressed by multitudes, he retired into the mountain again, or to an eminence in the plain, or to the side of the mountain, where the people might be more conveniently arranged and seated to hear him. There he *sat*, as recorded by Matthew, and delivered the discourse; for it is to be observed that Luke does *not* say that he delivered the sermon *on the plain*, but only that he *healed the sick there*. ¶ *Tyre and Sidon*. See Notes on Mat. xi. 21.

18. *Vexed.* The word *vex* with us means to provoke, or irritate by petty provocations. Here it means, however, to *afflict*, to *torment*—denoting deep and heavy trials. ¶ *Unclean spirits.* Demons that were impure and unholy, having a delight in tormenting, and in inflicting painful and loathsome diseases.

19. *Virtue.* Healing power. See Notes on Mar. v. 30.

his disciples, and said, Blessed *be*
ye [v]poor; for yours is the kingdom
of God.
21 Blessed *are ye* [w]that hunger
now; for ye [x]shall be filled. Blessed
are ye [y]that weep now; for ye shall
laugh.
22 Blessed are ye when men
shall [z]hate you, and when they
shall [a]separate you *from their com-*
pany, and shall reproach *you*, and
cast out your name as evil, for the
Son of man's sake.
23 Rejoice[b] ye in that day, and
leap for joy; for, behold, your reward *is* great in heaven; [c]for in the
like manner did their fathers unto
the prophets.
24 But woe unto [d]you that are
rich! for ye [e]have received your
consolation.
25 Woe unto [f]you that are full!
for ye shall hunger. Woe unto
you that [g]laugh now! for ye shall
mourn and weep.
26 Woe unto you when all men

v Ja.2.5. *w* Is.55.1. *x* Ps.107.9. *y* Is.61.3; Re.21.4. *z* Jn.17.14. *a* 1 Pe.2.19,20; 3.14; 4.14.

b Ac.5.41; Col.1.24; Ja.1.2. *c* Ac.7.52; He.11.32-39. *d* Hab.2.9; Ja.5.1. *e* ch.16.25. *f* Is.28.7; 65.13. *g* Pr.14.13; Ep.5.4.

20–49. See this passage fully illustrated in the sermon on the mount, in the 5th, 6th, and 7th chapters of Matthew.

21. *That hunger now.* Matthew has it, "that hunger and thirst after righteousness." Matthew has expressed *more fully* what Luke has briefly, but there is no contradiction.

24–26. These verses have been omitted by Matthew. They seem to have been spoken to the Pharisees. ¶ *Who are rich.* In this world's goods. They loved them; they had sought for them; they found their consolation in them. It implies, farther, that they would not seek or receive consolation from the gospel. They were proud, and would not seek it; satisfied, and did not desire it; filled with cares, and had no time or disposition to attend to it. All the consolation which they had reason to expect they *had received.* Alas! how poor and worthless is *such* consolation, compared with that which the gospel would give! ¶ *Woe unto you that are full!* Not hungry. Satisfied with their wealth, and not feeling their need of anything better than earthly wealth can give. Many, alas! are thus *full.* They profess to be satisfied. They desire nothing but wealth, and a sufficiency to satisfy the wants of the body. They have no anxiety for the riches that shall endure for ever. ¶ *Ye shall hunger.* Your property shall be taken away, or you shall see that it is of little value; and then you shall see the need of something better. You shall feel your want and wretchedness, and shall *hunger* for something to satisfy the desires of a dying, sinful soul. ¶ *That laugh now.* Are happy, or thoughtless, or gay, or filled with levity. ¶ *Shall mourn and weep.* The time is coming when you shall sorrow deeply. In sickness, in calamity, in the prospect of death, in the fear of eternity, your laughter shall be turned into sorrow. *There is* a place where you cannot laugh, and there you will see the folly of having passed the *proper time* of preparing for such scenes in levity and folly. Alas! how many thus spend their youth! and how many weep when it is too late! God gives them over, and *laughs at* THEIR *calamity*, and mocks when their fear comes, Pr. i. 26. To be happy in *such scenes*, it is necessary to be sober, humble, pious in early life. *Then* we need not weep in the day of calamity; then there will be no terror in death; then there will be nothing to fear in the grave.

26. *When all men shall speak well of you.* When they shall praise or applaud you. The men of the world will not praise or applaud *my* doctrine; they are *opposed* to it, and therefore, if they speak well of *you* and of *your teaching*, it is proof that you do not teach the true doctrine. If you do *not* do this, then there will be woe upon you. If men teach false doctrines for true; if they declare that God has spoken that which he has not spoken, and if they oppose what he *has* delivered, then heavy punishments will await them. ¶ *For so did their fathers.* The *fathers* or *ancestors* of this people; the ancient Jews. ¶ *To the false prophets.* Men who pretended to be of God—who delivered their *own* doctrines as the truth of God, and who accommodated themselves to the desires of the people. Of

shall [h]speak well of you! for so
did their fathers to the false prophets.
27 But I say unto you which
hear, [i]Love your enemies, do good
to them which hate you;
28 Bless them that curse you,
and [k]pray for them which despitefully use you.
29 And[l] unto him that smiteth
thee on the *one* cheek, offer also the
other; [m]and him that taketh away
thy cloak, forbid not *to take thy*
coat also.
30 Give[n] to every man that asketh of thee; and of him that taketh away thy goods, ask *them* not
again.
31 And[o] as ye would that men
should do to you, do ye also to
them likewise.
32 For if ye love them which
love you, what thank have ye? for
sinners also love those that love
them.
33 And if ye do good to them
which do good to you, what thank
have ye? for sinners also do even
the same.
34 And if ye lend *to them* of
whom ye hope to receive, what
thank have ye? for sinners also
lend to sinners, to receive as much
again.
35 But[p] love ye your enemies,
and do good, and [q]lend, hoping for
nothing again; and your reward
shall be great, and [r]ye shall be the
children of the Highest; for he is
kind unto the unthankful, and *to*
the evil.
36 Be ye therefore merciful, as
your Father also is merciful.
37 Judge[s] not, and ye shall not
be judged; condemn not, and ye
shall not be condemned; forgive,
and ye shall be forgiven:
38 Give, and it [t]shall be given
unto you; good measure, pressed
down, and shaken together, and
running over, shall men give [u]into
your bosom. For[v] with the same
measure that ye mete withal, it
shall be measured to you again.
39 And he spake a parable unto
them: [w]Can the blind lead the
blind? shall they not both fall
into the ditch?

h Jn.15.19; 1 Jn.4.5.
i Ex.23.4,5; Pr.25.21; Mat.5.44; ver.35; Ro.12.20.
k ch.23.24; Ac.7.60. *l* Mat.5.39. *m* 1 Co.6.7.
n De.15.7,8,10; Pr.19.17; 21.26; Mat.5.42,&c.
o Mat.7.12.
p ver.27. *q* Ps.37.26; 112.5. *r* Mat.5.45.
s Mat.7.1. *t* Pr.19.17; Mat.10.42. *u* Ps.79.12.
v Mat.7.2; Mar.4.24; Ja.2.13. *w* Mat.15.14.

this number were the prophets of Baal, the false prophets who appeared in the time of Jeremiah, &c.

27, 28. See Mat. v. 44, 45.

29. See Mat. v. 39, 40.

30. See Mat. v. 42.

31. See Mat. vii. 12.

32–36. See Mat. v. 46–48.

37–42. See Mat. vii. 1–9.

38. *Good measure.* They shall give you good measure, or *full* measure. ¶ *Pressed down.* As figs or grapes might be, and thus many more might be put into the measure. ¶ *Shaken together.* To make it more compact, and thus to give more. ¶ *Running over.* So full that the measure would overflow. ¶ *Shall men give.* This is said to be the reward of *giving* to the poor and needy; and the meaning is that the man who is liberal will find others liberal to him in dealing with them, and when he is also in circumstances of want. A man who is himself kind to the poor—who has that *character* established—will find many who are ready to help *him* abundantly when he is in want. He that is parsimonious, close, niggardly, will find few or none who will aid him. ¶ *Into your bosom.* That is, to you. The word *bosom* here has reference to a custom among Oriental nations of making the bosom or front part of their garments *large*, so that articles could be carried in them, answering the purpose of our pockets. Comp. Ex. iv. 6, 7; Pr. vi. 27; Ru. iii. 15.

39. *A parable.* A proverb or similitude. ¶ *Can the blind lead the blind?* See Notes on Mat. xv. 14.

40. *The disciple is not,* &c. The learner is not above his teacher, does not know more, and must expect to fare no better. This seems to have been spoken to show them that they

40 The[x] disciple is not above his master; but every one [1]that is perfect shall be as his master.

41 And why beholdest thou the mote that is in thy brother's eye, but perceivest not the beam that is in thine own eye?

42 Either how canst thou say to thy brother, Brother, let me pull out the mote that is in thine eye, when thou thyself beholdest not the beam that is in thine own eye? Thou hypocrite! [y]cast out first the beam out of thine own eye, and then shalt thou see clearly to pull out the mote that is in thy brother's eye.

43 For[z] a good tree bringeth not forth corrupt fruit; neither doth a corrupt tree bring forth good fruit.

44 For[a] every tree is known by his own fruit: for of thorns men do not gather figs, nor of a bramble-bush gather they [2]grapes.

45 A[b] good man, out of the good treasure of his heart, bringeth forth that which is good; and an evil man, out of the evil treasure of his heart, bringeth forth that which is evil; for of the abundance of the heart his mouth speaketh.

x Mat.10.24; Jn.13.16; 15.20.
1 or, *shall be perfected as his master.*
y Pr.18.17; Ro.2.1,21,&c. *z* Mat.7.16,17.
a Mat.12.33. 2 *a grape.* *b* Mat.12.35.

46 And why [c]call ye me, Lord, Lord, and do not the things which I say?

47 Whosoever cometh to me, and heareth my sayings, and doeth them, I will show you to whom he is like:

48 He[d] is like a man which built a house, and digged deep, and laid the foundation on a rock; and when the flood arose, the stream beat vehemently upon that house, and [e]could not shake it; for it was [f]founded upon a rock.

49 But he that [g]heareth, and doeth not, is like a man that without a foundation built an house upon the earth; against which the stream did beat vehemently, and immediately [h]it fell; and the ruin of that house was great.

CHAPTER VII.

NOW[a] when he had ended all his sayings in the audience of the people, he entered into Capernaum.

2 And a certain centurion's servant, who was [b]dear unto him, was sick, and ready to die.

3 And when he heard of Jesus,

c Mal.1.6; Mat.7.21; 25.11; ch.13.25; Ga.6.7.
d Mat.7.25,26. *e* 2 Pe.1.10; Jude 24.
f Ps.46.1-3; 62.2. *g* Ja.1.24-26.
h Pr.28.18; Ho.4.14.
a Mat.8.5,&c. *b* Job 31.15; Pr.29.21.

---

were not to expect that their disciples would go *beyond them* in attainments; that if *they* were blind, their followers would be also; and that therefore it was important for *them* to understand fully the doctrines of the gospel, and not to be blind leaders of the blind. ¶ *Every one that is perfect.* The word rendered *is perfect* means sometimes to *repair* or *mend*, and is thus applied to mending *nets*, Mat. iv. 21; Mar. i. 19. Hence it means to repair or amend in a moral sense, or to make whole or complete. Here it means, evidently, *thoroughly instructed* or *informed*. The Christian should be *like his Master*—holy, harmless, and undefiled, and separate from sinners. He should copy his example, and grow into the likeness of his Redeemer. Nor can any other be a Christian.

41, 42. See Notes on Mat. vii. 3-5.

43, 44. See Notes on Mat. vii. 16-18.

45. This verse is not found in the sermon on the mount as recorded by Matthew, but is recorded by him in ch. xii. 35. See Notes on that passage.

46-49. See Notes on Mat. vii. 21-27.

CHAPTER VII.

1-10. See Notes on Mat. viii. 5-13.

1. *In the audience of the people.* In the hearing of the people.

2. *Who was dear unto him.* That is, he was valuable, trusty, and honoured.

4. *They besought him instantly.* Urgently or earnestly. ¶ *He was worthy.* The centurion. He had showed favour to the Jews, and it was not improper to show him a kindness.

11. *A city called Nain.* This city was

he sent unto him the elders of the Jews, beseeching him that he would come and heal his servant.

4 And when they came to Jesus, they besought him instantly, saying, That he was worthy for whom he should do this:

5 For he [c]loveth our nation, and he hath built us a synagogue.

6 Then Jesus went with them. And when he was now not far from the house, the centurion sent friends to him, saying unto him, Lord, [d]trouble not thyself; for I am not worthy that thou shouldest enter under my roof:

7 Wherefore neither thought I myself worthy to come unto thee; but [e]say in a word, and my servant shall be healed.

8 For I also am a man set under authority, having under me soldiers; and I say unto [1]one, Go, and he goeth; and to another, Come, and he cometh; and to my servant, Do this, and he doeth *it*.

9 When Jesus heard these things, he marvelled at him, and turned him about, and said unto the people that followed him, I say unto you, I have not found so great faith, no, not in Israel.

10 And they that were sent, returning to the house, found the servant whole that had been sick.

11 And it came to pass the day after that he went into a city called Nain; and many of his disciples went with him, and much people.

12 Now when he came nigh to the gate of the city, behold, there was a dead man carried out, the only son of his mother, and she was a widow; and much people of the city was with her.

13 And when the Lord saw her, he had compassion on her, and said unto her, Weep not.

14 And he came and touched the [2]bier; and they that bare *him* stood still. And he said, Young man, I say unto thee, [f]Arise.

15 And he that was dead [g]sat up, and began to speak. And he delivered him to his mother.

16 And there came a fear on

c 1 Ki.5.1; Ga.5.6; 1 Jn.3.14; 5.1,2. d ch.8.49. e Ps.107.20. 1 *this man.*

2 or, *coffin.* f ch.8.54; Ac.9.40; Ro.4.17. g 2 Ki.4.32-37; 13.21; Jn.11.44.

---

in Galilee, in the boundaries of the tribe of Issachar. It was about two miles south of Mount Tabor, and not far from Capernaum. It is now a small village inhabited by Jews, Mohammedans, and Christians. Dr. Thomson (*The Land and the Book*, vol. ii. p. 158) locates it on the north-west corner of a mount now called Jebel ed Dûhy, one hour's ride from the foot of Mount Tabor. Of this place he says: "This mount is now called Jebel ed Dûhy, and that small hamlet on the north-west corner of it is Nain, famous for the restoration of the widow's son to life. It was once a place of considerable extent, but is now little more than a cluster of ruins, among which dwell a few families of fanatical Moslems. It is in keeping with the one historic incident that renders it dear to the Christian, that its only antiquities are tombs. These are situated mainly on the east of the village, and it was in that direction, I presume, that the widow's son was being carried on that memorable occasion. It took me just an hour to ride from the foot of Tabor to Nain."

12. *The gate of the city.* Cities were surrounded by walls, to defend them from their enemies. They were entered through *gates* placed at convenient distances from each other. In most cities it was not allowed to bury the dead within the walls; hence they were borne to some convenient burial-place in the vicinity of the city. ¶ *A dead man carried out.* A funeral procession. Anciently no Jews were buried within the walls of the city, except the kings and distinguished persons, 1 Sa. xxviii. 3; 2 Ki. xxi. 18. The custom of burying within cities, and especially within the walls of churches or in their vicinity, had its origin among Christians very early; yet perhaps few customs are more deleterious to health than burials within large cities, especially within the walls of frequented buildings. The effluvia from dead bodies is excessively unwhole-

all; and they glorified God, saying, That a [h]great prophet is risen
up among us; and, That [i]God
hath visited his people.
17 And this rumour of him went
forth throughout all Judea, and
throughout all the region round
about.
18 And the disciples of John
showed him of all these things.
19 And[k] John, calling *unto him*
two of his disciples, sent *them* to
Jesus, saying, Art thou [l]he that
should come, or look we for
another?
20 When the men were come
unto him, they said, John Baptist
hath sent us unto thee, saying, Art
thou he that should come, or look
we for another?
21 And in the same hour he
cured many of *their* infirmities
and plagues, and of evil spirits;
and unto many *that were* blind he
gave sight.
22 Then Jesus, answering, said
unto them, Go your way, and [m]tell
John what things ye have seen
and heard; how that [n]the blind
see, the lame walk, the lepers are
cleansed, the deaf hear, the dead
are raised, [o]to the poor the gospel
is preached.
23 And blessed is *he* whosoever
shall not be [p]offended in me.
24 And when the messengers of
John were departed, he began to
speak unto the people concerning
John, What went ye out into the
wilderness for to see? A reed
shaken with the wind?
25 But what went ye out for to

h ch.24.19. *i* ch.1.68. *k* Mat.11.2. *l* Zec.9.9. *m* Jn.1.46. *n* Is.35.5,6. *o* ch.4.18; Ja.2.5. *p* Is.8.14,15; Mat.11.6; 13.57; ch.2.34; Jn.6.66; 1 Co.1.21-28.

some. Burial-places should be in situations of retirement, far from the tread of the gay and busy world, where all the feelings may be still and calm, and where there can be no injury to health from the mouldering bodies of the dead.

16. *Came a fear on all.* An *awe* or solemnity at the presence of one who had power to raise the dead, and at the miracle which had been performed. ¶ *Glorified God.* Praised or honoured God that he had sent such a prophet. ¶ *And, That God hath visited his people.* Some said one thing and some another, but all expressing their belief that God had showed peculiar favour to the people. ¶ *Hath visited.* See Lu. i. 68.

The raising of this young man was one of the most decisive and instructive of our Lord's miracles. There was no doubt that he was dead. There could be no delusion, and no agreement to impose on the people. He came near to the city with no reference to this young man; he met the funeral procession, as it were, by accident, and by a word he restored him to life. All those who had the best opportunity of judging—the mother, the friends—believed him to be dead, and were about to bury him. The evidence that he came to life was decisive. He sat up, he spake, and *all* were impressed with the full assurance that God had raised him to life. Many witnesses were present, and none doubted that Jesus *by a word* had restored him to his weeping mother.

The whole scene was affecting. Here was a widowed mother who was following her only son, her stay and hope, to the grave. He was borne along—one in the prime of life and the only comfort of his parent—impressive proof that the young, the useful, the vigorous, and the lovely may die. Jesus met them, apparently a stranger. He approached the procession as if he had something important to say; he touched the bier, and the procession stood still. He was full of compassion for the weeping parent, and by a word restored the youth, stretched upon the bier, to life. He sat up, and spake. Jesus therefore had power over the dead. He also has power to raise sinners, dead in trespasses and sins, to life. He can speak the word, and, though in their death of sin they are borne along toward ruin, he can open their eyes, and raise them up, and restore them revived to *real* life or to their friends. Often he raises up children in this manner, and gives them, converted to God, to their friends, imparting as *real* joy as he gave to the widow of Nain by raising her son from the dead. And

see? A man clothed in soft raiment? Behold, they which are gorgeously apparelled, and live delicately, are [q]in kings' courts.

26 But what went ye out for to see? A [r]prophet? Yea, I say unto you, and much more than a prophet.

27 This is *he* of whom it is written, [s]Behold, I send my messenger before thy face, which shall prepare thy way before thee.

28 For I say unto you, Among those that are born of women, there is not a greater prophet than John the Baptist: but he that is least in the kingdom of God is greater than he.

29 And all the people that heard *him*, and the publicans, [t]justified God, being [u]baptized with the baptism of John.

30 But the Pharisees and lawyers [3]rejected the [v]counsel of God [4]against themselves, being not baptized of him.

31 And the Lord said, [w]Whereunto then shall I liken the men of this generation? and to what are they like?

32 They are like unto children sitting in the market-place, and calling one to another, and saying, We have piped unto you, and ye have not danced; we have mourned to you, and ye have not wept.

33 For John the Baptist [x]came neither eating bread nor drinking wine; and ye say, He hath a devil.

34 The[y] Son of man is come eating and drinking; and ye say, Behold, a gluttonous man, and a winebibber, a friend of publicans and sinners!

35 But[z] Wisdom is justified of all her children.

q 2 Sa.19.35; Es.1.3,11. r ch.1.76. s Mal.3.1; ch.1.15-17. t Ps.51.4; Ro.3.4. u Mat.3.5,6; ch.3.12.

3 or, *frustrated*. 4 or, *within themselves*. v Ac.20.27. w Mat.11.16,&c. x Mat.3.4; Mar.1.6; ch.1.15. y Jn.2.2; 12.2; ver.36. z Pr.8.32-36; 17.16.

every child should remember, if he has pious parents, that there is *no way* in which he can give so much joy to them as by embracing Him who is the resurrection and the life, and resolving to live to his glory.

19–35. See this passage explained in Mat. xi. 2–19.

29. *The people.* The common people. ¶ *That heard* him. That heard *John.* ¶ *The publicans.* The tax-gatherers, the worst kind of people, who had, however, been converted. ¶ *Justified God.* Considered God as *just* or *right* in the counsel which he gave by John —to wit, in calling men to repentance, and in denouncing future wrath on the impenitent. Comp. Mat. xi. 19. ¶ *Being baptized*, &c. They *showed* that they approved of the message of God by submitting to the ordinance which he commanded—the ordinance of baptism. This verse and the following are not to be considered as the words of *Luke*, but the continuation of the discourse of our Lord. He is saying what took place in regard to John. Among the common people he was approved and obeyed; among the rich and learned he was despised.

30. *But the Pharisees and lawyers rejected*, &c. It appears from Mat. iii. 7 that some of the Pharisees came to John to be baptized; but still this is entirely consistent with the supposition that the great mass of Pharisees and lawyers rejected him. ¶ *The counsel of God.* The *counsel of God* toward them was the solemn admonition by John to *repent* and be baptized, and be prepared to receive the Messiah. This was the command or revealed will of God in relation to them. When it is said that they *rejected* the counsel of God, it does not mean that they could frustrate his purposes, but merely that they violated his commands. Men cannot frustrate the *real* purposes of God, but they can contemn his messages, they can violate his commands, and thus they can reject the counsel which he gives them, and treat with contempt the desire which he manifests for their welfare. ¶ *Against themselves.* To their own hurt or detriment. God is wise and good. He knows what is best for us. He, therefore, that rejects what God commands, rejects it to his own injury. It *cannot* be well for any mortal to despise what God commands him to do.

31–35. See this passage explained in

36 And[a] one of the Pharisees desired him that he would eat with
him. And he went into the Pharisee's house, and sat down to meat.
37 And, behold, a woman in the
city, which was a [b]sinner, when
she knew that *Jesus* sat at meat in
the Pharisee's house, brought an
alabaster-box of ointment,
38 And stood at his feet behind
him weeping, and began to wash
his feet with tears, and did wipe
them with the hairs of her head,
and kissed his feet, and anointed
them with the ointment.
39 Now when the Pharisee which
had bidden him saw *it*, he spake
within himself, saying, [c]This man,
if he were a prophet, would have
known who and what manner of
woman *this is* that toucheth him;
for [d]she is a sinner.

a Mat.26.6,&c.; Mar.14.3,&c.; Jn.11.2,&c.
b ch.5.32; ver.34; 1 Ti.1.15.
c Jn.9.24. *d* ch.15.2.

---

the Notes on Mat. xi. 16-19. *And the Lord said.* This clause is wanting in almost all the manuscripts, and is omitted by the best critics.

36. *One of the Pharisees.* His name was Simon, ver. 10. Nothing more is known of him. It is not improbable, however, from what follows (ver. 40-47), that he had been healed by the Saviour of some afflictive disease, and made this feast to show his gratitude. ¶ *Sat down to meat.* The original word here means only that he placed himself or reclined at the table. The notion of *sitting* at meals is taken from modern customs, and was not practised by the Jews. See Notes on Mat. xxiii. 6. ¶ *Meat.* Supper. Food of any kind. Sat down to eat.

37. *In the city.* What city is meant is unknown. Some have supposed it was Nain; some Capernaum; some Magdala; and some Jerusalem. ¶ *Which was a sinner.* Who was depraved or wicked. This woman, it seems, was known to be a sinner—perhaps an abandoned woman or a prostitute. It is certain that she had much to be forgiven, and she had probably passed her life in crime. There is no evidence that this was the woman commonly called Mary Magdalene. ¶ *An alabaster-box*, &c. See Notes on Mar. xiv. 3.

38. *Stood at his feet behind* him. They reclined, at their meals, on their left side, and their feet, therefore, were extended *from* the table, so that persons could easily approach them. See Notes on Mat. xxiii. 6. ¶ *Began to wash his feet.* The Jews wore sandals. These were taken off when they entered a house. It was an act of hospitality and kindness to wash the feet of a guest. *She* therefore began to show her love for the Saviour, and at the same time her humility and penitence, by pouring forth a flood of tears, and washing his feet in the manner of a servant. ¶ *Kissed his feet.* The kiss was an emblem of love and affection. In this manner she testified her love for the Lord Jesus, and at the same time her humility and sense of sin by kissing his feet. There could be few expressions of penitence more deep and tender than were these. A sense of all her sins rushed over her mind; her heart burst at the remembrance of them, and at the presence of the pure Redeemer; with deep sorrow she humbled herself and sought forgiveness. She showed her love for him by a kiss of affection; her humility, by bathing his feet; her veneration, by breaking a costly box—perhaps procured by a guilty life—and anointing his feet. In this way we should all come, embracing him as the loved Redeemer, humbled at his feet, and offering *all* we have—all that we have gained in lives of sin, in our professions, by merchandise and toil, while we were sinners—offering *all* to his service. Thus shall we show the sincerity of our repentance, and thus shall we hear his gracious voice pronounce our sins forgiven.

39. *He spake within himself.* Thought. ¶ *If he were a prophet.* The word *prophet* here means, not one who predicts future events, but one who knows the hearts of men. If Jesus had been sent from God as a prophet, he supposed that he would have known the character of the woman and would have rebuked her. ¶ *Would have known*, &c. Because Jesus did not rebuke her and drive her from his presence, he inferred that he could not be acquainted with her character. The Pharisees considered it improper to hold communion with those who were notorious sinners.

40 And Jesus, answering, said unto him, Simon, I have somewhat to say unto thee. And he saith, Master, say on.

41 There was a certain creditor which had two debtors: the one owed five hundred [5]pence, and the other fifty:

42 And when they had [e]nothing to pay, he frankly forgave them both. Tell me, therefore, which of them will love him most?

43 Simon answered and said, I suppose that *he* to whom he forgave most. And he said unto him, Thou hast [f]rightly judged.

44 And he turned to the woman, and said unto Simon, Seest thou this woman? I entered into thine house, thou gavest me no water for my feet; but she hath washed my feet with tears, and wiped *them* with the hairs of her head.

45 Thou gavest me no kiss; but

5 See Mat.18.28. *e* Ps.49.7,8; Ro.5.6. *f* Ps.116.16-18; 1 Co.15.9; 2 Co.5.14; 1 Ti.1.13-16.

They judged our Saviour by their own rules, and supposed that *he* would act in the same way; and Simon therefore concluded that he did not know her character and could not be a prophet. Jesus did not refuse the society of the guilty. He came to save the lost; and no person ever came to him so sure of finding a *friend*, as those who came conscious that they were deeply depraved, and mourning on account of their crimes. ¶ *That toucheth him.* The *touch* of a Gentile, or a person singularly wicked, they supposed to be polluting, and the Pharisees avoided it. See Mat. ix. 11.

41. *A certain creditor.* A man who had lent money or sold property, the payment for which was yet due. ¶ *Five hundred pence.* About 69 dollars 26 cents, or £14, 11*s.* 8*d.* See Notes on Mat. xviii. 28. ¶ *Fifty.* About 7 dollars, or £1, 9*s.* 2*d.*

42. *Frankly forgave.* Freely forgave, or forgave entirely without any compensation. This is not designed to express anything about the way in which God forgives sinners. He forgives—forgives freely, but it is in connection with the *atonement* made by the Lord Jesus. If it was a mere *debt* which we owed to God, he might forgive, as this creditor did, without *any* equivalent. But it is *crime* which he forgives. He pardons as a moral governor. A parent might forgive a *debt* without any equivalent; but he cannot pardon an offending child without regarding his own *character* as a parent, the *truth* of his threatenings, the good order of his house, and the maintenance of his authority. So our sins against God, though they are called *debts*, are called so *figuratively*. It is not an affair of *money*, and God cannot forgive us without maintaining his word, the honour of his government, and law—in other words, without an *atonement*. It is clear that by the *creditor* here our Saviour meant to designate God, and by the *debtors*, sinners and the woman present. Simon, whose life had been comparatively upright, was denoted by the one that owed *fifty* pence; the woman, who had been an open and shameless sinner, was represented by the one that owed *five hundred*. Yet *neither* could pay. Both must be forgiven or perish. So, however much difference there is among men, *all* need the pardoning mercy of God, and *all*, without that, must perish.

43. *I suppose,* &c. He saw not *the point* of our Lord's parable. By thus saying, therefore, he condemned himself, and prepared the way for our Lord's reproof.

44. *Seest thou this woman?* You see what this woman has done to me, compared with what you have done. *She* has shown me expressions of regard which you, in your own house, have not shown. ¶ *I entered into thine house.* I came at your invitation, where I might expect all the usual rites of hospitality. ¶ *Thou gavest me no water for my feet.* Among Eastern people it was customary, before eating, to wash the feet; and to do this, or to bring water for it, was one of the rites of hospitality. See Ge. xviii. 4; Ju. xix. 21. The reasons for this were, that they wore *sandals*, which covered only the bottom of the feet, and that when they ate they reclined on couches or sofas. It became therefore necessary that the feet should be often washed.

45. *Thou gavest me no kiss.* The kiss was a token of affection or a common mode of salutation, and Simon had even neglected this mark of welcoming

this woman, since the time I came in, hath not ceased to kiss my feet.

46 My[g] head with oil thou didst not anoint; but this woman hath anointed my feet with ointment.

47 Wherefore I say unto thee, Her sins, which are many, are for-

g Ps.23.5.

---

him to his house. It was often used among *men* as a sign of salutation. Comp. Ge. xxxiii. 4; Ex. xviii. 7; Mat. xxvi. 49. ¶ *Hath not ceased to kiss my feet.* How striking the difference between the conduct of Simon and this woman! *He*, with all the richness of a splendid preparation, had omitted the common marks of regard and affection. *She*, in humility, had bowed at his feet, had watered them with tears, and had not ceased to kiss them. The most splendid entertainments do not always express the greatest welcome. There may be in such entertainments much insincerity—much seeking of popularity or some other motive; but no such motive could have operated in inducing a broken-hearted sinner to wash the Saviour's *feet* with tears.

46. *My head with oil.* The custom of pouring *oil* upon the head was universal among the Jews. The oil used was sweet oil or oil of olives, prepared in such a way as to give an agreeable smell. It was also used to render the hair more smooth and elegant. See Ru. iii. 3; 2 Sa. xii. 20; xiv. 2; Ps. xxiii. 5. ¶ *With ointment.* This *ointment* was a mixture of various aromatics, and was therefore far more costly and precious than the *oil* commonly used for anointing the head. Her conduct, compared with that of Simon, was therefore more striking. *He* did not give even the common oil *for his head* used on such occasions. *She* had applied to *his feet* a far more precious and valuable *unguent*. *He*, therefore, showed comparatively *little* love. *She* showed *much*.

47. *Wherefore I say unto thee.* As the result of this, or because she has done this; meaning by this that she had given *evidence* that her sins had been forgiven. The inquiry with Simon was whether it was proper for Jesus to *touch her* or to allow her to touch him, because she was such a sinner, ver. 39. Jesus said, in substance, to Simon, "Grant that she has been as great a sinner as you affirm, and even grant that if she had *continued so* it might be improper to suffer her to touch me, yet *her conduct* shows that her sins have been forgiven. She has evinced so much love for me as to show that she is no longer *such a sinner* as you suppose, and it is not, therefore, *improper* that she should be suffered to come near me." ¶ *For she loved much.* In our translation this would seem to be given as a reason why her sins had been forgiven—that she had loved much *before* they were pardoned; but this is clearly not the meaning. This would be contrary to the whole New Testament, which supposes that love *succeeds*, not *precedes* forgiveness; and which nowhere supposes that sins are forgiven *because* we love God. It would be also contrary to the design of the Saviour here. It was not to show *why* her sins had been forgiven, but to show that she had given evidence that they actually *had* been, and that it was proper, therefore, that she should come near to him and manifest this love. The meaning may be thus expressed: "That her sins, so many and aggravated, have been forgiven—that she is no longer such a sinner as you suppose, is manifest from her conduct. She shows deep gratitude, penitence, love. Her conduct is the *proper expression* of that love. While you have shown comparatively little evidence that you felt that *your sins* were great, and comparatively little love at their being forgiven, *she* has shown that she *felt* hers to be great, and has loved much." ¶ *To whom little is forgiven.* He who feels that little has been forgiven—that his sins were not as great as those of others. A man's love to God will be in proportion to the obligation he *feels* to him for forgiveness. God is to be *loved* for his perfections, apart from what he has *done* for us. But still it is proper that our love should be increased by a consideration of his goodness; and they who feel—as Christians do—that they are *the chief of sinners*, will feel under infinite obligation to love God and their Redeemer, and that no *expression* of attachment to him can be *beyond* what is due.

48. *Thy sins are forgiven.* What a gracious assurance to the weeping, loving penitent! How that voice, spoken to the troubled sinner, stills his anguish, allays his troubled feelings, and produces peace to the soul! And how manifest is it that he that could say

given, for she loved much; but to whom little is forgiven, *the same* loveth little.

48 And he said unto her, Thy sins are forgiven.

49 And they that sat at meat with him began to say within themselves, [h]Who is this that forgiveth sins also?

50 And he said to the woman, Thy[i] faith hath saved thee; go in peace.

CHAPTER VIII.

AND it came to pass afterward that he went throughout every city and village, preaching and showing the glad tidings of the kingdom of God; and the twelve *were* with him;

2 And[a] certain women which had been healed of evil spirits and infirmities, Mary called Magdalene, [b]out of whom went seven devils,

3 And Joanna the wife of Chuza, Herod's steward, and Susanna, and many others, which [c]ministered unto him of their substance.

4 And when much people were gathered together, and were come to him out of every city, he spake by a parable:

5 A[d] sower went out to sow his seed: and as he sowed, some

h Mat.9.2,3; Mar.2.7.
i Hab.2.4; Mat.9.22; Mar.5.34; 10.52; ch.8.48; 18.42; Ep.2.8.

a Mat.27.55. b Mar.16.9; ver.30. c 2 Co.8.9. d Mat.13.3,&c.; Mar.4.3,&c.

thus *must* be God! No man has a *right* to forgive sin. No man *can* speak peace to the soul, and give assurance that its transgressions are pardoned. Here, then, Jesus gave indubitable proof that he was God as well as man; that he was Lord of the conscience as well as the pitying friend; and that he was as able to read the heart and give peace there, as he was to witness the external expression of sorrow for sin.

49. *Who is this*, &c. A very pertinent question. Who *could* he be but God? Man could not do it, and there is no wonder that they were amazed.

50. *Thy faith hath saved thee; go in peace.* See Notes on Mar. v. 34.

CHAPTER VIII.

1. *Every city and village.* Of Galilee. ¶ *Preaching and showing the glad tidings of the kingdom of God.* That the kingdom of God was about to come, or that his reign in the gospel was about to be set up over men. See Notes on Mat. iii. 2. ¶ *The twelve.* The twelve apostles.

2. *Infirmities.* Sickness. ¶ *Mary called Magdalene.* So called from *Magdala*, the place of her residence. It was situated on the Sea of Galilee, south of Capernaum. To this place Jesus retired after feeding the four thousand. See Notes on Mat. xv. 39. ¶ *Out of whom went.* By the power of Jesus. ¶ *Seven devils.* The word *seven* is often used for an indefinite number, and *may* signify merely *many* devils. The expression is used to signify that she was grievously tormented, and rendered, doubtless, insane by the power of evil spirits. See Notes on Mat. iv. 24. It has been commonly supposed that Mary Magdalene was a woman of abandoned character, but of this there is not the least evidence. All that we know of her is that she was formerly grievously afflicted by the presence of those evil spirits, that she was perfectly cured by Jesus, and that afterward she became one of his most faithful and humble followers. She was at his crucifixion (Jn. xix. 25) and burial (Mar. xv. 47), and she was among those who had prepared the materials to embalm him (Mar. xvi. 1), and who first went to the sepulchre after the resurrection; and what is particularly interesting in her history, she was the first to whom the risen Redeemer appeared (Mar. xvi. 9), and his conversation with her is exceeded in interest and pathos by no passage of history, sacred or profane, Jn. xx. 11–18.

3. *Herod's steward.* Herod Antipas, who reigned in Galilee. He was a son of Herod the Great. The word *steward* means one who has charge of the domestic affairs of a family, to provide for it. This office was generally held by a *slave* who was esteemed the most faithful, and was often conferred as a reward of fidelity. ¶ *Ministered.* Gave for his support. ¶ *Of their substance.* Their property; their possessions. Christians then believed, when they professed to

fell by the way-side; and it was trodden[e] down, and fowls of the air devoured it.

6 And some fell upon a [f]rock: and as soon as it was sprung up it withered away, because it lacked moisture.

7 And some fell [g]among thorns: and the thorns sprang up with it, and choked it.

8 And other fell on good ground, and sprang up, and bare fruit [h]an hundred-fold. And when he had said these things, he cried, [i]He that hath ears to hear, let him hear.

9 And his disciples asked him, saying, What might this parable be?

10 And he said, Unto you it is given to know the mysteries of the kingdom of God, but to others in parables; [k]that seeing they might not see, and hearing they might not understand.

11 Now[l] the parable is this: The [m]seed is the word of God.

12 Those by the way-side are they that hear; then cometh the devil, and [n]taketh away the word out of their hearts, lest they should believe and be saved.

13 They on the rock *are they* which, when they hear, [o]receive the word with joy; and these have[p] no root, which for a while believe, and in time of temptation fall away.

14 And that which fell among thorns are they which, when they have heard, go forth, and [q]are choked with cares, and riches, and pleasures of *this* life, and [r]bring no fruit to perfection.

15 But that on the good ground are they which, in an [s]honest and good heart, having heard the word, keep *it,* and bring forth fruit with [t]patience.

16 No[u] man, when he hath lighted a candle, covereth it with a vessel, or putteth *it* under a bed; but setteth *it* on a candlestick, that they which enter in may see the light.

17 For[v] nothing is secret that shall not be made manifest, neither *any thing* hid that shall not be known and come abroad.

18 Take[w] heed, therefore, how ye hear; for [x]whosoever hath, to him shall be given; and whosoever hath not, from him shall be taken even that which he [1]seemeth to have.

19 Then[y] came to him *his* mother and his brethren, and could not come at him for the press.

20 And it was told him *by certain,* which said, Thy mother and thy brethren stand without, desiring to see thee.

21 And he answered and said unto them, My mother and my brethren are these which hear the word of God, and do it.

22 Now[z] it came to pass on a certain day that he went into a ship with his disciples; and he said unto them, Let us go over unto the other side of the lake. And they launched forth.

23 But as they sailed, he fell

e Ps.119.118; Mat.5.13. *f* Je.5.3. *g* Je.4.3.
h Ge.26.12. *i* Pr.20.12; Je.13.15; 25.4. *k* Is.6.9.
l Mat.13.18; Mar.4.14,&c. *m* 1 Pe.1.23.
n Pr.4.5; Is.65.11; Ja.1.23,24.
o Ps.106.12,13; Is.58.2; Ga.3.1,4; 4.15.
p Pr.12.3; Ho.6.4.
q 1 Ti.6.9,10; 2 Ti.4.10; 1 Jn.2.15-17.
r Jn.15.6. *s* Je.32.39. *t* He.10.36; Ja.1.4.
u Mat.5.15; Mar.4.21; ch.11.33.
v Ec.12.14; Mat.10.26; ch.12.2; 1 Co.4.5.
w Ja.1.21-25. *x* Mat.13.12; 25.29; ch.19.26.
1 or, *thinketh that he hath.*
y Mat.12.46,&c.; Mar.3.32,&c.
z Mat.8.23,&c.; Mar.4.35,&c.

---

follow Christ, that it was proper to give *all* up to him—their property as well as their hearts; and the same thing is still required—that is, to commit all that we have to his disposal; to be willing to part with it for the promotion of his glory, and to leave it when he calls us away from it.

4-15. See the parable of the sower explained in the Notes on Mat. xiii. 1-23.

16-18. See Notes on Mar. iv. 21-25.

asleep; and there came down a storm of wind on the lake; and they were filled *with water*, and were in jeopardy.

24 And they came to him [a]and awoke him, saying, Master, master, we perish! Then he arose, and rebuked the wind and the raging of the water; and they ceased, and there was a calm.

25 And he said unto them, Where is your faith? And they, being afraid, wondered, saying one to another, What manner of man is this? for he commandeth even the winds and water, and they obey him.

26 And[b] they arrived at the country of the Gadarenes, which is over against Galilee.

27 And when he went forth to land, there met him out of the city a certain man which had devils long time, and ware no clothes, neither abode in *any* house, but in the tombs.

28 When he saw Jesus, he cried out, and fell down before him, and with a loud voice said, What have I to do with thee, Jesus, *thou* Son of God most high? I beseech thee, torment[c] me not.

29 (For he had commanded the unclean spirit to come out of the man. For oftentimes it had caught him: and he was kept bound with chains and in fetters; and he brake the bands, and was driven of the devil into the wilderness.)

30 And Jesus asked him, saying, What is thy name? And he said, Legion; because many devils were entered into him.

31 And they besought him that he would not command them to go out into the [d]deep.

32 And there was there an herd of many swine feeding on the mountain; and they besought him that he would suffer them to enter into them; and he suffered them.

33 Then went the devils out of the man, and entered into the swine; and the herd ran violently down a steep place into the lake, and were choked.

34 When they that fed *them* saw what was done, [e]they fled, and went and told *it* in the city and in the country.

35 Then they went out to see what was done; and came to Jesus, and found the man out of whom the devils were departed, sitting at the feet of Jesus, clothed and in his [f]right mind; and they were afraid.

36 They also which saw *it* told them by what means he that was possessed of the devils was healed.

37 Then the whole multitude of the country of the Gadarenes round about [g]besought him to depart from them, for they were taken with great fear; and he went up into the ship, and returned back again.

38 Now the man out of whom the devils were departed [h]besought him that he might be with him; but Jesus sent him away, saying,

39 Return to [i]thine own house, and show how [k]great things God hath done unto thee. And he went his way, and published throughout the whole city how great things Jesus had done unto him.

40 And it came to pass, that, when Jesus was returned, the people *gladly* received him; for they were all waiting for him.

41 And behold, [l]there came a man named Jairus, and he was a ruler of the synagogue; and he fell

a Ps.44.23; Is.51.9,10. *b* Mat.8.28,&c.; Mar.5.1,&c. *c* Is.27.1; Ja.2.19; Re.20.10. *d* Re.20.3.
e Ac.19.16,17. *f* Ps.51.10. *g* Ac.16.39. *h* De.10.20,21; Ps.116.12,16. *i* 1 Ti.5.8. *k* Ps.126.2,3. *l* Mat.9.18,&c.; Mar.5.22,&c.

19–21. See Notes on Mat. xii. 46–50.

22–39. See this passage explained in the Notes on Mat. viii. 23–34, and Mar. v. 1–20.

down at Jesus' feet, and besought him that he would come into his house;

42 For he had one only daughter, about twelve years of age, and she lay a dying. But as he went the people thronged him.

43 And a woman having an issue of blood twelve years, which [m]had spent all her living upon [n]physicians, neither could be healed of any,

44 Came behind *him*, and touched the border of his garment; and immediately[o] her issue of blood stanched.

45 And Jesus said, Who touched me? When all denied, Peter, and they that were with him, said, Master, the multitude throng thee and press *thee*, and sayest thou, Who touched me?

46 And Jesus said, Somebody hath touched me; for I perceive that [p]virtue is gone out of me.

47 And when the woman saw that [q]she was not hid, she [r]came trembling, and falling down before him, she declared unto him, before all the people, for what cause she had touched him, and how she was healed immediately.

48 And he said unto her, Daughter, be of good comfort; thy faith hath made thee whole: go in peace.

49 While[s] he yet spake, there cometh one from the [t]ruler of the synagogue's *house*, saying to him, Thy daughter is dead; trouble not the Master.

50 But when Jesus heard *it*, he answered him, saying, [u]Fear not: believe only, and she shall be made whole.

51 And when he came into the house, he suffered no man to go in,

m 2 Ch.16.12; Is.55.2. *n* Job 13.4.
o Mat.8.3; 20.34; ch.13.13. *p* ch.6.19; 1 Pe.2.9.
q Ps.38.9; Ho.5.3. *r* Is.66.2; Ho.13.1; Ac.16.29.
s Mat.9.23,&c.; Mar.5.35,&c. *t* ver.41,42.
u Jn.11.25; Ro.4.17

40–56. See this passage explained in the Notes on Mat. ix. 18–26, and Mar. v. 21–43.

save Peter, and James, and John, and the father and the mother of the maiden.

52 And all wept, and bewailed her: but he said, Weep not; she is not dead, but [v]sleepeth.

53 And they [w]laughed him to scorn, knowing that she was dead.

54 And he put them all out, and took her by the hand, and called, saying, Maid, [x]arise.

55 And her spirit came again, and she arose straightway; and he commanded to give her meat.

56 And her parents were astonished; but he [y]charged them that they should tell no man what was done.

CHAPTER IX.

THEN[a] he called his twelve disciples together, and gave them power and authority over all devils, and to cure diseases.

2 And he sent them to preach the kingdom of God, and to heal the sick.

3 And he said unto them, [b]Take nothing for *your* journey, neither staves, nor scrip, neither bread, neither money; neither have two coats apiece.

4 And whatsoever house ye enter into, there abide, and thence depart.

5 And whosoever will not receive you, when ye go out of that city [c]shake off the very dust from your feet for a testimony against them.

6 And they departed, and went through the towns, preaching the gospel, and healing everywhere.

7 Now[d] Herod the tetrarch heard of all that was done by him; and

v Jn.11.11,13. *w* Ps.22.7; ch.16.14.
x ch.7.14; Jn.11.43. *y* Mat.8.4; 9.30; Mar.5.43.
a Mat.10.1,&c.; Mar.3.13,&c.; 6.7,&c.
b ch.10.4,&c.; 12.22. *c* Ne.5.13; Ac.13.51; 18.6.
d Mat.14.1,&c.; Mar.6.14,&c.

CHAPTER IX.

1–6. See Notes on Mat. x. 1–14.

7–9. See Notes on Mat. xiv. 1, 2. Comp. Mar. vi. 14–16.

he was perplexed, because that it was said of some that John was risen from the dead;

8 And of some, That Elias had appeared; and of others, That one of the old prophets was risen again.

9 And Herod said, John have I beheaded; but who is this of whom I hear such things? And he [e]desired to see him.

10 And the apostles, when they were returned, told him all that they had done. And he took them, and went aside privately into a desert place, belonging to the city called Bethsaida.

11 And the people, [f]when they knew *it*, followed him; and [g]he received them, and spake unto them of the [h]kingdom of God, and healed them that [i]had need of healing.

12 And[k] when the day began to wear away, then came the twelve, and said unto him, Send the multitude away, that they may go into the towns and country round about, and lodge, and get victuals; for we are here in a [l]desert place.

13 But he said unto them, Give ye them to eat. And they said, We have no more but five loaves and two fishes; except we should go and buy meat for all this people.

14 (For they were about five thousand men.) And he said to his disciples, [m]Make them sit down by fifties in a company.

15 And they did so, and made them all sit down.

16 Then he took the five loaves and the two fishes; and looking up to heaven, he blessed them, and brake, and gave to the disciples to set before the multitude.

17 And they did eat, and [n]were all filled; and there was taken up of fragments that remained to them, twelve baskets.

18 And[o] it came to pass, as he was alone praying, his disciples were with him; and he asked them, saying, Whom say the people that I am?

19 They answering, said, [p]John the Baptist; but some *say*, Elias; and others *say*, That one of the old prophets is risen again.

20 He said unto them, But whom say ye that I am? Peter [q]answering said, The Christ of God.

21 And he straitly charged them, and commanded *them* to tell no man that thing;

22 Saying, [r]The Son of man must suffer many things, and be rejected of the elders, and chief priests, and scribes, and be slain, and be raised the third day.

23 And he said to *them* all, [s]If any *man* will come after me, let him deny himself, and take up his cross daily, and follow me.

24 For whosoever will save his life shall lose it; but whosoever will lose his life for my sake, the same shall save it.

25 For what is a man advantaged if he gain the whole world and lose himself, or be cast away?

26 For[t] whosoever shall be ashamed of me and of my words, of him shall the Son of man be

e ch.23.8. *f* Ro.10.14,17. *g* Jn.6.37. *h* Ac.28.31. *i* ch.1.53; 5.31; He.4.16. *k* Mat.14.15,&c.; Mar.6.35,&c.; Jn.6.5,&c. *l* Ps.78.19,20; Eze.34.25; Ho.13.5. *m* 1 Co.14.40.

n Ps.107.9. *o* Mat.16.13,&c.; Mar.8.27,&c. *p* Mat.14.2; ver.7,8. *q* Jn.6.69. *r* Mat.16.21; 17.22. *s* Mat.10.38; 16.24; Mar.8.34; ch.14.27; Ro.8.13; Col.3.5. *t* Mat.10.33; Mar.8.38; 2 Ti.2.12.

10–17. See Notes on Mat. xiv. 13–21, and Mar. vi. 30–44.

10. *Bethsaida.* A city on the east bank of the river Jordan, near where the river enters into the Sea of Tiberias. In the neighbourhood of that city were extensive wastes or deserts.

12. *Day began to wear away.* To decline, or as it drew near toward evening.

18–26. See Notes on Mat. xvi. 13–27; Mar. viii. 27–38.

20. *The Christ of God.* The *Anointed* of God. The *Messiah* appointed by God,

ashamed when he shall come in
his own glory, and *in his* Father's,
and of the holy angels.
27 But[u] I tell you of a truth,
there be some standing here which
shall not [v]taste of death till they
see the kingdom of God.
28 And[w] it came to pass about
an eight days after these [1]sayings,
he took Peter, and John, and
James, and went up into a mountain to pray.
29 And as he prayed, the fashion
of his countenance was altered, and
his raiment *was* white *and* glistering.
30 And, behold, there talked with
him two men, which were Moses
and Elias,
31 Who appeared in glory, and
spake of his decease which he
should accomplish at Jerusalem.
32 But Peter and they that were
with him were [x]heavy with sleep;
and when they were awake, [y]they
saw his glory, and the two men
that stood with him.
33 And it came to pass, as they
departed from him, Peter said unto
Jesus, Master, [z]It is good for us to
be here: and let us make three
tabernacles; one for thee, and one
for Moses, and one for Elias; [a]not
knowing what he said.
34 While he thus spake, there
came a cloud and overshadowed
them; and they feared as they entered into the cloud.
35 And there came a voice out
of the cloud, saying, [b]This is my
beloved Son: [c]hear him.
36 And when the voice was past,
Jesus was found alone. And they
kept *it* close, and [d]told no man in
those days any of those things
which they had seen.
37 And[e] it came to pass, that on
the next day, when they were come
down from the hill, much people
met him.
38 And, behold, a man of the
company cried out, saying, Master, I beseech thee look upon my
son; for he is mine [f]only child:
39 And, lo, a spirit taketh him,
and he suddenly crieth out; and

u Mat.16.28; Mar.9.1. *v* Jn.8.52; He.2.9. *w* Mat.17.1,&c.; Mar.9.2,&c. 1 or, *things*. *x* Da.8.18; 10.9. *y* Jn.1.14.

z Ps.27.4; 73.28. *a* Mar.10.38. *b* Mat.3.17; 2 Pe.1.17,18. *c* De.18.15; Ac.3.22. *d* Ec.3.7. *e* Mat.17.14,&c.; Mar.9.17,&c. *f* Zec.12.10.

---

and who had been long promised by him. See Notes on Mat. i. 1.

28–36. See an account of the transfiguration in Mat. xvii. 1–13, and Mar. ix. 2–13.

29. *The fashion.* The *appearance.* ¶ *Glistering.* Shining like lightning—of a bright, dazzling whiteness. As Mark says, "more white than any fuller could make it."

31. *In glory.* Of a glorious appearance. Of an appearance like that which the saints have in heaven. ¶ *His decease.* Literally his *exit* or *departure.* The word translated here *decease*—that is, *exit,* or *going out*—is elsewhere used to denote death. See 2 Pe. i. 15. Death is a departure or going out from this life. In *this* word there may be an allusion to the *departure* of the children of Israel from Egypt. As that was going out from *bondage,* pain, and humiliation, so death, to a saint, is but going forth from a land of captivity and thraldom to one of plenty and freedom; to the land of promise, the Canaan in the skies. ¶ *He should accomplish.* Which was about to take place.

32. *Heavy with sleep.* Borne down with sleep—oppressed, overcome with sleep. It may seem remarkable that they should fall asleep on such an occasion; but we are to bear in mind that this may have been in the night, and that they were weary with the toils of the day. Besides, they did not *fall asleep* while the transfiguration lasted. While Jesus was praying, or perhaps after he closed, they fell asleep. *While* they were sleeping his countenance was changed, and Moses and Elias appeared. The first that *they* saw of it was after they awoke, having been probably awakened by the shining of the light around them.

36. *Jesus was found alone.* That is, the two men had left him. In respect to *them* he was alone.

it teareth him that he foameth
again; and, bruising him, hardly
departeth from him.
40 And I besought thy disciples
to cast him out, and [g]they could
not.
41 And Jesus answering said, O
faithless[h] and [i]perverse generation!
how long shall I be with you, and
suffer you? Bring thy son hither.
42 And as he was yet a coming,
the devil threw him down and tare
him. And Jesus [k]rebuked the unclean spirit, and healed the child,
and delivered him again to his
father.
43 And they were all [l]amazed
at the mighty power of God. But
while they wondered every one at
all things which Jesus did, he said
unto his disciples,
44 Let these sayings sink down
into your ears; [m]for the Son of man
shall be delivered [n]into the hands
of men.
45 But[o] they understood not this
saying, and it was hid from them,
that they perceived it not; and they
feared to ask him of that saying.
46 Then[p] there arose a reasoning
among them, which of them should
be greatest.
47 And Jesus, perceiving the
thought of their heart, took a
child, and set him by him,
48 And said unto them, [q]Who-
soever shall receive this child in
my name, receiveth me; and whosoever shall receive me, receiveth
him that sent me: [r]for he that is
least among you all, the same shall
be great.
49 And John answered and said,
Master, [s]we saw one casting out
devils in thy name; and we forbad
him, because he followeth not
with us.
50 And Jesus said unto him,
Forbid *him* not; [t]for he that is
not against us is for us.
51 And it came to pass, when
the time was come that he should

g Ac.19.13-16. *h* Jn.20.27; He.4.2.
i De.32.5; Ps.78.8. *k* Mar.1.27.
l Ps.139.14; Zec.8.6. *m* Mat.17.22. *n* 2 Sa.24.14.
o Mar.9.32; ch.2.50; 18.34.

p Mat.18.1,&c.; Mar.9.34,&c.
q Mat.10.40; Jn.12.44; 13.20.
r Mat.23.11,12; ch.14.11. *s* Nu.11.27-29.
t Mat.12.30; ch.16.13.

37-43. See this passage explained in the Notes on Mat. xvii. 14-21, and Mar. ix. 14-29.

44. *Let these sayings.* Probably this refers to the *sayings of the people,* who had seen his miracles, and who on that account had praised and glorified God. On that ground they had acknowledged him to be the Christ. As if he had said, "I am about to die. *You* will then be disconsolate, and perhaps doubtful about my being the Christ. *Then* do you remember these miracles, and the confessions of the people—the evidence which I gave you that I was from God." Or it may mean, "Remember that I am about to die, and let my sayings in regard to that sink down into your hearts, for it is a most important event; and you will have need of remembering, when it takes place, that I told you of it." This last interpretation, however, does not agree as well with the Greek as the former.

45. *It was hid from them.* They had imbibed the common notions of the Jews that he was to be a prince and a conqueror, to deliver the nation. They could not understand how that could be, if he was soon to be delivered into the hands of his enemies to die. In this way it was hid from them—not by God, but by their previous false belief. And from this we may learn that the plainest truths of the Bible are unintelligible to many because they have embraced some belief or opinion before which is erroneous, and which they are unwilling to abandon. The proper way of reading the Bible is to lay aside all previous opinions and submit entirely to God. The apostles should have supposed that their previous notions of the Messiah were wrong, and should have renounced them. They should have believed that what Jesus *then* said was consistent with his being the Christ. So *we* should believe that *all* that God says is consistent with truth, and should forsake all other opinions.

46-50. See Notes on Mat. xviii. 1-5. Comp. Mar. ix. 33-38.

be [u]received up, he stedfastly set his face to go to Jerusalem,
52 And sent messengers before his face; and they went, and entered into a village of the [v]Samaritans, to make ready for him.
53 And they did not receive him, because his face was as though he would go to Jerusalem.
54 And when his disciples, James and John, saw *this*, they said, Lord, wilt thou that we command fire to come down from heaven and consume them, even as [w]Elias did?

u Mar.16.19; Ac.1.2. v Jn.4.4. w 2 Ki.1.10,12.

51. *Should be received up.* The word here translated "received up" means literally a removal from a lower to a higher place, and here it refers evidently to the solemn ascension of Jesus to heaven. It is often used to describe that great event. See Ac. i. 11, 22; Mar. xvi. 19; 1 Ti. iii. 16. The time appointed for him to remain on the earth was about expiring, and he resolved to go to Jerusalem and die. And from this we learn that Jesus made a *voluntary* sacrifice; that he *chose* to give his life for the sins of men. Humanly speaking, had he remained in Galilee he would have been safe; but that it might appear that he did not shun danger, and that he was really a *voluntary* sacrifice—that no man had power over his life except as he was *permitted* (Jn. xix. 11)—he chose to put himself in the way of danger, and even to go into scenes which he knew would end in his death. ¶ *He stedfastly set his face.* He determined to go to Jerusalem, or he set out resolutely. When a man goes toward an object, he may be said to set his face toward it. The expression here means only that he *resolved* to go, and it implies that he was not appalled by the dangers—that he was determined to brave all, and go up into the midst of his enemies—to die.

52. *Sent messengers.* In the original the word is *angels;* and the use of that word here shows that the word *angel* in the Bible does not always mean heavenly beings. ¶ *To make ready.* To prepare a place, lodgings, refreshments. He had no reason to expect that he would experience any kind treatment from the Samaritans if he came suddenly among them, and if they saw that he was going to Jerusalem. He therefore made provision beforehand, and thus has shown us that it is not *improper* to look out beforehand for the supply of our wants, and to guard against want and poverty. ¶ *Samaritans.* See Notes on Mat. x. 5. They had no dealings with the Jews, Jn. iv. 9.

53. *They did not receive him.* Did not entertain him hospitably, or receive him with kindness. ¶ *Because his face was,* &c. Because they ascertained that he was going to Jerusalem. One of the subjects of dispute between the Jews and Samaritans pertained to the proper situation of the temple. The Jews contended that it should be at Jerusalem; the Samaritans, on Mount Gerizim, and accordingly they had built one there. They had probably heard of the miracles of Jesus, and that he claimed to be the Messiah. Perhaps they had hoped that he would decide that *they* were right in regard to the building of the temple. Had he decided the question in that way, they would have received him as the Messiah gladly; but when they saw that he was going among the Jews—that *by going* he would decide in their favour, they resolved to have nothing to do with him, and they rejected him. And from this we may learn—1st. That men wish all the teachers of religion to fall in with their own views. 2d. That if a doctrine does not accord with their selfish desires, they are very apt to reject it. 3d. That if a religious teacher or a doctrine favours a rival sect, it is commonly rejected without examination. And, 4th. That men, from a regard to their own views and selfishness, often reject the true religion, as the Samaritans did the Son of God, and bring upon themselves swift destruction.

54. *James and John.* They were called *Boanerges*—sons of thunder—probably on account of their energy and power in preaching the gospel, or of their vehement and rash zeal—a remarkable example of which we have in this instance, Mar. iii. 17. ¶ *Wilt thou,* &c. The insult had been offered to Jesus, their friend, and they felt it; but their zeal was rash and their spirit bad. Vengeance belongs to God: it was not theirs to attempt it. ¶ *Fire from*

55 But he turned and rebuked
them, and said, Ye know not what
manner of spirit ye are of.
56 For[x] the Son of man is not
come to destroy men's lives, but
to save *them*. And they went to
another village.
57 And[y] it came to pass, that,
as they went in the way, a certain
man said unto him, Lord, I will
follow thee whithersoever thou
goest.
58 And Jesus said unto him,
Foxes have holes, and birds of the
air *have* nests; but the Son of man
hath not where to lay *his* head.
59 And he said unto another,
Follow me. But he said, [z]Lord,
suffer me first to go and bury my
father.
60 Jesus said unto him, Let the
dead bury their dead; but go thou
and preach the kingdom of God.
61 And another also said, Lord,
I will follow thee; but let me first
go bid them farewell which are at
home at my house.
62 And Jesus said unto him,
No man, having put his hand to
the plough, and looking back, is
fit for the kingdom of God.

x Jn.3.17; 12.47. y Mat.8.19,&c. z 1 Ki.19.20.

---

heaven. Lightning, to consume them. ¶ *As Elias did.* By this they wished to justify their zeal. Perhaps, while they were speaking, they saw Jesus look at them with disapprobation, and to vindicate themselves they referred to the case of Elijah. The case is recorded in 2 Ki. i. 10–12.

55. *Ye know not what manner of spirit ye are of.* You suppose that you are actuated by a proper love for me; but you know not yourselves. It is rather a love of revenge; rather revengeful feelings toward the *Samaritans* than proper feelings toward *me*. We learn here—1st. That *apparent* zeal for God may be only improper opposition toward our fellow-men. 2d. That men, when they wish to honour God, should examine their spirit, and see if there is not lying at the bottom of their professed zeal for God some bad feeling toward their fellow-men. 3d. That the highest opposition which Jesus met with was not inconsistent with *his* loving those who opposed him, and with his seeking to do them good.

56. *For the Son of man*, &c. You should imitate, in your spirit, the Son of man. *He* came not to destroy. If he had come for that purpose, he would have destroyed these Samaritans; but he came to save. He is not soon angry. *He* bears patiently opposition to himself, and *you* should bear opposition to *him*. You should catch his spirit; temper your zeal like his; seek to do good to those who injure you and him; be mild, kind, patient, and forgiving.

57–60. See Notes on Mat. viii. 19–22.

61. *Bid them farewell.* To take leave, inform them of the design, and set things at home in order. Jesus did not suffer this, because he probably saw that he would be influenced by a love of his friends, or by their persuasions, not to return to him. The purpose to be a Christian requires *decision*. Men should not tamper with the world. They should not consult earthly friends about it. They should not even allow worldly friends to give them *advice* whether to be Christians or not. God is to be obeyed rather than man, and they should come forth boldly, and resolve at once to give themselves to his service.

62. *No man, having put his hand*, &c. To put one's hand to a plough is a proverbial expression to signify undertaking any business. In order that a ploughman may accomplish his work, it is necessary to look onward—to be intent on his employment—not to be looking back with regret that he undertook it. So in religion. He that enters on it must do it with his whole heart. He that comes still loving the world—still looking with regret on its pleasures, its wealth, and its honours—that has not *wholly* forsaken them as his portion, cannot be a Christian, and is not fit for the kingdom of God. How searching is this test to those who profess to be Christians! And how solemn the duty of all men to renounce all earthly objects, and to be not only *almost*, but *altogether*, followers of the Son of God! It is perilous to tamper with the world—to look at its pleasures or to seek its society. He that would enter heaven

CHAPTER X.

AFTER[a] these things the Lord appointed other seventy also, and sent them two and two before his face into every city and place, whither he himself would come.

2 Therefore said he unto them, [b]The harvest truly *is* great, but [c]the labourers *are* few: pray ye therefore the Lord of the harvest, that he would send forth labourers into his harvest.

3 Go your ways: behold, I send you forth as lambs among wolves.

a Mat.10.1,&c.; Mar.6.7,&c. b Mat.9.37; Jn.4.35. c 1 Co.3.9; 1 Ti.5.17.

must come with a heart full of love to God; giving *all* into his hands, and prepared always to give up all his property, his health, his friends, his body, his soul to God, when he demands them, or he cannot be a Christian. Religion is everything or nothing. He that is not willing to sacrifice *everything* for the cause of God, is really willing to sacrifice nothing.

CHAPTER X.

1. *After these things.* After the appointment of the twelve apostles, and the transactions recorded in the previous chapters. ¶ *Other seventy.* Seventy others besides the apostles. They were appointed for a different purpose from the apostles. The apostles were to be with him; to hear his instructions; to be witnesses of his miracles, his sufferings, his death, his resurrection and ascension, that they might *then* go and proclaim all these things to the world. The seventy were sent out to preach immediately, and chiefly where he himself was about to come. They were appointed for a temporary object. They were to go into the villages and towns, and prepare the way for his coming. The number *seventy* was a favourite number among the Jews. Thus the family of Jacob that came into Egypt consisted of seventy, Ge. xlvi. 27. The number of elders that Moses appointed to aid him was the same, Nu. xi. 16, 25. The number which composed the great Sanhedrim, or council of the nation, was the same. It is not improbable that our Saviour appointed this *number* with reference to the fact that it so often occurred among the Jews, or after the example of Moses, who appointed seventy to aid him in his work; but it is evident that the office was *temporary*—that it had a specific design—and of course that it would be improper to attempt to find now a *continuation* of it, or a parallel to it, in the Christian ministry. ¶ *Two and two.* There was much wisdom in sending them in this manner. It was done, doubtless, that they might aid one another by mutual counsel, and that they might sustain and comfort one another in their persecutions and trials. Our Lord in this showed the propriety of having *a religious friend*, who would be a confidant and help. Every Christian, and especially every Christian minister, needs such a friend, and should seek some one to whom he can unbosom himself, and with whom he can mingle his feelings and prayers.

2. See Notes on Mat. ix. 36, 37.

3. See Notes on Mat. x. 16.

4. *Purse—scrip—shoes.* See Notes on Mat. x. 10. ¶ *Salute no man by the way. Salutations* among the Orientals did not consist, as among us, of a slight bow or an extension of the hand, but was performed by many embraces and inclinations, and even prostrations of the body on the ground. All this required much *time;* and as the business on which the seventy were sent was urgent, they were required not to *delay* their journey by long and formal salutations of the persons whom they met. "If two Arabs of equal rank meet each other, they extend to each other the right hand, and having clasped, they elevate them as if to kiss them. Each one then draws back his hand and kisses it instead of his friend's, and then places it upon his forehead. The parties then continue the salutation by kissing each other's beard. They give thanks to God that they are once more permitted to see their friend—they pray to the Almighty in his behalf. Sometimes they repeat not less than ten times the ceremony of grasping hands and kissing." It may also be added, in the language of Dr. Thomson (*The Land and the Book*, vol. i. p. 534), that "there is such an amount of insincerity, flattery, and falsehood in the terms of salutation prescribed by etiquette, that our Lord, who is truth itself, desired his representatives to dispense with them as far as possible, perhaps tacitly

4 Carry[d] neither purse, nor scrip, nor shoes; and [e]salute no man by the way.

5 And into whatsoever house ye enter, first say, Peace *be* to this house.

6 And if the [f]son of peace be there, [g]your peace shall rest upon it; if not, it shall turn to you again.

7 And in the same house remain, eating and drinking such things as they give; for [h]the labourer is worthy of his hire. Go[i] not from house to house.

8 And into whatsoever city ye enter, and they receive you, [k]eat such things as are set before you;

9 And heal the sick that are therein, and say unto them, [l]The kingdom of God is come nigh unto you.

10 But into whatsoever city ye enter, and they receive you not, go your ways out into the streets of the same, and say,

d ch.9.3,&c. *e* Ge.24.33,56; 2 Ki.4.29; Pr.4.25. *f* Is.9.6. *g* 2 Th.3.16; Ja.3.18. *h* 1 Co.9.4-14; 1 Ti.5.18. *i* 1 Ti.5.13. *k* 1 Co.10.27. *l* Mat.3.2.

11 Even[m] the very dust of your city, which cleaveth on us, we do wipe off against you: notwithstanding, be ye sure of this, that the kingdom of God is come nigh unto you.

12 But I say unto you, that it shall be more tolerable in that day for Sodom than for that city.

13 Woe[n] unto thee, Chorazin! woe unto thee, Bethsaida! for [o]if the mighty works had been done in Tyre and Sidon which have been done in you, they had a great while ago repented, sitting in sackcloth and ashes.

14 But it shall be more tolerable for Tyre and Sidon at the judgment than for you.

15 And thou, Capernaum, [p]which art exalted to heaven, [q]shalt be thrust down to hell.

16 He[r] that heareth you, heareth me; and [s]he that despiseth you, despiseth me; and [t]he that de-

m ch.9.5. *n* Mat.11.21,&c. *o* Eze.3.6. *p* Is.14.13-15; Je.51.53; Am.9.2,3. *q* Eze.26.20; 31.18. *r* Jn.13.20. *s* Ac.5.4. *t* Jn.5.23.

---

to rebuke them. These 'instructions' were also intended to reprove another propensity which an Oriental can scarcely resist, no matter how urgent his business. If he meets an acquaintance, he must stop and make an endless number of inquiries and answer as many. If they come upon men making a bargain or discussing any other matter, they must pause and intrude their own ideas, and enter keenly into the business, though it in no wise concerns them; and more especially, an Oriental can never resist the temptation to assist *where accounts are being settled* or *money counted out.* The clink of coin has a positive fascination to them. Now the command of our Saviour strictly forbade all such loiterings. They would waste time, distract attention, and in many ways hinder the prompt and faithful discharge of their important mission." The salutation of friends, therefore, was a ceremony which consumed much time; and it was on this account that our Lord on this occasion forbade them to delay their journey to greet others. A similar direction is found in 2 Ki. iv. 29.

5. See Notes on Mat. x. 13.

6. *The son of peace.* That is, if the *house* or *family* be *worthy*, or be disposed to receive you in *peace* and kindness. See Mat. x. 13. *The son of peace* means one *disposed* to peace, or peaceful and kind in his disposition. Comp. Mat. i. 1.

7. See Notes on Mat. x. 11. On this passage Dr. Thomson (*The Land and the Book*, vol. i. p. 534) remarks: "The reason [for the command, 'Go not from house to house'] is very obvious to one acquainted with Oriental customs. When a stranger arrives in a village or an encampment, the neighbours, one after another, must invite him to eat with them. There is a strict etiquette about it, involving much ostentation and hypocrisy, and a failure in the due observance of this system of hospitality is violently resented, and often leads to alienations and feuds among neighbours; it also consumes much time, causes unusual distraction of mind, leads to levity, and every way counteracts the success of a spiritual mission."

spiseth me, despiseth him that sent me.

17 And the seventy returned again with joy, saying, Lord, even the devils are subject unto us through thy name.

18 And he said unto them, I beheld [u]Satan as lightning fall from heaven.

19 Behold, I give unto you power to [v]tread on serpents and scorpions, and over all the power of the enemy; and nothing shall by any means hurt you.

20 Notwithstanding, in this rejoice not, that the spirits are subject unto you; but rather rejoice because [w]your names are written in heaven.

21 In that hour Jesus rejoiced in spirit, and said, I thank thee, O Father, Lord of heaven and earth, that thou hast hid these things from the wise and prudent, and hast revealed them unto babes: even so, Father; for so it seemed good in thy sight.

22 [1]All [x]things are delivered to

u Re.12.8,9. *v* Mar.16.18; Ac.28.5.

w Ex.32.32; Ps.69.28; Is.4.3; Da.12.1; Phi.4.3; He. 12.23; Re.13.8; 20.12; 21.27.

1 Many ancient copies add, *And turning to his disciples, he said.* *x* Mat.28.18; Jn.3.35.

8–12. See Notes on Mat. x. 14, 15.

13–15. See Notes on Mat. xi. 21–24.

16. See Notes on Mat. x. 40.

17. *The devils are subject unto us.* The devils obey us. We have been able to cast them out. ¶ *Through thy name.* When commanded in thy name to come out of those who are possessed.

18. *I beheld Satan*, &c. *Satan* here denotes evidently the prince of the devils who had been cast out by the seventy disciples, for the discourse was respecting their power over evil spirits. *Lightning* is an image of *rapidity* or *quickness.* I saw Satan fall *quickly* or rapidly—as quick as lightning. The phrase "from heaven" is to be referred to the lightning, and does not mean that he saw *Satan* fall *from heaven*, but that he fell as quick as lightning from heaven or from the clouds. The whole expression then may mean, "I saw at your command devils immediately depart, as quick as the flash of lightning. I gave you this power—I saw it put forth—and I give also now, in addition to this, the power to tread on serpents," &c.

19. *To tread on serpents.* Preservation from danger. If you tread on a poisonous reptile that would otherwise injure you, *I* will keep you from danger. If you go among bitter and malignant enemies that would seek your life, *I* will preserve you. See Notes on Mar. xvi. 18. ¶ *Scorpions.* The scorpion is an animal with eight feet, eight eyes, and a long jointed tail, ending in a pointed weapon or sting. It is found in tropical climates, and seldom exceeds 4 inches in length. Its sting is extremely poisonous, and it is sometimes fatal to life. It is in Scripture the emblem of malicious and crafty men. When rolled up it has some resemblance to an egg, Lu. xi. 12; Eze. ii. 6. The

Scorpion.

annexed cut will give an idea of its usual form and appearance. ¶ *The enemy.* Satan. The meaning of this verse is, that Jesus would preserve them from the power of Satan and all his emissaries—from all wicked and crafty men; and this shows that he had divine power. He that can control Satan and his hosts—that can be present to guard from all their machinations, see all their plans, and destroy all their designs, must be clothed with no less than almighty power.

20. *Rather rejoice*, &c. Though it was an honour to work miracles, though it is an honour to be endowed with talents, and influence, and learning, yet it is a subject of *chief* joy that we are numbered among the people of God, and have a title to everlasting life. ¶ *Names are written in heaven.* The names of citizens of a city or state were accustomed to be written in a book or register, from which they were blotted out when they became unworthy, or forfeited the favour of their country. Comp. Ps. lxix. 28; Ex. xxxii. 32; De. ix. 14; Re. iii. 5. That their *names were written in heaven* means that

me of my Father; and [y]no man
knoweth who the Son is, but the
Father; and who the Father is,
but the Son, and *he* to whom the
Son will reveal *him*.
23 And he turned him unto *his*
disciples, and said privately, Blessed
are the eyes which see the things
that ye see:
24 For I tell you that [z]many
prophets and kings have desired
to see those things which ye see,
and have not seen *them;* and to
hear those things which ye hear,
and have not heard *them*.
25 And, behold, a certain lawyer
stood up, and tempted him, saying,
Master, [a]what shall I do to
[b]inherit eternal life?
26 He said unto him, What is
written in the law? how readest
thou?
27 And he answering said, [c]Thou
shalt love the Lord thy God with
all thy heart, and with all thy soul,
and with all thy strength, and with
all thy mind; and [d]thy neighbour
as thyself.
28 And he said unto him, Thou
hast answered right; [e]this do, and
thou shalt live.
29 But he, willing to [f]justify
himself, said unto Jesus, And who
is my [g]neighbour?

y Jn.6.44,46. *z* 1 Pe.1.10.

a Ac.16.30,31. *b* Ga.3.18. *c* De.6.5. *d* Le.19.18. *e* Le.18.5; Ne.9.29; Eze.20.11,21; Ro.10.5; Ga.3.12. *f* Job 32.2; ch.16.15; Ro.4.2; Ga.3.11; Ja.2.24. *g* Mat.5.43,44.

---

they were *citizens* of heaven; that they were friends of God and *approved* by him, and would be permitted to dwell with him. This was of far more value than all *earthly* honour, power, or wealth, and *in* this men should rejoice more than in eminent endowments of influence, learning, talents, or possessions.

21, 22. See Notes on Mat. xi. 25–27.

23, 24. See Notes on Mat. xiii. 16, 17.

25. *A certain lawyer.* One who professed to be well skilled in the laws of Moses, and whose business it was to explain them. ¶ *Stood up.* Rose—came forward to address him. ¶ *Tempted him.* Feigned a desire to be instructed, but did it to perplex him, or to lead him, if possible, to contradict some of the maxims of the law. ¶ *Inherit eternal life.* Be saved. This was the common inquiry among the Jews. *They* had said that man must keep the commandments—the written and oral law.

26. *What is written,* &c. Jesus referred him to the *law* as a safe rule, and asked him what was said there. The lawyer was doubtless endeavouring to justify himself by obeying the law. He trusted to his own works. To bring him off from that ground—to make him feel that it was an unsafe foundation, Jesus showed him what the law *required,* and thus showed him that he needed a better righteousness than his own. This is the proper use of the law. By comparing ourselves with *that* we see our own defects, and are thus prepared to welcome a better righteousness than our own—that of the Lord Jesus Christ. Thus the law becomes a schoolmaster to lead us to him, Ga. iii. 24.

27, 28. See this subject explained in the Notes on Mat. xxii. 37–40.

29. *To justify himself.* Desirous to appear blameless, or to vindicate himself, and show that he had kept the law. Jesus wished to lead him to a proper view of his own sinfulness, and his real departure from the law. The man was desirous of showing that he had kept the law; or perhaps he was desirous of justifying himself for asking the question; of showing that it could not be so easily settled; that a mere reference to the *words* of the law did not determine it. It was still a question what was meant by *neighbour.* The Pharisees held that the *Jews* only were to be regarded as such, and that the obligation did not extend at all to the Gentiles. The lawyer was probably ready to affirm that he had discharged faithfully his duty to his countrymen, and had thus kept the law, and could justify himself. Every sinner is desirous of *justifying himself.* He seeks to do it by his own works. For this purpose he perverts the meaning of the law, destroys its spirituality, and brings *down* the law to *his* standard, rather than attempt to frame his life by *its* requirements.

30. *Jesus answering.* Jesus answered him in a very different manner from

30 And Jesus answering said, A certain *man* went down from Jerusalem to Jericho, and fell among thieves, which stripped him of his raiment, and wounded *him*, and departed, leaving *him* half dead.

31 And by chance there came down a certain priest that way;

---

what he expected. By one of the most tender and affecting narratives to be found anywhere, he made the lawyer his own judge in the case, and constrained him to admit what at first he would probably have denied. He compelled him to acknowledge that a *Samaritan*—of a race most hated of all people by the Jews—had shown the kindness of a neighbour, while a *priest* and a *Levite* had denied it *to their own countrymen.* ¶ *From Jerusalem to Jericho.* Jericho was situated about 15 miles to the north-east of Jerusalem, and about 8 west of the river Jordan. See Notes on Mat. xx. 29. ¶ *Fell among thieves.* Fell among *robbers.* The word *thieves* means those who merely take *property.* These were highwaymen, and not merely took the property, but endangered the life. They were *robbers.* From Jerusalem to Jericho the country was rocky and mountainous, and in some parts scarcely inhabited. It afforded, therefore, among the rocks and fastnesses, a convenient place for highwaymen. This was also a very frequented road. Jericho was a large place, and there was much travelling to Jerusalem. At this time, also, Judea abounded with robbers. Josephus says that at one time Herod the Great dismissed forty thousand men who had been employed in building the temple, a large part of whom became highwaymen (Josephus' *Antiquities*, xv. 7). The following remarks of Professor Hackett, who visited Palestine in 1852, will furnish a good illustration of the scene of this parable. It is remarkable that a parable uttered more than eighteen hundred years ago might still be appropriately *located* in this region. Professor Hackett (*Illustrations of Scripture*, p. 215, 216) says of this region: "It is famous at the present day as the haunt of thieves and robbers. No part of the traveller's journey is so dangerous as the expedition to Jericho and the Dead Sea. The Oriental pilgrims who repair to the Jordan have the protection of an escort of Turkish soldiers; and others who would make the same journey must either go in company with them, or provide for their safety by procuring a special guard. I was so fortunate as to be able to accompany the great caravan at the time of the annual pilgrimage. Yet, in spite of every precaution, hardly a season passes in which some luckless wayfarer is not killed or robbed in 'going down from Jerusalem to Jericho.' The place derives its hostile character from its terrible wildness and desolation. If we might conceive of the ocean as being suddenly congealed and petrified when its waves are tossed mountain high, and dashing in wild confusion against each other, we should then have some idea of the aspect of the desert in which the Saviour has placed so truthfully the parable of the good Samaritan. The ravines, the almost inaccessible cliffs, the caverns, furnish admirable lurking-places for robbers. They can rush forth unexpectedly upon their victims, and escape as soon almost beyond the possibility of pursuit.

"Every circumstance in this parable, therefore, was full of significance to those who heard it. The Saviour delivered it near Bethany, on the border of the frightful desert, Lu. x. 25, 38. Jericho was a sacerdotal city. The passing of priests and Levites between that place and Jerusalem was an everyday occurrence. The idea of a caravanserai or 'inn' on the way was not invented, probably, for the sake of the allegory, but borrowed from the landscape. There are the ruins now of such a shelter for the benighted or unfortunate on one of the heights which overlook the infested road. Thus it is that the instructions of our Lord derive often the form and much of their pertinence from the accidental connections of time and place."

31. *By chance.* Accidentally, or as it happened. It means that he did not do it with a *design* to aid the man that was wounded. ¶ *A certain priest.* It is said that not less than twelve thousand priests and Levites dwelt at Jericho; and as their business was at Jerusalem, of course there would be many of them constantly travelling on that road. ¶ *When he saw him.* He saw him lie, but came not near him. ¶ *Passed by on the other side.* On the farther side of the way. Did not turn out of his course even to come and see him.

and when he saw him, he [h]passed
by on the other side.
32 And likewise a Levite, when
he was at the place, [i]came and
looked *on him*, and passed by on
the other side.
33 But a certain [k]Samaritan, as
he journeyed, came where he was;
and when he saw him he had [l]compassion *on him*,
34 And went to *him*, and [m]bound
up his wounds, pouring in oil and
wine, and set him on his own beast,
and brought him to an inn, and
took care of him.
35 And on the morrow, when he
departed, he took out two [2]pence,
and gave *them* to the host, and
said unto him, Take care of him;
and whatsoever thou spendest
more, when I come again [n]I will
repay thee.

h Ps.38.11. *i* Ps.109.25; Pr.27.10. *k* Jn.4.9. *l* Ex.2.6. *m* Ps.147.3; Is.1.6.

[2] See Mat.20.2. *n* Pr.19.17; ch.14.14.

32. *A Levite.* The Levites, as well as the priests, were of the tribe of Levi, and were set apart to the duties of religion. The peculiar duty of the priest was *to offer sacrifice* at the temple; to present incense; to conduct the morning and evening services of the temple, &c. The office or duty of the *Levites* was to render assistance to the priests in their services. In the journey of the Israelites through the wilderness, it was their duty to transport the various parts of the tabernacle and the sacred utensils. It was their duty to see that the tabernacle and the temple were kept clean; to prepare supplies for the sanctuary, such as oil, incense, wine, &c. They had also the care of the sacred revenues, and after the time of David they conducted the sacred *music* of the temple service, Nu. viii. 5–22; 1 Ch. xxiii. 3–5, 24–32; xxiv. 27–31. ¶ *Came and looked on him.* It is remarked by critics, here, that the expression used does not denote, as in the case of the priest, that he accidentally saw him and took no farther notice of him, but that he *came and looked on him more attentively*, but still did nothing to relieve him.

33. *A certain Samaritan.* The Samaritans were the most inveterate foes of the Jews. They had no dealings with each other. See Notes on Mat. x. 5. It was this fact which rendered the conduct of this good man so striking, and which was thus set in strong contrast with the conduct of the priest and the Levite. *They* would not help their own afflicted and wounded countryman. *He*, who could not be expected to aid a Jew, overcame all the usual hostility between the people; saw in the wounded man a neighbour, a brother, one who needed aid; and kindly denied himself to show kindness to the stranger.

34. *Pouring in oil and wine.* These were often used in medicine to heal wounds. Probably they were mingled together, and had a highly sanative quality. How strikingly is his conduct contrasted with the priest and Levite! and how particularly as well as beautifully by this does our Saviour show what *we* ought to do to those who are in circumstances of need! He does not merely say *in general* that he showed him kindness, but he *told how* it was done. He stopped—came where he was—pitied him—bound up his wounds—set him on his own beast—conducted him to a tavern—passed the night with him, and then secured the kind attendances of the landlord, promising him to pay him for his trouble—and all this without desiring or expecting any reward. If this had been by a *Jew*, it would have been signal kindness; if it had been by a *Gentile*, it would also have been great kindness; but it was by a *Samaritan*—a man of a nation most hateful to the Jews, and therefore it most strikingly shows what *we* are to do to friends and foes when they are in distress.

35. *Two pence.* About 27 cents, or 1*s.* 2*d.* This may seem a small sum, but we are to remember that that sum was probably ten times as valuable then as now—that is, that it would purchase ten times as much food and the common necessaries of life as the same sum would now. Besides, it is probable that all the man wanted was *attention* and kindness, and for all these it was the purpose of the Samaritan to *pay* when he returned. ¶ *The host.* The innkeeper.

36. *Was neighbour.* Showed the kindness of a neighbour, or evinced the proper feelings of a neighbour. The lawyer had asked him who was his neighbour? Jesus in this beautiful nar-

36 Which now of these three, thinkest thou, was neighbour unto him that fell among the thieves?

37 And he said, [o]He that showed mercy on him. Then said Jesus unto him, Go, and do thou likewise.

38 Now it came to pass, as they went, that he entered into a certain village; and a certain woman, named [p]Martha, received him into her house.

39 And she had a sister called

o Pr.14.21; Ho.6.6; Mi.6.8; Mat.23.23.

p Jn.11.1; 12.2,3.

---

rative showed him who and what a neighbour was, and he did this in a way that disarmed his prejudice, deeply affected him in regard to his own duty, and evinced the beauty of religion. Had he *at first* told him that a Samaritan might be a neighbour to a Jew and deserve his kindness, he would have been at once revolted at it; but when, by a beautiful and affecting narrative, he brought the *man himself* to see that it might be, he was constrained to admit it. Here we see the beauty of a parable and its use. It disarmed prejudice, fixed the attention, took the mind gently yet irresistibly, and prevented the possibility of cavil or objection. Compare, also, the address of Nathan to David, 2 Sa. xii. 1-7.

37. *He that showed mercy.* His *Jewish* prejudice would not permit him *to name* the Samaritan, but there was no impropriety, even in his view, in saying that the man who showed so much mercy was really the neighbour to the afflicted, and not he who *professed* to be his neighbour, but who would *do nothing* for his welfare. ¶ *Go, and do thou likewise.* Show the same kindness to *all*—to friend and foe—and *then* you will have evidence that you keep the law, and not *till* then. Of this man we know nothing farther; but from this inimitably beautiful parable we may learn—1. That the knowledge of the law is useful to make us acquainted with our own sinfulness and need of a Saviour. 2. That it is not he who *professes* most kindness that really loves us most, but he who will most deny himself that he may do us good in times of want. 3. That religion requires us to do good to *all* men, however *accidentally* we may become acquainted with their calamities. 4. That we should do good to our enemies. Real love to them will lead us to deny ourselves, and to sacrifice our own welfare, that we may help them in times of distress and alleviate their wants. 5. That he is really our neighbour who does us the most good—who helps us in our necessities, and especially if he does this when there has been *a controversy or difference* between us and him. 6. We hence see the beauty of religion. Nothing else will induce men to surmount their prejudices, to overcome opposition, and to do good to those who are at enmity with them. True religion teaches us to regard every man as our neighbour; prompts us to do good to all, to forget all national or sectional distinctions, and to aid all those who are in circumstances of poverty and want. If religion were valuable for nothing *but this*, it would be the most lovely and desirable principle on earth, and all, especially in their early years, should seek it. Nothing that a young person can gain will be so valuable as the feeling that regards all the world as one great family, and to learn early to do good TO ALL. 7. The difference between the Jew and the Samaritan was a difference in *religion* and *religious opinion;* and from the example of the latter we may learn that, while men differ in *opinions* on subjects of religion, and while they are zealous for what they hold to be the truth, still they should treat each other kindly; that they should aid each other in necessity; and that they should thus show that religion is a principle superior to the love of sect, and that the cord which binds man to man is one that is to be sundered by no difference of opinion, that Christian kindness is to be marred by no forms of worship, and by no bigoted attachment for what we esteem the doctrines of the gospel.

38. *A certain village.* Bethany. See Jn. xi. 1. It was on the eastern declivity of the Mount of Olives. See Notes on Mat. xxi. 1. ¶ *Received him.* Received him kindly and hospitably. From this it would seem that *Martha* was properly the mistress of the house. Possibly she was a widow, and her brother Lazarus and younger sister Mary lived with her; and as *she* had the care of the household, this will also show why she was so diligently employed about domestic affairs.

Mary, which also [q]sat at Jesus' feet, and heard his word.

40 But Martha was cumbered about much serving, and came to him and said, Lord, dost thou not care that my sister hath left me to serve alone? Bid her, therefore, that she help me.

41 And Jesus answered and said unto her, Martha, Martha, [r]thou art careful and troubled about many things:

42 But [s]one thing is needful; and Mary hath chosen that good part, which shall not be taken away from her.

q ch.8.35; Ac.22.3.

r Mar.4.19; ch.21.34; 1 Co.7.32,35.

s Ps.27.4; 73.25; Ec.12.13; Mar.8.36; ch.18.22; 1 Co. 13.3.

---

39. *Sat at Jesus' feet.* This was the ancient posture of disciples or learners. They sat at the *feet* of their teachers—that is, beneath them, in a humble place. Hence Paul is represented as having been brought up at the *feet* of Gamaliel, Ac. xxii. 3. When it is said that Mary sat at Jesus' feet, it means that she was *a disciple* of his; that she listened attentively to his instructions, and was anxious to learn his doctrine.

40. *Martha was cumbered about much serving.* Was much distracted with the cares of the family, and providing suitably to entertain the Saviour. It should be said here that there is no evidence that Martha had a worldly or covetous disposition. Her anxiety was to provide suitable entertainment for the Lord Jesus. As mistress of the family, this care properly devolved on her; and the only fault which can be charged on her was too earnest a desire to make such entertainment, when she might have sat with Mary at his feet, and, perhaps, too much haste and fretfulness in speaking to Jesus about Mary. ¶ *Dost thou not care*, &c. This was an improper reproof of our Lord, as if *he* encouraged Mary in neglecting her duty. Or perhaps Martha supposed that Mary was sitting there to show him the proper expressions of courtesy and kindness, and that she would not think it proper to leave him without his direction and permission. She therefore *hinted* to Jesus her busy employments, her need of the aid of her sister, and requested that he would signify his wish that Mary should assist her.

41. *Thou art careful.* Thou art *anxious.* ¶ *Troubled.* Disturbed, distracted, very solicitous. ¶ *Many things.* The many objects which excite your attention in the family. This was probably designed as a slight reproof, or a tender hint that she was improperly anxious about those things, and that she should, with Mary, rather choose to hear the discourses of heavenly wisdom.

42. *But one thing is needful.* That is, religion, or piety. This is eminently and peculiarly needful. Other things are of little importance. This should be secured *first*, and then all other things will be added. See 1 Ti. iv. 8; Mat. vi. 33. ¶ *That good part.* The portion of the gospel; the love of God, and an interest in his kingdom. She had chosen to be a Christian, and to give up her time and affections to God. ¶ *Which shall not be taken away. God* will not take away his grace from his people, neither shall any man pluck them out of his hand, Jn. x. 28, 29.

From this interesting narrative we learn—1st. That the cares of this life are dangerous, even when they seem to be most lawful and commendable. Nothing of a worldly nature could have been more proper than to provide for the Lord Jesus and supply his wants. Yet even *for this*, because it too much engrossed her mind, the Lord Jesus gently reproved Martha. So a care for our families may be the means of our neglecting religion and losing our souls. 2d. It is of more importance to attend to the instructions of the Lord Jesus than to be engaged in the affairs of the world. The one will abide for ever; the other will be but for a little time. 3d. There *are* times when it is proper to suspend worldly employments, and to attend to the affairs of the soul. It *was* proper for Mary to do it. It would have been proper for Martha to have done it. It *is* proper for all—on the Sabbath and at other occasional seasons—seasons of prayer and for searching the word of God—to suspend worldly concerns and to attend to religion. 4th. If attention to religion be omitted at *the proper time*, it will always be omitted. If Mary had neglected to hear Jesus *then*, she might never have heard him. 5th. Piety is the chief thing needed. Other things will perish. We shall soon die. All that we can

CHAPTER XI.

AND it came to pass, that as he was praying in a certain place, when he ceased, one of his disciples said unto him, Lord, teach us to pray, as John also taught his disciples.

2 And he said unto them, When ye pray, say, [a]Our Father which art in heaven, Hallowed be thy name. Thy kingdom come. Thy will be done, as in heaven, so in earth.

3 Give us [1]day by day our daily bread.

a Mat.6.9,&c. [1] or, *for the day.*

4 And forgive us our sins; [b]for we also forgive every one that is indebted to us. And lead us not into temptation; but deliver us from evil.

5 And he said unto them, Which of you shall have a friend, and shall go unto him at midnight, and say unto him, Friend, lend me three loaves;

6 For a friend of mine [2]in his journey is come to me, and I have nothing to set before him:

7 And he from within shall answer and say, Trouble me not: the

b Mar.11.25,26. [2] or, *out of his way.*

---

gain we must leave. But the *soul* will live. There is a judgment-seat; there is a heaven; there is a hell; and *all* that is needful to prepare us to die, and to make us happy for ever, is to be a friend of Jesus, and to listen to his teaching. 6th. Piety is the chief ornament in a female. It sweetens every other virtue; adorns every other grace; gives new loveliness to the tenderness, mildness, and grace of the female character. Nothing is more lovely than a female sitting at the feet of the meek and lowly Jesus, like Mary; nothing more unlovely than entire absorption in the affairs of the world, like Martha. The most lovely female is she who has most of the spirit of Jesus; the least amiable, she who neglects her soul—who is proud, gay, thoughtless, envious, and unlike the meek and lowly Redeemer. At his feet are peace, purity, joy. Everywhere else an alluring and wicked world steals the affections and renders us vain, gay, wicked, proud, and unwilling to die.

CHAPTER XI.

1. *As he was praying.* Luke has taken notice of our Saviour's praying often. Thus, at his baptism (ch. iii. 21); in the wilderness (ch. v. 16); before the appointment of the apostles, he continued all night in prayer (ch. vi. 12); he was alone praying (ch. ix. 18); his transfiguration also took place when he went up to pray (ch. ix. 28, 29). ¶ *Teach us to pray.* Probably they had been struck with the excellency and fervour of his prayers, and, recollecting that *John* had taught his disciples to pray, they asked him also to teach *them.* We learn, therefore—1st. That the gifts and graces of others should lead us to desire the same. 2d. That the true method of praying can be learned only by our being properly taught. Indeed, we cannot pray acceptably at all unless God shall teach us how to pray. 3d. That it is proper for us to meditate beforehand what we are to ask of God, and to arrange our thoughts, that we may not come thoughtlessly into his presence.

2–4. See this passage explained in the Notes on Mat. vi. 9–13.

4. *For we also forgive,* &c. This is somewhat different from the expression in Matthew, though the sense is the same. The idea is, that unless we forgive others, God will not forgive us; and unless we come to him *really* forgiving all others, we cannot expect pardon. It does not mean that by forgiving others we *deserve* forgiveness ourselves, or *merit it,* but that this is a disposition or state of mind without which God cannot consistently pardon us. ¶ *Every one that is indebted to us.* Every one that has *injured* us. This does not refer to pecuniary transactions, but to offences similar to those which *we* have committed against God, and for which we ask forgiveness. Besides the variations in the *expressions* in this prayer, Luke has omitted the doxology, or close, altogether; and this shows that Jesus did not intend that we should always use just this *form,* but that it was a general direction how to pray; or, rather, that we were to pray for these *things,* though not always using the same words.

door is now shut, and my children
are with me in bed; I cannot rise
and give thee.
8 I say unto you, Though he
will not rise and give him because
he is his friend, yet [c]because of his
importunity he will rise and give
him as many as he needeth.
9 And I say unto you, [d]Ask, and
it shall be given you; seek, and ye
shall find; knock, and it shall be
opened unto you.
10 For every one that asketh,
receiveth; and he that seeketh,
findeth; and to him that knocketh,
it shall be opened.

c ch.18.1-8.

d Mat.7.7; 21.22; Jn.15.7; Ja.1.5; 1 Jn.3.22.

5-7. *And he said unto them*, &c. Jesus proceeds to show that, in order to obtain the blessing, it was necessary to *persevere* in asking for it. For this purpose he introduces the case of a friend's asking bread of another for one who had come to him unexpectedly. His design is solely to show the necessity of being *importunate* or persevering in prayer to God. ¶ *At midnight.* A time when it would be most inconvenient for his friend to help him; an hour when he would naturally be in bed and his house shut. ¶ *Three loaves.* There is nothing particularly denoted by the number *three* in this place. Jesus often threw in such particulars merely to fill up the story, or to preserve the consistency of it. ¶ *My children are with me in bed.* This does not necessarily mean that they were in the *same bed* with him, but that they were *all* in bed, the house was still, the door was shut, and it was troublesome for him to rise at that time of night to accommodate him. It should be observed, however, that the customs of Orientals differ in this respect from our own. Among them it is not uncommon—indeed it is the common practice—for a whole family—parents, children, and servants—to sleep in the same room. See *The Land and the Book*, vol. i. p. 180. This is *not* to be applied to God, as if it were troublesome to him to be sought unto, or as if *he* would ever reply to a sinner in that manner. All that is to be applied to God in this parable is simply that it is proper to *persevere* in prayer. As a *man* often gives because the request is *repeated*, and as one is not discouraged because the favour that he asks of his neighbour is *delayed*, so God often answers us after long and importunate requests.

8. *I tell you.* The Latin Vulgate here adds, "if he shall continue knocking." Though this is not in the Greek, yet it is indispensable that it should be understood in order to the sense. Knocking *once* would not denote *importunity*, but it was because he *continued* knocking. ¶ *His importunity.* His troublesome perseverance; his continuing to disturb the man, and refusing to take any denial. The word *importunity* denotes perseverance in an object, without any regard to time, place, or circumstances—an improper perseverance. By this the man was influenced. Rather than be disturbed, he would rise and give what was asked. This is to be applied to God in no other sense than that he often hears prayers and grants blessings even *long after* they appear to be unanswered or withheld. He does not promise to give blessings *at once.* He promises only that he will do it, or *will answer* prayer. But he often causes his people long to wait. He tries their faith. He leaves them to persevere for months or years, until they feel *entirely* their dependence on him, until they see that they can obtain the blessing in no other way, and until they are *prepared* to receive it. Often they are not *prepared* to receive it when they ask it at first. They may be proud, or have no just sense of their dependence, or they would not value the blessing, or it may *at that time* not be best for them to obtain it. But let no one despair. If the thing is for *our* good, and if it is proper that it *should* be granted, God will give it. Let us first ask aright; let us see that our minds are in a proper state; let us feel our need of the blessing; let us inquire whether God has *promised such* a blessing, and *then* let us persevere until God gives it. Again: men, when they ask anything of God, often give over seeking. They go *once*, and if it is not granted they are discouraged. It is not so when we ask anything of men. *Then* we persevere; we take no denial; we go again, and *press* the matter till we obtain it. So we should of God. We should go again and again, until the prayer is heard, and God grants what we ask of him.

11 If a son shall ask bread of any of you that is a father, will he give him a stone? or if *he ask* a fish, will he for a fish give him a serpent?

12 Or if he shall ask an egg, will he [3]offer him a scorpion?

13 If ye then, being evil, know how to give good gifts unto your children, how much more shall *your* heavenly Father give the Holy Spirit to them that ask him!

14 And[e] he was casting out a devil, and it was dumb. And it came to pass, when the devil was gone out, the dumb spake; and the people wondered.

15 But some of them said, He casteth out devils through [4]Beelzebub, the chief of the devils.

16 And others, [f]tempting *him*, sought of him a sign from heaven.

17 But he, [g]knowing their thoughts, said unto them, [h]Every kingdom divided against itself is brought to desolation; and a house *divided* against a house falleth.

18 If Satan also be divided against himself, how shall his kingdom stand? because ye say that I cast out devils through Beelzebub.

19 And if I by Beelzebub cast out devils, by whom do your sons cast *them* out? therefore shall they be your judges.

20 But if I with the [i]finger of God cast out devils, no doubt the kingdom of God is come upon you.

21 When a strong man armed keepeth his palace, his goods are in peace;

22 But when a [k]stronger than he shall come upon him, and overcome him, he taketh from him all his armour wherein he trusted, and divideth his spoils.

23 He that is not with me is against me; and he that gathereth not with me scattereth.

24 When the unclean spirit is gone out of a man, he walketh through dry places, seeking rest; and finding none, he saith, I will return unto my house whence I came out.

25 And when he cometh, he findeth *it* swept and garnished.

26 Then goeth he, and taketh *to him* seven other spirits more wicked than himself; and they enter in, and dwell there: and the last *state* of that man is [l]worse than the first.

27 And it came to pass, as he spake these things, a certain woman of the company lifted up her voice and said unto him, [m]Blessed *is* the womb that bare thee, and the paps which thou hast sucked.

28 But he said, [n]Yea, rather

3 *give*. 4 *Beelzebul*, so ver.18,19. e Mat.9.32; 12.22,&c. f Mat.12.38; 16.1. g Jn.2.25. h Mat.12.25; Mar.3.24.

i Ex.8.19. k Is.53.12; Col.2.15. l Jn.5.14; He.6.4; 10.26,27; 2 Pe.2.20,21. m ch.1.28,48. n Ps.119.1,2; Mat.7.21; ch.8.21; Ja.1.25.

9–12. See this explained in the Notes on Mat. vii. 7–11.

12. *A scorpion.* See Notes on Lu. x. 19. Dr. Thomson (*The Land and the Book*, vol. i. p. 379) says: "There is no imaginable likeness between an egg and the ordinary black scorpion of this country, neither in colour nor size, nor, when the tail is extended, in shape; but old writers speak of a *white* scorpion, and such a one, with the tail folded up, as in specimens of fossil trilobites, would not look unlike a small egg. Perhaps the contrast, however, refers only to the different properties of the egg and the scorpion, which is sufficiently emphatic."

Pliny (*N. H.*, xi. 25) says that in Judea the scorpions are about the size of an egg, and not unlike one in shape.

14–23. See this passage explained in the Notes on Mat. xii. 22–30.

24-26. See Notes on Mat. xii. 43-45.

27, 28. *A certain woman.* One of the crowd. ¶ *Blessed* is *the womb*, &c. She thought that the *mother* of such a person must be peculiarly happy in having such a son. ¶ *Yea, rather blessed*, &c. Jesus admits that she was happy—that

blessed *are* they that hear the
word of God, and keep it.
29 And when the people were
gathered thick together, he began
to say, This is an evil generation:
they seek a sign, and [o]there shall
no sign be given it but the sign of
Jonas the prophet.
30 For as [p]Jonas was a sign unto
the Ninevites, so shall also the Son
of man be to this generation.
31 The [q]queen of the south shall
rise up in the judgment with the
men of this generation, and condemn them; for she came from
the utmost parts of the earth to
hear the wisdom of Solomon; and,
behold, a greater than Solomon *is*
here.
32 The men of Nineveh shall
rise up in the judgment with this
generation, and shall condemn it;
for[r] they repented at the preaching of Jonas; and, behold, a greater
than Jonas *is* here.
33 No[s] man, when he hath
lighted a candle, putteth *it* in a
secret place, neither under a bushel,
but on a candlestick, that they
which come in may see the light.
34 The [t]light of the body is the
eye: therefore, when thine eye is
single, thy whole body also is full
of light; but when [u]*thine eye* is
evil, thy body also *is* full of darkness.
35 Take heed, therefore, that
the light which is in thee be not
darkness.
36 If thy whole body, therefore,
be [v]full of light, having no part
dark, the whole shall be full of
light, as when [5]the [w]bright shining
of a candle doth give thee light.
37 And as he spake, a certain
Pharisee besought him to dine

o Mat.12.40,&c.; Mar.8.12. p Jonah 1.17; 2.10.
q 1 Ki.10.1,&c. r Jonah 3.5,10.

s Mat.5.15,&c.; Mar.4.21; ch.8.16.
t Mat.6.22,&c. u Pr.28.22; Mar.7.22.
v Ps.119.105; Pr.6.23; Is.8.20; 2 Co.4.6.
5 *a candle by its bright shining.* w Pr.4.18; 20.27.

it was an honour to be his mother, but he says that the chief happiness, the highest honour, was to obey the word of God. Compared with this, all earthly distinctions and honours are as nothing. Man's greatest dignity is in keeping the holy commandments of God, and in being prepared for heaven. See Notes on ch. x. 20.

29-32. See Notes on Mat. xii. 38-42.

33-36. These verses are found in Matthew, but in a different connection. See Notes on Mat. v. 15; vi. 22, 23.

37. *And as he spake.* While he was addressing the people, and particularly while he was reproving that generation and declaring its crimes. ¶ *A certain Pharisee.* The Pharisees had been particularly referred to in the discourse of the Saviour recorded in the previous verses. This one, perhaps, having felt particularly the force of the remarks of Jesus, and being desirous of being alone with him, invited him to go home with him. There is little doubt that this was for the purpose of drawing him away from the people; that he did it with a malignant intention, perhaps with a design to confute Jesus in private, or to reprove him for thus condemning the whole nation as he did. He might have seen that those who attacked Jesus *publicly* were commonly unsuccessful, and he desired, probably, to encounter him more privately. ¶ *Besought him.* Asked him. ¶ *To dine with him.* The Jews, as well as the Greeks and Romans, had but two principal meals. The first was a slight repast, and was taken about ten or eleven o'clock of our time, and consisted chiefly of fruit, milk, cheese, &c. The second meal was partaken of about three o'clock P.M., and was their principal meal. The *first* is the one here intended. ¶ *He went in.* Though he knew the evil design of the Pharisee, yet he did not decline the invitation. He knew that it might afford him an opportunity to do good. These two things are to be observed in regard to our Saviour's conduct in such matters: 1st. That he did not decline an invitation to dine with a man simply because he was a Pharisee, or because he was a wicked man. Hence he was charged with being gluttonous, and a friend of publicans and sinners, Mat. xi. 19. 2d. He seized upon all occasions to do good. He never shrank from declaring the truth, and making such

with him; and he went in and
sat down to meat.

38 And[x] when the Pharisee saw
it, he marvelled that he had not
first washed before dinner.

39 And the Lord said unto him,
Now[y] do ye Pharisees make clean
the outside of the cup and the
platter, but [z]your inward part is
full of ravening and wickedness.

40 *Ye* fools, did not he that made
that which is without make that
which is within also?

41 But[a] rather give alms [6]of
such things as ye have; and, behold,
all things are clean unto you.

x Mar.7.3. *y* Mat.23.25.

z Tit.1.15. *a* Is.58.7; ch.12.33. [6] or, *as you are able.*

---

occasions the means of spreading the gospel. If Christians and Christian ministers would follow the example of the Saviour always, they would avoid all scandal, and might do even in such places a vast amount of good. ¶ *Sat down.* Reclined at the table. See Notes on Mat. xxiii. 6.

38. *Saw* it. Saw that he sat immediately down without washing. ¶ *Marvelled.* Wondered. Was amazed. It was so unusual, and in his view so improper. ¶ *Had not first washed.* He wondered particularly, as he had been among a mixed multitude, and they esteemed the *touch* of such persons polluting. They never ate, therefore, without such washing. The origin of the custom of washing with so much formality *before* they partook of their meals was that they did not use, as we do, knives and forks, but used their hands only. Hence, as their hands would be often in a dish on the table, it was esteemed proper that they should be washed clean before eating. Nor was their impropriety in the thing itself, but the Pharisees made it a matter of ceremony; they placed no small part of their religion in such ceremonies; and it was right, therefore, that our Lord should take occasion to reprove them for it. Comp. Mar. vii. 4.

39. See Mat. xxiii. 25. *Ravening.* Robbery, plunder. Here the sense is that the cup and platter were filled with what had been unjustly taken from others. That is, they lived by their wickedness; their food was procured by dishonesty and extortion. This was a most terrible charge; and as it was applied, among others, to the man who had invited the Saviour to dine with him, it shows that nothing would prevent his dealing faithfully with the souls of men. Even in the Pharisee's own house, and when expressly invited to partake of his hospitality, he loved his soul so much that he faithfully warned him of his crimes.

40. Ye *fools.* How unwise and wicked is your conduct! The word denotes not only *want of wisdom*, but also *wickedness.* Comp. Ps. xiv. 1; Pr. xiii. 19; xiv. 9. Your conduct is not merely *foolish*, but it is a cloak for sin—designed to countenance wickedness. ¶ *Did not he*, &c. Did not God, who made the *body*, make also the *soul?* You Pharisees take great pains to cleanse the *body*, under a pretence of pleasing *God.* Did *he* not also make the *mind?* and is it not of as much importance that *that* should be pure, as that the body should?

41. *Alms.* Charity. Benefactions to the poor. ¶ *Such things as ye have.* Your property; though it has been gained unjustly: though you have lived by rapine, and have amassed wealth in an improper manner, yet, *since you have it*, it is your duty to make the best of it and do good. By giving to the poor, you may show your repentance for your crimes in amassing money in this manner. You may show that you disapprove of your former course of life, and are disposed henceforward to live honestly. If this be the meaning of this passage, then it shows what is the duty of those who have by unjust gains become wealthy, and who are *then* converted to God. It may not be possible for them in every case to make exact restitution to those whom they have injured; thousands of instances of wrong they may have forgotten; many persons whom they have injured may have died; but still they may show, by giving to others, that they do not think their gains acquired honestly, and that they truly repent. They may devote their property to God; distribute it to the poor; or give it to send the gospel to the heathen world. Thus may they show that they disapprove of their former conduct; and thus may be seen one great principle of God's government —*that good finally comes out of evil.* ¶ *And behold*, &c. Doing this will show that you are a true penitent, and the

42 But [b]woe unto you, Pharisees! for ye tithe mint, and rue, and all manner of herbs, and pass over judgment and the love of God. These ought ye to have done, and not to leave the other undone.

43 Woe unto you, Pharisees! [c]for ye love the uppermost seats in the synagogues, and greetings in the markets.

44 Woe unto you, scribes and Pharisees, hypocrites! for ye are as [d]graves which appear not, and the men that walk over *them* are not aware *of them.*

45 Then answered one of the lawyers, and said unto him, Master, thus saying, thou reproachest us also.

46 And he said, Woe unto you also, *ye* lawyers! for ye lade men with burdens grievous to be borne, and ye yourselves [e]touch not the burdens with one of your fingers.

47 Woe unto you! for ye build the sepulchres of the prophets, and your fathers killed them.

48 Truly ye bear witness that [f]ye allow the deeds of your fathers: for [g]they indeed killed them, and ye build their sepulchres.

49 Therefore also said the wisdom of God, I will send them prophets and apostles, and *some* of them they shall slay and persecute;

50 That the blood of all the prophets, which was shed from

b Mat.23.23,27. *c* Mat.23.6; Mar.12.38. *d* Ps.5.9. *e* Is.58.6. *f* Eze.18.19. *g* He.11.35,37.

---

remainder of your property you will enjoy with a feeling that you have done your duty, and no longer be smitten with the consciousness of hoarding unjust gains. The object of the Saviour here seems to have been to bring the Pharisee to repentance. Repentance consists in sorrow for sin, and in forsaking it. This he endeavoured to produce by showing him—1st, the *evil* and hypocrisy of his conduct; and, 2d, by exhorting him to *forsake* his sins, and to *show* this by doing good. Thus doing, he would evince that the *mind* was clean as well the *body;* the *inside* as well as the *outside.*

42. See Mat. xxiii. 23. ¶ *Rue.* This is a small garden plant, and is used as a medicine. It has a rosy flower, a bitter, penetrating taste, and a strong smell.

43, 44. See Mat. xxiii. 6, 27.

45. *Lawyers.* Men learned in the law; but it is not known in what way the lawyers differed from the *scribes*, or whether they were Pharisees or Sadducees. ¶ *Thus saying, thou,* &c. He felt that the remarks of Jesus about loving the chief seats, &c., applied to them as well as to the Pharisees. His conscience told him that if *they* were to blame, *he* was also, and he therefore applied the discourse to himself. ¶ *Reproachest.* Accusest. Dost calumniate or blame *us*, for we do the same things. Sinners often consider *faithfulness* as *reproach*—they know not how to separate them. Jesus did *not* reproach or abuse them. He dealt faithfully with them; reproved them; told them the unvarnished truth. Such faithfulness is rare; but when it *is* used, we must expect that men will flinch, perhaps be enraged. Though their consciences tell them they are *guilty*, still they will consider it as abuse.

46. See Notes on Mat. xxiii. 4.

47–51. See Notes on Mat. xxiii. 29–36.

49. *The wisdom of God.* By the *wisdom of God*, here, is undoubtedly meant the Saviour himself. What he immediately says is not written in the Old Testament. Jesus is called *the word of God* (Jn. i. 1), because he is the medium by which God *speaks* or makes his will known. He is called *the wisdom of God*, because by him God makes his wisdom known in creation (Col. i. 13–18) and in redemption (1 Co. i. 30). Many have also thought that the Messiah was referred to in the 8th chapter of Proverbs, under the name of Wisdom. ¶ *I will send,* &c. See Lu. x. 3; Mat. x. 16. ¶ *Shall slay,* &c. Comp. Jn. xvi. 2; Ac. vii. 52, 59; Ja. v. 10; Ac. xii. 2; xxii. 19; 2 Co. xi. 24, 25; 2 Ch. xxxvi. 15, 16.

52. *Woe unto you, lawyers!* See Notes on Mat. xxiii. 13. ¶ *The key of knowledge.* A key is made to open a lock or door. By their false interpretation of the Old Testament they had taken away the true key or method of understanding it. They had hindered the people

the foundation of the world, may
be [h]required of this generation;
51 From the blood of [i]Abel unto
the blood of [k]Zacharias, which
perished between the altar and
the temple: verily I say unto you,
It shall be [l]required of this generation.
52 Woe unto you, lawyers! for
ye have taken away the [m]key of
knowledge: ye entered not in
yourselves, and them that were
entering in ye [7]hindered.
53 And as he said these things
unto them, the scribes and Pharisees began to urge *him* vehemently,
and to [n]provoke him to speak of
many things;
54 Laying wait for him, [o]and
seeking to catch something out of
his mouth, that they might accuse
him.

h Ex.20.5; Je.51.56. *i* Ge.4.8. *k* 2 Ch.24.20. *l* Je.7.28,29. *m* Mal.2.7.

7 or, *forbad*. *n* 1 Co.13.5. *o* Mar.12.13.

from understanding it aright. "You endeavour to prevent the people also from understanding the Scriptures respecting the Messiah, and those who were coming to *me* ye hindered." If there is any sin of peculiar magnitude, it is that of keeping the people in ignorance; and few men are so guilty as they who by false instructions prevent them from coming to a knowledge of the truth, and embracing it as it is in Jesus.

53. *To urge* him *vehemently*. To press upon him *violently*. They were enraged against him. They therefore pressed upon him; asked him many questions; sought to entrap him, that they might accuse him. ¶ *Provoke him*, &c. This means that they put many questions to him about various matters, without giving him proper time to answer. They proposed questions as fast as possible, and about as many things as possible, that they might get him, in the hurry, to say something that would be wrong, that they might thus accuse him. This was a remarkable instance of their cunning, malignity, and unfairness.

54. *Laying wait for him*. Or, rather, laying *snares* for him. It means that they endeavoured to entangle him in his talk; that they did as men do who catch birds—who lay snares, and deceive them, and take them unawares. ¶ *That they might accuse him*. Before the Sanhedrim, or great council of the nation, and thus secure his being put to death.

From this we may learn—1st. That faithful reproofs must be expected to excite opposition and hatred. Though the *conscience* may be roused, and may testify against the man that is reproved, yet that does not prevent his hating the reproof and the reprover. 2d. We see here the manner in which wicked men endeavour to escape the reproofs of conscience. Instead of repenting, they seek vengeance, and resolve to put the reprover to shame or to death. 3d. We see the exceeding malignity which men have against the Lord Jesus. Well was it said that he was set for the fall of many in Israel, that thereby the thoughts of many hearts might be revealed! Lu. ii. 34, 35. Men, *now*, are not by nature less opposed to Jesus than they were then. 4th. We see the wisdom, purity, and firmness of the Saviour. To their souls he had been faithful. He had boldly reproved them for their sins. They sought his life. Multitudes of the artful and learned gathered around him, to endeavour to draw out something of which they might accuse him, yet in vain. Not a word fell from his lips of which they could accuse him. Everything that he said was calm, mild, peaceful, wise, and lovely. Even his cunning and bitter adversaries were always confounded, and retired in shame and confusion. Here, surely, must have been something more than man. None but *God manifest in the flesh* could have known all their designs, seen all their wickedness and their wiles, and escaped the cunning stratagems that were laid to confound and entangle him in his conversation. 5th. The same infinitely wise Saviour can still meet and confound all his own enemies and those of his people, and deliver all his followers, as he did himself, from all the snares laid by a wicked world to lead them to sin and death.

CHAPTER XII.

1. *In the mean time*. While he was discoursing with the scribes and Pharisees, as recorded in the last chapter.

CHAPTER XII.

IN[a] the mean time, when there were gathered together an innumerable multitude of people, insomuch that they trode one upon another, he began to say unto his disciples first of all, Beware ye of the leaven of the Pharisees, which is hypocrisy.

2 For[b] there is nothing covered that shall not be revealed, neither hid that shall not be known.

3 Therefore whatsoever ye have spoken in darkness shall be heard in the light; and that which ye have spoken in the ear, in closets, shall be proclaimed upon the housetops.

4 And I say unto you, [c]my friends, [d]Be not afraid of them that kill the body, and after that have no more that they can do.

5 But I will forewarn you whom ye shall fear: Fear him which, after he hath killed, hath power to cast into hell; yea, I say unto you, Fear him.

6 Are not five sparrows sold for two [1]farthings? and not one of them is forgotten before God;

7 But even the very hairs of your head are all numbered. Fear not, therefore; ye are of more value than many sparrows.

8 Also I say unto you, [e]Whosoever shall confess me before men, him shall the Son of man also [f]confess before the angels of God;

9 But he that [g]denieth me before men, shall be [h]denied before the angels of God.

10 And whosoever shall speak a word against the Son of man, it shall be forgiven him; but unto

a Mat.16.6,&c.; Mar.8.15,&c.
b Mat.10.26; Mar.4.22; ch.8.17.
c Jn.15.14. d Is.51.7-13; Mat.10.28,&c.

1 See Mat.10.29.
e 1 Sa.2.30; Ps.119.46; 2 Ti.2.12; Re.2.10.
f Jude 24. g Ac.3.13,14; Re.3.8. h Mat.25.31.

¶ *An innumerable multitude.* The original word is *myriads*, or ten thousands. It is used here to signify that there was a great crowd or collection of people, who were anxious to hear him. Multitudes were attracted to the Saviour's ministry, and it is worthy of remark that he never had more to hear him than when he was most faithful and severe in his reproofs of sinners. Men's consciences are on the side of the faithful reprover of their sins; and though they deeply feel the reproof, yet they will still respect and hear him that reproves. ¶ *To his disciples first of all.* This does not mean that his disciples were, before all others, to avoid hypocrisy, but that this was the *first* or chief thing of which they were to beware. The meaning is this: "He said to his disciples, *Above all things beware,*" &c. ¶ *The leaven.* See Notes on Mat. xvi. 6. ¶ *Which is hypocrisy.* See Notes on Mat. vii. 5. Hypocrisy is like leaven or yeast, because—1st. It may exist without being immediately detected. Leaven mixed in flour is not known until it produces its effects. 2d. It is insinuating. Leaven will soon pervade the whole mass. So hypocrisy will, if undetected and unremoved, soon pervade all our exercises and feelings. 3d. It is swelling. It puffs us up, and fills us with pride and vanity. No man is more proud than the hypocrite, and none is more odious to God. When Jesus cautions them to beware of *the leaven of the Pharisees*, he means that they should be cautious about imbibing their spirit and becoming like them. The religion of Jesus is one of sincerity, of humility, of an entire want of disguise. The humblest man is the best Christian, and he who has the least disguise is most like his Master.

2-9. *Nothing covered.* See Notes on Mat. x. 26-32.

3. *Shall be proclaimed upon the housetops.* See Notes on Mat. x. 27. The custom of making proclamation from the tops or roofs of houses still prevails in the East. Dr. Thomson (*The Land and the Book*, vol. i. p. 51, 52) says: "At the present day, local governors in country districts cause their commands thus to be published. Their proclamations are generally made in the evening, after the people have returned from their labours in the field. The public crier ascends the highest roof at hand, and lifts up his voice in a long-drawn call upon all faithful subjects to give ear and obey. He then proceeds to announce, in a set form,

him that blasphemeth against the
Holy Ghost, [i]it shall not be forgiven.
11 And when they bring you unto
the synagogues, and *unto* magistrates and powers, [k]take ye no
thought how or what thing ye
shall answer, or what ye shall say;
12 For the [l]Holy Ghost shall
teach you in the same hour what
ye ought to say.
13 And one of the company said
unto him, [m]Master, speak to my
brother, that he divide the inheritance with me.
14 And he said unto him, [n]Man,
who made me a judge or a divider
over you?
15 And he said unto them, [o]Take
heed and beware of covetousness;
for a man's [p]life consisteth not in
the abundance of the things which
he possesseth.
16 And he spake a parable unto

i Mat.12.31; 1 Jn.5.16.
k Mat.10.19; Mar.13.11; ch.21.14. *l* Ac.6.10; 26.1,&c.
m Eze.33.31. *n* Jn.18.35.
o 1 Ti.6.7-10. *p* Job 2.4; Mat.6.25.

the will of their master, and demand obedience thereto."

10. See Notes on Mat. xii. 32.

11, 12. See Notes on Mat. x. 17–20.

13. *One of the company.* One of the multitude. This man had probably had a dispute with his brother, supposing that his brother had refused to do him justice. Conceiving that Jesus had power over the people—that what he said must be performed—he endeavoured to secure him on his side of the dispute and gain his point. From the parable which follows, it would appear that he had no *just* claim on the inheritance, but was influenced by covetousness. Besides, if he *had* any just claim, it might have been secured by the laws of the land. ¶ *Speak to my brother.* Command my brother. ¶ *Divide the inheritance.* An inheritance is the property which is left by a father to his children. Among the Jews the older brother had two shares, or twice as much as any other child, De. xxi. 17. The remainder was then equally divided among all the children.

14. *Who made me a judge?* It is not my business to settle controversies of this kind. They are to be settled by the magistrate. Jesus came for another purpose—to preach the gospel, and so to bring men to a *willingness to do* right. Civil affairs are to be left to the magistrate. There is no doubt that Jesus *could* have told him what was right in this case, but then it would have been interfering with the proper office of the magistrates; it might have led him into controversy with the Jews; and it was, besides, evidently apart from the proper business of his life. We may remark, also, that the appropriate business of ministers of the gospel is to attend to spiritual concerns. They should have little to do with the temporal matters of the people. If they can *persuade men* who are at variance to be reconciled, it is right; but they have no power to take the place of a magistrate, and to settle contentions in a legal way.

15. *Beware of covetousness.* One of these brothers, no doubt, was guilty of this sin; and our Saviour, as was his custom, took occasion to warn his disciples of its danger. ¶ *Covetousness.* An unlawful desire of the property of another; also a desire of gain or riches beyond what is necessary for our wants. It is a violation of the tenth commandment (Ex. xx. 17), and is expressly called idolatry (Col. iii. 5). Compare, also, Ep. v. 3, and He. xiii. 5. ¶ *A man's life.* The word *life* is sometimes taken in the sense of happiness or felicity, and some have supposed this to be the meaning here, and that Jesus meant to say that a man's comfort does not depend on affluence—that is, on more than is necessary for his daily wants; but this meaning does not suit the parable following, which is designed to show that property will not lengthen out a man's life, and therefore is not too ardently to be sought, and is of little value. The word *life*, therefore, is to be taken *literally.* ¶ *Consisteth not.* Rather, *dependeth* not on his possessions. His possessions will not prolong it. The passage, then, means: Be not anxious about obtaining wealth, for, however much you may obtain, it will not prolong your life. *That* depends on the will of God, and it requires something besides wealth to make us ready to meet him. This sentiment he proceeds to illustrate by a beautiful parable.

them, saying, The ground of a certain rich man brought forth plentifully;
17 And he thought within himself, saying, What shall I do, because I have no room where to bestow my fruits?
18 And he said, [q]This will I do: I will pull down my barns and build greater, and there will I bestow all my fruits and my goods.
19 And I will say to my soul, [r]Soul, thou hast much goods laid up for many years; [s]take thine ease, eat, drink, *and* be merry.
20 But God said unto him, *Thou* fool! [t]this night [2]thy soul shall be required of thee: then [u]whose shall those things be which thou hast provided?
21 So *is* he that [v]layeth up treasure for himself, and [w]is not rich toward God.
22 And he said unto his disci-

q Ja.4.15,16.
r Ps.49.18. s Ec.11.9; 1 Co.15.32; Ja.5.5.
t Job 20.20-23; 27.8; Ps.52.7; Ja.4.14.
2 or, *do they require thy soul.*
u Ps.39.6; 49.16,17; Je.17.11. v Hab.2.9.
w 1 Ti.6.18; Ja.2.5; ver.33.

16. *A parable.* See Notes on Mat. xiii. 3. ¶ *Plentifully.* His land was fertile, and produced even beyond his expectations, and beyond what he had provided for.

17. *He thought within himself.* He reasoned or inquired. He was anxious and perplexed. Riches increase thought and perplexity. Indeed, this is almost their only effect — to engross the thoughts and steal the heart away from better things, in order to take care of the useless wealth. ¶ *No room.* Everything was full. ¶ *To bestow.* To place, to hoard, to collect. ¶ *My fruits.* Our word *fruits* is not applied to *grain;* but the Greek word is applied to all the produce of the earth—not only *fruit*, but also grain. This is likewise the old meaning of the English word, especially in the plural number.

18. *I will pull down my barns.* The word *barns*, here, properly means, *granaries*, or places exclusively designed to put wheat, barley, &c. They were commonly made, by the ancients, *underground*, where grain could be kept a long time more safe from thieves and from vermin. If it be asked why he did not let the old ones remain and build new ones, it may be answered that it would be easier to *enlarge* those already excavated in the earth than to dig new ones.

19. *Much goods.* Much property. Enough to last a long while, so that there is no need of anxiety or labour. ¶ *Take thine ease.* Be free from care about the future. Have no anxiety about coming to want. ¶ *Eat, drink,* and *be merry.* This was just the doctrine of the ancient Epicureans and atheists, and it is, alas! too often the doctrine of those who are rich. They think that all that is valuable in life is to eat, and drink, and be cheerful or merry. Hence their chief anxiety is to obtain the "delicacies of the season"—the luxuries of the world; to secure the productions of every clime at any expense, and to be distinguished for splendid repasts and a magnificent style of living. What a portion is this for an immortal soul! What folly to think that *all* that a man lives for is to satisfy his sensual appetites; to forget that he has an intellect to be cultivated, a heart to be purified, a soul to be saved!

20. Thou *fool.* If there is any supreme folly, it is this. As though riches could prolong life, or avert for a moment the approach of pain and death. ¶ *This night*, &c. What an awful sentence to a man who, as he thought, had got just ready to live and enjoy himself! In a single moment all his hopes were blasted, and his soul summoned to the bar of his long-forgotten God. So, many are surprised as suddenly and as unprepared. They are snatched from their pleasures, and hurried to a world where there is no pleasure, and where all their wealth cannot purchase one moment's ease from the gnawings of the worm that never dies. ¶ *Shall be required of thee.* Thou shalt be required to die, to go to God, and to give up your account. ¶ *Then whose*, &c. Whose they may be is of little consequence to the man that lost his soul to gain them; but they are often left to heirs that dissipate them much sooner than the father procured them, and thus they secure *their* ruin as well as his own. See Ps. xxxix. 6; Ec. ii. 18, 19.

21. *So* is *he.* This is the portion or the doom. ¶ *Layeth up treasure for*

ples, Therefore I say unto you, Take[x] no thought for your life, what ye shall eat; neither for the body, what ye shall put on.

23 The life is more than meat, and the body *is more* than raiment.

24 Consider the [y]ravens; for they neither sow nor reap; which neither have store-house nor barn; and God feedeth them. How much more are ye better than the fowls?

25 And which of you, with taking thought, can add to his stature one cubit?

26 If ye, then, be not able to do that thing which is least, why take ye thought for the rest?

27 Consider the lilies, how they grow; they toil not, they spin not; and yet I say unto you, that Solomon in all his glory was not arrayed like one of these.

28 If, then, God so clothe the grass, which is to-day in the field, and to-morrow is cast into the oven, how much more *will he clothe* you, O ye of little faith!

29 And seek not ye what ye shall eat, or what ye shall drink, [3]neither be ye of doubtful mind.

30 For all these things do the nations of the world seek after; and your Father knoweth that ye have need of these things.

31 But[z] rather seek ye the kingdom of God, and [a]all these things shall be added unto you.

32 Fear not, [b]little flock; for [c]it is your Father's good pleasure to give you the kingdom.

x Mat.6.25,&c. y Job 38.41; Ps.147.9.

3 or, *live not in careful suspense.* z Mat.6.33.
a Ps.34.10; Is.33.16; Ro.8.31,32.
b Is.40.11; Jn.10.27,28.
c Mat.25.34; Jn.18.36; He.12.28; Ja.2.5; 2 Pe.1.11; Re.1.6; 22.5.

himself. Acquires riches for his own use—for *himself.* This is the characteristic of the covetous man. It is all for *himself.* His plans terminate there. He lives only for himself, and acts only with regard to his own interest. ¶ *Rich toward God.* Has no inheritance in the kingdom of God—no riches laid up in heaven. His affections are all fixed on this world, and he has none for God.

From this instructive parable we learn—1st. That wicked men are often signally prospered—their ground brings forth plentifully. God gives them their desire, but sends leanness into their souls. 2d. That riches bring with them always an increasing load of cares and anxieties. 3d. That they steal away the affections from God—are sly, insinuating, and dangerous to the soul. 4th. That the anxiety of a covetous man is not what *good* he may do with his wealth, but where he may hoard it, and keep it secure from doing any good. 5th. That riches cannot secure their haughty owners from the grave. Death will come upon them suddenly, unexpectedly, awfully. In the very midst of the brightest anticipations—in a moment—in the twinkling of an eye—it may come, and all the wealth that has been accumulated cannot alleviate one pang, or drive away one fear, or prolong life for one moment. 6th. That the man who is trusting to his riches in this manner is a fool in the sight of God. Soon, also, he will be a fool in his *own* sight, and will go to hell with the consciousness that his life has been one of eminent folly. 7th. That the path of true wisdom is to seek first the kingdom of God, and to be ready to die; and *then* it matters little what is our portion here, or how suddenly or soon we are called away to meet our Judge. If our affections are not fixed on our riches, we shall leave them without regret. If our treasures are laid up in heaven, death will be but *going home*, and happy will be that moment when we are called to our rest.

22–31. See this passage explained in the Notes on Mat. vi. 25–33.

32. *Little flock.* Our Saviour often represents himself as a shepherd, and his followers as a flock or as sheep. The figure was beautiful. In Judea it was a common employment to attend flocks. The shepherd was with them, defended them, provided for them, led them to green pastures and beside still waters. In all these things Jesus was and is eminently the Good Shepherd. His flock was small. Few *really* followed him, compared with the multitude who professed to love him. But, though small in number, they were not to fear. God was their Friend. He

33 Sell[d] that ye have, and
give alms: provide yourselves bags
which wax not old, a [e]treasure in
the heavens that faileth not, where
no thief approacheth, neither moth
corrupteth.
34 For where your treasure is,
there will your heart be also.
35 Let[f] your loins be girded
about, and [g]*your* lights burning;
36 And ye yourselves like unto
men that wait for their lord, when
he will return from the wedding;
that, when he cometh and knocketh, they may open unto him immediately.
37 Blessed[h] *are* those servants
whom the lord, when he cometh,
shall find watching: verily I say
unto you, that he shall gird himself, and make them to sit down
to meat, and will come forth and
serve them.
38 And if he shall come in the

d Mat.19.21; Ac.2.45; 4.34.
e Mat.6.20; 1 Ti.6.19. *f* Ep.6.14; 1 Pe.1.13.
g Mat.25.1,13.
h Mat.24.46,&c.

---

would provide for them. It was his *purpose* to give them the kingdom, and they had nothing to fear. See Mat. vi. 19-21.

33. *Sell that ye have.* Sell your property. Exchange it for that which you can use in distributing charity. This was the condition of their being disciples. Their property they gave up; they forsook it, or they put it into common stock, for the sake of giving alms to the poor, Ac. ii. 44; iv. 32; Jn. xii. 6; Ac. v. 2. ¶ *Bags which wax not old.* The word *bags*, here, means *purses*, or the bags attached to their girdles, in which they carried their money. See Notes on Mat. v. 38. By bags which wax not old Jesus means that we should lay up treasure in heaven; that our aim should be to be prepared to enter there, where all our wants will be for ever provided for. Purses, here, grow old and useless. Wealth takes to itself wings. Riches are easily scattered, or *we* must soon leave them; but that wealth which is in heaven abides for ever. It never is corrupted; never flies away; never is to be left. ¶ *Wax.* This word is from an old Saxon word, and in the Bible means *to grow.*

35,36. *Let your loins,* &c. This alludes to the ancient manner of dress. They wore a long flowing robe as their outer garment. See Notes on Mat. v. 38-41. When they laboured, or walked, or ran, it was necessary to *gird* or tie this up by a *sash* or girdle about the body, that it might not impede their progress. Hence, to gird up the loins means to be *ready*, to be active, to be diligent. Comp. 2 Ki. iv. 29; ix. 1; Je. i. 17; Ac. xii. 8. ¶ Your *lights burning.* This expresses the same meaning. Be ready at all times to leave the world and enter into rest, when your Lord shall call you. Let every obstacle be out of the way; let every earthly care be removed, and be prepared to follow him into his rest. Servants were expected to be ready for the coming of their lord. If in the night, they were expected to keep their lights trimmed and burning. When their master was away in attendance on a wedding, as they knew not the hour when he would return, they were to be continually ready. So we, as we know not the hour when God shall call us, should be *always* ready to die. Comp. Notes on Mat. xxv. 1-13.

37. *Shall gird himself.* Shall take the place of the servant himself. Servants who waited on the table were girded in the manner described above. ¶ *Shall make them sit,* &c. Shall place them at his table and feast them. This evidently means that if we are faithful to Christ, and are ready to meet him when he returns, he will receive us into heaven—will admit us to all its blessings, and make us happy there—as if *he* should serve us and minister to our wants. It will be as if a master, instead of sitting down at the table *himself*, should place his faithful *servants* there, and be himself the servant. This shows the exceeding kindness and condescension of our Lord. For *us*, poor and guilty sinners, he denied himself, took the form of a servant (Phi. ii. 7), and ministered to our wants. In our nature he has wrought out salvation, and he has done it in one of the humblest conditions of the children of men. How should our bosoms burn with gratitude to him, and how should *we* be willing to serve one another! See Notes on Jn. xiii. 1-17.

38-46. See Notes on Mat. xxiv. 42-51. ¶ *Second watch.* See Notes on Mat. xiv. 25.

second watch, or come in the third
watch, and find *them* so, blessed
are those servants.
39 And this know, that if the
goodman of the house had known
what hour [i]the thief would come,
he would have watched, and not
have suffered his house to be
broken through.
40 Be[k] ye therefore ready also;
for the Son of man cometh at an
hour when ye think not.
41 Then Peter said unto him,
Lord, speakest thou this parable
unto us, or even to all?
42 And the Lord said, Who, then,
is that [l]faithful and wise steward,
whom *his* lord shall make ruler
over his household, to give *them*
their portion of meat in due season?
43 Blessed[m] is that servant whom
his lord, when he cometh, shall find
so doing.
44 Of a truth I say unto you,
that he will make him ruler over
all that he hath.

i 1 Th.5.2; 2 Pe.3.10; Re.3.3; 16.15.
k ch.21.34,36. *l* 1 Co.4.2. *m* ver.37.

45 But and if that servant say
in his heart, My lord delayeth his
coming; and shall begin to [n]beat
the men-servants and maidens,
and to eat and drink, and to be
drunken;
46 The lord of that servant will
come in a day when he looketh
not for *him*, and at an hour when
he is not aware, and [o]will [4]cut
him in sunder, and will appoint
him his portion with the unbelievers.
47 And that servant [p]which
knew his lord's will, and prepared
not *himself*, neither did according
to his will, [q]shall be beaten with
many *stripes*.
48 But he [r]that knew not, and
did commit things worthy of
stripes, shall be beaten with few
stripes. For[s] unto whomsoever
much is given, of him shall be
much required; and to whom men
have [t]committed much, of him
they will ask the more.
49 I am come to send fire on

n Mat.22.6. *o* Ps.37.9; 94.14. [4] or, *cut him off*.
p Ja.4.17. *q* De.25.2. *r* Ac.17.30.
s Le.5.17; Jn.15.22; 1 Ti.1.13. *t* 1 Ti.6.20.

---

47. *Which knew his lord's will.* Who knew what his master wished him to do. He that knows what God commands and requires. ¶ *Many stripes.* Shall be severely and justly punished. They who have many privileges, who are often warned, who have the gospel, and do not repent and believe, shall be far more severely punished than others. They who are early taught in Sunday-schools, or by pious parents, or in other ways, and who grow up in sin and impenitence, will have much more to answer for than those who have no such privileges.

48. *Few* stripes. The Jews never inflicted more than forty stripes for one offence, De. xxv. 3. For smaller offences they inflicted only four, five, six, &c., according to the nature of the crime. In allusion to this, our Lord says that he *that knew not*—that is, he who had comparatively little knowledge—would suffer a punishment proportionally light. He refers, doubtless, to those who have fewer opportunities, smaller gifts, or fewer teachers. ¶ *Much is given.* They who have much committed to their disposal, as stewards, &c. See the parable of the talents in Mat. xxv. 14–30.

49. *I am come*, &c. The result of my coming will be that there will be divisions and contentions. He does not mean that he came *for* that purpose, or that he *sought* and *desired* it; but that such was the state of the human heart, and such the opposition of men to the truth, that that would be the *effect* of his coming. See Notes on Mat. x. 34. ¶ *Fire.* Fire, here, is the emblem of discord and contention, and consequently of calamities. Thus it is used in Ps. lxvi. 12; Is. xliii. 2. ¶ *And what will I*, &c. This passage might be better expressed in this manner: "And what would I, but that it were kindled. Since it is *necessary* for the advancement of religion that such divisions should take place; since the gospel cannot be established without conflicts, and strifes, and hatreds, I am even desirous that they should come. Since the greatest bless-

the earth; and what will I if it be
already kindled?
50 But I have a baptism to be
baptized with; and how am I
straitened[5] till it be accomplished!
51 Suppose [u]ye that I am come
to give peace on earth? I tell you,
Nay; but rather division:
52 For from henceforth there
shall be five in one house divided,
three against two, and two against
three.
53 The [v]father shall be divided
against the son, and the son against
the father; the mother against the
daughter, and the daughter against
the mother; the mother-in-law
against her daughter-in-law, and
the daughter-in-law against her
mother-in-law.
54 And he said also to the people,
When[w] ye see a cloud rise out of
the west, straightway ye say, There
cometh a shower; and so it is.
55 And when *ye see* the south
wind blow, ye say, There will be
heat; and it cometh to pass.
56 *Ye* hypocrites! ye can discern the face of the sky, and of
the earth; but how is it that ye
do not discern this time?
57 Yea, and why even [x]of yourselves judge ye not what is right?
58 When[y] thou goest with thine
adversary to the magistrate, [z]*as thou
art* in the way, give diligence that
thou mayest be delivered from
him; lest he hale thee to the
judge, and the judge deliver thee
to the officer, and the officer cast
thee into prison.
59 I tell thee, thou shalt not
depart thence till thou hast paid
the very last [6]mite.

5 or, *pained*. u Mat.10.34. v Mi.7.6. w Mat.16.2,&c.

x 1 Co.11.14. y Mat.5.25. z Is.55.6. 6 See Mar.12.42.

ing which mankind can receive must be attended with such unhappy divisions, I am willing, nay, desirous that they should come." He did not wish evil in itself; but, as it was the occasion of good, he was desirous, if it *must* take place, that it should take place soon. From this we learn—1st. That the promotion of religion may be expected to produce many contests and bitter feelings. 2d. That the heart of man must be exceedingly wicked, or it would not oppose a work like the Christian religion. 3d. That though God cannot look on evil with approbation, yet, for the sake of the benefit which may grow out of it, he is willing to permit it, and suffer it to come into the world.

50. *A baptism.* See Notes on Mat. xx. 22. ¶ *Am I straitened.* How do I earnestly desire that it were passed! Since these sufferings *must* be endured, how anxious am I that the time should come! Such were the feelings of the Redeemer in view of his approaching dying hour. We may learn from this—1st. That it is not improper to *feel deeply* at the prospect of dying. It is a sad, awful, terrible event; and it is impossible that we should look at it aright *without* feeling—scarcely without trembling. 2d. It is not improper to desire that the time should come, and that the day of our release should draw nigh, Phi. i. 23. To the Christian, death is but the entrance to life; and since the pains of death *must* be endured, and since they lead to heaven, it matters little how soon he passes through these sorrows, and rises to his eternal rest.

51–53. See Notes on Mat. x. 34–36.

54–57. See Notes on Mat. xvi. 2, 3. ¶ *South wind.* To the south and southwest of Judea were situated Arabia, Egypt, and Ethiopia, all warm or hot regions, and consequently the air that came from those quarters was greatly heated. ¶ *How is it that ye do not discern this time?* You see a cloud rise, and predict a shower; a south wind, and expect heat. These are regular events. So you see my miracles; you hear my preaching; you have the predictions of me in the prophets; why do you not, in like manner, infer that *this is the time* when the Messiah should appear?

58, 59. See Notes on Mat. v. 25, 26.

CHAPTER XIII.

1. *There were present.* That is, some persons who were present, and who had heard his discourse recorded in the previous chapter. There was probably a pause in his discourse, when they mentioned what had been done by Pilate to the Galileans. ¶ *At that sea-*

CHAPTER XIII.

THERE were present at that
season some that told him of
the [a]Galileans, whose blood Pilate
had [b]mingled with their sacrifices.
2 And Jesus, answering, said
unto them, Suppose ye that these
Galileans were sinners above all
the Galileans, because they suffered such things?
3 I tell you, Nay; but [c]except
ye repent, ye shall all likewise
perish.
4 Or those eighteen, upon whom

a Ac.5.37. *b* La.2.20. *c* Ac.3.19; Re.2.21,22.

---

son. At that time—that is the time mentioned in the last chapter. At what period of our Lord's ministry this was, it is not easy to determine. ¶ *Some that told him.* This was doubtless an event of recent occurrence. Jesus, it is probable, had not before heard of it. Why they told him of it can only be a matter of conjecture. It might be from the desire to get him to express an opinion respecting the conduct of Pilate, and thus to involve him in difficulty with the reigning powers of Judea. It might be as a mere matter of news. But, from the answer of Jesus, it would appear that *they* supposed that the Galileans *deserved* it, and that they meant to pass a judgment on the character of those men, a thing of which they were exceedingly fond. The answer of Jesus is a reproof of their habit of hastily judging the character of others. ¶ *Galileans.* People who lived in Galilee. See Notes on Mat. ii. 22. They were not under the jurisdiction of Pilate, but of Herod. The Galileans, in the time of Christ, were very wicked. ¶ *Whose blood Pilate had mingled,* &c. That is, while they were sacrificing at Jerusalem, Pilate came suddenly upon them and slew them, and *their* blood was mingled with the blood of the animals that they were slaying for sacrifice. It does not mean that Pilate *offered* their blood in sacrifice, but only that as they were sacrificing he slew them. The fact is not mentioned by Josephus, and nothing more is known of it than what is here recorded. We learn, however, from Josephus that the Galileans were very wicked, and that they were much disposed to broils and seditions. It appears, also, that Pilate and Herod had a quarrel with each other (Lu. xxiii. 12), and it is not improbable that Pilate might feel a particular enmity to the subjects of Herod. It is likely that the Galileans excited a tumult in the temple, and that Pilate took occasion to come suddenly upon them, and show his opposition to them and Herod by slaying them. ¶ *Pilate.* The Roman governor of Judea. See Notes on Mat. xxvii. 2.

2, 3. *Suppose ye,* &c. From this answer it would appear that they supposed that the fact that these men had been slain in this manner proved that they were very great sinners. ¶ *I tell you, Nay.* Jesus assured them that it was not right to draw such a conclusion respecting these men. The fact that men come to a sudden and violent death is not proof that they are peculiarly wicked. ¶ *Except ye repent.* Except you forsake your sins and turn to God. Jesus took occasion, contrary to their expectation, to make a practical use of that fact, and to warn them of their own danger. He never suffered a suitable occasion to pass without warning the wicked, and entreating them to forsake their evil ways. The subject of religion was always present to his mind. He introduced it easily, freely, fully. In this he showed his love for the souls of men, and in this he set us an example that we should walk in his steps. ¶ *Ye shall all likewise perish.* You shall all be destroyed in a similar manner. Here he had reference, no doubt, to the calamities that were coming upon them, when thousands of the people perished. Perhaps there was never any reproof more delicate and yet more severe than this. They came to him believing that these men who had perished were peculiarly wicked. He did not tell them that *they* were as bad as the Galileans, but left them to *infer* it, for if they did not repent, they must soon likewise be destroyed. This was remarkably fulfilled. Many of the Jews were slain in the temple; many while offering sacrifice; thousands perished in a way very similar to the Galileans. Comp. Notes on Mat. xxiv. From this account of the Galileans we may learn—(1.) That men are very prone to infer, when any great calamity happens to others, that they are peculiarly guilty.

the tower in Siloam fell, and slew them, think ye that they were sinners[1] above all men that dwelt in Jerusalem?

5 I tell you, Nay; but except ye repent, ye shall all likewise perish.

[1] or, *debtors.*

See the Book of Job, and the reasonings of his three "*friends.*" (2.) That that conclusion, in the way in which it is usually drawn, is erroneous. If we see a man bloated, and haggard, and poor, who is in the habit of intoxication, we may infer properly that he is guilty, and that God hates his sin and punishes it. So we may infer of the effects of licentiousness. But we should not thus infer when a man's house is burned down, or when his children die, or when he is visited with a loss of health; nor should we infer it of the nations that are afflicted with famine, or the plague, or with the ravages of war; nor should we infer it when a man is killed by lightning, or when he perishes by the blowing up of a steamboat. Those who thus perish may be far more virtuous than many that live. (3.) This is not a world of retribution. Good and evil are mingled; the good and the bad suffer, and all are exposed here to calamity. (4.) There is another world—a future state—a world where the good will be happy and the wicked punished. There all that is irregular on earth will be regulated; all that appears unequal will be made equal; all that is chaotic will be reduced to order. (5.) When men are disposed to speak about the great guilt of others, and the calamities that come upon them, they should inquire about *themselves.* What is *their* character? what is *their* condition? It *may be* that they are in quite as much danger of perishing as those are whom they regard as so wicked. (6.) WE MUST REPENT. We must ALL repent or we shall perish. No matter what befalls others, *we* are sinners; *we* are to die; *we* shall be lost unless we repent. Let us, then, think of *ourselves* rather than of *others;* and when we hear of any signal calamity happening to others, let us remember that there is calamity in another world as well as here; and that while our fellow-sinners are exposed to trials *here,* we may be exposed to more awful woes *there.* Woe *there* is eternal; here, a calamity like that produced by a falling tower is soon over.

4. *Or those eighteen.* Jesus himself adds another similar case, to warn them —a case which had probably occurred not long before, and which it is likely they judged in the same manner. ¶ *Upon whom the tower in Siloam fell.* The name Siloah or Siloam is found only three times in the Bible as applied to water—once in Is. viii. 6, who speaks of it as running water; once as a pool near to the king's garden, in Ne. iii. 15; and once as a pool, in the account of the Saviour's healing the man born blind, in Jn. ix. 7-11. Josephus mentions the fountain of Siloam frequently as situated at the mouth of the Valley of Tyropœon, or the Valley of Cheesemongers, where the fountain long indicated as that fountain is still found. It is on the south side of Mount Moriah, and between that and the Valley of Jehoshaphat. The water at present flows out of a small artificial basin under the cliff, and is received into a large reservoir 53 feet in length by 18 in breadth. The small upper basin or fountain excavated in the rock is merely the entrance, or rather the termination of a long and narrow subterranean passage beyond, by which the water comes from the Fountain of the Virgin. For what purpose the *tower* here referred to was erected is not known; nor is it known at what time the event here referred to occurred. It is probable that it was not far from the time when the Saviour made use of the illustration, for the manner in which he refers to it implies that it was fresh in the recollection of those to whom he spoke.

5. *I tell you, Nay.* It is improper to suppose that those on whom heavy judgments fall in this world are the worst of men. This is not a world of retribution. Often the most wicked are suffered to prosper here, and their punishment is reserved for another world; while the righteous are called to suffer much, and *appear* to be under the sore displeasure of God, Ps. lxxiii. This only we know, that the wicked will not *always* escape; that God is just; and that none who *do* suffer here or hereafter, suffer more than they deserve. In the future world, all that seems to be unequal here will be made equal and plain.

6 He spake also this parable:
A[d] certain *man* had a fig-tree
planted in his vineyard; and he
came and [e]sought fruit thereon,
and found none.
7 Then said he unto the dresser
of his vineyard, Behold, these
three years I come seeking fruit
on this fig-tree and find none: [f]cut
it down; why cumbereth it the
ground?
8 And he, answering, said unto
him, Lord, [g]let it alone this year
also, till I shall dig about it and
dung *it:*
9 And if it bear fruit, *well;* and
if not, *then* [h]after that thou shalt
cut it down.
10 And he was teaching in one
of the synagogues on the sabbath.
11 And, behold, there was a woman which had a [i]spirit of infirmity

d Is.5.1,&c.; Mat.21.19. *e* Jn.15.16; Ga.5.22; Phi.4.17. *f* Ex.32.10. *g* Ps.106.23; 2 Pe.3.9. *h* Jn.15.2; He.6.8. *i* Ps.6.2.

6. *This parable.* See Notes on Mat. xiii. 3. ¶ *Vineyard.* A place where vines were planted. It was not common to plant fig-trees in them, but our Lord represents it as having been sometimes done.

7. *The dresser of his vineyard.* The man whose duty it was to trim the vines and take care of his vineyard. ¶ *These three years.* These words are not to be referred to the time which Christ had been preaching the gospel, as if he meant to specify the exact period. They mean, as applicable to the vineyard, that the owner had been *a long time* expecting fruit on the tree. For three successive years he had been disappointed. In his view it was long enough to show that the tree was barren and would yield no fruit, and that therefore it should be cut down. ¶ *Why cumbereth it the ground?* The word *cumber* here means to render *barren* or *sterile.* By taking up the juices of the earth, this useless tree rendered the ground sterile, and prevented the growth of the neighbouring vines. It was not merely *useless*, but was doing mischief, which may be said of all sinners and all hypocritical professors of religion. Dr. Thomson (*The Land and the Book*, vol. i. p. 539) says of the barren fig-tree: "There are many such trees now; and if the ground is not properly cultivated, especially when the trees are young—as the one of the parable was, for only *three* years are mentioned—they do not bear at all; and even when full grown they quickly fail, and wither away if neglected. Those who expect to gather good crops of well-flavoured figs are particularly attentive to their culture — not only plough and dig about them frequently, and manure them plentifully, but they carefully gather out the stones from the orchards, contrary to their general slovenly habits."

This parable is to be taken in connection with what goes before, and with our Saviour's calling the Jewish nation to repentance. It was spoken to illustrate the dealings of God with them, and their own wickedness under all his kindness, and we may understand the different parts of the parable as designed to represent—1st. God, by the man who owned the vineyard. 2d. The vineyard as the Jewish people. 3d. The coming of the owner for fruit, the desire of God that they should produce good works. 4th. The barrenness of the tree, the wickedness of the people. 5th. The dresser was perhaps intended to denote the Saviour and the other messengers of God, pleading that God would spare the Jews, and save them from their enemies that stood ready to destroy them, as soon as God should permit. 6th. His waiting denotes the delay of vengeance, to give them an opportunity of repentance. And, 7th. The remark of the dresser that he might *then* cut it down, denotes the acquiescence of all in the belief that such a judgment would be just.

We may also remark that God treats sinners in this manner now; that he spares them long; that he gives them opportunities of repentance; that many live but to cumber the ground; that they are not only useless to the church, but pernicious to the world; that in due time, when they are fairly tried, they shall be cut down; and that the universe will bow to the awful decree of God, and say that their damnation is just.

11. *There was a woman which had a spirit of infirmity.* Was infirm, or was weak and afflicted. This was produced by Satan, ver. 16. ¶ *Eighteen years.* This affliction had continued a long time.

eighteen years, and was bowed together, and could in no wise lift
up *herself*.
12 And when Jesus saw her, he
called *her to him*, and said unto
her, Woman, [k]thou art loosed from
thine infirmity.
13 And [l]he laid *his* hands on
her; and immediately she was
made straight, and glorified God.
14 And the ruler of the synagogue answered with indignation,
because that Jesus had [m]healed on

k Joel 3.10. l Mar.16.18; Ac.9.17. m Mat.12.10; Mar.3.2; ch.6.7; 14.3; Jn.5.16.

the sabbath-day, and said unto
the people, [n]There are six days in
which men ought to work: in
them, therefore, come and be
healed, and not on the sabbath-
day.
15 The Lord then answered him,
and said, [o]*Thou* hypocrite! doth not
each one of you [p]on the sabbath
loose his ox or *his* ass from the
stall, and lead *him* away to watering?
16 And ought not this woman,

n Ex.20.9. o Pr.11.9; Mat.7.5; 23.13,28; ch.12.1. p ch.14.5.

This shows that the miracle was *real;* that the disease was not feigned. Though thus afflicted, yet it seems she was regular in attending the worship of God in the synagogue. There in the sanctuary, is the place where the afflicted find consolation; and there it was that the Saviour met her and restored her to health. It is in the sanctuary and on the Sabbath, also, that he commonly meets his people, and gives them the joys of his salvation.

12. *Thou art loosed from thine infirmity.* This was a remarkable declaration. It does not appear that the woman *applied* to him for a cure; yet Jesus addressed her, and the disease departed. How clear would be the proofs from such a case that he was the Messiah! And how mighty the power of him that by a word could restore her to health!

13. *Glorified God.* Praised God. Gave thanks to him for healing her. They who are restored to health from sickness owe it to God; and they should devote their lives to his service, as expressive of their sense of gratitude to him who has spared them.

14. *Answered with indignation, because,* &c. He considered this a violation of the Sabbath, doing work contrary to the fourth commandment. If he had reasoned aright, he would have seen that he who could perform such a miracle could not be a violator of the law of God. From this conduct of the ruler we learn—1st. That men are often opposed to good being done, because it is not done *in their own way* and *according to their own views.* 2d. That they are more apt to look at what they consider a violation of the law in others, than at the good which others may do. 3d. That this opposition is manifested not only against those who *do good,* but also against those who are *benefited.* The ruler of the synagogue seemed particularly indignant that *the people* would come to Christ to be healed. 4th. That this conduct is often the result of envy. In this case it was rather hatred that the people should follow Christ instead of the Jewish rulers, and therefore envy at the popularity of Jesus, than any real regard for religion. 5th. That opposition to the work of Jesus may put on the appearance of great professed regard for religion. Many men oppose revivals, missions, Bible societies, and Sunday-schools—strange as it may seem—*from professed regard to the purity of religion.* They, like the ruler here, have formed their notions of religion as consisting in something *very different from doing good,* and they oppose those who are attempting to spread the gospel throughout the world.

15. Thou *hypocrite!* You condemn *me* for an action, and yet you perform one exactly similar. You condemn *me* for doing to a woman what you do to a beast. To her I have done good on the Sabbath; you provide for your cattle, and yet blame me for working a miracle to relieve a sufferer on that day. ¶ *Stall.* A place where cattle are kept to be fed, and sheltered from the weather.

16. *A daughter of Abraham.* A descendant of Abraham. See Notes on Mat. i. 1. She was therefore a Jewess; and the ruler of the synagogue, professing a peculiar regard for the Jewish people, considering them as peculiarly favoured of God, should have rejoiced that she was loosed from this infirmity. ¶ *Whom Satan hath bound.* Satan is

being a [q]daughter of Abraham, whom Satan hath bound, lo, these eighteen years, be loosed from this bond on the sabbath-day?

17 And when he had said these things, [r]all his adversaries were ashamed: and all the people rejoiced for all the [s]glorious things that were done by him.

18 Then said he, [t]Unto what is the kingdom of God like? and whereunto shall I resemble it?

19 It is like a grain of mustard-seed, which a man took and cast into his garden; and it grew, and waxed a great tree; and the fowls

q ch.19.9. *r* Is.45.24; 1 Pe.3.16. *s* Ex.15.11; Ps.111.3; Is.4.2. *t* Mat.13.31; Mar.4.30,&c.

of the air lodged in the branches of it.

20 And again he said, Whereunto shall I liken the kingdom of God?

21 It is like leaven, which a woman took and hid in three [2]measures of meal, till the whole was leavened.

22 And he went through the cities and villages, teaching, and journeying toward Jerusalem.

23 Then said one unto him, Lord, are there few that be saved? And he said unto them,

24 Strive[u] to enter in at the

[2] See Mat.13.33. *u* Mat.7.13.

---

the name given to the prince or leader of evil spirits, called also the devil, Beelzebub, and the old serpent, Mat. xii. 24; Re. xii. 9; xx. 2. By his *binding* her is meant that he had inflicted this disease upon her. It was not properly a *possession* of the devil, for that commonly produced derangement; but God had suffered him to afflict her in this manner, similar to the way in which he was permitted to try Job. See Notes on Job i. 12; ii. 6, 7. It is no more *improbable* that God would suffer *Satan* to inflict pain, than that he would suffer a wicked *man* to do it; yet nothing is more common than for one *man* to be the occasion of bringing on a disease in another which may terminate only with the life. He that seduces a virtuous man and leads him to intemperance, or he that wounds him or strikes him, may disable him as much as Satan did this woman. If God permits it in one case, he may, for the same reason, in another.

17. *Adversaries.* The ruler of the synagogue, and those who felt as he did. ¶ *All the people.* The persons who attended the synagogue, and who had witnessed the miracle. It is to be remarked—1st. That those who opposed Christ were chiefly the *rulers.* They had an *interest* in doing it. Their popularity was at stake. They were afraid that he would draw off the people from them. 2d. The common people heard him gladly. Many of them believed in him. The condition of the poor, and of those in humble life, is by far the most favourable for religion, and most of the disciples of Jesus have been found there.

18-21. See these parables explained in the Notes on Mat. xiii. 31, 32.

22. *Cities and villages.* Chiefly of Galilee, and those which were between Galilee and Jerusalem. ¶ *Teaching and journeying.* This evinces the diligence of our Lord. Though on a journey, yet he remembered his work. He did not excuse himself on the plea that he was in haste. Christians and Christian ministers should remember that when their Master travelled he did not *conceal* his character, or think that he was then freed from obligation to do good.

23. *Then said one.* Who this was does not appear. It is probable that he was not one of the disciples, but one of the Jews, who came either to perplex him, or to involve him in a controversy with the Pharisees. ¶ *Are there few that be saved?* It was the prevalent opinion among the Jews that few would enter heaven. As but two of all the hosts that came out of Egypt entered into the land of Canaan, so some of them maintained that a proportionally small number would enter into heaven (Lightfoot). On this subject the man wished the opinion of Jesus. It was a question of idle curiosity. The answer to it would have done little good. It was far more important for the man to secure his own salvation, than to indulge in such idle inquiries and vain speculations. Our Lord therefore advised *him*, as he does *all*, *to strive* to enter into heaven.

24. *Strive.* Literally, *agonize.* The word is taken from the Grecian games.

strait gate; [v]for many, I say unto you, will seek to enter in, and shall not be able.

25 When[w] once the master of the house is risen up, and [x]hath shut to the door, and ye begin to stand without, and to knock at the door, saying, [y]Lord, Lord, open unto us; and he shall answer and say unto you, I know you not whence ye are;

26 Then shall ye begin to say, We have eaten and drunk in thy presence, and thou hast taught in our streets.

27 But[z] he shall say, I tell you,

v Jn.7.34; 8.21; Ro.9.31. w Ps.32.6; Is.55.6. x Mat.25.10. y ch.6.46.

z Mat.7.22,23; 25.12,41.

In their races, and wrestlings, and various athletic exercises, they *strove* or *agonized*, or put forth all their powers to gain the victory. Thousands witnessed them. They were long trained for the conflict, and the honour of victory was one of the highest honours among the people. So Jesus says that we should strive to enter in; and he means by it that we should be diligent, be active, be earnest; that we should make it our first and chief business to overcome our sinful propensities, and to endeavour to enter into heaven. This same figure or allusion to the Grecian games is often used in the New Testament, 1 Co. ix. 24–26; Phi. ii. 16; He. xii. 1. ¶ *Strait gate.* See Notes on Mat. vii. 13, 14. Dr. Thomson (*The Land and the Book*, vol. i. p. 32) says: "I have seen these strait gates and narrow ways, 'with here and there a traveller.' They are in retired corners, and must be sought for, and are opened only to those who knock; and when the sun goes down and the night comes on, they are shut and locked. It is then too late." ¶ *Will seek to enter in.* Many in various ways manifest some desire to be saved. They seek it, but do not agonize for it, and hence they are shut out. But a more probable meaning of this passage is that which refers this *seeking* to a time that shall be *too late;* to the time when the master has risen up, &c. In this life they neglect religion, and are engaged about other things. At death, or at the judgment, they will seek to enter in; but it will be too late—the door will be shut; and because they did not make religion the chief business of their life, they cannot *then* enter in. ¶ *Shall not be able.* This is not designed to affirm anything respecting the inability of the sinner, provided he seeks salvation in a proper time and manner. It means that at the time when many *will* seek—when the door is shut—they will not be able *then* to enter in, agreeable to Mat. vii. 22. In the proper time, when the day of grace was lengthened out, they *might* have entered in; but there *will be* a time when it will be too late. The day of mercy will be ended, and death will come, and the doors of heaven barred against them. How important, then, to strive to enter in while we have opportunity, and before it shall be too late!

25. *When once the master*, &c. The figure here used is taken from the conduct of a housekeeper, who is willing to see his friends, and who at the proper time keeps his doors open. But there is a proper time for closing them, when he will not see his guests. At night it would be improper and vain to seek an entrance—the house would be shut. So there is a proper time to seek an entrance into heaven; but there will be a time when it will be too late. At death the time will have passed by, and God will be no longer gracious to the sinner's soul.

26. *We have eaten*, &c. Comp. Mat. vii. 22, 23. To have eaten with one is evidence of acquaintanceship or friendship. So the sinner may allege that he was a professed follower of Jesus, and had some evidence that Jesus was his friend. There is no allusion here, however, to the sacrament. The figure is taken from the customs of men, and means simply that they had professed attachment, and perhaps supposed that Jesus was their friend. ¶ *In thy presence.* With thee—as one friend does with another. ¶ *Thou hast taught.* Thou didst favour us, as though thou didst love us. Thou didst not turn away from us, and we did not drive thee away. All this is alleged as proof of friendship. It shows us—1st. On how slight evidence men will suppose themselves ready to die. How slender is the preparation which even many professed friends of Jesus have for death! How easily they are satisfied about their

I know you not whence ye are;
depart from me, all [a]*ye* workers
of iniquity.

28 There[b] shall be weeping and
gnashing of teeth, when ye shall
see Abraham, and Isaac, and Jacob, and all the prophets, in the
kingdom of God, and you *yourselves* thrust out.

29 And[c] they shall come from
the east, and *from* the west, and
from the north, and *from* the
south, and shall sit down in the
kingdom of God.

30 And, behold, [d]there are last
which shall be first, and there are
first which shall be last.

31 The same day there came
certain of the Pharisees, saying
unto him, Get thee out and depart
hence; for Herod will kill thee.

32 And he said unto them, Go,
ye and tell [e]that fox, Behold, I cast
out devils, and I do cures to-day

a Ps.6.8; 101.8. *b* Mat.8.12; 13.42; 24.51. *c* Re.7.9,10. *d* Mat.19.30. *e* Zep.3.3.

---

own piety! A profession of religion, attendance on the preaching of the word or at the sacraments, or a decent external life, is all they have and all they seek. With this they go quietly on to eternity—go to disappointment, wretchedness, and woe! 2d. None of these things will avail in the day of judgment. It will be only true love to God, a real change of heart, and a life of piety, that can save the soul from death. And oh! how important it is that all should search themselves and see what is the real foundation of their hope that they shall enter into heaven!

27. See Notes on Mat. vii. 23.

28–30. See Notes on Mat. viii. 11, 12.

31. *Came certain of the Pharisees.* Their coming to him in this manner would have the appearance of friendship, as if they had conjectured or secretly learned that it was Herod's intention to kill him. Their suggestion had much appearance of probability. Herod had killed John. He knew that Jesus made many disciples, and was drawing away many of the people. He was a wicked man, and he might be supposed to fear the presence of one who had so strong a resemblance to John, whom he had slain. It might seem probable, therefore, that he intended to take the life of Jesus, and this might appear as a friendly hint to escape him. Yet it is more than possible that Herod might have sent these Pharisees to Jesus. Jesus was eminently popular, and Herod might not dare openly to put him to death; yet he desired his removal, and for this purpose he sent these men, as if in a friendly way, to advise him to retire. This was probably the reason why Jesus called him a fox. ¶ *Herod.* Herod Antipas, a son of Herod the Great. He ruled over Galilee and Perea, and wished Jesus to retire beyond these regions. See Notes on ch. iii. 1.

32. *Tell that fox.* A fox is an emblem of slyness, of cunning, and of artful mischief. The word is also used to denote a dissembler. Herod was a wicked man, but the *particular thing* to which Jesus here alludes is not his *vices*, but his *cunning*, his *artifice*, in endeavouring to remove him out of his territory. He had endeavoured to do it by stratagem—by sending these men who pretended great friendship for his life. ¶ *Behold, I cast out devils*, &c. Announce to him the fact that I am working miracles in his territory, and that I shall continue to do it. I am not afraid of his art or his enmity. I am engaged in my appropriate work, and shall continue to be as long as is proper, in spite of his arts and his threats. ¶ *To-day and to-morrow.* A little time. The words seem here to be used not strictly, but proverbially—to denote a short space of time. Let not Herod be uneasy. I am doing no evil; I am not violating the laws. I only cure the sick, &c. In a little time this part of my work will be done, and I shall retire from his dominions. ¶ *The third* day. After a little time. Perhaps, however, he meant *literally* that he would depart on that day for Jerusalem; that for two or three days more he would remain in the villages of Galilee, and then go on his way to Jerusalem. ¶ *I shall be perfected.* Rather, I shall have ended my course *here;* I shall have *perfected* what I purpose to do in Galilee. It does not refer to his *personal* perfection, for he was always perfect, but it means that he would have *finished* or *completed* what he purposed to do in the regions of

and to-morrow, and the third *day*
I shall be [f]perfected.
33 Nevertheless, I must walk
to-day, and to-morrow, and the *day*
following; for it cannot be that a
prophet perish out of Jerusalem.
34 O[g] Jerusalem, Jerusalem,
which killest the prophets, and
stonest them that are sent unto
thee; how often would I have
gathered thy children together, as
a hen *doth gather* her brood under
her wings, and ye would not!
35 Behold, [h]your house is left
unto you desolate; and verily I
say unto you, Ye shall not see me,
until *the time* come when ye shall
say, [i]Blessed *is* he that cometh in
the name of the Lord.

CHAPTER XIV.

AND it came to pass, as he went
into the house of one of the
chief Pharisees, to eat bread on
the sabbath-day, that [a]they watched him.

f He.2.10. g Mat.23.37.
h Le.26.31,32; Ps.69.25; Is.1.7; 5.5,6; Da.9.27; Mi.3.12. i ch.19.38; Jn.12.13.
a Ps.37.32; Is.29.20,21; Je.20.10,11.

Herod. He would have completed his work, and would be ready then to go.

33. *I must walk*, &c. I must remain here this short time. These three days I must do cures here, and then I shall depart, though not for fear of Herod. It will be because my time will have come, and I shall go up to Jerusalem to die. ¶ *For it cannot be that a prophet should perish out of Jerusalem.* I have no fear that *Herod* will put me to death in Galilee. I shall not depart on that account. *Jerusalem* is the place where the prophets die, and where *I* am to die. I am not at all alarmed, therefore, at any threats of *Herod*, for my life is safe until I arrive at Jerusalem. Go and tell him, therefore, that I fear him not. I shall work here as long as it is proper, and shall then go up to Jerusalem to die. The reason why he said that a prophet could not perish elsewhere than in Jerusalem might be—1st. That he knew that he would be tried on a charge of blasphemy, and no other court could have cognizance of that crime but the great council or Sanhedrim, and so he was not afraid of any threats of Herod. 2d. It *had been* the fact that the prophets had been chiefly slain there. The meaning is, "It cannot easily be done elsewhere; it is not usually done. Prophets have generally perished there, and there *I* am to die. I am safe, therefore, from the fear of Herod, and shall not take the advice given and leave his territory."

34, 35. See Notes on Mat. xxiii. 37–39.

From the message which Jesus sent to Herod we may learn—1st. That our lives are safe in the hands of God, and that wicked men can do no more to injure us than he shall permit. Compare Jn. xix. 11. 2d. That we should go on fearlessly in doing our duty, and especially if we are doing good. We should not regard the threats of men. God is to be obeyed; and even if obedience *should* involve us in difficulty and trials, still we should not hesitate to commit our cause to God and go forward. 3d. We should be on our guard against crafty and unprincipled men. They often *profess* to seek our good when they are only plotting our ruin. Even those professedly coming from our enemies to caution us are often also our enemies, and are secretly plotting our ruin or endeavouring to prevent our doing good. 4th. We see here the nature of religion. It shrinks at nothing which is duty. It goes forward trusting in God. It comes out boldly and faces the world. And, 5th. How beautiful and consistent is the example of Christ! How *wise* was he to detect the arts of his foes! how *fearless* in going forward, in spite of all their machinations, to do what God had appointed for him to do!

CHAPTER XIV.

1. *It came to pass.* It so happened or occurred. ¶ *As he went*, &c. It is probable that he was invited to go, being in the neighbourhood (ver. 12); and it is also probable that the Pharisee invited him for the purpose of getting him to say something that would involve him in difficulty. ¶ *One of the chief Pharisees.* One of the Pharisees who were *rulers*, or members of the great council or the Sanhedrim. See Notes on Mat. v. 22. It does not mean that he was the head of the *sect* of the Pharisees, but one of those who hap-

2 And, behold, there was a certain man before him which had
the dropsy.
3 And Jesus, answering, spake
unto the lawyers and Pharisees,
saying, [b]Is it lawful to heal on the
sabbath-day?
4 And they held their peace.
And he took *him*, and healed him,
and let him go;
5 And answered them, saying,

b ch.13.14.

[c]Which of you shall have an ass or
an ox fallen into a pit, and will
not straightway pull him out on
the sabbath-day?
6 And they could not answer
him again to these things.
7 And he put forth a parable to
those which were bidden, when he
marked how they chose out the
chief rooms; saying unto them,
8 When[d] thou art bidden of any

c ch.13.15. *d* Pr.25.6,7.

---

pened to be a member of the Sanhedrim. He was therefore a man of influence and reputation. ¶ *To eat bread.* To dine. To partake of the hospitalities of his house. ¶ *On the sabbath-day.* It may seem strange that our Saviour should have gone to dine with a man who was a stranger on the Sabbath; but we are to remember—1st. That he was travelling, having no home of his own, and that it was no more improper to go there than to any other place. 2d. That he did not go there for the purpose of feasting and amusement, but to do good. 3d. That as several of that class of persons were together, it gave him an opportunity to address them on the subject of religion, and to reprove their vices. If, therefore, the example of Jesus should be pled to authorize accepting an invitation to dine on the Sabbath, it should be pled JUST AS IT WAS. If we can go *just as he did*, it is right. If when away from home; if we go to do good; if we make it an occasion to discourse on the subject of religion and to persuade men to repent, then it is not improper. Farther than this we cannot plead the example of Christ. And surely this should be the last instance in the world to be adduced to justify dinner-parties, and scenes of riot and gluttony on the Sabbath. ¶ *They watched him.* They malignantly fixed their eyes on him, to see if he did anything on which they could lay hold to accuse him.

2. *A certain man before him.* In what way he came there we know not. He might have been one of the Pharisee's family, or might have been placed there by the Pharisees to see whether he would heal him. This last supposition is not improbable, since it is said in ver. 1 that they watched him. ¶ *The dropsy.* A disease produced by the accumulation of water in various parts of the body; very distressing, and commonly incurable.

3. *Jesus, answering.* To *answer*, in the Scriptures, does not always imply, as among us, that anything had been said before. It means often merely to *begin* or to take up a subject, or, as here, to remark on the case that was present. ¶ *Is it lawful*, &c. He knew that they were watching him. If he healed the man at once, they would accuse him. He therefore proposed the question to them, and when it was asked, they could not say that it was not lawful.

4. *They held their peace.* They were silent. They *could* not say it was not lawful, for the law did not forbid it. If it had they would have said it. Here was the time for them to make objections if they had any, and not after the man was healed; and as they *made* no objection *then*, they could not with consistency afterward. They were therefore effectually silenced and confounded by the Saviour. ¶ *He took* him. Took hold of the man, or perhaps took him apart into another room. By taking hold of him, or touching him, he showed that the power of healing went forth from himself.

5, 6. See Notes on Mat. xii. 11. ¶ *Which of you*, &c. In this way Jesus refuted the notion of the Pharisees. If it was lawful to save an ox on the Sabbath, it was also to save the life of a man. To this the Jews had nothing to answer.

7. *A parable.* The word parable, here, means rather a *precept*, an *injunction.* He gave a *rule* or *precept* about the proper manner of attending a feast, or about the humility which ought to be manifested on such occasions. ¶ *That were bidden.* That were invited by the Pharisee. It seems that he had invited

man to a wedding, sit not down in the highest room; lest a more honourable man than thou be bidden of him;

9 And he that bade thee and him come and say to thee, Give this man place; and thou begin with shame to take the lowest room.

10 But when thou art bidden, go and sit down in the lowest room; that when he that bade thee cometh, he may say unto thee, Friend, go up higher; then shalt thou have worship in the presence of them that sit at meat with thee.

11 For[e] whosoever exalteth himself shall be abased; and he that humbleth himself shall be exalted.

12 Then said he also to him that bade him, When thou makest a dinner or a supper, call not thy

e 1 Sa.15.17; Job 22.29; Ps.18.27; Pr.15.33; 29.23; Mat.23.12; ch.18.14; Ja.4.6; 1 Pe.5.5.

---

his friends to dine with him on that day. ¶ *When he marked.* When he observed or saw. ¶ *Chief rooms.* The word *rooms* here does not express the meaning of the original. It does not mean *apartments*, but *the higher places* at the table; those which were nearest the head of the table and to him who had invited them. See Notes on Mat. xxiii. 6. That this was the common character of the Pharisees appears from Mat. xxiii. 6.

8, 9. *Art bidden.* Art invited. ¶ *To a wedding.* A wedding was commonly attended with a feast or banquet. ¶ *The highest room.* The seat at the table nearest the head. ¶ *A more honourable man.* A more aged man, or a man of higher rank. It is to be remarked that our Saviour did not consider the courtesies of life to be beneath his notice. His chief design here was, no doubt, to reprove the pride and ambition of the Pharisees; but, in doing it, he teaches us that religion does not violate the courtesies of life. It does not teach us to be rude, forward, pert, assuming, and despising the proprieties of refined intercourse. It teaches humility and kindness, and a desire to make all happy, and a willingness to occupy our appropriate situation and rank in life; and this is true *politeness*, for true politeness is a desire to make all others happy, and a readiness to do whatever is necessary to make them so. They have utterly mistaken the nature of religion who suppose that because they are professed Christians, they must be rude and uncivil, and violate all the distinctions in society. The example and precepts of Jesus Christ were utterly unlike such conduct. He teaches us to be kind, and to treat men according to their rank and character. Comp. Mat. xxii. 21; Ro. xiii. 7; 1 Pe. ii. 17.

10. *The lowest room.* The lowest seat at the table; showing that you are not desirous of distinctions, or greedy of that honour which may properly belong to you. ¶ *Shalt have worship.* The word *worship* here means *honour*. They who are sitting with you shall treat you with respect. They will learn your rank by your being invited nearer to the head of the table, and it will be better to learn it thus than by putting yourself forward. They will do you honour because you have shown a humble spirit.

11. *Whosoever exalteth*, &c. This is universal among men, and it is also the way in which God will deal with men. *Men* will perpetually endeavour to bring down those who endeavour to exalt themselves; and it is a part of God's regular plan to abase the proud, to bring down the lofty, to raise up those that be bowed down, and show *his* favours to those who are poor and needy.

12. *Call not thy friends*, &c. This is not to be understood as commanding us not to entertain *at all* our relatives and friends; but we are to remember the *design* with which our Lord spoke. He intended, doubtless, to reprove those who sought the society of the wealthy, and particularly rich relatives, and those who claimed to be intimate with the great and honourable, and who, to show their intimacy, were in the habit of *seeking* their society, and making for them expensive entertainments. He meant, also, to commend charity shown to the poor. The passage means, therefore, call *not only* your friends, but call also the poor, &c. Comp. Ex. xvi. 8; 1 Sa. xv. 22; Jer. vii. 22, 23; Mat. ix. 13. ¶ *Thy kinsmen.* Thy relations. ¶ *A recompense.* Lest they feel themselves bound to treat you with the same kindness, and, in so doing, neither you nor they will show

friends, nor thy brethren, neither
thy kinsmen, [f]nor *thy* rich neighbours; lest they also bid thee
again, and a recompense be made
thee.
13 But when thou makest a
feast, [g]call the poor, the maimed,
the lame, the blind:
14 And thou shalt be blessed,
for they cannot recompense thee;
for thou shalt be recompensed at
the resurrection of the just.
15 And when one of them that
sat at meat with him heard these
things, he said unto him, [h]Blessed
is he that shall eat bread in the
kingdom of God.
16 Then said he unto him, [i]A
certain man made a [k]great supper,
and bade many;
17 And sent his servant at supper-time to say unto them that
were bidden, [l]Come, for all things
are now ready.

f Pr.22.16. g Ne.8.10,12.

h Re.19.9. i Mat.22.2,&c. k Is.25.6,7. l Pr.9.2,5; Ca.5.1; Is.55.1,2.

any kind spirit, or any disposition to do good beyond what is repaid.

13. *The poor.* Those who are destitute of comfortable food. ¶ *The maimed.* Those who are deprived of any member of their body, as an arm or a leg, or who have not the use of them so that they can labour for their own support.

14. *Shalt be blessed.* Blessed in the *act* of doing good, which furnishes more *happiness* than riches can give, and blessed or rewarded *by God* in the day of judgment. ¶ *They cannot recompense thee.* They cannot invite you again, and thus pay you; and by inviting *them* you show that you have a *disposition* to do good. ¶ *The resurrection of the just.* When the just or holy shall be raised from the dead. Then *God* shall reward those who have done good to the poor and needy from love to the Lord Jesus Christ, Mat. x. 42; xxv. 34–36.

15. *Blessed* is *he that shall eat bread in the kingdom of God.* The kingdom of God here means the kingdom which the Messiah was to set up. See Notes on Mat. iii. 2. The Jews supposed that he would be a temporal prince, and that his reign would be one of great magnificence and splendour. They supposed that the *Jews* then would be delivered from all their oppressions, and that, from being a degraded people, they would become the most distinguished and happy nation of the earth. To that period they looked forward as one of great happiness. There is some reason to think that they supposed that the ancient just men would then be raised up to enjoy the blessings of the reign of the Messiah. Our Saviour having mentioned the *resurrection of the just*, this man understood it in the common way of the Jews, and spoke of the peculiar happiness which they expected at that time. The Jews *only*, he expected, would partake of those blessings. Those notions the Saviour corrects in the parable which follows.

16. *A great supper.* Or great feast. It is said to be *great* on account of the number who were invited. ¶ *Bade many.* Invited many beforehand. There is little difficulty in understanding this parable. The man who made the supper is, without doubt, designed to represent God; the supper, the provisions which he has made for the salvation of men; and the invitation, the offers which he made to men, particularly to the Jews, of salvation. See a similar parable explained in the Notes on Mat. xxii. 1–14.

17. *Sent his servant.* An invitation had been sent before, but this servant was sent at the time that the supper was ready. From this it would seem that it was the custom to announce to those invited just the time when the feast was prepared. The custom here referred to still prevails in Palestine. Dr. Thomson (*The Land and the Book*, vol. i. p. 178) says: "If a sheikh, beg, or emeer invites, he always sends a servant to call you at the proper time. This servant often repeats the very formula mentioned in Lu. xiv. 17: Tefŭddŭlû, el 'asha hâder—Come, for the supper is ready. The fact that this custom is mainly confined to the wealthy and to the nobility is in strict agreement with the parable, where the certain man who made the great supper and bade many is supposed to be of this class. It is true now, as then, that to refuse is a high insult to the maker of the feast, nor would such excuses as those in the parable be more acceptable to a Druse emeer than they were to the lord of this 'great supper.'"

18 And they all with one *consent*
began to make excuse. The[m] first
said unto him, I have bought a
piece of ground, and I must needs
go and see it: I pray thee have
me excused.
19 And another said, I have
bought five yoke of oxen, and I
go to prove them: I pray thee
have me excused.
20 And another said, [n]I have
married a wife, and therefore I
cannot come.
21 So that servant came and
showed his lord these things.
Then the master of the house, [o]being angry, said to his servant,
Go out quickly [p]into the streets
and lanes of the city, and bring in
hither the [q]poor, and the maimed,
and the [r]halt, and the blind.
22 And the servant said, Lord, it

m ch.8.14. n ver.26; 1 Co.7.33.

o Ps.2.12. p Re.22.17. q 1 Sa.2.8; Ps.113.7,8. r Ps.38.7; Is.33.23; 35.6.

18. *I have bought a piece of ground.* Perhaps he had purchased it on condition that he found it as good as it had been represented to him. ¶ *I must needs go.* I have necessity, or am obliged to go and see it; possibly pleading a contract or an agreement that he would go soon and examine it. However, we may learn from this that sinners sometimes plead that they are under a *necessity* to neglect the affairs of religion. The affairs of the world, they pretend, are so pressing that they cannot find time to attend to their souls. They have no time to pray, or read the Scriptures, or keep up the worship of God. In this way many lose their souls. God cannot regard such an excuse for neglecting religion with approbation. He commands us to seek *first* the kingdom of God and his righteousness, nor can he approve any excuse that men may make for not doing it.

19. *I go to prove them.* To try them, to see if he had made a good bargain. It is worthy of remark that this excuse was very trifling. He could as easily have tried them at any other time as then, and his whole conduct shows that he was more disposed to gratify *himself* than to accept the invitation of his friend. He was selfish; just as all sinners are, who, to gratify their own worldliness and sins, refuse to accept the offers of the gospel.

20. *I have married a wife*, &c. Our Saviour here doubtless intends to teach us that the love of earthly relatives and friends often takes off the affections from God, and prevents our accepting the blessings which he would bestow on us. This was the most trifling excuse of all; and we cannot but be amazed that *such* excuses are suffered to interfere with our salvation, and that men can be satisfied for *such* reasons to exclude themselves from the kingdom of God.

21. *Showed his lord.* Told his master of the excuses of those who had been invited. Their conduct was remarkable, and it was his duty to acquaint him with the manner in which his invitation had been received. ¶ *Being angry.* Being angry at the men who had slighted his invitation; who had so insulted him by neglecting his feast, and preferring *for such reasons* their own gratification to his friendship and hospitality. So it is no wonder that God is angry with the wicked every day. So foolish as well as wicked is the conduct of the sinner, so trifling is his excuse for not repenting and turning to God, that it is no wonder if God cannot look upon their conduct but with abhorrence. ¶ *Go out quickly.* The feast is ready. There is no time to lose. They who partake of it must do it soon. So the gospel is ready; time flies; and they who partake of the gospel must do it soon, and they who preach it must give diligence to proclaim it to their fellow-men. ¶ *The streets and lanes of the city.* The places where the poor, &c., would be found. Those first invited were the rich, who dwelt at ease in their own houses. By these the Jews were intended; by those who were in the streets, the Gentiles. Our Lord delivered this parable to show the Jews that the Gentiles would be called into the kingdom of God. They despised the Gentiles, and considered them cast out and worthless, as they did those who were in the lanes of the city. ¶ *The maimed*, &c. See Notes on ver. 13.

22. *Yet there is room.* He went out and invited all he found in the lanes, and yet the table was not full. This

is done as thou hast commanded, and [s]yet there is room.

23 And the lord said unto the servant, Go out into the highways and hedges, and [t]compel *them* to come in, that my house may be filled.

24 For I say unto you, [u]that none of those men which were bidden shall taste of my supper.

s Ps.103.6; 130.7. t Ps.110.3. u Pr.1.24; Mat.21.43; He.12.25.

---

he also reported to his master. *There is room!* What a glorious declaration is this in regard to the gospel! There yet is room. Millions have been saved, but there yet is room. Millions have been invited, and have come, and have gone to heaven, but heaven is not yet full. There is a banquet there which no number can exhaust; there are fountains which no number can drink dry; there are harps there which other hands may strike; and there are seats there which others may occupy. Heaven is not full, and there yet is room. The Sabbath-school teacher may say to his class, there yet is room; the parent may say to his children, there yet is room; the minister of the gospel may go and say to the wide world, there yet is room. The mercy of God is not exhausted; the blood of the atonement has not lost its efficacy; heaven is not full. What a sad message it *would* be if we were compelled to go and say, "There is no more room—heaven is full—not another one can be saved. No matter what their prayers, or tears, or sighs, they cannot be saved. Every place is filled; every seat is occupied." But, thanks be to God, this is not the message which we are to bear; and if there yet is room, come, sinners, young and old, and enter into heaven. Fill up that room, that heaven may be full of the happy and the blessed. If any part of the universe is to be vacant, O let it be the dark world of woe!

23. *Go out into the highways.* Since enough had not been found in the lanes and streets, he commands the servant to go into the roads—the public highways *out* of the city, as well as to the streets *in* it—and invite them also. ¶ *Hedges.* A hedge is the inclosure around a field or vineyard. It was commonly made of thorns, which were planted thick, and which kept the cattle out of the vineyard. "A common plant for this purpose is the prickly pear, a species of cactus, which grows several feet high, and as thick as a man's body, armed with sharp thorns, and thus forming an almost impervious defence" (Professor Hackett, *Scripture Illustrations*, p. 174). Those in the hedges were poor labourers employed in planting them or trimming them—men of the lowest class and of great poverty. By his directing them to go first into the streets of the city and then into the highways, we are not to understand our Saviour as referring to different classes of men, but only as denoting the *earnestness* with which God offers salvation to men, and his willingness that the most despised should come and live. Some parts of parables are thrown in for the sake of *keeping*, and they should not be pressed or forced to obtain any obscure or fanciful signification. The great point in this parable was, that God would call in the Gentiles after the Jews had rejected the gospel. This should be kept always in view in interpreting all the parts of the parable. ¶ *Compel* them. That is, urge them, press them earnestly, one and all. Do not hear their excuses on account of their poverty and low rank of life, but urge them so as to overcome their objections and lead them to the feast. This expresses the *earnestness* of the man; his anxiety that his table should be filled, and his purpose not to reject any on account of their poverty, or ignorance, or want of apparel. So God is earnest in regard to the most polluted and vile. He commands his servants, his ministers, to *urge* them to come, to *press* on them the salvation of the gospel, and to use ALL the means in their power to bring into heaven poor and needy sinners.

24. *For I say unto you.* These may be considered as the words of Jesus, making an application of the parable to the Pharisees before him. ¶ *None of those men.* This cannot be understood as meaning that no *Jews* would be saved, but that none of those who had *treated him in that manner*—none who had so decidedly rejected the offer of the gospel—would be saved. We may here see how dangerous it is *once* to reject the gospel; how dangerous to grieve away the Holy Spirit. How often God

25 And there went great multitudes with him; and he turned and said unto them,
26 If any *man* come to me, [v]and hate not his father, and mother, and wife, and children, and brethren, and sisters, yea, and [w]his own life also, he cannot be my disciple.
27 And[x] whosoever doth not bear his cross, and come after me, cannot be my disciple.
28 For which of you, [y]intending to build a tower, sitteth not down first and counteth the cost, whether ye have *sufficient* to finish *it?*

v De.33.9; Mat.10.37. w Ac.20.24; Re.12.11. x Mat.16.24; Mar.8.34; ch.9.23; 2 Ti.3.12. y Pr.24.27.

29 Lest haply, after he hath laid the foundation, and is not able to finish *it*, all that behold *it* begin to mock him,
30 Saying, This man began to build, and [z]was not able to finish.
31 Or what king, going to make war against another king, sitteth not down first, and [a]consulteth whether he be able with ten thousand to meet him that cometh against him with twenty thousand?
32 Or else, while the other is yet a great way off, he sendeth an

z He.7.11. a Pr.20.18.

---

forsakes for ever the sinner who has been once awakened, and who grieves the Holy Spirit. The invitation is full and free; but when it is rejected, and men turn wilfully away from it, God leaves them to their chosen way, and they are drowned in destruction and perdition. How important, then, is it to embrace the gospel *at once;* to accept the gracious invitation, and enter without delay the path that conducts to heaven!

25, 26, 27. See Notes on Mat. x. 37, 38.

26. *And hate not.* The word *hate*, here, means simply to *love less.* See the meaning of the verse in Mat. x. 37. It may be thus expressed: "He that comes after me, and does not love his father *less* than he loves me, &c., cannot be my disciple." We are not at liberty literally to *hate* our parents. This would be expressly contrary to the fifth commandment. See also Ep. vi. 1-3; Col. iii. 20. But we are to love them *less* than we love Christ; we are to obey Christ rather than them; we are to be willing to forsake them if he calls us to go and preach his gospel; and we are to submit, without a murmur, to him when he takes them away from us. This is not an uncommon meaning of the word *hate* in the Scriptures. Comp. Mal. i. 2, 3; Ge. xxix. 30, 31; De. xxi. 15-17.

28. *Intending to build a tower.* See Mat. xxi. 33. A tower was a place of defence or observation, erected on high places or in vineyards, to guard against enemies. It was made *high*, so as to enable one to see an enemy when he approached; and *strong*, so that it could not be easily taken. ¶ *Counteth the cost.* Makes a calculation how much it will cost to build it.

29. *Haply.* Perhaps. ¶ *To mock him.* To ridicule him. To laugh at him.

31. *With ten thousand to meet*, &c. Whether he will be able, with the forces which he *has*, to meet his enemy. Christ here perhaps intends to denote that the enemies which we have to encounter in following him are many and strong, and that *our* strength is comparatively feeble. ¶ *To meet him.* To contend with him. To gain a victory over him.

32. *Or else.* If he is not able. If he is satisfied that he would be defeated. ¶ *An ambassage.* Persons to treat with an enemy and propose terms of peace. These expressions are not to be improperly pressed in order to obtain from them a spiritual signification. The general scope of the parable is to be learned from the connection, and may be thus expressed: 1st. Every man who becomes a follower of Jesus should calmly and deliberately look at all the consequences of such an act and be prepared to meet them. 2d. Men in other things act with prudence and forethought. They do not begin to build without a reasonable prospect of being able to finish. They do not go to war when there is every prospect that they will be defeated. 3d. Religion is a work of soberness, of thought, of calm and fixed purpose, and no man can properly enter on it who does not resolve by the grace of God to fulfil all its requirements and make it the business of his life. 4th. We are to expect diffi-

ambassage, and desireth conditions
of peace.
33 So likewise, whosoever he be
of you that [b]forsaketh not all that
he hath, he cannot be my disciple.
34 Salt[c] *is* good; but if the salt
have lost its savour, wherewith
shall it be seasoned?
35 It is neither fit for the land,
nor yet for the dunghill; [d]*but* men
cast it out. He that hath ears to
hear, let him hear.

b Phi.3.7,8. c Mat.5.13; Mar.9.50. d Jn.15.6.

CHAPTER XV.

THEN[a] drew near unto him all
the publicans and sinners, for
to hear him.
2 And the Pharisees and scribes
murmured, saying, This man receiveth sinners, and [b]eateth with
them.
3 And he spake this parable
unto them, saying,
4 What[c] man of you, having an
hundred sheep, if he lose one of

a Mat.9.10,&c. b Ac.11.3; 1 Co.5.9-11; Ga.2.12. c Mat.18.12.

---

culties in religion. It will cost us the mortification of our sins, and a life of self-denial, and a conflict with our lusts, and the enmity and ridicule of the world. Perhaps it may cost us our reputation, or possibly our lives and liberties, and all that is dear to us; but we must cheerfully undertake all this, and be prepared for it all. 5th. If we do not deliberately resolve to leave all things, to suffer all things that may be laid on us, and to persevere to the end of our days in the service of Christ, we cannot be his disciples. No man can be a Christian who, when he makes a profession, is resolved after a while to turn back to the world; nor can he be a true Christian if he *expects* that he *will* turn back. If he comes not with a *full* purpose *always* to be a Christian; if he means not to persevere, by the grace of God, through all hazards, and trials, and temptations; if he is not willing to bear his cross, and meet contempt, and poverty, and pain, and death, without turning back, he *cannot* be a disciple of the Lord Jesus.

34, 35. See Notes on Mat. v. 13; Mar. ix. 49, 50. ¶ *Salt* is *good.* It is useful. It is good to preserve life and health, and to keep from putrefaction. ¶ *His savour.* Its saltness. It becomes tasteless or insipid. ¶ *Be seasoned.* Be salted again. ¶ *Fit for the land.* Rather, it is not fit *for land*—that is, it will not bear fruit of itself. You cannot sow or plant on it. ¶ *Nor for the dunghill.* It is not good for manure. It will not enrich the land. ¶ *Cast it out.* They throw it away as useless. ¶ *He that hath ears,* &c. See Mat. xi. 15. You are to understand that he that has not grace in his heart; who merely makes a profession of religion, and who sustains the same relation to true piety that this insipid and useless mass does to good salt, is useless in the church, and will be rejected. *Real* piety, true religion, is of vast value in the world. It keeps it pure, and saves it from corruption, as salt does meat; but a mere *profession* of religion is fit for nothing. It does no good. It is a mere encumbrance, and all such professors are fit only to be cast out and rejected. All such *must* be rejected by the Son of God, and cast into a world of wretchedness and despair. Comp. Mat. vii. 22, 23; viii. 12; xxiii. 30; xxv. 30; Re. iii. 16; Job viii. 13; xxxvi. 13.

CHAPTER XV.

1. *Publicans and sinners.* See Notes on Mat. ix. 10.

2. *Murmured.* They affected to suppose that if Jesus treated sinners kindly he must be fond of their society, and be a man of similar character. *They* considered it disgraceful to be with them or to eat with them, and they therefore brought a charge against him for it. They *would* not suppose that he admitted them to his society for the purpose of doing them good; nor did they remember that the very object of his coming was to call the wicked from their ways and to save them from death. ¶ *Receiveth sinners.* Receives them in a tender manner; treats them with kindness; does not drive them from his presence. ¶ *And eateth with them.* Contrary to the received maxims of the scribes. By eating with them he showed that he did not despise or overlook them.

3. *This parable.* See Notes on Mat. xiii. 3.

4–6. See Notes on Mat. xviii. 12, 13.

7. *Likewise joy,* &c. It is a principle of human nature that the *recovery* of an

them, doth not leave the ninety
and nine in the wilderness, and go
after that which is lost, until he
find it?
5 And when he hath found *it*, he
layeth *it* on his shoulders, rejoicing.
6 And when he cometh home,
he calleth together *his* friends and
neighbours, saying unto them, Rejoice with me; [d]for I have found
my sheep which was lost.
7 I say unto you, that likewise
joy shall be in heaven over one
sinner that repenteth, more than
over ninety and nine just persons
which [e]need no repentance.
8 Either what woman having ten
[1]pieces of silver, if she lose one
piece, doth not light a candle, and
sweep the house, and seek diligently
till she find *it?*
9 And when she hath found *it*,
she calleth *her* friends and *her*
neighbours together, saying, Rejoice with me; for I have found
the piece which I had lost.
10 Likewise, I say unto you,

d Ps.119.176; 1 Pe.2.25.

e ch.5.32.

[1] *Drachma*, here translated *a piece of silver*, is the eighth part of an ounce, which cometh to sevenpence halfpenny, and is equal to the Roman penny. See Mat.18.28.

object in danger of being lost, affords much more intense joy than the quiet *possession* of many that are safe. This our Saviour illustrated by the case of the lost sheep and of the piece of silver. It might also be illustrated by many other things. Thus we rejoice most in our health when we recover from a dangerous disease; we rejoice over a child rescued from danger or disease more than over those who are in health or safety. We rejoice that property is saved from conflagration or the tempest more than over much more that has not been in danger. This feeling our Lord represents as existing in heaven. *Likewise*, in like manner, or on the same principle, there is joy. ¶ *In heaven.* Among the angels of God. Comp. ver. 10. Heavenly beings are thus represented as rejoicing over those who repent on earth. They see the guilt and danger of men; they know what God has done for the race, and they rejoice at the recovery of any from the guilt and ruins of sin. ¶ *One sinner.* One rebel against God, however great may be his sins or however small. If a sinner, he must perish unless he repents; and they rejoice at his repentance because it recovers him back to the love of God, and because it will save him from eternal death. ¶ *That repenteth.* See Notes on Mat. ix. 13. ¶ *Just persons.* The word *persons* is not in the original. It means simply *just ones*, or those who have not sinned. The word may refer to angels as well as to men. There are no *just* men on earth who need no repentance, Ec. vii. 20; Ps. xiv. 2, 3; Ro. iii. 10-18. Our Saviour did not mean to imply that there were any such. He was speaking of what took place *in heaven*, or among *angels*, and of *their* emotions when they contemplate the creatures of God; and he says that *they* rejoiced in the repentance of one *sinner* more than in the holiness of many who had not fallen. We are not to suppose that he meant to teach that there were just ninety-nine holy angels to one sinner. He means merely that they rejoice more over the *repentance* of one sinner than they do over many who have not fallen. By this he vindicated his own conduct. The Jews did not deny the existence of angels. They would not deny that their feelings were proper. If *they* rejoiced in this manner, it was not improper for *him* to show similar joy, and especially to seek their conversion and salvation. If they rejoice also, it shows how desirable is the repentance of a sinner. They know of how much value is an immortal soul. They see what is meant by eternal death; and they do not feel *too much*, or have *too much anxiety* about the soul that can never die. Oh that men saw it as *they* see it! and oh that they would make an effort, such as angels see to be proper, to save their own souls and the souls of others from eternal death!

8-10. *Ten pieces of silver.* In the original, ten *drachmas*. The drachma was about the value of fifteen cents, and consequently the whole sum was about a dollar and a half, or six shillings. The sum was small, but it was all she had. The loss of one piece, therefore, was severely felt. ¶ *There is joy in the presence*, &c. Jesus in this parable expresses the same sentiment which he

there[f] is joy in the presence of the
angels of God over one sinner that
repenteth.
11 And he said, A certain man
had two sons;
12 And the younger of them said
to *his* father, Father, give me the
portion of goods that falleth *to me.*
And[g] he divided unto them *his*
living.

f Eze.18.23,32; 33.11; Ac.11.18; Phile.15,16.
g Mar.12.44.

13 And not many days after, the
younger son gathered all together
and took his journey into a far
country, and there wasted his substance with riotous living.
14 And when he had spent all,
there arose a mighty [h]famine in
that land; and he began to be in
want.
15 And he went and joined him-

h Am.8.11,12.

---

did in the preceding. A woman would have more immediate, present joy at finding a lost piece, than she would in the possession of those which had not been lost. *So*, says Christ, there is joy among the angels at the recovery of a single sinner.

11. *And he said.* Jesus, to illustrate still farther the sentiment which he had uttered, and to show that it was proper to rejoice over repenting sinners, proceeds to show it by a most beautiful and instructive parable. We shall see its beauty and propriety by remembering that the *design* of it was simply to *justify his conduct in receiving sinners*, and to show that to rejoice over their return was proper. This he shows by the feelings of a *father* rejoicing over the *return* of an ungrateful and dissipated son.

12. *And the younger of them said.* By this younger son we are to understand the publicans and sinners to be represented. By the elder, the Pharisees and scribes. ¶ *Give me the portion.* The part. ¶ *Of goods.* Of property. ¶ *That falleth* to me. That is properly my share. There is no impropriety in supposing that he was of age; and, as he chose to leave his father's house, it was proper that his father should, if he chose, give him the part of the estate which would be his. ¶ *He divided unto them his living.* His property, or *means* of living. The division of property among the Jews gave the elder son twice as much as the younger. In this case it seems the younger son received only money or movable property, and the elder chose to remain with his father and dwell on the paternal estate. The lands and fixed property remained in their possession. Among the ancient Romans and Syrophœnicians, it was customary, when a son came to the years of maturity, if he demanded his part of the inheritance, for the father to give it to him. This the son might claim by law. It is possible that such a custom may have prevailed among the Jews, and that our Saviour refers to some such demand made by the young man.

13. *Gathered all together.* Collected his property. If he had received flocks or grain, he sold them and converted them into money. As soon as this arrangement had been made he left his father's house. ¶ *Took his journey.* Went, or travelled. ¶ *Into a far country.* A country far off from his father's house. He went probably to trade or to seek his fortune, and in his wanderings came at last to this dissipated place, where his property was soon expended. ¶ *Wasted his substance.* Spent his property. ¶ *In riotous living.* Literally, "Living without saving anything." He lived extravagantly, and in the most dissolute company. See ver. 30. By his wandering away we may understand that sinners wander far away from God; that they fall into dissolute and wicked company; and that their wandering so far off is the reason why they fall into such company, and are so soon and so easily destroyed.

14. *A mighty famine.* Famines were common in Eastern nations. They were caused by the failure of the crops—by a want of timely rains, a genial sun, or sometimes by the prevalence of the plague or of the pestilence, which swept off numbers of the inhabitants. In this case it is very naturally connected with the luxury, the indolence, and the dissipation of the people in that land.

15. *Joined himself.* Entered the service of that citizen. Hired himself out to him. It would seem that he engaged to do any kind of work, even of the lowest kind. ¶ *A citizen.* One of the inhabitants of one of the cities or towns

self to a citizen of that country; and he sent him into his fields to feed swine.

16 And he would fain have [i]filled his belly with the husks that [k]the swine did eat; and no man gave unto him.

17 And when he came to himself, he said, How many hired servants of my father's have bread enough

[i] Is.44.20; Ho.12.1. [k] Ps.73.22.

of that region, probably a man of property. ¶ *Into the fields.* Out of the city where the owner lived. ¶ *To feed swine.* This was a very low employment, and particularly so to a *Jew.* It was forbidden to the Jews to eat swine, and of course it was unlawful to keep them. To be compelled, therefore, to engage in such an employment was the deepest conceivable degradation. The *object* of this image, as used by the Saviour in the parable, is to show the loathsome employments and the deep degradation to which sin leads men, and no circumstance could possibly illustrate it in a more striking manner than he has done here. Sin and its results everywhere have the same relation to that which is noble and great, which the feeding of swine had, in the estimation of a Jew, to an honourable and dignified employment.

16. *He would fain.* He would gladly. He desired to do it. ¶ *The husks.* The word *husks* with us denotes the outward covering of corn. In this there is little nourishment, and it is evident that this is not intended here; but the word used here denotes not only *husks*, but also leguminous plants, as beans, &c. It is also used to denote the fruit of a tree called the *carob* or *kharub-tree*, which is common in Ionia, Syria, and Rhodes. The tree is more bushy and thick-set than the apple-tree, and the leaves are larger and of a much darker green. The following is Dr. Thomson's description of the fruit of this tree (*The Land and the Book*, vol. i. p. 22): "The 'husks'—a mistranslation—are fleshy pods, somewhat like those of the locust-tree, from six to ten inches long and one broad, laid inside with a gelatinous substance, not wholly unpleasant to the taste when thoroughly ripe. I have seen large orchards of this kharub in Cyprus, where it is still the food which the swine do eat. The kharub is often called St. John's Bread, and also Locust-tree, from a mistaken idea about the food of the Baptist in the wilderness." The cut will give an idea of these *pods*, or "*husks*," as they are called in our translation. ¶ *No man gave unto him.* Some have understood this as meaning "no one gave him anything—

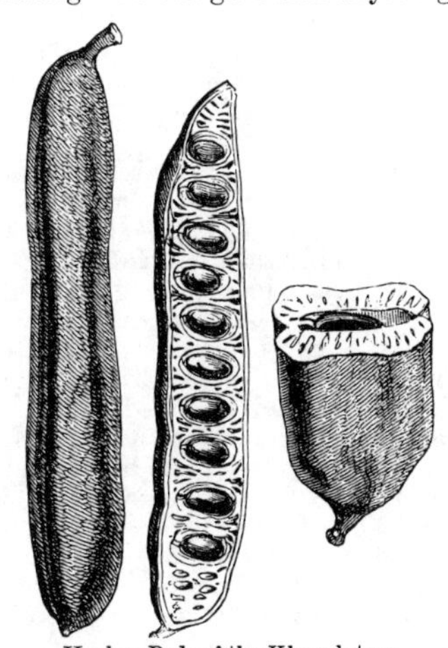

Husks—Pods of the Kharub-tree.

any bread or provisions;" but the connection requires us to understand it of the "husks." He did not go a begging—his master was bound to provide for his wants; but the provision which he made for him was so poor that he would have preferred the food of the swine. He desired a portion of *their* food, but that was not given him. A certain quantity was measured out for *them*, and *he* was not at liberty to eat it himself. Nothing could more strikingly show the evil of his condition, or the deep degradation, and pollution, and wretchedness of sin.

17. *He came to himself.* This is a very expressive phrase. It is commonly applied to one who has been *deranged*, and when he recovers we say he has *come to himself.* In this place it denotes that the folly of the young man was a kind of derangement—that he was insane. So it is of every sinner. Madness is in their hearts (Ec. ix. 3); they are estranged from God, and led, by the influence of evil passions, contrary to their better judgment and the decisions of a sound mind. ¶ *Hired servants.*

and to spare, and I perish with hunger!

18 I[l] will arise, and go to my father, and will say unto him, Father, I have sinned against heaven and before thee,

19 And am no more worthy to be called thy son: make me as one of thy hired servants.

20 And he arose, and came to his father. But when he was yet a [m]great way off, his father saw

l Ps.32.5.

m Ac.2.39; Ep.2.13,17.

Those in a low condition of life—those who were not born to wealth, and who had no friends to provide for them. ¶ *I perish.* I, who had property and a kind father, and who might have been provided for and happy.

18. *I will arise.* This is a common expression among the Hebrews to denote *entering on a piece of business.* It does not imply that he was *sitting*, but that he meant immediately to return. This should be the feeling of every sinner who is conscious of his guilt and danger. ¶ *To my father.* To his father, although he had offended him, and treated him unkindly, and had provoked him, and dishonoured him by his course of conduct. So the sinner. He has nowhere else to go but to *God.* He has offended him, but he may trust in his kindness. If *God* does not save him he cannot be saved. There is no other being that has an arm strong enough to deliver from sin; and though it is painful for a man to go to one whom he has offended—though he cannot go but with shame and confusion of face—yet, unless the sinner is willing to go to *God* and confess his faults, he can never be saved. ¶ *I have sinned.* I have been wicked, dissipated, ungrateful, and rebellious. ¶ *Against heaven.* The word *heaven* here, as it is often elsewhere, is put for God. I have sinned against *God.* See Mat. xxi. 25. It is also to be observed that one evidence of the genuineness of repentance is the feeling that our sins have been committed chiefly against *God.* Commonly we think most of our offences as committed against *man;* but when the sinner sees the true character of his sins, he sees that they have been aimed chiefly against *God*, and that the sins against *man* are of little consequence compared with those against God. So David, even after committing the crimes of adultery and murder—after having inflicted the deepest injury on *man*—yet felt that the sin as committed against *God* shut every other consideration out of view: *Against thee, thee* ONLY, *have I sinned*, &c., Ps. li. 4. ¶ *Before thee.* This means the same as *against* thee. The offences had been committed mainly against God, but they were to be regarded, also, as sins against his *father*, in wasting property which he had given him, in neglecting his counsels, and in plunging himself into ruin. He felt that he had *disgraced* such a father. A sinner will be sensible of his sins against his relatives and friends as well as against God. A true penitent will be as ready to *acknowledge* his offences against his fellow-men as those against his Maker.

19. *No more worthy*, &c. "Such has been my conduct that I have been a disgrace to my father. I am not fit to be honoured by being called the son of a man so kind and virtuous." ¶ *Make me as one*, &c. "Treat me as a servant. Let me come again into your family, but I do not ask to be treated *as a son.* I am willing to come in if you will give me only the support that you give to a servant." This evinced, 1st. Deep humility—such as a sinner should have. 2d. Love for his father's house—such as all penitents should have toward God's dwelling-place in heaven. 3d. Confidence in his father that he would treat him kindly, even if he treated him as a servant. Such confidence all returning penitents feel in God. They are assured that God will treat them kindly—that *whatever* he gives them will be more than they deserve, and they are therefore willing to be in his hands. Yet, 4th. He had no adequate sense of his father's kindness. He did not fully appreciate his character. He was far more kind than he had dared to hope he would be; just as all sinners undervalue the character of God, and find him always more kind than they had supposed. No sinner comes to God with a just and adequate view of his character, but *always* finds him more merciful than he had dared to hope.

20. *He arose, and came.* Was coming. But here is no indication of *haste.* He did not *run*, but came driven by his wants, and, as we may suppose, filled

him, and had compassion, and ran
and fell on his neck, and kissed
him.
21 And the son said unto him,
Father, [n]I have sinned against
heaven, and in thy sight, and am
no more worthy to be called thy
son.
22 But the father said to his
servants, [o]Bring forth the best
robe and put *it* on him; and put
a ring on his hand, and shoes on
his feet;
23 And bring hither the fatted
calf, and kill *it;* and let us eat and
be merry:
24 For[p] this my son [q]was dead,
and [r]is alive again; he [s]was lost,

n Ps.51.4.

o Zec.3.3-5. p ver.32. q Ep.2.1; 5.14; Re.3.1. r Ro.6.11,13. s Eze.34.4,16; ch.19.10.

with shame, and even with some doubts whether his father would receive him. ¶ *A great way off.* This is a beautiful description—the image of his father's happening to see him clad in rags, poor, and emaciated, and yet he recognized *his son*, and all the feelings of a father prompted him to go and embrace him. ¶ *Had compassion.* Pitied him. Saw his condition—his poverty and his wretched appearance—and was moved with compassion and love. ¶ *And ran.* This is opposed to the manner in which the son came. The beauty of the picture is greatly heightened by these circumstances. The son came slowly—the father *ran.* The love and joy of the old man were so great that he hastened to meet him and welcome him to his home. ¶ *Fell on his neck.* Threw his arms around his neck and embraced him. ¶ *And kissed him.* This was a sign at once of affection and reconciliation. This must at once have dissipated every doubt of the son about the willingness of his father to forgive and receive him. A kiss is a sign of affection, 1 Sa. x. 1; Ge. xxix. 13. This is evidently designed to denote the *readiness of God* to pity and pardon returning sinners. In this verse of inimitable beauty is contained the point of the parable, which was uttered by the Saviour to vindicate *his own conduct* in receiving sinners kindly. Who could *blame* this father for thus receiving his repenting son? Not even a Pharisee could blame him; and our Saviour thus showed them, so that *they* could not resist it, that *God* received returning sinners, and that it was right for *him* also to receive them and treat them with attention.

22. *The best robe.* The son was probably in rags. The joy of the father is expressed by clothing him in the best raiment, that he might appear well. The *robe* here mentioned is probably the outer garment; and the father told them to put on him the best one that was in the house—one reserved for festival occasions. See Ge. xxvii. 15. ¶ *A ring on his hand.* To wear a ring on the hand was one mark of wealth and dignity. The rich and those in office commonly wore them. Comp. Ja. ii. 2. To *give* a ring was a mark of favour, or of affection, or of conferring office. Comp. Ge. xli. 42; Es. viii. 2. Here it was expressive of the *favour* and affection of the father. ¶ *Shoes on* his *feet.* Servants, probably, did not usually wear shoes. The son returned, doubtless, without shoes—a condition very unlike that in which he was when he left home. When, therefore, the father commanded them to put shoes on him, it expressed his wish that he should not be treated *as a servant*, but *as a son.* The word *shoes* here, however, means no more than *sandals,* such as were commonly worn. And the meaning of all these images is the same—*that God will treat those who return to him with kindness and affection.* These images should not be attempted to be *spiritualized.* They are beautifully thrown in to fill up the narrative, and to express with more force the *general* truth that *God* will treat returning penitents with mercy and with love. To dress up the son in this manner was a proof of the father's affection. So God will bestow on sinners the marks of his confidence and regard.

23. *Be merry.* Literally, "eating, let us rejoice." The word *merry* does not quite express the meaning of the Greek. *Merriment* denotes a light, playful, jovial mirth. The Greek denotes simply *joy*—let us be *happy*, or *joyful.*

24. *Was dead.* This is capable of two significations: 1st. *I supposed* that he was dead, but I know now that he is alive. 2d. He was *dead* to *virtue*—he was sunk in pleasure and vice. The word is not unfrequently thus used. See 1 Ti. v. 6; Mat. viii. 22; Ro. vi. 13.

and is found. And they began to
be merry.
25 Now his elder son was in the
field: and as he came and drew
nigh to the house, he heard [t]music
and dancing.
26 And he called one of the
servants, and asked what these
things meant.
27 And he said unto him, Thy
brother is come; and thy father
hath killed the fatted calf, because
he hath received him safe and
sound.
28 And he was [u]angry, and
would not go in: therefore came
his father out and entreated him.
29 And he, answering, said to *his*
father, Lo, these many years do [v]I
serve thee, [w]neither transgressed
I at any time thy commandment;
and yet thou never gavest me a
kid, that I might make merry with
my friends;
30 But as soon as this thy son
was come, which hath devoured
thy living with harlots, thou hast
killed for him the fatted calf.
31 And he said unto him, [x]Son,

t Ps.30.11; 126.1,2. *u* Jonah 4.1-3; Ro.10.19.

v Is.65.5; ch.18.11. *w* Phi.3.6. *x* Ro.9.4; 11.1.

Hence to be restored to *virtue* is said to be restored again to life, Ro. vi. 13; Re. iii. 1; Ep. ii. 1. It is probable that this latter is the meaning here. See ver. 32. ¶ *Was lost.* Had wandered away from home, and we knew not where he was.

25. *In the field.* At work. This eldest son is designed to represent the Pharisees who had found fault with the Saviour. Their conduct is likened to that of this envious and unnatural brother. ¶ *Music and dancing.* Dancing was not uncommon among the Hebrews, and was used on various occasions. Thus Miriam celebrated the deliverance of the children of Israel from Egypt in dances as well as songs, Ex. xv. 20. David danced before the ark, 2 Sa. vi. 14. It was common at Jewish feasts (Ju. xxi. 19–21) and in public triumphs (Ju. xi. 34), and at all seasons of mirth and rejoicings, Ps. xxx. 11; Je. xxxi. 4, 13. It was also used in religious services by the idolaters (Ex. xxxii. 19), and also by the Jews, at times, in their religious services, Ps. cxlix. 3; cl. 4. In this case it was an expression of rejoicing. Our Lord expresses no opinion about its *propriety.* He simply states *the fact*, nor was there occasion for comment on it. His *mentioning it* cannot be pleaded for its lawfulness or propriety, any more than his mentioning the vice of the younger son, or the wickedness of the Pharisees, can be pleaded to justify their conduct. It is an expressive image, used in accordance with the known customs of the country, to express joy. It is farther to be remarked, that if the example of persons in Scripture be pleaded for dancing, it can be *only for just such dances as they practised*—for sacred or triumphal occasions.

26–28. *Safe and sound.* In health.

29. *A kid.* A young goat. This was of less value than the calf; and he complains that while his father had never given *him* a thing of so little value as *a kid*, he had now given his other son *the fatted calf.* ¶ *Make merry with.* Entertain them—give them a feast. This complaint was unreasonable, for his father had divided his property, and he *might* have had his portion, and his father had uniformly treated him with kindness. But it serves to illustrate the conduct of the scribes and Pharisees, and the folly of their complaint.

30. *This thy son.* This son of *thine.* This is an expression of great contempt. He did not call him *his brother*, but *his father's son*, to show at once his contempt for his younger brother, and for his father for having received him as he did. Never was there a more striking instance of petty malice, or more unjustifiable disregard of a father's conduct and will. ¶ *Thy living.* Thy property. This is still designed to irritate the father, and set him against his younger son. It was true that the younger son had been guilty, and foolish, and ungrateful; but he was penitent, and *that* was of more consequence to the father than all his property; and in the joy that he was penitent and was safe, he forgot his ingratitude and folly. So should the elder son have done.

31. *All I have is thine.* The property was divided. What remained was in reality the elder son's. He was heir to it all, and had a right, if he chose, to

thou art ever with me, and all that I have is thine.

32 It was [y]meet that we should [z]make merry and be glad; [a]for

y Jonah 4.10,11. z Ps.51.8; Is.35.10. a ver.24.

use it. He had therefore no right to complain.

This instructive and beautiful parable was designed to vindicate the conduct of Jesus—to show that it was right to receive sinners, and that the conduct of the Pharisees was unreasonable. The elder son represents the Pharisees; the younger, the returning sinner, whether Jew or Gentile; and the father, God, who is willing to receive them. The parable had the designed effect. It silenced the adversaries of Jesus and vindicated his own conduct. There is not, perhaps, anywhere to be found a more beautiful and touching narrative than this. Every circumstance is tender and happily chosen; every word has a meaning; every image is beautiful; and the narrative closes just where it is fitted to make the deepest impression. In addition to what has been suggested, we may learn from this parable the following lessons:—

1st. That the disposition of a sinner is selfish. He desires to get all that he can, and is impatient of delay, ver. 12.

2d. Sinners waste their blessings, and reduce themselves to a state of want and wretchedness, ver. 13. A life of sin brings on spiritual want and misery. It destroys the faculties, benumbs the mind, hardens the heart, abuses the beneficence of God, and makes us careless of him who gave us all that we have, and indifferent to the consequences of our own conduct.

3d. Sinners disregard the future woes that will come upon them. The young man cared not for any calamities that might be the result of his conduct. He went on heedlessly—like every sinner—to enjoy himself, and to squander what the toils of his father had procured for him.

4th. Afflictions are often the means of bringing sinners to reflection, ver. 14. While his property lasted the prodigal cared little about his father. When that was gone, and he was in the midst of a famine, he thought of his ways. When sinners are in prosperity they think little about God. When he takes away their mercies, and they are called to pass through afflictions, then they think of their ways, and remember that God can give them comfort.

5th. We have here an impressive exhibition of the wants and woes of a sinner. 1st. He had spent all. He had nothing. So the sinner. He has no righteousness, no comfort. 2d. He was far from God, away from his father, and in a land of strangers. The sinner has wandered, and has no friend. His miseries came upon him *because* he was so far away from God. 3d. His condition was wretched. He was needy, in famine, and without a friend. So the sinner. His condition is aptly denoted by that of the prodigal, who would gladly have partaken of the food of the swine. The sinner has taken the world for his portion, and it neither supplies the wants of his soul, nor gives him comfort when he is far away from his Father's home and from God.

6th. The sinner in this situation often applies to the wrong source for comfort, ver. 15. The prodigal should at once have returned to his father, but he rather chose to become a servant of a citizen of that region. The sinner, when sensible of his sins, should return at once to God; but he often continues still to wander. He tries new objects. He seeks new pleasures and new friends, and finds them equally unsatisfactory. He engages in new pursuits, but all in vain. He is still comfortless, and in a strange, a famished land.

7th. The repentance required in the gospel is a return to a right mind, ver. 17. Before his conversion the sinner was alienated from God. He was spiritually deranged. He saw not things as they are. Now he looks on the world as vain and unsatisfactory, and comes to himself. He thinks *aright* of God, of heaven, of eternity, and resolves to seek his happiness there. No man regards things as they are but he who sees the world to be vain, and eternity to be near and awful; and none acts with a *sane mind* but he who acts on the belief that he must soon die; that there is a God and a Saviour—a heaven and a hell.

8th. When the sinner returns he becomes sensible of the following things: 1st. That he is in danger of perishing, and must soon die but for relief—"I perish with hunger." 2d. That God is willing and able to save him—"How

this thy brother was dead, and is alive again; and was lost, and is found.

CHAPTER XVI.

AND he said also unto his disciples, There was a certain

---

many hired servants have bread enough *and to spare.*" There is abundance of mercy for all, and all may come. 3d. He begins to cherish a hope that this may be his. God is willing, and he feels that all that is needful is for him to go to him. 4th. He resolves to go to God—"I will arise and go." 5th. He comes to him willing to confess all his sins, and desirous of concealing none—"I will say, Father, I have sinned."

9th. True repentance is a voluntary act. It is not forced. It is the resolution of the sinner to go, and he cheerfully and cordially arises and goes, ver. 18.

10th. A real penitent feels that his sins have been committed against GOD, ver. 18.

11th. A true penitent also is willing to acknowledge his offences against his parents, brothers, friends, and all men, ver. 18.

12th. A real penitent is humble, ver. 18. He has no wish to conceal anything, or to be thought more highly of than he *ought* to be.

13th. God is willing to receive the true penitent, and has made the richest provision for his return and for his comfort. None need to hesitate to go. All who go, feeling that they are poor, and miserable, and blind, and naked, will find God willing to receive them, and none will be sent empty away.

14th. The joy at the return of sinners is great. Angels rejoice over it, and all holy beings are glad.

15th. We should not be envious at any favours that God may be pleased to bestow on others, ver. 32. He has given *us* more than we deserve; and if, by the sovereignty of his grace, he is pleased to endow others with more grace, or to give them greater talents, or to make them more useful, *we* have no cause to complain. We should rather rejoice that he is pleased to give such mercies to any of our race, and should praise him for the manifestation of his goodness, whether made to us or to other men.

16th. The sensible joy when the sinner returns to God is often greater than that which may be felt *after* the return, and yet the real *cause* of rejoicing be no greater. In times of revival, the sensible joy of Christians may be greater than in ordinary seasons. Their graces are quickened, their zeal kindled, and their hopes strengthened.

17th. If God is willing to receive sinners, if all holy beings rejoice, then how should Christians strive for their conversion, and seek for their return!

18th. If God is willing to receive sinners *now*, then all should at once return. There *will* be a time when he will not be willing to receive them. The day of mercy will be ended; and from the misery and want of this wretched world, they will go down to the deeper miseries and wants of a world of despair—where hope never comes; from whence the sinner can never return; and where the cheering thought can never enter the mind that in his Father's house there is bread enough and to spare, or where he must feel that if there *is*, it will be for ever untasted by the wretched prodigal in the land of eternal famine and death.

CHAPTER XVI.

1. *His disciples.* The word *disciples*, here, is not to be restricted to the twelve apostles or to the seventy. The parable appears to have been addressed to all the professed followers of the Saviour who were present when it was delivered. It is connected with that in the preceding chapter. Jesus had there been discoursing with the scribes and Pharisees, and vindicating his conduct in receiving kindly publicans and sinners. These *publicans and sinners* are here particularly referred to by the word *disciples.* It was with reference to *them* that the whole discourse had arisen. After Jesus had shown the Pharisees, in the preceding chapter, the propriety of his conduct, it was natural that he should turn and address his disciples. Among them there might have been some who were wealthy. The *publicans* were engaged in receiving taxes, in collecting money, and their chief danger arose from that quarter—from covetousness or dishonesty. Jesus always adapted his instructions to the circumstances of his hearers, and it was proper, therefore, that he should give *these disciples* instructions about their *peculiar* duties and dangers. He related this parable,

rich man which had a steward;
and the same was accused unto
him that he had wasted his goods.
2 And he called him, and said
unto him, How is it that I hear
this of thee? [a]give an account of
thy stewardship; for thou mayest
be no longer steward.
3 Then the steward said within
himself, What shall I do, for my

a ch.12.42; 1 Co.4.2; 1 Ti.4.14; 1 Pe.4.10.

therefore, to show them *the danger of the love of money;* the guilt it would lead to (ver. 1); the perplexities and shifts to which it would drive a man when once he had been dishonest (ver. 3-7); the necessity of using money aright, since it was their chief business (ver. 9); and the fact that if they would serve God aright they must give up supreme attachment to money (ver. 13); and that the first duty of religion demanded that they should resolve to serve God, and be honest in the use of the wealth intrusted to them. This parable has given great perplexity, and many ways have been devised to explain it. The above solution is the most simple of any; and if these plain principles are kept in view, it will not be difficult to give a consistent explanation of its particular parts. It should be borne in mind, however, that in this, as well as in other parables, we are not to endeavour to spiritualize every circumstance or allusion. We are to keep in view the great moral truth taught in it, that we cannot serve God and mammon, and that all attempts to do this will involve us in difficulty and sin. ¶ *A steward.* One who has charge of the affairs of a family or household; whose duty it is to provide for the family, to purchase provisions, &c. This is, of course, an office of trust and confidence. It affords great opportunity for dishonesty and waste, and for embezzling property. The master's eye cannot always be on the steward, and he may therefore squander the property, or hoard it up for his own use. It was an office commonly conferred on a slave as a reward for fidelity, and of course was given to him that, in long service, had shown himself most trustworthy. By the *rich man*, here, is doubtless represented God. By the *steward*, those who are his professed followers, particularly the *publicans* who were with the Saviour, and whose chief danger arose from the temptations to the improper use of the money intrusted to them. ¶ *Was accused.* Complaint was made. ¶ *Had wasted.* Had squandered or scattered it; had not been prudent and saving.

2. *Give an account.* Give a statement of your expenses and of your conduct while you have been steward. This is not to be referred to the day of judgment. It is a circumstance thrown into the parable to prepare the way for what follows. It is true that all will be called to give an account at the day of judgment, but we are not to derive that doctrine from such passages as this, nor are we to interpret this as teaching that our conscience, or the law, or any beings will *accuse us* in the day of judgment. All that will be indeed true, but it is not the truth that is taught in this passage.

3. *Said within himself.* Thought, or considered. ¶ *My lord.* My master, my employer. ¶ *I cannot dig.* This may mean either that his employment had been such that he could not engage in agriculture, not having been acquainted with the business, or that he was *unwilling* to stoop to so low an employment as to work daily for his support. *To dig*, here, is the same as to till the earth, to work at daily labour. ¶ *To beg.* These were the only two ways that presented themselves for a living—either to work for it, or to beg. ¶ *I am ashamed.* He was too proud for that. Besides, he was in good health and strength, and there was no good reason *why* he should beg—nothing which he could give as a cause for it. It is proper for the sick, the lame, and the feeble to beg; but it is *not* well for the able-bodied to do it, nor is it well to aid them, except by giving them employment, and compelling them to work for a living. He does a beggar who is able to work the most real kindness who sets him to work, and, as a general rule, we should not aid an able-bodied man or woman in any other way. Set them to work, and pay them a fair compensation, and you do them good in two ways, for the habit of labour may be of more value to them than the price you pay them.

4. *I am resolved.* He thought of his condition. He looked at the plans which occurred to him. He had been

lord taketh away from me the
stewardship? I cannot dig; to
beg I am ashamed.
4 I am resolved what to do, that
when I am put out of the stewardship they may receive me into
their houses.
5 So he called every one of his
lord's debtors *unto him*, and said
unto the first, How much owest
thou unto my lord?
6 And he said, An hundred
[1]measures of oil. And he said unto
him, Take thy bill, and sit down
quickly, and write fifty.
7 Then said he to another, And

1 The measure *Batos*, in the original, contained nine gallons three quarts. See Eze. 45.10-14.

dishonest, and knew that he must lose his place. It would have been better to have *considered before this*, and resolved on a proper course of life, and to be faithful to his trust; and his perplexity here teaches us that dishonesty will sooner or later lead us into difficulty, and that the path of honesty is not only the *right* path, but is the path that is filled with most comfort and peace. ¶ *When I am put out*, &c. When I lose my place, and have no home and means of support. ¶ *They may receive me*, &c. Those who are now under me, and whom I am resolved now to favour. He had been dishonest to his master, and, having *commenced* a course of dishonesty, he did not shrink from pursuing it. Having injured his master, and being now detected, he was willing still farther to injure him, to take revenge on him for removing him from his place, and to secure his own interest still at his expense. He was resolved to lay these persons under such obligations, and to show them so much kindness, that they could not well refuse to return the kindness to him and give him a support. We may learn here, 1st. That one sin leads on to another, and that one act of dishonesty will be followed by many more, if there is opportunity. 2d. Men who commit one sin cannot get along *consistently* without committing many more. One lie will demand many more to make it *appear* like the truth, and one act of cheating will demand many more to avoid detection. The beginning of sin is like the letting out of waters, and no man knows, if he indulges in one sin, where it will end. 3d. Sinners are selfish. They care more about *themselves* than they do either about God or truth. If they seek salvation, it is only for selfish ends, and because they desire a comfortable *abode* in the future world rather than because they have any regard to God or his cause.

5. *Called every one.* As he was *steward*, he had the management of all the affairs, and, of course, debts were to be paid to him. ¶ *Debtors.* Those who *owed* his master, or perhaps *tenants;* those who rented land of his master.

6. *An hundred measures.* The measure here mentioned is the *bath*, which contained, according to Dr. Arbuthnot's tables, 7½ gallons, or, according to the marginal note, about 9 gallons and 3 quarts. ¶ *Oil.* Oil of olives, or sweet oil. It was much used for lamps, as an article of food (Ex. xxix. 2), and also for anointing, and, of course, as an article of commerce, 1 Ki. v. 11. These were persons, doubtless, who had *rented* land of the rich man, and who were to give him a certain proportion of the produce. ¶ *Thy bill.* The contract, obligation, or *lease.* It was probably written as a *promise* by the debtor and signed by the steward, and thus became binding. Thus he had power to alter it, without supposing that his master would detect it. The bill or contract was in the hands of the steward, and he gave it back to him to write a new one. ¶ *Quickly.* He supposed that his master would soon remove him, and he was therefore in haste to have all things secure beforehand. It is worthy of remark, also, that *all* this was wrong. His master had called for the account; but, instead of rendering it, he engaged in other business, disobeyed his lord still, and, in contempt of his commands, sought his own interest. All sinners would be slow to give in their account to God if they could do it; and it is only because, when God calls them by death, they *cannot but go*, that they do not engage still in their own business and disobey him.

7. *Measures of wheat.* The measure here mentioned—the *kor*, or homer—contained, according to the tables of Dr. Arbuthnot, about 32 pecks, or 8 bushels; or, according to the marginal note, about 14 bushels and a *pottle.* A *pottle* is 4 pints. The Hebrew *kor*,

how much owest thou? And he said, An hundred [2] measures of wheat. And he said unto him, Take thy bill, and write fourscore.

8 And the lord commended the

[2] The measure here indicated contained about fourteen bushels and a pottle.

unjust steward because he had done wisely: for the children of this world are in their generation wiser than [b] the children of light.

9 And I say unto you, [c] Make

b Jn.12.36; Ep.5.8. *c* Ec.11.1; 1 Ti.6.18,19.

כֹּר—or *homer*, חֹמֶר—was equal to 10 baths or 70 gallons, and the actual amount of the measure, according to this, was not far from 8 gallons. Robinson (*Lex.*), however, supposes that the bath was 11½ gallons, and the kor or homer 14·45 bushels. The amount is not material to the proper understanding of the parable. ¶ *Fourscore.* Eighty.

8. *The lord commended.* Praised, or expressed admiration at his wisdom. These are not the words of Jesus, as commending him, but a part of the narrative or parable. His *master* commended him—saw that he was wise and considerate, though he was dishonest. ¶ *The unjust steward.* It is not said that his master commended him because he was *unjust*, but because he was *wise.* This is the only thing in his conduct of which there is any approbation expressed, and this approbation was expressed by *his master.* This passage cannot be brought, therefore, to prove that Jesus meant to commend his dishonesty. It was a commendation of his *shrewdness* or *forethought;* but the master could no more *approve* of his conduct as a moral act than he could the first act of cheating him. ¶ *The children of this world.* Those who are *devoted* to this world; who live for this world only; who are careful only to obtain property, and to provide for their temporal necessities. It does not mean that they are peculiarly wicked and profligate, but only that they are *worldly*, and anxious about earthly things. See Mat. xiii. 22; 2 Ti. iv. 10. ¶ *Are wiser.* More prudent, cunning, and anxious about their particular business. They show more skill, study more plans, contrive more ways to provide for themselves, than the children of light do to promote the interests of religion. ¶ *In their generation.* Some have thought that this means *in their manner of living*, or *in managing their affairs.* The word *generation* sometimes denotes the manner of life, Ge. vi. 9; xxxvii. 2. Others suppose that it means *toward* or *among the men of their own age.* They are more prudent and wise than Christians in regard to the people of their own time; they turn their connection with them to good account, and make it subserve their worldly interests, while Christians fail much more to use the world in such a manner as to subserve their spiritual interests. ¶ *Children of light.* Those who have been enlightened from above — who are Christians. This may be considered as the application of the parable. It does not mean that it is more wise to be a worldly man than to be a child of light, but that those who *are* worldly show much prudence in providing for themselves; seize occasions for making good bargains; are active and industrious; try to turn everything to the best account, and thus exert themselves to the utmost to advance their interests; while Christians often suffer opportunities of doing good to pass unimproved; are less steady, firm, and anxious about eternal things, and thus show less wisdom. Alas! this is too true; and we cannot but reflect here how different the world would be if all Christians were as anxious, and diligent, and prudent in religious matters as others are in worldly things.

9. *I say unto you.* I, Jesus, say to you, my disciples. ¶ *Make to yourselves friends.* Some have understood the word *friends*, here, as referring to the poor; others, to holy angels; and others, to God. Perhaps, however, the word should not be considered as referring to any particular *persons*, but is used in accordance with the preceding parable; for in the application our Saviour uses the *language* appropriated to the conduct of the steward to express the *general* truth that we are to make a proper use of riches. The steward had so managed his pecuniary affairs as to secure future comfort for himself, or so as to find friends that would take care of him *beyond* the time when he was put out of the office. That is, he would not be destitute, or cast off, or without comfort, when he was removed from his office. So, says our Saviour to the

to yourselves friends of the [3]mammon of unrighteousness; that, when ye fail, they may receive you into everlasting habitations.

10 He[d] that is faithful in that which is least, is faithful also in much; and he that is unjust in the least, is unjust also in much.

11 If, therefore, ye have not been faithful in the unrighteous [4]mam-

[3] or, *riches*. *d* Mat.25.21,23.

[4] or, *riches*.

---

publicans and those who had property, so use your property as *to secure* happiness and comfort beyond the time when you shall be removed from the present life. *Have reference*, in the use of your money, to the future. Do not use it so that it shall not avail you anything hereafter; but so employ it that, as the steward found friends, comfort, and a home by *his* wisdom in the use of it, so *you* may, after you are removed to another world, find friends, comfort, and a home—that is, may be happy in heaven. Jesus, here, does not say that we should do it *in the same way* that the steward did, for that was unjust; but only that we should *secure the result*. This may be done by using our riches as we *should do;* that is, by not suffering them to entangle us in cares and perplexities dangerous to the soul, engrossing the time, and stealing away the affections; by employing them in works of mercy and benevolence, aiding the poor, contributing to the advance of the gospel, bestowing them where they will do good, and in such a manner that God will *approve* the deed, and will bless us for it. Commonly riches are a *hindrance* to piety. To many they are snares; and, instead of positively *benefiting* the possessor, they are an injury, as they engross the time and the affections, and do not contribute at all to the eternal welfare of the soul. Everything may, by a proper use, be made to contribute to our welfare in heaven. Health, wealth, talents, and influence may be so employed; and this is what our Saviour doubtless means here. ¶ *Of the mammon. By means* of the mammon. ¶ *Mammon.* A Syriac word meaning riches. It is used, also, as an idol—the god of riches. ¶ *Of unrighteousness.* These words are an Hebrew expression for *unrighteous mammon*, the noun being used for an adjective, as is common in the New Testament. The word *unrighteous*, here, stands opposed to "*the true riches*" in verse 11, and means *deceitful, false, not to be trusted.* It has this meaning often. See 1 Ti. vi. 17; Lu. xii. 33; Mat. vi. 19; xix. 21. It does not signify, therefore, that they had acquired the property *unjustly*, but that property was *deceitful* and not to be trusted. The wealth of the steward was deceitful; he could not rely on its continuance; it was liable to be taken away at any moment. So the wealth of the world is deceitful. We cannot *calculate* on its continuance. It may give us support or comfort now, but it may be soon removed, or we taken from *it*, and we should therefore so use it as to derive benefit from it hereafter. ¶ *When ye fail.* When ye *are left*, or when ye *die*. The expression is derived from the parable as referring to the *discharge* of the steward; but it refers to *death*, as if God then *discharged* his people, or took them from their stewardship and called them to account. ¶ *They may receive you.* This is a form of expression denoting merely *that you may be received.* The plural form is used because it was used in the corresponding place in the parable, ver. 4. The direction is, so to use our worldly goods that *we may be received* into heaven when we die. *God* will receive us there, and we are to employ our property so that he will not cast us off for abusing it. ¶ *Everlasting habitations.* Heaven, the eternal *home* of the righteous, where all our wants will be supplied, and where there can be no more anxiety, and no more removal from enjoyments, 2 Co. v. 1.

10. *He that is faithful*, &c. This is a maxim which will almost universally hold true. A man that shows fidelity in small matters will also in large; and he that will cheat and defraud in little things will also in those involving more trust and responsibility. Fidelity is required in small matters as well as in those of more importance.

11. *Who will commit*, &c. If you are not faithful in the small matters pertaining to this world, if you do not use aright your property and influence, you cannot expect that God will commit to you the true riches of his grace. Men who are dishonest and worldly, and who do not employ the deceitful mam-

mon, who will commit to your trust
the true *riches?*
12 And if ye have not been
faithful in that which is another
man's, who shall give you that
which is your own?
13 No[e] servant can serve two
masters: for either he will hate
the one, and love the other; or
else he will hold to the one, and
despise the other. Ye cannot serve
God and mammon.
14 And the Pharisees also, [f]who
were covetous, heard all these
things; and they derided him.
15 And he said unto them, Ye
are they which [g]justify yourselves
before men; but [h]God knoweth
your hearts: for that which is
highly [i]esteemed among men is
abomination in the sight of God.
16 The[k] law and the prophets
were until John: since that time
the kingdom of God is preached,
and every man presseth into it.
17 And[l] it is easier for heaven

e Jos.24.15; Mat.6.24. f Mat.23.14.

g ch.10.29. h Ps.7.9; Je.17.10. i Pr.16.5; Mal.3.15. k Mat.11.12,13. l Ps.102.26; Is.40.8; 51.6.

---

mon as they ought, cannot expect to grow in grace. God does not confer grace upon them, and their being unfaithful in earthly matters is evidence that they *would be* also in much greater affairs, and would likewise *misimprove* the true riches. ¶ *True* riches. The graces of the gospel; the influences of the Spirit; eternal life, or religion. The riches of this world are false, deceitful, not to be trusted (ver. 9); the treasures of heaven are *true*, faithful, never-failing, Mat. vi. 19, 20.

12. *Another man's.* The word *man's* is not in the original. It is, "If ye have been unfaithful managers *for another.*" It refers, doubtless, to *God.* The wealth of the world is *his.* It is committed to us as his stewards. It is uncertain and deceitful, and at any moment he can take it away from us. It is still *his;* and if, while intrusted with *this*, we are unfaithful, we cannot expect that he will confer on us the rewards of heaven. ¶ *That which is your own.* The riches of heaven, which, if once given to us, may be considered as *ours*—that is, it will be permanent and fixed, and will not be taken away *as if* at the pleasure of another. We may *calculate* on it, and look forward with the assurance that it will *continue* to be *ours* for ever, and will not be taken away like the riches of this world, *as if* they were not ours. The meaning of the whole parable is therefore thus expressed: If we do not use the things of this world as we ought—with honesty, truth, wisdom, and integrity, we cannot have evidence of piety, and shall not be received into heaven. If we are true to that which is least, it is an evidence that we are the children of God, and he will commit to our trust that which is of infinite importance, even the eternal riches and glory of heaven.

13. See Notes on Mat. vi. 24.

14, 15. *They derided him.* The fact that they were "covetous" is here stated as the reason why they derided him, or, as it is literally, "they turned up the nose at him." They contemned or despised the doctrine which he had laid down, probably because it showed them that with their love of money they could not be the true friends of God, or that their profession of religion was really false and hollow. They were *attempting* to serve God and mammon, and they therefore looked upon his doctrine with contempt and scorn. ¶ *Justify yourselves. Attempt* to appear just; or, you aim to appear righteous in the sight of men, and do not regard the *heart.* ¶ *That which is highly esteemed.* That is, mere external works, or actions performed merely to *appear* to be righteous. ¶ *Is abomination.* Is abominable, or hateful. The word used here is the one that in the Old Testament is commonly given to *idols*, and denotes God's *abhorrence* of such conduct. These words are to be applied *chiefly* to what Jesus was discoursing about. There are many things esteemed among men which are *not* abomination in the sight of God; as, for example, truth, parental and filial affection, industry, &c. But many things, much sought and admired, *are* hateful in his sight. The love of wealth and show, ambition and pride, gay and splendid vices, and all the wickedness that men contrive to *gild* and to make appear like virtue—external acts that *appear* well while the heart is evil—are abominable in the sight of God, and

and earth to pass, than one tittle of the law to fail.

18 Whosoever [m]putteth away his wife, and marrieth another, committeth adultery; and whosoever marrieth her that is put away from *her* husband, committeth adultery.

19 There was a certain rich man, which was clothed in purple and fine linen, and fared sumptuously every day:

20 And there was a certain beggar named Lazarus, which was laid at his gate, full of sores,

m Mat.5.32; 1 Co.7.10,11.

---

should be in the sight of men. Comp. Lu. xviii. 11-14; 1 Sa. xvi. 7.

16. See Notes on Mat. xi. 12-14. ¶ *Every man.* Many men, or multitudes. This is an expression that is very common, as when we say everybody is engaged in a piece of business, meaning that it occupies general attention.

17. See Notes on Mat. v. 18.

18. See Notes on Mat. v. 32. These verses occur in Matthew in a different order, and it is not improbable that they were spoken by our Saviour at different times. The design, here, seems to be to reprove the Pharisees for not observing the law of Moses, notwithstanding their great pretensions to external righteousness, and to show them that they had *really* departed from the law.

19. *There was a certain rich man.* Many have supposed that our Lord here refers to a *real history*, and gives an account of some man who had lived in this manner; but of this there is no evidence. The probability is that this narrative is to be considered as a parable, referring not to any particular case which *had* actually happened, but teaching that such cases *might* happen. The *design* of the narrative is to be collected from the previous conversation. He had taught the danger of the love of money (ver. 1 and 2); the deceitful and treacherous nature of riches (ver. 9-11); that what was in high esteem on earth was hateful to God (ver. 15); that men who did not use their property aright could not be received into heaven (ver. 11, 12); that they ought to listen to Moses and the prophets (ver. 16, 17); and that it was the duty of men to show kindness to the poor. The design of the parable was to impress all these truths more vividly on the mind, and to show the Pharisees that, with all their boasted righteousness and their external correctness of character, they might be lost. Accordingly he speaks of no great fault in the rich man—no external, degrading vice—no open breach of the law; and leaves us to infer that *the mere possession of wealth* may be dangerous to the soul, and that a man surrounded with every temporal blessing may perish for ever. It is remarkable that he gave no *name* to this rich man, though the poor man is mentioned by name. If this was a parable, it shows us how unwilling he was to fix suspicion on anyone. If it was not a parable, it shows also that he would not drag out wicked men before the public, but would conceal as much as possible all that had any connection with them. The *good* he would speak well of by name; the evil he would not *injure* by exposing them to public view. ¶ *Clothed in purple.* A purple robe or garment. This colour was expensive as well as splendid, and was chiefly worn by princes, nobles, and those who were very wealthy. Comp. Mat. xxvii. 28. See Notes on Is. i. 18. ¶ *Fine linen.* This linen was chiefly produced of the flax that grew on the banks of the Nile, in Egypt, Pr. vii. 16; Eze. xxvii. 7. It was peculiarly soft and white, and was therefore much sought as an article of luxury, and was so expensive that it could be worn only by princes, by priests, or by those who were very rich, Ge. xli. 42; 1 Ch. xv. 27; Ex. xxviii. 5. ¶ *Fared sumptuously.* Feasted or lived in a splendid manner. ¶ *Every day.* Not merely occasionally, but constantly. This was a mark of great wealth, and, in the view of the world, evidence of great happiness. It is worthy of remark that Jesus did not charge on him any crime. He did not say that he had acquired this property by dishonesty, or even that he was unkind or uncharitable; but simply that he *was a rich man*, and that his riches did not secure him from death and perdition.

20, 21. *Beggar.* Poor man. The original word does not mean *beggar*, but simply that he was *poor*. It should have been so translated to keep up the contrast with the *rich man.* ¶ *Named Lazarus.* The word Lazarus is Hebrew,

21 And desiring to be fed with
the crumbs which fell from the
rich man's table: moreover, the
dogs came and licked his sores.
22 And it came to pass that the
beggar died, and was carried by
the angels into [n]Abraham's bosom:
[o]the rich man also died, and was
buried.
23 And[p] in hell he lifted up his

n Mat.8.11. o Pr.14.32. p Re.14.10,11.

and means a man destitute of help, a needy, poor man. It is a name given, therefore, to denote his needy condition. ¶ *Laid at his gate.* At the door of the rich man, in order that he might obtain aid. ¶ *Full of sores.* Covered with ulcers; afflicted not only with poverty, but with loathsome and offensive ulcers, such as often are the accompaniments of poverty and want. These circumstances are designed to show how different was his condition from that of the rich man. *He* was clothed in purple; the poor man was covered with sores; *he* fared sumptuously; the poor man was dependent even for the crumbs that fell from the rich man's table. ¶ *The dogs came.* Such was his miserable condition that even the dogs, as if moved by pity, came and licked his sores in kindness to him. These circumstances of his misery are very touching, and his condition, contrasted with that of the rich man, is very striking. It is not affirmed that the rich man was unkind to him, or drove him away, or refused to aid him. The narrative is designed simply to show that the possession of wealth, and all the blessings of this life, could not exempt from death and misery, and that the lowest condition among mortals may be connected with life and happiness beyond the grave. There was no provision made for the helpless poor in those days, and consequently they were often laid at the gates of the rich, and in places of public resort, for charity. See Ac. iii. 2. The gospel has been the means of all the public charity now made for the needy, as it has of providing hospitals for those who are sick and afflicted. No pagan nation ever had a hospital or an almshouse for the needy, the aged, the blind, the insane. Many heathen nations, as the Hindoos and the Sandwich Islanders, destroyed their aged people; and *all* left their poor to the miseries of public begging, and their sick to the care of their friends or to private charity.

22. *Was carried by the angels.* The Jews held the opinion that the spirits of the righteous were conveyed by angels to heaven at their death. Our Saviour speaks in accordance with this opinion; and as he expressly affirms the fact, it seems as proper that it should be taken literally, as when it is said the rich man died and was buried. Angels are ministering spirits sent forth to minister to those who are heirs of salvation (He. i. 14), and there is no more improbability in the supposition that they attend departing spirits to heaven, than that they attend them while on earth. ¶ *Abraham's bosom.* This is a phrase taken from the practice of reclining at meals, where the head of one lay on the bosom of another, and the phrase therefore denotes intimacy and friendship. See Notes on Mat. xxiii. 6. Also Jn. xiii. 23; xxi. 20. The Jews had no doubt that Abraham was in paradise. To say that Lazarus was in his bosom was therefore the same as to say that he was admitted to heaven and made happy there. The Jews, moreover, boasted very much of being the friends of Abraham and of being his descendants, Mat. iii. 9. To be his friend was, in their view, the highest honour and happiness. Our Saviour therefore showed them that this poor and afflicted man might be raised to the highest happiness, while the rich, who prided themselves on their being descended from Abraham, might be cast away and lost for ever. ¶ *Was buried.* This is not said of the poor man. Burial was thought to be an honour, and funerals were, as they are now, often expensive, splendid, and ostentatious. This is said of the rich man to show that he had *every* earthly honour, and all that the world calls happy and desirable.

23. *In hell.* The word here translated hell (*Hades*) means literally a dark, obscure place; the place where departed spirits go, but especially the place where *wicked* spirits go. See Notes on Job x. 21, 22; Is. xiv. 9. The following circumstances are related of it in this parable: 1st. It is *far off* from the abodes of the righteous. Lazarus was seen *afar off*. 2d. It is a place of torment. 3d. There is a great gulf fixed between that and heaven, ver. 26. 4th. The

eyes, being in torments, and seeth Abraham afar off, and Lazarus in his bosom:

24 And he cried and said, Father Abraham, have mercy on me, and send Lazarus, that he may dip the

---

suffering is great. It is represented by *torment* in a flame, ver. 24. 5th. There will be no escape from it, ver. 26. The word *hell* here means, therefore, that dark, obscure, and miserable place, far from heaven, where the wicked shall be punished for ever. ¶ *He lifted up his eyes.* A phrase in common use among the Hebrews, meaning *he looked*, Ge. xiii. 10; xviii. 2; xxxi. 10; Da. viii. 3; Lu. vi. 20. ¶ *Being in torment.* The word *torment* means *pain, anguish* (Mat. iv. 24); particularly the pain inflicted by the ancients in order to induce men to make confession of their crimes. These *torments* or tortures were the keenest that they could inflict, such as the rack, or scourging, or burning; and the use of the word here denotes that the sufferings of the wicked can be represented only by the extremest forms of human suffering. ¶ *And seeth Abraham*, &c. This was an aggravation of his misery. One of the first things that occurred in hell was to look up, and see the poor man that lay at his gate completely happy. What a contrast! Just now he was rolling in wealth, and the poor man was at his gate. He had no expectation of these sufferings: now they have come upon him, and Lazarus is happy and for ever fixed in the paradise of God. It is more, perhaps, than we are authorized to infer, that the wicked will *see* those who are in paradise. That they will *know* that they are there is certain; but we are not to suppose that they will be so near together as to be seen, or as to make conversation possible. These circumstances mean that there will be a *separation*, and that the wicked in hell will be conscious that the righteous, though on earth they were poor or despised, will be in heaven. Heaven and hell will be far from each other, and it will be no small part of the misery of the one that it is far and for ever removed from the other.

24. *Father Abraham.* The Jews considered it a signal honour that Abraham was their *father*—that is, that they were *descendants* from him. Though this man was now in misery, yet he seems not to have abandoned the idea of his relation to the father of the faithful. The Jews supposed that departed spirits might know and converse with each other. See Lightfoot on this place. Our Saviour speaks in conformity with that prevailing opinion; and as it was not easy to convey ideas about the spiritual world without some such representation, he therefore speaks in the language which was usual in his time. We are not, however, to suppose that this was *literally* true, but only that it was designed to represent more clearly the sufferings of the rich man in hell. ¶ *Have mercy on me.* Pity me. The rich man is not represented as calling on *God*. The mercy of God will be at an end when the soul is lost. Nor did he *ask* to be released from that place. Lost spirits *know* that their sufferings will have no end, and that it would be in vain to ask to escape the place of torment. Nor does he ask to be admitted where Lazarus was. He had no *desire* to be in a holy place, and he well knew that there was no restoration to those who once sink down to hell. ¶ *Send Lazarus.* This shows how low he was reduced, and how the circumstances of men change when they die. Just before, Lazarus was laid at his gate full of sores; now he is happy in heaven. Just before, he had nothing to give, and the rich man could expect to derive no benefit from him; now he asks, as the highest favour, that he might come and render him relief. Soon the poorest man on earth, if he is a friend of God, will have mercies which the rich, if unprepared to die, can never obtain. The rich will no longer despise such men; they would *then* be glad of their friendship, and would beg for the slightest favour at their hands. ¶ *Dip the tip*, &c. This was a small favour to ask, and it shows the greatness of his distress when so small a thing would be considered a great relief. ¶ *Cool my tongue.* The effect of great *heat* on the body is to produce almost insupportable thirst. Those who travel in burning deserts thus suffer inexpressibly when they are deprived of water. So *pain* of any kind produces thirst, and particularly if connected with fever. The sufferings of the rich man are therefore represented as producing burning *thirst*, so much that even a drop of water would be refreshing to his tongue. We can

tip of his finger in water and [q]cool my tongue; for I am [r]tormented in this flame.

25 But Abraham said, Son, remember that thou [s]in thy lifetime receivedst thy good things, and likewise Lazarus evil things; but now he is comforted, and thou art tormented.

26 And beside all this, between us and you there is a great gulf fixed; so that they which would

q Zec.14.12. r Is.66.24; Mar.9.44,&c. s Job 21.13; Ps.73.12-19; ch.6.24.

scarce form an idea of more distress and misery than where this is continued from one day to another without relief. We are not to suppose that he had been guilty of any particular wickedness with his *tongue* as the cause of this. It is simply an idea to represent the natural effect of great suffering, and especially suffering in the midst of great heat. ¶ *I am tormented.* I am in anguish—in insupportable distress. ¶ *In this flame.* The lost are often represented as suffering *in flames*, because *fire* is an image of the severest pain that we know. It is not certain, however, that the wicked will be doomed to suffer in *material* fire. See Notes on Mar. iv. 44.

25. *Son.* This is a representation designed to correspond with the word *father*. He was a descendant of Abraham—a Jew—and Abraham is represented as calling this thing to his remembrance. It would not lessen his sorrows to remember that he was a *son* of Abraham, and that he ought to have lived worthy of that relation to him. ¶ *Remember.* This is a cutting word in this place. One of the chief torments of hell will be the *remembrance* of what was enjoyed and of what was done in this world. Nor will it be any mitigation of the suffering to spend an *eternity* where there will be nothing else to do, day or night, but to *remember* what *was* done, and what *might have been*, if the life had been right. ¶ *Thy good things.* That is, property, splendour, honour. ¶ *Evil things.* Poverty, contempt, and disease. ¶ *But now*, &c. How changed the scene! How different the condition! And how much *better* was the portion of Lazarus, after all, than that of the rich man! It is probable that Lazarus had the most *real* happiness in the land of the living, for riches without the love of God can never confer happiness like the favour of God, even in poverty. But the comforts of the rich man are now gone for ever, and the joys of Lazarus have just commenced. *One* is to be comforted, and *the other* to be tormented, to all eternity. How much better, therefore, is poverty, with the friendship of God, than riches, with all that the world can bestow! And how foolish to seek our chief pleasures only in this life!

26. *A great gulf.* The word translated *gulf* means *chasm*, or the broad, yawning space between two elevated objects. In this place it means that there is no way of passing from one to the other. ¶ *Fixed.* Strengthened—made firm or immovable. It is so established that it will *never* be movable or passable. It will *for ever* divide heaven and hell. ¶ *Which would pass.* We are not to press this passage literally, as if those who are in heaven would *desire* to go and visit the wicked in the world of woe. The simple meaning of the statement is, that there can be no communication between the one and the other—there can be no passing from one to the other. It is impossible to conceive that the righteous would desire to leave their abodes in glory to go and dwell in the world of woe; nor can we suppose that they would wish to go for any reason unless it were possible to furnish relief. That will be out of the question. Not even a drop of water will be furnished as a relief to the sufferer. ¶ *Neither can they pass to us*, &c. There can be no doubt that the wicked will *desire* to pass the gulf that divides them from heaven. They would be glad to be in a state of happiness; but all such wishes will be vain. How, in the face of the solemn statement of the Saviour here, can men believe that there will be a *restoration* of all the wicked to heaven? He solemnly assures us that there can be no passage from that world of woe to the abodes of the blessed; yet, in the face of this, many Universalists hold that hell will yet be vacated of its guilty millions, and that all its miserable inhabitants will be received to heaven! Who shall conduct them across this gulf, when Jesus Christ says it *cannot* be passed? Who shall build a bridge over that yawning chasm which he says is "*fixed?*" No: if there

pass from hence to you cannot;
neither[t] can they pass to us that
would come from thence.
27 Then he said, I pray thee,
therefore, father, that thou wouldest send him to my father's house;
28 For I have five brethren; that
he may testify unto them, lest they
also come into this place of torment.
29 Abraham saith unto him,

t Eze.28.24.

[u]They have Moses and the prophets; let them hear them.
30 And he said, Nay, father
Abraham; but if one went unto
them from the dead, they will repent.
31 And he said unto him, [v]If
they hear not Moses and the prophets, [w]neither will they be persuaded though one rose from the
dead.

u Is.34.16; Jn.5.39. v 2 Co.4.3. w Jn.12.10,11.

---

is anything certain from the Scripture, it is that they who enter hell return no more; they who sink there sink for ever.

27, 28. *Five brethren.* The number *five* is mentioned merely to preserve the appearance of verisimilitude in the story. It is not to be spiritualized, nor are we to suppose that it has any hidden or inscrutable meaning. ¶ *May testify unto them.* May bear *witness* to them, or may inform them of what is my situation, and the dreadful consequences of the life that I have led. It is remarkable that he did not ask to go himself. He knew that he *could not* be released, even for so short a time. His condition was fixed. Yet he had no wish that his friends should suffer, and he supposed that if one went from the dead they would hear him.

29. *They have Moses.* The writings of Moses. The first five books of the Bible. ¶ *The prophets.* The remainder of the Old Testament. What the prophets had written. ¶ *Hear them.* Hear them speak in the Scriptures. Read them, or hear them read in the synagogues, and *attend* to what they have delivered.

30. *Nay.* No. They will *not hear* Moses and the prophets. They have heard them so long in vain, that there is no prospect now that they will attend to the message; but if one should go to them directly from the eternal world they would hear him. The novelty of the message would attract their attention, and they would listen to what he would say.

31. *Be persuaded.* Be convinced of the truth; of the danger and folly of their way; of the certainty of their suffering hereafter, and be induced to turn from sin to holiness, and from Satan unto God.

From this impressive and instructive parable we may learn—

1st. That the souls of men do not die with their bodies.

2d. That the soul is *conscious* after death; that it does not *sleep*, as some have supposed, till the morning of the resurrection.

3d. That the righteous are taken to a place of happiness immediately at death, and the wicked consigned at once to misery.

4th. That wealth does not secure from death.

"How vain are riches to secure
Their haughty owners from the grave!"

The rich, the beautiful, the gay, as well as the poor, go down to the grave. All their pomp and apparel, all their honours, their palaces, and their gold cannot save them. Death can as easily find his way into the splendid mansions of the rich as into the cottages of the poor; and the rich shall turn to the same corruption, and soon, like the poor, be undistinguished from common dust and be unknown.

5th. We should not envy the condition of the rich.

"On slippery rocks I see them stand,
And fiery billows roll below.

"Now let them boast how tall they rise,
I'll never envy them again;
There they may stand with haughty eyes,
Till they plunge deep in endless pain.

"Their fancied joys how fast they flee!
Like dreams, as fleeting and as vain;
Their songs of softest harmony
Are but a prelude to their pain."

6th. We should strive for a better inheritance than can be possessed in this life.

"Now I esteem their mirth and wine
Too dear to purchase with my blood:
Lord, 'tis enough that *thou* art mine—
My life, my portion, and my God."

7th. The sufferings of the wicked in hell will be indescribably great. Think

CHAPTER XVII.

THEN said he unto the disciples, [a]It is impossible but
that offences will come; but woe
unto him through whom they come!
2 It were better for him that a
millstone were hanged about his
neck, and he cast into the sea, than
that he should offend one of these
little ones.
3 Take heed to yourselves: If
thy brother trespass against thee,
[b]rebuke him; and if he repent,
forgive him.
4 And if he trespass against thee
seven times in a day, and seven
times in a day turn again to thee,
saying, I repent, [c]thou shalt forgive him.
5 And the apostles said unto the
Lord, [d]Increase our faith.
6 And the Lord said, [e]If ye had

a Mat.18.6,7; Mar.9.42.

b Le.19.17. *c* Mat.6.12,14; Col.3.13. *d* He.12.2. *e* Mat.17.20; 21.21; Mar.9.23; 11.23.

---

what is represented by *torment;* by burning flame; by insupportable thirst; by that state where a single *drop* of water would afford relief. Remember that *all this* is but a representation of the pains of the damned, and that this will have no intermission day or night, but will continue from year to year, and age to age, without any end, and you have a faint view of the sufferings of those who are in hell.

8th. There is a place of sufferings beyond the grave—a hell. If there is not, then this parable has no meaning. It is impossible to make *anything* of it unless it be designed to teach that.

9th. There will never be any escape from those gloomy regions. There is a gulf fixed—*fixed*, not movable. Nor can any of the damned beat a pathway across this gulf to the world of holiness.

10th. We see the amazing folly of those who suppose there may be an *end* to the sufferings of the wicked, and who, on that supposition, seem willing to go down to hell to suffer a long time, rather than go at once to heaven. If man were to suffer but a thousand years, or even *one* year, why should he be so foolish as to choose that suffering rather than go at once to heaven, and be happy at once when he dies?

11th. God gives us sufficient warning to prepare for death. He has sent his Word, his servants, his Son; he warns us by his Spirit and his providence; by the entreaties of our friends and by the death of sinners; he offers us heaven, and he threatens hell. If all this will not move sinners, what *would* do it? There is *nothing* that would.

12th. God will give us nothing farther to warn us. No dead man will come to life to tell us of what he has seen. If he *did*, we would not believe him. Religion appeals to man not by ghosts and frightful apparitions. It appeals to their reason, their conscience, their hopes, their fears. It sets life and death soberly before men, and if they *will not* choose the former, they must die. If you will not hear the Son of God and the warnings of the Scriptures, there is nothing which you *will* or *can* hear. You will *never* be persuaded, and will *never* escape the place of torment.

CHAPTER XVII.

1, 2. *It is impossible.* It cannot but happen. Such is the state of things that *it will be.* See these verses explained in the Notes on Mat. xviii. 6, 7.

3, 4. See Notes on Mat. xviii. 15, 21, 22. *Trespass against thee.* Sin against thee, or does anything that gives you an offence or does you an injury. ¶ *Rebuke.* Reprove. Go and tell him his fault, and seek an explanation. Acquaint him with what has been the effect of his conduct, and the state of your feelings, that he may acknowledge his error and repent.

5. *Increase our faith.* This duty of forgiving offences seemed so difficult to the disciples that they strongly felt the need of an increase of faith. They felt that they were prone themselves to harbour resentments, and that it required an additional increase of true religion to enable them to comply with the requirements of Jesus. We may learn from this—1st. That Jesus has *the power* of increasing the faith of his people. Strength comes from him, and especially strength to believe the gospel. Hence he is called the *Author* and *Finisher* of our faith, He. xii. 2. 2d. The duty of forgiving offences is one of the most difficult duties of the Christian religion. It is so contrary to our natural feelings; it implies such elevation above

faith as a grain of mustard-seed, ye might say unto the sycamine-tree, Be thou plucked up by the root, and be thou planted in the sea, and it should obey you.

7 But which of you, having a servant ploughing, or feeding cattle, will say unto him by and by, when he is come from the field, Go, and sit down to meat?

---

the petty feelings of malice and revenge, and is so contrary to the received maxims of the world, which teach us to *cherish* rather than to forgive the memory of offences, that it is no wonder our Saviour dwells much on this duty, and so strenuously insists on it in order to our having evidence that our hearts have been changed. Some have thought that this prayer that he would increase their faith refers to the power of working miracles, and especially to the case recorded in Mat. xvii. 16–20.

6. See Mat. xvii. 20. *Sycamine-tree.* This name, as well as sycamore, is given, among us, to the large tree commonly called the buttonwood; but the tree here mentioned is different. The Latin Vulgate and the Syriac versions translate it *mulberry-tree.* It is said to have been a tree that commonly grew in Egypt, of the size and appearance of a mulberry-tree, but bearing a species of

Sycamore (*Ficus Sycomorus*).

figs. This tree was common in Palestine. It is probable that our Lord was standing by one as he addressed these words to his disciples. Dr. Thomson (*The Land and the Book*, vol. i. p. 22–24) says of this tree: "It is generally planted by the wayside, in the open space where several paths meet." [Comp. Lu. xix. 4.] "This sycamore is a remarkable tree. It not only bears several crops of figs during the year, but these figs grow on short stems along the trunk and large branches, and not at the end of twigs, as in other fruit-bearing trees. The figs are small, and of a greenish-yellow colour. At Gaza and Askelon I saw them of a purple tinge, and much larger than they are in this part of the country. They were carried to market in large quantities, and appeared to be more valued there than with us. Still, they are, at best, very insipid, and none but the poorer classes eat them. It is easily propagated, merely by planting a stout branch in the ground, and watering it until it has struck its roots into the soil. This it does with great rapidity and to a vast depth. It was with reference to this latter fact that our Lord selected it to illustrate the power of faith. Now, look at this tree—its ample girth, its wide-spread arms branching off from the parent trunk only a few feet from the ground; then examine its enormous roots, as thick, as numerous, and as wide-spread into the deep soil below as the branches extend into the air above—the very best type of invincible steadfastness. What power on earth can pluck up such a tree? Heaven's thunderbolt may strike it down, the wild tornado may tear it to fragments, but nothing short of miraculous power can fairly pluck it up by the roots."

7. *Having a servant*, &c. This parable appears to have been spoken with reference to the rewards which the disciples were expecting in the kingdom of the Messiah. The occasion on which it was spoken cannot be ascertained. It does not seem to have any particular connection with what goes before. It may be supposed that the disciples were somewhat impatient to have the kingdom restored to Israel (Ac. i. 6)—that is, that he would assume his kingly power, and that they were impatient of the *delay*, and anxious to enter on *the rewards* which they expected, and which they not improbably were expecting in consequence of their devotedness to him. In answer to these expectations, Jesus spoke this parable, showing them, 1st. That they should be rewarded as a servant would be provided for; but, 2d. That this was not the *first* thing; that there was a proper *order* of things, and that thus the reward might be delayed,

8 And will not rather say unto
him, Make ready wherewith I may
sup, and gird thyself, and serve
me till I have eaten and drunken;
and afterward thou shalt eat and
drink?
9 Doth he thank that servant because he did the things that were
commanded him? I trow not.
10 So likewise ye, when ye shall
have done all those things which
are commanded you, say, [f]We are
unprofitable servants; we have
done that which was our duty to do.

f Job 22.3; 35.7; Ps.16.2,3; Is.64.6; Ro.11.35; 1 Co. 9.16,17.

11 And it came to pass, as he
went to Jerusalem, that he passed
through the midst of [g]Samaria
and Galilee.
12 And as he entered into a certain village, there met him ten
men that were lepers, which [h]stood
afar off:
13 And they lifted up *their*
voices, and said, Jesus, Master,
have mercy on us.
14 And when he saw *them*, he
said unto them, [i]Go show yourselves unto the priests. And it

g ch.9.51,52; Jn.4.4. h Le.13.46. i Le.13.2; 14.3; Mat.8.4; ch.5.14.

as a servant would be provided for, but at the proper time, and at the pleasure of the master; and, 3d. That this reward was not to be expected as a matter of *merit*, but would be given at the good pleasure of God, for they were but unprofitable servants. ¶ *By and by.* This should have been translated *immediately*. He would not, *as the first thing*, or *as soon as* he returned from the field, direct him to eat and drink. Hungry and weary he might be, yet it would be proper for him first to attend upon his master. So the apostles were not to be *impatient* because they did not *at once* receive the reward for which they were looking. ¶ *To meat.* To eat; or, rather, place thyself at the table.

8. *I may sup.* Make ready my supper. ¶ *Gird thyself.* See Notes on Lu. xii. 37.

9. *I trow not.* I *think* not; or I *suppose* not.

10. *Are unprofitable servants.* We have conferred no favour. We have *merited* nothing. We have not *benefited* God, or laid him under *obligation*. If he rewards us, it will be matter of unmerited favour. This is true in relation to Christians in the following respects: 1st. Our services are not *profitable* to God (Job xxii. 2); he *needs* not our aid, and his essential happiness will not be increased by our efforts. 2d. The grace to do his will comes from him only, and all the praise of that will be due to him. 3d. All that we do is what is our *duty;* we cannot lay claim to having rendered any service that will *bind* him to show us favour; and 4th. Our best services are mingled with imperfections. We come short of his glory (Ro. iii. 23); we do not serve him as sincerely, and cheerfully, and faithfully as we ought; we are far, very far from the example set us by the Saviour; and if we are saved and rewarded, it will be because God will be merciful to our unrighteousness, and will remember our iniquities no more, He. viii. 12.

11. *The midst of Samaria and Galilee.* He went from Galilee, and probably travelled through the chief villages and towns in it and then left it; and as Samaria was situated *between* Galilee and Jerusalem, it was necessary to pass through it; or it may mean that he passed along on the borders of each toward the river Jordan, and so passed in the midst, *i.e. between* Galilee and Samaria. This is rendered more probable from the circumstance that as he went from Galilee, there would have been no occasion for saying that he passed *through it*, unless it be meant through the *confines* or borders of it, or at least it would have been mentioned before Samaria.

12. *There met him.* They were in his way, or in his path, as he was entering the village. They were not allowed to enter the village while they were afflicted with the leprosy, Le. xiii. 46; Nu. v. 2, 3. ¶ *Lepers.* See Notes on Mat. viii. 2. ¶ *Stood afar off.* At a distance, as they were required by law. They were unclean, and it was not lawful for them to come near to those who were in health. As Jesus was travelling, they were also walking in the contrary way, and seeing him, and knowing that they were unclean, they stopped or turned aside, so that they might not expose others to the contagion.

came to pass that, [k]as they went, they were cleansed.

15 And one of them, when he saw that he was healed, turned back, and with a loud voice [l]glorified God.

16 And fell down on *his* face at his feet, giving him thanks: and he was a [m]Samaritan.

17 And Jesus answering said, Were there not ten cleansed? but where *are* the nine?

k 2 Ki.5.14; Is.65.24. *l* Ps.30.1,2. *m* Jn.4.39-42.

---

14. *Go show yourselves*, &c. See Notes on Mat. viii. 4. By this command he gave them an implied assurance that they would be healed; for the *design* for which they were to go was to exhibit the *evidence* that they were restored, and to obtain permission from the priest to mingle again in society. It may also be observed that this required no small measure of *faith* on their part, for he did not *first* heal them, and then tell them to go; he told them to go without *expressly* assuring them that they would be healed, and without, *as yet*, any evidence to show to the priest. So sinners, defiled with the leprosy of sin, should put faith in the Lord Jesus and obey his commands, with the fullest confidence that he is able to heal them, and that he *will* do it if they follow his directions; and that in due time they shall have the fullest evidence that their peace is made with God, and that their souls shall by him be declared free from the defilement of sin. ¶ *Were cleansed.* Were cured, or made whole.

15, 16. *One of them*, &c. This man, sensible of the power of God and grateful for his mercies, returned to express his gratitude to God for his goodness. Instead of obeying *at once* the *letter* of the command, he *first* expressed his thanks to God and to his Great Benefactor. There is no evidence, however, that he did not, *after* he had given thanks to God, and had poured out his joy at the feet of Jesus, go to the priest as he was directed; indeed, he could not have been restored to society without doing it; but he *first* poured out his thanks to God, and gave him praise for his wonderful recovery. The first duty of sinners, after they have been forgiven and have the hope of eternal life, is to prostrate themselves at the feet of their Great Benefactor, and to consecrate themselves to his service. *Then* let them go and show to others the evidence that they are cleansed. Let them go and mingle, like a restored leper, with their families and friends, and show by the purity and holiness of their lives how great is the mercy that has cleansed them. ¶ *He was a Samaritan.* See Notes on Mat. x. 5. This rendered his conduct more remarkable and striking in the sight of the Jews. *They* considered the Samaritans as peculiarly wicked, and *themselves* as peculiarly holy. This example showed them, like the parable of the good Samaritan, that in this they were mistaken; and one design of this seems to have been to break down the *opposition* between the Jews and Samaritans, and to bring the former to more charitable judgments respecting the latter.

17, 18. *Where* are *the nine?* Jesus had commanded them to go to the priest, and they were probably *literally* obeying the commandment. They were impatient to be healed and *selfish* in wishing it, and had no gratitude to God or their Benefactor. Jesus did not *forbid* their expressing gratitude to him for his mercy; he rather seems to reprove them for *not* doing it. One of the first feelings of the sinner cleansed from sin is a desire to praise his Great Benefactor; and a *real* willingness to obey his commandments is not inconsistent with a wish to render thanks to him for his mercy. With what singular propriety may this question now be asked, *Where are the nine?* And what a striking illustration is this of human nature, and of the ingratitude of man! One had come back to give thanks for the favour bestowed on him; the others were heard of no more. So now. When men are restored from dangerous sickness, here and there one comes to give thanks to God; but "where are the nine?" When men are defended from danger; when they are recovered from the perils of the sea; when a steamboat is destroyed, and a large part of crew and passengers perish, here and there one of those who are saved acknowledges the goodness of God and renders him praise; but where is the mass of them? They give no thanks; they offer no praise. They go about their usual employments, to

18 There are [n]not found that returned to give glory to God, save this stranger.

19 And he said unto him, Arise, go thy way: [o]thy faith hath made thee whole.

20 And when he was demanded of the Pharisees when the kingdom of God should come, he answered them and said, The kingdom of God cometh not [1]with observation.

21 Neither shall they say, Lo here! or, Lo there! for, behold, [p]the kingdom of God is [2]within you.

22 And he said unto the disci-

n Ps.106.13. *o* Mat.9.22.

1 or, *with outward show.* *p* Ro.14.17.
2 or, *among you*, Jn.1.26.

mingle in the scenes of pleasure and of sin as if nothing had occurred. Few, few of all who have been rescued from "threatening graves" feel their obligation to God, or ever express it. They forget their Great Benefactor; perhaps the mention of his name is unpleasant, and they scorn the idea that they are under any obligations to him. Such, alas! is man, ungrateful man! ¶ *This stranger.* This foreigner; or, rather, this alien, or this man of another tribe. In the *Syraic* version, "this one who is of a foreign people." This man, who might have been least *expected* to express gratitude to God. The most unlikely characters are often found to be most consistent and grateful. Men from whom we would expect *least* in religion, are often so entirely changed as to disappoint all our expectations, and to put to shame those who have been most highly favoured. The poor often thus put to shame the rich; the ignorant the learned; the young the aged.

19. *Go thy way.* To the *priest;* for without *his* certificate he could not again be restored to the society of his friends, or to the public worship of God. Having now appropriately expressed your gratitude, go to the priest and obey the law of God. Renewed sinners, while their hearts overflow with gratitude to Jesus, *express* that gratitude by obeying God, and by engaging in the appropriate duties of their calling and of religion.

20. *Was demanded.* Was asked. ¶ *Of the Pharisees.* This was a matter of much importance to them, and they had taught that it would come with parade and pomp. It is not unlikely that they asked this merely in *contempt*, and for the purpose of drawing out something that would expose him to ridicule. ¶ *The kingdom of God.* The *reign* of God; or the dispensation under the Messiah. See Notes on Mat. iii. 2. ¶ *With observation.* With scrupulous and attentive looking for it, or with such an appearance as to *attract* observation—that is, with pomp, majesty, splendour. He did not deny that, according to their views, the time was drawing near; but he denied that his kingdom would come in the *manner* in which they expected. The Messiah would *not* come with pomp like an earthly prince; perhaps not in such a manner as to be *discerned* by the eyes of sagacious and artful men, who were expecting him in a way agreeable to their own feelings. The kingdom of God is *within* men, and it makes its way, not by pomp and noise, but by silence, decency, and order, 1 Co. xiv. 40.

21. *Lo here! or, Lo there!* When an earthly prince visits different parts of his territories, he does it with pomp. His movements attract observation, and become the common topic of conversation. The inquiry is, Where is he? which way will he go? and it is a matter of important *news* to be able to say where he is. Jesus says that the Messiah would not come in that manner. It would not be with such pomp and public attention. It would be silent, obscure, and attracting comparatively little notice. Or the passage may have reference to the custom of the *pretended* Messiahs, who appeared in this manner. They said that in this place or in that, in this mountain or that desert, they would show signs that would convince the people that they were the Messiah. Comp. Notes on Ac. v. 36, 37. ¶ *Is within you.* This is capable of two interpretations. 1st. The reign of God is *in the heart.* It does not come with pomp and splendour, like the reign of temporal kings, merely to control the external *actions* and strike the senses of men with awe, but it reigns in the heart by the law of God; it sets up its dominion over the passions, and brings every thought into captivity to the obedience of Christ. 2d. It may mean

ples, [q]The days will come when ye
shall desire to see one of the days
of the Son of man, and ye shall
not see *it*.
23 And [r]they shall say to you,
See here; or, See there: go not
after *them*, nor follow *them*.
24 For as the lightning that
lighteneth out of the one *part* under heaven, shineth unto the other
part under heaven, so shall also
the Son of man be in his day.
25 But[s] first must he suffer many
things, and be rejected of this
generation.
26 And as it was [t]in the days
of Noe, so shall it be also in the
days of the Son of man.
27 They did eat, they drank, they
married wives, they were given in
marriage, until the day that Noe
entered into the ark, and the flood
came and destroyed them all.
28 Likewise also as it was in the
days of Lot; they did eat, they
drank, they bought, they sold, they
planted, they builded:
29 But the same day that [u]Lot
went out of Sodom, it rained fire
and brimstone from heaven, and
destroyed *them* all.
30 Even thus shall it be in the

q Mat.9.15. r Mat.24.23,&c.; Mar.13.21; ch.21.8. s Mar.8.31; ch.9.22. t Ge.7.11,23. u Ge.19.23,24.

---

the new dispensation is *even now among* YOU. The Messiah has come. John has ushered in the kingdom of God, and you are not to expect the appearance of the Messiah with great pomp and splendour, for he is now among you. Most critics at present incline to this latter interpretation. The ancient versions chiefly follow the former.

22. *The days will come.* He here takes occasion to direct the minds of his disciples to the days of vengeance which were about to fall on the Jewish nation. Heavy calamities will befall the Jewish people, and you will desire a deliverer. ¶ *Ye shall desire.* You who now number yourselves among my disciples. ¶ *One of the days of the Son of man.* The Son of man here means *the Messiah*, without affirming that *he* was the Messiah. Such will be the calamities of those times, so great will be the afflictions and persecutions, that you will greatly desire *a deliverer*—one who shall come to you in the character in which *you have expected* the Messiah would come, and who would deliver you from the power of your enemies; and at that time, in the midst of these calamities, men shall rise up pretending *to be* the Messiah, and to be able to deliver you. In view of this, he takes occasion to caution them against being led astray by them. ¶ *Ye shall not see* it. You shall not see such a day of deliverance—such a Messiah as the nation has expected, and such an interposition as you would desire.

23, 24. *And they shall say*, &c. Many false Christs, according to Josephus, appeared about that time, attempting to lead away the people. See Notes on Mat. xxiv. 23–27.

25. See Notes on Mar. viii. 31.

26, 27. See Notes on Mat. xxiv. 37–39.

28–30. *They did eat*, &c. They were busy in the affairs of this life, as if nothing were about to happen. ¶ *The same day*, &c. See Ge. xix. 23–25. ¶ *It rained.* The word here used *might* have been rendered *he* rained. In Genesis it is said that the *Lord* did it. ¶ *Fire and brimstone.* God destroyed Sodom on account of its great wickedness. He took vengeance on it for its sins; and the example of Sodom is set before men to deter them from committing great transgressions, and as a *full proof* that God will punish the guilty. See Jude 7; also Is. i. 10; Je. xxiii. 14. Yet, in overthrowing it, he used natural means. He is not to be supposed to have *created* fire and brimstone for the occasion, but to have *directed* the natural means at his disposal for their overthrow; as he did not *create* the waters to drown the world, but merely broke up the fountains of the great deep and opened the windows of heaven. Sodom and Gomorrah, Admah and Zeboim (De. xxix. 23), were four great cities, on a plain where is now the Dead Sea, at the south-east of Palestine, and into which the river Jordan flows. They were built on ground which abounded, doubtless, as all that region now does, in *bitumen* or *naphtha*, which is easily kindled, and which burns with great intensity. The phrase "fire and brim-

day [v]when the Son of man is revealed.
31 In that day, he which shall be
upon the house-top, and his stuff
in the house, let him not come
down to take it away; and he that
is in the field, let him likewise not
return back.
32 Remember [w]Lot's wife.
33 Whosoever[x] shall seek to save
his life shall lose it; and whosoever shall lose his life, shall preserve it.
34 I tell you, in that night [y]there
shall be two *men* in one bed; the
one shall be taken, and the other
shall be left.

v 2 Th.1.7. *w* Ge.19.26.
x Mat.16.25; Mar.8.35; ch.9.24; Jn.12.25.
y Mat.24.40,41.

35 Two *women* shall be grinding
together; the one shall be taken,
and the other left.
36 Two[3] *men* shall be in the
field; the one shall be taken, and
the other left.
37 And they answered and said
unto him, Where, Lord? And he
said unto them, [z]Wheresoever the
body *is*, thither will the eagles be
gathered together.

CHAPTER XVIII.

AND he spake a parable unto
them *to this end*, [a]that men
ought always to pray, and not to
faint;

3 Verse 36th is wanting in most Greek copies.
z Job 39.30; Mat.24.28.
a Ps.65.2; 102.17; ch.11.8; 21.36; Ro.12.12; Ep.6.18; Phi.4.6.

stone" is a Hebrew form of expression, denoting sulphurous fire, or fire having the smell of sulphur; and may denote a volcanic eruption, or any burning like that of naphtha. There is no improbability in supposing either that this destruction was accomplished by lightning, which ignited the naphtha, or that it was a volcanic eruption, which, by direction of God, overthrew the wicked cities. ¶ *From heaven.* By command of God, or from the sky. To the people of Sodom it had *the appearance* of coming from heaven, as all volcanic eruptions would have. Hundreds of towns have been overthrown in this way, and all by the agency of God. He rules the elements, and makes them his instruments, at his pleasure, in accomplishing the destruction of the wicked.

30. *Even thus*, &c. Destruction came upon the old world, and upon Sodom, *suddenly;* when they were engaged in other things, and little expecting this. *So* suddenly and unexpectedly, says he, shall destruction come upon the Jewish people. See Notes on Mat. xxiv.

31. See Notes on Mat. xxiv. 17, 18.

32. *Remember Lot's wife.* See Ge. xix. 26. *She* looked back—she delayed—perhaps she *desired* to take something with her, and God made her a monument of his displeasure. Jesus directed his disciples, when they saw the calamities coming upon the Jews, to flee to the mountains, Mat. xxiv. 16. He here charges them to be in haste—not to look back—not to delay—but to escape quickly, and to remember that by delaying the wife of Lot lost her life.

33. See Notes on Mat. x. 39.

34–36. See Notes on Mat. xxiv. 40, 41.

37. See Notes on Mat. xxiv. 26. ¶ *Where, Lord?* Where, or in what direction, shall these calamities come? The answer implies that it would be where there is the most *guilt* and *wickedness.* Eagles flock where there is prey. So, said he, these armies will flock to the place where there is the most wickedness; and by this their thoughts were directed at once to Jerusalem, the place of eminent wickedness, and the place, therefore, where these calamities might be expected to begin.

CHAPTER XVIII.

1. *A parable.* See Notes on Mat. xiii. 3. ¶ To this end. To show this. ¶ *Always.* At all times. That is, we must not neglect regular stated seasons of prayer; we must seize on occasions of remarkable providences—as afflictions or signal blessings—to seek God in prayer; we must *always* maintain a spirit of prayer, or be in a proper frame to lift up our hearts to God for his blessing, and we must not grow weary though our prayer seems not to be answered. ¶ *Not to faint.* Not to grow weary or give over. The parable is designed to teach us that, though our prayers should long appear to be unanswered, we should persevere, and not grow weary in supplication to God.

2 Saying, There was [1]in a city a
judge, which feared not God, neither regarded man:
3 And there was a widow in that
city; and she came unto him, saying, Avenge me of mine adversary.
4 And he would not for a while:
but afterward he said within himself, Though I fear not God, nor
regard man;
5 Yet, because this widow troub-
leth me, I will avenge her, lest by
her continual coming she weary me.
6 And the Lord said, Hear what
the unjust judge saith.
7 And shall not God [b]avenge his

1 *in a certain city.*

b Re.6.10.

---

2. *A judge which feared not God.* One appointed by law to determine causes brought before him. This judge had no reverence for God, and consequently no regard for the rights of man. These two things go together. He that has no regard for God can be expected to have none for man; and our Lord has here indirectly taught us what ought to be the character of a judge—that he *should* fear God and regard the rights of man. Comp. De. i. 16, 17. ¶ *Regarded man.* Cared not for man. Had no respect for the opinions or the rights of man.

3. *A widow.* This is a circumstance that gives increasing interest to the parable. Judges were bound to show peculiar attention to widows, Is. i. 17; Je. xxii. 3. The reason of this was that they were defenceless, were commonly poor, and were liable to be oppressed by those in power. ¶ *Avenge me.* This would have been better translated, "Do me justice against my adversary, or vindicate me from him." It does not denote vengeance or revenge, but simply that she wished to have *justice* done her—a thing which this judge was *bound* to do, but which it seems he had no disposition to do. ¶ *Adversary.* One opposed in law. In this case it seems that the judge was unwilling to do justice, and probably took advantage of her condition to oppress her.

4, 5. *For a while.* Probably this means for a *considerable* time. It was his duty to attend to the claims of justice, but this was long delayed. ¶ *Within himself.* He thought, or came to a conclusion. ¶ *Though I fear not*, &c. This contains the reason why he attended to the case at all. It was not from any regard to justice, or to the duties of his office. It was simply to avoid *trouble.* And yet his conduct in this case might have appeared very upright, and possibly might have been strictly according to law and to justice. How many actions are performed that *appear well*, when the doers of those actions know that they are mere hypocrisy! and how many actions are performed from the basest and lowest motives of *selfishness*, that have the appearance of external propriety and even of goodness! ¶ *She weary me.* The word used here, in the original, is that which was employed to denote the wounds and bruises caused by *boxers*, who beat each other, and blacken their eyes, and disable them. See Notes on 1 Co. ix. 27. Hence it means any vexatious and troublesome importunity that takes the time, and disables from other employment.

6. *Hear*, &c. Give attention to this, and derive from it practical instruction.

7. *Shall not God avenge*, &c. We are not to suppose that the character of God is at all represented by this judge, or that *his* principles of conduct are at all like those of the judge. This parable shows us conclusively that many *circumstances* of a parable are not to be interpreted closely: they are mere appendages to the narrative. The great truth which our Saviour *designed* to teach is what we ought to endeavour to find. In this case there can be no doubt what that truth is. He has himself told us that it is, that *men ought always to pray and not to faint.* This he teaches by the example in the parable; and the argument which it implies is this: 1st. A poor widow, by her perseverance only, obtained from an unjust man what otherwise she would *not* have obtained. 2d. God is not unjust. He is good, and disposed to do justice and to bestow mercy. If, therefore, this *wicked man* by persevering prayer was induced to do justice, how much more shall *God*, who is good, and who is not actuated by any such selfish and base principles, do justice to them who apply to him! ¶ *Avenge.* Do justice to or vindicate them. This may have a twofold reference. 1st. To the disciples

own elect which cry day and night unto him, though he bear long with them?
8 I tell you that [c]he will avenge
them speedily. Nevertheless, when the Son of man cometh, [d]shall he find faith on the earth?
9 And he spake this parable un-

c Ps.46.5; He.10.37; 2 Pe.3.8,9.

d Mat.24.12.

in the time of Jesus, who were about to be oppressed and persecuted, and over whom calamities were about to come, *as if* God did not regard their cries and had forsaken them. To them Jesus gives the assurance that God *would* hear their petitions and come forth to vindicate them; and that, notwithstanding all these calamities, he would yet appear for their deliverance. 2d. It may have a more *general* meaning. The people of God are often oppressed, calumniated, persecuted. They are few in number and feeble. They seem to be almost forsaken and cast down, and their enemies triumph. Yet in due time God will hear their prayers, and will come forth for their vindication. And even if it should not be *in this life*, yet he will do it in the day of judgment, when he will pronounce them blessed, and receive them for ever to himself. ¶ *His own elect.* People of God, saints, Christians; so called because God has *chosen* them to be his. The term is usually given in the Scriptures to the true followers of God, and is a term of affection, denoting his great and peculiar love in choosing them out of a world of sinners, and conferring on them grace, and mercy, and eternal life. See 1 Th. i. 4; Col. iii. 12; 1 Pe. i. 2; Ep. i. 4. It signifies here that they are peculiarly dear to him; that he feels a deep interest in their welfare, and that he will therefore be ready to come forth to their aid. The judge felt no special interest in that widow, yet he heard her; God feels a particular regard, a tender love for his elect, and therefore he will hear and save. ¶ *Which cry day and night.* This expresses one striking characteristic of the elect of God; they pray, and pray constantly. No one can have evidence that he is chosen of God who is not a man of prayer. One of the best marks by which the electing love of God is known is that it disposes us to pray. This passage supposes that when the elect of God are in trouble and pressed down with calamities, they *will* cry unto him; and it affirms that if they do, he will hear their cries and answer their requests. ¶ *Though he bear long with them.* This passage has been variously interpreted, and there is some variety of reading in the manuscripts. Some read, "Will not God avenge his elect? Will he linger in their cause?" But the most natural meaning is, "Although he defers long to avenge them, and greatly tries their patience, yet he will avenge them." He tries their faith; he suffers their persecutions and trials to continue a long time; and it almost *appears* as if he would not interpose. Yet he will do it, and will save them.

8. *Speedily.* Suddenly, unexpectedly. He will surely vindicate them, and that at a time, perhaps, when they were nearly ready to give over and to sink into despair. This may refer to the deliverance of the disciples from their approaching trials and persecutions among the Jews; or, in general, to the fact that God will interpose and aid his people. ¶ *Nevertheless.* But. Notwithstanding this. Though this is true that God will avenge his elect, yet will he find his elect *faithful?* The danger is not that *God* will be unfaithful—he will surely be true to his promises; but the danger is that his elect—his afflicted people—will be discouraged; will not persevere in prayer; will not continue to have confidence in him; and will, under heavy trials, sink into despondency. The sole meaning of this phrase, therefore, is, that *there is more danger that his people would grow weary, than that God would be found unfaithful and fail to avenge his elect.* For this cause Christ spoke the parable, and by the *design* of the parable this passage is to be interpreted. ¶ *Son of man cometh.* This probably refers to the approaching destruction of Jerusalem—the coming of the Messiah, by his mighty power, to abolish the ancient dispensation and to set up the new. ¶ *Faith.* The word *faith* is sometimes taken to denote the *whole* of religion, and it has been understood in this sense here; but there is a close connection in what Christ says, and it should be understood as referring to what he said before. The truth that he had been teaching was, that God would deliver his people from their calamities and save them, though he suffered them to be long tried. He asks

to certain [e] which trusted in themselves [2] that they were righteous, and despised others:

10 Two men went up into the temple to pray; the one a Pharisee, and the other a publican.

11 The Pharisee stood and prayed thus with himself: God, I thank

e ch.10.29. 2 or, *as being righteous.*

them here whether, when he came, he should find *this faith*, or a belief of *this truth*, among his followers? Would they be found persevering in prayer, and *believing* that God would yet avenge them; or would they cease to pray *always*, and *faint?* This is not to be understood, therefore, as affirming that when Christ comes to judgment there will be few Christians on the earth, and that the world will be overrun with wickedness. That *may be* true, but it is not the truth taught here. ¶ *The earth.* The land—referring particularly to the land of Judea. The discussion had particular reference to their trials and persecutions in that land. This question implies that *in* those trials many professed disciples might faint and turn back, and many of his *real* followers almost lose sight of this great truth, and begin to inquire whether God would interpose to save them. The same question may be asked respecting any other remarkable visitation of the Son of God in affliction. When tried and persecuted, do *we* believe that God will avenge us? Do *we* pray always and not faint? Have *we* faith to believe that, though clouds and darkness are round about him, yet righteousness and judgment are the habitation of his throne? And when storms of persecution assail us, can *we* go to God and confidently commit our cause to him, and believe that he will bring forth our righteousness as the light, and our judgment as the noon-day?

9. *Unto certain.* Unto some. ¶ *Which trusted in themselves.* Who confided in themselves, or who supposed that they were righteous. They did not trust to God or the Messiah for righteousness, but to their own works. They vainly supposed they had themselves complied with the demands of the law of God. ¶ *Despised others.* Others who were not as externally righteous as themselves. This was the character of the Pharisees. They trusted in their outward conformity to the ceremonies of the law. They considered all who did not do that as sinners. This, moreover, is the true character of self-righteousness. Men of that stamp always despise all others. They think they are far above them in holiness, and are disposed to say to them, Stand by thyself, for I am holier than thou, Is. lxv. 5. True religion, on the contrary, is humble. Those who trust in Christ for righteousness feel that *they* are, in themselves, poor, and miserable, and guilty, and they are willing to admit that others may be much better than themselves. Certain it is, they *despise* no one. They love all men; they regard them, however vile, as the creatures of God and as going to eternity, and are disposed to treat them well, and to aid them in their journey toward another world.

10. *The temple.* Into one of the courts of the temple—the court where prayer was commonly offered. See Notes on Mat. xxi. 12. ¶ *A Pharisee.* See Notes on Mat. iii. 7. ¶ *Publican.* See Notes on Mat. v. 46.

11. *Stood and prayed thus with himself.* Some have proposed to render this, "stood by himself" and prayed. In this way it would be characteristic of the sect of the Pharisees, who dreaded the contact of others as polluting, and who were disposed to say to all, Stand by yourselves. The Syraic so renders it, but it is doubtful whether the Greek will allow this construction. If not, it means, he said over to himself what he had done, and what was the ground on which he expected the favour of God. ¶ *God, I thank thee.* There was still in the prayer of the Pharisee an *appearance* of real religion. He did not profess to claim that he had made himself better than others. He was willing to acknowledge that God had done it for him, and that he had a right to his gratitude for it. Hypocrites are often the most orthodox in opinion of any class of men. They know the truth, and admit it. They use it frequently in their prayers and conversation. They will even persecute those who happen to differ from them in opinion, and who may be really wrong. We are not to judge of the *piety* of men by the fact that they admit the truth, or even that they use it often in their prayers. It is, however, not wrong to thank God that he has kept us from the gross sins which other men commit; but it should

thee that I am [f]not as other men *are*, extortioners, unjust, adulterers, or even as this publican:
12 I fast twice in the week, I give tithes of all that I possess.
13 And the publican, standing afar off, would not lift up so much as *his* eyes unto heaven, but [g]smote upon his breast, saying, God be merciful to me, a sinner.

f Is.65.5; Re.3.17.

g Je.31.19.

not be done in an ostentatious manner, nor should it be done forgetting still that we are great sinners and need pardon. These were the faults of the Pharisees. ¶ *Extortioners.* Rapacious; avaricious; who take away the goods of others by force and violence. It means, also, those who take advantage of the necessities of others, the poor and the oppressed, and extort their property. ¶ *Unjust.* They who are not fair and honest in their dealings; who get the property of others by *fraud.* They are distinguished from *extortioners* because they who are unjust may have the *appearance* of honesty; in the other case there is not.

12. *I fast twice*, &c. This was probably the Jewish custom. The Pharisees are said to have fasted regularly on the second and fifth days of every week in private. This was *in addition* to the public days of fasting required in the law of Moses, and they therefore made more a matter of *merit* of it because it was voluntary. ¶ *I give tithes.* A tithe means the tenth part of a thing. A tenth part of the possessions of the Jews was required for the support of the Levites, Nu. xviii. 21. In addition to the tithes required strictly by law, the Pharisees had tithed everything which they possessed—even the smallest matters—as mint, anise, cummin, &c., Lu. xi. 42. It was *this*, probably, on which he so particularly prided himself. As this could not be proved to be strictly *required* in the law, it had more the *appearance* of great piety, and therefore he particularly dwelt on it. ¶ *I possess.* This may mean either all which I *have*, or all which I *gain* or acquire. It is not material which meaning be considered the true one.

The religion of the Pharisee, therefore, consisted—1st. In abstaining from injustice to others; in pretending to live a harmless, innocent, and upright life; and 2d. In a regular observance of all the external duties of religion. His *fault* consisted in relying on this kind of righteousness; in not feeling and acknowledging that he was a sinner; in not seeking a religion that should dwell in the *heart* and regulate the feelings; and in making public and ostentatious professions of his own goodness. Most of all was this abominable in the sight of God, who *looks into the heart*, and who sees wickedness there when the external actions may be blameless. We may learn from the case of the Pharisee —1st. That it is not the man who has the most orthodox belief that has, of course, the most piety; 2d. That men may be externally moral, and not be righteous in the sight of God; 3d. That they may be very exact in the external duties of religion, and even go beyond the strict letter of the law; that they may assume a great appearance of sanctity, and still be strangers to true piety; and 4th. That ostentation in religion, or a *boasting* before God of what we are and of what we have done, is abominable in his sight. This spoils everything, even if the life *should be* tolerably blameless, and if there should be real piety.

13. *Standing afar off.* Afar off from the *temple.* The place where prayer was offered in the temple was the court of women. The Pharisee advanced to the side of the court nearest to the temple, or near as he could; the publican stood on the other side of the same court if he was a Jew, or in the court of the Gentiles if he was a pagan, as far as possible from the temple, being conscious of his unworthiness to approach the sacred place where God had his holy habitation. ¶ *So much as his eyes*, &c. Conscious of his guilt. He felt that he was a sinner, and shame and sorrow prevented his looking up. Men who are conscious of guilt always fix their eyes on the ground. ¶ *Smote upon his breast.* An expression of grief and anguish in view of his sins. It is a sign of grief among almost all nations. ¶ *God be merciful*, &c. The prayer of the publican was totally different from that of the Pharisee. He made no boast of his own righteousness toward God or man. He felt that he was a sinner, and, feeling it, was willing to acknowledge it. This is the kind of

14 I tell you, this man went down to his house justified *rather* than the other: [h]for every one that exalteth himself shall be abased; and he that humbleth himself shall be exalted.

15 And[i] they brought unto him also infants, that he would touch them; but when *his* disciples saw *it*, they rebuked them.

16 But Jesus called them *unto him*, and said, Suffer little children to come unto me, and forbid them not; for of such is the kingdom of God.

17 Verily I say unto you, Whosoever shall not receive the kingdom of God [k]as a little child, shall in no wise enter therein.

18 And[l] a certain ruler asked him, saying, Good Master, what shall I do to inherit eternal life?

19 And Jesus said unto him, Why callest thou me good? None *is* good save one, *that is*, God.

20 Thou knowest [m]the commandments, Do not commit adultery, Do not kill, Do not steal, Do not bear false witness, Honour thy father and thy mother.

21 And he said, All these have I kept from my youth up.

22 Now when Jesus heard these things, he said unto him, Yet lackest thou one thing: sell all that thou hast, and distribute unto the poor, and thou shalt have [n]treasure in heaven; and come, follow me.

23 And when he heard this he was very sorrowful; for he was very rich.

24 And when Jesus saw that he was very sorrowful, he said, [o]How hardly shall they that have riches enter into the kingdom of God!

25 For it is easier for a camel to go through a needle's eye, than for a rich man to enter into the kingdom of God.

26 And they that heard *it* said, Who, then, can be saved?

27 And he said, [p]The things which are impossible with men are possible with God.

28 Then Peter said, Lo, we have left all and followed thee.

29 And he said unto them, Verily I say unto you, There is no man that [q]hath left house, or parents, or brethren, or wife, or children, for the kingdom of God's sake,

30 Who shall not receive manifold more in this present time, and in the world to come [r]life everlasting.

31 Then he took *unto him* the

h Job 22.29; Mat.23.12.
i Mat.19.13; Mar.10.13,&c.
k Ps.131.2; Mar.10.15; 1 Pe.1.14.
l Mat.19.16,&c.; Mar.10.17,&c.
m Ex.20.12-16; De.5.16-20; Ro.13.9.
n Mat.6.19,20; 1 Ti.6.19. *o* Pr.11.28; 1 Ti.6.9.
p Je.32.17; Zec.8.6; ch.1.37. *q* De.33.9. *r* Re.2.10.

prayer that will be acceptable to God. When we are willing to confess and forsake our sins, we shall find mercy, Pr. xxviii. 13. The publican was willing to do this in any place; in the presence of any persons; amid the multitudes of the temple, or alone. He felt most that *God* was a witness of his actions, and he was willing, therefore, to confess his sins before him. While we should not *seek* to do this *publicly*, yet we should be willing at all times "to confess our manifold transgressions, to the end that we may obtain forgiveness of the same by God's infinite goodness and mercy." It is not dishonourable to make acknowledgment when we have done wrong. No man is so much dishonoured as he who is a sinner and is not willing to confess it; as he who has done wrong and yet attempts to *conceal* the fault, thus adding hypocrisy to his other crimes.

14. *I tell you.* The Pharisees would have said that the first man here was approved. Jesus assures them that they judged erroneously. God judges of this differently from men. ¶ *Justified.* Accepted or approved of God. The word *justify* means to declare or treat as righteous. In this case it means that in their prayers the one was approved and the other not; the one went down with the favour of God in answer to his petitions, the other not. ¶ *For every one*, &c. See Notes on Lu. xiv. 11.

15–30. See Notes on Mat. xix. 13–30.

twelve, and said unto them, Behold, we go up to Jerusalem, [s]and
all things that are written by the
prophets concerning the Son of
man shall be accomplished.
32 For he shall be [t]delivered
unto the Gentiles, and shall be
mocked, and spitefully entreated,
and spitted on:
33 And they shall scourge *him*,
and put him to death; and the
third day he shall rise again.
34 And[u] they understood none
of these things; and this saying
was hid from them, neither knew
they the things which were spoken.
35 And[v] it came to pass, that as
he was come nigh unto Jericho, a
certain blind man sat by the way-
side, begging:
36 And hearing the multitude
pass by, he asked what it meant.
37 And they told him that Jesus
of Nazareth passeth by.
38 And he cried, saying, Jesus,
thou son of David, [w]have mercy
on me.
39 And they which went before

s Ps.22.; Is.53.
t Mat.27.2; ch.23.1; Jn.18.28; Ac.3.13.
u Mar.9.32; Jn.12.16.
v Mat.20.29,&c.; Mar.10.46,&c. w Ps.62.12.

rebuked him, that he should hold
his peace; but he [x]cried so much
the more, *Thou* son of David,
have mercy on me.
40 And Jesus stood, and commanded him to be brought unto
him; and when he was come near,
he asked him,
41 Saying, What wilt thou that
I shall do unto thee? And he
said, Lord, that I may receive my
sight.
42 And Jesus said unto him,
Receive thy sight: [y]thy faith hath
saved thee.
43 And immediately he [z]received
his sight, and followed him, [a]glori-
fying God: and all the people,
when they saw *it*, gave praise unto
God.

CHAPTER XIX.

AND *Jesus* entered and passed
through [b]Jericho.
2 And, behold, *there was* a man
named Zaccheus, which was the
chief among the publicans, and he
was rich.

x Ps.141.1. y ch.17.19. z Ps.30.2.
a ch.5.26; Ac.4.21; 11.18; Ga.1.24.
b Jos.6.26; 1 Ki.16.34.

31–33. See Notes on Mat. xx. 17–19. ¶ *By the prophets.* Those who foretold the coming of the Messiah, and whose predictions are recorded in the Old Testament. ¶ *Son of man.* The Messiah. They predicted that certain things would take place respecting the Messiah that was to come. See Notes on Da. ix. 25–27; Is. liii. *These things*, Jesus said, would be accomplished *in him*, he being the Son of man, or the Messiah.

34. *Understood none of these things.* Though they were *plainly* revealed, yet such were their prejudices and their unwillingness to believe them that they did not understand them. They expected that he would be a temporal prince and a conqueror, and they were not *willing* to believe that he would be delivered into the hands of his enemies. They did not see how that could be consistent with the prophecies. To us now these things appear plain, and we may hence learn that those things which to us appear most mysterious may yet appear perfectly plain; and we should learn to trust in God, and *believe* just what he has spoken. See Mat. xvi. 21; xvii. 23.

35–43. See this passage explained in the Notes on Mat. xx. 29–34.

CHAPTER XIX.

1. *And* Jesus *entered*, &c. See Notes on Mat. xx. 29. This means, perhaps, *he was passing* through Jericho when Zaccheus saw him. His house was *in* Jericho.

2. *A man named Zaccheus.* The name Zaccheus is Hebrew, and shows that this man was a *Jew*. The Hebrew name properly means *pure*, and is the same as Zacchai in Ezr. ii. 9; Ne. vii. 14. The publicans, therefore, were not all foreigners. ¶ *Chief among the publicans.* Who presided over other tax-gatherers, or who *received* their collections and transmitted them to the Roman govern-

3 And he sought to see Jesus,
who he was; and could not for
the press, because he was little of
stature.
4 And he ran before, and climb-
ed up into a sycamore-tree to see
him; for he was to pass that *way*.
5 And when Jesus came to the
place, he looked up, and [b]saw him,
and said unto him, Zaccheus, make
haste and come down; for to-day
I must [c]abide at thy house.
6 And he made haste, and came
down, and received him joyfully.
7 And when they saw *it*, they
all murmured, saying, [d]That he
was gone to be guest with a man
that is a sinner.
8 And Zaccheus stood, and said
unto the Lord, Behold, Lord, the

b Ps.139.1-3. *c* Jn.14.23; Re.3.20. *d* Mat.9.11; ch.5.30.

ment. ¶ *He was rich.* Though this class of men was despised and often infamous, yet it seems that they were sometimes wealthy. They sustained, however, the general character of *sinners*, because they were particularly odious in the eyes of the Jews. See ver. 7. The evangelist has thought it worthy of record that he was rich, perhaps, because it was so unlikely that a *rich man* should follow so poor and despised a personage as Jesus of Nazareth, and because it was so unusual a thing during his personal ministry. Not many rich were called, but God chiefly chose the poor of this world. Comp. 1 Co. i. 26-29.

3. *Who he was.* Rather *what sort of person* he was, or how he appeared. He had that curiosity which is natural to men to see one of whom they have heard much. It would seem, also, that in this case mere *curiosity* led to his conversion and that of his family. Comp. 1 Co. xiv. 23-25. God makes use of every principle—of curiosity, or sympathy, or affection, or hope, or fear—to lead men in the way of salvation, and to impress truth on the minds of sinners. ¶ *The press.* The crowd; the multitude that surrounded Jesus. Earthly princes are often borne in splendid equipages, or even carried, as in Eastern nations, in palanquins on the shoulders of men. Jesus mingled with the multitude, not seeking distinctions of that sort, and perhaps, *in appearance*, not distinguished from thousands that followed him. ¶ *Little of stature.* Short. Not a tall man.

4. *A sycamore-tree.* See this described in the Notes on ch. xvii. 6.

5. *Abide at thy house.* Remain there, or put up with him. This was an honour which Zaccheus did not expect. The utmost, it seems, which he aimed at was to *see* Jesus; but, instead of that, Jesus proposed to remain with him, and to give him the benefit of his personal instruction. It is but one among a thousand instances where the Saviour goes, in bestowing mercies, far beyond the desert, the desire, or the expectation of men; and it is not improper to learn from this example that solicitude to behold the Saviour will not pass unnoticed by him, but will meet with his warm approbation, and be connected with his blessing. Jesus was willing to encourage efforts to come to him, and his benevolence prompted him to gratify the desires of the man who was solicitous to see him. He does not disdain the mansions of the rich any more than he does the dwelling-places of the poor, provided there be a humble heart; and he did not suppose there was *less* need of his presence in order to save in the house of the rich man than among the poor. He set an example to all his ministers, and was not afraid or ashamed to proclaim his gospel amid wealth. He was not awed by external splendour or grandeur.

7. *Murmured.* Found fault, complained. ¶ *To be a guest.* To remain with, or to be entertained by. ¶ *A man that is a sinner.* All publicans they regarded as great sinners, and the *chief* of the publicans, therefore, they regarded as peculiarly wicked. It would appear also from Zaccheus' confession that his character *had been* that of an oppressive man. But the people seemed to forget that he might be a penitent, and that the Messiah came to save that which was lost.

8. *The half of my goods I give to the poor.* It is not necessary to understand this as affirming that this *had* been his practice, or that he said this in the way of proclaiming his own righteousness. It may be understood rather as a purpose which he *then* formed under the teach-

half of my goods [e]I give to the poor; and if I have taken any thing from any man [f]by false accusation, I [g]restore *him* four-fold.

9 And Jesus said unto him, This day is salvation come to this house, forasmuch as he also is a [h]son of Abraham.

e Ps.41.1. *f* Ex.20.16; ch.3.14. *g* Ex.22.1; 2 Sa.12.6. *h* ch.13.16.

ing of Christ. He seems to have been sensible that he was a sinner. Of this he was convinced, as we may suppose, by the presence and discourse of Jesus. At first, attracted only by curiosity, or, it may be, by partial conviction that this was the Messiah, he had sought to see the Saviour; but his presence and conversation convinced him of his guilt, and he stood and openly confessed his sins, and expressed his purpose to give half his ill-gotten property to the poor. This was not a proclamation of his *own* righteousness, nor the *ground* of his righteousness, but it was the *evidence* of the sincerity of his repentance, and the confession which with the mouth is made unto salvation, Ro. x. 10. ¶ *And if I have taken.* His office gave him the power of oppressing the people, and it seems that he did not deny that it had been done. ¶ *By false accusation.* This is the same word which in Lu. iii. 14 is rendered "neither accuse any falsely." The accusation seems to have been so made that the person accused was obliged to pay much greater taxes, or so that his property came into the hands of the informer. There are many ways in which this might be done, but we do not know the exact manner. ¶ *I restore* him. We cannot suppose that this had been always his practice, for no man would wantonly extort money from another, and then restore him at once four times as much; but it means that he was made sensible of his guilt; perhaps that his mind had been a considerable time perplexed in the matter, and that now he was resolved to make the restoration. This was the *evidence* of his penitence and conversion. And here it may be remarked that this is *always* an indisputable evidence of a man's conversion to God. A man who has hoarded ill-gotten gold, if he becomes a Christian, will be disposed to do good with it. A man who has injured others—who has cheated them or defrauded them, *even by due forms of law*, must, if he be a Christian, be willing, as far as possible, to make restoration. Zaccheus, for anything that appears to the contrary, may have obtained this property by the decisions of courts of justice, but he now felt that it was wrong; and though the defrauded men could not *legally* recover it, yet his conscience told him that, in order to his being a true penitent, he must make restitution. One of the best evidences of true conversion is when it produces this result; and one of the surest evidences that a *professed* penitent is not a *true* one, is when he is *not* disposed to follow the example of this son of Abraham and make proper restitution. ¶ *Four-fold.* Four times as much as had been unjustly taken. This was the amount that was required in the Jewish law when a sheep had been stolen, and a man was convicted of the theft by trial at law, Ex. xxii. 1. If he *confessed* it himself, without being *detected* and tried, he had only to restore what was stolen, and add to it a fifth part of its value, Nu. v. 6, 7. The sincerity of Zaccheus' repentance was manifest by his being willing to make restoration as great as if it had been proved against him, evincing *his sense* of the wrong, and his purpose to make full restitution. The Jews were allowed to take *no interest* of their brethren (Le. xxv. 35, 36), and this is the reason why that is not mentioned as the measure of the restitution. When injury of this kind is done in other places, the least that is proper is to restore the principal and interest; for the injured person has a right *to all* that his property would have procured him if it had not been unjustly taken away.

9. *Salvation is come to this house.* This family. They have this day received the blessings of the gospel, and become interested in the Messiah's kingdom. Salvation *commences* when men truly receive Christ and their sins are pardoned; it is *completed* when the soul is sanctified and received up into heaven. ¶ *Forasmuch.* Because. For he has given *evidence* that he is a new man, and is disposed to forsake his sins and receive the gospel. ¶ *The son of Abraham.* Hitherto, although a Jew, yet he has been a sinner, and a great sinner. He was not worthy to be called a son of Abraham. Now, by repentance, and

10 For[i] the Son of man is come to seek and to save [k]that which was lost.

11 And as they heard these things, he added and spake a parable, because he was nigh to Jerusalem, and [l]because they thought that the kingdom of God should immediately appear.

12 He said, therefore, [m]A certain nobleman went into a far country, to receive for himself a kingdom, and to return.

13 And he called his ten ser-

i Mat.18.11. *k* Eze.34.16; Ro.5.6. *l* Ac.1.6. *m* Mat.25.14,&c.; Mar.13.34.

by receiving the Christ whose day Abraham saw and was glad (Jn. viii. 56), he has shown himself to be worthy to be called his son. Abraham was an example of distinguished piety; the father of the faithful (Ro. iv. 11), as well as the ancestor of the Jews. They were called his sons who were descended from him, and particularly they who *resembled* him. In this place the phrase is used in both senses.

10. See Notes on Mat. xviii. 11.

11. *He spake a parable.* This parable has in some respects a resemblance to the parable of the *talents* in Mat. xxv. 14–28, but it is not the same. They differ in the following respects: That was spoken *after* he had entered Jerusalem; this, while on his way there. That was delivered on the Mount of Olives; this, in the house of Zaccheus. That was delivered to teach them the necessity of *improving* the talents committed to them; this was for a different design. He was now near Jerusalem. A great multitude attended him. His disciples regarded him as the Messiah, and by this they understood a temporal prince who should deliver them from the dominion of the Romans and set them at liberty. They were anxious for that, and supposed that the time was at hand, and that *now*, as soon as he entered Jerusalem, he would assume the appearance of such a prince and set up his kingdom. To *correct that notion* seems to have been the main design of this parable. To do that, he tells them of a man who had a right to the kingdom, yet who, *before* taking possession of it, went into another kingdom to receive a confirmation of his title, thus intimating that *he* would also go away *before* he would completely set up his kingdom (ver. 12); he tells them that this nobleman left to his servants *property* to be improved in his absence, as *he* would leave to his disciples *talents* to be used in his service (ver. 12, 13); he tells them that this nobleman was rejected by his own citizens (ver. 14), as *he* would be by the Jews; and that he received the kingdom and called them to an account, as *he* also would his own disciples. ¶ *Because he was nigh to Jerusalem.* The capital of the country, and where they supposed he would probably set up his kingdom. ¶ *The kingdom of God should immediately appear.* That the reign of the Messiah would immediately commence. He spake the parable to *correct* that expectation.

12. *A certain nobleman.* A prince; a man descended from kings, and having a title, therefore, to succeed in the kingdom. ¶ *Went into a far country,* &c. This expression is derived from the state of things in Judea in the time of the Saviour. Judea was subject to the Romans, having been conquered by Pompey about sixty years before Christ. It was, however, governed by *Jews*, who held the government *under* the Romans. It was necessary that the prince or king should receive a recognition of his right to the kingdom by the Roman emperor, and, in order to this, that he should go to Rome; or, as it is said here, that he might receive to himself a kingdom. This actually occurred several times. Archelaus, a son of Herod the Great, about the time of the birth of Jesus, went to Rome to obtain a confirmation of the title which his father had left him, and succeeded in doing it. Herod the Great, his father, had done the same thing before to secure the aid and countenance of Antony. Agrippa the younger, grandson of Herod the Great, went to Rome also to obtain the favour of Tiberius, and to be confirmed in his government. Such instances, having frequently occurred, would make this parable perfectly intelligible to those to whom it was addressed. By the nobleman, here, is undoubtedly represented the Messiah, the Lord Jesus Christ; by his going into a far country is denoted his going to heaven, to the right hand of his Father, *before* he should *fully* set up his kingdom and establish his reign among men.

vants, and delivered them ten pounds,[1] and said unto them, Occupy till I come.

14 But[n] his citizens hated him, and sent a message after him, saying, We will not have this *man* to reign over us.

15 And it came to pass, that when he was returned, having received the kingdom, then he commanded those servants to be called unto him, to whom he had given the [2]money, that he might know how much every man had gained by trading.

16 Then came the first, saying, Lord, thy pound hath gained ten pounds.

17 And he said unto him, Well, thou good servant; because thou hast been [o]faithful in a very little, have thou authority over ten cities.

18 And the second came, saying, Lord, thy pound hath gained five pounds.

19 And he said likewise to him, Be thou also over five cities.

20 And another came, saying, Lord, behold, *here is* thy pound, which I have kept laid up in a napkin;

21 For I feared thee, because

1 *Mina*, here translated a *pound*, is 12 ounces and a half, which, at 5 shillings the ounce, is £3, 2*s*. 6*d*. *n* Jn.1.11; 15.18. 2 *silver*, and so ver.23.

o ch.16.10.

13. *Ten servants.* Nothing in particular is denoted by the number *ten*. It is a circumstance intended to keep up the narrative. In general, by these servants our Saviour denotes his disciples, and intends to teach us that talents are given us to be improved, for which we must give an account at his return. ¶ *Ten pounds.* The word translated *pound* here denotes the Hebrew *minah*, which was equal to about 15 dollars, or £3. The pounds here denote the talents which God has given to his servants on earth to improve, and for which they must give an account in the day of judgment. ¶ *Occupy till I come.* The word *occupy* here means not merely to *possess*, as it often does in our language, but to *improve*, to employ *in business*, for the purpose of increasing it or of making *profit* on it. The direction was to use this money so as to gain *more* against his return. So Jesus commands his disciples to *improve* their talents; to make the most of them; to increase their capability of doing good, and to do it *until* he comes to call us hence, by death, to meet him. See 1 Co. xii. 7; Ep. iv. 7.

14. *But his citizens.* His *subjects*, or the people whom he was desirous of ruling. ¶ *Hated him.* On account of his character, and their fear of oppression. This was, in fact, the case with regard to Archelaus, the Jewish prince, who went to Rome to be confirmed in his kingdom. ¶ *Sent a message, saying*, &c. His discontented subjects, fearing what would be the character of his reign, sent an embassy to remonstrate against his being appointed as the ruler. This actually took place. Archelaus went to Rome to obtain from Augustus a confirmation of his title to reign over that part of Judea which had been left him by his father, Herod the Great. The Jews, knowing his character (comp. Mat. ii. 22), sent an embassy of fifty men to Rome, to prevail on Augustus *not* to confer the title on him, but they could not succeed. He *received* the kingdom, and reigned in Judea in the place of his father. As this fact was *fresh* in the memory of the Jews, it makes this parable much more striking. By this part of it Christ designed to denote that the Jews would reject *him*—the Messiah, and would say that they did not desire him to reign over them. See Jn. i. 11. So it is true of all sinners that they do not *wish* Jesus to reign over them, and, if it were possible, would cast him off, and never submit to his reign.

15. See Notes on Mat. xxv. 19.

16–19. See Notes on Mat. xxv. 20, 21. ¶ *Ten cities.* We are not to suppose that this will be *literally* fulfilled in heaven. Christ teaches here that our reward in heaven will be *in proportion* to our faithfulness in improving our talents on earth.

20. *A napkin.* A towel. He means by it that he had not wasted it nor thrown it by carelessly, but had been *very careful* of it; so much so as to be at the pains to tie it up in a towel and put it in a safe place, as if he had been *very faithful* to his trust. So many

thou art an austere man: thou
takest up that thou layedst not
down, and reapest that thou didst
not sow.
22 And he saith unto him, [p]Out
of thine own mouth will I judge
thee, *thou* wicked servant. Thou
knewest that I was an austere man,
taking up that I laid not down,
and reaping that I did not sow:
23 Wherefore,[q] then, gavest not
thou my money into the bank, that
at my coming I might have required mine own with usury?
24 And he said unto them that
stood by, Take from him the
pound, and give *it* to him that
hath ten pounds.
25 (And they said unto him,
Lord, he hath ten pounds.)
26 For I say unto you, [r]That unto
every one which hath shall be
given; and from him that hath
not, even that he hath shall be
taken away from him.
27 But those [s]mine enemies,
which would not that I should
reign over them, bring hither, and
slay *them* before me.
28 And when he had thus spoken,
he went before, ascending up to
Jerusalem.

p 2 Sa.1.16; Job 15.6; Mat.12.37; 22.12; Ro.3.19.
q Ro.2.4,5.
r Mat.13.12; 25.29; Mar.4.25; ch.8.18.
s Ps.2.4,5,9; 21.8,9; Is.66.6,14; Na.1.2,8; He.10.13.

men employ their talents, their learning, their property, their influence. They *have* them; they *keep* them; but they never *use* them in the service of the Lord Jesus; and, in regard to their influence on the church or the world, it would be the same if God had never conferred on them these talents.

21. *An austere man.* Hard, severe, oppressive. The word is commonly applied to unripe fruit, and means *sour*, unpleasant, harsh. In this case it means that the man was taking every advantage, and, while *he* lived in idleness, was making his living out of the toils of others. ¶ *Thou takest up*, &c. Thou dost exact of others what thou didst not give. The phrase is applied to a man who *finds* what has been lost by another, and keeps it himself, and refuses to return it to the owner. All this is designed to show the sinner's view of God. He regards him as unjust, demanding more than man has *power* to render, and more, therefore, than God has a *right* to demand. See Notes on Mat. xxv. 24.

22. *Out of thine own mouth.* By your own statement, or your own views of my character. If you *knew* that this was my character, and *knew* that I would be rigid, firm, and even severe, it would have been the part of wisdom in you to have made the best use of the money in your power; but as you *knew* my character beforehand, and was well acquainted with the fact that I should demand a strict compliance with your obligation, you have no right to complain if you are condemned accordingly. We are not to suppose that God is *unjust* or *austere;* but what we are to learn from this is, that as men know that God will be *just*, and will call them to a strict account in the day of judgment, they ought to be prepared to meet him, and that they cannot then complain if God should condemn them.

23. *The bank.* The treasury, or the place of exchange. Why did you not loan it out, that it might be increased? ¶ *Usury.* Interest.

25. *And they said unto him.* Those standing around him said. ¶ *He hath*, &c. This was probably an observation made by some of the by-standers, as if surprised at such a decision. "He has already *ten pounds.* Why take away this *one*, and add to what he already possesses? Why should *his* property be increased at the expense of this man, who has but one pound?" The answer to this is given in the following verse, that every one that hath, to him shall be given; every man who is faithful, and improves what God gives him, shall receive much more.

26, 27. *For I say*, &c. These are the words of the *nobleman* declaring the principles on which he would distribute the rewards of his kingdom. ¶ *But those mine enemies.* By the punishment of those who would not that he should reign over them is denoted the ruin that was to come upon the Jewish nation for rejecting the Messiah, and also upon all sinners for not receiving him as their king. See Notes on the parable of the talents in Mat. xxv.

28–39. See Notes on Mat. xxi. 1–16.

29 And[t] it came to pass, when he was come nigh to Bethphage and Bethany, at the mount called *the mount* of Olives, he sent two of his disciples,

30 Saying, Go ye into the village over against *you;* in the which, at your entering, ye shall find a colt tied, whereon yet never man sat: loose him, and bring *him hither.*

31 And if any man ask you, Why do ye loose *him?* thus shall ye say unto him, [u]Because the Lord hath need of him.

32 And they that were sent went their way, and found even as he had said unto them.

33 And as they were loosing the colt, the owners thereof said unto them, Why loose ye the colt?

34 And they said, The Lord hath need of him.

35 And they brought him to Jesus; and they [v]cast their garments upon the colt, and they [w]set Jesus thereon.

36 And as he went they spread their clothes in the way.

37 And when he was come nigh, even now at the descent of the mount of Olives, the whole multitude of the disciples began to rejoice and praise God with a loud voice, for all the mighty works that they had seen;

38 Saying, [x]Blessed *be* the King that cometh in the name of the Lord; [y]peace in heaven, and glory in the highest.

39 And some of the Pharisees from among the multitude said unto him, Master, rebuke thy disciples.

40 And he answered and said unto them, I tell you, that if these should hold their peace, [z]the stones would immediately cry out.

41 And when he was come near, he beheld the city, and [a]wept over it,

42 Saying, If thou hadst known, even thou, at least in this [b]thy day, the things *which belong* unto thy peace! But now they are hid from thine eyes.

43 For the days shall come upon thee, that thine enemies shall [c]cast a trench about thee, and compass thee round, and keep thee in on every side,

44 And[d] shall lay thee even with the ground, and thy children with-

t Mat.21.1,&c.; Mar.11.1,&c.
u Ps.50.10. *v* 2 Ki.9.13. *w* Jn.12.14.

x Ps.118.26; ch.13.35. *y* ch.2.14; Ro.5.1; Ep.2.14.
z Hab.2.11; Mat.3.9.
a Ps.119.136; Je.9.1; 13.17; 17.16; Jn.11.35.
b Ps.95.7,8; He.3.7,13,15. *c* Is.29.2,3; Je.6.5,6.
d 1 Ki.9.7,8; Mi.3.12; Mat.23.37,38; ch.13.34,35.

40. *The stones would—cry out.* It is *proper* that they should celebrate my coming. Their acclamations *ought* not to be suppressed. So joyful is the event which they celebrate—the coming of the Messiah—that it is not fit that I should attempt to impose silence on them. The expression here seems to be *proverbial,* and is not to be taken literally. Proverbs are designed to express the truth *strongly,* but are not to be taken to signify as much as if they were to be interpreted literally. The sense is, that his coming was an event of so much importance that it *ought* to be celebrated in some way, and *would* be celebrated. It would be impossible to restrain the people, and improper to attempt it. The language here is strong proverbial language to denote that fact. We are not to suppose, therefore, that our Saviour meant to say that the stones were *conscious* of his coming, or that God would *make* them speak, but only that there was *great joy* among the people; that it was *proper* that they should express it in this manner, and that it was not fit that he should attempt to repress it.

41–44. *He wept over it.* Showing his compassion for the guilty city, and his strong sense of the evils that were about to come upon it. See Notes on Mat. xxiii. 37–39. As he entered the city he passed over the Mount of Olives. From that mountain there was a full and magnificent view of the city. See Notes on Mat. xxi. 1. The view of the splendid capital—the knowledge of its crimes—the remembrance of the mercies of God toward it—the certainty that it might have been spared if it had received the

in thee; and [e]they shall not leave in thee one stone upon another; because [f]thou knewest not the time of thy visitation.

45 And[g] he went into the temple, and began to cast out them that sold therein, and them that bought;

46 Saying unto them, It is written, [h]My house is the house of prayer, but ye have made it a [i]den of thieves.

47 And he [k]taught daily in the temple. But the chief priests and the scribes, and the chief of the people, sought to destroy him;

e Mat.24.2; Mar.13.2. f La.1.8; 1 Pe.2.12. g Mat.21.12,13; Mar.11.15-17; Jn.2.15,17. h Is.56.7. i Je.7.11. k Jn.18.20.

prophets and himself—the knowledge that it was about to put *him*, their long-expected Messiah, to death, and *for* that to be given up to utter desolation—affected his heart, and the triumphant King and Lord of Zion wept! Amid all *his* prosperity, and all the acclamations of the multitude, the heart of the Redeemer of the world was turned from the tokens of rejoicing to the miseries about to come on a guilty people. Yet they *might* have been saved. If thou hadst known, says he, even thou, with all thy guilt, the things that make for thy peace; if thou hadst repented, had been righteous, and had received the Messiah; if thou hadst not stained thy hands with the blood of the prophets, and shouldst not with that of the Son of God, then these terrible calamities would not come upon thee. But it is too late. The national wickedness is too great; the cup is full; mercy is exhausted; and Jerusalem, with all her pride and splendour, the glory of her temple, and the pomp of her service, *must perish!* ¶ *For the days shall come*, &c. This took place under Titus, the Roman general, A.D. 70, about thirty years after this was spoken. ¶ *Cast a trench about thee.* The word *trench* now means commonly a *pit* or *ditch*. When the Bible was translated, it meant also *earth thrown up to defend a camp* (Johnson's *Dictionary*). This is the meaning of the original here. It is not a pit or large *ditch*, but a pile of earth, stones, or wood thrown up to guard a camp, and to defend it from the approach of an enemy. This was done at the siege of Jerusalem. Josephus informs us that Titus, in order that he might compel the city to surrender by *famine*, built a wall around the whole circumference of the city. This wall was nearly 5 miles in length, and was furnished with thirteen castles or towers. This work was completed with incredible labour in ten days. The professed design of this wall was *to keep* the city *in on every side.* Never was a prophecy more strikingly accomplished. ¶ *Shall lay thee even with the ground*, &c. This was literally done. Titus caused a plough to pass over the place where the temple stood. See Notes on Mat. xxiv. All this was done, says Christ, because Jerusalem knew not the time of its visitation—that is, did not know, and *would not* know, that the Messiah had come. *His coming* was the time of their merciful visitation. That time had been predicted, and invaluable blessings promised as the result of his advent; but they would not know it. They rejected him, they put him to death, and it was just that they should be destroyed.

45, 46. See Notes on Mat. xxi. 12, 13.

47. *Daily in the temple.* That is, for five or six days before his crucifixion.

48. *Could not find*, &c. Were not able to accomplish their purpose; they did not know *how* to bring it about. ¶ *Very attentive.* Literally, *hung upon him* to hear him. The word denotes an anxious desire, a fixed attention, a cleaving to him, and an unwillingness to *leave* him, so that they might hear his words. This is always the case when men become anxious about their salvation. They manifest it by hanging on the preaching of the gospel; by fixed attention; and by an unwillingness to leave the place where the word of God is preached. In view of the fact that the Lord Jesus wept over Jerusalem, we may remark:

(1.) It was on account of the sins and danger of the inhabitants, and of the fact that they had rejected offered mercy.

(2.) There was *occasion* for weeping. Jesus would not have wept had there been no cause for it. If they were in no danger, if there was no punishment in the future world, why should he have wept? When the Lord Jesus weeps over sinners, it is the fullest proof that they are in danger.

48 And could not find what they might do; for all the people [3]were very attentive to hear him.

CHAPTER XX.

AND[a] it came to pass, *that* on one of those days, as he taught the people in the temple, and preached the gospel, the chief priests and the scribes came upon *him*, with the elders,

2 And spake unto him, saying, Tell us, [b]by what authority doest thou these things? or who is he that gave thee this authority?

3 And he answered and said unto them, I will also ask you one thing; and answer me:

4 The baptism of John, was it from heaven or of men?

5 And they reasoned with themselves, saying, If we shall say, From heaven, he will say, Why, then, believed ye him not?

6 But and if we say, Of men, all the people will stone us; [c]for they be persuaded that John was a prophet.

7 And they answered that they could not tell whence *it was*.

8 And Jesus said unto them, Neither tell I you by what authority I do these things.

9 Then began he to speak to the people this parable: [d]A certain man [e]planted a vineyard, and let it forth to husbandmen, and went into a far country for a long time.

10 And at the season he sent a servant to the husbandmen, that they should give him of the [f]fruit of the vineyard; but the husbandmen beat him, and sent *him* away empty.

11 And again he sent another servant; and they beat him also, and entreated *him* shamefully, and sent *him* away empty.

12 And again he sent a third; and they wounded him also, and cast *him* out.

13 Then said the lord of the vineyard, What shall I do? I will send my beloved son: it may be they will reverence *him*, when they see him.

14 But when the husbandmen saw him, they reasoned among themselves, saying, This is [g]the heir: come, [h]let us kill him, that the inheritance may be ours.

3 or, *hanged on him.*
a Mat.21.23,&c.; Mar.11.27,&c.
b Ac.4.7-10; 7.27. *c* Mat.14.5.
d Mat.21.33,&c.; Mar.12.1,&c.
e Ca.8.11,12; Is.5.1-7. *f* Jn.15.16; Ro.7.4.
g Ps.2.8; Ro.8.17; He.1.2.
h Mat.27.21-25; Ac.2.23; 3.15.

(3.) Sinners are in the same danger now. They reject Christ as sinners did then. They despise the gospel as they did then. They refuse now to come to him as the inhabitants of Jerusalem did. Why are they not then in the same danger?

(4.) Deep feeling, gushing emotions, lively affections, are proper in religion. If the Saviour wept, it is not improper for us to weep—it is right. Nay, can it be right *not* to weep over the condition of lost man.

(5.) Religion is tenderness and love. It led the Saviour to weep, and it teaches us to sympathize and to feel deeply. Sin hardens the heart, and makes it insensible to every pure and noble emotion; but religion teaches us to feel "for others' woes," and to sympathize in the danger of others.

(6.) Christians and Christian ministers should weep over lost sinners. They have souls just as precious as they had then; they are in the same danger; they are going to the judgment-bar; they are wholly insensible to their danger and their duty.

"Did Christ o'er sinners weep?
And shall our cheeks be dry?
Let floods of penitential grief
Burst forth from every eye.

"The Son of God in tears,
Angels with wonder see!
Be thou astonished, O my soul;
He shed those tears for thee.

"He wept that we might weep;
Each sin demands a tear;
In heaven alone no sin is found,
And there's no weeping there."

CHAPTER XX.

1-9. See this passage explained in the Notes on Mat. xxi. 23-27.

9-19. See this parable explained in the Notes on Mat. xxi. 33-45.

15 So they cast him out of the vineyard, and killed *him*. What, therefore, shall the lord of the vineyard do unto them?

16 He shall come and destroy these husbandmen, and shall [i]give the vineyard to others. And when they heard *it*, they said, God forbid.

17 And he beheld them, and said, What is this, then, that is written, The[k] stone which the builders rejected, the same is become the head of the corner?

18 Whosoever shall fall upon that stone shall be broken; [l]but on whomsoever it shall fall, it will grind him to powder.

19 And the chief priests and the scribes the same hour sought to lay hands on him; and they feared the people; for they perceived that he had spoken this parable against them.

20 And they watched *him*, and sent forth spies, which should feign themselves just men, [m]that they might take hold of his words, that so they might deliver him unto the power and authority of the governor.

21 And they asked him, saying, Master, we know that thou sayest and teachest rightly, neither acceptest thou the person *of any*, but teachest the way of God [1]truly:

22 Is it lawful for us to give tribute unto Cæsar, or no?

23 But he perceived their craftiness, and said unto them, Why tempt ye me?

24 Show me a [2]penny. Whose image and superscription hath it? They answered and said, Cæsar's.

25 And he said unto them, Render,[n] therefore, unto Cæsar the things which be Cæsar's, and unto God the things which be God's.

26 And they could not take hold of his words before the people; and they marvelled at his answer, and [o]held their peace.

27 Then[p] came to *him* certain of the [q]Sadducees, which deny that there is any resurrection; and they asked him,

28 Saying, Master, Moses wrote unto us, [r]If any man's brother die, having a wife, and he die without children, that his brother should take his wife, and raise up seed unto his brother.

29 There were therefore seven brethren; and the first took a wife and died without children.

30 And the second took her to wife, and he died childless.

31 And the third took her; and in like manner the seven also; and they left no children, and died.

32 Last of all the woman died also.

33 Therefore in the resurrection whose wife of them is she? for seven had her to wife.

34 And Jesus answering said unto them, The children of this world marry, and are given in marriage;

35 But they which shall be [s]accounted worthy to obtain that world, and the resurrection from the dead, neither marry nor are given in marriage:

36 Neither[t] can they die any more; for they are [u]equal unto the angels, and are [v]the children of God, being the children of the resurrection.

37 Now that the dead are raised, even Moses [w]showed at the bush, when he calleth the Lord the God of Abraham, and the God of Isaac, and the God of Jacob.

i Ne.9.36,37. *k* Ps.118.22. *l* Da.2.34,35. *m* Mat.22.15,&c.; Mar.12.13. 1 or, *of a truth*. 2 See Mat.18.28. *n* Ro.13.7.

o Tit.1.10,11. *p* Mat.22.23,&c.; Mar.12.18,&c. *q* Ac.23.6,8. *r* De.25.5-8. *s* ch.21.36; Re.3.4. *t* Re.21.4. *u* 1 Co.15.49,52; 1 Jn.3.2. *v* Ro.8.17. *w* Ex.3.2-6.

20–38. See this explained in the Notes on Mat. xxii. 15–33, and Mar. xii. 13-27.

39. See Notes on Mar. xii. 32.
40–44. See Notes on Mat. xxii. 41–46.
45–47. See Notes on Mat. xxiii. 1.

38 For he is not a God of the
dead, but of the living; [x]for all
live unto him.
39 Then certain of the scribes
answering, said, Master, thou hast
well said.
40 And after that they durst
not ask him any *question at all.*
41 And[y] he said unto them,
How say they that Christ is
David's son?
42 And David himself saith in
the book of Psalms, [z]The Lord
said unto my Lord, Sit thou on
my right hand,
43 Till I make thine enemies
thy footstool.
44 David therefore calleth him
Lord; how is he then his son?
45 Then, in the audience [a]of
all the people, he said unto his
disciples,
46 Beware[b] of the scribes, which
desire to walk in long robes, and
love [c]greetings in the markets, and
the highest seats in the synagogues,
and the chief rooms at feasts;
47 Which[d] devour widows'
houses, and for a [e]show make long
prayers: the same shall [f]receive
greater damnation.

CHAPTER XXI.

AND he looked up, [a]and saw
the rich men casting their
gifts into the treasury.
2 And he saw also a certain
poor widow casting in thither two
[1]mites.
3 And he said, Of a truth I
say unto you, that this poor
widow hath cast in [b]more than
they all;
4 For all these have of their
abundance cast in unto the offerings of God, but she of her penury
hath cast in all the living that
she had.
5 And[c] as some spake of the
temple, how it was adorned with
goodly stones and gifts, he said,
6 *As for* these things which ye
behold, the days will come in the
which [d]there shall not be left one
stone upon another that shall not
be thrown down.
7 And they asked him, saying,
Master, but when shall these things
be? and what sign *will there be*
when these things shall come to
pass?
8 And he said, [e]Take heed that
ye be not deceived; for many shall
come in my name, saying, I am
Christ; and [f]the time draweth near:
go ye not, therefore, after them.
9 But when ye shall hear of wars
and commotions, [g]be not terrified;
for these things must first come to
pass, but the end *is* not by and by.
10 Then said he unto them,
[h]Nation shall rise against nation,
and kingdom against kingdom;

x Ro.14.8,9. y Mat.22.42; Mar.12.35,&c. z Ps.110.1; Ac.2.34. a 1 Ti.5.20. b Mar.12.38,&c. c ch.11.43. d Is.10.2; Mat.23.14; 2 Ti.3.6. e 1 Th.2.5. f ch.10.12,14; Ja.3.1. a Mar.12.41.

1 See Mar.12.42. b 2 Co.8.12. c Mat.24.1,&c.; Mar.13.1,&c. d ch.19.44,&c. e 2 Th.2.3,9,10; 1 Jn.4.1; 2 Jn.7. f Re.1.3. g Pr.3.25,26. h Hag.2.22.

CHAPTER XXI.

1-4. See this explained in the Notes on Mar. xii. 41-44.

4. *Penury.* Poverty.

5. *Goodly stones.* Beautiful stones. Either referring to the large, square, and well-finished stones of which the eastern wall was built, or to the precious stones which might have been used in decorating the temple itself. See Notes on Mar. xiii. 1. ¶ *Gifts.* This word properly denotes anything devoted or dedicated to God. Anciently warriors dedicated to their gods the spoils of war—the shields, and helmets, and armour, and garments of those slain in battle. These were suspended in the temples. It would seem that something of this kind had occurred in the temple of Jerusalem, and that the people, to express their gratitude to God, had suspended on the pillars and porches of the temple gifts and offerings. Josephus mentions particularly a golden *vine* with which Herod the Great had adorned the columns of the temple (*Antiq.* xiii. 8). See also 2 Mac. v. 16; ix. 16.

11 And great earthquakes shall
be in divers places, and famines,
and pestilences; and fearful sights
and great signs shall there be from
heaven.
12 But before all these they shall
lay their hands on you, and persecute
you, delivering *you* up to the synagogues, and [i]into prisons, being
brought[k] before kings and rulers
for my name's sake.
13 And[l] it shall turn to you for
a testimony.
14 Settle *it*, therefore, in your
hearts [m]not to meditate before
what ye shall answer;
15 For I will give you a mouth and
wisdom which all your adversaries
shall [n]not be able to gainsay nor
resist.
16 And[o] ye shall be betrayed both
by parents, and brethren, and kins-

i Ac.4.3; 5.18; 12.4; 16.24; Re.2.10. *k* Ac.25.23. *l* Phi.1.28; 2 Th.1.5. *m* Mat.10.19; ch.12.11. *n* Ac.6.10. *o* Mi.7.5,6.

folks, and friends; [p]and *some* of you
shall they cause to be put to death.
17 And ye shall be [q]hated of all
men for my name's sake.
18 But[r] there shall not a hair of
your head perish.
19 In[s] your patience possess ye
your souls.
20 And when ye shall see Jerusalem compassed with armies, then
know that the desolation thereof is
nigh.
21 Then let them which are in
Judea flee to the mountains; and
let them which are in the midst of
it depart out; and let not them that
are in the countries enter thereinto.
22 For these be the days of vengeance, that [t]all things which are
written may be fulfilled.
23 But woe unto [u]them that are
with child, and to them that give

p Ac.7.59; 12.2; 26.10; Re.2.13; 6.9; 12.11. *q* Jn.17.14. *r* Mat.10.30. *s* Ro.5.3; He.10.36; Ja.1.4. *t* De.28.25,48; Da.9.26,27; Zec.11.6; 14.1,2. *u* La.4.10.

6. See Notes on Mat. xxiv. 2.

7–36. The account of the destruction of Jerusalem contained in this chapter has been fully considered in the Notes on Mat. xxiv. All that will be necessary here will be an explanation of a few words that did not occur in that chapter.

9. *Commotions.* Insurrections. Subjects rising against their rulers.

11. *Fearful sights.* See Mat. xxiv. 7.

12, 13. *Synagogues, and into prisons.* See Notes on Mar. xiii. 9, 10.

14. *Settle* it, *therefore, in your hearts.* Fix it firmly in your minds—so firmly as to become a settled principle—that you are always to depend on God for aid in all your trials. See Mar. xiii. 11.

15. *A mouth.* Eloquence, ability to speak as the case may demand. Comp. Ex. iv. 11. ¶ *Gainsay.* Speak against. They will not be able to *reply* to it, or to *resist* the force of what you shall say.

18. *A hair of your head perish.* This is a proverbial expression, denoting that they should not suffer any essential injury. This was strikingly fulfilled in the fact that in the calamities of Jerusalem there is reason to believe that no Christian suffered. Before those calamities came on the city they had fled to *Pella*, a city on the east of the Jordan. See Notes on Mat. xxiv. 18.

19. *In your patience.* Rather by your perseverance. The word *patience* here means constancy or perseverance in sustaining afflictions. ¶ *Possess ye your souls.* Some read here the *future* instead of the *present* of the verb rendered *possess.* The word *possess* means here to *preserve* or keep, and the word *souls* means *lives.* This passage may be thus translated: By persevering in bearing these trials you *will* save your lives, or you will be safe; or, by persevering *preserve* your lives; that is, do not yield to these calamities, but bear up under them, for he that endureth to the end, the same shall be saved. Comp. Mat. xxiv. 13.

22. *All things which are written may be fulfilled.* Judgment had been threatened by almost all the prophets against that wicked city. They had spoken of its crimes and threatened its ruin. Once God had destroyed Jerusalem and carried the people to Babylon; but their crimes had been repeated when they returned, and God had again threatened their ruin. Particularly was this very destruction foretold by Daniel,

suck in those days! for there shall be great distress in the land, and wrath upon this people.

24 And they shall fall by the edge of the sword, and shall be led away captive into all nations; [v]and Jerusalem shall be trodden down of the Gentiles [w]until the times of the Gentiles be fulfilled.

25 And there shall be signs in the sun, and in the moon, and in the stars; and upon the earth [x]distress of nations, with perplexity; the sea and the waves roaring;

v Da.12.7; Re.11.2. w Ro.11.25. x Da.12.1.

ch. ix. 26, 27: "And after threescore and two weeks shall Messiah be cut off, but not for himself; and the people of the prince that shall come *shall destroy the city and the sanctuary;* and the end thereof shall be with a flood, and unto the end of the war desolations are determined." See Notes on that passage.

24. *Shall fall*, &c. No less than one million one hundred thousand perished in the siege of Jerusalem. ¶ *Shall be led away captive.* More than ninety thousand were led into captivity. See Notes on Mat. xxiv. ¶ *Shall be trodden down by the Gentiles.* Shall be in possession of the Gentiles, or be subject to them. The expression also implies that it would be an *oppressive* subjection, as when a captive in war is trodden down under the feet of the conqueror. Anciently conquerors *trod on* the necks of those who were subdued by them, Jos. x. 24; 2 Sa. xxii. 41; Eze. xxi. 29. The bondage of Jerusalem has been long and very oppressive. It was for a long time under the dominion of the Romans, then of the Saracens, and is now of the Turks, and is aptly represented by a captive stretched on the ground whose neck is *trodden* by the foot of the conqueror. ¶ *Until the times of the Gentiles be fulfilled.* This passage has been understood very differently by different expositors. Some refer it to the time which the Romans who conquered it had dominion over it, as signifying that *they* should keep possession of it until a part of the pagans should be converted, when it should be rebuilt. Thus it was rebuilt by the Emperor Adrian. Others suppose that it refers to the end of the world, when all the Gentiles shall be converted, and they shall *cease* to be Gentiles by becoming Christians, meaning that it should *always* be desolate. Others, that Christ meant to say that in the times of the millennium, when the gospel should spread universally, he would reign personally on the earth, and that the *Jews* would return and rebuild Jerusalem and the temple. This is the opinion of the Jews and of many Christians. The meaning of the passage clearly is, 1st. That Jerusalem would be completely destroyed. 2d. That this would be done by Gentiles—that is, by the Roman armies. 3d. That this desolation would continue as long as God should judge it proper in a fit manner to express his abhorrence of the crimes of the nation—that is, until the times allotted to *them* by God for this desolation should be accomplished, without specifying how long that would be, or what would occur to the city after that. It *may* be rebuilt, and inhabited by converted Jews. Such a thing is *possible*, and the Jews naturally seek that as their home; but whether this be so or not, the time when the *Gentiles*, as such, shall have dominion over the city is limited. Like all other cities on the earth, it will yet be brought under the influence of the gospel, and will be inhabited by the true friends of God. Pagan, infidel, anti-Christian dominion shall cease there, and it will be again a place where God will be worshipped in sincerity—a place *even then* of peculiar interest from the recollection of the events which have occurred there. *How long* it is to be before this occurs is known only to Him "who hath put the times and seasons in his own power," Ac. i. 7.

25. See Notes on Mat. xxiv. 29. ¶ *Upon the earth distress of nations.* Some have proposed to render the word *earth* by *land*, confining it to Judea. It often has this meaning, and there seems some propriety in so using it here. The word translated *distress* denotes anxiety of mind—such an anxiety as men have when they do not know what to do to free themselves from calamities; and it means here that the calamities would be so great and overwhelming that they would not know what to do to escape. There would be a want of counsel, and deep anxiety at the impending evils. ¶ *With perplexity.* Rather *on account* of their perplexity,

26 Men's hearts failing them for
fear, and for looking after those
things which are coming on the
earth; for [y]the powers of heaven
shall be shaken.
27 And then shall they [z]see the
Son of man coming in a cloud with
power and great glory.
28 And when these things begin
to come to pass, then look up and
lift up your heads, for [a]your redemption draweth nigh.
29 And[b] he spake to them a
parable: Behold the fig-tree, and
all the trees;
30 When they now shoot forth,

y 2 Pe.3.10-12. *z* Re.1.7; 14.14. *a* Ro.8.23. *b* Mat.24.32; Mar.13.28.

ye see and know of your own selves
that summer is now nigh at hand.
31 So likewise ye, when ye see
these things come to pass, know ye
that the kingdom of God is nigh at
hand.
32 Verily I say unto you, This
generation shall not pass away till
all be fulfilled.
33 Heaven[c] and earth shall pass
away, but my word shall not pass
away.
34 And[d] take heed to yourselves,
lest at any time your hearts be
overcharged with [e]surfeiting, and
drunkenness, and cares of this life,

c Is.40.8; 51.6. *d* Ro.13.12,13; 1 Th.5.6-8; 1 Pe.4.7. *e* Is.28.1-3; 1 Co.6.10.

---

or the desperate state of their affairs. The Syriac has it, "perplexity or *wringing of hands*," which is a sign of deep distress and horror. ¶ *The sea and the waves roaring.* This is not to be understood literally, but as an image of great distress. Probably it is designed to denote that these calamities would come upon them like a deluge. As when in a storm the ocean roars, and wave rolls on wave and dashes against the shore, and each succeeding surge is more violent than the one that preceded it, so would the calamities come upon Judea. They would roll over the whole land, and each wave of trouble would be more violent than the one that preceded it, until the whole country would be desolate. The same image is also used in Is. viii. 7, 8, and Re. xviii. 15.

26. *Men's hearts failing them.* This is an expression denoting the highest terror. The word rendered *failing* commonly denotes *to die*, and here it means that the terror would be so great that men would faint and be ready to die in view of the approaching calamities. And if this was true in respect to the judgments about to come upon Judea, how much more so will it be in the day of judgment, when the wicked will be arraigned before the Son of God, and when they shall have before them the prospect of the awful sufferings of hell—the pains and woes which shall continue for ever! It will be no wonder, then, if they call on the rocks and mountains to hide them from the face of God, and if their hearts sink within them at the prospect of eternal suffering.

28. *Your redemption draweth nigh.* See Notes on Mat. xxiv. 33. This is expressed in the 31st verse thus: "the kingdom of God is nigh at hand"—that is, from that time God will signally build up his kingdom. It shall be fully established when the Jewish policy shall come to an end; when the temple shall be destroyed, and the Jews scattered abroad. Then the power of the Jews shall be at an end; they shall no longer be able to persecute you, and you shall be completely delivered from all these trials and calamities in Judea.

34. *Lest at any time your hearts be overcharged*, &c. The meaning of this verse is, "Be continually expecting these things. Do not forget them, and do not be *secure* and satisfied with this life and the good things which it furnishes. Do not suffer yourselves to be drawn into the fashions of the world; to be conformed to its customs; to partake of its feasts and revelry; and so these calamities shall come upon you when you least expect them." And from this we may learn—what alas! we may from the *lives* of many professing Christians—that there is need of cautioning the disciples of Jesus now that they do not indulge in the festivities of this life, and *forget* that they are to die and come to judgment. How many, alas! who bear the Christian name, have forgotten this caution of the Saviour, and live as if their lives were secure; as if they feared not death; as if there were no heaven and no judgment! Christians

and *so* that day come upon you
unawares.

35 For[f] as a snare shall it come
on all them that dwell on the face
of the whole earth.

36 Watch[g] ye, therefore, and pray
always, that ye may be [h]accounted
worthy to escape all these things
that shall come to pass, and [i]to stand
[k]before the Son of man.

37 And in the day-time he was
teaching in the temple; and at
night he went out, and abode in
the [l]mount that is called *the mount*
of Olives.

38 And all the people came
early in the morning to him in
the temple, for to hear him.

f 1 Th.5.2; 2 Pe.3.10; Re.16.15. *g* Mat.25.13. *h* ch.20.35.

i Ps.1.5. *k* Jude 24. *l* Jn.8.1,2.

---

should feel that they are soon to die, and that their portion is not in this life; and, feeling this, they should be *looking for and hasting unto the coming of the day of God.* ¶ *Overcharged.* Literally, *be made heavy*, as is the case with those who have eaten and drunken too much. ¶ *Surfeiting.* Excessive eating and drinking, so as to oppress the body; indulgence in the pleasures of the table. This word does not include *intoxication*, but merely indulgence in food and drink, though the food and drink should be in themselves lawful. ¶ *Drunkenness.* Intoxication, intemperance in drinking. The ancients were not acquainted with the poison that we chiefly use on which to become drunk. They had no distilled spirits. They became intoxicated on wine, and strong drink made of a mixture of dates, honey, &c. All nations have contrived some way to become intoxicated—to bring in folly, and disease, and poverty, and death, by drunkenness; and in nothing is the depravity of men more manifest than in thus endeavouring to hasten the ravages of crime and death.

35. *As a snare.* In Matthew and Mark Jesus compares the suddenness with which these calamities would come to the deluge coming in the days of Noah. Here he likens it to a snare. Birds are caught by a snare or net. It is sprung on them quickly, and when they are not expecting it. So, says he, shall these troubles come upon Judea. The figure is often used to denote the suddenness of calamities, Ps. lxix. 22; Ro. xi. 9; Ps. cxxiv. 7; Is. xxiv. 17.

36. *To stand before the Son of man.* These approaching calamities are represented as the *coming of the Son of man* to judge Jerusalem for its crimes. Its inhabitants were so wicked that they were not worthy to stand before him and would be condemned, and the city would be overthrown. To *stand before him* here denotes approbation, acquittal, favour, and is equivalent to saying that *they* would be free from these calamities, while they should come upon others. See Ro. xiv. 4; Ps. i. 5; cxxx. 3; Re. vi. 17. Perhaps, also, there is a reference here to the day of judgment. See Notes on Matthew xxiv.

37, 38. See Notes on Mat. xxi. 17. ¶ *Came early in the morning.* He returned early from the Mount of Olives, and taught in the temple. Our Saviour did not waste his mornings in idleness or sleep. He rose early and repaired to the temple. The people, also, flocked to the sanctuary to hear him. This example is at once an encouragement to early rising and to the early worship of God. It is a reproof of those who spend the part of the day best fitted for devotion in unnecessary sleep; and it shows the propriety, where it can be done, of assembling early in the morning for prayer and the worship of God. Early prayer-meetings have the countenance of the Saviour, and will be found to be eminently conducive to the promotion of religion. The whole example of Jesus goes to show the importance of beginning the day with God, and of lifting up the heart to him for direction, for the supply of our wants, and for preservation from temptation, before the mind is engrossed by the cares, and distracted by the perplexities, and led away by the temptations of this life. Commencing the day with God is like arresting evil at the fountain; prayer at any other time, without this, is an attempt to arrest it when it has swollen to a stream and rolls on like a torrent. Let the day be begun with God, and the work of piety is easy. Let the world have the ascendency in the morning, and it will be likely to have it also at noonday and at evening.

CHAPTER XXII.

NOW[a] the feast of unleavened
bread drew nigh, which is
called the Passover.

2 And[b] the chief priests and
scribes sought how they might kill
him; for they feared the people.

3 Then[c] entered Satan into Judas, surnamed Iscariot, being of the
number of the twelve.

4 And he went his way, and
communed with the chief priests
and captains how he might betray
him unto them.

5 And they were glad, [d]and
covenanted to give him money.

6 And he promised, and sought
opportunity to betray him unto
them [1]in the absence of the multitude.

7 Then came the [e]day of unleavened bread, when the passover must
be killed.

8 And he sent Peter and John,
saying, Go and prepare us the
passover, that we may eat.

9 And they said unto him,
Where wilt thou that we prepare?

10 And he said unto them, Behold, when ye are entered into the
city, there shall a man meet you,
bearing a pitcher of water: follow
him into the house where he entereth in.

11 And ye shall say unto the goodman of the house, The Master saith
unto thee, Where is the guest-
chamber, where I shall eat the
passover with my disciples?

12 And he shall show you a large
upper room furnished: there make
ready.

13 And they went, and found as
he had said unto them; and they
made ready the passover.

14 And[f] when the hour was

a Mat.26.2; Mar.14.1,&c. *b* Ps.2.2; Ac.4.27. *c* Mat.26.14; Mar.14.10,&c.; Jn.13.2,27. *d* Zec.11.12. [1] or, *without tumult.* *e* Ex.12. *f* Mat.26.20; Mar.14.17.

CHAPTER XXII.

1, 2. See Notes on Mat. xxvi. 1, 2.

3. *Then entered Satan into Judas.* It is not necessary to suppose that Satan entered personally into the body of Judas, but only that he brought him under his influence; he filled his mind with an evil passion, and led him on to betray his Master. The particular passion of which Satan made use was *avarice*—probably the besetting sin of Judas. To show its exceeding evil and baseness, it is only necessary to say that when it produced its *appropriate* effect in this case, it led to the betraying and crucifixion of the Son of God. We may learn, also, that when Satan *tempts* men, he commonly does it by exciting and raising to the highest pitch their native passions. He does not make them act contrary to their nature, but leads them on to *act out* their proper disposition. ¶ *Satan.* This word properly means an adversary or an accuser. It is the name which in the Scriptures is commonly given to the prince or leader of evil spirits, and is given to him because he is the *accuser* or *calumniator* of the righteous (see Re. xii. 10; comp. Job i. 6–9), as well as because he is the *adversary* of God. ¶ *Being of the number of the twelve.* One of the twelve apostles. This greatly aggravated his crime. He should have been bound by most tender ties to Jesus. He was one of his family—long with him, and treated by him with every mark of kindness and confidence; and nothing could more enhance his guilt than thus to make use of this confidence for the commission of one of the basest crimes.

4–6. *Chief priests and captains.* See Notes on Mat. xxvi. 14. See the account of the bargain which Judas made with them explained in the Notes on Mat. xxvi. 14–16, and Mar. xiv. 10, 11. ¶ *Absence of the multitude.* The multitude, *the people*, were then favourable to Jesus. He had preached in the temple, and many of them believed that he was the Messiah. It was a hazardous thing, therefore, to take him by force, and in their presence, as they might rise and rescue him. Hence they sought to take him when *he* was away from the multitude; and as Judas knew of a place where he could be found *alone*, they were glad of the opportunity of so easily securing him.

7–13. See this passage explained in the Notes on Mat. xxvi. 17–19, and Mar. xiv. 12–16.

come, he sat down, and the twelve
apostles with him.
15 And he said unto them, [2]With
desire I have desired to eat this
passover with you before I suffer.
16 For I say unto you, I will not
any more eat thereof, [g]until it be
fulfilled in the kingdom of God.
17 And he took the cup, and
gave thanks, and said, Take this
and divide *it* among yourselves;
18 For I say unto you, I will not
drink of the fruit of the vine until
the kingdom of God shall come.
19 And[h] he took bread, and gave
thanks, and brake *it*, and gave
unto them, saying, This is my

[2] or, *I have heartily desired.*
[g] ch.14.15; 1 Co.5.7,8; Re.19.9.
[h] 1 Co.10.16; 11.24,&c.

body, which is given for you: this
do in remembrance of me.
20 Likewise also the cup after
supper, saying, This cup *is* the new
testament in my blood, which is
shed for you.
21 But, behold, the hand of him
that betrayeth me *is* [i]with me on
the table.
22 And truly the Son of man
goeth [k]as it was determined; but
woe unto that man by whom he
is betrayed!
23 And they began to inquire
among themselves which of them
it was that should do this thing.
24 And[l] there was also a strife

[i] Ps.41.9; Jn.13.26.
[k] ch.24.46; Ac.2.23; 4.28; 1 Co.15.3.
[l] Mar.9.34; ch.9.46.

14. *When the hour was come.* The hour of eating the paschal lamb, which was in the evening. See Notes on Mat. xxvi. 20.

15. *With desire I have desired.* This is a Hebrew form of expression, and means *I have greatly desired.* The reasons why he desired this we may suppose to have been—1st. That, as he was about to leave them, he was desirous once of seeing them together, and of partaking with them of one of the religious privileges of the Jewish dispensation. Jesus was *man* as well as God, and he never undervalued the religious rites of his country, or the blessings of social and religious intercourse; and there is no impropriety in supposing that even *he* might feel that his human nature might be prepared by the service of religion for his great and terrible sufferings. 2d. He doubtless wished to take an opportunity to prepare *them* for his sufferings, and to impress upon them more fully the certainty that he was about to leave them, that they might be prepared for it. 3d. We may also suppose that he particularly desired it that he might institute for *their* use, and for the edification of all Christians, the supper which is called by his name—*the Lord's Supper.* All his sufferings were the expression of love to his people, and he was desirous of testifying *always* his regard for their comfort and welfare. ¶ *Before I suffer.* Before I die.

16. *Until it be fulfilled.* See Notes on Mat. xxvi. 29.

17. *And he took the cup and gave thanks.* This was not the *sacramental* cup, for that was taken *after* supper, ver. 20. This was one of the cups which were usually taken during the celebration of the Passover, and pertained to that observance. *After* he had kept this in the usual manner, he instituted the supper which bears his name, using the bread and wine which had been prepared for the Passover, and thus ingrafted the Lord's Supper on the Passover, or superseded the Passover by another ordinance, which was intended to be perpetual.

19, 20. See Notes on Mat. xxvi. 26-28.

21-23. See Notes on Mat. xxvi. 21-25.

24. *A strife.* A contention or debate. ¶ *Which of them should be the greatest.* The apostles, in common with the Jews generally, had supposed that the Messiah would come as a temporal prince, and in the manner of other princes of the earth—of course, that he would have officers of his government, ministers of state, &c. Their contention was founded on this expectation, and they were disputing which of them should be raised to the highest office. They had before had a similar contention. See Mat. xviii. 1; xx. 20-28. Nothing can be more humiliating than that the disciples should have had *such* contentions, and in such a time and place. That just as Jesus was contemplating his own death, and labouring to prepare them for it, they should strive and contend about office and rank,

among them which of them should be accounted the greatest.

25 And he said unto them, [m]The kings of the Gentiles exercise lordship over them; and they that exercise authority upon them are called benefactors.

26 But[n] ye *shall* not *be so;* but he that is greatest among you, let him be as the younger; and he that is chief, as he that doth serve.

27 For whether *is* greater, he that sitteth at meat, or he that serveth? *is* not he that sitteth at meat? [o]but I am among you as he that serveth.

28 Ye are they which have continued with me in [p]my temptations.

29 And I appoint unto you [q]a kingdom, as my Father hath appointed unto me;

30 That[r] ye may eat and drink at my table in my kingdom, and sit on thrones, [s]judging the twelve tribes of Israel.

31 And the Lord said, Simon, Simon, behold, [t]Satan hath desired

m Mat.20.25; Mar.10.42. *n* 1 Pe.5.3; 3 Jn.9,10.

o Jn.13.13,14; Phi.2.7. *p* He.4.15. *q* Mat.25.34; ch.12.32; 1 Co.9.25; 1 Pe.5.4. *r* Re.19.9. *s* Mat.19.28; 1 Co.6.2; Re.3.21. *t* 1 Pe.5.8.

---

shows how deeply seated is the love of power; how ambition will find its way into the most secret and sacred places; and how even the disciples of the meek and lowly Jesus are sometimes actuated by this most base and wicked feeling.

25. *The kings of the Gentiles.* The kings of the *nations*, or of the earth. They do this, and it is to be expected of them, and it is right. Our Lord does not mean to say that it was wrong that there should be such authority, but that *his* kingdom was to be of a different character, and they were not to expect it there. ¶ *Over them.* That is, over the *nations.* ¶ *Are called benefactors.* The word *benefactor* is applied to one who bestows *favour* on another. It was applied to kings by way of *compliment* or *flattery.* Some of them might have been truly benefactors of their people, but this was by no means true of *all.* Yet it was applied to all, and especially to the Roman emperors. It is found applied to them often in the writings of Josephus and Philo.

26, 27. *But ye* shall *not* be so. Christ here takes occasion to explain the nature of his kingdom. He assures them that it is established on different principles from those of the world; that his subjects were not to expect titles, and power, and offices of pomp in his kingdom. He that would be most advanced in *his* kingdom would be he that was most humble; and in order to show them this, he took a towel and girded himself after the manner of a servant, and washed their feet, to show them what ought to be their feelings toward each other. See Jn. xiii. 4–17. ¶ *He that sitteth at meat.* The master of the feast, or one of his guests. ¶ *But I am among you,* &c. This was said in connection with his washing their feet. He *showed* them how they ought to feel and act toward each other. *They* ought, therefore, not to aim at office and power, but to be humble, and serve and aid one another.

28. *My temptations.* My trials, my humiliations, and my assaults from the power of Satan and a wicked world. ¶ *And I appoint unto you a kingdom.* He assures them here that they should *have* a kingdom — their expectations would be realized. They had continued with him; they had seen how *he* had lived, and to what trials he had been subjected; they had all along expected a kingdom, and he assures them that they should not be disappointed. ¶ *As my Father,* &c. They had seen how God had appointed a kingdom to *him.* It was not with pomp, and splendour, and external glory, but it was in poverty, want, persecution, and trial. So would *he* appoint to them a kingdom. They should *surely* possess it; but it would be not with external splendour, but by poverty and toil. The original word *appoint* has the force of a *covenant* or compact, and means that it should be *surely* or certainly done, or that he pledged himself to do it. All Christians must enter into the kingdom of heaven after the manner of their Lord—through much tribulation; but, though it must be, as it was with him, by many tears and sorrows, yet they shall surely reach the place of their rest and the reward of heaven, for it is secured to them by the covenant pledge and faithfulness of their Lord and King.

30. See Notes on Mat. xix. 28.

31. *Simon.* Peter. Jesus, foreseeing the danger of Peter, and knowing that

to have you, that he may [u]sift *you*
as wheat;
32 But [v]I have prayed for thee,
that thy faith fail not; and when
thou art converted, [w]strengthen
thy brethren.
33 And he said unto him, Lord,
I am ready to go with thee both
into prison and to death.
34 And he said, I tell thee,
Peter, the cock shall not crow this
day before that thou shalt thrice
deny that thou knowest me.
35 And he said unto them, [x]When
I sent you without purse, and
scrip, and shoes, lacked ye any
thing? And they said, Nothing.
36 Then said he unto them, But

u Am.9.9. *v* Jn.17.9,15; He.7.25; 1 Jn.2.1. *w* Ps.51.13; Jn.21.15-17. *x* ch.9.3.

he was about to deny him, took occasion to forewarn him and put him on his guard, and also to furnish him with a solace when he should be brought to repentance. ¶ *Satan hath desired.* Satan is the prince of evil. One of his works is to try the faith of believers—to place temptations and trials in their way, that they may be tested. Thus God gave Job into his hands, that it might be seen whether he would be found faithful, or would apostatize. See Notes on Job i. 7-12. So Satan desired to have Peter in his hands, that he might also try him. ¶ *May sift* you *as wheat.* Grain was agitated or shaken in a kind of fan or sieve. The grain remained in the fan, and the chaff and dust were thrown off. So Christ says that Satan desired to try Peter; to place trials and temptations before him; *to agitate him;* to see whether anything of faith would remain, or whether all would not be found to be chaff—mere natural ardour and false professions.

32. *That thy faith fail not.* The word *faith,* here, seems to be used in the sense of religion, or attachment to Christ, and the words *fail not* mean *utterly fail* or fail altogether—that is, apostatize. It is true that the *courage* of Peter failed; it is true that he had not that immediate confidence in Jesus and reliance on him which he had before had; but the prayer of Jesus was that he might not altogether apostatize from the faith. God heard Jesus *always* (Jn. xi. 42); it follows, therefore, that *every* prayer which he ever offered was answered; and it follows, as he asked here for a specific thing, that that thing was granted; and as he prayed that Peter's faith might not utterly fail, so it follows that there was no time in which Peter was not really a pious man. Far as he wandered, and grievously as he sinned, yet he well knew that Jesus was the Messiah. He *did know* the man; and though his fears overcame him and led him to aggravated sin, yet the prayer of Christ was prevalent, and he was brought to true repentance. ¶ *When thou art converted.* The word *converted* means turned, changed, recovered. The meaning is, when thou art turned from this sin, when thou art recovered from this heinous offence, then use *your* experience to warn and strengthen those who are in danger of like sins. A man may be *converted* or *turned* from any sin, or any evil course. He is *regenerated* but once—at the beginning of his Christian life; he may be *converted* as often as he falls into sin. ¶ *Strengthen thy brethren.* Confirm them, warn them, encourage them. They are in continual danger, also, of sinning. Use your experience to warn them of their danger, and to comfort and sustain them in their temptations. And from this we learn—1st. That one design of permitting Christians to fall into sin is to show their own weakness and dependence on God; and, 2d. That they who have been overtaken in this manner should make use of their experience to warn and preserve others from the same path. The two epistles of Peter, and his whole life, show that *he* was attentive to this command of Jesus; and in his death he manifested his deep abhorrence of this act of dreadful guilt in denying his blessed Lord, by requesting to be crucified with his head downward, as unworthy to suffer in the same manner that Christ did. Comp. Notes on Jn. xxi. 18.

33, 34. See Notes on Mat. xxvi. 33-35.

35. *When I sent you,* &c. See Notes on Mat. x. 9, 10. ¶ *Lacked ye,* &c. Did you want anything? Did not God fully provide for you? He refers to this to convince them that his words were true; that their past experience should lead them to put confidence in him and in God.

now he that hath a purse, let him take *it*, and likewise *his* scrip; and he that hath no sword, let him sell his garment and buy one.

37 For I say unto you, that this that is written must yet be accomplished in me, [y] And he was reckoned among the transgressors; for the things concerning me have an end.

y Is.53.12.

---

36. *But now.* The Saviour says the times are changed. *Before*, he sent them out only for a little time. They were in their own country. Their journeys would be short, and there was no need that they should make preparation for a long absence, or for encountering great dangers. But *now* they were to go into the wide world, among strangers, trials, dangers, and wants. And as the time was near; as he was about to die; as these dangers pressed on, it was proper that they should make provision for what was before them. ¶ *A purse.* See Notes on Mat. x. 9. He intimates that they should *now* take money, as it would be necessary to provide for their wants in travelling. ¶ *Scrip.* See Notes on Mat. x. 10. ¶ *And he that hath no sword.* There has been much difficulty in understanding why Jesus directed his disciples to arm themselves, as if it was his purpose to make a defence. It is certain that the spirit of his religion is against the use of the sword, and that it was not his purpose to defend himself against Judas. But it should be remembered that these directions about the purse, the scrip, and the sword were not made with reference to his *being taken* in the garden, but with reference *to their future life.* The time of the trial in Gethsemane was just at hand; nor was there *time* then, if no other reason existed, to go and make the purchase. It altogether refers to their future life. They were going into the midst of dangers. The country was infested with robbers and wild beasts. It was customary to go armed. He tells them of those dangers—of the necessity of being prepared in the usual way to meet them. This, then, is not to be considered as a specific, positive *command* to procure a sword, but an intimation that great dangers were before them; that their manner of life would be changed, and that they would need the provisions *appropriate to that kind of life.* The *common* preparation for that manner of life consisted in money, provisions, and arms; and he foretells them of that manner of life by giving them directions commonly understood to be appropriate to it. It amounts, then, to a *prediction* that they would soon leave the places which they had been accustomed to, and go into scenes of poverty, want, and danger, where they would feel the necessity of money, provisions, and the means of defence. All, therefore, that the passage justifies is—1st. That it is proper for men to provide beforehand for their wants, and for ministers and missionaries as well as any others. 2d. That self-defence is lawful. Men encompassed with danger may lawfully *defend* their lives. It does not prove that it is lawful to make *offensive* war on a nation or an individual. ¶ *Let him sell his garment.* His *mantle* or his outer garment. See Notes on Mat. v. 40. The meaning is, let him procure one at any expense, even if he is obliged to sell his clothes for it—intimating that the danger would be very great and pressing.

37. *This that is written.* See Notes on Is. liii. 12. ¶ *Was reckoned among the transgressors.* Not reckoned *as* a transgressor, but *among* or *with* them—that is, he was treated as transgressors are. He was put to death in their company, and as he *would have been* if he had been a transgressor. He was innocent, holy, harmless, and undefiled, He. vii. 26. God knew this always, and could not *think* of him, or make him *to be* otherwise than he was; yet it pleased him to bruise him, and to give him into the hands of men who did reckon him as a transgressor, and who treated him accordingly. ¶ *Have an end.* This may either mean, "shall be surely accomplished," or "they are *about* to be fulfilled," or "are *now* fulfilled." The former is probably the meaning, denoting that *every* prophecy in regard to him would certainly be accomplished.

38. Are *two swords.* The Galileans, it is said, often went armed. The Essenes did so also. The reason was that the country was full of robbers and wild beasts, and it was necessary to carry, in their travels, some means of defence. It seems that the disciples followed the customs of the country, and had with

38 And they said, Lord, behold,
here *are* two swords; and he said
unto them, It is enough.
39 And[z] he came out, and went,
as he was wont, to the mount of
Olives, and his disciples also followed him.
40 And when he was at the
place, he said unto them, Pray
that ye enter not into temptation.
41 And he was withdrawn from
them about a stone's cast, and
kneeled down and prayed,
42 Saying, Father, if thou be
willing,[3] remove this cup from me;
nevertheless, not my will, but thine
be done.
43 And there appeared [a]an angel
unto him from heaven, strengthening him.
44 And[b] being in an agony, he
prayed more earnestly; and his
sweat was as it were great drops of
blood falling down to the ground.
45 And when he rose up from
prayer, and was come to his disciples, he found them sleeping for
sorrow,
46 And said unto them, Why
sleep ye? rise and [c]pray, lest ye
enter into temptation.
47 And while he yet spake, [d]be-
hold, a multitude, and he that was
called Judas, one of the twelve,
went before them, and drew near
unto Jesus to kiss him.

z Mat.26.36; Mar.14.32,&c.; Jn.18.1,&c.
3 *willing to remove.* a Mat.4.11.

b La.1.12; Jn.12.27; He.5.7. c ver.40.
d Mat.26.47,&c.; Mar.14.43,&c.; Jn.18.3,&c.

them some means of defence, though they had but two swords among the twelve. ¶ *It is enough.* It is difficult to understand this. Some suppose that it is spoken *ironically;* as if he had said, "You are bravely armed indeed, with two swords among twelve men, and to meet such a host!" Others, that he meant to reprove them for understanding him *literally*, as if he meant that they were *then* to procure swords for *immediate* battle. As if he had said, "This is absurd, or a perversion of my meaning. I did not *intend this*, but merely to foretell you of impending dangers *after* my death." It is to be observed that he did not say "*the two swords* are enough," but "*it* is enough;" perhaps meaning simply, enough has been said. Other matters press on, and you will yet understand what I mean.

39–46. See Notes on Mat. xxvi. 30–46; Mar. xiv. 26–42.

43. *Strengthening him.* His human nature, to sustain the great burden that was upon his soul. Some have supposed from this that he was not divine as well as human; for if he was *God*, how could an angel give any strength or comfort? and why did not the divine nature *alone* sustain the human? But the fact that he was *divine* does not affect the case at all. It might be asked with the same propriety, If he was, as all admit, the friend of God, and beloved of God, and holy, why, if he was a mere man, did not *God* sustain him alone, without an angel's intervening? But the objection in neither case would have any force. The *man, Christ Jesus*, was suffering. His human nature was in agony, and it is the *manner* of God to sustain the afflicted by the intervention of others; nor was there any more *unfitness* in sustaining the human nature of his Son in this manner than any other sufferer.

44. *In an agony.* See this verse explained in the Notes on Mat. xxvi. 42–44.

45. *Sleeping for sorrow.* On account of the greatness of their sorrow. See Notes on Mat. xxvi. 40.

47–53. See this explained in Mat. xxvi. 48–56.

48. *Betrayest thou the Son of man with a kiss?* By the *Son of man* was evidently meant *the Messiah.* Judas had had the most satisfactory evidence of that, and did not doubt it. A kiss was the sign of affection. By that slight artifice Judas thought to conceal his base purpose. Jesus with severity reproaches him for it. Every word is emphatic. *Betrayest* thou—dost thou violate all thy obligations of fidelity, and deliver thy Master up to death? Betrayest *thou*—thou, so long with him, so much favoured, so sure that this is the Messiah? Betrayest thou *the Son of man*—the Messiah, the hope of the nations, the desire of all people, the world's Redeemer? Betrayest thou the Son of man *with a kiss*—the sign of friendship

48 But Jesus said unto him, Judas, betrayest thou the Son of man with a kiss?

49 When they which were about him saw what would follow, they said unto him, Lord, shall we smite with the sword?

50 And one of them smote the servant of the high-priest, and cut off his right ear.

51 And Jesus answered and said, Suffer ye thus far. And he touched his ear, and healed him.

52 Then Jesus said unto the chief priests, and captains of the temple, and the elders, which were come to him, Be ye come out, as against a thief, with swords and staves?

53 When I was daily with you in the temple, ye stretched forth no hands against me; [e]but this is your hour and the power of darkness.

54 Then they took him, and led *him*, and brought him into the high-priest's house. And Peter followed afar off.

55 And when they had kindled a fire in the midst of the hall, and were set down together, Peter sat down among them.

56 But[f] a certain maid beheld him as he sat by the fire, and earnestly looked upon him, and said, This man was also with him.

57 And he denied him, saying, Woman, I know him not.

58 And[g] after a little while another saw him, and said, Thou art also of them. And Peter said, Man, I am not.

59 And about the space of one hour after, [h]another confidently affirmed, saying, Of a truth this *fellow* also was with him, for he is a Galilean.

60 And Peter said, Man, I know not what thou sayest. And immediately, while he yet spake, the cock crew.

61 And the Lord turned and looked upon Peter. And[i] Peter remembered the word of the Lord, how he had said unto him, [k]Before the cock crow, thou shalt deny me thrice.

62 And[l] Peter went out and wept bitterly.

63 And[m] the men that held Jesus mocked him and smote *him*.

64 And when they had blindfolded him, they struck him on the face, and asked him, saying, Prophesy, who is it that smote thee?

65 And many other things blasphemously spake they against him.

66 And[n] as soon as it was day, the elders of the people and the chief priests and the scribes came together, and led him into their council, saying,

67 Art[o] thou the Christ? tell us. And he said unto them, If I tell you, ye will not believe:

68 And if I also ask *you*, ye will not answer me nor let *me* go.

69 Hereafter shall the Son of man sit on the [p]right hand of the power of God.

70 Then said they all, Art thou, then, the Son of God? And he said unto them, Ye say that I am.

71 And they said, What need we any further witness? for we ourselves have heard of his own mouth.

e Job 20.5; Jn.12.27.
f Mat.26.69; Mar.14.66,69; Jn.18.17.
g Mat.26.71; Mar.14.69; Jn.18.25.
h Mat.26.73; Mar.14.70; Jn.18.26.

i Mat.26.75; Mar.14.72. *k* ver.34.
l Ps.130.1-4; 143.1-4; Je.31.18; Eze.7.16; 1 Co.10.12; 2 Co.7.10,11. *m* Mat.26.67,68; Mar.14.65.
n Mat.27.1; Ac.4.26-28.
o Mat.26.63,&c.; Mar.14.61,&c.
p He.1.3; 8.1; Re.3.21.

---

and affection employed in a base and wicked purpose, intending to add deceit, disguise, and the prostitution of a mark of affection to the *crime of treason?* Every word of this must have gone to the very soul of Judas. Perhaps few reproofs of crime more resemble the awful searchings of the souls of the wicked in the day of judgment.

54–62. See Notes on Mat. xxvi. 57–75.

63–71. See Notes on Mat. xxvi. 57–68.

CHAPTER XXIII.

AND[a] the whole multitude of
them arose, and led him unto
Pilate.
2 And they began to [b]accuse him,
saying, [c]We found this *fellow* perverting the nation, and [d]forbidding
to give tribute to Cæsar, saying
that [e]he himself is Christ a king.
3 And Pilate asked him, saying,
Art thou the King of the Jews?
And[f] he answered him, and said,
Thou sayest *it*.
4 Then said Pilate to the chief
priests and *to* the people, [g]I find no
fault in this man.
5 And they were the [h]more fierce,
saying, He stirreth up the people,
teaching throughout all Jewry, beginning from Galilee to this place.
6 When Pilate heard of Galilee,
he asked whether the man were a
Galilean.
7 And as soon as he knew that
he belonged unto [i]Herod's jurisdiction, he sent him to Herod, who
himself also was at Jerusalem at
that time.

a Mat.27.2,11,&c.; Mar.15.1,&c.; Jn.18.28, &c.
b Zec.11.8. *c* ver.5; Ac.16.20,21; 17.6,7.
d Mat.17.27; 22.21; Mar.12.17.
e Jn.18.36; 19.12. *f* 1 Ti.6.13.
g Jn.18.38; 19.4; He.7.26; 1 Pe.2.22.
h Ps.57.4. *i* ch.3.1.

CHAPTER XXIII.

1. See Notes on Mat. xxvii. 1, 2.

2. *This* fellow. The word *fellow* is not in the original. It conveys a notion of *contempt*, which no doubt they *felt*, but which is not expressed in the *Greek*, and which it is not proper should be expressed in the translation. It might be translated, "We found this man." ¶ *Perverting the nation.* That is, exciting them to sedition and tumults. This was a mere wanton accusation, but it was plausible before a Roman magistrate; for, 1st. The Galileans, as Josephus testifies, were prone to seditions and tumults. 2d. Jesus drew multitudes after him, and they thought it was easy to show that this was itself promoting tumults and seditions. ¶ *Forbidding,* &c. About their charges they were very cautious and cunning. They did not say that he *taught* that men should not give tribute—that would have been too gross a charge, and would have been easily refuted; but it was an *inference* which they drew. They said it *followed* from his doctrine. He professed to be a king. They *inferred*, therefore, if *he* was *a king*, that he must hold that it was not right to acknowledge allegiance to any foreign prince; and if they could make *this* out, they supposed that Pilate *must* condemn him of course. ¶ *Tribute.* Taxes. ¶ *Cæsar.* The Roman emperor, called also Tiberius. The name *Cæsar* was common to the Roman emperors, as *Pharaoh* was to the Egyptian kings. *All* the kings of Egypt were called Pharaoh, or *the* Pharaoh; so all the Roman emperors were called *Cæsar*.

3. See Notes on Mat. xxvii. 11.

4. *I find no fault.* I see no evidence that he is guilty of what you charge him with. This was *after* Pilate had taken Jesus into the judgment-hall by himself and examined him *privately*, and had been satisfied in regard to the nature of his kingdom. See Jn. xviii. 33–38. He was *then* satisfied that though he claimed to be *a king*, yet his kingdom was not of this world, and that *his* claims did not interfere with those of Cæsar.

5. *The more fierce.* The more urgent and pressing. They saw that there was a prospect of losing their cause, and they attempted to press on Pilate the point that would be most likely now to affect him. Pilate had, in fact, acquitted him of the charge of being an enemy to Cæsar, and they therefore urged the other point more vehemently. ¶ *Stirreth up the people.* Excites them to tumult and sedition. ¶ *All Jewry.* All Judea. ¶ *From Galilee to this place.* To Jerusalem—that is, throughout the whole country. It is not merely in one place, but from one end of the land to the other.

6. *Whether he were a Galilean.* He asked this because, if he was, he properly belonged to Herod's jurisdiction, who reigned over Galilee.

7. *Herod's jurisdiction.* Herod Antipas, a son of Herod the Great. This was the same Herod that put John the Baptist to death. Jesus had passed the most of his life in the part of the country where he ruled, and it was therefore considered that he belonged to his jurisdiction—that is, that it belonged to Herod, not to Pilate, to try this cause.

8 And when Herod saw Jesus he was exceeding glad, [k]for he was desirous to see him of a long *season*, [l]because he had heard many things of him; [m]and he hoped to have seen some miracle done by him.

9 Then he questioned with him in many words; [n]but he answered him nothing.

10 And the chief priests and scribes stood and vehemently accused him.

11 And Herod with his men of war [o]set him at nought, and mocked *him*, and arrayed him in a [p]gorgeous robe, and sent him again to Pilate.

k ch.9.9. *l* Mat.14.1; Mar.6.14. *m* 2 Ki.5.11.
n Ps.38.13,14; 39.1,9; Is.53.7.
o Is.49.7; 53.3. *p* Jn.19.5.

12 And the same day [q]Pilate and Herod were made friends together; for before they were at enmity between themselves.

13 And Pilate, when he had called together the chief priests, and the rulers, and the people,

14 Said unto them, Ye have brought this man unto me as one that perverteth the people; and, behold, [r]I, having examined *him* before you, have found no fault in this man touching those things whereof ye accuse him:

15 No, nor yet Herod; for I sent you to him; and, lo, nothing worthy of death is done unto him.

16 I will therefore [s]chastise him, and release *him*.

q Ac.4.27. *r* ver.4. *s* Is.53.5.

---

10. *Vehemently accused him.* Violently or unjustly accused him, endeavouring to make it appear that he had been guilty of sedition in Herod's province.

11. *Herod with his men of war.* With his soldiers, or his body-guard. It is probable that in travelling he had *a guard* to attend him constantly. ¶ *Set him at nought.* Treated him with contempt and ridicule. ¶ *A gorgeous robe.* A white or shining robe, for this is the meaning of the original. The Roman princes wore *purple* robes, and *Pilate* therefore put such a robe on Jesus. The Jewish kings wore a *white* robe, which was often rendered very shining or gorgeous by much tinsel or silver interwoven. Josephus says that the robe which Agrippa wore was so bright with silver that when the sun shone on it, it so dazzled the eyes that it was difficult to look on it. The Jews and Romans therefore decked him in the manner appropriate to their own country, for purposes of mockery. All this was unlawful and malicious, as there was not the least evidence of his guilt. ¶ *Sent him to Pilate.* It was by the interchange of these civilities that they were made friends. It would seem that Pilate sent him to Herod as a token of civility and respect, and with a design, perhaps, of putting an end to their quarrel. Herod returned the civility, and it resulted in their reconciliation.

12. *Made friends together*, &c. What had been the cause of their quarrel is unknown. It is commonly supposed that it was Pilate's slaying the Galileans in Jerusalem, as related in Lu. xiii. 1, 2. The occasion of their reconciliation seems to have been the civility and respect which Pilate showed to Herod in this case. It was not because they were united in *hating* Jesus, as is often the case with wicked men, for Pilate was certainly desirous of releasing him, and *both* considered him merely as an object of ridicule and sport. It is true, however, that wicked men, at variance in other things, are often united in opposing and ridiculing Christ and his followers; and that enmities of long standing are sometimes made up, and the most opposite characters brought together, simply to oppose religion. Comp. Ps. lxxxiii. 5–7.

15. *Nothing worthy of death is done unto him.* Deserving of death. The charges are not proved against him. They had had every opportunity of proving them, first before Pilate and then before Herod, unjustly subjecting him to trial before *two* men in succession, and thus giving them a double opportunity of condemning him, and yet, after all, he was declared by both to be innocent. There could be no better evidence that he *was* innocent.

16. *I will therefore chastise him.* The word *chastise* here means to *scourge* or to *whip*. This was usually done before capital punishment, to increase the sufferings of the man condemned. It is

17 (For of necessity he must release one unto them at the feast.)
18 And they cried out all at once,
saying, Away with this *man*, and
release unto us Barabbas:
19 (Who for a certain sedition
made in the city, and [t]for murder,
was cast into prison.)
20 Pilate therefore, willing to release Jesus, spake again to them.
21 But they cried, saying, Crucify *him*, crucify him.
22 And he said unto them the
third time, Why, what evil hath
he done? I have found no cause
of death in him: I will therefore
chastise him and let *him* go.
23 And they were [u]instant with
loud voices, requiring that he
might be crucified. And the voices
of them and of the chief priests
prevailed.
24 And Pilate [1]gave sentence
that it should be [v]as they required.
25 And he released [w]unto them
him that for sedition and murder
was cast into prison, whom they
had desired; but he delivered Jesus
to their will.
26 And[x] as they led him away,
they laid hold upon one Simon, a
Cyrenian, coming out of the country, and on him they laid the cross,
that he might bear *it* after Jesus.
27 And there followed him a
great company of people, and of
women, which also bewailed and
lamented him.
28 But Jesus, turning unto them,
said, Daughters of Jerusalem, weep
not for me, but weep for yourselves
and for your children:
29 For, behold, [y]the days are
coming, in the which they shall
say, Blessed *are* the barren, and
the wombs that never bare, and
the paps which never gave suck.
30 Then[z] shall they begin to say
to the mountains, Fall on us; and
to the hills, Cover us.

t Ac.3.14. *u* Ps.22.12; ver.5.
1 or, *assented*. *v* Ex.23.2. *w* Ac.3.14.
x Mat.27.32,&c.; Mar.15.21,&c.; Jn.19.17.
y Mat.24.19; ch.21.23.
z Is.2.19; Ho.10.8; Re.6.16; 9.6.

---

not easy to see the reason why, if Pilate supposed Jesus to be *innocent*, he should propose publicly to scourge him. It was as *really* unjust to do that as it was to crucify him. But probably he expected by this to conciliate the minds of his accusers; to show them that he was willing to gratify them if it *could* be done with propriety; and perhaps he expected that by seeing him whipped and disgraced, and condemned to ridicule, to contempt, and to suffering, they would be satisfied. It is farther remarked that among the Romans it was competent for a magistrate to inflict a *slight* punishment on a man when a charge of gross offence was not fully made out, or where there was not sufficient testimony to substantiate the precise charge alleged. All this shows, 1st, the palpable *injustice* of our Lord's condemnation; 2d, the persevering malice and obstinacy of the Jews; and, 3d, the want of firmness in Pilate. He should have released him at once; but the love of *popularity* led him to the murder of the Son of God. Man should do his duty in all situations; and he that, like Pilate, seeks only for public favour and popularity, will assuredly be led into crime.

17. See Notes on Mat. xxvii. 15.

18–23. See Notes on Mat. xxvii. 20–23.

23–25. See Notes on Mat. xxvii. 26.

26. See Notes on Mat. xxvii. 32. ¶ *After Jesus.* Probably to bear one end of the cross. Jesus was feeble and unable to bear it alone, and they compelled Simon to help him.

28. *Daughters of Jerusalem.* Women of Jerusalem. This was a common mode of speaking among the Hebrews. ¶ *Weep for yourselves,* &c. This refers to the calamities that were about to come upon them in the desolation of their city by the Romans.

30. *To the mountains, Fall on us,* &c. This is an image of great calamities and judgments. So great will be the calamities that they will seek for shelter from the storm, and will call on the hills to protect them. The same figure is used respecting the wicked in the day of judgment in Re. vi. 16, 17. Compare also Is. ii. 21.

31. *For if they do these things in a green tree,* &c. This seems to be a pro-

31 For[a] if they do these things
in a green tree, what shall be done
in the dry?
32 And there were also two
others, [b]malefactors, led with him
to be put to death.

a Pr.11.31; Je.25.29; Eze.20.47; 21.4; 1 Pe.4.17.
b Is.53.12.

33 And when they were come to
the place which is called [2]Calvary,
there they crucified him, and the
malefactors; one on the right hand,
and the other on the left.
34 Then said Jesus, [c]Father, for-

2 or, *the place of a skull.*
c Mat.5.44; Ac.7.60; 1 Co.4.12.

verbial expression. A *green* tree is not easily set on fire; a dry one is easily kindled and burns rapidly; and the meaning of the passage is—"If they, the Romans, do these things to *me*, who am innocent and blameless; if they punish me in this manner in the face of justice, what will they *not* do in relation to this guilty nation? What security have *they* that heavier judgments will not come upon them? What desolations and woes may not be expected when *injustice* and oppression have taken the place of justice, and have set up a rule over this wicked people?" Our Lord alludes, evidently, to the calamities that would come upon them by the Romans in the destruction of their city and temple. The passage may be applied, however, without impropriety, and with great beauty and force, to the punishment of the wicked in the future world. Thus applied, it means that the sufferings of the Saviour, as compared with the sufferings of the guilty, were like the burning of a green tree as compared with the burning of one that is dry. A green tree is not adapted to burn; a dry one is. So the Saviour —innocent, pure, and holy—stood in relation to suffering. There were sufferings which an innocent being could not endure. There was remorse of conscience, the sense of guilt, punishment properly so called, and the eternity of woes. He had the consciousness of innocence, and he would not suffer for ever. He had no passions to be enkindled that would rage and ruin the soul. The sinner is *adapted* to sufferings, like a dry tree to the fire. He is guilty, and will suffer all the horrors of remorse of conscience. He will be punished literally. He has raging and impetuous passions, and they will be enkindled in hell, and will rage for ever and ever. The meaning is, that if the innocent Saviour suffered *so much*, the sufferings of the sinner for ever in hell must be more unspeakably dreadful. Yet who could endure the sufferings of the Redeemer on the cross for a single day? Who could bear them for ever and ever, aggravated by all the horrors of a guilty conscience, and all the terrors of unrestrained anger, and hate, and fear, and wrath? *Why* WILL *the wicked die?*

32, 33. See Notes on Mat. xxvii. 35, 38.

34. *Father, forgive them.* This is a fulfilment of the prophecy in Is. liii. 12: *He made intercession for the transgressors.* The prayer was offered for those who were guilty of putting him to death. It is not quite certain whether he referred to the *Jews* or *to the Roman soldiers.* Perhaps he referred to both. The Romans knew not what they did, as they were really ignorant that he was the Son of God, and as they were merely obeying the command of their rulers. The Jews knew, indeed, that he was *innocent*, and they had evidence, if they would have looked at it, that he was the Messiah; but they did not know what would be the effect of their guilt; they did not know what judgments and calamities they were bringing down upon their country. It may be added, also, that, though they had abundant evidence, if they would look at it, that he was the Messiah, and enough to leave them without excuse, yet they did not, *in fact*, believe that he was the Saviour promised by the prophets, and had not, *in fact*, any proper sense of his rank and dignity as "the Lord of glory." If they had had, they would not have crucified him, as we cannot suppose that they would knowingly put to death their own Messiah, the hope of the nation, and him who had been so long promised to the fathers. See Notes on 1 Co. ii. 8. We may learn from this prayer—1st. The duty of praying for our enemies, even when they are endeavouring most to injure us. 2d. The thing for which we should pray for them is that *God* would pardon them and give them better minds. 3d. The power and excellence of the Christian religion. No other

give them, for they know not what
they do. And they parted his raiment, and cast lots.
35 And the people stood beholding. And the [d]rulers also with
them, derided *him*, saying, He
saved others; let him save himself,
if he be Christ, the chosen of God.
36 And the soldiers also mocked
him, coming to him and offering
him vinegar,
37 And saying, If thou be the
King of the Jews, save thyself.
38 And a superscription also
was written over him, in letters of
Greek, and Latin, and Hebrew,
THIS IS THE KING OF THE
JEWS.
39 And [e]one of the malefactors
which were hanged railed on him,
saying, If thou be Christ, save thyself and us.
40 But the other answering, rebuked him, saying, [f]Dost not thou
fear God, seeing thou art [g]in the
same condemnation?
41 And we indeed justly; for we
receive the due reward of our

d Ps.22.7. *e* ch.17.34-36. *f* Ps.36.1. *g* Je.5.3.

religion *teaches* men to pray for the forgiveness of enemies; no other *disposes* them to do it. Men of the world seek for *revenge;* the Christian bears reproaches and persecutions with patience, and prays that God would pardon those who injure them, and save them from their sins. 4th. The greatest sinners, through the intercession of Jesus, may obtain pardon. God heard him, and still hears him *always*, and there is no reason to doubt that many of his enemies and murderers obtained forgiveness and life. Comp. Ac. ii. 37, 42, 43; vi. 7; xiv. 1. ¶ *They know not what they do*. It was done through ignorance, Ac. iii. 17. Paul says that, "had they known it, they would not have crucified the Lord of glory," 1 Co. ii. 8. Ignorance does not excuse altogether a crime if the ignorance be wilful, but it diminishes its guilt. They *had* evidence; they *might* have learned his character; they *might* have known what they were doing, and they *might* be held answerable for all this. But Jesus here shows the compassion of his heart, and as they were *really* ignorant, whatever might have been the cause of their ignorance, he implores God to pardon them. He even urges it as a *reason* why they should be pardoned, that they were ignorant of what they were doing; and though men are often guilty for their ignorance, yet God often in compassion overlooks it, averts his anger, and grants them the blessings of pardon and life. So he forgave Paul, for he "did it in ignorance, in unbelief," 1 Ti. i. 13. So God *winked at* the ignorance of the Gentiles, Ac. xvii. 30. Yet this is no excuse, and no evidence of safety, for those who in our day contemptuously put away from them and their children the means of instruction.

35–39. See Notes on Mat. xxvii. 41–44.

38. *In letters of Greek*, &c. See Notes on Mat. xxvii. 37.

39. *One of the malefactors.* Matthew (ch. xxvii. 44) says "*the thieves—cast the same in his teeth.*" See the apparent contradiction in these statements reconciled in the Notes on that place. ¶ *If thou be Christ.* If thou art the Messiah; if thou art what thou dost pretend to be. This is a taunt or reproach of the same kind as that of the priests in ver. 35. ¶ *Save thyself and us.* Save our lives. Deliver us from the cross. This man did not seek for salvation truly; he asked not to be delivered from his sins; if he had, Jesus would also have heard him. Men often, in sickness and affliction, call upon God. They are earnest in prayer. They ask of God to save them, but it is only to save them from *temporal* death. It is not to be saved from their sins, and the consequence is, that when God *does* raise them up, they forget their promises, and live as they did before, as this robber *would* have done if Jesus had heard his prayer and delivered him from the cross.

40. *Dost not thou fear God*, &c. You are condemned to die as well as he. It is improper for you to rail on him as the rulers and Romans do. God is just, and you are hastening to his bar, and you should therefore fear him, and fear that he will punish you for railing on this innocent man. ¶ *Same condemnation.* Condemnation to death; not death for the same thing, but the same *kind* of death.

41. *Due reward of our deeds.* The pro-

deeds; but this man [h]hath done nothing amiss.
42 And he said unto Jesus, [i]Lord, remember me when thou comest into thy kingdom.
43 And Jesus said unto him,

h 1 Pe.1.19. *i* Ps.106.4,5; Ro.10.9,10; 1 Co.6.10,11.

per punishment for our crimes. They had been highwaymen, and it was just that they should die.

42. *Remember me.* This is a phrase praying for favour, or asking him to grant him an *interest* in his kingdom, or to acknowledge him as one of his followers. It implied that he believed that Jesus was what he claimed to be—the Messiah; that, though he was dying with them, yet he would set up his kingdom; and that he had full power to bless him, though about to expire. It is possible that this man might have heard him preach before his crucifixion, and have learned there the nature of his kingdom; or it may have been that while on the cross Jesus had taken occasion to acquaint them with the nature of his kingdom. While he might have been doing this, one of the malefactors may have continued to rail on him while the other became truly penitent. Such a result of preaching the gospel would not have been unlike what has often occurred since, where, while the gospel has been proclaimed, one has been "taken and another left;" one has been melted to repentance, another has been more hardened in guilt. The promise which follows shows that this prayer was answered. This was a case of repentance in the last hour, the trying hour of death; and it has been remarked that *one* was brought to repentance there, to show that no one should *despair* on a dying bed; and *but* one, that none should be presumptuous and delay repentance to that awful moment. ¶ *When thou comest*, &c. It is impossible now to fix the precise idea which this robber had of Christ's coming. Whether it was that he expected that he would rise from the dead, as some of the Jews supposed the Messiah would; or whether he referred to the day of judgment; or whether to an immediate translation to his kingdom in the heavens, we cannot tell. All that we know is, that he fully believed him to be the Messiah, and that he desired to obtain an interest in that kingdom which he knew he would establish.

43. *To-day*, &c. It is not probable that the dying thief expected that his prayer would be so soon answered. It is rather to be supposed that he looked to some *future* period when the Messiah would rise or would return; but Jesus told him that his prayer would be answered that very day, implying, evidently, that it would be *immediately* at death. This is the more remarkable, as those who were crucified commonly lingered for several days on the cross before they died; but Jesus foresaw that measures would be taken to *hasten* their death, and assured him that *that* day he should receive an answer to his prayer and be with him in his kingdom. ¶ *Paradise.* This is a word of *Persian* origin, and means *a garden*, particularly a garden of pleasure, filled with trees, and shrubs, and fountains, and flowers. In hot climates such gardens were peculiarly pleasant, and hence they were attached to the mansions of the rich and to the palaces of princes. The word came thus to denote any place of happiness, and was used particularly to denotes the abodes of the blessed in another world. The Romans spoke of their Elysium, and the Greeks of the gardens of Hesperides, where the trees bore golden fruit. The garden of Eden means, also, the garden of *pleasure*, and in Ge. ii. 8 the Septuagint renders the word *Eden* by *Paradise.* Hence this name in the Scriptures comes to denote the abodes of the blessed in the other world. See Notes on 2 Co. xii. 4. The Jews supposed that the souls of the righteous would be received into such a place, and those of the wicked cast down to Gehenna until the time of the judgment. They had many fables about this state which it is unnecessary to repeat. The plain meaning of the passage is, "To-day thou shalt be made happy, or be received to a state of blessedness with me after death." It is to be remarked that Christ says nothing about the *place where* it should be, nor of the condition of those there, excepting that it is a place of blessedness, and that its happiness is to commence immediately after death (see also Phi. i. 23); but from the narrative we may learn—1st. That the soul will exist separately from the body; for, while the thief and the Saviour would be in Paradise, their *bodies* would be on the cross or in the grave. 2d. That immediately after

Verily[k] I say unto thee, To-day
shalt thou be with me in [l]paradise.
44 And it was about the sixth
hour, and there was darkness over
all the [3]earth until the ninth hour.
45 And the sun was darkened,
and the veil of the temple was
rent in the midst.
46 And when Jesus had cried
with a loud voice, he said, [m]Father,
into thy hands I commend my
spirit; [n]and having said thus, he
gave up the ghost.
47 Now when the centurion saw
what was done, he glorified God,
saying, Certainly this was a righteous man.
48 And all the people that came
together to that sight, beholding
the things which were done, smote
their breasts and returned.
49 And all his acquaintance, and
the women that followed him from
Galilee, [o]stood afar off, beholding
these things.
50 And, behold, *there was* a man
named Joseph, a counsellor; *and
he was* a good man, and a just:
51 (The same had not consented
to the counsel and deed of them:)
he was of Arimathea, a city of the
Jews; [p]who also himself waited
for the kingdom of God.
52 This *man* went unto Pilate
and begged the body of Jesus.
53 And he took it down, and
wrapped it in linen, and laid it [q]in
a sepulchre that was hewn in
stone, wherein man never before
was laid.
54 And that day was [r]the preparation, and the sabbath drew on.
55 And the [s]women also, which
came with him from Galilee, followed after, and beheld the sepulchre, and how his body was laid.
56 And they returned, and [t]pre-
pared spices and ointments; and
rested the sabbath-day, [u]accord-
ing to the commandment.

CHAPTER XXIV.

NOW[a] upon the first *day* of the
week, very early in the morning, they came unto the sepulchre,
bringing the spices which they had
prepared, and certain *others* with
them.
2 And they found the stone
rolled away from the sepulchre.

k Ro.5.20,21. *l* 2 Co.12.4; Re.2.7. [3] or, *land*. *m* Ps.31.5; 1 Pe.2.23. *n* Mat.27.50,&c.; Mar.15.37,&c.; Jn.19.30. *o* Ps.38.11; 142.4.

p Mar.15.43; ch.2.25,38. *q* Is.53.9. *r* Mat.27.62. *s* ch.8.2; ver.49. *t* Mar.16.1. *u* Ex.20.8-10. *a* Mat.28.1,&c.; Mar.16.2,&c.; Jn.20.1,&c.

death—the same day—the souls of the righteous will be made happy. They will feel that they are secure; they will be received among the just; and they will have the assurance of a glorious immortality. 3d. That state will differ from the condition of the wicked. The promise was made to but one on the cross, and there is no evidence whatever that the other entered there. See also the parable of the rich man and Lazarus, Lu. xvi. 19–31. 4th. It is the chief glory of this state and of heaven to be permitted to see Jesus Christ and to be with him: "Thou shalt be *with me*." "I desire to depart and *to be with Christ*," Phi. i. 23. See also Re. xxi. 23; v. 9–14.

44–46. See Notes on Mat. xxvii. 45–50.

47–49. See Notes on Mat. xxvii. 52–55.

48. *The things which were done.* The earthquake, the darkness, and the sufferings of Jesus. ¶ *Smote their breasts.* In token of alarm, fear, and anguish. They saw the judgments of God; they saw the guilt of the rulers; and they feared the farther displeasure of the Almighty.

50–56. See Notes on Mat. xxvii. 57–61; Mar. xv. 42–47.

CHAPTER XXIV.

1–12. See Notes on Mat. xxviii. 1–11.

13. *Two of them.* Two of the disciples. The name of one of them was *Cleopas*, ver. 18. Many have supposed that the other was Luke, and that he omitted his own name from modesty. Others have supposed that it was Peter. See ver. 34; 1 Co. xv. 5. There is no evidence to guide us here. Dr. Lightfoot has shown that *Cleopas* is the same

3 And they entered in, and
found not the body of the Lord
Jesus.
4 And it came to pass, as they
were much perplexed thereabout,
behold, [b]two men stood by them
in shining garments:
5 And, as they were afraid, and
bowed down *their* faces to the
earth, they said unto them, Why
seek ye [1]the living among the
dead?
6 He is not here, but is risen:
remember how he [c]spake unto you
when he was yet in Galilee,
7 Saying, The Son of man
must be delivered into the hands
of sinful men, and be crucified,
and the third day rise again.
8 And they remembered his
words,
9 And returned from the sepulchre, and told all these things unto
the eleven, and to all the rest.
10 It was Mary Magdalene,
and [d]Joanna, and Mary *the mother*
of James, and other *women that
were* with them, which told these
things unto the apostles.
11 And their words [e]seemed
to them as idle tales, and they
believed them not.
12 Then[f] arose Peter, and ran
unto the sepulchre; and stooping
down, he beheld the linen clothes
laid by themselves, and departed,
wondering in himself at that which
was come to pass.
13 And, behold, [g]two of them
went that same day to a village
called Emmaus, which was from
Jerusalem *about* threescore furlongs.
14 And they talked together of

b Jn.20.12; Ac.1.10.
1 or, *him that liveth*, Re.1.18.
c Mat.16.21; 17.23; Mar.8.31; 9.31; ch.9.22; Jn.2.22.
d ch.8.3.
e Ge.19.14; 2 Ki.7.2; Job 9.16; Ps.126.1; Ac.12.9,15.
f Jn.20.3,6.
g Mar.16.12.

name as *Alpheus*, who was the father of the apostle James, Mat. x. 3. ¶ *Emmaus.* In regard to the locality of Emmaus, it seems quite probable that it is the same village which is referred to by Josephus (*Jewish Wars*, vii. 6, § 6), who states that, after the destruction of Jerusalem, Titus gave *Emmaus*, distant from Jerusalem threescore furlongs, to eight hundred of his troops, whom he had dismissed from his army, for their habitation. Dr. Thomson (*The Land and the Book*, vol. ii. p. 307, 540) regards it as the present Kuriet el 'Aineb, which Dr. Robinson identifies with Kirjath-jearim. Of this place he says: "Kuriet el 'Aineb itself would be the proper distance from Jerusalem, and being on the road to Jaffa, and on the dividing ridge between the plain and the mountains, the Roman emperor might have deemed it an advantageous post for a colony made up of his disbanded soldiers, who could keep in check the surrounding country. Certain it is that in these later ages the occupants of this place have controlled the whole adjacent region, and for many a generation exercised their lawless tyranny upon helpless pilgrims.

"It took just three hours' moderate riding from Kuriet el 'Aineb to Jerusalem: first, a long descent into Wady Hanîna, which passes between it and Soba; then a similar ascent, succeeded by a very steep pass, and a very slippery path down to Kulonia. At this place are some heavy foundations of church, convent, or castle by the road-side, which may be of almost any age, and also gardens of fruit-trees, irrigated by a fountain of excellent water. Kulonia is on a hill north of the road, and appears in a fair way to become a ruin itself before long. The path then winds up a valley, and stretches over a dreary waste of bare rocks until within a mile of the city, when the view opens upon its naked ramparts and the mysterious regions toward the Dead Sea." ¶ *Threescore furlongs.* Sixty furlongs, or about seven or eight miles. It is not certain that these were apostles, but the contrary seems to be implied in ver. 33. See Notes on that verse. If they were not, it is probable that they were intimate disciples, who may have been much with the Saviour during the latter part of his ministry and the closing scenes of his life. But it is wholly unknown why they were going to Emmaus. It may have been that this was their native place, or that they had friends in the vicinity. They seem to have

all these things which had happened.
15 And it came to pass that,
while they [h]communed *together*
and reasoned, Jesus himself drew
near and went with them.
16 But their [i]eyes were holden,
that they should not know him.
17 And he said unto them,
What manner of communications

h Mal.3.16; Mat.18.20; ver.36.
i Jn.20.14,15; 21.4.

are these that ye have one to
another, as ye walk and are sad?
18 And the one of them, whose
name was [k]Cleopas, answering,
said unto him, Art thou only a
stranger in Jerusalem, and hast
not known the things which are
come to pass there in these days?
19 And he said unto them,
What things? And they said unto

k Jn.19.25.

---

given up all for lost, and to have come to the conclusion that Jesus was not the Messiah, though they naturally conversed about it, and there were many things which they could not explain. Their Master had been crucified contrary to their expectation, their hopes dashed, their anticipation disappointed, and they were now returning in sadness, and very naturally conversed, in the way, of the things which had happened in Jerusalem.

15. *Communed* together. Talked together. ¶ *And reasoned.* They reasoned, doubtless, about the probability or improbability that Jesus was the Messiah; about the evidence of his resurrection; about what was to be done in the present state of things. ¶ *Jesus himself drew near*, &c. The disciples were properly employed. Their minds were anxious about the state of things, and they endeavoured to arrive at the truth. In this state of things Jesus came to solve their doubts, and to establish them in the belief that he was the Christ; and we may learn from this that Christ will guide those who are sincerely endeavouring to know the truth. They who candidly and seriously endeavour to ascertain what is true and right he will direct; and often in an unexpected manner he will appear, to dissipate their doubts and to scatter all their perplexities. *Our* duty is sincerely to strive to ascertain the truth, and to do his will; and if his people do this, he will not leave them to perplexity and wandering.

16. *Their eyes were holden.* This expression is used merely to denote that they did not *know* who he was. It does not appear that there was anything supernatural or miraculous in it, or that God used any power to blind them. It may easily be accounted for without any such supposition; for, 1st. Jesus appeared *in another form* (Mar. xvi. 12)—that is, different from his *usual* appearance. 2d. They were not *expecting* to see him—indeed, they did not suppose that he was alive, and it required the strongest evidence to convince them that he was really risen from the dead.

17. *What manner of communications*, &c. What is the subject of your conversation? What is it that has so much affected your minds? They were deeply affected in the recollection of the death of Jesus; and, as became all Christians, they were conversing about him, and were sad at the overwhelming events that had come upon them.

18. *Art thou only a stranger?* &c. This is an expression of surprise that he should be unacquainted with an affair that had made so much noise, and that had been attended with so remarkable circumstances. The word *stranger* here denotes one who had come to reside at a place only for a *time*, not a permanent inhabitant. Many Jews came up from all parts of the world to Jerusalem, to keep the Passover there. They appear to have taken Jesus to be such a stranger or foreigner. The meaning of this verse may be thus expressed: "The affair concerning which we are sad has been well known, and has made a great talk and noise, so that all, even the strangers who have come up to remain there but a little time, are well acquainted with it. Art thou the *only one* of them who has not heard it? Is everybody so well acquainted with it, and thou hast not heard of it? It is a matter of surprise, and we cannot account for it."

19. *A prophet.* A teacher sent from God. They did not now call him the *Messiah*, for his *death* had led them to doubt that, but they had no doubt that he was a distinguished *prophet*. The

him, Concerning Jesus of Nazareth,
which was [l]a prophet [m]mighty in
deed and word before God and all
the people;
20 And [n]how the chief priests
and our rulers delivered him to be
condemned to death, and have
crucified him.
21 But we trusted that [o]it had
been he which should have redeemed Israel; and, beside all this,
to-day is the third day since these
things were done.
22 Yea, and [p]certain women
also of our company made us
astonished, which were early at
the sepulchre;
23 And when they found not his
body, they came, saying that they
had also seen a vision of angels,
which said that he was alive.
24 And [q]certain of them which
were with us went to the sepulchre, and found *it* even so as the
women had said; but him they
saw not.
25 Then he said unto them, [r]O
fools, and slow of heart to believe
all that the prophets have spoken!
26 Ought[s] not Christ to have

l ch.7.16; Jn.3.2; Ac.2.22. *m* Ac.7.22. *n* ch.23.1; Ac.13.27,28. *o* ch.1.68; Ac.1.6. *p* ver.9,10. *q* ver.12. *r* He.5.11,12. *s* ver.46; Ac.17.3; He.9.22,23.

evidence of that was so clear that they *could* not call it in question. ¶ *Mighty in deed.* Powerful in working miracles, in raising the dead, healing the sick, &c. ¶ *In word.* In teaching. ¶ *Before God and all the people.* Manifestly; publicly. So that *God* owned him, and the people regarded him as a distinguished teacher.

20. See Notes on Mat. xxvi. 59–66.

21. *We trusted.* We hoped and expected. ¶ *Should have redeemed Israel.* That he was the Messiah, who would have delivered the nation from the Romans. ¶ *Besides all this.* It is to be observed that Cleopas states things just as they occurred to his own mind. There is little connection. His mind is confused and distracted. There were so many things that were remarkable in Jesus; there was so much evidence that he was the Messiah; their hopes had been so suddenly dashed by his death, and the succeeding events had been so wonderful, that his mind was confused, and he knew not what to think. The things which he now stated served to increase his perplexity. The expressions here are perfectly natural. They bespeak an agitated mind. They are simple touches of nature, which show that the book was not forged. If the book had been the work of imposture, this artless and perplexed narrative would not have been thought of. ¶ *To-day is the third day,* &c. Jesus had foretold them that he would rise on the third day. This they did not understand; but it is not improbable that they looked to this day expecting something wonderful, and that the visit to the sepulchre had called it to their recollection, and they were more and more amazed when they put all these things together. As if they had said, "The third day is come, and we have not seen him. Yet we begin to remember his promise—the angels have informed us that he is alive—but we do not know how to put these things together, or what to make of them."

22, 23. *Certain women.* See Mat. xxviii. 1–7; Jn. xx. 12. ¶ *A vision of angels.* An appearance of angels, or they had seen angels. See Jn. xx. 12.

24. *Certain of them which were with us.* Peter and John. See Jn. xx. 2–9.

25. *O fools.* The word *fool* sometimes is a term of reproach denoting *wickedness.* In this sense we are forbidden to employ it in addressing another, Mat. v. 22. That, however, is a different word in the Greek from the one which occurs here. The one there used implies contempt, but the one employed in this place denotes *weakness* or *dulness.* He reproached them for not seeing what he had himself so clearly predicted, and what had been foretold by the prophets. The word used in the original does not imply as much *reproach* as the word *fool* does among us. It was not an expression of *contempt;* it was an expression denoting merely that they were *thoughtless,* and that they did not properly *attend to* the evidence that he must die and rise again. ¶ *Slow of heart to believe.* Not quick to perceive. Dull of learning. They had suffered their previous opinions and prejudices to prevent their seeing the evidence that he must die

suffered these things, [t]and to enter
into his glory?

27 And beginning at [u]Moses,
and all [v]the prophets, he expounded
unto them in all the scriptures the
things concerning himself.

28 And they drew nigh unto the
village whither they went; [w]and he
made as though he would have gone
further.

29 But they constrained him,
saying, Abide with us; for it is
toward evening, and the day is far
spent. And he went in to tarry
with them.

30 And it came to pass as he
sat at meat with them, [x]he took
bread, and blessed *it*, and brake,
and gave to them.

31 And their eyes were opened,

t 1 Pe.1.3,11. *u* ver.44; Ac.3.22. *v* Ac.10.43; 26.22. *w* Ge.32.26; Mar.6.48.

x Mat.14.19.

---

and rise from the dead. ¶ *All that the prophets have spoken.* Respecting the character and sufferings of the Messiah. See Notes on ver. 27.

26. *Ought not Christ*, &c. Ought not the *Messiah.* Was there not evidence that he would do it? and was it not indispensable that he should, in order to fulfil the prophecies? The *necessity* of his suffering these things referred to *here* was that it was foretold that he *would.* The reason why it was predicted, and why it was necessary that it should occur, was that it was proper that God should manifest his justice, and do honour to his law, and secure the due regard for his government, while he pardoned the guilty.

27. *Beginning at Moses.* At the *writings* of Moses, or at the beginning of the Old Testament; or rather the word *beginning* should be separated from what follows, denoting simply that he *commenced* his discourse, and not that he began at the prophets as well as at Moses; thus, "And commencing his discourse, or replying to them, he expounded from Moses and the prophets," &c. ¶ *All the prophets.* The books of the Old Testament generally. ¶ *He expounded.* He explained or interpreted it to them. Probably he showed them that *their* notions of the Messiah were not according to the Scriptures. *They* expected a temporal prince; they were perplexed because Jesus had not assumed the regal power, but had been put to death. He showed them that according to the prophecies he ought to suffer, and that his *death*, therefore, was no argument that he was not the Messiah. ¶ *In all the scriptures.* In all the *writings* of the Old Testament. They were called *scriptures* because they were *written*, the art of printing being then unknown. ¶ *The things concerning himself.* Concerning the Messiah. It does not appear that he *applied* them to himself, but left them, probably, to make the application. He showed what the Scriptures foretold, and *they* saw that these things applied to Jesus of Nazareth, and began to be satisfied that he was the Messiah. The most striking passages foretelling the character and sufferings of Christ are the following, which we may suppose it possible our Saviour dwelt upon to convince them that, though he was crucified, yet he was the Christ: Ge. iii. 15; De. xviii. 15; Ge. xlix. 10; Nu. xxi. 8, 9; Is. liii.; Da. ix. 25–27; Is. ix. 6, 7; Ps. cx.; xvi.; xxii.; Mal. iv. 2–6.

28. *He made as though he would have gone further.* He did not *say* he would go farther, but he kept on as if it was not his intention to stop, and doubtless he *would* have gone on if they had not constrained him to tarry.

29. *Constrained him.* They urged him, or pressingly invited him. They did not yet perceive that it was Jesus, but they had been charmed and delighted with his discourse, and they wished to hear him farther. Christians are delighted with communion with the Saviour. They seek it as the chief object of their desire, and they find their chief pleasure in fellowship with him. The two disciples felt it a privilege to entertain the stranger, as they supposed, who had so charmed them with his discourse; and so those to whom the gospel is preached, and who love it, feel it a privilege, and not a burden, to show kindness to those who bear to them the message of salvation. ¶ *Abide with us.* Remain with us, or pass the night in our house.

30. *Sat at meat.* Reclined at the table, or while he was at supper. ¶ *He took bread and blessed* it, &c. This was the office of the master of a feast, and perhaps this first attracted particularly their attention. Though he was in *their*

and they knew him; and he [2]vanished out of their sight.

32 And they said one to another, Did not our heart [y]burn within us while he talked with us by the way, and while he opened to us the scriptures?

33 And they rose up the same hour and returned to Jerusalem, and found the eleven gathered

[2] or, *ceased to be seen of them.*
[y] Ps.39.3; Je.20.9; 23.29.

house, yet he acted as *master* of the feast, as he used to do with them before his death. Perhaps, also, as he *gave* them the bread, they observed the *prints* in his hands, and they knew that it was Jesus. This was not a *sacramental*, but a common supper; yet our Saviour sought a blessing on the food, and thus set an example to all his followers to acknowledge God in their daily gifts, and to seek his benediction in all their enjoyments.

31. *Their eyes were opened.* The obscurity was removed. They saw him to be the Messiah. Their doubts were gone, and they saw clearly that he was risen, and was truly, as they had long hoped, the Saviour of men. It is not meant that they were before *blind*, but that they did not know till then who he was. ¶ *He vanished out of their sight.* He suddenly departed. It does not appear that there was anything miraculous in this, but, during their surprise, he took the opportunity suddenly to withdraw from them.

32. *Our heart burn within us.* This is an expression denoting the deep interest and pleasure which they had felt in his discourse before they knew who he was. They now recalled his instruction; they remembered how his words reached the *heart* as he spoke to them; how convincingly he had showed them that the Messiah ought to suffer, and how, while he talked to them of the Christ that they so much loved, their hearts glowed with intense love. This feeling was not confined to them alone. All the followers of Jesus know how precious and tender are the communications of the Saviour, and how the heart glows with love as they think or hear of his life, and sufferings, and death. ¶ *He opened to us.* He *explained* to us the Scriptures. See ver. 27.

This narrative shows us, 1st. How blind men may be to the plainest doctrines of the Scriptures until they are explained to them. These disciples had often read or heard the Scriptures, but never, till then, did they fully understand that the Messiah must suffer. 2d. It is proper there should be those whose office it is to explain the Scriptures. Jesus did it while on earth; he does it now by his Spirit; and he has appointed his ministers, whose business it is to explain them. 3d. If men attempt to explain the Bible, they should themselves understand it. They should give their time and talents to a suitable preparation to understand the sacred volume. Preaching should consist in *real*, and not *fancied* explanations of the Scriptures; the real doctrines which *God* has taught in his word, and not the doctrines that *men* have taught in their systems. 4th. Here was convincing evidence that Jesus was the Messiah. This was but one of many instances where Jesus convinced his disciples, contrary to their previous belief. In this case the evidence was abundant. He first satisfied them from the Old Testament that the very things which had happened were foretold; he then dissipated every doubt by showing *himself* to them and convincing them that he was truly the Christ. There was no chance here for deception and juggling. Who would have met them and talked with them in this way but the real Saviour? Who would have thought of writing this narrative to help an imposture? What impostor would have recorded the dulness of the disciples as to the plain declarations of the Old Testament, and *then* have thought of this device to prop up the narrative? Everything about this narrative—its simplicity—its tenderness—its particularity—its perfect nature—its freedom from all appearance of trick—shows that it was taken from real life; and if so, then the Christian religion is true, for here is evidence that Jesus rose from the dead.

33. *The same hour.* Though it was late, and they had stopped, as they thought, for the night, yet such was their joy that they hastened to tell it to their companions and friends. This was natural and proper, and it shows how quick and ready they who have found the Saviour are to tell it to others. Comp. Jn. i. 41-45. Young converts to Christ *should* hasten to tell

together, and them that were with them,

34 Saying, The Lord is risen indeed, and [z]hath appeared to Simon.

35 And they told what things *were done* in the way, and how he was known of them in breaking of bread.

36 And[a] as they thus spake, Jesus himself stood in the midst of them, and saith unto them, Peace *be* unto you.

37 But they were terrified and affrighted, and [b]supposed that they had seen a spirit.

38 And he said unto them, Why are ye troubled? and why do thoughts arise in your hearts?

39 Behold my hands and my feet, that it is I myself: handle me, and see; for a spirit hath not flesh and bones, as ye see me have.

40 And when he had thus spoken, he showed them *his* hands and *his* feet.

z 1 Co.15.5. a Mar.16.14,&c.; Jn.20.19,&c. b Mar.6.49.

---

their joy, and should not shrink at self-denial to proclaim to others what God hath done for the soul, Ps. lxvi. 16.

"My lips and cheerful heart, prepare
To make his mercies known:
Come, ye that fear my God, and hear
The wonders he hath done.

"When on my head huge sorrows fell,
I sought his heavenly aid;
He saved my sinking soul from hell,
And death's eternal shade."

¶ *The eleven.* The eleven apostles. Judas was now dead. This shows that the two that went to Emmaus were not apostles.

34. *Saying.* The eleven said this. ¶ *Hath appeared to Simon.* To Peter. It is not known precisely when this happened, as the time and place are not mentioned. Paul has referred to it in 1 Co. xv. 5, from which it appears that he appeared to *Cephas* or *Peter* before he did to any other of the apostles. This was a mark of special love and favour, and particularly, after Peter's denial, it showed how ready he was to pardon, and how willing to impart comfort to those who are penitent, though their sins are great.

36, 37. *Jesus stood in the midst of them.* This was when the apostles were assembled, and when they had closed the doors for fear of the Jews, Jn. xx. 19. It was this fact, as well as his sudden and unexpected appearance, that alarmed them. The doors were shut, and the suddenness of his appearance led them to suppose they had seen a spirit. ¶ *Peace* be *unto you.* This was a form of salutation among the Hebrews denoting a wish of peace and prosperity. See Ge. xliii. 23. It was peculiarly appropriate for Jesus, as he had said before his death that he left *his peace* with them as their inheritance (Jn. xiv. 27), and as they were now alarmed and fearful at their state, and trembling for fear of the Jews, Jn. xx. 19.

38. *Why are ye troubled?* Why are you alarmed or frightened? ¶ *And why do thoughts,* &c. The word *thoughts* here means *doubts* or suspicions. It is used in this sense also in 1 Ti. ii. 8. The doubts which they had were whether he was the Christ. He reproves them for doubting this; for, 1st. The Scriptures had foretold his death; 2d. He had himself repeatedly done it; and, 3d. They had now the testimony of Peter that he had seen Jesus alive, and of the angels that he was risen. After all this evidence, Jesus reproves them for doubting whether he was truly the Messiah.

39–43. *Behold my hands,* &c. Jesus proceeds to give them evidence that he was truly the same person that had been crucified. He first showed them his hands and his feet—still pierced, and with the wounds made by the nails still open. Comp. Jn. xx. 27. He told them to handle him and see him. He ate before them. All this was to satisfy them that be was not, as they supposed, a spirit. Nor could better evidence have been given. He appealed to their senses, and peformed acts which a disembodied spirit could not do. ¶ *Handle me.* Or touch me; feel of me. Comp. Jn. xx. 27. ¶ *And see.* Be convinced, for you could not thus handle a spirit. The object here was to convince them that his body had really come to life. ¶ *For a spirit,* &c. He appeals here to what they well knew; and this implies that the spirit may exist separate from the body. That was the view of the apostles, and our Saviour distinctly countenances that belief.

41 And while they yet [c]believed not for joy, and wondered, he said unto them, [d]Have ye here any meat?

42 And they gave him a piece of a broiled fish, and of an honey-comb.

43 And he took *it*, and did [e]eat before them.

44 And he said unto them, [f]These *are* the words which I spake unto you while I was yet with you, [g]that all things must be fulfilled which were written in the law of Moses, and *in* [h]the prophets, and *in* [i]the psalms, concerning me.

45 Then opened he their understanding, that they might understand the scriptures,

46 And said unto them, Thus it

c Ge.45.26. *d* Jn.21.5,&c.
e Ac.10.41. *f* Mat.16.21.
g ch.21.22; Ac.3.18; 13.27,33.
h ver.27. *i* Ps.22.1,&c.

---

41. *Believed not for joy.* Their joy was so great, and his appearance was so sudden and unexpected, that they were bewildered, and still sought more evidence of the truth of what they *wished* to believe. This is nature. We have similar expressions in our language. *The news is too good to be true;* or, *I cannot believe it; it is too much for me.* ¶ *Any meat.* This word does not mean *meat* in our sense of it, but in the old English sense, denoting *anything to eat.*

42. *Honey-comb.* Honey abounded in Palestine, and was a very common article of food. Bees lived in caves of the rocks, in the hollows of trees, and were also kept as with us. The disciples gave, probably, just what was their own common fare, and what was ready at the time.

44. *These* are *the words.* Or this is the *fulfilment* of what I before told you respecting my death. See Lu. xviii. 33; Mar. x. 33. ¶ *While I was yet with you.* Before my death. While I was with you as a teacher and guide. ¶ *In the law of Moses.* The five books of Moses—Genesis, Exodus, Leviticus, Numbers, Deuteronomy. Among the Jews this was the first division of the Old Testament, and was called the *law.* ¶ *The prophets.* This was the second and largest part of the Hebrew Scriptures. It comprehended the books of Joshua, Judges, 1st and 2d Samuel, 1st and 2d Kings, which were called the *former prophets;* and Isaiah, Jeremiah, Ezekiel, and the twelve smaller books from Daniel to Malachi, which were called the *latter prophets.* ¶ *The psalms.* The word here used probably means what were comprehended under the name of *Hagiographa*, or holy writings. This consisted of the Psalms, Proverbs, Job, Song of Solomon, Ruth, Lamentations, Ecclesiastes, Esther, Daniel, Ezra, and Nehemiah, and the two books of Chronicles. This division of the Old Testament was in use long before the time of Christ, and was what he referred to here; and he meant to say that in *each of* these divisions of the Old Testament there were prophecies respecting himself. The *particular* subject before them was his *resurrection from the dead.* A most striking prediction of this is contained in Ps. xvi. 9–11. Compare it with Ac. ii. 24–32; xiii. 35–37.

45. *Opened he their understanding.* Enabled them fully to comprehend the meaning of the prophecies which foretold his death and resurrection. They had seen him die, they now saw him risen. Their prejudices were now, by his instructions, and by the facts which they could no longer call in question, removed, and they no longer doubted that he was the Messiah, and that all the *facts* in the case which had before confounded them could be easily accounted for. Hence we may learn—1st. That *facts*, or the farther disclosure of truth, will yet remove the *mysteries* that we now see in religion. 2d. That our prejudices and our preconceived opinions are one cause of our seeing so many mysteries in the Bible. If a man is willing to take the plain declarations of the Bible, he will commonly be little perplexed with mysteries. 3d. That God only can open the mind so as fully to comprehend the Scriptures. He only can overcome our prejudices, open our hearts, and dispose us to receive the ingrafted word with meekness, and with the simplicity of a child. See Ac. xvi. 14; Ja. i. 21; Mar. x. 15. 4th. The design of God's opening the understanding is that we may be acquainted with the Scriptures. It is not that we may be made wise above what is written, but that we may submit ourselves wholly to the Word of God.

46. *It behoved.* It became; it was

is written, and thus [k]it behoved
Christ to suffer, and [l]to rise from
the dead the third day;
47 And that [m]repentance and remission of sins should be preached
in his name among all nations, beginning at Jerusalem.
48 And ye are [n]witnesses of these
things.
49 And, behold, I send the promise of my Father upon you; but
tarry ye in the city of Jerusalem
until ye be [o]endued with power
from on high.
50 And he led them out as far
as to Bethany; and he lifted up
his hands and blessed them.
51 And it came to pass, while
he blessed them, he was parted
from them, and [p]carried up into
heaven.
52 And[q] they worshipped him,

k Is.53.3,5; Ac.4.12. *l* 1 Pe.1.3. *m* Ac.5.31; 13.38. *n* Ac.1.8.

o Is.44.3; Joel 2.28,&c.; Ac.2.1-21; 1.8. *p* Ac.1.9; He.4.14. *q* Mat.28.9,17.

---

proper or necessary that the Messiah should thus suffer. It was predicted of him, and all things have happened as it was foretold.

47. *Repentance.* Sorrow for sin and forsaking of it. It was proper that the *necessity* of repentance should be preached among all nations, for all were sinners. See Ac. xvii. 30. ¶ *Remission of sins.* Pardon or forgiveness of sins. It should be proclaimed that all men should repent, and that those who are penitent may be pardoned. ¶ *In my name.* By my command it should be proclaimed that men should repent, and by my merit that they may be pardoned. Pardon is offered by the authority of Christ to ALL nations, and this is a sufficient warrant to offer the gospel *to every man.* ¶ *Beginning at Jerusalem.* This was the dwelling of his murderers, and it shows his readiness to forgive the vilest sinners. It was the holy place of the temple, the habitation of God, the place of the solemnities of the ancient dispensation, and it was proper that pardon should be first proclaimed there. This was done — the gospel was first preached there. See Ac. ii. Paul also, in his travels, preached the gospel *first* to the Jews, the ancient people of God, offering them pardon through their own Messiah; and, when *they* rejected it, turned to the Gentiles, Ac. xiii. 46.

48. *Are witnesses of these things.* Of my life, my sufferings, my death, and my resurrection. How solemn was their office—to *testify* these things to the world, and, in the face of suffering and death, to go and proclaim them to all nations! In like manner, *all* Christians are witnesses for Christ. They are the *evidences* of his mercy and his love, and they should so live that others may be brought to see and love the Saviour.

49. *The promise of my Father.* The promise which the Father had made to them *through* the Saviour. See Mat. x. 19; Jn. xiv. 16, 17, 26. The promise was, that they should be aided by the power of the Holy Ghost. He also doubtless referred to the promise of God, made in the days of Joel, respecting the outpouring of the Holy Ghost. See Joel ii. 28, 29, compared with Ac. ii. 16–21. ¶ *Endued with power from on high.* The power which would be given them by the descent of the Holy Ghost —the power of speaking with tongues, of working miracles, and of preaching the gospel with the attending blessing and aid of the Holy Ghost. This was accomplished in the gift of the Holy Spirit on the day of Pentecost. See Ac. ii.

50, 51. *To Bethany.* See Notes on Mar. xvi. 19. Bethany was on the eastern declivity of the Mount of Olives, from which our Lord was taken up to heaven, Ac. i. 12. Bethany was a favoured place. It was the abode of Martha, and Mary, and Lazarus, and our Saviour delighted to be there. From this place, also, he ascended to his Father and our Father, and to his God and our God. ¶ *While he blessed them.* While he commanded his benediction to rest upon them; while he assured them of his favour, and commended them to the protection and guidance of God, in the dangers, trials, and conflicts which they were to meet in a sinful and miserable world.

52. *They worshipped him.* The word *worship* does not *always* denote religious homage. See Notes on Mat. ii. 11. Comp. Lu. xiv. 10. But here it is to be remarked, 1st. That they offered this worship to an *absent* Saviour. It was *after* he left them and had vanished out of their sight. It was therefore an act of religion, and was the *first* religious

and returned to Jerusalem with great joy;
53 And were continually in the temple, [r]praising and blessing God. Amen.

r Ac.2.46,47; 5.42.

homage that was paid to Jesus after he had left the world. 2d. If *they* worshipped an absent Saviour—a Saviour unseen by the bodily eye, it is right for *us* to do it. It was an example which we *may* and *should* follow. 3d. If worship may be rendered to Jesus, he is divine. See Ex. xx. 4, 5.

53. *Were continually in the temple.* Until the day of Pentecost—that is, about ten days after. See Ac. ii. ¶ *Praising and blessing God.* Chiefly for the full proof that the Messiah had come; had redeemed them, and had ascended to heaven. "Thus the days of their mourning were ended." They were filled with happiness at the assurance of redemption, and expressed what every Christian should feel—fulness of joy at the glad tidings that a Saviour has died, and risen, and ascended to God; and an earnest desire to pour forth in the sanctuary prayers and thanksgivings to the God of grace for his mercy to a lost and ruined world.

PREFACE

TO THE GOSPEL ACCORDING TO JOHN

JOHN, the writer of this Gospel, was the son of Zebedee and Salome; compare Mat. xxvii. 56 with Mar. xv. 40, 41. His father was a fisherman of Galilee, though it would appear that he was not destitute of property, and was not in the lowest condition of life. He had hired men in his employ, Mar. i. 20. Salome is described as one who attended our Saviour in his travels, and ministered to his wants, Mat. xxvii. 55; Mar. xv. 41. Jesus commended his own mother Mary, on the cross, to John, and he took her to his own home (Jn. xix. 26, 27), with whom, history informs us, she lived until her death, about fifteen years after the crucifixion of Christ; and John was known to Caiaphas, the high-priest, Jn. xviii. 15. From all this it would seem not improbable that John had some property, and was better known than any of the other apostles.

He was the youngest of the apostles when called, and lived to the greatest age, and is the only one who is supposed to have died a peaceful death. He was called to be a follower of Jesus while engaged with his father and his elder brother James mending their nets at the Sea of Tiberias, Mat. iv. 21; Mar. i. 19; Lu. v. 10.

John was admitted by our Saviour to peculiar favour and friendship. One of the ancient fathers (Theophylact) says that he was related to him. "Joseph," he says, "had seven children by a former wife, four sons and three daughters, Martha, Esther, and *Salome*, whose son John was; therefore Salome was reckoned our Lord's sister, and John was his nephew." If this was the case it may explain the reason why James and John sought and expected the first places in his kingdom, Mat. xx. 20, 21. These may also possibly be the persons who were called our Lord's "brethren" and "sisters," Mat. xiii. 55, 56. This may also explain the reason why our Saviour committed his mother to the care of John on the cross, Jn. xix. 27.

The two brothers, James and John, with Peter, were several times admitted to peculiar favours by our Lord. They were the only disciples that were permitted to be present at the raising of the daughter of Jairus, Mar. v. 37; Lu. viii. 51; they only were permitted to attend the Saviour to the mount where he was transfigured, Mat. xvii. 1; Mar. ix. 2. The same three were permitted to be present at his sufferings in the garden of Gethsemane, Mat. xxvi. 36–45; Mar. xiv. 32–42. And it was to *these* disciples, together with Andrew, to whom the Saviour specially addressed himself when he made known the desolations that were coming upon Jerusalem and Judea; compare Mat. xxiv. 12; Mar. xiii. 3, 4. John was also admitted to *peculiar* friendship with the Lord Jesus. Hence he is mentioned as "that disciple whom Jesus loved" (Jn. xix. 26), and he is represented (Jn. xiii. 23) as leaning on his bosom at the institution of the Lord's Supper—an evidence of peculiar friendship. See Notes on that place. Though the Redeemer was attached to *all* his disciples, yet there is no improbability in supposing that *his* disposition was congenial with that of the meek and amiable John—thus authorizing and setting the example of special friendships among Christians.

To John was committed the care of Mary, the mother of Jesus. After the ascension of Christ he remained some time at Jerusalem, Ac. i. 14; iii. 1; iv. 13. John is also mentioned as having been sent down to Samaria to preach the gospel there with Peter (Ac. viii. 14–25); and from Ac. xv. it appears that he was present at the council at Jerusalem, A.D. 49 or 50. All this agrees with what is said by Eusebius, that he lived at Jerusalem till the death of Mary, fifteen years after the crucifixion of Christ. Till this time it is probable that he had not been engaged in preaching the gospel among the Gentiles.

At what time he went first among the Gentiles to preach the gospel is not certainly known. It has commonly been supposed that he resided in Judea and the neighbourhood until the war broke out with the Romans, and that he came into Asia Minor about the year 69 or 70. It is clear that he was not at Ephesus at the time that Paul visited those regions, as in all the travels of Paul and Luke there is no mention made of John.

Ecclesiastical history informs us that he spent the latter part of his life in Asia Minor, and that he resided chiefly at Ephesus, the chief city of that country. Of his residence there little is certainly known. In the latter part of his life he was banished to Patmos, a small desolate island in the Ægean Sea, about twenty miles in circumference. This is commonly supposed to have been during the persecution of Domitian, in the latter part of his reign. Domitian died A.D. 96. It is probable that he returned soon after that, in the reign of the Emperor Trajan. In that island he wrote the book of Revelation. See Notes on Rev. i. 9. After his return from Patmos he lived peaceably at Ephesus until his death, which is supposed to have occurred not long after. He was buried at Ephesus; and it has been commonly thought that he was the only one of the apostles who did not suffer martyrdom. It is evident that he lived to a very advanced period of life. We know not his age, indeed, when Christ called him to follow him, but we cannot suppose it was less than twenty-five or thirty. If so, he must have been not far from one hundred years old when he died.

Many anecdotes are related of him while he remained at Ephesus, but there is no sufficient evidence of their truth. Some have said that he was taken to Rome in a time of persecution and thrown into a caldron of boiling oil, and came out uninjured. It has been said also that, going into a bath one day at Ephesus, he perceived *Cerinthus*, who denied the divinity of the Saviour, and that he fled from him hastily, to express his disapprobation of his doctrine. It is also said, and of this there can be no doubt, that during his latter years he was not able to make a long discourse. He was carried to the church, and was accustomed to say nothing but this, "Little children, love one another." At length his disciples asked him why he always dwelt upon the same thing. He replied, "Because it is the Lord's command; and if this be done, it is sufficient."

Learned men have been much divided about the *time* when this Gospel was written. Wetstein supposed it was written just after our Saviour's ascension; Mill and Le Clerc, that it was written in 97; Dr. Lardner, that it was about the year 68, just before the destruction of Jerusalem. The common opinion is that it was written at Ephesus after his return from Patmos, and of course as late as the year 97 or 98. Nothing can be determined with certainty on the subject, and it is a matter of very little consequence.

There is no doubt that it was written by John. This is abundantly confirmed by the ancient fathers, and was not questioned by Celsus, Porphyry, or Julian, the acutest enemies of revelation in the early ages. It has never been extensively questioned to have been the work of John, and is one of the books of the New Testament whose canonical authority was never disputed. See Lardner, or Paley's *Evidences.*

The design of writing it John himself states, ch. xx. 31. It was to show that Jesus was the Christ, the Son of God, and that those who believed might have life through his name. *This design is kept in view through the whole Gospel, and should be remembered in our attempts to explain it.* Various attempts have been made to show that he wrote it to confute the followers of Cerinthus and the Gnostics, but no satisfactory evidence of such a design has been furnished.

As he wrote after the other evangelists, he has recorded many things which they omitted. He dwells much more fully than they do on the *divine character* of Jesus; relates many things pertaining to the early part of his ministry which they had omitted; records many more of his discourses than they have done, and particularly the interesting discourse at the institution of the Supper. See ch. xiv. xv. xvi. xvii.

It has been remarked that there are evidences in this Gospel that it was not written for the Jews. The author explains words and customs which to a Jew would have needed no explanation. See ch. i. 38, 41; v. 1, 2; vii. 2; iv. 9. The style in the Greek indicates that he was an unlearned man. It is simple, plain, unpolished, such as we should *suppose* would be used by one in his circumstances. At the same time it is dignified, containing pure and profound sentiments, and is on many accounts the most difficult of all the books of the New Testament to interpret. It contains more about *Christ*, his person, design, and work, than any of the other Gospels. The other evangelists were employed more in recording the *miracles*, and giving *external* evidence of the divine mission of Jesus. John is employed chiefly in telling us what he was, and what was his peculiar doctrine. His aim was to show, 1st, That Jesus was the Messiah. 2d. To show, *from the words of Jesus himself*, what the Messiah was. The other evangelists record his parables, his miracles, his debates with the Scribes and Pharisees; John records chiefly his discourses about *himself*. If anyone wishes to learn the true doctrine respecting the *Messiah, the Son of God*, expressed in simple language, but with most sublime conceptions; to learn the true nature and character of God, and the way of approach to his mercy-seat; to see the true nature of Christian piety, or the source and character of religious consolation; to have perpetually before him the purest model of character the world has seen, and to contemplate the purest precepts that have ever been delivered to man, he cannot better do it than by a prayerful study of the Gospel by John. It may be added that this Gospel is of itself proof that cannot be overthrown of the truth of revelation. John was a fisherman, unhonoured and unlearned, Ac. iv. 13. What man in that rank of life *now* could compose a book like this? Can it be conceived that any man of that rank, unless under the influence of inspiration, could conceive so sublime notions of God, could present so pure views of morals, and could draw a character so inimitably lovely and pure as that of Jesus Christ? To ask these questions is to answer them. And this Gospel will stand to the end of time as an unanswerable demonstration that the fisherman who wrote it was under a more than human guidance, and was, according to the promise that he has recorded (xvi. 13; comp. xiv. 26), *guided into all truth*. It will also remain as an unanswerable proof that the character which he has described—the character of the Lord Jesus—was real. It is a perfect character. It has not a flaw. How has this happened? The attempt has often been made to draw a perfect character—and as often, in every other instance, failed. How is it, when Homer and Virgil, and the ancient historians, have all failed to describe a perfect character, with the purest models before them, and with all the aid of imagination, that in every instance they have failed? How is it that this has at last been accomplished only by a Jewish fisherman? The difficulty is vastly increased if another idea is borne in mind. John describes one who he believed had a divine nature, ch. i. 1. It is an attempt to describe *God in human nature*, or to show how the Divine Being acts when united with man, or when appearing in human form. And the description is complete. There is not a word expressed by the Lord Jesus, or an emotion ascribed to him, inconsistent with such a supposition. But this same attempt was often made, and as often failed. Homer and Virgil, and all the ancient poets, have undertaken to show what the gods would be if they came down and conversed with man. And what were they? What were Jupiter, and Juno, and Venus, and Mars, and Vulcan? Beings of lust, and envy, and contention, and blood. How has it happened that the only successful account which has been given of the divine nature united with the human, and of living and acting as became such a union, has been given by a Jewish fisherman? How, unless the character was *real*, and the writer under a guidance far superior to the genius of Homer and the imagination of Virgil—the guidance of the Holy Spirit?

THE

GOSPEL ACCORDING TO JOHN

CHAPTER I.

IN[a] the beginning was the [b]Word,
and the Word was [c]with God,
and the Word [d]was God.

a Pr.8.22-31; Col.1.16,17; 1 Jn.1.1. *b* Re.19.13. *c* ch.17.5. *d* Phi.2.6; He.1.8-13; 1 Jn.5.7.

2 The same was in the beginning with God.
3 All[e] things were made by him;
and without him was not any thing
made that was made.

e Ps.33.6; Ep.3.9.

---

1. *In the beginning.* This expression is used also in Ge. i. 1. To that place John evidently has allusion here, and means to apply to "the Word" an expression which is there applied *to God.* In both places it clearly means "before creation," "before the world was made," "when as yet there was nothing." The meaning is, that the *Word* had an existence before the world was created. This is not spoken of the *man* Jesus, but of that which *became* a man, or was incarnate, ver. 14. The Hebrews, by expressions like this, commonly denoted eternity. Thus the *eternity* of God is described (Ps. xc. 2): *Before the mountains were brought forth,* &c.; and eternity is commonly expressed by the phrase, *before the foundation of the world.* Whatever is meant by the term "Word," it is clear that it had an existence before *creation.* It is not, then, a *creature* or created being, and must be, therefore, uncreated and eternal. There is but *one* Being that is uncreated, and Jesus must be therefore divine. Compare the Saviour's own declarations respecting himself in the following places: Jn. viii. 58; xvii. 5; vi. 62; iii. 13; vi. 46; viii. 14; xvi. 28. ¶ *Was the Word.* Greek, "was the *Logos.*" This name is given to him who afterward became *flesh,* or was incarnate (ver. 14)—that is, to the Messiah. Whatever is meant by it, therefore, is applicable to the Lord Jesus Christ. There have been many opinions about the reason why this name was given to the Son of God. Those opinions it is unnecessary to repeat. The opinion which seems most plausible may be expressed as follows: 1st. A *word* is that by which we communicate our will; by which we convey our thoughts; or by which we issue commands—the medium of communication with others. 2d. The Son of God may be called "the Word," because he is the medium by which God promulgates his will and issues his commandments. See He. i. 1-3. 3d. This term was in use before the time of John. (*a*) It was used in the Chaldee translation of the Old Testament, as, *e. g.*, Is. xlv. 12: "I have made the earth, and created man upon it." In the Chaldee it is, "I, *by my word,* have made," &c. Is. xlviii. 13: "Mine hand also hath laid the foundation of the earth." In the Chaldee, "*By my word* I have founded the earth." And so in many other places. (*b*) This term was used by the Jews as applicable to the Messiah. In their writings he was commonly known by the term "Mimra"—that is, "Word;" and no small part of the interpositions of God in defence of the Jewish nation were declared to be by "the Word of God." Thus, in their Targum on De. xxvi. 17, 18, it is said, "Ye have appointed THE WORD OF GOD a king over you this day, that he may be your God." (*c*) The term was used by the Jews who were scattered among the Gentiles, and especially those who were conversant with the Greek philosophy. (*d*) The term was used by the followers of Plato among the Greeks, to denote the second person of the *Trinity.* The term *nous,* or *mind,* was commonly given to this second person, but it was said that this *nous* was *the word* or *reason* of the first person. The term was therefore extensively in use among the Jews and Gentiles before John wrote his Gospel, and it was certain that it *would be* applied to the second person of the Trinity by Christians, whether converted from Judaism or Paganism. It was important, therefore, that the *meaning* of the term should be settled by an inspired man, and accordingly John, in the com-

mencement of his Gospel, is at much pains to state clearly what is the true doctrine respecting the Logos, or Word. It is *possible*, also, that the doctrines of the Gnostics had begun to spread in the time of John. They were an Oriental sect, and held that the *Logos* or *Word* was one of the *Æons* that had been created, and that this one had been united to the man Jesus. If that doctrine had begun then to prevail, it was of the more importance for John to settle the truth in regard to the rank of the Logos or Word. This he has done in such a way that there need be no doubt about its meaning. ¶ *Was with God.* This expression denotes friendship or intimacy. Comp. Mar. ix. 19. John affirms that he was *with God* in the beginning—that is, before the world was made. It implies, therefore, that he was partaker of the divine glory; that he was blessed and happy with God. It proves that he was intimately united with the Father, so as to partake of his glory and to be appropriately called by the name God. He has himself explained it. See Jn. xvii. 5: *And now, O Father, glorify thou me with thine own self, with the glory which I had with thee before the world was.* See also Jn. i. 18: *No man hath seen God at any time; the only-begotten Son, which* IS IN THE BOSOM OF THE FATHER, *he hath declared him.* See also Jn. iii. 13: *The Son of man, which is in heaven.* Comp. Phi. ii. 6, 7. ¶ *Was God.* In the previous phrase John had said that the Word was *with God.* Lest it should be supposed that he was a different and *inferior* being, he here states that *he was God.* There is no more unequivocal declaration in the Bible than this, and there *could* be no stronger proof that the sacred writer meant to affirm that the Son of God was equal with the Father; for, 1st. There is no doubt that by the *Logos* is meant Jesus Christ. 2d. This is not an *attribute* or quality of God, but is a real subsistence, for it is said that the Logos was made *flesh*—that is, became a man. 3d. There is no variation here in the manuscripts, and critics have observed that the Greek will bear no other construction than what is expressed in our translation—that the Word *was God.* 4th. There is no evidence that John intended to use the word *God* in an *inferior* sense. It is not "the Word was *a* god," or "the Word was *like* God," but the Word *was God.* He had just used the word *God* as evidently applicable to Jehovah, the true God; and it is absurd to suppose that he would *in the same verse*, and without any indication that he was using the word in an inferior sense, employ it to denote a being altogether inferior to the true God. 5th. The name *God* is elsewhere given to him, showing that he is the supreme God. See Ro. ix. 5; He. i. 8, 9, 10–12; 1 Jn. v. 20; Jn. xx. 28. The meaning of this important verse may then be thus summed up: 1st. The name Logos, or Word, is given to Christ in reference to his becoming the Teacher or Instructor of mankind; the medium of communication between God and man. 2d. The name was in use at the time of John, and it was his design to state the correct doctrine respecting the Logos. 3d. The *Word*, or Logos, existed *before creation*—of course was not a *creature*, and must have been, therefore, from eternity. 4th. He was *with God*—that is, he was united to him in a most intimate and close union *before* the creation; and, as it could not be said that God was *with himself*, it follows that the Logos was in some sense *distinct* from God, or that there was a *distinction* between the Father and the Son. When we say that one is *with another*, we imply that there is some sort of distinction between them. 5th. Yet, lest it should be supposed that he was a *different* and *inferior* being—a creature—he affirms that he was God—that is, was equal with the Father. This is the foundation of the doctrine of the Trinity: 1. That the second person is in some sense *distinct* from the first. 2. That he is intimately united with the first person in essence, so that there are not two or more Gods. 3. That the second person may be called by the same name; has the same attributes; performs the same works; and is entitled to the same honours with the first, and that therefore he is "the same in substance, and equal in power and glory," with God.

2. *The same.* The Word, or the Logos, ¶ *Was in the beginning with God.* This seems to be a repetition of what was said in the first verse; but it is stated over again *to guard the doctrine*, and to prevent the possibility of a mistake. John had said that he existed before the creation, and that he was *with God;* but he had *not* said in the first verse *that the union with God existed in the beginning.* He now expresses that idea,

4 In[f] him was life; and the life was [g]the light of men.

f ch.5.26; 1 Jn.5.11. *g* ch.8.12.

5 And the light shineth [h]in darkness, and the darkness [i]comprehended it not.

h ch.3.19. *i* 1 Co.2.14.

and assures us that that *union* was not one which was commenced *in time*, and which might be, therefore, a mere union of *feeling*, or a *compact*, like that between any other beings, but was one which existed in *eternity*, and which was therefore a union of *nature or essence*.

3. *All things.* The universe. The expression cannot be limited to any part of the universe. It appropriately expresses everything which exists—all the vast masses of material worlds, and all the animals and things, great or small, that compose those worlds. See Re. iv. 11; He. i. 2; Col. i. 16. ¶ *Were made.* The original word is from the verb *to be*, and signifies "*were*" by him; but it expresses the idea of creation here. It does not alter the sense whether it is said "*were* by him," or "were *created* by him." The word is often used in the sense of *creating*, or forming from nothing. See Ja. iii. 9; and Ge. ii. 4, Is. xlviii. 7, in the Septuagint. ¶ *By him.* In this place it is affirmed that *creation* was effected by *the Word*, or the Son of God. In Ge. i. 1, it is said that the Being who created the heavens and the earth was God. In Ps. cii. 25–28, this work is ascribed to Jehovah. The *Word*, or the Son of God, is therefore appropriately called *God.* The work of *creation* is uniformly ascribed in the Scriptures to the second person of the Trinity. See Col. i. 16; He. i. 2, 10. By this is meant, evidently, that he was the agent, or the efficient cause, by which the universe was made. There is no higher proof of *omnipotence* than the work of *creation;* and hence God often appeals to that work to prove that he is the *true* God, in opposition to idols. See Is. xl. 18–28; Je. x. 3–16; Ps. xxiv. 2; xxxix. 11; Pr. iii. 19. It is absurd to say that God can invest a creature with *omnipotence.* If he can make a *creature omnipotent*, he can make him *omniscient*, and can in the same way make him omnipresent, and infinitely wise and good; that is, he can invest a creature with all his own attributes, or make another being like himself, or, which is the same thing, there could be two Gods, or as many Gods as he should choose to make. But this is absurd. The Being, therefore, that *created* all things must be divine; and as this work is ascribed to Jesus Christ, and as it is uniformly in the Scriptures declared to be the work of God, Jesus Christ is therefore *equal with the Father.* ¶ *Without him.* Without his agency; his notice; the exertion of his power. Comp. Mat. x. 29. This is a strong way of speaking, designed to confirm, beyond the possibility of doubt, what he had just said. He says, therefore, in general, that all things were made by Christ. In this part of the verse he shuts out all doubt, and affirms that there was *no exception;* that there was not a single thing, however minute or unimportant, which was not made by him. In this way he confirms what he said in the first verse. Christ was not merely *called* God, but he did the *works* of God, and therefore the name is used in its proper sense as implying supreme divinity. To this same test Jesus himself appealed as proving that he was divine. Jn. x. 37: *If I do not* THE WORKS *of my Father, believe me not.* Jn. v. 17: MY FATHER *worketh hitherto, and I work.*

4. *In him was life.* The evangelist had just affirmed (ver. 3) that by the *Logos* or *Word* the world was originally created. One part of that creation consisted in *breathing into man the breath of life*, Ge. ii. 7. God is declared to be *life*, or the *living* God, because he is the source or fountain of life. This attribute is here ascribed to Jesus Christ. He not merely made the *material* worlds, but he also gave *life.* He was the agent by which the *vegetable* world became animated; by which *brutes* live; and by which *man* became a living soul, or was endowed with immortality. This was a *higher* proof that the "Word was God," than the creation of the material worlds; but there is another sense in which he was *life.* The *new creation*, or the renovation of man and his restoration from a state of sin, is often compared with the *first creation;* and as the Logos was the source of *life* then, so, in a similar but higher sense, he is the source of life to the soul dead in trespasses and sins, Ep. ii. 1. And it is probably in reference to this that he is so often called *life* in the writings of John. "For as the Father hath life in himself, so hath

6 There was a [k]man sent from God, whose name *was* John.

7 The same came for a witness, to bear witness of the Light, that

k Lu.3.2,3.

he given to the Son to have life in himself," Jn. v. 26; "He giveth life unto the world," Jn. vi. 33; "I am the resurrection and the life," Jn. xi. 25; "This is the true God and eternal life," 1 Jn. v. 20. See also 1 Jn. i. 1, 2; v. 11; Ac. iii. 15; Col. iii. 4. The meaning is, that he is the source or the fountain of both natural and spiritual life. Of course he has the attributes of God. ¶ *The life was the light of men. Light* is that by which we see objects distinctly. The light of the sun enables us to discern the form, the distance, the magnitude, and the relation of objects, and prevents the perplexities and dangers which result from a state of darkness. Light is in all languages, therefore, put for *knowledge*—for whatever enables us to discern our duty, and that saves us from the evils of ignorance and error. "Whatsoever doth make manifest is light," Ep. v. 13. See Is. viii. 20; ix. 2. The Messiah was predicted as the *light* of the world, Is. ix. 2, compared with Mat. iv. 15, 16; Is. lx. 1. See Jn. viii. 12: "I am the light of the world;" xii. 35, 36, 46: "I am come a light into the world." The meaning is, that the Logos or Word of God is the *instructor* or *teacher* of mankind. This was done before his advent by his direct agency in giving man reason or understanding, and in giving his law, for the "law was ordained by angels *in the hand of a mediator*" (Ga. iii. 19); after his advent by his personal ministry when on earth, by his Spirit (Jn. xiv. 16, 26), and by his ministers since, Ep. iv. 11; 1 Co. xii. 28.

5. *The light shineth in darkness.* Darkness, in the Bible, commonly denotes ignorance, guilt, or misery. See Is. ix. 1, 2; Mat. iv. 16; Ac. xxvi. 18; Ep. v. 8, 11; Ro. xiii. 12. It refers here to a wicked and ignorant people. When it is said that "the light shineth in darkness," it is meant that the Lord Jesus came to teach an ignorant, benighted, and wicked world. This has always been the case. It was so when he sent his prophets; so during his own ministry; and so in every age since. His efforts to enlighten and save men have been like light struggling to penetrate a thick, dense cloud; and though a few rays may pierce the gloom, yet the great mass is still an impenetrable shade. ¶ *Comprehended it not.* This word means *admitted* it not, or *received* it not. The word *comprehend*, with us, means to *understand.* This is not the meaning of the original. The darkness did not *receive* or *admit* the rays of light; the shades were so thick that the light could not penetrate them; or, to drop the figure, men were so ignorant, so guilty, so debased, that they did not appreciate the value of his instructions; they despised and rejected him. And so it is still. The great mass of men, sunk in sin, will not receive his teachings, and be enlightened and saved by him. Sin always blinds the mind to the beauty and excellency of the character of the Lord Jesus. It indisposes the mind to receive his instructions, just as *darkness* has no affinity for *light;* and if the one exists, the other must be displaced.

6. *A man sent from God.* See Mat. iii. The evangelist proceeds now to show that John the Baptist was not the Messiah, and to state the true nature of his office. Many had supposed that he was the Christ, but this opinion he corrects; yet he admits that he was *sent from God*—that he was divinely commissioned. Though he denied that he was *the Messiah*, yet he did not deny that he was sent from or by heaven on an important errand to men. Some have supposed that the sole design of this gospel was to show that John the Baptist was not the Messiah. Though there is no foundation for this opinion, yet there is no doubt that *one* object was to show this. The *main* design was to show that *Jesus was the Christ*, ch. xx. 31. To do this, it was proper, in the beginning, to prove that *John* was not the Messiah; and this might have been at that time an important object. John made many disciples, Mat. iii. 5. Many persons supposed that he might be the Messiah, Lu. iii. 15; Jn. i. 19. *Many of these disciples of John remained* AT EPHESUS, *the very place where John is supposed to have written this gospel, long after the ascension of Jesus*, Ac. xix. 1–3. It is not improbable that there might have been many others who adhered to John, and perhaps many who supposed that he was the Messiah. On these accounts it was important for the evan-

all *men* through him might believe.

8 He[l] was not that Light, but *was sent* to bear witness of that Light.

9 *That* was the true [m] Light,

l Ac.19.4.

m Is.49.6.

gelist to show that John *was not the Christ*, and to show, also, that he, who was extensively admitted to be a prophet, was an important *witness* to prove that Jesus of Nazareth was the Christ. The evangelist in the first four verses stated that "the Word" was divine; he now proceeds to state the proof that he was *a man*, and was the Messiah. The *first* evidence adduced is the testimony of John the Baptist.

7, 8. *For a witness.* To give testimony. He came to prepare the minds of the people to receive him (Mat. iii.; Lu. iii.); to lead them by repentance to God; and to point out the Messiah to Israel when he came, Jn. i. 31. ¶ *Of the Light.* That is, of the Messiah. Comp. Is. lx. 1. ¶ *That all* men, &c. It was the object of John's testimony that *all* men might believe. He designed to prepare them for it; to announce that the Messiah was about to come, to direct the minds of men *to* him, and thus to fit them to believe on him when he came. Thus he baptized them, saying "That they should believe on him who should come after him" (Ac. xix. 4), and thus he produced a very general expectation that the Messiah was about to come. The testimony of John was peculiarly valuable on the following accounts: 1st. It was made when he had no *personal* acquaintance with Jesus of Nazareth, and of course there could have been no *collusion* or agreement to deceive them, Jn. i. 31. 2d. It was sufficiently long before he came to excite general attention, and to fix the mind on it. 3d. It was that of a man acknowledged by all to be a prophet of God—"for all men held John to be a prophet," Mat. xxi. 26. 4th. It was *for the express purpose* of declaring beforehand that he was about to appear. 5th. It was *disinterested.* He was himself extremely popular. Many were disposed to receive *him* as the Messiah. It was evidently in his *power* to form a large party, and to be regarded extensively as the Christ. This was the highest honour to which a Jew could aspire; and it shows the value of John's testimony, that he was willing to lay all his honours at the feet of Jesus, and to acknowledge that he was unworthy to perform for him the office of the humblest servant, Mat. iii. 11. ¶ *Through him.* Through John, or by means of his testimony. ¶ *Was not that Light.* Was not *the Messiah.* This is an explicit declaration designed to satisfy the disciples of John. The *evidence* that he was not the Messiah he states in the following verses.

From the conduct of John here we may learn, 1st. The duty of laying *all* our honours at the feet of Jesus. 2d. As John came that all might believe, so it is no less true of the ministry of Jesus himself. He came for a similar purpose, and we may ALL, therefore, trust in him for salvation. 3d. We should not rely too much on ministers of the gospel. They cannot save us any more than John could; and *their* office, as *his* was, is simply to direct men *to the Lamb of God that taketh away the sin of the world.*

9. That *was the true Light.* Not John, but the Messiah. He was not a false, uncertain, dangerous guide, but was one that was true, real, steady, and worthy of confidence. A false light is one that leads to danger or error, as a false beacon on the shores of the ocean may lead ships to quicksands or rocks; or an *ignis fatuus* to fens, and precipices, and death. A true light is one that does not deceive us, as the true beacon may guide us into port or warn us of danger. Christ does not lead astray. All false teachers do. ¶ *That lighteth.* That enlightens. He removes darkness, error, ignorance, from the mind. ¶ *Every man.* This is an expression denoting, in general, the whole human race—Jews and Gentiles. John preached to the Jews. Jesus came *to be a light to lighten the Gentiles*, as well as to be the *glory of the people of Israel*, Lu. ii. 32. ¶ *That cometh into the world.* The phrase in the original is ambiguous. The word translated "that cometh" may either refer to the *light*, or to the word *man;* so that it may mean either "this *true light that cometh* into the world enlightens all," or "it enlightens every *man that cometh* into the world." Many critics, and, among the fathers, Cyril and Augustine, have preferred the former, and translated it, "The true light was he who, coming into the world, enlightened

which lighteth every man that cometh into the world.

10 He was in the world, and the world was made by him, [n]and the world knew him not.

n ver.5.

11 He[o] came unto his own, and his own received him not.

12 But [p]as many as received him, to them gave he [1]power to become

o Ac.3.26; 13.46. *p* Is.56.4,5; Ro.8.15; 1 Jn.3.1.
1 or, *the right;* or, *privilege.*

---

every man." The principal reasons for this are, 1st. That the Messiah is often spoken of as he that cometh into the world. See ch. vi. 14; xviii. 37. 2d. He is often distinguished as "*the light that cometh into the world.*" Ch. iii. 19: "This is the condemnation, that *light* is come into the world." Ch. xii. 46: "I am come *a light* into the world." Christ may be said *to do* what is accomplished by his command or appointment. This passage means, therefore, that by his own personal ministry, and by his Spirit and apostles, light or teaching is afforded to all. It does not mean that every individual of the human family is enlightened with the knowledge *of the gospel*, for this never yet *has been;* but it means, 1st. That this light is not confined to the *Jews*, but is extended to *all*—Jews and Gentiles. 2d. That it is provided for all and offered to all. 3d. It is not affirmed that at the time that John wrote all *were actually enlightened*, but the word "lighteth" has the form of the *future*. *This is that light so long expected and predicted, which, as the result of its coming into the world, will ultimately enlighten all nations.*

10. *He was in the world.* This refers, probably, not to his pre-existence, but to the fact that he became incarnate; that he dwelt among men. ¶ *And the world was made by him.* This is a repetition of what is said in ver. 3. Not only *men*, but all material things, were made by him. These facts are mentioned here to make what is said immediately after more striking, to wit, that men did not receive him. The proofs which he furnished that they *ought* to receive him were, 1st. Those given while he was *in the world*—the miracles that he wrought and his instructions; and, 2d. The fact that the *world was made by him.* It was remarkable that the world did not *know* or approve its own maker. ¶ *The world knew him not.* The word *knew* is sometimes used in the sense of *approving* or *loving*, Ps. i. 6; Mat. vii. 23. In this sense it may be used here. The world did not love or approve him, but rejected him and put him to death. Or it may mean that they did not understand or know that he was the Messiah; for had the Jews *known* and *believed* that he was the Messiah, they would not have put him to death, 1 Co. ii. 8: "Had they known it, they would not have crucified the Lord of glory." Yet they *might* have known it, and therefore they were not the less to blame.

11. *He came unto his own.* His own *land* or *country*. It was called *his* land because it was the place of his birth, and also because it was the chosen land where God delighted to dwell and to manifest his favour. See Is. v. 1–7. Over that land the laws of God had been extended, and that land had been regarded as peculiarly his, Ps. cxlvii. 19, 20. ¶ *His own.* His own *people.* There is a distinction here in the original words which is not preserved in the translation. It may be thus expressed: "He came to his own *land*, and his own people received him not." They were *his* people, because God had chosen them to be his above all other nations; had given to them his laws; and had signally protected and favoured them, De. vii. 6; xiv. 2. ¶ *Received him not.* Did not acknowledge him to be the Messiah. They rejected him and put him to death, agreeably to the prophecy, Is. liii. 3, 4. From this we learn, 1st. That it is reasonable to expect that those who have been peculiarly favoured should welcome the message of God. God had a right to expect, after all that had been done for the Jews, that they would receive the message of eternal life. So he has a right to expect that *we* should embrace him and be saved. Yet, 2d. It is not the abundance of mercies that incline men to seek God. The Jews had been signally favoured, but they rejected him. So, many in Christian lands live and die rejecting the Lord Jesus. 3d. Men are alike in every age. All would reject the Saviour if left to themselves. All men are by nature wicked. There is no more certain and universal proof of this than the universal rejection of the Lord Jesus.

12. *To as many as received him.* The great mass; the people; the scribes and

the sons of God, *even* to [q]them that
believe on his name:
13 Which were [r]born, not of
blood, nor of the will of the flesh,
nor of the will of man, but of God.
14 And the [s]Word was made

q Ga.3.26. r Ja.1.18. s Lu.1.35; 1 Ti.3.16.

Pharisees rejected him. A few in his lifetime received him, and many more after his death. To *receive him*, here, means to *believe* on him. This is expressed at the end of the verse. ¶ *Gave he power.* This is more appropriately rendered in the margin by the word *right* or *privilege.* Comp. Ac. i. 7; v. 4; Ro. ix. 21; 1 Co. vii. 37; viii. 9; ix. 4, 5. ¶ *Sons of God.* Children of God by adoption. See Notes on Mat. i. 1. Christians are called sons of God—1st. Because they are *adopted* by him, 1 Jn. iii. 1. 2d. Because they are *like him;* they resemble him and have his spirit. 3d. They are united to the Lord Jesus, the Son of God—are regarded by *him* as his brethren (Mat. xxv. 40), and are therefore regarded as the children of the Most High. ¶ *On his name.* This is another way of saying believeth in *him.* The *name* of a person is often put for the person himself, ch. ii. 23; iii. 18; 1 Jn. v. 13. From this verse we learn, 1st. That to be a child of God is a privilege—far more so than to be the child of any man, though in the highest degree rich, or learned, or honoured. Christians are therefore more honoured than any other men. 2d. God *gave* them this privilege. It is not by their own works or deserts; it is because God chose to impart this blessing to them, Ep. ii. 8; Jn. xv. 16. 3d. This favour is given only to those who believe on him. All others are the children of the wicked one, and no one who has not *confidence in God* can be regarded as his child. No parent would acknowledge one for his child, or approve of him, who had no *confidence* in him, who *doubted* or denied all he said, and who despised his character. Yet this the sinner constantly does toward God, and he cannot, therefore, be called his son.

13. *Which were born.* This doubtless refers to the *new birth,* or to the great change in the sinner's mind called regeneration or conversion. It means that they did not become the children of God in virtue of their natural birth, or because they were the children of *Jews,* or because they were descended from pious parents. The term "to be born" is often used to denote this change. Comp. Jn. iii. 3–8; 1 Jn. ii. 29. It illustrates clearly and beautifully this great change. The natural birth introduces us to life. The new birth is the beginning of spiritual life. Before, the sinner is *dead* in sins (Ep. ii. 1); now he begins truly to live. And as the natural birth is the beginning of life, so to be born of God is to be introduced to *real* life, to light, to happiness, and to the favour of God. The term expresses at once the *greatness* and the *nature* of the change. ¶ *Not of blood.* The Greek word is plural; not of *bloods*—that is, not of *man.* Comp. Mat. xxvii. 4. The Jews prided themselves on being the descendants of Abraham, Mat. iii. 9. They supposed that it was proof of the favour of God to be descended from such an illustrious ancestry. In this passage this notion is corrected. It is not because men are descended from an illustrious or pious parentage that they are entitled to the favour of God; or perhaps the meaning may be, not because there is a *union* of illustrious lines of ancestry or *bloods* in them. The law of Christ's kingdom is different from what the Jews supposed. Comp. 1 Pe. i. 23. It was necessary to be *born of God* by regeneration. Possibly, however, it may mean that they did not become children of God by the bloody rite of *circumcision,* as many of the Jews supposed they did. This is agreeable to the declaration of Paul in Ro. ii. 28, 29. ¶ *Nor of the will of the flesh.* Not by natural generation. ¶ *Nor of the will of man.* This *may* refer, perhaps, to the will of man in *adopting* a child, as the former phrases do to the natural birth; and the design of using these three phrases *may* have been to say that they became the children of God neither in virtue of their descent from illustrious parents like Abraham, nor by their natural birth, nor by being *adopted* by a pious man. None of the ways by which we become entitled to the privileges of *children* among men can give us a title to be called the sons of God. It is not by human power or agency that men become children of the Most High. ¶ *But of God.* That is, God produces the change, and confers the privilege of being called his children.

flesh, and dwelt among us, ([t]and we beheld his glory, the glory as of the only-begotten of the Father,) [u]full of grace and truth.

t 2 Pe.1.17; 1 Jn.1.1,2. *u* Ps.45.2; Col.2.3,9.

The heart is changed by his power. No unaided effort of man, no works of ours, can produce this change. At the same time, it is true that no man is renewed who does not himself *desire* and *will* to be a believer; for the effect of the change is on his *will* (Ps. cx. 3), and no one is changed who does not strive to enter in at the strait gate, Phi. ii. 12. This important verse, therefore, teaches us, 1st. That if men are saved they must be born again. 2d. That their salvation is not the result of their birth, or of any honourable or pious parentage. 3d. That the children of the rich and the noble, as well as of the poor, must be born of God if they will be saved. 4th. That the children of pious parents must be born again, or they cannot be saved. None will go to heaven simply because their *parents* are Christians. 5th. That this work is the work of God, and *no man* can do it for us. 6th. That we should forsake all human dependence, cast off all confidence in the flesh, and go at once to the throne of grace, and beseech of God to adopt us into his family and save our souls from death.

14. *And the Word was made flesh.* The word *flesh*, here, is evidently used to denote *human nature* or *man.* See Mat. xvi. 17; xix. 5; xxiv. 22; Lu. iii. 6; Ro. i. 3; ix. 5. The "Word" was made *man.* This is commonly expressed by saying that he became *incarnate.* When we say that a being becomes *incarnate*, we mean that one of a higher order than man, and of a different nature, assumes the appearance of man or becomes a man. Here it is meant that "the Word," or the second person of the Trinity, whom John had just proved to be equal with God, became a man, or was united with the man Jesus of Nazareth, so that it might be said that he *was made flesh.* ¶ *Was made.* This is the same word that is used in ver. 3: "All things *were made* by him." It is not simply affirmed that he *was* flesh, but that he was *made* flesh, implying that he had pre-existence, agreeably to ver. 1. This is in accordance with the doctrine of the Scriptures elsewhere. He. x. 5: "A *body* hast thou prepared me." He. ii. 14: "As the children are partakers of flesh and blood, he also himself likewise took part of the same." 1 Jn. iv. 2: "Jesus Christ is come in the flesh." See also 1 Ti. iii. 16; Phi. ii. 6; 2 Co. viii. 9; Lu. i. 35. The expression, then, means that he became a man, and that he became such by the power of God providing for him a body. It cannot mean that the divine nature was *changed* into the human, for that could not be; but it means that the Logos, or "Word," became so intimately *united* to Jesus that it might be said that the Logos, or "Word" *became* or *was* a man, as the *soul* becomes so *united* to the body that we may say that it is *one person* or *a man.* ¶ *And dwelt among us.* The word in the original denotes "dwelt as in a tabernacle or tent;" and some have supposed that John means to say that the human body was a tabernacle or tent for the Logos to abide in, in allusion to the tabernacle among the Jews, in which the Shechinah, or visible symbol of God, dwelt; but it is not necessary to suppose this. The object of John was to prove that "the Word" became *incarnate.* To do this he appeals to various evidences. One was that he *dwelt* among them; sojourned with them; ate, drank, slept, and was with them for years, so that they "saw him with their eyes, they looked upon him, and their hands handled him," 1 Jn. i. 1. To *dwell in a tent with one* is the same as to be in his family; and when John says he *tabernacled* with them, he means that he was with them as a friend and as one of a family, so that they had full opportunity of becoming familiarly acquainted with him, and could not be mistaken in supposing that *he was really a man.* ¶ *We beheld his glory.* This is a new proof of what he was affirming—*that* THE WORD OF GOD *became man.* The first was, that they had seen him *as a man.* He now adds that they had seen him in his proper glory *as God and man united in one person*, constituting him the unequalled Son of the Father. There is no doubt that there is reference here to the transfiguration on the holy mount. See Mat. xvii. 1–9. To this same evidence Peter also appeals, 2 Pe. i. 16–18. John was one of the witnesses of that scene, and hence he says, "WE *beheld his glory*," Mar. ix. 2. The word *glory* here means majesty, dignity,

15 John[v] bare witness of him, and cried, saying, This was he of whom I spake, He that cometh after me is preferred before me; for he was before me.

v Mat.3.13,&c.

splendour. ¶ *The glory as of the only-begotten of the Father.* The dignity which was appropriate to the only-begotten Son of God; such glory or splendour as could belong to no other, and as properly expressed his rank and character. This glory was seen eminently on the mount of transfiguration. It was also seen in his miracles, his doctrine, his resurrection, his ascension; all of which were such as to illustrate the perfections, and manifest the glory that belongs only to the Son of God. ¶ *Only-begotten.* This term is never applied by John to any but Jesus Christ. It is applied by him five times to the Saviour, ch. i. 14, 18; iii. 16, 18; 1 Jn. iv. 9. It means literally an only child. Then, as an only child is peculiarly dear to a parent, it means one that is especially beloved. Comp. Ge. xxii. 2, 12, 16; Je. vi. 26; Zec. xii. 10. On *both* these accounts it is bestowed on the Saviour. 1st. As he was eminently the Son of God, sustaining a peculiar relation to him in his divine nature, exalted above all men and angels, and thus worthy to be called, by way of eminence, his only Son. Saints are called his *sons* or children, because they are born of his Spirit, or are like him; but the Lord Jesus is exalted far above all, and deserves eminently to be called his only-begotten Son. 2d. He was peculiarly dear to God, and therefore this appellation, implying tender affection, is bestowed on him. ¶ *Full of grace and truth.* The word *full* here refers to the *Word made flesh*, which is declared to be full of grace and truth. The word *grace* means *favours*, gifts, acts of beneficence. He was kind, merciful, gracious, doing good to all, and seeking man's welfare by great sacrifices and love; so much so, that it might be said to be characteristic of him, or he *abounded* in favours to mankind. He was also *full of truth.* He declared the truth. In him was no falsehood. He was not like the false prophets and false Messiahs, who were wholly impostors; nor was he like the emblems and shadows of the old dispensation, which were only types of the true; but he was truth itself. He *represented things as they are*, and thus became the *truth* as well as *the way and the life.*

15. *John bare witness of him.* The evangelist now returns to the testimony of John the Baptist. He had stated that the Word became incarnate, and he now appeals to the testimony of John to show that, thus incarnate, he was the Messiah. ¶ *He that cometh after me.* He of whom I am the forerunner, or whose way I am come to prepare. See Notes on Mat. iii. 3. ¶ *Is preferred before me.* Is superior to me. Most critics have supposed that the words translated "is preferred" relate to *time*, and not to *dignity;* meaning that though he came *after* him publicly, being six months younger than John, as well as entering on his work *after* John, yet that he had existed long before him. Most, however, have understood it more correctly, as our translators seem to have done, as meaning, He was worthy of more *honour* than I am. ¶ *He was before me.* This can refer to nothing but his pre-existence, and can be explained only on the supposition that he *existed* before John, or, as the evangelist had before shown, from the beginning. He came *after* John in his public ministry and in his human nature, but in his divine nature he had existed long before John had a being—from eternity. We may learn here that it is one mark of the true spirit of a minister of Christ to desire and feel that Christ is always to be preferred to ourselves. We should keep ourselves out of view. The great object is to hold up the Saviour; and however much ministers may be honoured or blessed, yet they should lay all at the feet of Jesus, and direct all men to him as the undivided object of affection and honour. It is the business of every Christian, as well as of every Christian minister, to be a *witness* for Christ, and to endeavour to convince the world that he is worthy of confidence and love.

16. *Of his fulness.* In the 14th verse the evangelist has said that Christ was *full of grace and truth.* Of that *fulness* he now says that all the disciples had received; that is, they derived from his abundant truth and mercy grace to understand the plan of salvation, to preach the gospel, to live lives of holiness; they *partook* of the numerous blessings which he came to impart by his instructions

16 And of his [w]fulness have all
we received, and grace for grace.
17 For the law was given by
Moses, *but* [x]grace and truth came
by Jesus Christ.
18 No[y] man hath seen God at

w ch.3.34.

x Ps.85.10; Ro.5.21. y Ex.33.20; 1 Ti.6.16.

and his death. These are undoubtedly not the words of John the Baptist, but of the evangelist John, the writer of this gospel. They are a continuation of what he was saying in the 14th verse, the 15th verse being evidently thrown in as a parenthesis. The declaration had not exclusive reference, probably, to the apostles, but it is extended to *all* Christians, for all believers have received of the *fulness of grace and truth* that is in Christ. Comp. Ep. i. 23; iii. 19; Col. i. 19; ii. 9. In all these places our Saviour is represented as the fulness of God—as *abounding* in mercy, as exhibiting the divine attributes, and as possessing in himself all that is necessary to fill his people with truth, and grace, and love. ¶ *Grace for grace.* Many interpretations of this phrase have been proposed. The chief are briefly the following: 1st. "We have received, under the gospel, grace or favour, *instead* of those granted under the law; and God has *added* by the gospel important favours to those which he gave under the law." This was first proposed by Chrysostom. 2d. "We, Christians, have received grace *answering to*, or corresponding to that which is in Jesus Christ. We are *like* him in meekness, humility," &c. 3d. "We have received grace *as grace*—that is, freely. We have not purchased it nor deserved it, but God has conferred it on us *freely*" (Grotius). 4th. The meaning is, probably, simply that we have received through him *abundance* of grace or favour. The Hebrews, in expressing the *superlative* degree of comparison, used simply to *repeat* the word—thus, "pits, pits," meaning many pits (Hebrew in Ge. xiv. 10). So here grace for grace may mean *much* grace; superlative favours bestowed on man; favours superior to all that had been under the law —superior to all other things that God can confer on men. These favours consist in pardon, redemption, protection, sanctification, peace here, and heaven hereafter.

17. *The law was given.* The Old Testament economy. The institutions under which the Jews lived. ¶ *By Moses.* By Moses, as the servant of God. He was the great legislator of the Jews, by whom, under God, their polity was formed. The *law* worketh wrath (Ro. iv. 15); it was attended with many burdensome rites and ceremonies (Ac. xv. 10); it was preparatory to another state of things. The gospel succeeded that and took its place, and thus showed the *greatness* of the gospel economy, as well as its grace and truth. ¶ *Grace and truth came by Jesus Christ.* A system of religion full of favours, and the *true* system, was revealed by him. The old system was one of *law*, and *shadows*, and *burdensome rites; this* was full of mercy to mankind, and was true in all things. We may learn from these verses—1st. That all our mercies come from Jesus Christ. 2d. "All true believers receive from Christ's fulness; the best and greatest saints cannot live without him, the meanest and weakest may live by him. This excludes proud boasting that we have nothing but *we have received it*, and silenceth perplexing fears that we want nothing but *we may receive it.*"

18. *No man hath seen God at any time.* This declaration is probably made to show the superiority of the revelation of Jesus above that of any previous dispensation. It is said, therefore, that Jesus *had an intimate knowledge of God*, which neither Moses nor any of the ancient prophets had possessed. God is invisible; no human eyes have seen him; but Christ had a knowledge of God which might be expressed to *our* apprehension by saying that he *saw* him. He knew him intimately and completely, and was therefore fitted to make a fuller manifestation of him. See Jn. v. 37; vi. 46; 1 Jn. iv. 12; Ex. xxxiii. 20; Jn. xiv. 9. This passage is not meant to deny that men had witnessed *manifestations* of God, as when he appeared to Moses and the prophets (comp. Nu. xii. 8; Is. vi.); but it is meant that no one has seen the essence of God, or has *fully known God.* The prophets delivered what they *heard* God speak; Jesus what he *knew* of God as his equal, and as understanding fully his nature. ¶ *The only-begotten Son.* See Notes on ver. 14. This verse shows John's sense of the meaning of that phrase, as denoting an intimate and

any time; [z]the only-begotten Son,
which is in the bosom of the Father, he hath declared *him*.

19 And this is [a]the record of
John, when the Jews sent priests and Levites from Jerusalem to ask him, Who art thou?

20 And he confessed, and denied
not; but confessed, I am not the Christ.

21 And they asked him, What
then? Art thou Elias? And he saith, I am not. Art thou [2]that prophet? And he answered, No.

22 Then said they unto him,
Who art thou? that we may give

z 1 Jn.4.9. a Lu.3.15,&c.

2 or, *a prophet.*

---

full knowledge of God. ¶ *In the bosom of the Father.* This expression is taken from the custom among the Orientals of reclining at their meals. See Notes on Mat. xxiii. 6. It denotes intimacy, friendship, affection. Here it means that Jesus had a knowledge of God such as one friend has of another—knowledge of his character, designs, and nature which no other one possesses, and which renders him, therefore, qualified above all others to make him known. ¶ *Hath declared* him. Hath fully revealed him or made him known. Comp. He. i. 1, 4. This verse proves that Jesus had a knowledge of God above that which any of the ancient prophets had, and that the fullest revelations of his character are to be expected in the gospel. By his Word and Spirit he can enlighten and guide us, and lead us to the true knowledge of God; and there is no true and full knowledge of God which is not obtained through his Son. Comp. ch. xiv. 6; 1 Jn. ii. 22, 23.

19. *This is the record.* The word *record* here means *testimony*, in whatever way given. The word *record* now commonly refers to *written* evidence. This is not its meaning here. John's testimony was given without writing. ¶ *When the Jews sent.* John's fame was great. See Mat. iii. 5. It spread from the region of Galilee to Jerusalem, and the nation seemed to suppose, from the character of his preaching, that he was the Messiah, Lu. iii. 15. The great council of the nation, or the Sanhedrim, had, among other things, the charge of religion. They felt it to be their duty, therefore, to inquire into the character and claims of John, and to learn whether he was the Messiah. It is not improbable that they *wished* that he might be the long-expected Christ, and were prepared to regard him as such. ¶ *When the Jews sent priests and Levites.* See Notes on Lu. x. 31, 32. These were probably members of the Sanhedrim.

20. *I am not the Christ.* This confession proves that John was not an impostor. He had a wide reputation. The nation was expecting that the Messiah was about to come, and multitudes were ready to believe that John was he, Lu. iii. 15. If John had been an impostor he would have taken advantage of this excited state of public feeling, proclaimed himself to be the Messiah, and formed a large party in his favour. The fact that he did *not* do it is full proof that he did not intend to *impose* on men, but came only as the forerunner of Christ; and his example shows that all Christians, and especially all Christian ministers, however much they may be honoured and blessed, should be willing to lay all their honours at the feet of Jesus; to keep *themselves* back and to hold up before the world only the Son of God. To do this is one eminent mark of the true spirit of a minister of the gospel.

21. *Art thou Elias?* This is the Greek way of writing Elijah. The Jews expected that Elijah would appear before the Messiah came. See Notes on Mat. xi. 14. *They* supposed that it would be the *real* Elijah returned from heaven. In this sense John denied that he *was* Elijah; but he did not deny that he was the Elias or Elijah which the prophet intended (Mat. iii. 3), for he immediately proceeds to state (ver. 23) that he was sent, as it was predicted that Elijah would be, to prepare the way of the Lord; so that, while he corrected their false notions about Elijah, he so clearly stated to them his true character that they might understand that he was really the one predicted as Elijah. ¶ *That prophet.* It is possible that the Jews supposed that not only *Elijah* would reappear before the coming of the Messiah, but also *Jeremiah*. See Notes on Mat. xvi. 14. Some have supposed, however, that this question has reference to the prediction of Moses in De. xviii. 15.

an answer to them that sent us. What sayest thou of thyself?

23 He[b] said, I *am* the voice of one crying in the wilderness, Make straight the way of the Lord, as said the prophet [c]Esaias.

24 And they which were sent were of the Pharisees.

25 And they asked him, and said unto him, Why baptizest thou then, if thou be not that Christ, nor Elias, neither that prophet?

26 John answered them, saying, I baptize with water; but [d]there standeth one among you whom ye know not:

b Mat.3.3; Mar.1.3; Lu.3.4; ch.3.28. *c* Is.40.3. *d* Mal.3.1.

23. *I* am *the voice*, &c. See Notes on Mat. iii. 3.

24. *Were of the Pharisees.* For an account of this sect, see Notes on Mat. iii. 7. Why *they* are particularly mentioned is not certainly known. Many of the *Sadducees* came to his baptism (Mat. iii. 7), but it seems that they did not join in sending to him to know what was the design of John. This circumstance is one of those incidental and delicate allusions which would occur to no impostor in forging a book, and which show that the writers of the New Testament were honest men and knew what they affirmed. For, 1st. The Pharisees composed a great part of the Sanhedrim, Ac. xxiii. 6. It is probable that a deputation from the Sanhedrim would be of that party. 2d. The Pharisees were very tenacious of rites and customs, of traditions and ceremonies. They observed many. They believed that they were lawful, Mar. vii. 3, 4. Of course, they believed that those rites might be increased, but they did not suppose that it could be done except by the authority of a prophet or of the Messiah. When, therefore, John came *baptizing*—adding a rite to be observed by his followers—baptizing not only *Gentiles*, but also *Jews*—the question was whether he had *authority* to institute a new rite; whether it was to be received among the ceremonies of religion. In this question the *Sadducees* felt no interest, for they rejected *all* such rites at once; but the *Pharisees* thought it was worth inquiry, and it was a question on which *they* felt themselves specially called on to act as the guardians of the ceremonies of religion.

25. *Why baptizest thou then*, &c. Baptism on receiving a proselyte from *heathenism* was common before the time of John, but it was not customary to baptize a *Jew*. John had changed the custom. He baptized *all*, and they were desirous of knowing by what authority he made such a change in the religious customs of the nation. They presumed, from the fact that he *introduced* that change, that he claimed to be a prophet or the Christ. They supposed that no one would attempt it without *pretending*, at least, authority from heaven. As he disclaimed the character of Christ and of the prophet Elijah, they asked whence he derived his authority. As he had just before applied to himself a prediction that they all considered as belonging to the forerunner of Christ, they *might* have understood *why* he did it; but they were blind, and manifested, as all sinners do, a remarkable slowness in understanding the plainest truths in religion.

26. *I baptize.* He did not deny it; nor did he condescend to state his authority. *That* he had given. He *admitted* that he had introduced an important *change* in the rites of religion, and he goes on to tell them that *this* was not all. Greater and more important changes would soon take place without *their* authority. The Messiah was about to come, and the *power* was about to depart from *their* hands. ¶ *There standeth one.* There *is* one. ¶ *Among you.* In the midst of you. He is undistinguished among the multitude. The Messiah had already come, and was about to be manifested to the people. It was not until the next day (ver. 29) that Jesus was manifested or proclaimed as the Messiah; but it is not improbable that he was *then* among the people that were assembled near the Jordan, and mingled with them, though he was undistinguished. He had gone there, probably, with the multitudes that had been drawn thither by the fame of John, and had gone without attracting attention, though his real object was to receive baptism in this public manner, and to be exhibited and proclaimed as the Messiah. ¶ *Whom ye know not.* Jesus was not yet declared publicly to be the Christ. Though it is probable

27 He it is, who, coming after
me, is preferred before me, whose
shoe's latchet I am not worthy to
unloose.
28 These things were done [e]in
Bethabara, beyond Jordan, where
John was baptizing.
29 The next day John seeth
Jesus coming unto him, and saith,
Behold the [f]Lamb of God, [g]which
[3]taketh away the sin of the world!
30 This is he of whom I said,
After me cometh a man which is
preferred before me; for he was
before me.
31 And I knew him not; but

e Ju.7.24.

f Ex.12.3; Is.53.7,11; Re.5.6.
g Ac.13.39; 1 Pe.2.24; Re.1.5. 3 or, *beareth*, He.9.28.

that he was then among the multitude, yet he was not known as the Messiah. We may hence learn, 1st. That there is often great excellency in the world that is obscure, undistinguished, and unknown. Jesus was *near* to all that people, but they were not conscious of his presence, for he was retired and obscure. Though the greatest personage ever in the world, yet he was not externally distinguished from others. 2d. Jesus may be near to men of the world, and yet they know him not. He is everywhere by his Spirit, yet few know it, and few are *desirous* of knowing it.

27. *Whose shoe's latchet.* See Notes on Mat. iii. 11. The *latchet* of sandals was the string or thong by which they were fastened to the feet. To unloose them was the office of a servant, and John means, therefore, that he was unworthy to perform the lowest office for the Messiah. This was remarkable humility. John was well known; he was highly honoured; thousands came to hear him. Jesus was at that time unknown; but John says that he was unworthy to perform the humblest office for Jesus. So we all should be willing to lay all that we have at the feet of Christ, and feel that we are unworthy to be his lowest servants.

28. *In Bethabara.* Almost all the ancient manuscripts and versions, instead of *Bethabara* here, have *Bethany*, and this is doubtless the true reading. There was a Bethany about 2 miles east of Jerusalem, but there is said also to have been another in the tribe of Reuben, on the east side of the river Jordan, and in this place, probably, John was baptizing. It is about 12 miles above Jericho. The word *Bethabara* means *house* or *place of a ford.* The reading *Bethabara*, instead of *Bethany*, seems to have arisen from the conjecture of Origen, who found in his day no such place as *Bethany*, but saw a town called *Bethabara*, where John was said to have baptized, and therefore took the liberty of changing the former reading.—Rob., *Lex.* ¶ *Beyond Jordan.* On the east side of the river Jordan.

29. *The next day.* The day after the Jews made inquiry whether he was the Christ. ¶ *Behold the Lamb of God.* A *lamb*, among the Jews, was killed and eaten at the Passover to commemorate their deliverance from Egypt, Ex. xii. 3–11. A lamb was offered in the tabernacle, and afterward in the temple, every morning and evening, as a part of the daily worship, Ex. xxix. 38, 39. The Messiah was predicted as a lamb led to the slaughter, to show his patience in his sufferings, and readiness to die for man, Is. liii. 7. A lamb, among the Jews, was also an emblem of patience, meekness, gentleness. On *all* these accounts, rather than on any one of them alone, Jesus was called *the Lamb.* He was innocent (1 Pe. ii. 23-25); he was a sacrifice for sin—the substance represented by the daily offering of the lamb, and slain at the usual time of the evening sacrifice (Lu. xxiii. 44–46); and he was what was represented by the Passover, turning away the anger of God, and saving sinners by his blood from vengeance and eternal death, 1 Co. v. 7. ¶ *Of God.* Appointed by God, approved by God, and most dear to him; the sacrifice which he *chose*, and which he *approves* to save men from death. ¶ *Which taketh away.* This denotes his *bearing* the sins of the world, or the sufferings which made an atonement for sin. Comp. Is. liii. 4; 1 Jn. iii. 5; 1 Pe. ii. 24. He takes away sin by *bearing* in his own body the sufferings which God appointed to show his sense of the evil of sin, thus magnifying the law, and rendering it consistent for him to pardon. See Notes on Ro. iii. 24, 25. ¶ *Of the world.* Of all mankind, Jew and Gentile. His work was not to be confined to the Jew, but was also to

that he should be made manifest
to Israel, therefore am I come baptizing with water.
32 And John bare record, saying,
I saw the Spirit descending from
heaven like a dove, and it abode
upon him.
33 And I knew him not: but he
that sent me to baptize with water, the same said unto me, Upon
whom thou shalt see the Spirit descending and [h]remaining on him,

h ch.3.34.

the same is he which [i]baptizeth
with the Holy Ghost.
34 And I saw, and bare record
that this is the Son of God.
35 Again, the next day after,
John stood, and two of his disciples;
36 And looking upon Jesus as
he walked, he saith, Behold the
Lamb of God!
37 And the two disciples heard

i Ac.1.5; 2.4.

---

benefit the Gentile; it was not confined to any one part of the world, but was designed to open the way of pardon to all men. He was the propitiation for the sins of the whole world, 1 Jn. ii. 2. See Notes on 2 Co. v. 15.

31. *I knew him not.* John was not *personally* acquainted with Jesus. Though they were remotely related to each other, yet it seems that they had had heretofore no personal acquaintance. John had lived chiefly in the hill country of Judea. Jesus had been employed with Joseph at Nazareth. Until Jesus came to be baptized (Mat. iii. 13, 14), it seems that John had no acquaintance with him. He understood that he was to announce that the Messiah was about to appear. He was sent to proclaim his coming, but he did not personally know Jesus, or that *he* was to be the Messiah. This proves that there could have been no *collusion* or *agreement* between them to impose on the people. ¶ *Should be made manifest.* That the Messiah should be *exhibited*, or made known. He came to prepare the way for the Messiah, and it *now* appeared that the Messiah was Jesus of Nazareth. ¶ *To Israel.* To the Jews.

32. *Bare record.* Gave testimony. ¶ *I saw the Spirit*, &c. See Notes on Mat. iii. 16, 17.

33, 34. *The same said*, &c. This was the sign by which he was to know the Messiah. He was to see the Spirit descending like a dove and abiding on him. It does not follow, however, that he had no *intimation* before this that Jesus was the Christ, but it means that by this he should *infallibly know it.* From Mat. iii. 13, 14, it seems that John supposed, before the baptism of Jesus, that he *claimed* to be the Messiah, and that he believed it; but the *infallible, certain* testimony in the case was the descent of the Holy Spirit on him at his baptism. ¶ *That this is the Son of God.* This was distinctly declared by a voice from heaven at his baptism, Mat. iii. 17. This John heard, and he testified that he had heard it.

35. *The next day.* The day after his remarkable testimony that Jesus was the Son of God. This testimony of John is reported because it was the main design of this evangelist to show that Jesus was the Messiah. See the Introduction. To do this, he adduces the decided and repeated testimony of John the Baptist. This was impartial evidence in the case, and hence he so particularly dwells upon it. ¶ *John stood.* Or was standing. This was probably apart from the multitude. ¶ *Two of his disciples.* One of these was Andrew (ver. 40), and it is not improbable that the other was the writer of this gospel.

36. *Looking upon Jesus*, &c. Fixing his eyes intently upon him. Singling him out and regarding him with special attention. Contemplating him as the long-expected Messiah and Deliverer of the world. In this way should all ministers fix the eye on the Son of God, and direct all others to him. ¶ *As he walked.* While *Jesus* was walking.

37. *They followed Jesus.* They had been the disciples of John. *His* office was to point out the Messiah. When that was done, they left at once their master and teacher, John, and followed the long-expected Messiah. This shows that John was sincere; that he was not desirous of forming a party or of building up a sect; that he was willing that all those whom he had attracted to himself by his ministry should become followers of Christ. The object of minis-

him speak, and they followed Jesus.

38 Then Jesus turned, and saw them following, and saith unto them, What seek ye? They said unto him, Rabbi, (which is to say, being interpreted, Master,) where dwellest[4] thou?

39 He saith unto them, Come and see. They came and saw where he dwelt, and abode with him that day; for it was [5]about the tenth hour.

40 One of the two which heard John *speak*, and followed him, was Andrew, Simon Peter's brother.

[4] or, *abidest*.

[5] *That was two hours before night.*

---

ters should *not* be to build up their own interests or to extend their own fame. It is to point men to the Saviour. Ministers, however popular or successful, should be willing that their disciples should look to Christ rather than to them; nay, should *forget* them and look away from them, to tread in the footsteps of the Son of God; and the conduct of these disciples shows us that we should forsake *all* and follow Jesus when he is pointed out to us as the Messiah. We should not delay nor debate the matter, but leave at once all our old teachers, guides and companions, and follow the Lamb of God. And we should do that, too, though *to the world* the Lord Jesus may appear, as he did to the multitude of the Jews, as poor, unknown, and despised. Reader, have *you* left all and followed him? Have you forsaken the guides of false philosophy and deceit, of sin and infidelity, and committed yourself to the Lord Jesus Christ.

38. *What seek ye?* This was not asked to obtain *information.* Comp. ver. 48. It was not a harsh reproof, forbidding them to follow him. Comp. Mat. xi. 28–30. It was a kind inquiry respecting their desires; an invitation to lay open their minds, to state their wishes, and to express all their feelings respecting the Messiah and their own salvation. We may learn, 1st. That Jesus regards the first inclinations of the soul to follow him. He *turned* toward these disciples, and he will incline his ear to all who begin to approach him for salvation. 2d. Jesus is ready to hear their requests and to answer them. 3d. Ministers of the gospel, and all other Christians, should be accessible, kind, and tender toward all who are inquiring the way to life. In conformity with their Master, they should be willing to aid all those who look to them for guidance and help in the great work of their salvation. ¶ *Rabbi.* This was a Jewish title conferred somewhat as literary degrees now are, and meaning literally *a great one*, and was applied to a teacher or master in the Jewish schools. It corresponded with the title *Doctor*. Our Saviour solemnly forbade his disciples to wear that title. See Notes on Mat. xxiii. 8. The fact that John *interpreted* this word shows that he wrote his gospel not for the Jews only, but for those who did not understand the Hebrew language. It is supposed to have been written at Ephesus. ¶ *Where dwellest thou?* This question they probably asked him in order to signify their wish to be with him and to be instructed by him. They desired more fully to listen to him than they could now by the wayside. They were unwilling to interrupt him in his travelling. Religion teaches men true politeness, or a disposition to consult the convenience of others, and not improperly to molest them, or to break in upon them when engaged. It also teaches us to *desire to be with Christ;* to seek every opportunity of communion with him, and chiefly to desire *to be with him where he is* when we leave this world. Comp. Phi. i. 23.

39. *Come and see.* This was a kind and gracious answer. He did not put them off to some future period. Then, as now, he was willing that they should come at once and enjoy the full opportunity which they desired of his conversation. Jesus is ever ready to admit those who seek him to his presence and favour. ¶ *Abode with him.* Remained with him. This was probably the dwelling of some friend of Jesus. His usual home was at Nazareth. ¶ *The tenth hour.* The Jews divided their day into twelve equal parts, beginning at sunrise. If John used their mode of computation, this was about four o'clock P.M. The Romans divided time as we do, beginning at midnight. If John used their mode, it was about ten o'clock in the forenoon. It is not certain which he used.

41. *He first findeth.* He found him

41 He first findeth his own
brother Simon, and saith unto him,
We have found the Messias, which
is, being interpreted, [6]the Christ.
42 And he brought him to Jesus.
And when Jesus beheld him he
said, Thou art Simon, the son of
Jonas: [k]thou shalt be called Cephas,
which is, by interpretation, [7] A
stone.
43 The day following, Jesus
would go forth into Galilee, and
findeth Philip, and saith unto
him, Follow me.
44 Now Philip was of Bethsaida, the city of Andrew and
Peter.
45 Philip findeth Nathanael,
and saith unto him, We have
found him of whom [l]Moses in the
law, and the prophets, did write,
Jesus of Nazareth, the son of
Joseph.
46 And Nathanael said unto

[6] or, *the anointed.* [k] Mat.16.18. [7] or, *Peter.*

[l] Lu.24.27,44.

---

and *told him about Jesus* before he brought him to Jesus. ¶ *We have found the Messias.* They had learned from the testimony of John, and now had been more fully convinced from conversation with Jesus, that he was the Messiah. The word Messiah, or Messias, is Hebrew, and means the same as the Greek word Christ, *anointed.* See Notes on Mat. i. 1. From the conduct of Andrew we may learn that it is the nature of religion to desire that others may possess it. It does not lead us to monopolize it or to hide it under a bushel, but it seeks that others also may be brought to the Saviour. It does not *wait* for them to come, but it goes *for* them; it seeks them out, and tells them that a Saviour is found. Young converts should *seek* their friends and neighbours, and tell them of a Saviour; and not only their relatives, but all others as far as possible, that all may come to Jesus and be saved.

42. *Cephas.* This is a Syriac word, meaning the same as the Greek word Peter, a stone. See Notes on Mat. xvi. 17. The stone, or rock, is a symbol of firmness and steadiness of character—a trait in Peter's character *after* the ascension of Jesus that was very remarkable. *Before* the death of Jesus he was rash, headlong, variable; and it is one proof of the omniscience of Jesus that he saw that Peter *would* possess a character that would be expressed appropriately by the word *stone* or *rock.* The word *Jonas* is a Hebrew word, whose original signification is *a dove.* It may be that Jesus had respect to that when he gave Simon the name Peter. "You now bear a name emblematic of timidity and inconstancy. You shall be called by a name denoting firmness and constancy."

43. *Would go forth.* Was about to go. ¶ *Into Galilee.* He was now in Judea, where he went to be baptized by John. He was now about to return to his native country. ¶ *Findeth Philip.* This does not refer to his calling these disciples to be *apostles,* for that took place at the Sea of Tiberias (Mat. iv. 18), but it refers to their being convinced that he was the Christ. This is the object of this evangelist, to show how and when they were convinced of this. Matthew states the time and occasion in which they were called to be *apostles;* John, the time in which they first became acquainted with Jesus, and were convinced that he was the Messiah. There is, therefore, no contradiction in the evangelists.

44. *Of Bethsaida.* See Notes on Mat. xi. 21. ¶ *The city of.* The place where Andrew and Peter dwelt.

45. *Moses, in the law.* Moses, in that part of the Old Testament which he wrote, called by the Jews *the law.* See De. xviii. 15, 18; Ge. xlix. 10; iii. 15. ¶ *And the prophets,* Is. liii.; ix. 6, 7; Da. ix. 24-27; Je. xxiii. 5, 6; &c. ¶ *Jesus of Nazareth,* &c. They spoke according to common apprehension. They spoke of him as the son of Joseph because he was commonly supposed to be. They spoke of him as dwelling at Nazareth, though they might not have been ignorant that he was born at Bethlehem.

46. *Can any good thing,* &c. The character of Nazareth was proverbially bad. To be a Galilean or a Nazarene was an expression of decided contempt, Jn. vii. 52. See Notes on Mat. ii. 23. Nathanael asked, therefore, whether it was possible that the Messiah should come from a place proverbially wicked. This was a mode of judging in the case not uncommon. It is not by examining *evidence,* but by prejudice. Many per-

him, [m]Can there any good thing
come out of Nazareth? Philip
saith unto him, Come and see.
47 Jesus saw Nathanael coming
to him, and saith of him, [n]Behold,
an Israelite indeed, in whom is no
guile!
48 Nathanael saith unto him,
Whence knowest thou me? Jesus
answered and said unto him, Before that Philip called thee, when
thou wast under the fig-tree, [o]I
saw thee.
49 Nathanael answered and

m ch.7.41. *n* Ps.32.2; Ro.2.28,29. *o* Ps.139.1,2.

---

sons suffer their minds to be filled with prejudice against religion, and then pronounce at once without examination. They refuse to examine the subject, for they have set it down that it *cannot* be true. It matters not where a teacher comes from, or what is the place of his birth, provided he be authorized of God and qualified for his work. ¶ *Come and see.* This was the best way to answer Nathanael. He did not sit down to *reason* with him, or speculate about the possibility that a good thing could come from Nazareth; but he asked him to go and examine for himself, to see the Lord Jesus, to hear him converse, to lay aside his prejudice, and to judge from a fair and candid personal inquiry. So we should beseech sinners to lay aside their prejudices against religion, and *to be Christians*, and thus make trial for themselves. If men can be persuaded to come to Jesus, all their petty and foolish objections against religion will vanish. They will be satisfied from their *own experience* that it is true, and in this way only *will* they ever be satisfied.

47. *An Israelite indeed.* One who is really an Israelite—not by birth only, but one worthy of the name. One who possesses the spirit, the piety, and the integrity which become a man who is really a Jew, who fears God and obeys his law. Comp. Ro. ix. 6; ii. 28, 29. ¶ *No guile.* No deceit, no fraud, no hypocrisy. He is really what he professes to be—a Jew, a descendant of the patriarch Jacob, fearing and serving God. He makes no profession which he does not live up to. He does not say that Nathanael was without guilt or sin, but that he had no disguise, no trick, no deceit—he was sincere and upright. This was a most honourable testimony. How happy would it be if he, who knows the hearts of all as he did that of Nathanael, could bear the same testimony of all who profess the religion of the gospel!

48. *Whence knowest thou me?* Nathanael was not yet acquainted with the divinity of Christ, and supposed that he had been a stranger to him. Hearing him express a favourable opinion of him, he naturally inquired by what means he had any knowledge of him. His conscience testified to the truth of what Jesus said—that he had no guile, and he was anxious to know whence he had learned his character. ¶ *Before that Philip called thee.* See ver. 45. ¶ *When thou wast under the fig-tree.* It is evident that it was from something that had occurred under the fig-tree that Jesus judged of his character. What that was is not recorded. It is not improbable that Nathanael was accustomed to retire to the shade of a certain tree, perhaps in his garden or in a grove, for the purpose of meditation and prayer. The Jews were much in the habit of selecting such places for private devotion, and in such scenes of stillness and retirement there is something peculiarly favourable for meditation and prayer. Our Saviour also worshipped in such places. Comp. Jn. xviii. 2; Lu. vi. 12. In that place of retirement it is not improbable that Nathanael was engaged in private devotion. ¶ *I saw thee.* It is clear, from the narrative, that Jesus did not mean to say that he was bodily present with Nathanael and saw him; but he knew his thoughts, his desires, his secret feelings and wishes. In this sense Nathanael understood him. We may learn —1st. That Jesus sees what is done in secret, and is therefore divine. 2d. That he sees us when we little think of it. 3d. That he sees us especially in our private devotions, hears our prayers, and marks our meditations. And 4th. That he judges of our *character* chiefly by our private devotions. Those are secret; the world sees them not; and in our closets we show what we are. How does it become us, therefore, that our secret prayers and meditations should be without *guile* and hypocrisy, and such as Jesus will approve!

saith unto him, Rabbi, thou art
the[p] Son of God; thou art [q]the
King of Israel.
50 Jesus answered and said
unto him, Because I said unto
thee, I saw thee under the fig-tree, believest thou? Thou shalt see greater things than these.
51 And he saith unto him,
Verily, verily, I say unto you,

p Mat.14.33; ch.20.28,29. q Mat.21.5; 27.11.

49. *Rabbi.* Master. Applied appropriately to Jesus, and to no one else, Mat. xxiii. 10. ¶ *The Son of God.* By this title he doubtless meant that he was the Messiah. His conscience told him that he had judged right of his character, and that therefore he must know the heart and the desires of the mind. If so, he could not be a mere man, but must be the long-expected Messiah. ¶ *The King of Israel.* This was one of the titles by which the Messiah was expected, and this was the title which was affixed to his cross, Jn. xix. 18. This case of Nathanael John adduces as another evidence that Jesus was the Christ. The great object he had in view in writing this gospel was to collect the evidence that he was the Messiah, ch. xx. 31. A case, therefore, where Jesus searched the heart, and where his knowledge of the heart convinced a pious *Jew* that he was the Christ, is very properly adduced as important testimony.

50. *Greater things.* Fuller proof of his Messiahship, particularly what is mentioned in the following verse.

51. *Verily, verily.* In the Greek, *Amen, amen.* The word *amen* means *truly, certainly, so be it*—from the verb to confirm, to establish, to be true. It is often used in this gospel. When repeated it expresses the speaker's sense of the *importance* of what he is saying, and the *certainty* that it is as he affirms. ¶ *Ye shall see.* Not, perhaps, with the bodily eyes, but you shall have *evidence* that it is so. The thing shall take place, and you shall be a witness of it. ¶ *Heaven open.* This is a figurative expression, denoting *the conferring of favours.* Ps. lxxviii. 23, 24: "He opened the doors of heaven, and had rained down manna." It also denotes that God was about to work a miracle in attestation of a particular thing. See Mat. iii. 16. In the *language*, here, there is an evident allusion to the ladder that Jacob saw in a dream, and to the angels ascending and descending on it, Ge. xxviii. 12. It is not probable that Jesus referred to any particular instance in which Nathanael should literally see the heavens opened. The baptism of Jesus had taken place, and no other instance occurred in his life in which it is said that the *heavens were* opened. ¶ *Angels of God.* Those pure and holy beings that dwell in heaven, and that are employed as ministering spirits to our world, He. i. 14. Good men are represented in the Scriptures as being under their protection, Ps. xci. 11, 12; Ge. xxviii. 12. They are the agents by which God often expressed his will to men, He. ii. 2; Ga. iii. 19. They are represented as strengthening the Lord Jesus, and ministering unto him. Thus they aided him in the wilderness (Mar. i. 13), and in the garden (Lu. xxii. 43), and they were present when he rose from the dead, Mat. xxviii. 2–4; Jn. xx. 12, 13. By their ascending and descending upon him it is probable that he meant that Nathanael would have evidence that they came to his aid, and that he would have *the* KIND of protection and assistance from God which would show *more fully that he was the Messiah.* Thus his life, his many deliverances from dangers, his wisdom to confute his skilled and cunning adversaries, the scenes of his death, and the attendance of angels at his resurrection, may all be represented by the angels descending upon him, and *all* would show to Nathanael and the other disciples most clearly that he was the Son of God. ¶ *The Son of man.* A term by which he often describes himself. It shows his humility, his love for man, his willingness to be esteemed *as a man*, Phi. ii. 6, 7.

From this interview with Nathanael we may learn, 1st. That Jesus searches the heart. 2d. That he was truly the Messiah. 3d. That he was under the protection of God. 4th. That if we have faith in Jesus, it will be continually strengthened—the evidence will grow brighter and brighter. 5th. That if we believe his *word*, we shall yet see full proof that his word is true. 6th. As Jesus was under the protection of God, so will all his friends be. God will defend and save us also if we put our trust in him. 7th. Jesus applied to himself terms expressive of humility. He was not solicitous even to be called by titles

Hereafter ye shall see [r]heaven
open, and [s]the angels of God ascending
and descending upon the
Son of man.

CHAPTER II.

AND the third day there was
a marriage in [a]Cana of Galilee;
and the mother of Jesus was
there:
2 And both Jesus was called,
and his disciples, to [b]the marriage.
3 And [c] when they wanted
wine, the mother of Jesus saith
unto him, They have no wine.
4 Jesus saith unto her, Woman,

r Eze.1.1. *s* Ge.28.12; Da.7.9,10; Ac.1.10,11. *a* Jos.19.28; ch.4.46.

b He.13.4. *c* Ec.10.19; Is.24.11.

which he *might* claim. So we should not be ambitious of titles and honours. Ministers of the gospel most resemble him when they seek for the fewest titles, and do not aim at distinctions from each other or their brethren. See Notes on Mat. xxiii. 8.

CHAPTER II.

1. *And the third day.* On the third day after his conversation with Nathanael. ¶ *Cana.* This was a small town about 15 miles north-west of Tiberias and 6 miles north-east of Nazareth. It is now called Kefr Kenna, is under the government of a Turkish officer, and contains perhaps three hundred inhabitants, chiefly Catholics. The natives still pretend to show the place where the water was turned into wine, and even one of the large stone water-pots. "A Greek church," says Professor Hackett (*Illustrations of Scripture*, p. 322), "stands at the entrance of the town, deriving its special sanctity, as I understood, from its being supposed to occupy the site of the house in which the marriage was celebrated to which Jesus and his friends were invited. A priest to whom we were referred as the custodian soon arrived, in obedience to our call, and unlocked the doors of the church. It is a low stone building, wretchedly neglected and out of repair." "The houses," says Dr. Thomson (*The Land and the Book*, vol. ii. p. 126), "were built of limestone, cut and laid up after the fashion still common in this region, and some of them may have been inhabited within the last fifty years. There are many ancient cisterns about it, and fragments of water-jars in abundance, and both reminded us of the 'beginning of miracles.' Some of my companions gathered bits of these water-jars as mementoes — witnesses they could hardly be, for those of the narrative were of *stone*, while these were baked earth." The place is now quite deserted. Dr. Thomson (*ibid.*) says: "There is not now a habitable house in the humble village where our blessed Lord sanctioned, by his presence and miraculous assistance, the all-important and world-wide institution of marriage." It was called *Cana of Galilee* to distinguish it from another Cana in the tribe of Ephraim, Jos. xvi. 9. This was the native place of Nathanael, Jn. xxi. 2. ¶ *The mother of Jesus.* Mary. It is not improbable that she was a relative of the family where the marriage took place.

2. *His disciples.* Those that he had made when in Judea. These were Peter, Andrew, Philip, and Nathanael. They were not yet called to be *apostles*, but they believed that he was the Messiah. The miracle wrought here was doubtless to convince them more fully that he was the Christ.

3. *When they wanted wine.* A marriage feast among the Jews was commonly observed for seven or eight days. It is not probable that there would be a want of wine at the marriage itself, and it is possible, therefore, that Jesus came there some time during the marriage feast. ¶ *They have no wine.* It is not known why Mary told this to Jesus. It would seem that she had a belief that he was able to supply it, though he had as yet worked no miracle.

4. *Woman.* This term, as used here, seems to imply reproof, as if she was interfering in that which did not properly concern her; but it is evident that no such reproof or disrespect was intended by the use of the term *woman* instead of *mother*. It is the same term by which he tenderly addressed Mary Magdalene after his resurrection (ch. xx. 15), and his mother when he was on the cross, ch. xix. 26. Comp. also Mat. xv. 28; Jn. iv. 21; 1 Co. vii. 16. ¶ *What have I to do with thee?* See Notes on Mat. viii. 29. This expression is sometimes used to denote indignation or contempt. See Ju. xi. 12; 2 Sa. xvi.

what have I to do with thee?
Mine hour is not yet come.
5 His mother saith unto the
servants, [d] Whatsoever he saith
unto you, do *it*.
6 And there were set there
six water-pots of stone, after the
manner of the purifying of the
Jews, containing two or three
firkins apiece.
7 Jesus saith unto them, Fill
the water-pots with water. And
they filled them up to the brim.
8 And he saith unto them,

d Lu.5.5,6.

10; 1 Ki. xvii. 18. But it is not probable that it denoted either in this place; if it did, it was a mild reproof of Mary for attempting to control or direct him in his power of working miracles. Most of the ancients supposed this to be the intention of Jesus. The words sound to us harsh, but they might have been spoken in a *tender* manner, and not have been intended as a reproof. It is clear that he did not intend to *refuse* to provide wine, but only to *delay* it a little; and the design was, therefore, to compose the anxiety of Mary, and to prevent her being solicitous about it. It may, then, be thus expressed: "My mother, be not anxious. To you and to me this should not be a matter of solicitude. The proper time of my interfering has not yet come. When that is come I will furnish a supply, and in the meantime neither you nor I should be solicitous." Thus understood, it is so far from being *a harsh reproof*, that it was a mild exhortation for her to dismiss her fears and to put proper trust in him. ¶ *Mine hour*, &c. My time. The proper time for my interposing. Perhaps the wine was not yet *entirely* exhausted. The wine had begun to fail, but he would not work a miracle until it was entirely gone, that the miracle might be free from all possibility of suspicion. It does not mean that the proper time for his working a miracle, or entering on his public work had not come, but that the proper time for his interposing *there* had not arrived.

5. *His mother saith*, &c. It is evident from this verse that his mother did not understand what he had said as a harsh reproof and repulse, but as an indication of his willingness at the proper time to furnish wine. In all this transaction he evinced the appropriate feelings of a son toward a mother.

6. *Six water-pots of stone.* Made of stone; or, as we should say, stoneware. ¶ *After the manner.* After the usual custom. ¶ *Of the purifying.* Of the *washings* or ablutions of the Jews. They were for the purpose of washing the hands before and after eating (Mat. xv. 2), and for the formal washing of vessels, and even articles of furniture, Lu. xi. 39; Mar. vii. 3, 4. ¶ *Two or three firkins.* It is not quite certain what is meant here by the word *firkins*. It is probable that the measure intended is the Hebrew *bath*, containing about 7½ gallons.

7. *With water.* This was done by the servants employed at the feast. It was done by *them*, so that there might be no opportunity of saying that the disciples of Jesus had filled them with wine to produce the *appearance* of a miracle. In this case there could be no deception. The quantity was very considerable. The servants would know whether the *wine* or *water* had been put in these vessels. It could not be believed that *they* had either the power or the disposition to impose on others in this manner, and the way was therefore clear for the proof that Jesus had really changed what was known to be *water* into *wine*. ¶ *To the brim.* To the top. So full that no *wine* could be *poured in* to give the *appearance* of a mixture. Farther, vessels were used for this miracle in which wine had not been kept. These pots were never used to put wine in, but simply to keep *water* in for the various purposes of ablution. A large number was used on this occasion, because there were many guests.

8. *Draw out now.* This command was given to the servants. It showed that the miracle had been *immediately* wrought. As soon as they were filled the servants were directed to take to the governor of the feast. Jesus made no parade about it, and it does not even appear that he approached the water-pots. He willed it, and it was done. This was a clear exertion of divine power, and made in such a manner as to leave no doubt of its reality. ¶ *The governor.* One who presided on the occasion. The one who stood at the *head* or upper end of the table. He had the charge of the entertainment,

Draw[e] out now and bear unto the governor[f] of the feast. And they bare *it*.

9 When the ruler of the feast had tasted the water that was made wine, and knew not whence it was, (but the [g]servants which drew the water knew,) the governor of the feast called the bridegroom,

10 And saith unto him, Every man at the beginning doth set forth good wine; and when men have well drunk, then that which

e Ec.9.7. f Ro.13.7. g Ps.119.100; ch.7.17.

---

provided the food, gave directions to the servants, &c.

9. *And knew not whence it was.* This is said, probably, to indicate that his judgment was not biased by any favour, or any *want* of favour, toward Jesus. Had he known what was done, he would have been less likely to have judged impartially. As it is, we have his testimony that this was *real* wine, and of so fine a body and flavour as to surpass that which had been provided for the occasion. Everything in this miracle shows that there was no collusion or understanding between Jesus and any of the persons at the feast.

10. *Every man.* It is customary, or it is generally done. ¶ *When men have well drunk.* This word does not of necessity mean that they were *intoxicated*, though it is usually employed in that sense. It may mean when they have drunk sufficient, or to satiety; or have drunk so much as to produce hilarity, and to destroy the keenness of their taste, so that they could not readily distinguish the good from that which was worse. But this cannot be adduced in favour of drunkenness, even if it means to be intoxicated; for, 1st. It is not said of those who were present *at that feast*, but of what *generally* occurred. For anything that appears, at that feast all were perfectly temperate and sober. 2d. It is not the saying of Jesus that is here recorded, but of the governor of the feast, who is declaring what usually occurred as a fact. 3d. There is not any expression of opinion in regard to its *propriety*, or in approval of it, even by that governor. 4th. It does not appear that our Saviour even *heard* the observation. 5th. Still less is there any evidence that he *approved* such a state of things, or that he designed that it should take place here. Farther, the word translated "well drunk" cannot be shown to mean intoxication; but it *may* mean when they had drunk as much as they judged proper or as they desired, then the other was presented. It is clear that neither our Saviour, nor the sacred writer, nor the speaker here expresses any *approbation* of intemperance, nor is there the least evidence that anything of the kind occurred here. It is not proof that *we* approve of intemperance when we mention, as this man did, what occurs usually among men at feasts. ¶ *Is worse.* Is of an inferior quality. ¶ *The good wine.* This shows that this had all the qualities of real wine. We should not be deceived by the phrase "*good wine.*" *We* often use the phrase to denote that it is good in proportion to its strength and its power to intoxicate; but no such sense is to be attached to the word here. Pliny, Plutarch, and Horace describe wine as *good*, or mention that as *the best wine*, which was *harmless* or *innocent*—poculo vini *innocentis*. The most useful wine—*utilissimum vinum*—was that which had little strength; and the most wholesome wine—*saluberrimum vinum*—was that which had not been adulterated by "the addition of anything to the *must* or juice." Pliny expressly says that a "good wine" was one that was destitute of spirit (lib. iv. c. 13). It should not be assumed, therefore, that the "good wine" was *stronger* than the other: it is rather to be presumed that it was milder. The wine referred to here was doubtless such as was commonly drunk in Palestine. That was the pure juice of the grape. It was not brandied wine, nor drugged wine, nor wine compounded of various substances, such as we drink in this land. The common wine drunk in Palestine was that which was the simple juice of the grape. *We* use the word *wine* now to denote the kind of liquid which passes under that name in this country—always containing a considerable portion of alcohol—not only the alcohol produced by fermentation, but alcohol *added* to keep it or make it stronger. But we have no right to take *that* sense of the word, and go with it to the interpretation of the Scriptures. We should endeavour to place ourselves in

is worse; *but* thou hast kept [h]the good wine until now.

11 This beginning of miracles did Jesus in Cana of Galilee, [i]and

h Ps.104.15; Pr.9.2,5.

i ch.1.14.

the exact circumstances of those times, ascertain precisely what idea the word would convey to those who used it then, and apply *that* sense to the word in the interpretation of the Bible; and there is not the slightest evidence that the word so used would have conveyed any idea but that of the pure juice of the grape, nor the slightest circumstance mentioned in this account that would not be fully met by such a supposition. No man should adduce *this* instance in favour of drinking wine unless he can prove that the wine made in the "water-pots" of Cana was *just like* the wine which he proposes to drink. The Saviour's example may be always pleaded JUST AS IT WAS; but it is a matter of obvious and simple justice that we should find out exactly what the example was before we plead it. There is, moreover, no evidence that any other part of the water was converted into wine than that which was *drawn out* of the water-casks for the use of the guests. On this supposition, certainly, all the circumstances of the case are met, and the miracle would be more striking. All that was needed was to furnish a *supply* when the wine that had been prepared was nearly exhausted. The object was not to furnish a large quantity for future use. The miracle, too, would in this way be more apparent and impressive. On this supposition, the casks would *appear* to be filled with water *only;* as it was drawn out, it was pure wine. Who could doubt, then, that there was the exertion of miraculous power? All, therefore, that has been said about the Redeemer's furnishing a large quantity of wine for the newly-married pair, and about his benevolence in doing it, is wholly gratuitous. There is no evidence of it whatever; and it is not necessary to suppose it in order to an explanation of the circumstances of the case.

11. *This beginning of miracles.* This his first public miracle. This is declared by the sacred writer to be a *miracle*—that is, an exertion of divine power, producing a change of the substance of water into wine, which no human power could do. ¶ *Manifested forth.* Showed; exhibited. ¶ *His glory.* His power, and proper character as the Messiah; showed that he had divine power, and that God had certainly commissioned him. This is shown to be a *real* miracle by the following considerations: 1st. Real water was placed in the vessels. This the servants believed, and there was no possibility of deception. 2d. The water was placed where it was not *customary* to keep wine. It could not be *pretended* that it was merely a *mixture* of water and wine. 3d. It was judged to be wine without knowing whence it came. There was no agreement between Jesus and the governor of the feast to impose on the guests. 4th. It was a change which nothing but divine power could effect. He that can change *water* into a substance like the juice of the grape must be clothed with divine power. ¶ *Believed on him.* This does not mean that they did not *before* believe on him, but that their faith was *confirmed* or strengthened. They saw a miracle, and it satisfied them that he was the Messiah. *Before this* they *believed* on the testimony of John, and from conversation with Jesus (ch. i. 35–51); *now* they saw that he was invested with almighty power, and their faith was established.

From this narrative we may learn, 1st. That marriage is honourable, and that Jesus, if sought, will not refuse his presence and blessing on such an occasion. 2d. On such an occasion the presence and approbation of Christ *should* be sought. No compact formed on earth is more important; none enters so deeply into our comfort in this world; perhaps none will so much affect our destiny in the world to come. It should be entered into, then, in the fear of God. 3d. On all such occasions our conduct should be such that the presence of Jesus would be no interruption or disturbance. He is holy. He is always present in every place; and on all festival occasions our deportment should be such as that we should welcome the presence of the Lord Jesus Christ. *That is not a proper state of feeling or employment which would be interrupted by the presence of the Saviour.* 4th. Jesus delighted to do good. In the very beginning of his ministry he worked a miracle to show his benevolence. This was the appropriate commencement of a life in which he was to go about doing

manifested forth his glory; [k]and his disciples believed on him.

12 After this he went down to Capernaum, he, and his mother, and his brethren, and his disciples; and they continued there not many days.

k 1 Jn.5.13.

13 And the Jews' [l]passover was at hand, and [m]Jesus went up to Jerusalem,

14 And[n] found in the temple those that sold oxen, and sheep, and doves, and the changers of money sitting;

l Ex.12.14. *m* ver.23; ch.5.1; 6.4; 11.55. *n* Mat.21.12; Mar.11.15; Lu.19.45.

good. He seized every opportunity of doing it; and at a marriage feast, as well as among the sick and poor, he showed the character which he always sustained —that of a benefactor of mankind. 5th. An argument *cannot* be drawn from this instance in favour of intemperate drinking. There is no evidence that any who were present on that occasion drank too freely. 6th. Nor can an argument be drawn from this case in favour even of drinking wine such as we have. The common wine of Judea was the pure juice of the grape, without any mixture of alcohol, and was harmless. It was the common drink of the people, and did not tend to produce intoxication. *Our* wines are a *mixture* of the juice of the grape and of brandy, and often of infusions of various substances to give it colour and taste, and the appearance of wine. Those wines are little less injurious than brandy, and the habit of drinking them should be classed with the drinking of all other liquid fires.

The following table will show the danger of drinking the wines that are in common use:—

Brandy has fifty-three parts and 39 hundredths in a hundred of alcohol, or	53·39	per cent.
Rum	53·68	,,
Whisky, Scotch	54·32	,,
Holland Gin	51·60	,,
Port Wine, highest kind	25·83	,,
,, lowest ,,	21·40	,,
Madeira, highest ,,	29·42	,,
,, lowest ,,	19·34	,,
Lisbon	18·94	,,
Malaga	17·26	,,
Red Champagne	11·30	,,
White ,,	12·80	,,
Currant Wine	20·25	,,

It follows that a man who drinks two glasses of most of the wines used has taken as much alcohol as if he had taken one glass of brandy or whisky, and why should he not as well drink the alcohol in the brandy as in the wine? What difference can it make in morals? what difference in its effects on his system? The experience of the world has shown that water, pure water, is the most wholesome, safe, and invigorating drink for man.

12. *To Capernaum.* See Notes on Mat. iv. 13. ¶ *Not many days.* The reason why he remained there no longer was that the Passover was near, and they went up to Jerusalem to attend it.

13. *The Jews' passover.* The feast among the Jews called the Passover. See Notes on Mat. xxvi. 2-17. ¶ *And Jesus went up to Jerusalem.* Every male among the Jews was required to appear at this feast. Jesus, in obedience to the law, went up to observe it. This is the *first* Passover on which he attended after he entered on the work of the ministry. It is commonly supposed that he observed three others—one recorded Lu. vi. 1, another Jn. vi. 4, and the last one on the night before he was crucified, Jn. xi. 55. As his baptism when he entered on his ministry had taken place some time before this —probably not far from six months— it follows that the period of his ministry was not far from three years and a half, agreeably to the prophecy in Da. ix. 27.

14. *Found in the temple*, &c. The transaction here recorded is in almost all respects similar to that which has been explained in the Notes on Mat. xxi. 12. This took place at the *commencement* of his public ministry; that *at the close.* On each occasion he showed that his great regard was for the *pure worship* of his Father; and one great design of his coming was to reform the abuses which had crept into that worship, and to bring man to a proper regard for the glory of God. If it be asked how it was that those engaged in this traffic so readily *yielded* to Jesus of Nazareth, and that they left their gains and their property, and fled from the temple at the command of one so obscure as he was, it may be replied, 1st. That their *consciences* reproved them for their impiety, and they could not set up the *appearance* of self-defence. 2d. It was customary in the nation to cherish a profound regard for the authority of a

15 And when he had made a scourge of small cords, he drove them all out of the temple, and the sheep, and the oxen; and poured out the changers' money, and overthrew the tables;

16 And said unto them that sold doves, Take these things hence; make not my Father's house an house of merchandise.

17 And his disciples remembered that it was written, [o]The zeal of thine house hath eaten me up.

18 Then answered the Jews

o Ps.69.9.

prophet; and the appearance and manner of Jesus—so fearless, so decided, so authoritative—led them to suppose *he* was a prophet, and they were afraid to resist him. 3d. He *had* even then a wide reputation among the people, and it is not improbable that many supposed him to be the Messiah. 4th. Jesus on all occasions had a most wonderful control over men. None could resist him. There was something in his *manner*, as well as in his doctrine, that awed men, and made them tremble at his presence. Comp. Jn. xviii. 5, 6. On this occasion he had the *manner* of a prophet, the authority of God, and the testimony of their own consciences, and they could not, therefore, resist the authority by which he spoke.

Though Jesus thus purified the temple at the commencement of his ministry, yet in three years the same scene was to be repeated. See Mat. xxi. 12. And from this we may learn, 1st. How soon men forget the most solemn reproofs, and return to evil practices. 2d. That no sacredness of time or place will guard them from sin. In the very temple, under the very eye of God, these men soon returned to practices for which their consciences reproved them, and which they knew God disapproved. 3d. We see here how strong is the love of gain—the ruling passion of mankind. Not even the sacredness of the temple, the presence of God, the awful ceremonials of religion, deterred them from this unholy traffic. So wicked men and hypocrites will always turn *religion*, if possible, into gain; and not even the sanctuary, the Sabbath, or the most awful and sacred scenes, will deter them from schemes of gain. Comp. Am. viii. 5. So strong is this grovelling passion, and so deep is that depravity which fears not God, and regards not his Sabbaths, his sanctuary, or his law.

15. *A scourge.* A whip. ¶ *Of small cords.* This whip was made as an emblem of authority, and also for the purpose of driving from the temple the cattle which had been brought there for sale. There is no evidence that he used any violence to the men engaged in that unhallowed traffic. The original word implies that these *cords* were made of twisted *rushes* or *reeds*—probably the ancient material for making ropes.

17. *It was written*, &c. This is recorded in Ps. lxix. 9. Its meaning is, that he was affected with great zeal or concern for the pure worship of God. ¶ *The zeal of thine house. Zeal* is intense ardour in reference to any object. The *zeal of thine house* means extraordinary concern for the temple of God; intense solicitude that the worship there should be pure, and such as God would approve. ¶ *Hath eaten me up.* Hath absorbed me, or engaged my entire attention and affection; hath surpassed all other feelings, so that it may be said to be the one great absorbing affection and desire of the mind. Here is an example set for ministers and for all Christians. In Jesus this was the great commanding sentiment of his life. In us it should be also. In this manifestation of zeal he began and ended his ministry. In this we should begin and end our lives. We learn, also, that ministers of religion should aim to purify the church of God. Wicked men, conscience-smitten, will tremble when they see proper zeal in the ministers of Jesus Christ; and there is no combination of wicked men, and no form of depravity, that can stand before the faithful, zealous, pure preaching of the gospel. The preaching of every minister should be such that wicked men will feel that they must either become Christians or leave the house of God, or spend their lives there in the consciousness of guilt and the fear of hell.

18. *What sign*, &c. What *miracle* dost thou work? He assumed the character of a prophet. He was reforming, by his authority, the temple. It was natural to ask by what *authority* this was done; and as they had been accustomed

and said unto him, [p] What sign showest thou unto us, seeing that thou doest these things?

19 Jesus answered and said unto them, [q] Destroy this temple, and in three days I will raise it up.

20 Then said the Jews, Forty

p Mat.12.38,&c.; ch.6.30.

q Mat.26.61; 27.40.

to miracles in the life of Moses, and Elijah, and the other prophets, so they demanded evidence that *he* had authority thus to cleanse the house of God. ¶ *Seeing that thou doest.* Rather "by what *title* or *authority* thou doest these things." Our translation is ambiguous. They wished to know *by what miracle* he had shown, or could show, his right to do those things.

19. *Destroy this temple.* The evangelist informs us (ver. 21) that by *temple*, here, he meant his body. It is not improbable that he pointed with his finger to his body as he spoke. The word *destroy*, used here in the *imperative*, has rather the force of the *future.* Its meaning may thus be expressed: "You are now profaners of the temple of God. You have defiled the sanctuary; you have made it a place of traffic. You have also despised my authority, and been unmoved by the miracles which I have already wrought. But your wickedness will not end here. You will oppose me more and more; you will reject and despise me, until in your wickedness you will take my life and *destroy* my body." Here was therefore a distinct prediction both of his death and the cause of it. The word *temple*, or *dwelling*, was not unfrequently used by the Jews to denote the *body* as being the residence of the spirit, 2 Co. v. 1. Christians are not unfrequently called the temple of God, as being those in whom the Holy Spirit dwells on earth, 1 Co. iii. 16, 17; vi. 19; 2 Co. vi. 16. Our Saviour called his body a temple in accordance with the common use of language, and more particularly because *in him the fulness of the Godhead dwelt bodily*, Col. ii. 9. The *temple* at Jerusalem was the appropriate dwelling-place of God. His visible presence was there peculiarly manifested, 2 Ch. xxxvi. 15; Ps. lxxvi. 2. As the Lord Jesus was divine—as the fulness of the Godhead dwelt in him—so his body might be called a *temple.* ¶ *In three days I will raise it up.* The Jews had asked a *miracle* of him in proof of his authority—that is, a proof that he was the Messiah. He tells them that a full and decided proof of that would be his *resurrection from the dead.* Though they would not be satisfied by any other miracle, yet by this they ought to be convinced that he came from heaven, and was the long-expected Messiah. To the same evidence that he was the Christ he refers them on other occasions. See Mat. xii. 38, 39. Thus early did he foretell his death and resurrection, for at the beginning of his work he had a clear foresight of all that was to take place. This knowledge shows clearly that he came from heaven, and it evinces, also, the extent of his love—that he was *willing* to come to save us, knowing clearly what it would cost him. Had he come *without* such an expectation of suffering, his love might have been far less; but when he fully knew all that was before him, when he saw that it would involve him in contempt and death, it shows compassion "worthy of a God" that he was willing to endure the load of all our sorrows, and die to save us from death everlasting. When Jesus says, "*I* will raise it up," it is proof, also, of divine power. A mere *man* could not say this. No deceased *man* can have such power over his body; and there must have been, therefore, in the person of Jesus a nature superior to human to which the term "I" could be applied, and which had power to raise the dead—that is, which was divine.

20. *Then said the Jews*, &c. The Jews, either from the ambiguity of his language, or more probably from a design to cavil, understood him as speaking of the temple at Jerusalem. What he said here is all the evidence that they could adduce on his trial (Mat. xxvi. 61; Mar. xiv. 58), and they reproached him with it when on the cross, Mat. xxvii. 40. The Jews frequently perverted our Saviour's meaning. The language which he used was often that of parables or metaphor; and as they *sought* to misunderstand him and pervert his language, so he often left them to their own delusions, as he himself says, "that seeing they might not see, and hearing they might not understand," Mat. xiii. 13. This was a case

and six years was this temple in
building, and wilt thou rear it up
in three days?
21 But he spake of the [r]temple
of his body.
22 When, therefore, he was risen
from the dead, [s]his disciples remembered that he had said this
unto them; and they believed the
scripture, and the word which Jesus had said.
23 Now when he was in Jerusalem, at the passover, in the feast-
day, many believed in his name

r Ep.2.21,22; Col.2.9; He.8.2. s Lu.24.8.

---

which they *might*, if they had been disposed, have easily understood. They were in the temple; the conversation was about the temple; and though he probably pointed to his body, or designated it in some plain way, yet they *chose* to understand him as referring to the temple itself; and as it appeared so improbable that he could raise up that in three days, they sought to pervert his words and pour ridicule on his pretensions. ¶ *Forty and six years*, &c. The temple in which they then were was that which was commonly called *the second temple*, built after the return of the Jews from Babylon. See Notes on Mat. xxi. 12. This temple Herod the Great commenced repairing, or began to rebuild, in the eighteenth year of his reign—that is, *sixteen years* before the birth of Christ (Jos. *Ant.*, b. xv. § 1). The main body of the temple he completed in *nine years and a half* (Jos. *Ant.*, xv. 5, 6), yet the temple, with its outbuildings, was not entirely complete in the time of our Saviour. Herod continued to ornament it and to perfect it even till the time of Agrippa (Jos. *Ant.*, b. xx. ch. viii. § 11). As Herod began to rebuild the temple sixteen years before the birth of Jesus, and as what is here mentioned happened in the thirtieth year of the age of Jesus, so the time which had been occupied in it was *forty-six years*. This circumstance is one of the many in the New Testament which show the accuracy of the evangelists, and which prove that they were well acquainted with what they recorded. It demonstrates that their narration is true. Impostors do not trouble themselves to be very accurate about names and dates, and there is nothing in which they are more liable to make mistakes. ¶ *Wilt thou*, &c. This is an expression of contempt. Herod, with all his wealth and power, had been engaged in this work almost half a century. Can you, an obscure and unknown Galilean, accomplish it in three days? The thing, in their judgment, was ridiculous, and showed, as *they* supposed, that he had no authority to do what he had done in the temple.

22. *When he was risen from the dead*, &c. This saying of our Saviour at that time seemed obscure and difficult. The disciples did not understand it, but they treasured it up in their memory, and the event showed what was its true meaning. Many prophecies are obscure when spoken which are perfectly plain when the event takes place. We learn from this, also, the importance of treasuring up the truths of the Bible *now*, though we may not perfectly understand them. Hereafter they may be plain to us. It is therefore important that *children* should learn the truths of the sacred Scriptures. Treasured up in their memory, they may not be understood *now*, but hereafter they may be clear to them. Every one engaged in teaching a Sunday-school, therefore, may be imparting instruction which may be understood, and may impart comfort, long after the teacher has gone to eternity. ¶ *They believed.* That is, *after* he rose from the dead. ¶ *The scripture.* The Old Testament, which predicted his resurrection. Reference here must be made to Ps. xvi. 10, comp. Ac. ii. 27–32, xiii. 35–37; Ps. ii. 7, comp. Ac. xiii. 33. They understood those Scriptures in a sense different from what they did before. ¶ *The word which Jesus had said.* The prediction which he had made respecting his resurrection in this place and on other occasions. See Mat. xx. 19; Lu. xviii. 32, 33.

23. *Feast*-day. Feast. During the celebration of the Passover, which continued eight days. ¶ *Miracles which he did.* These miracles are not particularly recorded. Jesus took occasion to work miracles, and to preach at that time, for a great multitude were present from all parts of Judea. It was a favourable opportunity for making known his doctrines and showing the evidence that he was the Christ, and he embraced it.

when they saw the miracles which
he did.
24 But Jesus did not commit
himself unto them, because [t]he
knew all *men*,
25 And needed not that any
should testify of man; for he knew
what was in man.

t 1 Sa.16.7; 1 Ch.28.9; 29.17; Je.17.9,10; Mat.9.4; ch. 16.30; Ac.1.24; Re.2.23.

CHAPTER III.

THERE was a man of the Pharisees, named [a]Nicodemus, a
ruler of the Jews:
2 The same came to Jesus by
night, and said unto him, Rabbi,
we know that thou art a teacher
come from God; [b]for no man can

a ch.7.50,51; 19.39. *b* ch.9.16,33; Ac.2.22.

We should always seek and embrace opportunities of doing good, and we should not be *deterred*, but rather *excited*, by the multitude around us to make known our real sentiments on the subject of religion.

24. *Did not commit himself.* The word translated *commit* here is the same which in ver. 23 is translated *believed.* It means to put *trust* or *confidence in.* Jesus did not put *trust* or *reliance* in them. He did not leave himself in their hands. He acted cautiously and prudently. The proper time for him to die had not come, and he secured his own safety. The *reason* why he did not commit himself to them is *that he knew all men.* He knew the *inconstancy* and *fickleness* of the multitude. He knew how easily they might be turned against him by the Jewish leaders, and how unsafe he would be if they should be moved to sedition and tumult.

25. *Should testify of man.* Should give him the character of any man. ¶ *He knew what was in man.* This he did because he had made all (ch. i. 3), and because he was God, ch. i. 1. There can be no higher evidence than this that he was omniscient, and was therefore divine. To search the heart is the prerogative of God alone (Je. xvii. 10); and as Jesus knew what was in *these disciples*, and as it is expressly said that he knew what was in *man*—that is, in *all men*—so it follows that he must be equal with God. As he knows *all*, he is acquainted with the *false* pretentions and professions of hypocrites. None can deceive him. He also knows the wants and desires of all his *real* friends. He hears their groans, he sees their sighs, he counts their tears, and in the day of need will come to their relief.

CHAPTER III.

1. *A man of the Pharisees.* A Pharisee. See Notes on Mat. iii. 7. ¶ *Nicodemus, a ruler of the Jews.* One of the *Sanhedrim*, or great council of the nation. He is twice mentioned after this as being friendly to our Saviour; in the first instance as advocating his cause, and defending him against the unjust suspicion of the Jews (ch. vii. 50), and in the second instance as one who came to aid in embalming his body, ch. xix. 39. It will be recollected that the design of *John* in writing this gospel was to show that Jesus was the *Messiah.* To do this he here adduces the testimony of one of the *rulers* of the Jews, who early became convinced of it, and who retained the belief of it until the death of Jesus.

2. *The same came to Jesus.* The design of his coming seems to have been to inquire more fully of Jesus what was the doctrine which he came to teach. He seems to have been convinced that he was the Messiah, and desired to be farther instructed *in private* respecting his doctrine. It was not usual for a man of rank, power, and riches to come to inquire of Jesus in this manner; yet we may learn that the most favourable opportunity for teaching such men the nature of personal religion is when they are alone. Scarcely any man, of any rank, will refuse to converse on this subject when addressed respectfully and tenderly *in private.* In the midst of their companions, or engaged in business, they may refuse to listen or may cavil. When *alone*, they will hear the voice of entreaty and persuasion, and be willing to converse on the great subjects of judgment and eternity. Thus Paul says (Ga. ii. 2), "*privately to them which are of reputation;*" evincing his consummate prudence, and his profound knowledge of human nature. ¶ *By night.* It is not mentioned why he came by night. It might have been that, being a member of the Sanhedrim, he was engaged all the day; or it may have been because the Lord Jesus was occupied all the day in teaching publicly and in working miracles, and that there was no oppor-

do these miracles that thou doest
except [c]God be with him.

[c] Ac.10.38.

3 Jesus answered and said unto
him, Verily, verily, I say unto thee,

---

tunity for conversing with him as freely as he desired; or it may have been that he was afraid of the ridicule and contempt of those in power, and fearful that it might involve him in danger if publicly known; or it may have been that he was afraid that if it were publicly known that he was disposed to favour the Lord Jesus, it might provoke more opposition against *him* and endanger his life. As no *bad* motive is imputed to him, it is most in accordance with Christian charity to suppose that his motives were such as God would approve, especially as the Saviour did not reprove him. We should not be disposed to blame men where Jesus did not, and we should desire to find *goodness* in every man rather than be ever on the search for evil motives. See 1 Co. xiii. 4–7. We may learn here, 1st. That our Saviour, though engaged during the day, did not refuse to converse with an inquiring sinner at night. Ministers of the gospel at all times should welcome those who are asking the way to life. 2d. That it is *proper* for men, even those of elevated rank, to *inquire* on the subject of religion. Nothing is so important as religion, and no temper of mind is more lovely than a disposition to ask the way to heaven. *At all times* men should seek the way of salvation, and especially in times of great religious excitement they should make inquiry. At Jerusalem, at the time referred to here, there was great solicitude. Many believed on Jesus. He wrought miracles, and preached, and many were converted. There was what would now be called *a revival of religion*, having all the features of a work of grace. At such a season it was proper, as it is now, that not only the poor, but the rich and great, should inquire the path to life. ¶ *Rabbi.* This was a title of respect conferred on distinguished Jewish teachers, somewhat in the way that the title *doctor of divinity* is now conferred. See Notes on ch. i. 38. Our Saviour forbade his disciples to wear that title (see Notes on Mat. xxiii. 8), though it was proper for *him* to do it, as being the great *Teacher* of mankind. It literally signifies *great*, and was given by Nicodemus, doubtless, because Jesus gave distinguished proofs that he came as a teacher from God. ¶ *We know.* I know, and those with whom I am connected. Perhaps he was acquainted with some of the Pharisees who entertained the same opinion about Jesus that he did, and *he* came to be more fully confirmed in the belief. ¶ *Come from God.* Sent by God. This implies his *readiness* to hear him, and his *desire* to be instructed. He acknowledges the divine mission of Jesus, and delicately asks him to instruct him in the truth of religion. When we read the words of Jesus in the Bible, it should be with a belief that he came from God, and was therefore qualified and authorized to teach us the way of life. ¶ *These miracles.* The miracles which he wrought in the temple and at Jerusalem, ch. ii. 23. ¶ *Except God be with him.* Except God *aid* him, and except his instructions are *approved* by God. Miracles show that a prophet or religious teacher comes from God, because God would not work a miracle in attestation of a falsehood or to give countenance to a false teacher. If God gives a man power to work a miracle, it is proof that he approves the teaching of that man, and the miracle is the proof or the credential that he came from God.

3. *Verily, verily.* An expression of strong affirmation, denoting the *certainty* and the *importance* of what he was about to say. Jesus proceeds to state one of the fundamental and indispensable doctrines of his religion. It may seem remarkable that he should introduce this subject in this manner; but it should be remembered that Nicodemus acknowledged that he was a *teacher* come from God; that he *implied* by that his readiness and desire to receive instruction; and that it is not wonderful, therefore, that Jesus should *commence* with one of the fundamental truths of his religion. It is no part of Christianity to *conceal* anything. Jesus declared to every man, high or low, rich or poor, the most humbling truths of the gospel. Nothing was kept back for fear of offending men of wealth or power; and for them, as well as the most poor and lowly, it was declared to be indispensable to experience, as the first thing in religion, a change of heart and of life. ¶ *Except a man.* This is a universal form of expression de-

Except[d] a man be born [1]again, he cannot see the kingdom of God.

4 Nicodemus saith unto him, How can a man be born when he

d ch.1.13; Ga.6.15; Ep.2.1; Tit.3.5; Ja.1.18; 1 Pe.1. 23; 1 Jn.2.29; 3.9. 1 or, *from above.*

signed to include all mankind. Of *each and every* man it is certain that unless he is born again he cannot see the kingdom of God. It includes, therefore, men of every character and rank, and nation, moral and immoral, rich and poor, in office and out of office, old and young, bond and free, the slave and his master, Jew and Gentile. It is clear that our Saviour intended to convey to *Nicodemus* the idea, also, that *he* must be born again. It was not sufficient to be a Jew, or to acknowledge him to be a teacher sent by God—that is, the Messiah; it was necessary, in addition to this, to experience in his own soul that great change called the *new birth* or regeneration. ¶ *Be born again.* The word translated here *again* means also *from above*, and is so rendered in the margin. It is evident, however, that Nicodemus understood it not as referring to a birth *from above*, for if he had he would not have asked the question in ver. 4. It is probable that in the language which he used there was not the same ambiguity that there is in the Greek. The ancient versions all understood it as meaning *again*, or *the second time*. Our natural birth introduces us to light, is the commencement of life, throws us amid the works of God, and is the beginning of our existence; but it also introduces us to a world of sin. We early go astray. All men transgress. The imagination of the thoughts of the heart is evil from the youth up. We are conceived in sin and brought forth in iniquity, and there is none that doeth good, no, not one. The carnal mind is enmity against God, and by nature we are dead in trespasses and sins, Ge. viii. 21; Ps. xiv. 2, 3; li. 5; Ro. i. 29-32; iii. 10-20; viii. 7. All sin exposes men to misery here and hereafter. To escape from sin, to be happy in the world to come, it is necessary that man should be changed in his principles, his feelings, and his manner of life. This change, or the beginning of this new life, is called the *new birth*, or *regeneration*. It is so called because in many respects it has a striking analogy to the natural birth. It is the beginning of spiritual life. It introduces us to the light of the gospel. It is the moment when we really begin to live to any purpose. It is the moment when God reveals himself to us as our reconciled Father, and we are adopted into his family as his sons. And as every man is a sinner, it is necessary that each one should experience this change, or he cannot be happy or saved. This doctrine was not unknown to the Jews, and was particularly predicted as a doctrine that would be taught in the times of the Messiah. See De. x. 16; Je. iv. 4; xxxi. 33; Eze. xi. 19; xxxvi. 25; Ps. li. 12. The change in the New Testament is elsewhere called the *new creation* (2 Co. v. 17; Ga. vi. 15), and *life from the dead*, or a resurrection, Ep. ii. 1; Jn. v. 21, 24. ¶ *He cannot see.* To *see*, here, is put evidently for enjoying—or he cannot be fitted for it and partake of it. ¶ *The kingdom of God.* Either in this world or in that which is to come—that is, heaven. See Notes on Mat. iii. 2. The meaning is, that the kingdom which Jesus was about to set up was so pure and holy that it was indispensable that every man should experience this change, or he could not partake of its blessings. This is solemnly declared by the Son of God by an affirmation equivalent to an oath, and there can be no possibility, therefore, of entering heaven without experiencing the change which the Saviour contemplated by the *new birth*. And it becomes every man, as in the presence of a holy God before whom he must soon appear, to ask himself whether he has experienced this change, and if he has not, to give no rest to his eyes until he has sought the mercy of God, and implored the aid of his Spirit that his heart may be renewed.

4. *How can a man*, &c. It may seem remarkable that Nicodemus understood the Saviour *literally*, when the expression *to be born again* was in common use among the Jews to denote a change from *Gentilism* to *Judaism* by becoming a proselyte by *baptism*. The word with them meant a change from the state of a heathen to that of a Jew. But they never used it as applicable to *a Jew*, because they supposed that by his birth every Jew was entitled to all the privileges of the people of God. When, therefore, our Saviour used it of *a Jew*, when he affirmed its necessity of *every*

is old? Can he enter the second time into his mother's womb and be born?

5 Jesus answered, Verily, verily, I say unto thee, Except a man be born of [e]water and *of* [f]the Spirit, he cannot enter into the kingdom of God.

6 That[g] which is born of the

e Mar.16.16; Ac.2.38. f Ro.8.2; 1 Co.2.12. g 1 Co.15.47-49; 2 Co.5.17.

---

man, Nicodemus supposed that there was an absurdity in the doctrine, or something that surpassed his comprehension, and he therefore asked whether it was possible that Jesus could teach so absurd a doctrine—as he could conceive no other sense as applicable to a Jew—as that he should, when old, enter a second time into his mother's womb and be born. And we may learn from this—1st. That prejudice leads men to misunderstand the plainest doctrines of religion. 2d. That things which are at first incomprehensible or apparently absurd, may, when explained, become clear. The doctrine of regeneration, so difficult to Nicodemus, is plain to a *child* that is born of the Spirit. 3d. Those in high rank in life, and who are learned, are often most ignorant about the plainest matters of religion. It is often wonderful that they exhibit so little acquaintance with the most simple subjects pertaining to the soul, and so much absurdity in their views. 4th. A doctrine is not to be *rejected* because the rich and the great do not believe or understand it. The doctrine of regeneration was not *false* because Nicodemus did not comprehend it.

5. *Be born of water.* By *water*, here, is evidently signified *baptism.* Thus the word is used in Ep. v. 26; Tit. iii. 5. Baptism was practised by the Jews in receiving a Gentile as a proselyte. It was practised by John among the Jews; and Jesus here says that it is an ordinance of his religion, and the sign and seal of the renewing influences of his Spirit. So he said (Mar. xvi. 16), "He that believeth *and is baptized* shall be saved." It is clear from these places, and from the example of the apostles (Ac. ii. 38, 41; viii. 12, 13, 36, 38; ix. 18; x. 47, 48; xvi. 15, 33; xviii. 8; xxii. 16; Ga. iii. 27), that they considered this ordinance as binding on all who professed to love the Lord Jesus. And though it cannot be said that none who are not baptized can be saved, yet Jesus meant, undoubtedly, to be understood as affirming that this was to be the regular and uniform way of entering into his church; that it was the appropriate mode of making a profession of religion; and that a man who neglected this, when the duty was made known to him, neglected a plain command of God. It is clear, also, that any other command of God might as well be neglected or violated as this, and that it is the duty of everyone not only to love the Saviour, but to make an acknowledgment of that love by being baptized, and by devoting himself thus to his service. But, lest Nicodemus should suppose that this was all that was meant, he added that it was necessary that he should *be born of the Spirit* also. This was predicted of the Saviour, that he should *baptize with the Holy Ghost and with fire*, Mat. iii. 11. By this is clearly intended that the heart must be changed by the agency of the Holy Spirit; that the love of sin must be abandoned; that man must repent of crime and turn to God; that he must renounce all his evil propensities, and give himself to a life of prayer and holiness, of meekness, purity, and benevolence. This great change is in the Scripture ascribed uniformly to the Holy Spirit, Tit. iii. 5; 1 Th. i. 6; Ro. v. 5; 1 Pe. i. 22. ¶ *Cannot enter into.* This is the way, the appropriate way, of entering into the kingdom of the Messiah here and hereafter. He cannot enter into the true church here, or into heaven in the world to come, except in connection with a change of heart, and by the proper expression of that change in the ordinances appointed by the Saviour.

6. *That which is born of the flesh.* To show the *necessity* of this change, the Saviour directs the attention of Nicodemus to the natural condition of man. By *that which is born of the flesh* he evidently intends man as he is by nature, in the circumstances of his natural birth. Perhaps, also, he alludes to the question asked by Nicodemus, whether a man could be born when he was old? Jesus tells him that if this could be, it would not answer any valuable purpose; he would still have the same propensities and passions. Another change was therefore indispensable. ¶ *Is flesh.*

flesh is flesh; and that which is born of the Spirit is spirit.

7 Marvel not that I said unto thee, Ye must be born [2]again.

8 The wind bloweth where it listeth, and thou hearest the sound thereof, but canst not tell whence it cometh and whither it goeth; [h]so is every one that is born of the Spirit.

2 or, *from above*.

h 1 Co.2.11.

Partakes of the nature of the parent. Comp. Ge. v. 3. As the parents are corrupt and sinful, so will be their descendants. See Job xiv. 4. And as the parents are *wholly* corrupt by nature, so their children will be the same. The word *flesh* here is used as meaning *corrupt, defiled, sinful*. The *flesh* in the Scriptures is often used to denote the sinful propensities and passions of our nature, as those propensities are supposed to have their seat in the animal nature. "The works of the flesh are manifest, which are these: adultery, fornication, uncleanness, lasciviousness," &c., Ga. v. 19, 20. See also Ep. ii. 3; 1 Pe. iii. 21; ii. 18; 1 Jn. ii. 16; Ro. viii. 5. ¶ *Is born of the Spirit*. Of the Spirit of God, or by the agency of the Holy Ghost. ¶ *Is spirit*. Is spiritual, *like* the spirit, that is, holy, pure. Here we learn, 1st. That all men are by nature sinful. 2d. That none are renewed but by the Spirit of God. If man did the work himself, it would be still carnal and impure. 3d. That the effect of the new birth is to make men *holy*. And, 4th. That no man can have evidence that he is born again who is not holy, and just in proportion as he becomes pure in his life will be the evidence that he is born of the Spirit.

7. *Marvel not*. Wonder not. It is possible that Nicodemus in some way still expressed a doubt of the doctrine, and Jesus took occasion in a very striking manner to illustrate it.

8. *The wind bloweth*, &c. Nicodemus had objected to the doctrine because he did not understand how it *could be*. Jesus shows him that he ought not to reject it on that account, for he constantly believed things quite as difficult. It might appear incomprehensible, but it was to be judged of by its *effects*. As in this case of the wind, the *effects* were seen, the sound was heard, important *changes* were produced by it, trees and clouds were moved, yet the wind is *not seen*, nor do we know whence it comes, nor by what laws it is governed; so it is with the operations of the Spirit. We see the changes produced. Men just now sinful become holy; the thoughtless become serious; the licentious become pure; the vicious, moral; the moral, religious; the prayerless, prayerful; the rebellious and obstinate, meek, and mild, and gentle. When we see such changes, we ought no more to doubt that they are produced by some *cause*—by some mighty agent, than when we see the trees moved, or the waters of the ocean piled on heaps, or feel the cooling effects of a summer's breeze. In those cases we attribute it to the *wind*, though we see it not, and though we do not understand its operations. We may learn, hence, 1st. That the proper evidence of conversion is the *effect* on the life. 2d. That we are not too curiously to search for the *cause* or *manner* of the change. 3d. That God has power over the most hardened sinner to change him, as he has power over the loftiest oak, to bring it down by a sweeping blast. 4th. That there may be great *variety* in the modes of the operation of the Spirit. As the *wind* sometimes sweeps with a tempest, and prostrates all before it, and sometimes breathes upon us in a mild evening zephyr, so it is with the operations of the Spirit. The sinner sometimes trembles and is prostrate before the truth, and sometimes is sweetly and gently drawn to the cross of Jesus. ¶ *Where it listeth*. Where it *wills* or *pleases*. ¶ *So is every one*, &c. Every one that is born of the Spirit is, in some respects, like the effects of the wind. You see it not, you cannot discern its laws, but you see *its effects*, and you know therefore that it does exist and operate. Nicodemus's objection was, that he could not *see* this change, or perceive *how* it could be. Jesus tells him that he should not reject a doctrine merely because he could not understand it. Neither could the *wind* be seen, but its effects were well known, and no one doubted the existence or the power of the agent. Comp. Ec. xi. 5.

9. *How can these things be?* Nicodemus was still unwilling to admit the doctrine unless he understood it; and we have here an instance of a man of rank stum-

9 Nicodemus answered and said
unto him, How can these things
be?
10 Jesus answered and said unto
him, Art thou a master of Israel,
and knowest not these things?
11 Verily, verily, I say unto thee,
[i] We speak that we do know, and

i 1 Jn.1.1-3.

bling at one of the plainest doctrines of religion, and unwilling to admit a truth because he could not understand *how* it could be, when he daily admitted the truth of facts in other things which he could as little comprehend. And we may learn, 1st. That men will often admit facts on other subjects, and be greatly perplexed by similar facts in religion. 2d. That no small part of men's difficulties are because they cannot understand *how* or *why* a thing is. 3d. That men of rank and learning are as likely to be perplexed by these things as those in the obscurest and humblest walks of life. 4th. That this is one reason why such men, particularly, so often reject the truths of the gospel. And, 5th. That this is a very *unwise* treatment of truth, and a way which they do not apply to other things. If the wind cools and refreshes me in summer—if it prostrates the oak or lashes the sea into foam—if it destroys my house or my grain, it matters little *how* it does this; and so of the Spirit. If it renews my heart, humbles my pride, subdues my sin, and comforts my soul, it is a matter of little importance *how* it does all this. Sufficient for me is it to know that it *is* done, and to taste the blessings which flow from the renewing and sanctifying grace of God.

10. *A master of Israel.* A *teacher* of Israel; the same word that in the second verse is translated *teacher.* As such a *teacher* he ought to have understood this doctrine. It was not *new*, but was clearly taught in the Old Testament. See particularly Ps. li. 10, 16, 17; Eze. xi. 19; xxxvi. 26. It may seem surprising that a man whose business it was to teach the people should be a stranger to so plain and important a doctrine; but when worldly-minded men are placed in offices of religion—when they seek those offices for the sake of ease or reputation, it is no wonder that they are strangers to the plain truths of the Bible; and there have been many, and there are still, who are in the ministry itself, to whom the plainest doctrines of the gospel are obscure. No man can understand the Bible fully unless he is a humble Christian, and the easiest way to comprehend the truths of religion is to give the heart to God and live to his glory. A child thus may have more *real* knowledge of the way of salvation than many who are pretended masters and teachers of Israel, Jn. vii. 17; Mat. xi. 25; Ps. viii. 2, compared with Mat. xxi. 16. ¶ *Of Israel.* Of the Jews; of the Jewish nation.

11. *We speak.* Jesus here speaks in the *plural* number, including himself and those engaged with him in preaching the gospel. Nicodemus had said (ver. 2), "*We* know that thou art," &c., including himself and those with whom he acted. Jesus in reply said, *We*, who are engaged in spreading the new doctrines about which you have come to inquire, speak what we know. We do not deliver doctrines which we do not *practically* understand. This is a positive affirmation of Jesus, which he had a right to make about his new doctrine. *He* knew its truth, and those who came into his kingdom knew it also. We learn here, 1st. That the Pharisees taught doctrines which they did not practically understand. They taught much truth (Mat. xxiii. 2), but they were deplorably ignorant of the plainest matters in their practical application. 2d. Every minister of the gospel ought to be able to appeal to his own experience, and to say that he *knows* the truth which he is communicating to others. 3d. Every Sunday-school teacher should be able to say, "I *know* what I am communicating; I have experienced what is meant by the new birth, and the love of God, and the religion which I am teaching." ¶ *Testify.* Bear witness to. ¶ *That we have seen.* Jesus had seen by his omniscient eye all the operations of the Spirit on the hearts of men. His ministers have seen its effects as we see the effects of the wind, and, having seen men changed from sin to holiness, they are qualified to bear witness to the truth and reality of the change. Every successful minister of the gospel thus becomes a witness of the saving power of the gospel. ¶ *Ye receive not.* Ye Pharisees. Though we give evidence of the truth of the new religion; though miracles are wrought, and proof is given that this doctrine

testify that we have seen; and ye receive not our witness.

12 If I have told you earthly things and ye believe not, how shall ye believe if I tell you *of* heavenly things?

13 And[k] no man hath ascended up to heaven, but he that came

k Ep.4.9,10.

came from heaven, yet you reject it. ¶ *Our witness.* Our testimony. The *evidence* which is furnished by miracles and by the saving power of the gospel. Men reject revelation though it is attested by the strongest evidence, and though it is constantly producing the most desirable changes in the hearts and lives of men.

12. *If I have told you earthly things.* Things which *occur* on earth. Not *sensual* or *worldly* things, for Jesus had said nothing of these; but he had told him of *operations of the Spirit* which had occurred *on earth*, whose effects were visible, and which *might* be, therefore, believed. These were the *plainest* and most obvious of the doctrines of religion. ¶ *How shall ye believe.* How *will* you believe. Is there any probability that you will understand them? ¶ *Heavenly things.* Things pertaining to the government of God and his doings in the heavens; things which are removed from human view, and which cannot be subjected to human sight; the more profound and inscrutable things pertaining to the redemption of men. Learn hence, 1st. The height and depth of the doctrines of religion. There is much that we cannot yet understand. 2d. The feebleness of our understandings and the corruptions of our hearts are the real causes why doctrines of religion are so little understood by us. 3d. There is before us a vast eternity, and there are profound wonders of God's government, to be the study of the righteous, and to be seen and admired by them for ever and ever.

13. *And no man hath ascended into heaven.* No man, therefore, is qualified to speak of heavenly things, ver. 12. To speak of those things requires intimate acquaintance with them—demands that we have *seen* them; and as no one has ascended into heaven and returned, so no one is qualified to speak of them but He who came down from heaven. This does not mean that no one had *gone* to heaven or had been saved, for Enoch and Elijah had been borne there (Ge. v. 24; comp. He. xi. 5; 2 Ki. ii. 11), and Abraham, Isaac, and Jacob, and others were there; but it means that no one had ascended and *returned*, so as to be qualified to speak of the things there. ¶ *But he that came down*, &c. The Lord Jesus. He is represented as coming down, because, being equal with God, he took upon himself our nature, Jn. i. 14; Phi. ii. 6, 7. He is represented as *sent* by the Father, Jn. iii. 17, 34; Ga. iv. 4; 1 Jn. iv. 9, 10. ¶ *The Son of man.* Called thus from his being *a man;* from his interest in man; and as expressive of his regard for man. It is a favourite title which the Lord Jesus gives to himself. ¶ *Which is in heaven.* This is a very remarkable expression. Jesus, the Son of man, was then bodily on earth conversing with Nicodemus; yet he declares that he is *at the same time* in heaven. This can be understood only as referring to the fact that he had two natures—that his *divine nature* was in heaven, and his *human nature* on earth. Our Saviour is frequently spoken of in this manner. Comp. Jn. vi. 62; xvii. 5; 2 Co. viii. 9. As Jesus was *in* heaven—as his proper abode was there—he was fitted to speak of heavenly things, and to declare the will of God to man. And we may learn, 1st. That the truth about the deep things of God is not to be learned of *men.* No one has ascended to heaven and returned to tell us what is there; and no infidel, no mere man, no prophet, is qualified of himself to speak of them. 2d. That all the light which we are to expect on those subjects is to be sought in the Scriptures. It is only Jesus and his inspired apostles and evangelists that can speak of those things. 3d. It is not wonderful that some things in the Scriptures are mysterious. They are about things which we have not seen, and we must receive them on the *testimony* of one who *has* seen them. 4th. The Lord Jesus is divine. He was in heaven while on earth. He had, therefore, a nature far above the human, and is equal with the Father, ch. i. 1.

14. *And as Moses.* Jesus proceeds in this and the following verses to state the reason why he came into the world; and, in order to this, he illustrates his design, and the efficacy of his coming, by a reference to the case of the brazen

down from heaven, *even* the Son of man which is in heaven.

14 And[l] as Moses lifted up the serpent in the wilderness, even so must the Son of man be lifted up;

15 That[m] whosoever believeth in him should not perish, but have eternal life.

16 For[n] God so loved the world that he gave his only-begotten

l Nu.21.9. *m* ver.36; He.7.25. *n* 1 Jn.4.9.

serpent, recorded in Nu. xxi. 8, 9. The people were bitten by flying fiery serpents. There was no cure for the bite. Moses was directed to make an *image* of the serpent, and place it in sight of the people, that they might look on it and be healed. There is no evidence that this was intended to be a *type* of the Messiah, but it is used by Jesus as strikingly *illustrating* his work. Men are sinners. There is no cure by human means for the maladies of the soul; and as the people who were bitten might look on the image of the serpent and be healed, so may sinners look to the Saviour and be cured of the moral maladies of our nature. ¶ *Lifted up.* Erected on a pole. Placed on high, so that it might be seen by the people. ¶ *The serpent.* The *image* of a serpent made of brass. ¶ *In the wilderness.* Near the land of Edom. In the desert and desolate country to the south of Mount Hor, Nu. xxi. 4. ¶ *Even so.* In a similar *manner* and with a similar *design.* He here refers, doubtless, to his own death. Comp. Jn. xii. 32; viii. 28. The points of resemblance between *his* being lifted up and that of the brazen serpent seem to be these: 1st. In each case those who are to be benefited can be aided in no other way. The bite of the serpent was deadly, and could be healed only by looking on the brazen serpent; and sin is deadly in its nature, and can be removed only by looking on the cross. 2d. The mode of their being lifted up. The brazen serpent was in the sight of the people. So Jesus was exalted from the earth—raised on a tree or cross. 3d. The design was similar. The one was to save the life, the other the soul; the one to save from temporal, the other from eternal death. 4th. The manner of the cure was similar. The people of Israel were *to look* on the serpent and be healed, and so sinners are to look on the Lord Jesus that they may be saved. ¶ *Must.* It is proper; necessary; indispensable, if men are saved. Comp. Lu. xxiv. 26; xxii. 42. ¶ *The Son of man.* The Messiah.

15. *That whosoever.* This shows the fulness and freeness of the gospel. All may come and be saved. ¶ *Believeth in him.* Whosoever puts *confidence* in him as able and willing to save. All who feel that they are sinners, that they have no righteousness of their own, and are willing to look to him as their only Saviour. ¶ *Should not perish.* They are in danger, by nature, of *perishing*—that is, of sinking down to the pains of hell; of "being *punished with everlasting destruction* from the presence of the Lord and from the glory of his power," 2 Th. i. 9. All who believe on Jesus shall be saved from this condemnation and be raised up to eternal life. And from this we learn, 1st. That there is salvation in no other. 2d. That salvation is here full and free for all who will come. 3d. That it is easy. What was more easy for a poor, wounded, dying Israelite, bitten by a poisonous serpent, than to *look up* to a brazen serpent? So with the poor, lost, dying sinner. And what more foolish than for such a wounded, dying man to *refuse* to look on a remedy so easy and effectual? So nothing is more foolish than for a lost and dying sinner to *refuse* to look on God's only Son, exalted on a cross to die for the sins of men, and able to save to the uttermost *all* who come to God by him.

16. *For God so loved.* This does not mean that God *approved* the conduct of men, but that he had *benevolent* feelings toward them, or was *earnestly desirous* of their happiness. God hates wickedness, but he still desires the happiness of those who are sinful. *He hates the sin, but loves the sinner.* A parent may love his child and desire his welfare, and yet be strongly opposed to the conduct of that child. When we approve the *conduct* of another, this is the love of *complacency;* when we desire simply their *happiness*, this is the love of *benevolence.* ¶ *The world.* All mankind. It does not mean any particular *part* of the world, but *man as man—the race* that had rebelled and that deserved to die. See Jn. vi. 33; xvii. 21. His love for the world, or for all mankind, in giving his Son, was shown by these circumstances: 1st. All the world was in

Son, that whosoever believeth in
him should not perish, but have
everlasting life.
17 For[o] God sent not his Son
into the world to condemn the
world, but that the world through
him might be saved.
18 He[p] that believeth on him is
not condemned; but he that believeth not is condemned already,

o Lu.9.56.

p ch.6.40,47.

ruin, and exposed to the wrath of God. 2d. All men were in a hopeless condition. 3d. God *gave* his Son. Man had no *claim* on him; it was a gift—an undeserved gift. 4th. He gave him up to extreme sufferings, even the bitter pains of death on the cross. 5th. It was for all the world. He tasted "death for every man," He. ii. 9. He "died for all," 2 Co. v. 15. "He is the propitiation for the sins of the whole world," 1 Jn. ii. 2. ¶ *That he gave.* It was a free and unmerited gift. Man had no claim; and when there was no eye to pity or arm to save, it pleased God to *give* his Son into the hands of men to die in their stead, Ga. i. 4; Ro. viii. 32; Lu. xxii. 19. It was the mere movement of love; the expression of eternal compassion, and of a desire that sinners should not perish for ever. ¶ *His only-begotten Son.* See Notes on Jn. i. 14. This is the highest expression of love of which we can conceive. A parent who should give up his only son to die for others who are guilty—if this could or might be done—would show higher love than could be manifested in any other way. So it shows the depth of the love of God, that he was willing to give his only Son into the hands of sinful men that he might be slain, and thus redeem them from eternal sorrow.

17. *To condemn the world.* Not to *judge*, or pronounce sentence on mankind. God *might* justly have sent him for this. Man deserved condemnation, and it would have been right to have pronounced it; but God was willing that there should be an offer of pardon, and the sentence of condemnation was delayed. But, although Jesus did not come *then* to condemn mankind, yet the time is coming when he will return to judge the living and the dead, Ac. xvii. 31; 2 Co. v. 10; Mat. xxv. 31-46.

18. *He that believeth.* He that has confidence in him; that relies on him; that trusts to his merits and promises for salvation. To believe on him is to *feel* and *act* according to truth—that is, to go as lost sinners, and act toward him as a Saviour from sins; relying on him, and looking to him *only* for salvation. See Notes on Mar. xvi. 16. ¶ *Is not condemned.* God pardons sin, and delivers us from deserved punishment, *because* we believe on him. Jesus died in our stead; he suffered for us, and by his sufferings our sins are expiated, and it is *consistent* for God to forgive. When a sinner, therefore, believes on Jesus, he trusts in him as having died in his place, and God having accepted the offering which Christ made in our stead, as being an equivalent for *our* sufferings in hell, there is now no farther condemnation, Ro. viii. 1. ¶ *He that believeth not.* All who do not believe, whether the gospel has come to them or not. All men by nature. ¶ *Is condemned already.* By conscience, by law, and in the judgment of God. God disapproves of their character, and this feeling of disapprobation, and the expression of it, is the condemnation. There is no condemnation so terrible as this—that *God disapproves* our conduct, and that he will *express* his disapprobation. He will judge according to truth, and woe to that man whose conduct God *cannot* approve. ¶ *Because.* This word does not imply that the *ground* or *reason* of their condemnation is that they have not believed, or that they are condemned *because* they do not believe on him, for there are millions of sinners who have never heard of him; but the meaning is this: There is but *one* way by which men can be freed from condemnation. All men without the gospel are condemned. They who do not believe are still under this condemnation, not having embraced the *only way* by which they can be delivered from it. The verse may be thus paraphrased: "All men are by nature condemned. There is but one way of being delivered from this state—by believing on the Son of God. They who do *not* believe or *remain* in that state are still condemned, FOR they have not embraced the only way in which they can be freed from it." Nevertheless, those to whom the gospel comes greatly heighten their guilt and condemnation by rejecting the offers of mercy, and trampling under foot the blood of the

because he hath not believed in the name of the only-begotten Son of God.

19 And this is the condemnation, that [q]light is come into the world, and men loved darkness rather than light, because their deeds were evil.

20 For every one that doeth evil hateth the light, [r]neither cometh to the light, lest his deeds should be [3]reproved.

21 But he that [s]doeth truth cometh to the light, that his deeds may be made manifest that [t]they are wrought in God.

q ch.1.4,9-11.

r Job 24.13,17; Pr.4.18,19.
3 or *discovered*. *s* 1 Jn.1.6. *t* 3 Jn.11.

Son of God, Lu. xii. 47; Mat. xi. 23; He. x. 29; Pr. i. 24–30. And there are thousands going to eternity under this *double* condemnation—1st. For positive, open sin; and, 2d. For rejecting God's mercy, and despising the gospel of his Son. This it is which will make the doom of sinners in Christian lands so terrible.

19. *This is the condemnation.* This is the *cause* of condemnation; or this is the reason why men are punished. ¶ *That light is come.* Light often denotes instruction, teaching, doctrine, as that by which we see clearly the path of duty. *All* the instruction that God gives us by conscience, reason, or revelation may thus be called light; but this word is used peculiarly to denote the Messiah or the Christ, who is often spoken of as *the light.* See Is. lx. 1; ix. 2. Compare Mat. iv. 16; also Notes on Jn. i. 4. It was doubtless this light to which Jesus had particular reference here. ¶ *Men loved darkness.* Darkness is the emblem of ignorance, iniquity, error, superstition—whatever is opposite to truth and piety. Men are said to love darkness more than they do light when they are better pleased with error than truth, with sin than holiness, with Belial than Christ. ¶ *Because their deeds are evil.* Men who commit crime commonly choose to do it in the night, so as to escape detection. So men who are wicked prefer false doctrine and error to the truth. Thus the Pharisees cloaked their crimes under the errors of their system; and, amid their false doctrines and superstitions, they attempted to convince others that they had great zeal for God. ¶ *Deeds.* Works; actions.

20. *That doeth evil.* Every wicked man. ¶ *Hateth the light.* This is true of all wicked men. They choose to practise their deeds of wickedness in darkness. They are afraid of the light, because they could be easily detected. Hence most crimes are committed in the night. So with the sinner against God. He hates the gospel, for it condemns his conduct, and his conscience would trouble him if it were enlightened. ¶ *His deeds should be reproved.* To *reprove* here means not only to *detect* or make manifest, but also includes the idea of *condemnation* when his deeds are detected. The gospel would make his wickedness manifest, and his conscience would condemn him. We learn from this verse, 1st. That one design of the gospel is *to reprove* men. It convicts them of sin in order that it may afford consolation. 2d. That men by nature *hate* the gospel. No man who is a sinner loves it; and no man by nature is disposed to come to it, any more than an adulterer or thief is disposed to come to the daylight, and do his deeds of wickedness there. 3d. The reason why the gospel is hated is that men are sinners. "Christ is hated because sin is loved." 4th. The sinner must be convicted or convinced of sin. If it be not in this world, it will be in the next. There is no escape for him; and the only way to avoid condemnation in the world to come is to come humbly and acknowledge sin here, and seek for pardon.

21. *He that doeth truth.* He who does right, or he that *obeys* the truth. *Truth* here is opposed to error and to evil. The sinner acts from falsehood and error. The good man acts according to truth. The sinner believes a lie—that God will not punish, or that there is no God, or that there is no eternity and no hell. The Christian believes all these, and acts *as if* they were true. This is the difference between a Christian and a sinner. ¶ *Cometh to the light.* Loves the truth, and seeks it more and more. By prayer and searching the Scriptures he endeavours to ascertain the truth, and yield his mind to it. ¶ *May be made manifest.* May be made clear or plain; or that it may be made plain that his deeds *are* wrought

22 After these things came Jesus and his disciples into the land of Judea; and there he tarried with them, [u]and baptized.

u ch.4.2.

23 And John also was baptizing in Enon, near to [v]Salim, because there was much water there; [w]and they came and were baptized:

v 1 Sa.9.4. w Mat.3.5,6.

in God. He searches for truth and light that he may have evidence that his actions are right. ¶ *Wrought in God.* That they are performed according to the will of God, or perhaps by the assistance of God, and are such as God will approve. The actions of good men are performed by the influence and aid of God, Phi. ii. 12. Of course, if they are performed by his aid, they are such as he will approve. Here is presented the character of a good man and a sincere Christian. We learn respecting that character, 1st. He does truth. He loves it, seeks it, follows it. 2d. He comes to the light. He does not attempt to deceive himself or others. 3d. He is willing to know himself, and aims to do it. He desires to know the true state of his heart before God. 4th. An especial object of his efforts is that his deeds may be *wrought in God.* He *desires* to be a good man; to receive continual aid from God, and to perform such actions as he will approve.

This is the close of our Lord's discourse with Nicodemus—a discourse condensing the gospel, giving the most striking exhibition and illustration of truth, and representing especially the fundamental doctrine of regeneration and the evidence of the change. It is clear that the Saviour regarded this as lying at the foundation of religion. Without it we cannot possibly be saved. And now it becomes every reader, as in the presence of God, and in view of the judgment-seat of Christ, solemnly to ask himself whether he has experienced this change? whether he knows by experience what it is to be born of that Spirit? If he does he will be saved. If not, he is in the gall of bitterness and in the bond of iniquity, and should give no sleep to his eyes till he has made his peace with God.

22. *Land of Judea.* The region round about Jerusalem. ¶ *And baptized.* Jesus did not *himself* administer the ordinance of baptism, but his disciples did it by his direction and authority, Jn. iv. 2.

23. *In Enon.* The word *Enon,* or *Ænon,* means *a fountain,* and was doubtless given to this place because of the *fountains* there. On the situation of the place nothing certain has been determined. Eusebius places it 8 Roman miles south of Scythopolis or Bethshan, and 53 north-east of Jerusalem. ¶ *Near to Salim.* It would seem from this that Salim was better known then than Enon, but nothing can be determined now respecting its site. These places are believed to have been on the west side of the Jordan. ¶ *Because there was much water there.* John's preaching attracted great multitudes. It appears that they remained with him probably many days. In many parts of that country, particularly in the hilly region near where John preached, it was difficult to find water to accommodate the necessities of the people, and perhaps, also, of the camels with which those from a distance would come. To meet their necessities, as well as for the purpose of baptizing, he selected a spot that was well watered, probably, with springs and rivulets. Whether the ordinance of baptism was performed by immersion or in any other mode, the selection of a place well watered was proper and necessary. The mention of the fact that there was much water there, and that John selected that as a convenient place to perform his office as a baptizer, proves nothing in regard to the *mode* in which the ordinance was administered, since he would naturally select such a place, whatever was the mode. Where numbers of people came together to remain any time, it is necessary to select such a place, whatever their employment. An encampment of soldiers is made on the same principles, and in every camp-meeting that I have ever seen, a place is selected where there is a good supply of water, though not one person should be *immersed* during the whole services. As all the facts in the case are fully met by the supposition that John might have baptized in some other way besides immersion, and as it is easy to conceive *another* reason that is sufficient to account for the fact that such a place was selected, *this* passage certainly should not be adduced to prove that he performed baptism only in that manner.

24 For[x] John was not yet cast
into prison.
25 Then there arose a question
between *some* of John's disciples
and the Jews about purifying.
26 And they came unto John,
and said unto him, Rabbi, he that
was with thee beyond Jordan,
[y] to whom thou barest witness,
behold, the same baptizeth, and
[z]all *men* come to him.
27 John answered and said, [a]A

x Mat.14.3.

y ch.1.7,15,&c. z Ps.65.2; Is.45.23. a 1.Co.2.12-14; 4.7; He.5.4; Ja.1.17.

---

24. *For John was not yet cast into prison.* See Lu. iii. 20. The mention of this shows that John was not imprisoned till some time after our Lord entered on his ministry. The design of John was to call men to repentance, and to prepare them for the Messiah, and this he continued to do after our Saviour commenced *his* work. It shows that a minister of religion should be industrious to the day of his death. John still toiled in his work not the *less* because the Messiah had come. So ministers should not labour less when Christ appears by his Spirit, and takes the work into his own hands, and turns many to himself.

25. *A question.* Rather a controversy—a dispute. ¶ *John's disciples.* Those who had been baptized by him, and who attached great efficacy and importance to the teaching of their master. Comp. Notes on Ac. xix. 1-5. ¶ *And the Jews.* Many manuscripts, some of the fathers, and the ancient Syriac version, read this in the singular number—"with *a Jew*," one who, it is commonly supposed, had been baptized by the disciples of Jesus. ¶ *About purifying.* What the precise subject of this dispute was we do not know. From what follows, it would seem probable that it was about the comparative value and efficacy of the baptism performed by John and by the disciples of Jesus. The word *purifying* may be applied to baptism, as it was an emblem of repentance and purity, and was thus used by the Jews, by John, and by Jesus. About this subject it seems that a dispute arose, and was carried to such a length that complaint was made to John. From this we may learn, 1st. That even in the time of Jesus, when the gospel began to be preached, there was witnessed—what has been ever since—unhappy disputings on the subject of religion. Even young converts may, by overheated zeal and ignorance, fall into angry discussion. 2d. That such discussions are commonly about some unimportant matter of religion—something which they may not yet be qualified to understand, and which does not materially affect them if they could. 3d. That such disputes are often connected with a spirit of proselytism—with boasting of the superior excellence of the sect with which *we* are connected, or in connection with whom *we* have been converted, and often with a desire to persuade others to join with us. 4th. That such a spirit is eminently improper on such occasions. Love should characterize the feelings of young converts; a disposition to *inquire* and not to *dispute;* a willingness that all should follow the dictates of their own consciences, and not a desire to *proselyte* them to *our* way of thinking or to *our* church. It may be added that there is scarcely anything which so certainly and effectually arrests a revival of religion as such a disposition to *dispute*, and to make proselytes to particular modes of faith, and of administering the ordinances of the gospel.

26. *Came unto John.* Came to him with their complaint; envious and jealous at the success of Jesus, and evidently irritated from the discussion, as if their master was about to lose his popularity. ¶ *Rabbi.* Master. See Notes on Mat. xxiii. 7. Acknowledging him as their master and teacher. ¶ *That was with thee.* Who was baptized by thee. ¶ *Thou barest witness.* See ch. i. 29-35. ¶ *All* men *come to him.* This was the source of their difficulty. It was that Jesus was gaining popularity; that the people flocked to him; that they feared that John would be forsaken, and his followers be diminished in numbers and influence. Thus many love their *sect* more than they do Christ, and would be more rejoiced that a man became a Presbyterian, a Methodist, a Baptist, than that he became a sincere and humble Christian. This is not the spirit of the gospel. True piety teaches us to rejoice that sinners turn to Christ and become holy, whether they follow *us* or not. See Mar. ix. 38, 39. Let Jesus be exalted, and let men turn to *him*, is the

man can [4]receive nothing, except
it be given him from heaven.
28 Ye yourselves bear me witness
that I said, [b]I am not the Christ,
but that [c]I am sent before him.
29 He that hath the [d]bride is
the bridegroom; but the [e]friend
of the bridegroom, which standeth

4 or, *take unto himself*. *b* ch.1.20,27. *c* Lu.1.17. *d* Ca.4.8-12; Je.2.2; Eze.16.8; Ho.2.19,20; Mat.22.2; 2 Co.11.2; Ep.5.25,27; Re.21.9. *e* Ca.5.1.

and heareth him, rejoiceth greatly
because of the bridegroom's voice.
This my joy, therefore, is fulfilled.
30 He must increase, but I *must*
decrease.
31 He that cometh [f]from above
is above all: [g]he that is of the
earth is earthly, and speaketh of

f ch.6.33; 8.23; Ep.1.20,21. *g* 1 Co.15.47.

language of religion, whatever denomination they may feel it their duty to follow.

27. *John answered*, &c. John did not enter into their feelings or sympathize with their love of party. He came to honour Jesus, not to build up a sect. He rejoiced at the success of the Messiah, and began to teach them to rejoice in it also. ¶ *A man can receive nothing*, &c. All success is from heaven. All *my* success was from God. All the success of Jesus is from God. As success comes from the *same* source, we ought not to be envious. It is designed to answer the same end, and, by whomsoever accomplished, the hand of God is in it, and we should rejoice. If Jesus and his disciples are successful, if all men flee to him, it is proof that God favours him, and you should rejoice.

28. *Bear me witness*. You remember that at first I told you I was not the Messiah. As he had been *witness* to Jesus—as he came for no other end but to point him out to the Jews, they ought not to suppose that he was his superior. It was but reasonable to expect that Christ himself would be more successful than his forerunner. "I came, not to form *a separate party*, a peculiar sect, but to prepare the way that *he* might be more successful, and that the people might be ready for his coming, and that he might have the success which he has actually met with. You should rejoice, therefore, at that success, and not envy it, for *his success* is the best proof of the greatness of *my* word, and of *its success* also."

29. *He that hath the bride*, &c. This is an illustration drawn from marriage. The bride belongs to her husband. So the church, the bride of the Messiah, belongs to him. It is *to be expected*, therefore, and *desired*, that the people should flock to him. ¶ *But the friend of the bridegroom*. He whose office it is to attend him on the marriage occasion. This was commonly the nearest friend, and was a high honour. ¶ *Rejoiceth greatly*. Esteems himself highly honoured by the proof of friendship. ¶ *The bridegroom's voice*. His commands, requests, or conversation. ¶ *This my joy*, &c. "I sustain to the Messiah the relation which a groomsman does to the groom. The chief honour and the chief joy is not mine, but his. It is to be expected, therefore, that the people will come to him, and that his success will be great." The relation of Christ to the church is often compared with the marriage relation, denoting the tenderness of the union, and his great love for his people. Comp. Is. lxii. 5; Re. xxi. 2, 9; xxii. 17; Ep. v. 26, 27, 32; 2 Co. xi. 2.

30. *He must increase*. *His* authority and influence among the people must grow. *His* doctrine shall continue to spread till it extends through all the earth. ¶ *I must decrease*. "The purpose of my ministry is to point men to him. When that is done my work is done. I came not to form a party of my own, nor to set up a religion of my own; and my teaching must *cease* when he is fully established, as the light of the morning star fades away and is lost in the beams of the rising sun." This evinced John's humility and willingness to be esteemed as nothing if he could honour Christ. It shows us, also, that it is sufficient honour for man if he may be permitted to point sinners to the Lord Jesus Christ. No work is so honourable and joyful as the ministry of the gospel; none are so highly honoured as those who are permitted to stand near the Son of God, to hear his voice, and to lead perishing men to his cross. Comp. Da. xii. 3.

31. *He that cometh from above*. The Messiah, represented as coming down from heaven. See ver. 13; ch. vi. 33; viii. 23. It has been doubted whether the remainder of this chapter contains

the earth: he that cometh from heaven is above all.

32 And what he hath seen and heard, that he testifieth; and [h]no man receiveth his testimony.

33 He that hath received his testimony hath [i]set to his seal that God is true.

34 For[k] he whom God hath sent speaketh the words of God; [l]for God giveth not the Spirit by measure *unto him.*

h ch.1.11.

i 1 Jn.5.10. *k* ch.7.16.
l Ps.45.7; Is.11.2; 59.21; ch.1.16; Col.1.19.

---

the words of *John the Baptist* or of *the evangelist.* The former is the more probable opinion, but it is difficult to decide it, and it is of very little consequence. ¶ *Is above all.* In nature, rank, and authority. Is *superior to all prophets* (He. i. 1, 2); *to all angels* (He. i. 4–14), *and is over all the universe as its sovereign Lord,* Ro. ix. 5; Ep. i. 21, 22; Col. i. 15–19; 1 Co. xv. 25. ¶ *He that is of the earth.* He who has no higher nature than the human nature. The prophets, apostles, and John were men like others, born in the same way, and sinking, like others, to the dust. See Ac. xiv. 15. Jesus had a nature superior to man, and *ought,* therefore, to be exalted above all. ¶ *Is earthly.* Is human. Is *inferior* to him who comes from heaven. Partakes of his *origin,* which is inferior and corrupt. ¶ *Speaketh of the earth.* His teaching is inferior to that of him who comes from heaven. It is comparatively obscure and imperfect, not full and clear, like the teaching of him who is from above. This was the case with all the prophets, and even with John the Baptist, as compared with the teaching of Christ.

32. *And what he hath seen,* &c. See ver. 11. ¶ *No man receiveth his testimony.* The words *no man* are here to be understood in the sense of *few.* Though his doctrine is pure, plain, sublime, yet *few,* comparatively, received it in faith. Though multitudes came to him, drawn by various motives (Jn. vi. 26), yet *few* became his *real* disciples, Mat. xxvi. 56; vii. 22. ¶ *His testimony.* His doctrine. The truth to which he bears *witness* as having *seen* and *known* it, ver. 11. Often many persons *appear* for a time to become the followers of Christ, who in the end are seen to have known nothing of religion, Mat. xiii. 6; Lu. viii. 13.

33. *He that hath received his testimony.* Hath received and fully believed his doctrine. Hath yielded his heart to its influence. ¶ *Hath set to his seal.* To *seal* an instrument is to make it sure; to acknowledge it as *ours;* to pledge our veracity that it is true and binding, as when a man seals a bond, a deed, or a will. Believing a doctrine, therefore, in the heart, is expressed by *sealing it,* or by believing it we express *our firm conviction* that it is true, and that God who has spoken it is true. We vouch for the veracity of God, and assume *as our own* the proposition that it is the truth of God. ¶ *God is true.* Is faithful; is the author of the system of doctrines, and will fulfil all that he has promised. We learn here, 1st. That to be a true believer is something more than to hold a mere speculative belief of the truth. 2d. That to be a believer is to *pledge ourselves* for the truth, to seal it as our own, to adopt it, to choose it, and solemnly assent to it, as a man does in regard to an instrument of writing that is to convey his property, or that is to dispose of it when he dies. 3d. Every Christian is a witness for God, and it is his business to show by his life that he believes that God is true to his threatenings and to his promises. See Notes on Is. xliii. 10. 4th. It is a solemn act to become a Christian. It is a surrender of all to God, or giving away body, soul, and spirit to him, with a belief that he is *true,* and alone is able to save. 5th. The man that does not do this—that is not willing to pledge his belief that God is true, sets to *his* seal that God is *a liar* and unworthy of confidence, 1 Jn. v. 10.

34. *Whom God hath sent.* The Messiah. ¶ *Speaketh the words of God.* The *truth,* or commands of God. ¶ *For God giveth not the Spirit.* The Spirit of God. Though Jesus was God as well as man, yet, *as Mediator,* God anointed him, or endowed him with the influences of his Spirit, so as to be completely qualified for his great work. ¶ *By measure.* Not in a small degree, but fully, completely. The prophets were inspired on *particular* occasions to deliver special messages. The Messiah was *continually* filled with the Spirit of God. "The Spirit dwelt in him, not as a vessel, but

35 The[m] Father loveth the Son, and hath given all things into his hand.

36 He[n] that believeth on the Son hath everlasting life; and he that believeth not the Son shall not see life, but the [o]wrath of God abideth on him.

m Mat.28.18. *n* Hab.2.4; ver.15,16. *o* Ro.1.18.

CHAPTER IV.

WHEN, therefore, the Lord knew how the Pharisees had heard that Jesus made and [a]baptized more disciples than John,

2 (Though Jesus himself baptized not, but his disciples,)

a ch.3.22,26.

as in a fountain, as in a bottomless ocean" (Henry).

35. *Loveth the Son.* Loves him eminently, above all the prophets and all the other messengers of God. ¶ *Hath given all things into his hand.* See Notes on Mat. xxviii. 18.

36. *Hath everlasting life.* Has or is in possession of that which is a recovery from spiritual death, and which will result in eternal life in heaven. Piety here is the same that it will be there, except that it will be expanded, matured, purified, made more glorious. It is here life begun—the first breathings and pantings of the soul for immortality; yet it is life, though at first feeble and faint, which is eternal in its nature, and which shall be matured in the full and perfect bliss of heaven. The Christian here has a foretaste of the world of glory, and enjoys the same *kind* of felicity, though not the same *degree*, that he will there. ¶ *Shall not see life.* Shall neither enjoy true *life* or happiness here nor in the world to come. Shall never enter heaven. ¶ *The wrath of God.* The anger of God for sin. His opposition to sin, and its terrible effects in this world and the next. ¶ *Abideth on him.* This implies that he is *now* under the wrath of God, or under condemnation. It implies, also, that it will *continue* to remain on him. It will *abide* or *dwell* there as its appropriate habitation. As there is no way of escaping the wrath of God but by the Lord Jesus Christ, so those who will not believe must go to eternity *as they are*, and bear alone and unpitied all that God may choose to inflict as the expression of *his* sense of sin. Such is the miserable condition of the sinner! Yet thousands choose to remain in this state, and to encounter *alone* all that is terrible in the wrath of Almighty God, rather than come to Jesus, who has borne their sins in his own body on the tree, and who is willing to bless them with the peace, and purity, and joy of immortal life.

CHAPTER IV.

1. *The Lord knew.* When Jesus knew. *How* he knew this we are not informed; whether by that power of omniscience by which he knew all things, or whether some person had informed him of it. ¶ *How the Pharisees had heard.* The *Pharisees*, here, seem to denote either the members of the Sanhedrim or those who were in authority. They claimed the authority to regulate the rites and ceremonies of religion, and hence they supposed they had a right to inquire into the conduct of both John and our Lord. They had on a former occasion sent to inquire of John to know by what authority he had introduced such a rite into the religion of the Jewish people. See Notes on ch. i. 25. ¶ *More disciples than John.* Though many of the Pharisees came to his baptism (Mat. iii.), yet those who were in authority were displeased with the success of John, Jn. i. 25. The reasons of this were, probably, the severity and justness of his reproofs (Mat. iii. 7), and the fact that by drawing many after him he weakened their authority and influence. As they were displeased with *John*, so they were with *Jesus*, who was doing the same thing on a larger scale—not only making disciples, but *baptizing* also without their authority, and drawing away the people after him.

2. *Though Jesus himself baptized not.* The reason why Jesus did not baptize was probably because, if *he* had baptized, it might have made unhappy divisions among his followers: those might have considered themselves most worthy or honoured who had been baptized by *him*. Comp. 1 Co. i. 17.

3. *He left Judea.* The envy and malice of the Pharisees he might have known were growing so rapidly as to endanger his life. As his time to die had not yet come, he retired to Galilee, a country farther from Jerusalem, and much less under their control than Judea. See

3 He left Judea, and departed again into Galilee.

4 And he [b]must needs go through Samaria.

5 Then cometh he to a city of Samaria which is called Sychar, near to the parcel of ground that Jacob [c]gave to his son Joseph.

6 Now Jacob's well was there. Jesus therefore, being wearied with *his* journey, sat thus on the well; *and* it was about the sixth hour.

7 There cometh a woman of Samaria to draw water. Jesus saith unto her, Give me to drink.

8 For his disciples were gone away unto the city to buy meat.

9 Then saith the woman of

b Lu.2.49. c Ge.33.19; 48.22; Jos.24.32.

Mar. ii. 22; Lu. iii. 1. Though he feared not death and did not shrink from suffering, yet he did not *needlessly* throw himself into danger or provoke opposition. He could do as much *good* in Galilee, probably, as in Judea, and he therefore withdrew himself from immediate danger.

4. *And he must needs go through Samaria.* Samaria was between Judea and Galilee. The *direct* and usual way was to pass through Samaria. Sometimes, however, the Jews took a circuitous route on the east side of the Jordan, See Notes on Mat. ii. 22.

5. *Sychar.* This city stood about eight miles south-east of the city called Samaria, between Mount Ebal and Mount Gerizim. It was one of the oldest cities of Palestine, and was formerly known by the name of *Shechem*, or Sichem, Ge. xxxiii. 18; xii. 6. The city was in the tribe of Ephraim, Jos. xxi. 21. It was at this place that Joshua assembled the people before his death, and here they renewed their covenant with the Lord, Jos. xxiv. After the death of Gideon it became a place of idolatrous worship, the people worshipping *Baal-berith*, Ju. ix. 46. It was destroyed by Abimelech, who beat down the city and sowed it with salt, Ju. ix. 45. It was afterward rebuilt, and became the residence of Jeroboam, the King of Israel, 1 Ki. xii. 25. It was called by the Romans *Flavia Neapolis*, and this has been corrupted by the Arabs into *Nablûs*, its present name. It is still a considerable place, and its site is remarkably pleasant and productive. ¶ *The parcel of ground.* The *piece* of ground; or the *land*, &c. ¶ *That Jacob gave*, &c. Jacob bought one piece of ground near to Shalem, a city of Shechem, of the children of Hamor, the father of Shechem, for an hundred pieces of silver, Ge. xxxiii. 19. In this place the bones of Joseph were buried when they were brought up from Egypt, Jos. xxiv. 32. He also gave to Joseph an additional piece of ground which he took from the hand of the Amorite by his own valour, "with his sword and his bow," as a portion above that which was given to his brethren, Ge. xlviii. 22. Possibly these pieces of ground lay near together, and were a part of the *homestead* of Jacob. The well was "near" to this. There is now, the Rev. E. Smith mentioned to me in conversation, a place near this well called *Shalem.*

6. *Jacob's well.* This is not mentioned in the Old Testament. It was called *Jacob's well*, probably, either because it was handed down by tradition that he dug it, or because it was near to the land which he gave to Joseph. There is still a well a few miles to the east of Nablûs, which is said by the people there to be the same. The Rev. Eli Smith, missionary to Syria, stated to me that he had visited this well. It is about 100 feet deep. It is cut through solid rock of limestone. It is now dry, probably from having been partly filled with rubbish, or perhaps because the water has been diverted by earthquakes. The well is covered with a large stone, which has a hole in the centre large enough to admit a man. It is at the foot of Mount Gerizim, and has a plain on the east. ¶ *Sat thus.* Jesus was weary, and, being *thus* weary, sat down on the well. The word translated *on* here may denote also *by*—he sat down *by* the well, or near it. ¶ *The sixth hour.* About twelve o'clock. This was the common time of the Jewish meal, and this was the reason why his disciples were gone away to buy food.

7. *Of Samaria.* Not of the *city* of Samaria, for this was at a distance of 8 miles, but a woman who was a Samaritan, and doubtless from the city of Sychar. ¶ *Give me to drink.* This was in the heat of the day, and when Jesus was weary with his journey. The request was also made that it might give him occasion to discourse with her on

Samaria unto him, How is it
that thou, being a Jew, askest
drink of me, which am a woman
of Samaria? [d]for the Jews have
no dealings with the Samaritans.
10 Jesus answered and said
unto her, If thou knewest [e]the
gift of God, and who it is that
saith to thee, Give me to drink;
thou wouldest have asked of him,
and he would have given thee
[f]living water.
11 The woman saith unto him,
Sir, thou hast nothing to draw
with, and the well is deep; from
whence, then, hast thou that living
water?
12 Art thou greater than our

d Ac.10.28. e Ep.2.8.

f Is.12.3; 41.17,18; Je.2.13; Zec.13.1; 14.8; Re.22.17.

the subject of religion, and in this instance we have a specimen of the remarkably happy manner in which he could lead on a conversation so as to introduce the subject of religion.

8. *Buy meat.* Buy food.

9. *No dealings with the Samaritans.* For an account of the Samaritans, and of the differences between them and the Jews, see Notes on Mat. x. 5.

10. *The gift of God.* The word *gift*, here denotes *favour*. It may refer to Jesus *himself*, as the *gift* of God to the world, given to save men from death (ch. iii. 16; 2 Co. ix. 15), or it may refer to the *opportunity* then afforded her of seeking salvation. If thou knewest how favourable an opportunity God now gives thee to gain a knowledge of himself, &c. ¶ *And who it is*, &c. If thou knewest that the Messiah was speaking. ¶ *Living water.* The Jews used the expression *living water* to denote springs, fountains, or running streams, in opposition to dead and stagnant water. Jesus here means to denote by it his doctrine, or his grace and religion, in opposition to the impure and dead notions of the Jews and the Samaritans. See ver. 14. This was one of the many instances in which he took occasion from common topics of conversation to introduce religious discourse. None ever did it so happily as he did, but, by studying his example and manner, *we* may learn also to do it. One way to acquire the art is to have the mind *full* of the subject; to make religion our first and main thing; to carry it with us into all employments and into all society; to look upon everything in a religious light, and out of the abundance of the heart the mouth will speak, Mat. xii. 34.

11. *Hast nothing to draw with.* It seems that there were no means of drawing water *affixed* to the well, as with us. Probably each one took a pail or pitcher and a cord for the purpose. In travelling this was indispensable. The woman, seeing that Jesus had no *means* of drawing water, and not yet understanding his design, naturally inquired whence he could obtain the water. ¶ *The well is deep.* If the same one that is there now, it was about 100 feet deep.

12. *Art thou greater?* Art thou wiser, or better able to find water, than Jacob was? It seems that she supposed that he meant that he could direct her to some living spring, or to some better well in that region, and that this implied more knowledge or skill than Jacob had. To find water and to furnish a good well was doubtless considered a matter of signal skill and success. It was a subject of great importance in that region. This shows how ready sinners are to misunderstand the words of Christ, and to pervert the doctrines of religion. If she had had any proper anxiety about her soul, she would at least have *suspected* that he meant to direct her thoughts to spiritual objects. ¶ *Our father Jacob.* The Samaritans were composed partly of the remnant of the ten tribes, and partly of people sent from Chaldea; still, they considered themselves descendants of Jacob. ¶ *Which gave us.* This was doubtless the tradition, though there is no evidence that it was true. ¶ *And drank thereof*, &c. This was added in commendation of the water of the well. A well from which Jacob, and his sons, and cattle had drank must be pure, and wholesome, and honoured, and quite as valuable as any that Jesus could furnish. Men like to commend that which their ancestors used as superior to anything else. The world over, people love to speak of that which *their* ancestors have done, and boast of titles and honours that have been handed down from them, even if it is nothing better than existed here—because Jacob's *cattle* had drunk of the water.

father Jacob, which gave us the well, and drank thereof himself, and his children, and his cattle?

13 Jesus answered and said unto her, Whosoever drinketh of this water shall thirst again;

14 But[g] whosoever drinketh of the water that I shall [h]give him shall never thirst; but the water that I shall give him shall be [i]in him a well of water springing up into everlasting life.

15 The woman saith unto him, Sir, give me this water, that I thirst not, neither come hither to draw.

16 Jesus saith unto her, Go call thy husband, and come hither.

17 The woman answered and

g ch.6.35,58. h ch.17.2,3; Ro.6.23. i ch.7.38.

13. *Shall thirst again.* Jesus did not directly answer her question, or say that he was *greater* than Jacob, but he gave her an answer by which she might infer that he was. He did not despise or undervalue Jacob or his gifts; but, however great might be the value of that well, the water could not altogether remove thirst.

14. *The water that I shall give him.* Jesus here refers, without doubt, to his own *teaching*, his *grace*, his *spirit*, and to the benefits which come into the soul that embraces his gospel. It is a striking image, and especially in Eastern countries, where there are vast deserts, and often a great want of water. The soul by nature is like such a desert, or like a traveller wandering through such a desert. It is thirsting for happiness, and seeking it everywhere, and finds it not. It looks in all directions and tries all objects, but in vain. Nothing meets its desires. Though a sinner seeks for joy in wealth and pleasures, yet he is not satisfied. He still thirsts for more, and seeks still for happiness in some new enjoyment. To such a weary and unsatisfied sinner the grace of Christ is *as cold waters to a thirsty soul.* ¶ *Shall never thirst.* He shall be *satisfied* with this, and will not have a sense of want, a distressing feeling that it is not adapted to him. He who drinks this will not wish to seek for happiness in other objects. *Satisfied* with the grace of Christ, he will not desire the pleasures and amusements of this world. And this will be for ever—in this world and the world to come. *Whosoever* drinketh of this—all who partake of the gospel—shall be *for ever* satisfied with its pure and rich joys. ¶ *Shall be in him.* The grace of Christ shall be in his heart; or the principles of religion shall abide with him. ¶ *A well of water.* There shall be a constant supply, an unfailing fountain; or religion shall *live* constantly with him. ¶ *Springing up.* This is a beautiful image. It shall bubble or spring up like a fountain. It is not like a stagnant pool—not like a deep well, but like an ever-living fountain, that flows at all seasons of the year, in heat and cold, and in all external circumstances of weather, whether foul or fair, wet or dry. So religion always lives; and, amid all changes of external circumstances—in heat and cold, hunger and thirst, prosperity and adversity, life, persecution, contempt, or death—it still lives on, and refreshes and cheers the soul. ¶ *Into everlasting life.* It is not *temporary*, like the supply of our natural wants; it is not changing in its nature; it is not like a natural fountain or spring of water, to play a while and then die away, as all natural springs will at the end of the world. It is eternal in its nature and supply, and will continue to live on for ever. We may learn here—1st. That the Christian has a never-failing source of consolation adapted to all times and circumstances. 2d. That religion has its seat in the heart, and that it should constantly *live* there. 3d. That it sheds its blessings on a world of sin, and is manifest by a continual *life* of piety, like a constant flowing spring. 4th. That its end is everlasting life. It will continue for ever; and *whosoever drinks of this shall never thirst*, but his piety shall be in his heart a pure fountain *springing up to eternal joy.*

15. *The woman said*, &c. It may seem strange that the woman did not yet understand him, but it shows how slow sinners are to understand the doctrines of religion.

16. *Go call thy husband.* We may admire the manner which our Saviour took to lead her to perceive that he was the Christ. His instructions she did not understand. He therefore proceeded to show her that he was acquainted with her life and with her sins. His object, here, was to lead her

said, I have no husband. Jesus said unto her, Thou hast well said, I have no husband;

18 For thou hast had five husbands; and he whom thou now hast is not thy husband: in that saidst thou truly.

19 The woman saith unto him, Sir, I [k]perceive that thou art a prophet.

20 Our fathers worshipped in [l]this mountain; and ye say that in [m]Jerusalem is the place where men ought to worship.

k ch.1.48,49. *l* Ju.9.7. *m* De.12.5-11; 1 Ki.9.3.

to consider her own state and sinfulness—a delicate and yet pungent way of making her see that she was a sinner. By showing her, also, that he knew her life, though a stranger to her, he convinced her that he was qualified to teach her the way to heaven, and thus prepared her to admit that he was the Messiah, ver. 29.

17. *I have no husband.* This was said, evidently, to evade the subject. Perhaps she feared that if she came there with the man that she lived with, the truth might be exposed. It is not improbable that by this time she began to suspect that Jesus was a prophet. ¶ *Hast well said.* Hast said the truth.

18. *Hast had five husbands.* Who have either died; or who, on account of your improper conduct, have divorced you; or whom you have left improperly, without legal divorce. Either of these might have been the case. ¶ *Is not thy husband.* You are not lawfully married to him. Either she might have left a former husband without divorce, and thus her marriage with this man was unlawful, or she was living with him without the form of marriage, in open guilt.

19. *A prophet.* One sent from God, and who understood her life. The word here does not denote one who *foretells future events*, but one who *knew her heart* and life, and who must therefore have come from God. She did not yet suppose him to be the Messiah, ver. 25. Believing him now to be a man sent from God, she proposed to him a question respecting the proper place of worship. This point had been long a matter of dispute between the Samaritans and the Jews. She submitted it to him because she thought he could settle the question, and perhaps because she wished to divert the conversation from the unpleasant topic respecting her husbands. The conversation about her manner of life was a very unpleasant topic to her—as it is always unpleasant to sinners to talk about their lives and the necessity of religion—and she was glad to *turn the conversation* to something else. Nothing is more common than for sinners to *change* the conversation when it begins to bear too hard upon their consciences; and no way of doing it is more common than to direct it to some *speculative* inquiry having *some sort of connection with religion*, as if to show that they are willing to talk *about* religion, and do not wish to appear to be opposed to it. Sinners do not love direct religious conversation, but many are too well-bred to refuse altogether to talk about it; yet they choose to converse about some speculative matter, or something pertaining to the mere *externals* of religion, rather than the salvation of their own souls. So sinners often now change the conversation to some inquiry about a preacher, or about some doctrine, or about building or repairing a place of worship, or about a Sabbath-school, in order to *seem* to talk *about* religion, and yet to evade close and faithful appeals to their own consciences.

20. *Our fathers.* The Samaritans; perhaps also meaning to intimate that the patriarchs had done it also. See Ge. xii. 6; xxxiii. 20. ¶ *Worshipped.* Had a place of worship. ¶ *In this mountain. Mount Gerizim*, but a little way from Sychar. On this mountain they had built a temple somewhat similar to the one in Jerusalem. This was one of the main subjects of controversy between them and the Jews. The old Samaritan Pentateuch, or five books of Moses, has the word *Gerizim* instead of *Ebal* in De. xxvii. 4. On this account, as well as because the patriarchs are mentioned as having worshipped in Shechem, they supposed that that was the proper place on which to erect the temple. ¶ *Ye say.* Ye Jews. ¶ *In Jerusalem.* The place where the temple was built. This was built in accordance with the promise and command of God, De. xii. 5, 11. In building this, David and Solomon were under the divine direction, 2 Sa. vii. 2, 3, 13; 1 Ki. v. 5, 12; viii. 15-22.

21 Jesus saith unto her, Woman, believe me, the hour cometh [n]when ye shall neither in this mountain, nor yet at Jerusalem, worship the Father.

22 Ye[o] worship ye know not what: we know what we worship; [p]for salvation is of the Jews.

23 But the hour cometh, and now is, when the true worshippers

n Mal.1.11; Mat.18.20.

o 2 Ki.17.29. p Is.2.3; Ro.9.5.

As it was contemplated in the law of Moses that there should be but *one* place to offer sacrifice and to hold the great feasts, so it followed that the Samaritans were in error in supposing that *their* temple was the place. Accordingly, our Saviour decided in favour of the Jews, yet in such a manner as to show the woman that the question was of much *less* consequence than *they* supposed it to be.

21. *Believe me.* As she had professed to believe that he was a prophet, it was right to require her to put faith in what he was about to utter. It also shows the importance of what he was about to say. ¶ *The hour cometh.* The *time* is coming, or is near. ¶ *When neither in this mountain*, &c. Hitherto the public solemn worship of God has been confined to one place. It has been a matter of dispute whether that place should be Jerusalem or Mount Gerizim. That controversy is to be of much less importance than you have supposed. The old dispensation is about to pass away. The *peculiar* rites of the Jews are to cease. The worship of God, so long confined to a single place, is soon to be celebrated everywhere, and with as much acceptance in one place as in another. He does not say that there would be *no* worship of God in that place or in Jerusalem, but that the worship of God would not be *confined* there. He would be worshipped in other places as well as there.

22. *Ye worship ye know not what.* This probably refers to the comparative ignorance and corruption of the Samaritan worship. Though they received the five books of Moses, yet they rejected the prophets, and of course all that the prophets had said respecting the true God. Originally, also, they had joined the worship of idols to that of the true God. See 2 Ki. xvii. 26–34. They had, moreover, no *authority* for building their temple and conducting public worship by sacrifices there. On all these accounts they were acting in an unauthorized manner. They were not obeying the true God, nor offering the worship which he had commanded or would approve. Jesus thus *indirectly* settled the question which she had proposed to him, yet in such a way as to show her that it was of much less importance than she had supposed. ¶ *We know.* We Jews. This they knew because God had commanded it; because they worshipped in a place appointed by God, and because they did it in accordance with the direction and teaching of the prophets. ¶ *Salvation is of the Jews.* They have the true religion and the true form of worship; and the *Messiah*, who will bring salvation, is to proceed from them. See Lu. ii. 30; iii. 6. Jesus thus affirms that the Jews had the true form of the worship of God. At the same time he was sensible how much they had corrupted it, and on various occasions reproved them for it.

23. *But the hour cometh, and now is.* The old dispensation is about to pass away, and the new one to commence. *Already* there is so much light that God may be worshipped acceptably in any place. ¶ *The true worshippers.* All who truly and sincerely worship God. They who do it with the *heart*, and not merely *in form.* ¶ *In spirit.* The word *spirit*, here, stands opposed to rites and ceremonies, and to the pomp of external worship. It refers to the *mind*, the *soul*, the *heart.* They shall worship God with a sincere *mind;* with the simple offering of gratitude and prayer; with a *desire* to glorify him, and without external pomp and splendour. *Spiritual* worship is that where the *heart* is offered to God, and where we do not depend on external forms for acceptance. ¶ *In truth.* Not through the medium of shadows and types, not by means of sacrifices and bloody offerings, but in the manner represented or typified by all these, He. ix. 9, 24. In the *true* way of direct access to God through Jesus Christ. ¶ *For the Father seeketh*, &c. Jesus gives two reasons why this kind of worship should take place. *One* is that God *sought* it, or desired it. He had appointed the old mode, but he did it because he sought to lead the mind to himself even *by those forms*, and to pre-

shall worship the Father [q]in spirit
and in truth; for the Father seeketh
such to worship him.
24 God[r] *is* a spirit; and they
that worship him must worship
him in spirit and in truth.
25 The woman saith unto him,
I know that Messias cometh, which
is called Christ: when he is come, he
will tell us all things.
26 Jesus saith unto her, [s]I that
speak unto thee am *he*.
27 And upon this came his
disciples, and marvelled that he

q Phi.3.3. *r* 2 Co.3.17. *s* ch.9.37.

---

pare the people for the purer system of the gospel, and *now* he sought or *desired* that those who worshipped him should worship him in that manner. He intimated his will by Jesus Christ.

24. *God* is *a spirit*. This is the *second* reason why men should worship him in spirit and in truth. By this is meant that God is without a body; that he is not material or composed of parts; that he is invisible, in every place, pure and holy. This is one of the first truths of religion, and one of the sublimest ever presented to the mind of man. Almost all nations have had some idea of God as gross or material, but the Bible declares that he is a pure spirit. As he is such a spirit, he dwells not in temples made with hands (Ac. vii. 48), neither is worshipped with men's hands as though he needed anything, seeing he giveth to all life, and breath, and all things, Ac. xvii. 25. A pure, a holy, a spiritual worship, therefore, is such as he seeks—the offering of the *soul* rather than the formal offering of *the body*—the homage of the *heart* rather than that of the *lips*.

25. *I know that Messias cometh.* As the Samaritans acknowledged the five books of Moses, so they expected, also, the coming of the Messiah. ¶ *Which is called Christ.* These are probably the words of the evangelist, as it is not likely that the woman would explain the name on such an occasion. ¶ *Will tell us all things.* Jesus had decided the question proposed to him (ver. 20) in favour of the Jews. The woman does not seem to have been satisfied with this answer, and said that the Messiah would tell them all about this question. Probably she was expecting that he would soon appear.

26. *I that speak unto thee am* he. I am the Messiah. This was the first time that he openly professed it. He did not do it yet to the Jews, for it would have excited envy and opposition. But nothing could be apprehended in Samaria; and as the woman seemed reluctant to listen to him as a prophet, and professed her willingness to listen to the Messiah, he openly declared that he was the Christ, that by some means he might save her soul. From this we may learn, 1st. The great wisdom of the Lord Jesus in leading the thoughts along to the subject of practical personal religion. 2d. His knowledge of the heart and of the life. He must be therefore divine. 3d. He gave evidence here that he was the Messiah. This was the design of John in writing this gospel. He has therefore recorded this narrative, which was omitted by the other evangelists. 4th. We see *our* duty. It is to seize on all occasions to lead sinners to the belief that Jesus is the Christ, and to make use of all topics of conversation to teach them the nature of religion. There never was a model of so much wisdom in this as the Saviour, and we shall be successful only as we diligently study his character. 5th. We see the nature of religion. It does not consist merely in external forms. It is pure, spiritual, active—an ever-bubbling fountain. It is the worship of a pure and holy God, where the *heart* is offered, and where the desires of an humble soul are breathed out for salvation.

27. *Upon this.* At this time. ¶ *Marvelled.* Wondered. They wondered because the Jews had no intercourse with the Samaritans, and they were surprised that Jesus was engaged with her in conversation. ¶ *Yet no man said.* No one of the disciples. They had such respect and reverence for him that they did not dare to ask him the reason of his conduct, or even to appear to reprove him. We should be confident that Jesus is right, even if we cannot fully understand all that he does.

28. *Left her water-pot.* Her mind was greatly excited. She was disturbed, and hastened to the city in great agitation to make this known. She seems to have been convinced that he was the Messiah, and went immediately to make

talked with the woman; yet no
man said, What seekest thou? or,
Why talkest thou with her?
28 The woman then left her
water-pot, and went her way into
the city, and saith to the men,
29 Come, see a man which told
me all things that ever I did. Is
not this the Christ?
30 Then they went out of the
city and came unto him.
31 In the mean while his disciples
prayed him, saying, Master, eat.
32 But he said unto them, I have
meat to eat that ye know not of.
33 Therefore said the disciples
one to another, Hath any man
brought him *aught* to eat?
34 Jesus saith unto them, [t]My
meat is to do the will of him that
sent me, and to [u]finish his work.
35 Say not ye, There are yet four

t Job 23.12; ch.6.38. *u* ch.17.4.

---

it known to others. Our first business, when we have found the Saviour, should be to make him known also to others.

29. *Is not this the Christ?* Though she probably believed it, yet she proposed it modestly, lest she should appear to dictate in a case which was so important, and which demanded so much attention. The evidence on which *she* was satisfied that he was the Messiah was that he had told her all things that she had done—perhaps much more than is here recorded. The question which she submitted to them was whether this was not satisfactory proof that he was the Messiah.

30. *They went out of the city.* The men of the city left it and went to Jesus, to hear and examine for themselves.

31. *Prayed him.* Asked him.

32. *I have meat to eat.* See ver. 34.

33. *Hath any man brought him*, &c. This is one of the many instances in which the disciples were slow to understand the Saviour.

34. *My meat*, &c. Jesus here explains what he said in ver. 32. His great object—the great design of his life—was to do the will of God. He came to that place weary and thirsty, and at the usual time of meals, probably an hungered; yet an opportunity of doing good presented itself, and he forgot his fatigue and hunger, and found comfort and joy in doing good—in seeking to save a soul. This one great object absorbed all his powers, and made him forget his weariness and the wants of nature. The mind may be so absorbed in doing the will of God as to forget all other things. Intent on this, we may rise above fatigue, and hardship, and want, and bear all with pleasure in seeing the work of God advance. See Job xxiii. 12: "I have esteemed the words of his mouth more than my necessary food." We may learn, also, that the main business of life is not to avoid fatigue or to seek the supply of our temporal wants, but to do the will of God. The mere supply of our temporal necessities, though most men make it an object of their chief solicitude, is a small consideration in the sight of him who has just views of the great design of human life. ¶ *The will of him that sent me.* The will of God in regard to the salvation of men. See Jn. vi. 38. ¶ *To finish his work.* To *complete* or fully to do the work which he has commanded in regard to the salvation of men. It is *his* work to provide salvation, and his to redeem, and his to apply the salvation to the heart. Jesus came to *do it* by teaching, by his example, and by his death as an expiation for sin. And he shows us that *we* should be diligent. If *he* was so diligent for *our* welfare, if he bore fatigue and want to benefit *us*, then *we* should be diligent, also, in regard to our *own* salvation, and also in seeking the salvation of others.

35. *Say not ye.* This seems to have been a proverb. Ye say—that is, men say. ¶ *Four months and*, &c. The common time from sowing the seed to the harvest, in Judea, was about *four months.* The meaning of this passage may be thus expressed: "The husbandman, when he sows his seed, is compelled to wait a considerable period before it produces a crop. He is encouraged in sowing it; he expects fruit; his labour is lightened by that expectation; but it is not *immediate*—it is remote. But it is not so with *my* preaching. The seed has already sprung up. Scarce was it sown before it produced an abundant harvest. The gospel was just preached to a woman, and see how many of the Samaritans come to hear

months, and *then* cometh harvest?
Behold, I say unto you, Lift up
your eyes, and look on the fields,
for they are [v]white already to
harvest.
36 And he that reapeth receiveth
wages, and [w]gathereth fruit unto
life eternal; that [x]both he that
soweth and he that reapeth may
rejoice together.
37 And herein is that saying true,
[y]One soweth, and another reapeth.
38 I sent you to reap that whereon
ye bestowed no labour: [z]other men

v Mat.9.37. *w* Ro.6.22. *x* 1 Co.3.5-9. *y* Mi.6.15. *z* 1 Pe.1.12.

---

it also. There is therefore more encouragement to labour in this field than the farmer has to sow his grain." ¶ *Lift up your eyes.* See the Samaritans coming to hear the gospel. ¶ *They are white.* Grain, when ripe, turns from a green to a yellow or light colour, indicating that it is time to reap it. So here were indications that the gospel was effectual, and that the harvest was to be gathered in. Hence we may learn, 1st. That there is as much encouragement to attempt to save souls as the farmer has to raise a crop. 2d. That the gospel is fitted to make an *immediate* impression on the minds of men. We are to expect that it will. We are not to *wait* to some future period, as if we could not expect immediate results. This wicked and ignorant people—little likely, apparently, to be affected—turned to God, heard the voice of the Saviour, and came in multitudes to him. 3d. We are to expect *revivals* of religion. Here was one instance of it under the Saviour's own preaching. Multitudes were excited, moved, and came to learn the way of life. 4th. We know not how much good may be done by conversation with even a single individual. This conversation with a woman resulted in a deep interest felt throughout the city, and in the conversion of many of them to God. So a single individual may often be the means, in the hand of God, of leading many to the cross of Jesus. 5th. What evils may follow from *neglecting* to do our duty! How easily might Jesus have alleged, if he had been like many of his professed disciples, that he was weary, that he was hungry, that it was esteemed improper to converse with a woman alone, that she was an abandoned character, and there could be little hope of doing her good! How many consciences of ministers and Christians would have been satisfied with reasoning like this? Yet Jesus, in spite of his fatigue and thirst, and all the difficulties of the case, seriously set about seeking the conversion of this woman. And behold what a glorious result! The city was moved, and a great harvest was found ready to be gathered in! *Let us not be weary in well-doing, for in due season we shall reap if we faint not.*

36. *He that reapeth.* He that gathers the harvest, or he who so preaches that souls are converted to Christ. ¶ *Receiveth wages.* The labourer in the harvest receives his hire. Jesus says it shall be thus with those who labour in the ministry—he will not suffer them to go unrewarded. See Da. xii. 3; Mat. xix. 28. ¶ *Gathereth fruit unto life eternal.* Converts souls, who shall inherit eternal life. The harvest is not temporary, like gathering grain, but shall result in eternal life. ¶ *That both he that soweth,* &c. It is a united work. It matters little whether we sow the seed or whether we reap the harvest. It is part of the same work, and whatever part we may do, we should rejoice. God gives the increase, while Paul may plant and Apollos water. The teacher in the Sunday-school, who sows the seed in early life, shall rejoice with the minister of the gospel who may gather in the harvest, and both join in giving all the praise to God.

37. *That saying.* That proverb. This proverb is found in some of the *Greek* writers (Grotius). Similar proverbs were in use among the Jews. See Is. lxv. 21, 22; Le. xxvi. 16; Mi. vi. 15. ¶ *One soweth,* &c. One man may preach the gospel, and with little apparent effect; another, succeeding him, may be crowned with eminent success. The seed, long buried, may spring up in an abundant harvest.

38. *I sent you.* In the commission given you to preach the gospel. You have not laboured or toiled in preparing the way for the great harvest which is now to be gathered in. ¶ *Other men laboured.* (1.) The prophets, who long laboured to prepare the way for the coming of the Messiah. (2.) The teachers among the Jews, who have read and

laboured, and ye are entered into
their labours.
39 And many of the Samaritans
of that city believed on him [a]for the
saying of the woman, which testified, He told me all that ever I did.
40 So when the Samaritans were
come unto him, they besought him
that he would tarry with them;
and he abode there two days.
41 And many more believed
because of his own word;
42 And said unto the woman,
Now we believe, not because of
thy saying; [b]for we have heard
him ourselves, and know that this
is indeed the Christ, the Saviour
of the world.
43 Now after two days he
departed thence, and went into
Galilee.
44 For Jesus himself testified
that [c]a prophet hath no honour
in his own country.
45 Then, when he was come
into Galilee, the Galileans received
him, [d]having seen all the things
that he did at Jerusalem at the
feast; [e]for they also went unto the
feast.
46 So Jesus came again into
Cana of Galilee, where he [f]made

a ver.29. *b* ch.17.8; 1 Jn.4.14.

c Mat.13.57; Mar.6.4; Lu.4.24. *d* ch.2.23. *e* De.16.16. *f* ch.2.1,11.

explained the law and taught the people. (3.) John the Baptist, who came to prepare the way. And, (4.) The Saviour himself, who by his personal ministry taught the people, and prepared them for the success which was to attend the preaching of the apostles. Especially did Jesus lay the foundation for the rapid and extensive spread of the gospel. *He* saw comparatively little fruit of his ministry. He confined his labours to Judea, and even there he was occupied in sowing seed which chiefly sprang up after his death. From this we may learn, 1st. That the man who is crowned with eminent success has no cause of *boasting* over others, any more than the man who *reaps* a field of grain should *boast* over the man who sowed it. The labour of both is equally necessary, and the labour of both would be useless if GOD did not give the increase. Comp. 1 Co. iii. 6. 2d. We should not be discouraged if we do not meet with immediate success. The man that *sows* is not disheartened because he does not see the harvest *immediately* spring up. We are to sow our seed in the morning, and in the evening we are not to withhold our hand, for we know not whether shall prosper, this or that; and we are to go forth bearing precious seed, though *weeping*, knowing that we shall come again rejoicing, bearing our sheaves with us, Ec. xi. 4; Ps. cxxvi. 6. 3d. Every part of the work of the ministry and of teaching men is needful, and we should rejoice that we are permitted to bear any part, however humble, in bringing sinners to the knowledge of our Lord and Saviour Jesus Christ, 1 Co. xii. 21–24.

39–42. *And many of the Samaritans of that city believed on him*, &c. There is seldom an instance of so remarkable success as this. From a single conversation, in circumstances, in a place, and with an individual little likely to be attended with such results, many sinners were converted; many believed on the testimony of the woman; many more came to hear, and believed because they heard him themselves. We should never despair of doing good in the most unpromising circumstances, and we should seize upon every opportunity to converse with sinners on the great subject of their souls' salvation.

43. *Into Galilee.* Into some of the parts of Galilee, though evidently not into Nazareth, but probably direct to *Cana*, ver. 46.

44. *For Jesus himself testified*, &c. See Notes on Mat. xiii. 57. The connection of this verse with the preceding may be thus explained: "Jesus went to Galilee, *but not* to Nazareth, for he testified," &c. Or, "Jesus went to Galilee, *although* he had said that a prophet had no honour in his own country; yet, because he foreknew that the Galileans would many of them believe on him, he went at this time."

45. *Received him.* Received him kindly, or as a messenger of God. They had seen his miracles, and believed on him.

46. *A certain nobleman.* One who was of the royal family, connected by

the water wine. And there was
a certain [1]nobleman, whose son
was sick at Capernaum.
47 When he heard that Jesus
was come out of Judea into
Galilee, he went unto him, and
besought him that he would come
down and heal his son, for he was
at the point of death.
48 Then said Jesus unto him,
Except ye see [g]signs and wonders,
ye will not believe.
49 The nobleman saith unto him,
Sir, come down ere my child die.

[1] or, *courtier;* or, *ruler.* [g] 1 Co.1.22.

50 Jesus saith unto him, [h]Go
thy way; thy son liveth. And the
man believed the word that Jesus
had spoken unto him, and he went
his way.
51 And as he was now going
down, his servants met him, and
told *him*, saying, Thy son liveth.
52 Then inquired he of them the
hour when he began to amend.
And they said unto him, Yesterday at the seventh hour the fever
left him.
53 So the father knew that

[h] Mat.8.13; Mar.7.29,30; Lu.17.14.

birth with Herod Antipas; or one of the officers of the court, whether by birth allied to him or not. It seems that his ordinary residence was at Capernaum. Capernaum was about a day's journey from Cana, where Jesus then was.

47. *He went unto him.* Though high in office, yet he did not refuse to go personally to Jesus to ask his aid. He felt as a father; and believing, after all that Jesus had done, that he could cure his son, he travelled to meet him. If men receive benefits of Christ, they must come in the same manner. The rich and the poor, the high and the low, must come personally as humble suppliants, and must be willing to bear all the reproach that may be cast on them for thus coming to him. This man showed strong faith in being willing thus to *go* to Jesus, but he erred in supposing that Jesus could heal only by his being present with his son. ¶ *Would come down.* It is probable that the miracles of Jesus heretofore had been performed only on those who were *present* with him, and this nobleman seems to have thought that this was necessary. One design of Jesus in working this miracle was to show him that this was not necessary. Hence he did not go down to Capernaum, but healed him where he was.

48. *Except ye see signs*, &c. This was spoken not to the nobleman only, but to the Galileans generally. The Samaritans had believed without any miracle. The Galileans, he said, were less disposed to believe him than even they were; and though he had wrought miracles *enough* to convince them, yet, unless they continually saw them, they would not believe.

49. *Come down*, &c. The earnestness of the nobleman evinces the deep and tender anxiety of a father. So anxious was he for his son that he was not willing that Jesus should delay a moment—not even to address the people. He still seems to have supposed that Jesus had no power to heal his son except he was *present* with him.

50. *Go thy way.* This was a kind and tender address. It was designed to convince him that he could word a miracle though not personally present. ¶ *Thy son liveth.* Thy son shall recover; or he shall be restored to health, according to thy request. ¶ *The man believed.* The manner in which Jesus spoke it, and the assurance which he gave, convinced the man that he could heal him there as well as to go to Capernaum to do it. This is an instance of the power of Jesus to convince the mind, to soothe doubts, to confirm faith, and to meet our desires. He blesses not always in the *manner* in which we ask, but he grants us our *main* wish. The father wished his son healed by Jesus *going down* to Capernaum. Jesus healed him, but not in *the way* in which he asked it to be done. God will hear our prayers and grant our requests, but often not in the precise *manner* in which we ask it. It is *his* to judge of the best way of doing us good.

52. *The seventh hour.* About one o'clock in the afternoon.

53. *The same hour.* The very time when Jesus spoke. ¶ *The fever left him.* It seems that it left him suddenly and entirely; so much so that his friends went to inform the father, and to comfort him, and also, doubtless, to apprise him that it was not necessary to ask aid

it was at the [i]same hour in the which Jesus said unto him, Thy son liveth: [k]and himself believed, and his whole house.

54 This *is* again the second miracle *that* Jesus did when he was come out of Judea into Galilee.

i Ps.107.20. *k* Ac.16.34; 18.8.

CHAPTER V.

AFTER this there was a [a]feast of the Jews; and Jesus went up to Jerusalem.

2 Now there is at Jerusalem, by the sheep-[1]*market*, a pool, which is called in the Hebrew

a Le.23.2,&c.; De.16.16; ch.2.13.
1 or, gate, Ne.3.1; 12.39.

from Jesus. From this miracle we may learn, 1st. That Jesus has an intimate knowledge of all things. He knew the case of this son—the extent of his disease—where he was—and thus had power to heal him. 2d. That Jesus has almighty power. Nothing else could have healed this child. Nor could it be pretended that he did it by any natural means. He was far away from him, and the child knew not the source of the power that healed him. It could not be pretended that there was any collusion or jugglery. The father came in deep anxiety. The servants saw the cure. Jesus was at a distance. Everything in the case bears the mark of being the simple energy of God—put forth with equal ease to heal, whether far or near. Thus he can save the sinner. 3d. We see the benevolence of Jesus. Ever ready to aid, to heal, or to save, he may be called on at all times, and will never be called on in vain. ¶ *Himself believed.* This miracle removed all his doubts, and he became a real disciple and friend of Jesus. ¶ *His whole house.* His whole family. We may learn from this, 1st. That sickness or any deep affliction is often the means of great good. Here the sickness of the son resulted in the faith of all the family. God often takes away earthly blessings that he may impart rich spiritual mercies. 2d. The father of a family may be the means of the salvation of his children. Here the effort of a parent resulted in their conversion to Christ. 3d. There is great beauty and propriety when sickness thus results in piety. For that it is sent. God does not willingly grieve or afflict the children of men; and when afflictions thus terminate, it will be cause of eternal joy, of ceaseless praise. 4th. There is a peculiar charm when piety thus comes into the families of the rich and the noble. It is so unusual; their example and influence go so far; it overcomes so many temptations, and affords opportunities of doing so much good, that there is no wonder that the evangelist selected this instance as one of the effects of the power and of the preaching of the Lord Jesus Christ.

CHAPTER V.

1. *A feast.* Probably the Passover, though it is not certain. There were two other feasts—the Pentecost and the Feast of Tabernacles—at which all the males were required to be present, and it might have been one of them. It is of no consequence, however, which of them is intended.

2. *The sheep*-market. This might have been rendered the *sheep-gate*, or the gate through which the sheep were taken into the city for sacrifice. The marginal rendering is *gate*, and the word "*market*" is not in the original, nor is a "*sheep-market*" mentioned in the Scriptures or in any of the Jewish writings. A *sheep-gate* is repeatedly mentioned by Nehemiah (ch. iii. 1, 32; xii. 39), being that by which sheep and oxen were brought into the city. As these were brought mainly for sacrifice, the gate was doubtless near the temple, and near the present place which is shown as the pool of Bethesda. ¶ *A pool.* This word may either mean a small lake or pond in which one can swim, or a place for fish, or any waters collected for bathing or washing. ¶ *Hebrew tongue.* Hebrew language. The language then spoken, which did not differ essentially from the ancient Hebrew. ¶ *Bethesda.* The house of mercy. It was so called on account of its strong healing properties—the property of restoring health to the sick and infirm. ¶ *Five porches.* The word *porch* commonly means a covered place surrounding a building, in which people can walk or sit in hot or wet weather. Here it probably means that there were five covered places, or apartments, in which the sick could remain, from each one of which they could have access to the water. This "pool" is thus described by Professor Hackett (*Illustra-*

tongue Bethesda, having five porches.

3 In these lay a great multitude of impotent folk, of blind, halt, withered, waiting for the moving of the water.

4 For an angel went down at a certain season into the pool,

---

tions of Scripture, p. 291, 292): "Just to the east of the Turkish garrison, and under the northern wall of the mosque, is a deep excavation, supposed by many to be the ancient pool of Bethesda, into which the sick descended 'after the troubling of the water,' and were healed, Jn. v. 1, sq. It is 360 feet long, 130 feet wide, and 75 deep. The evangelist says that this pool was near the sheep-gate, as the Greek probably signifies, rather than sheep-market, as rendered in the English version. That gate, according to Ne. iii. 1, sq., was on the north side of the temple, and hence the situation of this reservoir would agree with that of Bethesda. The present name, Birket Israil, Pool of Israil, indicates the opinion of the native inhabitants in regard to the object of the excavation. The general opinion of the most accurate travellers is that the so-called pool was originally part of a trench or fosse which protected the temple on the north. Though it contains no water at present except a little which trickles through the stones at the west end, it has evidently been used at some period as a reservoir. It is lined with cement, and adapted in other respects to hold water." Dr. Robinson established by personal inspection the fact of the subterranean connection of the pool of *Siloam* with the *Fountain of the Virgin*, and made it probable that the fountain under the mosque of Omar is connected with them. This spring is, as he himself witnessed, an *intermittent* one, and there *may* have been some artificially constructed basin in connection with this spring to which was given the name of *Bethesda*. He supposes, however, that there is not the slightest evidence that the place or reservoir now pointed out as *Bethesda* was the Bethesda of the New Testament (*Bib. Res.*, i. 501, 506, 509). In the time of Sandys (1611) the spring was found running, but in small quantities; in the time of Maundrell (1697) the stream did not run. Probably in his time, as now, the water which had formerly filtered through the rocks was dammed up by the rubbish.

3. *Impotent folk.* Sick people; or people who were *weak* and feeble by long disease. The word means those who were *feeble* rather than those who were afflicted with *acute* disease. ¶ *Halt.* Lame. ¶ *Withered.* Those who were afflicted with one form of the palsy that *withered* or dried up the part affected. See Notes on Mat. iv. 24. ¶ *Moving of the water.* It appears that this pool had medicinal properties only when it was *agitated* or *stirred*. It is probable that at regular times or intervals the fountain put forth an unusual quantity of water, or water of peculiar properties, and that *about* these times the people assembled in multitudes who were to be healed.

4. *An angel.* It is not affirmed that the angel did this *visibly*, or that they *saw* him do it. They judged by the *effect*, and when they saw the waters agitated, they concluded that they had healing properties, and descended to them. The Jews were in the habit of attributing all favours to the ministry of the angels of God, Ge. xix. 15; He. i. 14; Mat. iv. 11; xviii. 10; Lu. xvi. 22; Ac. vii. 53; Ga. iii. 19; Ac. xii. 11. This fountain, it seems, had strong medicinal properties. Like many other waters, it had the property of healing certain diseases that were incurable by any other means. Thus the waters of Bath, of Saratoga, &c., are found to be highly medicinal, and to heal diseases that are otherwise incurable. In the case of the waters of Bethesda there does not appear to have been anything *miraculous*, but the waters seem to have been endued with strong medicinal properties, especially after a periodical agitation. All that is peculiar about them in the record is that this was produced by the ministry of an angel. This was in accordance with the common sentiment of the Jews, the common doctrine of the Bible, and the belief of the sacred writers. Nor can it be shown to be absurd or improbable that such blessings should be imparted to man by the ministry of an angel. There is no more absurdity in the belief that a pure spirit or holy *angel* should aid man, than that a physician or a parent should; and no more absurdity in supposing that the healing

and troubled the water: whosoever then [b]first after the troubling of the water stepped in, [c]was made whole of whatsoever disease he had.

5 And a certain man was there which [d]had an infirmity thirty and eight years.

6 When Jesus saw him lie, [e]and knew that he had been now a long time in *that case*, he saith unto him, Wilt thou be made whole?

7 The impotent man answered him, Sir, [f]I have no man, when the water is troubled, to put me

b Pr.8.17; Ec.9.10; Mat.11.12.
c Eze.47.8,9; Zec.13.1. *d* Lu.8.43; 13.16.
e Ps.142.3.
f De.32.36; Ps.72.12; 142.4; Ro.5.6; 2 Co.1.9,10.

---

properties of such a fountain should be produced by his aid, than that any other blessing should be, He. i. 12. What man can *prove* that all his temporal blessings do not come to him through the medium of others—of parents, of teachers, of friends, of *angels?* And who can prove that it is unworthy the *benevolence* of angels to minister to the wants of the poor, the needy, and the afflicted, when *man* does it, and Jesus Christ did it, and God himself does it daily? ¶ *Went down.* Descended to the pool. ¶ *At a certain season.* At a certain time; periodically. The people knew *about* the time when this was done, and assembled in multitudes to partake of the benefits. Many medicinal springs are more strongly impregnated at some seasons of the year than others. ¶ *Troubled the water.* Stirred or *agitated* the water. There was probably an increase, and a bubbling and agitation produced by the admission of a fresh quantity. ¶ *Whosoever then first.* This does not mean that but *one* was healed, and that the *first* one, but that those who first descended into the pool were healed. The strong medicinal properties of the waters soon subsided, and those who could not at first enter into the pool were obliged to wait for the return of the agitation. ¶ *Stepped in.* Went in. ¶ *Was made whole.* Was healed. It is not implied that this was done *instantaneously* or *by a miracle.* The water had such properties that he was healed, though probably gradually. It is not less the gift of God to suppose that this fountain restored gradually, and in accordance with what commonly occurs, than to suppose, what is not affirmed, that it was done at once and in a miraculous manner.

In regard to this passage, it should be remarked that the account of the angel in the 4th verse is wanting in many manuscripts, and has been by many supposed to be spurious. There is not conclusive evidence, however, that it is not a part of the genuine text, and the best critics suppose that it should not be rejected. One difficulty has been that no such place as this spring is mentioned by Josephus. But John is as good a historian, and as worthy to be believed as Josephus. Besides, it is known that many important places and events have not been mentioned by the Jewish historian, and it is no evidence that there was no such place as this because *he* did not mention it. When this fountain was discovered, or how long its healing properties continued to be known, it is impossible now to ascertain. All that we know of it is what is mentioned here, and conjecture would be useless. We may remark, however, that *such* a place anywhere is an evidence of the great goodness of God. Springs or fountains having healing properties abound on earth, and nowhere more than in our own country. Diseases are often healed in such places which no human skill could remove. The Jews regarded such a provision as proof of the mercy of God. They gave this healing spring the name of a "house of mercy." They regarded it as under the care of an angel. And there is no place where man should be more sensible of the goodness of God, or be more disposed to render him praise as *in* a "house of mercy," than when at such a healing fountain. And *yet* how lamentable is it that such places—watering places—should be mere places of gaiety and thoughtlessness, of balls, and gambling, and dissipation! How melancholy that amid the very places where there is most evidence of the goodness of God, and of the misery of the poor, the sick, the afflicted, men should forget all the goodness of their Maker, and spend their time in scenes of dissipation, folly, and vice!

5. *An infirmity.* A weakness. We know not what his disease was. We

into the pool; but while I am coming, another steppeth down before me.

8 Jesus saith unto him, [g]Rise, take up thy bed, and walk.

9 And immediately the man was made whole, and took up his bed, and walked; [h]and on the same day was the sabbath.

10 The Jews therefore said unto him that was cured, [i]It is the sabbath-day; it is not lawful for thee to carry *thy* bed.

11 He answered them, He that

g Mat.9.6; Mar.2.11; Lu.5.24. *h* ch.9.14. *i* Je.17.21,&c.; Mat.12.2,&c.

---

know only that it disabled him from walking, and that it was of very long standing. It was doubtless regarded as incurable.

7. *Sir, I have no man*, &c. The answer of the man implied that he *did* wish it, but, in addition to all his other trials, he had no *friend* to aid him. This is an additional circumstance that heightened his affliction.

8. *Rise, take up*, &c. Jesus not only restored him to health, but he gave evidence to those around him that this was a real miracle, and that he was really healed. For almost forty years he had been afflicted. He was not even able to walk. Jesus commanded him not only to *walk*, but to take up his *bed* also, and carry that as proof that he was truly made whole. In regard to this we may observe, 1st. That it was a remarkable command. The poor man had been long infirm, and it does not appear that he expected to be healed except by being put into the waters. Yet Jesus, when he gives a commandment, can give strength to obey it. 2d. It is our business to obey the commands of Jesus, however feeble we feel ourselves to be. His grace will be sufficient for us, and his burden will be light. 3d. The weak and helpless sinner should put forth his efforts in obedience to the command of Jesus. Never was a sinner more *helpless* than was this man. If God gave *him* strength to do his will, so he can all others; and the plea that we can do nothing could have been urged with far more propriety by this man than it can be by any impenitent sinner. 4th. This narrative should not be *abused*. It should not be supposed as intended to teach that a sinner should delay repentance, as if *waiting for God*. The narrative neither teaches nor implies *any such thing*. It is a simple record *of a fact* in regard to a man who had no power to heal himself, and who was under no obligation to heal himself. There is no reference in the narrative to the difficulties of a sinner—no intimation that it was intended to refer to his condition; and to make this example an excuse for *delay*, or an argument for *waiting*, is to abuse and pervert the Bible. Seldom is more mischief done than by attempting to draw from the Bible what it was not intended to teach, and by an effort to make that convey spiritual instruction which God has not declared designed for that purpose. ¶ *Thy bed*. Thy couch; or the mattress or clothes on which he lay.

9. *The Sabbath*. To carry burdens on the Sabbath was forbidden in the Old Testament, Je. xvii. 21; Ne. xiii. 15; Ex. xx. 8–10. If it be asked, then, why Jesus commanded a man to do on the Sabbath what was understood to be a violation of the day, it may be answered, 1st. That the Son of man was Lord of the Sabbath, and had a right to declare what *might* be done, and even to dispense with a *positive* law of the Jews, Mat. xii. 8; Jn. v. 17. 2d. This was a poor man, and Jesus directed him to secure his property. 3d. The Jews extended the obligation of the Sabbath beyond what was intended by the appointment. They observed it superstitiously, and Jesus took every opportunity to convince them of their error, and to restore the day to its proper observance, Mat. xii. 6–11; Lu. vi. 9; xiii. 14; xiv. 5. This method he took to show them what the law of God really *permitted* on that day, and that works of necessity and mercy were lawful.

10. *Not lawful*. It was forbidden, they supposed, in the Old Testament. The Jews were very strenuous in the observation of the external duties of religion.

11. *He that made me whole*. The man reasoned correctly. If Jesus had power to work so signal a miracle, he had a right to explain the law. If he had conferred so great a favour on him, he had a right to expect obedience; and we may learn that the mercy of God

made me whole, the same said
unto me, Take up thy bed and
walk.
12 Then asked they him, What
man is that which said unto thee,
Take up thy bed and walk?
13 And he that was healed
wist[k] not who it was; [l]for Jesus
had conveyed himself away, [2]a
multitude being in *that* place.
14 Afterward Jesus findeth him
in the temple, and said unto him,
Behold, thou art made whole:
[m]sin no more, lest a worse thing
come unto thee.
15 The man departed, and told

k ch.14.9. *l* Lu.4.30.

2 or, *from the multitude that was.* *m* ch.8.11.

in pardoning our sins, or in bestowing any signal blessing, imposes the obligation to obey him. We should yield obedience to him according to what we *know* to be his will, whatever may be the opinions of men, or whatever interpretation *they* may put on the law of God. *Our* business is a simple, hearty, child-like obedience, let the men of the world say or think of us as they choose.

12. *What man is he*, &c. In this verse there is a remarkable instance of the *perverseness* of men, of their want of candour, and of the manner in which they often look at a subject. Instead of looking at the *miracle*, and at the man's statement of the manner in which he was healed, they look only at what they thought to be a violation of the law. They assumed it as certain that nothing could make his conduct, in carrying his bed on the Sabbath-day, proper; and they meditated vengeance, not only on the man who was carrying his bed, but on him, also, who had told him to do it. Thus men often assume that a certain course or opinion is proper, and when anyone differs from them they look only *at the difference*, but not *at the reasons* for it. One great source of dispute among men is that they look only at the points in which they *differ*, but are unwilling to listen to the reasons why others do not believe as they do. It is always enough to condemn one in the eyes of a bigot that he differs from *him*, and he looks upon him who holds a different opinion, as the Jews did at this man, *as certainly wrong;* and such a bigot looks at the reasons why others differ from him just as the Jews did at the reason why this man bore his bed on the Sabbath—as not worth regarding or hearing, or as if they could not possibly be right.

13. *Wist not.* Knew not. ¶ *Had conveyed himself away.* Was lost in the crowd. He had silently mingled with the multitude, or had passed on with the crowd unobserved, and the man had been so rejoiced at his cure that he had not even inquired the *name* of his benefactor.

14. *Findeth him.* Fell in with him, or saw him. ¶ *In the temple.* The man seems to have gone at once to the temple—perhaps a privilege of which he had been long deprived. They who are healed from sickness should seek the sanctuary of God and give him thanks for his mercy. Comp. Notes on Is. xxxviii. 20. There is nothing more improper, when we are raised up from a bed of pain, than to forget God our benefactor, and neglect to praise him for his mercies. ¶ *Thou art made whole.* Jesus calls to his remembrance the fact that he was healed, in order that he might admonish him not to sin again. ¶ *Sin no more.* By this expression it was implied that the infirmity of this man was caused by sin—perhaps by vice in his youth. His crime or dissipation had brought on him this long and distressing affliction. Jesus shows him that he knew the *cause* of his sickness, and takes occasion to warn him not to repeat it. No man who indulges in vice can tell what may be its consequences. It must always end in evil, and not unfrequently it results in loss of health, and in long and painful disease. This is always the case with intemperance and all gross pleasures. Sooner or later, sin will always result in misery. ¶ *Sin no more.* Do not repeat the vice. You have had dear-bought experience, and if repeated it will be worse. When a man has been restored from the effects of sin, he should learn to avoid the very appearance of evil. He should shun the place of temptation; he should not mingle again with his old companions; he should touch not, taste not, handle not. God visits with heavier judgment those who have been once restored from the ways of sin and who return again to it. The drunkard that has been reformed, and

the Jews that it was Jesus which had made him whole.

16 And therefore did the Jews persecute Jesus, and sought to slay him, because he had done these things on the sabbath-day.

17 But Jesus answered them, [n]My Father worketh hitherto, and I work.

18 Therefore the Jews sought the more [o]to kill him, because he not only had broken the sabbath,

n ch.9.4; 14.10. *o* ch.7.19.

---

that returns to his habits of drinking, becomes more beastly; the man that professes to have experienced a change of heart, and who then indulges in sin, sinks deeper into pollution, and is seldom restored. The only way of safety in all such cases is to *sin no more;* not to be in the way of temptation; not to expose ourselves; not to touch or approach that which came near to working our ruin. The man who has been intemperate and is reformed, if he tastes the poison *at all*, may expect to sink deeper than ever into drunkenness and pollution. ¶ *A worse thing.* A more grievous disease, or the pains of hell. "The doom of apostates is a worse thing than thirty-eight years' lameness" (Henry).

16. *Persecuted Jesus.* They opposed him; attempted to ruin his character; to destroy his popularity; and probably held him up before the people as a violator of the law of God. Instead of making inquiry whether he had not given proof that he was the Messiah, they *assumed* that he must be wrong, and ought to be punished. Thus every bigot and persecutor does in regard to those who differ from them. ¶ *To slay him.* To put him to death. This they attempted to do because it was directed in the law of Moses, Ex. xxxi. 15; xxxv. 2. See Lu. vi. 7, 11; xiii. 14. We see here, 1st. How full of enmity and how bloody was the purpose of the Jews. All that Jesus had done was to restore an infirm man to health—a thing which *they* would have done for their cattle (Lu. vi. 7), and yet they sought his life because he had done it for a sick *man.* 2d. Men are often extremely envious because good is done by others, especially if it is not done according to the way of *their* denomination or party. 3d. Here was an instance of the common feelings of a hypocrite. He often covers his enmity against the *power* of religion by great zeal for the *form* of it. He hates and persecutes those who do good, who seek the conversion of sinners, who love revivals of religion and the spread of the gospel, because it is not according to some matter of form which has been established, and on which he supposes the whole safety of the church to hang. There was nothing that Jesus was more opposed to than hypocrisy, and nothing that he set himself more against than those who suppose all goodness to consist in *forms*, and all piety in the *shibboleths* of a party.

17. *My Father.* God. ¶ *Worketh hitherto.* Worketh *until now*, or till this time. God has not ceased to work on the Sabbath. He makes the sun to rise; he rolls the stars; he causes the grass, the tree, the flower to grow. He has not suspended his operations on the Sabbath, and the obligation to *rest* on the Sabbath does not extend to him. He *created* the world in six days, and ceased the work of *creation;* but he has not ceased to *govern* it, and to carry forward, by his providence, his great plans on the Sabbath. ¶ *And I work.* "As God does good on that day; as he is not bound by the law which requires his creatures to rest on that day, so *I* do the same. The law on that subject may be dispensed with, also, in my case, for the Son of man is Lord of the Sabbath." In this reply it is implied that he was equal with God from two circumstances: 1st. Because he called God his Father, ver. 18. 2d. Because he claimed the same *exemption* from law which God did, asserting that the law of the Sabbath did not bind him or his Father, thus showing that he had a right to impose and repeal laws in the same manner as God. He that has a right to do this must be God.

18. *The more to kill him.* The answer of Jesus was fitted greatly to irritate them. He did not *deny* what he had done, but he *added* to that what he well knew would highly offend them. That he should claim the right of *dispensing* with the law, and affirm that, in regard to its observance, he was in the same condition with God, was eminently fitted to enrage them, and he doubtless knew that it might endanger his life. We may learn from his answer, 1st.

but said also that God was his
Father, [p] making himself equal
with God.
19 Then answered Jesus and
said unto them, Verily, verily, I
say unto you, [q] The Son can do
nothing of himself, but what he
seeth the Father do; for what
things soever he doeth, these also
doeth the Son likewise.
20 For [r] the Father loveth the
Son, and showeth him all things

p Zec.13.7; ch.10.30,33; Phi.2.6. q ver.30. r Mat.3.17; ch.3.35; 17.26.

That we are not to keep back truth because it may endanger us. 2d. That we are not to keep back truth because it will irritate and enrage sinners. The fault is not in the *truth*, but in the *sinner*. 3d. That when any one portion of truth enrages hypocrites, they will be enraged the more they hear. ¶ *Had broken the sabbath.* They *supposed* he had broken it. ¶ *Making himself equal with God.* This shows that, in the view of the Jews, the name Son of God, or that calling God his Father, implied equality with God. The Jews were the best interpreters of their own language, and as Jesus did not deny the correctness of their interpretations, it follows that he meant to be so understood. See ch. x. 29-38. The interpretation of the Jews was a very natural and just one. He not only said that God was his Father, but he said that he had the same right to work on the Sabbath that God had; that by the same authority, and in the same manner, he could dispense with the obligation of the day. They had now *two* pretences for seeking to kill him—one for making himself equal with God, which they considered blasphemy, and the other for violating the Sabbath. For each of these the law denounced death, Nu. xv. 35; Le. xxiv. 11-14.

19. *The Son can do nothing of himself.* Jesus, having stated the *extent* of his authority, proceeds here to show its *source and nature*, and to *prove* to them that what he had said was true. The first explanation which he gives is in these words: *The Son*—whom he had just impliedly affirmed to be equal with God—did nothing *of himself;* that is, nothing without the appointment of the Father; nothing contrary to the Father, as he immediately explains it. When it is said that he CAN *do nothing* OF HIMSELF, it is meant that such is the union subsisting between the Father and the Son that he can do nothing *independently* or separate from the Father. Such is the nature of this union that he can do nothing which has not the concurrence of the Father, and which he does not command. In all things he must, from the necessity of his nature, act in accordance with the nature and will of God. Such is the intimacy of the union, that the fact that *he* does anything is proof that it is by the concurring agency of God. There is no separate action—no separate existence; but, alike in being and in action, there is the most perfect oneness between him and the Father. Comp. Jn. x. 30; xvii. 21. ¶ *What he seeth the Father do.* In the works of creation and providence, in making laws, and in the government of the universe. There is a peculiar force in the word *seeth* here. No *man* can see God acting in his works; but the word here implies that the Son sees him act, as we see our fellow-men act, and that he has a knowledge of him, therefore, which no mere mortal could possess. ¶ *What things soever.* In the works of creation and of providence, and in the government of the worlds. The word is without limit—ALL that the Father does the Son likewise does. This is as high an assertion as possible of his being *equal* with God. If one does *all* that another does or can do, then there must be equality. If the Son does all that the Father does, then, like him, he must be almighty, omniscient, omnipresent, and infinite in every perfection; or, in other words, he must be God. If he had *this* power, then he had authority, also, to do on the Sabbath-day what God did.

20. *The Father loveth the Son.* This authority he traces to the love which the Father has for him—that peculiar, ineffable, infinite love which God has for his only-begotten Son, feebly and dimly illustrated by the love which an earthly parent has for an only child. ¶ *Showeth him.* Makes him acquainted with. Conceals nothing from him. From apostles, prophets, and philosophers no small part of the doings of God are concealed. From the *Son* nothing is. And as God shows him *all* that he does, he must be possessed of omniscience, for to no finite mind could be imparted a

that himself doeth; and he will
show him greater works than
these, that ye may marvel.
21 For as the Father raiseth up
the dead, and quickeneth *them*,
even so [s]the Son quickeneth whom
he will.

s Lu.8.54; ch.11.25; 17.2.

22 For the Father judgeth no
man, but [t]hath committed all
judgment unto the Son;
23 That all *men* should honour
the Son, even as they honour the
Father. He that honoureth not

t Mat.11.27; Ac.17.31; 2 Co.5.10.

---

knowledge of *all* the works of God. ¶ *Will show him.* Will appoint and direct him to do greater works than these. ¶ *Greater works than these.* Than healing the impotent man, and commanding him to carry his bed on the Sabbath-day. The greater works to which he refers are those which he proceeds to specify—he will raise the dead and judge the world, &c. ¶ *May marvel.* May wonder, or be amazed.

21. *As the Father raiseth up the dead.* God has power to raise the dead. By his power it had been done in at least two instances—by the prophet Elijah, in the case of the son of the widow of Sarepta (1 Ki. xvii. 22), and by the prophet Elisha, in the case of the Shunamite's son, 2 Ki. iv. 32–35. The Jews did not doubt that God had power to raise the dead. Jesus here expressly affirms it, and says he has the same power. ¶ *Quickeneth* them. Gives them *life.* This is the sense of the word *quickeneth* throughout the Bible. ¶ *Even so.* In the same manner. By the same authority and power. The power of raising the dead must be one of the highest attributes of the divinity. As Jesus affirms that he has the power to do this *in the same manner* as the Father, so it follows that he must be equal with God. ¶ *The Son quickeneth.* Gives life to. This may either refer to his raising the dead from their graves, or to his giving spiritual life to those who are dead in trespasses and sins. The former he did in the case of Lazarus and the widow's son at Nain, Jn. xi. 43, 44; Lu. vii. 14, 15. The latter he did in the case of all those who were converted by his power, and still does it in any instance of conversion. ¶ *Whom he will.* It was in the power of Jesus to raise up any of the dead as well as Lazarus. It depended on his will whether Lazarus and the widow's son should come to life. So it depends on his will whether sinners shall live. He has power to renew them, and the renewing of the heart is as much the result of his *will* as the raising of the dead.

22. *Judgeth no man.* Jesus in these verses is showing his *equality with God.* He affirmed (ver. 17) that he had the same power over the Sabbath that his Father had; in ver. 19, that he *did* the same things as the Father; in ver. 21 particularly that he had the same power to raise the dead. He now adds that God has given him the authority to *judge* men. The Father pronounces judgment on no one. This office he has committed to the Son. The power of judging the world implies ability to search the heart, and omniscience to understand the motives of all actions. This is a work which none but a divine being can do, and it shows, therefore, that the Son is equal to the Father. ¶ *Hath committed,* &c. Hath appointed him to be the judge of the world. In the previous verse he had said that he had power *to raise the dead;* he here adds that it will be his, also, to *judge* them when they are raised. See Mat. xxv.; Ac. xvii. 31.

23. *That all* men *should honour,* &c. To honour is to esteem, reverence, praise, do homage to. We honour one when we ascribe to him in our hearts, and words, and actions the praise and obedience which are due to him. We honour God when we obey him and worship him aright. We honour the Son when we esteem him to be as he is; when we have right views and feelings toward him. As he is declared to be God (Jn. i. 1), as he here says he has power and authority equal with God, so we honour him when we regard him as such. The primitive Christians are described by Pliny, in a letter to the Emperor Trajan, as meeting together to sing hymns to Christ *as God.* So we honour him aright when we regard him as possessed of wisdom, goodness, power, eternity, omniscience—equal with God. ¶ *Even as.* To the same extent; in the same manner. Since the Son is to be honoured EVEN AS the Father, it follows that he must be equal

the Son, honoureth not the Father which hath sent him.

24 Verily, verily, I say unto you, [u]He that heareth my word, and believeth on him that sent me, hath everlasting life, and shall

u ch.6.40,47.

with the Father. To *honour the Father* must denote *religious* homage, or the rendering of that honour which is due to God; so to honour the Son must also denote *religious* homage. If our Saviour here did not intend to teach that he ought to be *worshipped*, and to be esteemed as *equal* with God, it would be difficult to teach it by any language which we could use. ¶ *He that honoureth not the Son.* He that does not believe on him, and render to him the homage which is his due as the equal of God. ¶ *Honoureth not the Father.* Does not worship and obey the Father, the first person of the Trinity—that is, does not worship *God.* He may imagine that he worships God, but there *is* no God but the God subsisting as Father, Son, and Holy Ghost. He that withholds proper homage from one, withholds it from all. He that should refuse to honour *the Father*, could not be said to honour *God;* and in the like manner, he that honoureth not *the Son*, honoureth not *the Father.* This appears farther from the following considerations:—1st. The Father wills that the Son should be honoured. He that refuses to do it disobeys the Father. 2d. They are equal. He that denies the one denies also the other. 3d. The same feeling that leads us to honour the *Father* will also lead us to honour the *Son*, for he is "the brightness of his glory, and the express image of his person," He. i. 3. 4th. The evidence of the existence of the Son is the same as that of the Father. He has the same wisdom, goodness, omnipresence, truth, power.

And from these verses we may learn —1st. That those who do not render proper homage to Jesus Christ do not worship the true God. 2d. There is no such God as the infidel professes to believe in. There can be but one God; and if the God of the Bible be the true God, then all other gods are false gods. 3d. Those who withhold proper homage from Jesus Christ, who do not honour him EVEN AS they honour the Father, cannot be Christians. 4th. One evidence of piety is when we are willing to render proper praise and homage to Jesus Christ —to love him, and serve and obey him, with all our hearts. 5th. *As a matter of fact*, it may be added that they who do not honour the Son do not worship God at all. The infidel has no form of worship; he has no place of secret prayer, no temple of worship, no family altar. Who ever yet heard of an infidel that prayed? Where do such men build houses of worship? Where do they meet to praise God? Nowhere. As certainly as we hear the name *infidel*, we are certain at once that we hear the name of a man who has no form of religion in his family, who never prays in secret, and who will do nothing to maintain the public worship of God. Account for it as men may, it is a fact that no one can dispute, that it is only they who do honour to the Lord Jesus that have any form of the worship of God, or that honour him; *and their veneration for God is just in proportion to their love for the Redeemer—just as they honour him.*

24. *He that heareth my word.* To *hear*, in this place, evidently denotes not the outward act of hearing, but to receive in a proper manner; to suffer it to make its proper impression on the mind; to obey. The word *hear* is often used in this sense, Mat. xi. 15; Jn. viii. 47; Ac. iii. 23. Many persons outwardly hear the gospel who neither understand nor obey it. ¶ *My word.* My doctrine, my teaching. All that Jesus taught about *himself*, as well as about the Father. ¶ *On him that sent me.* On the Father, who, in the plan of redemption, is represented as *sending* his Son to save men. See Jn. iii. 17. Faith in God, who sent his Son, is here represented as being connected with everlasting life; but there can be no faith in him who *sent* his Son, without faith also in him who is *sent.* The belief of *one* of the true doctrines of religion is connected with, and will lead to, the belief of *all.* ¶ *Hath everlasting life.* The state of man by nature is represented as death in sin, Ep. ii. 1. Religion is the opposite of this, or is *life.* The *dead* regard not anything. They are unaffected by the cares, pleasures, amusements of the world. They hear neither the voice of merriment nor the tread of the living over their graves. So with sinners. They are unmoved with the things of

not come into condemnation, but is[v] passed from death unto life.

25 Verily, verily, I say unto you, The hour is coming, and now is, when [w]the dead shall hear the voice of the Son of God; and they that hear shall live.

26 For as the Father hath life

v 1 Jn.3.14.

w ver.28; Ep.2.1.

religion. They hear not the voice of God; they see not his loveliness; they care not for his threatenings. But religion is *life*. The Christian *lives* with God, and feels and acts as if there was a God. Religion, and its blessings here and hereafter, are one and the same. The happiness of heaven is *living* unto God—being sensible of his presence, and glory, and power—and rejoicing in that. There shall be no more *death* there, Re. xxi. 4. This *life*, or this religion, whether on earth or in heaven, is the same—the same joys extended and expanded for ever. Hence, when a man is converted, it is said that he *has* everlasting life; not merely *shall have*, but is already *in possession* of that life or happiness which shall be everlasting. It is life begun, expanded, ripening for the skies. He has already entered on his inheritance—that inheritance which is everlasting. ¶ *Shall not come into condemnation.* He was by nature under condemnation. See Jn. iii. 18. Here it is declared that he shall not return to that state, or he will not be again condemned. This promise is sure; it is made by the Son of God, and there is no one that can pluck them out of his hand, Jn. x. 28. Comp. Notes on Ro. viii. 1. ¶ *But is passed from death unto life.* Has *passed over* from a state of spiritual death to the life of the Christian. The word translated *is passed* would be better expressed by *has passed*. It implies that he has done it voluntarily; that none compelled him; and that the passage is made unto *everlasting* life. Because Christ is the *author* of this life in the soul, he is called the *life* (Jn. i. 4); and as he has *always* existed, and is the source of *all life*, he is called the *eternal life*, 1 Jn. v. 20.

25. *The hour.* The time. ¶ *Is coming.* Under the preaching of the gospel, as well as in the resurrection of the dead. ¶ *Now is.* It is now taking place. Sinners were converted under his ministry and brought to spiritual life. ¶ *The dead.* Either the dead in sins, or those that are in their graves. The words of the Saviour will apply to either. Language, in the Scriptures, is often so used as to describe two *similar* events. Thus the destruction of Jerusalem and the end of the world are described by Jesus in the same language, Mat. xxiv. xxv. The return of the Jews from Babylon, and the coming of the Messiah, and the spread of his gospel, are described in the same language by Isaiah, Is. xl.-lxi. Comp. Notes on Is. vii. 14. The renewal of the heart, and the raising of the dead at the judgment, are here also described in similar language, because they so far resemble each other that the same language will apply to both. ¶ *The voice of the Son of God.* The voice is that by which we give command. Jesus raised up the dead by his command, or by his authority. When he did it he spoke, or commanded it to be done. Mar. v. 41: "He took the damsel by the hand, and *said*, Talitha cumi." Lu. vii. 14: "And he came and touched the bier, and *said*, Young man, I say unto thee, Arise." Jn. xi. 43: "He cried with a loud voice, Lazarus, come forth." So it is by his command that those who are dead in sins are quickened or made alive, ver. 21. And so at the day of judgment the dead will be raised by his command or voice, though there is no reason to think that his voice will be audibly heard, ver. 28. ¶ *Shall live.* Shall be restored to life.

26. *As the Father hath life.* God is the source of all life. He is thence called the *living* God, in opposition to idols which have no life. Ac. xiv. 15: "We preach unto you that ye should turn from these vanities (idols) *unto the living God*," Jos. iii. 10; 1 Sa. xvii. 26; Je. x. 10. See also Is. xl. 18-31. ¶ *In himself.* This means that life in God, or existence, is not *derived* from any other being. *Our* life is derived from God. Gen. ii. 7: God "breathed into his nostrils the breath of life, and man became a living soul"—that is, a living being. All other creatures derive their life from him. Ps. civ. 30, 29: "Thou sendest forth thy spirit, they are created; thou takest away their breath, they die and return to their dust." But God is underived. He always existed as he is. Ps. xc. 2: "From everlasting to everlasting thou art God." He is unchangeably the same, Ja. i. 17. It

in himself, so hath he given to the Son to have [x]life in himself;

x 1 Co.15.45.

27 And hath given him [y]authority to execute judgment also, because he is the Son of man.

y ver.22.

cannot be said that he is *self-existent*, because that is an absurdity; no being can originate or create himself; but he is not dependent on any other for *life*. Of course, no being can take away his existence; and of course, also, no being can take away his *happiness*. He has *in himself* infinite sources of happiness, and no other being, no change in his universe can destroy that happiness. ¶ *So*. In a manner like his. It corresponds to the first "as," implying that one is the same as the other; life in the one is the *same*, and possessed in the *same manner*, as in the other. ¶ *Hath he given*. This shows that the power or authority here spoken of was *given* or committed to the Lord Jesus. This evidently does not refer to the manner in which the second person of the Trinity exists, for the power and authority of which Christ here speaks is that which he exercises as *Mediator*. It is the power of raising the dead and judging the world. In regard to his *divine nature*, it is not affirmed here that it is in any manner derived; nor does the fact that God is said to have *given* him this power prove that he was inferior in his nature or that his existence was derived. For, 1st. It has reference merely *to office*. As Mediator, he may be said to have been appointed by the Father. 2d. Appointment to office does not prove that the one who is appointed is inferior in nature to him who appoints him. A son may be appointed to a particular work by a parent, and yet, in regard to talents and every other qualification, may be equal or superior to the father. He sustains the relation of a son, and in this relation there is an official inferiority. General Washington was not inferior in nature and talents to the men who commissioned him. He simply derived *authority* from them to do what he was otherwise fully *able* to do. So the Son, *as Mediator*, is subject to the Father; yet this proves nothing about *his nature*. ¶ *To have life*. That is, the right or authority of imparting life to others, whether dead in their graves or in their sins. ¶ *In himself*. There is much that is remarkable in this expression. It is IN *him* as it is IN *God*. He has the control of it, and can exercise it as he will. The prophets and apostles are never represented as having such power in themselves. They were dependent; they performed miracles in the name of God and of Jesus Christ (Ac. iii. 6; iv. 30; xvi. 18); but Jesus did it by his own name, authority, and power. He had but to speak, and it was done, Mar. v. 41; Lu. vii. 14; Jn. xi. 43. This wonderful commission he bore from God to raise up the dead as he pleased; to convert sinners when and where he chose; and finally to raise up *all* the dead, and pronounce on them an eternal doom according to the deeds done in the body. None could do this but he who had the power of creation—equal in omnipotence to the Father, and the power of searching *all* hearts—equal in omniscience to God.

27. *Hath given him authority*. Hath appointed him to do this. Has made him to be judge of all. This is represented as being the appointment of the Father, Ac. xvii. 31. The word *authority* here (commonly rendered *power*) implies all that is necessary to execute judgment—all the physical power to raise the dead, and to investigate the actions and thoughts of the life; and all the *moral right* or authority to sit in judgment on the creatures of God, and to pronounce their doom. ¶ *To execute judgment*. To *do* judgment—that is, to judge. He has appointment to *do justice;* to see that the universe suffers no wrong, either by the escape of the guilty or by the punishment of the innocent. ¶ *Because he is the Son of man*. The phrase *Son of man* here seems to be used in the sense of "because he is a man," or because he has human nature. The term is one which Jesus often gives to himself, to show his union with man and his interest in man. See Notes on Mat. viii. 19, 20. It is to be remarked here that the word *son* has not the article before it in the original: "Because he is *a* Son of man"—that is, because he is a man. It would seem from this that there is a propriety that one in our nature should judge us. What this propriety is we do not certainly know. It may be, 1st. Because one who has experienced our infirmities, and who possesses our nature, may be supposed by those *who are judged* to be

28 Marvel not at this; for the hour is coming, in the which all that are in the graves shall hear his voice,
29 And shall come forth; [z]they that have done good unto the resurrection of life, and they that have done evil unto [a]the resurrection of damnation.
30 I[b] can of mine own self do

z Da.12.2. a Mat.25.46. b ver.19.

better qualified than one in a different nature. 2d. Because he is to decide between *man* and *God*, and it is proper that *our* feelings, and nature, and views should be represented in the judge, as well as those of God. 3d. Because Jesus has all the feelings of compassion we could ask—all the benevolence we could desire in a judge; because he has *shown* his disposition to defend us by giving his life, and it can never be alleged by those who are condemned that their judge was a distant, cold, and unfriendly being. Some have supposed that the expression *Son of man* here means the same as *Messiah* (see Da. vii. 13, 14), and that the meaning is that God hath made him judge because he was the Messiah. Some of the ancient versions and fathers connected this with the following verse, thus: "Marvel not because I am a man, or because this great work is committed to a man apparently in humble life. You shall see greater things than these." Thus the Syriac version reads it, and Chrysostom, Theophylact, and some others among the fathers.

28. *Marvel not.* Do not wonder or be astonished at this. ¶ *The hour is coming.* The *time* is approaching or will be. ¶ *All that are in the graves.* All the dead, of every age and nation. They are described as *in the graves.* Though many have turned to their native dust and perished from human view, yet God sees them, and can regather their remains and raise them up to life. The phrase *all that are in the graves* does not prove that the same particles of matter will be raised up, but it is equivalent to saying *all the dead.* See Notes on 1 Co. xv. 35–38. ¶ *Shall hear his voice.* He will restore them to life, and command them to appear before him. This is a most sublime description, and this will be a wonderful display of almighty power. None but God can *see* all the dead, none but he could remould their frames, and none else could command them to return to life.

29. *Shall come forth.* Shall come out of their graves. This was the language which he used when he raised up Lazarus, Jn. xi. 43, 44. ¶ *They that have done good.* That is, they who are righteous, or they who have by their good works *shown* that they were the friends of Christ. See Mat. xxv. 34–36. ¶ *Resurrection of life.* Religion is often called life, and everlasting life. See Notes on ver. 24. In the resurrection the righteous will be raised up to the full enjoyment and perpetual security of that life. It is also called the resurrection of life, because there shall be no more *death*, Re. xxi. 4. The enjoyment of God himself and of his works; of the society of the angels and of the redeemed; freedom from sickness, and sin, and dying, will constitute the *life* of the just in the resurrection. The resurrection is also called the resurrection of the just (Lu. xiv. 14), and the first resurrection, Re. xx. 5, 6. ¶ *The resurrection of damnation.* The word *damnation* means the sentence passed on one by a judge—judgment or condemnation. The word, as we use it, applies only to the judgment pronounced by God on the wicked; but this is not its meaning always in the Bible. Here it has, however, that meaning. Those who have done evil will be raised up *to be condemned* or *damned.* This will be the object in raising them up—this the sole design. It is elsewhere said that they shall then be condemned to everlasting punishment (Mat. xxv. 46), and that they shall be punished with everlasting destruction (2 Th. i. 8, 9); and it is said of the unjust that they are reserved unto the day of judgment to be punished, 2 Pe. ii. 9. That this refers to the future judgment—to the resurrection then, and not to anything that takes place in this life—is clear from the following considerations: 1st. Jesus had just spoken of what would be done in this life—of the power of the gospel, ver. 25. He adds here that something still more wonderful—something *beyond* this—would take place. *All that are in the graves* shall hear his voice. 2d. He speaks of those who are in their graves, evidently referring to the dead. Sinners are sometimes said to be dead

nothing: as I hear I judge; and my judgment is just, because I seek not mine own will, but [c]the will of the Father which hath sent me.

31 If[d] I bear witness of myself, my witness is not true.

32 There is [e]another that beareth witness of me; and I know that the witness which he witnesseth of me is true.

33 Ye sent unto John, and [f]he bare witness unto the truth.

34 But I receive not testimony

c Ps.40.7,8; Mat.26.39; ch.4.34; 6.38. d Ps.27.2; ch.8.14; Re.3.14.

e ch.8.18; Ac.10.43; 1 Jn.5.7-9. f ch.1.7,32.

---

in sin, but sinners are not said to be *in a grave.* This is applied in the Scriptures only to those who are deceased. 3d. The language used here of the *righteous* cannot be applied to anything in this life. When God converts men, it is not because they *have been good.* 4th. Nor is the language employed of the evil applicable to anything here. In what condition among men can it be said, with any appearance of sense, that they are brought forth from their graves to the resurrection of damnation? The doctrine of those Universalists who hold that all men will be saved immediately at death, therefore, cannot be true. This passage proves that at the day of judgment the wicked will be condemned. Let it be added that if *then* condemned they will be lost for ever. Thus (Mat. xxv. 46) it is said to be *everlasting* punishment; 2 Th. i. 8, 9, it is called *everlasting* destruction. There is no account of redemption in hell—no Saviour, no Holy Spirit, no offer of mercy there.

30. *Of mine own self.* See ver. 19. The Messiah, the Mediator, does nothing without the concurrence and the authority of God. Such is the nature of the union subsisting between them, that he does nothing *independently* of God. Whatever he does, he does according to the will of God. ¶ *As I hear I judge.* To *hear* expresses the condition of one who is commissioned or instructed. Thus (Jn. viii. 26), "I speak to the world those things which I have *heard* of him;" viii. 28, "As the Father hath taught me, I speak those things." Jesus here represents himself as commissioned, taught, or sent of God. When he says, "as I *hear*," he refers to those things which the Father had *showed* him (ver. 20)—that is, he came to communicate the will of God; to show to man what God wished man to know. ¶ *I judge.* I determine or decide. This was true respecting the institutions and doctrines of religion, and it will be true respecting the sentence which he will pass on mankind at the day of judgment. He will decide their destiny according to what the Father wills and wishes—that is, according to justice. ¶ *Because I seek,* &c. This does not imply that his own judgment would be wrong if he sought his own will, but that he had no *private* ends, no selfish views, no improper bias. He came not to aggrandize himself, or to promote his own views, but he came to do the will of God. Of course his decision would be impartial and unbiased, and there is every security that it will be according to truth. See Lu. xxii. 42, where he gave a memorable instance, in the agony of the garden, of his submission to his Father's will.

31. *If I bear witness of myself.* If I have no other evidence than my own testimony about myself. ¶ *My witness.* My testimony; my evidence. The proof would not be decisive. ¶ *Is not true.* The word *true,* here, means worthy of belief, or established by suitable evidence. See Mat. xxii. 16: "We *know* that thou art *true*"—that is, worthy of confidence, or that thou hast been truly sent from God, Lu. xx. 21; Jn. viii. 13, 17. The law did not admit a man to testify in his own case, but required *two* witnesses, De. xvii. 6. Though what Jesus said was *true* (ch. viii. 13, 17), yet he admitted it was not sufficient testimony *alone* to claim their belief. They had a right to expect that his statement that he came from God would be confirmed by other evidence. This evidence he gave in the miracles which he wrought as proof that God had sent him.

32. *There is another.* That is, God. See ver. 36.

33. *Ye sent unto John.* See ch. i. 19. ¶ *He bare witness,* &c. See ch. i. 26, 29, 36. This testimony of John *ought* to have satisfied them. John was an eminent man; many of the Pharisees believed on him; he was candid, unambitious, sincere, and his evidence was impartial. On this Jesus *might* have

from man; [g]but these things I
say that ye might be saved.
35 He was a burning and a
shining light, and [h]ye were willing
for a season to rejoice in his light.
36 But I have greater witness
than *that* of John; for [i]the works
which [k]the Father hath given me
to finish, the same works that I
do, bear witness of me that the
Father hath sent me.
37 And [l] the Father himself,

g ch.20.31; Ro.3.3. *h* Mat.21.26; Mar.6.20.
i ch.10.25; 15.24; Ac.2.22. *k* ch.17.4. *l* Mat.3.17; 17.5.

---

rested the proof that he was the Messiah, but he was willing, also, to adduce evidence of a higher order.

34. *I receive not testimony from men.* I do not depend for proof of my Messiahship on the testimony of men, nor do I pride myself on the commendations or flattery of men. ¶ *But these things,* &c. "This testimony of John I adduce that you might be convinced. It was evidence of your own seeking. It was clear, full, explicit. You *sent* to make inquiry, and he gave you a candid and satisfactory answer. Had you believed that, you would have believed in the Messiah and been saved." Men are often dissatisfied with the very evidence of the truth of religion which they sought, and on which they professed themselves willing to rely.

35. *He was.* It is probable that John had been cast into prison before this. Hence his public ministry had ceased, and our Saviour says he *was* such a light. ¶ *Light.* The word in the original properly means a *lamp,* and is not the same which in Jn. i. 4, 5 is translated *light.* That is a word commonly applied to the sun, the fountain of light; this means a *lamp,* or a light that is lit up or kindled artificially from oil or tallow. A teacher is often called a *light,* because he guides or illuminates the minds of others. Ro. ii. 19: "Thou art confident that thou art a guide of the blind, *a light* of them that sit in darkness;" Jn. viii. 12; xii. 46; Mat. v. 14. ¶ *A burning.* A lamp lit up that burns with a steady lustre. ¶ *Shining.* Not dim, not indistinct. The expression means that he was an eminent teacher; that his doctrines were clear, distinct, consistent. ¶ *Ye were willing.* You willed, or you chose; you went out voluntarily. This shows that some of those whom Jesus was now addressing were among the great multitudes of Pharisees that came unto John in the wilderness, Mat. iii. 7. As *they* had at one time admitted John to be a prophet, so Jesus might with great propriety adduce his testimony in his favour. ¶ *For a season.* In the original, for an *hour*—denoting only a short time. They did it, as many others do, while he was popular, and it was the *fashion* to follow him. ¶ *To rejoice in his light.* To rejoice in his doctrines, and in admitting that he was a distinguished prophet; perhaps, also, to rejoice that he professed to be sent to introduce the Messiah, until they found that he bore testimony to Jesus of Nazareth.

36. *Greater witness.* Stronger, more decisive evidence. ¶ *The works.* The miracles—healing the sick and raising the dead. ¶ *Hath given me.* Hath committed to me, or appointed me to do. Certain things he intrusted in his hands to accomplish. ¶ *To finish.* To do or to perform until the task is completed. The word is applied to the *termination* of anything, as we say a task is *ended* or a work is completed. So Jesus said, when he expired, It is "*finished,*" Jn. xix. 30. From this it appears that Jesus came to *accomplish* a certain work; and hence we see the reason why he so often guarded his life and sought his safety until the task was fully completed. These works or miracles bore witness of him; that is, they showed that he was sent from God, because none but God could perform them, and because God would not give such power to any whose life and doctrines he did not approve. They were more decisive proof than the testimony of John, because, 1st. John worked no miracles, Jn. x. 41. 2d. It was possible that *a man* might be deceived or be an impostor. It was *not* possible for *God* to deceive. 3d. The miracles which Jesus wrought were such as no *man* could work, and no angel. He that could raise the dead must have all power, and he who commissioned Jesus, therefore, must be God.

37. *The Father himself—hath borne witness of me.* This God had done, 1st. By the miracles which Jesus had wrought, and of which he was conversing. 2d. At the baptism of Jesus, where he said, "This is my beloved

which hath sent me, hath borne witness of me. Ye[m] have neither heard his voice at any time, nor seen his shape.

m De.4.12; 1 Ti.6.16.

38 And[n] ye have not his word abiding in you; for whom he hath sent, him ye believe not.

39 Search[o] the scriptures; for in

n 1 Jn.2.14. o Is.8.20; 34.16; Lu.16.29.

Son," Mat. iii. 17. 3d. In the prophecies of the Old Testament. It is not easy to say here to which of these he refers. Perhaps he has reference to all. ¶ *Ye have neither heard his voice.* This difficult passage has been interpreted in various ways. The main design of it seems to be clear—to reprove the Jews for not believing the evidence that he was the Messiah. In doing this he says that they were indisposed to listen to the testimony of God. He affirmed that God had given sufficient evidence of his divine mission, but they had disregarded it. The *first thing* that he notices is that they had not heard his voice. The word *hear*, in this place, is to be understood in the sense of *obey* or listen to. See Notes on ver. 25. The voice of God means his *commands* or his declarations, however made; and the Saviour said that it had been the *characteristic* of the Jews that they had not listened to the voice or command of God. As this had been their *general* characteristic, it was not wonderful that they disregarded now his testimony in regard to the Messiah. The voice of God *had been* literally heard on the mount. See De. iv. 12: "Ye heard the voice of the words." ¶ *At any time.* This has been the uniform characteristic of the nation that they have disregarded and perverted the testimony of God, and it was as true of that generation as of their fathers. ¶ *Nor seen his shape.* No man hath seen *God* at any time, Jn. i. 18. But the word *shape*, here, does not mean *God himself.* It refers to the visible *manifestation* of himself; to the *appearance* which he assumed. It is applied in the Septuagint to his manifesting himself to Moses, Nu. xii. 8: "With him will I speak mouth to mouth, *even apparently;*" in Greek, *in a form* or *shape*—the word used here. It is applied to the visible symbol of God that appeared in the cloud and that rested on the tabernacle, Nu. ix. 15, 16. It is the same word that is applied to the Holy Spirit appearing in bodily *shape* like a dove, Lu. iii. 22. Jesus does not here deny that God had *appeared* in this manner, but he says they had not seen—that is, had not *paid attention to*, or *regarded*, the appearance of God. He had manifested himself, but they disregarded it, and, in particular, they had disregarded his manifestations in attestation of the Messiah. As the word *hear* means to obey, to listen to, so the word *see* means to pay attention to, to regard (2 Jn. 8; 1 Jn. iii. 6), and thus throws light on Jn. xiv. 9: "He that hath seen me hath seen the Father." "I am a *manifestation* of God—God appearing in human flesh, as he appeared formerly in the symbol of the cloud; and he that *regards me*, or attends to me, regards the Father."

38. *His word abiding in you.* His law does not abide in you—that is, you do not regard or obey it. This was the *third* thing that he charged them with. 1st. They had not obeyed the command of God. 2d. They had not regarded his manifestations, either in the times of the old dispensation, or now through the Messiah. 3d. They did not yield to what he had said in the revelation of the Old Testament. ¶ *For whom he hath sent.* God had foretold that the Messiah would come. He had now given evidence that Jesus was he; but now they rejected him, and this was proof that they did not regard the word of God.

39. *Search the scriptures.* The word translated *search* here means to *search diligently* or anxiously. It is applied to miners, who search for precious metals—who look anxiously for the *bed* of the ore with an intensity or anxiety proportionate to *their sense* of the value of the metal. Comp. Notes on Job xxviii. 3. It is applied by Homer to a lioness robbed of her whelps, and who *searches* the plain to *trace out* the footsteps of the man who has robbed her. It is also applied by him to dogs tracing their game by searching them out by the scent of the foot. It means a diligent, faithful, anxious investigation. The word *may be* either in the indicative or imperative mood. In our translation it is in the imperative, as if Jesus *commanded* them to search the Scriptures. Cyril, Erasmus, Beza, Bengel,

them ye think ye have eternal life; and [p] they are they which testify of me.

40 And [q] ye will not come to me, that ye might have life.

41 I receive not honour [r] from men.

42 But I know you, that ye have not the love of God in you.

43 I am come in my Father's name, and ye receive me not: if another shall come in his own name, him ye will receive.

44 How can ye believe, [s] which

p Lu.24.27; 1 Pe.1.10,11. q ch.3.19. r ver.34; 1 Th.2.6. s ch.12.43.

Kuinoel, Tholuck, De Wette, and others, give it as in the indicative; Chrysostom, Augustine, Luther, Calvin, Wetstein, Stier, Alford, and others, regard it as in the imperative, or as a command. It is impossible to determine which is the true interpretation. Either of them makes good sense, and it is proper to use the passage in either signification. There is abundant evidence that the Jews *did* search the books of the Old Testament. It is equally clear that all men *ought* to do it. ¶ *The scriptures.* The writings or books of the Old Testament, for those were all the books of revelation that they then possessed. ¶ *In them ye think ye have eternal life.* The meaning of this is: "Ye think that by studying the Scriptures you will obtain eternal life. You suppose that they teach the way to future blessedness, and that by diligently studying them you will attain it." We see by this—1. That the Jews in the time of Jesus were expecting a future state. 2. The Scriptures teach the way of life, and it is our duty to study them. The Bereans are commended for searching the Scriptures (Ac. xvii. 11); and Timothy is said from a child to have "known the holy scriptures, which are able to make us wise unto salvation," 2 Ti. iii. 15. Early life is the proper time to search the Bible, for they who seek the Lord early shall find him. ¶ *They are they,* &c. They bear witness to the Messiah. They predict his coming, and the manner of his life and death, Is. liii.; Da. ix. 26, 27, &c. See Notes on Lu. xxiv. 27.

40. *And ye will not come,* &c. Though the Old Testament bears evidence that I am the Messiah; though you professedly search it to learn the way to life, and though my works prove it, yet you will not come to me to obtain life. From this we may learn, 1st. That life is to be obtained in Christ. He is the way, the truth, and the life, and he only can save us. 2d. That, in order to do that, we must *come to him*—that is, must come in the way appointed, as lost sinners, and be willing to be saved by him alone. 3d. That the reason why sinners are not saved lies in the will. "The only reason why sinners die is because *they will not come* to Christ for life and happiness: it is not because they *cannot*, but because they *will not*" (Henry). 4th. Sinners have a particular opposition to going to *Jesus Christ* for eternal life. They would prefer any other way, and it is commonly not until all other means are tried that they are willing to submit to him.

41, 42. *I receive not honour,* &c. "I do not say these things because I am desirous of human applause, but to account for the fact that you do not believe on me. The reason is, that you have not the love of God in you." In this passage we see, 1st. That we should not seek for human applause. It is of very little value, and it often keeps men from the approbation of God, ver. 44. 2d. They who will not believe on Jesus Christ give evidence that they have no love for God. 3d. The reason why they do not believe on him is because they have no regard for his character, wishes, or law. ¶ *Love of God.* Love to God. ¶ *In you.* In your hearts. You do not love God.

43. *I am come in my Father's name.* By the authority of God; or giving proof that I am sent by him. ¶ *If another shall come in his own name.* A false teacher setting up himself, and not even pretending to have a divine commission. The Jews were much accustomed to receive and follow particular teachers. In the time of Christ they were greatly divided between the schools of Hillel and Shammai, two famous teachers. ¶ *Ye will receive.* You will follow, or obey him as a teacher.

44. *Which receive honour one of another.* Who are studious of praise, and live for pride, ambition, and vainglory. This desire, Jesus says, was the great reason why they would not believe on him.

receive honour one of another, and[t] seek not the honour that *cometh* from God only?

45 Do not think that I will accuse you to the Father: [u]there is *one* that accuseth you, *even* Moses, in whom ye trust.

46 For had ye believed Moses, ye would have believed me; for [v]he wrote of me.

t Ro.2.10. u Ro.2.12. v Ge.3.15; 22.18; De.18.15,18; Ac.26.22.

They were unwilling to renounce their worldly honours, and become the followers of one so humble and unostentatious as he was. They expected a Messiah of pomp and splendour, and would not submit to one so despised and of so lowly a rank. Had the Messiah come, as they expected, with pomp and power, it would have been an honour, in their view, to follow him; as it was, they despised and rejected him. The great reason why multitudes do not believe is their attachment to human honours, or their pride, and vanity, and ambition. These are so strong, that while they continue they cannot and will not believe. They might, however, renounce these things, and then, the obstacles being removed, they would believe. Learn, 1. A man *cannot* believe the gospel while he is wholly under the influence of ambition. The two are not compatible. The religion of the gospel is humility, and a man who has not that *cannot* be a Christian. 2. Great numbers are deterred from being Christians by pride and ambition. Probably there is no single thing that prevents so many young men from becoming Christians as this passion. The proud and ambitious heart refuses to bow to the humiliating terms of the gospel. 3. Though while a man is under this governing principle he *cannot* believe the gospel, yet this proves nothing about his *ability* to lay that aside, and to yield to truth. *That* is another question. A child CANNOT open a trunk when he gets on the lid and attempts to raise his own weight and the cover of the trunk too; but that settles nothing about the inquiry whether he might not get off and then open it. The true question is whether a man can or cannot lay aside his ambition and pride, and about that there ought not to be any dispute. No one doubts that it may be done; and if that can be done, he can become a Christian. ¶ *Seek not the honour.* The praise, the glory, the approbation of God. The honour which comes from men is their praise, flattery, commendation; the honour that comes from God is his approbation for doing his will. God alone can confer the honours of heaven—the reward of having done our duty here. That we should seek, and if we seek that, we shall come to Christ, who is the way and the life.

45, 46. *Do not think that I will accuse you.* Do not suppose that I intend to follow your example. They had accused Jesus of breaking the law of God, ver. 16. He says that he will not imitate their example, though he implies that he *might* accuse them. ¶ *To the Father.* To God. ¶ *There is* one *that accuseth you.* Moses might be said to accuse or reprove them. He wrote of the Messiah, clearly foretold his coming, and commanded them to hear him. As they did *not* do it, it might be said that they had disregarded his command; and as Moses was divinely commissioned and had a right to be obeyed, so his command reproved them: they were disobedient and rebellious. ¶ *He wrote of me.* He wrote of the Messiah, and I am the Messiah, Ge. iii. 15; xii. 3; comp. Jn. viii. 56; Ge. xlix. 10; De. xviii. 15.

47. *If ye believe not his writings.* If you do not credit what he has written which you *profess* to believe, it is not to be expected that you will believe my declarations. And from this we may learn, 1st. That many men who *profess* to believe the Bible have really no regard for it when it crosses their own views and inclinations. 2d. It is our duty to study the Bible, that we may be established in the belief that Jesus is the Messiah. 3d. The prophecies of the Old Testament are conclusive proofs of the truth of the Christian religion. 4th. He that rejects one part of the Bible, will, for the same reason, reject all. 5th. The Saviour acknowledged the truth of the writings of Moses, built his religion upon them, appealed to them to prove that he was the Messiah, and commanded men to search them. We have the testimony of Jesus, therefore, that the Old Testament is a revelation from God. He that rejects his testimony on *this* subject must reject his authority altogether; and it is vain for any man to profess to believe in

47 But[w] if ye believe not his writings, how shall ye believe my words?

CHAPTER VI.

AFTER[a] these things Jesus went over the sea of Galilee, which is *the sea* of Tiberias.

2 And a great multitude followed him, because they saw his miracles which he did on them that were diseased.

3 And Jesus went up into a mountain, and there he sat with his disciples.

4 And the passover, a feast of the Jews, was nigh.

5 When Jesus then lifted up *his* eyes, and saw a great company come unto him, he saith unto Philip, Whence shall we buy bread, that these may eat?

6 And this he said to prove him; for he himself knew what he would do.

7 Philip answered him, [b]Two hundred pennyworth of bread is not sufficient for them, that every one of them may take a little.

8 One of his disciples, Andrew, Simon Peter's brother, saith unto him,

9 There is a lad here which hath five barley-loaves and two small fishes; but what are they among so many?

10 And Jesus said, Make the men sit down. Now there was much grass in the place. So the men sat down, in number about five thousand.

11 And Jesus took the loaves; and when he had given thanks, he distributed to the disciples, and the disciples to them that were set down; and likewise of the fishes as much as they would.

12 When they were [c]filled, he said unto his disciples, Gather up the fragments that remain, [d]that nothing be lost.

13 Therefore they gathered *them*

w Lu.16.31.
a Mat.14.15,&c.; Mar.6.34,&c.; Lu.9.12,&c.
b Nu.11.21,22; 2 Ki.4.43.
c Ne.9.25.
d Ne.8.10.

---

the New Testament, or in the Lord Jesus, without also acknowledging the authority of the Old Testament and of Moses.

We have in this chapter an instance of the profound and masterly manner in which Jesus could meet and silence his enemies. There is not anywhere a more conclusive argument, or a more triumphant meeting of the charges which they had brought against him. No one can read this without being struck with his profound wisdom; and it is scarcely possible to conceive that there could be a more distinct declaration and proof that he was equal with God.

CHAPTER VI.

1. *Jesus went over.* Went to the east side of the sea. The place to which he went was Bethsaida, Lu. ix. 10. The account of this miracle of feeding the five thousand is recorded also in Mat. xiv. 13-21; Mar. vi. 32-44; Lu. ix. 10-17. John has added a few circumstances omitted by the other evangelists.

2. *Because they saw his miracles,* &c. They saw that he had the power to supply their wants, and they therefore followed him. See ver. 26. Comp. also Mat. xiv. 14.

4. *The passover.* See Notes on Mat. xxvi. 2, 17. ¶ *A feast of the Jews.* This is one of the circumstances of explanation thrown in by John which show that he wrote for those who were unacquainted with Jewish customs.

6. *To prove him.* To try him; to see if he had faith, or if he would show that he believed that Jesus had power to supply them.

12. *Gather up the fragments.* This command is omitted by the other evangelists. It shows the care of Jesus that there should be no waste. Though he had power to provide any quantity of food, yet he has here taught us that the bounties of Providence are not to be squandered. In all things the Saviour set us an example of frugality, though he had an infinite supply at his disposal; he was himself economical, though he was Lord of all. If *he* was thus saving, it becomes *us* dependent creatures not to waste the bounties of a

together, and filled twelve baskets with the fragments of the five barley-loaves, which remained over and above unto them that had eaten.

14 Then those men, when they had seen the miracle that Jesus did, said, This is of a truth [e]that Prophet that should come into the world.

15 When Jesus therefore perceived that they would come and take him by force, to make him a king, he departed again into a mountain himself alone.

16 And[f] when even was *now* come, his disciples went down unto the sea,

17 And entered into a ship, and went over the sea toward Capernaum. And it was now dark, and Jesus was not come to them.

18 And[g] the sea arose, by reason of a great wind that blew.

19 So when they had rowed about five and twenty or thirty furlongs, they see Jesus walking on the sea, and drawing nigh unto the ship; and they were afraid.

20 But he saith unto them, [h]It is I; be not afraid.

21 Then they willingly received him into the ship; and immediately the ship was at the land whither they went.

22 The day following, when the people which stood on the other side of the sea saw that there was

e Ge.49.10; De.18.15-18. *f* Mat.14.23; Mar.6.47,&c. *g* Ps.107.25. *h* Ps.35.3; Is.43.1,2; Re.1.17,18.

---

beneficent Providence. And it especially becomes the rich not to squander the bounties of Providence. They often *feel* that they are rich. They have enough. They have no fear of want, and they do not feel the necessity of studying economy. Yet let them remember that what they have is the gift of God—just as certainly as the loaves and fishes created by the Saviour were his gift. It is not given them to waste, nor to spend in riot, nor to be the means of injuring their health or of shortening life. It is given to sustain life, to excite gratitude, to fit for the active service of God. Everything should be applied to its appropriate end, and nothing should be squandered or lost.

14. *That Prophet*, &c. The Messiah. The *power* to work the miracle, and the benevolence manifested in it, showed that he was the long-expected Messiah.

15. *When Jesus perceived*, &c. They were satisfied by the miracle that he was the Messiah. They supposed that the Messiah was to be a temporal prince. They saw that Jesus was retiring, unambitious, and indisposed to assume the ensigns of office. They thought, therefore, that they would proclaim him as the long-expected king, and constrain him to assume the character and titles of an earthly prince. Men often attempt to dictate to God, and suppose that they understand what is right better than he does. They are fond of pomp and power, but Jesus sought retirement, and evinced profound humility. Though he had *claims* to the honour and gratitude of the nation, yet he sought it not in this way; nor did it evince a proper spirit in his followers when they sought to advance him to a place of external splendour and regal authority.

16–21. See this miracle of walking on the sea explained in the Notes on Mat. xiv. 22–33. Comp. Mar. vi. 45–52.

21. *Immediately*. Quickly. Before a long time. How far they were from the land we know not, but there is no evidence that there was a *miracle* in the case. The word translated *immediately* does not of necessity imply that there was no interval of time, but that there was not a long interval. Thus in Mat. xiii. 5, in the parable of the sower, "and *forthwith* (the same word in Greek) they sprung up," &c., Mar. iv. 17; Mat. xxiv. 29; 3 Jn. 14.

22. *The people which stood on the other side of the sea*. That is, on the *east* side, or on the same side with Jesus. The country was called the region *beyond* or *on the other side* of the sea, because the writer and the people lived on the west side. ¶ *Jesus went not with his disciples.* He had gone into a mountain to pray alone, ver. 15. Comp. Mar. vi. 46.

23. *There came other boats*. After the disciples had departed. This is added because, from what follows, it appears that they supposed that he had entered one of those boats and gone to Capernaum after his disciples had departed.

none other boat there, save that one whereinto his disciples were entered, and that Jesus went not with his disciples into the boat, but *that* his disciples were gone away alone:

23 (Howbeit there came other boats from Tiberias, nigh unto [i]the place where they did eat bread, after that the Lord had given thanks:)

24 When the people, therefore, saw that Jesus was not there, neither his disciples, they also took shipping and came to Capernaum, seeking for Jesus.

25 And when they had found him on the other side of the sea, they said unto him, Rabbi, when camest thou hither?

26 Jesus answered them and said, Verily, verily, I say unto you,

i ver.11.

¶ *From Tiberias.* This town stood on the western borders of the lake, not far from where the miracle had been wrought. It was so called in honour of the Emperor Tiberius. It was built by Herod Antipas, and was made by him the capital of Galilee. The city afterward became a celebrated seat of Jewish learning. It is now called *Tabaria*, and is a considerable place. It is occupied chiefly by Turks, and is very hot and unhealthy. Mr. Fisk, an American missionary, was at Tiberias (Tabaria) in 1823. The old town is surrounded by a wall, but within it is very ruinous, and the plain for a mile or two south is strewed with ruins. The Jordan, where it issues from the lake, was so shallow that cattle and asses forded it easily. Mr. Fisk was shown a house called the house of Peter, which is used as the Greek Catholic church, and is the only church in the place. The number of Christian families is thirty or forty, all Greek Catholics. There were two sects of Jews, each of whom had a synagogue. The Jewish population was estimated at about one thousand. On the 1st of January, 1837, Tiberias was destroyed by an earthquake. Dr. Thomson (*The Land and the Book*, vol. ii. p. 76, 77) says of this city: "Ever since the destruction of Jerusalem, it has been chiefly celebrated in connection with the Jews, and was for a long time the chief seat of rabbinical learning. It is still one of their four holy cities. Among the Christians it also early rose to distinction, and the old church, built upon the spot where our Lord gave his last charge to Peter, is a choice bit of ecclesiastical antiquity. The present city is situated on the shore, at the north-east corner of this small plain. The walls inclose an irregular parallelogram, about 100 rods from north to south, and in breadth not more than 40. They were strengthened by ten round towers on the west, five on the north, and eight on the south. There were also two or three towers along the shore to protect the city from attack by sea. Not much more than one-half of this small area is occupied by buildings of any kind, and the north end, which is a rocky hill, has nothing but the ruins of the old palace. The earthquake of 1837 prostrated a large part of the walls, and they have not yet been repaired, and perhaps never will be. There is no town in Syria so utterly filthy as Tiberias, or so little to be desired as a residence. Being *600 feet* below the level of the ocean, and overhung on the west by a high mountain, which effectually shuts off the Mediterranean breezes, it is fearfully hot in summer. The last time I was encamped at the Baths the thermometer stood at 100° *at midnight*, and a steam went up from the surface of the lake as from some huge smouldering volcano. Of course it swarms with all sorts of vermin. What can induce human beings to settle down in such a place? And yet some two thousand of our race make it their chosen abode. They are chiefly Jews, attracted hither either to cleanse their leprous bodies in her baths, or to purify their unclean spirits by contact with her traditionary and ceremonial holiness."

24. *Took shipping.* Went into the boats. ¶ *Came to Capernaum.* This was the ordinary place of the residence of Jesus, and they therefore expected to find him there.

26. *Ye seek me, not because*, &c. The *miracles* which Jesus wrought were proofs that he came from God. To seek him because they had seen them, and were convinced by them that he was the Messiah, would have been proper; but to follow him simply because

Ye seek me, not because ye saw
the miracles, but because ye did
eat of the loaves and were filled.

27 Labour[1] not for the meat
which perisheth, but for [k]that meat
which endureth unto everlasting
life, which the Son of man shall
give unto you; for [l]him hath God
the Father sealed.

1 or, *Work not.* *k* Je.15.16; ch.4.14; ver.54,58. *l* Ps.2.7; 40.7; Is.42.1; ch.8.18; Ac.2.22; 2 Pe.1.17.

28 Then said they unto him,
What shall we do, that we might
work the works of God?

29 Jesus answered and said unto
them, [m]This is the work of God,
that ye believe on him whom he
hath sent.

30 They said, therefore, unto
him, What [n]sign showest thou

m 1 Jn.3.23. *n* Mat.12.38; 1 Co.1.22.

their wants were supplied was mere selfishness of a gross kind. Yet, alas! many seek religion from no better motive than this. They suppose that it will add to their earthly happiness, or they seek *only* to escape from suffering or from the convictions of conscience, or they seek for heaven *only* as a place of enjoyment, and regard religion as valuable *only* for this. All this is mere selfishness. Religion does not *forbid* our regarding our own happiness, or seeking it in any proper way; but when this is the *only* or the *prevailing* motive, it is evident that we have never yet sought God aright. We are aiming at the loaves and fishes, and not at the honour of God and the good of his kingdom; and if this is the only or the main motive of our entering the church, we *cannot* be Christians.

27. *Labour not.* This does not mean that we are to make *no effort* for the supply of our wants (comp. 1 Ti. v. 1; 2 Th. iii. 10), but that we are not to manifest anxiety, we are not to make this the main or supreme object of our desire. See Notes on Mat. vi. 25. ¶ *The meat that perisheth.* The food for the supply of your natural wants. It perishes. The strength you derive from it is soon exhausted, and your wasted powers need to be reinvigorated. ¶ *That meat which endureth.* The supply of your spiritual wants; that which supports, and nourishes, and strengthens the soul; the doctrines of the gospel, that are to a weak and guilty soul what needful food is to the weary and decaying body. ¶ *To everlasting life.* The strength derived from the doctrines of the gospel is not exhausted. It endures without wasting away. It nourishes the soul to everlasting life. "They that wait upon the Lord shall renew their strength; they shall run and not be weary, and shall walk and not faint," Is. xl. 31. ¶ *Him hath God the Father sealed.* To *seal* is to confirm or approve as *ours.* This is done when we set our seal to a compact, or deed, or testament, by which we ratify it as *our act.* So God the Father, by the miracles which had been wrought by Jesus, had shown that he had sent him, that he approved his doctrines, and ratified his works. The *miracles* were to his doctrine what *a seal* is to a written instrument. See Notes on Jn. iii. 33.

28. *What shall we do, that we might work the works of God?* That is, such things as God will approve. This was the earnest inquiry of men who were seeking to be saved. They had crossed the Sea of Tiberias to seek him; they supposed him to be the Messiah, and they sincerely desired to be taught the way of life; yet it is observable that they expected to find that way as other sinners commonly do—by *their works.* The idea of doing something to *merit* salvation is one of the last that the sinner ever surrenders.

29. *This is the work of God.* This is the thing that will be acceptable to God, or which you are to do in order to be saved. Jesus did not tell them they had *nothing to do,* or that they were to sit down and wait, but that there *was* a work to perform, and that was a duty that was imperative. It was to believe on the Messiah. This is the work which sinners are to do; and doing this they will be saved, for Christ is the end of the law for righteousness to every one that believeth, Ro. x. 4.

30. *What sign showest thou?* On the word *sign,* comp. Notes on Is. vii. 14. What miracle dost thou work to prove that thou art the Messiah? They had just seen the miracle of the loaves in the desert, which was sufficient to show that he was the Messiah, and it would seem from the preceding narrative that those who crossed the lake to see him supposed that he was the Christ. It seems wonderful that they should so

then, that we may see and believe
thee? what dost thou work?
31 Our[o] fathers did eat manna
in the desert; as it is written, [p]He
gave them bread from heaven to
eat.
32 Then Jesus said unto them,
Verily, verily, I say unto you, Moses gave you not that bread from
heaven; but [q]my Father giveth
you the true bread from heaven.
33 For the [r]bread of God is he
which cometh down from heaven,
and giveth life unto the world.

o Ex.16.15; Nu.11.7; 1 Co.10.3.
p Ne.9.15; Ps.78.24,25.
q Ga.4.4. r ver.48,58.

soon ask for farther evidence that he was sent from God; but it is not improbable that this question was put by *other Jews*, rulers of the synagogue, who happened to be present, and who had not witnessed his miracles. Those men were continually asking for *signs* and proofs that he was the Messiah. See Mat. xii. 38, 39; Mar. viii. 11; Lu. xi. 29. As Jesus claimed the right of teaching them, and as it was manifest that he would teach them differently from what *they* supposed Moses to teach, it was natural to ask him by what authority he claimed the right to be heard.

31. *Our fathers.* The Jews who were led by Moses through the wilderness. ¶ *Did eat manna.* This was the name given by the Jews to the food which was furnished to them by God in their journey. It means literally, "What is this?" and was the question which they asked when they first saw it, Ex. xvi. 14, 15. It was small like frost, and of the size of coriander-seed, and had a sweetish taste like honey. It fell in great quantities, and was regarded by the Jews as proof of a continued miracle during forty years, and was incontestable evidence of the interposition of God in favour of their fathers. The manna which is sold in the shops of druggists is a different substance from this. It is obtained from the bark of certain trees in Armenia, Georgia, Persia, and Arabia. It is procured, as resin is, by making an incision in the bark, and it flows out or distils from the tree. ¶ *As it is written.* The substance of this is written in Ps. lxxviii. 24, 25. ¶ *He gave them.* This was regarded as a miraculous interference in their behalf, and an attestation of the divine mission of Moses, and hence they said familiarly that *Moses* gave it to them. ¶ *Bread from heaven.* The word *heaven*, in the Scriptures, denotes often the region of the *air*, the atmosphere, or that region in which the clouds are. See Mat. xvi. 3: "The sky (heaven) is red and lowering." Also Mat. iii. 16; Lu. iv. 15; v. 18. The Jews, as appears from their writings (see Lightfoot), expected that the Messiah would provide his followers with plenty of delicious food; and as *Moses* had provided for the Jews in the wilderness, so they supposed that Christ would make provision for the temporal wants of his friends. This was *the sign*, probably, which they were now desirous of seeing.

32. *Moses gave you not that bread from heaven.* This might be translated, "Moses gave you not *the* bread of heaven." The word "that," which makes some difference in the sense, is not necessary to express the meaning of the original. It does not appear that Jesus intended to call in question the fact that their fathers were fed by the instrumentality of Moses, but to state that he did not give them the true bread that was adapted to the wants of the *soul.* He fed the body, although his food did not keep the body alive (ver. 49), but he did not give that which would preserve the soul from death. God gave, in his Son Jesus, the true bread from heaven which was fitted to man, and of far more value than any supply of their temporal wants. He tells them, therefore, that they are not to seek from him any such supply of their temporal wants as they had supposed. A better gift had been furnished in *his* being given for the life of the world. ¶ *My father giveth you.* In the gospel; in the gift of his Son. ¶ *The true bread.* The *true* or *real* support which is needed to keep the soul from death. It is not false, deceitful, or perishing. Christ is called *bread*, because, as bread supports life, so his doctrine supports, preserves, and saves the soul from death. He is the *true* support, not only in opposition to the mere supply of *temporal* wants such as Moses furnished, but also in opposition to all false religion which deceives and destroys the soul.

33. *The bread of God.* The means of

34 Then said they unto him, Lord, evermore give us this bread.

35 And Jesus said unto them, I am the bread of life: [s]he that cometh to me shall never hunger, and [t]he that believeth on me shall never thirst.

36 But I said unto you, [u]That ye also have seen me, and believe not.

37 All[v] that the Father giveth me shall come to me; and [w]him that cometh to me I will in no wise cast out.

s Re.7.16. t ch.4.14; 7.38.

u ver.64. v ver.45; ch.17.6,8,&c. w Ps.102.17; Is.1.18; 55.7; Mat.11.28; Lu.23.42,43; 1 Ti.1.15,16; Re.22.17.

support which God furnishes. That which, in his view, is needful for man. ¶ *Is he*, &c. Is the Messiah who has come from heaven. ¶ *And giveth life*, &c. See Notes on Jn. i. 4.

35. *I am the bread of life.* I am the *support* of spiritual life; or my doctrines will give life and peace to the soul. ¶ *Shall never hunger.* See Notes on Jn. iv. 14.

36. *But I said unto you.* This he said, not in so many words, but *in substance*, in ver. 26. Though they saw him, and had full proof of his divine mission, yet they did not believe. Jesus then proceeds to state that, although *they* did not believe on him, yet his work would not be in vain, for others would come to him and be saved.

37. *All.* The original word is in the neuter gender, but it is used, doubtless, for the masculine, or perhaps refers to his people considered as a *mass* or *body*, and means that *every individual* that the Father had given him should come to him. ¶ *The Father giveth me.* We here learn that those who come to Christ, and who will be saved, are *given* to him by God. 1st. God promised him that he should see of the travail of his soul—that is, "the fruit of his wearisome toil" (Lowth), and should be satisfied, Is. liii. 11. 2d. All men are sinners, and none have any *claim* to mercy, and he may therefore bestow salvation on whom he pleases. 3d. All men of themselves are disposed to reject the gospel, Jn. v. 40. 4th. God enables those who do believe to do it. He draws them to him by his Word and Spirit; he opens their hearts to understand the Scriptures (Ac. xvi. 14); and he grants to them repentance, Ac. xi. 18; 2 Ti. ii. 25. 5th. All those who become Christians may therefore be said to be *given* to Jesus as the reward of his sufferings, for his death was the price by which they were redeemed. Paul says (Ep. i. 4, 5) that, "he hath chosen us in him (that is, in Christ) before the foundation of the world, that we should be holy and without blame before him in love; having predestinated us unto the adoption of children to himself, according to the good pleasure of his will." ¶ *Shall come to me.* This is an expression denoting that they would *believe* on him. To *come to* one implies our need of help, our confidence that he can aid us, and our readiness to trust to him. The sinner comes to Jesus feeling that he is poor, and needy, and wretched, and casts himself on his mercy, believing that he alone can save him. This expression also proves that men are not *compelled* to believe on Christ. Though they who believe are *given* to him, and though his Spirit works in them faith and repentance, yet they are made *willing* in the day of his power, Ps. cx. 3. No man is *compelled* to go to heaven against his will, and no man is *compelled* to go to hell against his will. The Spirit of God inclines the will of one, and he *comes* freely as a moral agent. The other *chooses* the way to death; and, though God is constantly using means to save him, yet he prefers the path that leads down to woe. ¶ *Him that cometh.* Every one that comes—that is, every one that comes in a proper manner, feeling that he is a lost and ruined sinner. This invitation is wide, and full, and free. It shows the unbounded mercy of God; and it shows, also, that the reason, and the only reason, why men are not saved, is that they will not come to Christ. Of any sinner it may be said that if he had been willing to come to Christ he *might* have come and been saved. As he *chooses not* to come, he cannot blame God because he saves others who *are* willing, no matter from what cause, and who thus are made partakers of everlasting life. ¶ *In no wise.* In no manner, or at no time. The original is simply, "I will *not* cast out." ¶ *Cast out.* Reject, or refuse to save. This expression does not refer to the doctrine of perseverance of the saints, but

38 For I came down from heaven, not to do mine own will, [x]but the will of him that sent me.

39 And this is the [y]Father's will which hath sent me, that of all which he hath given me I should lose nothing, but should raise it up again at the last day.

40 And this is the will of him that sent me, [z]that every one which seeth the Son, and believeth on him, may have everlasting life; and [a]I will raise him up at the last day.

41 The Jews then murmured at him because he said, I am the

x Ps.40.7,8; ch.5.30.
y Mat.18.14; ch.10.28; 17.12; 18.9; 2 Ti.2.19.
z ver.47,54; ch.3.15,16. a ch.11.25.

to the fact that Jesus will not *reject* or *refuse* any sinner who comes to him.

38. *For I came down*, &c. This verse shows that he came for a specific purpose, which he states in the next verse, and means that, as he came to do his Father's will, he would be faithful to the trust. Though his hearers should reject him, yet the will of God would be accomplished in the salvation of some who should come to him. ¶ *Mine own will.* See Notes on Jn. v. 30.

39. *Father's will.* His purpose; desire; intention. As this is the Father's will, and Jesus came to execute his will, we have the highest security that it will be done. God's will is always right, and he has power to execute it. Jesus was always faithful, and all power was given to him in heaven and on earth, and he will therefore most certainly accomplish the will of God. ¶ *Of all which.* That is, of every one who believes on him, or of all who become Christians. See ver. 37. ¶ *I should lose nothing.* Literally, "I should not *destroy.*" He affirms here that he will keep it to life eternal; that, though the Christian will die, and his body return to corruption, yet he will not be *destroyed.* The Redeemer will watch over him, though in his grave, and keep him to the resurrection of the just. This is affirmed of all who are given to him by the Father; or, as in the next verse, "*Every one* that believeth on him shall have everlasting life." ¶ *At the last day.* At the day of judgment. The Jews supposed that the *righteous* would be raised up at the appearing of the Messiah. See Lightfoot. Jesus directs them to a *future* resurrection, and declares to them that they will be raised at the *last* day—the day of judgment. It is also supposed and affirmed by some Jewish writers that they did not believe that the *wicked* would be raised. Hence, to speak of being raised up in the last day was the same as to say that one was righteous, or it was spoken of as the peculiar privilege of the righteous. In accordance with this, Paul says, "If by any means I might attain *unto the resurrection of the dead,*" Phi. iii. 11.

40. *Every one which seeth the Son, and believeth on him.* It was not sufficient to see him and hear him, but it was necessary, also, to *believe* on him. Many of the Jews had *seen* him, but few believed on him. Jesus had said in the previous verse that all that the Father *had given him* should be saved. But he never left a doctrine so that men *must* misunderstand it. Lest it should be supposed that if a man was *given* to him this was all that was needful, and lest anyone should say, "If I am to be saved I shall be, and my efforts will be useless," he states here that it is necessary that a man should *believe* on him. This would be the *evidence* that he was given to God, and this would be evidence conclusive that he would be saved. If this explanation of the Saviour had always been attended to, the doctrine of election would not have been abused as it has been. Sinners would not sit down in unconcern, saying that if they are *given* to Christ all will be well. They would have arisen like the prodigal, and would have gone to God; and, having *believed* on the Saviour, they would *then* have had evidence that they were *given* to him—the evidence resulting from an humble, penitent, believing heart—and *then* they might rejoice in the assurance that Jesus would lose none that were given to him, but would raise it up at the last day. All the doctrines of Jesus, as *he* preached them, are safe, and pure, and consistent; as *men* preach them, they are, unhappily, often inconsistent and open to objection, and are either fitted to produce despair on the one hand, or presumptuous self-confidence on the other. Jesus teaches men to strive to enter heaven, as if they could do the work themselves; and yet to depend on the help

bread which came down from heaven.

42 And they said, [b]Is not this Jesus, the son of Joseph, whose father and mother we know? How is it then that he saith, I came down from heaven?

43 Jesus therefore answered and said unto them, Murmur not among yourselves.

44 No man can come to me except the Father, which hath sent me, [c]draw him; and I will raise him up at the last day.

45 It is written [d]in the prophets, And they shall be all taught of God. Every[e] man, therefore, that hath heard, and hath learned of the Father, cometh unto me.

46 Not[f] that any man hath seen

b Mat.13.55; Mar.6.3; Lu.4.22.

c Ca.1.4. d Is.54.13; Je.31.34; Mi.4.2. e Mat.11.27. f ch.5.37.

---

of God, and give the glory to him, as if he had done it all.

44. *No man can come to me.* This was spoken by Jesus to reprove their murmurings—"Murmur not among yourselves." They objected to his doctrine, or murmured against it, because he claimed to be greater than Moses, and because they supposed him to be a mere man, and that what he said was impossible. Jesus does not deny that these things appeared difficult, and hence he said that if any man believed, it was proof that God had inclined him. It was not to be expected that *of themselves* they would embrace the doctrine. If any man believed, it would be because he had been influenced by God. When we inquire what the reasons were why they did not believe, they appear to have been—1st. Their improper regard for Moses, as if no one could be superior to him. 2d. Their unwillingness to believe that Jesus, whom they knew to be the reputed son of a carpenter, should be superior to Moses. 3d. The difficulty was explained by Jesus (Jn. v. 40) as consisting in the opposition of their will; and (Jn. v. 44) when he said that their love of *honour* prevented their believing on him. The difficulty in the case was not, therefore, a want of natural faculties, or of power to do their duty, but erroneous opinions, pride, obstinacy, self-conceit, and a deep-felt contempt for Jesus. The word "*cannot*" is often used to denote a strong and violent opposition of the *will.* Thus we say a man is so great a liar that he cannot speak the truth, or he is so profane that he cannot but swear. We mean by it that he is so wicked that while he has that disposition the other effects will follow, but we do not mean to say that he could not break off from the habit. Thus it is said (Ge. xxxvii. 4) of the brethren of Joseph that they *hated him, and could not speak peaceably to him.* Thus (Mat. xii. 34), "How *can* ye, being evil, speak good things?" See Lu. xiv. 33; 1 Sa. xvi. 2. ¶ *Come to me.* The same as believe on me. ¶ *Draw him.* This word is used here, evidently, to denote such an influence from God as to secure the result, or as to incline the mind to believe; yet the *manner* in which this is done is not determined by the use of the word. It is used in the New Testament six times. Once it is applied to a compulsory drawing of Paul and Silas to the market-place, Ac. xvi. 19. Twice it is used to denote the drawing of a net, Jn. xxi. 6, 11. Once to the drawing of a sword (Jn. xviii. 10); and once in a sense similar to its use here (Jn. xii. 32): "And I, if I be lifted up from the earth, will *draw* all men unto me." What is its meaning here must be determined by the *facts* about the sinner's conversion. See Notes on ver. 40. In the conversion of the sinner God enlightens the mind (ver. 45), he inclines the will (Ps. cx. 3), and he influences the soul by motives, by just views of his law, by his love, his commands, and his threatenings; by a desire of happiness, and a consciousness of danger; by the Holy Spirit applying truth to the mind, and urging him to yield himself to the Saviour. So that, while God inclines him, and will have all the glory, man yields without compulsion; the obstacles are removed, and he becomes a willing servant of God.

45. *In the prophets.* Is. liv. 13. A similar sentiment is found in Mi. iv. 1–4, and Je. xxxi. 34; but by the *prophets,* here, is meant *the book of the prophets,* and it is probable that Jesus had reference only to the place in Isaiah, as this was the usual way of quoting the prophets. ¶ *Shall be all taught of God.*

the Father, [g]save he which is of
God; he hath seen the Father.
47 Verily, verily, I say unto you,
He[h] that believeth on me hath
everlasting life.
48 I[i] am that bread of life.
49 Your fathers did eat manna
in the wilderness, and [k]are dead.
50 This is the bread which
cometh down from heaven, that a
man may eat thereof, and [l]not die.

g Lu.10.22. h ver.40. i ver.33,35,51. k Zec.1.5. l ver.58.

51 I am the living bread which
came down from heaven. If any
man eat of this bread he shall live
for ever; and the bread that I will
give is [m]my flesh, which I will give
for [n]the life of the world.
52 The Jews therefore strove
among themselves, saying, [o]How
can this man give us *his* flesh to
eat?
53 Then Jesus said unto them,

m He.10.5,10,20. n ch.3.16; 1 Jn.2.2. o ch.3.9.

This explains the preceding verse. It is by the *teaching* of his Word and Spirit that men are *drawn* to God. This shows that it is not *compulsory*, and that there is no obstacle in the way but a strong voluntary ignorance and unwillingness.

46. *Not that any man hath seen the Father.* Jesus added this, evidently, to guard against mistake. He had said that all who came to him were *taught* of God. The *teacher* was commonly *seen* and *heard* by the pupil; but, lest it should be supposed that he meant to say that a man to come to him must *see* and *hear* God, visibly and audibly, he adds that he did not intend to affirm this. It was still true that no man had seen God at any time. They were not, therefore, to *expect* to see God, and his words were not to be *perverted* as if he meant to teach that. ¶ *Save he which is of God.* Jesus here evidently refers to himself as the Son of God. He had just said that no *man* had seen the Father. When he affirms that *he* has seen the Father, it implies that he is more than man. He is the only-begotten Son who is in the bosom of the Father, Jn. i. 18; the brightness of his glory, and the express image of his person, He. i. 3; God over all, blessed for ever, Ro. ix. 5. By his being *of God* is meant that he is the only-begotten Son of God, and sent as the Messiah into the world. ¶ *Hath seen.* Hath intimately known or perceived him. He knows his nature, character, plans. This is a claim to knowledge superior to what man possesses, and it cannot be understood except by supposing that Jesus is equal with God.

48. *I am that bread of life.* My doctrines and the benefits of my mediation are that *real* support of spiritual life of which the manna in the wilderness was the faint emblem. See ver. 32, 33.

49. *Your fathers did eat manna.* There was a real miracle wrought in their behalf; there was a perpetual interposition of God which showed that they were his chosen people. ¶ *And are dead.* The bread which they ate could not save them from death. Though God interfered in their behalf, yet they died. We may learn, 1st. That that is not the most valuable of God's gifts which merely satisfies the temporal wants. 2d. That the most distinguished temporal blessings will not save from death. Wealth, friends, food, raiment, will not preserve life. 3d. There is need of something better than mere earthly blessings; there is need of that bread which cometh down from heaven, and which giveth life to the world.

51. *The bread that I will give is my flesh.* That is, his body would be offered as a sacrifice for sin, agreeably to his declaration when he instituted the Supper: "This is my body which is broken for you," 1 Co. xi. 24. ¶ *Life of the world.* That sinners might, by his atoning sacrifice, be recovered from spiritual death, and be brought to eternal life. The use of the word *world* here shows that the sacrifice of Christ was full, free, ample, and designed for all men, as it is said in 1 Jn. ii. 2, "He is the propitiation for our sins, and not for ours only, but also for the sins of the whole world." In this verse Jesus introduces the subject of his *death* and atonement. It may be remarked that in the language which he used the transition from *bread* to his *flesh* would appear more easy than it does in our language. The same word which in Hebrew means *bread*, in the Syriac and Arabic means also *flesh*.

53–55. In these verses Jesus repeats

Verily, verily, I say unto you, [p]Except ye eat the flesh of the Son of man, and drink his blood, ye have no life in you.
54 Whoso[q] eateth my flesh, and drinketh my blood, hath eternal life, and I will raise him up at the last day.
55 For my flesh is [r]meat indeed, and my blood is drink indeed.
56 He that [s]eateth my flesh, and drinketh my blood, [t]dwelleth in me, and I in him.
57 As the living Father hath sent me, and I live by the Father, [u]so he that eateth me, even he shall live by me.
58 This is that bread which came down from heaven: [v]not as your fathers did eat manna, and are dead: he that eateth of this bread shall live for ever.

p Mat.26.26,28. *q* ver.40. *r* Ps.4.7. *s* La.3.24. *t* ch.15.4; 1 Jn.3.24; 4.15,16. *u* 1 Co.15.22. *v* ver.49–51.

---

what he had in substance said before. ¶ *Except ye eat the flesh,* &c. He did not mean that this should be understood *literally,* for it was never done, and it is absurd to suppose that it was intended to be so understood. Nothing can *possibly* be more absurd than to suppose that when he instituted the Supper, and gave the bread and wine to his disciples, they literally ate his flesh and drank his blood. Who *can* believe this? There he stood, a living man—his body yet alive, his blood flowing in his veins; and how can it be believed that this body was eaten and this blood drunk? Yet this absurdity must be held by those who hold that the bread and wine at the communion are "changed into the body, blood, and *divinity* of our Lord." So it is taught in the decrees of the Council of Trent; and to such absurdities are men driven when they depart from the simple meaning of the Scriptures and from common sense. It may be added that if the bread and wine used in the Lord's Supper were not changed into his literal body and blood when it was first instituted, they have never been since. The Lord Jesus would institute it just as he meant it should be observed, and there is nothing *now* in that ordinance which there was not when the Saviour first appointed it. His body was offered on the cross, and was raised up from the dead and received into heaven. Besides, there is no evidence that he had any reference in this passage to the Lord's Supper. That was not yet instituted, and in that there was no literal eating of his flesh and drinking of his blood. The plain meaning of the passage is, that by his bloody death—his body and his blood offered in sacrifice for sin—he would procure pardon and life for man; that they who partook of that, or had an interest in that, should obtain eternal life. He uses the figure of eating and drinking because that was the subject of discourse; because the Jews prided themselves much on the fact that their fathers had eaten *manna;* and because, as he had said that he was the *bread* of life, it was natural and easy, especially in the language which he used, to *carry out the figure,* and say that bread must be eaten in order to be of any avail in supporting and saving men. To eat and to drink, among the Jews, was also expressive of *sharing in* or *partaking of* the privileges of friendship. The happiness of heaven and all spiritual blessings are often represented under this image, Mat. viii. 11; xxvi. 29; Lu. xiv. 15, &c.

55. *Is meat indeed.* Is truly food. My doctrine is truly that which will give life to the soul.

56. *Dwelleth in me.* Is truly and intimately connected with me. To dwell or abide in him is to remain in the belief of his doctrine, and in the participation of the benefits of his death. Comp. Jn. xv. 1–6; xvii. 21–23. ¶ *I in him.* Jesus dwells in believers by his Spirit and doctrine. When his Spirit is given them to sanctify them; when his temper, his meekness, his humility, and his love pervade their hearts; when his doctrine is received by them and influences their life, and when they are supported by the consolations of the gospel, it may be said that he *abides* or dwells in them.

57. *I live by the Father.* See Notes on Jn. v. 26.

58. *This is that bread,* &c. This is *the* true bread that came down. The word "that" should not be in the translation. ¶ *Shall live for ever.* Not on

59 These things said he in the synagogue, as he taught in Capernaum.

60 Many, therefore, of his disciples, when they had heard *this*, said, This is an hard saying; who can hear it?

61 When Jesus knew in himself that his disciples murmured at it, he said unto them, Doth this offend you?

62 *What* and if ye shall see the Son of man [w]ascend up where he was before?

63 It[x] is the Spirit that quickeneth; the flesh profiteth nothing: the words that I speak unto you, *they* are spirit and *they* are life.

w ch.3.13; Mar.16.19; Ep.4.8-10. *x* 2 Co.3.6.

the earth, but in the enjoyments of a better world.

60. *Many of his disciples.* The word *disciple* means *learner.* It was applied to the followers of Christ because they were *taught* by him. It does not imply, of necessity, that those to whom it was given were real Christians, but simply that they were under his *teaching*, and were professed learners in his school. See Mat. xvii. 16; Mar. ii. 18; Jn. ix. 28; Mat. x. 24. It is doubtless used in this sense here. It is, however, often applied to those who are real Christians. ¶ *This is an hard saying.* The word *hard* here means *offensive, disagreeable* —that which they could not bear. Some have understood it to mean "difficult to be understood," but this meaning does not suit the connection. The doctrine which he delivered was opposed to their prejudices; it seemed to be absurd, and they therefore rejected it. ¶ *Saying.* Rather *doctrine* or *speech*—Greek, *logos.* It does not refer to any *particular part* of the discourse, but includes the whole. ¶ *Who can hear it?* That is, who can hear it *patiently*—who can stay and listen to such doctrine or believe it. The effect of this is stated in ver. 66. The doctrines which Jesus taught that were so offensive appear to have been, 1st. That he was superior to Moses. 2d. That God would save all that he had chosen, and those only. 3d. That he said he was the bread that came from heaven. 4th. That it was necessary to partake of that; or that it was necessary that an *atonement* should be made, and that they should be saved by that. These doctrines have always been among the most offensive that men have been called on to believe, and many, rather than trust in them, have chosen to draw back to perdition.

62. What *and if*, &c. Jesus does not say that those who were then present would see him ascend, but he implies that he would ascend. They had taken offence because he said he came down from heaven. Instead of explaining that away, he proceeds to state another doctrine quite as offensive to them—that he would reascend to heaven. The apostles only were present at his ascension, Ac. i. 9. As Jesus was to *ascend* to heaven, it was clear that he could not have intended *literally* that they should eat his flesh.

63. *It is the Spirit that quickeneth.* These words have been understood in different ways. The word "Spirit," here, evidently does not refer to the Holy Ghost, for he adds, "The words that I speak unto you, they are *spirit.*" He refers here, probably, to the doctrine which *he* had been teaching in opposition to *their* notions and desires. "*My* doctrine is spiritual; it is fitted to quicken and nourish the soul. It is from heaven. Your doctrine or your views are *earthly*, and may be called *flesh*, or fleshly, as pertaining only to the support of the body. You place a great value on the doctrine that Moses fed the *body;* yet that did not permanently *profit*, for your fathers are dead. You seek also food from me, but your views and desires are gross and earthly." ¶ *Quickeneth.* Gives life. See Notes on ch. v. 21. ¶ *The flesh.* Your carnal views and desires, and the *literal* understanding of my doctrine. By this Jesus shows them that he did not intend that his words should be taken literally. ¶ *Profiteth nothing.* Would not avail to the *real* wants of man. The bread that Moses gave, the food which you seek, would not be of *real* value to man's highest wants. ¶ They *are spirit.* They are spiritual. They are not to be understood *literally*, as if you were really to eat my flesh, but they are to be understood as denoting the need of that provision for the soul which God has made by my coming into the world. ¶ *Are life.* Are fitted to produce or give life to the soul dead in sins.

64 But there are some of you that believe not. For Jesus [y]knew from the beginning who they were that believed not, and who should betray him.

65 And he said, Therefore [z]said I unto you, that no man can come unto me except it were given unto him of my Father.

66 From that *time* many of his disciples [a]went back, and walked no more with him.

67 Then said Jesus unto the twelve, Will ye also go away?

68 Then Simon Peter answered him, Lord, to whom shall we go? thou hast [b]the words of eternal life.

y Ro.8.29; 2 Ti.2.19. *z* ver.44,45.

a Zep.1.6; Lu.9.62; He.10.38. *b* Ac.5.20; 7.38.

64. *Jesus knew from the beginning*, &c. As this implied a knowledge of the *heart*, and of the secret principles and motives of men, it shows that he must have been omniscient.

66. *Many of his disciples.* Many who had followed him professedly as his disciples and as desirous of learning of him. See Notes on ver. 60. ¶ *Went back.* Turned away from him and left him. From this we may learn, 1st. Not to wonder at the apostasy of many who profess to be followers of Christ. Many are induced to become his professed followers by the prospect of some temporal benefit, or under some public excitement, as these were; and when that temporal benefit is not obtained, or that excitement is over, they fall away. 2d. Many may be expected to be offended by the doctrines of the gospel. Having no spirituality of mind, and really understanding nothing of the gospel, they may be expected to take offence and turn back. The best way to understand the doctrines of the Bible is to be a sincere Christian, and aim to do the will of God, Jn. vii. 17. 3d. We should examine ourselves. We should honestly inquire whether we have been led to make a profession of religion by the hope of any temporal advantage, by any selfish principle, or by mere excited animal feeling. If we have it will profit us nothing, and we shall either *fall away* of ourselves, or be *cast away* in the great day of judgment.

67. *The twelve.* The twelve apostles. ¶ *Will ye also go away?* Many apostatized, and it was natural now for Jesus to submit the question to the twelve. "Will *you*, whom I have chosen, on whom I have bestowed the apostleship, and who have seen the evidence of my Messiahship, will you now also leave me?" This was the time to try them; and it is always a time to try *real* Christians when many professed disciples become cold and turn back; and *then* we may suppose Jesus addressing *us*, and saying, Will ye ALSO go away? Observe here, it was submitted to their choice. God compels none to remain with him against their will, and the question in such trying times is submitted to every man whether he will or will not go away.

68. *Simon Peter answered him.* With characteristic ardour and promptness. Peter was probably one of the oldest of the apostles, and it was his character to be *first* and most ardent in his professions. ¶ *To whom shall we go?* This implied their firm conviction that Jesus was the Messiah, and that he alone was able to save them. It is one of Peter's noble confessions—the instinctive promptings of a pious heart and of ardent love. There was no one else who could teach them. The Pharisees, the Sadducees, and the scribes were corrupt, and unable to guide them aright; and, though the doctrines of Jesus were mysterious, yet they were the *only* doctrines that could instruct and save them. ¶ *Thou hast*, &c. The meaning of this is, *thou teachest the doctrines which lead to eternal life.* And from this we may learn, 1st. That we are to expect that some of the doctrines of the Bible will be mysterious. 2d. That, though they are difficult to be understood, yet we should not therefore reject them. 3d. That nothing would be *gained* by rejecting them. The atheist, the infidel—nay, the philosopher, believes, or professes to believe, propositions quite as mysterious as any in the Bible. 4th. That poor, lost, sinful man has nowhere else to go but to Jesus. He is the way, the truth, and the life, and if the sinner betakes himself to any other way he will wander and die. 5th. We should, therefore, on no account forsake the teachings of the Son of God. The words that he speaks are spirit and are life.

69. *We are sure*, &c. See a similar confession of Peter in Mat. xvi. 16, and

69 And[c] we believe and are sure that thou art that Christ, the Son of the living God.

70 Jesus answered them, Have not I chosen you twelve, and one of you is [d]a devil?

71 He spake of Judas Iscariot, *the son* of Simon; for he it was that should betray him, being one of the twelve.

c Mat.16.16; ch.1.29; 11.27.

d ch.13.27.

---

the Notes on that place. Peter says *we* are sure, in the name of the whole of the apostles. Jesus immediately cautions him, as he did on other occasions, not to be too confident, for *one* of them actually had no such feelings, but was a traitor.

70. *Have not I chosen you twelve?* There is much emphasis in these words. Have not *I*—I, the Saviour, the Messiah, chosen you in mercy and in love, and therefore it will be a greater sin to betray me? *Chosen.* Chosen to the apostolic office; conferred on you marks of peculiar favour, and treason is therefore the greater sin. *You twelve.* So small a number. Out of such a multitude as follow for the loaves and fishes, it is to be expected there should be apostates; but when the number is so small, chosen in such a manner, then it becomes every one, however confident he may be, to be on his guard and examine his heart. ¶ *Is a devil.* Has the spirit, the envy, the malice, and the treasonable designs of a devil. The word *devil* here is used in the sense of an *enemy*, or one hostile to him.

71. *He spake of Judas*, &c. There is no evidence that Jesus *designated* Judas so that the disciples *then* understood that it was he. It does not appear that the apostles even suspected Judas, as they continued to treat him afterward with the same confidence, for he carried the *bag*, or the purse containing their little property (Jn. xii. 6; xiii. 29); and at the table, when Jesus said that one of them would betray him, the rest did not suspect Judas until Jesus pointed him out particularly, Jn. xiii. 26. Jesus spoke of *one*, to put them on their guard, to check their confidence, and to lead them to self-examination. So in every church, or company of professing Christians, we may know that it is probable that there may be some one or more deceived; but we may not know who it may be, and should therefore inquire prayerfully and honestly, "Lord, is it *I*?" ¶ *Should betray.* Would betray. If it be asked why Jesus called a man to be an apostle who he knew had no love for him, who would betray him, and who had from the beginning the spirit of a "devil," we may reply, 1st. It was that Judas might be an important witness for the innocence of Jesus, and for the fact that he was not an impostor. Judas was with him more than three years. He was treated with the same confidence as the others, and in some respects even with superior confidence, as he had "the bag" (Jn. xii. 6), or was the treasurer. He saw the Saviour in public and in private, heard his public discourses and his private conversation, and he would have been just the witness which the high-priests and Pharisees would have desired, if he had known any reason why he should be condemned. Yet he alleged nothing against him. Though he betrayed him, yet he afterward said that he was *innocent*, and, under the convictions of conscience, committed suicide. If Judas had known anything *against* the Saviour he would have alleged it. If he had known that he was an impostor, and had alleged it, he would have saved his own life and been rewarded. If Jesus was an impostor, he *ought* to have made it known, and to have been rewarded for it. 2d. It *may* have been, also, with a foresight of the necessity of having such a man among his disciples, in order that his own death might be brought about in the manner in which it was predicted. There were several prophecies which would have been unfulfilled had there been no such man among the apostles. 3d. It showed the knowledge which the Saviour had of the human heart, that he could thus discern character before it was developed, and was able so distinctly to predict that he would betray him. 4th. We may add, what benevolence did the Saviour evince—what patience and forbearance—that he had with him for more than three years a man who he knew hated him at heart, and who would yet betray him to be put to death on a cross, and that during all that time he treated him with the utmost kindness!

CHAPTER VII.

AFTER these things Jesus walked in Galilee; for he would not walk in Jewry, because the Jews sought to kill him.

2 Now the Jews' [a]feast of tabernacles was at hand.

3 His brethren therefore said unto him, Depart hence, and go into Judea, that thy disciples also may see the works that thou doest.

4 For *there is* no man *that* doeth any thing in secret, and he himself seeketh to be known openly. If thou do these things, show thyself to the world.

5 For neither did his [b]brethren believe in him.

6 Then Jesus said unto them, [c]My time is not yet come; but your time is alway ready.

7 The[d] world cannot hate you;

a Le.23.34. *b* Mar.3.21. *c* ch.2.4; 8.20; ver.8,30. *d* ch.15.19.

CHAPTER VII.

1. *After these things.* After the transactions which are recorded in the last chapters had taken place, and after the offence he had given the Jews. See ch. v. 18. ¶ *Jesus walked.* Or Jesus *lived*, or *taught*. He travelled around Galilee teaching. ¶ *In Jewry.* In Judea, the southern division of Palestine. Comp. Notes on ch. iv. 3. ¶ *The Jews sought.* That is, the *rulers* of the Jews. It does not appear that the common people ever attempted to take his life.

2. *The Jews' feast of tabernacles.* Or the feast of *tents.* This feast was celebrated on the fifteenth day of the month *Tisri*, answering to the last half of our month September and the first half of October, Nu. xxix. 12; De. xvi. 13-15. It was so called from the *tents* or tabernacles which on that occasion were erected in and about Jerusalem, and was designed to commemorate their dwelling in *tents* in the wilderness, Ne. viii. 16-18. During the continuance of this feast they dwelt in *booths* or tents, as their fathers did in the wilderness, Le. xxiii. 42, 43. The feast was continued *eight* days, and the eighth or last day was the most distinguished, and was called the *great day* of the feast, ver. 37; Nu. xxix. 35. The Jews on this occasion not only dwelt in *booths*, but they carried about the branches of palms, willows, and other trees which bore a thick foliage, and also branches of the olive-tree, myrtle, &c., Ne. viii. 15. Many sacrifices were offered on this occasion (Nu. xxix. 12-39; De. xvi. 14-16), and it was a time of general joy. It is called by Josephus and Philo the *greatest* feast, and was one of the three feasts which every male among the Jews was obliged to attend.

3. *His brethren.* See Notes on Mat. xii. 47. ¶ *Thy disciples.* The disciples which he had made when he was before in Judea, Jn. iv. 1-3. ¶ *The works.* The miracles.

4, 5. *For* there is *no man*, &c. The brethren of Jesus supposed that he was influenced as others are. As it is a common thing among men to seek popularity, so they supposed that he would also seek it; and as a great multitude would be assembled at Jerusalem at this feast, they supposed it would be a favourable time to make himself known. What follows shows that this was said, probably, not in sincerity, but in derision; and to the other sufferings of our Lord was to be added, what is so common to Christians, *derision* from his relatives and friends on account of his pretensions. If our Saviour was derided, we also may expect to be by our relatives; and, having his example, we should be content to bear it. ¶ *If thou do*, &c. It appears from this that they did not really believe that he wrought miracles; or, if they *did* believe it, they did not suppose that he was the Christ. Yet it seems hardly credible that they could suppose that his miracles were *real*, and yet not admit that he was the Messiah. Besides, there is no evidence that these relatives had been present at any of his miracles, and all that they knew of them might have been from report. See Notes on Mar. iii. 21. On the word *brethren* in ver. 5, see Notes on Mat. xiii. 55, and Ga. i. 19.

6. *My time*, &c. The proper time for my going up to the feast. We know not *why* it was not yet a proper time for him to go. It might be because if he went *then*, in their company, while multitudes were going, it would have too much the appearance of parade and ostentation; it might excite too much notice, and be more likely to expose him to the envy and opposition of the

but me it hateth, because I testify of it, that the works thereof are evil.

8 Go ye up unto this feast: I go not up yet unto this feast; for my time is not yet full come.

9 When he had said these words unto them he abode *still* in Galilee.

10 But when his brethren were gone up, then went he also up unto the feast, not openly, but as it were in secret.

11 Then[e] the Jews sought him at the feast, and said, Where is he?

12 And[f] there was much murmuring among the people concerning him; for some said, He is a good man; others said, Nay, but he deceiveth the people.

13 Howbeit, no man spake openly of him, for fear of the Jews.

14 Now about the midst of the feast, Jesus went up into the temple and taught.

15 And[g] the Jews marvelled, saying, How knoweth this man [1]letters, having never learned?

e ch.11.56.

f ch.9.16. g Mat.13.54. 1 or, *learning.*

rulers. ¶ *Your time*, &c. It makes no difference to you when you go up. Your going will excite no tumult or opposition; it will not attract attention, and will not endanger your lives. Jesus therefore chose to go up more privately, and to remain until the multitude had gone. They commonly travelled to those feasts in large companies, made up of most of the families in the neighbourhood. See Notes on Lu. ii. 44.

7. *The world cannot hate you.* You profess no principles in opposition to the world. You do not excite its envy, or rouse against you the civil rulers. As you possess the same spirit and principles with the men of the world, they cannot be expected to hate you. ¶ *I testify of it.* I bear witness against it. This was the main cause of the opposition which was made to him. He proclaimed that men were depraved, and the result was that they hated him. We may expect that all who preach faithfully against the wickedness of men will excite opposition. Yet this is not to deter us from doing our duty, and, after the example of Jesus, from proclaiming to men their sins, whatever may be the result.

8. *I go not up yet.* Jesus remained until about the middle of the feast, ver. 14. That is, he remained about four days after his brethren had departed, or until the mass of the people had gone up, so that his going might excite no attention, and that it might not be said he chose such a time to excite a tumult. We have here a signal instance of our Lord's prudence and opposition to parade. Though it would have been *lawful* for him to go up at that time, and though it would have been a favourable period to make himself known, yet he chose to forego these advantages rather than to afford an occasion of envy and jealousy to the rulers, or to *appear* even to excite a tumult among the people.

12. *Murmuring.* Contention, disputing. ¶ *He deceiveth the people.* That is, he is *deluding* them, or drawing them away by pretending to be the Messiah.

13. *Spake openly of him.* The word translated *openly*, here, is commonly rendered *boldly.* This refers, doubtless, to those who really believed on him. His enemies were not silent; but his friends had not confidence to speak of him *openly* or *boldly*—that is, to speak what they really thought. Many supposed that he was the Messiah, yet even this they did not dare to profess. All that they could say in his favour was that he *was a good man.* There are always many such friends of Jesus in the world who are desirous of saying *something* good about him, but who, from fear or shame, refuse to make a full acknowledgement of him. Many will praise his *morals*, his *precepts*, and his *holy life*, while they are ashamed to speak of his *divinity* or his *atonement*, and still more to acknowledge that they are dependent on him for salvation.

14. *About the midst.* Or about the middle of the feast. It continued eight days. ¶ *The temple.* See Notes on Mat. xxi. 12. ¶ *And taught.* Great multitudes were assembled in and around the temple, and it was a favourable time and place to make known his doctrine.

15. *Knoweth this man letters.* The

16 Jesus answered them and
said, My doctrine is [h] not mine,
but his that sent me.
17 If[i] any man will do his will,
he shall know of the doctrine
whether it be of God, or *whether*
I speak of myself.
18 He[k] that speaketh of him-

h ch.8.28; 12.49. i ch.8.43. k ch.8.50.

Jewish *letters* or science consisted in the knowledge of their Scriptures and traditions. Jesus exhibited in his discourses such a profound acquaintance with the Old Testament as to excite their amazement and admiration. ¶ *Having never learned.* The Jews taught their law and tradition in celebrated schools. As Jesus had not been instructed in those schools, they were amazed at his learning. What early human teaching the Saviour had we have no means of ascertaining, farther than that it was customary for the Jews to teach their children to read the Scriptures. 2 Ti. iii. 15: "From a child thou (Timothy) hast known the holy scriptures."

16. *My doctrine.* My *teaching*, or what I teach. This is the proper meaning of the word *doctrine.* It is what is *taught* us, and, as applied to religion, it is what is *taught* us by God in the holy Scriptures. ¶ *Is not mine.* It is not *originated* by me. Though I have not learned in your schools, yet you are not to infer that the doctrine which I teach is *devised* or *invented* by me. I teach nothing that is contrary to the will of God, and which he has not appointed me to teach. ¶ *His that sent me.* God's. It is such as he approves, and such as he has commissioned me to teach. The doctrine is divine in its origin and in its nature.

17. *If any man will do his will.* Literally, if any man *wills* or is *willing* to do the will of God. If there is a *disposition* in anyone to do that will, though he should not be able perfectly to keep his commandments. To do the *will* of God is to obey his commandments; to yield our hearts and lives to his requirements. A disposition to do his will is a readiness to yield our intellects, our feelings, and all that we have entirely to him, to be governed according to his pleasure. ¶ *He shall know.* He shall have *evidence*, in the very attempt to do the will of God, of the truth of the doctrine. This evidence is *internal*, and to the individual it is satisfactory and conclusive. It is of two kinds. 1st. He will find that the doctrines which Jesus taught are such as commend themselves to his reason and conscience, and such as are consistent with all that we know of the perfections of God. His doctrines commend themselves to us as fitted to make us pure and happy, and of course they are such as must be from God. 2d. An honest desire to obey God will lead a man to embrace the great doctrines of the Bible. He will find that his heart is depraved and inclined to evil, and he will see and feel the truth of the doctrine of *depravity;* he will find that he is a sinner and needs to be *born again;* he will learn his own weakness, and see his need of *a Saviour*, of an atonement, and of pardoning mercy; he will feel that he is polluted, and needs the purifying influence of the Holy Spirit. Thus we may learn, 1st. That an honest effort to obey God is the easiest way to become acquainted with the doctrines of the Bible. 2d. Those who *make* such an effort will not *cavil* at *any* of the doctrines of the Scriptures. 3d. This is evidence of the truth of revelation which every man can apply to his own case. 4th. It is such evidence as to lead to *certainty.* No man who has ever made an honest effort to live a pious life, and to do all the will of God, has ever had any doubt of the truth of the Saviour's doctrines, or any doubt that his religion is true and is fitted to the nature of man. They only doubt the truth of religion who wish to live in sin. 5th. We see the goodness of God in giving us evidence of his truth that may be within every man's reach. It does not require great learning to be a Christian, and to be convinced of the truth of the Bible. It requires an *honest* heart, and a willingness to obey God. ¶ *Whether it be of God.* Whether it be *divine.* ¶ *Or* whether *I speak of myself.* Of myself without being commissioned or directed by God.

18. *That speaketh of himself.* This does not mean *about* or *concerning* himself, but he that speaks by *his own authority*, without being sent by God, as mere human teachers do. ¶ *Seeketh his own glory.* His own *praise*, or seeks for reputation and applause. This is the case with mere human teachers,

self seeketh his own glory; [l]but
he that seeketh his glory that
sent him, the same is true, and
no unrighteousness is in him.
19 Did not [m]Moses give you
the law, and *yet* [n]none of you
keepeth the law? Why go ye
about [o]to kill me?
20 The people answered and
said, [p]Thou hast a devil; who
goeth about to kill thee?

l Pr.25.27. m Jn.1.17; Ga.3.19. n Ro.3.10-19. o Mat.12.14; ch.5.16,18. p ch.8.48.

21 Jesus answered and said
unto them, I have done one work,
and ye all marvel.
22 Moses[q] therefore gave unto
you circumcision; (not because it
is of Moses, [r]but of the fathers;)
and ye on the sabbath-day circumcise a man.
23 If a man on the sabbath-
day receive circumcision, [2]that
the law of Moses should not be

q Le.12.3. r Ge.17.10. 2 or, *without breaking the law of Moses.*

---

and as Jesus in his discourses manifestly sought to honour *God*, they ought to have supposed that he was sent by him. ¶ *No unrighteousness.* This word here means, evidently, there is no *falsehood*, no *deception* in him. He is not an impostor. It is used in the same sense in 2 Th. ii. 10–12. It is true that there was no *unrighteousness*, no *sin* in Jesus Christ, but that is not the truth taught here. It is that he was not an *impostor*, and the evidence of this was that he sought not his own glory, but the honour of God. This evidence was furnished, 1st. In his retiring, unobtrusive disposition; in his not seeking the applause of men. 2d. In his teaching such doctrines as tended to exalt God and humble man. 3d. In his ascribing all glory and praise to God.

19. *Did not Moses give you the law?* This they admitted, and on this they prided themselves. Every violation of that law they considered as deserving of death. They had accused Jesus of violating it because he had healed a man on the Sabbath, and for that they had sought his life, ch. v. 10–16. He here recalls that charge to their recollection, and shows them that, though they pretended great reverence for that law, yet they were really its violators in having sought his life. ¶ *None of you*, &c. None of you Jews. They had sought to kill him. This was a pointed and severe charge, and shows the great faithfulness with which he was accustomed to proclaim the truth. ¶ *Why go ye about to kill me?* Why do ye *seek* to kill me? See ch. v. 16.

20. *The people.* Perhaps some of the people who were not aware of the designs of the rulers. ¶ *Thou hast a devil.* Thou art deranged or mad. See ch. x. 20. As they saw no effort to kill him, and as they were ignorant of the designs of the rulers, they supposed that this was the effect of derangement.

21. *One work.* The healing of the man on the Sabbath, Jn. v. ¶ *Ye all marvel.* You all wonder or are amazed, and particularly that it was done on the Sabbath. This was the *particular* ground of astonishment, that he should dare to do what they esteemed a violation of the Sabbath.

22. *Moses therefore gave unto you circumcision.* Moses commanded you to circumcise your children, Le. xii. 3. The word "therefore" in this place—literally "*on account of this*"—means, "Moses *on this account* gave you circumcision, not because it is of Moses, but of the fathers;" that is, the reason was not that he himself appointed it as a new institution, but he found it already in existence, and incorporated it in his institutions and laws. ¶ *Not because*, &c. Not *that* it is of Moses. Though Jesus spoke in accordance with the custom of the Jews, who ascribed the appointment of circumcision to Moses, yet he is careful to remind them that it was in observance long before Moses. So, also, the *Sabbath* was kept before Moses, and alike in the one case and the other they ought to keep in mind the *design* of the appointment. ¶ *Of the fathers.* Of the patriarchs, Abraham, Isaac, and Jacob, Ge. xvii. 10. ¶ *Ye on the sabbath-day*, &c. The law required that the child should be circumcised on the *eighth* day. If that day happened to be the *Sabbath*, yet they held that he was to be circumcised, as there was a positive law to that effect; and as this was *commanded*, they did not consider it a breach of the Sabbath. ¶ *A man.* Not an *adult* man, but a man-child. See Jn. xvi. 21:

broken, are ye angry at me [s]be-
cause I have made a man every
whit whole on the sabbath-day?
24 Judge[t] not according to the
appearance, but judge righteous
judgment.
25 Then said some of them of

s Jn.5.8. t De.1.16,17.

Jerusalem, Is not this he whom
they seek to kill?
26 But, lo, he speaketh boldly,
and they say nothing unto him.
Do[u] the rulers know indeed that
this is the very Christ?
27 Howbeit[v] we know this man

u ver.48. v Mat.13.55.

"She remembereth no more the anguish, for joy that *a man* is born into the world."

23. *That the law of Moses should not be broken.* In order that the law requiring it to be done at a specified time, though that might occur on the Sabbath, should be kept. ¶ *Are ye angry,* &c. The argument of Jesus is this: "You yourselves, in interpreting the law about the Sabbath, allow a work of necessity to be done. You do that which is necessary as an ordinance of religion denoting *separation* from other nations, or external purity. As you allow this, you ought also, for the same reason, to allow that a man should be completely restored to health—that a work of much more importance should be done." We may learn here that it would be happy for all if they would not condemn others in that thing which they allow. Men often accuse others of doing things which they themselves do in other ways. ¶ *Every whit whole.* Literally, "I have restored the whole man to health," implying that the man's *whole body* was diseased, and that he had been *entirely* restored to health.

24. *Judge not according to the appearance.* Not as a thing first offers itself to you, without reflection or candour. In *appearance,* to circumcise a child on the Sabbath might be a violation of the law; yet you do it, and it is right. So, to *appearance,* it might be a violation of the Sabbath to heal a man, yet it is right to do works of necessity and mercy. ¶ *Judge righteous judgment.* Candidly; looking at the law, and inquiring what its *spirit* really requires.

26. *Do the rulers know indeed,* &c. It seems from this that they supposed that the *rulers* had been convinced that Jesus was the Messiah, but that from some cause they were not willing yet to make it known to the people. The reasons of this opinion were these: 1st. They knew that they *had* attempted to kill him. 2d. They now saw him speaking boldly to the people without interruption from the rulers. They concluded, therefore, that some change had taken place in the sentiments of the rulers in regard to him, though they had not yet made it public. ¶ *The rulers.* The members of the *Sanhedrim,* or great council of the nation, who had charge of religious affairs. ¶ *Indeed.* Truly; certainly. Have they certain evidence, as would appear from their suffering him to speak without interruption? ¶ *The very Christ.* Is *truly* or *really* the Messiah.

27. *Howbeit.* But. They proceeded to state a reason why *they* supposed that he could *not* be the Messiah, whatever the *rulers* might think. ¶ *We know this man whence he is.* We know the place of his birth and residence. ¶ *No man knoweth whence he is.* From Mat. ii. 5, it appears that the common expectation of the Jews was that the Messiah would be born at Bethlehem; but they had also feigned that after his birth he would be *hidden* or taken away in some mysterious manner, and appear again from some unexpected quarter. We find allusions to this expectation in the New Testament, where our Saviour *corrects* their common notions, Mat. xxiv. 23: "Then if any man shall say unto you, Lo, here is Christ, or there, believe it not." And again (ver. 26), "If they shall say unto you, Behold, he is in the desert, go not forth; behold, he is in the secret chambers, believe it not." The following extracts from Jewish writings show that this was the common expectation: "The Redeemer shall manifest himself, and afterward be hid. So it was in the redemption from Egypt. Moses showed himself and then was hidden." So on the passage, Ca. ii. 9—"My beloved is like a roe or a young hart"—they say: "A roe appears and then is hid; so the Redeemer shall first appear and then be concealed, and then again be concealed and then again appear." "So the Redeemer shall first appear and then be hid, and then, at the end of forty-five days, shall reap-

whence he is; but when Christ
cometh, no man knoweth whence
he is.
28 Then cried Jesus in the
temple as he taught, saying, Ye
both know me, and ye know
whence I am; [w]and I am not
come of myself, but [x]he that sent
me is true, [y]whom ye know not.
29 But[z] I know him; for I am
from him, and he hath sent me.
30 Then[a] they sought to take
him, but no man laid hands on
him, because his hour was not yet
come.

w ch.5.43. x Ro.3.4. y ch.1.18; 8.55.
z Mat.11.27; ch.10.15.
a Mar.11.18; Lu.20.19; ch.8.37.

31 And [b]many of the people
believed on him, and said, When
Christ cometh, will he do more
miracles than these which this
man hath done?
32 The Pharisees heard that
the people murmured such things
concerning him; and the Pharisees
and the chief priests sent officers
to take him.
33 Then said Jesus unto them,
[c]Yet a little while am I with
you, and *then* I go unto him that
sent me.
34 Ye[d] shall seek me, and shall

b ch.4.39. c ch.13.33; 16.16. d Ho.5.6; ch.8.21.

pear, and cause *manna* to descend." See Lightfoot. Whatever may have been the source of this opinion, it explains this passage, and shows that the writer of this gospel was well acquainted with the opinions of the Jews, however improbable those opinions were.

28. *Ye know whence I am.* You have sufficient evidence of my divine mission, and that I am the Messiah. ¶ *Is true.* Is worthy to be believed. He has given evidence that I came from him, and he is worthy to be believed. Many read this as a question—Do ye know me, and know whence I am? I am not come of myself, &c.

30. *Then they sought to take him.* The rulers and their friends. They did this —1st. Because of his reproof; and, 2d. For professing to be the Messiah. ¶ *His hour.* The proper and the appointed *time* for his death. See Mat. xxi. 46.

31. *Will he do more miracles?* It was a common expectation that the Messiah would work many miracles. This opinion was founded on such passages as Is. xxxv. 5, 6, &c.: "Then the eyes of the blind shall be opened, and the ears of the deaf shall be unstopped; then shall the lame man leap as an hart," &c. Jesus had given abundant evidence of his power to work such miracles, and they therefore believed that he was the Messiah.

32. *The people murmured such things.* That is, that the question was agitated whether he was the Messiah; that it excited debate and contention; and that the consequence was, he made many friends. They chose, therefore, if possible, to remove him from them.

33. *Yet a little while am I with you.* It will not be long before my death. This is supposed to have been about six months before his death. This speech of Jesus is full of tenderness. They were seeking his life. He tells them that he is fully aware of it; that he will not be long with them; and *implies* that they should be diligent to seek him while he was yet with them. He was about to die, but they might now seek his favour and find it. When we remember that this was said to his persecutors and murderers; that it was said even while they were seeking his life, we see the peculiar tenderness of his love. Enmity, and hate, and persecution did not prevent his offering salvation to them. ¶ *I go unto him that sent me.* This is one of the intimations that he gave that he would *ascend* to God. Comp. ch. vi. 62.

34. *Ye shall seek me.* This probably means simply, Ye shall seek *the Messiah.* Such will be your troubles, such the calamities that will come on the nation, that you will earnestly desire the coming of *the Messiah.* You will seek for a deliverer, and will look for *him* that he may bring deliverance. This does not mean that they would seek for *Jesus* and not be able to find him, but that they would desire the aid and comfort of *the Messiah*, and would be disappointed. Jesus speaks of *himself* as the Messiah, and his own name as synonymous with the Messiah. See Notes on Mat. xxiii. 39. ¶ *Shall not find* me. Shall not find the Messiah. He will not come, according to your expectations, to aid you. See Notes on Mat. xxiv. ¶ *Where I am.* This whole

not find *me;* and where I am,
thither ye cannot come.
35 Then said the Jews among
themselves, Whither will he go,
that we shall not find him? Will
he go unto the [e]dispersed among
the [3]Gentiles, and teach the Gentiles?
36 What *manner of* saying is
this that he said, Ye shall seek
me, and shall not find *me;* and
where I am, *thither* ye cannot
come?
37 In the [f]last day, that great
day of the feast, Jesus stood and
cried, saying, [g]If any man thirst,
let him come unto me and drink.
38 He that believeth on me, as

e Is.11.12; Ja.1.1; 1 Pe.1.1. 3 or, *Greeks*.

f Le.23.36. g Is.55.1; Re.22.17.

clause is to be understood as future, though the words "am" and "cannot" are both in the present tense. The meaning is, Where I shall be you will not be able to come. That is, he, the Messiah, would be in heaven; and though they would earnestly desire his presence and aid to save the city and nation from the Romans, yet they would not be able to obtain it—represented here by their not being able to *come to him*. This does not refer to their *individual* salvation, but to the deliverance of their nation. It is not true of individual sinners that they seek Christ in a proper manner and are not able to find him; but it *was* true of the Jewish nation that they *looked for* the Messiah, and sought his coming to deliver them, but he did not do it.

35. *The dispersed among the Gentiles.* To the *Jews* scattered among the Gentiles, or living in distant parts of the earth. It is well known that at that time there were Jews dwelling in almost every land. There were multitudes in Egypt, in Asia Minor, in Greece, in Rome, &c., and in all these places they had synagogues. The question which they asked was whether he would leave an ungrateful country, and go into those distant nations and teach them. ¶ *Gentiles.* In the original, *Greeks*. All those who were not *Jews* were called *Greeks*, because they were chiefly acquainted with those heathens only who spake the Greek language. It is remarkable that Jesus returned no answer to these inquiries. He rather chose to turn off their minds from a speculation about the place to which he was going, to the great affairs of their own personal salvation.

37. *In the last day.* The eighth day of the festival. ¶ *That great* day. The day of the holy convocation or solemn assembly, Le. xxiii. 36. This seems to have been called the *great* day, 1st. Because of the solemn assembly, and because it was the closing scene. 2d. Because, according to their traditions, on the previous days they offered sacrifices for the *heathen* nations as well as for themselves, but on this day for the Jews only (Lightfoot). 3d. Because on this day they abstained from all servile labour (Le. xxiii. 39), and regarded it as a *holy* day. 4th. On this day they finished the reading of the law, which they commenced at the beginning of the feast. 5th. Because on this day probably occurred the ceremony of drawing water from the pool of Siloam. On the last day of the feast it was customary to perform a solemn ceremony in this manner: The priest filled a golden vial with water from the fount of Siloam (see Notes on Jn. ix. 7), which was borne with great solemnity, attended with the clangour of trumpets, through the gate of the temple, and being mixed with wine, was poured on the sacrifice on the altar. What was the origin of this custom is unknown. Some suppose, and not improbably, that it arose from an improper understanding of the passage in Is. xii. 3: "With joy shall ye draw water out of the wells of salvation." It is certain that no such ceremony is commanded by Moses. It is supposed to be probable that Jesus *stood and cried* while they were performing this ceremony, that he might, 1st, *illustrate* the nature of his doctrine by this; and 2d, call off their attention from a rite that was uncommanded, and that could not confer eternal life. ¶ *Jesus stood.* In the temple, in the midst of thousands of the people. ¶ *If any man thirst.* Spiritually. If any man feels his need of salvation. See Jn. iv. 13, 14; Mat. v. 6; Re. xxii. 17. The invitation is full and free to all. ¶ *Let him come unto me,* &c. Instead of depending on *this* ceremony of drawing water let him come to me, the Messiah, and he shall find an ever-abundant supply for all the wants of his soul.

the scripture hath said, [h]out of his belly shall flow rivers of living water.

39 (But this he spake of [i]the Spirit, which they that believe on him should receive; for the Holy Ghost was not yet *given*, because that Jesus was not yet glorified.)

40 Many of the people, therefore, when they heard this saying, said, Of a truth this is [k]the Prophet.

41 Others said, This is [l]the

h Pr.18.4; Is.58.11; ch.4.14.
i Is.44.3; Joel 2.28; ch.16.7; Ac.2.17,33.
k De.18.15,18; ch.6.14. *l* ch.4.42; 6.69.

38. *He that believeth on me.* He that acknowledges me as the Messiah, and trusts in me for salvation. ¶ *As the scripture hath said.* This is a difficult expression, from the fact that no such expression as follows is to be found literally in the Old Testament. Some have proposed to connect it with what precedes—"He that believeth on me, as the Old Testament has *commanded* or required"—but to this there are many objections. The natural and obvious meaning here is, doubtless, the true one; and Jesus probably intended to say, not that there was any *particular* place in the Old Testament that affirmed this in so many words, but that this was the *substance* of what the Scriptures taught, or this was the *spirit* of their declarations. Hence the *Syriac* translates it in the plural—the *Scriptures.* Probably there is a reference more particularly to Is. lviii. 11, than to any other single passage: "Thou shalt be like a watered garden, and like a spring of water whose waters fail not." See also Is. xliv. 3, 4; Joel iii. 18. ¶ *Out of his belly.* Out of his midst, or out of his heart. The word belly is often put for the midst of a thing, the centre, and the heart, Mat. xii. 40. It means here that from the *man* shall flow; that is, his piety shall be of such a nature that it will extend its blessings to others. It shall be like a running fountain—perhaps in allusion to statues or ornamented reservoirs in gardens, in which pipes were placed from which water was continually flowing. The Jews used the same figure: "His two reins are like fountains of water, from which the law flows." And again: "When a man turns himself to the Lord, he shall be as a fountain filled with living water, and his streams shall flow to all the nations and tribes of men" (Kuinoel). ¶ *Rivers.* This word is used to express *abundance*, or a full supply. It means here that those who are Christians shall diffuse large, and liberal, and constant blessings on their fellow-men; or, as Jesus immediately explains it, that they shall be the *instruments* by which the Holy Spirit shall be poured down on the world. ¶ *Living water.* Fountains, ever-flowing streams. That is, the gospel shall be constant and life-giving in its blessings. We learn here, 1st. That it is the nature of Christian piety to be diffusive. 2d. That no man can believe on Jesus who does not desire that others should also, and who will not seek it. 3d. That the desire is large and liberal—that the Christian desires the salvation of all the world. 4th. That the *faith* of the believer is to be connected with the influence of the Holy Spirit, and *in that way* Christians are to be like rivers of living water.

39. *Of the Spirit.* Of the Holy Spirit, that should be sent down to attend their preaching and to convert sinners. ¶ *For the Holy Ghost was not yet given.* Was not given in such full and large measures as should be after Jesus had ascended to heaven. Certain measures of the influences of the Spirit had been always given in the conversion and sanctification of the ancient saints and prophets; but that *abundant* and *full* effusion which the apostles were permitted afterward to behold had not yet been given. See Ac. ii.; x. 44, 45. ¶ *Jesus was not yet glorified.* Jesus had not yet ascended to heaven—to the glory and honour that awaited him there. It was a part of the arrangement in the work of redemption that the influences of the Holy Spirit should descend chiefly after the death of Jesus, as that death was the procuring cause of this great blessing. Hence he said (Jn. xvi. 7), "It is expedient for you that I go away; for if I go not away the Comforter will not come unto you; but if I depart I will send him unto you." See also ver. 8–12, and ch. xiv. 15, 16, 26. Comp. Ep. iv. 8–11.

40. *The Prophet.* That is, the prophet whom they expected to *precede* the coming of the Messiah—either Elijah or Jeremiah. See Mat. xvi. 14.

41, 42. See Notes on Mat. ii. 4–6. ¶ *Where David was.* 1 Sa. xvi. 1–4.

Christ. But some said, [m]Shall
Christ come out of Galilee?
42 Hath not the scripture said,
That [n]Christ cometh of the seed
of David, and out of [o]the town of
Bethlehem, [p]where David was?
43 So there was a division among
the people because of him.
44 And some of them would
have taken him, but no man laid
hands on him.

m ch.1.46; ver.52. *n* Ps.132.11; Je.23.5. *o* Mi.5.2; Lu.2.4. *p* 1 Sa.16.1,4.

45 Then came the officers to the
chief priests and Pharisees; and
they said unto them, Why have
ye not brought him?
46 The officers answered, [q]Never
man spake like this man.
47 Then answered them the
Pharisees, Are ye also deceived?
48 Have any of [r]the rulers or
of the Pharisees believed on him?

q Lu.4.22. *r* Je.5.4,5; ch.12.42; 1 Co.1.26.

45, 46. *The officers.* Those who had been appointed (ver. 32) to take him. It seems that Jesus was in the midst of the people addressing them, and that they happened to come at the very time when he was speaking. They were so impressed and awed with what he said that they dared not take him. There have been few instances of eloquence like this. His speaking had so much evidence of truth, so much proof that he was from God, and was so impressive and persuasive, that they were convinced of his innocence, and they *dared* not touch him to execute their commission. We have here, 1st. A remarkable testimony to the commanding eloquence of Jesus. 2d. Wicked men may be awed and restrained by the presence of a good man, and by the evidence that he speaks that which is true. 3d. God can preserve his friends. Here were men sent for a particular purpose. They were armed with power. They were commissioned by the highest authority of the nation. On the other hand, Jesus was without arms or armies, and without external protection. Yet, in a manner which the officers and the high-priests would have little expected, he was preserved. So, in ways which *we* little expect, God will defend and deliver us when in the midst of danger. 4th. No prophet, apostle, or minister has ever spoken the truth with as much power, grace, and beauty as Jesus. It should be *ours*, therefore, to listen to his words, and to sit at his feet and learn heavenly wisdom.

47. *Are ye also deceived?* They set down the claims of Jesus as of course an imposture. They did not examine, but were, like thousands, determined to believe that he was a deceiver. Hence they did not ask them whether they were *convinced*, or had seen evidence that he was the Messiah; but, with mingled contempt, envy, and anger, they asked if they were also *deluded.* Thus many assume religion to be an imposture; and when one becomes a Christian, they *assume* at once that he is deceived, that he is the victim of foolish credulity or superstition, and treat him with ridicule or scorn. Candour would require them to inquire whether such changes were not proof of the *power* and *truth* of the gospel, as candour in the case of the rulers required them to inquire whether Jesus had not given them evidence that he was from God.

48. *The rulers.* The members of the Sanhedrim, who were supposed to have control over the religious rites and doctrines of the nation. ¶ *The Pharisees.* The sect possessing wealth, and office, and power. The name *Pharisees* sometimes denotes those who were high in honour and authority. ¶ *Believed on him.* Is there any instance in which those who are high in rank or in office have embraced him as the Messiah? This shows the rule by which *they* judged of religion. 1st. They claimed the right of regulating the doctrines and rites of religion. 2d. They repressed the liberty of private judgment, stifled investigation, assumed that a *new* doctrine *must* be heresy, and laboured to keep the people in inglorious bondage. 3d. They treated the new doctrine of Jesus with *contempt*, and thus attempted to put it down, not by argument, but by *contempt*, and especially because it was embraced by the common people. This is the way in which doctrines contrary to the truth of God have been uniformly supported in the world; this is the way in which new views of truth are met; and this the way in which those in ecclesiastical power often attempt to *lord it over*

49 But this people, who knoweth not the law, are cursed.

50 Nicodemus saith unto them, ([s]he that came [4]to Jesus by night, being one of them,)

51 Doth[t] our law judge *any man* before it hear him, and know what he doeth?

52 They answered and said unto him, Art thou also of Galilee?

s ch.3.2. 4 *to him.* t De.17.8; Pr.18.13.

God's heritage, and to repress the investigation of the Bible.

49. *This people.* The word here translated *people* is the one commonly rendered *the multitude.* It is a word expressive of contempt, or, as we would say, *the rabble.* It denotes the scorn which they felt that the *people* should presume to judge for themselves in a case pertaining to their own salvation. ¶ *Who knoweth not the law.* Who have not been *instructed* in the schools of the Pharisees, and been taught to interpret the Old Testament as they had. They supposed that any who believed on the humble and despised Jesus must be, *of course*, ignorant of the true doctrines of the Old Testament, as they held that a very *different* Messiah from him was foretold. Many instances are preserved in the writings of the Jews of the great contempt in which the Pharisees held the common people. It may here be remarked that Christianity is the only system of religion ever presented to man that in a proper manner regards the poor, the ignorant, and the needy. Philosophers and Pharisees, in all ages, have looked on them with contempt. ¶ *Are cursed.* Are execrable; are of no account; are worthy only of contempt and perdition. Some suppose that there is reference here to their being worthy to be cut off from the people for believing on him, or worthy to be put out of the synagogue (see ch. ix. 22); but it seems to be an expression only of *contempt;* a declaration that they were a rabble, ignorant, unworthy of notice, and going to ruin. Observe, however, 1st. That of this despised people were chosen most of those who became Christians. 2d. That if the people were ignorant, it was the fault of the Pharisees and rulers. It was their business to see that they were taught. 3d. There is no way so common of attempting to oppose Christianity as by ridiculing its friends as poor, and ignorant, and weak, and credulous. As well might food, and raiment, and friendship, and patriotism be held in contempt because the poor need the one or possess the other.

50. *Nicodemus.* See ch. iii. 1. ¶ *One of them.* That is, one of the great council or Sanhedrim. God often places one or more pious men in legislative assemblies to vindicate his honour and his law; and he often gives a man grace on such occasions boldly to defend his cause; to put men *upon their proof*, and to confound the proud and the domineering. We see in this case, also, that a man, at one time timid and fearful (comp. ch. iii. 1), may on other occasions be bold, and fearlessly defend the truth as it is in Jesus. This example should lead every man intrusted with authority or office fearlessly to defend the truth of God, and, when the rich and the mighty are pouring contempt on Jesus and his cause, to stand forth as its fearless defender.

51. *Doth our law*, &c. The law required *justice* to be done, and gave every man the right to claim a fair and impartial trial, Le. xix. 15, 16; Ex. xxiii. 1, 2; De. xix. 15, 18. Their condemnation of Jesus was a violation of every rule of right. He was not arraigned; he was not heard in self-defence, and not a single witness was adduced. Nicodemus demanded that *justice* should be done, and that he should not be condemned until he had had a fair trial. Every man should be presumed to be innocent until he is proved to be guilty. This is a maxim of law, and a most just and proper precept in our judgments in private life.

52. *Art thou also of Galilee?* Here is another expression of contempt. To be a *Galilean* was a term of the highest reproach. They knew well that he was not of Galilee, but they meant to ask whether *he* also had become a follower of the despised Galilean. Ridicule is not argument, and there is no demonstration in a gibe; but, unhappily, this is the only weapon which the proud and haughty often use in opposing religion. ¶ *Ariseth no prophet.* That is, there is no prediction that any prophet should come out of Galilee, and especially no

Search and look; for [u]out of Galilee ariseth no prophet.

53 And every man went unto his own house.

CHAPTER VIII.

JESUS went unto the mount of Olives.

2 And early in the morning he came again into the temple, and all the people came unto him; and he sat down and taught them.

3 And the scribes and Pharisees brought unto him a woman taken in adultery; and when they had set her in the midst,

4 They say unto him, Master, this woman was taken in adultery, in the very act.

5 Now[a] Moses in the law commanded us that such should be stoned; but what sayest thou?

6 This they said, tempting him, that they might have to accuse him.

u Is.9.1,2.

a Le.20.10.

---

prophet that was to attend or precede the Messiah. Comp. Jn. i. 46. They assumed, therefore, that Jesus could not be the Christ.

53. *And every man went unto his own house.* There is every mark of confusion and disorder in this breaking up of the Sanhedrim. It is possible that some of the Sadducees might have joined Nicodemus in opposing the Pharisees, and thus increased the disorder. It is a most instructive and melancholy exhibition of the influence of pride, envy, contempt, and anger, when brought to bear on an inquiry, and when they are manifestly opposed to candour, to argument, and to truth. So wild and furious are the passions of men when they oppose the person and claims of the Son of God! It is remarkable, too, how God accomplishes his purposes. *They* wished to destroy Jesus. God suffered their passions to be excited, a tumult to ensue, the assembly thus to break up in disorder, and Jesus to be safe, for his time had not yet come. "The wrath of man shall praise thee; the remainder of wrath shalt thou restrain," Ps. lxxvi. 10.

CHAPTER VIII.

1. *Mount of Olives.* The mountain about a mile directly east of Jerusalem. See Notes on Mat. xxi. 1. This was the place in which he probably often passed the night when attending the feasts at Jerusalem. The Garden of Gethsemane, to which he was accustomed to resort (ch. xviii. 2), was on the western side of that mountain, and Bethany, the abode of Martha and Mary, on its east side, ch. xi. 1.

5. *Moses in the law,* &c. The punishment of adultery commanded by Moses was death, Le. xx. 10; De. xxii. 22. The particular manner of the death was not specified in the law. The Jews had themselves, in the time of Christ, determined that it should be by stoning. See this described in the Notes on Mat. xxi. 35, 44. The punishment for adultery varied. In some cases it was strangling. In the time of Ezekiel (ch. xvi. 38–40) it was stoning and being thrust through with a sword. If the adulteress was the daughter of a priest, the punishment was being burned to death.

6. *Tempting him.* Trying him, or laying a plan that they might have occasion to accuse him. If he decided the case, they expected to be able to bring an accusation against him; for if he decided that she ought to die, they might accuse him of claiming power which belonged to the Romans—the power of life and death. They might allege that it was not the giving an opinion about an abstract case, but that she was formally before him, that he decided her case *judicially*, and that without authority or form of trial. If he decided otherwise, they would have alleged that he denied the authority of the law, and that it was his intention to abrogate it. They had had a controversy with him about the authority of the Sabbath, and they perhaps supposed that he would decide this case as he did that—against them. It may be farther added that they knew that Jesus admitted publicans and sinners to eat with him; that one of their charges was that he was friendly to sinners (see Lu. xv. 2); and they wished, doubtless, to make it appear that he was *gluttonous*, and a *winebibber*, and a *friend of sinners,* and disposed to relax all the laws of morality, even in the case of adultery. Seldom was there a plan more artfully laid, and *never* was more wisdom and knowledge

But Jesus stooped down, and with
his finger wrote on the ground, *as
though he heard them not.*
7 So when they continued asking him, he lifted up himself, and
said unto them, [b]He that is without sin among you, let him first
cast a stone at her.
8 And again he stooped down
and wrote on the ground.
9 And they which heard *it*, being convicted by *their own* conscience, went out one by one, beginning at the eldest, *even* unto the
last; and Jesus was left alone, and
the woman standing in the midst.
10 When Jesus had lifted up
himself, and saw none but the
woman, he said unto her, Woman,
where are those thine accusers?
Hath no man condemned thee?
11 She said, No man, Lord. And

b De.17.7; Ro.2.1,22.

---

of human nature displayed than in the manner in which it was met. ¶ *Wrote on the ground.* This took place in the *temple.* The "ground," here, means the *pavement*, or the dust on the pavement. By this Jesus showed them clearly that he was not *solicitous* to pronounce an opinion in the case, and that it was not his wish or intention to intermeddle with the civil affairs of the nation. ¶ As though he heard them not. This is added by the translators. It is not in the original, and should not have been added. There is no intimation in the original, as it seems to be implied by this addition, that the *object* was to convey the impression that he did not hear them. What was his object is unknown, and conjecture is useless. The most probable reason seems to be that he did not wish to intermeddle; that he designed to show no solicitude to decide the case; and that he did not mean to decide it unless he was *constrained* to.

7. *They continued asking him.* They pressed the question upon him. They were determined to extort an answer from him, and showed a perseverance in evil which has been unhappily often imitated. ¶ *Is without sin.* That is, without this particular sin; he who has not himself been guilty of this very crime—for in this place the connection evidently demands this meaning. ¶ *Let him first cast a stone at her.* In the punishment by death, one of the witnesses threw the culprit from the scaffold, and the other threw the first stone, or rolled down a stone to crush him. See De. xvii. 6, 7. This was in order that the witness might feel his responsibility in giving evidence, as he was also to be the executioner. Jesus therefore put them to the test. Without pronouncing on her case, he directed them, if any of them were innocent, to perform the office of executioner. This was said, evidently, well knowing their guilt, and well knowing that no one would dare to do it.

9. *Beginning at the eldest.* As being conscious of more sins, and, therefore, being desirous to leave the Lord Jesus. The word *eldest* here probably refers not to *age*, but to *honour*—from those who were in highest reputation to the lowest in rank. This consciousness of crime showed that the state of the public morals was exceedingly corrupt, and justified the declaration of Jesus that it was an *adulterous and wicked generation*, Mat. xvi. 4. ¶ *Alone.* Jesus *only* was left with the woman, &c. ¶ *In the midst.* Her *accusers* had gone out, and left Jesus and the woman; but it is by no means probable that *the people* had left them; and, as this was in the temple on a public occasion, they were doubtless surrounded still by many. This is evident from the fact that Jesus immediately (ver. 12) addressed a discourse to the people present.

10. *Hath no man condemned thee?* Jesus had directed them, if innocent, to cast a stone, thus *to condemn her*, or to use the power which he gave them to condemn her. No one of them had done that. They had *accused* her, but they had not proceeded to the act expressive of *judicial condemnation.*

11. *Neither do I condemn thee.* This is evidently to be taken in the sense of *judicial* condemnation, or of passing sentence as a *magistrate*, for this was what they had arraigned her for. It was not to obtain his *opinion* about adultery, but to obtain the *condemnation* of the woman. As he claimed no *civil* authority, he said that he did not exercise it, and should not *condemn her to die.* In this sense the word is used in the previous verse, and this is the only

Jesus said unto her, [c]Neither do I condemn thee; go, [d]and sin no more.

12 Then spake Jesus again unto them, saying, [e]I am the light of the world. He[f] that followeth me shall not walk in darkness, but shall have the light of life.

13 The Pharisees therefore said unto him, [g]Thou bearest record of thyself; thy record is not true.

14 Jesus answered and said unto them, Though I bear record of myself, *yet* my record is true; for I know whence I came, and whither I go; [h]but ye cannot tell whence I come, and whither I go.

15 Ye judge after the flesh; [i]I judge no man.

c ch.3.17. d ch.5.14. e ch.1.4; 9.5. f ch.12.35,46.

g ch.5.31. h ch.7.28; 9.29,30. i ch.3.17; 12.47.

sense which the passage demands. Besides, what follows shows that this was his meaning. ¶ *Go, and sin no more.* You have sinned. You have been detected and accused. The sin is great. But I do not claim power to condemn you to die, and, as your *accusers* have left you, my direction to you is that you *sin* no more. This passage therefore teaches us, 1st. That Jesus claimed no *civil* authority. 2d. That he regarded the action of which they accused her as *sin*. 3d. That he knew the *hearts* and *lives* of men. 4th. That men are often very zealous in accusing others of that of which they themselves are guilty. And, 5th. That Jesus was endowed with wonderful wisdom in meeting the devices of his enemies, and eluding their deep-laid plans to involve him in ruin.

It should be added that this passage, together with the last verse of the preceding chapter, has been by many critics thought to be spurious. It is wanting in many of the ancient manuscripts and versions, and has been rejected by Erasmus, Calvin, Beza, Grotius, Wetstein, Tittman, Knapp, and many others. It is not easy to decide the question whether it be a genuine part of the New Testament or not. Some have supposed that it was not *written* by the evangelists, but was often *related* by them, and that after a time it was recorded and introduced by Papias into the sacred text.

12. *I am the light of the world.* See Notes on ch. i. 4, 9.

13. *Thou bearest record of thyself.* Thou art a *witness* for thyself, or in thy own case. See ch. v. 31. The law required two witnesses in a criminal case, and they alleged that as the only evidence which Jesus had was his own assertion, it could not be entitled to belief. ¶ *Is not true.* Is not worthy of belief, or is not substantiated by sufficient evidence.

14. *Jesus answered,* &c. To this objection Jesus replied by saying, first, that the case was such that his testimony *alone* ought to be received; and, secondly, that he had the evidence given him by his Father. Though, in common life, in courts, and in mere human transactions, it was true that a man ought not to give evidence in his own case, yet in this instance, such was the nature of the case that his word was worthy to be believed. ¶ *My record.* My evidence, my testimony. ¶ *Is true.* Is worthy to be believed. ¶ *For I know whence I came—but ye,* &c. I know by what authority I act; I know by whom I am sent, and what commands were given me; but you cannot determine this, for you do not know these unless *I* bear witness of them to you. We are to remember that Jesus came not of himself (ch. vi. 38); that he came not to do his own will, but the will of his Father. He came as a *witness* of those things which he had seen and known (ch. iii. 11), and no man could judge *of those things*, for no man had seen them. As he came from heaven; as he knew his Father's will; as he had *seen* the eternal world, and known the counsels of his Father, so his testimony was worthy of confidence. As *they* had not seen and known these things, they were not qualified to judge. An ambassador from a foreign court knows the will and purposes of the sovereign who sent him, and is competent to bear witness of it. The court to which he is sent has no way of judging but by *his* testimony, and he is therefore competent to testify in the case. All that can be demanded is that he give his *credentials* that he is appointed, and this Jesus had done both by the nature of his doctrine and his miracles.

15. *After the flesh.* According to appearance; according to your carnal and corrupt mode; not according to the

16 And yet, if I judge, [k]my judgment is true; [l]for I am not alone, but I and the Father that sent me.

17 It is also [m]written in your law that the testimony of two men is true.

18 I am one that bear witness of myself, and [n]the Father that sent me beareth witness of me.

19 Then said they unto him, Where is thy Father? Jesus answered, [o]Ye neither know me, nor

k 1 Sa.16.7; Ps.45.6,7; 72.2. *l* ver.29; ch.16.32. *m* De.17.6; 19.15. *n* ch.5.37. *o* ver.55; ch.16.3; 17.25.

---

spiritual nature of the doctrines. By your preconceived opinions and prejudices you are determined not to believe that I am the Messiah. ¶ *I judge no man.* Jesus came not to *condemn* the world, ch. iii. 17. *They* were in the habit of judging rashly and harshly of all; but this was not the purpose or disposition of the Saviour. This expression is to be understood as meaning that he judged no one *after their manner;* he did not come to censure and condemn men *after the appearance*, or in a harsh, biassed, and unkind manner.

16. *And yet, if I judge.* If I should express my judgment of men or things. He was not *limited*, nor forbidden to do it, nor restrained by any fear that his judgment would be erroneous. ¶ *My judgment is true.* Is worthy to be regarded. ¶ *For I am not alone.* I concur with the Father who hath sent me. His judgment *you* admit would be right, and *my* judgment would accord with his. He was commissioned by his Father, and his judgment would coincide with all that God had purposed or revealed. This was shown by the evidence that God gave that he had sent him into the world.

17. *In your law.* De. xvii. 6; xix. 15. Comp. Mat. xviii. 16. This related to cases in which the life of an individual was involved. Jesus says that if, in such a case, the testimony of two men were sufficient to *establish* a fact, his own testimony and that of his Father ought to be esteemed ample evidence in the case of religious doctrine. ¶ *Two men.* If two *men* could confirm a case, the evidence of *Jesus* and of *God* ought not to be deemed insufficient. ¶ *Is true.* In Deuteronomy, "*established.*" This means the same thing. It is confirmed; is worthy of belief.

18. *I am one that bear witness of myself.* In human courts a man is not allowed to bear witness of himself, because he has a personal interest in the case, and the court could have no proof of the *impartiality* of the evidence; but in the case of Jesus it was otherwise. When one has no party ends to serve; when he is willing to deny himself; when he makes great sacrifices; and when, by his life, he gives every evidence of sincerity, his own testimony may be admitted in evidence of his motives and designs. This was the case with Jesus and his apostles. And though in a *legal* or *criminal* case such testimony would not be admitted, yet, in an argument on *moral* subjects, about the will and purpose of him who sent him, it would not be right to reject the testimony of one who gave so many proofs that he came from God. ¶ *The Father—beareth witness of me.* By the voice from heaven at his baptism (Mat. iii. 17), and by the miracles which Jesus wrought, as well as by the prophecies of the Old Testament. We may here remark, 1st. That there is a distinction between the Father and the Son. They are both represented as bearing testimony; yet, 2d. They are not divided. They are not different beings. They bear testimony to the same thing, and are *one* in counsel, in plan, in essence, and in glory.

19. *Where is thy Father?* This question was asked, doubtless, in derision. Jesus had often given them to understand that by his Father he meant God, ch. v. vi. They *professed* to be ignorant of this, and probably looked round in contempt for his Father, that he might adduce him as a witness in the case. ¶ *If ye had known me,* &c. If you had listened to my instructions, and had received me as the Messiah, you would also, at the same time, have been acquainted with God. We may here observe, 1st. The *manner* in which Jesus answered them. He gave no heed to their cavil; he was not *irritated* by their contempt; he preserved his *dignity*, and gave them an answer worthy of the Son of God. 2d. We should meet the *cavils* and sneers of sinners in the same manner. We should not render railing for railing, but "in meekness instruct those that oppose themselves, if God peradventure will give them repentance to the acknow-

my Father: [p]if ye had known me,
ye should have known my Father
also.

20 These words spake Jesus in
the [q]treasury, as he taught in the
temple; and no man laid hands on
him, [r]for his hour was not yet come.

21 Then said Jesus again unto
them, I go my way, and [s]ye shall
seek me, [t]and shall die in your
sins: whither I go [u]ye cannot come.

22 Then said the Jews, Will he
kill himself? because he saith,
Whither I go ye cannot come.

23 And he said unto them, Ye
are from beneath, I am from above;
ye are of this world, I am not of
this world.

24 I [v]said therefore unto you,
that ye shall die in your sins; [w]for
if ye believe not that I am *he*, ye
shall die in your sins.

25 Then said they unto him,
Who art thou? And Jesus saith

p ch.14.7,9. q Mar.12.41. r ch.7.30. s ch.7.34. t Job 20.11; Ps.73.18-20; Pr.14.32; Is.65.20; Ep.2.1. u Lu.16.26.

v ver.21. w Mar.16.16.

ledging of the truth," 2 Ti. ii. 25. 3d. The way to know God is to know Jesus Christ. "No man hath seen God at any time. The only-begotten Son which is in the bosom of the Father, he hath *declared* him," Jn. i. 18. No sinner can have just views of God but in Jesus Christ, 2 Co. iv. 6.

20. *The treasury.* See Notes on Mat. xxi. 12. ¶ *His hour was not yet come.* The time for him to die had not yet arrived, and God restrained them, and kept his life. This proves that God has power over wicked men to control them, and to make them accomplish his own purposes.

21. *I go my way.* See Notes on ch. vii. 33. ¶ *Ye shall die in your sins.* That is, you will seek the Messiah; you will desire his coming, but the Messiah that *you* expect will not come; and, as you have rejected me, and there is no other Saviour, you must die in your sins. You will die unpardoned, and as you did not seek me where you might find me, you cannot come where I shall be. Observe, 1st. All those who reject the Lord Jesus must die unforgiven. There is no way of pardon but by him. See Notes on Ac. iv. 12. 2d. There will be a time when sinners will seek for a Saviour but will find none. Often this is done too late, in a dying moment, and in the future world they may seek a deliverer, but not be able to find one. 3d. Those who reject the Lord Jesus *must* perish. Where he is they cannot come. Where he is is heaven. Where he is not, with his favour and mercy, there is hell; and the sinner that has *no Saviour* must be wretched for ever.

22. *Will he kill himself?* It is difficult to know whether this question was asked from ignorance or malice. Self-murder was esteemed then, as it is now, as one of the greatest crimes; and it is not improbable that they asked this question with mingled hatred and contempt. "He is a *deceiver;* he has broken the law of Moses; he is mad, and it is probable he *will* go on and kill himself." If this was their meaning, we see the wonderful patience of Jesus in enduring the contradiction of sinners; and as *he* bore contempt without rendering railing for railing, so should we.

23. *Ye are from beneath.* The expression *from beneath*, here, is opposed to the phrase *from above.* It means, You are *of the earth*, or are influenced by earthly, sensual, and corrupt passions. You are governed by the lowest and vilest views and feelings, such as are opposed to heaven, and such as have their origin in earth or in hell. ¶ *I am from above.* From heaven. My views are heavenly, and my words should have been so interpreted. ¶ *Ye are of this world.* You think and act like the corrupt men of this world. ¶ *I am not of this world.* My views are above these earthly and corrupt notions. The meaning of the verse is: "Your reference to *self-murder* shows that you are earthly and corrupt in your views. You are governed by the mad passions of men, and can think only of these." We see here how difficult it is to excite wicked men to the contemplation of heavenly things. They interpret all things in a low and corrupt sense, and suppose all others to be governed as they are themselves.

24. *That I am* he. That I am the Messiah.

25. *Who art thou?* As Jesus did not *expressly* say in the previous verse that he was the Messiah, they professed still

unto them, Even *the same* that I said unto you from the beginning.

26 I have many things to say and to judge of you; but [x]he that sent me is true, and I speak to the world those things which I have heard of him.

27 They understood not that he spake to them of the Father.

28 Then said Jesus unto them, When ye have [y]lifted up the Son of man, then shall ye know that I am *he*, and *that* I do nothing of myself; but as my Father hath taught me, I speak these things.

29 And he that sent me is with me: the Father hath not left me

x ch.7.28.

y ch.3.14; 12.32.

---

not to understand him. In great contempt, therefore, they asked him who *he* was. As if they had said, "Who art thou that undertakest to threaten us in this manner?" When we remember that they regarded him as a mere pretender from Galilee; that he was poor and without friends; and that he was persecuted by those in authority, we cannot but admire the patience with which all this was borne, and the coolness with which he answered them. ¶ *Even* the same, &c. What he had professed to them was that he was the light of the world; that he was the bread that came down from heaven; that he was sent by his Father, &c. From all this they might easily gather that he claimed to be the Messiah. He assumed no *new* character; he made no *change* in his professions; he is the same yesterday, to-day, and for ever; and as he had once professed to be the light of the world, so, in the face of contempt, persecution, and death, he adhered to the profession. ¶ *The beginning.* From his first discourse with them, or *uniformly.*

26. *I have many things to say.* There are many things which I *might* say to reprove and expose your pride and hypocrisy. By this he implied that he understood *well* their character, and that he was able to expose it. This, indeed, he had shown them in his conversations with them. ¶ *And to judge of you.* To reprove in you. There are many things in you which I might condemn. ¶ *But he that sent me is true.* Is worthy to be believed, and his declarations about men are to be credited. The meaning of this verse may be thus expressed: "I have indeed many things to say blaming or condemning you. I have already said many such things, and there are many more that I might say; but I speak only those things which God has commanded. I speak not of myself I come to execute his commission, and he is worthy to be heard and feared. Let it not be thought, therefore, that my judgment is rash or harsh. It is such as is commanded by God."

27. *They understood not.* They knew not, or they were unwilling to receive him as a messenger from God. They doubtless understood that he *meant* to speak of God, but they were unwilling to acknowledge that he *really* came from God.

28. *When ye have lifted up.* When you have crucified. See Notes on ch. iii. 14; also ch. xii. 32. ¶ *The Son of man.* See Notes on Mat. viii. 19, 20. ¶ *Then shall ye know.* Then shall you have *evidence* or *proof.* ¶ *That I am* he. Am the Messiah, which I have professed to be. ¶ *And* that *I do nothing of myself.* That is, you shall have proof that God has sent me; that I am the Messiah; and that God concurs with me and approves my doctrine. This proof was furnished by the miracles that attended the death of Jesus —the earthquake and darkness; but chiefly by his resurrection from the dead, which proved, beyond a doubt, that he was what he affirmed he was— the Messiah.

29. *Is with me.* In working miracles, &c. ¶ *Hath not left me alone.* Though *men* had forsaken and rejected him, yet God attended him. ¶ *Those things that please him.* See Mat. iii. 17: "This is my beloved Son, in whom I am well pleased," Phi. ii. 8; Is. liii. 10, 11, 12; 2 Pe. i. 17; Lu. iii. 22; Mat. xvii. 5. His *undertaking* the work of redemption was pleasing to God, and he had the consciousness that in *executing* it he did those things which God approved. It is a small matter to have *men* opposed to us, if we have a conscience void of offence, and evidence that we please God. Comp. He. xi. 5: "Enoch —before his translation had this testimony that he *pleased* God." See also 1 Co. iv. 3.

alone, for I do always those things
that please him.
30 As he spake these words
many[z] believed on him.
31 Then said Jesus to those Jews
which believed on him, If ye [a]con-
tinue in my word, *then* are ye my
disciples indeed;
32 And ye shall [b]know the truth,
and [c]the truth shall make you free.
33 They answered him, We be
Abraham's seed, and were [d]never in

z ch.10.42. a Ro.2.7; Col.1.23; He.10.38,39.

b Ho.6.3.
c Ps.119.45; ch.17.17; Ro.6.14,18,22; Ja.1.25; 2.12.
d Le.25.42.

30. *Many believed on him.* Such was the convincing nature and force of the truths which he presented, that they believed he was the Messiah and received his doctrine. While there were many that became more obstinate and hardened under his preaching, there were many, also, who by the same truth were made penitent and believing. "The same sun that hardens the clay, softens the wax" (Clarke).

31. *If ye continue in my word.* If you continue to obey my commandments and to receive my doctrines. ¶ Then *are ye*, &c. This is the true test of Christian character. Jn. xiv. 21: "He that hath my commandments and keepeth them, he it is that loveth me." See 1 Jn. ii. 4; iii. 24; 2 Jn. 6. In this place Jesus cautions them against *too much confidence* from their present feelings. They were just converted—converted under a single sermon. They had had no time to test their faith. Jesus assures them that if their faith should abide the test, if it should produce obedience to his commandments and a holy life, it would be proof that their faith was genuine, for the tree is known by its fruit. So we may say to all new converts, Do not repress your love or your joy, but do not be too confident. Your faith has not yet been tried, and if it does not produce a holy life it is vain, Ja. ii. 17–26.

32. *Shall know the truth.* See Notes on ch. vii. 17. ¶ *The truth shall make you free.* The *truth* here means the Christian religion. Comp. Ga. iii. 1; Col. i. 6. The doctrines of the true religion shall make you free—that is, it will free you from the *slavery* of evil passions, corrupt propensities, and grovelling views. The condition of a sinner is that of a *captive* or a *slave* to sin. He is one who serves and obeys the dictates of an evil heart and the promptings of an evil nature, Ro. vi. 16, 17: "Ye were the *servants* of sin;" —19: "Ye have yielded your members *servants* unto iniquity;"—20; vii. 6, 8, 11; viii. 21; Ac. viii. 23: "Thou art in the —*bond* of iniquity;" Ga. iv. 3, 9. The effect of the gospel is to break this hard bondage to sin and to set the sinner free. We learn from this that religion is not slavery or oppression. It is true freedom.

"He is the freeman whom the truth makes free,
And all are slaves beside."—*Cowper.*

The service of God is freedom from degrading vices and carnal propensities; from the slavery of passion and inordinate desires. It is a cheerful and delightful surrender of ourselves to Him whose yoke is easy and whose burden is light.

33. *They answered him.* Not those who believed on him, but some who stood by and heard him. ¶ *We be Abraham's seed.* We are the children or descendants of Abraham. Abraham was not a slave, and they pretended that they were his real descendants, inheriting his freedom as well as his spirit. They meant that they were the direct descendants of Abraham by Isaac, his heir. Ishmael, also Abraham's son, was the son of a bondwoman (Ga. iv. 21–23), but *they* were descended in a direct line from the acknowledged heir of Abraham. ¶ *Were never in bondage to any man.* This is a most remarkable declaration, and one evidently false. Their fathers had been slaves in Egypt; their nation had been enslaved in Babylon; it had repeatedly been subject to the Assyrians; it was enslaved by Herod the Great; and was, at the very time they spoke, groaning under the grievous and insupportable bondage of the Romans. But we see here, 1st. That Jesus was right when he said (ver. 44), "Ye are of your father the devil; he is a liar, and the father of it." 2d. Men will say anything, however false or ridiculous, to avoid and oppose the truth. 3d. Men groaning under the most oppressive bondage are often unwilling to acknowledge it in any manner, and are indignant at being charged with it. This is the case with all sinners. 4th. Sin, and the bondage

bondage to any man; how sayest
thou, Ye shall be made free?
34 Jesus answered them, Verily,
verily, I say unto you, [e]Whosoever
committeth sin is the servant of
sin.
35 And the [f]servant abideth not
in the house for ever, *but* the Son
abideth ever.
36 If[g] the Son, therefore, shall
make you free, [h]ye shall be free
indeed.
37 I know that ye are Abraham's
seed; but ye seek to kill me, because my word hath no place in
you.
38 I[i] speak that which I have
seen with my Father, and ye do
that which ye have seen with your
father.

e Ro.6.16,20; 2 Pe.2.19. f Ga.4.30. g Is.61.1. h Ro.8.2; Ga.5.1. i ch.14.10,24.

---

to sin, produces passion, irritation, and a troubled soul; and a man under the influence of passion regards little what he says, and is often a liar. 5th. There is need of the gospel. That only can make men free, calm, collected, meek, and lovers of truth; and as every man is by nature the servant of sin, he should without delay seek an interest in that gospel which can alone make him free.

34. *Whosoever committeth sin*, &c. In this passage Jesus shows them that he did not refer to *political* bondage, but to the slavery of the soul to evil passions and desires. ¶ *Is the servant.* Is the *slave* of sin. He is bound to it as a slave is to his master.

35. *The servant abideth not*, &c. The servant does not, of course, remain for ever, or till his death, with his master. If he is disobedient and wicked, the master sells him or turns him away. He is not the heir, and may at any time be expelled from the house of his master. But a son is the heir. He cannot be in this manner cast off or sold. He is privileged with the right of remaining in the family. This takes place in common life. So said the Saviour to the Jews: "You, if you are disobedient and rebellious, may at any time be rejected from being the people of God, and be deprived of your peculiar privileges as a nation. You are in the condition of servants, and unless you are made *free* by the gospel, and become entitled to the privilege of the sons of God, you will be cast off like an unfaithful slave." Comp. He. iii. 5, 6. ¶ *Abideth not.* Remains not, or has not the legal right to remain. He may at any time be rejected or sold. ¶ *In the house.* In the family of his master. ¶ *For ever.* During the whole time of his life. ¶ *The Son.* The heir. He remains, and cannot be sold or cast off. ¶ *Ever.* Continually. Till the day of his death. This is the privilege of a son, to inherit and dispose of the property.

36. *If the Son*, &c. The Son of God—heir of all things—who is for ever with God, and who has therefore the right and power to liberate men from their thraldom. ¶ *Shall make you free.* Shall deliver you from the bondage and dominion of sin. ¶ *Free indeed.* Truly and really free. You shall be blessed with the most valuable freedom; not from the chains and oppressions of earthly masters and monarchs, but from the bondage of sin.

37. *I know*, &c. I admit that you are the descendants of Abraham. Jesus did not wish to call that in question, but he endeavoured to show them that they might be his descendants and still lack entirely his spirit. See Notes on Mat. iii. 9. ¶ *Ye seek to kill me.* Ch. v. 16; vii. 32. ¶ *Because my word.* My *doctrine;* the principles of my religion. You have not the spirit of my doctrine; you hate it, and you therefore seek to kill me. ¶ *Hath no place.* That is, you do not embrace my doctrine, or it exerts no influence over you. The original word conveys the notion that there was no *room* for his doctrine in their minds. It met with *obstructions*, and did not penetrate into their hearts. They were so filled with pride, and prejudice, and false notions, that they would not receive his truth; and as they had not his truth or spirit, and could not bear it, they sought to kill him.

38. *I speak*, &c. Jn. iii. 11–13. ¶ *My Father.* God. ¶ *Your father.* The devil. See ver. 44. To *see* here means *to learn of.* They had learned of or been taught by the devil, and *imitated* him.

39. *Abraham is our father.* We are descended from Abraham. Of this the Jews boasted much, as being descended from such an illustrious man. See

39 They answered and said unto him, [k]Abraham is our father. Jesus saith unto them, [l]If ye were Abraham's children, ye would do the works of Abraham.

40 But now ye seek to kill me, a man that hath told you the truth, which I have heard of God: [m]this did not Abraham.

41 Ye do the deeds of your father. Then said they to him, We be not born of fornication; [n]we have one Father, *even* God.

42 Jesus said unto them, [o]If God were your Father, ye would love me; for I proceeded forth and came from God; neither came I of myself, but [p]he sent me.

k Mat.3.9. *l* Ro.2.28,29; 9.7; Ga.3.7,29. *m* Ro.4.12.
n Is.63.16; 64.8. *o* Mal.1.6; 1 Jn.5.1. *p* ch.17.8,25.

Notes on Mat. iii. 9. As Jesus did not expressly say who he meant (ver. 38) when he said they did the works of their father, they obstinately persisted in pretending not to understand him, as if they had said, "We acknowledge no other father but Abraham, and to charge us with being the offspring of another is slander and calumny." ¶ *If ye were Abraham's children.* The words *sons* and *children* are often used to denote those who *imitate* another or who have his spirit. See Notes on Mat. i. 1. Here it means, "if you were worthy to be called the children of Abraham, or if you had his spirit."

40. *Ye seek to kill me.* See ver. 37. ¶ *This did not Abraham.* Or *such* things Abraham did not do. There are two things noted here in which they differed from Abraham: 1st. In seeking to kill him, or in possessing a murderous and bloody purpose. 2d. In rejecting the truth as God revealed it. Abraham was distinguished for love to man as well as God. He liberated the captives (Ge. xiv. 14–16); was distinguished for hospitality to strangers (Ge. xviii. 1–8); and received the revelations of God to him, however mysterious, or however trying their observance, Ge. xii. 1–4; xv. 4–6; xxii. It was for these things that he is so much commended in the New Testament (Ro. iv. 9; ix. 9; Ga. iii. 6); and, as the Jews sought to *kill* Jesus instead of treating him hospitably and kindly, they showed that they had none of the spirit of Abraham.

41. *The deeds of your father.* See ver. 38. Jesus repeats the charge, and yet repeats it as if unwilling to *name* Satan as their father. He chose that they should *infer* whom he meant, rather than bring a charge so direct and repelling. When the Saviour delivered an awful or an offensive truth, he always approached the mind so that the truth might make the deepest impression. ¶ *We be not born of fornication.* The people still professed not to understand him; and since Jesus had denied that they were the children of *Abraham*, they affected to suppose that he meant they were a mixed, spurious race; that they had no right to the covenant privileges of the Jews; that they were not worshippers of the true God. Hence they said, We are not thus descended. We have the evidence of our genealogy. We are worshippers of the true God, descended from those who acknowledged him, and we acknowledge no other God and Father than him. To be *children of fornication* is an expression denoting in the Scriptures *idolatry*, or the worship of other gods than the true God, Is. i. 21; lvii. 3; Ho. i. 2; ii. 4. This they denied. They affirmed that they acknowledged no God for their Father but the true God.

42. *If God were your Father.* If you had the spirit of God, or love to him, or were worthy to be called his children. ¶ *Ye would love me.* Jesus was "the brightness of the Father's glory and the express image of his person," He. i. 3. "Every one that loveth him that begat, loveth him also that is begotten of him," 1 Jn. v. 1. From this we see, 1st. That all who truly love God, love his Son Jesus Christ. 2d. That men that *pretend* that they love God, and reject his Son, have no evidence that they are the friends of God. 3d. That those who reject the Bible cannot be the friends of God. If they loved God, they would love Him who came from him, and who bears his image.

43. *Why do ye not*, &c. My meaning is clear, if you were disposed to understand me. ¶ Even *because ye cannot hear my word.* The word "hear" in this place is to be understood in the sense of *bear* or *tolerate*, as in ch. vi. 60. His doctrine was offensive to them. They hated it, and hence they perverted his meaning, and were resolved *not* to understand him. Their pride, vanity,

43 Why do ye not understand
my speech? *even* [q]because ye cannot hear my word.
44 Ye[r] are of *your* father the
devil, and the lusts of your father
ye will do. He was a murderer
from the beginning, and [s]abode
not in the truth, because there is
no truth in him. When he speaketh a lie, he speaketh of his own;
for he is a liar, and the father of it.
45 And [t]because I tell *you* the
truth, ye believe me not.
46 Which of you [u]convinceth me

q Is.6.9. r Mat.13.38; 1 Jn.3.8. s Jude 6. t Ga.4.16; 2 Th.2.10. u He.4.15.

and wickedness opposed it. The reason why sinners do not understand the Bible and its doctrines is because they cannot *bear* them. They hate them, and their hatred produces want of candour, a disposition to cavil and to pervert the truth, and an obstinate purpose that it *shall not* be applied to their case. Hence they embrace every form of false doctrine, and choose error rather than truth, and darkness rather than light. A *disposition to believe God* is one of the best helps for understanding the Bible.

44. *Ye are of* your *father the devil.* That is, you have the temper, disposition, or spirit of the devil. You are influenced by him, you imitate him, and ought therefore to be called his children. See also 1 Jn. iii. 8, 9, 10; Ac. xiii. 10: "Thou child of the devil." ¶ *The devil.* See Nôtes on Mat. iv. 1. ¶ *The lusts.* The *desires* or *the wishes.* You do what pleases him. ¶ *Ye will do.* The word *will*, here, is not an auxiliary verb. It does not simply express *futurity*, or that such a thing *will* take place, but it implies an act of *volition.* This you *will* or *choose* to do. The same mode of speech occurs in Jn. v. 40. In what *respects* they showed that they were the children of the devil he proceeds to state: 1st, in their murderous disposition; 2d, in rejecting the truth; 3d, in being favourable to falsehood and error. ¶ *He was a murderer from the beginning.* That is, from the beginning of the world, or in the first records of him he is thus represented. This refers to the seduction of Adam and Eve. Death was denounced against sin, Ge. ii. 17. The devil deceived our first parents, and they became subject to death, Ge. iii. As he was the *cause* why death came into the world, he may be said to have been a *murderer* in that act, or from the beginning. We see here that the tempter mentioned in Ge. iii. was Satan or the devil, who is here declared to have been the murderer. Comp. Ro. v. 12, and Re. xii. 9: "And the great dragon was cast out, that old serpent called the devil, and Satan, which deceiveth the whole world." Besides, Satan has in all ages *deceived* men, and been the cause of their spiritual and eternal death. His work has been to destroy, and in the worst sense of the word he may be said to have been *a murderer.* It was by his instigation, also, that Cain killed his brother, 1 Jn. iii. 12: "Not as Cain, who was of that wicked one, and slew his brother." As the Jews endeavoured to *kill* the Saviour, so they showed that they had the spirit of the devil. ¶ *Abode not in the truth.* He departed from the truth, or was false and a liar. ¶ *No truth in him.* That is, he is a liar. It is his nature and his work to deceive. ¶ *He speaketh of his own.* The word "own" is in the *plural* number, and means *of the things that are appropriate to him*, or that belong to his nature. His speaking falsehood is originated by his own propensities or disposition; he utters the expressions of his genuine character. ¶ *He is a liar.* As when he *deceived* Adam, and in his deceiving, as far as possible, the world, and dragging man down to perdition. ¶ *The father of it.* The father or *originator of falsehood.* The word "it" refers to *lie* or *falsehood* understood. From him falsehood first proceeded, and all liars possess his spirit and are under his influence. As the Jews refused to hear the truth which Jesus spoke, so they showed that they were the children of the father of lies.

46. *Which of you convinceth me?* To *convince*, with us, means to satisfy a *man's own mind* of the truth of anything; but this is not its meaning here. It rather means to *convict.* Which of you can *prove* that I am guilty of sin? ¶ *Of sin.* The word *sin* here evidently means *error, falsehood*, or *imposture.* It stands opposed to *truth.* The argument of the Saviour is this: A doctrine might be rejected if it could be proved that he that delivered it was an *impostor;*

of sin? And if I say the truth, why do ye not believe me?

47 He that is of God heareth God's words; ye, therefore, hear *them* not, because ye are not of God.

48 Then answered the Jews and said unto him, Say we not well, that thou art a Samaritan, [v]and hast a devil?

49 Jesus answered, I have not a devil; but I honour my Father, and ye do dishonour me.

50 And [w]I seek not mine own glory: there is one that seeketh and judgeth.

v ch.7.20. w ch.5.41.

---

but as you cannot prove this of me, you are bound to receive my words.

47. *He that is of God.* He that loves, fears, and honours God. ¶ *Heareth God's words.* Listens to, or attends to the doctrines or commandments of God, as a child who loves his parent will regard and obey his commandments. This is an evidence of true piety. A willingness to receive all that God teaches us, and to obey all his commandments, is an undoubted proof that we are his friends, Jn. xiv. 21; 1 Jn. ii. 4; iii. 24. As the Jews did *not* show a readiness to obey the commands of God, it proved that they were not of him, and to this was owing their rejection of the Lord Jesus.

48. *Say we not well.* Say we not *truly.* ¶ *Thou art a Samaritan.* This was a term of contempt and reproach. See Notes on ch. iv. 9. It had the force of charging him with being a *heretic* or a *schismatic*, because the Samaritans were regarded as such. ¶ *And hast a devil.* See ch. vii. 20. This charge they brought against him because he had said that they were not of God, or were not the friends of God. This they regarded as the same as taking sides with the Samaritans, for the question between the Jews and Samaritans was, which of them worshipped God aright, ch. iv. 20. As Jesus affirmed that the *Jews* were not of God, and as he, contrary to all *their* views, had gone and preached to the Samaritans (ch. iv.), they regarded it as a proof that he was disposed to take part with them. They also regarded it as evidence that he had a devil. The *devil* was an *accuser* or *calumniator;* and as Jesus charged them with being opposed to God, they considered it as proof that he was influenced by such an evil spirit. ¶ *Devil.* In the original, *demon.* Not the prince or chief of the devils, but an evil spirit.

49. *I have not a devil.* To the first part of the charge, that he was a Samaritan, he did not reply. To the other part he replied by saying that he *honoured his Father.* He taught the doctrines that tended to exalt God. He taught that he was holy and true. He sought that men should love him and obey him. All his teaching proved this. An evil spirit would not do this, and this was sufficient proof that he was not influenced by such a spirit.

50. *Mine own glory.* My own praise or honour. In all his teaching this was true. He did not seek to exalt or to vindicate himself. He was willing to lie under reproach and to be despised. He regarded little, therefore, their taunts and accusations; and *even now*, he says, he would not seek to *vindicate himself.* ¶ *There is one that seeketh and judgeth.* God will take care of my reputation. He seeks my welfare and honour, and I may commit my cause into his hands without attempting my own vindication. From these verses (46–50) we may learn—1st. That where men have no sound arguments, they attempt to overwhelm their adversaries by calling odious and reproachful names. Accusations of heresy and schism, and the use of reproachful terms, are commonly proof that men are not only under the influence of unchristian feeling, but that they have no sound reasons to support their cause. 2d. It is right to vindicate ourselves from such charges, but it should not be done by rendering railing for railing. "In meekness we should instruct those that oppose themselves, if God peradventure will give them repentance to the acknowledging of the truth," 2 Ti. ii. 25. 3d. We should not regard it as necessarily dishonourable if we lie under reproach. If we have a good conscience, if we have examined for ourselves, if we are conscious that we are seeking the glory of God, we should be willing, as Jesus was, to bear reproach, believing that God will in due time avenge us, and bring forth our righteousness as the light, and our judgment as the noonday, Ps. xxxvii. 6.

51 Verily, verily, I say unto you,
If a man keep my saying, he shall
never see death.
52 Then said the Jews unto him,
Now we know that thou hast a
devil. Abraham [x]is dead, and the
prophets; and thou sayest, If a
man keep my saying, he shall
never taste of death.
53 Art thou greater than our
father Abraham, which is dead?
And the prophets are dead: whom
makest thou thyself?

x Zec.1.5.

54 Jesus answered, [y]If I honour
myself, my honour is nothing: [z]it
is my Father that honoureth me,
of whom ye say that he is your
God;
55 Yet ye have not known him;
but I know him; and if I should
say I know him not, I shall be a
liar like unto you; but I know
him, and keep his saying.
56 Your father Abraham rejoiced
to see my day, and [a]he saw *it* and
was glad.

y ch.5.31,41. z ch.17.1. a Ge.22.13,14; He.11.13.

---

51. *If a man keep my saying.* If he believes on me and obeys my commandments. ¶ *He shall never see death.* To *see death*, or to *taste of death*, is the same as *to die*, Lu. ii. 26; Mat. xvi. 28; Mar. ix. 1. The sense of this passage is, "He shall obtain eternal life, or he shall be raised up to that life where there shall be no death." See ch. vi. 49, 50; iii. 36; v. 24; xi. 25, 26.

52. *Hast a devil.* Art deranged. Because he affirmed a thing which they supposed to be contrary to all experience, and to be impossible.

53. *Whom makest thou thyself?* Or, who dost thou pretend to be? Although the greatest of the prophets have died, yet *thou*—a Nazarene, a Samaritan, and a devil — pretendest that thou canst keep thy followers from dying! It would have been scarcely possible to ask a question implying more contempt and scorn.

54. *If I honour myself.* If I commend or praise myself. If I had no other honour and sought no other honour than that which proceeds from a desire to glorify myself. ¶ *My honour is nothing.* My commendation or praise of myself would be of no value. See Notes on ch. v. 31.

56. *Your father Abraham.* The testimony of Abraham is adduced by Jesus because the Jews considered it to be a signal honour to be his descendants, ver. 39. As they regarded the sayings and deeds of Abraham as peculiarly illustrious and worthy of their imitation, so they were bound, in consistency, to listen to what he had said of the Messiah. ¶ *Rejoiced.* This word includes the notion of *desire* as well as *rejoicing.* It denotes that act when, impelled with strong desire for an object, we *leap forward* toward its attainment with joy; and it expresses—1st. The fact that this was an object that filled the heart of Abraham with joy; and 2d. That he *earnestly desired* to see it. We have no single word which expresses the meaning of the original. In Mat. v. 12 it is rendered "be exceeding glad." ¶ *To see.* Rather, he earnestly and joyfully desired *that he might see.* To see here means to have *a view* or *distinct conception of.* It does not imply that Abraham *expected* that the Messiah would appear during his life, but that he might have a representation of, or a clear description and foresight of the times of the Messiah. ¶ *My day.* The day of the Messiah. The word "day," here, is used to denote the *time*, the appearance, the advent, and the manner of life of the Messiah. Lu. xvii. 26: "As it was in the *days* of Noah, so shall it be also *in the days* of the Son of man." See Jn. ix. 4; Mat. xi. 12. The day of judgment is also called *the day* of the Son of man, because it will be a remarkable *time* of his manifestation. Or perhaps in both those cases it is called HIS *day* because *he* will act the most conspicuous part; his person and work will *characterize the times;* as we speak of the *days* of Noah, &c., because he was the most conspicuous person of the age. ¶ *He saw* it. See He. xi. 13: "These all died in faith, not having received (obtained the fulfilment of) the promises, *but having seen them afar off*, and were persuaded of them," &c. Though Abraham was not permitted to live to see the times of the Messiah, yet he was permitted to have a prophetic view of him, and also of the design of his coming; for, 1st. God foretold his

57 Then said the Jews unto him, Thou art not yet fifty years old, and hast thou seen Abraham?

58 Jesus said unto them, Verily, verily, I say unto you, Before Abraham was, [b]I am.

b Ex.3.14; Is.43.13; ch.1.1,2; Col.1.17; Re.1.8.

advent clearly to him, Ge. xii. 3; xviii. 18. Comp. Ga. iii. 16: "Now to Abraham and his seed were the promises made. He saith not, And to seeds, as of many; but as of one, and to thy seed, which is Christ." 2d. Abraham was permitted to have a view of the death of the Messiah as a sacrifice for sin, represented by the command to offer Isaac, Ge. xxii. 1–13. Comp. He. xi. 19. The death of the Messiah as a sacrifice for the sins of men was that which characterized his work—which distinguished his times and his advent, and this was represented to Abraham clearly by the command to offer his son. From this arose the proverb among the Jews (Ge. xxii. 14), "In the mount of the Lord it shall be seen," or it shall be provided for; a proverb evidently referring to the offering of the Messiah on the mount for the sins of men. By this event Abraham was impressively told that a parent would not be required to offer in sacrifice his sons for the sins of his soul—a thing which has often been done by heathen; but that God would provide a victim, and in due time an offering would be made for the world. ¶ *Was glad.* Was glad in view of the promise, and that he was permitted so distinctly to see it represented. If the father of the faithful rejoiced so much to see him afar off, how should we rejoice that he has come; that we are not required to look into a distant futurity, but know that he has appeared; that we may learn clearly the manner of his coming, his doctrine, and the design of his death! Well might the eyes of a patriarch rejoice to be permitted to look in any manner on the sublime and glorious scene of the Son of God dying for the sins of men. And *our* chief honour and happiness is to contemplate the amazing scene of man's redemption, where the Saviour groaned and died to save a lost and ruined race.

57. *Fifty years old.* Jesus is supposed to have been at this time about thirty-three. It is remarkable that when he was so young they should have mentioned the number fifty, but they probably designed to prevent the possibility of a reply. Had they said *forty* they might have apprehended a reply, or could not be so certain that they were correct. ¶ *Hast thou seen Abraham?* It is remarkable, also, that they perverted his words. His affirmation was not that *he* had seen Abraham, but that *Abraham* had seen his day. The design of Jesus was to show that he was greater than Abraham, ver. 53. To do this, he says that Abraham, great as he was, earnestly desired to see his time, thus acknowledging his *inferiority* to the Messiah. The Jews perverted this, and affirmed that it was impossible that he and Abraham should have seen each other.

58. *Verily, verily.* This is an expression used only in John. It is a strong affirmation denoting particularly the great importance of what was about to be affirmed. See Notes on ch. iii. 5. ¶ *Before Abraham was.* Before Abraham *lived.* ¶ *I am.* The expression I *am*, though in the *present* tense, is clearly designed to refer to a *past* time. Thus, in Ps. xc. 2, "From everlasting to everlasting thou *art* God." Applied to God, it denotes *continued* existence without respect to time, so far as *he* is concerned. *We* divide time into the past, the present, and the future. The expression, applied to God, denotes that *he* does not measure his existence in this manner, but that the word by which we express the *present* denotes his *continued* and *unchanging* existence. Hence he assumes it as his name, "I AM," and "I AM THAT I AM," Ex. iii. 14. Comp. Is. xliv. 6; xlvii. 8. There is a remarkable similarity between the expression employed by Jesus in this place and that used in Exodus to denote the name of God. The *manner* in which Jesus used it would strikingly *suggest* the application of the same language to God. The question here was about his pre-existence. The objection of the Jews was that he was not fifty years old, and could not, therefore, have seen Abraham. Jesus replied to that that he *existed before Abraham.* As in his human nature he was *not* yet fifty years old, and could not, as a man, have existed before Abraham, this declaration must be referred to another nature; and the passage proves that, while he was *a man,* he was also endowed with *another nature*

59 Then took they up stones to cast at him; but Jesus hid himself and went out of the temple, going through the midst of them, and so passed by.

CHAPTER IX.

AND as *Jesus* passed by, he saw a man which was blind from *his* birth.

2 And his disciples asked him, saying, Master, who did sin, this man, or his parents, that he was born blind?

3 Jesus answered, Neither hath this man sinned, nor his parents, but [a]that the works of God should be made manifest in him.

4 I must work the works of him that sent me while it is day: the

a ch.11.4.

existing before Abraham, and to which he applied the term (familiar to the Jews as expressive of the existence of God) I AM; and this declaration corresponds to the affirmation of John (ch. i. 1), that he was in the beginning with God, and was God. This affirmation of Jesus is one of the proofs on which John relies to prove that he was the Messiah (ch. xx. 31), to establish which was the design of writing this book.

59. *Then took they up stones.* It seems *they* understood him as blaspheming, and proceeded, even without a form of trial, to stone him as such, because this was the punishment prescribed in the law for blasphemy, Le. xxiv. 16. See ch. x. 31. The fact that the *Jews* understood him in this sense is strong proof that his words *naturally* conveyed the idea that he was divine. This was in the temple. Herod the Great had not yet completed its repairs, and Dr. Lightfoot has remarked that stones would be lying around the temple in repairing it, which the people could easily use in their indignation. ¶ *Jesus hid himself.* See Lu. iv. 30. That is, he either by a miracle rendered himself invisible, or he so mixed with the multitude that he was concealed from them and escaped. Which is the meaning cannot be determined.

CHAPTER IX.

1. *As* Jesus *passed by.* As he was leaving the temple, ch. viii. 59. This man was in the way in which Jesus was going to escape from the Jews.

2. *Master, who did sin?* &c. It was a universal opinion among the Jews that *calamities* of all kinds were the effects of sin. See Notes on Lu. xiii. 1-4. The case, however, of this man was that of one that was blind from his *birth*, and it was a question which the disciples could not determine whether it was *his* fault or that of his parents. Many of the Jews, as it appears from their writings (see Lightfoot), believed in the doctrine of the *transmigration* of souls; or that the soul of a man, in consequence of sin, might be compelled to pass into other bodies, and be punished there. They also believed that an infant might sin before it was born (see Lightfoot), and that consequently this blindness might have come upon the child as a consequence of that. It was also a doctrine with many that the crime of the parent might be the cause of deformity in the child, particularly the violation of the command in Le. xx. 18.

3. *Neither hath this man sinned,* &c. That is, his blindness is not the effect of his sin, or that of his parents. Jesus did not, evidently, mean to affirm that he or his parents were without any sin, but that this blindness was not the effect of sin. This answer is to be interpreted by the nature of the question submitted to him. The sense is, "his blindness is not to be traced to any fault of his or of his parents." ¶ *But that the works of God.* This thing has happened that it might appear how great and wonderful are the works of God. By the *works of God*, here, is evidently intended the miraculous power which God would put forth to heal the man, or rather, perhaps, the *whole* that happened to him in the course of divine providence—first his blindness, as an act of his providence, and then his *healing* him, as an act of mercy and power. It has *all* happened, not by the fault of his parents or of himself, but by the wise arrangement of God, that it *might be seen* in what way calamities come, and in what way God meets and relieves them. And from this we may learn, 1st. To pity and not to despise and blame those who are afflicted with any natural deformity or calamity. While the Jews regarded it as the effect of *sin*, they looked upon it without compassion. Jesus tells us that it

night cometh, when no man can work.

5 As long as I am in the world, I[b] am the light of the world.

6 When he had thus spoken, [c]he spat on the ground, and made clay of the spittle, and he [1]anointed

b ch.1.5,9; 8.12; 12.35,46.

c Mar.8.23.

1 or, *spread the clay upon the eyes of the blind man.*

---

is not the fault of man, but proceeds from the wise arrangement of God. 2d. All suffering in the world is not the effect of sin. In this case it is expressly so declared; and there may be many modes of suffering that cannot be traced to any particular transgression. We should be cautious, therefore, in affirming that there can be no calamity in the universe but by transgression. 3d. We see the wise and wonderful arrangement of Divine Providence. It is a part of his great plan to adapt his mercies to the woes of men; and often calamity, want, poverty, and sickness are permitted, that he may show the provisions of his mercy, that he may teach us to prize his blessings, and that deep-felt gratitude for deliverance may bind us to him. 4th. Those who are afflicted with blindness, deafness, or any deformity, should be submissive to God. It is his appointment, and is right and best. God does no wrong, and the universe will, when *all* his works are seen, feel and know that he is just.

4. *The works of him*, &c. The works of beneficence and mercy which God has commissioned me to do, and which are expressive of his goodness and power. This was on the Sabbath-day (ver. 14); and though Jesus had endangered his life (ch. v. 1-16) by working a similar miracle on the Sabbath, yet he knew that this was the will of God that he should do good, and that he would take care of his life. ¶ *While it is day.* The *day* is the proper time for work—night is not. This is the general, the universal sentiment. While the day lasts it is proper to labour. The term *day* here refers to the *life* of Jesus, and to the opportunity thus afforded of working miracles. His life was drawing to a close. It was probably but about six months after this when he was put to death. The meaning is, My life is near its close. While it continues I must employ it in doing the works which God has appointed. ¶ *The night cometh. Night* here represents death. It was drawing near, and he must therefore do what he had to do soon. It is not improbable, also, that this took place near the close of the Sabbath, as the sun was declining, and the shades of evening about to appear. This supposition will give increased beauty to the language which follows. ¶ *No man can work.* It is literally true that *day* is the appropriate time for toil, and that the *night of death* is a time when nothing can be done. Ec. ix. 10: "There is no work, nor device, nor knowledge, nor wisdom in the grave." From this we may learn, 1st. That it is our duty to employ all our time in doing the will of God. 2d. That we should seek for opportunities of doing good, and suffer none to pass without improving it. *We go but once through the world, and we cannot return to correct errors, and recall neglected opportunities of doing our duty.* 3d. We should be especially diligent in doing our Lord's work from the fact that the night of death is coming. This applies to the aged, for they *must* soon die; and to the young, for they *may* soon be called away from this world to eternity.

5. *As long as I am in the world*, &c. As the sun is the natural light of the world, even while it sinks away to the west, so am I, although my days are drawing to a close, the light of the spiritual world. What a sublime description is this! Jesus occupied the same place, filled the same space, shed his beams as far, in the moral world, as the sun does on natural objects; and as all is dark when that sun sinks to the west, so when he withdraws from the souls of men all is midnight and gloom. When we look on the sun in the firmament or in the west, let us remember that such is the great Sun of Righteousness in regard to our souls; that his shining is as necessary, and his beams as mild and lovely on the soul, as is the shining of the natural sun to illumine the material creation. See Notes on ch. i. 4.

6. *And made clay*, &c. Two reasons may be assigned for making this clay, and anointing the eyes with it. One is, that the Jews regarded *spittle* as medicinal to the eyes when diseased, and that they forbade the use of medicines

the eyes of the blind man with
the clay,
7 And said unto him, Go, wash
in the [d]pool of Siloam, (which is,
by interpretation, Sent.) He[e] went
his way, therefore, and washed, and
came seeing.
8 The neighbours, therefore,
and they which before had seen
him that he was blind, said, Is
not this he that sat and begged?
9 Some said, This is he; others
said, He is like him; *but* he said,
I am *he*.
10 Therefore said they unto
him, How were thine eyes opened?
11 He answered and said,[f] A man
that is called Jesus made clay, and
anointed mine eyes, and said unto
me, Go to the pool of Siloam, and
wash; and I went and washed, and
I received sight.

d Ne.3.15. *e* 2 Ki.5.14. *f* ver.6,7.

---

on the Sabbath. They regarded the Sabbath so strictly that they considered the preparation and use of medicines as contrary to the law. Especially it was particularly forbidden among them to use spittle on that day to heal diseased eyes. See instances in Lightfoot. Jesus, therefore, by making this spittle, showed them that their manner of keeping the day was superstitious, and that he dared to do a thing which they esteemed unlawful. He showed that *their* interpretation of the law of the Sabbath was contrary to the intention of God, and that his disciples were not bound by *their* notions of the sacredness of that day. Another reason may have been that it was common for prophets to use some symbolical or expressive action in working miracles. Thus Elisha commanded his *staff* to be laid on the face of the child that he was about to restore to life, 2 Ki. iv. 29. Compare Notes on Is. viii. 18. In such instances the prophet showed that the miracle was wrought by power communicated through *him;* so, in this case, Jesus by this act showed to the blind man that the power of *healing* came from him who anointed his eyes. He could not *see* him, and the act of anointing convinced him of what might have been known without such an act, could he have *seen* him—that Jesus had power to give sight to the blind.

7. *Wash in the pool.* In the *fountain.* ¶ *Of Siloam.* See Notes on Lu. xiii. 4. ¶ *By interpretation, Sent.* From the Hebrew verb *to send*—perhaps because it was regarded as a blessing *sent* or *given* by God. *Why* Jesus sent him to wash there is not known. It is clear that the waters had no efficacy themselves to open the eyes of a blind man, but it is probable that he directed him to go there to *test his obedience,* and to see whether he was disposed to obey him in a case where he could not see the reason of it. An instance somewhat similar occurs in the case of Naaman, the Syrian leper, 2 Ki. v. 10. The proud Syrian despised the direction; the humble blind man obeyed and was healed. This case shows us that we should obey the commands of God, however unmeaning or mysterious they may appear. God has always a reason for all that he directs us to do, and our faith and willingness to obey him are often tried when we can see little of the reason of his requirements. In the first edition of these Notes it was remarked that the word *Siloam* is from the same verb as *Shiloh* in Ge. xlix. 10. "The sceptre shall not depart from Judah—until Shiloh (that is, the Sent of God; the Messiah) come," and that John in this remark probably had reference to this prophecy. This was incorrect; and there is no evidence that John in this passage had reference to that prophecy, or that this fountain was emblematic of the Messiah. The original words *Siloam* and *Shiloh* are from different roots and mean different things. The former, *Siloam* (שִׁלֹחַ), is derived from שָׁלַח (*to send*); the latter, *Shiloh* (שִׁילֹה), means *rest* or *quiet*, and was given to the Messiah, probably, because he would bring *rest*—that is, he would be the "prince of peace." Comp. Is. ix. 6.

8. *The neighbours,* &c. This man seems to have been one who attracted considerable attention. The number of persons totally blind in any community is very small, and it is possible that this was the only blind beggar in Jerusalem. The case was one, therefore, likely to attract attention, and one where there

12 Then said they unto him, Where is he? He said, I know not.
13 They brought to the Pharisees him that aforetime was blind.
14 And it was the sabbath-day when Jesus made the clay and opened his eyes.
15 Then again the Pharisees also asked him how he had received his sight. He said unto them, He put clay upon mine eyes, and I washed, and do see.
16 Therefore said some of the Pharisees, This man is not of God, because he keepeth not the sabbath-day. Others said, [g] How can a man that is a sinner do such miracles? And[h] there was a division among them.
17 They say unto the blind man again, What sayest thou of

[g] ver.31; ch.3.2. [h] ch.7.12,43.

could be no imposture, as he was generally known.

13. *To the Pharisees.* To the members of the Sanhedrim. They did this, doubtless, to accuse Jesus of having violated the Sabbath, and not, as they ought to have done, to examine into the evidence that he was from God.

15. *The Pharisees asked him how,* &c. The proper question to have been asked in the case was whether he had *in fact* done it, and not *in what way.* The question, also, about a sinner's conversion is whether in fact it has been done, and not about the *mode* or *manner* in which it is effected; yet it is remarkable that no small part of the disputes and inquiries among men are about the *mode* in which the Spirit renews the heart, and not about the evidence that it is done.

16. *This man is not of God.* Is not *sent* by God, or cannot be a *friend* of God. ¶ *Because he keepeth not the sabbath-day.* They assumed that *their views* of the Sabbath were correct, and by *those views* they judged others. It did not occur to them to inquire whether the interpretation which they put on the law might not be erroneous. Men often assume their own interpretations of the Scriptures to be infallible, and then judge and condemn all others by those interpretations. ¶ *A sinner.* A deceiver; an impostor. They reasoned conclusively that God would not give the power of working such miracles to an impostor. The miracles were such as could not be denied, nor did even the enemies of Jesus attempt to deny them or to explain them away. They were open, public, frequent. And this shows that they *could* not deny their reality. Had it been possible, they would have done it; but the reality and power of those miracles had already made a party in favour of Jesus, even in the Sanhedrim (ch. vii. 50; xii. 42), and those opposed to them could not deny their reality. It may be added that the early opponents of Christianity never denied the *reality* of the miracles performed by the Saviour and his apostles. Celsus, Porphyry, and Julian—as acute foes of the gospel as perhaps have ever lived—never call this in question. They attempted to show that it was by some evil influence, or to account for the miracles in some other way than by admitting the divine origin of the Christian religion, but about the *facts* they had no question. Were they not as well qualified to judge about those *facts* as men are now? They lived near the time; had every opportunity to examine the evidence; were skilful and talented disputants; and if they *could* have denied the reality of the miracles they would have done it. It is scarcely possible to conceive of more conclusive proof that those miracles were really performed, and, if so, then the Lord Jesus was sent by God. ¶ *A division.* Greek, "*A schism.*" A separation into two parties.

17. *What sayest thou of him?* &c. The translation here expresses the sense obscurely. The meaning is, "What sayest thou of him for giving thee sight?" (Campbell); or, "What opinion of him hath this work of power and mercy to thee wrought in thee?" (Hammond). ¶ *He is a prophet.* That is, "I think that the power to work such a miracle proves that he is sent from God. And though this has been done on the Sabbath, yet it proves that he must have been sent by God, for such a power could never have proceeded from man." We see here, 1st. A noble confession made by the man who was healed, in the face of the rulers of the people, and when he doubtless knew

him, that he hath opened thine
eyes? He said, [i]He is a prophet.
18 But the Jews [k]did not believe
concerning him, that he had been
blind, and received his sight, until
they called the parents of him that
had received his sight.
19 And they asked them, saying,
Is this your son, who ye say was
born blind? How then doth he
now see?
20 His parents answered them
and said, We know that this is
our son, and that he was born
blind;
21 But by what means he now
seeth we know not, or who hath
opened his eyes we know not: he
is of age, ask him; he shall speak
for himself.
22 These *words* spake his parents,
because [l]they feared the Jews; for
the Jews had agreed already that
if any man did confess that he was
Christ, [m]he should be put out of the
synagogue.
23 Therefore said his parents,
He is of age, ask him.
24 Then again called they the
man that was blind, and said unto

i ch.4.19. *k* Is.26.11. *l* Pr.29.25; ch.7.13; 12.42. *m* ver.34; ch.16.2.

---

that they were opposed to Jesus. We should never be ashamed, before any class of men, to acknowledge the favours which we have received from Christ, and to express our belief of his power and of the truth of his doctrine. 2d. The works of Jesus were such as to prove that he came from God, however much he may have appeared to oppose the previous notions of men, the interpretation of the law by the Pharisees, or the deductions of reason. Men should *yield* their own views of religion to the teachings of God, and believe that he that could open the eyes of the blind and raise the dead was fitted to declare his will.

18, 19. *Is this your son?* &c. The Pharisees proposed *three* questions to the parents, by which they hoped to convict the man of falsehood. 1st. Whether he was their son? 2d. Whether they would affirm that he was *born* blind? and, 3d. Whether they knew by what means he now saw? They evidently intended to intimidate the parents, so that they might give an answer to *one* of these questions that would convict the man of deception. We see here the *art* to which men will resort rather than admit the truth. Had they been half as much *disposed* to believe on Jesus as they were to disbelieve, there would have been no difficulty in the case. And so with all men: were they as much *inclined* to embrace the truth as they are to reject it, there would soon be an end of cavils.

20–22. *His parents answered,* &c. To the first *two* questions they answered without hesitation. They knew that he was their son, and that he was born blind. The third question they *could not* positively answer, as they had not witnessed the means of the cure, and were afraid to express their belief. It appears that they had themselves no doubt, but they were not eye-witnesses, and could not be therefore legal evidence. ¶ *He is of age.* He is of sufficient age to give testimony. Among the Jews this age was fixed at thirteen years. ¶ *If any man did confess that he was Christ.* Did acknowledge that he was *the Messiah.* They had prejudged the case, and were determined to put down all free inquiry, and *not* to be convinced by *any* means. ¶ *Put out of the synagogue.* This took place in the *temple,* or near the temple. It does not refer, therefore, to any *immediate* and violent putting forth from the place where they were. It refers to *excommunication* from the synagogue. Among the Jews there were two grades of excommunication; the one for lighter offences, of which they mentioned twenty-four causes; the other for greater offences. The first excluded a man for thirty days from the privilege of entering a synagogue, and from coming nearer to his wife or friends than 4 cubits. The other was a solemn exclusion for ever from the worship of the synagogue, attended with awful maledictions and curses, and an exclusion from all intercourse with the people. This was called *the curse,* and so thoroughly excluded the person from all communion whatever with his countrymen, that they were not allowed to sell to him anything, even the necessaries of life (Buxtorf). It is probable that this *latter* punishment was what they intended to inflict if anyone should

him, [n]Give God the praise: we
know that this man is a sinner.
25 He answered and said,
Whether he be a sinner *or no*, I
know not: one thing I know, that
whereas I was blind, now I see.
26 Then said they to him again,

n Jos.7.19; Ps.50.14,15.

What did he to thee? how opened
he thine eyes?
27 He answered them, I have
told you already, and ye did not
hear; wherefore would ye hear *it*
again? will ye also be his disciples?
28 Then they [o]reviled him, and

o 1 Pe.2.23.

---

confess that Jesus was the Messiah; and it was the fear of this terrible punishment that deterred his parents from expressing their opinion.

24. *Give God the praise.* This expression seems to be a form of administering an oath. It is used in Jos. vii. 19, when Achan was put on his oath and entreated to confess his guilt. Joshua said, "My son, give, I pray thee, glory to the Lord God of Israel (in the Greek of the Septuagint, the very expression used in John, 'Give God the praise'), and make confession unto him." It is equivalent to an adjuration in the presence of God to acknowledge the truth; as the *truth* would be giving God praise, confessing the case before him, and trusting to his mercy. Comp. 1 Sa. vi. 5. The meaning here is not "give God praise for *healing* you," for they were not willing to admit that *he had been cured* (ver. 18), but *confess* that there is imposture in the case; that you have declared to us a falsehood, that you have endeavoured to impose on us; and by *thus* confessing your sin, give praise and honour to God, who condemns all imposture and falsehood, and whom you will thus acknowledge to be *right* in your condemnation. To induce him to do this, they added that they *knew*, or were satisfied that Jesus was a sinner. As they considered *that point* settled, they urged him to confess that *he* had attempted to impose on them. ¶ *We know.* We have settled that. He has broken the Sabbath, and that leaves no doubt. ¶ *A sinner.* A violator of the law respecting the Sabbath, and an impostor. See ver. 16.

25. *Whether he be a sinner* or no, *I know not.* The man had just said that he believed Jesus to be *a prophet*, ver. 17. By his saying that he did not know whether he was a sinner *may be* meant that *though* he might be a prophet, yet that he might not be perfect; or that it did not become him, being an obscure and unlearned man, to attempt to determine that question. What follows shows that he did not believe that he was a sinner, and these words were probably spoken in *irony* to deride the Pharisees. They were perverse and full of cavils, and were determined not to believe. The man reminded them that the question was not whether Jesus was a sinner; that, though that *might* be, yet it did not settle the other question about opening his eyes, which was the chief point of the inquiry. ¶ *One thing I know*, &c. About this *he* could have no doubt. He disregarded, therefore, their cavils. We may learn, also, here, 1st. That this declaration may be made by every converted sinner. He may not be able to meet the cavils of others. He may not be able to tell *how* he was converted. It is enough if he can say, "I *was* a sinner, but now love God; I *was* in darkness, but have now been brought to the light of truth." 2d. We should not be *ashamed* of the fact that we are made to see by the Son of God. No cavil or derision of men should deter us from such an avowal. 3d. Sinners are perpetually shifting the *real* point of inquiry. They do not inquire into *the facts*. They *assume* that a thing *cannot* be true, and then argue as if *that* was a conceded point. The proper way in religion is first to inquire *into the facts*, and then account for them as we can.

26. *How opened he thine eyes?* The reason why they asked this so often was doubtless to attempt to draw him into a contradiction; either to intimidate him, or throw him off his guard, so that he might be detected in denying what he had before affirmed. But God gave to this poor man grace and strength to make a bold confession of the truth, and sufficient common sense completely to confound his proud and subtle examiners.

28. *Thou art his disciple.* This they cast at him as a reproach. His defence of Jesus they regarded as proof that he was his follower, and this they now attempted to show was inconsistent with being a friend of Moses and his law. Moses had given the law respecting the

said, Thou art his disciple, but we
are Moses' disciples.
29 We[p] know that God spake
unto Moses; *as for* this *fellow*,
we[q] know not from whence he is.
30 The man answered and said
unto them, [r]Why, herein is a marvellous thing, that ye know not
from whence he is, and *yet* [s]he
hath opened mine eyes.
31 Now we know that [t]God
heareth not sinners; [u]but if any
man be a worshipper of God, and
doeth his will, him he heareth.
32 Since the world began was it

p Ps.103.7; He.3.5. q ch.8.14. r ch.3.10.

s Ps.119.18; Is.29.18,19; 35.5; 2 Co.4.6.
t Job 27.9; Ps.66.18; Pr.28.9; Is.1.15; Je.11.11; Eze.8.18; Mi.3.4; Zec.7.13. u Ps.34.15; Pr.15.29.

Sabbath; Jesus had healed a man contrary, in *their* view, to the law of Moses. They therefore held Jesus to be a violater and contemner of the law of Moses, and of course that his followers were also. ¶ *We are Moses' disciples.* We acknowledge the authority of the law of Moses, which they alleged Jesus has broken by healing on that day.

29. *We know*, &c. We know that God commanded Moses to deliver the law. In that they were correct; but they assumed *their* interpretation of the law to be infallible, and hence condemned Jesus. ¶ As for *this* fellow. The word *fellow* is not in the original. It is simply "*this.*" The word *fellow* implies contempt, which it cannot be proved they intended to express. ¶ *Whence he is.* We know not his origin, his family, or his home. The contrast with the preceding member of the sentence shows that they intended to express their belief that he was not from God. They knew not whether he was mad, whether he was instigated by the devil, or whether he spoke of himself. See ch. vii. 27; viii. 48–52.

30. *A marvellous thing.* This is wonderful and amazing. ¶ *Know not from whence he is.* That you cannot perceive that he who has wrought such a miracle *must* be from God.

31. *Now we know.* That is, it is an admitted or conceded point. No one calls it into question. ¶ *God heareth not.* When a miracle was performed it was customary to invoke the aid of God. Jesus often did this himself, and it was by his power only that prophets and apostles could perform miracles. The word "*heareth*" in this place is to be understood as referring to such cases. God will not *hear*—that is, answer. ¶ *Sinners.* Impostors. False prophets and pretenders to divine revelation. See ver. 24. The meaning of this verse is, therefore, "It is well understood that God will not give miraculous aid to impostors and false prophets." We may remark here, 1st. That the passage has no reference to the prayers which *sinners* make for salvation. 2d. If it had it would not be of course true. It was the mere opinion of this man, in accordance with the common sentiment of the Jews, and there is no evidence that *he* was inspired. 3d. The only prayers which God will not hear are those which are offered in mockery, or when the man loves his sins and is unwilling to give them up. Such prayers God will not hear, Ps. lxvi. 18: "If I regard iniquity in my heart, the Lord will not hear me;" Is. i. 14, 15; Job xxvii. 9; Je. xi. 11; Eze. viii. 18; Mi. iii. 4; Zec. vii. 13. ¶ *A worshipper.* A sincere worshipper; one who fears, loves, and adores him. ¶ *Doeth his will.* Obeys his commandments. This is infallibly true. The Scripture abounds with promises to such that God will hear their prayer. See Ps. xxxiv. 15; Mat. vii. 7, 8.

32. *Since the world began.* Neither Moses nor any of the prophets had ever done this. No instance of this kind is recorded in the Old Testament. As this was a miracle which had *never* been performed, the man argued justly that he who had done it must be from God. As Jesus did it not by surgical operations, but by *clay*, it showed that he had power of working miracles by any means. It may be also remarked that the restoration of sight to the blind by surgical operations was never performed until the year 1728. Dr. Cheselden, an English surgeon, was the first who attempted it successfully, who was enabled to remove a *cataract* from the eye of a young man, and to restore sight. This fact shows the difficulty of the operation when the most skilful natural means are employed, and the greatness of the miracle performed by the Saviour.

33. *Could do nothing.* Could do no such work as this. This reasoning was conclusive. The fact that Jesus could

not heard that any man opened the
eyes of one that was born blind.
33 If this man were not of God,
he could do nothing.
34 They answered and said unto
him, [v]Thou wast altogether born
in sins, and dost thou teach us?
And [w]they [2]cast him out.
35 Jesus heard that they had
cast him out; and when he had
found him, he said unto him,
Dost thou [x]believe on the Son of
God?
36 He answered and said, Who
is he, Lord, that I might believe
on him?
37 And Jesus said unto him,
Thou hast both seen him, [y]and it
is he that talketh with thee.
38 And he said, Lord, I believe.
And[z] he worshipped him.
39 And Jesus said, [a]For judg-

v ver.2. *w* Is.66.5.
2 or, *excommunicated him.*
x 1 Jn.5.13. *y* ch.4.26. *z* Mat.14.33.
a ch.5.22,27; 12.47.

perform miracles like this was full proof that he was commissioned by God—proof that never has been and never can be refuted. One such miracle proves that he was from God. But Jesus gave *many* similar proofs, and thus put his divine mission beyond the possibility of doubt.

34. *Wast born in sins.* That is, thou wast born in a state of blindness—a state which proved that either thou or thy parents had sinned, and that this was the punishment for it. See ver. 2. Thou wast cursed by God with blindness for crime, and yet thou dost set up for a religious teacher! When men have no arguments, they attempt to supply their place by revilings. When they are *pressed* by argument, they reproach their adversaries with crime, and especially with being *blind, perverse, heretical, disposed to speculation, and regardless of the authority of God.* And especially do they consider it great presumption that one of an inferior *age* or *rank* should presume to advance an argument in opposition to prevailing opinions. ¶ *They cast him out.* Out of the synagogue. They *excommunicated* him. See Notes on ver. 22.

35. *Dost thou believe on the Son of God?* Hitherto he had understood little of the true character of Jesus. He believed that he had *power* to heal him, and he *inferred* that he must be a prophet, ver. 17. He believed according to the *light he had*, and he *now* showed that he was prepared to believe *all* that Jesus said. This is the nature of true faith. It believes all that God *has* made known, and it is *prepared* to receive all that he *will* teach. The phrase *Son of God* here is equivalent to *the Messiah.* See Notes on Mat. viii. 29.

36. *Who is he?* It is probable that the man did not know that he who now addressed him was the same who had healed him. He had not yet *seen him* (ver. 7), but he was prepared to acknowledge him when he did see him. He inquired, therefore, *who* the person was, or wished that he might be pointed out to him, that he *might* see him. This passage shows that he was *disposed* to believe, and had a strong desire to see and hear the Son of God. ¶ *Lord.* This word here, as in many other instances in the New Testament, means "Sir." It is clear that the man did not know that it was the *Lord Jesus* that addressed him, and he therefore replied to him in the common language of respect, and asked him to point out to him the Son of God. The word translated "Lord" here is rendered "Sir" in Jn. iv. 11; xx. 15; xii. 21; Ac. xvi. 30; Mat. xxvii. 63. It should have been also here, and in many other places.

38. *I believe.* This was the overflowing expression of gratitude and faith. ¶ *And he worshipped him.* He did homage to him as the Messiah and as his gracious benefactor. See Notes on Mat. ii. 2. This shows, 1st. That it is right and natural to express thanks and praise for mercies. 2d. All blessings should lead us to pour out our gratitude to Jesus, for it is from him that we receive them. 3d. Especially is this true when the *mind* has been enlightened, when our spiritual eyes have been opened, and we are permitted to see the glories of the heavenly world. 4th. It is right to pay homage or worship to Jesus. He forbade it not. He received it on earth, and for all mercies of providence and redemption we should pay to him the tribute of humble and grateful hearts. The Syriac renders the phrase, "he worshipped him," thus: "and, casting himself down, he adored him." The Persic, "and he bowed

ment I am come into this world, that [b]they which see not might see, and that [c]they which see might be made blind.

40 And *some* of the Pharisees which were with him heard these words, and said unto him, [d]Are we blind also?

41 Jesus said unto them, [e]If ye were blind, ye should have no sin: but now ye say, We see; [f]therefore your sin remaineth.

CHAPTER X.

VERILY, verily, I say unto you, [a]He that entereth not

b 1 Pe.2.9. c Mat.13.13; ch.3.19. d Ro.2.19; Re.3.17.
e ch.15.22,24. f Is.5.21; Lu.18.14; 1 Jn.1.8-10. a Ro.10.15; He.5.4.

---

down and adored Christ." The Arabic, "and he adored him." The Latin Vulgate, "and, falling down, he adored him."

39. *For judgment.* The word *judgment*, here, has been by some understood in the sense of *condemnation*—"The effect of my coming is to condemn the world." But this meaning does not agree with those places where Jesus says that he came not to condemn the world, Jn. iii. 17; xii. 47; v. 45. To *judge* is to express *an opinion in a judicial manner*, and also to express any sentiment about any person or thing, Jn. vii. 24; v. 30; Lu. viii. 43. The meaning here may be thus expressed: "I came to *declare the condition* of men; to show them their duty and danger. My coming will have this effect, that some will be reformed and saved, and some more deeply condemned." ¶ *That they*, &c. The Saviour does not affirm that this was the *design* of his coming, but that such would be the *effect* or *result.* He came to declare the truth, and the effect *would be*, &c. Similar instances of expression frequently occur. Comp. Mat. xi. 25; x. 34: "I came not to send peace, but a sword"—that is, such will be the effect of my coming. ¶ *That they which see not.* Jesus took this illustration, as he commonly did, from the case before him; but it is evident that he meant it to be taken in a *spiritual* sense. He refers to those who are blind and ignorant by sin; whose minds have been darkened, but who are desirous of seeing. ¶ *Might see.* Might discern the path of truth, of duty, and of salvation, ch. x. 9. ¶ *They which see.* They who *suppose* they see; who are proud, self-confident, and despisers of the truth. Such were evidently the Pharisees. ¶ *Might be made blind.* Such would be *the effect* of his preaching. It would exasperate them, and their pride and opposition to him would confirm them more and more in their erroneous views. This is always the effect of truth. Where it does not *soften* it *hardens* the heart; where it does not convert, it sinks into deeper blindness and condemnation.

41. *If ye were blind.* If you were *really* blind—had had no *opportunities* of learning the truth. If you were truly ignorant, and were willing to confess it, and to come to me for instruction. ¶ *No sin.* You would not be guilty. Sin is measured by the *capacities* or *ability* of men, and by their opportunities of knowing the truth. If men had no *ability* to do the will of God, they could incur no blame. If they have all proper *ability*, and no *disposition*, God holds them to be guilty. This passage teaches conclusively, 1st. That men are not condemned for what they cannot do. 2d. That the reason why they are condemned is that they are not disposed to receive the truth. 3d. That pride and self-confidence are the sources of condemnation. 4th. That if men are condemned, they, and not God, will be to blame. ¶ *We see.* We have knowledge of the law of God. This they had pretended when they professed to understand the law respecting the Sabbath better than Jesus, and had condemned him for healing on that day. ¶ *Your sin remaineth.* You *are* guilty, and your sin is unpardoned. Men's sins will *always* be unpardoned while they are proud, and self-sufficient, and confident of their own wisdom. If they will come with humble hearts and confess their ignorance, God will forgive, enlighten, and guide them in the path to heaven.

CHAPTER X.

1. *Verily, verily.* See Notes on Jn. iii. 3. ¶ *I say unto you.* Some have supposed that what follows here was delivered on some other occasion than the one mentioned in the last chapter; but the expression *verily, verily*, is one which is not used at the *commencement*

by the door into the sheepfold,
but climbeth up some other way,
the same is a thief and a robber.
2 But he that entereth in by
[b]the door is the shepherd of the
sheep.
3 To[c] him the porter openeth,
and the sheep hear his voice; and

b ver.7,9. c Re.3.20.

of a discourse, and the discourse itself seems to be a continuation of what was said before. The Pharisees professed to be the *guides* or *shepherds* of the people. Jesus, in the close of the last chapter, had charged them with being *blind*, and of course of being unqualified to lead the people. He proceeds here to state the character of a *true* shepherd, to show what was a hireling, and to declare that *he* was the true shepherd and guide of his people. This is called (ver. 6) *a parable*, and it is an eminently beautiful illustration of the office of the Messiah, drawn from an employment well known in Judea. The Messiah was predicted under the image of a *shepherd*, Eze. xxxiv. 23; xxxvii. 24; Zec. xiii. 7. Hence at the close of the discourse they asked him whether he were the Messiah, ver. 24. ¶ *Into the sheepfold.* The sheepfold was an inclosure made in fields where the sheep were collected by night to defend them from robbers, wolves, &c. It was not commonly covered, as the seasons in Judea were mild. By the figure here we are to understand the Jewish people, or the church of God, which is often likened to a flock, Eze. xxxiv. 1–19; Je. xxiii. 1–4; Zec. xiii. By the *door*, here, is meant the Lord Jesus Christ, ver. 7, 9. He is "the way, the truth, and the life," Jn. xiv. 6. And, as the only proper way of entering the fold was by the door, so the only way of entering the church of God is by believing on him and obeying his commandments. The particular application of this place, however, is to *religious teachers*, who cannot enter properly on the duties of teaching and guarding the flock except by the Lord Jesus—that is, in the way which he has appointed. The Pharisees claimed to be *pastors*, but not under his appointment. They entered some other way. The true *pastors* of the church are those who enter by the influences of the Spirit of Jesus, and in the manner which he has appointed. ¶ *Some other way.* Either at a window or over the wall. ¶ *A thief.* One who *silently* and *secretly* takes away the property of another. ¶ *A robber.* One who does it by *violence* or *bloodshed.* Jesus here designates those pastors or ministers of religion who are influenced not by love to *him*, but who seek the office from ambition, or the love of power, or wealth, or ease; who come, not to promote the welfare of the church, but to promote their own interests. Alas! in all churches there have been many—many who for no better ends have sought the pastoral office. To all such Jesus gives the names of *thieves* and *robbers.*

2. *He that entereth by the door.* This was the way in which a *shepherd* had access to his flock. In ver. 7 Jesus says *he* is the door. In this place he refers to those who *by him*—that is, in accordance with his spirit and law—become ministers of religion. ¶ *Is the shepherd of the sheep.* Christ does not here refer *to himself*, for he is the way or door by which *others* enter; but he refers to all the ministers of the gospel who have access to the church *by* him. In the original, the article "the" is wanting before the word shepherd—"is *a* shepherd." By his entering in this manner he shows that he is a *shepherd*—one who cares for his flock, and does not come to kill and destroy.

3. *To him the porter openeth.* The *porter* is the *doorkeeper*. It seems that the more wealthy Jews who owned flocks employed some person to take charge of the flock. At first *all* shepherds attended their flocks personally by day and by night, and this continued to be commonly the practice, but not always. ¶ *The sheep hear his voice.* The voice of the shepherd. A flock will readily discern the well-known voice of one who is accustomed to attend them. The meaning is, that the people of God will be found disposed to listen to the instructions of those who are appointed by Christ, who preach his pure doctrines, and who show a real love for the church of God. There is scarcely any better test of fidelity in the pastoral office than the approbation of the humble and obscure people of God, when they discern in the preacher the very manner and spirit of the doctrines of the Bible. ¶ *He calleth his own sheep by name.* It was customary, and is still, we are told by travellers, for shepherds to give particular *names* to their sheep,

he [d]calleth his own sheep by name, and [e]leadeth them out.
4 And when he putteth forth his own sheep, he goeth before them, and the sheep follow him, for [f]they know his voice.
5 And a stranger will they not follow, [g]but will flee from him;

d Eze.34.11; Ro.8.30. *e* Is.40.11. *f* Ca.2.8; 5.2. *g* 2 Ti.3.5; Re.2.2.

by which they soon learned to regard the voice of the shepherd. By this our Saviour indicates, doubtless, that it is the duty of a minister of religion to seek an intimate and personal acquaintance with the people of his charge; to feel an interest in them as *individuals*, and not merely to address them *together;* to learn their private wants; to meet them in their individual trials, and to administer to them personally the consolations of the gospel. ¶ *Leadeth them out.* He leads them from the fold to pasture or to water. Perhaps there is here intended the care of a faithful pastor to provide suitable *instruction* for the people of his charge, and to feed them with the bread of life. See a beautiful and touching description of the care of the Great Shepherd in Ps. xxiii.

4. *He putteth forth.* Or leads them out of the fold. ¶ *He goeth before them.* He leads them, and guides them, and does not leave them. A shepherd spent his time with his flocks. He went before them to seek the best pastures and watering-places, and to defend them from danger. In this is beautifully represented the tender care of him who watches for souls as one that must give account.

5. *A stranger*, &c. This was literally true of a flock. Accustomed to the voice and presence of a kind shepherd, they would not regard the command of a stranger. It is also true spiritually. Jesus by this indicates that the true people of God will not follow false teachers—those who are proud, haughty, and self-seeking, as were the Pharisees. Many *may* follow such, but humble and devoted Christians seek those who have the mild and self-denying spirit of their Master and Great Shepherd. It is also true in reference to those who are *pastors* in the churches. They have an influence which no stranger or wandering minister can have. A church learns to put confidence in a pastor; he knows the wants of his people, sees their danger, and can adapt his instructions to them. A stranger, however eloquent, pious, or learned, can have few of these advantages; and it is more absurd to commit the churches to the care of wandering strangers, of those who have no permanent relation to the church, than it would be for a flock to be committed to a foreigner who knew nothing of it, and who had no particular interest in it. The *pastoral office* is one of the wisest institutions of heaven. The following extract from *The Land and the Book* (Thomson) will show how strikingly this whole passage accords with what actually occurs at this day in Palestine: "This is true to the letter. They are so tame and so trained that they *follow* their keeper with the utmost docility. He leads them forth from the fold, or from their houses in the villages, just where he pleases. As there are many flocks in such a place as this, each one takes a different path, and it is his business to find pasture for them. It is necessary, therefore, that they should be taught to follow, and not to stray away into the unfenced fields of corn which lie so temptingly on either side. Any one that thus wanders is sure to get into trouble. The shepherd calls sharply from time to time to remind them of his presence. They know his voice and follow on; but if a stranger call, they stop short, lift up their heads in alarm, and, if it is repeated, they turn and flee, because they know not the voice of a stranger. This is not the fanciful costume of a parable; it is simple fact. I have made the experiment repeatedly. The shepherd goes before, not merely to point out the way, but to see that it is practicable and safe. He is armed in order to defend his charge, and in this he is very courageous. Many adventures with wild beasts occur not unlike that recounted by David, and in these very mountains; for, though there are now no lions here, there are wolves in abundance; and leopards and panthers, exceedingly fierce, prowl about these wild wadies. They not unfrequently attack the flock in the very presence of the shepherd, and he must be ready to do battle at a moment's warning. I have listened with intense interest to their graphic descriptions of downright and desperate fights with these savage beasts. And when

for they know not the voice of
strangers.
6 This parable spake Jesus unto
them; but they understood not
what things they were which he
spake unto them.
7 Then said Jesus unto them
again, Verily, verily, I say unto
you, [h] I am the door of the sheep.
8 All that ever came before me
are thieves and robbers; but the
sheep did not hear them.
9 I am the door: by me, if any
man enter in, he shall be saved,
and shall go in and out, and find
pasture.
10 The thief cometh not but
for to steal, and to kill, and to
destroy; I am come that they

h Ep.2.18.

---

the thief and the robber come (and come they do), the faithful shepherd has often to put his life in his hand to defend his flock. I have known more than one case in which he had literally to lay it down in the contest. A poor faithful fellow last spring, between Tiberias and Tabor, instead of fleeing, actually fought three Bedawin robbers until he was hacked to pieces with their khanjars, and died among the sheep he was defending."

6. *This parable.* See Notes on Mat. xiii. 3. ¶ *They understood not*, &c. They did not understand the *meaning* or *design* of the illustration.

7. *I am the door.* I am the way by which ministers and people enter the true church. It is by his merits, his intercession, his aid, and his appointment that they enter. ¶ *Of the sheep.* Of the church.

8. *All that ever came before me.* This does not refer to the prophets, but to those who came *pretending* to be the pastors or guides of the people. Some have supposed that he referred to those who pretended to be the Messiah before him; but there is not evidence that *any* such person appeared before the coming of Jesus. It is probable that he rather refers to the scribes and Pharisees, who claimed to be instructors of the people, who claimed the right to regulate the affairs of religion, and whose only aim was to aggrandize themselves and to oppress the people. See Notes on Jn. i. 18. When the Saviour says that "*all*" were thieves, he speaks in a popular sense, using the word "all" as it is often used in the New Testament, to denote the great *mass* or the *majority*. ¶ *Thieves and robbers.* See ver. 1; also Je. xxiii. 1: "Woe be unto the pastors that destroy and scatter the sheep of my pasture;" Eze. xxxiv. 2, 3: "Woe be to the shepherds of Israel that do feed themselves! Ye eat the fat, and ye clothe you with the wool, ye kill them that are fed; but ye feed not the flock." This had been the *general* character of the Pharisees and scribes. They sought wealth, office, ease at the expense of the people, and thus deserved the character of thieves and robbers. They insinuated themselves slyly as a *thief*, and they oppressed and spared not, like a robber. ¶ *The sheep.* The people of God—the pious and humble portion of the Jewish nation. Though the great *mass* of the people were corrupted, yet there were always *some* who were the humble and devoted people of God. Comp. Ro. xi. 3, 4. So it will be always. Though the great mass of teachers may be corrupt, yet the true friends of God will mourn in secret places, and refuse to "listen to the instruction that causeth to err."

9. *By me.* By my instruction and merits. ¶ *Shall be saved.* See ch. v. 24. ¶ *Shall go in and out*, &c. This is language applied commonly to flocks. It meant that he shall be well supplied, and defended, and led "beside the still waters of salvation."

10. *The thief cometh not*, &c. The thief has no other design in coming but to plunder. So false teachers have no other end in view but to enrich or aggrandize themselves. ¶ *I am come that they might have life.* See Notes on Jn. v. 24. ¶ *Might have* it *more abundantly.* Literally, that they may have *abundance*, or that which abounds. The word denotes that which is not absolutely essential to *life*, but which is superadded to make life happy. They shall not merely have *life*—simple, bare *existence*—but they shall have all those superadded things which are needful to make that life eminently blessed and happy. It would be vast mercy to keep men merely from annihilation or hell; but Jesus will give them eternal joy, peace, the society of the blessed, and all those exalted means of felicity which are prepared for them in the world of glory.

might have life, and that they
might have *it* more abundantly.

11 I[i] am the good shepherd:
the good shepherd giveth his life
for the sheep.

12 But he that is an hireling,
and not the shepherd, whose own
the sheep are not, seeth the wolf
coming, and [k]leaveth the sheep,
and fleeth; and the wolf catcheth
them, and scattereth the sheep.

13 The hireling fleeth because
he is an hireling, and careth not
for the sheep.

14 I am the good shepherd, [l]and
know my *sheep*, [m]and am known
of mine.

15 As[n] the Father knoweth
me, even so know I the Father;
and [o]I lay down my life for the
sheep.

16 And[p] other sheep I have,
which are not of this fold: them
also I must bring, and they shall

i He.13.20; 1 Pe.2.25. *k* Eze.34.2-6; Zec.11.17.

l 2 Ti.2.19. *m* 1 Jn.5.20. *n* Mat.11.27. *o* ch.15.13; Is.53.4,5. *p* Is.49.6; 56.8.

---

11. *The good shepherd.* The faithful and true shepherd, willing to do *all* that is necessary to defend and save the flock. ¶ *Giveth his life.* A shepherd that regarded his flock would hazard his own life to defend them. When the wolf comes, he would still remain to protect them. To *give his life*, here, means the same as *not to fly*, or to forsake his flock; to be willing to expose his life, if necessary, to defend them. Comp. Ju. xii. 3: "I put my life in my hands and passed over," &c.; 1 Sa. xix. 5; xxviii. 21. See ver. 15. The Messiah was often predicted under the character of a shepherd.

12. *A hireling.* A man employed to take care of the sheep, to whom wages is paid. As he does not *own* the sheep, and guards them merely for pay, rather than risk his life he would leave the flock to the ravages of wild beasts. The word translated *hireling* is often employed in a good sense; but here it denotes one who is unfaithful to his trust; and especially those ministers who preach *only* for support, and who are unwilling to encounter any danger or to practise any self-denial for the welfare of the church of God. They are those who have no *boldness* in the cause of their Master, but who, rather than lose their reputation or place, would see the church corrupted and wasted by its spiritual foes. ¶ *Whose own the sheep are not.* Who does not own the sheep.

13. *Because he is a hireling.* Because he regards only his wages. He feels no special interest in the flock.

14. *Know my* sheep. Know my people, or my church. The word *know* here is used in the sense of *affectionate regard* or *love.* It implies such a knowledge of their wants, their dangers, and their characters, as to result in a *deep interest* in their welfare. Thus the word "knoweth," in ver. 15, is in ver. 17 explained by the word "loveth." Jesus *knows* the hearts, the dangers, and the wants of his people, and his kindness as their shepherd prompts him to defend and aid them. ¶ *Am known of mine.* That is, he is known and loved as their Saviour and Friend. They have seen their sins, and dangers, and wants; they have felt their need of a Saviour; they have come to him, and they have found him and his doctrines to be such as they need, and they have loved him. And as a flock follows and obeys its kind shepherd, so they follow and obey him who leads them beside the still waters, and makes them to lie down in green pastures.

15. *As the Father knoweth me*, &c. See Notes on Mat. xi. 27; also Lu. x. 22. ¶ *I lay down my life for the sheep.* That is, I give my life as an atoning sacrifice for their sins. I die in their place, to redeem them from sin, and danger, and death. See ver. 17, 18.

16. *Other sheep.* There are others who shall be members of my redeemed church. ¶ *I have.* This does not imply that they were *then* his friends, but that they *would* be. There were others whom it was his *purpose* and *intention* to call to the blessings of the gospel and salvation. The purpose was so sure, and the fact that they would believe on him so certain, that he could use the present tense as if they were already his own. This purpose was in accordance with the promise (Is. liii. 11), "He shall see of the travail of his soul, and shall be satisfied." An instance of a parallel expression occurs in Ac. xviii. 10, "I *have much people* in this city" (Corinth). That is, it was the *purpose* of God to bless the preaching of Paul, and give

hear my voice; [q]and there shall be one fold *and* one shepherd.

17 Therefore doth my Father love me, [r]because I lay down my life, that I might take it again.

18 No man taketh it from me, but [s]I lay it down of myself. I have power to lay it down, and [t]I have power to take it again. [u]This commandment have I received of my Father.

19 There was a division, there-

q Eze.37.22; Ep.2.14. r Is.53.7-12; He.2.9. s Phi.2.6-8. t ch.2.19. u ch.6.38.

him many souls as the seals of his ministry. It was so *certain* that they would believe in the Saviour, that it could be spoken of as if it were already done. This certainty could have existed only in consequence of the *intention* of God that it *should be* so. It did not consist in any disposition to embrace the gospel which was foreseen, for they were the most corrupt and licentious people of antiquity, and it must have been because God *meant* that it should be so. Declarations like these are full proof that God has a *plan* in regard to the salvation of men, and that the number is known and determined by him. Learn—1. That it is not a question of chance or uncertainty whether men shall be saved. 2. That there is encouragement for preaching the gospel. There are those whom God *means* to save, and if he *intends* to do it it will be done. ¶ *Not of this fold.* Not Jews. This is a distinct intimation that the gospel was to be preached to the Gentiles—a doctrine extremely offensive to the Jews. This prediction of the Saviour has been strikingly confirmed in the conversion of millions of the Gentiles to the gospel. ¶ *Them also I must bring.* Bring into the church and kingdom of heaven. This was to be done, not by his personal ministry, but by the labour of his apostles and other ministers. ¶ *One fold.* One church; there shall be no distinction, no peculiar national privileges. The partition between the Jews and the Gentiles shall be broken down, and there shall be no pre-eminence of rank or honour, Ep. ii. 14: "Christ hath broken down the middle wall of partition between us;" Ro. x. 12: "There is no difference between the Jew and the Greek." ¶ *One shepherd.* That is, the Lord Jesus—the common Saviour, deliverer, and friend of all true believers, in whatever land they were born and whatever tongue they may speak. This shows that Christians of all denominations and countries should feel that they are *one*—redeemed by the same blood, and going to the same eternal home. Comp. 1 Co. xii. 13; Ga. iii. 28; Col. iii. 11; Ac. xvii. 26.

17. *I lay down my life.* I give myself to die for my people, in Jewish and pagan lands. I offer myself a sacrifice to show the willingness of my Father to save them; to provide an atonement, and thus to open the way for their salvation. This proves that the salvation of man was an object dear to God, and that it was a source of peculiar gratification to him that his Son was *willing* to lay down his life to accomplish his great purposes of benevolence. ¶ *That I might take it again.* Be raised up from the dead, and glorified, and still carry on the work of redemption. See this same sentiment sublimely expressed in Phi. ii. 5–11.

18. *No man taketh it from me.* That is, no one could take it by force, or unless I was willing to yield myself into his hands. He had power to preserve his life, as he showed by so often escaping from the Pharisees; he voluntarily went up to Jerusalem, knowing that he would die; he knew the approach of Judas to betray him; and he expressly told Pilate at his bar that he could have no power at all against him except it were given him by his Father, Jn. xix. 11. Jesus had a right to lay down his life for the good of men. The patriot dies for his country on the field of battle; the merchant exposes his life for gain; and the Son of God had a right to put himself in the way of danger and of death, when a dying world *needed* such an atoning sacrifice. This shows the peculiar love of Jesus. His death was voluntary. His *coming* was voluntary—the fruit of love. His death was the fruit of love. He was permitted to choose the *time* and *mode* of his death. He did. He chose the most painful, lingering, ignominious manner of death then known to man, and THUS showed his love. ¶ *I have power.* This word often means *authority.* It includes all necessary power in the case, and the commission or *authority* of his Father

fore, again among the Jews for
these sayings.
20 And many of them said,
He[v] hath a devil, and is mad;
why hear ye him?
21 Others said, These are not
the words of him that hath a devil.
Can a devil [w]open the eyes of the
blind?
22 And it was at Jerusalem the
feast of the dedication, and it was
winter.
23 And Jesus walked in the
temple, in [x]Solomon's porch.
24 Then came the Jews round
about him, and said unto him,
How long dost thou [1]make us to
doubt? If thou be the Christ,
tell us plainly.
25 Jesus answered them, I told

v ch.7.20. w ch.9.6,&c. x Ac.3.11; 5.12. 1 or, *hold us in suspense.*

---

to do it. ¶ *Power to take it again.* This shows that he was divine. A *dead* man has no power to raise himself from the grave. And as Jesus had this power *after* he was deceased, it proves that there was some other nature than that which had expired, to which the term "I" might be still applied. None but God can raise the dead; and as Jesus had this power over his own body it proves that he was divine. ¶ *This commandment.* My Father has appointed this, and commissioned me to do it.

20. *He hath a devil.* Ch. vii. 20. ¶ *Is mad.* Is deranged, or a maniac. His words are incoherent and unintelligible.

21. *Not the words,* &c. His words are sober, grave, pious, full of wisdom. The preaching of Jesus always produced effect. It made bitter enemies or decided friends. So will all faithful preaching. It is not the fault of the *gospel* that there are divisions, but of the unbelief and mad passions of men.

22. *The feast of the dedication.* Literally, the feast of the *renewing*, or of the *renovation.* This feast was instituted by Judas Maccabæus, in the year 164 B.C. The temple and city were taken by Antiochus Epiphanes in the year 167 B.C. He slew forty thousand inhabitants, and sold forty thousand more as slaves. In addition to this, he sacrificed a sow on the altar of burnt-offerings, and a broth being made of this, he sprinkled it all over the temple. The city and temple were recovered three years afterward by Judas Maccabæus, and the temple was *purified* with great pomp and solemnity. The ceremony of purification continued through eight days, during which Judas presented magnificent victims, and celebrated the praise of God with hymns and psalms (Josephus, *Ant.*, b. xii. ch. 11). "They decked, also, the forefront of the temple with crowns of gold and with shields, and the gates and chambers they *renewed* and hanged doors upon them," 1 Mac. iv. 52–59. On this account it was called the feast of renovation or dedication. Josephus calls it the feast of *lights*, because the city was illuminated, as expressive of joy. The feast began on the twenty-fifth day of *Chisleu*, answering to the fifteenth day of December. The festival continued for eight days, with continued demonstrations of joy. ¶ *It was winter.* The feast was celebrated in the winter. The word here implies that it was cold and inclement, and it is given as a reason why he walked in Solomon's porch. ¶ *Solomon's porch.* The porch or covered way on the east of the temple. See Notes on Mat. xxi. 12.

24. *Tell us plainly.* The Messiah was predicted as a *shepherd.* Jesus had applied that prediction to himself. They supposed that that was an evidence that he claimed to be the Messiah. He also wrought miracles, which they considered as evidence that he was the Christ, ch. vii. 31. Yet the rulers made a difficulty. They alleged that he was from Galilee, and that the Messiah could not come from thence, ch. vii. 52. He was poor and despised. He came contrary to the common expectation. A splendid prince and conqueror had been expected. In this perplexity they came to him for a plain and positive declaration that he was the Messiah.

25. *I told you.* It is not recorded that Jesus had told them in so many words that he was the Christ, but he had used expressions designed to convey the same truth, and which many of them understood as claiming to be the Messiah. See ch. v. 19; viii. 36, 56; x. 1. The expression "the Son of God" they understood to be equivalent to the Messiah. This he had often used of himself in a sense not to be mistaken. ¶ *The works.* The

you, and ye believed not: [y]the
works that I do in my Father's
name, they bear witness of me.
26 But[z] ye believe not, because
ye are not of my sheep, as I said
unto you.
27 My[a] sheep hear my voice,
and I know them, and they follow me;
28 And I give unto them eternal
life; and [b]they shall never perish,
neither shall any *man* pluck them
out of my hand.
29 My[c] Father, which [d]gave

y ch.5.36. z ch.8.47; 1 Jn.4.6. a ver.4. b ch.17.12; 18.9; He.7.25. c ch.14.28. d ch.17.2.

---

miracles, such as restoring the blind, curing the sick, &c. ¶ *In my Father's name.* By the power and command of God. Jesus was either the Messiah or an impostor. The Pharisees charged him with being the latter (Mat. xxvi. 60, 61; xxvii. 63; Jn. xviii. 36); but God would not give such power to an impostor. The power of working miracles is an attestation of God to what is taught. See Notes on Mat. iv. 24.

26. *Are not of my sheep.* Are not my people, my followers. You do not possess the spirit of meek and humble disciples. Were it not for pride, and prejudice, and vainglory—for your false notions of the Messiah, and from a determination *not* to believe, you would have learned from my declarations and works that I am the Christ. ¶ *As I said unto you.* Comp. ch. viii. 47.

27. *My sheep.* My church, my people, those who have the true spirit of my followers. The name is given to his people because it was an illustration which would be well understood in a country abounding in flocks. There is also a striking resemblance, which he proceeds to state, between them. ¶ *Hear my voice.* See ver. 3, 4. Applied to Christians, it means that they hear and obey his commandments. ¶ *I know them.* See ver. 14. ¶ *They follow me.* A flock follows its shepherd to pastures and streams, ver. 3. Christians not only *obey* Christ, but they *imitate* him; they go where his Spirit and providence lead them; they yield themselves to his guidance, and seek to be led by him. When Jesus was upon earth many of his disciples *followed* or *attended* him from place to place. Hence Christians are called his *followers*, and in Re. xiv. 4 they are described as "they that follow the Lamb."

28. *I give unto them eternal life.* See ch. v. 24. ¶ *Shall never perish.* To *perish* here means to be *destroyed*, or to be punished in hell. Mat. x. 28: "Which is able to *destroy* (the same word) both soul and body in hell." Mat. xviii. 14: "It is not the will of your Father which is in heaven that one of these little ones should *perish.*" Jn. iii. 15: "That whosoever believeth in him should not *perish.*" Ro. ii. 12: "They who have sinned without law shall also *perish* without law." Jn. xvii. 12; 1 Co. i. 18. In all these places the word refers to *future punishment*, and the declaration of the Saviour is that his followers, his true disciples, shall never be cast away. The original is expressed with remarkable strength: "They shall not be destroyed for ever." Syriac: "They shall not perish to eternity." This is spoken of all Christians—that is, of all who ever possess the character of true followers of Christ, and who can be called his flock. ¶ *Shall any.* The word *any* refers to any power that might *attempt* it. It will apply either to men or to devils. It is an affirmation that no man, however eloquent in error, or persuasive in infidelity, or cunning in argument, or mighty in rank; and that no devil with all his malice, power, cunning, or allurements, shall be able to pluck them from his hand. ¶ *Pluck them.* In the original to *rob;* to seize and bear away as a robber does his prey. Jesus holds them so secure and so certainly that no foe can *surprise* him as a robber does, or overcome him *by force.* ¶ *My hand.* The *hand* is that by which we *hold* or *secure* an object. It means that Jesus has them safely in his own care and keeping. Comp. Ro. viii. 38, 39.

29. *Which gave them me.* See ch. vi. 37. ¶ *Is greater.* Is more powerful. ¶ *Than all.* Than all others—men, angels, devils. The word includes *everything*—everything that could *attempt* to pluck them away from God; in other words, it means that God is *supreme.* It implies, farther, that God will keep them, and will so control *all* other beings and things that they shall be safe. ¶ *None is able.* None has power to do it. In these two verses we are taught the following important truths:

them me, is greater than all, and
no *man* is able to pluck *them* out
of my Father's hand.
30 I[e] and *my* Father are one.
31 Then[f] the Jews took up
stones again to stone him.
32 Jesus answered them, Many
good works have I showed you
from my Father; for which of
those works do ye stone me?
33 The Jews answered him,
saying, For a good work we stone

e ch.17.11,22. f ch.8.59.

1st. That Christians are *given* by God the Father to Christ. 2d. That *Jesus* gives to them eternal life, or *procures* by his death and intercession, and *imparts* to them by his Spirit, that religion which shall result in eternal life. 3d. That both the Father and the Son are pledged to keep them so that they shall never fall away and perish. It would be impossible for any language to teach more explicitly that the saints will persevere. 4th. That there is no power in man or devils to defeat the purpose of the Redeemer to save his people. We also see our safety, if we truly, humbly, cordially, and *daily* commit ourselves to God the Saviour. In no other way can we have evidence that we are his people than by such a persevering resignation of ourselves to him, to obey his law, and to follow him through evil report or good report. If we do that we are safe. If we do not that we have no evidence of piety, and are not, cannot be safe.

30. *I and* my *Father are one.* The word translated "one" is not in the *masculine*, but in the *neuter* gender. It expresses *union*, but not the precise nature of the union. It *may* express any union, and the particular kind intended is to be inferred from the connection. In the previous verse he had said that he and his Father were *united* in the same object—that is, in redeeming and preserving his people. It was *this* that gave occasion for this remark. Many interpreters have understood this as referring to union of design and of plan. The words may bear this construction. In this way they were understood by Erasmus, Calvin, Bucer, and others. Most of the Christian fathers understood them, however, as referring to the *oneness* or *unity of nature* between the Father and the Son; and that this was the design of Christ appears probable from the following considerations: 1st. The question in debate was not about his being united with the Father in *plan* and *counsel*, but in *power*. He affirmed that he was able to rescue and keep his people from *all* enemies, or that he had *power* superior to men and devils—that is, that he had *supreme* power over all creation. He affirmed the same of his Father. *In this*, therefore, they were *united*. But this was an attribute only of God, and they thus understood him as claiming equality to God in regard to *omnipotence*. 2d. The Jews understood him as affirming his equality with God, for they took up stones to punish him for blasphemy (ver. 31, 33), and they said *to him* that they understood him as affirming that he was God, ver. 33. 3d. Jesus did not *deny* that it was his intention to be so understood. See Notes on ver. 34–37. 4th. He *immediately* made another declaration implying the same thing, leaving the same impression, and which they attempted to punish in the same manner, ver. 37–39. If Jesus had not *intended* so to be understood, it cannot be easily reconciled with moral honesty that he did not distinctly *disavow* that such was his intention. The Jews were well acquainted with their own language. They understood him in this manner, and he left this impression on their minds.

31. *The Jews took up stones.* Stoning was the punishment of a blasphemer, Le. xxiv. 14–16. They considered him guilty of blasphemy because he made himself equal with God, ver. 33. ¶*Again.* They had before plotted against his life (ch. v. 16, 18), and once at least they had taken up stones to destroy him, ch. viii. 59.

32. *Many good works.* Many miracles of benevolence—healing the sick, &c. His miracles were *good works*, as they tended to promote the happiness of men, and were proofs of his benevolence. He had performed no other works than those of benevolence; he knew that they could charge him with no other, and he confidently appealed to *them* as witnesses of that. Happy would it be if all, when they are opposed and persecuted, could appeal even to their persecutors in proof of their own innocence.

33. *For blasphemy.* See Notes on Mat.

thee not; but for blasphemy; [g]and
because that thou, being a man,
makest thyself God.
34 Jesus answered them, Is it
not written in your law, I said,
Ye are gods?
35 If he called them gods, unto

g ch.5.18; ver.30; Ps.82.6; Ro.13.1.

whom the word of God came, and
the scripture cannot be broken;
36 Say ye of him, whom the
Father [h]hath sanctified and sent
into the world, Thou blasphemest;
because I said, [i]I am the Son of
God?

h Is.11.2,3; 49.1,3; ch.6.27. i Phi.2.6.

---

ix. 3. ¶ *Makest thyself God.* See Notes on ch. v. 18. This shows how *they* understood what he had said. ¶ *Makest thyself.* Dost *claim* to be God, or thy language implies this.

34–38. *Jesus answered them.* The answer of Jesus consists of two parts. The first (ver. 34–36) shows that *they* ought not to object to his use of the word God, *even if* he were no more than a man. The second (ver. 37, 38) repeats substantially what he had before said, left the same impression, and in proof of it he appealed to his works.

34. *In your law.* Ps. lxxxii. 6. The word *law* here, is used to include the Old Testament. ¶ *I said.* The Psalmist said, or God said by the Psalmist. ¶ *Ye are gods.* This was said of *magistrates* on account of the dignity and honour of their office, and it shows that the word translated "god" in that place *might* be applied to man. Such a use of the word is, however, rare. See instances in Ex. vii. 1; iv. 16.

35. *Unto whom the word of God came.* That is, who were his servants, or who received their dignity and honour *only* because the law of God was intrusted to them. The *word of God* here means the *command of God;* his commission to them to do justice. ¶ *The scripture cannot be broken.* See Mat. v. 19. The authority of the Scripture is final; it *cannot be set aside.* The meaning is, "If, therefore, the Scripture uses the word *god* as applied to magistrates, it settles the question that it is *right* to apply the term to those in office and authority. If applied to *them*, it may be to others in similar offices. It cannot, therefore, be *blasphemy* to use this word as applicable to a personage so much more exalted than mere magistrates as the Messiah."

36. *Whom the Father hath sanctified.* The word *sanctify* with us means to *make holy;* but this is not its meaning here, for the Son of God was always holy. The original word means to set apart from a common to a sacred use; to devote to a sacred purpose, and to designate or consecrate to a holy office. This is the meaning here. God has *consecrated* or appointed his Son to be his Messenger or Messiah to mankind. See Ex. xxviii. 41; xxix. 1, 44; Le. viii. 30. ¶ *And sent into the world.* As the Messiah, an office far more exalted than that of magistrates. ¶ *I am the Son of God.* This the Jews evidently understood as the same as saying that he was equal with God. This expression he had often applied to himself. The meaning of this place may be thus expressed: "You charge me with blasphemy. The foundation of that charge is the use of the name *God*, or the *Son of God*, applied to myself; yet *that same term* is applied in the Scriptures to magistrates. The use of it there shows that it is *right* to apply it to those who sustain important offices. And especially *you*, Jews, ought not to attempt to found a charge of blasphemy on the application of a word to the *Messiah* which in *your own Scriptures* is applied to *all* magistrates." And we may remark here, 1st. That Jesus did not deny that he meant to apply the term to himself. 2d. He did not deny that it was *properly* applied to him. 3d. He did not deny that it implied that he *was* God. He affirmed only that *they* were *inconsistent*, and *were not authorized* to bring a charge of blasphemy for the application of the *name* to himself.

37. *The works of my Father.* The very works that my Father does. See ch. v. 17: "My Father worketh hitherto, and I work." See the Note on that place. *The works of his Father* are those which God only can do. As Jesus *did* them, it shows that the *name* "*Son of God*," implying *equality* with God, was properly applied to him. This shows conclusively that he *meant* to be understood as claiming to be equal with God. So the Jews naturally understood him (ver. 39), and they were left with this impression on their minds.

38. *Believe the works.* Though you do

37 If[k] I do not the works of my
Father, believe me not.
38 But if I do, though ye believe
not me, believe the works; that ye
may know and believe that the
Father *is* in me, and I in him.
39 Therefore they sought again
to take him; but he escaped out of
their hand,
40 And went away again beyond
Jordan, into [l]the place where
John at first baptized; and there
he abode.
41 And many resorted unto him,
and said, John did no miracle; but
[m]all things that John spake of this
man were true.
42 And many believed on him
there.

CHAPTER XI.

NOW a certain *man* was sick,
named Lazarus, of Bethany,
the town of [a]Mary and her sister
Martha.
2 (It was *that* Mary [b]which
anointed the Lord with ointment,
and wiped his feet with her hair,
whose brother Lazarus was sick.)
3 Therefore his sisters sent unto

k ch.14.10,11; 15.24. l ch.1.28. m ch.3.30-36. a Lu.10.38,39. b Mar.14.3; ch.12.3.

---

not credit *me*, yet consider my *works*, for they prove that I came from God. No one could do them unless he was sent of God. ¶ *Father* is *in me*, &c. Most intimately connected. See Jn. v. 36. This expression denotes most intimate union—such as can exist in no other case. See Mat. xi. 27. Notes on Jn. xvii. 21.

39. *Sought again to take him.* They evidently understood him as still claiming equality with God, and under this impression Jesus left them. Nor can it be doubted that he *intended* to leave them with this impression; and if so, then he is divine. ¶ *He escaped.* See ch. viii. 59.

40. *Where John at first baptized.* At Bethabara, or Bethany, ch. i. 28.

41. *No miracle.* He did not confirm his mission by working *miracles*, but he showed that he was a *prophet* by foretelling the character and success of Jesus. Either miracle or prophecy is conclusive proof of a divine mission, for no man can foretell a future event, or work a miracle, except by the special aid of God. It may be remarked that the people of that place were properly prepared by the ministry of John for the preaching of Jesus. The persecution of the Jews was the occasion of his going there, and thus the wrath of man was made to praise him. It has commonly happened that the opposition of the wicked has resulted in the increased success of the cause which they have persecuted. God takes the wise in their own craftiness, and brings glory to himself and salvation to sinners out of the pride, and passions, and rage of wicked men.

CHAPTER XI.

1. *A certain* man *was sick.* The resurrection of Lazarus has been recorded only by John. Various reasons have been conjectured why the other evangelists did not mention so signal a miracle. The most probable is, that at the time they wrote Lazarus was still living. The miracle was well known, and yet to have recorded it might have exposed Lazarus to opposition and persecution from the Jews. See ch. xii. 10, 11. Besides, John wrote for Christians who were out of Palestine. The other gospels were written chiefly for those who were in Judea. There was the more need, therefore, that he should enter minutely into the account of the miracle, while the others did not deem it necessary or proper to record an event so well known. ¶ *Bethany.* A village on the eastern declivity of the Mount of Olives. See Notes on Mat. xxi. 1. ¶ *The town of Mary.* The place where she lived. At that place also lived Simon the leper (Mat. xxvi. 6), and there our Lord spent considerable part of his time when he was in Judea. The transaction recorded in this chapter occurred nearly four months after those mentioned in the previons chapter. Those occurred in December, and these at the approach of the Passover in April.

2. *It was* that *Mary*, &c. See Notes on Mat. xxvi. 6; Lu. vii. 36-50.

3. *Whom thou lovest*, ver. 5. The members of this family were among the few peculiar and intimate friends of our Lord. He was much with them, and showed them marks of special friendship (Lu. x. 38–42), and they bestowed upon him peculiar proofs of affection in

him, saying, Lord, behold, [c]he whom
thou lovest is sick.
4 When Jesus heard *that*, he said,
This sickness is not unto death,
but [d]for the glory of God, that
the Son of God might be glorified
thereby.
5 Now Jesus loved Martha, and
her sister, and Lazarus.
6 When he had heard, therefore,
that he was sick, he abode two
days still in the same place where
he was.
7 Then after that saith he to *his*
disciples, Let us go into Judea
again.
8 *His* disciples say unto him,
Master, the Jews [e]of late sought
to stone thee; and [f]goest thou
thither again?
9 Jesus answered, Are there not
twelve hours in the day? If[g] any
man walk in the day he stumbleth
not, because he seeth the light of
this world.

c He.12.6; Re.3.19. *d* ch.9.3; ver.40. *e* ch.10.31. *f* Ac.20.24. *g* ch.12.35.

return. This shows that *special* attachments are lawful for Christians, and that those friendships are peculiarly lovely which are tempered and sweetened with the spirit of Christ. *Friendships* should always be cemented by religion, and one main end of those attachments should be to aid one another in the great business of preparing to die. ¶ *Sent unto him.* They believed that he had power to heal him (ver. 21), though they did not *then* seem to suppose that he could raise him if he died. Perhaps there were two reasons why they sent for him; one, because they supposed he would be desirous of *seeing* his friend; the other, because they supposed he could restore him. In sickness we should implore the aid and presence of Jesus. He only can restore us and our friends; he only can perform for us the office of a friend when all other friends fail; and he only can cheer us with the hope of a blessed resurrection.

4. *This sickness is not unto death.* The word *death* here is equivalent to *remaining under death*, Ro. vi. 23: "The wages of sin is *death*"—permanent or unchanging death, opposed to *eternal* life. Jesus evidently did not intend to deny that he would die. The words which he immediately adds show that he would expire, and that he would raise him up to show forth the power and glory of God. Comp. ver. 11. Those words cannot be understood on any other supposition than that he *expected* to raise him up. The Saviour often used expressions similar to this to fix the attention on what he was about to say in explanation. The sense may be thus expressed: "His sickness is not *fatal*. It is not *designed* for his death, but to furnish an opportunity for a signal display of the glory of God, and to furnish a standing proof of the truth of religion. It is intended to exhibit the power of the Son of God, and to be a proof at once of the truth of his mission; of his friendship for this family; of his mild, tender, peculiar love as a man; of his power and glory as the Messiah; and of the great doctrine that the dead will rise. ¶ *For the glory of God.* That God may be honoured. See ch. ix. 3. ¶ *That the Son of God*, &c. The glory of God and of his Son is the same. That which promotes the one promotes also the other. Few things could do it more than the miracle which follows, evincing at once the lovely and tender character of Jesus as a man and a friend, and his power as the equal with God.

6. *He abode two days.* Probably Lazarus died soon after the messengers left him. Jesus knew that (ver. 11), and did not hasten to Judea, but remained two days longer where he was, that there might not be the possibility of doubt that he was dead, so that when he came there he had been dead four days, ver. 39. This shows, moreover, that he *intended* to raise him up. If he had not, it could hardly be reconciled with friendship thus to remain, without any reason, away from an afflicted family. ¶ *Where he was.* At Bethabara (ch. i. 28; x. 40), about 30 miles from Bethany. This was about a day's journey, and it renders it probable that Lazarus died soon after the message was sent. One day would be occupied before the message came to him; two days he remained; one day would be occupied by him in going to Bethany; so that Lazarus had been dead four days (ver. 39) when he arrived.

8. *Of late.* About four months before, ch. x. 31.

10 But if a man [h]walk in the night, he stumbleth, because there is no light in him.

11 These things said he; and after that he saith unto them, Our friend Lazarus [i]sleepeth; but I go that I may awake him out of sleep.

12 Then said his disciples, Lord, if he sleep, he shall do well.

13 Howbeit Jesus spake of his death; but they thought that he had spoken of taking of rest in sleep.

14 Then said Jesus unto them plainly, Lazarus is dead;

h Ec.2.14. *i* De.31.16; Ac.7.60; 1 Co.15.18,51.

9, 10. *Twelve hours.* The Jews divided the day from sunrise to sunset into twelve equal parts. A similar illustration our Saviour uses in ch. ix. 4, 5. See the Notes on that place. ¶ *If any man walk.* If any man *travels.* The illustration here is taken from a *traveller.* The conversation was respecting a *journey* into Judea, and our Lord, as was his custom, took the illustration from the case before him. ¶ *He stumbleth not.* He is able, having light, to make his journey safely. He sees the obstacles or dangers and can avoid them. ¶ *The light of this world.* The light by which the world is illuminated —that is, the light of the sun. ¶ *In the night.* In darkness he is unable to see danger or obstacles, and to avoid them. His journey is unsafe and perilous, or, in other words, it is not a proper time to travel. ¶ *No light in him.* He sees no light. It is dark; his eyes admit no light within him to direct his way. This description is figurative, and it is difficult to fix the meaning. Probably the intention was the following: 1st. Jesus meant to say that there was an allotted or appointed time for him to live and do his Father's will, represented here by the *twelve hours of the day.* 2d. Though his life was *nearly* spent, yet it was not entirely; a remnant of it was left. 3d. A traveller journeyed on till night. It was as proper for him to travel the *twelfth* hour as any other. 4th. So it was proper for Jesus to labour until the close. It was the proper time for him to work. The night of death was coming, and no work could then be done. 5th. God would defend him in this until the appointed time of his death. He had nothing to fear, therefore, in Judea from the Jews, until it was the will of God that he should die. He was safe in his hand, and he went fearlessly into the midst of his foes, trusting in him. This passage teaches us that we should be diligent to the end of life; fearless of enemies when we know that God requires us to labour, and confidently committing ourselves to Him who is able to shield us, and in whose hand, if we have a conscience void of offence, we are safe.

11. *Lazarus sleepeth.* Is dead. The word *sleep* is applied to death, 1st. Because of the *resemblance* between them, as sleep is the "*kinsman of death.*" In this sense it is often used by pagan writers. But, 2d. In the Scriptures it is used to intimate that death will not be *final:* that there will be an awaking out of this sleep, or a resurrection. It is a beautiful and tender expression, removing all that is dreadful in death, and filling the mind with the idea of calm repose after a life of toil, with a reference to a future resurrection in increased vigour and renovated powers. In this sense it is applied in the Scriptures usually to the saints, 1 Co. xi. 30; xv. 51; 1 Th. iv. 14; v. 10; Mat. ix. 24.

12. *If he sleep, he shall do well.* Sleep was regarded by the Jews, in sickness, as a favourable symptom; hence it was said among them, "Sleep in sickness is a sign of recovery, because it shows that the violence of the disease has abated" (Lightfoot). This seems to have been the meaning of the disciples. They intimated that if he had *this* symptom, there was no need of his going into Judea to restore him.

15. *I am glad,* &c. The meaning of this verse may be thus expressed: "If I had been there during his sickness, the entreaties of his sisters and friends would have prevailed with me to restore him to health. I could not have refused them without appearing to be unkind. Though a restoration to *health* would have been a miracle, and sufficient to convince you, yet the miracle of raising him after being four days dead will be far more impressive, and on that account I rejoice that an opportunity is thus given so strikingly to confirm your faith." ¶ *To the intent.* To furnish you *evidence* on which you might be

15 And I am glad for your sakes that I was not there, to the intent ye may believe; nevertheless, let us go unto him.

16 Then said Thomas, which is called Didymus, unto his fellow-disciples, Let us also go, that we may die with him.

17 Then when Jesus came, he found that he had *lain* in the grave four days already.

18 Now Bethany was nigh unto Jerusalem, [1]about fifteen furlongs off;

19 And many of the Jews came to Martha and Mary, [k]to comfort them concerning their brother.

20 Then Martha, as soon as she

[1] i.e. *about two miles.*
[k] 1 Ch.7.22; Job 2.11; 42.11; Ro.12.15; 1 Th.4.18.

established in the belief that I am the Messiah.

16. *Thomas, which is called Didymus.* These names express the same thing. One is Hebrew and the other Greek. The name means *a twin.* ¶ *Die with him.* It has been much doubted by critics whether the word *him* refers to Lazarus or to Jesus. They who refer it to *Lazarus* suppose this to be the meaning: "Let us go and die, for what have we to hope for if Jesus returns into Judea? Lately they attempted to stone him, and now they will put him to death, and *we* also, like Lazarus, shall be dead." This expression is supposed to be added by John to show the *slowness* with which Thomas believed, and his readiness to doubt without the fullest evidence. See ch. xx. 25. Others suppose, probably more correctly, that it refers to Jesus: "He is about to throw himself into danger. The Jews lately sought his life, and will again. They will put him to death. But let us not forsake him. Let us attend him and die with him." It may be remarked that this, not less than the other mode of interpretation, expresses the *doubts* of Thomas about the *miracle* which Jesus was about to work.

17. *In the grave.* It was sometimes the custom to *embalm* the dead, but in this case it does not seem to have been done. He was probably buried soon after death.

18. *Nigh unto Jerusalem.* This is added to show that it was easy for many of the Jews to come to the place. The news that Jesus was there, and the account of the miracle, would also be easily carried to the Sanhedrim. ¶ *Fifteen furlongs.* Nearly two miles. It was directly east from Jerusalem. Dr. Thomson (*The Land and the Book*, vol. ii. p. 599) says of Bethany: "It took half an hour to walk over Olivet to Bethany this morning, and the distance from the city, therefore, must be about two miles. This agrees with what John says: 'Now Bethany was nigh unto Jerusalem, about fifteen furlongs off.' The village is small, and appears never to have been large, but it is pleasantly situated near the south-eastern base of the mount, and has many fine trees about and above it. We, of course, looked at the remains of those old edifices which may have been built in the age of Constantine, and repaired or changed to a convent in the time of the Crusades. By the dim light of a taper we also descended very cautiously, by twenty-five slippery steps, to the reputed sepulchre of Lazarus, or El Azariyeh, as both tomb and village are now called. But I have no description of it to give, and no questions about it to ask. It is a wretched cavern, every way unsatisfactory, and almost disgusting."

19. *Many of the Jews.* Probably their distant relatives or their friends. ¶ *To comfort.* These visits of consolation were commonly extended to seven days (Grotius; Lightfoot).

20. *Then Martha,* &c. To Martha was intrusted the management of the affairs of the family, Lu. x. 40. It is probable that she first heard of his coming, and, without waiting to inform her sister, went immediately out to meet him. See ver. 28. ¶ *Sat* still *in the house.* The word *still* is not in the original. It means that she remained sitting in the house. The common posture of grief among the Jews was that of *sitting*, Job ii. 8; Eze. viii. 14. Often this grief was so excessive as to fix the person in astonishment, and render him immovable, or prevent his being affected by any external objects. It is possible that the evangelist meant to intimate this of Mary's grief. Comp. Ezr. ix. 3, 4; Ne. i. 4; Is. xlvii. 1.

22. *Whatsoever thou wilt ask of God.* Whatever is necessary to our consolation that thou wilt ask, thou canst ob-

heard that Jesus was coming, went
and met him; but Mary sat *still* in
the house.
21 Then said Martha unto Jesus,
Lord, if thou hadst been here, my
brother had not died.
22 But I know that even now,
whatsoever[l] thou wilt ask of God,
God will give *it* thee.
23 Jesus saith unto her, Thy
brother shall rise again.
24 Martha saith unto him, I know
that he shall rise again [m]in the
resurrection at the last day.
25 Jesus said unto her, I am
[n]the resurrection and [o]the life: he
that believeth in me, [p]though he
were dead, yet shall he live;
26 And [q]whosoever liveth and
believeth in me shall never die.
Believest thou this?
27 She saith unto him, Yea,
Lord; I believe that thou art
the Christ, the Son of God, which
should come into the world.
28 And when she had so said,
she went her way, and [r]called Mary
her sister secretly, saying, [s]The

l ch.9.31. *m* ch.5.29.

n ch.6.40,44. *o* Is.38.16; ch.14.6; 1 Jn.1.2. *p* Job 19.26; Is.26.19; Ro.4.17. *q* ch.3.15; 4.14. *r* ch.21.7. *s* ch.13.13.

tain. It is possible that she meant gently to intimate that he could raise him up and restore him again to them.

23. *Thy brother shall rise again.* Martha had spoken of the power of Jesus. He said nothing of *himself* in reply. It was not customary for him to speak of himself, unless it was demanded by necessity. It cannot be doubted that by *rising again*, here, Jesus referred to the act which he was about to perform; but as Martha understood it, referring to the future resurrection, it was full of consolation. The idea that departed friends shall rise to glory is one that fills the mind with joy, and one which we owe only to the religion of Christ.

24. *At the last day.* The day of judgment. Of this Martha was fully convinced; but this was not all which she desired. She in this manner delicately hinted what she did not presume expressly to declare—her wish that Jesus might even *now* raise him up.

25. *I am the resurrection.* I am the *author* or the *cause* of the resurrection. It so depends on my power and will, that it may be said that I *am* the resurrection itself. This is a most expressive way of saying that the whole doctrine of the resurrection came from him, and the whole power to effect it was his. In a similar manner he is said to be made of God unto us "*wisdom, and righteousness, and sanctification, and redemption*," 1 Co. i. 30. ¶ *And the life.* Jn. i. 4. As the resurrection of *all* depends on him, he intimated that it was not indispensable that it should be deferred to the *last day*. He had power to do it now as well as then. ¶ *Though he were dead.* Faith does not save from *temporal* death; but although the believer, as others, will die a temporal death, yet he will hereafter have life. *Even if he dies*, he shall hereafter live. ¶ *Shall he live.* Shall be restored to life in the resurrection.

26. *Whosoever liveth.* He had just spoken of the prospects of the pious dead. He now says that the same prospects are before the living who have like faith. Greek, "Every one living and believing on me." ¶ *Shall never die.* As the dead, though dead, shall yet *live*, so the living shall have the same kind of life. They shall never come into eternal death. See ch. vi. 50, 51, 54, 58. Greek, "Shall by no means die for ever." ¶ *Believest thou this?* This question was doubtless asked because it implied that he was then able to raise up Lazarus, and because it was a proper time for her to test her own faith. The time of affliction is a favourable period to try ourselves to ascertain whether we have faith. If we still have confidence in God, if we look to him for comfort in such seasons, it is good evidence that we are his friends. He that loves God when he takes away his comforts, has the best evidence possible of true attachment to him.

27. *Yea, Lord.* This was a noble confession. It showed her full confidence in him as the Messiah, and her full belief that all that he said was true. See Mat. xvi. 16.

28. *She went her way.* Jesus probably directed her to go, though the evangelist has not recorded it, for she said to Mary, *The Master calleth for thee.* ¶ *Secretly.* Privately. So that the others did not hear her. This was done, per-

Master is come, and [t] calleth for
thee.
29 As soon as she heard *that*, she
arose quickly and came unto him.
30 Now Jesus was not yet come
into the town, but was in that
place where Martha met him.
31 The[u] Jews, then, which were
with her in the house, and comforted her, when they saw Mary
that she rose up hastily and went
out, followed her, saying, She goeth
unto the grave, to weep there.
32 Then when Mary was come
where Jesus was, and saw him, she
fell down at his feet, saying unto
him, [v] Lord, if thou hadst been
here, my brother had not died.
33 When Jesus therefore saw
her weeping, and the Jews also
weeping which came with her,
he groaned in the spirit and [2] was
troubled,
34 And said, Where have ye
laid him? They say unto him,
Lord, come and see.
35 Jesus[w] wept.

t Mar.10.49. *u* ver.19.

v ch.4.49; ver.21,37. [2] *he troubled himself.*
w Is.63.9; Lu.19.41; He.2.16,17.

haps, to avoid confusion, or because it was probable that if they knew Jesus was coming they would have made opposition. Perhaps she doubted whether Jesus desired it to be known that he had come. ¶ *The Master is come.* This appears to have been the appellation by which he was known to the family. It means, literally, *teacher*, and was a title which he claimed for himself: "One is your Master, even Christ," Mat. xxiii. 8, 10. The Syriac has it, "*Our* Master."

31. *Saying, She goeth unto the grave.* Syriac, "They *thought* that she went to weep." They had not heard Martha call her. The first days of mourning among the Jews were observed with great solemnity and many ceremonies of grief.

33. *He groaned in the spirit.* The word rendered *groaned*, here, commonly denotes to be angry or indignant, or to reprove severely, denoting violent agitation of mind. Here it also evidently denotes violent agitation — not from *anger*, but from *grief*. He saw the sorrow of others, and he was also moved with sympathy and love. The word *groan* usually, with us, denotes an *expression* of internal sorrow by a peculiar sound. The word here, however, does not mean that *utterance* was given to the internal emotion, but that it was deep and agitating, though internal. ¶ *In the spirit.* In the mind. See Ac. xix. 21: "Paul purposed *in the spirit*"—that is, in his mind, Mat. v. 3. ¶ *Was troubled.* Was affected with grief. Perhaps this expression denotes that his countenance was troubled, or gave indications of sorrow (Grotius).

34. *Where have ye laid him?* Jesus spoke as a man. In all this transaction he manifested the deep sympathies of a man; and though he who could raise the dead man up could also know where he was, yet he chose to lead them to the grave by inducing them to point the way, and hence he asked this question.

35. *Jesus wept.* It has been remarked that this is the shortest verse in the Bible; but it is exceedingly important and tender. It shows the Lord Jesus as a friend, a tender friend, and evinces his character as a man. And from this we learn, 1st. That the most tender personal friendship is not inconsistent with the most pure religion. Piety binds stronger the ties of friendship, makes more tender the emotions of love, and seals and sanctifies the affections of friends. 2d. It is right, it is natural, it is indispensable for the Christian to sympathize with others in their afflictions. Ro. xii. 15: "Rejoice with them that do rejoice, and weep with them that weep." 3d. Sorrow at the death of friends is not improper. It is right to weep. It is the expression of nature, and religion does not forbid or condemn it. All that religion does in the case is to *temper* and chasten our grief; to teach us to mourn with submission to God; to weep without murmuring, and to seek to banish tears, not by *hardening the heart* or forgetting the friend, but by bringing the soul, made tender by grief, to receive the sweet influences of religion, and to find calmness and peace in the God of all consolation. 4th. We have here an instance of the tenderness of the character of Jesus. The same Saviour *wept* over Jerusalem, and felt deeply for poor dying sinners. To the same tender and compassionate Saviour Christians may now come (He. iv. 15);

36 Then said the Jews, Behold, how he loved him!

37 And some of them said, Could not this man, [x]which opened the eyes of the blind, have caused that even this man should not have died?

38 Jesus therefore, again groaning in himself, cometh to the grave. It was a cave, and a stone lay upon it.

39 Jesus said, [y]Take ye away the stone. Martha, the sister of him that was dead, saith unto him, Lord, [z]by this time he stinketh; for he hath been *dead* four days.

40 Jesus saith unto her, [a]Said I not unto thee, that if thou wouldest believe, thou shouldest see the glory of God?

41 Then they took away the stone *from the place* where the dead was laid. And Jesus lifted up *his* eyes, and said, [b]Father, I thank thee that thou hast heard me.

42 And I knew that thou hearest me always; but because of the people which stand by, I said *it*, that they may believe that thou hast sent me.

43 And when he thus had spoken, he cried with a loud voice, Lazarus, come forth!

x ch.9.6. *y* Mar.16.3. *z* Ps.49.7,9; Ac.2.27. *a* ver.4,23. *b* ch.12.28-30.

---

and to him the penitent sinner may also come, knowing that he will not cast him away.

38. *It was a cave.* This was a common mode of burial. See Notes on Mat. viii. 28. ¶ *A stone lay upon it.* Over the mouth of the cave. See Mat. xxvii. 60.

39. *Four days.* This proves that there could be no deception, for it could not have been a case of suspended animation. All these circumstances are mentioned to show that there was no imposture. Impostors do not mention minute *circumstances* like these. They deal in *generals* only. Every part of this narrative bears the marks of truth.

40. *Said I not unto thee.* This was *implied* in what he had said about the resurrection of her brother, ver. 23–25. There would be a manifestation of the glory of God in raising him up which *she* would be permitted, with all others, to behold. ¶ *The glory of God.* The power and goodness displayed in the resurrection. It is probable that Martha did not really expect that Jesus would raise him up, but supposed that he went there merely to see the corpse. Hence, when he directed them to take away the stone, she suggested that by that time the body was offensive.

41. *Lifted up* his *eyes.* In an attitude of prayer. See Lu. xviii. 13; Mat. xiv. 19. ¶ *I thank thee that thou hast heard me.* It is possible that John has recorded only the sum or substance of the prayer on this occasion. The thanks which Jesus renders here are evidently in view of the fact that power had been committed to him to raise up Lazarus. On account of the people, and the signal proof which would be furnished of the truth of his mission, he expressed his thanks to God. In all his doings he recognized his *union* to the Father, and his dependence on him as Mediator.

42. *And I knew.* "As for me. So far as *I* am concerned. I had no anxiety, no doubt as to myself, that I should always be heard; but the particular ground of gratitude is the benefit that will result to those who are witnesses." Jesus never prayed in vain. He never attempted to work a miracle in vain; and in all his miracles the ground of his joy was, not that *he* was to be praised or honoured, but that *others* were to be benefited and God glorified.

43. *A loud voice.* Greek, "A *great* voice." Syriac, "A *high* voice." This was distinctly asserting *his* power. He uttered a distinct, audible voice, that there might be no suspicion of charm or *incantation.* The ancient magicians and jugglers performed their wonders by whispering and muttering. See Notes on Is. viii. 19. Jesus spake openly and audibly, and asserted thus his power. So, also, in the day of judgment he will call the dead with a *great sound* of a trumpet, Mat. xxiv. 31; 1 Th. iv. 16. ¶ *Lazarus, come forth!* Here we may remark, 1st. That Jesus did this by his own power. 2d. The power of raising the dead is the highest of which we can conceive. The ancient heathen declared it to be even beyond the power of God. It implies not merely giving life to the deceased body, but the power of enter-

44 And[c] he that was dead came forth, bound hand and foot with grave-clothes; and [d]his face was bound about with a napkin. Jesus saith unto them, Loose him, and let him go.

45 Then many of the Jews which came to Mary, and [e]had seen the

c 1 Ki.17.22; 2 Ki.4.34,35; Lu.7.14,15; Ac.20.9-12. d ch.20.7.

e ch.2.23; 10.41,42; 12.11,18.

ing the world of spirits, of recalling the departed soul, and of reuniting it with the body. He that could do this must be omniscient as well as omnipotent; and if Jesus did it by his own power, it proves that he was divine. 3d. This is a striking illustration of the general resurrection. In the same manner Jesus will raise *all* the dead. This miracle shows that it is possible; shows the way in which it will be done—by the voice of the Son of God; and demonstrates the certainty that he will do it. Oh how important it is that *we* be prepared for that moment when his voice shall be heard in *our* silent tombs, and he shall call *us* forth again to life!

44. *He that was dead.* The same man, body and soul. ¶ *Bound hand and foot.* It is not certain whether the whole body and limbs were bound together, or each limb separately. When they embalmed a person, the whole body and limbs were *swathed* or bound together by strips of linen, involved around it to keep together the aromatics with which the body was embalmed. This is the condition of Egyptian mummies. See Ac. v. 6. But it is not certain that this was always the mode. Perhaps the body was simply involved in a winding-sheet. The custom still exists in western Asia. No coffins being used, the body itself is more carefully and elaborately wrapped and swathed than is common or desirable where coffins are used. In this method the body is stretched out and the arms laid straight by the sides, after which the whole body, from head to foot, is wrapped round tightly in many folds of linen or cotton cloth; or, to be more precise, a great length of cloth is taken and rolled around the body until the whole is enveloped, and every part is covered with several folds of the cloth. The ends are then sewed, to keep the whole firm and compact; or else a narrow bandage is wound over the whole, forming, ultimately, the exterior surface. The body, when thus enfolded and swathed, retains the profile of the human form; but, as in the Egyptian mummies, the legs are not folded separately, but together; and the arms also are not distinguished, but confined to the sides in the general envelope. Hence it would be clearly impossible for a person thus treated to move his arms or legs, if restored to existence.

The word rendered "grave-clothes" denotes also the bands or clothes in which new-born infants are involved. He went forth, but his walking was impeded by the bands or clothes in which he was involved. ¶ *And his face,* &c. This was a common thing when they buried their dead. See ch. xx. 7. It is not known whether the whole face was covered in this manner, or only the forehead. In the Egyptian mummies it is only the forehead that is thus bound. ¶ *Loose him.* Remove the bandages, so that he may walk freely. The effect of this miracle is said to have been that many believed on him. It may be remarked in regard to it that there could not be a more striking proof of the divine mission and power of Jesus. There could be here no possibility of deception. 1st. The friends of Lazarus *believed* him to be dead. In this they could not be deceived. There *could* have been among them no design to deceive. 2d. He was four days dead. It could not be a case, therefore, of suspended animation. 3d. Jesus was at a distance at the time of his death. There was, therefore, no *agreement* to attempt to impose on others. 4th. No higher power can be conceived than that of raising the dead. 5th. It was not *possible* to impose on his sisters, and to convince them that he was restored to life, if it was not really so. 6th. There were *many* present who were convinced also. God had so ordered it in his providence that to this miracle there should be many witnesses. There was no concealment, no jugglery, no secrecy. It was done publicly, in open day, and was witnessed by many who followed them to the grave, ver. 31. 7th. Others, who saw it, and did not believe that Jesus was the Messiah, went and told it to the Pharisees. But they did not *deny* that Jesus had raised up Lazarus. They could not deny it. The very ground of their alarm—the very *reason* why they went—was that he had *actually done it.*

things which Jesus did, believed on him.
46 But some of them went their ways to the Pharisees, and told them what things Jesus had done.
47 Then[f] gathered the chief priests and the Pharisees a council, and said, [g]What do we? for this man doeth many miracles.
48 If we let him thus alone, [h]all *men* will believe on him; and the Romans shall come, and take away both our place and nation.
49 And one of them, [i]*named*

f Ps.2.2.

g Ac.4.16. *h* ch.12.19. *i* Lu.3.2; ch.18.14; Ac.4.6.

Nor did the Pharisees dare to call the fact in question. If they *could* have done it, they would. But it was not possible; for, 8th. Lazarus was yet alive (ch. xii. 10), and the fact of his resurrection could not be denied. Every circumstance in this account is plain, simple, consistent, bearing all the marks of truth. But if Jesus performed this miracle his religion is true. God would not give such power to an impostor; and unless it can be *proved* that this account is false, the Christian religion *must be* from God.

46. *Some of them*, &c. We see here the different effect which the word and works of God will have on different individuals. Some are converted and others are hardened; yet the *evidence* of this miracle was as clear to the one as the other. But they *would not* be convinced.

47. *A council.* A meeting of the Sanhedrim, or great council of the nation. See Notes on Mat. ii. 4. They claimed the right of regulating all the affairs of religion. See Notes on Jn. i. 19. ¶ *What do we?* What measures are we taking to arrest the progress of his sentiments? ¶ *For this man doeth many miracles.* If they admitted that he performed *miracles*, it was clear what they *ought* to do. They should have received him as the Messiah. It may be asked, If they really believed that he worked miracles, why did they not believe on him? To this it may be replied that they did not doubt that *impostors* might work miracles. See Mat. xxiv. 24. To this opinion they were led, probably, by the wonders which the magicians performed in Egypt (Ex. vii., viii.), and by the passage in De. xiii. 1. As they regarded the tendency of the doctrines of Jesus to draw off the people from the worship of God, and from keeping his law (ch. ix. 16), they did not suppose themselves bound to follow him, even *if he did* work miracles.

48. *All* men. That is, all men among the Jews. The whole nation. ¶ *And the Romans shall come.* They were then subject to the Romans—tributary and dependent. Whatever privileges they had they held at the will of the Roman emperor. They believed, or feigned to believe, that Jesus was intending to set up a *temporal* kingdom. As he claimed to be the Messiah, so they supposed, of course, that he designed to be a temporal prince, and they professed to believe that this claim was, *in fact*, hostility to the Roman emperor. They supposed that it would involve the nation in war if he was not arrested, and that the effect would be that they would be vanquished and destroyed. It was on this charge that they at last arraigned him before Pilate, Lu. xxiii. 2, 3. ¶ *Will take away.* This expression means to *destroy*, to ruin, to overthrow, Lu. viii. 12; Ac. vi. 13, 14. ¶ *Our place.* This probably refers to the *temple*, Ac. vi. 13, 14. It was called "*the place*" by way of eminence, as being the chief or principal place on earth—being the seat of the peculiar worship of God. This place *was* utterly destroyed by the Romans. See Notes on Mat. xxiv. ¶ *And nation.* The nation or *people* of the Jews.

49. *Caiaphas.* See Notes on Lu. iii. 2. ¶ *Being high-priest that same year.* It is probable that the office of high-priest was at first for life, if there was no conduct that rendered the person unworthy the office. In that case the incumbent was removed. Thus Abiathar was removed by Solomon, 1 Ki. ii. 27. Subsequently the kings, and especially the conquerors of Judea, claimed and exercised the right of removing the high-priest at pleasure, so that, in the time of the Romans, the office was held but a short time. (See the Chronological Table at the end of this volume.) Caiaphas held the office about ten years. ¶ *Ye know nothing at all.* That is, you know nothing respecting the subject under consideration. You are fools to *hesitate* about so plain a case. It is probable that there was a party, even in

Caiaphas, being the high-priest that same year, said unto them, Ye know nothing at all,

50 Nor consider that [k]it is expedient for us that one man should die for the people, and that the whole nation perish not.

51 And this spake he not of himself; but, being high-priest that year, he prophesied that Jesus should die for that nation;

k Lu.24.46.

---

the Sanhedrim, that was secretly in favour of Jesus as the Messiah. Of that party Nicodemus was certainly one. See ch. iii. 1; vii. 50, 51; xi. 45; xii. 42: "Among the chief rulers, also, many believed on him," &c.

50. *It is expedient for us.* It is *better* for us. Literally, "It is *profitable* for us." ¶ *That one man should die.* Jesus they regarded as promoting sedition, and as exposing the nation, if he was successful, to the vengeance of the Romans, ver. 48. If *he* was put to death they supposed *the people* would be safe. This is all, doubtless, that he meant by his dying for the people. He did not *himself* intend to speak of his dying as an *atonement* or a *sacrifice;* but his *words* might also express that, and, though he was unconscious of it, he was expressing a *real truth.* In the sense in which *he* intended it there was no truth in the observation, nor occasion for it, but in the sense which the words *might convey* there was *real* and most important truth. It *was* expedient, it was infinitely desirable, that Jesus should die for that people, and for all others, to save them from perishing.

51. *Not of himself.* Though he uttered what proved to be a *true prophecy*, yet it was accomplished in a way which *he* did not intend. He had a wicked design. He was plotting murder and crime. Yet, wicked as he was, and little as he intended it, God so ordered it that he delivered a most precious truth respecting the atonement. Remark, 1st. God may fulfil the words of the wicked in a manner which they do not wish or intend. 2d. He may make even *their* malice and wicked plots the very means of accomplishing his purposes. What they regard as the fulfilment of *their* plans God may make the fulfilment of *his*, yet so as directly to overthrow *their* designs, and prostrate *them* in ruin. 3d. Sinners should tremble and be afraid when they lay plans against God, or seek to do unjustly to others. ¶ *Being high-priest that year.* It is not to be supposed that Caiaphas was a *true prophet*, or was conscious of the meaning which John has affixed to his words; but his words *express* the truth about the atonement of Jesus, and John records it *as a remarkable circumstance* that the high-priest of the nation should unwittingly deliver a sentiment which turned out to be the truth about the death of Jesus. Great importance was attached to the opinion of the high-priest by the Jews, because it was by him that the judgment by Urim and Thummim was formerly declared in cases of importance and difficulty, Nu. xxvii. 21. It is not certain or probable that the high-priest ever was endowed with the gift of prophecy; but he sustained a high office, the authority of his name was great, and it was thence remarkable that he uttered a declaration which the result showed to be *true*, though not in the sense that he intended. ¶ *He prophesied.* He uttered words which proved to be prophetic; or he expressed at that time a sentiment which turned out to be true. It does not mean that he was *inspired*, or that he deserved to be ranked among the true prophets; but his words were such that they accurately expressed a future event. The word *prophecy* is to be taken here not in the strict sense, but in a sense which is not uncommon in the sacred writers. Ac. xxi. 9: "And the same man had four daughters, virgins, which did *prophesy*." See Notes on Ro. xii. 6; 1 Co. xiv. 1; comp. Mat. xxvi. 68; Lu. xxii. 64. ¶ *That Jesus should die.* Die in the *place* of men, or as an atonement for sinners. This is evidently the meaning which John attaches to the words. ¶ *For that nation.* For the Jews. As a sacrifice for their sins. In no other sense whatever could it be said that he died for them. His death, so far from *saving* them in the sense in which the high-priest understood it, was the very occasion of their destruction. They invoked the vengeance of God when they said, "His blood be on us and on our children" (Mat. xxvii. 25), and all these calamities came upon them because they *would*

52 And [l]not for that nation only, but that also he should gather together in one the children of God that were [m]scattered abroad.

53 Then from that day forth they[n] took counsel together for to put him to death.

54 Jesus therefore walked no more [o]openly among the Jews, but went thence into a country near to the wilderness, into a city called Ephraim,[p] and there continued with his disciples.

55 And[q] the Jews' passover was nigh at hand; and many went out of the country up to Jerusalem before the passover to purify themselves.

56 Then[r] sought they for Jesus, and spake among themselves as they stood in the temple, What think ye, that he will not come to the feast?

57 Now both the chief priests and the Pharisees had given a commandment, that if any man knew where he were, he should show *it*, that they might take him.

l Is.49.6; Ro.3.29; 1 Jn.2.2. m ch.10.16; Ep.2.14-17. n Ps.109.4,5. o ch.7.1; 18.20. p 2 Sa.13.23; 2 Ch.13.19. q ch.2.13; 5.1; 6.4.

r ch.5.16,18; ver.8.

not come to him and be saved—that is, because they rejected him and put him to death, Mat. xxiii. 37-39.

52. *Should gather together in one.* All his chosen among the Jews and Gentiles. See ch. x. 16. ¶ *The children of God.* This is spoken not of those who *were then* Christians, but of all whom God should bring to him; all who *would be*, in the mercy of God, called, chosen, sanctified among all nations, ch. x. 16.

53. *They took counsel.* The judgment of the high-priest silenced opposition, and they began to devise measures to put him to death without exciting tumult among the people. Comp. Mat. xxvi. 5.

54. *No more openly.* No more publicly, in the cities and towns. Jesus never exposed his life unnecessarily to hazard. Although the time of his death was determined in the counsel of God, yet this did not prevent his using proper means to preserve his life. ¶ *The wilderness.* See Notes on Mat. iii. 1. ¶ *A city called Ephraim.* This was probably a small town in the tribe of Ephraim, about five miles west of Jericho.

55. *Jews' passover.* See Notes on Mat. xxvi. 2-17. Its being called the *Jews'* Passover shows that John wrote this gospel among people who were not Jews, and to whom it was necessary, therefore, to explain their customs. ¶ *To purify themselves.* This purifying consisted in preparing themselves for the proper observation of the Passover, according to the commands of the law. If any were defiled in any manner by contact with the dead or by any other ceremonial uncleanness, they were required to take the prescribed measures for purification, Le. xxii. 1-6. For want of this, great inconvenience was sometimes experienced. See 2 Ch. xxx. 17, 18. Different periods were necessary in order to be cleansed from ceremonial pollution. For example, one who had been polluted by the touch of a dead body, of a sepulchre, or by the bones of the dead, was sprinkled on the third and seventh days, by a clean person, with hyssop dipped in water mixed in the ashes of the red heifer. After washing his body and clothes he was then clean. These persons who went up *before* the Passover were doubtless those who had in some manner been ceremonially polluted.

56. *Will not come to the feast?* They doubted whether he would come. On the one hand, it was required by law that all males should come. On the other, his coming was attended with great danger. This was the cause of their doubting. It was in this situation that our Saviour, like many of his followers, was called to act. Danger was on the one hand, and duty on the other. He chose, as all should, to do his duty, and leave the event with God. He preferred to do it, though he *knew* that death was to be the consequence; and we should not shrink, when we have reason to apprehend danger, persecution, or death, from an honest attempt to observe all the commandments of God.

CHAPTER XII.

1. *Then Jesus came to Bethany.* This was near to Jerusalem, and it was from

CHAPTER XII.

THEN Jesus, six days before the passover, came to Bethany, where [a]Lazarus was which had been dead, whom he raised from the dead.

2 There they made him a supper, and [b]Martha served; but Lazarus was one of them that sat at the table with him.

3 Then[c] took Mary a pound of ointment of spikenard, very costly, and anointed the feet of Jesus, and wiped his feet with her hair; and the house was filled with the odour of the ointment.

4 Then saith one of his disciples, Judas Iscariot, Simon's *son*, which should betray him,

5 Why was not this ointment sold for three hundred pence, and given to the poor?

6 This he said, not that he cared for the poor, but because [d]he was a thief, and [e]had the bag, and bare what was put therein.

a ch.11.1,43. b Lu.10.38-42. c Mat.26.6,&c.; Mar.14.3,&c.; ch.11.2.

d 2 Ki.5.20-27; Ps.50.18. e ch.13.29.

---

this place that he made his triumphant entry into the city. See Notes on Mat. xxi. 1

2-8. See this passage explained in the Notes on Mat. xxvi. 3-16.

2. *A supper.* At the house of Simon the leper, Mat. xxvi. 6. ¶ *Lazarus was*, &c. The names of Martha and Lazarus are mentioned because it was not in their own house, but in that of Simon. Lazarus is particularly mentioned, since it was so remarkable that one who had been once dead should be enjoying again the endearments of friendship. This shows, also, that his resurrection was no illusion—that he was *really* restored to the blessings of life and friendship. Calmet thinks that this was about two months after his resurrection, and it is the last that we hear of him. How long he lived is unknown, nor is it recorded that he made any communication about the world of spirits. It is remarkable that none who have been restored to life from the dead have made any communications respecting that world. See Lu. xvi. 31, and Notes on 2 Co. xii. 4.

4. *Which should betray him.* Greek, "who was to betray him"—that is, who *would* do it.

5. *Three hundred pence.* About forty dollars, or £8, 10*s*. ¶ *And given to the poor.* The *avails* or value of it given to the poor.

6. *Had the bag.* The word translated *bag* is compounded of two words, meaning "tongue," and "to keep or preserve." It was used to denote the bag in which musicians used to keep the *tongues* or reeds of their pipes when travelling. Hence it came to mean any bag or purse in which travellers put their money or their most precious articles. The disciples appear to have had such a bag or purse in common, in which they put whatever money they had, and which was designed especially for the poor, Lu. viii. 3; Mat. xxviii. 55; Ac. ii. 44. The keeping of this, it seems, was intrusted to Judas; and it is remarkable that the only one among them who appears to have been naturally avaricious should have received this appointment. It shows us that every man is tried according to his native propensity. This is the object of trial—to bring out man's native character; and every man will find *opportunity* to do evil according to his native disposition, if he is inclined to it. ¶ *And bare*, &c. The word translated *bare* means literally to *carry* as a burden. Then it means to *carry away*, as in Jn. xx. 15: "If thou hast *borne* him hence." Hence it means to carry away *as a thief does*, and this is evidently its meaning here. It has this sense often in classic writers. Judas was a *thief*, and *stole* what was put into the bag. The money he desired to be intrusted to him, that he might secretly enrich himself. It is clear, however, that the disciples did not at this time *know* that this was his character, or they would have remonstrated against him. They learned it afterward. We may learn here, 1st. That it is not a new thing for members of the church to be covetous. Judas was so before them. 2d. That *such* members will be those who complain of the *great waste* in spreading the gospel. 3d. That this deadly, mean, and grovelling passion will work all evil in a church. It brought down the curse of God on the children of Israel in the case of Achan (Jos. vii.), and it betrayed our Lord to death. It

7 Then said Jesus, Let her alone;
against the day of my burying
hath she kept this.
8 For[f] the poor always ye have
with you, but [g]me ye have not always.
9 Much people of the Jews therefore knew that he was there; and
they came not for Jesus' sake
only, but that they might see Lazarus also, whom he had raised from
the dead.
10 But the chief priests consulted
that they might [h]put Lazarus also
to death;
11 Because[i] that by reason of
him many of the Jews went away
and believed on Jesus.
12 On[k] the next day, much people that were come to the feast,
when they heard that Jesus was
coming to Jerusalem,
13 Took branches of palm-trees,
and went forth to meet him, and
cried, [l]Hosanna! Blessed *is* the
King of Israel, that cometh in the
name of the Lord!
14 And Jesus, when he had found
a young ass, sat thereon; as it is
written,
15 Fear[m] not, daughter of Sion.
Behold, thy King cometh, sitting
on an ass's colt.
16 These [n]things understood not
his disciples at the first; but [o]when
Jesus was glorified, then [p]remem-
bered they that these things were
written of him, and *that* they had
done these things unto him.
17 The people, therefore, that
was with him when he called Lazarus out of his grave, and raised
him from the dead, bare record.
18 For[q] this cause the people
also met him, for that they heard
that he had done this miracle.
19 The Pharisees therefore said
among themselves, [r]Perceive ye
how ye prevail nothing? behold,
the world is gone after him.
20 And there were [s]certain

f De.15.11; Mat.26.11; Mar.14.7.
g Ca.5.6; ch.8.21; ver.35; ch.13.33; 16.5-7.
h Lu.16.31. i ch.11.45; ver.18.
k Mat.21.8,&c.; Mar.11.8,&c.; Lu.19.36,&c.
l Ps.118.25,26.
m Zec.9.9. n Lu.18.34. o ch.7.39.
p ch.14.26. q ver.11.
r ch.11.47,48. s Ac.17.4; Ro.1.16.

has often since brought blighting on the church; and many a time it has *betrayed* the cause of Christ, and drowned men in destruction and perdition, 1 Ti. vi. 9.

10. *That they might put Lazarus also to death.* When men are determined not to believe the gospel, there is no end to the crimes to which they are driven. Lazarus was alive, and the evidence of his resurrection was so clear that they could not resist it. They could neither deny it, nor prevent its effect on the people. As it was determined to kill Jesus, so they consulted about the propriety of removing Lazarus first, that the number of his followers might be lessened, and that the death of Jesus might make less commotion. Unbelief stops at no crime. Lazarus was innocent; they could bring no charge against him; but they deliberately plotted *murder* rather than believe on the Lord Jesus Christ.

12–19. See this passage explained in the Notes on Mat. xxi. 1–16. Also Mar. xi. 1–11; Lu. xix. 29–44.

16. *Was glorified.* Was raised from the dead, and had ascended to heaven.

17. *Bare record.* Testified that he had raised him, and, as was natural, spread the report through the city. This excited much attention, and the people came out in multitudes to meet one who had power to work such miracles.

19. *Prevail nothing.* All your efforts are ineffectual to stop the progress of his opinions, and to prevent the people from believing on him. ¶ *The world.* As we should say, "Everybody—all the city has gone out." The fact that he met with such success induced them to hasten their design of putting him to death, ch. xi. 53.

20. *Certain Greeks.* In the original, "some Hellenists"—the name commonly given to the Greeks. The same name was commonly used by the Jews to denote *all* the pagan nations, because most of those whom they knew spoke the Greek language, Jn. vii. 34; Ro. i. 16; ii. 9, 10; iii. 9. "Jews and Greeks." The Syriac translates this place, "Some

Greeks among [t]them that came up
to worship at the feast:
21 The same came therefore [u]to
Philip, which *was* of Bethsaida of
Galilee, and desired him, saying,
Sir, we would see Jesus.
22 Philip cometh and telleth
Andrew; and again Andrew and
Philip tell Jesus.
23 And Jesus answered them,
saying, [v]The hour is come that the
Son of man should be glorified.
24 Verily, verily, I say unto you,
Except a corn of wheat [w]fall into

t 1 Ki.8.41,42. *u* ch.1.44. *v* ch.13.32; 17.1. *w* 1 Co.15.36.

---

of the Gentiles." There are three opinions in regard to these persons: 1st. That they were *Jews* who spoke the Greek language, and dwelt in some of the Greek cities. It is known that Jews were scattered in Asia Minor, Greece, Macedonia, Egypt, &c., in all which places they had synagogues. See Notes on ch. vii. 35. 2d. That they were *proselytes* from the Greeks. 3d. That they were still Gentiles and idolaters, who came to bring offerings to Jehovah to be deposited in the temple. Lightfoot has shown that the surrounding pagans were accustomed not only to send presents, sacrifices, and offerings to the temple, but that they also frequently attended the great feasts of the Jews. Hence the outer court of the temple was called *the court of the Gentiles.* Which of these opinions is the correct one cannot be determined.

21. *Bethsaida of Galilee.* See Notes on ch. i. 44. ¶ *Would see Jesus.* It is probable that the word *see*, here, implies also a desire to converse with him, or to hear his doctrine about the nature of his kingdom. They had seen or heard of his triumphal entry into Jerusalem, and, either by curiosity or a desire to be instructed, they came and interceded with his disciples that they might be permitted to see him. In this there was nothing wrong. Christ made the *curiosity* of Zaccheus the means of his conversion, Lu. xix. 1-9. If we wish to find the Saviour, we must seek for him and take the proper means.

22. *Telleth Andrew.* Why he did not at once tell Jesus is not known. Possibly he was doubtful whether Jesus would wish to converse with *Gentiles*, and chose to consult with Andrew about it. ¶ *Tell Jesus.* Whether the Greeks were with them cannot be determined. From the following discourse it would seem probable that they were, or at least that Jesus admitted them to his presence and delivered the discourse to them.

23. *The hour is come.* The *time* is come. The word *hour* commonly means a definite part or a division of a day; but it also is used to denote a brief period, and a *fixed, definite, determined* time. It is used in this sense here. The appointed, fixed time is come—that is, is so near at hand that it may be said *to be come.* ¶ *The Son of man.* This is the favourite title which Jesus gives to himself, denoting his union with man, and the interest he felt in his welfare. The title is used here rather than "The Son of God," because as a *man* he had been humble, poor, and despised; but the time had come when, as a man, he was to receive the appropriate honours of the Messiah. ¶ *Be glorified.* Be honoured in an appropriate way--that is, by the testimony which God would give to him at his death, by his resurrection, and by his ascension to glory. See ch. vii. 39.

24. *Verily, verily.* An expression denoting the great importance of what he was about to say. We cannot but admire the wisdom by which he introduces the subject of his death. They had seen his triumph. They supposed that he was about to establish his kingdom. He told them that the time *had* come in which he was to be glorified, but not in the manner in which *they* expected. It was to be by his death. But as they would not at once see how this could be, as it would appear to dash their hopes, he takes occasion to illustrate it by a beautiful comparison. All the beauty and richness of the *harvest* results from the fact that the grain had *died.* If it had not died it would never have germinated or produced the glory of the yellow harvest. So with him. By this he still keeps before them the truth that he was to be glorified, but he delicately and beautifully introduces the idea still that he *must die.* ¶ *A corn.* A grain. ¶ *Of wheat.* Any kind of grain—wheat, barley, &c. The word includes all grain of this kind. ¶ *Into the ground.* Be buried in the earth, so as to be accessible by the proper moisture. ¶ *And*

the ground and die, it abideth alone; but if it die, it bringeth forth much fruit.

25 He[x] that loveth his life shall lose it; and he that hateth his life in this world shall keep it unto life eternal.

26 If[y] any man serve me, let him follow me; and [z]where I am, there shall also my servant be: [a]if any man serve me, him will *my* Father honour.

27 Now[b] is my soul troubled; and what shall I say? Father, save

x Mat.10.39; 16.25; Mar.8.35; Lu.9.24; 17.33.

y Lu.6.46; ch.14.15; 1 Jn.5.3.
z ch.14.3; 17.24; 1 Th.4.17. *a* 1 Sa.2.30; Pr.27.18.
b Mat.26.38,39; Lu.12.50; ch.13.21.

die. The whole *body* or substance of the grain, except the germ, dies in the earth or is decomposed, and this decomposed substance constitutes the first nourishment of the tender germ—a nutriment wonderfully adapted to it, and fitted to nourish it until it becomes vigorous enough to derive its support entirely from the ground. In this God has shown his wisdom and goodness. No one thing could be more *evidently* fitted for another than this provision made in the grain itself for the future wants of the tender germ. ¶ *Abideth alone.* Produces no fruit. It remains without producing the rich and beautiful harvest. So Jesus intimates that it was *only* by his death that he would be glorified in the salvation of men, and in the honours and rewards of heaven, He. ii. 9: "We see Jesus, who was made a little lower than the angels *for the suffering of death*, crowned with glory and honour." Phi. ii. 8, 9: "He humbled himself, and became obedient unto death, even the death of the cross; *wherefore* God also hath highly exalted him," &c. He. xii. 2: "Who, *for the joy* that was set before him, endured the cross, despising the shame, and is set down at the right hand of the throne of God." See also Ep. i. 20–23.

25. *He that loveth his life*, &c. This was a favourite principle, a sort of *axiom* with the Lord Jesus, which he applied to himself as well as to his followers. See Notes on Mat. x. 39; Lu. ix. 24.

26. *Serve me.* Will be my disciple, or will be a Christian. Perhaps this was said to inform the Greeks (ver. 20) of the nature of his religion. ¶ *Let him follow me.* Let him imitate me; do what I do, bear what I bear, and love what I love. He is discoursing here particularly of his own sufferings and death, and this passage has reference, therefore, to calamity and persecution. "You see me triumph—you see me enter Jerusalem, and you supposed that my kingdom was to be set up without opposition or calamity; but it is not. I am to die; and if *you* will serve me, you must follow me even in these scenes of calamity; be willing to endure trial and to bear shame, looking for future reward." ¶ *Where I am.* See ch. xiv. 3; xvii. 24. That is, he shall be in heaven, where the Son of God then *was* in his divine nature, and where he *would* be as the glorified Messiah. See Notes on Jn. iii. 13. The natural and obvious meaning of the expression "I am" implies that he was then in heaven. The design of this verse is to comfort them in the midst of persecution and trial. They were to *follow* him to any calamity; but, as *he* was to be glorified as the result of his sufferings, so *they* also were to look for their reward in the kingdom of heaven, Re. iii. 21: "To him that *overcometh* will I grant to sit with me in my throne."

27. *Now is my soul troubled.* The mention of his death brought before him its approaching horrors, its pains, its darkness, its unparalleled woes. Jesus was full of acute sensibility, and his human nature shrunk from the scenes through which he was to pass. See Luke xxiii. 41–44. ¶ *What shall I say?* This is an expression denoting intense anxiety and perplexity. *As if* it were a subject of debate whether he *could* bear those sufferings; or whether the work of man's redemption should be abandoned, and he should call upon God to save him. Blessed be his name that he was willing to endure these sorrows, and did not forsake man when he was *so near* being redeemed! On the decision of that moment—the fixed and unwavering purpose of the Son of God—depended man's salvation. If Jesus had forsaken his purpose then, all would have been lost. ¶ *Father, save me.* This ought undoubtedly to have been read as a question—"Shall I say, Father, save me?" Shall I apply to God to rescue me? or shall I go forward to bear these trials? As it is in our translation, it represents him as

me from this hour; [c]but for this
cause came I unto this hour.
28 Father, glorify thy name.
Then came there [d]a voice from
heaven, *saying*, I have both glorified *it*, and will glorify *it* again.
29 The people, therefore, that
stood by and heard *it*, said that it
thundered; others said, An angel
spake to him.
30 Jesus answered and said, This
voice came not because of me, [e]but
for your sakes.
31 Now is the judgment of this

c ch.18.37. d Mat.3.17. e ch.11.42.

actually offering the prayer, and then checking himself. The Greek will bear either interpretation. The whole verse is full of deep feeling and anxiety. Comp. Mat. xxvi. 38; Lu. xii. 50. ¶ *This hour.* These *calamities.* The word *hour*, here, doubtless has reference to his approaching sufferings—the appointed *hour* for him to suffer. Shall I ask my Father to save me from this *hour* —that is, from these approaching sufferings? That it *might* have been done, see Mat. xxvi. 53. ¶ *But for this cause.* That is, to suffer and die. As this was the *design* of his coming—as he did it deliberately—as the salvation of the world depended on it, he felt that it would not be proper to pray to be delivered from it. He came to suffer, and he submitted to it. See Lu. xxiii. 42.

28. *Glorify thy name.* The meaning of this expression in this connection is this: "I am willing to bear any trials; I will not shrink from any sufferings. Let thy name be honoured. Let thy character, wisdom, goodness, and plans of mercy be manifested and promoted, whatever sufferings it may cost me." Thus Jesus showed us that *God's glory* is to be the great end of our conduct, and that we are to seek that, whatever sufferings it may cost us. ¶ *I have both glorified* it. The word *it* is not here in the original, but it is not improperly supplied by the translators. There can be no doubt that when God says here that he *had* glorified his name, he refers to what had been done by Christ, and that this was to be understood as an *attestation* that he attended him and approved his work. See ver. 30. He *had* honoured his name, or had glorified *him*, by the pure instructions which he had given to man through him; by the power displayed in his miracles; by proclaiming his mercy through him; by appointing him to be the Messiah, &c. ¶ *Will glorify* it *again.* By the death, the resurrection, and ascension of his Son, and by extending the blessings of the gospel among all nations. It was thus that he sustained his Son in view of approaching trials; and we may learn, 1st. That God will minister grace to us in the prospect of suffering. 2d. That the fact that God will be honoured by our afflictions should make us willing to bear them. 3d. That whatever was done by Christ tended to honour the name of God. This was what he had in view. He lived and suffered, not for himself, but to glorify God in the salvation of men.

29. *The people.* A part of the people. ¶ *It thundered.* The unexpected sound of the voice would confound and amaze them; and though there is no reason to doubt that the words were spoken distinctly (Mat. iii. 17), yet some of the people, either from amazement or envy, would suppose that this was a mere natural phenomenon. ¶ *An angel spake.* It was the opinion of many of the Jews that God did not speak to men except by the ministry of angels, He. ii. 2: "The word spoken *by angels;*" Ga. iii. 19: "It was ordained *by angels* in the hand of a mediator."

30. *Came not because of me.* Not to strengthen or confirm me; not that *I* had any doubts about my course, or any apprehension that God would *not* approve me and glorify his name. ¶ *For your sakes.* To give you a striking and indubitable proof that I am the Messiah; that you may remember it when I am departed, and be *yourselves* comforted, supported, and saved.

31. *Now is the judgment of this world.* Greek, "crisis." This expression, doubtless, has reference to his approaching death, and whatever he means by *judgment* here relates to something that was to be accomplished *by* that death. It cannot mean that then was to be the time in which the world was to be finally judged, for he says that he did not come then to judge the world (ch. xii. 47; viii. 15), and he has clearly declared that there shall be a *future* day when he will judge all mankind. The meaning of it may be thus expressed:

world; now shall [f]the prince of this world be cast out.

32 And I, if I be [g]lifted up from the earth, [h]will draw all *men* unto me.

33 This he said, [i]signifying what death he should die.

34 The people answered him, [k]We have heard [l]out of the law that Christ abideth for ever; and

f Lu.10.18; ch.16.11; Ac.26.18; Ep.2.2. *g* ch.8.28. *h* Ro.5.18.

i ch.18.32. *k* Ps.89.36,37; 110.4; Is.9.7. *l* Ro.5.18; Ps.72.17-19.

"Now is approaching the decisive scene, the eventful period—*the crisis*—when it shall be determined who shall rule this world. There has been a long conflict between the powers of light and darkness — between God and the devil. Satan has so effectually ruled that he may be said to be the prince of this world; but my approaching death will destroy his kingdom, will break down his power, and will be the means of setting up the kingdom of God over man." The death of Christ was to be the most grand and effectual of all means that could be used to establish the authority of the law and the government of God, Ro. viii. 3, 4. This it did by showing the regard which God had for his law; by showing his hatred of sin, and presenting the strongest motives to induce man to leave the service of Satan; by securing the influences of the Holy Spirit, and by his putting forth his own direct power in the cause of virtue and of God. The death of Jesus was the determining cause, the grand crisis, the concentration of all that God had ever done, or ever will do, to break down the kingdom of Satan, and set up his power over man. Thus was fulfilled the prediction (Ge. iii. 15), "I will put enmity between thee and the woman, and between thy seed and her seed; it shall bruise thy head, and thou shalt bruise his heel." ¶ *Now shall the prince of this world.* Satan, or the devil, ch. xiv. 30; xvi. 11. He is also called the *god of this world*, 2 Co. iv. 4; Ep. vi. 12: "The rulers of the darkness of this world"—that is, the rulers of this *dark world*—a well-known Hebraism. He is also called "the prince of the power of the air, the spirit that now worketh in the children of disobedience," Ep. ii. 2. All these names are given him from the influence or power which he has over the men of this world, because the great mass of men have been under his control and subject to his will. ¶ *Be cast out.* His kingdom shall be destroyed; his empire shall come to an end. It does not mean that his reign over all men would entirely cease then, but that then would be the *crisis*, the grand conflict in which *he* would be vanquished, and from that time his kingdom begin to decline, until it would finally cease, and then be free altogether from his dominion. See Lu. x. 18; Col. i. 18–20; Ac. xxvi. 18; 1 Co. xv. 25, 26; Re. xx. 14.

32. *Be lifted up.* See ch. iii. 14; viii. 28. ¶ *Will draw.* Ch. vi. 44. The same word is used in both places. ¶ *All* men. I will incline all kinds of men; or will make the way open by the cross, so that all men may come. I will provide a way which shall present a strong motive or inducement—the strongest that *can* be presented—to all men to come to me.

34. *We have heard out of the law.* Out of the Old Testament; or rather we have been so taught by those who have interpreted the law to us. ¶ *That Christ.* That *the* Messiah. ¶ *Abideth for ever.* Will *remain* for ever, or will live for ever. The doctrine of many of them certainly was that the Messiah would not die; that he would reign as a prince for ever over the people. This opinion was founded on such passages of Scripture as these: Ps. cx. 4, "Thou art a priest for ever;" Da. ii. 44; viii. 13, 14. In the interpretation of these passages they had overlooked such places as Is. liii.; nor did they understand how the fact that he would reign for ever could be reconciled with the idea of his death. To us, who understand that his reign does not refer to a *temporal*, an *earthly* kingdom, it is easy. ¶ *How sayest thou*, &c. *We* have understood by the title "the Son of man" the same as the Messiah, and that he is to reign for ever. How can he be put to death? ¶ *Who is this Son of man?* "The Son of man *we* understand to be the Messiah spoken of by Daniel, who is to reign for ever. To *him*, therefore, you cannot refer when you say that he must be lifted up, or must die. Who is it—what *other Son of man* is referred to but the Messiah?" Either ignorantly or wilfully, they supposed he

how sayest thou, The Son of man must be lifted up? who is this Son of man?

35 Then Jesus said unto them, Yet a little while is [m]the light with[n] you. Walk while ye have the light, lest darkness come upon you; [o]for he that walketh in darkness knoweth not whither he goeth.

36 While ye have light believe in the light, that ye may be [p]the children of light. These things spake Jesus, and departed, and did hide himself from them.

37 But, though he had done so many miracles before them, yet they believed not on him;

38 That the saying of Esaias the prophet might be fulfilled which he spake, [q]Lord, who hath believed

m ch.8.12. n Je.13.16. o ch.11.10. p Ep.5.8. q Is.53.1.

---

referred to some one else than the Messiah.

35. *Yet a little while is the light with you.* Jesus did not reply directly to their question. He saw that they were offended by the mention of his death, and he endeavoured to arrive at the same thing *indirectly*. He tells them, therefore, that the light would be with them a little while, and that they ought to improve the opportunity while they had it to listen to his instructions, to inquire with candour, and thus to forsake their false notions respecting the Messiah. ¶ *The light.* Ch. i. 4. It is probable that they understood this as denoting the Messiah. See ch. viii. 12: "I am the light of the world;" ch. ix. 4. ¶ *Walk*, &c. Ch. xi. 9. Whatever you have to do, do it while you enjoy this light. Make good use of your privileges before they are removed. That is, while the Messiah is with you, avail yourselves of his instructions and learn the way to life. ¶ *Lest darkness.* Lest God should take away all your mercies, remove all light and instruction from you, and leave you to ignorance, blindness, and woe. This was true that darkness and calamity were to come upon the Jewish people when the Messiah was removed; and it is also true that God leaves a sinner to darkness and misery when he has long rejected the gospel. ¶ *For he*, &c. See ch. xi. 10.

36. *While ye have light.* This implied two things—1st. That *he* was the light, or was the Messiah. 2d. That he was soon to be taken away by death. In this manner he answered their question —not *directly*, but in a way to convey the truth to their minds, and at the same time to administer to them a useful admonition. Jesus never aroused the prejudices of men unnecessarily, yet he never shrank from declaring to them the truth *in some way*, however unpalatable it might be. ¶ *Believe in the light.* That is, in the Messiah, who is the light of the world. ¶ *That ye may be the children*, &c. That ye may be the friends and followers of the Messiah. See Notes on Mat. i. 1. Comp. Jn. viii. 12; Ep. v. 8: "Now are ye light in the Lord; walk as children of light." ¶ *Did hide himself from them.* Ch. viii. 59. He went out to Bethany, where he commonly passed the night, Lu. xxi. 37.

37. *So many miracles.* This does not refer to any miracles wrought on this occasion, but to all his miracles wrought in view of the nation, in healing the sick, opening the eyes of the blind, raising the dead, &c. John here gives the *summary* or the result of all his works. Though Jesus had given the most undeniable proof of his being the Messiah, yet the nation did not believe on him. ¶ *Before them.* Before the Jewish nation. Not in the presence of the people whom he was then addressing, but before the Jewish people. ¶ *They believed not.* The Jewish nation did not believe *as a nation*, but rejected him.

38. *The saying.* The *word* of Isaiah, or that which Isaiah predicted. This occurs in Is. liii. 1. ¶ *Might be fulfilled.* That the same effect should occur which occurred in the time of Isaiah. This does not mean that the Pharisees rejected Christ *in order* that the prophecy of Isaiah should be fulfilled, but that *by* their rejection of him the same thing had occurred which took place in the time of Isaiah. *His* message was despised by the nation, and he himself put to death. And it was also true—by the same causes, by the same nation—that the same gospel message was rejected by the Jews in the time of Christ. The same language of the prophet would express *both* events, and no doubt it was

our report? and to whom hath the arm of the Lord been revealed?
39 Therefore they could not believe, because that Esaias said again,
40 He[r] hath blinded their eyes,

r Is.6.9,10.

intended by the Holy Spirit to mark both events. In this way it was completely fulfilled. See Notes on Is. liii. 1. ¶ *Our report.* Literally, by *report* is meant "what is heard." Our speech, our message. That is, few or none have received the message. The form of the question is an emphatic way of saying that it was rejected. ¶ *The arm of the Lord.* The *arm* is a symbol of power, as it is the instrument by which we execute our purposes. It is put for the power of God, Is. li. 9; lii. 10. Thus he is said to have brought out the children of Israel from Egypt with *a high arm*—that is, with great power. It hence means God's power in defending his people, in overcoming his enemies, and in saving the soul. In this place it clearly denotes the power displayed by the miracles of Christ. ¶ *Revealed.* Made known, seen, understood. Though the power of God was *displayed*, yet the people did not see and understand it.

39. *They could not believe.* See Mark vi. 5: "He could there do no mighty works," &c. The works *can* and *could* are often used in the Bible to denote the existence of such obstacles as to make a result certain, or as affirming that while one thing exists another thing cannot follow. Thus, Jn. v. 44: "How *can* ye believe which receive honour one of another." That is, while this propensity to seek for honour exists, it will effectually prevent your believing. Thus (Ge. xxxvii. 4) it is said of the brethren of Joseph that they "*could* not speak peaceably unto him." That is, while their hatred continued so strong, the other result would follow. See also Mat. xii. 34; Ro. viii. 7; Jn. vi. 60; Am. iii. 3. In this case it means that there was some obstacle or difficulty that made it certain that while it existed they would not believe. What that was is stated in the next verse; and while that blindness of mind and that hardness of heart existed, it was impossible that they should believe, for the two things were incompatible. But this determines nothing about their power of *removing that blindness*, or of yielding their heart to the gospel. It simply affirms that while one exists the other cannot follow. Chrysostom and Augustine understand this of a *moral inability*, and not of any *natural* want of power. "They could not, because they would not" (Chrysostom *in loco*). So on Je. xiii. 23, "Can the Ethiopian change his skin," &c., he says, "he does not say it is impossible for a wicked man to do well, but, BECAUSE *they will not, therefore they cannot.*" Augustine says on this place: "If I be asked why they *could* not believe, I answer without hesitation, because they *would* not: because God foresaw their *evil will*, and he annouuced it beforehand by the prophet." ¶ *Said again*, Is. vi. 9, 10.

40. *He hath blinded their eyes.* The expression in Isaiah is, "Go, make the heart of this people fat, and shut their eyes." That is, go and proclaim truth to them—truth that will *result* in blinding their eyes. Go and proclaim the law and the will of God, and the *effect will be*, owing to the hardness of their heart, that their eyes will be blinded and their hearts hardened. As God knew that this would be the result—as it was to be the effect of the message, his commanding Isaiah to go and proclaim it was the same *in effect*, or *in the result*, as if he had commanded him to blind their eyes and harden their hearts. It is this *effect* or *result* to which the evangelist refers in this place. He states that God did it—that is, he did it in the manner mentioned in Isaiah, for we are limited to that in our interpretation of the passage. In that case it is clear that the mode specified is not a *direct* agency on the part of God in blinding the mind—which we cannot reconcile with any just notions of the divine character—but *in suffering the truth to produce a regular effect on sinful minds, without putting forth any positive supernatural influence to prevent it.* The effect of truth on such minds is to irritate, to enrage, and to harden, unless counteracted by the grace of God. See Ro. vii. 8, 9, 11; 2 Co. ii. 15, 16. And as God *knew* this, and, knowing it, still sent the message, and suffered it to produce the *regular* effect, the evangelist says "*he* hath blinded their minds," thus retaining the *substance* of the passage in Isaiah without quoting the precise language; but in proclaiming the *truth* there was nothing *wrong*

and hardened their heart; that
they should not see with *their*
eyes, nor understand with *their*
heart, and be converted, and I
should heal them.
41 These things said Esaias[s] when
he saw his glory, and spake of
him.

42 Nevertheless, among the chief
rulers also many believed on him;
but [t] because of the Pharisees they
did not confess *him*, lest they should
be put out of the synagogue;
43 For[u] they loved the praise of
men more than the praise of God.
44 Jesus cried and said, [v] He that

s Is.6.1. *t* ch.9.22. *u* ch.5.44; Ro.2.29. *v* Mar.9.37; 1 Pe.1.21.

on the part of God or of Isaiah, nor is there any indication that God was unwilling that *they* should believe and be saved. ¶ *That they should not see*, &c. This does not mean that it was the *design* of God that they should not be converted, but that it was the *effect* of their rejecting the message. See Notes on Mat. xiii. 14, 15.

41. *When he saw his glory*, Is. vi. 1–10. Isaiah saw the LORD (in Hebrew, JEHOVAH) sitting on a throne and surrounded with the seraphim. This is perhaps the only instance in the Bible in which Jehovah is said to have been seen by man, and *for* this the Jews affirm that Isaiah was put to death. God had said (Ex. xxxiii. 20), "No man shall see me and live;" and as Isaiah affirmed that he had seen Jehovah, the Jews, for that and other reasons, put him to death by sawing him asunder. See Introduction to Isaiah, § 2. In the prophecy Isaiah is said expressly to have seen JEHOVAH (ver. 1); and in ver. 5, "Mine eyes have seen the King JEHOVAH of hosts." By his *glory* is meant the manifestation of him—the *shechinah*, or visible cloud that was a representation of God, and that rested over the mercy-seat. This was regarded as equivalent to seeing God, and John here expressly applies this to the Lord Jesus Christ; for he is not affirming that the people did not believe *in God*, but is assigning the reason why they believed not on Jesus Christ as the Messiah. The whole discourse has respect to the Lord Jesus, and the natural construction of the passage requires us to refer it to him. John affirms that it was the glory *of the Messiah* that Isaiah saw, and yet Isaiah affirms that it was JEHOVAH; and from this the inference is irresistible that John regarded Jesus as the Jehovah whom Isaiah saw. The name Jehovah is never, in the Scriptures, applied to a man, or an angel, or to any creature. It is the peculiar, incommunicable name of God. So great was the reverence of the Jews for that name that they would not even *pronounce* it. This passage is therefore conclusive proof that Christ is equal with the Father. ¶ *Spake of him.* Of the Messiah. The connection requires this interpretation.

42. *The chief rulers.* Members of the Sanhedrim—Nicodemus, Joseph, and others like them. ¶ *Because of the Pharisees.* The Pharisees were a majority of the council. ¶ *Put out of the synagogue.* Excommunicated. See Notes on ch. ix. 22.

43. *The praise of men.* The approbation of men. It does not appear that they had a living, active faith, but that they were convinced in their understanding that he was the Messiah. They had that kind of faith which is so common among men—a speculative acknowledgment that religion is true, but an acknowledgment which leads to no self-denial, which shrinks from the active duties of piety, and fears man more than God. True faith is active. It overcomes the fear of man; it prompts to self-denying duties, He. xi. Nevertheless, it was no unimportant proof that Jesus was the Messiah, that *any part* of the great council of the Jews were even speculatively convinced of it: and it shows that the evidence could not have been slight when it overcame their prejudices and pride, and constrained them to admit that the lowly and poor man of Nazareth was the long-expected Messiah of their nation. ¶ *Did not confess him.* Did not openly avow their belief that he was the Messiah. Two of them, however, did afterward evince their attachment to him. These were Joseph and Nicodemus, ch. xix. 38, 39. That Joseph was one of them appears from Mar. xv. 43; Lu. xxiii. 50, 51.

44. *Jesus cried and said.* John does not say *where* or *when* this was; it is probable, however, that it was a continuation of the discourse recorded in ver. 30–36. Jesus saw their unbelief,

believeth on me, believeth not on me, but on him that sent me.

45 And he that seeth me, seeth him that sent me.

46 I[w] am come a light into the world, that whosoever believeth on me should not abide in darkness.

47 And if any man hear my words and believe not, I judge him not; [x]for I came not to judge the world, but to save the world.

48 He that rejecteth me, and [y]receiveth not my words, hath one that judgeth him: the word that I have spoken, the same shall judge him in the last day.

49 For I have not spoken of myself; but the Father which sent me, he gave me a commandment, what I should say, and what I should speak.

50 And I know that [z]his com-

w ch.1.5; 3.19. *x* ch.3.17.

y De.18.19; Lu.9.26. *z* 1 Jn.3.23.

---

and proceeded to state the consequence of believing on him, and of rejecting him and his message. ¶ *Believeth not on me.* That is, not on me *alone*, or his faith does not *terminate* on me. Comp. Mat. x. 20; Mar. ix. 37. It *involves*, also, belief in him that sent me. Jesus uniformly represents the union between himself and God as so intimate that there could not be faith in *him* unless there was also faith in God. *He* did the *same* works (ch. v. 17, 20, 36; x. 25, 37), and taught the very doctrine which God had commissioned him to do, ch. viii. 38; v. 30, 20–23.

45. *Seeth me*, &c. This verse is a strong confirmation of his equality with God. In no other way can it be true that he who saw Jesus saw him that sent him, unless he were the same in essence. Of no *man* could it be affirmed that he who saw him saw God. To say this of Paul or Isaiah would have been blasphemy. And yet Jesus uses this language familiarly and constantly. It shows that he had a consciousness that he was divine, and that it was the *natural* and proper way of speaking when speaking of himself. Comp. ch. v. 17.

46. *A light into the world.* Ch. viii. 12; i. 9; iii. 19. ¶ *Walk in darkness.* In gross and dangerous errors. Darkness is put for error as well as for sin, Jn. iii. 19; 1 Jn. i. 5. It is also used to denote the state when the *comforts* of religion are withdrawn from the soul, Is. viii. 22; Joel ii. 2; Is. lix. 9; Jn. viii. 12.

47. *I judge him not*, &c. Ch. viii. 15. It was not his *present* purpose to condemn men. He would come to *condemn* the guilty at a future time. At present he came to save them. Hence he did not now even pronounce decisively on the condition of those who rejected him, but still gave them an opportunity to be saved.

48. *He that rejecteth me.* Lu. x. 16. The word *reject* means to *despise*, or to refuse to receive him. ¶ *Hath one.* That is, he needs not my voice to condemn him. He will carry his own condemnation with him, even should I be silent. His own conscience will condemn him. The words which I have spoken will be remembered and will condemn him, if there were nothing farther. From this we learn, 1st. That a guilty conscience needs no accuser. 2d. That the words of Christ, and the messages of mercy which the sinner has rejected, will be remembered by him. 3d. That this will be the source of his condemnation. This will make him miserable, and there will be no possibility of his being happy. 4th. That the conscience of the sinner will *concur* with the sentence of Christ in the great day, and that he will go to eternity *self-condemned.* It is this which will make the pains of hell so intolerable to the sinner. 5th. The word that Christ has spoken, the doctrines of his gospel, and the messages of mercy, will be that by which the sinner will be judged in the last day. Every man will be judged by that message, and the sinner will be punished according to the frequency and clearness with which the rejected message has been presented to his mind, Mat. xii. 41.

49. *Of myself.* Ch. vii. 16–18.

50. *Is life everlasting.* Is the *cause* or *source* of everlasting life. He that *obeys* the commandment of God shall obtain everlasting life; and this is his commandment, that we believe in the name of his only-begotten Son, 1 Jn. iii. 22. We see here the reason of the earnestness and fidelity of the Lord Jesus. It was because he saw that *eternal life* depended on the faithful preaching of the message of God. He therefore pro-

mandment is life everlasting: whatsoever I speak, therefore, even as the Father said unto me, so I speak.

CHAPTER XIII.

NOW[a] before the feast of the passover, when Jesus knew that [b]his hour was come that he should depart out of this world unto the Father, [c]having loved his own which were in the world, he loved them unto the end.

2 And supper being ended, [d]the devil having now put into the heart of Judas Iscariot, Simon's *son*, to betray him,

3 Jesus [e]knowing that the Fa-

a Mat.26.2,&c. *b* ch.17.1,11.

c Je.31.3; Ep.5.2; 1 Jn.4.19; Re.1.5.
d Lu.22.3,53; ch.6.70. *e* Mat.28.18; He.2.8.

---

claimed it in the face of all opposition, contempt, and persecution. And we see also, 1st. That every minister of religion should have a deep and abiding conviction that he delivers a message that is to be connected with the eternal welfare of his hearers. And, 2d. Under the influence of this belief, he should fearlessly deliver his message in the face of bonds, poverty, contempt, persecution, and death.

It may not be improper to remark here that this is the *close* of the public preaching of Christ. The rest of his ministry was employed in the private instruction of his apostles, and in preparing them for his approaching death. It is such a close as all his ministers should desire to make—a solemn, deliberate, firm exhibition of the truth of God, under a belief that on it was depending the eternal salvation of his hearers, and uttering without fear the solemn message of the Most High to a lost world.

CHAPTER XIII.

1. *The feast of the passover.* See Notes on Mat. xxvi. 2, 17. ¶ *His hour was come.* The hour appointed in the purpose of God for him to die, ch. xii. 27. ¶ *Having loved his own.* Having given to them decisive and constant proofs of his love. This was done by his calling them to follow him; by patiently teaching them; by bearing with their errors and weaknesses; and by making them the heralds of his truth and the heirs of eternal life. ¶ *He loved them unto the end.* That is, he *continued* the proofs of his love until he was taken away from them by death. Instances of that love John proceeds immediately to record in his washing their feet and in the institution of the Supper. We may remark that Jesus is the same yesterday, to-day, and for ever. He does not change; he always loves the same traits of character; nor does he *withdraw* his love from the soul. If his people walk in darkness and wander from him, the fault is *theirs*, not *his*. His is the character of a friend that never leaves or forsakes us; a friend that sticketh closer than a brother. Ps. xxxvii. 28: "The Lord—forsaketh not his saints." Is. xlix. 14–17; Pr. xviii. 24.

2. *Supper being ended.* This translation expresses too much. The original means *while they were at supper;* and that this is the meaning is clear from the fact that we find them still eating after this. The Arabic and Persic translations give it this meaning. The Latin Vulgate renders it like the English. ¶ *The devil.* The leader or prince of evil spirits. ¶ *Having now put it into the heart.* Literally, having *cast it* into the heart. Comp. Ep. vi. 16: "The fiery darts of the wicked." See Ac. v. 3; Lu. xxii. 3. The meaning of this passage is that Satan inclined the mind of Judas to do this, or he tempted him to betray his Master. We know not precisely how this was done, but we know that it was by means of his *avarice.* Satan *could* tempt no one unless there was some inclination of the mind, some natural or depraved propensity that he could make use of. He presents objects in alluring forms fitted to that propensity, and under the influence of a strong or a corrupt inclination the soul yields to sin. In the case of Judas it was the love of money; and it was necessary to present to him only the possibility of obtaining money, and it *found* him ready for any crime.

3. *Jesus knowing,* &c. With the full understanding of his dignity and elevation of character, he yet condescended to wash their feet. The evangelist introduces his washing their feet by saying that he was fully conscious of his elevation above them, as being intrusted with all things, and this made his humi

ther had given all things into his hands, and that [f]he was come from God, and went to God;

4 He riseth from supper, and laid aside his garments, and took a towel and girded himself.

5 After that he poureth water into a basin, and began to wash the disciples' feet, and to wipe *them* with the towel wherewith he was girded.

6 Then cometh he to Simon Peter; and [1]Peter said unto him, Lord, [g]dost thou wash my feet?

7 Jesus answered and said unto him, What I do thou knowest not now; but thou shalt know hereafter.

f ch.17.11. 1 *he.* g Mat.3.14.

liation the more striking and remarkable. Had he been a mere human teacher or a prophet, it would have been remarkable; but when we remember the dignity of his nature, it shows how low he would stoop to teach and save his people. ¶ *Had given all things,* &c. See Notes on Mat. xxviii. 18. ¶ *Was come from God.* See Notes on ch. viii. 42. ¶ *Went to God.* Was about to return to heaven. See ch. vi. 61, 62.

4. *He riseth from supper.* Evidently while they were eating. See ver. 2. ¶ *Laid aside his garments.* His outer garment. See Notes on Mat. v. 40. This was his *mantle* or robe, which is said to have been without seam. It was customary to lay this aside when they worked or ran, or in the heat of summer. ¶ *Took a towel and girded himself.* This was the manner of a servant or slave. See Notes on Lu. xvii. 8.

5. *Began to wash,* &c. It was uniformly the office of a servant to wash the feet of guests, 1 Sa. xxv. 41. It became a matter of necessity where they travelled without shoes, and where they reclined on couches at meals. It should be remembered here that the disciples were not *sitting* at the table, as we do, but were lying with their feet extended from the table, so that Jesus could easily have access to them. See Notes on Mat. xxiii. 6.

6. *Dost thou wash my feet?* Every word here is emphatic. Dost *thou*—the Son of God, the Messiah—perform the humble *office of a servant*—toward *me*, a sinner? This was an expression of Peter's humility, of his reverence for Jesus, and also a refusal to allow him to do it. It is *possible*, though not certain from the text, that he came to Simon Peter first.

7. *Thou knowest not now.* Though he saw the action of Jesus, yet he did not fully understand the *design* of it. It was a symbolical action, inculcating a lesson of humility, and intended to teach it to them in such a manner that it would be impossible for them ever to forget it. Had he simply *commanded* them to be humble, it would have been far less forcible and impressive than when they saw him actually performing the office of a servant. ¶ *Shalt know hereafter.* Jesus at that time partially explained it (ver. 14, 15); but he was teaching them by this expressive act a lesson which they would continue to learn all their lives. Every day they would see more and more the necessity of humility and of kindness to each other, and would see that *they* were the servants of Christ and of the church, and ought not to aspire to honours and offices, but to be willing to perform the humblest service to benefit the world. And we may remark here that God often does things which we do not fully understand now, but which we may hereafter. He often afflicts us; he disappoints us; he frustrates our plans. Why it is we do not know now, but we yet shall learn that it was for our good, and designed to teach us some important lesson of humility and piety. So he will, in heaven, scatter all doubts, remove all difficulties, and show us the reason of the whole of his mysterious dealings in his leading us in the way to our future rest. We ought also, in view of this, to submit ourselves to him; to hush every murmur, and to believe that he does all things well. It is one evidence of piety when we are willing to receive affliction at the hand of God, the *reason* of which we cannot see, content with the belief that we *may* see it hereafter; or, even if we never do, still having so much confidence in God as to believe that WHAT HE DOES IS RIGHT.

8. *Thou shalt never wash my feet.* This was a decided and firm expression of his reverence for his Master, and yet it was improper. Jesus had just declared that it had a meaning, and that he

8 Peter saith unto him, Thou shalt never wash my feet. Jesus answered him, [h]If I wash thee not, thou hast no part with me.

9 Simon Peter saith unto him, Lord, not my feet only, but also *my* hands and *my* head.

10 Jesus saith to him, He that is

h 1 Co.6.11; Ep.5.26; Tit.3.5.

ought to submit to it. We should yield to all the plain and positive requirements of God, even if we cannot *now* see how obedience would promote his glory. ¶ *If I wash thee not.* This had *immediate* reference to the act of washing his feet; and it denotes that if Peter had not so much confidence in him as to believe that an act which he performed was proper, though he could not see its propriety—if he was not willing to submit *his* will to that of Christ and implicitly obey him, he had no evidence of piety. As Christ, however, was accustomed to pass from temporal and sensible objects to those which were spiritual, and to draw instruction from whatever was before him, some have supposed that he here took occasion to state to Peter that if his soul was not made pure by him he could not be his follower. Washing is often thus put as an emblem of moral purification, 1 Co. vi. 11; Tit. iii. 5, 6. This is the meaning, also, of baptism. If this was the sense in which Jesus used these words, it denotes that unless Christ should purify Peter, he could have no evidence that he was his disciple. "Unless by my doctrine and spirit I shall purify you, and remove your *pride* (Mat. xxvi. 33), your want of constant watchfulness (ver. 40), your anger (ver. 51), your timidity and fear (ver. 70, 74), you can have no part in me" (Grotius). ¶ *Hast no part with me.* Nothing *in common* with me. No evidence of possessing my spirit, of being interested in my work, and no participation in my glory.

9. *Not my feet only*, &c. Peter, with characteristic readiness and ardour, saw now that everything depended on this. His whole salvation, the entire question of his attachment to his Master, was involved. If to refuse to have his feet washed was to be regarded as evidence that he had no part with Jesus, he was not only *willing*, but *desirous* that it should be done; not only anxious that his *feet* should be cleansed, but his hands and his head—that is, that he should be cleansed *entirely*, *thoroughly*. Perhaps he saw the spiritual meaning of the Saviour, and expressed his ardent wish that his whole soul might be made pure by the work of Christ. A true Christian is desirous of being cleansed from all sin. He has no reserve. He wishes not merely that *one* evil propensity should be removed, but all; *that every thought should be brought into captivity to the obedience of Christ* (2 Co. x. 5); and *that his whole body, soul, and spirit should be sanctified wholly and be preserved blameless unto the coming of the Lord Jesus Christ*, 1 Th. v. 23. His intellect, his will, his affections, his fancy, memory, judgment, he desires should be *all* brought under the influence of the gospel, and every power of the body and mind be consecrated unto God.

10. *He that is washed.* This is a difficult passage, and interpreters have been divided about its meaning. Some have supposed that it was customary to *bathe* before eating the paschal supper, and that the apostles did it; Jesus having said, "he that hath bathed his body is clean except in regard to his *feet*—to the dirt contracted in returning from the bath, and that there was need *only* that the feet should be washed in order to prepare them properly to receive the supper." They suppose, also, that the *lesson* which Jesus meant to teach was that they were really pure (ch. xv. 3); that they were qualified to partake of the ordinances of religion, and needed only to be purified from *occasional* blemishes and impurities (Grotius). Others say that there is not evidence that the Jews *bathed* before partaking of the paschal supper, but that reference is made to the custom of washing their *hands* and their *face.* It is known that this was practised. See Notes on Mat. xv. 2; Mar. vii. 3, 4. Peter had requested him to wash his hands and his head. Jesus told him that as that had been done, it was unnecessary to repeat it; but to wash the feet was an act of hospitality, the office of a servant, and that all that was needed now was for him to show this condescension and humility. Probably reference is had here to *internal purity*, as Jesus was fond of drawing illustrations from every quarter to teach them spiritual doctrine; as if he had said, "You are clean by my word and ministry (ch. xv. 3); you are my followers, and are prepared for the

washed needeth not save to wash
his feet, but is clean every whit;
and ye are clean, but not all.
11 For[i] he knew who should betray him; therefore said he, Ye are
not all clean.
12 So after he had washed their
feet, and had taken his garments,
and was set down again, he said
unto them, Know ye what I have
done to you?
13 Ye[k] call me Master and Lord;
and ye say well, for *so* I am.
14 If I, then, *your* Lord and
Master, have washed your feet, ye
also ought to wash one another's
feet.
15 For[l] I have given you an example, that ye should do as I have
done to you.
16 Verily, verily, I say unto you,
The servant is not greater than his
lord; neither he that is sent greater than he that sent him.
17 If[m] ye know these things,
happy are ye if ye do them.
18 I speak not of you all; I know
whom I have chosen; but that the

i ch.6.64. *k* Mat.23.8-10; Phi.2.11. *l* 1 Pe.2.21. *m* Ja.1.25.

scene before you. But one thing remains. And as, when we come to this rite, having washed, there remains no need of washing except to wash the feet, so there is now nothing remaining but for *me* to show you an example that you will always remember, and that shall *complete* my public instructions to you." ¶ *Is clean.* This word may apply to the *body* or the *soul.* ¶ *Every whit.* Altogether, wholly. ¶ *Ye are clean.* Here the word has doubtless reference to the mind and heart. ¶ *But not all.* You are not all my true followers, and fitted for the ordinance before us.

11. *Who should betray him.* Greek, "He knew him who was about to betray him."

12. *Know ye what,* &c. Do you know the *meaning* or *design* of what I have done unto you?

13. *Ye call me Master.* Teacher. ¶ *And Lord.* This word is applied to one who *rules,* and is often given to God as being the *Proprietor* and *Ruler* of all things. It is given to Christ many hundred times in the New Testament. ¶ *Ye say well,* &c. Mat. xxiii. 8, 10. ¶ So *I am.* That is, he was their *Teacher* and Instructor, and he was their Sovereign and King.

14, 15. *Ye also ought to wash,* &c. Some have understood this *literally as instituting a religious rite* which we ought to observe; but this was evidently not the design; for, 1st. There is no evidence that Jesus intended it as a *religious* observance, like the Lord's Supper or the ordinance of baptism. 2d. It was not observed by the apostles or the primitive Christians as a religious rite. 3d. It was a rite of hospitality among the Jews, a common, well-known thing, and performed by servants. 4th. It is the manifest design of Jesus here to inculcate a lesson of humility; to teach them by his example that they ought to condescend to the most humble offices for the benefit of others. They ought not to be proud, and vain, and unwilling to occupy a low place, but to regard themselves as the servants of each other, and as willing to befriend each other in every way. And especially as they were to be founders of the church, and to be greatly honoured, he took this occasion of warning them against the dangers of ambition, and of teaching them, by an example that they *could not forget,* the duty of humility.

16, 17. *The servant is not,* &c. This was universally true, and this they were to remember always, that *they* were to manifest the same spirit that he did, and that they were to expect the same treatment from the world. See Notes on Mat. x. 24, 25.

18. *I speak not of you all.* That is, in addressing you as *clean,* I do not mean to say that you *all* possess this character. ¶ *I know whom I have chosen.* He here means evidently to say that he had not chosen them all, implying that Judas had not been chosen. As, however, this word is applied to Judas in one place (Jn. vi. 70), "Have not I *chosen* you twelve, and one of you is a devil?" it must have a different meaning here from that which it has there. *There* it evidently refers to the *apostleship.* Jesus *had* chosen him to be an *apostle,* and had treated him as such. *Here* it refers to purity *of heart,* and Jesus implies that, though Judas had been chosen to the office of apostleship,

scripture may be fulfilled, [n]He that eateth bread with me hath lifted up his heel against me.

19 Now[2] I [o]tell you before it come, that when it is come to pass ye may believe that I am *he*.

20 Verily, verily, I say unto you, [p]He that receiveth whomsoever I send, receiveth me; and he that receiveth me, receiveth him that sent me.

21 When[q] Jesus had thus said,

n Ps.41.9. [2] or, *From henceforth.* *o* ch.14.29; 16.4. *p* Mat.10.40. *q* Mat.26.21; Mar.14.18; Lu.22.21.

---

yet he had not been chosen to purity of heart and life. The remaining eleven *had* been, and would be saved. It was not, however, the fault of Jesus that Judas was not saved, for he was admitted to the same teaching, the same familiarity, and the same office; but his execrable love of gold gained the ascendency, and rendered vain all the means used for his conversion. ¶ *But that the scripture*, &c. These things have occurred in order that the prophecies may receive their completion. It does not mean that Judas was *compelled* to this course in order that the Scripture might be fulfilled, but that this was foretold, and that *by this* the prophecy *did* receive a completion. ¶ *The scripture.* This is written in Ps. xli. 9. It is commonly understood of Ahithophel, and of the enemies of David who had been admitted to his friendship, and who had now proved ungrateful to him. ¶ *May be fulfilled.* See Notes on Mat. i. 22. It is difficult to tell whether this prophecy had a primary reference to Judas, or whether it be meant that it received a more complete fulfilment in his case than in the time of David. The cases were similar; the same words would describe both events, for there was an exhibition of similar ingratitude and baseness in both cases, so that the same words would fitly describe both events. ¶ *He that eateth bread with me.* To eat with one was a proof of friendship. See 2 Sa. ix. 11; Mat. ix. 11; Ge. xliii. 32. This means that Judas had been admitted to all the privileges of friendship, and had partaken of the usual evidences of affection. It was this which greatly aggravated his offence. It was base ingratitude as well as murder. ¶ *Hath lifted up his heel. Suidas* says that this figure is taken from those who are running in a race, when one attempts to trip the other up and make him fall. It was a base and ungrateful return for kindness to which the Lord Jesus referred, and it means that he who had been admitted to the intimacies of friendship had ungratefully and maliciously injured him. Some suppose the expression means to lay *snares* for one; others, to kick or injure a man after he is cast down (Calvin on Ps. xli. 9). It is clear that it denotes great injury, and injury aggravated by the fact of professed friendship. It was not merely the common people, the open enemies, the Jewish nation that did it, but one who had received all the usual proofs of kindness. It was this which greatly aggravated our Saviour's sufferings.

19. *Now I tell you before it come*, &c. They would see by that that he had a knowledge of the heart and the power of foretelling future events, and must therefore have been sent by God. This does not imply that they had no faith *before* this, but that their faith would be increased and strengthened by it.

20. *He that receiveth*, &c. This sentiment is found in the instructions which Jesus gave to his disciples in Mat. x. 40. Why he repeats it at this time cannot now be known. It is certain that it is not closely connected with the subject of his conversation. Perhaps, however, it was to show how intimately united he, his Father, his apostles, and all who received them were. They who received *them* received *him*, and they who received *him* received *God*. So he who betrayed *him*, betrayed, for the same reason, *God*. Hence Judas, who was about to betray *him*, was also about to betray the cause of religion in the world, and to betray God and his cause. Everything pertaining to religion is connected together. A man cannot do dishonour to one of the institutions of religion without injuring *all;* he cannot dishonour its ministers or the Saviour without dishonouring God. And this shows that one prominent ground of the Saviour's solicitude was that his Father might be honoured, and one source of his deep grief at the treason of Judas was that it would bring injury upon the whole cause of religion in the world.

21. *Troubled in spirit.* See ch. xii. 27. The reason of his trouble here was that Judas, a professed friend, was about to

he was troubled in spirit, and testified, and said, Verily, verily, I
say unto you that one of you shall
betray me.
22 Then the disciples looked one
on another, doubting of whom he
spake.
23 Now there was leaning on
Jesus' bosom [r] one of his disciples,
whom Jesus loved.
24 Simon Peter therefore beckoned to him that he should ask who
it should be of whom he spake.
25 He then, lying on Jesus'
breast, saith unto him, Lord, who
is it?
26 Jesus answered, He it is to
whom I shall give a [3] sop when I
have dipped *it*. And when he had
dipped the sop, he gave *it* to Judas
Iscariot, *the son* of Simon.
27 And after the sop, [s] Satan en-

r ch.20.2; 21.7,20.

3 or, *morsel*. s Lu.22.3.

---

betray him. He doubtless foresaw the deep and dreadful sorrows of his approaching death, and was also deeply affected with the ingratitude and wickedness of a professed friend. Jesus was *man* as well as *God*, and he felt like other men. His human nature shrank from suffering, and his tender sensibilities were affected not less deeply than would be those of other men by baseness and treason. ¶ *Testified.* He bore witness to the truth; openly declared what he had before intimated—that one of them would betray him.

22. *Doubting of whom*, &c. The word translated *doubting* denotes that kind of anxiety which a man feels when he is in perplexity, and knows not what to say or do. We should say they were *at a loss*. See Notes on Mat. xxvi. 22.

23. *Leaning on Jesus' bosom.* This does not mean that he was at that time *actually* lying on his bosom, but that he occupied a situation *next* to him at the table, so that his head naturally fell back on his bosom when he spoke to him. See Notes on Mat. xxiii. 6. ¶ *Whom Jesus loved.* This was doubtless John himself. The evangelists are not accustomed to mention their own *names* when any mark of favour or any good deed is recorded. They did not seek publicity or notoriety. In this case the appellation is more tender and honourable than any mere *name*. John was admitted to peculiar friendship, perhaps, because the natural disposition of our Saviour was more nearly *like* the amiableness and mildness of John than any of the other disciples (Robert Hall). The highest honour that can be conferred on any man is to say that Jesus *loved him*. Yet this is an honour which *all may* possess, but which none *can* inherit without his spirit and without loving him. It is an honour which cannot be won by wealth or learning, by beauty or accomplishments, by rank or earthly honours, but only by the possession of a meek and quiet spirit, which is in the sight of God of great price, 1 Pe. iii. 4; comp. Ro. viii. 9.

25. *He then lying on Jesus' breast.* This is a different word from the one rendered (ver. 23) *leaning*. It means *falling back* or *reclining* on the bosom of Jesus. When Peter spake, John *laid his head back* on the bosom of Jesus, so that he could speak to him privately without being heard by others.

26. *Jesus answered.* That is, he answered *John*. It does not appear that either Judas or the other apostles heard him. ¶ *Shall give a sop.* The word translated *sop* means a *morsel*, a piece of bread, or anything else eaten—as much as we are accustomed to take at a mouthful. Jesus was about to *dip it* in the sauce which was used at the Passover. The word *dip*, in the original, is that from which is derived the word *baptize*. It means here that Jesus would dip it into the sauce as we do a piece of bread. It is probable that it was not an unusual thing for the master of a feast to help others in this way, as it does not appear to have attracted the attention of the others as at all remarkable. It was an indication to *John* who the betrayer was, and a hint which *Judas* also probably understood.

27. *After the sop.* After he had taken and probably eaten it. By this Judas saw that Jesus knew his design, and that he could not conceal his plan. He saw, also, that the other disciples would be acquainted with it; and, aroused by sudden anger, or with the apprehension that he should lose his reward, or that Jesus might escape, he resolved on executing his plan at once. ¶ *Satan entered into him.* The devil had *before*

tered into him. Then said Jesus unto him, That thou doest, do quickly.

28 Now no man at the table knew for what intent he spake this unto him.

29 For some *of them* thought, because [t]Judas had the bag, that Jesus had said unto him, Buy *those things* that we have need of against the feast; or that he should give something to the poor.

30 He then, having received the sop, went immediately out; and it was night.

31 Therefore, when he was gone out, Jesus said, [u]Now is the Son of man glorified, and [v]God is glorified in him.

32 If God be glorified in him,

t ch.12.6.

u ch.12.23; 17.1-6. v ch.14.13; 1 Pe.4.11.

---

this put it into his heart to betray Jesus (ver. 2), but he now excited him to a more decided purpose. See Lu. xxii. 3; also Ac. v. 3: "Why hath Satan filled thine heart," &c. ¶ *What thou doest, do quickly.* This showed to Judas that Jesus was acquainted with his design. He did not *command* him to betray him, but he left him to his own purpose. He had used means enough to reclaim him and lead him to a holy life, and now he brought him to a decision. He gave him to understand that he was acquainted with his plan, and submitted it to the *conscience* of Judas to do quickly what he would do. If he relented, he called on him to do it at once. If he could still pursue his wicked plan, could go forward when he was conscious that the Saviour knew his design, he was to do it at once. God adopts all means to bring men to a decision. He calls upon them to act decisively, firmly, immediately. He does not allow them the privilege to *deliberate* about wicked deeds, but calls on them to act at once, and to show whether they will obey or disobey him; whether they will serve him, or whether they will betray his cause. He knows *all* their plans, as Jesus did that of Judas, and he calls on men to act under the full conviction that *he* knows all their soul. Sin thus is a vast evil. When men can sin knowing that God sees it all, it shows that the heart is *fully* set in them to do evil, and that there is nothing that *will* restrain them.

28, 29. *No man at the table knew.* This shows that Jesus had signified to *John* only who it was that should betray him. ¶ *The bag.* The travelling-bag in which they put their common property. See Notes on ch. xii. 6. ¶ *Have need of against the feast.* The feast of the Passover. This feast continued seven days, and they supposed that Jesus had directed him to make preparation for their wants on those days.

30. *It was night.* It was in the evening, or early part of the night. What is recorded in the following chapters took place the same night.

31. *Now is the Son of man glorified.* The last deed is done that was necessary to secure the death of the Son of man, the glory that shall result to him from that death, the wonderful success of the gospel, the exaltation of the Messiah, and the public and striking attestation of God to him in the view of the universe. See Notes on ch. xii. 32.

32. *If God be glorified in him.* If God be honoured by him. If the life and death of the Messiah be such as to lead to the honour of God, such as shall manifest its perfections, and show his goodness, truth, and justice, then he will *show* that he thus approves his work. ¶ *God shall also glorify him.* He will honour the Messiah. He will not suffer him to go without a proper attestation of his acceptance, and of the honour that God puts on him. Jesus here confidently anticipated that the Father *would* show that he was pleased with what he had done. He did it in the miracles that attended his death, in his resurrection, ascension, exaltation, and in the success of the gospel. We may remark that God *will always*, in the proper time and way, *manifest* his approbation of those who live so as to promote the honour of his name. ¶ *In himself.* Or *by* himself; by a direct and public expression of his approbation. Not by the ministry of *angels* or by any other *subordinate* attestation, but by an expression that shall be *direct* from him. This was done by his *direct* interposition in his resurrection and ascension to heaven. ¶ *Shall straightway.* Immediately, or without *delay.* This refers to the fact that the time when God

God shall also glorify him in himself, and shall straightway glorify him.

33 Little children, yet a little while I am with you. Ye shall seek me; and, [w]as I said unto the Jews, Whither I go ye cannot come; so now I say to you.

34 A[x] new commandment I give unto you, that ye love one

w ch.7.34; 8.21.
x Le.19.18; ch.15.12,17; Ep.5.2; 1 Th.4.9; Ja.2.8; 1 Pe.1.22; 1 Jn.2.7,8; 3.11,23; 4.20,21.

would put this honour on him was at hand. His death, resurrection, and ascension were near.

33. *Little children.* An expression of great tenderness, denoting his deep interest in their welfare. As he was about to leave them, he endeavours to mitigate their grief by the most tender expressions of attachment, showing that he felt for them the deep interest in their welfare which a parent feels for his children. The word *children* is often given to Christians as implying—1st. That God is their Father, and that they sustain toward him that endearing relation, Ro. viii. 14, 15. 2d. As denoting their need of teaching and guidance, as children need the aid and counsel of a father. See the corresponding term *babes* used in 1 Co. iii. 1; 1 Pe. ii. 2. 3d. It is used, as it is here, as an expression of *tenderness* and affection. See Ga. iv. 19; 1 Jn. ii. 1, 12, 28; iii. 7, 18; iv. 4; v. 21. ¶ *Yet a little while I am with you.* He did not conceal the fact that he was soon to leave them. There is something exceedingly tender in this address. It shows that he loved them to the end; that as their friend and guide, *as a man*, he felt deeply at the thoughts of parting from them, and leaving them to a cold and unfeeling world. A parting scene at death is always one of tenderness; and it is well when, like this, there is the presence of the Saviour to break the agony of the parting pang, and to console us with the words of his grace. ¶ *As I said unto the Jews.* See ch. vii. 34. ¶ *So now I say to you.* That is, they could not follow him *then*, ver. 36; ch. xiv. 2. He was about to die and return to God, and for a time they must be willing to be separated from him. But he consoled them (ver. 36) with the assurance that the separation would be only temporary, and that they should afterward follow him.

34. *A new commandment.* This command he gave them as he was about to leave them, to be a *badge* of discipleship, by which they might be known as his friends and followers, and by which they might be *distinguished* from all others. It is called *new,* not because there was no command before which required men to love their fellow-men, for one great precept of the law was that they should love their neighbour as themselves (Le. xix. 18); but it was *new* because it had never before been made that by which any class or body of men had been *known* and *distinguished.* The *Jew* was known by his external rites, by his peculiarity of dress, &c.; the philosopher by some other mark of distinction; the military man by another, &c. In none of these cases had love *for each other* been the distinguishing and peculiar badge by which they were known. But in the case of Christians they were *not* to be known by distinctions of wealth, or learning, or fame; they were not to aspire to earthly honours; they were not to adopt any peculiar style of dress or *badge,* but they were to be distinguished by tender and constant attachment to each other. This was to surmount all distinction of country, of colour, of rank, of office, of sect. Here they were to feel that they were on a level, that they had common wants, were redeemed by the same sacred blood, and were going to the same heaven. They were to befriend each other in trials; be careful of each other's feelings and reputation; deny themselves to promote each other's welfare. See 1 Jn. iii. 23; 1 Th. iv. 9; 1 Pe. i. 22; 2 Th. i. 3; Ga. vi. 2; 2 Pe. i. 7. In all these places the command of Jesus is repeated or referred to, and it shows that the first disciples considered this indeed as the peculiar law of Christ. This command or law was, moreover, *new* in regard to the *extent* to which this love was to be carried; for he immediately adds, "*As I have loved you, that ye also love one another.*" His love for them was strong, continued, unremitting, and he was now about to show his love for them in death. Ch. xv. 13: "Greater love hath no man than this, that a man lay down his life for his friends." So in 1 Jn. iii. 16 it is said that "we ought also to lay down our lives for the brethren." This

another; as I have loved you, that ye also love one another.

35 By this shall all *men* know that ye are my disciples, if ye have love one to another.

36 Simon Peter said unto him, Lord, whither goest thou? Jesus answered him, Whither I go thou canst not follow me now; [y]but thou shalt follow me afterward.

37 Peter said unto him, Lord, why cannot I follow thee now? [z]I will lay down my life for thy sake.

38 Jesus answered him, Wilt thou lay down thy life for my sake? Verily, verily, I say unto thee, The cock shall not crow till thou hast denied me thrice.

CHAPTER XIV.

LET[a] not your heart be troubled; ye believe in God, [b]believe also in me.

y ch.21.18; 2 Pe.1.14.
z Mat.26.33,&c.; Mar.14.29,&c.; Lu.22.33,&c.
a Is.43.1,2; ver.27; 2 Th.2.2.
b Is.12.2,3; Ep.1.12,13; 1 Pe.1.21.

---

was a *new* expression of love; and it showed the strength of attachment which *we* ought to have for Christians, and how ready we should be to endure hardships, to encounter dangers, and to practise self-denial, to benefit those for whom the Son of God laid down his life.

35. *By this shall all* men, &c. That is, your love for each other shall be so decisive evidence that you are like the Saviour, that all men shall see and know it. It shall be the thing by which you shall be known among all men. You shall not be known by peculiar rites or habits; not by a peculiar form of dress or manner of speech; not by peculiar austerities and unusual customs, like the Pharisees, the Essenes, or the scribes, but by deep, genuine, and tender affection. And it is well known it was this which eminently distinguished the first Christians, and was the subject of remark by the surrounding pagans. "See," said the heathen, "see how they love one another! They are ready to lay down their lives for each other." Alas! how changed is the spirit of the Christian world since then! Perhaps, of all the commands of Jesus, the observance of this is that which is least apparent to a surrounding world. It is not so much that they are divided into different sects, for this *may be* consistent with love for each other; but it is the want of deep-felt, genuine love toward Christians even of our own denomination; the absence of genuine self-denial; the pride of rank and wealth; and the fact that professed Christians are often known by *anything* else rather than by true attachment to those who bear the same Christian name and image. The true Christian loves religion wherever it is found—equally in a prince or in a slave, in the mansion of wealth or in the cottage of poverty, on the throne or in the hut of want. He overlooks the distinction of sect, of colour, and of nations; and wherever he finds a man who bears the Christian *name* and *manifests the Christian spirit*, he loves him. And this, more and more as the millennium draws near, will be the peculiar badge of the professed children of God. Christians will love their own denominations *less* than they love the spirit and temper of *the Christian*, wherever it may be found.

CHAPTER XIV.

1. *Let not your heart be troubled.* The disciples had been greatly distressed at what Jesus had said about leaving them. Comp. ch. xvi. 6, 22. Perhaps they had indicated their distress to him in some manner by their countenance or their expressions, and he proceeds now to administer to them such consolations as their circumstances made proper. The discourse in *this* chapter was delivered, doubtless, while they were sitting at the table partaking of the Supper (see ver. 31); that in the two following chapters, and the prayer in the 17th chapter, were while they were on their way to the *Mount of Olives.* There is nowhere to be found a discourse so beautiful, so tender, so full of weighty thoughts, and so adapted to produce comfort, as that which occurs in these three chapters of John. It is the *consolatory* part of our religion, where Christ brings to bear on the mind full of anxiety, and perplexity, and care, the tender and inimitably beautiful truths of his gospel—truths fitted to allay every fear, silence every murmur, and give every needed consolation to

2 In my Father's house are many mansions: if *it were* not *so* I would have told you. I[c] go to prepare a place for you.

3 And if I go and prepare a place for you, [d]I will come again, and receive you unto myself; that [e]where I am, *there* ye may be also.

c He.6.20; 9.8,24; Re.21.2.

d He.9.28. e ch.12.26; 17.24; 1 Th.4.17.

the soul. In the case of the disciples there *was* much to *trouble* them. They were about to part with their beloved, tender friend. They were to be left alone to meet persecutions and trials. They were without wealth, without friends, without honours. And it is not improbable that they felt that *his death* would demolish all their schemes, for they had not yet fully learned the doctrine that the Messiah must suffer and die, Lu. xxiv. 21. ¶ *Ye believe in God.* This may be read either in the indicative mood or the imperative. Probably it should be read in the imperative—"Believe on God, and believe on me." If there were no other reason for it, this is sufficient, that there was no more evidence that they *did* believe in God than that they believed in Jesus. All the ancient versions except the Latin read it thus. The Saviour told them that their consolation was to be found at this time in confidence in God and in him; and he intimated what he had so often told them and the Jews, that there was an *indissoluble union* between him and the Father. This union he takes occasion to explain to them more fully, ver. 7-12. ¶ *Believe in.* Put confidence in, rely on for support and consolation.

2, 3. *In my Father's house.* Most interpreters understand this of heaven, as the peculiar dwelling-place or *palace* of God; but it *may* include the *universe*, as the abode of the omnipresent God. ¶ *Are many mansions.* The word rendered *mansions* means either the *act* of dwelling in any place (ver. 23, "we will make our *abode* with him"), or it means *the place* where one dwells. It is taken from the verb *to remain*, and signifies the place where one dwells or remains. It is applied by the Greek writers to the *tents* or temporary habitations which soldiers pitch in their marches. It denotes a dwelling of less *permanency* than the word *house.* It is commonly understood as affirming that in heaven there is *ample room* to receive all who will come; that therefore the disciples might be sure that they would not be excluded. Some have understood it as affirming that there will be different *grades* in the joys of heaven; that some of the mansions of the saints will be nearer to God than others, agreeably to 1 Co. xv. 40, 41. But perhaps this passage may have a meaning which has not occurred to interpreters. Jesus was consoling his disciples, who were affected with grief at the idea of his separation. To comfort them he addresses them in this language: "The universe is the dwelling-place of my Father. All is his *house.* Whether on earth or in heaven, we are still in his habitation. In that vast abode of God there are many mansions. The earth is one of them, heaven is another. Whether here or there, we are still in the house, in one of the mansions of our Father, in one of the *apartments* of his vast abode. This we ought continually to feel, and to rejoice that we are permitted to occupy *any part* of his dwelling-place. Nor does it differ much whether we are in *this* mansion or another. It should not be a matter of grief when we are called to pass from one part of this vast habitation of God to another. I am indeed about to leave you, but I am going only to another part of the vast dwelling-place of God. I shall still be in the same universal habitation with you; still in the house of the same God; and am going for an important purpose—to fit up another abode for your eternal dwelling." If this be the meaning, then there is in the discourse true consolation. We see that the *death* of a Christian is not to be dreaded, nor is it an event over which we should immoderately weep. It is but removing from *one apartment* of God's universal dwelling-place to another—one where we shall still be in his house, and still feel the same interest in all that pertains to his kingdom. And especially the removal of the Saviour from the earth was an event over which Christians should rejoice, for he is still in the house of God, and still preparing mansions of rest for his people. ¶ *If it were not* so, &c. "I have concealed from you no truth. You have been cherishing this hope of a future abode with God. Had it been ill founded I would have told you plainly, as I have told you

4 And whither I go ye know,
and the way ye know.
5 Thomas saith unto him, Lord,
we know not whither thou goest,
and how can we know the way?
6 Jesus saith unto him, I am

---

other things. Had any of you been deceived, as Judas was, I would have made it known to you, as I did to him." ¶ *I go to prepare a place for you.* By his *going* is meant his death and ascent to heaven. The figure here is taken from one who is on a journey, who goes before his companions to provide a place to lodge in, and to make the necessary preparations for their entertainment. It evidently means that he, by the work he was yet to perform in heaven, would *secure* their admission there, and obtain for them the blessings of eternal life. That work would consist mainly in his *intercession*, He. x. 12, 13, 19–22; vii. 25–27; iv. 14, 16. ¶ *That where I am.* This language could be used by no one who was not *then* in the place of which he was speaking, and it is just such language as one would naturally use who was both God and man—in reference to his human nature, speaking of his *going* to his Father; and in reference to his divine nature, speaking as if he was *then* with God. ¶ *Ye may be also.* This was language eminently fitted to comfort them. Though about to leave them, yet he would not *always* be absent. He would come again at the day of judgment and gather all his friends to himself, and they should be ever with him, He. ix. 28. So shall *all* Christians be with him. And so, when we part with a beloved Christian friend by death, we may feel assured that the separation will not be *eternal.* We shall meet again, and dwell in a place where there shall be no more separation and no more tears.

4. *Whither I go ye know.* He had so often told them that he was to die, and rise, and ascend to heaven, that they could not but understand it, Mat. xvi. 21; Lu. ix. 22; xviii. 31, 32. ¶ *The way ye know.* That is, the way that leads to the dwelling-place to which he was going. The way which they were to tread was to obey his precepts, imitate his example, and follow him, ver. 6.

5. *We know not whither thou goest.* Though Jesus had so often told them of his approaching death and resurrection, yet it seems they did not understand him, nor did they fully comprehend him until after his resurrection. See Lu. xxiv. 21. They entertained the common notions of a *temporal kingdom;* they supposed still that he was to be an earthly prince and leader, and they did not comprehend the reason why he should die. Thomas confessed his ignorance, and the Saviour again patiently explained his meaning. All this shows the difficulty of believing when the mind is full of prejudice and of contrary opinions. Had Thomas *laid aside* his previous opinions—had he been willing to receive the truth as Jesus plainly spoke it, there would have been no difficulty. Faith would have been an easy and natural exercise of the mind. And so with the sinner. If he were *willing* to receive the plain and unequivocal doctrines of the Bible, there would be no difficulty; but his mind is full of opposite opinions and plans, occupied with errors and vanities, and these are the reasons, and the only reasons, why he is not a Christian. Yet who would say that, after the plain instructions of Jesus, Thomas *might not* have understood him? And who will dare to say that any sinner *may not* lay aside his prejudices and improper views, and receive the plain and simple teaching of the Bible?

6. *I am the way.* See Is. xxxv. 8. By this is meant, doubtless, that they and all others were to have access to God only by obeying the instructions, imitating the example, and depending on the merits of the Lord Jesus Christ. He was the *leader* in the road, the guide to the wandering, the teacher of the ignorant, and the example to all. See ch. vi. 68: "Thou hast the words of eternal life;" 1 Pe. ii. 21: "Christ—suffered for us, leaving us an example that ye should follow his steps;" He. ix. 8, 9. ¶ *The truth.* The source of truth, or he who originates and communicates truth for the salvation of men. Truth is a representation of things as they are. The life, the purity, and the teaching of Jesus Christ was the most complete and perfect representation of the things of the eternal world that has been or can be presented to man. The ceremonies of the Jews were shadows; the life of Jesus was the truth. The opinions of men are fancy, but the doctrines of Jesus were nothing more than a representation of *facts* as they

the[f] way, and [g] the truth, and
the[h] life, [i] no man cometh unto the
Father but by me.

7 If ye had known me, ye should
have known my Father also; and
from henceforth ye know him and
have seen him.

8 Philip saith unto him, Lord,
show us the Father, and it sufficeth
us.

9 Jesus saith unto him, Have I
been so long with you, and yet
hast thou not known me, Philip?
[k] he that hath seen me hath seen

f Is.35.8,9; ch.10.9; He.10.19,20. *g* ch.1.17; 15.1. *h* ch.1.4; 11.25. *i* Ac.4.12.

k Col.1.15.

exist in the government of God. It is implied in this, also, that Jesus was the fountain of all truth; that by *his* inspiration the prophets spoke, and that by him all truth is communicated to men. See Notes on ch. i. 17. ¶ *The life.* See ch. xi. 25, and Notes on ch. i. 4. ¶ *No man cometh to the Father but by me.* To come to the Father is to obtain his favour, to have access to his throne by prayer, and finally to enter his kingdom. No man can obtain any of these things except by the merits of the Lord Jesus Christ. By coming *by him* is meant coming in his name and depending on his merits. We are ignorant, and he alone can guide us. We are sinful, and it is only by his merits that we can be pardoned. We are blind, and he only can enlighten us. God has appointed him as the Mediator, and has ordained that all blessings shall descend to this world through him. Hence he has put the world under his control; has given the affairs of men into his hand, and has appointed him to dispense whatever may be necessary for our peace, pardon, and salvation, Ac. iv. 12; v. 31.

7. *If ye had known me.* By this Jesus does not intend to say that they were not truly his disciples, but that they had not a *full* and *accurate* knowledge of his character and designs. They still retained, to a large extent, the Jewish notions respecting a temporal Messiah, and did not fully understand that he was to die and be raised from the dead. ¶ *Ye should have known my Father also.* You would have known the *counsels* and *designs* of my Father respecting my death and resurrection. If you had been divested of your Jewish prejudices about the Messiah, if you had understood that it was proper for me to die, you would also have understood the purposes and plans of God in my death; and, *knowing that,* you would have seen that it was wise and best. We see here that a correct knowledge of the character and work of Christ is the same as a correct knowledge of the counsels and plans of God; and we see, also, that the reasons why we have not such a knowledge are our previous prejudices and erroneous views. ¶ *From henceforth.* From this time. From my death and resurrection you shall understand the plans and counsels of God. ¶ *Ye know him.* You shall have just views of his plans and designs. ¶ *Have seen him.* That is, they had seen Jesus Christ, his *image,* and the *brightness of his glory* (He. i. 3), which was *the same* as having seen the Father, ver. 9.

8. *Lord, show us the Father.* Philip here referred to some outward and visible manifestation of God. God had manifested himself in various ways to the prophets and saints of old, and Philip affirmed that if some such manifestation should be made to them they would be satisfied. It was right to desire evidence that Jesus was the Messiah, but such evidence *had been* afforded abundantly in the miracles and teaching of Jesus, and that *should* have sufficed them.

9. *So long time.* For more than three years Jesus had been with them. He had raised the dead, cast out devils, healed the sick, done those things which no one could have done who had not come from God. In that time they had had full opportunity to learn his character and his mission from God. Nor was it needful, after so many proofs of his divine mission, that God should *visibly manifest* himself to them in order that they might be convinced that he came from him. ¶ *He that hath seen me.* He that has seen my works, heard my doctrines, and understood my character. He that has given *proper attention* to the proofs that I have afforded that I came from God. ¶ *Hath seen the Father.* The word *Father* in these passages seems to be used with reference to the divine nature, or to God represented *as a Father,* and not particularly to the distinction in the Trinity of Father and Son. The idea is that God, *as* God, or

the Father; and how sayest thou, *then*, Show us the Father?

10 Believest thou not that I am in the Father, and the Father in me? The words that I speak unto you I speak not of myself; but the Father that dwelleth in me, he doeth the works.

11 Believe me that I *am* in the Father, and the Father in me; or else believe me for the very works' sake.

12 Verily, verily, I say unto you, [l] He that believeth on me, the works that I do shall he do also; and greater *works* than these shall he do, because I go unto my Father.

l Mat.21.21.

---

as a Father, had been manifested in the incarnation, the works, and the teachings of Christ, so that they who had seen and heard him might be said to have had a real view of God. When Jesus says, "hath *seen* the Father," this cannot refer to the *essence* or *substance* of God, for he is invisible, and in that respect no man has seen God at any time. All that is meant when it is said that *God is seen*, is that some *manifestation* of him has been made, or some such *exhibition* as that we may learn his *character*, his *will*, and his *plans*. In this case it cannot mean that he that had seen Jesus with the bodily eyes had *in the same sense* seen God; but he that had been a witness of his miracles and of his transfiguration—that had heard his doctrines and studied his character—had had full evidence of his divine mission, and of the *will and purpose* of the Father in sending him. The knowledge of the Son was itself, of course, the knowledge of the Father. There was such an intimate *union* in their nature and design that he who understood the one understood also the other. See Notes on Mat. xi. 27; also Lu. x. 22; Jn. i. 18.

10. *I am in the Father.* See Notes on ch. x. 38. ¶ *The words that I speak*, &c. See Notes on ch. vii. 16, 17. ¶ *The Father that dwelleth in me.* Literally, "The Father *remaining* in me." This denotes most *intimate union*, so that the works which Jesus did might be said to be done by the Father. It implies a more intimate union than can subsist between a mere *man* and *God.* Had Jesus been a mere *man*, like the prophets, he would have said, "The Father who *sent* or *commissioned* me doeth the works;" but here there is reference, doubtless, to that mysterious and peculiar union which subsists between the Father and the Son. ¶ *He doeth the works.* The miracles which had been wrought by Jesus. The Father could be said to do them on account of the intimate union between him and the Son. See ch. v. 17, 19, 36; x. 30.

11. *Believe me*, &c. Believe my declarations that I am in the Father, &c. There were two grounds on which they might believe; one was his *own testimony*, the other was *his works.* ¶ *Or else.* If credit is not given to my *words*, let there be to my miracles. ¶ *For the very works' sake.* On account of the works; or, be convinced by the miracles themselves. Either his own testimony was sufficient to convince them, or the many miracles which he had wrought in healing the sick, raising the dead, &c.

12. *He that believeth on me.* This promise had doubtless peculiar reference to the apostles themselves. They were full of grief at his departure, and Jesus, in order to console them, directed them to the great honour which was to be conferred on them, and to the assurance that God would not leave them, but would attend them in their ministry with the demonstrations of his mighty power. It cannot be understood of *all* his followers, for the circumstances of the promise do not require us to understand it thus, and it has not been a matter of fact that *all* Christians have possessed power to do greater works than the Lord Jesus. It is a general promise that greater works than he performed should be done by his followers, without specifying that *all* his followers would be instrumental in doing them. ¶ *The works that I do.* The miracles of healing the sick, raising the dead, &c. This was done by the apostles in many instances. See Ac. v. 15; xix. 12; xiii. 11; v. 1-10. ¶ *Greater* works *than these shall he do.* Interpreters have been at a loss in what way to understand this. The most probable meaning of the passage is the following: The word "greater" cannot refer to the miracles themselves, for the works of the apostles did not exceed

13 And[m] whatsoever ye shall ask in my name, that will I do, that the Father may be glorified in the Son.
14 If ye shall ask any thing in my name, I will do *it*.

m 1 Jn.5.14.

15 If[n] ye love me, keep my commandments.
16 And I will pray the Father, and he shall give you [o]another Comforter, that he may abide with you for ever;

n ch.15.10,14; ver.21,23; 1 Jn.5.3. o ch.15.26.

---

those of Jesus in *power*. No higher exertion of power was put forth, or could be, than raising the dead. But, though not greater *in themselves considered*, yet they were greater *in their effects*. They made a deeper impression on mankind. They were attended with more extensive results. They were the means of the conversion of more sinners. The works of Jesus were confined to Judea. They were seen by few. The works of the apostles were witnessed by many nations, and the effect of their miracles and preaching was that thousands from among the Jews and Gentiles were converted to the Christian faith. The word *greater* here is used, therefore, not to denote the *absolute exertion of power*, but the *effect* which the miracles would have on mankind. The word "works" here probably denotes not merely *miracles*, but *all things that the apostles did* that made an impression on mankind, including their travels, their labours, their doctrine, &c. ¶ *Because I go unto my Father.* He would there intercede for them, and especially by his going to the Father the Holy Spirit would be sent down to attend them in their ministry, ver. 26, 28; xvi. 7-14. See Mat. xxviii. 18. By his going to the Father is particularly denoted his exaltation to heaven, and his being placed as head over all things to his church, Ep. i. 20-23; Phi. ii. 9-11. By his being exalted there the Holy Spirit was given (ch. xvi. 7), and by his power thus put forth the Gentiles were brought to hear and obey the gospel.

13. *Whatsoever ye shall ask.* This promise referred particularly to the apostles in their work of spreading the gospel; it is, however, true of all Christians, if what they ask is in *faith*, and according to the will of God, Ja. i. 6; 1 Jn. v. 14. ¶ *In my name.* This is equivalent to saying *on my account*, or *for my sake*. If a man who has money in a bank authorizes us to draw it, we are said to do it in his name. If a son authorizes us to apply to his father for aid because we are his friends, we do it in the name of the son, and the favour will be bestowed on us from the regard which the parent has to his son, and through him to all his friends. So we are permitted to apply to God in the name of his Son Jesus Christ, because God is in him well pleased (Mat. iii. 17), and because we are the friends of his Son he answers our requests. Though *we* are undeserving, yet he loves us on account of his Son, and because he sees in us his image. No privilege is greater than that of approaching God in the name of his Son; no blessings of salvation can be conferred on any who do not come in his name. ¶ *That will I do.* Being exalted, he will be possessed of all power in heaven and earth (Mat. xxviii. 18), and he therefore could fulfil all their desires. ¶ *That the Father may be glorified in the Son.* See Notes on ch. xiii. 31.

15. *If ye love me.* Do not show your love by grief at my departure merely, or by profession, but by obedience. ¶ *Keep my commandments.* This is the only proper evidence of love to Jesus, for mere profession is no proof of love; but that love for him which leads us to do all his will, to love each other, to deny ourselves, to take up our cross, and to follow him through evil report and through good report, is true attachment. The evidence which we have that a child loves its parents is when that child is willing, without hesitation, gainsaying, or murmuring, to do *all* that the parent requires him to do. So the disciples of Christ are required to show that they are attached to him supremely by yielding to all his requirements, and by patiently doing his will in the face of ridicule and opposition, 1 Jn. v. 2, 3.

16. *I will pray the Father.* This refers to his intercession after his death and ascension to heaven, for this prayer was to be connected with their keeping his commandments. In what *way* he makes *intercession* in heaven for his people we do not know. The *fact*, however, is

17 *Even* the Spirit of truth; whom[p] the world cannot receive, because it seeth him not, neither knoweth him; but ye know him,

p 1 Co.2.14.

---

clearly made known, Ro. viii. 34; He. iv. 14, 15; vii. 25. It is as the result of his intercession in heaven that we obtain all our blessings, and it is through him that our prayers are to be presented and made efficacious before God. ¶ *Another Comforter.* Jesus had been to them a counsellor, a guide, a friend, while he was with them. He had instructed them, had borne with their prejudices and ignorance, and had administered consolation to them in the times of despondency. But he was about to leave them now to go alone into an unfriendly world. The *other* Comforter was to be given as a compensation for his absence, or to perform the offices toward them which *he* would have done if he had remained personally with them. And from this we may learn, in part, what is the office of the Spirit. *It is to furnish to all Christians the instruction and consolation which would be given by the personal presence of Jesus*, ch. xvi. 14. To the apostles it was particularly to inspire them with the knowledge of all truth, ch. xiv. 26; xv. 26. Besides this, he came to convince men of sin. See Notes on ch. xvi. 8-11. It was proper that such an agent should be sent into the world—1st. Because it was a part of the plan that Jesus should ascend to heaven after his death. 2d. Unless some heavenly agent should be sent to carry forward the work of salvation, man would reject it and perish. 3d. Jesus could not be personally and bodily present in all places with the vast multitudes who should believe on him. The Holy Spirit is omnipresent, and can reach them all. See Notes on ch. xvi. 7. 4th. It was manifestly a part of the plan of redemption that each of the persons of the Trinity should perform his appropriate work—the Father in sending his Son, the Son in making atonement and interceding, and the Spirit in applying the work to the hearts of men.

The word translated *Comforter* is used in the New Testament five times. In four instances it is applied to the Holy Spirit—Jn. xiv. 16, 26; xv. 26; xvi. 7. In the other instance it is applied to the Lord Jesus—1 Jn. ii. 1: "We have an *advocate* (Paraclete—Comforter) with the Father, Jesus Christ the righteous." It is used, therefore, only by John. The verb from which it is taken has many significations. Its proper meaning is to *call one* to us (Ac. xxvii. 20); then to call one *to aid us*, as an advocate in a court; then to exhort or entreat, to pray or implore, as an advocate does, and to comfort or console, by suggesting *reasons* or *arguments* for consolation. The word "comforter" is frequently used by Greek writers to denote *an advocate* in a court; one who intercedes; a monitor, a teacher, an assistant, a helper. It is somewhat difficult, therefore, to fix the precise meaning of the word. It may be translated either advocate, monitor, teacher, or helper. What the office of the Holy Spirit in this respect is, is to be learned from what we are elsewhere told he does. We learn particularly from the accounts that our Saviour gives of his work that that office was, 1st. To comfort the disciples; to be with them in his absence and to supply his place; and this is properly expressed by the word *Comforter.* 2d. To *teach them*, or remind them of truth; and this might be expressed by the word *monitor* or *teacher*, ver. 26; xv. 26, 27. 3d. To *aid* them in their work; to advocate their cause, or to assist them in advocating the cause of religion in the world, and in bringing sinners to repentance; and this may be expressed by the word *advocate*, ch. xvi. 7-13. It was also by the Spirit that they were enabled to stand before kings and magistrates, and boldly to speak in the name of Jesus, Mat. x. 20. These seem to comprise all the meanings of the word in the New Testament, but no *single* word in our language expresses fully the sense of the original. ¶ *That he may abide with you for ever.* Not that he should remain with you for a few years, as I have done, and then leave you, but be with you in all places to the close of your life. He shall be your constant guide and attendant.

17. *The Spirit of truth.* He is thus called here because he would teach them the truth, or would guide them into all truth, ch. xvi. 13. He would keep them from all error, and teach them the truth, which, either by writing or preaching, they were to communicate to others. ¶ *The world.* The term *world* is often used to denote all who are entirely under

for he dwelleth with you, [q] and shall be in you.
18 I will not leave you [1] comfortless; [r] I will come to you.

19 Yet a little while, and the world seeth me no more; but ye see me: [s] because I live, ye shall live also.

q Ro.8.9; 1 Jn.2.27. [1] or, *orphans*. *r* ver.3,28.

s He.7.25.

the influence of the things of this world —pride, ambition, and pleasure; all who are not Christians, and especially all who are addicted to gross vices and pursuits, 1 Co. i. 21; xi. 32; Jn. xii. 31; 2 Co. iv. 4. ¶ *Cannot receive.* Cannot admit as a teacher or comforter, or cannot receive in his offices of enlightening and purifying. The reason why they *could not* do this is immediately added. ¶ *Because it seeth him not.* The men of the world are under the influence of the senses. They walk by *sight*, and not by *faith*. Hence what they cannot perceive by their senses, what does not gratify their sight, or taste, or feeling, makes no impression on them. As they cannot *see* the operations of the Spirit (Jn. iii. 8), they judge that all that is said of his influence is delusive, and hence they cannot receive him. They have an erroneous mode of judging of what is for the welfare of man. ¶ *Neither knoweth him.* To *know*, in the Scriptures, often means more than the act of the mind in simply *understanding* a thing. It denotes *every* act or *emotion* of the mind that is requisite in receiving the proper *impression* of a truth. Hence it often includes the idea of *approbation*, of *love*, of *cordial feeling*, Ps. i. 6; xxxvii. 18; cxxxviii. 6; Na. i. 7; 2 Ti. ii. 19. In this place it means the approbation of the heart; and as the people of the world do not *approve* of or *desire* the aid of the Spirit, so it is said they cannot receive him. They have no love for him, and they reject him. Men often consider his work in the conversion of sinners and in revivals as delusion. They love the world so much that they cannot understand his work or embrace him. ¶ *He dwelleth in you.* The Spirit dwells in Christians by his sacred influences. There is no personal union, no physical indwelling, for God is essentially present in one place as much as in another; but he works in us repentance, peace, joy, meekness, &c. He teaches us, guides us, and comforts us. See Notes on Ga. v. 22–24. Thus he is said to *dwell in us* when we are made pure, peaceable, holy, humble; when we become *like him*, and cherish his sacred influences. The word "dwelleth" means to *remain* with them. Jesus was to be taken away, but the Spirit would remain. It is also implied that they would *know* his presence, and have assurance that they were under his guidance. This was true of the apostles as *inspired men*, and it is true of all Christians that by ascertaining that they have the *graces of the Spirit*—joy, peace, long-suffering, &c.—they *know* that they are the children of God, 1 Jn. iii. 24; v. 10.

18. *Comfortless.* Greek, *orphans.* Jesus here addresses them as children, ch. xiii. 33. He says that he would show them the kindness of a *parent*, and, though he was going away, he would provide for their future welfare. And even while *he* was absent, yet they would sustain to him *still* the relation of children. Though he was to die, yet he would live again; though absent in body, yet he would be present with them by his Spirit; though he was to go away to heaven, yet he would return again to them. See ver. 3.

19. *A little while.* This was the day before his death. ¶ *Seeth me no more.* No more until the day of judgment. The men of the world would not see him *visibly*, and they had not the eye of faith to discern him. ¶ *But ye see me.* Ye shall continue to see me by faith, even when the world cannot. You will continue to see me by the eye of faith as still your gracious Saviour and Friend. ¶ *Because I live.* Though the Saviour was about to die, yet was he also about to be raised from the dead. He was to *continue* to live, and though absent from them, yet he would feel the same interest in their welfare as when he was with them on earth. This expression does not refer *particularly* to his *resurrection*, but his *continuing to live.* He had a nature which could not die. As Mediator also he would be raised and continue to live; and he would have both power and inclination to give them also life, to defend them, and bring them with him. ¶ *Ye shall live also.* This doubtless refers to their future life. And we learn from this, 1st. That the life of the Christian depends on that of Christ. They are united; and if they

20 At that day ye shall know that I *am* in my Father, and ye in me, and I in you.

21 He[t] that hath my commandments, and keepeth them, he it is that loveth me; and he that loveth me shall be loved of my Father; and I will love him, and will manifest myself to him.

22 Judas[u] saith unto him, (not Iscariot,) Lord, how is it that thou wilt manifest thyself unto us, and not unto the world?

23 Jesus answered and said unto him, If a man love me he will keep my words; and my Father will love him, [v]and we will come unto him, and make our abode with him.

t ver.15,23. *u* Lu.6.16. *v* 1 Jn.2.24; Re.3.20.

---

were separated, the Christian could neither enjoy spiritual life here nor eternal joy hereafter. 2d. The fact that Jesus lives is a pledge that all who believe in him shall be saved. He has power over all our spiritual foes, and he can deliver us from the hands of our enemies, and from all temptations and trials.

20. *At that day.* In the time when my life shall be fully manifested to you, and you shall receive the assurance that I live. This refers to the time *after* his resurrection, and to the manifestations which in various ways he would make that he was alive. ¶ *That I* am *in my Father*, &c. That we are most intimately and indissolubly united. See Notes on ch. x. 38. ¶ *Ye in me.* That there is a union between us which can never be severed. See Notes on ch. xv. 1-7.

21. *He that hath*, &c. This intimate union is farther manifested by these facts: 1st. That true love to Jesus will produce obedience. See ver. 15. 2d. That those who love *him* will be loved of the *Father*, showing that there is a union between the Father and the Son. 3d. That Jesus also will love them, evincing still the same union. Religion is love. The love of one holy being or object is the love of all. The kingdom of God is one. His people, though called by different names, are one. They are united to each other and to God, and the bond which unites the whole kingdom in one is love. ¶ *Will manifest myself to him.* To *manifest* is to show, to make appear, to place before the eyes so that an object may be seen. This means that Jesus would so *show* himself to his followers that they should *see* and *know* that he was their Saviour. In what way this is done, see ver. 23.

22. *Judas saith unto him.* This was the same as Lebbeus or Thaddeus. See Mat. x. 3. He was the brother of James, and the author of the Epistle of Jude. ¶ *How is it*, &c. Probably Judas thought that he spake *only* of his resurrection, and he did not readily see how it could be that he could show himself to them, and not be seen also by others.

23. *Will keep my words.* See ver. 15. ¶ *We will come to him.* We will come to him with the manifestation of pardon, peace of conscience, and joy in the Holy Ghost. It means that God will manifest himself to the soul as a Father and Friend; that Jesus will manifest himself as a Saviour; that is, that there will be shed abroad in the heart just views and proper feelings toward God and Christ. The Christian will rejoice in the perfections of God and of Christ, and will delight to contemplate the glories of a present Saviour. The condition of a sinner is represented as one who has gone astray from God, and from whom God has withdrawn, Ps. lviii. 3; Pr. xxviii. 10; Eze. xiv. 11. He is *alienated* from God, Ep. ii. 12; Is. i. 4; Ep. iv. 18; Col. i. 21. Religion is represented as God returning to the soul, and manifesting himself as reconciled through Jesus Christ, 2 Cor. v. 18; Col. i. 21. ¶ *Make our abode.* This is a figurative expression implying that God and Christ would *manifest* themselves in no *temporary* way, but that it would be the privilege of Christians to enjoy their presence continually. They would take up their residence in the heart as their dwelling-place, as a temple fit for their abode. See 1 Cor. iii. 16: "Ye are the temple of God;" vi. 19: "Your body is the temple of the Holy Ghost;" 2 Co. vi. 16: "Ye are the temple of the living God." This does not mean that there is any *personal union* between Christians and God—that there is any peculiar indwelling of the *essence* of God in us—for God is essentially present in all places in the same way; but it is a figurative mode of speaking, denoting that the Christian is under the influence of

24 He that loveth me not, keepeth
not my sayings; and the word
which ye hear is not mine, but
the Father's which sent me.
25 These things have I spoken
unto you, being *yet* present with
you.
26 But[w] the Comforter, *which is*
the Holy Ghost, whom the Father
will send in my name, [x]he shall
teach you all things, and bring all
things to your remembrance, whatsoever I have said unto you.
27 Peace[y] I leave with you, my
peace I give unto you: not as the
world giveth, give I unto you.

w ver.16.

x ch.16.13; 1 Jn.2.20,27. *y* Ep.2.14-17; Phi.4.7.

God; that he rejoices in his presence, and that he has the views, the feelings, the joys which God produces in a redeemed soul, and with which he is pleased.

24. *The word which ye hear is not mine.* See Notes on ch. v. 19; vii. 16.

25. *Have I spoken.* For your consolation and guidance. But, though he had said so many things to console them, yet *the Spirit* would be given also as their Comforter and Guide.

26. *Will send in my name.* On my account. To perfect my work. To execute it as I would in applying it to the hearts of men. See ver. 13. ¶ *Shall teach you all things.* All things which it was needful for them to understand in the apostolic office, and particularly those things which they were not prepared then to hear or could not then understand. See ch. xvi. 12. Comp. Notes on Mat. x. 19, 20. This was a full promise that they would be inspired, and that in organizing the church, and in recording the truths necessary for its edification, they would be under the infallible guidance of the Holy Ghost. ¶ *Bring all things to your remembrance.* This probably refers to two things: 1st. He would seasonably remind them of the sayings of Jesus, which they might otherwise have forgotten. In the organization of the church, and in composing the sacred history, he would preside over their *memories*, and recall such truths and doctrines as were necessary either for their comfort or the edification of his people. Amid the multitude of things which Jesus spake during a ministry of more than three years, it was to be expected that many things which he had uttered, that would be important for the edification of the church, would be forgotten. We see, hence, the nature of their inspiration. The Holy Spirit made use of their *memories*, and doubtless of all their natural faculties. He so presided *over* their memories as to recall what they had forgotten, and *then* it was recorded as a thing which they distinctly remembered, in the same way as we remember a thing which would have been forgotten had not some friend recalled it to our recollection. 2d. The Holy Spirit would teach them the *meaning* of those things which the Saviour had spoken. Thus they did not understand that he ought to be put to death till after his resurrection, though he had repeatedly told them of it, Lu. xxiv. 21, 25, 26. So they did not till then understand that the gospel was to be preached to the Gentiles, though this was also declared before. Comp. Mat. iv. 15, 16; xii. 21, with Ac. x. 44-48.

27. *Peace I leave with you.* This was a common form of benediction among the Jews. See Notes on Mat. x. 13. It is the invocation of the blessings of peace and happiness. In this place it was, however, much more than a mere *form* or an empty wish. It came from Him who had power to make peace and to confer it on all, Ep. ii. 15. It refers here particularly to the consolations which he gave to his disciples in view of his approaching death. He had exhorted them not to be troubled (ver. 1), and he had stated *reasons* why they should not be. He explained to them why he was about to leave them; he promised them that he would return; he assured them that the Holy Ghost would come to comfort, teach, and guide them. By all these truths and promises he provided for their peace in the time of his approaching departure. But the expression refers also, doubtless, to the *peace* which is given to all who love the Saviour. They are by nature enmity against God, Ro. viii. 7. Their minds are like the troubled sea, which cannot rest, whose waters cast up mire and dirt, Is. lvii. 20. They were at war with conscience, with the law and perfections of God, and with all the truths of religion. Their state after conversion is described as a state *of peace*. They are *reconciled* to God;

Let not your heart be troubled,
neither let it be afraid.
28 Ye have heard how I said
unto you, I go away, and come
again unto you. If ye loved me,
ye would rejoice, because I said,
[z]I go unto the Father; [a]for my
Father is greater than I.
29 And now I have told you
before it come to pass, that when it
is come to pass ye might believe.
30 Hereafter I will not talk much

z ver.12. a 1 Co.15.27,28.

they acquiesce in all his claims; and they have a joy which the world knows not in the word, the promises, the law, and the perfections of God, in the plan of salvation, and in the hopes of eternal life. See Ro. i. 7; v. 1; viii. 6; xiv. 7; Ga. v. 22; Ep. ii. 17; vi. 15; Phi. iv. 7; Col. iii. 15. ¶ *My peace.* Such as I only can impart. The peculiar peace which my religion is fitted to impart. ¶ *Not as the world.* 1st. Not as the objects which men commonly pursue—pleasure, fame, wealth. They leave care, anxiety, remorse. They do not meet the desires of the immortal mind, and they are incapable of affording that peace which the soul needs. 2d. Not as the men of the world give. They salute you with empty and flattering words, but their professed friendship is often feigned and has no sincerity. You cannot be sure that they are sincere, but I am. 3d. Not as systems of philosophy and false religion give. They profess to give peace, but it is not real. It does not still the voice of conscience; it does not take away sin; it does not reconcile the soul to God. 4th. My peace is such as meets all the wants of the soul, silences the alarms of conscience, is fixed and sure amid all external changes, and will abide in the hour of death and for ever. How desirable, in a world of anxiety and care, to possess this peace! and how should all who have it not, seek that which the world can neither give nor take away! ¶ *Neither let it be afraid.* Of any pain, persecutions, or trials. You have a Friend who will never leave you; a peace that shall always attend you. See ver. 1.

28. *Ye have heard*, &c. Ver. 2, 3. ¶ *If ye loved me.* The expression is not to be construed as if they had then no love to him, for they evidently had; but they had also low views of him as the Messiah; they had many Jewish prejudices, and they were slow to believe his plain and positive declarations. This is the slight and tender reproof of a friend, meaning manifestly if you had *proper* love for me; if you had the *highest* views of my character and work; if you would lay aside your Jewish prejudices, and put *entire, implicit* confidence in what I say. ¶ *Ye would rejoice.* Instead of grieving, you would rejoice in the completion of the plan which requires me to return to heaven, that greater blessings may descend on you by the influences of the Holy Spirit. ¶ *Unto the Father.* To heaven; to the immediate presence of God, from whom all the blessings of redemption are to descend. ¶ *For my Father is greater than I.* The object of Jesus here is not to compare his *nature* with that of the Father, but his *condition.* Ye would rejoice that I am to leave this state of suffering and humiliation, and resume that glory which I had with the Father before the world was. You ought to rejoice at my exaltation to bliss and glory with the Father (Professor Stuart). The object of this expression is to *console* the disciples in view of his absence. This he does by saying that *if* he goes away, the Holy Spirit will descend, and great success will attend the preaching of the gospel, ch. xvi. 7–10. In the plan of salvation the Father is represented as *giving* the Son, the Holy Spirit, and the various blessings of the gospel. As the *Appointer*, the *Giver*, the *Originator*, he may be represented as in office superior to the Son and the Holy Spirit. The discourse has no reference, manifestly, to the *nature* of Christ, and cannot therefore be adduced to prove that he is not divine. Its whole connection demands that we interpret it as relating solely to the imparting of the blessings connected with redemption, in which the Son is represented all along as having been *sent* or *given*, and in this respect as sustaining a relation subordinate to the Father.

29. *Before it come to pass.* Before my death, resurrection, and ascension. ¶ *Ye might believe.* You might be confirmed or strengthened in faith by the evidence which I gave that I came from God—the power of foretelling future events.

30. *Will not talk much.* The time of

with you; for the [b]prince of this world cometh, and [c]hath nothing in me.

31 But that the world may know that I love the Father; and as[d] the Father gave me commandment, even so I do. Arise, let us go hence.

b ch.16.11; Ep.2.2. c 2 Co.5.21; He.4.15; 1 Jn.3.5. d Ps.40.8; Phi.2.8.

CHAPTER XV.

I AM the [a]true vine, and my Father is the [b]husbandman.

a Is.4.2. b Ca.8.12.

my death draws nigh. It occurred the next day. ¶ *The prince of this world.* See Notes on ch. xii. 31. ¶ *Cometh.* Satan is represented as approaching him to try him in his sufferings, and it is commonly supposed that no small part of the pain endured in the garden of Gethsemane was from some dreadful conflict with the great enemy of man. See Lu. xxii. 53: "This is your hour *and the power of darkness.*" Comp. Lu. iv. 13. ¶ *Hath nothing in me.* There is in me no principle or feeling that accords with his, and nothing, therefore, by which he can prevail. Temptation has only power because there are some principles in us which accord with the designs of the tempter, and which may be *excited* by presenting corresponding objects till our virtue be overcome. Where there is no such propensity, temptation has no power. As the principles of Jesus were wholly on the side of virtue, the meaning here may be that, though he had the natural appetites of man, his virtue was so supreme that Satan "had nothing in him" which could constitute any danger that he would be led into sin, and that there was no fear of the result of the conflict before him.

31. *That the world may know that I love the Father.* That it might not be alleged that his virtue had not been subjected to *trial.* It *was* subjected. He was tempted in all points like as we are, yet without sin, He. iv. 15. He passed through the severest forms of temptation, that it might be seen and known that his holiness was proof to *all* trial, and that human nature *might be* so pure as to resist *all* forms of temptation. This *will* be the case with all the saints in heaven, and it *was* the case with Jesus on earth. ¶ *Even so I do.* In all things he obeyed; and he showed that, in the face of calamities, persecutions, and temptations, he was still disposed to obey his Father. This he did that the world might know that he loved the Father. So should we bear trials and resist temptation; and so, through persecution and calamity, should we show that we are actuated by the love of God. *Arise, let us go hence.* It has been commonly supposed that Jesus and the apostles now rose from the paschal supper and went to the Mount of Olives, and that the remainder of the discourse in ch. xv., xvi., together with the prayer in ch. xvii., was delivered while on the way to the garden of Gethsemane; but some have supposed that they merely rose from the table, and that the discourse was finished before they left the room. The former is the more correct opinion. It was now probably toward midnight, and the moon was at the full, and the scene was one, therefore, of great interest and tenderness. Jesus, with a little band, was himself about to die, and he went forth in the stillness of the night, counselling his little company in regard to their duties and dangers, and invoking the protection and blessing of God his Father to attend, to sanctify, and guide them in the arduous labours, the toils, and the persecutions they were yet to endure, ch. xvii.

CHAPTER XV.

1. *I am the true vine.* Some have supposed that this discourse was delivered in the room where the Lord's Supper was instituted, and that, as they had made use of *wine*, Jesus took occasion from that to say that he was the true vine, and to intimate that his blood was the real wine that was to give strength to the soul. Others have supposed that it was delivered in the temple, the entrance to which was adorned with a golden vine (Josephus), and that Jesus took occasion thence to say that he was the *true* vine; but it is most probable that it was spoken while they were going from the paschal supper to the Mount of Olives. Whether it was suggested by the sight of *vines* by the way, or by the wine of which they had just partaken, cannot now be determined. The comparison was frequent among the Jews, for Palestine abounded in

2 Every[c] branch in me that beareth not fruit he taketh away; and every *branch* [d]that beareth fruit, he purgeth it, that it may bring forth more fruit.

3 Now[e] ye are clean through

c Mat.15.13. d He.12.15; Re.3.19. e ch.17.17; Ep.5.26; 1 Pe.1.22.

vineyards, and the illustration was very striking. Thus the Jewish people are compared to a vine which God had planted, Is. v. 1-7; Ps. lxxx. 8-16; Joel i. 7; Je. ii. 21; Eze. xix. 10. When Jesus says he was the *true* vine, perhaps allusion is had to Je. ii. 21. The word *true*, here, is used in the sense of *real, genuine*. He really and truly gives what is emblematically represented by a vine. The point of the comparison or the meaning of the figure is this: A *vine* yields proper juice and nourishment to all the branches, whether these are large or small. All the nourishment of each branch and tendril passes through the main stalk, or the vine, that springs from the earth. So Jesus is the source of all real strength and grace to his disciples. He is their leader and teacher, and imparts to them, as they need, grace and strength to bear the fruits of holiness. ¶ *And my Father is the husbandman.* The word *vine-dresser* more properly expresses the sense of the original word than *husbandman*. It means one who has the care of a vineyard; whose office it is to nurture, trim, and defend the vine, and who of course feels a deep interest in its growth and welfare. See Notes on Mat. xxi. 33. The figure means that God gave, or appointed his Son *to be*, the source of blessings to man; that all grace descends *through* him; and that God takes care of all the branches of this vine—that is, of all who are by faith united to the Lord Jesus Christ. In Jesus and all his church he feels the deepest interest, and it is an object of great solicitude that his church *should* receive these blessings and bear much fruit.

2. *Every branch in me.* Every one that is a true follower of me, that is united to me by faith, and that truly derives grace and strength from me, as the branch does from the vine. The word *branch* includes all the boughs, and the smallest tendrils that shoot out from the parent stalk. Jesus here says that he sustains the same relation to his disciples that a parent stalk does to the branches; but this does not denote any *physical* or incomprehensible union. It is a union formed by *believing* on him; resulting from our feeling our dependence on him and our need of him; from embracing him as our Saviour, Redeemer, and Friend. We become united to him in all our interests, and have common feelings, common desires, and a common destiny with him. We seek the same objects, are willing to encounter the same trials, contempt, persecution, and want, and are desirous that *his* God shall be ours, and his eternal abode ours. It is a union of friendship, of love, and of dependence; a union of weakness with strength; of imperfection with perfection; of a dying nature with a living Saviour; of a lost sinner with an unchanging Friend and Redeemer. It is the most tender and interesting of all relations, but not more mysterious or more *physical* than the union of parent and child, of husband and wife (Ep. v. 23), or friend and friend. ¶ *That beareth not fruit.* As the vine-dresser will remove all branches that are dead or that bear no fruit, so will God take from his church all professed Christians who give no evidence by their lives that they are truly united to the Lord Jesus. He here refers to such cases as that of Judas, the apostatizing disciples, and all false and merely *nominal Christians* (Dr. Adam Clarke). ¶ *He taketh away.* The vine-dresser cuts it off. God removes such in various ways: 1st. By the discipline of the church. 2d. By suffering them to fall into temptation. 3d. By persecution and tribulation, by the deceitfulness of riches, and by the cares of the world (Mat. xiii. 21, 22); by suffering the man to be placed in such circumstances as Judas, Achan, and Ananias were—such as to show what *they were*, to bring their characters *fairly out*, and to let it be *seen* that they had no true love to God. 4th. By death, for God has power thus at any moment to remove unprofitable branches from the church. ¶ *Every branch that beareth fruit.* That is, all true Christians, for all such bear fruit. To *bear fruit* is to show by our lives that we are under the influence of the religion of Christ, and that that religion produces in us its appropriate effects, Ga. v. 22, 23. Notes on Mat. vii. 16-20. It is also to live so as to be useful to others. As a vineyard is worthless un-

the word which I have spoken unto you.

4 Abide[f] in me, and I in you. As[g] the branch cannot bear fruit of itself except it abide in the vine, no more can ye, except ye abide in me.

5 I am the vine, ye *are* the branches: he that abideth in me, and I in him, the same bringeth

f 1 Jn.2.6. *g* Ho.14.8; Ga.2.20; Phi.1.11.

less it bears fruit that may promote the happiness or subsistence of man, so the Christian principle would be worthless unless Christians should live so that others may be made holy and happy by their example and labours, and so that the *world* may be brought to the cross of the Saviour. ¶ *He purgeth it.* Or rather he *prunes* it, or cleanses it by pruning. There is a use of words here — a *paronomasia* — in the original which cannot be retained in the translation. It may be imperfectly seen by retaining the Greek words — "Every branch in me that beareth not fruit he *taketh away* (*airei*); every branch that beareth fruit, he purgeth it (*kathairei*); now ye *are clean* (*katharoi*)," &c. The same Greek word in different forms is still retained. God purifies all true Christians so that they may be more useful. He takes away that which hindered their usefulness; teaches them; quickens them; revives them; makes them more pure in motive and in life. This he does by the regular influences of his Spirit in sanctifying them, purifying their motives, teaching them the beauty of holiness, and inducing them to devote themselves more to him. He does it by taking away what opposes their usefulness, however much they may be attached to it, or however painful to part with it; as a vine-dresser will often feel himself compelled to lop off a branch that is large, apparently thrifty, and handsome, but which bears no fruit, and which *shades* or injures those which do. So God often takes away the *property* of his people, their children, or other idols. He removes the objects which bind their affections, and which render them inactive. He takes away the things around man, as he did the valued gourds of Jonah (Jonah iv. 5–11), so that he may feel his dependence, and live more to the honour of God, and bring forth more proof of humble and active piety.

3. *Now ye are clean.* Still keeping up the figure (*katharoi*). It does not mean that they were *perfect*, but that they had been under a process of *purifying* by his instructions all the time he had been with them. He had removed their erroneous notions of the Messiah; he had gradually reclaimed them from their fond and foolish views respecting earthly honours; he had taught them to be willing to forsake all things; and he had so trained and disciplined them that immediately after his death they would be ready to go and bear fruit among all nations to the honour of his name. In addition to this, *Judas* had been removed from their number, and they were now *all* true followers of the Saviour. See Notes on ch. xiii. 10. ¶ *Through the word.* By means of the *teachings* of Jesus while he had been with them.

4. *Abide in me.* Remain united to me by a living faith. Live a life of dependence on me, and obey my doctrines, imitate my example, and constantly exercise faith in me. ¶ *And I in you.* That is, if you remain attached to me, I will remain with you, and will teach, guide, and comfort you. This he proceeds to illustrate by a reference to the vine. If the branch should be cut off an instant, it would die and be fruitless. As long as it is in the vine, *from the nature of the case*, the parent stock imparts its juices, and furnishes a constant circulation of sap adapted to the growth and fruitfulness of the branch. So our piety, if we should be separate from Christ, or if we cease to feel our union to him and dependence on him, withers and droops. While we are united to him by a living faith, *from the nature of the case*, strength flows from him to us, and we receive help as we need. Piety then, manifested in good works, in love, and self-denial, is as natural, as easy, as unconstrained, and as lovely as the vine covered with fruitful branches is at once useful and enticing.

5. *I am the vine*, ver. 1. ¶ *Without me ye can do nothing.* The expression "without me" denotes the same as *separate from me.* As the branches, if separated from the parent stock, could produce no fruit, but would immediately wither and die, so Christians, if separate from Christ, could do nothing. The expression is one, therefore, strongly implying dependence. The Son of God

forth much fruit; for [1]without me
ye can do nothing.
6 If[h] a man abide not in me, he
is cast forth as a branch, and is
withered; and men gather them,
and cast *them* into the fire, and
they are burned.

7 If ye abide in me, and my
words abide in you, [i]ye shall ask
what ye will, and it shall be done
unto you.
8 Herein is my Father glorified,
that ye bear much fruit; so shall
ye be my disciples.

1 or, *severed from me*. h Mat.3.10; 7.19. i ch.16.23.

was the original source of life, Jn. i. 4. He also, by his work as Mediator, gives life to the world (Jn. vi. 33), and it is by the same grace and agency that it is continued in the Christian. We see hence, 1st. That to him is due all the praise for all the good works the Christian performs. 2d. That they will perform good works just in proportion as they feel their dependence on him and look to him. And 3d. That the reason why others fail of being holy is because they are unwilling to look to him, and seek grace and strength from him who alone is able to give it.

6. *If a man abide not in me*. See ver. 4. If a man is not truly united to him by faith, and does not live with a continual sense of his dependence on him. This doubtless refers to those who are professors of religion, but who have never known anything of true and real connection with him. ¶ *Is cast forth*. See Notes on ver. 2. Also Mat. viii. 12; xxii. 13. ¶ *Is withered*. Is dried up. A branch cut off withers. So of a soul unconnected with Christ, however fair it may have appeared, and however flourishing when a profession of religion was first made, yet when it is tried, and it is seen that there was no true grace, everything withers and dies. The zeal languishes, the professed love is gone, prayer is neglected, the sanctuary is forsaken, and the soul becomes like a withered branch reserved for the fire of the last great day. See a beautiful illustration of this in Eze. xv. ¶ *Men gather them*. The word *men* is not in the original, and should not have been in the translation. The Greek is "they gather them," a form of expression denoting simply *they are gathered*, without specifying by whom it is done. From Mat. xiii. 40–42, it seems that it will be done by the angels. The expression means, as the withered and useless branches of trees are gathered for fuel, so shall it be with all hypocrites and false professors of religion. ¶ *Are burned*. See Mat. xiii. 42.

7. *My words*. My doctrine; my commandments. ¶ *Abide in you*. Not only are *remembered*, but are suffered to remain in you as a living principle, to regulate your affections and life. ¶ *Ye shall ask*, &c. See ch. xiv. 13. This promise had particular reference to the apostles. It is applicable to other Christians only so far as they are in circumstances similar to the apostles, and only so far as they possess their spirit. We learn from it that it is only when we keep the commandments of Christ—only when we live by faith in him, and his words are suffered to control our conduct and affections, that our prayers will be heard. Were we *perfect* in all things, he would always hear us, and we should be kept from making an improper petition; but just so far as men regard iniquity in their heart, the Lord will not hear them, Ps. lxvi. 18.

8. *Herein*. In this—to wit, in your bearing much fruit. ¶ *Glorified*. Honoured. ¶ *Bear much fruit*. Are fruitful in good works; are faithful, zealous, humble, devoted, always abounding in the work of the Lord. This honours God, 1st. Because it shows the excellence of his law which requires it. 2d. Because it shows the power of his gospel, and of that grace which can overcome the evil propensities of the heart and *produce* it. 3d. Because the Christian is restored to the divine image, and it shows how excellent is the character after which they are formed. They imitate God, and the world sees that the whole tendency of the divine administration and character is to make man holy; to produce in us that which is lovely, and true, and honest, and of good report. Comp. Mat. vii. 20; Phi. iv. 8. ¶ *So*. That is, in doing this. ¶ *Shall ye be my disciples*. This is a true test of character. It is not by profession, but it is by a holy life, that the character is tried. This is a test which it is easy to apply, and one which decides the case. It is worthy of re-

9 As the Father hath loved me,
so have I loved you: continue ye
in my love.
10 If[k] ye keep my commandments, ye shall abide in my love;
even as I have kept my Father's
commandments, and abide in his
love.
11 These things have I spoken
unto you, that my joy might re-

k ch.14.21,23.

mark that the Saviour says that those who bear MUCH *fruit* are they who are his disciples. The design and tendency of his religion is to excite men to do *much* good, and to call forth *all* their strength, and time, and talents in the work for which the Saviour laid down his life. Nor should anyone take comfort in the belief that he is a Christian who does not aim to do *much* good, and who does not devote to God *all* that he has in an honest effort to glorify his name, and to benefit a dying world. The apostles obeyed this command of the Saviour, and went forth preaching the gospel everywhere, and aiming to bring all men to the knowledge of the truth; and it is this spirit only, manifested in a proper manner, which can constitute any certain evidence of piety.

9. *As the Father hath loved me.* The love of the Father toward his only-begotten Son is the highest affection of which we can conceive. Comp. Mat. iii. 17; xvii. 5. It is the love of God toward his coequal Son, who is like him in all things, who always pleased him, and who was willing to endure the greatest sacrifices and toils to accomplish his purpose of mercy. Yet this love is adduced to illustrate the tender affection which the Lord Jesus has for all his friends. ¶ *So have I loved you.* Not to the same degree, for this was impossible, but with the same *kind* of love—deep, tender, unchanging; love prompting to self-denials, toils, and sacrifices to secure their welfare. ¶ *Continue ye.* The reason which he gives for their doing this is the *strength* of the love which he had shown for them. His love was so great for them that he was about to lay down his life. This constitutes a strong reason why *we* should continue in his love. 1st. Because the love which he shows for us is unchanging. 2d. It is the love of our best friend—love whose strength was expressed by toils, and groans, and blood. 3d. As he is unchanging in the character and strength of his affection, so should *we* be. Thus only can we properly express our gratitude; thus only show that we are his true friends. 4th. Our happiness here and for ever depends altogether on our *continuing* in the love of Christ. We have no source of permanent joy but in that love. ¶ *In my love.* In love to me. Thus it is expressed in the Greek in the next verse. The connection also demands that we understand it of *our* love to him, and not of *his* love to us. The latter cannot be the subject of a command; the former may. See also Lu. xi. 42; 1 Jn. ii. 5; Jude 21.

10. See ch. xiv. 23, 24.

11. *These things.* The discourse in this and the previous chapter. This discourse was designed to comfort them by the promise of the Holy Spirit and of eternal life, and to direct them in the discharge of their duty. ¶ *My joy.* This expression probably denotes the happiness which Jesus had, and would continue to have, by their obedience, love, and fidelity. Their obedience was to him a source of joy. It was that which he sought and for which he had laboured. He now clearly taught them the path of duty, and encouraged them to persevere, notwithstanding he was about to leave them. If they obeyed him, it would continue to him to be a source of joy. Christ rejoices in the obedience of all his friends; and, though his happiness is not dependent on them, yet their fidelity is an object which he desires and in which he finds delight. The same sentiment is expressed in ch. xvii. 13. ¶ *Your joy might be full.* That you might be delivered from your despondency and grief at my departure; that you might see the reason why I leave you, be comforted by the Holy Spirit, and be sustained in the arduous trials of your ministry. See 1 Jn. i. 4; 2 Jn. 12. This promise of the Saviour was abundantly fulfilled. The apostles with great frequency speak of the fulness of their joy—joy produced in just the manner promised by the Saviour—by the presence of the Holy Spirit. And it showed his great love, that he promised such joy; his infinite knowledge, that, in the midst of their many trials and persecutions, he knew that

main in you, and *that* [l]your joy
might be full.
12 This[m] is my commandment,
That ye love one another, as I have
loved you.
13 Greater[n] love hath no man
than this, that a man lay down
his life for his friends.
14 Ye[o] are my friends if ye do
whatsoever I command you.

l ch.16.24; 17.13. *m* ch.13.34. *n* Ro.5.7,8. *o* ver.10.

15 Henceforth I call you not
servants, for the servant knoweth
not what his lord doeth; but I
have called you [p]friends, for all
things that I have heard of my
Father I have made known unto
you.
16 Ye[q] have not chosen me, but
I have chosen you, and [r]ordained
you, that ye should go and bring

p Ja.2.23. *q* 1 Jn.4.10,19. *r* Ep.2.10.

they would possess it; and the glorious power and loveliness of his gospel, that it could impart such joy amid so many tribulations. See instances of this joy in Ac. xiii. 52; Ro. xiv. 17; 2 Co. ii. 3; Ga. v. 22; 1 Th. i. 6; ii. 19, 20; iii. 9; 1 Pe. i. 8; Ro. v. 11; 2 Co. vii. 4.

12. *This is my commandment.* The peculiar law of Christianity, called hence the *new* commandment. See Notes on ch. xiii. 34. ¶ *As I have loved you.* That is, with the same tender affection, willing to endure trials, to practise self-denials, and, if need be, to lay down your lives for each other, 1 Jn. iii. 16.

13. *Greater love hath,* &c. No higher expression of love could be given. Life is the most valuable object we possess; and when a man is willing to lay that down for his friends or his country, it shows the utmost extent of love. Even this love for friends has been rarely witnessed. A *very few* cases—like that of Damon and Pythias—have occurred where a man was willing to save the life of his friend by giving his own. It greatly enhances the love of Christ, that while the instances of those who have been willing to die for *friends* have been so rare, *he* was willing to die for enemies—bitter foes, who rejected his reign, persecuted him, reviled him, scorned him, and sought his life, 1 Jn. iv. 10; Ro. v. 6, 10. It also shows us the extent of his love that he gave himself up, not to *common* sufferings, but to the most bitter, painful, and protracted sorrows, not for himself, not for friends, but for a thoughtless and unbelieving world.

"O Lamb of God, was ever *pain*,
Was ever LOVE like thine!"

15. *I call you not servants.* This had been the *common* title by which he addressed them (Mat. x. 24, 25; Jn. xii. 26; xiii. 13); but he *had* also before this, on one occasion, called them friends (Lu. xii. 4), and on one occasion after this he called them servants, Jn. xv. 20. He here means that the *ordinary* title by which he would henceforth address them would be that of friends. ¶ *The servant knoweth not,* &c. He receives the command of his master without knowing the reason why this or that thing is ordered. It is one of the conditions of slavery not to be let into the counsels and plans of the master. It is the privilege of friendship to be made acquainted with the plans, wishes, and wants of the friend. This instance of friendship Jesus had given them by making them acquainted with the reasons why he was about to leave them, and with his secret wishes in regard to them. As he had given them this *proof* of friendship, it was proper that he should not withhold from them the *title* of friends. ¶ *His lord.* His master. ¶ *I have called you friends.* I have given you the name of friends. He does not mean that the usual appellation which he had given them had been than of friends, but that such was the title which he had now given them. ¶ *For all things,* &c. The reason why he *called* them friends was that he had now treated them *as* friends. He had opened to them his mind; made known his plans; acquainted them with the design of his coming, his death, his resurrection, and ascension; and, having thus given them the clearest *proof* of friendship, it was proper that he should give them the *name.* ¶ *That I have heard,* &c. Jesus frequently represents himself as commissioned or sent by God to accomplish an important work, and as being instructed by him in regard to the nature of that work. See Notes on Jn. v. 30. By what he had *heard of the Father,* he doubtless refers to the *design* of God in his coming and his death. This he had made known to them.

forth fruit, and *that* your fruit should remain; that [s]whatsoever ye shall ask of the Father in my name, he may give it you.

s ver.7; ch.14.13.

16. *Ye have not chosen me.* The word here translated *chosen* is that from which is derived the word *elect*, and means the same thing. It is frequently thus translated, Mar. xiii. 20; Mat. xxiv. 22, 24, 31; Col. iii. 12. It refers here, doubtless, to his choosing or electing them to be apostles. He says that it was not because *they* had chosen *him* to be their teacher and guide, but because *he* had designated them to be his apostles. See Jn. vi. 70; also Mat. iv. 18–22. He thus shows them that his love for them was pure and disinterested; that it commenced when they had no affection for him; that it was not a matter of obligation on his part, and that therefore it placed them under more tender and sacred obligations to be entirely devoted to his service. The same may be said of all who are endowed with talents of any kind, or raised to any office in the church or the state. It is not that they have originated these talents, or laid God under obligation. What they have they owe to his sovereign goodness, and they are bound to devote all to his service. Equally true is this of all Christians. It was not that by nature they were more *inclined* than others to seek God, or that they had any native goodness to recommend them to him, but it was because he graciously inclined them by his Holy Spirit to seek him; because, in the language of the Episcopal and Methodist articles of religion, "The grace of Christ PREVENTED them;" that is, *went before them*, *commenced* the work of their personal salvation, and thus God in sovereign mercy chose them as his own. Whatever Christians, then, possess, they owe to God, and by the most tender and sacred ties they are bound to be his followers. ¶ *I have chosen you.* To be apostles. Yet all whom he now addressed were true disciples. Judas had left them; and when Jesus says he had chosen them *to bear fruit*, it may mean, also, that he had "chosen them to salvation, through sanctification of the Spirit and belief of the truth," 2 Th. ii. 13. ¶ *Ordained you.* Literally, I have *placed you*, appointed you, set you apart. It does not mean that he had done this by any formal public act of the imposition of hands, as we now use the word, but that he had *designated* or appointed them to this work, Lu. vi. 13–16; Mat. x. 2–5. ¶ *Bring forth fruit.* That you should be rich in good works; faithful and successful in spreading my gospel. This was the great business to which they were set apart, and this they faithfully accomplished. It may be added that this is the great end for which Christians are chosen. It is not to be idle, or useless, or simply to seek enjoyment. It is to do good, and to spread as far as possible the rich temporal and spiritual blessings which the gospel is fitted to confer on mankind. ¶ *Your fruit should remain.* This probably means, 1st. That the effect of their labours would be *permanent* on mankind. Their efforts were not to be like those of false teachers, the result of whose labours soon vanish away (Ac. v. 38, 39), but their gospel was to spread—was to take a deep and permanent hold on men, and was ultimately to fill the world, Mat. xvi. 18. The Saviour knew this, and never was a prediction more cheering for man or more certain in its fulfilment. 2d. There is included, also, in this declaration the idea that their labours were to be *unremitted*. They were sent forth to be diligent in their work, and untiring in their efforts to spread the gospel, until the day of their death. Thus their fruit, the continued *product* or *growth* of religion in their souls, was to *remain*, or to be continually produced, until God should call them from their work. The Christian, and especially the Christian minister, is devoted to the Saviour for life. He is to toil without intermission, and without being weary of his work, till God shall call him home. The Saviour never called a disciple to serve him merely for a part of his life, nor to feel himself at liberty to relax his endeavours, nor to suppose himself to be a Christian when his religion produced no fruit. He that enlists under the banners of the Son of God does it for life. He that *expects* or *desires* to grow weary and cease to serve him, has never yet put on the Christian armour, or known anything of the grace of God. See Lu. ix. 62. ¶ *That whosoever*, &c. See ver. 7.

18. *If the world hate you.* The friendship of the world they were not to ex-

17 These[t] things I command
you, that ye love one another.
18 If[u] the world hate you, ye
know that it hated me before *it*
hated you.
19 If ye were of the world, the
world would love his own; but
because ye are not of the world,
but I have chosen you out of the
world, [v]therefore the world hateth
you.
20 Remember[w] the word that I
said unto you, The servant is not
greater than his lord. If they
have persecuted me, they will also
persecute you; [x]if they have kept
my saying, they will keep yours
also.
21 But[y] all these things will they
do unto you for my name's sake,
because they know not him that
sent me.
22 If[z] I had not come and
spoken unto them, they had not

t ver.12. *u* 1 Jn.3.13. *v* ch.17.14. *w* Mat.10.24; Lu.6.40; ch.13.16.

x Eze.3.7. *y* Mat.10.22; 24.9; ch.16.3. *z* ch.9.41.

---

pect, but they were not to be deterred from their work by its hatred. They had seen the example of Jesus. No opposition of the proud, the wealthy, the learned, or the men of power, no persecution or gibes, had deterred him from his work. Remembering this, and having his example steadily in the eye, they were to labour *not less* because wicked men should oppose and deride them. It is enough for the disciple to be as his Master, and the servant as his Lord, Mat. x. 25.

19. *If ye were of the world.* If you were actuated by the principles of the world. If, like them, you were vain, earthly, sensual, given to pleasure, wealth, ambition, they would not oppose you. ¶ *Because ye are not of the world.* Because you are influenced by different principles from men of the world. You are actuated by the love of God and holiness; they by the love of sin. ¶ *I have chosen you out of the world.* I have, by choosing you to be my followers, separated you from their society, and placed you under the government of my holy laws. ¶ *Therefore,* &c. A Christian may esteem it as one evidence of his piety that he is hated by wicked men. Often most decided evidence is given that a man is the friend of God by the opposition excited against him by the profane, by Sabbath-breakers, and by the dissolute, 1 Jn. iii. 13; Jn. vii. 7.

20. *Remember the word that I said,* &c. At their first appointment to the apostolic office. See Mat. x. 24, 25.

21. *My name's sake.* On my account. Because you are my followers and possess my spirit. See Notes on ch. xiv. 13. ¶ *Because they know not him that sent me.* They will not believe that God has sent me. They do not so understand his character, his justice, or his law, as to see that it was fit that he should send his Son to die. They are so opposed to it, so filled with pride and opposition to a plan of salvation that is so humbling to men, as to be resolved *not* to believe it, and thus they persecute me, and will also you.

22. *And spoken unto them.* Declared unto them the will of God, and made known his requirements. Jesus had not less certainly shown by his own *arguments* that he was the Messiah than by his miracles. By *both* these kinds of proof their guilt was to be measured. See ver. 26. No small part of the gospel of John consists of arguments used by the Saviour to convince the Jews that he came from God. He here says if he had not used these arguments, and proved to them his divine mission, they had not had sin. ¶ *Had not had sin.* This is evidently to be understood of the particular sin of persecuting and rejecting him. Of this he was speaking; and though, if he had not come, they would have been guilty of many other sins, yet of this, their great crowning sin, they would not have been guilty. We may understand this, then, as teaching, 1st. That they would not have been guilty of this *kind of sin.* They would not have been chargeable with rejecting the signal grace of God if Jesus had not come and made an offer of mercy to them. 2d. They would not have been guilty of the same *degree of sin.* The rejection of the Messiah was the crowning act of rebellion which brought down the vengeance of God, and led on their peculiar national calamities. By way of eminence, therefore, this might be called *the sin*—the peculiar sin of their age and nation. Comp. Mat. xxiii. 34–39; xxvii. 25. And this shows us, what

had sin; [a]but now they have no
cloak[2] for their sin.
23 He that hateth me, hateth
my Father also.
24 If I had not done among
them the [b]works which none other
man did, they had not had sin;
but now have they both seen and
hated both me and my Father.
25 But *this cometh to pass,* that
the word might be fulfilled that is
written in their law, [c]They hated
me without a cause.
26 But when the [d]Comforter is
come, whom I will send unto you
from the Father, *even* the Spirit
of truth, which proceedeth from
the Father, [e]he shall testify of me;

a Ja.4.17. 2 or, *excuse.* b ch.7.31. c Ps.35.19; 69.4. d ch.14.17. e 1 Jn.5.6.

is so often taught in the Scriptures, that our guilt will be in proportion to the light that we possess and the mercies that we reject, Mat. xi. 20–24; Lu. xii. 47, 48. If it was such a crime to reject the Saviour *then*, it is a crime now; and if the rejection of the Son of God brought such calamities on the Jewish nation, the same rejection will involve the sinner now in woe, and vengeance, and despair. ¶ *No cloak.* No covering, no excuse. The proof has been so clear that they cannot plead ignorance; it has been so often presented that they cannot allege that they had no opportunity of knowing it. It is still so with all sinners.

23. *He that hateth me*, &c. To show them that this was no slight crime, he reminds them that a rejection of himself is also a rejection of God. Such is the *union* between them, that no one can hate the one without also hating the other. See ch. v. 19, 20; xiv. 7, 9.

24. *The works which none other man did.* The miracles of Jesus surpassed those of Moses and the prophets—1st. In their number. He healed great multitudes, and no small part of his life was occupied in doing good by miraculous power. 2d. In their nature. They involved a greater exertion of power. He healed *all* forms of disease. He showed that his power was superior to all kinds of pain. He raised Lazarus after he had been four days dead. He probably refers also to the fact that he had performed miracles of a different *kind* from all the prophets. 3d. He did all this by his *own power;* Moses and the prophets by the invoked power of God. Jesus spake and it was done, showing that he had power of himself to do more than all the ancient prophets had done. It may be added that his miracles were done in a short time. They were constant, rapid, continued, in all places. Wherever he was, he showed that he had this power, and in the short space of three years and a half it is probable that he wrought *more* miracles than are recorded of Moses and Elijah, and all the prophets put together.

25. *In their law*, Ps. xxxv. 19. All the Old Testament was sometimes called *the law.* The meaning here is that the same thing happened to him which did to the psalmist. The same words which David used respecting his enemies would express, also, the conduct of the Jews and their treatment of the Messiah. In both cases it was without cause. Jesus had broken no law, he had done no injury to his country or to any individual. It is still true that sinners hate him in the same way. He injures no one, but, amid all their hatred, he seeks their welfare; and, while they reject him in a manner for which they *can give no reason in the day of judgment*, he still follows them with mercies and entreats them to return to him. Who has ever had any reason to *hate* the Lord Jesus? What injury has he ever done to any one of the human race? What evil has he ever said or thought of any one of them? What cause or reason had the Jews for putting him to death? What reason has the sinner for hating him now? What reason for neglecting him? No one can give a reason for it that will satisfy his own conscience, none that has the least show of plausibility. Yet no being on earth has ever been more hated, despised, or neglected, and in every instance it has been "without a cause." Reader, do *you* hate him? If so, I ask you WHY? Wherein has he injured you? or why should you think or speak reproachfully of the benevolent and pure Redeemer?

27. *Ye also shall bear witness.* You shall be witnesses to the world to urge on them the evidences that the Lord Jesus is the Messiah. ¶ *Have been with me.* They had for more than three years seen his works, and were therefore qualified to bear witness of his character and

27 And[f] ye also shall bear witness, because [g]ye have been with me from the beginning.

CHAPTER XVI.

THESE things have I spoken unto you, that ye should not be offended.

2 They shall put you out of the synagogues; yea, the time cometh, that [a]whosoever killeth you will think that he doeth God service.

3 And[b] these things will they do unto you, because [c]they have not known the Father, nor me.

4 But these things have I told you, that, when the time shall come, ye may remember that I

f Lu.24.48; Ac.2.32; 4.20,33; 2 Pe.1.16. *g* 1 Jn.1.2.

a Ac.26.9-11. *b* ch.15.21. *c* 1 Co.2.8; 1 Ti.1.13.

doctrines. ¶ *From the beginning.* From his entrance on the public work of the ministry, Mat. iv. 17–22. Comp. Ac i. 21, 22.

CHAPTER XVI.

1. *These things.* The things spoken in the two previous chapters, promising them divine aid and directing them in the path of duty. ¶ *Be offended.* For the meaning of the word *offend*, see Notes on Mat. v. 29. It means here the same as to *stumble* or *fall*—that is, to apostatize. He proceeds immediately to tell them, what he had often apprised them of, that they would be subject to great persecutions and trials. He was also himself about to be removed by death. They were to go into an unfriendly world. All these things were in themselves greatly fitted to shake their faith, and to expose them to the danger of apostasy. Comp. Lu. xxiv. 21. If they had not been apprised of this, if they had not known *why* Jesus was about to die, and if they had not been encouraged with the promised aid of the Holy Ghost, they would have sunk under these trials, and forsaken him and his cause. And we may learn hence, 1st. That if Christians were left to themselves they would fall away and perish. 2d. That God affords means and helps *beforehand* to keep them in the path of duty. 3d. That the instructions of the Bible and the help of the Holy Spirit are all granted to keep them from apostasy. 4th. That Jesus beforehand *secured* the fidelity and made certain the continuance in faith of his apostles, seeing all their dangers and knowing all their enemies. And, in like manner, we should be persuaded that "he is able to keep that which we commit to him against that day," 2 Ti. i. 12.

2. *Out of the synagogues.* See Notes on ch. ix. 22. They would *excommunicate* them from their religious assemblies. This was often done. Comp. Ac. vi. 13, 14; ix. 23, 24; xvii. 5; xxi. 27–31. ¶ *Whosoever killeth you.* This refers principally to the Jews. It is also true of the Gentiles, that in their persecution of Christians they supposed they were rendering acceptable service to their gods. ¶ *God service.* The Jews who persecuted the apostles regarded them as blasphemers, and as seeking to overthrow the temple service, and the system of religion which God had established. Thus they supposed they were rendering service to God in putting them to death, Ac. vi. 13, 14; xxi. 28–31. Sinners, especially hypocrites, often cloak enormous crimes under the pretence of great zeal for religion. Men often suppose, or profess to suppose, that they are rendering God service when they persecute others; and, under the pretence of great zeal for truth and purity, evince all possible bigotry, pride, malice, and uncharitableness. The people of God have suffered most from those who have been *conscientious persecutors;* and some of the most malignant foes which true Christians have ever had have been *in* the church, and have been professed ministers of the gospel, persecuting them under pretence of great zeal for the cause of purity and religion. It is no evidence of piety that a man is full of zeal against those whom he supposes to be heretics; and it is one of the best proofs that a man knows nothing of the religion of Jesus when he is eminent for self-conceit in his own views of orthodoxy, and firmly fixed in the opinion that all who differ from him and his sect *must* of course be wrong.

3. See ch. xv. 21.

4. *These things.* These things which are about to happen, ver. 1, 2. He had foretold them that they would take place. ¶ *Ye may remember*, &c. By calling to mind that he had foretold these things they would perceive that

told you of them. And these
things I said not unto you at the
beginning, because I was with you.
5 But now I go my way to him
that sent me; and none of you
asketh me, Whither goest thou?
6 But because I have said these
things unto you, [d]sorrow hath filled
your heart.
7 Nevertheless I tell you the
truth; It is expedient for you that
I go away; for if I go not away,

d ver.21.

he was omniscient, and would remember, also, the consolations which he had afforded them and the instructions which he had given them. Had these calamities come upon them without their having been foretold, their faith might have failed; they might have been tempted to suppose that Jesus was not aware of them, and of course that he was not the Messiah. God does not suffer his people to fall into trials without giving them sufficient warning, and without giving all the grace that is needful to bear them. ¶ *At the beginning.* In the early part of the ministry of Jesus. The expression *these things* here refers, probably, to *all* the topics contained in these chapters. He had, in the early part of his ministry, forewarned them of calamities and persecutions (Mat. x. 16; v. 10–12; ix. 15), but he had not so fully acquainted them with the nature, and design, and sources of their trials; he had not so fully apprised them of the fact, the circumstances, and the object of his death and of his ascension to heaven; he had not revealed to them so clearly that the Holy Spirit would descend, and sanctify, and guide them; and especially he had not, in one continued discourse, *grouped* all these things together, and placed their sorrows and consolations so fully before their minds. All these are included, it is supposed, in the expression "these things." ¶ *Because I was with you.* This is the reason which he gives why he had not *at first* made known to them clearly the certainty of their calamities and their joys; and it implies, 1st. That it was not needful to do it at once, as he was to be with them for more than three years, and could have abundant opportunity *gradually* to teach these things, and to prepare them for the more full announcement when he was about to leave them. 2d. That while he was with them he would go before them, and the weight of calamities would fall on *him*, and consequently they did not so much then need the presence and aid of the Holy Spirit as they would when he was gone. 3d. That his presence was to them what the presence of the Holy Spirit would be after his death, ver. 7. He could teach them all needful truth. He could console and guide them. Now that he was to leave them, he fully apprised them of what was before them, and of the descent of the Holy Spirit to do for them what *he* had done when with them.

5, 6. *Now I go my way.* Now I am about to die and leave you, and it is proper to announce all these things to you. ¶ *None of you asketh me*, &c. They gave themselves up to grief instead of inquiring why he was about to leave them. Had they made the inquiry, he was ready to answer them and to comfort them. When we are afflicted we should not yield ourselves to excessive grief. We should inquire *why* it is that God thus tries us; and we should never doubt that if we come to him, and spread out our sorrows before him, he will give us consolation.

7. *It is expedient for you*, &c. The reason why it was expedient for them that he should go away, he states to be, that in this way only would the Comforter be granted to them. Still, it may be asked why the presence of the Holy Spirit was more valuable to them than that of the Saviour himself? To this it may be answered, 1st. That by his departure, his death, and ascension—by having these great *facts* before their eyes—they would be led by the Holy Spirit to see more fully the design of his coming than they would by his presence. While he was with them, notwithstanding the plainest teaching, their minds were filled with prejudice and error. They still adhered to the expectation of a temporal kingdom, and were unwilling to believe that he was to die. When he should have actually left them they could no longer doubt on this subject, and would be *prepared* to understand why he came. And this was done. See the Acts of the Apostles everywhere. It is often needful that God should visit us with severe afflic-

the Comforter will not come unto
you; but if I depart, I will send
him unto you.
8 And when he is come, he will
[1]reprove the world of sin, and of
righteousness, and of judgment:
9 Of [e]sin, because they believe
not on me;

1 or, *convince*, Ac.2.37. *e* Ro.3.20; 7.9.

tion before our pride will be humbled and we are willing to understand the plainest truths. 2d. While on the earth the Lord Jesus could be bodily present but in one place at one time. Yet, in order to secure the great design of saving men, it was needful that there should be some agent who could be in all places, who could attend all ministers, and who could, at the same time, apply the work of Christ to men in all parts of the earth. 3d. It was an evident arrangement in the great plan of redemption that each of the persons of the Trinity should perform a part. As it was not the work of the Spirit to make an atonement, so it was not the work of the Saviour to apply it. And until the Lord Jesus had performed this great work, the way was not open for the Holy Spirit to descend to perform his part of the great plan; yet, when the Saviour had completed *his* portion of the work and had left the earth, the Spirit would carry forward the same plan and apply it to men. 4th. It was to be expected that far more signal success would attend the preaching of the gospel when the atonement was actually made than before. It was the office of the Spirit to carry forward the work only when the Saviour had died and ascended; and this was actually the case. See Ac. ii. Hence it was expedient that the Lord Jesus should go away, that the Spirit might descend and apply the work to sinners. The departure of the Lord Jesus was to the apostles a source of deep affliction, but had they seen *the whole case* they would not have been thus afflicted. So God often takes away from us one blessing that he may bestow a greater. All affliction, if received in a proper manner, is of this description; and could the afflicted people of God always *see the whole case* as God sees it, they would think and feel, as *he* does, that it was *best* for them to be thus afflicted. ¶ *It is expedient.* It is *better* for you. ¶ *The Comforter.* See Notes on ch. xiv. 16.

8. *He will reprove.* The word translated *reprove* means commonly to demonstrate by argument, to prove, to persuade anyone to do a thing by presenting reasons. It hence means also to *convince* of anything, and particularly to *convince of crime.* This is its meaning here. He will *convince* or *convict* the world of sin. That is, he will so apply the truths of God to men's own minds as to *convince* them by fair and sufficient arguments that they are sinners, and cause them to *feel* this. This is the nature of conviction always. ¶ *The world.* Sinners. The men of the world. All men are by nature sinners, and the term *the world* may be applied to them all, Jn. i. 10; xii. 31; 1 Jn. v. 19.

9. *Of sin.* The first thing specified of which the world would be convinced is *sin.* Sin, in general, is any violation of a law of God, but the particular sin of which men are here said to be convinced is that of rejecting the Lord Jesus. This is placed *first*, and is deemed the sin of chief magnitude, as it is the principal one of which men are guilty. This was particularly true of the Jews who had rejected him and crucified him; and it was the great crime which, when brought home to their consciences by the preaching of the apostles, overwhelmed them with confusion, and filled their hearts with remorse. It was their rejection of the Son of God that was made the great truth that was instrumental of their conversion, Ac. ii. 22, 23, 37; iii. 13-15; iv. 10, 26-28; comp. ver. 31-33. It is also true of other sinners. Sinners, when awakened, often feel that it has been the great crowning sin of their lives that they have rejected the tender mercy of God, and trampled on the blood of his Son; and that they have for months and years refused to submit to him, saying that they would not have him to reign over them. Thus is fulfilled what is spoken by Zechariah, xii. 10: "And they shall look upon me whom they have pierced, and mourn." Throughout the New Testament this is regarded as the sin that is pre-eminently offensive to God, and which, if unrepented of, will certainly lead to perdition, Mar. xvi. 16; Jn. iii. 36. Hence it is placed *first* in those sins of which the Spirit will convince men; and hence, if we have not yet been brought to see

10 Of [f]righteousness, because I go to my Father, and ye see me no more;

11 Of [g]judgment, because [h]the prince of this world is judged.

12 I have yet many things to say

f Is.42.21; Ro.1.17.

g Ac.17.31; Ro.2.2; Re.20.12,13. *h* ch.12.31.

---

our guilt in rejecting God's tender mercy through his Son, we are yet in the gall of bitterness and under the bond of iniquity.

10. *Of righteousness.* This seems clearly to refer to the righteousness or *innocence* of Jesus himself. He was now persecuted. He was soon to be arraigned on heavy charges, and condemned by the highest authority of the nation as guilty. Yet, though condemned, he says that the Holy Spirit would descend and *convince* the world that he was innocent. ¶ *Because I go to my Father.* That is, the amazing miracle of his resurrection and ascension to God would be a demonstration of his innocence that would satisfy the Jews and Gentiles. God would not raise up an impostor. If he had been truly *guilty*, as the Jews who condemned him pretended, God would not have set his seal to the imposture by raising him from the dead; but when he did raise him up and exalt him to his own right hand, he gave his attestation to his *innocence;* he showed that he approved his work, and gave evidence conclusive that Jesus was sent from God. To this proof of the *innocence* of Jesus the apostles often refer, Ac. ii. 22–24; xvii. 31; Ro. i. 4; 1 Co. xv. 14, &c.; 1 Ti. iii. 16. This same proof of the *innocence* or righteousness of the Saviour is as satisfactory now as it was then. One of the deepest feelings which an awakened sinner has, is his conviction of the righteousness of Jesus Christ. He sees that he is holy; that his own opposition to him has been unprovoked, unjust, and base; and it is this which so often overwhelms his soul with the conviction of his own unworthiness, and with earnest desires to obtain a better righteousness than his own. ¶ *And ye see me no more.* That is, he was to be taken away from them, and they would not see him till his return to judgment; yet this source of grief to *them* would be the means of establishing his religion and greatly blessing others.

11. *Of judgment.* That God is just, and will execute judgment. This is proved by what he immediately states. ¶ *The prince of this world.* Satan. See Notes on ch. xii. 31. The death of Christ was a judgment or a condemnation of Satan. In this struggle Jesus gained the victory and subdued the great enemy of man. This proves that God will execute judgment or justice on all his foes. If he vanquished his great enemy who had so long triumphed in this world, he will subdue all others in due time. All sinners in like manner may expect to be condemned. Of this great truth Jesus says the Holy Spirit will convince men. God showed himself to be *just* in subduing his great enemy. He showed that he was resolved to vanquish his foes, and that *all* his enemies in like manner must be subdued. This is deeply felt by the convicted sinner. He knows that he is guilty. He learns that God is just. He fears that he will condemn him, and trembles in the apprehension of approaching condemnation. From this state of alarm there is no refuge but to flee to Him who subdued the great enemy of man, and who is able to deliver him from the vengeance due to his sins. Convinced, then, of the righteousness of Jesus Christ, and of his ability and willingness to save him, he flees to his cross, and seeks in him a refuge from the coming storm of wrath.

In these verses we have a condensed and most striking view of the work of the Holy Spirit. These three things comprise the whole of his agency in the conversion of sinful men; and in the accomplishment of this work he still awakens, convinces, and renews. He attends the preaching of the gospel, and blesses the means of grace, and manifests his power in revivals of religion. He thus imparts to man the blessings purchased by the death of Jesus, carries forward and extends the same plan of mercy, and will yet apply it to all the kingdoms and tribes of men. Have *we* ever felt his power, and been brought by his influence to mourn over our sins, and seek the mercy of a dying Saviour?

12. *I have yet many things to say*, &c. There were many things pertaining to the work of the Spirit and the establishment of religion which might be said. Jesus had given them the outline; he had presented to them the great doctrines of the system, but he had not

unto you, but [i]ye cannot bear them
now.
13 Howbeit, when he, the Spirit
of truth, is come, [k]he will guide
you into all truth; for he shall not
speak of himself; but whatsoever
he shall hear, *that* shall he speak;
and [l]he will show you things to
come.
14 He shall glorify me; for he
shall receive of mine, and shall
show *it* unto you.
15 All things that the Father
hath are mine; therefore said I

i He.5.12. k ch.14.26. l Re.1.1,19.

gone into details. These were things which they could not then bear. They were still full of Jewish prejudices, and were not prepared for a full development of his plans. Probably he refers here to the great *changes* which were to take place in the Jewish system—the abolition of sacrifices and the priesthood, the change of the Sabbath, the rejection of the Jewish nation, &c. For these doctrines they were not prepared, but they would in due time be taught them by the Holy Spirit.

13. *The Spirit of truth.* So called because he would teach them all needful truth. ¶ *Will guide you into all truth.* That is, truth which pertained to the establishment of the Christian system, which they were not then prepared to hear. We may here remark that this is a full promise that they would be inspired and guided in founding the new church; and we may observe that the plan of the Saviour was replete with wisdom. Though they had been long with him, yet they were not prepared *then* to hear of the changes that were to occur; but his death would open their eyes, and the Holy Spirit, making use of the striking and impressive scenes of his death and ascension, would carry forward with vast rapidity their views of the nature of the Christian scheme. Perhaps in the few days that elapsed, of which we have a record in the first and second chapters of the Acts of the Apostles, they learned more of the true nature of the Christian plan than they would have done in months or years even under the teaching of Jesus himself. The more we study the plan of Christ, the more shall we admire the profound wisdom of the Christian scheme, and see that it was eminently fitted to the great design of its Founder—to introduce it in such a manner as to make on man the deepest impression of its wisdom and its truth. ¶ *Not speak of himself.* Not as *prompted* by himself. He shall declare what is communicated to him. See Notes on ch. vii. 18. ¶ *Whatsoever he shall hear.* What he shall receive of the Father and the Son; represented by *hearing,* because in this way instruction is commonly received. See Notes on ch. v. 30. ¶ *Things to come.* Probably this means *the meaning of things* which were to take place *after* the time when he was speaking to them—to wit, the design of his death, and the nature of the changes which were to take place in the Jewish nation. It is also true that the apostles were inspired by the Holy Spirit to predict future events which would take place in the church and the world. See Ac. xi. 28; xx. 29; xxi. 11; 1 Ti. iv. 1-3; 2 Ti. iii.; 2 Pe. i. 14; and the whole book of Revelation.

14. *Shall glorify me.* Shall honour me. The nature of his influence shall be such as to exalt my character and work in view of the mind. ¶ *Shall receive of mine.* Literally, "shall take of or from me." He shall receive his commission and instructions as an ambassador from me, to do my will and complete my work. ¶ *Shall show* it. Shall announce or communicate it to you. This is always the work of the Spirit. All serious impressions produced by him lead to the Lord Jesus (1 Co. xii. 3), and by this we may easily test our feelings. If we have been truly convicted of sin and renewed by the Holy Ghost, the tendency of all his influences has been to lead us to the Saviour; to show us our need of him; to reveal to us the loveliness of his character, and the fitness of his work to our wants; and to incline us to cast our eternal interests on his almighty arm, and commit all to his hands.

15. *All things,* &c. See Mat. xxviii. 18; xi. 27. No one could have said this who was not *equal* with the Father. The union was so intimate, though mysterious, that it might with propriety be said that whatever was done in relation to the Son, was also done in regard to the Father. See ch. xiv. 9.

16. *A little while* His death would

that he shall take of mine, and shall show *it* unto you.

16 A little while, and ye shall not see me; and again a little while, and ye shall see me, because I go to the Father.

17 Then said *some* of his disciples among themselves, What is this that he saith unto us, A little while, and ye shall not see me; and again a little while, and ye shall see me; and, Because I go to the Father?

18 They said, therefore, What is this that he saith, A little while? We cannot tell what he saith.

19 Now[m] Jesus knew that they were desirous to ask him, and said unto them, Do ye inquire among yourselves of that I said, [n]A little while, and ye shall not see me; and again a little while, and ye shall see me?

20 Verily, verily, I say unto you, That [o]ye shall weep and lament, but the world shall rejoice; and ye shall be sorrowful, but your sorrow shall be turned into joy.

21 A[p] woman when she is in travail hath sorrow, because her hour is come; but as soon as she is delivered of the child, she remembereth no more the anguish, for joy that a man is born into the world.

22 And[q] ye now therefore have sorrow; but [r]I will see you again, and your heart shall rejoice, [s]and your joy no man taketh from you.

m ch.2.24,25. *n* ver.16; ch.7.33; 13.33; 14.19.

o Lu.24.17,21. *p* Is.26.17. *q* ver.6. *r* Lu.24.41,52; ch.20.20. *s* 1 Pe.1.8.

---

occur in a short time. It took place the next day. See ch. xiv. 19. ¶ *Ye shall not see me.* That is, he would be concealed from their view in the tomb. ¶ *And again a little while.* After three days he would rise again and appear to their view. ¶ *Because I go,* &c. Because it is a part of the plan that I should ascend to God, it is necessary that I should rise from the grave, and then you will see me, and have evidence that I am still your Friend. Comp. ch. vii. 33. Here are three important events foretold for the consolation of the disciples, yet they were stated in such a manner that, in *their* circumstances and with *their* prejudices, it appeared difficult to understand him.

20. *Ye shall weep,* &c. At my crucifixion, sufferings, and death. Comp. Lu. xxiii. 27. ¶ *The world.* Wicked men. The term *world* is frequently used in this sense. See ver. 8. It refers particularly, here, to the Jews who sought his death, and who would rejoice that their object was obtained. ¶ *Shall be turned into joy.* You will not only rejoice at my resurrection, but even my death, now the object of so much grief to you, will be to you a source of unspeakable joy. It will procure for you peace and pardon in this life, and eternal joy in the world to come. Thus their greatest apparent calamity would be to them, finally, the source of their highest comfort; and though *then* they could not see *how* it could be, yet if they had known *the whole case* they would have seen that they might rejoice. As it was, they were to be consoled by the assurance of the Saviour that it would be for their good. And thus, in our afflictions, if we could see the whole case, we should rejoice. As it is, when they appear dark and mysterious, we may trust in the promise of God that they will be for our welfare. We may also remark here that the apparent triumphs of the wicked, though they may produce grief at present in the minds of Christians, will be yet overruled for good. *Their* joy shall be turned into mourning, and the mourning of Christians into joy; and wicked men may be doing the very thing—as they were in the crucifixion of the Lord Jesus—that shall yet be made the means of promoting the glory of God and the good of his people, Ps. lxxvi. 10.

22. *I will see you again.* After my resurrection. ¶ *Your joy no man taketh from you.* You shall be so firmly persuaded that I have risen and that I am the Messiah, that neither the threats nor persecutions of men shall ever be able to shake your faith and produce doubt or unbelief, and thus take away your joy. This prediction was remarkably fulfilled. It is evident that after his ascension not one of the apostles ever *doubted* for a moment that he had risen from the dead. No persecution or trial was able to shake their faith;

23 And in that day ye shall ask
me nothing. Verily, verily, I say
unto you, Whatsoever ye shall ask
the Father in my name, he will
give *it* you.
24 Hitherto have ye asked nothing in my name: [t]ask, and ye
shall receive, [u]that your joy may
be full.

t Mat.7.7,8; Ja.4.2,3. *u* ch.15.11.

25 These things have I spoken
unto you in [2]proverbs; but the
time cometh when I shall no more
speak unto you in [2]proverbs, but
I shall show you plainly of the
Father.
26 At[v] that day ye shall ask in
my name; and I say not unto you
that I will pray the Father for you;

2 or, *parables*. *v* ver.23.

and thus, amid all their afflictions, they had an unshaken source of joy.

23. *In that day.* After my resurrection and ascension. ¶ *Ye shall ask me nothing.* The word rendered *ask* here may have two significations, one to ask by way of inquiry, the other to ask for assistance. Perhaps there is reference here to both these senses. While he was with them they had been accustomed to depend on him for the supply of their wants, and in a great degree to propose their trials to him, expecting his aid. See Mat. viii. 25; Jn. xi. 3. They were also dependent on his personal instructions to explain to them the mysteries of his religion, and to remove their perplexities on the subject of his doctrines. They had not sought to God through him *as the Mediator*, but they had directly applied to the Saviour himself. He now tells them that henceforward their requests were to be made to God in his name, and that *he*, by the influences of his Spirit, would make known to them what Jesus would himself do if bodily present. The emphasis in this verse is to be placed on the word "*me*." Their requests were not to be made to *him*, but to the *Father*. ¶ *Whatsoever ye shall ask*, &c. See ch. xiv. 13.

24. *Hitherto.* During his ministry, and while he was with them. ¶ *Have ye asked*, &c. From the evangelists, as well as from this declaration, it seems that they had presented their requests for instruction and aid to Jesus himself. If they had prayed to God, it is probable that they had not done it in his name. This great truth—that we must approach God in the name of the Mediator—was reserved for the last that the Saviour was to communicate to them. It was to be presented at the close of his ministry. Then they were prepared in some degree to understand it; and then, amid trials, and wants, and a sense of their weakness and unworthiness, they would see its preciousness, and rejoice in the privilege of being thus permitted to draw near to God. Though he would be bodily absent, yet their blessings would still be given through the same unchanging Friend. ¶ *Ask*, &c. Now they had the assurance that they might approach God in his name; and, amid all their trials, they, as well as all Christians since, might draw near to God, knowing that he would hear and answer their prayers. ¶ *That your joy*, &c. See ch. xv. 11.

25. *In proverbs.* In a manner that appears obscure, enigmatical, and difficult to be understood. It is worthy of remark, that though his declarations in these chapters about his death and resurrection appear to *us* to be plain, yet to the apostles, filled with Jewish prejudices, and unwilling to believe that he was about to die, they would appear exceedingly obscure and perplexed. The plainest declarations to them on the subject would appear to be involved in mystery. ¶ *The time cometh.* This refers, doubtless, to the time *after* his ascension to heaven, when he would send the Holy Spirit to teach them the great truths of religion. It does not appear that he himself, after his resurrection, gave them any more clear or full instruction than he had done before. ¶ *I shall show you plainly.* As Jesus said that *he* would send the Holy Spirit (ver. 7), and as he came to carry forward the work of Christ, so it may be said that the teachings of the Holy Spirit were the teachings of Christ himself. ¶ *Of the Father.* *Concerning* the will and plan of the Father; particularly his plan in the establishment and spread of the Christian religion, and in organizing the church. See Ac. x.

26. *I say not unto you that I will pray*, &c. In ch. xiv. 16, Jesus says that he would pray the Father, and that he would send the Comforter. In ch. xvii. he offered a memorable prayer for them. In He. vii. 25, it is said that

27 For[w] the Father himself loveth you, because ye have loved me, and have believed that [x]I came out from God.

28 I came forth from the Father, and am come into the world; again, I leave the world and go to the Father.

29 His disciples said unto him, Lo, now speakest thou plainly, and speakest no [3]proverb.

w ch.14.21,23. x ver.30; ch.17.8. 3 or, *parable.*

30 Now are we sure that thou knowest all things, and needest not that any man should ask thee. By this we believe that thou camest forth from God.

31 Jesus answered them, Do ye now believe?

32 Behold,[y] the hour cometh, yea, is now come, that ye shall be scattered, every man to [4]his own, and shall leave me alone; and yet

y Mat.26.31; Mar.14.27. 4 or, *his own home.*

Jesus ever liveth to make intercession for us; and it is constantly represented in the New Testament that it is by his intercession in heaven now that we obtain the blessings of pardon, peace, strength, and salvation. Comp. He. ix. 24. This declaration of Jesus, then, does not mean that he *would not* intercede for them, but that there was *no need* then of his mentioning it to them again. They knew that; and, in *addition* to that, he told them that God was ready and willing to confer on them all needful blessings.

27. See ch. xiv. 21, 23.

28. *I came forth from the Father.* I came sent by the Father. ¶ *And am come into the world.* See ch. iii. 19; vi. 14, 62; ix. 39.

29. *Now speakest thou plainly.* What he had said that perplexed them was that which is contained in ver. 16. Comp. ver. 17–19: "A little while and ye shall not see me," &c. This he had now explained by saying (ver. 28), "Again, I *leave the world,* and go to the Father." In this there was no ambiguity, and they expressed themselves satisfied with this explanation.

30. *Now are we sure that thou knowest,* &c. Their difficulty had been to understand what was the meaning of his declaration in ver. 16. About this they conversed among themselves, ver. 17–19. It is evident that they had not mentioned their difficulty to him, and that he had not even heard their conversation among themselves, ver. 19. When, therefore, by his answers to them (ver. 20–28), he showed that he clearly understood their doubts; and when he gave them an answer so satisfactory without their having *inquired* of him, it satisfied them that he knew the heart, and that he assuredly came from God. They were convinced that there was *no need that any man should ask him,* or propose his difficulties to him, since he knew them all and could answer them.

31. *Do ye now believe?* Do you truly and really believe? This question was evidently asked to put them on a full examination of their hearts. Though they supposed that they had unshaken faith—faith that would endure every trial, yet he told them that they were about to go through scenes that would test them, and where they would need all their confidence in God. When we feel strong in the faith we should examine ourselves. It may be that we are deceived; and it may be that God may even then be preparing trials for us that will shake our faith to its foundation. The Syriac and Arabic read this in the indicative as an affirmation—"Ye do now believe." The sense is not affected by this reading.

32. *The hour cometh.* To wit, on the next day, when he was crucified. ¶ *Ye shall be scattered.* See Mat. xxvi. 31. ¶ *Every man to his own.* That is, as in the margin, to his own home. You shall see me die, and suppose that my work is defeated, and return to your own dwellings. It is probable that the two disciples going to Emmaus were on their way to their dwellings, Lu. xxiv. After his death all the disciples retired into Galilee, and were engaged in their common employment of fishing, Jn. xxi. 1–14; Mat. xxviii. 7. ¶ *Leave me alone.* Leave me to die without human sympathy or compassion. See Notes on Mat. xxvi. 31, 56. ¶ *Because the Father is with me.* His Father was his friend. He had all along trusted in God. In the prospect of his sufferings he could still look to him for support. And though in his dying moments he suffered so much as to use the language, "Why hast thou forsaken me?" yet it

I[z] am not alone, because the Father is with me.
33 These things have I spoken
unto you, that [a]in me ye might
have peace. In[b] the world ye shall
have tribulation; but be of good
cheer; I have overcome the world.

z Is.50.7,9; ch.8.29. a ch.14.27; Ro.5.1; Ep.2.14. b ch.15.19-21; 2 Ti.3.12.

CHAPTER XVII.

THESE words spake Jesus, and
lifted up his eyes to heaven,
and said, Father, [a]the hour is
come: glorify thy Son, that thy
Son also may glorify thee;
2 As thou hast given him power

a ch.12.23; 13.32.

was language addressed to him still as *his* God—"*My* God, *my* God." Even then he had confidence in God—confidence so strong and unwavering that he could say, "Into *thy* hands I commend my spirit," Lu. xxiii. 46. In all these sufferings he had the assurance that God was his friend, that he was doing his will, that he was promoting his glory, and that he looked on him with approbation. It matters little who else forsakes us if God be with us in the hour of pain and of death; and though poor, forsaken, or despised, yet, if we have the consciousness of his presence and his favour, then we may fear no evil. His rod and his staff, they will comfort us. Without his favour then, death will be full of horrors, though we be surrounded by weeping relatives, and by all the honour, and splendour, and wealth which the world can bestow. The Christian can die saying, I am not alone, because the Father is with me. The sinner dies without a friend that can alleviate his sufferings —without one source of real joy.

33. *In me.* In my presence, and in the aid which I shall render you by the Holy Spirit. ¶ *In the world.* Among the men to whom you are going. You must expect to be persecuted, afflicted, tormented. ¶ *I have overcome the world.* He overcame the prince of this world by his death, Jn. xii. 31. He vanquished the great foe of man, and triumphed over all that would work our ruin. He brought down aid and strength from above by his death; and by procuring for us the friendship of God and the influence of the Spirit; by his own instructions and example; by revealing to us the glories of heaven, and opening our eyes to see the excellence of heavenly things, he has furnished us with the means of overcoming all our enemies, and of triumphing in all our temptations. See Notes on Jn. xiv. 19; also Ro. viii. 34–37; 1 Jn. iv. 4; v. 4; Re. xii. 11. Luther said of this verse "that it was worthy to be carried from Rome to Jerusalem upon one's knees." The world is a vanquished enemy; Satan is a humbled foe; and all that believers have to do is to put their trust in the Captain of their salvation, putting on the whole armour of God, assured that the victory is theirs, and that the church shall yet shine forth fair as the moon, clear as the sun, and terrible as an army with banners, Ca. vi. 10.

CHAPTER XVII.

1. *These words.* The words addressed to them in the preceding chapters. They were proceeding to the garden of Gethsemane. It adds much to the interest of this prayer that it was offered in the stillness of the night, in the open air, and in the peculiarly tender circumstances in which Jesus and his apostles were. It is the *longest* prayer recorded in the New Testament. It was offered on the most tender and solemn occasion that has ever occurred in our world, and it is perhaps the most sublime composition to be found anywhere. Jesus was about to die. Having expressed his love to his disciples, and made known to them his last desires, he now commends them to the protection and blessing of the God of grace. This prayer is moreover a specimen of the manner of his *intercession*, and evinces the interest which he felt in behalf of all who should become his followers in all ages of the world. ¶ *Lifted up his eyes.* This was the common attitude of prayer. Comp. Lu. xviii. 13. ¶ *The hour is come.* That is, the appointed *time* for his sufferings and death. Comp. Notes on ch. xii. 27. ¶ *Glorify thy Son. Honour* thy Son. See ch. xi. 4. Give to the world demonstration that I am thy Son. So sustain me, and so manifest thy power in my death, resurrection, and ascension, as to afford indubitable evidence that I am the Son of God. ¶ *That thy Son also may glorify thee.* This refers clearly to the manifestation of the hon-

over all flesh, [b]that he should give eternal life to as many as thou hast given him.

b ch.5.27; ver.24.

3 And [c]this is life eternal, that they might [d]know thee, [e]the only

c 1 Jn.5.11. d Je.9.23,24. e 1 Th.1.9.

our of God which would be made by the spread of the gospel among men, ver. 2. Jesus prayed that God would so honour him in his death that striking proof might be furnished that he was the Messiah, and men thus be brought to honour God. By his death the law, the truth, and the mercy of God were honoured. By the spread of his gospel and the conversion of sinners; by all that Christ will do, now that he is glorified, to spread his gospel, God will be honoured. The conversion of a single sinner honours God; a revival of religion is an eminent means of promoting his honour; and the spread of the gospel among all nations shall yet do more than all other things to promote the honour of God among men. Whatever honours the Saviour honours God. Just as he is exalted in view of the mind, so will God be honoured and obeyed.

2. *As thou hast given him power.* It was on the ground of this power given to Christ that the apostles were commanded to go and teach all nations. See Notes on Mat. xxviii. 18, 19. ¶ *All flesh.* All men, Mat. xxiv. 22; Lu. iii. 6. ¶ *That he should give eternal life.* See Notes on Jn. v. 24. ¶ *To as many as thou hast given him.* See Notes on Jn. x. 16; vi. 37. To all on whom the Father has purposed to bestow the blessings of redemption through his Son. God has a plan in all he does, extending to men as well as to other objects. One part of his plan was that the atonement of Christ should not be in vain. Hence he promised him that he should see of the travail of his soul and should be satisfied (Is. liii. 11); and hence the Saviour had the assurance that the Father had given him a portion of the human family, and would apply this great work to them. It is to be observed here that the Saviour in this prayer makes an important distinction between "all flesh" and those who were "given him." He has *power* over all. He can control, direct, restrain them. Wicked men are so far under his universal dominion, and so far restrained by his power, that they will not be *able* to prevent his bestowing redemption on those were given him—that is, all who will believe on him. Long ago, if they had been able, they would have banished religion from the world; but they are under the power of Christ, and it is his purpose that there shall be "a seed to serve him," and that "the gates of hell shall not prevail" against his church. Men who oppose the gospel should therefore feel that they *cannot* prevent the salvation of Christians, and should be alarmed lest they be found "fighting against God."

3. *This is life eternal.* This is *the source* of eternal life; or it is in this manner that it is to be obtained. The knowledge of God and of his Son Jesus Christ *is itself* a source of unspeakable and eternal joy. Comp. ch. xi. 25; vi. 63; xii. 50. ¶ *Might know thee.* The word *know* here, as in other places, expresses more than a mere speculative acquaintance with the character and perfections of God. *It includes all the impressions on the mind and life which a just view of God and of the Saviour is fitted to produce.* It includes, of course, love, reverence, obedience, honour, gratitude, supreme affection. To *know God as he is* is to know and regard him as a lawgiver, a sovereign, a parent, a friend. It is to yield the whole soul to him, and strive to obey his law. ¶ *The only true God.* The only God, in opposition to all false gods. What is said here is in opposition to idols, not to Jesus himself, who, in 1 Jn. v. 20, is called "the true God and eternal life." ¶ *And Jesus Christ.* To know Jesus Christ is to have a practical impression of him *as he is*—that is, to suffer his character and work to make their due impression on the heart and life. Simply to have *heard* that there is a Saviour is not to *know* it. To have been taught in childhood and trained up in the belief of it is not to know it. To know him is to have a just, practical view of him in all his perfections—as God and man; as a mediator; as a prophet, a priest, and a king. It is to feel our need of such a Saviour, to see that we are sinners, and to yield the whole soul to him, *knowing* that he is a Saviour fitted to our wants, and that in his hands our souls are safe. Comp. Ep. iii. 19; Tit. i. 16; Phi. iii. 10; 1 Jn. v. 20. In this

true God, and Jesus Christ, [f] whom
thou hast sent.
4 I[g] have glorified thee on the
earth; [h] I have finished the work
which thou gavest me to do.
5 And now, O Father, glorify
thou me with thine own self, [i] with
the glory which I had with thee
before the world was.
6 I[k] have manifested thy name
unto [l] the men which thou gavest
me out of the world: thine they

f ch.10.36. *g* ch.14.13. *h* ch.19.30; 2 Ti.4.7. *i* ch.1.1,2; Phi.2.6; He.1.3,10. *k* Ps.22.22; ver.26. *l* Ro.8.30; ver.2,9,11.

verse is contained the sum and essence of the Christian religion, as it is distinguished from all the schemes of idolatry and philosophy, and all the false plans on which men have sought to obtain eternal life. The Gentiles worshipped many gods; the Christian worships one —the living and the true God; the Jew, the Deist, the Mohammedan, the Socinian, profess to acknowledge one God, without any atoning sacrifice and Mediator; the true Christian approaches him through the great Mediator, equal with the Father, who for us became incarnate, and died that he might reconcile us to God.

4. *Have glorified thee.* In my instructions and life. See his discourses everywhere, the whole tendency of which is to put honour on God. ¶ *I have finished the work.* Comp. ch. xix. 30. When he says "I *have* finished," he probably means to include also his death. All the *preparations* for that death were made. He had preached to the Jews; he had given them full proof that he was the Messiah; he had collected his disciples; he had taught them the nature of his religion; he had given them his parting counsel, and there was nothing remaining to be done but to return to God. We see here that Jesus was careful that his great and important work should be done *before* his dying hour. He did not postpone it to be performed just as he was leaving the world. So completely had he done his work, that even *before* his death he could say, "*I have finished* the work." How happy would it be if men would imitate his example, and not leave their great work of life to be done on a dying bed! Christians should have their work accomplished, and when that hour approaches, have nothing to do but to die, and return to their Father in heaven.

5. *With thine own self.* In heaven, granting me a participation of the same honour which the Father has. He had just said that he *had* glorified God *on the earth;* he now prays that God would glorify him *in heaven.* ¶ *With the glory.* With the honour. This word also includes the notion of happiness, or everything which could render the condition blessed. ¶ *Before the world was.* There could not be a more distinct and clear declaration of the pre-existence of Christ than this. It means before the *creation* of the world; before there was any world. Of course, the speaker here must have existed then, and this is equivalent to saying that he existed from eternity. See Jn. i. 1, 2; vi. 62; iii. 13; xvi. 28. The glory which he had then was that which was proper to the Son of God, represented by the expression *being in the bosom of the Father* (Jn. i. 18), denoting intimacy, friendship, united felicity. The Son of God, by becoming incarnate, is represented as *humbling himself* (Greek, he "emptied himself"), Phi. ii. 8. He laid aside for a time the external aspect of honour, and consented to become despised, and to assume the form of a servant. He now prays that God would raise him up to the dignity and honour which he had before his incarnation. This is the state to which he is now exalted, with the *additional* honour of having made atonement for sin, and having opened the way to save a race of rebels from eternal death. The lowest condition on earth is frequently connected with the highest honours of heaven. Man looks on the outward appearance. God looks to him that is humble and of a contrite spirit.

6. *Have manifested thy name.* The word *name* here includes the attributes or character of God. Jesus had made known his character, his law, his will, his plan of mercy—or, in other words, he had revealed GOD to them. The word *name* is often used to designate the *person*, Jn. xv. 21; Mat. x. 22; Ro. ii. 24; 1 Ti. vi. 1. ¶ *Which thou gavest me.* God gave them to him in his purpose. He gave them by his providence. He so ordered affairs that they heard him preach and saw his miracles; and he gave them by disposing them to follow him when he called them. ¶ *Thine*

were, and thou gavest them me, and [m]they have kept thy word.

7 Now they have known that all things whatsoever thou hast given me are of thee.

8 For I have given unto them the[n] words which thou gavest me; and they have received *them*, and have known surely that I came out from thee, and they have believed that thou didst send me.

9 I pray for them: [o]I pray not for the world, but for them which thou hast given me; for they are thine.

10 And[p] all mine are thine, and thine are mine; and [q]I am glorified in them.

11 And now I am no more in the world, but these are in the world, and I come to thee. Holy Father, [r]keep through [s]thine own

m He.3.6. n ch.6.68; 14.10.
o 1 Jn.5.19. p ch.16.15. q Ga.1.24; 1 Pe.2.9. r 1 Pe.1.5; Jude 1,24. s Pr.18.10.

they were. All men are God's by creation and by preservation, and he has a right to do with them as seemeth good in his sight. These men he chose to designate to be the apostles of the Saviour; and he committed them to him to be taught, and then commissioned them to carry his gospel, though amid persecutions, to the ends of the world. God has a right to the services of all; and he has a right to appoint us to any labour, however humble, or hazardous, or wearisome, where we may promote his glory and honour his name.

7. *They have known.* They have been *taught* that and have believed it. ¶ *Hast given me.* This refers, doubtless, to the *doctrine* of Christ, ver. 8. They are assured that all my instructions are of God.

8. *The words.* The doctrines. Christ often represented himself as *instructed* and *sent* to teach certain great truths to men. Those he taught, and no others. See Notes on Jn. v. 30.

9, 10. *I pray for them.* In view of their dangers and trials, he sought the protection and blessing of God on them. His prayer was always answered. ¶ *Not for the world.* The term *world* here, as elsewhere, refers to wicked, rebellious, vicious men. The meaning of this expression here seems to be this: Jesus is praying for his disciples. As a *reason* why God should bless them, he says that they were not of the world; that they had been taken out of the world; that they belonged unto God. The petition was not offered for wicked, perverse, rebellious men, but for those who were the friends of God and were disposed to receive his favours. This passage, then, settles nothing about the question whether Christ prayed for sinners. He *then* prayed for his disciples, who were not those who hated him and disregarded his favours. He *afterward* extended the prayer for all who should become Christians, ver. 20. When on the cross he prayed for his crucifiers and murderers, Lu. xxiii. 34. ¶ *For they are thine.* This is urged as a *reason* why God should protect and guide them. His honour was concerned in keeping them; and we may always *fill our mouths with* such *arguments* when we come before God, and plead that his honour will be advanced by keeping *us* from evil, and granting us all needful grace. ¶ *I am glorified in them.* I am honoured by their preaching and lives. The sense of this passage is, "Those who are my disciples are thine. That which promotes my honour will also promote thine. I pray, therefore, that they may have needful grace to honour my gospel, and to proclaim it among men."

11. *I am no more in the world.* I have finished my work among men, and am about to leave the world. See ver. 4. ¶ *These are in the world.* They will be among wicked men and malignant foes. They will be subject to trials and persecutions. They will *need* the same protection which *I* could give them if I were with them. ¶ *Keep.* Preserve, defend, sustain them in trials, and save them from apostasy. ¶ *Through thine own name.* Our translators seem to have understood this expression as meaning "keep by thy power," but this probably is not its meaning. It is literally "keep *in* thy name." And if the term *name* be taken to denote God himself and his perfections (see Note on ver. 6), it means "keep in the knowledge of thyself. Preserve them in obedience to thee and to thy cause. Suffer them not to fall away from thee and to become apostates." ¶ *That they may be one.* That they may be united. ¶ *As we* are. This refers not to a union

name those whom thou hast given
me, that they may be one, as we *are*.
12 While I was with them in the
world, I kept them in thy name:
those that thou gavest me I have
kept; and none of them is lost but
the son of perdition; [t]that the
scripture might be fulfilled.
13 And now come I to thee; and
these things I speak in the world,
that they might have my joy fulfilled in themselves.

t Ps.109.8; Ac.1.20.

14 I have given them thy word;
and [u]the world hath hated them,
because they are not of the world,
even as I am not of the world.
15 I pray not that thou shouldest take them out of the world,
but [v]that thou shouldest keep them
from the evil.
16 They are not of the world,
even as I am not of the world.
17 Sanctify[w] them through thy
truth; [x]thy word is truth.

u ch.15.18,19. *v* Ga.1.4. *w* Ac.15.9; Ep.5.26; 2 Th.2.13. *x* Ps.119.151.

---

of *nature*, but of feeling, plan, purpose. Any other union between Christians is impossible; but a union *of affection* is what the Saviour sought, and this he desired might be so strong as to be an illustration of the unchanging love between the Father and the Son. See ver. 21–23.

12. *While I was with them in the world.* While I was engaged with them among other men—surrounded by the people and the temptations of the world. Jesus had now finished his work among the men of the world, and was performing his last offices with his disciples. ¶ *I kept them.* By my example, instructions, and miracles. I preserved them from apostasy. ¶ *In thy name.* In the knowledge and worship of thee. See ver. 6–11. ¶ *Those that thou gavest me*, &c. The word "gavest" is evidently used by the Saviour to denote not only to give to him to be his real followers, but also as apostles. It is here used, probably, in the sense of giving as apostles. God had so ordered it by his providence that they had been given to him to be his apostles and followers; but the terms "thou gavest me" do not of necessity prove that they were true believers. Of Judas Jesus knew that he was a deceiver and a devil, Jn. vi. 70: "Have not I *chosen* you twelve, and one of you is a devil?" Judas is there represented as having been *chosen* by the Saviour to the apostleship, and this is equivalent to saying that he was given to him for this work; yet at the same time he knew his character, and understood that he had never been renewed. ¶ *None of them.* None of those chosen to the apostolic office. ¶ *But the son of perdition.* See Notes on Mat. i. 1. The term *son* was given by the Hebrews to those who possessed the character described by the word or name following. Thus, sons of Belial—those who possessed his character; children of wisdom—those who were wise, Mat. xi. 19. Thus Judas is called a son of perdition because he had the character of a *destroyer.* He was a traitor and a murderer. And this shows that he who knew the heart regarded his character as that of a wicked man—one whose appropriate name was that of a son of perdition. ¶ *That the scripture*, &c. See Notes on ch. xiii. 18. Comp. Ps. xli. 9.

13. *My joy fulfilled*, &c. See Notes on ch. xv. 11. The expression "my joy" here probably refers to the joy of the apostles respecting the Saviour—the joy which would result from his resurrection, ascension, and intercession in heaven.

14. *I have given them*, &c. See ver. 8. ¶ *The world hath hated them*, &c. Ch. xv. 18–21.

15. *That thou shouldest take them out of the world.* Though they were going into trials and persecutions, yet Jesus did not pray that they might be removed soon from them. It was better that they should endure them, and thus spread abroad the knowledge of his name. It would be easy for God to remove his people at once to heaven, but it is better for them to remain, and show the power of religion in supporting the soul in the midst of trial, and to spread his gospel among men. ¶ *Shouldest keep them from the evil.* This may mean either from the evil one—that is, the devil, or from evil in general—that is, from apostasy, from sinking in temptation. Preserve them from that evil, or give them such grace that they may endure all trials and be sustained amid them. See Notes on Mat. vi. 13. It

18 As thou hast sent me into the
world, even so have I also sent
them into the world.
19 And[y] for their sakes I sanctify myself, that they also might
be [1]sanctified through the truth.
20 Neither pray I for these alone,

y 1 Co.1.2,30.

1 or, *truly sanctified.*

matters little how long we are in this world if we are kept in this manner.

16. See ch. xv. 19.

17. *Sanctify them.* This word means to render pure, or to cleanse from sins, 1 Th. v. 23; 1 Co. vi. 11. Sanctification in the heart of a Christian is progressive. It consists in his becoming more like God and less attached to the world; in his getting the ascendency over evil thoughts, and passions, and impure desires; and in his becoming more and more weaned from earthly objects, and attached to those things which are unseen and eternal. The word also means to *consecrate*, to set apart to a holy office or purpose. See ver. 19; also Notes on ch. x. 36. When Jesus prayed here that God would *sanctify* them, he probably included both these ideas, that they might be made personally more holy, and might be truly consecrated to God as the ministers of his religion. Ministers of the gospel will be *really* devoted to the service of God just in proportion as they are personally pure. ¶ *Through thy truth.* Truth is a representation of things as they are. The Saviour prayed that through those just views of God and of themselves they might be made holy. To see things as they are is to see God to be infinitely lovely and pure; his commands to be reasonable and just; heaven to be holy and desirable; his service to be easy, and religion pleasant, and sin odious; to see that life is short, that death is near; that the pride, pomp, pleasures, wealth, and honours of this world are of little value, and that it is of infinite importance to be prepared to enter on the eternal state of being. He that sees all this, or *that looks on things as they are*, will desire to be holy. He will make it his great object to live near to God and to glorify his name. In the sanctification of the soul God makes use of *all truth*, or of everything fitted to make a representation of things as they are to the mind. His Word states that and no more; his Spirit and his providence do it. The earth and the heavens, the seasons, the sunshine and the rain, are all fitted to teach us his goodness and power, and lead us to him. His daily mercies tend to the same end, and afflictions have the same design. Our own sickness teaches us that we are soon to die. The death of a friend teaches us the instability of all earthly comforts, and the necessity of seeking better joys. All these things are fitted to make *just representations* to the mind, and thus to sanctify the soul. As the Christian is constantly amid these objects, so he should be constantly growing in grace, and daily and hourly gaining new and deeper impressions of the great truths of religion. ¶ *Thy word is truth.* All that thou hast *spoken*—that is, all that is contained in the Bible. All the commands and promises of God; his representations of his own character and that of man; his account of the mission and death of his Son; of the grave, the resurrection, judgment, and eternity, all tend to *represent things as they are*, and are thus fitted to sanctify the soul. We have here also the testimony of the Saviour that the revelation which God has given is true. *All* that God has spoken is true, and the Christian should rejoice and the sinner should tremble. See Ps. xix. 7-14.

19. *I sanctify myself.* I consecrate myself exclusively to the service of God. The word *sanctify* does not refer here to *personal* sanctification, for he had no sin, but to setting himself apart entirely to the work of redemption. ¶ *That they also*, &c. 1st. That they might have an *example* of the proper manner of labouring in the ministry, and might learn of me *how* to discharge its duties. Ministers will understand their work best when they most faithfully study the example of their great model, the Son of God. 2d. That they might be made pure by the *effect* of my sanctifying myself—that is, that they might be made pure by the shedding *of that blood which cleanses from all sin.* By this only can men be made holy; and it was because the Saviour *so* sanctified himself, or set himself to this work so unreservedly as to shed his own blood, that any soul can be made pure and fit for the kingdom of God.

20, 21. *Neither pray I for these alone*, &c. Not for the apostles only, but for all who shall be converted under the

but for them also which shall believe on me through their word;
21 That[z] they all may be one; as thou, Father, *art* in me, and I in thee, that they also may be one in us; that the world may believe that thou hast sent me.
22 And[a] the glory which thou gavest me I have given them; that they may be one, even as we are one;
23 I in them, and thou in me, that they may be made perfect in one; and that the world may know

z Ro.12.5.

a 2 Co.3.18.

---

preaching of the gospel. They will all need similar grace and be exposed to similar trials. It is a matter of unspeakable joy that *each* Christian, however humble or unknown to men—however poor, unlearned, or despised, can reflect that he was remembered in prayer by *him whom God heareth always.* We value the prayers of pious friends. How much more should we value this petition of the Son of God! To that single prayer we who are Christians owe infinitely more real benefits than the world can ever bestow; and in the midst of any trials we may remember that the Son of God *prayed for us,* and that the prayer was assuredly heard, and will be answered in reference to all who truly believe. ¶ *All may be one.* May be united as brethren. Christians are all redeemed by the same blood, and are going to the same heaven. They have the same wants, the same enemies, the same joys. Though they are divided into different denominations, yet they will meet at last in the same abodes of glory. Hence they *should* feel that they belong to the same family, and are children of the same God and Father. There are no ties so tender as those which bind us in the gospel. There is no friendship so pure and enduring as that which results from having the same attachment to the Lord Jesus. Hence Christians, in the New Testament, are represented as being indissolubly united—parts of the same body, and members of the same family, Ac. iv. 32–35; 1 Co. xii. 4–31; Ep. ii. 20–22; Ro. xii. 5. On the ground of this union they are exhorted to love one another, to bear one another's burdens, and to study the things that make for peace, and things wherewith one may edify another, Ep. iv. 3; Ro. xii. 5–16. ¶ *As thou, Father,* art *in me.* See ch. xiv. 10. This does not affirm that the union between Christians should be *in all respects* like that between the Father and the Son, but only in the points in which they *are capable of being compared.* It is not the union of *nature* which is referred to, but the union of plan, of counsel, of purpose—seeking the same objects, and manifesting attachment to the same things, and a desire to promote the same ends. ¶ *That they also may be one in us.* To be *in* God and *in* Christ is to be *united to* God and Christ. The expression is common in the New Testament. The phrase here used denotes *a union among all Christians founded on and resulting from a union to the same God and Saviour.* ¶ *That the world may believe,* &c. That the world, so full of animosities and fightings, may see the power of Christian principle in overcoming the sources of contention and producing love, and may thus see that a religion that could produce this *must* be from heaven. See Notes on ch. xiii. 34. This was done. Such was the attachment of the early Christians to each other, that a heathen was constrained to say, "See how these Christians love one another!"

22. *And the glory,* &c. The *honour* which thou hast conferred on *me* by admitting me to *union* with thee, the same honour I have conferred on them by admitting them to *like union* with me. ¶ *May be one, even as we are one.* Not in *nature,* or in the mode of existence—for this was not the subject of discourse, and would be impossible—but in feeling, in principle, in purpose. Evincing, as the Father and the Son had always done, the same great aim and plan; not pursuing different interests, or counteracting each other's purposes, or forming parties, but seeking the same ends by the same means. This is the union between the Father and the Son. Always, in the creation, preservation, and redemption of the world, the Father and the Son have sought the same object, and this is to be the model on which Christians should act.

23. *May be made perfect in one.* That their union may be complete. That there may be no jars, discords, or contentions. A machine is perfect or com-

that thou hast sent me, and hast
loved them as thou hast loved me.
24 Father, I will that they also
whom thou hast given me [b]be with
me where I am, that they may behold my glory which thou hast
given me; for thou lovedst me before the foundation of the world.
25 O righteous Father, the world
hath not known thee; but I have
known thee, and these have known
that thou hast sent me.
26 And I have declared unto

b 1 Th.4.17.

plete when it has all its parts and is in good order—when there is no portion of it wanting. So the union of Christians, for which the Saviour prayed, would be complete or perfect if there were no controversies, no envyings, no contentions, and no heart-burnings and jealousies. It is worthy of remark here how entirely *the union of his people* occupied the mind of Jesus as he drew near to death. He saw the danger of strifes and contentions in the church. He knew the imperfections of even the best of men. He saw how prone they would be to passion and ambition; how ready to mistake love of sect or party for zeal for pure religion; how selfish and worldly men in the church might divide his followers, and produce unholy feeling and contention; and he saw, also, how much this would do to dishonour religion. Hence he took occasion, when he was about to die, to impress the importance of union on his disciples. By solemn admonition, and by most tender and affecting appeals to God in supplication, he showed *his* sense of the value of this union. He used the most sublime and impressive illustration; he adverted to the eternal union between the Father and himself; he reminded them of his love, and of the effect that their union would have on the world, to fix it more deeply in their hearts. The effect has shown the infinite wisdom of the Saviour. The contentions and strifes of Christians have shown his knowledge in foreseeing it. The effect of all this on religion has shown that *he* understood the value of union. Christians have contended long enough. It is time that they should hear the parting admonitions of their Redeemer, and go unitedly against their common foe. The world still lies in wickedness; and the friends of Jesus, bound by the cords of eternal love, should advance together against the common enemy, and spread the triumphs of the gospel around the globe. All that is needful now, under the blessing of God, to convince the world *that God sent the Lord Jesus, is that very union among all Christians for which he prayed;* and when that union of feeling, and purpose, and action shall take place, the task of sending the gospel to all nations will be soon accomplished, and the morning of the millennial glory will dawn upon the world.

24. *I will.* This expression, though it commonly denotes *command*, is here only expressive of *desire.* It is used in *prayer*, and it was not the custom of the Saviour to use language of *command* when addressing God. It is often used to express *strong* and *earnest* desire, or a pressing and importunate *wish*, such as we are exceedingly anxious should not be denied, Mar. vi. 25; x. 35; Mat. xii. 38; xv. 28. ¶ *Where I am.* In heaven. The Son of God was still in the bosom of the Father, Jn. i. 18. See Notes on Jn. vii. 34. Probably the expression here means where *I shall be.* ¶ *My glory.* My honour and dignity when exalted to the right hand of God. The word "behold" implies more than simply *seeing;* it means also to *participate*, to *enjoy.* See Notes on ch. iii. 3; Mat. v. 8. ¶ *Thou lovedst me*, &c. This is another of the numerous passages which prove that the Lord Jesus existed before the creation of the world. It is not possible to explain it on any other supposition.

25. *Hath not known thee.* See Notes on ver. 3.

26. *Thy name.* See Notes on ver. 6. ¶ *And will declare* it. After my resurrection, and by the influence of the Holy Spirit, Lu. xxiv. 45; Ac. i. 3. ¶ *I in them.* By my doctrines and the influences of my Spirit. That my religion may show its power, and produce its proper fruits in their minds, Ga. iv. 19.

The discourse in the xivth, xvth, and xvith chapters is the most tender and sublime that was ever pronounced in our world. No composition can be found anywhere so fitted to sustain the soul in trial or to support it in death. This

them thy name, and will declare *it;*
that the love wherewith thou hast
loved me may be in them, and I
in them.

CHAPTER XVIII.

WHEN Jesus had spoken these
words, he went forth with
his disciples over the brook [a]Ce-
dron, where was a garden, into the
which he entered, and his disciples.
2 And Judas also, which betrayed him, knew the place; for Jesus
ofttimes resorted thither with his
disciples.
3 Judas[b] then, having received
a band *of men* and officers from the
chief priests and Pharisees, cometh
thither with lanterns, and torches,
and weapons.
4 Jesus therefore, [c]knowing all
things that should come upon him,
went forth, and said unto them,
Whom seek ye?
5 They answered him, [d]Jesus of
Nazareth. Jesus saith unto them,

a 2 Sa.15.23.

b Mat.26.47,&c.; Mar.14.43,&c.; Lu.22.47,&c. *c* ch.10.17,18; Ac.2.28. *d* Mat.2.23; ch.19.19.

sublime and beautiful discourse is appropriately closed by a solemn and most affecting prayer—a prayer at once expressive of the profoundest reverence for God and the tenderest love for men—simple, grave, tender, sublime, and full of consolation. It is the model for our prayers, and with like reverence, faith, and love we should come before God. This prayer for the church will yet be fully answered; and he who loves the church and the world cannot but cast his eyes onward to that time when all believers shall be one; when contentions, bigotry, strife, and anger shall cease; and when, in perpetual union and love, Christians shall show forth the power and purity of that holy gospel with which the Saviour came to bless mankind. Soon may that happy day arise!

CHAPTER XVIII.

1. *The brook Cedron.* This was a small stream that flowed to the east of Jerusalem, through the valley of Jehoshaphat, and divided the city from the Mount of Olives. It was also called *Kidron* and *Kedron.* In summer it is almost dry. The word used here by the evangelist—χειμάῤῥου—denotes properly a water-stream (from χεῖμα, *shower* or *water*, and ῥέω, ῥόος, to *flow, flowing*), and the idea is that of a stream that was swollen by rain or by the melting of the snow (Passow, *Lex.*). This small rivulet runs along on the east of Jerusalem till it is joined by the water of the pool of Siloam, and the water that flows down on the west side of the city through the valley of Jehoshaphat, and then goes off in a south-east direction to the Dead Sea. (See the Map of the Environs of Jerusalem in vol. i.) Over this brook David passed when he fled from Absalom, 2 Sa. xv. 23. It is often mentioned in the Old Testament, 1 Ki. xv. 13; 2 Ch. xv. 16; xxx. 14; 2 Ki. xxiii. 6, 12. ¶ *Where was a garden.* On the west side of the Mount of Olives. This was called *Gethsemane.* See Notes on Mat. xxvi. 36. It is probable that this was the property of some wealthy man in Jerusalem—perhaps some friend of the Saviour. It was customary for the rich in great cities to have country-seats in the vicinity. This, it seems, was so accessible that Jesus was accustomed to visit it, and yet so retired as to be a suitable place for devotion.

2. *Jesus ofttimes resorted thither.* For what purpose he went there is not declared, but it is probable that it was for retirement and prayer. He had no home in the city, and he sought this place, away from the bustle and confusion of the capital, for private communion with God. Every Christian should have some place—be it a grove, a room, or a garden—where he may be alone and offer his devotions to God. We are not told much of the private habits of Jesus, but we are permitted to know so much of him as to be assured that he was accustomed to seek for a place of retirement, and during the great feasts of the Jews the Mount of Olives was the place which he chose, Lu. xxi. 37; Mat. xxi. 17; Jn. viii. 1.

3. *A band.* See Notes on Mat. xxvi. 47; xxvii. 27. John passes over the agony of Jesus in the garden, probably because it was so fully described by the other evangelists. ¶ *Lanterns,* &c. This was the time of the full moon, but it might have been cloudy, and their taking lights with them shows their determination to find him.

I am *he*. And Judas also, which
betrayed him, stood with them.
6 As soon then as he had said
unto them, I am *he*, [e]they went
backward and fell to the ground.
7 Then asked he them again,
Whom seek ye? And they said,
Jesus of Nazareth.
8 Jesus answered, I have told
you that I am *he;* [f]if, therefore, ye
seek me, let these go their way;
9 That the saying might be fulfilled which he spake, [g]Of them
which thou gavest me have I lost
none.
10 Then[h] Simon Peter, having
a sword, drew it, and smote the
high-priest's servant, and cut off
his right ear. The servant's name
was Malchus.
11 Then said Jesus unto Peter,
Put up thy sword into the sheath:
[i]the cup which my Father hath
given me, shall I not drink it?
12 Then the band, and the captain, and officers of the Jews took
Jesus, and bound him,
13 And led him away to [k]Annas
first; for he was father-in-law to
Caiaphas, which was the high-
priest that same year.[1]
14 Now Caiaphas was he which

e Ps.27.2; 40.14. *f* Is.53.6; Ep.5.25. *g* ch.17.12. *h* Mat.26.51; Mar.14.47; Lu.22.49,50.

i Mat.20.22; 26.39,42. *k* Lu.3.2.
1 *And Annas sent Christ bound unto Caiaphas, the high-priest*, ver.24.

6. *They went backward*, &c. The *cause* of their retiring in this manner is not mentioned. Various things might have produced it. The frank, open, and fearless *manner* in which Jesus addressed them may have convinced them of his innocence, and deterred them from prosecuting their wicked attempt. His disclosure of himself was sudden and unexpected; and while they perhaps anticipated that he would make an effort to escape, they were amazed at his open and bold profession. Their consciences reproved them for their crimes, and probably the firm, decided, and yet mild manner in which Jesus addressed them, the expression of his unequalled power in knowing how to find the way to the consciences of men, made them feel that they were in the presence of more than mortal man. There is no proof that there was here any miraculous power, any mere physical force, and to suppose that there was greatly detracts from the moral sublimity of the scene.

8. *Let these go their way*. These apostles. This shows his care and love even in the hour of danger. *He* expected to die. *They* were to carry the news of his death to the ends of the earth. Hence he, the faithful Captain of salvation, went foremost into trials; he, the Good Shepherd, secured the safety of the flock, and went before them into danger. By the *question* which he asked those who came out against him, he had secured the safety of his apostles. He was answered that they sought for *him*. He demanded that, agreeably to their declaration, they should take *him* only, and leave his followers at liberty. The wisdom, caution, and prudence of Jesus forsook him in no peril, however sudden, and in no circumstances, however difficult or trying.

9. *The saying*. Ch. xvii. 12. As he *had* kept them for more than three years, so he still sought their welfare, even when his death was near.

10, 11. See Notes on Mat. xxvi. 51, 52. ¶ *The servant's name was Malchus.* His name is mentioned by neither of the other evangelists, nor is it said by the other evangelists who was the disciple that gave the blow. It is probable that both Peter and the servant were alive when the other gospels were written.

12. See Mat. xxvi. 50.

13. *To Annas first*. Probably his house was nearest to them, and he had great authority and influence in the Jewish nation. He had been himself a long time high-priest; he had had five sons who had successively enjoyed the office of high-priest, and that office was now filled by his son-in-law. It was of importance, therefore, to obtain his sanction and counsel in their work of evil. ¶ *That same year*. Ch. xi. 49.

14. *Which gave counsel*, &c. Ch. xi. 49, 50. This is referred to here, probably, to show how little prospect there was that Jesus would have *justice* done him in the hands of a man who had already pronounced on the case.

15-18. See Notes on Mat. xxvi. 57,

gave[l] counsel to the Jews that it
was expedient that one man should
die for the people.

15 And[m] Simon Peter followed
Jesus, and *so did* another disciple.
That disciple was known unto the
high-priest, and went in with Jesus
into the palace of the high-priest.

16 But Peter stood at the door
without. Then went out that other
disciple, which was known unto
the high-priest, and spake unto her
that kept the door, and brought
in Peter.

17 Then saith the damsel that
kept the door unto Peter, Art not
thou also *one* of this man's disciples? He saith, I am not.

18 And the servants and officers
stood there, who had made a fire
of coals, for it was cold; and they
warmed themselves; and Peter
stood with them and warmed himself.

19 The high-priest then asked
Jesus of his disciples, and of his
doctrine.

20 Jesus answered him, [n]I spake
openly to the world: I ever taught
in the synagogue, and in the temple, whither the Jews always resort; and [o]in secret have I said
nothing.

21 Why askest thou me? Ask
them which heard me what I have

l ch.11.49,50. *m* Mat.26.58,&c.; Mar.14.54; Lu.22.54.

n Lu.4.15; ch.7.14,26,28; 8.2. *o* Ac.26.26.

58. ¶ *Another disciple.* Not improbably John. Some critics, however, have supposed that this disciple was one who dwelt at Jerusalem, and who, not being a Galilean, could enter the palace without suspicion. John, however, mentions the circumstance of his being *known* to them, to show why it was that he was not questioned as Peter was. It is not probable that any danger resulted from its being known that he was a follower of Jesus, or that any harm was meditated on *them* for this. The questions asked *Peter* were not asked by those in authority, and his apprehensions which led to his denial were groundless.

19. *The high-priest then asked Jesus of his disciples.* To ascertain their *number* and *power*. The charge on which they wished to arraign him was that of sedition, or of rebellion against Cæsar. To make that plausible, it was necessary to show that he had made *so many* disciples as to form a strong and dangerous faction; but, as they had no direct proof of that, the high-priest insidiously and improperly attempted to draw the Saviour into a confession. Of this he was aware, and referred him to the proper source of evidence—his open, undisguised conduct before the world. ¶ *His doctrine.* His teaching. The sentiments that he inculcated. The object was doubtless to convict him of teaching sentiments that tended to subvert the Mosaic institutions, or that were treasonable against the Roman government. Either would have answered the design of the Jews, and they doubtless expected that he—an unarmed and despised Galilean, now completely in their power—would easily be drawn into confessions which art and malice could use to procure his condemnation.

20. *Openly to the world.* If his doctrine had tended to excite sedition and tumult, if he had aimed to overthrow the government, he would have trained his friends in secret; he would have retired from public view, and would have laid his plans in private. This is the case with all who attempt to subvert existing establishments. Instead of that, he had proclaimed his views to all. He had done it in every place of public concourse—in the synagogue and in the temple. He here speaks the language of one conscious of innocence and determined to insist on his rights. ¶ *Always resort.* Constantly assemble. They were required to assemble there three times in a year, and great multitudes were there constantly. ¶ *In secret*, &c. He had taught no private or concealed doctrine. He had taught nothing to his disciples which he had not himself taught in public and commanded them to do, Mat. x. 27; Lu. xii. 3.

21. *Why askest thou me? Ask them*, &c. Jesus here insisted on his *rights*, and reproves the high-priest for his unjust and illegal manner of extorting a confession from him. If he had done wrong, or taught erroneous and seditious doctrines, it was easy to prove it, and the course which he had a right to

said unto them; behold, they know
what I said.
22 And when he had thus spoken, one of the officers which stood
by [p]struck Jesus [2]with the palm of
his hand, saying, Answerest thou
the high-priest so?
23 Jesus answered him, If I have
spoken evil, bear witness of the
evil; [q]but if well, why smitest
thou me?
24 Now[3] Annas had sent him
bound unto Caiaphas the high-
priest.

p Job 16.10; Je.20.2; Ac.23.2,3. q 1 Pe.2.19-23. 2 or, *with a rod.* 3 See ver.13.

25 And Simon Peter stood and
warmed himself. They said, therefore, unto him, Art not thou also
one of his disciples? He denied
it, and said, I am not.
26 One of the servants of the
high-priest, being *his* kinsman
whose ear Peter cut off, saith, Did
not I see thee in the garden with
him?
27 Peter then denied again; [r]and
immediately the cock crew.
28 Then[s] led they Jesus from
Caiaphas unto [4]the hall of judg-

r Mat.26.74; Mar.14.72; Lu.22.60; ch.13.38.
s Mat.27.2,&c.; Mar.15.1,&c.; Lu.23.1,&c.
4 or, *Pilate's house.*

demand was that they should establish the charge by fair and incontrovertible evidence. We may here learn, 1st. That, though Jesus was willing to be reviled and persecuted, yet he also insisted that *justice* should be done him. 2d. He was conscious of innocence, and he had been so open in his conduct that he could appeal to the vast multitudes which had heard him as witnesses in his favour. 3d. It is proper for us, when persecuted and reviled, meekly but firmly to insist on our rights, and to demand that justice shall be done us. Laws are made to *protect* the innocent as well as to condemn the guilty. 4th. Christians, like their Saviour, should so live that they may confidently appeal to all who have known them as witnesses of the sincerity, purity, and rectitude of their lives, 1 Pe. iv. 13-16.

22. *One of the officers.* One of the *inferior* officers, or those who attended on the court. ¶ *With the palm of his hand.* This may mean, "Gave him a blow either with the open hand or with a rod"—the Greek does not determine which. In whatever way it was done, it was a violation of all law and justice. Jesus had showed no disrespect for the office of the high-priest, and if he had, *this* was not the proper way to punish it. The Syriac reads thus: "Smote the *cheek* of Jesus." The Vulgate and Arabic: "Gave him a blow."

23. *Spoken evil.* In my answer to the high-priest. If there was any disrespect to the office, and want of regard for the law which appointed him, then testify to the fact, and let punishment be inflicted according to the law; comp. Ex. xxii. 28. ¶ *But if well,* &c. While an accused person is on trial he is under the protection of the court, and has a right to *demand* that all *legal* measures shall be taken to secure his rights. On this right Jesus insisted, and thus showed that, though he had no disposition to take revenge, yet he claimed that, when arraigned, strict justice should be done. This shows that his precept that *when we are smitten on one cheek we should turn the other* (Mat. v. 39), is consistent with a firm demand that justice should be done us. That precept refers, besides, rather to *private* matters than to judicial proceedings. It does not demand that, when we are unjustly arraigned or assaulted, and when the law is in our favour, we should sacrifice our rights to the malignant accuser. Such a surrender would be injustice to the law and to the community, and be giving *legal* triumph to the wicked, and destroying the very *end* of all law. In private matters this effect would not follow, and we should there bear injuries without reviling or seeking for vengeance.

24. Comp. ver. 13 with Mat. xxvi. 57.

25, 26. See Notes on Mat. xxvi. 72-74.

28. See Mat. xxvii. 1, 2. ¶ *Hall of judgment.* The *prætorium*—the same word that in Mat. xxvii. 27, is translated *common hall.* See Notes on that place. It was the place where the Roman *prætor*, or governor, heard and decided cases brought before him. Jesus had been condemned by the Sanhedrim, and pronounced guilty of death (Mat. xxvi. 66); but they had not power to carry their sentence into execution (ver. 31), and they therefore sought that he

ment; and it was early; and they
themselves went not into the judgment-hall, [t]lest they should be defiled, but that they might eat the
passover.
29 Pilate then went out unto
them, and said, What accusation
bring ye against this man?

30 They answered and said unto
him, If he were not a malefactor,
we would not have delivered him
up unto thee.
31 Then said Pilate unto them,
Take ye him, and judge him according to your law. The Jews
therefore said unto him, [u]It is

t Ac.10.28.

u Ge.49.10; Eze.21.27.

---

might be condemned and executed by Pilate. ¶ *Lest they should be defiled.* They considered the *touch* of a Gentile to be a defilement, and on this occasion, at least, seemed to regard it as a pollution to enter the *house* of a Gentile. They took care, therefore, to guard themselves against what they considered ceremonial pollution, while they were wholly unconcerned at the enormous crime of putting the innocent Saviour to death, and imbruing their hands in their Messiah's blood. Probably there is not anywhere to be found among men another such instance of petty regard to the mere ceremonies of the law and attempting to keep from pollution, at the same time that their hearts were filled with malice, and they were meditating the most enormous of all crimes. But it shows us how much more concerned men will be at the violation of the mere *forms* and *ceremonies* of religion than at real crime, and how they endeavour to keep their consciences at ease amid their deeds of wickedness by the observance of some of the outward ceremonies of religion—by mere sanctimoniousness. ¶ *That they might eat the passover.* See Notes on Mat. xxvi. 2, 17. This defilement, produced by contact with *a Gentile*, they considered as equivalent to that of the contact of a dead body (Le. xxii. 4–6; Nu. v. 2), and as disqualifying them to partake of the passover in a proper manner. The word translated *passover* means properly the paschal lamb which was slain and eaten on the observance of this feast. This rite Jesus had observed with his disciples the day before this. It has been supposed by many that he *anticipated* the usual time of observing it one day, and was crucified on the day on which the Jews observed it; but this opinion is improbable. The *very day* of keeping the ordinance was specified in the law of Moses, and it is not probable that the Saviour departed from the commandment. All the circumstances, also, lead us to suppose that he observed it at the usual time and manner, Mat. xxvi. 17, 19. The only passage which has led to a contrary opinion is this in John; but here the word *passover* does not, of necessity, mean the *paschal lamb.* It probably refers to the *feast* which followed the sacrifice of the lamb, and which continued seven days. Comp. Nu. xxviii. 16, 17. *The whole feast* was called the Passover, and they were unwilling to defile themselves, even though the paschal lamb had been killed, because it would disqualify them for participating in the remainder of the ceremonies (Lightfoot).

30. *If he were not a malefactor.* A violator of the law. If we had not *determined* that he was such, and was worthy of death, Mat. xxvi. 66. From this it appears that they did not deliver him up to be *tried*, but hoped that Pilate would *at once* give sentence that he should be executed according to their request. It is probable that in ordinary cases the Roman governor was not accustomed to make very strict inquiry into the justice of the sentence. The Jewish Sanhedrim tried causes and pronounced sentence, and the sentence was usually approved by the governor; but in this case Pilate, evidently contrary to their expectations, proceeded *himself* to rehear and retry the cause. He had doubtless heard of the miracles of Jesus. He seems to have been strongly prepossessed with the belief of his innocence. He knew that they had delivered him from mere envy (Mat. xxvii. 18), and hence he inquired of them the nature of the case, and the kind of charge which they expected to substantiate against him.

31. *Judge him*, &c. The Jews had not directly *informed* him that they *had* judged him and pronounced him worthy of death. Pilate therefore tells them to inquire into the case; to ascertain the proof of his guilt, and to decide on what

not lawful for us to put any man
to death:
32 That[v] the saying of Jesus
might be fulfilled which he spake,
signifying what death he should
die.
33 Then Pilate entered into the

v Mat.20.19; Lu.18.32,33.

the law of Moses pronounced. It has been doubted whether this gave them the power of putting him to death, or whether it was not rather a direction to them to inquire into the case, and inflict on him, if they judged him guilty, the mild punishment which they were yet at liberty to inflict on criminals. Probably the former is intended. As they had already determined that in their view this case demanded the punishment of death, so in their answer to Pilate they *implied* that they *had* pronounced on it, and that he ought to die. They still, therefore, *pressed* it on his attention, and refused to obey his injunction to judge him. ¶ *It is not lawful*, &c. The Jews were accustomed to put persons to death still in a popular tumult (Ac. vii. 59, 60), but they had not the power to do it in any case in a regular way of justice. When they first laid the plan of arresting the Saviour, they did it *to kill him* (Mat. xxvi. 4); but whether they intended to do this secretly, or in a tumult, or by the concurrence of the Roman governor, is uncertain. The Jews themselves say that the power of inflicting capital punishment was taken away about forty years before the destruction of the temple; but still it is probable that in the time of Christ they had the power of determining on capital cases in instances that pertained to religion (Josephus, *Antiq.*, b. xiv. ch. 10, § 2; comp. *Jewish Wars*, b. vi. ch. 2, § 4). In this case, however, it is supposed that their sentence was to be *confirmed* by the Roman governor. But it is admitted on all hands that they had *not* this power in the case of seditions, tumults, or treason against the Roman government. If they had this power in the case of blasphemy and irreligion, they did not dare to exert it here, because they were afraid of tumult among the people (Mat. xxvi. 5); hence they sought to bring in the authority of Pilate. To do this, they endeavoured to make it appear that it was a case of *sedition* and *treason*, and one which

judgment-hall again, and called
Jesus, and said unto him, Art
thou the King of the Jews?
34 Jesus answered him, Sayest
thou this thing of thyself, or did
others tell it thee of me?
35 Pilate answered, Am I a Jew?

therefore *demanded* the interference of the Roman governor. Hence it was on *this charge* that they arraigned him, Lu. xxiii. 2. Thus a tumult might be avoided, and the *odium* of putting him to death they expected would fall, not on themselves, but on Pilate.

32. *That the saying of Jesus*, &c. To wit, that he would be delivered into the hands of the *Gentiles* and be *crucified*, Mat. xx. 19. Neither of these things would have happened if he had been put to death in the way that the Jews first contemplated, Mat. xxvi. 4. Though it should be admitted that they had the power, in *religious cases*, to do this, yet in such a case it would not have been done, as Jesus predicted, by the Gentiles; and even if it should be admitted that they had the right to take life, yet they had *not* the right to do it by *crucifixion*. This was particularly a Roman punishment. And thus it was ordered, in the providence of God, that the prediction of Jesus in both these respects was fulfilled.

33. *Art thou the King of the Jews?* This was *after* they had accused him of perverting the nation, and forbidding to give tribute to Cæsar, Lu. xxiii. 2, 3.

34. *Of thyself.* From any conviction of your own mind, or any apprehension of danger. During all the time in which you have been prætor, have you seen anything in me that has led you to apprehend sedition or danger to the Roman power? This evidently was intended to remind Pilate that nothing was proved against him, and to caution him against being influenced by the malicious accusations of others. Jesus demanded a just trial, and claimed that Pilate should not be influenced by any *reports* that he might have heard of him.

35. *Am I a Jew?* Am I likely to be influenced by Jewish prejudices and partialities? Am not I, being a Roman, likely to judge impartially, and to decide on the accusations without being biassed by the malignant charges of the accusers? ¶ *Thine own nation*, &c. In this Pilate denies that it was from any-

Thine [w]own nation and the chief
priests have delivered thee unto
me: what hast thou done?
36 Jesus [x]answered, [y]My kingdom is not of this world. If my
kingdom were of this world, then
would my servants fight, that I
should not be delivered to the
Jews; but now is my kingdom
not from hence.

w ch.19.11; Ac.3.13. x 1 Ti.6.13.
y Ps.45.3,6; Is.9.6,7; Da.2.44; 7.14; Zec.9.9; Lu.12.14; ch.6.15; Ro.14.17; Col.1.13.

37 Pilate therefore said unto him,
Art thou a king then? Jesus
answered, Thou sayest that I am
a king. To this end was I born,
and for this cause came I into the
world, that I should [z]bear witness
unto the truth. Every[a] one that is
of the truth heareth my voice.
38 Pilate saith unto him, What
is truth? And when he had said
this, he went out again unto the

z Is.55.4; Re.1.5; 3.14. a ch.8.47; 1 Jn.4.6.

---

thing that *he* had observed that Jesus was arraigned. He admits that it was from the accusation of others; but then he tells the Saviour that the charge was one of moment, and worthy of the deepest attention. It had come from the *very nation* of Jesus, from his own countrymen, and from the highest authority among the people. As such it demanded consideration, and Pilate besought him to tell him *what he had done*—that is, what there had been in his conduct that had given occasion for this charge.

36. *My kingdom*, &c. The charge on which Jesus was arraigned was that of laying claim to the office of a king. He here substantially admits that he *did* claim to be a king, but not in the sense in which the Jews understood it. *They* charged him with attempting to set up an *earthly* kingdom, and of exciting sedition against Cæsar. In reply to this, Jesus says that *his kingdom is not of this world*—that is, it is not of the same nature as earthly kingdoms. It was not originated for the same purpose, or conducted on the same plan. He immediately adds a circumstance in which they differ. The kingdoms of the world are defended by arms; they maintain armies and engage in wars. If the kingdom of Jesus had been of *this* kind, he would have excited the multitudes that followed him to prepare for battle. He would have armed the hosts that attended him to Jerusalem. He would not have been alone and unarmed in the garden of Gethsemane. But though he *was* a king, yet his dominion was over the heart, subduing evil passions and corrupt desires, and bringing the soul to the love of peace and unity. ¶ *Not from hence.* That is, not from *this world*.

37. *Art thou a king then?* Dost thou *admit* the charge in any sense, or dost thou lay claim to a kingdom of any kind? ¶ *Thou sayest*, &c. This is a form of expression denoting *affirmation*. It is equivalent to *yes*. ¶ *That I am a king*. This does not mean simply that Pilate *affirmed* that he was a king; it does not appear that he had done this; but it means, "Thou affirmest the truth; thou declarest what is correct, *for* I am a king." I *am* a king in a certain sense, and do not deny it. ¶ *To this end*, &c. Comp. ch. iii. 11, 12, &c. Jesus does not here affirm that he was born to *reign*, or that this was the *design* of his coming; but it was to bear witness to and to exhibit *the truth*. By this he showed what was the *nature* of his kingdom. It was not to assert power; not to collect armies; not to subdue nations in battle. It was simply to present *truth* to men, and to exercise dominion only *by* the truth. Hence the only power put forth in restraining the wicked, in convincing the sinner, in converting the heart, in guiding and leading his people, and in sanctifying them, is that which is produced by applying *truth* to the mind. Men are not *forced* or *compelled* to be Christians. They are made to *see* that they are sinners, that God is merciful, that they need a Redeemer, and that the Lord Jesus is fitted to their case, and yield themselves then wholly to his reign. This is all the *power* ever used in the kingdom of Christ, and no men in his church have a right to use any other. Alas! how little have persecutors remembered this! And how often, under the pretence of great regard for the kingdom of Jesus, have bigots attempted by force and flames to make all men think as *they* do! We see here the importance which Jesus attached to *truth*. It was his *sole* business in coming into the world. He had no

Jews, and saith unto them, I find
in him no fault *at all.*
39 But ye have a custom, that I
should release unto you one at the
passover; will ye, therefore, that I
release unto you the King of the
Jews?
40 Then cried they all again,
saying, Not this man, but Barabbas.
Now Barabbas was a robber.

CHAPTER XIX.

THEN [a] Pilate therefore took
Jesus and [b]scourged *him.*
2 And the soldiers platted a
crown of thorns, and put *it* on his
head, and they put on him a purple
robe,
3 And said, Hail, King of the
Jews! and they smote him with
their hands.
4 Pilate therefore went forth
again, and saith unto them, Behold,
I bring him forth to you,
that ye may know that [c]I find no
fault in him.
5 Then came Jesus forth, wearing
the crown of thorns, and the

a Mat.27.26,&c.; Mar.15.15,&c. *b* Is.53.5. *c* ch.18.38; ver.6.

other end than to establish it. *We* therefore should value it, and seek for it as for hid treasures, Pr. xxiii. 23. ¶ *Every one*, &c. See ch. viii. 47.

38. *What is truth?* This question was probably asked in *contempt*, and hence Jesus did not answer it. Had the question been sincere, and had Pilate *really* sought it as Nicodemus had done (ch. iii.), Jesus would not have hesitated to explain to him the nature of his kingdom. They were now alone in the judgment-hall (ver. 33), and as soon as Pilate had asked the question, without waiting for an answer, he went out. It is evident that he was satisfied, from the answer of Jesus (ver. 36, 37), that he was not a king in the sense in which the Jews accused him; that he would not endanger the Roman government, and consequently that he was *innocent* of the charge alleged against him. He regarded him, clearly, as a *fanatic*—poor, ignorant, and deluded, but innocent and not dangerous. Hence he sought to release him; and hence, in *contempt*, he asked him this question, and immediately went out, not expecting an answer. This question had long agitated the world. It was the great subject of inquiry in all the schools of the Greeks. Different sects of philosophers had held different opinions, and Pilate now, in derision, asked him, whom *he* esteemed an ignorant fanatic, whether *he* could solve this long-agitated question. He *might* have had an answer. Had he patiently waited in sincerity, Jesus would have told him what it was. Thousands ask the question in the same way. They have a fixed contempt for the Bible; they deride the instructions of religion; they are unwilling to *investigate* and to wait at the gates of wisdom; and hence, like Pilate, they remain ignorant of the great Source of truth, and die in darkness and in error. *All might* find truth if they would seek it; none ever *will* find it if they do not apply for it to the great source of light—the God of truth, and seek it patiently in the way in which he has chosen to communicate it to mankind. How highly should we prize the Bible! And how patiently and prayerfully should we *search* the Scriptures, that we may not err and die for ever! See Notes on ch. xiv. 6. ¶ *I find in him no fault.* See Lu. xxiii. 4.

39, 40. See Notes on Mat. xxvii. 15–21.

CHAPTER XIX.

1–3. See Notes on Mat. xxvii. 26–30.

4. *Behold, I bring him forth*, &c. Pilate, after examining Jesus, had gone forth and *declared* to the Jews that he found no fault in him, ch. xviii. 38. At that time Jesus remained in the judgment-hall. The Jews were not satisfied with that, but demanded still that he should be put to death, ver. 39, 40. Pilate, disposed to gratify the Jews, returned to Jesus and ordered him to be scourged, as if preparatory to death, ch. xix. 1. The patience and meekness with which Jesus bore this seem to have convinced him still more that he was innocent, and he *again* went forth to *declare* his conviction of this; and, to do it more effectually, he said, "Behold, I bring him forth to you, that ye may know," &c.—that they might themselves *see*, and be satisfied, as he had been, of his innocence.

purple robe. And *Pilate* saith unto them, Behold the man!

6 When the chief priests, therefore, and officers saw him, they cried out, saying, Crucify *him*, crucify *him!* Pilate saith unto them, Take ye him, and crucify *him:* for I find no fault in him.

7 The Jews answered him, [d]We have a law, and by our law he ought to die, [e]because he made himself the Son of God.

[d] Le.24.16. [e] ch.5.18; 10.33.

All this shows his anxiety to release him, and also shows that the meekness, purity, and sincerity of Jesus had power to convince a Roman governor that he was not guilty. Thus the highest evidence was given that the charges were false, even when he was condemned to die.

5. *Behold the man!* It is probable that Pilate *pointed* to the Saviour, and his object evidently was to move them to compassion, and to convince them, by a sight of the Saviour himself, that he was innocent. Hence he brought him forth with the crown of thorns, and the purple robe, and with the marks of scourging. Amid all this Jesus was meek, patient, and calm, giving evident proofs of innocence. The conduct of Pilate was as if he had said, "See! The man whom you accuse is arrayed in a gorgeous robe, as if a king. He has been scourged and mocked. All this he has borne with patience. See! How calm and peaceful! Behold his countenance! How mild! His body scourged, his head pierced with thorns! Yet in all this he is meek and patient. This is the man that you accuse; and he is now brought forth, that you may *see* that he is not guilty."

6. *They cried out, saying, Crucify* him, &c. The view of the Saviour's meekness only exasperated them the more. They had *resolved* on his death; and as they saw Pilate disposed to acquit him, they redoubled their cries, and endeavoured to gain by tumult, and clamour, and terror, what they saw they could not obtain by justice. When men are *determined* on evil, they cannot be reasoned with. Every *argument* tends to defeat their plans, and they press on in iniquity with the more earnestness in proportion as sound reasons are urged to stay their course. Thus sinners go in the way of wickedness down to death. They make up in firmness of purpose what they lack in reason. They are more fixed in their plans in proportion as God faithfully warns them and their friends admonish them. ¶ *Take ye him*, &c. These are evidently the words of a man *weary* with their importunity and with the subject, and yet resolved not to sanction their conduct. It was not the act of a *judge* delivering him up according to the forms of the law, for they did not understand it so. It was equivalent to this: "*I* am satisfied of his innocence, and shall not pronounce the sentence of death. If *you* are bent on his ruin—if you are determined to put to death an innocent man—if *my* judgment does not satisfy you—take him and put him to death *on your own responsibility*, and take the consequences. It cannot be done with my consent, nor in the due form of law; and *if* done, it must be by *you*, without authority, and in the face of justice." See Mat. xxvii. 24.

7. *We have a law.* The law respecting blasphemy, Le. xxiv. 16; De. xiii. 1-5. They had arraigned Jesus on that charge before the Sanhedrim, and condemned him for it, Mat. xxvi. 63-65. But *this* was not the charge on which they had arraigned him before Pilate. They had accused him of *sedition*, Lu. xxiii. 2. On *this charge* they were now convinced that they could not get Pilate to condemn him. He declared him innocent. Still bent on his ruin, and resolved to gain their purpose, they now, contrary to their first intention, adduced the *original* accusation on which they had already pronounced him guilty. If they could not obtain his condemnation as *a rebel*, they now sought it as *a blasphemer*, and they appealed to Pilate to sanction what they believed was required in their law. Thus to Pilate himself it became more manifest that he was innocent, that they had attempted to *deceive* HIM, and that the charge on which they had arraigned him was a mere pretence to obtain *his* sanction to their wicked design. ¶ *Made himself.* Declared himself, or claimed to be. ¶ *The Son of God.* The law did not forbid this, but it forbade *blasphemy*, and they considered the assumption of this title as the same as blasphemy (Jn. x. 30, 33, 36), and therefore condemned him.

8 When Pilate therefore heard that saying, he was the more afraid;

9 And went again into the judgment-hall, and saith unto Jesus, Whence art thou? But [f] Jesus gave him no answer.

10 Then saith Pilate unto him, Speakest thou not unto me? knowest thou not that [g] I have power to crucify thee, and have power to release thee?

11 Jesus answered, [h] Thou couldest have no power *at all* against me

f Ps.38.13; Is.53.7; Mat.27.12,14; Phi.1.28.

g Da.3.14,15. *h* Lu.22.53; ch.7.30.

8. *When Pilate therefore heard that saying.* That they had accused him of blasphemy. As this was not the charge on which they had arraigned him before his bar, he had not before heard it, and it now convinced him more of their malignity and wickedness. ¶ *He was the more afraid.* What was the ground of his *fear* is not declared by the evangelist. It was probably, however, the alarm of his *conscience*, and the fear of *vengeance* if he suffered such an act of injustice to be done as to put an innocent man to death. He was convinced of his innocence. He saw more and more clearly the design of the Jews; and it is not improbable that a *heathen*, who believed that the *gods* often manifested themselves to men, dreaded their vengeance if he suffered one who *claimed* to be divine, and who *might* be, to be put to death. It is clear that Pilate was convinced that Jesus was innocent; and in this state of agitation between the convictions of his own conscience, and the clamours of the Jews, and the fear of vengeance, and the certainty that he would do wrong if he gave him up, he was thrown into this state of alarm, and resolved again to question Jesus, that he might obtain satisfaction on the subjects that agitated his mind.

9. *Whence art thou?* See Notes on ch. vii. 27. Pilate knew that he was a Galilean, but this question was asked to ascertain whether he claimed to be the Son of God—whether a mere man, or whether divine. ¶ *Jesus gave him no answer.* Probably for the following reasons: 1st. He had already told him his design, and the nature of his kingdom, ch. xviii. 36, 37. 2d. He had said enough to satisfy him of his innocence. Of that Pilate was convinced. His duty was clear, and if he had had firmness to do it, he would not have asked this. Jesus, by his silence, therefore *rebuked* him for his want of firmness, and his unwillingness to do what his conscience told him was right. 3d. It is not probable that Pilate would have understood him if he had declared to him the truth about his origin, and about his being the Son of God. 4th. After what had been done—after he had satisfied Pilate of his innocence, and then had been beaten and mocked by his permission—he had no reason to expect justice at his hands, and therefore properly declined to make any farther defence. By this the prophecy (Is. liii. 7) was remarkably fulfilled.

10. *Speakest thou not*, &c. This is the expression of a man of pride. He was not accustomed to be met with silence like this. He endeavoured, therefore, to address the *fears* of Jesus, and to appal him with the declaration that his life was at his disposal, and that his safety depended on his favour. This arrogance called forth the reply of the Saviour, and he told him that he had *no* power except what was given him from above. Jesus was not, therefore, to be intimidated by any claim of *power* in Pilate. His life was not in his hands, and he could not stoop to ask the *favour* of a *man*.

11. *No power.* No such power as you claim. You have not *originated* the power which you have. You have just as much as is *given*, and your ability extends no farther. ¶ *Except it were given thee.* It has been conceded or granted to you. God has ordered your life, your circumstances, and the extent of your dominion. This was a reproof of a proud man in office, who was forgetful of the great Source of his authority, and who supposed that by his own talents or fortune he had risen to his present place. Alas! how many men *in office* forget that *God* gives them their rank, and vainly think that it is owing to their own talents or merits that they have risen to such an elevation. Men of office and talent, as well as others, should remember that *God* gives them what they have, and that they have no influence except as it is conceded to

except[i] it were given thee from above; therefore [k]he that delivered me unto thee hath [l]the greater sin.

12 And from thenceforth Pilate sought to release him; but the Jews cried out, saying, If thou let this man go thou art not Cæsar's friend: [m]whosoever maketh himself a king, speaketh against Cæsar.

13 When[n] Pilate therefore heard that saying, he brought Jesus forth, and sat down in the judgment-seat, in a place that is called the Pavement, but in the Hebrew, Gabbatha.

i Ps.39.9. *k* Mar.14.44; ch.18.3. *l* He.6.4-8; Ja.4.17. *m* Lu.23.2; Ac.17.7. *n* Pr.29.25; Ac.4.19.

them from on high. ¶ *From above.* From God, or by his direction, and by the arrangements of his providence. Ro. xiii. 1: "There is no power but of God; the powers that be are ordained of God." The words "from above" often refer to *God* or to *heaven*, Ja. i. 17; iii. 15, 17; Jn. iii. 3 (in the Greek). The providence of God was remarkable in so ordering affairs that a man, flexible and yielding like Pilate, should be intrusted with power in Judea. Had it been a man firm and unyielding in his duty—one who could not be terrified or awed by the multitude—Jesus would *not* have been delivered to be crucified, Ac. ii. 23. God thus brings about his wise ends; and while Pilate was *free*, and *acted out his nature* without compulsion, yet the purposes of God, long before predicted, were fulfilled, and Jesus made an atonement for the sins of the world. Thus God overrules the wickedness and folly of men. He so orders affairs that the *true character* of men shall be *brought out*, and makes use of that character to advance his own great purposes. ¶ *Therefore.* On this account. "You are a magistrate. Your power, as such, is given you by God. You are not, indeed, guilty for *accusing* me, or malignantly arraigning me; but you have power *intrusted* to you over my life; and the Jews, who *knew* this, and who knew that the power of a magistrate was given to him by God, have the *greater sin* for seeking my condemnation before a tribunal *appointed by God*, and for endeavouring to obtain so solemn a sanction to their own malignant and wicked purposes. They have endeavoured to avail themselves of the civil power, the sacred appointment of God, and *on this account* their sin is greater." This does not mean that their sin was greater than that of Pilate, though that was true; but their sin was greater *on account* of the fact that they perseveringly and malignantly endeavoured to obtain the sanction of the magistrate to their wicked proceedings. Nor does it mean, because God had *purposed* his death (Ac. ii. 23), and given power to Pilate, that *therefore* their sin was greater, for *God's purpose* in the case made it neither more nor less. It did not change the *nature* of their free acts. This passage teaches no such doctrine, but that their sin was *aggravated* by malignantly endeavouring to obtain the sanction of a *magistrate* who was invested with authority *by God*, and who wielded the power that *God* gave him. By this Pilate *ought* to have been convinced, and *was* convinced, of their wickedness, and hence he sought more and more to release him. ¶ *He that delivered me.* The singular here is put for the plural, including Judas, the high-priests, and the Sanhedrim.

12. *Sought to release him.* He was more and more convinced of his innocence, and more unwilling to yield him to mere malice and envy in the face of justice. ¶ *But the Jews cried out*, &c. This moved Pilate to deliver Jesus into their hands. He feared that he would be accused of unfaithfulness to the interests of the Roman emperor if he did not condemn a man whom *his own nation* had accused of sedition. The Roman emperor then on the throne was exceedingly jealous and tyrannical, and the *fear* of losing his favour induced Pilate to deliver Jesus into their hands. ¶ *Cæsar's friend.* The friend of the Roman emperor. The name of the reigning emperor was Tiberius. After the time of Julius Cæsar all the emperors were called *Cæsar*, as all the kings of Egypt were called *Pharaoh.* This emperor was, during the latter part of his reign, the most cruel, jealous, and wicked that ever sat on the Roman throne.

13. *Judgment-seat.* The tribunal or place of pronouncing sentence. He came here to deliver him, in due form of law, into the hands of the Jews. ¶ *Pavement.* This was an area or room of the judgment-hall whose floor was made of small square stones of various

14 And[o] it was the preparation of the passover, and about the sixth hour; and he saith unto the Jews, Behold your King!

15 But they cried out, Away with *him*, away with *him;* crucify him! Pilate saith unto them, Shall I crucify your King? The chief priests answered, [p]We have no king but Cæsar.

16 Then[q] delivered he him, therefore, unto them to be crucified. And they took Jesus, and led *him* away.

17 And he, bearing his cross, went[r] forth into a place called *the place* of a skull, which is called in the Hebrew, Golgotha;

18 Where they crucified him, and two others with him, on either side one, and Jesus in the midst.

19 And[s] Pilate wrote a title, and put *it* on the cross. And the writing was, JESUS OF NAZARETH, THE KING OF THE JEWS.

o Mat.27.62. *p* Ge.49.10.
q Mat.27.26,&c.; Mar.15.15,&c.; Lu.23.24,&c.
r Nu.15.36; He.13.12.
s Mat.27.37; Mar.15.26; Lu.23.38.

20 This title then read many of the Jews; for the place where Jesus was crucified was nigh to the city; and it was written in Hebrew, *and* Greek, *and* Latin.

21 Then said the chief priests of the Jews to Pilate, Write not, The King of the Jews; but that he said, I am King of the Jews.

22 Pilate answered, What I have written I have written.

23 Then the soldiers, when they had crucified Jesus, took his garments, and made four parts, to every soldier a part; and also *his* coat: now the coat was without seam, [1]woven[t] from the top throughout.

24 They said, therefore, among themselves, Let us not rend it, but cast lots for it, whose it shall be; that the scripture might be fulfilled which saith, [u]They parted my raiment among them, and for my vesture they did cast lots. These things, therefore, the soldiers did.

1 or, *wrought.* *t* Ex.39.22. *u* Ps.22.18.

colours. This was common in palaces and houses of wealth and splendour. See Notes on Mat. ix. 2. ¶ *Gabbatha.* This word is not elsewhere used. It comes from a word signifying to be *elevated.* The name given to the place by the Hebrews was conferred from its being the place of the *tribunal*, as an *elevated* place.

14. *The preparation of the passover.* See Notes on Mar. xv. 42. ¶ *The sixth hour.* Twelve o'clock. Mark says (ch. xv. 25) that it was the *third* hour. See the difficulty explained in the Notes on that place.

16–22. See Notes on Mat. xxvii. 32–37.

22. *What I have written*, &c. This declaration implied that he would make no change. He was impatient, and weary of their solicitations. He had yielded to them contrary to the convictions of his own conscience, and he now declared his purpose to yield no farther.

23. *His garments.* The plural here is used to denote the *outer garment.* It was made, commonly, so as to be easily thrown on or off, and when they laboured or walked it was girded about the loins. See Notes on Mat. v. 40. ¶ *Four parts.* It seems, from this, that there were *four* soldiers employed as his executioners. ¶ His *coat.* His under garment, called the *tunic.* ¶ *Was without seam.* Josephus (*Antiq.*, b. iii. ch. 8, § 4) says of the garment or coat of the high-priest that "this vesture was not composed of two pieces, nor was it sewed together upon the shoulders and the sides; but it was one long vestment, so woven as to have an aperture for the neck. It was also parted where the hands were to come out." It seems that the Lord Jesus, the great High-priest of his people, had also a coat made in a similar manner. Comp. Ex. xxxix. 22.

24. *Let us not rend it.* It would then have been useless. The *outer* garment, being composed of several parts — fringes, borders, &c. (De. xii. 12)—could be easily divided. ¶ *That the scripture*, &c. Ps. xxii. 18.

25 Now there stood by the
cross of Jesus his mother, and
his mother's sister, Mary the *wife*
of [2]Cleophas, [v]and Mary Magdalene.
26 When Jesus therefore saw his
mother, and [w]the disciple standing
by whom he loved, he saith unto
his mother, [x]Woman, behold thy
son!
27 Then saith he to the disciple,
Behold thy [y]mother! And from
that hour that disciple took her
unto [z]his own *home*.
28 After this, Jesus, knowing
that all things were now accomplished, that the [a]scripture might
be fulfilled, saith, I thirst.
29 Now there was set a vessel
full of vinegar: and they filled a
sponge with vinegar, and put *it*
upon hyssop, and put *it* to his
mouth.
30 When Jesus therefore had

2 or, *Clopas*. v Lu.24.18. w ch.13.23. x ch.2.4. y 1 Ti.5.2. z ch.16.32. a Ps.69.21.

26. *The disciple—whom he loved.* See ch. xiii. 23. ¶ *Woman.* This appellation certainly implied no disrespect. See Notes on ch. ii. 4. ¶ *Behold thy son!* This refers to *John*, not to Jesus himself. Behold, my beloved disciple shall be to you *a son*, and provide for you, and discharge toward you the duties of an affectionate child. Mary was poor. It would even seem that now she had no home. Jesus, in his dying moments, filled with tender regard for his mother, secured for her an adopted son, obtained for her a home, and consoled her grief by the prospect of attention from him who was the most beloved of all the apostles. What an example of filial attention! What a model to all children! And how lovely appears the dying Saviour, thus remembering his afflicted mother, and making *her* welfare one of his last cares on the cross, and even when making atonement for the sins of the world!

27. *Behold thy mother!* One who is to be to thee *as* a mother. The fact that she was the mother of Jesus would secure the kindness of John, and the fact that she was now intrusted to him demanded of him affectionate regard and tender care. ¶ *From that hour*, &c. John seems to have been in better circumstances than the other apostles. See ch. xviii. 16. Tradition says that she continued to live with him in Judea till the time of her death, which occurred about fifteen years after the death of Christ.

28–30. See Notes on Mat. xxvii. 46–50. ¶ *That the scripture might be fulfilled, saith, I thirst.* See Ps. lxix. 21. *Thirst* was one of the most distressing circumstances attending the crucifixion. The wounds were highly inflamed, and a raging fever was caused, usually, by the sufferings on the cross, and this was accompanied by insupportable thirst. See Notes on Mat. xxvii. 35. A Mameluke, or Turkish officer, was crucified, it is said in an Arabic manuscript recently translated, on the banks of the river Barada, under the castle of Damascus. He was nailed to the cross on Friday, and remained till Sunday noon, when he died. After giving an account of the crucifixion, the narrator proceeds: "I have heard this from one who witnessed it; and he thus remained till he died, patient and silent, without wailing, but looking around him to the right and the left, upon the people. But he begged for water, and none was given him; and the hearts of the people were melted with compassion for him, and with pity on one of God's creatures, who, yet a boy, was suffering under so grievous a trial. In the meantime the water was flowing around him, and he gazed upon it, and longed for one drop of it; and he complained of thirst all the first day, after which he was silent, for God gave him strength."—Wiseman's *Lectures*, p. 164, 165, ed. Andover.

30. *It is finished.* The sufferings and agonies in redeeming man are over. The work long contemplated, long promised, long expected by prophets and saints, is done. The toils in the ministry, the persecutions and mockeries, and the pangs of the garden and the cross, are ended, and man is redeemed. What a wonderful declaration was this! How full of consolation to man! And how should this dying declaration of the Saviour reach every heart and affect every soul!

31. *The preparation.* Ver. 14. ¶ *That the bodies*, &c. The law required that the bodies of those who were hung

received the vinegar, he said, [b]It is finished; and he bowed his head and [c]gave up the ghost.

31 The Jews, therefore, because it was [d]the preparation, that [e]the bodies should not remain upon the cross on the sabbath-day, ([f]for that sabbath-day was an high day,) besought Pilate that their legs might be broken, and *that* they might be taken away.

32 Then came the soldiers and brake the legs of the first, and of the other which was crucified with him.

33 But when they came to Jesus, and saw that he was dead already, they brake not his legs;

34 But one of the soldiers with a spear pierced his side, and forthwith came thereout [g]blood and [h]water.

b ch.17.4. *c* Is.53.10,12; He.2.14,15. *d* ver.42. *e* De.21.23. *f* Le.23.7,8.

g He.9.22,23; 1 Jn.5.6,8. *h* 1 Pe.3.21.

---

should not remain suspended during the night. See De. xxi. 22, 23. That law was made when the punishment by crucifixion was unknown, and when those who were suspended would almost immediately expire. In the punishment by crucifixion, life was lengthened out for four, five, or eight days. The Jews therefore requested that their death might be hastened, and that the land might not be polluted by their bodies remaining suspended on the Sabbath-day. ¶ *Was an high day.* It was, 1st. The Sabbath. 2d. It was the day on which the paschal feast properly commenced. It was called a *high day* because that year the feast of the Passover *commenced* on the Sabbath. Greek, "*Great day.*" ¶ *Their legs might be broken.* To hasten their death. The effect of this, while they were suspended on the cross, would be to increase their pain by the *act* of breaking them, and to deprive their body of the support which it received from the feet, and to throw the whole weight on the hands. By this increased torment their lives were soon ended. Lactantius says that this was commonly done by the Romans to persons who were crucified. The common period to which persons crucified would live was several days. To *compensate* for those *lingering* agonies, so that the full amount of suffering might be endured, they *increased* their sufferings by breaking their limbs, and thus hastening their death.

33. *Saw that he was dead.* Saw by the indications of death on his person, and perhaps by the testimony of the centurion, Mat. xxvii. 54. The death of Jesus was doubtless hastened by the intense agony of the garden, and the peculiar sufferings endured as an atonement for sin on the cross. Comp. Mat. xxvii. 46.

34. *One of the soldiers.* One of those appointed to watch the bodies till they were dead. This man appears to have doubted whether he was dead, and, in order to see whether he was not yet sensible, he pierced him with his spear. The Jews designed that his legs should be broken, but this was prevented by the providence of God; yet in another way more satisfactory proof was obtained of his death than would have been by the breaking of his legs. This was so ordered, no doubt, that there might be the *fullest proof* that he was truly dead; that it could not be pretended that he had swooned away and revived, and so, therefore, that there could not be the least doubt of his resurrection to life. ¶ *With a spear.* The common spear which soldiers used in war. There can be no doubt that such a stroke from the strong arm of a Roman soldier would have caused death, if he had not been already dead; and it was, doubtless, to furnish this conclusive proof that he was *actually dead*, and that an atonement had thus been made for mankind, that John mentions so particularly this fact. Let the following circumstances be remembered, showing that death *must* have ensued from such a wound: (1.) The Saviour was elevated but a little from the ground, so as to be easily reached by the spear of a soldier. (2.) The wound must have been *transversely upward*, so as to have penetrated into the body, as he could not have stood directly under him. (3.) It was probably made with a strong arm and with violence. (4.) The spear of the Roman soldier was a lance which tapered very gently to a point, and would penetrate easily. (5.) The wound was comparatively a *large* wound. It was so large *as to admit the hand* (Jn. xx. 27); but for a lance thus tapering to have

35 And[i] he that saw *it* bare
record, and his record is true; and
he knoweth that he saith true,
that ye might believe.
36 For these things were done
that the [k]scripture should be fulfilled, A bone of him shall not be
broken.
37 And again [l]another scripture saith, They shall look on him
whom they pierced.
38 And after this, Joseph of Ari-

i 1 Jn.1.1-3. *k* Ex.12.46; Nu.9.12; Ps.34.20. *l* Ps.22.16; Zec.12.10; Re.1.7.

---

made a wound so wide as to admit the hand, it must have been *at least* four or five inches in depth, and must have been such as to have made death certain. If it be remembered that this blow was *probably* in the left side, the conclusion is inevitable that death would have been the consequence of such a blow. To make out this fact was of special importance, probably, in the time of John, as the reality of the death of Jesus was denied by the Gnostics, many of whom maintained that he died *in appearance only*. ¶ *Pierced his side.* Which side is not mentioned, nor can it be certainly known. The common opinion is that it was the left side. Car. Frid. Gruner (*Commentatio Antiquaria Medica de Jesu Christi Morte*, p. 30–36) has attempted to show that it must have been the left side. See Wiseman's *Lectures*, p. 161, 162, and Kuinoel on Jn. xix. 34, where the arguments of Gruner are fully stated. It is clear that the spear pierced to the region of the heart. ¶ *And forthwith came*, &c. This was evidently a *natural* effect of thus piercing the side. Such a flowing of blood and water makes it probable that the spear reached the heart, and if Jesus had not before been dead, this would have closed his life. The heart is surrounded by a membrane called the *pericardium*. This membrane contains a serous matter or liquor resembling water, which prevents the surface of the heart from becoming dry by its continual motion (Webster). It was this which was pierced and from which the water flowed. The point of the spear also reached one of the ventricles of the heart, and the blood, yet warm, rushed forth, either mingled with or followed by the water of the pericardium, so as to *appear* to John to be blood and water flowing together. This was a natural effect, and would follow in any other case. Commentators have almost uniformly supposed that this was significant; as, for example, that the blood was an emblem of the eucharist, and the water of baptism, or that the blood denoted justification, and the water sanctification; but that this was the design there is not the slightest evidence. It was strictly a natural result, adduced by John to establish *one* fact on which the whole of Christianity turns —*that he was truly dead.* On this depends the doctrine of the atonement, of his resurrection, and all the prominent doctrines of religion. This fact it was of importance to prove, that it might not be pretended that he had only suffered a *syncope*, or had fainted. This John establishes. He shows that those who were sent to hasten his death *believed* that he had expired; that then a soldier inflicted a wound which *would* have terminated life if he had not been already dead; and that the infliction of this wound was followed by the fullest proof that he had truly expired. On this *fact* he dwells with the interest which became a subject of so much importance to the world, and thus laid the foundation for undoubted assurance that the Lord Jesus *died* for the sins of men.

35. *He that saw* it. John himself. He is accustomed to speak of himself in the third person. ¶ *His record is true.* His testimony is true. Such was the *known* character of this writer, such his sacred regard for truth, that he could appeal to that with full assurance that all would put confidence in him. He often appeals thus to the fact that his testimony was *known* to be true. It would be well if *all* Christians had such a character that their *word* would be assuredly believed.

36. *That the scripture should be fulfilled.* See Ex. xii. 46. John here regards the paschal lamb as an emblem of Christ; and as in the law it was commanded that a bone of that lamb should not be broken, so, in the providence of God, it was ordered that a bone of the Saviour should not be broken. The Scripture thus received a complete fulfilment respecting both the type and the antitype. Some have supposed, however, that John referred to Ps. xxxiv. 20.

mathea, being a disciple of Jesus,
but secretly [m]for fear of the Jews,
besought Pilate that he might
take away the body of Jesus; and
Pilate gave *him* leave. He came,
therefore, and took the body of
Jesus.
39 And there came also [n]Nico-
demus, (which at the first came to
Jesus by night,) and [o]brought a
mixture of myrrh and aloes, about
an hundred pound *weight*.
40 Then took they the body of
Jesus, and [p]wound it in linen
clothes with the spices, as the
manner of the Jews is to bury.
41 Now in the place where he
was crucified there was a garden,
and in the garden a new sepulchre, wherein was never man yet
laid.
42 There[q] laid they Jesus, therefore, [r]because of the Jews' preparation *day;* for the sepulchre was
nigh at hand.

CHAPTER XX.

THE[a] first *day* of the week
cometh Mary Magdalene
early, when it was yet dark, unto
the sepulchre, and seeth the stone
taken away from the sepulchre.
2 Then she runneth, and cometh
to Simon Peter, and to the other
disciple [b]whom Jesus loved, and
saith unto them, They have taken
away the Lord out of the sepulchre, and we know not where they
have laid him.
3 Peter[c] therefore went forth,
and that other disciple, and came
to the sepulchre.
4 So they ran both together;
and the other disciple did [d]outrun
Peter, and came first to the sepulchre.
5 And he, stooping down, *and
looking in,* saw [e]the linen clothes
lying; yet went he not in.
6 Then cometh Simon Peter
following him, and went into the
sepulchre, and seeth the linen
clothes lie;
7 And the [f]napkin that was
about his head, not lying with
the linen clothes, but wrapped
together in a place by itself.
8 Then went in also that other
disciple which came first to the
sepulchre, and he saw and believed.
9 For as yet they knew not [g]the
scripture, that he must rise again
from the dead.
10 Then the disciples went away
again unto their own home.
11 But Mary stood without at
the sepulchre, weeping; and as
she wept she stooped down, *and*
[h]*looked* into the sepulchre.
12 And seeth two angels in white,
sitting, the one at the head and the

m ch.9.22; 12.42. *n* ch.3.1,2; 7.50. *o* 2 Ch.16.14. *p* Ac.5.6. *q* Is.53.9; 1 Co.15.4. *r* ver.31. *a* Mat.28.1,&c.; Mar.16.1,&c.; Lu.24.1,&c. *b* ch.13.23; 19.26; 21.7,24.

c Lu.24.12. *d* Lu.13.30. *e* ch.19.40. *f* ch.11.44. *g* Ps.16.10; Ac.2.25-31; 13.34,35. *h* Mar.16.5.

37. *Another scripture*, Zec. xii. 10. We must here be struck with the wonderful providence of God, that so *many* scriptures were fulfilled in his death. All these things happened without any such *design* on the part of the men engaged in these scenes; but whatever was done by Jew or Gentile tended to the fulfilment of prophecies long on record, and with which the Jews themselves ought to have been familiar. Little did they suppose, when delivering him to Pilate—when he was mocked—when they parted his garments—when they pierced him—that they were fulfilling ancient predictions. But in this way God had so ordered it that the firmest foundation should be laid for the belief that he was the true Messiah, and that the designs of wicked men should all be overruled to the fulfilment of the great plans which God had in sending his Son.

38–42. See Notes on Mat. xxvii. 57–61.

CHAPTER XX.

1-12. For an account of the resurrection of Christ, see Notes on Mat. xxviii.

9. *The scripture.* See Lu. xxiv. 26, 46. The sense or meaning of the various predictions that foretold his death, as, for example, Ps. ii. 7, comp. Ac. xiii. 33;

other at the feet, where the body of Jesus had lain.

13 And they say unto her, Woman, why weepest thou? She saith unto them, Because they have taken away my Lord, and I know not where they have laid him.

14 And when she had thus said, she turned herself back, and [i]saw Jesus standing, and [k]knew not that it was Jesus.

15 Jesus saith unto her, Woman, why weepest thou? whom seekest thou? She, supposing him to be the gardener, saith unto him, Sir, if thou have borne him hence, tell me where thou hast laid him, [l]and I will take him away.

16 Jesus saith unto her, [m]Mary. She[n] turned herself, and saith unto him, Rabboni; which is to say, Master.

17 Jesus saith unto her, Touch me not; for I am not yet ascended to my Father; but go to [o]my brethren, and say unto them, [p]I ascend unto my Father and [q]your Father, and *to* [r]my God and [s]your God.

18 Mary[t] Magdalene came and

i Mat.28.9; Mar.16.9. *k* Lu.24.16,31; ch.21.4.

l Ca.3.2. *m* Is.43.1; ch.10.3. *n* Ca.3.4. *o* Ps.22.22; Ro.8.29; He.2.11. *p* ch.16.28. *q* Ro.8.14,15; 2 Co.6.18; Ga.3.26; 4.6,7. *r* Ep.1.17. *s* Ge.17.7,8; Ps.43.4,5; 48.14; Is.41.10; Je.31.33; Eze. 36.28; Zec.13.9; He.11.16; Re.21.3. *t* Mat.28.10.

Ps. xvi. 9, 10, comp. Ac. ii. 25-32; Ps. cx. 1, comp. Ac. ii. 34, 35.

13. *They have taken away.* That is, the disciples or friends of Jesus who had laid him there. Perhaps it was understood that the body was deposited there only to remain over the Sabbath, with an intention then of removing it to some other place of burial. Hence they hastened *early* in the morning to make preparation, and Mary supposed they had arrived before her and had taken him away.

14. *Knew not that it was Jesus.* She was not *expecting* to see him. It was yet also twilight, and she could not see distinctly.

16. *Jesus saith unto her, Mary.* This was spoken, doubtless, in a tone of voice that at once recalled him to her recollection. ¶ *Rabboni.* This is a Hebrew word denoting, literally, *my great master.* It was one of the titles given to Jewish teachers. This title was given under three forms: (*a*) *Rab*, or master—the lowest degree of honour. (*b*) *Rabbi*, my master—a title of higher dignity. (*c*) *Rabboni*, my great master—the most honourable of all. This title, among the Jews, was only given to seven persons, all persons of great eminence. As given by Mary to the Saviour, it was at once an expression of her joy, and an acknowledgment of him as her Lord and Master. It is not improbable that she, filled with joy, was about to cast herself at his feet.

17. *Touch me not*, &c. This passage has given rise to a variety of interpretations. Jesus required Thomas to touch him (ver. 27), and it has been difficult to ascertain why he forbade this now to Mary. The reason why he directed Thomas to do this was, that he doubted whether he had been restored to life. Mary did not doubt that. The reason why he forbade her to touch him now is to be sought in the circumstances of the case. Mary, filled with joy and gratitude, was about to prostrate herself at his feet, disposed to *remain* with him, and offer him there her homage as her risen Lord. This is probably included in the word *touch* in this place; and the language of Jesus may mean this: "Do not approach me *now* for this purpose. Do not *delay* here. Other opportunities will yet be afforded to see me. I have not yet ascended—that is, I am not *about* to ascend *immediately*, but shall remain yet on earth to afford opportunity to my disciples to enjoy my presence." From Mat. xxviii. 9, it appears that the women, when they met Jesus, *held him by the feet and worshipped him.* This species of adoration it was probably the intention of Mary to offer, and this, *at that time,* Jesus forbade, and directed her to go at once and give his disciples notice that he had risen. ¶ *My brethren.* See ch. xv. 15. ¶ *My Father and your Father*, &c. Nothing was better fitted to afford them consolation than this assurance that *his* God was *theirs,* and that, though he had been slain, they were still indissolubly united in attachment to the same Father and God.

19. *The same day at evening.* On the first day of the week, the day of the

told the disciples that she had
seen the Lord, and *that* he had
spoken these things unto her.
19 Then[u] the same day at evening,
being the first *day* of the week, when
the doors were shut where the disciples were assembled for fear of the
Jews, came Jesus, and stood in the
midst, and saith unto them, Peace
be unto you.
20 And when he had so said, he
showed unto them *his* hands and his
side. Then[v] were the disciples glad
when they saw the Lord.
21 Then said Jesus to them again,
[w]Peace *be* unto you: as *my* Father
hath sent me, even [x]so send I you.
22 And when he had said this, he
breathed on *them*, and saith unto
them, [y]Receive ye the Holy Ghost.

u Mar.16.14; Lu.24.36; 1 Co.15.5.

v ch.16.22. *w* ch.14.27. *x* Mat.28.19; ch.17.18; 2 Ti.2.2; He.3.1. *y* Ac.2.4,38.

resurrection of Christ. ¶ *When the doors were shut.* This does not mean that the doors were *fastened*, though that might have been the case, but only that they were closed. Jesus had been taken from them, and it was natural that they should apprehend that the Jews would next attempt to wreak their vengeance on his followers. Hence they met in the evening, and with closed doors, lest the Jews should bring against them the same charge of sedition that they had against the Lord Jesus. It is not certainly said what was the *object* of their assembling, but it is not unreasonable to suppose that it was to talk over the events which had just occurred, to deliberate about their condition, and to engage in acts of worship. Their minds were doubtless much agitated. They had seen their Master taken away and put to death; but a part of their number also had affirmed that they had seen him alive. In this state of things they naturally came together in a time and place of safety. It was not uncommon for the early Christians to hold their meetings for worship in the *night*. In times of persecution they were forbidden to assemble during the day, and hence they were compelled to meet in the night. Pliny the younger, writing to Trajan, the Roman emperor, and giving an account of Christians, says that "they were wont to meet together on a stated day before it was light, and sing among themselves alternately a hymn to Christ as God." True Christians will love to meet together for worship. Nothing will prevent this; and one of the evidences of piety is a desire to assemble to hear the Word of God, and to offer to him prayer and praise. It is worthy of remark that this is the first assembly that was convened for worship on the Lord's day, and in that assembly Jesus was present. Since that time, the day has been observed in the church as the Christian Sabbath, particularly to commemorate the resurrection of Christ. ¶ *Came Jesus*, &c. There is no evidence that he came into their assembly in any *miraculous* manner. For anything that appears to the contrary, Jesus entered in the usual way and manner, though *his* sudden appearance alarmed them. ¶ *Peace be unto you.* The *sudden* manner of his appearance, and the fact that most of them had not before seen him since his resurrection, tended to alarm them. Hence he addressed them in the usual form of salutation to allay their fears, and to assure them that it was their *own* Saviour and Friend.

20. *He showed unto them* his *hands*, &c. In this manner he gave them indubitable proofs of his identity. He showed them that he was the *same* Being who had suffered; that he had truly risen from the dead, and had come forth with the same body. That body had not yet put on its glorified form. It was necessary *first* to establish the proof of his resurrection, and that could be done *only* by his appearing *as he was* when he died.

21. *As* my *Father hath sent me.* As God sent me to preach, to be persecuted, and to suffer; to make known his will, and to offer pardon to men, so I send you. This is the design and the extent of the commission of the ministers of the Lord Jesus. He is their model; and they will be successful only as they *study* HIS *character* and imitate his example. This commission he proceeds to confirm by endowing them all with the gift of the Holy Ghost.

22. *He breathed on* them. It was customary for the prophets to use some significant act to *represent* the nature of their message. See Je. xiii., xviii., &c. In this case the act of *breathing*

23 Whose[z] soever sins ye remit,
they are remitted unto them; *and*
whose soever *sins* ye retain, they
are retained.
24 But [a]Thomas, one of the
twelve, called Didymus, was not
with them when Jesus came.
25 The other disciples therefore
said unto him, We have seen the
Lord. But [b]he said unto them,
Except I shall see in his hands
the print of the nails, and put my
finger into the print of the nails,
and thrust my hand into his side,
I will not believe.
26 And after eight days, again

z Mat.16.19; 18.18. a ch.11.16. b Ps.78.11,32.

was used to represent the *nature* of the influence that would come upon them, and the *source* of that influence. When man was created, God *breathed* into him the breath of life, Ge. ii. 7. The word rendered *spirit* in the Scriptures denotes *wind*, *air*, *breath*, as well as Spirit. Hence the operations of the Holy Spirit are compared to the wind, Jn. iii. 8; Ac. ii. 2. ¶ *Receive ye the Holy Ghost.* His breathing on them was a certain sign or pledge that they would be endowed with the influences of the Holy Spirit. Comp. Ac. i. 4; ch. ii.

23. *Whose soever sins*, &c. See Notes on Mat. xvi. 19; xviii. 18. It is worthy of remark here that Jesus confers the same power on *all* the apostles. He gives to no one of them any peculiar authority. If *Peter*, as the Papists pretend, had been appointed to any peculiar authority, it is wonderful that the Saviour did not here hint at any such pre-eminence. This passage conclusively proves that they were invested with equal power in organizing and governing the church. The authority which he had given Peter to preach the gospel *first* to the Jews and the Gentiles, does not militate against this. See Notes on Mat. xvi. 18, 19. This authority given them was full proof that they were inspired. The meaning of the passage is not that *man* can forgive sins—that belongs only to God (Is. xliii. 23), but that they should be *inspired;* that in founding the church, and in declaring the will of God, they should be taught by the Holy Ghost to *declare on what terms*, *to what characters*, and *to what temper of mind* God would extend forgiveness of sins. It was not authority to *forgive individuals*, but to establish in all the churches the *terms* and *conditions* on which men might be pardoned, with a promise that God would *confirm* all that they taught; that all might have assurance of forgiveness who would comply with those terms; and that those who did not comply should not be forgiven, but that their sins should be retained. This commission is *as far as possible* from the authority which the Roman Catholic claims of remitting sin and of pronouncing pardon.

25. *Except I shall see*, &c. It is not known what was the ground of the incredulity of Thomas. It is probable, however, that it was, in part, at least, the effect of deep grief, and of that despondency which fills the mind when a long-cherished hope is taken away. In such a case it requires proof of uncommon clearness and strength to overcome the despondency, and to convince us that we *may* obtain the object of our desires. Thomas has been much blamed by expositors, but he asked only for proof that would be satisfactory in his circumstances. The testimony of *ten* disciples *should* have been indeed sufficient, but an opportunity was thus given to the Saviour to convince the last of them of the truth of his resurrection. This incident shows, what all the conduct of the apostles proves, that they had not *conspired* together to impose on the world. Even they were slow to believe, and one of them refused to rely even on the testimony of *ten* of his brethren. How unlike this to the conduct of men who *agree* to impose a story on mankind! Many are like Thomas. Many *now* are unwilling to believe because they do not *see* the Lord Jesus, and with just as little reason as Thomas had. The *testimony* of those eleven men—including Thomas—who saw him alive after he was crucified; who were willing to lay down their lives to attest that they had seen him alive; who had nothing to gain by imposture, and whose conduct was removed as far as possible from the appearance of imposture, should be regarded as ample proof of the fact that he rose from the dead.

26. *And after eight days again.* That is, on the return of the first day of the

his disciples were within, and
Thomas with them. *Then* came
Jesus, the doors being shut, and
stood in the midst, and said, [c]Peace
be unto you.
27 Then saith he to Thomas,
Reach hither thy finger, and behold my hands; and reach hither
thy [d]hand, and thrust *it* into my
side; and [e]be not faithless, but
believing.
28 And Thomas answered and
said unto him, [f]My Lord and my
God.
29 Jesus saith unto him, Thomas,
because thou hast seen me, thou
hast believed; [g]blessed *are* they
that have not seen, and *yet* have
believed.
30 And[h] many other signs truly
did Jesus in the presence of his
disciples, which are not written in
this book.
31 But[i] these are written that ye

c Is.26.12. d 1 Jn.1.1. e 1 Ti.1.14. f Ps.118.28; ch.5.23; 1 Ti.3.16. g 1 Pe.1.8. h ch.21.25. i Lu.1.4.

week. From this it appears that they thus early set apart this day for assembling together, and Jesus countenanced it by appearing twice with them. It was *natural* that the apostles should observe this day, but not probable that they would do it without the sanction of the Lord Jesus. His repeated presence gave such a sanction, and the historical fact is indisputable that from this time this day was observed as the Christian Sabbath. See Ac. xx. 7; 1 Co. xvi. 2; Re. i. 10.

28. *My Lord and my God.* In this passage the name *God* is expressly given to Christ, in his own presence and by one of his own apostles. This declaration has been considered as a clear proof of the divinity of Christ, for the following reasons: 1st. There is no evidence that this was a mere expression, as some have supposed, of surprise or astonishment. 2d. The language was addressed to Jesus himself—"*Thomas—said* UNTO HIM." 3d. The Saviour did not *reprove* him or *check* him as using any improper language. If he had *not* been divine, it is impossible to reconcile it with his *honesty* that he did not rebuke the disciple. No *pious man* would have allowed such language to be addressed to him. Comp. Ac. xiv. 13-15; Re. xxii. 8, 9. 4th. The Saviour proceeds immediately to *commend* Thomas for believing; but what was the *evidence* of his believing? It was this declaration, and this only. If this was a mere exclamation of *surprise*, what proof was it that Thomas believed? Before this he doubted. Now he believed, and gave utterance to his belief, *that Jesus was his Lord and his God.* 5th. If this was *not* the meaning of Thomas, then his exclamation was a mere act of profaneness, and the Saviour would not have commended him for taking the name of the Lord his God in vain. The passage proves, therefore, that it is proper to apply to Christ the name *Lord* and GOD, and thus accords with what John affirmed in ch. i. 1, and which is established throughout this gospel.

29. *Because thou hast seen me.* Because you have looked upon my body, and seen the proofs that I am the same Saviour that was crucified. Jesus here *approves* the faith of Thomas, but more highly commends the faith of those who should believe without having seen. ¶ *Blessed.* Happy, or worthy of the divine approbation. The word has here the force of the comparative degree, signifying that they would be in some respects *more* blessed than Thomas. They would evince higher faith. ¶ *That have not seen*, &c. Those who should be convinced by the testimony of the apostles, and by the influences of the Spirit. They would evince *stronger faith*. *All* faith is of things not seen; and God blesses those most who most implicitly rely on his word.

30. *Other signs.* Other miracles. Many were recorded by the other evangelists, and many which he performed were never recorded, ch. xxi. 25.

31. *These are written.* Those recorded in this *gospel.* ¶ *That ye might believe*, &c. This is a *clue* to the design which John had in view in writing this gospel. The whole *scope* or *end* of the book is to accomplish two objects: 1st. To prove that Jesus was the Messiah; and, 2d. That they who looked at the proof might be convinced and have eternal life. This design is kept in view throughout the book. The miracles, facts, arguments, instructions, and conversations of our Lord all tend to this. This

might believe that Jesus is the Christ, the Son of God; [k]and that, believing, ye might have life through his name.

CHAPTER XXI.

AFTER these things Jesus showed himself again to the disciples at the sea of Tiberias; and on this wise showed he *himself*.

2 There were together Simon Peter, and Thomas called Didymus, and [a]Nathanael of Cana in Galilee, and [b]the *sons* of Zebedee, and two other of his disciples.

3 Simon Peter saith unto them, I go a fishing. They say unto him, We also go with thee. They went forth, and entered into a ship immediately; and that night they caught nothing.

4 But when the morning was now come, Jesus stood on the shore; but the disciples [c]knew not that it was Jesus.

5 Then[d] Jesus saith unto them, [1]Children, have ye any meat? They answered him, No.

6 And he said unto them, [e]Cast the net on the right side of the ship, and ye shall find. They cast,

k ch.3.15,16; 5.24; 10.10; 1 Pe.1.9. *a* ch.1.45. *b* Mat.4.21.

c ch.20.14. *d* Lu.24.41. 1 or, *Sirs*. *e* Lu.5.4-7.

point had not been kept in view so directly by either of the other evangelists, and it was reserved for the last of the apostles to collect those arguments, and make out a connected demonstration *that Jesus was the Messiah*. If this design of John is kept steadily in view, it will throw much light on the book, and the argument is unanswerable, framed after the strictest rules of reasoning, infinitely beyond the skill of man, and having throughout the clearest evidence of demonstration.

CHAPTER XXI.

1. *The sea of Tiberias.* Called also the Sea of Galilee, being situated in Galilee. See Notes on Mat. iv. 18. In this place Jesus had promised to meet them, Mar. xiv. 28; xvi. 7; Mat. xxvi. 32; xxviii. 10. This interview of Jesus is but just mentioned by Matthew (ch. xxviii. 16), and is omitted by both Mark and Luke. This is the reason why John relates so particularly what occurred there. Galilee was a retired place where they would be free from danger, and was therefore a safe and convenient situation for Jesus to meet them, in order to give them his last instructions. ¶ *On this wise.* Thus. In this manner.

2. *There were together.* Probably residing in the same place. While they were waiting for the promise of the Holy Spirit, they still found it proper to be usefully employed. Their Master had been taken away by death, and the promised Spirit had not descended on them. In the interval—before the promised Spirit was poured upon them—they chose not to be idle, and therefore returned to their former employment. It is to be remarked, also, that they had no other means of support. While with Jesus, they were commonly supplied by the kindness of the people; but now, when the Saviour had died, they were cut off from this means of support, and returned to the honest labour of their early lives. Moreover, they had been directed by the Saviour to repair to a mountain in Galilee, where he would meet them, Mat. xxviii. 10. This was probably not far from the Sea of Galilee, so that, until he came to them, they would naturally be engaged in their old employment. Ministers of the gospel should be willing to labour, if necessary, for their own support, and should not esteem such labour dishonourable. God has made *employment* indispensable to man, and if the field of labour is not open in one way, they should seek it in another. If at any time the people withhold the supply of their wants, they should be able and willing to seek support in some other honest occupation.

3. *That night they caught nothing.* This was so ordered in the providence of God that the miracle which was wrought might appear more remarkable.

4. *Knew not that it was Jesus.* Probably it was yet twilight, and in the distance they could not distinctly recognize him.

5. *Children.* A term of affection and friendship, 1 Jn. ii. 18. ¶ *Any meat.* This word (Greek) means anything

therefore, and now they were not
able to draw it for the multitude
of fishes.
7 Therefore that disciple whom
Jesus loved saith unto Peter, It
is the Lord. Now when Simon
Peter heard that it was the Lord,
he girt *his* fisher's coat *unto him*,
(for he was naked,) and did cast
himself into the sea.
8 And the other disciples came
in a little ship, (for they were not
far from land, but as it were two
hundred cubits,) dragging the net
with fishes.
9 As soon, then, as they were
come to land, they saw a fire of
coals there, and fish laid thereon,
and bread.
10 Jesus saith unto them, Bring
of the fish which ye have now
caught.
11 Simon Peter went up, and
drew the net to land full of great
fishes, an hundred and fifty and
three; and, for all there were so
many, yet was not the net broken.
12 Jesus saith unto them, Come
and dine. And none of the disciples durst ask him, Who art thou?
knowing that it was the Lord.
13 Jesus[f] then cometh, and taketh

f Ac.10.41.

eaten with bread. It was used by the Greeks especially to denote *fish* (Schleusner).

6. *On the right side.* Why the *right* side is mentioned is not known. Grotius supposes that it was the side nearest the shore, where there was *less* probability of taking fish. It does not appear that they yet recognized the Lord Jesus, but from some cause they had sufficient confidence in him to make another trial. Perhaps they judged that he was one skilled in that employment, and knew where there was the greatest probability of success.

7. *Therefore that disciple whom Jesus loved.* John, ch. xiii. 23. ¶ *It is the Lord.* He was convinced, perhaps, by the apparent miracle, and by looking more attentively on the person of one who had been the means of such unexpected and remarkable success. ¶ His *fisher's coat.* His upper or outer garment or tunic, in distinction from the inner garment or tunic which was worn next the skin. In the case of Peter it may have been made of coarse materials such as fishermen commonly wore, or such as Peter usually wore when he was engaged in this employment. Such garments are common with men of this occupation. This outer garment he probably had laid aside. ¶ *He was naked.* He was *undressed*, with nothing on but the under garment or tunic. The word does not require us to suppose a greater degree of nakedness than this. See Notes on Mar. xiv. 51; also 1 Sa. xix. 24. ¶ *Did cast himself into the sea.* With characteristic ardour, desirous of meeting again his Lord, and showing his affection for him.

8. *Two hundred cubits.* About 350 feet, or a little more than 20 rods.

9. *They saw a fire*, &c. We have no knowledge whence this was produced--whether it was, as Grotius supposes, by a miracle, or whether it was a place occupied by other fishermen, where *they* also might cook the fish which they had caught. As no miracle is mentioned, however, there is no reason for supposing that any existed in the case.

11. *An hundred and fifty and three.* The number is mentioned because it seems to have been a very unusual draught, and it was particularly gratifying and striking to them after they had spent the whole night and had caught *nothing*. This convinced them that it was no other than the same Saviour who had so often worked wonders before them that was now with them.

12. *Come* and *dine.* The word in the original means the meal which is taken in the *morning*, or breakfast.

13. *Jesus then cometh, and taketh bread*, &c. It is not said that Jesus himself *ate* with them, but he gave them food. The design of this interview seems to have been to convince them that he had truly risen from the dead. Hence he performed a miracle *before* they suspected that it was he, that there might be no room to say that they had ascribed to him the power of the miracle through friendship and collusion with him. The miracle was such as to satisfy them of its truth, and was, in accordance with all his works, not for mere display, but

bread, and giveth them, and fish likewise.

14 This[g] is now the third time that Jesus showed himself to his disciples after that he was risen from the dead.

15 So when they had dined, Jesus saith to Simon Peter, Simon, *son* of Jonas, lovest thou me [h]more than these? He saith unto him, Yea, Lord; thou knowest that I love thee. He saith unto him, [i]Feed my lambs.

16 He saith to him again the

g ch.20.19,26.

h Mat.26.33,35.
i Is.40.11; Je.3.15; Eze.34.2-10; Ac.20.28; 1 Pe.5.2,4.

---

for utility. He remained with them, was with them at their meal, conversed with them, and thus convinced them that he was the same Friend who had died.

14. *The third time.* See the "Harmony of the Accounts of the Resurrection of Jesus" at the end of Matthew.

15. *Lovest thou me more than these?* There is a slight ambiguity here in the original, as there is in our translation. The word *these* may be in the *neuter* gender, and refer to these *things*—his boat, his fishing utensils, and his employments; or it may be in the masculine, and refer to the apostles. In the former sense it would mean, "Lovest thou me more than thou lovest these objects? Art thou now willing, from love to me, to forsake all these, and go and preach my gospel to the nations of the earth?" In the other sense, which is probably the true sense, it would mean, "Lovest thou me more than these other apostles love me?" In this question Jesus refers to the profession of superior attachment to him which Peter had made before his death (Mat. xxvi. 33): "Though all men shall be offended because of thee, yet will I never be offended." Comp. Jn. xiii. 37. Jesus here slightly reproves him for that confident assertion, reminds him of his sad and painful denial, and now puts this direct and pointed question to him to know what was the *present* state of his feelings. After all that Peter had had to humble him, the Saviour inquired of him what had been the *effect* on his mind, and whether it had tended to prepare him for the arduous toils in which he was about to engage. This question we should all put to ourselves. It is a matter of much importance that we should ourselves know what is the effect of the dealings of divine Providence on our hearts, and what is our *present* state of feeling toward the Lord Jesus Christ. ¶ *Thou knowest that I love thee.* Peter now made no pretensions to love superior to his brethren. His sad denial had convinced him of the folly of that claim; but still he could appeal to the Searcher of the heart, and say that he *knew* that he loved him. Here is the expression of a humbled soul—a soul made sensible of its weakness and need of strength, yet with evidence of true attachment to the Saviour. It is not the most confident pretensions that constitute the highest proof of love to Christ; and the happiest and best state of feeling is when we can with humility, yet with confidence, look to the Lord Jesus and say, "Thou *knowest* that I love thee." ¶ *Feed my lambs.* The word *here* rendered *feed* means the care afforded by furnishing *nutriment* for the flock. In the next verse there is a change in the Greek, and the word rendered *feed* denotes rather the *care*, *guidance*, and *protection* which a shepherd extends to his flock. By the use of both these words, it is supposed that our Saviour intended that a shepherd was both to offer the proper food for his flock and to govern it; or, as we express it, to exercise the office of a pastor. The expression is taken from the office of a *shepherd*, with which the office of a minister of the gospel is frequently compared. It means, as a good shepherd provides for the wants of his flock, so the pastor in the church is to furnish food for the soul, or so to exhibit truth that the faith of believers may be strengthened and their hope confirmed. ¶ *My lambs.* The church is often compared to a flock. See ch. x. 1-16. Here the expression *my lambs* undoubtedly refers to the *tender* and the *young* in the Christian church; to those who are young in years and in Christian experience. The Lord Jesus saw, what has been confirmed in the experience of the church, that the success of the gospel among men depended on the care which the ministry would extend to those in early life. It is in obedience to this command that Sunday-schools have been established, and no means of fulfilling this command

second time, Simon, *son* of Jonas,
lovest thou me? He saith unto
him, Yea, Lord; thou knowest
that I love thee. He saith unto
him, [k]Feed my sheep.
17 He saith unto him the third
time, Simon, *son* of Jonas, lovest
thou me? Peter was [l]grieved
because he said unto him the third
time, Lovest thou me? and he said
unto him, Lord, [m]thou knowest all
things; thou knowest that I love
thee. Jesus saith unto him, Feed
my sheep.
18 Verily, verily, I say unto
thee, [n]When thou wast young,
thou girdedst thyself, and walkedst
whither thou wouldest; but when
thou shalt be old, thou shalt stretch
forth thy hands, and another [o]shall

k He.13.20; 1 Pe.2.25. *l* La.3.33. *m* ch.16.30. *n* ch.13.36; Ac.12.3,4. *o* Ac.21.11.

---

of the Saviour have been found so effectual as to extend patronage to those schools. It is not merely, therefore, the *privilege*, it is the solemn *duty* of ministers of the gospel to countenance and patronize those schools.

16. *Feed my sheep.* The word here rendered *feed*, as has been remarked, is different from the word in the previous verse. It has the sense of *governing*, *caring for*, *guiding*, *protecting*—the kind of faithful vigilance which a shepherd uses to guide his flock, and to make provision against their wants and dangers. It *may* be implied here that the care needed for the young in the church is to *instruct* them, and for those in advanced years *both* to instruct and govern them. ¶ *My sheep.* This term commonly denotes the church in general, without respect to age, ch. x.

17. *The third time.* It is probable that Jesus proposed this question three times because Peter had thrice denied him. Thus he tenderly admonished him of his fault and reminded him of his sin, while he solemnly charged him to be faithful and vigilant in the discharge of the duties of the pastoral office. The reason why the Saviour addressed *Peter* in this manner was doubtless because he had just denied him—had given a most melancholy instance of the instability and weakness of his faith, and of his liability to fall. As he had thus been prominent in forsaking him, he took this occasion to give to him a *special* charge, and to *secure* his future obedience. Hence he so administered the charge as to remind him of his fault; and he made him so prominent as to show the solicitude of the Saviour that henceforward he might not be left to dishonour his high calling. This same charge, in substance, he had on other occasions given to the apostles (Mat. xviii. 18), and there is not the slightest evidence here that Christ intended, as the Papists pretend, to give Peter any *peculiar* primacy or eminence in the church. The charge to Peter arose, manifestly, from his prominent and melancholy act in denying him, and was the kind and tender means used by a faithful Saviour to keep him from similar acts in the future dangers and trials of life. It is worthy of remark that the admonition was effectual. Henceforward Peter was one of the most firm and unwavering of all the apostles, and thus fully justified the appellation of *a rock*, which the Saviour by anticipation had given him. See Notes on Jn. i. 42.

18. *When thou wast young.* When in early life thou didst gird *thyself*, &c. The Jews, in walking or running, *girded* their outer garments around them, that they might not be impeded. See Notes on Mat. v. 38-41. ¶ *Thou girdedst.* The expression here denotes *freedom*. He did as he pleased—he girded himself or not—he went or remained, as he chose. Perhaps the expression refers rather *to that time* than to the previous period of Peter's life. "Thou being now young or in the vigour of life, hast just girded thyself and come freely to the shore." In either case the Saviour intimates that at the end of his life he would not be thus free. ¶ *When thou shalt be old.* Ancient writers say that Peter was put to death about thirty-four years after this. His precise age at that time is not known. ¶ *Thou shalt stretch forth thy hands.* When Peter was put to death, we are told that he requested that he might be crucified with his head downward, saying that he who had denied his Lord as he had done was not *worthy* to die as he did. This expression of Christ may intimate the *readiness* of Peter thus to die. Though he was not at liberty as when he was

gird thee, and carry *thee* whither thou wouldest not.

19 This spake he, signifying by what [p]death he should glorify God. And when he had spoken this, he saith unto him, [q]Follow me.

20 Then Peter, turning about, seeth the disciple whom Jesus loved following, which also leaned on his breast at supper, and said, Lord, which is he that betrayeth thee?

21 Peter, seeing him, saith to Jesus, Lord, and what *shall* this man *do?*

22 Jesus saith unto him, If I

p 2 Pe.1.14.
q Nu.14.24; 1 Sa.12.20; Mat.19.28; ch.12.26.

---

young, though bound by others, yet he *freely* stretched out his hands on the cross, and was ready to give up his life. ¶ *Another shall gird thee.* Another shall *bind* thee. The limbs of persons crucified were often *bound* instead of being *nailed*, and even the *body* was sometimes girded to the cross. See Notes on Mat. xxvii. 35. ¶ *Carry* thee, &c. Shall *bear* thee, or shall *compel* thee to go to prison and to death. This is not said to intimate that Peter would be unwilling to suffer martyrdom, but it stands opposed to the freedom of his early life. Though willing when compelled to do it, yet he would not *seek it;* and though he would not needlessly expose himself to it, yet he would not shrink from it when it was the will of God.

19. *By what death*, &c. In these words two things are implied: 1st. That Peter would die a violent death; and, 2d. That his death would be such as to honour God. The ancients say that Peter was crucified at Rome, about thirty-four years after this, with his head downward. Clemens says that he was led to the crucifixion with his wife, and sustained her in her sufferings by exhorting her to remember the example of her Lord. He also adds that he died, not as the philosophers did, but with a firm hope of heaven, and patiently endured the pangs of the cross (*Strom.* vii.). This declaration of the Saviour was doubtless continually before the mind of Peter, and to the hour of his death he maintained the utmost constancy and fidelity in his cause, thus justifying the appellation which the Lord Jesus gave him—*a rock.*

20. *Which also leaned*, &c. See ch. xiii. 24, 25.

21. *What* shall *this man* do? This question probably means, "What death shall he die?" But it is impossible to ascertain certainly why Peter asked this question. John was a favourite disciple, and *perhaps* Peter suspected that he would have a happier lot, and not be put to death in this manner. Peter was *grieved* at the question of Jesus; he was probably deeply affected with the account of his own approaching sufferings; and, with *perhaps* a mixture of grief and *envy*, he asked what would be *his* lot. But it is *possible*, also, that it was from *kindness* to John—a deep solicitude about him, and a wish that he might not die in the same manner as one who had denied his Lord. Whatever the motive was, it was a curiosity which the Lord Jesus did not choose to gratify.

22. *That he tarry.* That he *live.* The same word is used to express life in Phi. i. 24, 25; 1 Co. xv. 6. ¶ *Till I come.* Some have supposed this to refer to the destruction of Jerusalem; others to the day of judgment; others to signify that he would not die a violent death; but the plain meaning is, "If I will that he should not *die at all*, it is nothing to thee." In this way the apostles evidently understood it, and hence raised a report that he would *not* die. It is remarkable that John *was* the last of the apostles; that he lived to nearly the close of the first century, and then died a peaceful death at Ephesus, being the only one, as is supposed, of the apostles who did not suffer martyrdom. The testimony of antiquity is clear on this point; and though there have been many idle *conjectures* about this passage and about the fate of John, yet no fact of history is better attested than that John died and was buried at Ephesus. ¶ *What* is that *to thee?* From this passage we learn, 1st. That our main business is to follow the Lord Jesus Christ. 2d. That there are many subjects of religion on which a vain and impertinent curiosity is exercised. All such curiosity Jesus here reproves. 3d. That Jesus will take care of *all* his true disciples, and that we should not be unduly solicitous about them. 4th. That we should go forward to whatever he calls

will that he tarry till [r] I come,
what *is that* to thee? [s] Follow
thou me.
23 Then went this saying abroad
among the brethren, that that disciple should not die; yet Jesus said
not unto him, He shall not die; but,

If I will that he tarry till I come,
what *is that* to thee?
24 This is the disciple which
testifieth of these things, and wrote
these things; [t] and we know that
his testimony is true.
25 And [u] there are also many

r Mat.25.31; Re.1.7; 22.20. s ver.19. t ch.19.35; 3 Jn.12. u ch.20.30.

us—to persecution or death—not envying the lot of any other man, and anxious only to do the will of God.

23. *Then went this saying*, &c. This mistake arose very naturally—1st. From the *words* of Jesus, which might be easily misunderstood to mean that he should not die; and, 2d. It was probably confirmed when it was seen that John survived *all* the other apostles, had escaped all the dangers of persecution, and was leading a peaceful life at Ephesus. This mistake John deemed it proper to correct before he died, and has thus left on record what Jesus *said* and what he *meant*.

24. *This is the disciple*, &c. This *proves* that the beloved disciple was John. ¶ *We know.* That is, *it is known;* it is universally admitted. It was so decidedly his character that he always declared the truth, that it had become *known* and was unquestioned, so that *he himself* might appeal to the universal testimony in his behalf. In this case, therefore, we have the testimony of a man whose character for nearly *a century* was that of a man of truth—so much so that it had become, in a manner, proverbial, and was put beyond a doubt. It is impossible to believe that such a man would sit down deliberately to *impose* on mankind, or to write a book which was false; and if not, then *this* book is true, and that is the same as saying that Christianity is a religion from heaven.

25. *Many other things.* Many miracles, ch. xx. 30. Many discourses delivered, &c. ¶ *I suppose*, &c. This is evidently the figure of speech called a *hyperbole.* It is a mode of speech where the *words* express more or less than is *literally* true. It is common among all writers; and as the sacred writers, in recording a revelation to men, used human language, it was proper that they should express themselves as men ordinarily do if they wished to be understood. This figure of speech is commonly the effect of *surprise*, or having the mind *full* of some object, and not having words to express the ideas: at the same time, the words convey no *falsehood.* The statement is to be taken *as it would be understood* among the persons to whom it is addressed; and as no one *supposes* that the author means to be understood *literally*, so there is no deception in the case, and consequently no impeachment of his veracity or inspiration. Thus, when Longinus said of a man that "he was the owner of a piece of ground not larger than a Lacedæmonian letter," no one understood him literally. He meant, evidently, a *very small* piece of land, and no one would be deceived. So Virgil says of a man, "he was so tall as to reach the stars," and means only that he was *very tall.* So when John says that the world could not contain the books that would be written if *all* the deeds and sayings of Jesus were recorded, he clearly intends nothing more than that *a great many* books would be required, or that it would be extremely difficult to record them all; intimating that his life was active, that his discourses were numerous, and that *he* had not *pretended* to give them all, but only such as would go to establish the main point for which he wrote—that he was the Messiah, ch. xx. 30, 31. The figure which John uses here is not uncommon in the Scriptures, Ge. xi. 4; xv. 5; Nu. xiii. 33; Da. iv. 20.

This gospel contains in itself the clearest proof of inspiration. It is the work of a fisherman of Galilee, without any proof that he had any unusual advantages. It is a connected, clear, and satisfactory *argument* to establish the great truth that Jesus was the Messiah. It was written many years after the ascension of Jesus. It contains the record of the Saviour's profoundest discourses, of his most convincing arguments with the Jews, and of his declarations respecting himself and God. It contains the purest and most elevated views of God to be found anywhere,

other things which Jesus did, the which, if they should be written every one, I suppose that even [v]the world itself could not contain the books that should be written. Amen.

v Am.7.10.

as far exceeding all the speculations of philosophers as the sun does the blaze of a taper. It is in the highest degree absurd to suppose that an unlettered fisherman could have *originated* this book. Anyone may be convinced of this by comparing it with what *would be* the production of a man in that rank of life now. But if John has preserved the record of what has occurred so many years before, then it shows that he was under the divine guidance, and is himself a proof, a full and standing proof, of the fulfilment of the promise which he has recorded—that the Holy Spirit would guide the apostles into all truth, Jn. xiv. 26. Of this book we may, in conclusion, apply the words spoken by John respecting his vision of the future events of the church: "Blessed is he that readeth and they that hear the words of this" book, "and keep those things which are written therein, for the time is at hand," Re. i. 3.

A CHRONOLOGICAL TABLE

OF THE

PRINCIPAL EVENTS OCCURRING IN JUDEA, AND THE CORRESPONDING EVENTS IN THE ROMAN EMPIRE,

FROM THE

CONQUEST OF JUDEA BY POMPEY TO THE DESTRUCTION OF JERUSALEM BY TITUS.

BEFORE CHRIST.

77–68. ALEXANDRA QUEEN OF THE JEWS. She leaves two sons, Hyrcanus and Aristobulus. Both claim the crown—Aristobulus seizing upon it by force, and Hyrcanus being placed on the throne by the Pharisees. In a battle between the two brothers Hyrcanus is overcome, and Aristobulus secures the crown.

70. Pompey and Crassus consuls in Rome.

66. Pompey conquers Mithridates and reduces Pontus.

65. In Syria the dynasty of the Seleucidæ ends with Antiochus XII., who is overcome by Pompey. Syria becomes a Roman province.

67–63. ARISTOBULUS II. KING OF THE JEWS. He had been high-priest under the reign of his mother nine years. Was then king and high-priest. Was afterward priest nineteen years. Then ethnarch four years. Then Herod's captive and sport eight years. Hyrcanus, at the instigation of Antipater, the father of Herod the Great, seeks the aid of Aretas, the king of Arabia. Antipater, or Antipas, was an Idumean by birth, but had adopted the Jewish religion, and was governor of Idumea during the reign of Alexander Janneus and his widow Alexandra. Antipater joins the party of Hyrcanus. He and Hyrcanus flee to Aretas, king of Arabia. Aretas agrees to place him on the throne, and conducts him to Judea with an army of 50,000 men. Takes Jerusalem, and restores him to the throne. Aristobulus flees to the temple, and then appeals to Scaurus, the Roman general at Damascus, for aid. Scaurus writes to Aretas; threatens to declare him an enemy of the Roman people if he does not withdraw. He withdraws, and Aristobulus pursues him, and defeats him in a battle.

63. Pompey the Great, who had come to Damascus, commands the two brothers to appear before him. The two brothers appear before him, and urge their respective claims—Hyrcanus pleading his birth, Aristobulus the necessity of the case. Aristobulus, foreseeing that the decision would be against him, withdraws, and fortifies himself in Jerusalem. Aristobulus surrenders himself to Pompey, but his party shut the gates against the Romans, and Pompey puts Aristobulus in chains, and begins a siege. The city is taken by the Romans because the Jews would not fight on the Sabbath, and is brought under the Roman power, according to Calmet 59 years, according to Hales 63 years, and according to Jahn 63 years before Christ. Pompey confirms Hyrcanus in the high-priesthood.

63–55. HYRCANUS II. PRINCE AND HIGH-PRIEST OF THE JEWS. JUDEA A ROMAN PROVINCE.

60. THE FIRST TRIUMVIRATE—Pompey, Crassus, and Julius Cæsar.

58. Clodius procures the banishment of Cicero.

55. Cæsar invades Britain.

54. Alexander, son of Aristobulus, escapes from those who were carrying him to Rome, and returns to Judea and raises soldiers. Hyrcanus, not being able to defend himself, applies to Gabinius, the Roman general. Antipater, the father

of Herod the Great, joins the Roman army. Alexander is defeated. Gabinius confirms Hyrcanus in the high-priesthood, but changes the form of the government to an ARISTOCRACY. This continues until the year 44 B.C., when Cæsar comes to Judea and restores Hyrcanus to his former power.

53. Aristobulus escapes from Rome, and comes to Judea with his younger son, Antigonus. They are taken prisoners and sent to Rome.

54. Gabinius is removed from Judea. Crassus is made proconsul of Syria, and comes to Syria. He comes to Jerusalem, and robs the temple of 8000 talents of gold, equal to about £40,000,000. Makes war with the Parthians, and is put to death. Cassius Longinus succeeds him in the command of the army; brings the remainder of the army over the Euphrates, and takes about 30,000 Jewish captives.

53. Augustus, afterward the Roman emperor, is born.

48. Calpurnius Bibulus made governor of Syria.

48. About this time Ptolemy Auletes, king of Egypt, died.

46–44. Hyrcanus II. high-priest.

46. Civil war between Cæsar and Pompey.

45. Battle of Pharsalia, in Thessaly, where Pompey is defeated. Pompey flees to Egypt, and is beheaded.

45. ANTIPATER, THE FATHER OF HEROD THE GREAT, IS MADE GOVERNOR OF JUDEA. He is appointed to this office by Julius Cæsar. Cæsar confirms Hyrcanus in the high-priesthood, and gives him permission to build the walls of Jerusalem, which had been demolished by Pompey.

44. Hyrcanus sends to Rome a golden shield, and the Jews are, by a decree of the Senate, acknowledged as the allies of the Romans.

44. Antipater rebuilds the walls of Jerusalem. He makes his eldest son, Phazael, governor of Jerusalem, and HEROD, afterward Herod the Great, governor of Galilee.

44. Cæsar subdues all Egypt, and gives it into the hands of Cleopatra. Is again made dictator.

Herod attacks and subdues the robbers in Galilee.

Herod is summoned before the Sanhedrim on the charge of the exercise of arbitrary power. He appears before them in a purple robe, and attended by his life-guard, and defies them. He departs from Jerusalem, and goes to Sextus Cæsar at Damascus, and obtains the government of all Cœle-Syria.

43. The Roman calendar reformed by Julius Cæsar. This year was called the *Year of Confusion*, and consisted of 445 days.

41. Julius Cæsar restores to the Jews all that they had formerly possessed, and confirms them in the enjoyment of all their privileges.

Cæsar is put to death in the senate-house.

40. TRIUMVIRATE — Octavianus Cæsar (afterward Augustus), Antony, and Lepidus.

40. Jewish ambassadors appear at Rome to pray that their privileges may be confirmed. Their request is granted.

39. Malichus causes Antipater, the father of Herod, to be poisoned.

38. Herod causes Malichus to be killed to revenge the death of his father.

39. Battle of Philippi, in which Brutus and Cassius are defeated.

39. Herod and Phazael tetrarchs of Judea. They are accused by the Jews before Antony. More than a thousand Jews appear with these complaints. Antony regards it as rebellion, and causes many of them to be slain, and confirms the brothers as tetrarchs of the Jews.

Antigonus, son of Aristobulus, prevails on the Parthians to place him on the throne of Judea. The Parthians seize Hyrcanus and Phazael, and deliver them up to Antigonus.

Phazael beats out his own brains. Antigonus cuts off the ears of Hyrcanus and sends him beyond the Euphrates.

37. *Herod is forced to flee to Jerusalem, and thence to Rome, to implore the aid of*

Antony. He obtains the grant of the KINGDOM *of Judea from the Senate, and the governors of Syria are required to aid him in securing it.* He is conducted to the Capitol at Rome by Antony and Octavianus, and there crowned king with idolatrous sacrifices. He reigned thirty-seven years.

37. HEROD KING OF JUDEA. He was the second son of Antipater, an Idumean by birth, who had been governor of Judea.

37. Ventidius, a Roman, has command of the forces in the East. Appointed by Antony.

Herod returns to Judea, having been absent but three months. He raises an army. Hastens to relieve his family in the fortress of Massada, where they were besieged by Antigonus. Goes to Idumea, and takes possession of a strong fortress by the name of Ressa, and then returns and lays siege to Jerusalem. Unable to take the city, he is obliged to decamp. Marches to Galilee, and endeavours to clear the country of robbers.

36. Herod renews his attacks on the robbers. Is obliged to let down his soldiers in chests by ropes over the mouth of the caves, and to fight them there. Having subdued the robbers, he marches to Samaria against Antigonus, but is obliged to return to Galilee to quell the robbers.

The brother of Herod, Joseph, is surrounded and slain by the army of Antigonus near Jericho.

36. Antony leads an army against the Parthians. Commits the government of Syria to Sosius, and returns to Italy.

The Roman Triumvirate continues, and Antony has assigned to him the affairs of the East.

35. Herod marches against Jerusalem, and lays siege again to the city.

He is married to Mariamne, to whom he had been betrothed four years. She was the daughter of Alexander, the son of King Aristobulus, by Alexandra, the daughter of Hyrcanus II., and was thus granddaughter to both these brothers. Herod hoped by this marriage to reconcile the Jews to him, as the Asmonean family, from which she was descended, was in high favour with the Jews. She was a woman of uncommon beauty. Herod is joined by the Roman general, Sosius.

34. Jerusalem is taken by Herod, and Antigonus surrenders himself. He is treated with the greatest indignity. Is sent to Antioch, and beheaded by the command of Antony, and thus the reign of the Asmoneans, which had lasted 126 years, is ended, and HEROD IS CONFIRMED IN THE KINGDOM.

REIGN OF HEROD THE GREAT.

34. Herod condemns to death all the members of the Sanhedrim except Sameas and Pollio.

32. He appoints to the office of high-priest Ananel, of Babylon, a common priest, but a descendant of the ancient high-priests.

He invites Hyrcanus II. to come to Jerusalem from Seleucia, where he had been kindly entertained by the Oriental Jews. Hyrcanus comes to Jerusalem, where he is treated by Herod with great respect.

32. Herod, at the earnest solicitations of Alexandra and Mariamne, deprives Ananel of the high-priesthood, and confers it on Aristobulus, the brother of Mariamne, then only seventeen years old. Herod is displeased with the interference of Alexandra in this business, and she and her son Aristobulus attempt to escape to Cleopatra in Egypt. Aristobulus is drowned by order of Herod in a lake near Jericho on account of the affection shown for him by the people.

32. Antony comes into Syria, but goes then into Egypt, where he spends a whole year with Cleopatra. Lepidus and Octavianus come to an open rupture, and Lepidus retires as a private man, and the Roman power is left in the hands of Antony and Octavianus, afterward Augustus.

31. Herod is sent for by Antony to justify himself against the charge of having murdered Aristobulus. Gives his kingdom to the care of his uncle Joseph. Charges him, in case *he* is condemned, to put Mariamne to death, that she might not be possessed by Antony. Joseph informs her of the charge of Herod, and is imprisoned on his return.

30. Ananel high-priest the second time.

War between Augustus and Antony. Herod sides with Antony.

Antony gives to Cleopatra the most fertile part of Judea, but Herod agrees to pay her a yearly tribute of two hundred talents.

Cleopatra visits Herod at Jerusalem, and attempts in vain to entangle him in her snares.

Antony makes war on Armenia. Appoints Cæsario, son of Julius Cæsar by Cleopatra, king of Egypt. Makes his eldest son, Alexander, king of Armenia and Parthia.

27. Herod makes war with the Arabians at the command of Antony. Is defeated near Cana. A great earthquake in Judea.

27. THE BATTLE OF ACTIUM, between Antony and Octavianus, which decides the destiny of the Roman world. Antony is defeated.

26. Antony and Cleopatra kill themselves.

26. Hyrcanus, then eighty years of age, attempts to escape, and Herod gladly embraces this opportunity to put him to death. Goes to Rome to pay court to Augustus and to conciliate his favour. Places Mariamne and her mother Alexandra in the castle of Alexandrium, with orders to the keepers to put them to death if he is slain. Confesses to Augustus all that he had done for Antony, and is confirmed in his kingdom.

25. Augustus visits Judea, and is magnificently entertained by Herod.

24. Mariamne becomes irreconcilably opposed to Herod. Herod becomes jealous. Orders the most faithful servant of Mariamne to be put to the torture. Accuses Mariamne of adultery before judges of his own selection. She is condemned, in accordance with the wishes of Herod, and immediately executed. Herod, filled with remorse, loses all self-command.

23. Herod puts to death the sons of Babas, at the instigation of his sister Salome, and thus cuts off the last remains of the Asmonean race. They were the descendants of Hyrcanus, and Herod now felt himself secure from any claimant to the throne.

21. Plague and famine in Judea. Herod lays the foundation of a palace on Mount Zion.

He marries Mariamne, the daughter of the priest Simon.

21. Augustus is made emperor. He was the nephew of Julius Cæsar.

19. Herod builds Cæsarea in Palestine, and fortifies Samaria. Sends to Rome his two sons, Alexander and Aristobulus, whom he had by the murdered Mariamne. Agrippa, the favourite of Augustus, is made Governor of the East.

18. Augustus visits Antioch, and, at the request of Herod, raises his brother Pheroras to the dignity of a tetrarch.

17. Agrippa comes into Asia. Herod visits him.

16. Herod, in order to conciliate the affection of the Jews, resolves on rebuilding the temple in a style of much greater magnificence than the former temple. Two years are spent in collecting materials. The old temple is taken down by degrees, as fast as its parts could be replaced by the new building. The main body of the edifice completed in nine years and a half, but the whole not completed until long after the death of Herod. (Notes on Jn. ii. 20.)

13. Herod goes to Rome. Takes his two sons with him on his return, and marries them, the one to a daughter of the king of Cappadocia and the other to a daughter of his sister Salome.

12. Agrippa visits the East, and is magnificently entertained by Herod at Jerusalem.

8. Herod goes to Rome, and accuses his two sons, Alexander and Aristobulus, of a design against his life. To this he is instigated principally by his brother Pheroras and his sister Salome, on account of their hatred of Mariamne.

7. Cæsarea, a city built in honour of Augustus, is dedicated with great pomp.

Herod is finally reconciled to his sons by the influence of Archelaus, king of

Cappadocia, whose daughter Alexander had married. He goes into Arabia, takes the fortress of Repta, and puts the garrison to the sword.

5. He breaks open the tomb of David, and takes out a large amount of treasures.

3. The suspicions of Herod are again excited against his two sons, Alexander and Aristobulus. They are arrested, tried, condemned, and sent to Samaria, where they are strangled by order of their father.

1. Pheroras, the brother of Herod, and Antipater, the son of Herod, form a conspiracy against his life. The plan is to poison him. Pheroras is taken sick and dies. Antipater at the time is in Rome. The whole plot is discovered by the widow of Pheroras, and Herod divorces his wife Mariamne, daughter of Simon, for being an accomplice, strikes the name of Antipater from his will, deposes Simon from the high-priesthood, and puts many persons to death. All this is kept secret from Antipater at Rome, and Herod sends for him to come home, with many expressions of his paternal love.

Augustus the Roman Emperor. The Temple of Janus shut as a sign of universal peace.

The birth of Christ four years before the common Christian era. That era began to be used about A.D. 526, being first employed by Dionysius, and is supposed to have been placed about four years too late. Some make the difference two, others three, four, five, and even eight years. He was born at the commencement of the last year of the reign of Herod, or at the close of the year preceding. Herod had been king thirty-seven years, Augustus emperor about sixteen.

Antipater returns from Rome. Is accused and convicted of a design to murder Herod, and is put to death by his order. The flight into Egypt, Mat. ii. 13–15. The murder of the innocents at Bethlehem, Mat. ii. 16.

Herod dies at Jericho five days after his son Antipater, in the seventieth year of his age, of a most loathsome and painful disease. He called around him the principal men of the nation, and charged his sister Salome and her husband to confine them in the Hippodrome, and to massacre them as soon as he had breathed his last, that the Jews might have some cause to mourn when he died.

By the will of Herod, Archelaus is appointed his successor in the kingdom, Herod Antipas made tetrarch of Perea and Galilee, and Philip tetrarch of Batanea, Gaulonitis, Trachonitis, and Paneas. To his sister Salome he gives Jamnia and some other places. As soon as Herod was dead, his sister Salome dismissed all the Jewish nobles who had been confined in the Hippodrome, and who had been ordered to be put to death.

AFTER CHRIST.

2–11. ARCHELAUS. Goes to Rome to obtain the confirmation of his title as king from Augustus. The decision of Augustus is delayed. Archelaus takes the high-priesthood from Joazer and gives it to Eleazar.

Great tumult in Judea. The nation in arms against the Roman power. The temple is attacked, but the Romans are repulsed.

Augustus confirms Archelaus in the kingdom, but with the title of *ethnarch* instead of *king*. Archelaus rebuilds Jericho. Is accused by the Jews and Samaritans of tyranny before Augustus, and is banished to Vienne, in Gaul, in the tenth year of his reign.

12–26. JUDEA A ROMAN PROVINCE. In the year 12 A.D. Augustus united Judea and Samaria to Syria, and appointed Publius Sulpitius Quirinus (*Cyrenius*, Lu. ii. 2) governor of the province. At the same time Coponius is made procurator of Judea.

14. The temple at Jerusalem is polluted by some Samaritans, who entered it by night and strewed there the bones of dead men.

17. Augustus dies at Rola, in Campania, in the seventy-sixth year of his age and the fifty-seventh year of his reign. He is succeeded by Tiberius, the son of his wife Julia.

18. Valerius Gratus made procurator of Judea by Tiberius. He deposes Ananus and makes Ismael high-priest. Afterward he gives the office to Eleazar, son of Ananus; then to Simeon, and at last to Joseph, called in the New Testament *Caiaphas.*

Herod Antipas builds the city of Tiberias.

26. PONTIUS PILATE MADE PROCURATOR OF JUDEA BY TIBERIUS.

He attempts to set up Roman colours and ensigns in Jerusalem, but is opposed by the Jews.

29. John the Baptist begins to preach.

30. Jesus is baptized by John.

Tiberius banishes all who professed the Jewish religion from Rome.

About this time hostilities existed between Herod Antipas and Aretas, king of Arabia. Herod Antipas had married a daughter of Aretas. On his way to Rome he saw and fell in love with Herodias, the wife of his brother, and agreed to marry her and put away the daughter of Aretas. She, hearing this, fled to her father, and the consequence was a war, in which Herod was defeated and his army dispersed.

30. John the Baptist declares this marriage unlawful, and is imprisoned by Herod.

31. John the Baptist in prison. Sends a deputation to Jesus to know if he was the Messiah.

32. Is slain by the order of Herod, at the instigation of Herodias.

33. Jesus is crucified on Friday, April 3. Supposed to have been at about three o'clock P.M.

34. Stephen put to death. Paul converted on his way to Damascus.

35. Agrippa the Younger, being involved in debt, resolves to go to Rome. Attaches himself to the party of Caius, and incurs the displeasure of Tiberius. This year died Philip, tetrarch of Trachonitis, &c., a son of Herod the Great. He was mild and equitable in his government, and had ruled thirty-seven years. The countries over which he had presided were at his death united to the province of Syria.

37. Tiberius dies a most profligate and abandoned man. He is succeeded by Caius Caligula.

37. Pilate is recalled by Caligula, and banished to Vienne, in Gaul, where he is said to have put an end to his own life.

38-45. AGRIPPA THE YOUNGER, KING OF THE JEWS. He was the son of Aristobulus and grandson of Mariamne. Shortly before the death of Herod the Great (his grandfather) he goes to Rome, squanders his property there, and is reduced to want. Goes to Idumea, and resolves to commit suicide. Persuaded to abandon his plan by his wife. Obtains the government from Tiberius. Is accused by his half-brother Aristobulus, and goes again to Rome. Is favourably received by Tiberius. Is accused, however, of having made a treasonable remark respecting Tiberius, and imprisoned till the death of that emperor. Is released by Caligula from prison, and made king of Gaulonitis, Batanea, and Trachonitis.

42. Herod Antipas, at the instigation of Agrippa, is banished to Lyons, and his tetrarchy given to King Agrippa.

Caligula orders Petronius to place his statue in the temple at Jerusalem. It is delayed at the instance of Agrippa.

42. Caligula is assassinated at Rome, and succeeded by Claudius.

42. Agrippa is raised by Claudius to the rank of consul; Samaria and Judea are given him, and thus he obtains the entire kingdom of Herod the Great.

42. Agrippa arrives at Jerusalem.

43. Deprives the high-priest Matthias of the priesthood, and bestows it on Elioneus.

Causes the Apostle James the Greater to be put to death (Ac. xii. 1), and imprisons Peter. Soon afterward dies at Cæsarea in great misery, Ac. xii. 21–23.

A famine at Rome.

45. Cuspius Fadus is sent into Judea as governor or procurator. He continues in the office two years.

A great famine in Judea.

Fadus demands that the vestments of the high-priest should be placed under Roman custody. Longinus comes to Jerusalem to enforce this order.

Claudius places Herod, the brother of the deceased Agrippa, over the temple and the treasury.

A celebrated false Messiah appears. He persuades the people to follow him to the Jordan. Promises to stop the river by a word, and to lead them over on dry ground. Is pursued by the Roman cavalry and beheaded.

A second famine in the reign of Claudius. This was in Palestine, Ac. xi. 28.

46. Fadus is recalled. Tiberius, an apostate Jew, is made governor of Judea in his place.

47. Claudius takes away the authority of Herod and gives it to Agrippa, the son of King Agrippa, who died at Cæsarea. *This* was the Agrippa before whom Paul afterward appeared, Ac. xxvi.

47. Tiberius is recalled, and Cumanus is made procurator of Judea. Violent disturbances in Judea.

53. Cumanus is recalled and expelled from Rome. Claudius appoints FELIX procurator of Judea. Felix was a freedman of Claudius. Claudius gives to Agrippa the tetrarchy which had formerly belonged to Philip—Gaulonitis, Batanea, and Trachonitis.

Claudius expels the Jews from Rome, because, in expectation of the Messiah, they are constantly exciting disturbances.

55. Claudius dies, being poisoned by the Empress Agrippina, the mother of Nero. Nero succeeds him. Nero soon put many persons to death, and, among others, his own mother.

56. Nero gives to Agrippa the cities Tiberias, Tarichæa, Abila, and Julias, and the districts belonging to them.

Felix captures a number of robbers and crucifies them.

The *Sicarii*, or robbers with short swords, appear and abound in Judea. Felix hires one of them to assassinate the high-priest Jonathan. Many false prophets appear in Judea.

58. Paul goes into Judea to carry contributions. Is seized in the temple at Jerusalem, and sent to Cæsarea. Ishmael made high-priest. Paul makes his defence before Felix (Ac. xxiv.) at Cæsarea. Is imprisoned two years.

60. PORCIUS FESTUS MADE GOVERNOR OF JUDEA. Felix is accused at Rome.

Paul appeals to the emperor. Makes his speech before Agrippa (Ac. xxvi.), and is put on shipboard to be sent to Rome. Is shipwrecked at Malta.

Festus finds the country overrun with robbers. A false Messiah is taken and slain. Agrippa at Jerusalem builds a high apartment in the palace of Herod, by which he can overlook all that is done in the temple. The Jews build a high wall on the west side of the temple to intercept his view. The case is submitted to Nero. Nero allows the wall to stand.

63. FESTUS DIES IN JUDEA, AND ALBINUS MADE HIS SUCCESSOR.

64. Martyrdom of James the Less at Jerusalem. According to Josephus, he was stoned.

64. Herod's temple at Jerusalem is completed, and about 18,000 workmen are discharged from employment, many of whom become robbers.

65. GESSIUS FLORUS MADE PROCURATOR OF JUDEA—a man *worse* than any of his predecessors. He was cruel, tyrannical, and insatiably avaricious.

Josephus says that at that time there were 3,000,000 Jews in Jerusalem.

Rome set on fire—probably by order of Nero. He charges it on the Christians, several of whom are put to death by being inclosed in pitch and set on fire, to illuminate the gardens of the emperor.

66. BEGINNING OF THE JEWISH WAR.

The probable year of the martyrdom of Paul and Peter at Rome.

An edict of the emperor is issued by which the Syrian and Greek inhabitants of Cæsarea are raised above the Jews. The dissatisfaction which this occasions is the first cause of the war. The Syrians and Greeks at Cæsarea sacrifice birds on the bottom of an earthen vessel, in order to irritate the Jews. A tumult is excited. Florus demands seventeen talents from the temple for the use of the emperor. The Jews are exasperated, and take possession of the lower city. They attack the castle of Antonia, and take it after two days.

The Christians in Jerusalem, seeing that a war is about to break out, retire to Pella, in the kingdom of Agrippa, beyond Jordan.

67. Vespasian is appointed by Nero to prosecute the Jewish war. Comes to Antioch, and forms a numerous army. Division in Jerusalem, and general revolt in Judea. Titus, the son of Vespasian, is sent to Alexandria to collect an army, and to proceed to Palestine in aid of his father. Vespasian subdues Galilee.

Josephus besieged in Jotapata. Jotapata taken, and Josephus surrenders to Vespasian.

The Zealots in Jerusalem seize the temple, and depose Theophilus from being high-priest, and put Phannias in his place. They send for the Idumeans to aid them.

68. Vespasian takes all the places of strength in Judea, around Jerusalem. Nero dies. Galba succeeds him.

69. Josephus set at liberty.

Eleazar, son of Simon, forms a third party, and makes himself master of the inner temple.

Galba dies. Otho declared emperor. Otho dies. Vitellius proclaimed emperor by the German legions. Vespasian proclaimed by the army in the East. Vespasian secures the throne.

70. Titus marches against Jerusalem to besiege it. Approaches it some days before the Passover.

The factions in Jerusalem at first unite against the Romans, but afterward divide again.

The Romans make a wall all around Jerusalem, to reduce it to famine.

July 17. The perpetual daily sacrifice ceases.

A Roman soldier sets the temple on fire, notwithstanding the orders of Titus to the contrary.

71. Titus demolishes the temple to its foundation, and also the city, reserving the towers of Hippicus, Phazael, and Mariamne.

Titus returns to Rome, to his father, Vespasian. A triumph decreed them, and the arch erected in Rome, which is still standing.

The Jewish war ended; Bassus sent into Judea as lieutenant, and Judea is subdued.

CHRONOLOGICAL ARRANGEMENT AND HARMONY OF THE FOUR GOSPELS.

[*From Dr. Townsend's Historical and Chronological Arrangement of the Old and New Testaments.*]

PERIOD I.—FROM THE BIRTH OF CHRIST TO THE TEMPTATION.

DATE.	EVENTS.	SCRIPTURES.
B. C.		
—	General Preface, - - - - - - -	Mar. i. 1; Lu. i. 1-4.
—	The Divinity, Humanity, and Office of Christ, -	Jn. i. 1-18.
6	Birth of John the Baptist, - - - - -	Lu. i. 5-25.
5	The Annunciation, - - - - - - - -	Lu. i. 26-38.
...	Interview between Mary and Elizabeth, - -	Lu. i. 39-56.
...	Birth and Naming of John the Baptist, - -	Lu. i. 57, to end.
...	An Angel appears to Joseph, - - - - -	Mat. i. 18-25.
...	Birth of Christ at Bethlehem, - - - - -	Lu. ii. 1-7.
...	The Genealogies of Christ, - - - -	Mat. i. 1-17; Lu. iii. 23, to end.
...	The Angels appear to the Shepherds, - -	Lu. ii. 8-20.
...	The Circumcision, - - - - - - - -	Lu. ii. 21.
...	The Purification. Presentation of Christ in the Temple, where he is acknowledged by Simeon and Anna, - - - - - - - -	Lu. ii. 22-39.
...	The Offering of the Magi, - - - - - -	Mat. ii. 1-12.
...	The Flight into Egypt, - - - - - -	Mat. ii. 13-15.
...	Slaughter of the Children at Bethlehem, - -	Mat. ii. 16-18.
A.D.		
3	Joseph returns from Egypt, - - - -	Mat. ii. 19, to end; Lu. ii. 40.
7	History of Christ at the age of 12 years, - -	Lu. ii. 41, to end.
26	Commencement of the Ministry of John the Baptist, - - - - - - - -	Mat. iii. 1-12; Mar. i. 2-8; Lu. iii. 1-18.
...	The Baptism of Christ, - - - - -	Mat. iii. 13, to end; Mar. i. 9-11; Lu. iii. 21, 22, and part of 23.
...	The Temptation of Christ, - - - -	Mat. iv. 1-11; Mar. i. 12, 13; Lu. iv. 1-13.

PERIOD II.—FROM THE TEMPTATION OF CHRIST TO THE COMMENCEMENT OF HIS MORE PUBLIC MINISTRY AFTER THE IMPRISONMENT OF JOHN.

DATE.	EVENTS.	SCRIPTURES.
26	Further Testimony of John the Baptist, - -	Jn. i. 19-34.
...	Christ obtains his first Disciples from John, -	Jn. i. 35, to end.
27	Marriage at Cana, in Galilee, - - - - -	Jn. ii. 1-11.
...	Christ goes down to Capernaum, and continues there some short time, - - - - -	Jn. ii. 12.
...	The Buyers and Sellers driven from the Temple,	Jn. ii. 13, to end.
...	Conversation of Christ with Nicodemus, - -	Jn. iii. 1-21.
...	John's last Testimony to Christ, - - - -	Jn. iii. 22, to end.
...	Imprisonment of John the Baptist, - -	Mat. xiv. 3-5; Mar. vi. 17-20; Lu. iii. 19, 20.

Period III.—From the Commencement of the more public Ministry of Christ to the Mission of the Twelve Apostles.

Date.	Events.	Scriptures.
A.D. 27	General Introduction to the History of Christ's more public ministry, - - - -	Mat. iv. 12–17; Mar. i. 14, 15; Lu. iv. 14, 15.
...	Christ's Conversation with the Woman of Samaria,	Jn. iv. 1–42.
...	Second Miracle at Cana in Galilee, - - -	Jn. iv. 43, to end.
...	First public Preaching of Christ in the Synagogue at Nazareth, and his Danger there,	Lu. iv. 16–30.
...	Christ sojourns at Capernaum, - - - -	Lu. iv. 31, 32.
...	The Miraculous Draught of Fishes, and the Calling of Andrew and Peter, James and John,	Mat. iv. 18–22; Mar. i. 16–20; Lu. v. 1–11.
...	The Demoniac healed at Capernaum, -	Mar. i. 21–28; Lu. iv. 33–37.
...	Peter's Mother-in-law cured of a Fever, -	Mat. viii. 14, 15; Mar. i. 29–31; Lu. iv. 38, 39.
...	Christ teaches, and performs Miracles and Cures throughout Galilee, - - -	Mat. iv. 23–25; viii. 16, 17; Mar. i. 32–39; Lu. iv. 40, to end.
...	Christ Cures a Leper, - - - - -	Mat. viii. 2–4; Mar. i. 40, to end; Lu. v. 12–16.
...	The Paralytic cured; and the Power of Christ to forgive Sins asserted, - - - -	Mat. ix. 2–8; Mar. ii. 1–12; Lu. v. 17–26.
...	The Calling of Matthew, - - - -	Mat. ix. 9; Mar. ii. 13, 14; Lu. v. 27, 28.
...	The Infirm Man healed at the Pool of Bethesda,	Jn. v. 1–15.
...	Christ vindicates the Miracle, and asserts the Dignity of his Office, - - - - -	Jn. v. 16, to end.
...	Christ defends his Disciples for plucking the Ears of Corn on the Sabbath-day, - -	Mat. xii. 1–8; Mar. ii. 23, to end; Lu. vi. 1–5.
...	Christ heals the Withered Hand, - -	Mat. xii. 9–14; Mar. iii. 1–6; Lu. vi. 6–11.
...	Christ is followed by great Multitudes, whose Diseases he heals, - - - - - -	Mat. xii. 15–21; Mar. iii. 7–12.
...	Preparation for the Sermon on the Mount—Election of the Twelve Apostles, - -	Mar. iii. 13–19; Lu. vi. 12–19.
...	The Sermon on the Mount, - - -	Mat. v. 6, 7; and viii. 1; Lu. vi. 20, to end.
...	The Centurion's Servant healed, - -	Mat. viii. 5–13; Lu. vii. 1–10.
...	The Widow's Son at Nain is raised to Life, -	Lu. vii. 11–18.
...	Message from John, who was still in Prison, to Christ, - - - - - - - -	Mat. xi. 2–6; Lu. vii. 19–23.
...	Christ's Testimony concerning John, -	Mat. xi. 7–15; Lu. vii. 24–30.
...	Christ reproaches the Jews for their Impenitence and Insensibility, - - - - - -	Mat. xi. 16–24; Lu. vii. 31–35.
...	Christ invites all to come to him, - - -	Mat. xi. 25, to end.
...	Christ forgives the Sins of a female Penitent, at the House of a Pharisee, - - -	Lu. vii. 36, to end.
...	Christ preaches again throughout Galilee, -	Lu. viii. 1–3.
...	Christ cures a Demoniac—Conduct of the Scribes and Pharisees, - - - - - -	Mat. xii. 22–45; Mar. iii. 19–30; Lu. xi. 14–28.
...	Christ declares his faithful Disciples to be his real Kindred, - - - - - -	Mat. xii. 46, to end; Mar. iii. 31, to end; Lu. viii. 19–21.
...	Parable of the Sower, - - - - -	Mat. xiii. 1–9; Mar. iv. 1–9; Lu. viii. 4–8.

Date.	Events.	Scriptures.
A.D. 27	Reasons for Teaching by Parables, - -	Mat. xiii. 10–17; Mar. iv. 10–12; Lu. viii. 9, 10.
...	Explanation of the Parable of the Sower, -	Mat. xiii. 18–23; Mar. iv. 13–23; Lu. viii. part of ver. 9, and 11–17.
...	Christ directs his Hearers to practise what they hear, - - - - - - - -	Mar. iv. 24, 25; Lu. viii. 18.
...	Various Parables descriptive of Christ's kingdom,	Mat. xiii. 24–53; Mar. iv. 26–34.
...	Christ crosses the Sea of Galilee, and calms the Tempest, - - - - - - -	Mat. viii. 18–27; Mar. iv. 35, to end; Lu. viii. 22-25.
...	Christ heals the Gadarene Demoniac, -	Mat. viii. 28, to end; Mar. v. 1–20; Lu. viii. 26–40.
...	Christ dines with Matthew, - - -	Mat. ix. 10–17; Mar. ii. 15–22; Lu. v. 29, to end.
...	Jairus' Daughter is healed, and the Infirm Woman, - - - - - - -	Mat. ix. 1, 18–26; Mar. v. 21, to end; Lu. viii. 40, to end.
...	Christ restores two Blind Men to sight, - -	Mat. ix. 27–31.
...	Christ casts out a Dumb Spirit, - - -	Mat. ix. 32–34.
...	Christ returns to Nazareth, and is again ill-treated there, - - - - - -	Mat. xiii. 54, to end; Mar. vi. 1–6.
28	Christ preaches again throughout Galilee, -	Mat. ix. 35, to end.

Period IV.—From the Mission of the Twelve Apostles to the Mission of the Seventy.

Date.	Events.	Scriptures.
28	Christ's Mission of the Twelve Apostles, -	Mat. x. and xi. 1; Mar. vi. 7–13; Lu. ix. 1–6.
...	Death of John the Baptist—Herod desires to see Christ, - - - - - - - -	Mat. xiv. 1–12; Mar. vi. 14–29; Lu. ix. 7–9.
...	The Twelve return, and Jesus retires with them to the Desert of Bethsaida, - - -	Mat. xiv. 13, 14; Mar. vi. 30–34; Lu. ix. 10, 11; Jn. vi. 1, 2.
...	Five thousand are fed miraculously, - -	Mat. xiv. 15–21; Mar. vi. 35–44; Lu. ix. 12–17; Jn. vi. 3–14.
...	Christ sends the Multitude away, and prays alone, - - - - - - - -	Mat. xiv. 22, 23; Mar. vi. 45, 46; Jn. vi. 15.
...	Christ walks on the Sea to his Disciples, who are overtaken with a Storm, - - -	Mat. xiv. 24–33; Mar. vi. 47–52; Jn. vi. 16–21.
...	Christ heals many People, - - -	Mat. xiv. 34–36; Mar. vi. 53, to end.
...	Christ teaches in the Synagogue of Capernaum —His Conversation there, - - -	Jn. vi. 22, to end; and vii. 1.
...	Christ converses with the Scribes and Pharisees on the subject of Jewish Traditions, -	Mat. xv. 1–20; Mar. vii. 1–23.
...	Christ heals the Daughter of the Canaanite, or Syro-Phœnician Woman, - - -	Mat. xv. 21–28; Mar. vii. 24–30.
...	Christ goes through Decapolis, healing and teaching, - - - - - - -	Mat. xv. 29–31; Mar. vii. 31, to end.
...	Four thousand Men are fed miraculously,	Mat. xv. 32, to end; Mar. viii. 1–10.
...	The Pharisees require other Signs—Christ charges them with hypocrisy, - -	Mat. xvi. 1–12; Mar. viii. 11–21.
...	Christ heals a blind Man at Bethsaida, - -	Mar. viii. 22–26.
...	Peter confesses Christ to be the Messiah, -	Mat. xvi. 13-20; Mar. viii. 27–30; Lu. ix. 18–21.

DATE.	EVENTS.	SCRIPTURES.
A.D. 28	Christ astonishes the Disciples by declaring the necessity of his Death and Resurrection,	Mat. xvi. 21, to end; Mar. viii. 31, to end, and ix. 1; Lu. ix. 22-27.
...	The Transfiguration of Christ, - - -	Mat. xvii. 1-13; Mar. ix. 2-13; Lu. ix. 28-36.
...	The Deaf and Dumb Spirit cast out, -	Mat. xvii. 14-21; Mar. ix. 14-29; Lu. ix. 37-42, and part of 43.
...	Christ again foretells his Death and Resurrection, - - - - - - - -	Mat. xvii. 22, 23; Mar. ix. 30-32, and part of 33; Lu. ix. 43-46.
...	Christ works a Miracle to pay the Half-shekel for the Temple Service, - - - - -	Mat. xvii. 24, to end.
...	The Disciples contend for superiority, - .	Mat. xviii. 1, to end; Mar. ix. part of 33, to end; Lu. ix. 47-50.

PERIOD V.—FROM THE MISSION OF THE SEVENTY DISCIPLES TO THE TRIUMPHAL ENTRY OF CHRIST INTO JERUSALEM, SIX DAYS BEFORE THE CRUCIFIXION.

DATE.	EVENTS.	SCRIPTURES.
28	The Mission of the Seventy Disciples, - -	Lu. x. 1-16.
...	Christ goes up to the Feast of Tabernacles,	Mat. xix. 1; Mar. x. 1; Jn. vii. 2-10.
...	Agitation of the Public Mind at Jerusalem concerning Christ, - - - - - -	Jn. vii. 11-52.
...	Conduct of Christ to the Adulteress and her Accusers, - - - - - - - -	Jn. vii. 53; viii. 1-11.
...	Christ declares himself to be the Son of God, -	Jn. viii. 12-20.
...	Christ declares the Manner of his Death, - -	Jn. viii. 21, to end.
...	The Seventy return with joy, - - - -	Lu. x. 17-24.
...	Christ directs the Lawyer how he may attain Eternal Life, - - - - - - -	Lu. x. 25-28.
...	The Parable of the Good Samaritan, - -	Lu. x. 29-37.
...	Christ in the House of Martha, - - -	Lu. x. 38, to end.
...	Christ teaches his Disciples to pray, - - -	Lu. xi. 1-13.
...	Christ reproaches the Pharisees and Lawyers, -	Lu. xi. 37, to end.
...	Christ cautions his Disciples against Hypocrisy,	Lu. xii. 1-12.
...	Christ refuses to act as Judge, - - - -	Lu. xii. 13, 14.
...	Christ cautions the Multitude against Worldly-mindedness, - - - - - - -	Lu. xii. 15-34.
...	Christ exhorts to Watchfulness, Fidelity, and Repentance, - - - - - - -	Lu. xii. 35, to end xiii. 1-9.
...	Christ cures an Infirm Woman in the Synagogue,	Lu. xiii. 10-17.
...	Christ begins his journey towards Jerusalem, to be present at the Feast of the Dedication,	Lu. xiii. 22, 18-21.
...	Christ restores to sight a Blind Man, who is summoned before the Sanhedrim, - -	Jn. ix. 1-34.
...	Christ declares that he is the True Shepherd,	Jn. ix. 35, to end; x. 1-21.
...	Christ publicly asserts his Divinity, - - -	Jn. x. 22-38.
...	In consequence of the opposition of the Jews, Christ retires beyond Jordan, - -	Jn. x. 39, to end.
...	Christ, leaving the City, laments over Jerusalem,	Lu. xiii. 23, to end.
...	Christs dines with a Pharisee—Parable of the Great Supper, - - - - - -	Lu. xiv. 1-24.
...	Christ's Disciples must forsake the World, -	Lu. xiv. 25, to end.

Date.	Events.	Scriptures.
A.D. 28	Parables of the Lost Sheep, and of the Lost Piece of Silver, - - - - - - -	Lu. xv. 1-10.
...	Parable of the Prodigal Son, - - - -	Lu. xv. 11, to end.
...	Parable of the Unjust Steward, - - -	Lu. xvi. 1-13.
...	Christ reproves the Pharisees, - - - - -	Lu. xvi. 14-17.
...	Christ answers the Question concerning Divorce and Marriage, - - - - - -	Mat. xix. 3-12; Mar. x. 2-12; Lu. xvi. 18.
...	Christ receives and blesses little Children,	Mat. xix. 13-15; Mar. x. 13-17; Lu. xviii. 15-17.
...	Parable of the Rich Man and Lazarus, - -	Lu. xvi. 19, to end.
...	On Forgiveness of Injuries, - - - - -	Lu. xvii. 1-10.
...	Christ journeys towards Jerusalem, - - -	Lu.ix.51,to end; xvii.11.
...	Christ heals ten Lepers, - - - - - -	Lu. xvii. 12-19.
...	Christ declares the Lowliness of his Kingdom and the sudden Destruction of Jerusalem,	Lu. xvii. 20, to end.
...	Christ teacheth the true Nature of Prayer, -	Lu. xviii. 1-8.
...	Parable of the Publican and Pharisee, - -	Lu. xviii. 9-14.
...	From the Conduct of the young Ruler, Christ cautions his Disciples on the Dangers of Wealth,	Mat. xix. 16-29; Mar. x. 17-30; Lu. xviii. 18-30.
...	Parable of the Labourers in the Vineyard, -	Mat. xix. 30; xx. 1-16; Mar. x. 31.
...	Christ is informed of the Sickness of Lazarus, -	Jn. xi. 1-16.
29	Christ again predicts his Sufferings and Death,	Mat. xx. 17-19; Mar. x. 32-34; Lu. xviii. 31-34.
...	Ambition of the Sons of Zebedee, - -	Mat. xx. 20-28; Mar. x. 35-45.
...	Two Blind Men healed at Jericho, - -	Mat. xx. 29, to end; Mar. x. 46, to end; Lu. xviii. 35, to end.
...	Conversion of Zaccheus, and the Parable of the Pounds, - - - - - - - -	Lu. xix. 1-28.
...	The Resurrection of Lazarus, - - - - -	Jn. xi. 17-46.
...	The Sanhedrim assemble to deliberate concerning the Resurrection of Lazarus, - -	Jn. xi. 47, 48.
...	Caiaphas prophesies, - - - - - - - -	Jn. xi. 49-52.
...	The Sanhedrim resolves to put Christ to death,	Jn. xi. 53.
...	Christ retires to Ephraim, or Ephrata, - -	Jn. xi. 54.
...	State of the Public Mind at Jerusalem, immediately preceding the last Passover, at which Christ attended, - - - - - -	Jn. xi. 55, to end.
...	Christ comes to Bethany, where he is anointed by Mary, - - - - - - -	Mat. xxvi. 6-13; Mar. xiv. 3-9; Jn. xii. 1-11.
...	Christ prepares to enter Jerusalem, - -	Mat. xxi. 1-7; Mar. xi. 1-7; Lu. xix. 29-40; Jn. xii. 12-18.

Period VI.—From Christ's Triumphant Entry into Jerusalem, to His Apprehension—Sunday, the Fifth Day before the last Passover.

Date.	Events.	Scriptures.
29	The people meet Christ with Hosannahs. Christ approaches Jerusalem, - - - - -	Mat. xxi. 8, 9; Mar. xi. 8-10; Lu. xix. 36-40; Jn. xii. 19.
...	Christ's Lamentation over Jerusalem, and the Prophecy of its Destruction, - - -	Lu. xix. 41-44.
...	Christ, on entering the City, casts the Buyers and Sellers out of the Temple, - -	Mat. xxi. 10-13; Mar. xi. part of ver. 11; Lu. xix. 45, 46.

DATE.	EVENTS.	SCRIPTURES.
A.D. 29	Christ heals the Sick in the Temple, and reproves the Chief Priests, - - - - - -	Mat. xxi. 14-16.
...	Some Greeks at Jerusalem desire to see Christ. The Bath Col [Voice from Heaven] is heard,	Jn. xii. 20-43.
...	Christ declares the Object of his Mission, - -	Jn. xii. 44, to end.
...	Christ leaves Jerusalem in the Evening, and goes to Bethany, - - - - - - - -	Mat. xxi. 17; Mar. xi. part of ver. 11.
...	Monday—Fourth Day before the Passover. Christ, entering Jerusalem, again curses the barren Fig-tree, - - - - - -	Mat. xxi. 18, 19; Mar. xi. 12-14.
...	Christ again casts the Buyers and Sellers out of the Temple, - - - - - - -	Mar. xi. 15-17.
...	The Scribes and Chief Priests seek to destroy Jesus, - - - - - - - - -	Mar. xi. 18; Lu. xix. 47, 48.
...	Christ retires in the Evening from the City, -	Mar. xi. 19.
...	Tuesday—Third Day before the Passover. The Fig-tree is now withered, - - - -	Mat. xxi. 20-22; Mar. xi. 20-26.
...	Christ answers the Chief Priests who inquire concerning the Authority by which he acted. Parables of the Vineyard and Marriage Feast,	Mat. xxi. 23, to end; xxii. 1-14; Mar. xi. 27, to end; xii. 1-12; Lu. xix. 1-19.
...	Christ replies to the Herodians, - - -	Mat. xxii. 15-22; Mar. xii. 13-17; Lu. xx. 20-26.
...	Christ replies to the Sadducees, - -	Mat. xxii. 23-33; Mar. xii. 18-27; Lu. xx. 27-40.
...	Christ replies to the Pharisees, - - -	Mat. xxii. 34-40; Mar. xii. 28-35.
...	Christ inquires of the Pharisees concerning the Messiah, - - - - - - -	Mat. xxii. 41, to end; Mar. xii. 35-37; Lu. xx. 41-44.
...	Christ severely reproves the Pharisees, -	Mat. xxiii. 1, to end; Mar. xii. 38-40; Lu. xx. 45, to end.
...	Christ applauds the Liberality of the poor Widow, - - - - - - - - -	Mar. xii. 41, to end; Lu. xxi. 1-4.
...	Christ foretells the Destruction of Jerusalem, the End of the Jewish Dispensation, and of the World, - - - - - - -	Mat. xxiv. 1-35; Mar. xiii. 1-31; Lu. xxi. 5-33.
...	Christ compares the Suddenness of his Second Advent to the Coming of the Deluge, -	Mat. xxiv. 36, to end; Mar. xiii. 32, to end; Lu. xxi. 34-36.
...	The Parable of the Wise and Foolish Virgins, - - - - - - - - -	Mat. xxv. 1-13.
...	The Parable of the Servants and the Talents, -	Mat. xxv. 14-30.
...	Christ declares the Proceedings at the Day of Judgment, - - - - - - - -	Mat. xxv. 31, to end.
...	Christ retires from the City to the Mount of Olives, - - - - - - - - -	Lu. xxi. 37, 38.
...	Wednesday—Second Day before the Crucifixion. Christ foretells his approaching Death, -	Mat. xxvi. 1, 2; Mar. xiv. part of ver. 1.
...	The Rulers consult how they may take Christ,	Mat. xxvi. 3-5; Mar. xiv. part of ver. 1, ver. 2; Lu. xxii. 1, 2.
...	Judas agrees with the Chief Priests to betray Christ, - - - - - - - -	Mat. xxvi. 14-16; Mar. xiv. 10, 11; Lu. xxii. 3-6.

DATE.	EVENTS.	SCRIPTURES.
A.D. 29	Thursday — The day before the Crucifixion. Christ directs two of his Disciples to prepare the Passover, - - - - - -	Mat. xxvi. 17-19; Mar. xiv. 12-16; Lu. xxii. 7-13.
...	Christ partakes of the last Passover, -	Mat. xxvi. 20; Mar. xiv. 17; Lu. xxii. 14-18; Jn. xiii. 1.
...	Christ again reproves the Ambition of his Disciples, - - - - - - -	Lu. xxii. 24-27; Jn. xiii. 2-16.
...	Christ, sitting at the Passover, and continuing the Conversation, speaks of his Betrayer,	Mat. xxvi. 21-25; Mar. xiv. 18-21; Lu. xxii. 21-23; Jn. xiii. 17-30.
...	Judas goes out to betray Christ, who predicts Peter's Denial of him, and the Danger of the rest of the Apostles, - - - -	Lu. xxii. 28-38; Jn. xiii. 31, to end.
...	Christ institutes the Eucharist, - -	Mat. xxvi. 26-29; Mar. xiv. 22-25; Lu. xxii. 19, 20.
...	Christ exhorts the Apostles, and consoles them on his approaching Death, - - -	Jn. xiv.
...	Christ goes with his Disciples to the Mount of Olives, - - - - - - - - -	Mat. xxvi. 30; Mar. xiv. 26; Lu. xxii. 39.
...	Christ declares himself to be the True Vine, -	Jn. xv. 1-8.
...	Christ exhorts his Apostles to mutual Love, and to prepare for Persecution, - - -	Jn. xv. 9, to end; xvi. 1-4.
...	Christ promises the Gifts of the Holy Spirit, -	Jn. xvi. 5, to end.
...	Christ intercedes for all his Followers, - -	Jn. xvii.
..	Christ again predicts Peter's Denial of him,	Mat. xxvi. 31-35; Mar. xiv. 27-31.
...	Christ goes into the Garden of Gethsemane—His agony there, - - - - -	Mat. xxvi. 36-46; Mar. xiv. 32-42; Lu. xxii. 40-46; Jn. xviii. 1, 2.
...	Christ is betrayed and apprehended. The Resistance of Peter, - - - - -	Mat. xxvi. 47-56; Mar. xiv. 43-50; Lu. xxii. 47-53; Jn. xviii. 3-11.

PERIOD VII.—FROM THE APPREHENSION OF CHRIST TO THE CRUCIFIXION.

DATE.	EVENTS.	SCRIPTURES.
29	Christ is taken to Annas, and to the Palace of Caiaphas, - - - - - - -	Mat. xxvi. 57; Mar. xiv. 51-53; Lu. xxii. 54; Jn. xviii. 12-14.
...	Peter and John follow their Master, -	Mat. xxvi. 58; Mar. xiv. 54; Lu. xxii. 55; Jn. xviii. 15, 16.
...	Christ is first examined and condemned in the House of the High Priest, - - -	Mat. xxvi. 59-66; Mar. xiv. 55-64; Jn. xviii. 19-24.
...	Twelve at Night. Christ is struck and insulted by the Soldiers, - - - - -	Mat. xxvi. 67, 68; Mar. xiv. 65; Lu. xxii. 63-65.
...	Peter's First Denial of Christ, at the fire, in the Hall of the High Priest's Palace, . -	Mat. xxvi. 69, 70; Mar. xiv. 66-68; Lu. xxii. 56, 57; Jn. xviii. 17, 18, 25-27.
...	After Midnight. Peter's Second Denial of Christ, at the Porch of the Palace of the High Priest, - - - - - -	Mat. xxvi. 71, 72; Mar. xiv. 69, part of 70; Lu. xxii. 58.

Date.	Events.	Scriptures.
A.D. 29	Friday, the day of the Crucifixion—Time, about three in the Morning. Peter's Third Denial of Christ, in the Room where Christ was waiting among the Soldiers till the Dawn of Day,	Mat. xxvi. 73, to end; Mar. xiv. part of 70, to end; Lu. xxii. 59–61.
...	Christ is taken before the Sanhedrim, and condemned, - - - - - - -	Mat. xxvii. 1; Mar. xv. part of 1; Lu. xxii. 66, to end.
...	Judas declares the Innocence of Christ, - -	Mat. xxvii. 3–10.
...	Christ is accused before Pilate, and is by him also declared to be innocent, - - -	Mat. xxvii. 2, 11–14; Mar. xv. 1–5; Lu. xxiii. 1–4; Jn. xviii. 28–38.
...	Christ is sent by Pilate to Herod, - - -	Lu. xxiii. 5–12.
...	Christ is brought back again to Pilate, who again declares him innocent, and endeavours to persuade the people to ask for his release, -	Mat. xxvii. 15–20; Mar. xv. 6–11; Lu. xxiii. 13–19; Jn. xviii. 39.
...	Pilate three times endeavours again to release Christ, - - - - - - - -	Mat. xxvii. 21–23; Mar. xv. 12–14; Lu. xxiii. 20–23; Jn. xviii. 40.
...	The Jews imprecate the punishment of Christ's Death upon themselves, - - -	Mat. xxvii. 24, 25.
...	Pilate releases Barabbas, and delivers Christ to be Crucified, - - - - - - -	Mat. xxvii. 26–30; Mar. xv. 15–19; Lu. xxiii. 24, 25; Jn. xix. 1–16.
...	Christ is led away from the Judgment-hall of Pilate to Mount Calvary, - - -	Mat. xxvii. 31, 32; Mar. xv. 20, 21; Lu. xxiii. 26–32; Jn. xix. part of 16, and 17.
...	Christ arrives at Mount Calvary, and is Crucified, - - - - - - - -	Mat. xxvii. 33, 34, 37, 38; Mar. xv. 22, 23, 26–28; Lu. xxiii. 33–38; Jn. xix. 18–22.
...	Christ prays for his Murderers, - - -	Lu. xxiii. part of 34.
...	The Soldiers divide and cast Lots for the Raiment of Christ, - - - - - -	Mat. xxvii. 35, 36; Mar. xv. 24, 25; Lu. xxiii. part of 34; Jn. xix. 23, 24.
...	Christ is reviled, when on the Cross, by the Chief Priests, the Rulers, the Soldiers, the Passengers, and the Malefactors, - -	Mat. xxvii. 39–44; Mar. xv. 29–32; Lu. xxiii. 35–37.
...	Christ, when Dying as a Man, asserts his Divinity, in his Answer to the Penitent Thief,	Lu. xxiii. 39–43.
...	Christ commends his Mother to the care of John,	Jn. xix. 25–27.
...	The Death of Christ and its attendant circumstances, - - - - - - - -	Mat. xxvii. 45–51, 54–56; Mar. xv. 33-41; Lu. xxiii. 44–49; Jn. xix. 28–37.

Period VIII.—From the Death of Christ till his Ascension into Heaven.

Date.	Events.	Scriptures.
29	Joseph of Arimathea and Nicodemus bury the Body of Christ, - - - - - -	Mat. xxvii. 57–60; Mar. xv. 42–46; Lu. xxiii. 50–54; Jn. xix. 38, to end.
...	Mary Magdalene, and the other Mary, and the Women from Galilee, observe where the body of Christ was laid, - - - - - -	Mar. xv. 47; Lu. xxiii. 55.
...	The Women from Galilee hasten to return Home before the Sabbath began, to prepare Spices,	Lu. xxiii. 56.
...	Mary Magdalene and the other Mary continue to sit opposite the Sepulchre till it is too late to prepare their Spices, - - - -	Mat. xxvii. 61.

DATE.	EVENTS.	SCRIPTURES.
A.D. 29	The Sabbath being ended, the Chief Priests prepare a Guard of Soldiers to watch the Sepulchre,	Mat. xxvii. 62, to end.
...	The Sabbath being over, Mary Magdalene, the other Mary, and Salomé, purchase their Spices to anoint the Body of Christ, - -	Mar. xvi. 1.
...	The Morning of Easter-day. Mary Magdalene, the other Mary, and Salomé, leave their homes very early to go to the Sepulchre, -	Mat. xxviii. 1; Mar. xvi. part of 2; Jn. xx. part of 1.
...	After they had left their Homes, and before their arrival at the Sepulchre, Christ rises from the Dead, - - - - - -	Mat. xxviii. 2–4.
...	The Bodies of many come out of their Graves, and go to Jerusalem, - - - - -	Mat. xxvii. part of 52, and 53.
...	Mary Magdalene, the other Mary, and Salomé, arrive at the Sepulchre, and find the Stone rolled away, - - - - - - -	Mar. xvi. part of 2, and 3, 4; Jn. xx. part of 1.
...	Mary Magdalene leaves the other Mary and Salomé to tell Peter, - - - - -	Jn. xx. 2.
...	Salomé and the other Mary, during the absence of Mary Magdalene, enter the porch of the Sepulchre, and see one Angel, who commands them to inform the Disciples that Jesus was risen, - - - - - - - -	Mat. xxviii. 5–7; Mar. xvi. 5–7.
...	Salomé and the other Mary leave the Sepulchre,	Mat.xxviii.8;Mar.xvi.8.
...	Peter and John, as soon as they hear the report of Mary Magdalene, hasten to the Sepulchre, which they inspect, and immediately depart,	Jn. xx. 3–10.
...	Mary Magdalene, having followed Peter and John, remains at the Sepulchre after their departure, - - - - - - -	Jn. xx. part of 11.
...	Mary Magdalene looks into the Tomb, and sees two Angels, - - - - - - -	Jn. xx. part of 11, 12, 13, and part of 14.
...	Christ first appears to Mary Magdalene, and commands her to inform the Disciples that he has risen, - - - - - - -	Mar. xvi. 9; Jn. xx. part of 14, and 15–17.
...	Mary Magdalene, when going to inform the Disciples that Christ had risen, meets again with Salomé and the other Mary. Christ appears to the three Women, - -	Mat. xxviii. 9, 10; Jn. xx. 18.
...	The Soldiers, who had fled from the Sepulchre, report to the High Priests the Resurrection of Christ, - - - - - - -	Mat. xxviii. 11–15.
...	The Second Party of Women, from Galilee, who had bought their Spices on the evening previous to the Sabbath, having had a longer way to come to the Sepulchre, arrive after the departure of the others, and find the Stone rolled away, - - - - - - -	Lu. xxiv. 1–3.
...	Two Angels appear also to the Second Party of Women, from Galilee, assuring them that Christ was risen, and reminding them of his foretelling this fact, - - - - -	Lu. xxiv. 4–9.
...	Mary Magdalene unites her Testimony to that of the Galilean Women, - - - -	Mar. xvi. 10; Lu. xxiv. 10.
...	The Apostles are still incredulous, - - -	Mar.xvi.11;Lu.xxiv.11.
...	Peter goes again to the Sepulchre, - - -	Lu. xxiv. part of 12.
...	Peter, who had probably seen Christ, departs from the Sepulchre, - - - - -	Lu. xxiv. part of 12.

Date.	Events.	Scriptures.
A.D. 29	Christ appears to Cleopas and another disciple, going to Emmaus, - - - - - -	Mar. xvi. 12; Lu. xxiv. 13–32.
...	Cleopas and his Companion return to Jerusalem, and assure the Apostles that Christ had certainly risen, - - - - - - -	Mar. xvi. 13; Lu. xxiv. 33–35.
...	Christ appears to the assembled Apostles, Thomas only being absent, convinces them of the Identity of his Resurrection Body, and blesses them, - - - - - -	Lu. xxiv. 36–43; Jn. xx. 19–23.
...	Thomas is still incredulous, - - - - -	Jn. xx. 24, 25.
...	Christ appears to the Eleven, Thomas being present, - - - - - - -	Mar. xvi. 14; Jn. xx. 26–29.
...	Christ appears to a large number of his Disciples on a Mountain in Galilee, - -	Mat. xxviii. 16, 17, and part of 18.
...	Christ appears again at the Sea of Tiberias—His Conversation with St. Peter, - -	Jn. xxi. 1–24.
...	Christ appears to his Apostles at Jerusalem, and commissions them to convert the World,	Lu. xxiv. 44–49; Ac. i. 4, 5.
...	Christ leads out his Apostles to Bethany, within sight of Jerusalem, gives them their final commission, blesses them, and ascends visibly into Heaven; from whence he will come to judge the living and the dead, - -	Mat. xxviii. part of 18–20; Mar. xvi. 15, to end; Lu. xxiv. 50, to end; Ac. i. 6–12.
...	St. John's Conclusion to the Gospel History of Jesus Christ, - - - - - - -	Jn. xx. 30, 31, and xxi. 25.

SCRIPTURE WEIGHTS, MEASURES, AND MONEY.

I.—Scriptural Measures of Length, reduced to English Measure.

								Feet.	Inches.
A Digit,								0	0·912
4	A Palm,							0	3·648
12	3	A Span,						0	10·944
24	6	3	A Cubit,					1	9·888
96	24	6	2	A Fathom,				7	3·552
144	36	12	6	1·5	Ezekiel's Reed,			10	11·328
192	48	16	8	2	1·3	An Arabian Pole,		14	7·104
1920	480	160	80	20	13·3	10	A *Schœnus*, or Measuring Line,	145	11·04

II.—The Long Scripture Measures.

						Miles.	Paces.	Feet.
A Cubit,						0	0	1·824
400	A Stadium, or Furlong,					0	145	4·6
2000	5	A Sabbath Day's Journey,				0	729	3
4000	10	2	An Eastern Mile,			1	403	1
12000	30	6	3	A Parasang,		4	153	3
96000	240	48	24	8	A Day's Journey,	33	172	4

III.—Jewish Money reduced to our Standard.

					£	s.	d.
A Gerah,					0	0	1·2687
10	A Bekah,				0	1	1·6875
20	2	A Shekel,			0	2	3·375
1200	120	50	A Maneh, or Mina,		5	14	0·75
60000	6000	3000	60	A Talent of silver,	342	3	9
A gold Shekel was worth					1	16	6
A Talent of gold was worth					5475	0	0

IV.—Roman Money, mentioned in the New Testament, reduced to our Standard.

A Mite, about three-eighths of a farthing.
A Farthing, about three-fourths of a farthing.
A Penny or Denarius, sevenpence three farthings.
A Pound or Mina, three pounds two shillings and sixpence.

INDEX

TO THE NOTES ON THE GOSPELS BY

LUKE AND JOHN.